VISITING

P9-CAS-938

The Caribb

TRUST US.
WORLDWIDE.

READ THIS!
The advice below is designed to help you if you are travelling to the Caribbean.

The US Dollar is the principally accepted foreign currency.
However, you may also use Sterling Pounds in the English Caribbean, French
Francs in the French Caribbean and Dutch Guilders in the Dutch Caribbean.
Black or free market rates are normally better than official market rates.
Be careful, because in some countries the black market is illegal.
Shop around for Bank rates.
Hotel exchange rates are seldom better than official rates.
On many islands only certain Banks, and even only certain branches,
may deal in exchange. You may even find yourself in a town where no Bank
deals in exchange. Take a supply of local currency if travelling outside large
cities or to the smaller islands.
Finally, although exchange rates are marginally better for US Dollar bills
than for travellers cheques make sure that the bulk of your money is in US$
Thomas Cook MasterCard® Travellers Cheques.
These can be refunded in case of loss or theft, cash is lost forever.
Avoid taking along the large denomination cheque,
for example $500 and $1,000.

*See the lists at the end of this book
for Refund locations.*

1993

CARIBBEAN ISLANDS HANDBOOK

FOURTH EDITION

Editors
Sarah Cameron & Ben Box

"Open the map. More islands there, man,
than peas on a tin plate, all different size,
one thousand in the Bahamas alone,
from mountains to low scrub with coral keys,
and from this bowsprit, I bless every town,
the blue smell of smoke in hills behind them,
and the one small road winding down them like
twine to the roofs below ..."
Derek Walcott *From Canto II, 'After the Storm' of The
Schooner Flight in The Star-Apple Kingdom*

TRADE & TRAVEL PUBLICATIONS

2

Trade & Travel Publications Limited
6 Riverside Court, Riverside Road
Bath BA2 3DZ
England
Tel 0225 469141 Fax 0225 462921

©Trade & Travel Publications Ltd., September 1992

ISBN 0 900751 38 X

CIP DATA: A catalogue record for this book is available from the British Library

Published in the United States of America and Canada by
Prentice Hall General Reference
A division of Simon & Schuster Inc.
15 Columbus Circle
New York, NY 10023-7780

PRENTICE HALL and colophon are registered trademarks of Simon & Schuster, Inc.

In North America, ISBN   0-13-116971-8
Library of Congress Catalogue Card Number   90-661355

WARNING: Whilst every endeavour is made to ensure that the facts printed in this book are correct at the time of going to press, travellers are cautioned to obtain authoritative advice from consulates, airlines, etc concerning current travel and visa requirements and conditions before embarking. The publishers cannot accept legal responsibility for errors, however caused, which are printed in this book.

Cover illustration by Jeremy Pyke
Printed and bound in Great Britain by Clays Ltd., Bungay, Suffolk.

Preface

Although the *Caribbean Islands Handbook* was originally intended to deal solely with islands, for the first time this year we include the Guianas (Guyana, Suriname and French Guyane). Culturally, the links between these three countries is stronger with the Caribbean than with the mainland and transport connections with the islands are reasonably good. Guyana's political and trading connections are with the Caricom countries and its cricketing ties are undoubtedly Caribbean. Guyane, as an overseas department of France, is on a par with Guadeloupe and Martinique. From the visitor's point of view, the upsurge in nature tourism is benefiting the Guianas since their forested interiors have been invaded to a far lesser degree than those of their neighbours. Jungle lodges are opening up in Guyana and Suriname's national parks are once again accessible after several years of civil war.

In July 1992, the First Caribbean Conference on Ecotourism was held in Belize City. Further ecotourism conferences were held in Belize and St John (US Virgin Islands) in April and May 1992, indicating that this sector of the travel market is gathering momentum. Mass tourism has suffered from the worldwide recession and tourist arrivals to the more established destinations, such as Bermuda, the Bahamas, Barbados, the Cayman Islands and Puerto Rico, have fallen sharply. Conversely, smaller islands which can offer more intimate nature tourism on land or under water, have seen an increase in visitors and these include the Turks and Caicos Islands, Bonaire, Grenada, Martinique, St Kitts and Nevis and others.

Several chapters in this year's Handbook have been expanded as a result of editorial visits. In March 1992, Sarah Cameron went to the Turks and Caicos Islands, a growing market of particular interest to scuba divers. Thanks are due to Ruth Buckmaster, of the Turks and Caicos Islands' office in London (now unfortunately closed), for her help in organizing the trip, to Clifford Hamilton, Director of Tourism, for many hours of conversation, to Norma Outten, formerly of the Tourist Office in Providenciales, for setting up meetings and making travel arrangements. In addition, invaluable assistance and hospitality was received from Louise Fletcher on Providenciales, who helped to revise the whole chapter, while Jo Anne James Selver of North Caicos kindly commented on the North and Middle Caicos sections. Patrick Dawson, of Trade and Travel Publications, and his family travelled in St Kitts and Nevis, St Lucia and Barbados in October 1991 and came back with much new information to improve those chapters. Revision of the Belize Cayes chapter was aided by Ben Box's attendance at the First Ecotourism Conference and much help with the text was received from Neil Rogers of Chaa Creek Cottages, Cayo, Belize.

We should also like to thank our regular correspondents: Rachel Cartwright (the Family Islands), Huw Clough and Kate Hennessy (Jamaica, Cuba, the Bay Islands), Kathy Coombes (Montserrat), Frank Eelens (Aruba), Dianne Erdos (Sosúa, Dominican Republic), Pamela Gaffin (the Virgin Islands), Dania Goris (Santo Domingo, Dominican Republic), Lars Karlsson (the 3 S's, Anguilla, Antigua and the French Antilles), Jan Murray of Traveller's Tree (Dominica), David Renwick (Trinidad), Tony Thorne (Guyana), Jorge Valle-Aguiluz (the Bay Islands) and Mark Wilson (peripatetic). For transferring all the new and corrected material to disk, we are extremely grateful to Debbie Wylde, to Janet Krengel for providing statistics, to Katherine Jarvis for updating maps and to Sebastian Ballard for drawing new maps. We are delighted that so many of our readers take the trouble to write to us and we are always glad to receive travellers' comments. A list of those who have contributed to this edition is at the end of the section How To Use This Handbook.

The Editors

Contents

Contents

How To Use This Handbook

The Caribbean Islands Handbook is the most complete and up-to-date package of information for independent travellers on all the Caribbean islands. Its text is updated every year for the new edition which is published on 1 September. The text is based on the editors' personal travels, extensive information from correspondents living in the region, material and maps which travellers send us, contributions from national tourist authorities, and the many sources of information on the Caribbean available in the UK and elsewhere.

Editorial Logic
Users of the *Handbook* will find that we employ a logical system of arrangement, which we believe is the most convenient for travellers.

Introduction and Hints
This first section in the book gives information and hints that apply generally to all the islands we cover, including:

- ❏ Travel to and in the Caribbean
- ❏ Documents
- ❏ Language
- ❏ Money
- ❏ Travel in the Eastern Caribbean
- ❏ Further Reading

Miami
A guide to one of the major gateways to the Caribbean by Mark Wilson, teacher of geography and journalist, currently based in Barbados.

Health Information
This major section by Dr David Snashall of St Thomas's Hospital Medical School, London, gives details of the health risks common in the Caribbean, and the sensible precautions travellers should take to combat them.

Watersports and Sailing in the Caribbean
Rosie Mauro, an experienced sailor from Barbados, has compiled this section to give an idea of variety of the aquatic activities that can be enjoyed in the region.

Scuba Diving in the Caribbean
Martha Watkins Gilkes, a freelance diving journalist based in Antigua, outlines the best dive sites with general advice for divers.

Walking in the Caribbean
Written by Mark Wilson.

Responsible Tourism and Flora and Fauna
These two sections have been contributed by Mark Eckstein of David Bellamy Associates, Durham, UK.

Island Sections
Information is set out island by island in a constant sequence as follows:

- ❏ List of contents
- ❏ Description of geography and details on the people
- ❏ History
- ❏ Government
- ❏ The Economy
- ❏ Culture
- ❏ Flora and Fauna
- ❏ Marine Life and Diving
- ❏ Beaches and Watersports
- ❏ Other Sports
- ❏ Festivals
- ❏ Excursions

In smaller islands the capital is usually treated as an excursion. In larger islands, the capital and other major towns and districts are treated as separate sections, each with its own description, excursions and local information. **Local Information** sections include accommodation, where to eat, transport and other services.

In cases where a group of islands constitute a chapter, separate islands may have an **Island Information** section which will contain much the same details as the local information sections just mentioned.

Information for Visitors concludes each chapter. This section comprises how to get there, what documents are necessary, clothing, food, which is the best time to visit, currency regulations and other essential information. Where accommodation and restaurants have not been covered in the descriptive part, they will appear in Information for Visitors.

All those who have assisted in the preparation of chapters are listed with our thanks at the end.

Map Symbols

Roads	————	Capital Cities	■SANTIAGO
Railways	+++++++++	Cities/Towns	●córdoba
Trails/Paths/Tracks	– – – –	Archaeological sites	▲
Rivers	RÍO ARUÑA	Mountains	⌂
Ferries	. . . .	Streets	SAN MARTÍN
Waterfall	⫶⫶	Parks	
Barrier Reef	～～～	Train station	T
Borders		Bus Station	B
Country Subdivisions	/////	Airport	✕
Metropolitan areas	▨	Key Numbers	6
Major Highway	═══		

Maps
Each island chapter is accompanied by maps of the relevant islands and of the major towns.

Prices
A wide cross section of hotel rates and transport costs is listed in each chapter. Prices are either given in US dollars, or the local currency, whichever is appropriate. (A list of exchange rates is given in the book.) Unless otherwise stated, hotel prices quoted are for a double room in high season; rates are subject to change without notice and therefore those given in this book should only be taken as representative. High season is normally referred to as "winter", running from roughly mid-December to mid-April. "Summer" is low season, the remainder of the year.

Certain abbreviations are used in relation to hotel prices. These are:
  EP—European Plan, room only
  CP—Continental Plan, room and breakfast
  MAP—Modified American Plan, room, breakfast and dinner
  AP—American Plan, room with three daily meals
  FAP—Full American Plan, room and all meals (including afternoon tea, etc).

Other abbreviations used in the text are: pp = per person; d = double; s = single; a/c = air conditioned; Tel: = telephone.

In addition to those thanked at the end of each chapter, we should like to express our gratitude to the following who have given us advice and assistance in the preparation of this volume: John Alton (Weider Travel, London WC2), Frank Bellamy and the staff at Transatlantic Wings (London W8), Rod Prince and Trevor Petch (*Caribbean Insight*).

We should also like to thank the following travellers who wrote to us about their experiences in the Caribbean: J P F M van Aalst (Utrecht), Ian Alexander (Madrid), Tim Armstrong (Rochester, Kent), Simon Bailey (Derby), Harrie Balthussen (The Netherlands), Georg Bannat (Berlin 44), John Beattie (Chester), Vanessa M Bennett-Dixon (Montserrat), Phillip Bishop and Caroline Harman (Belmont, Australia), Gerhard Borchert (Wolfsburg, Germany), Brigitte Braatz (Munich 70), Julia Cairns (Dominica), Andrew Clarke (Bucaramanga), Nan M Cobbey (New York), Graham R Cox (Port Pirie, South Australia), G M Devlin (Burton-on-Trent), Kees-Jan Donkers (Amsterdam), Jackson Elizondo (Caracas), Kit Faith (Jamaica), Cathy Farnworth (London N16), Ingrid Finsterer (Moosthenning, Germany), Louise Fletcher (Providenciales), Evert N Fowle (Southport, ME), Rosalie Fox and Lawrence Wolofsky (Ottawa, Ontario), Nadia Fusager (Frederiksberg, Denmark), Marie Gomez and Tomas Roztocil (Geneva), Paul and Peggy Grebstad (Port Orchard, WA), D W and J M Guiver (Lymington, Hants), Marcel W Gut (Niederhasli, Switzerland), A Halbach (Geneva), Bronwyn Hanna and Gary Williams (Bondi Junction, Australia), Gill Harrison (Barbados), Eva Hauge and Helen de Bellis (Oslo, Norway), Bengt Hellstrom and Elisabet Andersson (Gothenburg, Sweden), Bernadette van Houten (Amsterdam), Andrew Humphreys (Upholland, Lancashire), Catarina Johansson (Göteborg, Sweden), Barrie M Jones (Hawthorn, Victoria, Australia), Fiona and Christian Jurtan (Berlin 31), V A Kerns (Williamsburg, VA), John W Kirpestein (Geldermalsen, Netherlands), Gordon Koizumi (Batavia, IL), Werner Kroer (Vienna), Pierre Lavanchy (Lutry, Switzerland),

Dave and Linda Mallard (Bristol 14), Kathryn E Nairne (West Vancouver), Dr Robert G Neville (Oxford, UK), Amoy Ong (Toronto) Anthony Overman (Montserrat), Mark Pafko (Minneapolis), Jenny Paltney (Southampton), John Raspey (Montevideo), Lo Reizevoort (Deventer, Netherlands), Jacquie Ruan (Sandy Ground, Anguilla), Toru Sasaki (Kainan City, Wakayama, Japan), Alexander von Schuckmann (Caracas), Sabine Schmitt (Bonn, Germany), Claudia Schaerer (Castries, St Lucia), Dr André Siraa (Panama City), Inger Lyhne Sorensen (Herlev, Denmark), Pat Stocker (London NW10), Birgit Stürzl (Basel, Switzerland), David Tither (Washington, DC), Leigh Turner (London), Bela and Susan Vastag (Salt Lake City), Pia Vinther (Denmark), Patrick Warner (Hadley, MA), Wolfgang von Wartburg (Rosenheim), Barbara and Paul Watson (London SW12), C Weems (New York City), Marlies Wilmsen and Hans-Peter Gemmel (Worms), Haltom Wray (New York), David and Helene Zagier (Montreux), Peter-Paul Zahl (Long Bay, Jamaica), Mag Martin Zausner and Dr Waltraud Zausner (Vienna).

Introduction and Hints

Travel to and in the Caribbean

By Air All the main airlines flying to each island are given in the Information for Visitors sections. In addition to the scheduled flights listed, there are a great many charter flights from Europe and North America. For details on both types of service, you are advised to consult a good travel agent. An agent will also be able to tell you if you qualify for any student or senior citizen discount on offer.

The most extensive links between islands are by air, either with the scheduled flights on the regional and international carriers (again given in the text), or by chartered plane. If you are in a group, or family, the latter option may not cost very much more than a scheduled flight. It often has the advantage of linking the charter direct to your incoming or homeward flight.

The regional carriers with most routes in the Caribbean are Liat (co-owned by 11 Caribbean states, with its headquarters in Antigua) and BWIA (based in Trinidad). Each offers air passes. Liat's are called Explorer tickets: the Liat Explorer costs US$169 basic, US$199 peak (1 July—31 August, 15 December—31 January), valid for 21 days, maximum 3 stops between San Juan, Puerto Rico and Trinidad; the Liat Super Explorer costs US$357 for a 30-day ticket, allowing unlimited stop overs in 25 destinations between San Juan and Caracas (do not overload your itinerary, a lot of time can be spent waiting at airports for flights). The Super Explorer should be bought in the West Indies, but Transatlantic Wings (see below) are permitted to sell it. Notice, though, that Liat distance tickets (for example between Grenada and San Juan) permit intermediate stop overs and may well work out cheaper than an Explorer pass. Liat operates an airpass in which each flight costs US$55 midweek (Monday-Thursday), US$65 at weekends, valid for 21 days; minimum 3 stop overs, maximum 6. These tickets may only be purchased in conjunction with an international flight to a Caribbean gateway, the itinerary must be settled in advance, with no changes permitted, and the fares must be paid for in Europe (including the UK and Eire). Travellers from the UK should note that Liat is represented in the UK by British Airways, but it is best to go to Transatlantic Wings, 70 Pembroke Road, London W8 6NX, Tel: 071-602 4021, Fax: 071-603 6101, who have experience in arranging Liat flights. Liat has no representation in Europe outside the UK, so here again Transatlantic Wings in London should be contacted for details. In the USA, contact a specialist travel agent. Liat's telephone number on Antigua is (809) 462 0700, or 462 2682 for Fax. For those who fly regularly within the Caribbean, Liat runs a frequent flyer club, organized in Antigua.

BWIA's intra-Caribbean unlimited mileage fare is US$356; no destination may be visited more than once, except for making a connection and the entire journey must be fixed at the time of payment (changes are subject to a US$20 surcharge). This airpass is valid for 30 days and is not valid on flights to or from Georgetown. No refunds are given for unused sectors.

Airlines will only allow a certain weight of luggage without a surcharge; this is normally 30 kg for first class and 20 kg for business and economy classes, but these limits may not be strictly enforced if it is known that the plane is not going to be full. On the other hand, weight limits for inter-island flights are often lower; it is best to enquire beforehand.

Note that departure tax is payable on leaving every island; make sure you know what this is in advance so that you do not get caught out.

In Switzerland, Globetrotter Travel Service, Rennweg, 8001 Zürich, has been recommended for arranging cheap flights to the region. At certain times of the year, Air France and Aéromaritime have flights at very advantageous prices from several southern French cities and Paris to Guadeloupe and Martinique; travellers from France, Switzerland and southern Germany should be able to use them. Air France flights can also be combined with Liat air passes. From the USA, Puerto Rico and Antigua are the only island to which student fares are available; it is worth checking these out since it may be cheaper to take a student flight then continue to your destination rather than flying direct to the island of your choice (contact CIEE in the USA). For those over 65, Delta Airlines sells a Senior Citizen Young at Heart booklet of four coupons for US$472, each one good for a one-way ticket for a domestic flight on Delta between any US cities (except in Alaska or Hawaii) including San Juan, Puerto Rico. You can carry on from there on another airline.

By Sea The most popular way of visiting the Caribbean by ship is on a cruise liner, as the figures given in the Economy sections below attest. A travel agent will advise on this mode of transport. For cargo ships which carry passengers, it is best to enquire in your own country. In general it is very difficult to secure a passage on a cargo ship from Europe to the Caribbean without making full arrangements in advance.

The Geest Line runs a weekly cargo/passenger service from Barry, South Wales, to the Windwards and Leewards. There are weekly sailings to St Lucia and St Vincent, fortnightly to Barbados, Trinidad, Dominica, Grenada, Antigua and St Kitts. A return fare from the UK depends on which island you are going to and what standard of accommodation you choose, but prices range from £2,480 to £2,860 per person. Geest Line will also take packages; speak to the freight clerk at the agent's office. Geest's head office is at PO Box 20, Barry, South Glamorgan, CF6 8XE, Tel: 0446 700333, Fax: 0446 700623 (may be moving to Southampton early in 1993).

MV *Author* and MV *Adviser* of the Harrison Line makes a 7-week round trip from Liverpool, returning to Felixstowe, calling at the following ports: Ponce (Puerto Rico), La Guaira and Puerto Cabello (Venezuela), Bridgetown, Port of Spain, Willemstad, Oranjestad, Río Haina (Dominican Republic), Port-au-Prince, Kingston, Belize, Santo Tomás de Castilla (Guatemala), Puerto Cortés (Honduras), Puerto Limón (Costa Rica), then returning through Kingston, Río Haina and Ponce. The voyage costs approximately £65 per day, full board, or £3,127 per person in a double cabin, £3,180 in a single cabin, £3,445 in a suite, for the entire trip. In all, six passengers can be accommodated. Preference is given to those buying round trips; one-way passages are impossible to buy for autumn and winter months but may be available in (European) summer. Full details are available from Weider Travel, Charing Cross Shopping Concourse, The Strand, London WC2N 4HZ, Tel: 071-836-6363, Fax: 071-497 0078.

Weider Travel can also advise on the Compagnie Générale Maritime's 4 sailings a month from Dunkerque or Le Havre to Fort-de-France and

Pointe-à-Pitre, 21-25 days voyage (£650 one way with wine at dinner and lunch, good cuisine, greater availability of one-way tickets).

For those with 1,000 miles offshore sailing experience, a cheap way to get to the Caribbean is crewing on a yacht being delivered from Europe or the USA to the region; seek information from Compass Yacht Services (Alan Toone, Director), Holly Cottage, Heathley End, Chislehurst, Kent, BR7 6AB, Tel: 081-467 2450, UK.

Island-hopping by boats with scheduled services is fairly limited. Boat services are more common between dependent islands, eg St Vincent and the Grenadines, Trinidad and Tobago, Belize City and Caye Caulker. Again, full details are given in the relevant sections below. In 1992 Windward Lines Limited began a weekly passenger and cargo ferry service: Trinidad-Venezuela-Trinidad-St Vincent-Barbados-St Lucia-Barbados-St Vincent-Trinidad. For information and tickets contact United Caribbean Shipping Agency, Suite 106, Furness Building, 86B Independence Square, Port of Spain, Trinidad, Tel: 625 6328, Fax: 624 6865.

Irregular passenger services on cargo boats (with basic accommodation, usually a hammock on deck, no meals supplied), schooners, crewing or hitching on yachts can only be discovered by asking around when you are in port. Crewing on yachts is not difficult in winter (in the hurricane season yachtsmen stay away). If you are looking for a job on a yacht, or trying to hitch a ride, it will be easier to make contact if you are living at the yacht harbour. Boat owners often advertise bunks for rent, which is a very cheap form of accommodation (US$10-30); ask around, or look on the bulletin boards. If arriving by sea, make sure you are aware of the island's entry requirements before setting out.

Travel on Land Buses are cheap, but services tend not to be very convenient, in the sense that they often involve a night away from the point of departure, even on small islands. This is because buses start in outlying towns in the early morning and return from the capital in the afternoon. Another limiting factor to public transport is a shortage of funds for spare parts, so buses may be scarce and crowded.

Taxis are plentiful, but generally not cheap. Some islands, eg Trinidad, have route taxis, which are inexpensive and travel only on set routes. On many islands, taxi fares are set by the tourist office or government.

Renting a car gives the greatest flexibility, but is also hardest on the pocket. You can expect to pay more than in the USA or Europe. A number of islands require drivers to take out a temporary, or visitor driver's licence (these are mentioned in the text), but some places will not issue a licence to those over 70 years of age without a medical certificate. In small places, to rent a motorcycle, scooter or bicycle is a good idea.

Finances
The Caribbean is not a cheap area to visit. Transport is expensive (unless you are staying in one place and using only buses), but if you book your flights in advance, taking advantage of whatever air pass or stopovers are suitable, that expenditure at least will be out of the way.

Accommodation is generally expensive, too, even at the lower end of the market. There is no shortage of luxury resorts and beach hotels throughout the price range. In a number of instances you can book all-inclusive packages which are often good value and let you know in advance almost exactly what your expenditure will be. However, you will not see much of your chosen island outside your enclave. To find cheaper accommodation you need mobility, probably a hired car. One option is renting a self-catering apartment, villa or house, the range of which is also vast, and here the advantage is that a group of people can share the cost (this is not an economical prospect for single travellers).

Since, on a number of islands, resort-type hotels form the majority, turning up at a cheaper place may not always yield a room because competition is great. The term guest house is usually applied to places at the lower end of the market; they tend, but by no means in all cases, to be basic. Note also that, if booking ahead, tourist office lists may not include the cheapest establishments, so you may have to reserve a dearer room, then look around. This is probably what you will have to do in any event, time permitting, to find the best value. In the main, tourist offices publish accurate, up-to-date lists of accommodation, which are a great help for making preliminary bookings. Remember that in Cuba particular rules apply and that the Dominican Republic has the most hotel rooms in the Caribbean, so there is no real problem in finding a space there; see each island section for details. Some islands, such as the French Antilles, have well-organized camp sites, but on many camping is actually prohibited, eg Antigua.

The following tips on economizing were sent by Steve Wilson and Debra Holton of San Francisco: even if not travelling with a tent, take a cooking stove and prepare your own food; much cheaper than eating in restaurants. Look out for bunk rentals on boats (see above). "Happy Hours" in bars often have free food, couples sharing costs can often take advantage of "Ladies' Night" in a bar or nightclub, which either permits free entry or cheap drinks.

High and Low Season
High season in the Caribbean is usually called "winter"; in other words it comes in the Northern Hemisphere's colder months. Dates vary a little but the season is roughly from mid-December to mid-April. At this time air fares, room rates and other costs rise. In addition, air fares are also increased at European and US holiday times, ie July, August and September if flying from the UK, July and August from the USA, etc. Flights to the Caribbean from the UK are at a premium in the pre-Christmas period.

Money
In general, the US dollar is the best currency to take, in cash or travellers' cheques. The latter are the most convenient and, if you follow the issuer's instructions, can be replaced if lost or stolen. On the most frequently-visited holiday islands, eurocurrencies can be exchanged without difficulty but US dollars are preferred. In some places, the US dollar is accepted alongside local currency (but make sure in which currency prices are being quoted). In others, eg Jamaica, only the local currency is accepted. Credit cards are widely used. Remember to keep your money, credit cards, etc, safely on your person, or in a hotel safe.

A list of currencies and exchange rates is provided, **see pages 806-807**.

Documents
Individual island entry requirements are given in the relevant chapters under Information for Visitors. North Americans, British and Commonwealth citizens in some cases need only show proof of identity. If intending to visit Puerto Rico or the US Virgin Islands, or making connections through Miami or another US gateway, a visa for the United States will not be necessary if your home country and the airline on which you are travelling are part of the US Visa Waiver Program. A US consulate will supply all relevant details. An onward ticket is a common prerequisite for entry. Australians and New Zealanders should note that many islands impose strict entry laws on holders

of the above passports. Satisfying visa and other requirements, if not done at home, can take at least a day, usually involve expense, and passport photographs will be needed: be prepared.

On all forms, refer to yourself as a "visitor" rather than a "tourist".

You should always carry your passport in a safe place about your person, or if not going far, leave it in the hotel safe. If staying in a place for several weeks, it is worth while registering at your Embassy or Consulate. Then, if your passport is stolen or lost, the process of replacing it is simplified and speeded up. Keeping photocopies of essential documents, and some additional passport-sized photographs, is recommended.

Travel in the Eastern Caribbean

Certain conditions are common to the former British colonies, or still British dependencies, in the Leewards and Windwards, including Barbados. At immigration on arrival, say you want to stay longer than planned because getting an extension is time-consuming and difficult. If asked where you are staying and you have not booked in advance, say any hotel (they do not usually check), but do not say you are going to camp and do not say that you are going to arrange accommodation later. Do not imagine that you can go to the Eastern Caribbean to work. Make sure that you have a ticket home: in Barbados, Trinidad, St Lucia and Dominica, the immigration laws state that visitors will not be allowed to enter without a ticket back to the home country shown on the passport. Tickets to other countries will not suffice. This becomes a problem if you are not going home for 12 months since airline tickets become void after a year. Some airlines sell tickets on the 6-12 month extended payment plan; these can be credited when you have left the islands with restrictive entry requirements.

In this part of the Caribbean, including the French islands, it is difficult to buy single tickets between islands because of the entry requirements mentioned above. This is a problem if you enter the region on a one-way ticket, intending to continue to South America and fly home from there, buying the tickets en route. You may be required to buy at once all the tickets up to the point of departure for home. This would be more expensive than buying all flight tickets at home so, even if you propose to take some boat trips between islands, we recommend that you purchase flights in advance and refund those that have not been used later.

Telephones
Many airport lounges and phone companies in the region have AT&T's "USA Direct" phones by which the USA and Canada may be called using a charge card (which bills your home phone account), or by calling collect. The service is not available to Europe. Public card phones have been introduced by Cable and Wireless on those islands where it operates. Phone cards usually come in several denominations, with a tax added on, and can be useful for local and international calls, particularly as you then avoid the extra charges made by hotels on phone calls.

Language
In the majority of cases, English is widely spoken and understood (although non-native speakers of English may have difficulty understanding some of the local dialects). In the French Antilles and Haiti, French is the main language. However, in these last, and on English islands which at one time belonged to France, Créole is spoken. On English islands the population is bilingual, so the English-speaking traveller will have no problems with communication. On the French islands, knowledge of French is of great benefit (in the French Antilles English and Spanish speakers may find assistance from the Commonwealth of Dominica and Dominican Republic citizens who work on the islands). The Netherlands Antilles speak Dutch, English and Papiamento. English and Spanish are both spoken on Puerto Rico and the Bay Islands. The principal language in the Dominican Republic, Cuba, the Mexican and Venezuelan islands is Spanish. If visiting non-English islands, a basic knowledge of the main language is a great advantage.

Sport
Information on sport is given under each island, but for those visiting the former British colonies, British dependencies and even the US Virgin Islands, an understanding of cricket is an advantage. It is more than a national game, having become a symbol of achievement and a unifying factor (baseball and basketball serve much the same function in Puerto Rico). Spectating at a match is entertaining both for the cricket itself and for the conversation that arises.

Further Reading
A number of books are suggested for further reading, these will be found in the Culture, Tourist Information and other sections. Similarly, maps that may be consulted are indicated. With regard to maps, for the British and ex-British islands the Directorate of Overseas Surveys in the UK (now merged with the Ordnance Survey, Southampton) has prepared, and sells, a wide selection at 1:25,000 or 1:50,000 scale. Similarly, the French Institut Géographique National publishes good maps of Martinique and Guadeloupe/St-Martin/St-Barthélémy.

By no means all the writers of history, fiction, poetry and other topics will be found below. There is no room to talk of the many authors who have

been inspired by aspects of the Caribbean for their fiction, eg Robert Louis Stevenson, Graham Greene, Ernest Hemingway, Gabriel García Márquez. Nor have the travellers been mentioned: Patrick Leigh Fermor, *The Traveller's Tree*, Quentin Crewe, *Touch the Happy Isles*, Trollope, *Travels in the West Indies and the Spanish Main*, Alec Waugh, *The Sugar Isles*, James Pope-Hennessy, among others. Of the histories of the region, *A Short History of The West Indies*, by J H Parry, P M Sherlock and Anthony Maingot (Macmillan, 1987) is very accessible; also *From Columbus to Castro: The History of the Caribbean 1492-1969*, Eric Williams (Harper and Row, 1970). For an introduction to the geography of the Caribbean, Mark Wilson's *The Caribbean Environment* (Oxford University Press, 1989), prepared for the Caribbean Examinations Council, is a fascinating text book (Wilson is preparing a book for the Latin American Bureau on Tourism in the Caribbean, due for publication in 1992). Another introductory book is *Far from Paradise, An Introduction to Caribbean Development*, by James Ferguson (Latin American Bureau, 1990). A recent economic study is *The Poor and the Powerless, Economic Policy and Change in the Caribbean*, by Clive Y Thomas (Latin American Bureau, 1988).

The work of a great many English-speaking poets is collected in *The Penguin Book of Caribbean Verse in English*, edited by Paula Burnett (1986); see also *Hinterland: Caribbean Poetry From the West Indies and Britain*, edited by E A Markham (Bloodaxe, 1990). For a French verse anthology, see *La Poésie Antillaise*, collected by Maryse Condé (Fernand Nathan, 1977). There are a number of prose anthologies of stories in English, eg *Stories from the Caribbean*, introduced by Andrew Salkey (Paul Elek, 1972), or *West Indian Narrative: an Introductory Anthology*, by Kenneth Ramchand (Nelson, 1966). *The Story of English*, by Robert McCrumb, William Cran and Robert MacNeil (Faber and Faber/BBC, 1986) has an interesting section on the development of the English language in the Caribbean. The Commonwealth Institute in London publishes useful checklists on Caribbean writing: No 4 on literature, 1986; No 6 on general topics, 1987, both compiled by Roger Hughes.

FT Caribbean publishes *The Caribbean Handbook*, a business and reference guide, with a useful bibliography on all Caribbean topics, and the inflight magazines of BWIA International (*BWIA Sunjet*) and Liat (*Liat Islander*). FT Caribbean also publishes *The Antiguan Visitors Guide* and *The Official St Kitts and Nevis Tourist Guide* (FT Caribbean, Head Office, PO Box 1037, St John's, Antigua, or 3A Sloane Avenue, London SW3 3JD). A rival to *The Caribbean Handbook* is *The Caribbean Business Directory* and *Caribbean Yellow Pages Telephone Directory* (Antigua: Caribbean Publishing Cos, 2 vols), a good source of current information on telephone and fax numbers, key companies, economic statistics, business and government information. The *Business Directory* contains a section on each island in the Caribbean, plus Florida, North America and selected South American countries; the *Yellow Pages* volume is a listing of telephone and fax numbers for companies. *Caribbean Insight*, published monthly in London by the West India Committee in association with Caribbean Publishing Company (Tel: 071 976 1493, Fax: 071 976 1541) is an informative newsletter covering the entire region and Central America.

Finally, a generally excellent series of Caribbean books is published by Macmillan Caribbean; this includes island guides, natural histories, books on food and drink, sports and pirates, and wall maps (for a full catalogue, write to Macmillan Caribbean, Houndmills, Basingstoke, Hampshire, RG21 2XS, England).

This list is not exhaustive, concentrating mainly on books in English, published (or readily available) in the UK. For any favourites omitted, we apologize.

Miami

Journeys to (and between) the Caribbean Islands often involve a change of planes in Miami. A five hour transfer in the middle of a tiring journey may seem like a daunting prospect, but Miami airport is surprisingly user-friendly and there is quite a lot to do in the city if you have a longer stopover.

The airport is rather like a big, horseshoe-shaped suburban shopping mall. The upper level has shops and airline check-in counters; the lower level has other services like car rentals and baggage claim. The airport is divided into a series of concourses labelled B to H.

On Arrival
Immigration queues are long, and can take 30-50 minutes. Heavy hand luggage is more of a nuisance than at most airports, both in the queues and because of the long walk up and down the fingers which lead to the planes. Customs is crowded, but the queue moves faster.

Passengers arriving from the Bahamas pre-clear in Nassau, which saves time. Pre-clearance is also possible in Aruba. From London, Delta Airlines arrange pre-clearance for immigration and customs.

Baggage There are baggage carts in customs, but these must be left behind when you have been cleared. From this point on there are *skycaps* (tip around US$1-2 per large bag). Skycaps can also be called from the *paging phones* which are thick on the ground in the concourses and entrances.

There are luggage lockers at all entrances to the airport and at various other points. They cost US$1 in quarters (25 cents - look for change machines, or ask information counters). After 24 hours, bags are taken to a storage facility next to the *lost and found* office in concourse E. The charge for storage here is US$2 per day.

For very large items there is a left luggage office (baggage service office) on the lower level of concourse G and on the second level of concourse B. Charges are US$2-6 per day, depending on the size of the item.

Filling In Time
The concourses are chocabloc with snackbars, duty free shops, and gift shops selling overpriced garbage. **Note** A 6% sales tax is added to the marked price. Watch out if you are fine-tuning your US currency before departure. The best place to pass the time and relax is probably the *Hotel MIA*, in the middle of the horseshoe on concourse E. The Lobby Lounge, open 1000-0100, is on the same floor as flight check in. The upper floors have a sundeck (free), an open air swimming pool, gym and sauna area (US$5 per day), racquetball courts (US$8 per hour), snackbar, lounge bar (the happy hour, 1700-1900, has drinks on special and complimentary snacks). There is also the *Top of The Port* restaurant, with pleasant surroundings and much better food than on the concourses (open 0700-2300; full breakfast US$7.75, lunch specials from US$8, dinner specials from US$15). The hotel has special day rates between 0800 and 1800.

Information There are very helpful information counters in concourse E and just outside customs. They can also be contacted from any paging phone. (Counters open 0630-2230; paging phone service 24 hours.) They will advise on ground transport, airport services, and the Miami area generally.

Nursery Mainly for changing or feeding babies, on concourse E. If locked, the information office in this concourse has a key.

Banking Barnett Bank on concourse C, Monday to Friday 0900-1600, Saturday 0900-1200. Visa and Mastercard cash advances (US$25 minimum, US$2,000 maximum) on production of passport and one other piece of identification. 24-hour cashpoint on concourse outside the bank. Several foreign exchange counters, including a 24-hour one on concourse E.

Service Centre between concourses B and C has stamp machines, credit card phones, TDD phone for deaf or mute passengers, and another cashpoint.

Post Office Leave the building at the lower level of concourse B and walk a couple of metres along the airport road. Open Monday to Friday 0830-2100 and 0930-1330 on Saturday. Also sells bubble packing, padded envelopes, mailing tubes for posters etc. Express mail service in the post office is open 24 hours.

Leaving The Airport
If you want to venture into the real world, you can use:

Rental Cars This works out at around US$30 per day for a small car. Many companies have offices on the lower level concourses. It can take an hour or more to book a car, take the company bus to its main office, fill out all the forms, and pick up a car. Leaving the car can take just as long. The information counters have a full list of companies. Some car hire firms may offer lower rates to passengers booking in advance through a Caribbean travel agent, or flying with certain airlines. Check in advance.

Buses Miami has a good bus service. Fare is US$1.25, with US$0.25 for a transfer to another route. Buses stop outside concourse E. Route 37 runs north-south every 30 minutes in the day, every hour late evenings and weekends; Route 42 also runs north-south, every hour. Route J runs every 20-30 minutes or every hour on Sundays to Miami Beach; Route 7 runs every 20-40 minutes. Eastbound buses go downtown, westbound buses go to the Mall of the Americas and the International Mall, two big shopping complexes.

Routes J and 42 connect with the *Greyhound* bus terminal at Coral Gables.

Metrorail All of the airport bus routes connect with stations on the Metrorail line. This gives a quick service every 15 minutes from 0600 to 2400 between downtown Miami and many suburban areas.

Metromover Metrorail tickets give a free connection to Metromover, a 1.9 mile (3 km) elevated track which whizzes round downtown Miami. The connection is at Government Center station.

Tri-Rail is another rail system which connects Miami and points north. The full journey to West Palm Beach takes 1 hour 39 minutes. Connecting buses leave from outside concourse E; it is a five-minute ride to the station. Departures at 0500, 0600, 0700, 0745, 1200, 1530, 1632, 1730, 1830, 1930.

Supershuttle is a minibus running to and from the airport. You can book ahead to be picked up from a hotel or private house. The fare is US$7 for downtown, US$8 for south Miami Beach, US$13 to Fort Lauderdale airport.

Taxis are more expensive. Approximate fares are US$13 for downtown, US$18 for Miami Beach, US$42 to south Fort Lauderdale.

Hotels Rooms at the *Miami International Airport Hotel (MIA)* in the airport start at US$159 plus 12.5% tax for a double, US$104 s corporate rate. Rooms quite small but double glazing keeps out aircraft noise, very impersonal, Tel: 1-800-327-1276 from within the USA, or 305-871-4100 from elsewhere. Fax: 305-871-0800. Information has a good listing of downtown hotels, starting from the cheapest (*Bayman International*, Flagler Street, Tel: 266-5098 and *Miami Springs Hotel*, 661 E Drive, Tel: 888-8421) and ending with the most expensive (*Miami Airport Hilton*, 5101 Blue Lagoon Drive, Tel: 262-1000, and *Marriott Hotel*, 1202 NW LeJeune Road, Tel: 649-5000).

Information also has a separate listing of Miami Beach hotels (alphabetical, not by price). Best value in Miami Beach is the *Clay Hotel*, 1438 Washington Avenue, which has a youth hostel attached. Single rooms are US$17, hostel accommodation is less, Tel: 305-534-2988, Fax: 305-673-0346. *Clay Hotel* has young and friendly staff and caters for many young European tourists. There are direct free phone lines to several hotels next to the baggage check in on lower level concourse F.

There are also reservations services which will make reservations for you. Try CRS (Toll free 1-800-683-3311), Express Reservation (Toll free 1-800-627-1356), or Room with a View (305-433-4343).

Shopping For bargains, try Flagler Street in downtown Miami, it's crowded and full of action. The suburban malls are more expensive and more relaxed: Mall of the Americas and International Mall are easiest to reach by bus.

Things To See In Miami
This guide is not the place for a full listing. The airport information office has a useful booklet, *Destination Miami*, which gives details of a wide range of cultural events.

Miami is about the nearest that the continental USA gets to a tropical environment. Many attractions are designed for visitors from the north. The Monkey Jungle, Orchid Jungle, Parrot Jungle, etc may not be that exciting if you have just seen the real thing. With half a day to spare, however, you should be able to visit any of these, or the Metrozoo, or the Seaquarium. Museums include Vizcaya, a Renaissance-style villa with formal gardens, and the Spanish Monastery in North Miami Beach, brought to America in pieces by William Randolph Hearst from Segovia in Spain, where it was first built in 1141. That, in a way, makes it the oldest building in the USA.

Miami Beach is probably the best place for a short stay. There are plenty of interesting Art Deco buildings, with restaurants and cafes along the sea front. Shops, hotels, nightclubs, etc are all within walking distance. Moreover, you can walk around at night without getting mugged. It also has the Bass Museum, with a good collection of European paintings.

If you have a full day in Miami, there would be time to rent a car and drive to the *Everglades National Park*, a huge freshwater swamp with interesting wildlife and an excellent network of interpretative centres and nature trails. The nearer Florida Keys would be an alternative, but are probably not so exciting if you have just been in the Caribbean.

Caribbean Festivals at a Glance

	Page	Jan	Feb	Mar	Easter	Apr	May	Jun	Jul	Aug	Sept	Oct	Nov	Dec
Aruba	707	F	C	F				F,M		C,R			S,A	
Anguilla	396				R	R								
Antigua	362								C					
Bahamas	68							C	F			F		C
Barbados	567		F						F	F		F	M	
Bermuda	62	M	M	M	F				F			M		
Bay Islands (Honduras)	745				F									
Belize Cays	758			F							F			
Bonaire	675		C	R				F			F	R/F		
British Virgin Islands	342			R	F				F			F		
Carriacou	554		C		F			F,A		R		R/F		
Cayman Islands	164				F	C						R/F		
Corn Islands (Nicaragua)	727	F			F									
Cuba	121		C				F		C			F	M	
Curaçao	690		C		F				F			M		
Dominica	489		C									F		
Dominican Republic	257	A	C		R			A	M	C,F			F	
Grenada	549		F					F	F					
Guadeloupe	444		C			C						F		
Guyana	630		F											
Haiti	233	F			F									
Isla de Margarita	658		C											
Jamaica	176					C				E,M	A			
Martinique	468		C		F				F		F		F	
Montserrat	406													C
Nevis	378				F			F	C					C

	Page	Jan	Feb	Mar	Easter	Apr	May	Jun	Jul	Aug	Sept	Oct	Nov	Dec
Providencia	736							C						
Puerto Rico	292							F	F		F			
Saba	418													F
San Andrés	736						M		C				F	
San Blas Islands (Panama)	719		C											
Sint Maarten	429					C,F						F		
St Eustatius	424		R						C				F	
St Kitts	378							F					F	
St Lucia	505		C,F				R		F	F				C,F
St Vincent	526							C			R		F	
Bequia	530				R									
Union Island	533				S									
St-Barthélémy	460		C					F	F			F	F	
St-Martin	455		R,C					F	F	F		F		
Tobago	596		C,A						M	R	M	F		
Trinidad	596		C,F		F				F	F	F			
Turks & Caicos: Grand Turk	209								A					
: Providenciales	218								C,R					
: South Caicos	213						R							
USVI: St Thomas	324								C					
: St John	329					C								
: St Croix	335		F											F
Yucatán/Mexican Islands	781													
Isla Mujeres	786		C											F

Health Information

The following information has been very kindly compiled for us by Dr David Snashall, who is presently Senior Lecturer in Occupational Health at St Thomas's Hospital Medical School in London and Chief Medical Advisor of the British Foreign and Commonwealth Office. He has travelled extensively in Central and South America, worked in Peru and in East Africa and keeps in close touch with developments in preventative and tropical medicine. The publishers have every confidence that the following information is correct, but cannot assume any direct responsibility in this connection.

The traveller to the Caribbean is inevitably exposed to health risks not encountered in North America or Western Europe. Most of the islands have a tropical climate but this does not mean that tropical diseases as such are an enormous problem or even the main problem for visitors. The problems of infectious disease still predominate in most of the islands, but vary in severity between town and rural areas and from island to island depending on the state of economic development and the attention paid to public health. Thus there are few hard and fast rules. You will often have to make your own judgements on the healthiness or otherwise of your surroundings.

Language is not on the whole a problem and throughout the islands there are well-qualified doctors who speak good English. Medical practises vary from those you may be used to, but there is likely to be better experience at dealing with locally occurring disease.

A certain amount of self medication may be necessary and you will find that many of the drugs available have familiar names. However, always check the date stamping and buy from reputable pharmacies because the shelf life of some items, especially vaccines and antibiotics, is markedly reduced in tropical conditions.

With the following precautions and advice you should keep as healthy as usual. Make local enquiries about health risks if you are apprehensive and take the general advice of European and North American families who have lived or are living in the country.

Before You Go
Take out medical insurance. You should have a dental check-up, obtain a spare glasses prescription and if you suffer from a chronic disease such as diabetes, high blood pressure, cardio-pulmonary disease, or a nervous disorder, arrange for a check-up with your doctor who can at the same time provide you with a letter explaining details of your disability. Check the current practice for malaria prophylaxis (prevention) if you are going to the Dominican Republic or Haiti.

Inoculations
Smallpox vaccination is no longer required. Neither is yellow fever vaccination unless you are going to or are coming from South America. As of mid-1992 the cholera epidemic in South and Central America had not spread to any of the Caribbean islands but they were all on the alert for the

possibility. Although cholera vaccination is largely ineffective, immigration officers may ask for proof of such vaccination if coming from a country where the epidemic is rife. The following vaccinations are recommended: Typhoid (monovalent): one dose, followed by a booster in one month's time (an oral preparation may be recommended). Immunity from this course lasts two to three years. Poliomyelitis: this is a live vaccine generally given orally and a full course consists of three doses with a booster in tropical regions, every three to five years. Tetanus: one dose should be given with a booster at six weeks and another at six months and ten yearly boosters thereafter are recommended. Children should in addition be properly protected against diphtheria, against whooping cough, mumps and measles. Teenage girls, if they have not had the disease, should be given Rubella (german measles) vaccination. Consult your doctor for advice on tuberculosis inoculation; the disease is still present in the British Virgin Islands, Grenada, Guadeloupe, Haiti, and Martinique.

Infectious Hepatitis (Jaundice) is of some concern throughout the Caribbean, more so in Cuba, Dominica, Haiti, and Montserrat. It seems to be frequently caught by travellers. The main symptoms are pains in the stomach, lack of appetite, lassitude, and the typical yellow colour of the eyes and skin. Medically speaking there are two different types: the less serious, but more common, is Hepatitis A for which the best protection is the careful preparation of food, the avoidance of contaminated drinking water and scrupulous attention to toilet hygiene. Human normal immunoglobulin (gamma-globulin) confers considerable protection against the disease and is particularly useful in epidemics. It should be obtained from a reputable source and is certainly recommended for travellers who intend to live rough. The injection should be given as close as possible to your departure and, as the dose depends on the likely time you are to spend in infected areas, the manufacturer's instructions should be taken as to dose. At last vaccination against Hepatitis A has been developed and is generally available. Three shots over six months would seem to give excellent protection lasting up to ten years.

The other, more serious, version is Hepatitis B, which is acquired usually from injections with unclean needles, blood transfusion, as a sexually transmitted disease and possibly by insect bites. You may have had jaundice before, or you may have had hepatitis of either type before without becoming jaundiced in which case you may be immune to either Hepatitis A or B. This can be tested for before you travel. If you are not immune to Hepatitis B a vaccine is available (three shots over six months) and if you are not immune to Hepatitis A, then you should consider having gamma-globulin.

AIDS

Aids in the Caribbean is increasing in its prevalence, as in most countries, but is not wholly confined to the well known high risk sections of the population, ie homosexual men, intravenous drug abusers, prostitutes and children of infected mothers. Heterosexual transmission is now the dominant mode and so the main risk to travellers is from casual sex. The same precautions should be taken as when encountering any sexually transmitted disease. The AIDS virus (HIV) can be passed via unsterile needles which have been previously used to inject an HIV positive patient but the risk of this is very small indeed. It would however be sensible to check that needles have been properly sterilized or disposable needles used. Be wary of carrying disposable needles yourself: customs officials find them suspicious. The risk of receiving a blood transfusion with blood infected with the HIV virus is greater than from dirty needles because of the amount of fluid exchanged. Supplies of blood for transfusion should now be screened for HIV in all reputable hospitals so again the risk must be very small indeed. Catching the AIDS virus does not usually produce an illness in itself; the only way to be sure if you feel you have been put at risk is to have a blood test for HIV antibodies on your return to a place where there are reliable laboratory facilities. The test does not become positive for many weeks. Presently the higher risks are probably in Haiti, Dominican Republic, Trinidad, Bahamas and Bermuda.

Common Problems
Heat And Cold Full acclimatization to high temperatures takes about two weeks and during this period it is normal to feel relatively apathetic, especially if the relative humidity is high. Drink plenty of water (up to 15 litres a day are required when working physically hard in the tropics), use salt on your food and avoid extreme exertion. Tepid showers are more cooling than hot or cold ones. Large hats do not cool you down, but prevent sunburn. Remember that, especially in the mountains, there can be a large and sudden drop in temperature between sun and shade and between night and day, so dress accordingly. Loose fitting cotton clothes are still the best for hot weather.

Intestinal Upsets
Most of the time these are due to the insanitary preparation of food so do not eat uncooked fish or vegetables or meat (especially pork), fruit with the skin off (always peel your fruit yourself) or food that is exposed to flies (especially salads.) Tap water may be unsafe outside the major cities especially in the rainy season and the same goes for stream water. Filtered or bottled water is usually available and safe. If your hotel has a central hot water supply this is safe to drink after cooling. Ice for drinks should be made from boiled water but rarely is, so stand your glass on the ice cubes instead of putting them in the drink. Dirty water should first be strained through a filter bag (available from camping shops) and then boiled or treated. Boiling water for five minutes at sea level is sufficient or you can add sterilizing tablets based on Chlorine or Iodine.

Pasteurized or heat-treated milk is now widely available as is ice cream and yoghurt. Unpasteurized milk products including cheese are sources of Tuberculosis, Brucellosis, Listeria and food poisoning germs. You can render fresh milk safe by heating it to 62 degrees centigrade for 30 minutes followed by rapid cooling, or by boiling it. Matured or processed cheeses are safer than fresh varieties.

The most effective treatment for simple diarrhoea is rest and plenty to drink. Seek medical advice if there is no improvement after three days. Much of the exhaustion of traveller's diarrhoea derives from the fact that water and salts are lost from the body and not replaced. This can be done by proprietory preparations of salts which are dissolved in water or simply adding a tablespoonful of sugar and a teaspoonful of salt to a litre of water. If rest is not possible, or stomach cramps are particularly bad then the following drugs may help: Loperamide (Imodium, Janssen or Arret) up to 8 capsules a day—this is now available in the UK without prescription. Diphenoxylate with atropine (Lomotil, Searle) up to 16 tablets in 24 hours—not really recommended unless cramps are really severe and never to be used in children. Codeine Phospate 30 mgs one tablet every 4 hours. Kaolin and Morphine or Paregoric as directed by the pharmacist. Severe vomiting may be calmed by metaclopramide (Maxolon, Beechams Primperan, Berk) 10 mg tablet or injection every eight hours but not more frequently.

The vast majority of cases of diarrhoea and/or vomiting are due to microbial infections of the bowel plus an effect from strange food and drink. They represent no more than a temporary inconvenience which you learn to live with and need no special treatment. Fasting, peculiar diets and the consumption of large quantities of yoghurt have not been found useful in calming traveller's diarrhoea or in rehabilitating inflamed bowels. Oral rehydration (replacement of salt and water) by mouth has, in contrast, been well proven to save the lives of thousands of children with diarrhoea throughout the developing world. There is some evidence that alcohol and milk might prolong diarrhoea so they should probably be avoided during and immediately after an attack. If in addition to cramps and diarrhoea you pass blood in the bowel motion, have severe abdominal pain, fever and feel really terrible you may well have dysentery and a doctor should be consulted at once. If this is not possible the recommended treatment for Bacillary Dysentery is Ciprofloxacin 500 mg every 12 hours, or tetracycline 500 mg every six hours plus replacement of water and salts. If you catch amoebic dysentery which has rather similar symptoms do not try to self-treat but put yourself in proper medical hands. The treatment can be complex and self medication may just damp down the symptons with the risk of serious liver involvement later on. The same goes for infection with the organism called Giardia. Enterovioform (CIBA) and Mexaform give some protection against amoebic dysentery but are useless in the general prevention of diarrhoea and can have serious side-effects if taken for long periods.

Insects
These can be a great nuisance and some of course are carriers of serious diseases such as malaria, dengue fever, filariasis and various worm infections. The best way of keeping mosquitos away at night is to sleep off the ground with a mosquito net and to burn mosquito coils containing Pyrethrum. Aerosol sprays or a "flit" gun may be effective as are insecticidal tablets which are heated on a mat which is plugged into the wall socket (if taking your own, check the voltage of the area you are visiting so that you can take an appliance that will work; similarly check that your electrical adaptor is suitable for the repellent's plug-Ed) The best repellents contain a high concentration of di-ethyl-toluamide. Clothes impregnated with the insecticide Permethrin are now becoming available, as are wide-meshed mosquito nets impregnated with the same substance. They are lighter to carry and less claustrophobic to sleep in.

Liquid is best for arms and face (care around eyes and make sure they don't dissolve the plastic of your spectacles or watch glass), aerosol spray on clothes and ankles deter mites and ticks. Liquid DET suspended in water can be used to impregnate cotton clothes and mosquito nets. If you are bitten, itching may be relieved by baking soda baths, anti-histamine tablets (care with alcohol or driving), corticosteroid creams (great care—never use if any hint of sepsis) or by judicious scratching. Calamine lotion and cream have limited effectiveness and anti-histamine creams (Anthisan) have a tendency to cause skin allergies and are therefore not generally recommended. Bites which become infected (commonly in the tropics) should be treated with a local antiseptic or antibiotic cream such as Cetrimide (Savlon ICI), as should infected scratches. Skin infestation with body lice, crabs and scabies are unfortunately easy to pick up. Use gamma benzene hexachloride for lice, and benzyl benzoate for scabies. Crotamiton cream (Eurax CIBA) alleviates itching and also kills a number of skin parasites. Malathion lotion 5% (Prioderm) is good for lice but avoid the highly toxic full strength Malathion.

Malaria

in the West Indies is confined to the island of Hispaniola, being more prevalent in Haiti than the Dominican Republic. It remains a serious disease and you are advised to protect yourself against mosquito bites as above, and to take prophylactic (preventive) drugs. Start taking the tablets a few days before exposure and continue to take six weeks after leaving the malaria zone. Remember to give drugs to babies and children also. The subject of malaria prevention is becoming more complex as the malaria parasite becomes immune to some of the older drugs. However, at the present time Proguanil (Paludrine), 100 mgs two tablets a day, should give sufficient protection. You can catch malaria even when taking these drugs, though it is unlikely. If you do develop symptoms (high fever, shivering, headaches), seek medical advice immediately.

If this is not possible and the likelihood of malaria is high the treatment is Chloroquine a single dose of 4 tablets (600 mgs) followed by two tablets (300 mgs) in six hours and 300 mgs each day following. Pregnant women are particularly prone to malaria and should stick to Proguanil for prophylaxis. Chloroquine can also be used to prevent malaria on a weekly basis. The risk of malaria is obviously greater the further you move from cities and into rural areas with primitive facilities and standing water.

Sunburn

The burning power of the tropical sun is phenomenal. Always wear a wide brimmed hat and use some form of sun cream lotion on untanned skin. Normal temperate zone suntan lotions (protection factor up to 7) are not much good. You need to use the type designed specifically for the tropics or for mountaineers or skiers, with a protection factor between 7 and 15. Lotions with a factor of 25 or 30 can be found on some islands. They are waterproof and well worth using for sailing or golf. Glare from the sun can cause conjunctivitis so wear sunglasses especially on tropical beaches.

Snakebite

If you are unlucky enough to be bitten by a venomous snake, spider, scorpion, centipede or sea creature, try (within limits) to catch the animal for identification. The reactions to be expected are: fright, swelling, pain and bruising around the bite, soreness of the regional lymph glands, nausea, vomiting and fever. If any of the following symptoms supervene get the victim to a doctor without delay: numbness, tingling of the face, muscular spasms, convulsions, shortness of breath and haemorrhage. Commercial snake bite or scorpion sting kits are available, but are only useful for the specific type of snake or scorpion for which they are designed. The serum has to be given intravenously so is not much good unless you have had some practice in making injections into veins. If the bite is on a limb, immobilize the limb and apply a tight bandage between the bite and the body, releasing it for ninety seconds every 15 minutes. Reassurance of the bitten person is very important because death from snake bite is in fact very rare. Do not slash the bite area and try to suck out the poison because this sort of heroism does more harm than good. Hospitals usually hold stocks of snakebite serum. Best precaution: do not walk in snake territory with bare feet, sandals, or shorts. If swimming in an area where there are poisonous fish, such as stone or scorpion fish (also called by a variety of local names) or sea urchins on rocky coasts, tread carefully or wear plimsoles. The sting of such fish is intensely painful and this can be helped by immersing the stung part in water as hot as you can bear for as long as it remains painful. This is not always very practical and you must take care not to scald yourself, but it does work. Avoid spiders and scorpions by keeping your bed away from the wall, look under lavatory seats and inside your shoes in the morning. In the rare event of being bitten, consult a doctor.

Other Afflictions
Remember that **rabies** is endemic in some countries including Trinidad and Tobago, Puerto Rico, Haiti, Grenada, and possibly more so in the Dominican Republic and Cuba. If you are bitten by a domestic animal try to have it captured for observation and see a doctor at once. Treatment with human diploid vaccine is now extremely effective and worth seeking out if the likelihood of having contracted rabies is high. A course of anti rabies vaccine might be a good idea before you go.

   Dengue fever is present in all the islands with a higher prevalence in Barbados, Cuba, Dominican Republic, Haiti and Puerto Rico; there is no treatment, you must just avoid mosquito bites.

   Intestinal worms are common and the more serious ones such as **hookworm** can be contracted from walking bare foot on infested earth or beaches.

   Schistosomiasis (Bilharzia) is caused by a parasite which lurks in lakes and slow-moving rivers infested with snails and can have serious consequences later. The main problem is in St Lucia.

   Leptospirosis: Various forms of leptospirosis occur in most of the Caribbean islands, transmitted by a bacterium which is excreted in rodent urine. Fresh water and moist soil harbour the organisms which enter the body through cuts and scratches. If you suffer from any form of prolonged fever, consult a doctor.

   Prickly heat, a very common itchy rash, is avoided by frequent washing and by wearing loose clothing. It is helped by the use of talcum powder to allow the skin to dry thoroughly after washing. **Athletes Foot** and other fungal infections are best treated with sunshine and a proprietory preparation such as Tinaderm.

When You Return Home
Remember to take your anti malaria tablets for six weeks. If you have had attacks of diarrhoea it is worth having a stool specimen tested, in case you have picked up amoebic dysentery. If you have been living rough a blood test may be worthwhile to detect worms and other parasites.

Basic Supplies
The following items you may find useful to take with you from home; sunglasses, earplugs, suntan cream, insect repellent, flea powder, mosquito net, and coils or tablets, tampons, contraceptives, water-sterilizing tablets, anti-malaria tablets, anti-infective ointment, dusting powder for feet, travel-sickness pills, antacid tablets, anti-diarrhoea tablets, sachets of

rehydration salts eg "Electrosol", "Rehidrat" and first-aid kit.

The following organizations give information regarding well-trained English-speaking physicians in the Caribbean; International Association for Medical Assistance to Travellers, 745 5th Avenue, New York 10022. Intermedic, 777 3rd Avenue, New York 10017. Information regarding country by country malaria risk can be obtained from the World Health Organization (WHO), or the ROSS Institute, The London School of Hygiene and Tropical Medicine, Keppel Street, London WC1E 7HT, which publishes a book, strongly recommended, entitled *Preservation of Personal Health in Warm Climates*.

The organization MASTA (Medical Advisory Services for Travellers Abroad, also based at the London School of Hygiene and Tropical Medicine, Tel: 071-631 4408, telex 8953474) will provide country by country information on up-to-date health risks.

Additional Hints On the coasts of the islands beware of the manchineel tree whose fruits look very like small green apples; they are poisonous. Do not shelter under them as the dripping oil from the leaves during and after rain can cause blisters.

If travelling with very young children, use an umbrella to protect the child from the rain and sun and protect the baby's ears from the wind with a cap. This is especially important on buses or short-hop flights on which there is a lot of draught. Both these precautions are common practice in the region (Ed).

Recommended Reading Richard Dawood, *Travellers' Health. How to Stay Healthy Abroad* (3rd edition, Oxford/New York/Tokyo: Oxford University Press, 1992).

Watersports and Sailing in the Caribbean

The crystal clear waters of the sunny Caribbean combined with the constant northeast Trade winds make the islands a paradise for watersports enthusiasts. The great increase in tourism in the area has brought a corresponding development in watersports and every conceivable watersport is now available. For a full range of watersports with all arrangements, if not at hotel reception at only a short walk down the beach, some of the best islands to head for are Barbados, Jamaica, Antigua, Martinique, the Bahamas, Cayman Islands, Puerto Rico and the Virgin Islands.

On these islands you can find hobie-cats and sunfishes for rent, windsurfers, water skiing, glass-bottomed boats plying the reefs, charter yachts and booze cruises, scuba diving, snorkelling and deep sea fishing. Prices for such watersports vary from island to island and often increase by about 30% in the peak tourist season (December to April). It is worth knowing that prices can often be reduced for regular or long term rentals and that bargaining with individual beach operators is definitely worth trying.

Swimming
If all you want is sea and sand, these abound on nearly every island. The coral islands have the white postcard-perfect beaches and some of the islands of the Grenadines are nothing more than this. Swimming is safe on almost all Caribbean coasts, but do be careful on the exposed Atlantic coasts where waves are big at times and currents rip. Swimming in the Atlantic can be dangerous and in some places it is actually forbidden.

Water Skiing
This is almost always available in developed resort areas and beginners are looked after well. If you are a serious water skier it may be worth bringing your own slalom ski as many boats only cater for beginners.

Surfing
Good breaks for surfing and boogey-boarding can be found on the north shores of Puerto Rico, the Dominican Republic, Tobago and in Barbados. In both Puerto Rico and Barbados, custom-made surfboards can be bought and several competitions are organized every year. There are several good surf spots in Puerto Rico and the most consistent break in Barbados is at Bathsheba. In the Dominican Republic and Tobago, the sport is less developed. Waves tend to be bigger and more consistent in winter.

Windsurfing
For intermediate to advanced board sailors the best islands are Aruba and Barbados, although most islands will have windsurfers available in resort areas for beginners. In Barbados there are 15-25 knot winds from December to June and the added attraction of windsurfing on waves (2-5 metres is

average wave height in winter). Silver Sands on the south coast is the best area for short-board sailing and wave-jumping.

For windsurfers bringing their own equipment, check first with the airlines as some refuse boards and others may charge a fee. A deposit of 25% of the value of the board must be left with customs at the airport.

Aruba has very steady winds of about 15 knots and is good for speed sailing. Caribasurf operates from the Manchebo Beach Hotel which is a slalomboard area on the most beautiful beach in the island. Fisherman's Hut is a shallow water spot which allows standing up to 300 metres off shore and is an ideal area for practising manoeuvres. Sailboards Aruba operate from here. Boca Grandi sometimes offers the challenge of wave-riding.

Fishing

Sportfishing is excellent in many of the islands of the northern Caribbean. Almost every variety of deep-sea game fish: marlin, swordfish, tuna, mackerel and dorado abound in the waters. Over 50 world record catches have been made off the Bahamas alone. In the reefs and shallows there are big barracuda, tarpon and bonefish. There are areas for all methods of fishing: surf fishing, bottom fishing or trolling. Spearfishing, however, is banned in many islands. Although most fish seem to run between November and March, there is really no off-season in most islands and a good local captain will always know where to find the best fishing grounds. Note, fishermen should beware of eating large predators (eg grand barracuda) and other fish which accumulate the ciguatera toxin by eating coral-browsing smaller fish.

Fishing is very well organized in such islands as the Bahamas where Bimini, lying close to the Gulf Stream, is devoted entirely to game fishing. Exciting game fishing is also available very close to the shore off Puerto Rico, especially in the area which has become known to the enthusiasts as Blue Marlin Alley. Fishing is also very good off the Cayman Islands, Jamaica and the US Virgin Islands. The barrier reef off Belize harbours a huge variety of game fish. In many islands there are annual fishing tournaments open to all, such as the Million Dollar Month Fishing Tournament held in June in the Caymans. Deep-sea fishing boats can be chartered for a half or full day and some are available on a weekly basis. Anglers can also pay individually on split charters. When arranging a charter, be careful to clarify all details in advance.

Sailing

Exploring the Caribbean has never been easier. Many of the islands have developed new facilities, new marinas and anchorages to cater for the increasing number of yachts which have made the Caribbean their home. Many of the islands, especially the gems of the Grenadines, have no airstrips and the only way to see these islands is by boat. While travelling between the islands, be careful to clear immigration, especially on arrival, as failing to do this can lead to heavy fines.

For yachts crossing the Atlantic along the Trade Wind route, Barbados, the most easterly island, is a natural first landfall. Although there is no marina yet in Barbados, mooring facilities are available at the Shallow Draft next to the Deep Water Harbour or there are calm anchorages in Carlisle Bay. All boat needs can be met from the Boatyard on Carlisle Bay.

Following the wind, the next stop from Barbados is Grenada. Grenada Yacht Services on a sheltered lagoon next to one of the most picturesque Caribbean capitals, St George's, is one of the oldest yachting headquarters in the Southern Caribbean. There is also a friendly little marina on the south coast at Lance aux Épines.

Lying between Grenada and St Vincent over 45 miles of prime Caribbean sailing waters are the beautiful Grenadine Islands. Off the beaten track, they are a favourite cruising ground for sailors. There are few moorings or docks, but countless perfect anchorages. Many of the islands are uninhabited and you can anchor close to the shore and barbecue your own fish. Bequia is one of the two places in the world where whales are still hunted with harpoons and it is a centre for traditional boatbuilding. There are many sea orientated festivals in the Grenadines and a major one is the Bequia Regatta in April where traditional fishing boats compete.

In St Vincent, the best place to anchor is just off Young Island (which is private) opposite the Blue Lagoon which is home to a CSY charter fleet. It is difficult to enter the lagoon which has a very narrow channel and should only be attempted by the experienced. An enterprising taxi-driver, Charlie Tango, can be called on the VHF and he will go and do your shopping in Kingstown.

It is an easy sail through the Windward Island chain. Land is almost always in sight. It is well worth putting into Rodney Bay in St Lucia, where an ultra modern marina has been opened. It is storm-proof, being under the shadow of Pigeon Island and there are complete services for yachts and "yachties". Several charter companies are based here including Stevens Yachts and Tradewind Yacht Charters. South of Castries there is a small marina in Marigot Bay where the Moorings charter fleet is based. Further south, one can anchor close to the impressive Pitons. Here lives what must be the only elephant in the Caribbean. The next stop is Martinique where sailors can stock up with French goods from the hypermarkets. Charter yachts abound. Fort-de-France is one of the best places to dry dock (along with Antigua and St Martin). There is a small, relaxed marina, Trois Islets, across the bay from Fort-de-France.

The Atlantic Rally for Cruisers offers support and entertainment for any sailors contemplating an Atlantic crossing. Departure is from Gran Canaria at the end of November and the yachts arrive in St Lucia to a warm welcome for Christmas. A major regatta on the Caribbean racing circuit is held around April.

Heading further north, the Saints off the southern tip of Guadeloupe offer peaceful anchorages. Guadeloupe has a very large marina just outside the capital, Point-à-Pitre, which is crowded with wandering French yachts. There is a slipway here with a modern 50-ton travel lift and crews can do their own work. The multi-hulls of the professional racing circuit congregate here once a year. Favourable French tax laws for boat owners have led to a proliferation of yachts and fierce competition in the charter market from the French islands of Guadeloupe, Martinique, St Martin and St Lucia.

Antigua is the mecca of the Caribbean yachting world and it is likely that the Atlantic Rally for Cruisers will end here in the future. The hurricane-proof English Harbour is one of the most distinctive ports in the Caribbean with its restored Royal Naval Dockyard which was once the haunt of Admiral Nelson.

The major marina facilities are the Catamaran Club Marina, Crabbs Marina in the Parham Sound on the northern coast and the elegant St James Club Marina in Mamora Bay. There are also dozens of coves and anchorages, a large charter fleet (home to Nicholsons Yacht Charters) and almost every spare part is available. Antigua Sailing Week in April is the biggest yachting event in the Caribbean and the island takes on a carnival atmosphere to cater for the yachts which arrive from all over the Caribbean as well as other parts of the world.

Further north, the small island of St-Barthélémy is also worth a visit. Somewhat resembling St Tropez in the 50's, St-Barts is expensive and exclusive. Yachts can use the quay in Gustavia Harbours. Lively St Maarten, half-French and half-Dutch, with good marina facilities, is a favourite stop for sailors stocking up on duty-free goods for an Atlantic crossing.

The British Virgin Islands are home to the largest bareboat charter fleet in the world although the recession has forced several companies to cease operations. The main sailing area between the islands, the Sir Francis Drake Channel, is protected from the open seas, making the waters calm and particularly well suited to novice sailors. There are numerous marinas with many in places that only boats can reach as at Bitter End and the Virgin Gorda Marina.

If sailing in the northern Caribbean and in Bahamian waters, you should be aware of a risk of piracy by drug runners. Boats have been reported seized, crews have disappeared. Seek advice about local conditions.

Yacht Charters
Large charter fleets operate from the British Virgin Islands, Antigua, Martinique and St Lucia. Yachts can be chartered on a daily or term basis either bareboat or with skipper and crew. CSY also offers "Sail-'n-Learn" cruises. Among the more established charter companies are:
    CSY (St Vincent), Blue Lagoon, St Vincent.
    Stevens Yachts, Rodney Bay, St Lucia.
    Tradewinds Yachts, Rodney Bay, St Lucia.
    Nicholson's Yacht Charters, PO Box 103, St John's, Antigua (Tel: 809 463-1530, Fax: 463-1531; in USA, 432 Columbia Street, Cambridge MA 02138, Tel: 617-225-0555, Fax: 225-0190).

Hitching Yachts
Hitching and working on yachts is an ideal way of seeing the islands for the adventurous person with time on his/her hands. The variety of yachts is endless. Many yachts charter in the Caribbean in winter and go north to the United States or Mediterranean for the charter season there. Other yachts are cruisers passing through on their way around the world. "Yachties" are friendly people and if you ask around in the right places, frequent the "yachtie" bars and put up a few notices, crew positions can be found, either on a charter yacht or a cruiser. Some of the easiest places to join boats are in Martinique (Fort-de-France and Trois Islets), St Lucia (Rodney Bay and Marigot Bay), Antigua (English Harbour) and in the Grenadines from Bequia (Admiralty Bay) and Union Island (Anchorage). The end of Antigua Week sees many boats looking for crew as does the end of the Atlantic Rally for Cruisers.

Rosie Mauro, Barbados

Scuba Diving in the Caribbean

Scuba diving has become the "in sport" with the numbers of divers having increased dramatically in recent years. The epitome of a scuba dive is in clear, tropical waters on a colourful reef abounding with life. The Caribbean is a scuba diver's paradise, for there is a conglomeration of islands surrounded by living reefs providing different types of diving to suit everyone's dreams. Unfortunately, some of the islands have turned into a "diving clrcus", as in some of the more developed northern Caribbean islands where 30 or 40 divers are herded onto large dive boats and dropped on somewhat packaged dive sites where "tame" fish come for handouts. Other islands in the Caribbean region are still virginal in the diving sense, which can lead to an exciting undersea adventure. Nevertheless, this can also be frustrating on a diving holiday as on the more remote islands facilities are not often available and diving can be more difficult and basic.

The **Cayman Islands** are among the most developed for scuba diving and there is a fine organization of over 20 dive operations, including live aboard boats. There is also a well-run decompression facility on Grand Cayman, which is an added safety factor. The Caymans are very conservation minded and it is a criminal offence to take ANY form of marine life while scuba diving. In fact, it is illegal on Cayman Brac, the smaller sister island, even to wear gloves while scuba diving. This helps ensure that divers will not hold or damage the delicate coral formations and other marine life.

Underwater photographic facilities are well developed in the Caymans and several outfits offer comprehensive courses for the beginner as well as the experienced photographer.

Belize is becoming well-known for the spectacular diving available on its barrier reef. Thirty miles offshore, Lighthouse Reef offers pristine dive sites in addition to the incredible Blue Hole, a sinkhole exceeding 400 feet. Massive stalagmites and stalactites are found along overhangs down the sheer vertical walls of the Blue Hole. The outer reef lies beyond the access of land-based diving resorts and even beyond most fishermen, so the marine life is undisturbed. An exciting marine phenomenon takes place during the full moon each January in the waters around Belize when thousands of the Nassau groupers gather to spawn at Glory Cay on Turneff Reef. The gathering occurs at other locations in the Caribbean also. These more remote areas around Belize are now accessible on a comfortable live aboard boat which has opened up diving on these sites.

The **British Virgin Islands**, with an array of some 50 coral islands, are well worth a mention as the diving is exciting and varied. Both live aboard and land-based operations are available with well-developed facilities for divers. Popular diving sites include the wreck of the *HMS Rhone*, a 310-foot British mail ship sunk in 1867 in a hurricane. She was the site for the

Hollywood movie *The Deep*, which is what really made her famous. Other interesting sites include Turtle Cave in Brewers Bay which offers a spiral arch divers can swim through beginning at a depth of 45 feet and winding up to 15 feet. Many sites lie in the string of islands to the south between Tortola and the island of Virgin Gorda. To the north lies Mosquito Island, the site of The Cousteau Society's Project Ocean Search. Hosted annually by Jean-Michel Cousteau, the expedition gives a small number of participants the chance to find out what it is like to be on a Cousteau expedition (The Cousteau Society, 930 West 21st St, Norfolk, Virginia, USA 23517).

Other especially spectacular diving destinations with abundant marine life include Saba, Dominica and the Turks and Caicos. **Saba**, a tiny Dutch island, only fives miles long, is truly one of the most protected places for divers. The entire reef surrounding the island was established as a marine park in 1987 and this conservation effort has led to an abundance of "tame" fish. Saba diving is known for several deep pinnacles including Third Encounter, Twilight Zone and Shark Shoal. For the less adventurous and experienced, sites like Diamond Rock and Tent Reef offer the thrill of seeing large French Angels swimming up to the divers. The sport of diving has been developing with both land-based and live aboard diving boat facilities available, as well as a decompression chamber facility.

Dominica, "The Nature Island", is a lush, mountainous island with rugged topside and underwater terrain. It is diving for the adventurous and not for the diver who wants easy diving. For the more experienced the Atlantic East coast offers some spectacular wall dives. Dominica has just been introduced to the diving world and there are only a few dive shops.

The **Turks and Caicos Islands**, which consist of over 40 lovely sand islands and cays, are located on the Turks Island Passage, a 22-mile channel which is 7,000 feet deep connecting the Atlantic Ocean and the Caribbean Sea. This contributes to the abundance of marine life and large pelagic fish seen in these waters and spectacular wall diving in the channel. The islands are surrounded by coral reefs that cover over 200 square miles. Visibility is usually 100 feet or more and marine life plentiful. There are several dive shops on Providenciales and Grand Turk, mostly catering for small groups of divers, and there are three or four liveaboard boats in the islands' waters at any one time.

The **Grenadines** in the South Eastern Caribbean offer pristine diving, although facilities are limited. Grenada and tiny sister island of Carriacou offer limited diving facilities, as does Bequia, although nearby St Vincent is more developed for scuba diving.

Barbados is among the more developed islands in the Caribbean and the surrounding reef life is not as unspoiled as on some of the less developed islands. However, there are some thriving reefs and within the last few years the island has become known as a wreck diving destination. Five shipwrecks have been intentionally sunk as diving sites, offering interesting underwater photography. In addition, the island is the base for the regional organization, **The Eastern Caribbean Safe Diving Association**. This association helps to maintain a decompression facility for the Leeward and Windward islands and is attempting to establish minimum safe operating standards for dive shops, initially in the Eastern Caribbean and eventually, regionally. For more information write ECSDA, Box 86 WRD, Welches Post Office, Barbados.

Bonaire, just off the South American coast, has long been known as a "hot spot" for diving, and is one of the few islands (like the Caymans) which has devoted itself to scuba diving. A far-sighted government established a marine park way back in 1979 when conservation was not even being discussed by most diving destinations. Neighbouring Curaçao has now joined her in this reputation, with an expansion of diving facilities and exciting diving sites. Aruba is not likely to equal her sister islands as she lacks the reefs which surround Bonaire and Curaçao, although diving is available.

Bonaire, being very experienced in offering diving, has a wide selection of about a dozen dive operations, including photo and marine life education facilities. Diving sites are also varied with reef, wreck and wall dives. In fact, the Marine Park Guide for Bonaire lists over 50 dive sites. The town pier, right off the capital, has long been a favourite night dive and the pilings are covered in soft sponges and invertebrate life.

Curaçao offers the reef diving of Bonaire and a couple of wreck dives of interest. The freighter, *Superior Producer* (rather deep at 100 feet) is intact and has a variety of growth including beautiful orange tubastera sponges.

While the reefs of **Aruba** may not be as prolific as her sister islands, there is an interesting wreck site, with which few other sites around the island compare in marine life. The *Antilla*, a 400-foot German ship, is in 70 feet (and less) of water. Her massive hull has provided a home for an amazing variety and size of fish life and night dives are truly a thrill on this site.

Most Caribbean destinations offer some form of scuba diving, although not all operations are safety minded. While scuba diving is exciting and thrilling, it can also be dangerous, particularly for beginners who are not aware of what to look for in a safe diving operation. Proper instruction from a recognized scuba instructor is a must. Not all diving shops in the Caribbean adhere to the recommended safety standards, so it is important to ensure the level of training an instructor has and request to see certificates of instructor training if they are not displayed.

Good health is a must, but the myth that one needs to be a super man or super woman is not true. Important health aspects are healthy lungs, sinus and the ability to equalize your ears (by gently blowing air into the eustachian tube while blocking your nose). A medical exam by a physician trained in hyperbaric (diving) medicine is recommended and required by many instructors. A good basic swimming ability is necessary, although you do not need to be an Olympic swimmer. For female divers, smaller, lighter scuba tanks are available at some dive shops which makes the cumbersome, heavy gear easier to handle.

Most scuba training organizations offer several types of diving courses. A "resort course" provides diving instruction in a condensed version (about three hours) with a minimum of academic knowledge, one confined water session (usually in a swimming pool) and one scuba dive. This type of course is done by many tourists who do not have the time to do a full certification course, which requires written exams, classroom lectures, several confined water sessions and several scuba dives. For the serious diver, however, a full certification course should be taken.

It is not possible to provide here a comprehensive list of diving facilities on each island; see the **Diving and Marine Life** sections of the country chapters for further information and addresses. For information on the live aboard boats mentioned for Belize, and the Cayman Islands, contact The Aggressor Fleet, PO Drawer K, Morgan City, LA 70881-000K, Tel: (504) 385-2416, Fax: (504) 384-0817 or (USA & Canada) (800) 348-2628.

Martha Watkins Gilkes, Antigua

Walking in the Caribbean

The Caribbean provides ideal conditions for medium-distance walking in the tropics. Small islands avoid the very high temperatures which are common in India, Africa, or the South American mainland. Distances are manageable; a hard day's walk will take you from coast to coast on the smaller islands, and a few days is enough for a complete circuit. The scenery is varied: peasant farms with fruit trees, rain forests, and high mountains. Mountain streams and waterfalls which would be ice-cold in temperate countries are perfect for bathing. The sea is never far away. Nor are road transport, comfortable accommodation, rum shops and restaurants. Nevertheless, the illusion of remoteness can sometimes be complete. And much of the nastier *mainland* wildlife can't swim, so there are no large carnivores and few poisonous snakes on the islands.

There are some tips to note for people more used to walking in temperate countries.

Maps Good large scale maps (1: 25,000 or 1: 50,000) are available for all the Commonwealth islands. These can be obtained from the local Lands and Surveys department on each island; and usually from Edward Stanford Ltd, 12/14 Long Acre, London WC2E 9LP, or The Map Shop, 15 High Street, Upton-upon-Severn, Worcestershire, (Tel: 06846 3146). The Ordnance Survey (Romsey Road, Southampton, UK, Tel: 0703 792792) publishes a series of colourful World Maps which includes some holiday destinations. They contain comprehensive tourist information ranging from hotels and beaches to climbing and climate. Each map is produced in association with the country concerned. Relevant titles so far are: Barbados, St Lucia, Cayman Islands, Belize (Ambergris Caye), British Virgin Islands, St Vincent, Dominica. There are also good large scale maps of Guadeloupe and Martinique. Footpath information on maps is not always reliable, however.

Clothing Lightweight cotton clothing, with a wide brimmed hat to keep off the sun. Shorts are more comfortable, but can leave the legs exposed to sunburn or sharp razor grasses; ditto short sleeved shirts. It is best to carry short and long, and change en route as appropriate. Rain comes in intense bursts. Raincoats are not particularly comfortable. A better technique is to strip down to light clothes and dry off when the rain stops.

Timing An early start is ideal, preferably just before sunrise. This will give several hours walking before the sun becomes too hot. Public transport starts running surprisingly early in most places.

Water Carry a large thermos. This can keep water ice-cold through a full day. Refilling from mountain streams is generally safe if purification tablets are used, but be careful of streams *below* villages especially in islands like St Lucia and Martinique where there is some bilharzia, and of springs in cultivated areas where generously applied pesticides may have leached into the groundwater.

Sunburn Remember that the angle of the sun in the sky is what counts, not the temperature. So you may get burnt at midday even if you feel cool, but are unlikely to have trouble before 1000 or after 1500. Forearms can get burnt, and so can the back of your legs if you are walking away from the sun. It is a good idea to walk west in the morning and east in the afternoon to avoid strong sun on the face.

Snakes The only islands where these are a worry are Trinidad, St Lucia, and Martinique. Trinidad has several dangerous species, and also has African killer bees. All three islands have the venomous Fer de Lance. This snake, however, is usually frightened off by approaching footsteps, so snakebites are rare, but they can be fatal. The Fer de Lance prefers bush country in dry coastal areas. Ask and accept local advice on where to go, and stick to well marked trails. Some other islands have boa constrictors, which can bite but are not poisonous. Large centipedes (sometimes found in dry coastal areas) can also give a very nasty bite.

Marijuana Farmers In remote mountain areas in most islands these people are likely to assume that outsiders have come either to steal the crop or as police spies. On most islands they are armed, and on some they set trap guns for the unwary. Again, the best way to avoid them is to keep to well marked trails, and accept local advice about where to go.

Details of walks are to be found in each country chapter, but here is an indication of what is possible on a selection of islands:

Jamaica Spectacular scenery especially in the Blue Mountains and in the

Cockpit country. Marijuana growers are a real problem in the remote areas, but the main trails in the Blue Mountains are safe. Jamaica Camping and Hiking Association and Ministry of Tourism have a useful *Hikers Guide to the Blue Mountains*.

Haiti Another story altogether. Walking is the normal means of transport in rural areas, so there are masses of well-trodden trails. Haiti is fairly safe, but it is better to walk with a group. Maps are rudimentary and small scale. Few people speak French in remote areas—try to pick up some Créole. Make sure you carry basic supplies, particularly water. Hiring a guide should be no problem.

Guadeloupe Network of waymarked trails on the mountainous half (Basse Terre).

Martinique The *Parc Naturel Régional* (Caserne Bouillé, Rte de la Redoute de Matouba, Tel: 72 19 30) organizes group hikes, usually on Sundays, and publishes a useful *Guide des Sentiers Pedestres à la Martinique*. Good trails on Mont Pelée and along the north coast.

Dominica Probably has the best unspoiled mountain scenery in the Caribbean. Some of the long distance trails are hard to follow, though. Guides readily available. Try the path via Laudat to the Boiling Lake.

St Lucia Very well marked east-west trail through Quilesse forest reserve. Other walks organized by the Forestry Department. Also a good trail up Gros Piton. See St Lucia chapter for details.

St Vincent Spectacular but sometimes difficult trail across the Soufrière volcano from Orange Hill to Richmond. Guide advisable. North coast trail past Falls of Baleine is spectacular, but hard to follow. Marijuana growers.

Grenada Very accessible mountain and rainforest scenery. Good network of signposted trails linking Grand Etang, Concord waterfall, and other points.

Barbados Very safe and pleasant walking, especially on the east coast, but little really wild scenery. Barbados National Trust (Tel: 426 2421) organizes regular Sunday hikes, morning at 0600, afternoon at 1500.

Trinidad Some fine scenery, but marijuana growers are a real problem, particularly in the Northern Range. Well marked trails are safe. Those at the Asa Wright Nature Centre are recommended (Tel: 667-4655, Fax: 667-0493). Trinidad Field Naturalists Club (1 Errol Park Road, St Anns, Port of Spain, Tel: 624-3321, Louisa Zuniaga) organizes long distance hikes, and visits to caves etc.

Tobago Safe and pleasant walking; distances are not too great. The scenery is varied: hills, woodland and unspoilt beaches.

Useful Addresses For groups organizing a serious hiking/camping expedition in the Caribbean, contact Mr David Clarke, Caribbean Regional Consultant, Duke of Edinburgh's Award, The Garrison, Bridgetown, Barbados (Tel: 436 8954, Fax: 431 0076). He is generally able to provide advice and to supply the address of a local organization on most islands with expedition experience.

Mark Wilson, Barbados

Responsible Tourism

Much has been written about the adverse impacts of tourism on the environment and local communities. It is usually assumed that this only applies to the more excessive end of the travel industry such as the Spanish Costas and Bali. However travellers can have an impact at almost any density and this is especially true in areas "off the beaten track" where local people may not be used to western conventions and lifestyles, and natural environments may be very sensitive.

Of course, tourism can have a beneficial impact and this is something to which every traveller can contribute. Many National Parks are part funded by receipts from people who travel to see exotic plants and animals, El Yunque (Puerto Rico) and the Asa Wright Centre (Trinidad) are good examples of such sites. Similarly, travellers can promote patronage and protection of valuable archaeological sites and heritages through their interest and entrance fees.

However, where visitor pressure is high and/or poorly regulated, damage can occur. This is especially so in parts of the Caribbean where some tour operators are expanding their activities with scant regard for the environment or local communities. It is also unfortunately true that many of the most popular destinations are in ecologically sensitive areas easily disturbed by extra human pressures. Eventually the very features that tourists travel so far to see may become degraded and so we seek out new sites, discarding the old, and leaving someone else to deal with the plight of local communities and the damaged environment. Fortunately, there are signs of a new awareness of the responsibilities that the travel industry and its clients need to endorse. For example, some tour operators fund local conservation projects and travellers are now more aware of the impact they may have on host cultures and environments. We can all contribute to the success of what is variously described as responsible, green or alternative tourism. All that is required is a little forethought and consideration. It would be impossible to identify all the potential impacts that might need to be addressed by travellers, but it is worthwhile noting the major areas in which we can all take a more responsible attitude in the countries we visit. These include changes to natural ecosystems (air, water, land, ecology and wildlife), cultural values (beliefs and behaviour) and the built environment (sites of antiquity and archaeological significance).

At an individual level, travellers can reduce their impact if greater consideration is given to their activities. For example in most Caribbean countries dress codes are fairly strictly adhered to; shorts and T shirts are OK on the beach but less so when shopping or cashing cheques. Avoid topless or nude bathing except where it is expressly allowed. Do not take photographs of people without permission. Recognition of these cultural cues goes a long way towards reducing the friction that can develop between host and visitor. Collecting or purchasing wildlife curios might have an effect on local ecosystems and may well be illegal under either local or international legislation (see below). Similarly, some tourist establishments have protected wildlife (especially turtle) on the menu, don't add to the problem by buying it. Some environmental impacts are caused by factors beyond the direct control of travellers, such as the management and operation of a hotel chain. However, even here it is possible to voice concern about damaging activities and an increasing number of hotels and travel operators are taking "green concerns" seriously, even if it is only to protect their share of the market.

Environmental Legislation
Legislation may have been enacted to control damage to the environment, and in some cases this can have a bearing on travellers. The establishment of National Parks may involve rules and guidelines for visitors and these should always be followed. In addition there may be local or national laws controlling behaviour and use of natural resources (especially wildlife) that are being increasingly enforced. If in doubt, ask. Finally, international legislation, principally the Convention on International Trade in Endangered Species of Wild Fauna and Flora (CITES), may affect travellers.

CITES aims to control the trade in live specimens of endangered plants and animals and also "recognizable parts or derivatives" of protected species. Sale of black coral, turtle shells, rare orchids and other protected wildlife is strictly controlled by signatories of the convention. The full list of protected wildlife varies, so if you feel the need to purchase souvenirs and trinkets derived from wildlife, it would be prudent to check whether they are protected. CITES parties in the Caribbean include: Dominican Republic, Trinidad and Tobago, St Lucia, St Vincent, the Bahamas and Cuba. Puerto Rico and the US Virgin Islands are included in the US ratification of CITES. The UK dependencies (Anguilla, Bermuda, British Virgin Islands, Cayman and Turks and Caicos Islands) all look to the UK government for advice and support in the implementation of international wildlife legislation and in particular CITES regulation as the UK is a party to the convention. In addition, most European countries, the USA and Canada are all signatories. Importation of CITES protected species into these countries can lead to heavy fines, confiscation of goods and even imprisonment. Information on the status of legislation and protective measures can be obtained from Traffic International (Fax: UK 0223 277237).

Green Travel Companies and Information
The increasing awareness of the environmental impact of travel and tourism has led to a range of advice and information services as well as spawning specialist travel companies who claim to provide "responsible travel" for clients. This is an expanding field and the veracity of claims needs to be substantiated in some cases. The following organizations and publications can provide useful information for those with an interest in pursuing responsible travel opportunities.

International Organizations
Green Flag International aims to work with travel industry and conservation bodies to improve environments at travel destinations and also to promote conservation programmes at resort destinations; provides a travellers guide for "green" tourism as well as advice on destinations, Tel: UK 0223 893587.

Tourism Concern aims to promote a greater understanding of the impact of tourism on host communities and environments, Tel: UK 081-878 9053.

Centre for Responsible Tourism (CRT) co-ordinates a North American network and advises on North American sources of information on responsible tourism: CRT, 2 Kensington Rd, San Anselmo, California USA.

Centre for the Advancement of Responsive Travel (CART) has a range of publications available as well as information on alternative holiday destinations, Tel: UK 0732 352757.

Caribbean Conservation Organizations

The conservation organizations described below may also be able to provide advice on sites of historical or wildlife interest and possibly provide guides. The use of local experts as guides can of course provide an important source of income for small conservation bodies. In addition, they are often far more sensitive to the cultural taboos and ecological constraints of sites whose long term survival they can help to ensure.

Anguilla Archeological and Historical Society, PO Box 252, The Valley, Anguilla.
Antigua Archeological and Historical Society, PO Box 103, English Harbour, Antigua.
Bahamas National Trust, PO Box N 4105, Nassau, Bahamas.
Barbados National Trust, 10th Avenue, Belleville, St Michael, Barbados.
Bermuda Audubon Society, PO Box 1328, Hamilton 5, Bermuda.
Bermuda National Trust, PO Box 61, Hamilton 5, Bermuda.
British Virgin Islands National Parks Trust, c/o Ministry of Natural Resources, Road Town, Tortola, BVI.
Caribbean Conservation Association, Savannah Lodge, The Garrison, St Michael, Barbados.
Dominica Conservation Association, PO Box 71, Roseau, Dominica.
Grenada Historical Society, St George's, Grenada.
Jamaica Conservation and Development Trust, PO Box 1225, Kingston 8, Jamaica.
Montserrat National Trust, PO Box 54, Plymouth, Montserrat.
Natural History Society of Puerto Rico Inc.
Netherlands Antilles National Parks Foundation (STINA PA), PO Box 2090, Curaçao.
Nevis Historical and Conservation Society, c/o Mr S Byron, PO Box 476, Charlestown, Nevis.
Pointe à Pierre Wildfowl Trust (Trinidad), 18 Grove Road, Valsayn Park North, Trinidad.
St Lucia National Trust, PO Box 525, Castries, St Lucia.
St Lucia Naturalists Society, PO Box 783, Castries.
Trinidad and Tobago Field Naturalists Club, 1 Errol Park Road, St Ann's, Port of Spain.
Union Régionale des Associations du Patrimoine et de l'Environment de Guadeloupe, BP82L, Pointe-à-Pitre, Leder 97112, Guadeloupe.
Union Régionale des Associations du Patrimoine et de l'Environment de Martinique, Centre du PNRM, Caserne Bouille, Rue Redoute de Matouba, Fort de France 97200, Martinique.
Virgin Islands Conservation Society, PO Box 12379, St Thomas, US Virgin Islands 00801 USA. **Environmental Association**, PO Box 3839, Christiansted, St Croix, US Virgin Islands 00822.

Publications

The Good Tourist by Katie Wood and Syd House (1991: Mandarin Paperbacks), addresses issues surrounding environmental impacts of tourism, suggests ways in which damage can be minimized, suggests a range of environmentally sensitive holidays and projects. *Independent Guide to Real Holidays Abroad* by Frank Barrett (1991: available from the Independent Newspaper), suggestions for a range of special interest holidays.

Flora and Fauna of the Caribbean

For many travellers, a trip to the Caribbean offers a first glimpse of the tropics, complete with luxuriant vegetation and exotic wildlife. Images of untouched beaches and rainforest form a major selling point of many travel brochures. In fact there is very little "untouched" wilderness left and what visitors see is an environment that has been affected by the activities of man. Forestry, agriculture, fisheries and increasingly tourism have all helped to mould the modern landscape and natural heritage of the Caribbean. However, there is still much of interest to see, and it is true to say that small islands can combine a variety of habitats within a limited area. On many islands, it is possible to move between the coastal reefs and beaches through thorn scrub and plantation into rainforest within a matter of miles. Increasingly, the complexity and fragility of island ecosystems is being appreciated and fortunately most countries have recognized the value of balancing development and the protection of the natural environment and have begun to develop national parks and protected areas programmes. Many islands also have active conservation societies or national wildlife trusts (see above).

Wildlife
Over long periods of time, islands tend to develop their own unique flora and fauna. These "endemic" species add to the interest of wildlife and natural history tours. The St Lucia parrot and Dominica's sisserou have become a regular part of the tour circuit of these islands, and have undoubtedly benefited from the interest that tourists have shown in their plight. Details of National Parks and wildlife are included under the specific island chapter headings (Fauna and Flora). This section provides a broad overview of the range of animals, plants and habitats that are to be found in the region.

Mammals
Mammals are not particularly good colonizers of small islands and this has resulted in a general scarcity of species in the Caribbean. Many of the more commonly seen species (mongoose, agouti, opossum, and some of the monkeys) were introduced by man. Bats are the one exception to this rule and most islands have several native species.

Mongoose were introduced to many islands to control snakes, they have also preyed on many birds, reptiles and other animals and have had a devastating effect on native fauna.

Of the monkeys, the green monkeys of Barbados, Grenada and St Kitts and Nevis were introduced from West Africa in the 17th century. Similarly, rhesus monkeys have been introduced to Desecheo Island off Puerto Rico. The red howler monkeys on Trinidad are native to the island as are several other mammals including the brocket deer, squirrel and armadillo. These species have managed to colonize from nearby Venezuela.

There are endemic mammals on some islands for example the pygmy racoon, a species of coati and "jabli" in Cozumel and possibly the Guadeloupe racoon.

Sailors may encounter marine mammals including dolphin, porpoise and whales. Between November and December hump back whales migrate through the Turks and Caicos Passage on their way to the Silver Banks breeding grounds off the Dominican Republic. The ungainly manatee, or sea cow, can still be seen in some coastal areas in the Greater Antilles (especially Jamaica, Cozumel, Cuba—Zapata Peninsula—and Puerto Rico) although it is becoming increasingly uncommon.

Birds

It is the birds perhaps more than any other group of animals that excite the most interest from visitors to the region. Many islands have their own endemic species such as the Grenada dove, yellow-billed parrot and 24 other species in Jamaica and Guadeloupe woodpecker. The islands also act as important stepping stones in the migration of many birds through the Americas. As a result, the region is highly regarded by ornithologists and there are several internationally important nature reserves.

Trinidad and Tobago demonstrate the influence of the nearby South American mainland. While they have no endemic species they still support at least 400 species and the Asa Wright Centre is regarded as one of the premier bird watching sites in the World. At the other end of the Caribbean, Inagua (Bahamas) is the site of the world's largest flamingo colony at Lake Windsor. There is also an important flamingo colony on Bonaire in the southern Caribbean.

Many of the endemic species have become rare as a result of man's activities. Habitat destruction, introduction of new species (especially the mongoose) and hunting for food and the international pet trade have all had an effect. Parrots in particular have suffered as a result of these activities. Fortunately, measures are now being undertaken to protect the birds and their habitats on many islands (eg Bahamas, Jamaica, Dominica, Puerto Rico and St Lucia).

Reptiles

Lizards and geckos are common on virtually all the islands in the region and may even be seen on very small offshore islets. There are also a number of species of snakes, iguanas and turtles scattered throughout the region. Many are restricted to one island and Jamaica has at least 27 island endemics including several species of galliwasp. The vast majority of reptiles found in the region are completely harmless to man although there are strong superstitions about the geckos (*mabouya*) and of course the snakes. For example, the skin and fat of boa constrictors (*tête chien*) are used for bush remedies on some of the Windward Islands.

The fer de lance snake (St Lucia, Martinique and also South America), deserves to be treated with extreme caution; although the bite is not usually lethal, hospitalization is required. It is found in isolated areas of dry scrubland and river valley. The best protection is to wear long trousers and stout boots and to avoid walking in these areas at night. Local advice should be sought if in doubt.

Iguanas are still found on many islands although they have declined as a result of hunting throughout the region. Although of fearsome appearance, they are herbivorous and spend much of their time in trees and low scrub feeding on leaves and trying to avoid man.

Marine turtles including the loggerhead, leatherback, hawksbill and green turtles are found throughout Caribbean waters and they may occasionally be seen by divers and snorkellers. Females come ashore on isolated sandy beaches between the months of May and August to lay eggs. There may be opportunities for assisting natural history and wildlife societies (St Lucia Naturalists Society, Fish and Wildlife Dept in the US Virgin Islands) in their turtle watches, to record numbers and locations of nests and to protect the turtles from poachers. There is a large commercial breeding programme for green turtles in the Cayman Islands. Freshwater turtles are also found on some islands including Jamaica and Cat Island (Bahamas). Caiman have been introduced to Puerto Rico and are also found on Cuba and the Dominican Republic.

Many species of reptile are now protected in the region (especially the marine turtles and iguana) and reserves have been specifically established to protect them. For example, the Maria Islands Nature Reserve on St Lucia is home to the St Lucia ground lizard and grass snake. The latter is possibly the rarest snake in the world with an estimated population of 150 individuals.

Amphibians

Frogs and toads are common in a variety of shapes and colours. There are generally more species on the larger islands (Greater Antilles and Trinidad). The Cuban pygmy frog is described as the world's smallest frog, while at the other end of the scale, the mountain chicken of Dominica and Montserrat is probably the largest frog on the region. Its name relates to its supposed flavour. The call of the piping frogs (*eleutherodactylus spp*) is often mistaken for a bird and these small animals are common throughout the Lesser Antilles, becoming especially vocal at night and after rain. The largest and most visible amphibian is probably the marine toad which has been introduced to islands throughout the region in an attempt to control insects and other invertebrate pests. The male toads use flat exposed areas from which to display, often roads. Unfortunately, they have not evolved to deal with the car yet and as a result many are killed.

Invertebrates

This group includes the insects, molluscs, spiders and a host of other animals that have no backbones. For first time travellers to the tropics, the huge range of invertebrates can seem daunting and it is estimated that there are at least 290 species of butterfly in the Caribbean. No one knows how many species of beetles, bugs or mollusc there are.

Of the butterflies, the swallowtails are perhaps the most spectacular, with several species being found in the Greater Antilles (especially Cuba). However the other islands also have large colourful butterflies including the monarch and flambeau which are present throughout the region. Another insect of note is the hercules beetle, reportedly the world's largest beetle which may reach a length of 12cm and is occasionally found in rainforest in the Lesser Antilles.

Land and freshwater crabs inhabit a range of environments from the rainforest (eg bromeliad crab from Jamaica) to the dry coastal areas (many species of hermit crab). Tarantula spiders are also fairly common, although they are nocturnal and rarely seen. Their bite is painful but, in most of the species found in the region, no worse than a bee sting. Of far more concern are the large centipedes (up to 15 cm long) that can inflict a nasty and painful bite with their pincers. They are mostly restricted to the dry coastal areas and are most active at night. Black widow spiders are also present on some of the islands in the Greater Antilles. Fortunately they are rarely encountered by the traveller.

Marine Environments (Beaches, Coral Reef, Sea Cliffs)

A diving or snorkelling trip over a tropical reef allows a first hand experience of this habitat's diversity of wildlife. There are a number of good field guides to reef fish and animals (see book list) and some are even printed on waterproof paper. Alternatively, glass bottomed boats sail over some sites (Buccoo Reef, Tobago), and there are underwater trails which identify types of corals and marine habitats (eg Buck Island, US Virgin Islands, and one in Saba under construction).

Amongst the commonest fish are the grunts, butterfly, soldier, squirrel and angel fish. Tiny damsel fish are very territorial and may even attempt to nip swimmers who venture too close to their territories (more surprising than painful).

There are over fifty species of hard coral (the form that builds reefs) with a variety of sizes and colours. Amongst the most dramatic are the stagshorn and elkhorn corals which are found on the more exposed outer reefs. Brain coral forms massive round structures up to 2 metres high and Pillar coral forms columns that may also reach 2 metres in height. Soft corals, which include black corals, sea fans and gorgonians, colonize the surface of the hard coral adding colour and variety. Associated with these structures is a host of animals and plants. Spiny lobsters may be seen lurking in holes and crevices along with other crustaceans and reef fish. The patches of sand between outcrops of coral provide suitable habitat for conch and other shellfish. Some islands now restrict the collection and sale of corals (especially black corals) and there are also legal restrictions on the sale of black corals under CITES.

The delights of swimming on a coral reef need to be tempered by a few words of caution: Many people assume the water will be seething with sharks, however these animals are fairly uncommon in nearshore waters and the species most likely to be encountered is the nurse shark, which is harmless unless provoked or cornered. Other fish to keep an eye open for include the scorpion fish with its poisonous dorsal spines; it frequently lies stationary on coral reefs onto which the incautious can blunder. Finally moray eels may be encountered, a fearsome looking fish, but harmless unless provoked at which point they can inflict serious bites. Of far more concern should be the variety of stinging invertebrates that are found on coral reefs. The most obvious is fire coral which comes in a range of shapes and sizes but is recognizable by the white tips to its branches. In addition, many corals have sharp edges and branches that can graze and cut. Another common group of stinging invertebrates are the fire worms which have white bristles along the sides of their bodies. As with the fire coral, these can inflict a painful sting if handled or brushed against. Large black sea urchins are also common on some reefs and their spines can penetrate unprotected skin very easily. Probably the best advice when observing coral reefs and their wildlife is to look, but don't touch.

Other coastal habitats that may have interesting wildlife include beaches and sea cliffs. Some islands, especially those in the southern part of the Caribbean, have spectacular cliffs and offshore islets. These are home to large flocks of sea birds including the piratical frigate bird which chases

smaller birds, forcing them to disgorge their catch; another notable species
is the tropic bird with its streamer like tail feathers. The cliffs may also provide
dry sandy soils for the large range of Caribbean cacti, including prickly pear
(*opuntia sp*) and the Turks head cactus.

Wetlands (Rivers, Swamps, Mangroves)

Wetlands include a wide range of fresh and brackish water habitats such as
rivers, marsh and mangroves. They are important for many species of bird,
as well as fish. Unfortunately they are also home to an array of biting insects,
including mosquitos which can be unpleasant though only a serious problem
in Hispaniola where malaria is still present.

Important coastal wetlands include the Baie de Fort de France
(Martinique), the Cabrits Swamp (Dominica), Caroni (Trinidad), Negril and
Black Morass (Jamaica). These sites all support large flocks of migratory and
resident birds including waders, herons, egrets and ducks. In addition, some
of the mangroves in the Greater Antilles also provide habitats for manatee,
and the Negril and Black Morass has a population of American crocodiles.
Large freshwater lakes are less common although Grenada, Dominica and
St Vincent all have volcanic crater lakes and these are used by migratory
waders and ducks as well as kingfishers.

Woodland and Forest (Thorn Scrub, Plantations, Rainforest)

There is little if any primary rainforest left in the Caribbean, although there
may be small patches in Guadeloupe. Nevertheless, many of the islands still
have large areas of good secondary forest which has only suffered from a
limited amount of selective felling for commercially valuable wood (eg
gommier, balata and blue mahoe).

Martinique has some of the largest tracts of forest left in the Caribbean
(eg rainforest at Piton du Carbet, cloud forest on Mt Pelée, dry woodland
in the south). Many other islands also have accessible forest, although you
should always use a local guide if venturing off the beaten track.

The Caribbean rainforests are not as diverse as those on the South and
Central American mainland, however they still support a very large number
of plant species many of which are endemic (Jamaica has over 3,000 species
of which 800 are endemic). The orchids and bromeliads are particularly
impressive in many forests and it is not unusual to see trees festooned with
both these groups. The wildlife of the rainforest includes both native and
introduced species, although they are often difficult to see in the rather
shady conditions. Agouti, boa constrictor, monkeys and opossum may be
seen, but it is the bird life that is most evident. Hummingbirds, vireos,
thrashers, todies and others are all found along with parrots, which are
perhaps the group most associated with this habitat. Early morning and
evening provide the best times for birdwatching.

Plantations of commercial timber (blue mahoe, Caribbean pine, teak,
mahogany and others) have been established in many places. These reduce
pressure on natural forest and help to protect watersheds and soil. They are
also valuable for wildlife and some species have adapted to them with
alacrity (eg hummingbirds in blue mahoe plantation).

Closer to the coasts, dry scrub woodland often predominates. The trees
may lose their leaves during the dry season. One of the most recognizable
of the trees in this woodland is the turpentine tree, also known as the tourist
tree because of its red peeling bark.

Bush medicines and herbal remedies are still used in the countryside although less so than previously. Leaves and bark can be seen for sale in markets.

Books: Field Guides

There are not many good books on Caribbean wildlife. The following are worth looking for: *Tropical Wild Flowers*, V E Graham (Hulton Educational Publications); *Caribbean Wild Plants and their Uses*, P Honeychurch (Macmillan); *Birds of the West Indies*, J Bond (Collins); *A Guide to the Birds of Trinidad and Tobago*, Richard Ffrench (Horowood); *Flora and Fauna of the Caribbean*, P Bacon (Key Caribbean Publications, PO Box 21, Port of Spain, Trinidad); *Fishwatchers Guide to West Atlantic Coral Reefs*, C C Chaplin (Horowood Books—some printed on plastic paper for use underwater); *Guide to Corals and Fishes of Florida, the Bahamas and the Caribbean*, I Greenberg (Seahawk Press).

Macmillan also produce short field guides on *The Flowers of the Caribbean*, *The Fishes of the Caribbean*, *Fishes of the Caribbean Reefs*, *Marine Life of the Caribbean*, *Butterflies and Other Insects of the Caribbean*; and the *Ephemeral Isles, a Natural History of the Bahamas*.

Specialist Reading

For the more serious naturalist, there are several detailed reviews of the natural history and conservation of wildlife in the Caribbean. Among the best and most widely available are the *Floristic Inventory of Tropical Countries* (World Wide Fund for Nature) which contains a short report on the Caribbean; *Biodiversity and Conservation in the Caribbean*, Profiles of selected islands (includes Cozumel, Dominica, Grenada, Guadeloupe, Jamaica, Martinique, Montserrat, Puerto Rico, St Lucia, St Vincent, San Andrés) published by the International Council for Bird Preservation, ISBN 0 946888 14 0; *Fragments of Paradise* which covers conservation issues in the UK dependencies (Pisces Publications, ISBN 0 9508245 5 0). *A Field Guide to the Coral Reefs of the Caribbean and Florida including Bermuda and the Bahamas*, Peterson Field Guides Series no. 27 (Houghton Mifflin Company). *Coral Reefs of the World*—Volume I, S Wells et al (IUCN)

The Natural History Book Service (Tel: UK 0803 865913) holds a very large stock of wildlife and conservation books on the Caribbean.

Mark Eckstein, with additional information from Mark Wilson

Pre-Columbian Civilizations

The recorded history of the Caribbean islands begins with the arrival of Christopher Columbus' fleet in 1492. Our knowledge of the native peoples who inhabited the islands before and at the time of his arrival is largely derived from the accounts of contemporary Spanish writers and from archaeological examinations as there is no evidence of indigenous written records.

The Amerindians encountered by Columbus in the Greater Antilles had no overall tribal name but organized themselves in a series of villages or local chiefdoms, each of which had its own tribal name. The name now used, Arawak, was not in use then. The term Arawak was used by the Indians of the Guianas, a group of whom had spread into Trinidad, but their territory was not explored until nearly another century later. The use of the generic term, Arawak, to describe the Indians Columbus encountered, arose because of linguistic similarities with the Arawaks of the mainland. It is therefore surmised that migration took place many centuries before Columbus' arrival, but the two groups were not in contact at that time. The time of the latest migration from the mainland, and consequently the existence of the island Arawaks, is in dispute, with some academics tracing it to about the time of Christ (the arrival of the Saladoids) and others to AD 1000 (the Ostionoids).

    The inhabitants of the Bahamas were generally referred to as Lucayans, and those of the Greater Antilles as Tainos, but there were many sub-groupings. The inhabitants of the Lesser Antilles were, however, referred to as Carib and were described to Columbus as an aggressive tribe which sacrificed and sometimes ate the prisoners they captured in battle. It was from them that the Caribbean gets its name and from which the word cannibal is derived.

    The earliest known inhabitants of the region, the Siboneys, migrated from Florida and spread throughout the Bahamas and the major islands. Most archaeological evidence of their settlements has been found near the shore, along bays or streams, where they lived in small groups. The largest discovered settlement has been one of 100 inhabitants in Cuba. They were hunters and gatherers, living on fish and other seafood, small rodents, iguanas, snakes and birds. They gathered roots and wild fruits, such as guava, guanabana and mamey, but did not cultivate plants. They worked with primitive tools made out of stone, shell, bone or wood, for hammering, chipping or scraping, but had no knowledge of pottery. The Siboneys were eventually absorbed by the advance of the Arawaks migrating from the south, who had made more technological advances in agriculture, arts and crafts.

    The people now known as Arawaks migrated from the Guianas to Trinidad and on through the island arc to Cuba. Their population expanded because of the natural fertility of the islands and the abundance of fruit and seafood, helped by their agricultural skills in cultivating and improving wild plants and their excellent boatbuilding and fishing techniques. They were healthy, tall, good looking and lived to a ripe old age. It is estimated that up to 8 million may have lived on the island of Hispaniola alone, but there was always plenty of food for all.

Their society was essentially communal and organized around families. The smaller islands were particularly egalitarian, but in the larger ones, where village communities of extended families numbered up to 500 people, there was an incipient class structure. Typically, each village had a headman, called a *cacique*, whose duty it was to represent the village when dealing with other tribes, to settle family disputes and organize defence. However, he had no powers of coercion and was often little more than a nominal head. The position was largely hereditary, with the eldest son of the eldest sister having rights of succession, but women could and did become *caciques*. In the larger communities, there was some delegation of responsibility to the senior men, but economic activities were usually organized along family lines, and their power was limited.

The division of labour was usually based on age and sex. The men would clear and prepare the land for agriculture and be responsible for defence of the village, while women cultivated the crops and were the major food producers, also making items such as mats, baskets, bowls and fishing nets. Women were in charge of raising the children, especially the girls, while the men taught the boys traditional customs, skills and rites.

The Tainos hunted for some of their food, but fishing was more important and most of their settlements were close to the sea. Fish and shellfish were their main sources of protein and they had many different ways of catching them, from hands, baskets or nets to poisoning, shooting or line fishing. Cassava was a staple food, which they had successfully learned to leach of its poisonous juice. They also grew yams, maize, cotton, arrowroot, peanuts, beans, cocoa and spices, rotating their crops to prevent soil erosion. It is documented that in Jamaica they had three harvests of maize annually, using maize and cassava to make breads, cakes and beer.

Cotton was used to make clothing and hammocks (never before seen by Europeans), while the calabash tree was used to make ropes and cords, baskets and roofing. Plants were used for medicinal and spiritual purposes, and cosmetics such as face and body paint. Also important, both to the Arawaks and later to the Europeans, was the cultivation of tobacco, as a drug and as a means of exchange.

They had no writing, no beasts of burden, no wheeled vehicles and no hard metals, although they did have some alluvial gold for personal ornament. The abundance of food allowed them time to develop their arts and crafts and they were skilled in woodwork and pottery. They had polished stone tools, but also carved shell implements for manioc preparation or as fishhooks. Coral manioc graters have also been found. Their boatbuilding techniques were noted by Columbus, who marvelled at their canoes of up to 75 feet in length, carrying up to 50 people, made of a single tree trunk in one piece. It took two months to fell a tree by gradually burning and chipping it down, and many more to make the canoe.

The Arawaks had three main deities, evidence of which have been found in stone and conch carvings in many of the Lesser Antilles as well as the well populated Greater Antilles, although their relative importance varied according to the island. The principal male god was Yocahú, *yoca* being the word for cassava and *hú* meaning "giver of". It is believed that the Indians associated this deity's power to provide cassava with the mystery of the volcanoes, for all the carvings, the earliest out of shells and the later ones of stone, are conical. The Yocahú cult was wiped out in the Lesser Antilles by the invading Caribs, and in the Greater Antilles by the Spaniards, but it is thought to have existed from about 200 AD.

The main female diety was a fertility goddess, often referred to as Atabeyra, but she is thought to have had several names relating to her other roles as goddess of the moon, mother of the sea, the tides and the springs, and the goddess of childbirth. In carvings she is usually depicted as a squatting figure with her hands up to her chin, sometimes in the act of giving birth.

A third deity is a dog god, named Opiyel-Guaobiran, meaning "the dog deity who takes care of the souls of the immediately deceased and is the son of the spirit of darkness." Again, carvings of a dog's head or whole body have been found of shell or stone, which were often used to induce narcotic trances. Many of the carvings have holes and Y-shaped passages which would have been put to the nose to snuff narcotics and induce a religious trance in the shaman or priest, who could then ascertain the status of a departed soul for a recently bereaved relative.

One custom which aroused interest in the Spaniards was the ball game, not only for the sport and its ceremonial features, but because the ball was made of rubber and bounced, a phenomenon which had not previously been seen in Europe. Catholicism soon eradicated the game, but archaeological remains have been found in several islands, notably in Puerto Rico, but also in Jamaica and Hispaniola. Excavations in the Greater Antilles have revealed earth embankments and rows of elongated upright stones surrounding plazas or courts, pavements and stone balls. These are called *bateyes, juegos de indios, juegos de bola, cercados* or *corrales de indios. Batey* was the aboriginal name for the ball game, the rubber ball itself and also the court where it was played. The word is still used to designate the cleared area in front of houses in the country.

The ball game had religious and ceremonial significance but it was a sport and bets and wagers were important. It was played by two teams of up to 20 or 30 players, who had to keep the ball in the air by means of their hips, shoulders, heads, elbows and other parts of their body, but never with their hands. The aim was to bounce the ball in this manner to the opposing team until it hit the ground. Men and women played, but not usually in mixed sex games. Great athleticism was required and it is clear that the players practised hard to perfect their skill, several, smaller practice courts having been built in larger settlements. The game was sometimes played before the village made an important decision, and the prize could be a sacrificial victim, usually a prisoner, granted to the victor.

In 1492 Arawaks inhabited all the greater islands of the Caribbean, but in Puerto Rico they were being invaded by the Caribs who had pushed north through the Lesser Antilles, stealing their women and enslaving or killing the men. The Caribs had also originated in South America, from around the Orinoco delta. In their migration northwards through the Caribbean islands they proved to be fierce warriors and their raids on the Arawak settlements were feared. Many of their women were captured Arawaks, and it was they who cultivated the land and performed the domestic chores. Polygamy was common, encouraged by the surplus of women resulting from the raids, and the Arawak female influence on Carib culture was strong.

Despite rumours of cannibalism reported to Columbus by frightened Arawaks, there appears to be no direct evidence of the practice, although the Spaniards took it seriously enough to use it as an excuse to justify taking slaves. After some unfortunate encounters, colonizers left the Caribs alone for many years. The Arawaks, on the other hand, were soon wiped out by disease, cruelty and murder. The Spanish invaders exacted tribute and forced labour while allowing their herds of cattle and pigs to destroy the Indians' unfenced fields and clearings. Transportation to the mines resulted in shifts in the native population which could not be fed from the surrounding areas and starvation became common. Lack of labour in the Greater Antilles led to slave raids on the Lucayans in the Bahamas, but they also died or committed collective suicide. They felt that their gods had deserted them and there was nowhere for them to retreat or escape. Today there are no full-blooded Arawaks and only a handful of Caribs is left on Dominica. The 500 years since Columbus' arrival have served to obliterate practically all the evidence of the indigenous civilization.

The Contemporary Caribbean

The decisive date in the shaping of the modern Caribbean was 1492, when Christopher Columbus successfully crossed the Atlantic to make landfall in the Antilles. Although Spain did not exert its influence here to the same degree as on the American mainland, the way was open for Europeans to follow Columbus, take possession of, fight over and exploit the islands for profit. Over the following five centuries, the population of the region has been imported and almost all traces of the precolumbian past have been removed. Similarly, the majority of food and cash crops grown have been transplanted from elsewhere.

At one stage, the islands were some of the most valuable colonies ever known, but little of the wealth they generated stayed in the region. Being for the most part small, the territories still depend on the outside world for their prosperity (commodity exports, tourism), but with limited regional organization and economic imbalances there is great inequality of reward. Politically the region is disunited. Its own major events, like the Haitian and Cuban Revolutions, the movement towards black consciousness, have had tremendous, lasting impact outside their immediate realm, but at the same time have been engulfed in wider, global concerns.

The culture that the immigrants brought with them is now confronted by influences of global media systems. Ease of travel has also brought cultural pressures, not solely from the incoming tourist, but also from the large number of emigrants who, having sought work abroad, bring home the culture of their adopted countries. Conversely, emigration, the result of the unemployment which followed the decline of labour intensive agriculture, takes Caribbean culture to Europe and North America. At the same time, though, it causes a social structure which is heavily biased towards female heads of families when the men go elsewhere to work.

Yet for all the new cultural clashes, which build up on top of older ones (French spoken on "English" islands, islands divided between nations), the struggle for a Caribbean identity continues, particularly in the work of writers and artists. Different colours and faiths coexist; the African and European mix to make some of the most vibrant music; the goal of the Jamaican national motto applies to all: "Out of many, one people".

BERMUDA

Introduction

ONE OF BRITAIN'S OLDEST, now self-governing, dependent territories is Bermuda. It comprises over 150 small islands and islets in the western Atlantic, 775 miles southeast of New York, and 900 miles northeast of Nassau, Bahamas. The ten largest islands form the main land mass of 21 square miles. They are linked by causeways and bridges to create a narrow chain which, seen from the air, takes the shape of a fish hook. Under one of its earliest governors, Daniel Tucker, Bermuda was divided into eight tribes, now called the parishes of Hamilton, Smiths, Devonshire, Pembroke, Paget, Warwick, Southampton and Sandys, with the "public land" at St George.

Bermuda sits on a cap of rock made up of tiny coral creatures, accumulated over millions of years, surmounting an extinct volcano which rises sharply from the seabed. The land is hilly, but too porous for streams to form. The mild, semi-tropical climate brings high yearly rainfall and sunshine, which sustains the attractive hedgerows and trees lining long stretches of narrow road. Most fresh water in buildings is provided by rainfall, on which all rely. The rainwater is collected from the white, furrowed roofs characteristic of Bermudian houses, channelled into underground storage tanks, then pumped into the houses. Bermuda's rural aspect is being transformed into a more urban environment as development has been fuelled by rising property values.

Around the islands are some notoriously treacherous coral reefs which are the graveyard of many seafarers and their ships. Paradoxically, the reefs protect the inshore waters, which are the feeding grounds throughout the year for a wealth of marine flora and fauna.

The civilian population in 1990 stood at approximately 59,300, about 60% of whom were of African origin, the remainder being mainly of European descent. Currently there are several thousand guest "contract" workers, whose skills are required to maintain the islands' business and environmental development. Population density is extremely high, at 2,824 per square mile, with the entire population classed as urban. The United States, Canada and the United Kingdom have had established military bases as, for many years, Bermuda has been considered strategically important. The US presence is the greatest, with its substantial Air Force base adjacent to Kindley Field Airport used by both military and commercial air transport. However, personnel at the US naval air force station are to be reduced from 850 to 300 by end-1993, while the Canadian navy communications base, employing 70 people, closed in 1992. The Royal Navy's base is visited

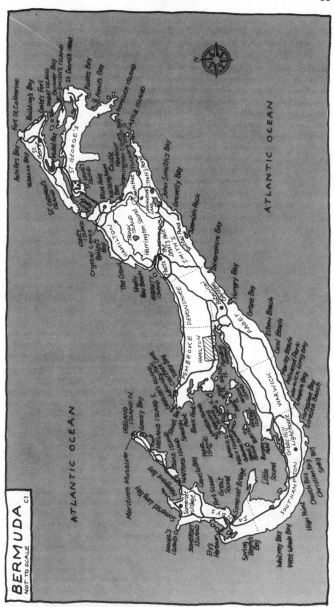

regularly by NATO frigates- and destroyer-class vessels, which call in for refuelling and provisioning.

History

Evidence suggests that Bermuda was first discovered by the Spanish explorer Juan Bermúdez, early in the 16th century. Apart from one or two subsequent landings by seafarers, notably in 1543 at Spittal Pond by the Portuguese, Bermuda was not inhabited until 1609 when the British ship *Sea Venture*, bound for Virginia, ran into a storm and foundered on the coral reef. The *Sea Venture*'s company, headed by Admiral Sir George Somers, struggled ashore at St Catherine's beach. With an abundant supply of Bermuda cedar timber and food, principally fish and birds, the ship's company was able to settle for nearly a year before resuming its voyage after building the *Deliverance*, a replica of which stands on Ordnance Island, St George.

In 1612 a charter was granted by King James I to the Virginia Company to include the Bermudas as part of its dominions, but in 1684 Charles II dissolved the Virginia Company charter and Bermuda became a Royal colony.

The 1968 elections were won by the multi-racial United Bermuda Party (UBP), but racial tensions dominated politics at the time and race riots erupted in 1972-73 and again in 1977. The main opposition party is the left wing, mostly black, Progressive Labour Party. In 1989, the UBP, led by John Swan, was elected to a third term of office, but with a much reduced majority. Its representation in the House of Assembly fell from 31 seats to 23, while the PLP increased its share from 7 to 15. The National Liberal Party and an Independent hold one seat each. Independence from the UK had been an election issue, but as a result of the vote, Premier John Swan dropped his plans for increased autonomy.

Government

Bermuda is a Crown Colony of the United Kingdom. The British Government has responsibility for foreign affairs, defence and national security and is represented by a Governor. In 1992 Lord Waddington, former UK Home Secretary and latterly Conservative leader in the House of Lords, was appointed Governor. The country remains today one of the oldest self-governing British dependent territories, the Bermuda constitution becoming effective in June 1968.

The Economy

The main engine of economic growth in Bermuda is tourism, which accounts for half of gdp and is the major employer and source of foreign exchange revenues. About 85% of all tourists come from the USA and Bermuda is therefore highly susceptible to fluctuations in US demand. Three good years in 1985-87 were followed by a slump of 8% in 1988 after the end-1987 US stock market crash and a further fall of 6% in visitors in 1989. In 1990 air arrivals rose by 4% but cruise ship passengers fell by 14% with the number of ships calling dropping to 121 from 165 in 1989 in line with a government decision to limit them. In 1991 air arrivals fell again by 11% to 384,046 as the US market slumped a further 12%, but a slight increase was noted in cruise ship passengers. Cruise ship passengers account for 23% of all visitors and the island is generally a high cost tourist destination.

Bermuda is also a leading offshore business centre and is the largest centre for captive insurance and reinsurance. Over 6,200 companies are registered, including more than 1,200 captive and other insurance corporations, which have benefited from US tax concessions. While growth in the offshore business has slowed, Bermuda has gained from offshore companies transferring out of Hong Kong before 1997 and, to a lesser extent, from the troubles in Panama. The shipping register rose sharply from 1.58m gross registered tons in 1986 to over 3.5m tons by end-1988, and is the fifth largest free flag merchant fleet in the world.

There is little agriculture on Bermuda and only 800 acres are devoted to farming for domestic consumption, market gardening and dairy produce. Pressure on land is intense and the island's size imposes development constraints. The population is close to the maximum tolerable although unemployment is virtually non-existent and per capita income is one of the highest in the world. Environmental issues have become important for the electorate, as have high housing costs, scarce low-cost housing, the office development boom, traffic congestion and the high level of immigration, which has brought about 8,000 foreign professionals to the island, equivalent to nearly 23% of the total employed.

The lack of an export industry and scarce farming land means that Bermuda suffers from large, persistent trade deficits, as virtually all its needs are met by imports. However, this is offset by the well-developed service sector and the current account of the balance of payments usually shows a small surplus. The Gulf crisis and the downturn in the US economy was keenly felt in 1990-92 as the flow of tourists slowed, higher oil prices pushed up inflation to around 6% and tax increases were necessary to cover budget spending proposals.

Flora and Fauna

The rural parts of the island are covered by vegetation apart from breaks and rocky protrusions which pierce the thin layers of top soil. The endemic plants include olivewod bark, which is rare, and the cedar. The cedar tree with its exceptionally pleasant smelling timber once covered the island but in 1945 it was severely blighted by an insect pest. Native plants transported by natural means to the islands are the palmetto and bermudiana. Other trees introduced from different parts of the world include the pimento, the poinciana, fiddlewood, the Surinam cherry, the casuarina, the Norfolk Island pine, the coconut and royal palms. Bananas, loquats, guavas and citrus fruits which are sold from roadside stalls grow quite plentifully alongside other "allotment" type vegetable crops. The Easter Lily is cultivated for local sale. It was one of Bermuda's agricultural exports. Other shrubs include oleander and hibiscus, often grown as hedgerows. Geraniums, fennel and other herbs grow plentifully while in the sandier beach soil the prickly pear is common. Two endemic varieties of fern survive, the pretty maidenhair and the tough sword fern.

Bermuda has few wild animals, the largest are rodents and lizards and the saucer-sized toad introduced to help control pests. The whistling tree frogs have a leading voice in the continual orchestral background which reaches almost crescendo proportions after heavy rain. Other singers are the yellow kis-k-dee, the red coloured cardinal, the endemic blue bird and the European starling and sparrow. The white seagoing longtail gull is the flying favourite of the Bermudians as it glides through the summer skies during its regular visits to the islands. Jewellery models of the longtail are very popular with holiday visitors.

Of the insect "nasties" there are very few of the stinging variety. The principal beast to avoid is the two- to four-inch centipede which has poisonous pincers. These fortunately are come across very infrequently. Cockroaches, which are much more prevalent, especially near dampness or where food is stored, are relatively harmless. There is an interesting variety of spiders, moths, butterflies and the less interesting mosquito, which can irritate but does not usually pose a problem.

Diving and Marine Life

The extensive coral reef barrier combined with the warmth of the gulf stream provides excellent feeding and breeding grounds for varieties of colourful tropical and reef fish. Beyond the reef some of the most popular game fish can be found. Although commercial fishing is restricted to holders of fishing licences, and the catching of lobster and conch is regulated, in recent years concern has been expressed, not least by the conservation organizations (Friends of Fish), that fish stocks are decreasing at an alarming rate. In 1990 the Government announced a ban, effective 31 March, on pot fishing, together with limits on permitted catches by fishing boats. For information on fishing contact Tom Smith (Tel: 238 0112), secretary of the Bermuda Game Fishing Association and representative of the International Game Fish Association.

The reefs together with the carcasses of many wrecked ships, ranging from Spanish and French galleons to more recent paddleships and steamers, provide memorable scuba-diving. A number of well trained operators run daily excursions and give guidance to novice and experienced divers. All equipment is available for hire. Among the several local diving operators are Blue Water Divers Ltd at Robinson's Marina, Somerset Bridge, Sandys (Tel: 234 1034, Fax: 234 3561), two tank dive US$60, half day snorkelling US$28, and Nautilus Diving Ltd at *Southampton Princess Hotel* (Tel: 238 2332, Fax: 236 4284), two tank dive US$65, snorkelling US$25, both dive shops offer resort courses for US$75. Other companies with similar rates include Dive Bermuda, 6 Dockyard Terrace, Sandys (Tel: 234 0225, Fax 234 0723), Fantasea Diving, 6 Fairylands Road, Pembroke (Tel: 295 3052), South Side Scuba Watersports, at *Grotto Beach Hotel*, Hamilton Parish, and at *Sonesta Beach*, Southampton (Tel: 293 2915). Two operators offer helmet diving, which you do by walking, not swimming, underwater at a depth of 10 feet (the open-bottomed helmet is like a glass inverted in water, creating a vacuum, fresh air is pumped in through the top and bubbles escape at the bottom, your hair stays dry and you can reach inside, the helmet appears weightless): Bronson Hartley, Flatt's Village, Smith's (Tel: 292 4434) and Greg Hartley, Sandys (Tel/Fax: 234 2861), both do three-hour glass bottomed boat tour and shallow dive for US$36.

The local branch of the British Sub Aqua Club (BSAC), based in Admiralty Park, Pembroke, has been operating and training novices since 1971. Members of BSAC visiting Bermuda are recommended to contact the dive leader for information and advice for favoured in-shore and off-shore diving sites. The shallowness of some of the reef areas and rock formations in clear, relatively calm inshore waters make excellent snorkelling conditions. Recommended diving sites include South West Breaker (off *Sonesta Beach Hotel*), John Smith's Bay and L'Hermione (from Somerset Bridge).

Beaches and Watersports

The beach-going and water sport season for Bermudians traditionally runs from 24 May (Queen Victoria's birthday: Empire Day, now Bermuda Day) to October when sea temperatures can reach a maximum of 32°C (average in July/August 26°C). Sea temperatures rarely fall below 19°C at any time during the year. The blue and turquoise tones of the sea are striking, and the pink-tinted coral beaches of soft powdery sand are exceptional. Horseshoe Bay, Church Bay, Warwick Long Bay and Elbow Beach are favourites and are cleaned regularly. Lifeguards are on duty at certain times at Horseshoe Beach and John Smith's Bay. Unleashed dogs are not allowed on public beaches. It is important for swimmers to be aware of under-currents which can be strong. They should· also watch for portuguese-man-of-war jelly fish, fortunately only a threat during February and March. The unmistakable floating 2-8 inch long cigar shaped wind bag supports up to ten foot long tentacles which can give nasty multiple stings.

Several operators, centred mainly in Hamilton and St George, run glass-bottomed boat tours, game fishing, snorkelling, wind surfing, parasailing (US$40), water ski-ing (US$40-50/30 minutes) and a host of other activities. Prices for glass-bottomed boat cruises with snorkelling are US$30-37 for 3½-4 hours. Boardsailing rentals at Mangrove Marina (Tel: 234 0914) or Watlington's Windsurfing Bermuda at Glencoe Harbour Club, Paget (Tel: 236 5274) are US$15/hour, US$50/day, but at South Side Scuba Watersports boards cost US$20/hour, US$80/day. Sailing is one of the most popular watersports for residents. Sunfish and other craft can be rented for US$25-35 for two hours from Mangrove Marina, Harbour Road Marina, Rance's Boatyard, Robinson's Charter Boat Marina, Salt Kettle Boat Rentals and South Side Scuba Watersports, the last two also offering sailing instruction. Chartered yachts with licensed skippers are available from US$200-250/half day. Visitors with some previous crewing experience can seek crewing opportunities at the Royal Hamilton Yacht Club and Dinghy Club. As well as casual sailing in and around the islands, there are substantial numbers of week-end racing events which take place in the Great Sound for various classes of boats.

Other Sports

The principal land sport (competitive and part time) is **golf**. "Make your friends green with envy at one easy stroke" from a choice of eight scenic golf courses providing a stimulating variety of play for the beginner or the professional. An introduction can be arranged through the visitor's hotel or guest house. Port Royal is owned and operated by the government and the green fee is US$36 compared with about US$70 at a private club. Bermudians generally take a break from golf from May until September when it gets cooler again. A useful tip to bear in mind is that from 1600 green fees on some courses are reduced by fifty per cent. Reseeding is done late September to early November, depending on the weather; some courses use temporary greens. The Bermuda Golf Guide published by the Bermuda Department of Tourism tells you all you need to know about the clubs, courses and fees.

Running and **cycling** are popular and a number of marathon and triathlon events are held annually. Walking the old railway trail is a relaxing and pleasurable way of exploring the heart of Bermuda's countryside, and you can appreciate the flowers, trees, birds and small creatures in their natural setting. *The Bermuda Railway Trail Guide* is available from the Visitor's Service Bureau. The Guide describes the trail in sections of 1¾-3¾ miles, some of which are suitable for bicycles and motor bikes, but most can be walked only. Some parks are available for picnics.

The larger hotels have **tennis** courts, (rates vary considerably from free to US$10 for house guests) and fresh water swimming pools. There is a Government Tennis Stadium at Pembroke (Tel: 292 0105) with teaching pro, US$5 on clay, US$4 on asphalt; the private Coral Beach and Tennis Club, South Road, Paget (Tel: 236 2233), several pros, 8 clay courts, introduction by member only, US$3 guest fee, US$6 court rental; the Pomander Gate

Tennis Club, Paget (Tel: 236 5400), has 4 hard courts, US$10; the Port Royal Club, Southampton (Tel: 234 0974), has 4 flexipave courts, US$5, pro on request. Proper tennis clothes are required everywhere. Tournaments are held throughout the year, for details contact the Bermuda Lawn Tennis Association, PO Box HM 341, Hamilton HM BX, Bermuda. There are two English size squash courts at the Coral Beach and Tennis Club and four international size courts at the Bermuda Squash Racquets Club next to the National's Sports Club, Middle Road, Devonshire (Tel: 292 6881), open 0900-2300 by reservation, US$5 pp for 40 minutes, including towel, racquet and ball. There is a strong **rugby union** following, particularly amongst British ex-patriots. The principal local teams are called the Mariners, Police, Renegades and Teachers. Bermuda has a national side that competes in a number of international fixtures at home or abroad. League football and cricket are also very popular, with the highlight of the **cricket** calendar being Cup Match Day, which is a national holiday. **Horse riding** is strictly controlled and you must be accompanied by a qualified instructor. Lee Bow Riding Centre, Tribe Road 1, Devonshire (Tel: 236 4181), lessons available daily by reservation, trail rides US$25/hour. Spicelands Riding Centre, Middle Road, Warwick (Tel: 238 8212), trail rides US$25/hour, 0700 ride along South Shore followed by breakfast US$37.50, lessons available on request. For information on horse shows, gymkhanas etc, contact the Bermuda Equestrian Federation, PO Box DV 583, Devonshire DV BX, Bermuda.

Hamilton

Hamilton, in the parish of Pembroke (population approximately 6,000) is the capital, located centrally in the island chain. Traditionally a harbour town, it is laid out almost geometrically, on rising ground. In recent years its development as a business centre has been phenomenal and building projects have proliferated. At the present time, there is a government restriction on the height of buildings. Most of the duty-free shops are located along Front Street facing the water. Bermuda has the third oldest parliament in the world and the **Sessions House** was built in 1817, when the seat of Government was moved from St George's, where Parliament had sat for two centuries. The Golden Jubilee clocktower and terracotta colonnade were added in 1887. Open Monday-Friday 0900-1700, you can watch debates from the Visitors' Gallery when Parliament meets, October-July on Fridays at 1000. The Supreme Court, also in the Sessions House, meets most of the year. The Cabinet Building and Senate Chamber, opposite, are also open to the public Monday-Friday 0900-1700, and you can watch Senate debates on Wednesdays. **The Library**, Queens Street Hamilton is a well-maintained and stocked library, in a quiet attractive building where the international press can be read freely. Open Monday-Friday 0930-1800, Saturday 0930-1700. It is situated next to the Par-la-Ville Gardens, originally the private garden to the town house, Par-la-Ville, now the Bermuda Historical Society Museum, open Monday, Tuesday, Friday, Saturday 0930-1230, 1400-1630.

Island Excursions

St George (population approximately 3,000) was the capital until 1815. This old harbour town is located at the north end of the island, not far from Kindley Field airport. The town with its quaint old houses, walled gardens and picturesque alleyways was said to have been the setting of Shakespeare's *The Tempest*: "the vexed Bermouthes". Bermudians and visitors have worshipped undisturbed in the Anglican **St Peter's Church**, Kings Square, St George since the present church was built in 1713, which represents the longest continued use in the Western Hemisphere. The original church, built in 1612, was wooden and thatched with palmetto leaf; a stone structure replaced it in 1619. The tower was added to the 1713 building in 1814. Donations welcome. The State House (open 1000-1600 most Wednesdays), at the top of King Street, is the oldest building in Bermuda. It was built by Governor Nathaniel Butler in 1620 and while St George was the capital the House of Assembly and the principal court met here. It is currently rented to a Masonic Lodge for one peppercorn a year; the Peppercorn Ceremony in April is a highlight of the town's annual festivities. Bridge House, also on King Street, dates from the beginning of the 18th century and was the home of several governors, now owned by the Bermuda National Trust and used as an art gallery, open Monday-Saturday, 1000-1700. Cedar furniture and Bermudan antiquities can be seen at St George's Historical Society Museum on Duke of Kent Street, open Monday-Friday except holidays, 1000-1600, entrance US$1, children 6-16 half price, under 6 free. Other museums include three owned by the Bermuda National Trust: Tucker House, on Water Street, containing cedar furniture and items collected by the prominent Bermudan Tucker family, open Monday-Saturday except holidays, 1000-1700, entrance US$2 or by combination ticket; The Old Rectory, off Church Street, open Wednesdays and Fridays, 1000-1700, donations welcome; and the Confederate Museum, King's Square, built in 1700 by Governor Samuel Day, now housing memorabilia from the American Civil War, open Monday-Saturday, 1000-1700, entrance US$2 or by combination ticket.

Some of the most attractive and interesting places to visit can be reached relatively easily by moped (see below on moped hire). A selection of sights worth visiting are: **Fort St Catherine** at the northeast tip of St George's. The restored fort that once defended Bermuda contains exhibits and military memorabilia covering the island's history. Open daily except Christmas Day, 1000-1630, entrance US$2.50, children under 12 free. **Fort Hamilton**, overlooking Hamilton, designed by the Duke of Wellington to protect the Royal Naval Dockyard from land attack. Underground passages were cut through rock in the 1870s but the moat is now a pleasant garden. There are so many fortifications on Bermuda that the Tourist Board has a leaflet just on forts, some of which are easily accessible and in good condition.

The Royal Naval Dockyard was built on Ireland Island North as a winter anchorage and major dockyard to repair Royal Naval ships used to protect trans-Atlantic shipping. Work began in 1809 and the hard labour was carried out by slaves and thousands of British convicts, many of whom died of yellow fever. H M Dockyard was opened to the public in 1951 when Royal Navy operations ceased, and there are many fine stone buildings, fortifications and wharfs, some of which have been converted for other uses. **The Bermuda Maritime Museum** in the fortified keep displays Bermuda's nautical heritage over the last four centuries (entrance US$5, children under 12 US$1, open 1000-1700, last admission 1630, daily except Christmas Day. Other things to visit at the dockyard include the Victualling Yard and the Cooperage, a secure area for storing food that was preserved in barrels made by the cooper; the Bermuda Arts Centre, open Tuesday-Friday 1000-1630,

Saturday-Sunday 1100-1630, entrance US$1, half price children under 12, exhibitions change every month and feature Bermudian and foreign artists, photographers, sculptors and craftsmen; the Craft Market, open daily 1000-1600 except Christmas Day and Boxing Day, demonstrations begin at 1100 in the Cooperage. Guided walking tours at 1200 and 1430, US$2 adults, children free, starting at the Cooperage.

Spittal Pond, near John Smith's Bay in Smiths parish, is the island's largest nature reserve comprising 60 acres of lush parkland, home of much of Bermuda's wildlife. **Aquarium at Flatt's**, Smith's parish. Located at the seaward entrance to Harrington Sound, the aquarium has a wide selection of healthy-looking marine life in a natural environment (entrance approximately US$5 per person). **Crystal and Leamington Caves**, Smith's Parish: stunning tours through rock and salt formations in underground caves.

Botanical Gardens, South Road, Paget. This is a quiet and uncrowded 36-acre park where visitors may stroll or picnic amid sub-tropical floral gardens and bird song. There is an orchid house, an aviary, formal gardens, a hibiscus garden containing 150 varieties, a palm garden, sub-tropical fruit garden and a garden for the blind with scented plants and herbs. Open sunrise to sunset, guided tours Tuesday, Wednesday (except in November-March) and Friday at 1030 from the main car park. Also in the Gardens is Camden, the official residence of the Premier, an 18th century mansion containing some superb cedar furniture and paintings, open Tuesday and Friday 1200-1400 unless there are official functions.

Gibbs Hill Lighthouse, off Lighthouse Road, Southampton. Shining since 1846, its 185 steps lead up one of the few cast-iron constructed lighthouses. It has a commanding view of the islands and the Great Sound.

Festivals
The principal festival is now the spring "cultural" festival running between January and March. Sailing regattas during the summer, in particular the fitted dinghy race series, are held in Hamilton and St George harbour, cricket match cup day and Gombeys dancing are the main occasions. The military brass band adds colour to a number of celebrations and anniversary proceedings.

Information for Visitors

Documents
All visitors must be able to present a return ticket or onward ticket, or other document of onward transportation. Visitors from the United Kingdom and Western Europe are required to present a valid Passport. Visitors from the United States are required to present either a passport (if recently expired the photograph should resemble bearer) or birth certificate issued by a competent municipal authority with a raised seal (or certified copy), or a US Re-entry Permit, US Naturalization Certificate, or US Alien Registration card. Visitors from Canada are required by the Bermuda Immigration Authorities to present either a valid passport, a Birth Certificate, or a Canadian Certificate of Citizenship. Visas are required for visitors from Albania, Algeria, Bulgaria, China (People's Republic of), Cuba, Czechoslovakia, Haiti, Hungary, Iran, Iraq, Jordan, Kampuchea (Cambodia), Laos, Lebanon, Libya, Mongolia, Morocco, Nigeria, North Korea, Philippines, Poland, Romania, South Africa, the former Soviet Union, Sri Lanka, Syria, Tunisia and Vietnam.

All bona fide visitors may stay in Bermuda for a reasonable period of time, usually up to 3 or 4 weeks. Passengers arriving with an open return ticket will have a time limit imposed. Permission to stay longer may have to be sought from the Immigration Department.

Bermuda has a very strict immigration control policy over non-Bermudian workers. Only nationals who have acquired "status" can freely look for employment.

How To Get There

Air links from the United Kingdom, United States and Canada are good. British Airways operates direct services twice a week from London (Gatwick) with a flight time of approximately 7 hours. There are also direct links and regular scheduled flights from New York, Boston, Atlanta, Baltimore, Charlotte, Detroit, Hartford, Orlando, Washington DC, Raleigh/ Durham, Pittsburgh, Philadelphia, Providence, Syracuse, Toronto and Halifax by American Airlines, Air Canada, Delta, North West Airlines, Continental and US Air. Look out for budget-priced tours advertized in major US weekend papers.

There are connections to a number of Caribbean islands via the USA.

The international airport at Kindley Field is 12 miles (20 km) from Hamilton. A US$15 departure tax is charged on visitors and residents alike. Children under 2 year exempt, children between 2 and 11 years US$5. Be prepared for handlers who will expect a gratuity tip somewhere in the region of US$1 to US$2 for carrying baggage the short distance between the baggage collections, through customs, to the taxi rank. The cost of a taxi ride to cover the 35 minute journey to Hamilton is approximately US$15. During the daytime the journey provides an excellent introduction to Bermuda's countryside and the cab driver will have the weather predictions at hand.

By Sea: The Royal Caribbean Cruise Line and the Chandris Line operate a weekly cruise service between New York and Hamilton. Additionally a number of cruise liners, Holland American, Kloster Cruises, Regency Cruises, including *Queen Elizabeth II*, visit the islands throughout the summer. Some of the larger liners have to drop anchor in the Great Sound when passengers continue their journey by ferry. The government levies a US$60 tax on all visitors collected by tour operators.

Customs

Visitors may bring into Bermuda duty-free, all clothing and articles for their personal use, including sports equipment, cameras, golf bags etc. Also 50 cigars, 200 cigarettes, 1lb of tobacco, 1 quart of wine and 1 quart of spirit. On all other items duty will be charged at approximately 30% of market value estimates.

When departing, visitors may take back merchandise duty-free to the following values: US citizens, cleared by US customs at Bermuda's airport are permitted US$400 after 48 hours and every 31 days; Canadians are allowed US$100 after 48 hours and any number of trips or US$300 after 7 days once every calendar year. British visitors are allowed £32. US customs pre-clearance is available in Bermuda for all scheduled flights. Declaration forms are stocked by hotels, travel agencies and airlines.

Local Travel

Motor cars were not admitted until 1947 and they are limited to size and number (one car per registered household). The official traffic speed limit is 22 mph (35 kph). Vehicles drive on the left along narrow roads which, in some places, are unpaved. Serious penalties are imposed on drivers recklessly exceeding the speed limit. International Driving Licences are not valid and car users must have a valid Bermuda driver's licence which can only be obtained after taking a practical and written test. Consequently there are no car-hire facilities whatsoever.

There is a regular **bus** service network to most parts of the island along the 125 miles of road. Buses depart from the main terminal in Hamilton from approximately 0600 to 1830. The only exception being the number 8 which travels along the middle road to Dockyard.

The cost of a bus from Hamilton to the airport is US$2.50 while shorter trips under 6 miles cost US$1.25 (children half-price). Exact change is required. Some saving can be made if you purchase a booklet of 15 tickets from the main terminal in Hamilton for US$16 (for trips over 6 miles) and US$9 (for trips under 6 miles). Multi-day passes are available from the Hamilton bus terminal and the Visitors Service Bureau. Bus timetables are readily available.

Taxis are common, but hard to find in bad weather. Radio cabs should be called in advance of important journeys. Taxis are metered and cost approximately US$4 for the first mile and US$1.40 each mile beyond. From midnight to 0600 there is a surcharge. Parcels carried in the boot or on the roof are US$0.25 each. Hourly/daily rates can be arranged for island tours.

Ferry boats run frequently from Hamilton to Paget, Salt Kettle, Warwick, Somerset, Watford Bridge and Dockyard.

Mopeds are the most popular form of transport for residents and tourists aged 16 and over. Machines can be hired relatively easily for about US$75 per week, inclusive of helmet and insurance, and without having had previous driving experience. Gasoline stations are open 0700-1900 Mon-Sat (although a few open until 2200), with limited opening hours on Sundays and holidays. Bicycles can also be hired. The charge for a horse-drawn carriage is approximately US$30 per hour.

Where To Stay

There is a wide selection of hotels, guest houses, "self catering" and private houses and condominiums where visitors can make arrangements to stay. Most hotels are in the luxury class, but cheaper accommodation can be found. No camping facilities exist and camping on the beaches is not allowed. The peak holiday season commences in May and visitors are advised to make their bookings well in advance. High season rates for the most expensive hotels can be around US$400 per person per night plus tax and service. Accommodation at the cheaper end of the range is unlikely to be less than US$100 per night. Summer 1992 rates are quoted here. All room rates are subject to a 6% government tax and service charges will also be added to your bill. Some hotels and apartments levy an energy surcharge.

In Hamilton, the principal hotels include the *Hamilton Princess* (US$175-265d, 456 rooms, private beach, fresh and salt water pools, sports facilities, convention centre, Tel: 295 3000, Fax: 295 1914) and the *Rosedon* (US$65-97 pp double occupancy EP, 43 rooms in main house or garden section, no credit cards, pool, breakfast and light meals in rooms, on verandahs or poolside, Tel: 295-1640, Fax: 295 5904). Out of town, along Harbour Road, Paget are *Palm Reef* (US$140-180d EP, 94 rooms, use of *Elbow Beach's* private beach, salt water pool, dining room and coffee shop, Tel: 236 1000, Fax: 236 6392), Middle Road Warwick, the *White Sands and Cottages* (US$225d EP for room, US$250-375 cottage, overlooking Grape Bay, 32 rooms, 3 cottages on waterfront, pool, 6 minutes' walk to beach, Tel: 236 2023, Fax: 236 2486), the *Stonington Beach* (US$112-184, 64 rooms, 1 room with facilities for handicapped, prefer no children under 5, private beach, pool, tennis, serviced by students of hotel technology, Tel: 236 5416, Fax: 236 0371) and the *Belmont Hotel Golf and Country Club* (US$200-280d, 154 rooms, resort type hotel, shuttle bus to beach, salt water pool, tennis, golf, watersports arranged, Tel: 236 1301, Fax: 236 6867), and on South Shore Road the *Elbow Beach* (US$228- 524d, 298 rooms and suites, resort type hotel, tennis, health club, private beach, salt water pool, games room, Tel: 236 3535, Fax: 236 8043), *Sonesta* (US$210-345d EP, 403 rooms and suites, 3 private beaches, indoor and outdoor pools, health spa, games room, children's playground, tennis, scuba on site, Tel: 238 8122, Fax: 238 8463), *Coral Beach* (US$200-400d, introduction by club member required, 66 rooms and cottages, no credit cards, private beach, tennis, squash, putting green, croquet, bowls, pool, Tel: 236 2233, Fax: 236 1876), *Southampton Princess* (US$326-475d MAP, 600 rooms, indoor and outdoor pool, tennis, golf course, scuba diving, private beach, Tel: 238 8000, Fax: 238 8245), and *The Reefs* (US$252-316d, 65 rooms and cottage suites, no credit cards, tennis, scuba diving next door, pool, beach, Tel: 238 0222, Fax: 238 8372). *Horizons*, German-managed, main house and cottages, (US$220-372d or cottage for four US$460-800, no credit cards, pool, tennis, mashie golf, Tel: 236 0048, Fax: 236 1981). Nearer to the Airport is the *Marriott's Castle Harbour* (US$230- 330d EP, 402 rooms and suites, championship golf course, tennis, watersports, convention centre, beach, 3 pools, Tel: 293 2040, Fax: 293 8288).

The larger guesthouses are often old Bermuda mansions which have been converted, some have dining rooms and pools. *Fordham Hall* on Pitt's Bay Road in Pembroke Parish, Tel: 295 1551, Fax: 295 3906, within walking distance of Hamilton, US$96d CP summer, 12 rooms with bathroom, fans; *Loughlands*, 79 South Road, Paget, Tel: 236 1253, set in 9 acres in the middle of the island, a/c, tennis, pool, US$90-110d CP, 25 rooms, no credit cards, single rooms available; *Oxford House*, close to bus and ferry terminals in Hamilton, family run, a/c, US$112d CP, 12 rooms, triples, quads, no credit cards, Tel: 295 0503, Fax: 295 0250; *Hillcrest Guest House*, Nea's Alley, off Old Maid's Lane, St George's, Tel: 297 1630, lovely old building, lawns and gardens, US$65d EP all year, 11 rooms, singles available, no credit cards; *Edgehill Manor*, Rosemont Avenue, near Hamilton, Tel: 295 7124, Fax: 295 3850, 9 large rooms, good breakfast, pool, US$98-110d CP, no credit cards. At the cheapest end of the scale, *Wainwright Guest House*, 2 Slip Point Lane, St George's, 4 rooms, Tel: 297 0254, US$40s, US$60d EP all year, no service charge, no credit cards. A full list of current tourist accommodation prices and service charges can be obtained from the Tourist Board of Bermuda and Travel Agencies. Not all hotels and guest houses accept credit cards; check beforehand.

What And Where To Eat And Drink

When dining out it is advisable to dress smartly. There is a wide choice of quality restaurants serving international gourmet and Bermuda specialities. Lobster and fish chowder with sherry peppers is a special favourite, while mussel pie, conch stew, shark, wahoo and tuna steaks are also popular dishes. Local desserts include sweet potato pudding, bay grape jelly, syllabub and guava jelly. The price of a three course dinner for two will vary between US$65 and US$85 (plus gratuities of 15%) depending upon which bottle of wine is chosen from the usually comprehensive selection of US and European wines. A meal in one of the very top restaurants with a superior wine may cost up to US$150.

Some restaurant chains promote seasonal "dine about" offers which represent extremely good value, for example, vouchers can sometimes be purchased and exchanged for a three course evening meal exclusive of wine and service at each of *The Little Venice*, *La Trattoria* and *The Harbour Front* in Hamilton. The vouchers also give free entry to the *Club* discothèque situated above *The Little Venice* restaurant, Bermudiana Road.

The Sunday brunch offered by some hotels and restaurants between noon and mid afternoon is a veritable feast costing US$25 per head plus 15% service. You can eat what you like from a wide and generous selection of salads, vegetables and hot and cold meat dishes and desserts.

King Henry VIII and *The Palmetto*, near Gibbs Hill Lighthouse and the Aquarium at Flatts, respectively, are recommended as good value, in pleasant surroundings and close to a place of interest to visit afterwards (keep your receipt from your meal at the *Palmetto* to gain free entry to the Aquarium).

Good restaurants are too numerous to list in full. The most expensive are *Tom Moore's Cabin*, *The Plantation*, *Newport Room*, *Once Upon a Table*, *Fourways Inn*, *Lantarnas* and *Romanoff's*. A magazine called *Dining out in Bermuda*, which can be purchased for US$2, sets out the menus of most leading restaurants.

For those who require a quick snack there are a number of cheaper, café-style places which can be found easily and where a hamburger, pizza or sandwich and a beer will cost less than US$15.

Supermarkets sell a wide selection of quality food and drinks, mainly imported from North America and Europe. Because most food is imported it is more costly than in the country of origin. As a guide, a loaf of bread costs US$2.50 and a pint of milk is US$0.75.

Tap-water is safe but it is fool-hardy to drink well-water. All kinds of rum punches and cocktails are served and bottled lager is drunk straight from the bottle. A number of bars have "happy hour" between 1700 and 1900 when the price of drinks is reduced from approximately US$4.50 to US$2.50. *The Robin Hood* in Hamilton is recommended for those who like a lively environment. *The Hood's* pizzas are some of Bermuda's best. The *Beer Garden*, off Washington Mall. Other "watering holes" on Front Street, Hamilton, worth a visit are *Rum Runners*, *Loquats*, *The Cock and Feathers* and, if you prefer traditional (but travelled) English real ale, *The Docksider*. For local atmosphere, try *Casey's Bar*, Queen Street.

Entertainment

In Hamilton are two modern cinemas which show recent US and British films. There is also a cinema in Dock Yard. There are periodical theatrical and other shows performed principally at the City Hall, Hamilton, particularly during the Spring Festival when a range of shows are promoted, from jazz to opera. In recent years, programmes have included the hilarious productions of the Harvard University dramatic society's *Hasty Pudding*. In November look out for the very popular satirical production of *Not the Um Um Show*, performed at the Clayhouse Inn, North Shore Road. ("Um Um" is a sort of speech impediment peculiar to many Bermudians.) After dinner, many people go to the discotheque or stroll along the harbour front.

Best Buys

Bermuda is famous for its local artwork. During the off season the major stores, Triminghams, Coopers, Smiths and

Pearman Watlington, Marks and Spencers have genuine reductions on a range of quality goods. Particularly popular are Italian and Scottish wool and cotton pullovers. For US visitors British and European glass, china and perfumes are good buys. At duty-free shopping outlets minimum purchase is two 1-litre bottles of spirit or fortified wine.

Banks

The majority of international banks have representation in Hamilton. The three Bermuda banks are The Bank of Bermuda Ltd, 6 Front Street, Hamilton HM 11 (with branches in Par-La-Ville and Church Street, Hamilton and in Somerset and St George and the Civil Air Terminal Building); The Bank of N T Butterfield and Son Ltd, 65 Front Street, Hamilton HM 12 (with branches at the Rosebank Building, Bermudiana Road, Hamilton, Somerset and St George and *Southampton Princess Hotel*); and Bermuda Commercial Bank Ltd, affiliated to Barclays Bank, Church Street, Hamilton HM12 (which has a cashing facility at the Airport). Bank hours are 0930 to 1500 Monday to Friday and 1630 to 1730 Friday only.

Currency

The legal currency is the Bermuda Dollar (Bd$) which bears the head of Queen Elizabeth II. US dollars are accepted virtually everywhere and are interchangeable with the Bermuda dollar at par (ie 1 Bermuda dollar = US$1). Canadian currency is also accepted, but not so widely. There are exchange control regulations designed to prevent the transfer of dollars out of the country. Exchange rates for all currencies are available from any bank, US travellers' cheques can be cashed everywhere and international bank credit cards are widely accepted. Better rates of exchange currently can be obtained in Bermuda itself, although it is advisable to have some US or Bermudan currency on arrival.

Health

Sanitation is good and the standard of hygiene and health care extremely high, but expensive. Medical insurance is therefore recommended. King Edward VII memorial hospital in Point Finger Road just outside Hamilton is well-equipped and operates the only civilian recompression chamber. There are a number of general practitioners and clinics principally in Hamilton, but also around the island.

Mosquitoes no longer present a problem and there are very few stinging insects. Repellent sprays are not therefore essential but if needed can be purchased locally from a number of well-stocked pharmacies. The main hazards for visitors are over-exposure to the sun, moped accidents and irresponsible diving. Should you be stung by jelly fish, a solution of ammonia will relieve the pain. Rain water is collected for drinking, washing and cooking although some of the large hotels operate their own desalination plants.

Climate

The climate is sub-tropical, with sunshine averaging between 7 and 8 hours a day. High rainfall of approximately 65 inches per year falls mainly between October and March. The summer season runs from May to October but in February, the coolest month, temperatures rarely drop below 60°F (15°C). The peak temperatures are in July and August when they can average 85°F (30°C). Humidity reaches a peak in August and September when sporadic winds can sometimes reach hurricane force. The last major hurricane was "Emily" in September 1987 which hit the island by surprise. In the summer months, the sun rises at approximately 0600 and sets at about 2000.

Clothing

As a rule always dress conventionally. Bathing suits, abbreviated tops, trunks or bare feet are only appropriate on the beach or pool side. There is no nudism on the beaches. It is an offence to ride a cycle or appear in public without a shirt or just wearing a bathing suit. Casual sports-style clothes are fine for day time, but you should be prepared to wear jacket and tie in the evening in some very formal restaurants. Local smart and office wear, for men, is the tailored Bermuda shorts, blazer and knee-length socks. Holiday visitors should bring light-weight clothes and shower proof rain gear. An umbrella could be useful, but it's likely to be too windy to use satisfactorily.

National Holidays

New Year's Day (1 January), Good Friday, Bermuda Day (24 May), the Queen's Birthday (12 June), Cup Match and Somer's Day (late July), Labour Day (4 September), Remembrance Day (12 November), Christmas and Boxing Day (25 and 26 December). When a public holiday falls on a Saturday, the following Monday is usually a holiday.

Time Zone

Atlantic Standard Time, 4 hours behind GMT, 1 ahead of EST.

Post

The Bermuda Post Office has its headquarters at Church and Parliament Streets, Hamilton 5-24. Sub-post offices can be found throughout the parishes.

Telecommunications

Bermuda has a modern automated telephone and cable system operated with the assistance of Cable and Wireless Plc which links Bermuda with the rest of the world by satellite and submarine cable to the USA. International telephone, telex, data transmission and facsimile facilities are available and most countries can be dialled directly. Cable and Wireless Plc's Administrative Office is in Church Street, Hamilton, Tel: 295 1815.

If telephoning Bermuda from the USA, the international prefix for Bermuda is 809 followed by the local seven digit number; from the UK the international dialling prefix is 0101 (USA) then 809 followed by the local seven digit number.

Press

The *Royal Gazette* is the only daily (not Sunday) newspaper. The *Bermudan Sun* and *Mid Ocean News* are weeklies published on Fridays.

Bermuda Department Of Tourism

For further tourist information, contact the following: in **Bermuda**, Bermuda Department of Tourism, Global House, 43 Church Street, Hamilton, Bermuda HM12, Tel: 292 0023, Fax: 292 7537 (PO Box HM 465, Hamilton HM BX, Bermuda); Visitors' Service Bureau, Chamber of Commerce Building, Front Street, Hamilton, Bermuda, Tel: 295 1480. There are Visitor's Information Centres in Hamilton, St George and the Naval Dockyard.

In the **USA**: Bermuda Department of Tourism, Suite 201, 310 Madison Avenue, New York, NY 10017, Tel: (212) 818-9800, Fax: (212) 983-5289; Suite 2008, 235 Peachtree Street NE, Atlanta, Georgia 30303, Tel: (404) 524-1541, Fax: (404) 586-9933; Suite 1010, 44 School Street, Boston, MA 02108, Tel: (617) 742-0405, Fax: (617) 723-7786; Suite 1070, Randolph-Wacker Building, 150 N Wacker Drive, Chicago, IL 60606, Tel: (312) 782-5486, Fax: (312) 704-6996; John A Tetley Inc, Suite 601, 3075 Wilshire Blvd, Los Angeles, CA 90010-1293, Tel: (213) 388-1151, Fax: (213) 487-5467.

In **Canada**: Bermuda Department of Tourism, Suite 1004, 1200 Bay Street, Toronto, Ontario M5R 2A5, Tel: (416) 923-9600, Fax: (416) 923-4840.

In the **UK** (European Representative): Bermuda Tourism BCB Ltd, 1 Battersea Church Road, London SW11 3LY Tel: 071-734 8813, Fax: 071-352 6501.

BAHAMAS

Introduction

THE BAHAMAS is a coral archipelago consisting of some 700 low-lying islands, and over 2,000 cays (pronounced "keys"). The highest hills, on Cat Island, are less than 400 feet and most islands have a maximum height of 100 feet. The total area of the islands is about 5,400 square miles, roughly the same as Jamaica. The whole archipelago extends for about 600 miles southeast from the Mantanilla shoal off the coast of Florida to 50 miles north of Haiti. Some of the smaller cays are privately owned but most of them are uninhabited. Nassau, the capital, on New Providence Island, is 184 miles by air from Miami. The other islands, known as the "Family Islands", include Grand Bahama (60 miles from Florida), Bimini, the Berry Islands, Abaco, Eleuthera (these two are particularly attractive), the Exumas, Andros, Cat Island, Long Island, San Salvador, Rum Cay, the Inaguas, Acklins and Crooked Island.

The islands are made up of limestone over 5,000 metres deep, most of it Oolite, laid down for more than 150 million years on a gradually sinking sea bed. New material accumulated constantly and the seas of the Bahamas Platform remained remarkably shallow, often only a few metres deep. From the air, the different shades of turquoise, ultramarine and blue in these shallow waters are spectacular. On land, the soil is thin and infertile. In many places, bare limestone rock is exposed at the surface while much land is swampy, impenetrable and uninhabitable. There are many large cave systems, including the impressive blue holes, formed when sea levels were lower and since flooded. There are no rivers or streams on any of the islands,

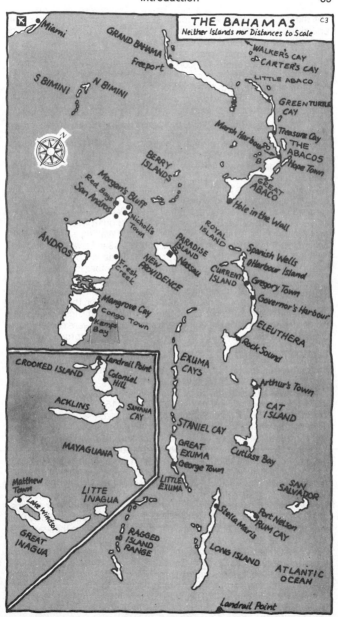

THE BAHAMAS
Neither Islands nor Distances to Scale

but there is some fresh water, found close to the surface but resting on underlying salt water. If wells are drilled too deep, they produce brackish or salt water. Most people drink bottled water.

About 15 island areas have been developed. They have a total population of about 255,000; about 172,000 live in New Providence and 41,000 in Grand Bahama. The weather can be pleasant in the winter season although cold fronts from the North American continent can bring strong north winds, heavy rain and surprisingly low temperatures. The summer months are hot, humid and often windless, with frequent thunderstorms.

History

The first inhabitants were probably the Siboneys, fishermen who migrated from Florida and the Yucatán. The Indians Columbus found in the southern Bahamas were Arawaks, practising a culture called Tainan. They called themselves Lukku-cairi, island people, and became known as Lucayans. They were primitive farmers and fishermen, but produced the best cotton known to the Arawaks. The island of Guanahani is generally credited with Columbus' first landfall in the New World on 12 October 1492. Columbus called Guanahani San Salvador but it was not until 1926 that the Bahamas Parliament officially renamed Watling Island, an island which best fitted his rather vague description, as San Salvador. Columbus visited Rum Cay, which he named Santa María de la Concepción, Long Island, which he called Fernandina, and several other islands and cays, but finding no gold he set off for brighter horizons. The lack of mineral deposits meant that the islands held little interest for the Spanish and there is no evidence of permanent settlement. However, the development of Hispaniola and Cuba led to shortages of labour on those islands and to the depopulation of the Bahamas as the Lucayans were captured and carried off as slaves. By 1520 about 20,000 had been captured for use in the plantations, mines or pearl fisheries in the Spanish colonies and the Bahamas were uninhabited. The islands and cays became feared by navigators and many ships were wrecked there, including a whole fleet of 17 Spanish ships off Abaco in 1595.

It was after founding their first colonies in Virginia that the English realized the strategic importance of the Bahamas, and in 1629 the islands received their first constitution as part of the Carolinas. In fact, the first settlers came from Bermuda with the aim of founding a colony free from the religious and constitutional troubles of Charles I's England. Then William Sayle, who had been Governor of Bermuda, published in London in 1647 *A Broadside Advertising Eleuthera and the Bahama Islands*. As a result of this publicity, a company of Eleutherian Adventurers was formed and a party of about 70 settlers and 28 slaves, led by Sayle himself, set out for Eleuthera. Their ship was wrecked on the reefs. The party managed to land but most of the stores were lost and the settlers barely managed to survive by trading ambergris.

From this time on, the life of the Bahamas was largely influenced by their proximity to the North American mainland and their place on the sea routes. Piracy, buccaneering and the slave trade were features of the next two centuries. Pirates began to make the Bahamas their base after 1691 when they were thrown out of Tortuga. Conditions there were perfect, with creeks, shallows, headlands, rocks and reefs for hiding or making surprise attacks. By 1715 there were about 1,000 pirates active in the Bahamas, of whom the most notorious was Blackbeard, who wore his beard in plaits and was renowned for his cruelty. The colony was very poor and survived on the fortunes of shipping, both legal and illicit. In 1739 during the War of Jenkins' Ear, privateering brought a boom in trading activity but peace returned the islands to poverty. A revival of trade during the Seven Years' War was welcomed but peace once more brought depression to Nassau. When not involved in piracy or privateering, many of the inhabitants lived off wrecks, and great was their enthusiasm when whole fleets were destroyed.

A new form of piracy began after the abolition of the British slave trade, when illegal slave traders used the Bahamas as a base to supply the southern states of the mainland. This was followed during the 1861-65 American Civil War by the advent of blockade runners, shipowners and adventurers drawn by the prospect of vast profits. New, fast ships were developed which were unable to carry large cargoes and needed to find a safe, neutral port within two or three days' steaming. Nassau was again ideal, and the port prospered, the harbour and shops being packed with merchandise. The captains and pilots of the blockade running ships became as famous as their pirate predecessors. The end of the war provoked a severe and prolonged recession, with the cotton warehouses lying empty for 50 years. The inhabitants turned again to wrecking but even this livelihood was denied them when lighthouses and beacons were introduced, leaving few stretches of dangerous waters.

In 1919, with the advent of Prohibition in the United States, Nassau became a bootleggers' paradise, but with the repeal of Prohibition, this source of wealth dried up and the islands had little to fall back on. The Thirties, a time of severe depression, ended in disaster in 1939 when disease killed off the sponges which had provided some means of livelihood. Once again, it was war which brought prosperity back. This time, however, foundations were laid for more stable conditions in the future and the two bases of prosperity, tourism and offshore finance, became firmly established. Nevertheless, the Bahamas' location and the enormous difficulty in policing thousands of square miles of ocean has attracted both drug trafficking and the laundering of the resulting profits. About 11% of the cocaine entering the USA is officially estimated to pass through the Bahamas. The Bahamas Government, in full cooperation with the US anti-narcotics agencies, has stepped up efforts to eradicate the trade.

For three centuries the merchant class elite of Nassau, known as the "Bay Street Boys", influenced government and prevented universal adult suffrage until 1961. In the 1967 elections, an administration supported by the black majority came to power, led by Lynden (later Sir Lynden) Pindling, of the Progressive Liberal Party (PLP). Sir Lynden is still Prime Minister, and also currently Minister of Finance. In the first half of the 1980s allegations were made that he was involved in the drugs trade, but they were never conclusively proven. This and subsequent scandals have led to the resignation or removal of a number of public officials. The major opposition party is the Free National Movement (FNM), with 17 seats in the 49-seat House of Assembly, compared with the PLP's 32. At the end of 1991, 25 out of the country's 49 Congressmen reported assets of over US$1 million.

Government

The Bahamas became independent, within the Commonwealth, in July 1973. The new Constitution provided for a Governor General to represent the British monarch who is head of state, a nominated 16-member Senate and an elected, 49-member House of Assembly, with a parliamentary life of a maximum of five years. Elections are due by December 1992.

The Economy
The economy of the Bahamas is based on tourism, financial services and shipping registration. Visitors are attracted throughout the year and since 1986, total arrivals have exceeded three million a year, mostly from the USA, of which just over half are cruise ship passengers or day trippers. Also, since 1986, annual total visitor expenditure has exceeded US$1,100m, about 16% of all tourist spending in the Caribbean region. Stopover tourists spend an average of US$735 per head while cruise ship passengers average US$60-70. In 1988 there were 12,480 licensed rooms in hotels, villas or apartments. In1990 and 1991 the Gulf war and US recession took their toll on the Bahamian tourist industry with many airlines and hotels shedding staff and fiscal problems becoming more acute. Average hotel occupancy fell to 62% in 1990 and 56% in 1991 as US stopover visitors (82% of the total) declined by 11%. Agriculture is less important than tourism. Emphasis is on fruit farming, taking advantage of the lack of frost and competing with the Florida citrus growers. Economic activity is principally restricted to the two main islands although on the Family Islands tourist facilities are being developed and agriculture extended.

Some steps have been taken to encourage light industries, notably salt, pharmaceuticals, rum and beer production, and substantial investment has taken place in the free-trade zone of Freeport, Grand Bahama. The financial sector, with its banks, insurance companies and finance companies, has developed since the 1920s, but since the mid-1980s has suffered from competition from other offshore centres such as the Cayman Islands and Barbados and from pressure from US bank regulators to reduce secrecy. As far as foreign trade is concerned, exports are mostly re-exports of oil products and there are also sales of rum, pharmaceuticals, crawfish, fishery products, fruits and vegetables. Imports are of food, consumer goods and crude oil (mainly kept in bunkers for re-export).

Further Reading
Out-island Doctor by Evans Cottman (Hodder and Stoughton) gives a picture of the 1940s; an interesting comparison can be made with *Cocaine Wars* by Paul Eddy et al (Bantam), a fascinating study of the 1980s.

New Providence

New Providence is in the centre of the Bahamas archipelago, surrounded by Andros to the west, the Berry Islands to the north, the arc of the Eleutheran cays starting off the northeastern tip and the Exuma Cays to the east and southeast. It is one of the smallest major islands, at only 80 square miles, yet over half of the population lives here. The centre of Nassau has some fine historic buildings and there are some good beaches, but most of the island is covered by sprawling suburbia, scrubby woodland or swamp. Tourism is the principal industry, followed by banking, with the main developments at Nassau, Cable Beach and Paradise Island. Paradise Island, just off the north coast, is 750 acres of tourist resort. Once known as Hog Island, a legacy of New Providence settlers who used it as a pig farm, it was developed in the 1950s by Huntington Hartford as a resort. The name was changed after a bridge was built to connect the island with Nassau and the first casino licence was granted.

Diving and Marine Life
The variety of reefs and cays makes the Bahamas ideal for new or experienced divers. A great number of wrecks add spice to life underwater,

including some that have been planted by film crews off the southwest corner of New Providence, which attract scuba divers eager to see where the underwater scenes of James Bond films, or Walt Disney's "20,000 Leagues Under the Sea", were filmed. Just off Paradise Island there is a series of caves and a 19th century wreck, while to the west of New Providence there are dramatic walls and drops leading to the mile-deep "Tongue of the Ocean". There are seven dive operations, all offering PADI certification courses and trips to wrecks, reefs and walls, as well as other activities. Peter Hughes Dive South Ocean is particularly recommended (Tel: 326 4391), but the others include Bahama Divers Ltd (Tel: 326 5644), Dive, Dive, Dive Ltd (Tel: 362 1143), Nassau Undersea Adventures Ltd (Tel: 326 4171), Sun Divers Ltd (Tel: 325 8927), Diver's Haven and Sunskiff Divers Ltd. The cost of a two tank scuba dive with all equipment and transport included is about US$50. A learn-to-dive package costs much the same. Boats and diving equipment can also be hired at shops by the Paradise Island Bridge.

Beaches and Watersports

Beaches are best near the hotels, where the seaweed is cleaned off. The nicest ones are Love Beach (west), the eastern end of Paradise Island beach (hotel security guards often try to keep people off the beach at weekends; use hotel car park and walk through hotel as if you are a guest), Divi Beach (the sea here is very shallow) and beaches on the small islands off New Providence. One of the best and longest beaches is Lyford Cay, which is behind barriers in an expatriate housing area in the west, but not impossible to enter with enough confidence. It is unwise to go to a beach where you might be on your own. Watersports include waterskiing (no tuition), parasailing, windsurfing and snorkelling. Some of the larger hotels, such as the Carnival's *Crystal Palace*, *Ramada South Ocean* and the *Sheraton Grand Paradise Island*, offer full facilities to guests and non-guests. Prices about US$25 for 15 minutes for waterskiing, while windsurfing can be US$12 an hour. Parasailing is US$30 for seven minutes and jet skiing US$25. Snorkelling equipment hire is US$25 for the day. For those who prefer a less active encounter with the sea, glass-bottomed boats leave several times a day from Prince George Wharf in downtown Nassau. Hartley's Undersea Walk, for those not keen to dive but wanting to see coral reefs up close, at 0930 and 1330, US$35 (Tel: 393 8234). For island cruises, the Calypso Blue Lagoon trip and Rose Island excursions are recommended (daily at 1000 except Wednesday and Sunday, Tel: 363 3577, US$40 for the day with lunch, although it is unlikely to be as good as in the brochure pictures, no complimentary snorkelling equipment). Boat hire is US$140 a day for up to 4 people with a deposit of US$250 and insurance of US$10 (East Bay Tel: 393 3950). Powerboat Adventures (Tel: 322 4527/ 327 7747) go further in a faster boat; day trip with lavish picnic to the Exuma Cays for US$139. A captained boat for fishing trips is US$300 for 4 hours or US$500 for a day for up to 6 people (Tel: 363 2335), or arranged through hotel tour desks for US$50 per person for a half day. A ferry goes from the docks at Cable Beach across to Discovery Island every half hour for US$5 return, with the first boat at 1000 and the last boat coming back at 1600.

Other Sports

The most popular and well-developed sport on dry land is probably golf. There are four world class courses on New Providence: *Crystal Palace, Ramada, Paradise Island* and *Lyford Cay Golf Course*. Green fees vary but are around US$45 per person plus US$20 for a golf cart and US$20 for hire of clubs. Guests of *Crystal Palace* get US$10 off green fees.

There are over 100 **tennis** courts in the Nassau/Cable Beach/Paradise Island area and many of them are lit for night time play until 2200 (with an extra charge). Most of the larger hotels have tennis courts, usually free for guests. The Racquets Club, on Independence Drive (Tel: 323 1854) has squash courts at about US$7 per hour. Very popular with Bahamians, it has European-sized squash courts. The Crystal Palace Sports Centre charges US$8 an hour and has racquet-ball available. Smarter, but the squash courts are smaller, being converted racquet-ball courts.

You can go **horse riding** for US$40 an hour, including transport, along the beach at Happy Trails, Coral Harbour (Tel: 362 1820).

Gambling at Paradise Island and *Crystal Palace* casinos, 1000-0400. Enquire about lessons free of charge. Fascinating to see the massed ranks of flashing fruit machines and the many games tables. Bahamians are not allowed to gamble in the casinos.

Festivals

Junkanoo is a loud and boisterous national festivity loosely derived from African customs, celebrated on New Providence at 0300 on 26 December and 1 January (see under Grand Bahama for details of celebrations on that island). While the exact origins of Junkanoo are unknown, it is thought to have its roots in slave celebrations on their only days off in the year, at Christmas. John Canoe is said to have been a popular slave leader. Wild costumed "rushers" dance in Bay Street until dawn beating cowbells and shak-shaks, and blowing whistles. As in Carnival in many countries, local businesses sponsor groups who spend the whole year making their costumes. **Goombay** is an all long summer festival with a series of events, the highlight of which is a fair of music and food every Wednesday on Bay Street. Parades with a military spirit and fireworks celebrate **Independence Day** on 10 July.

Nassau

Nassau is the capital of the Bahamas. It looks comfortably old-fashioned with its white and pink houses: by-laws forbid skyscrapers. **Parliament Square** is typical of the colonial architecture with the Houses of Assembly, the old Colonial Secretary's Office and the Supreme Court clustered around a statue of Queen Victoria. On the northern side of the square, more government buildings overlook the bust of Sir Milo B Butler, the first Bahamian Governor-General. To the right, surrey rides can be taken through the town for US$5 pp (horses rest 1300-1500 May-October, 1300-1400 November-April). Walking up Parliament Street you pass the Cenotaph on the left and the *Parliament Hotel*, built in the 1930s, on the right. The octagonal pink building bordering on Shirley Street is the **Public Library**, built in 1798, which was once used as a prison. Inside you can climb stairs and look out from the balcony, but unfortunately the old dungeons below are no longer open to the public.

Opposite the library are the burnt out ruins of the *Royal Victoria Hotel*, the first hotel in the Bahamas, built in 1859-61, which closed in 1971. On Elizabeth Avenue is the Bahamas Historical Society, which organizes monthly talks and houses a small museum (open Tues 1000-1600 and Wed 1000-1400). Nearby is the **Queen's Staircase**. The 66 steps (102-foot climb) at the end of a gorge (thought to have been cut out of the limestone by slaves in 1790) lead to the ruined **Fort Fincastle**. Be careful to ignore men offering information on the history of the area unless you want to pay for it. The Fort itself was built in 1793 in the shape of a ship's bow. Take the lift

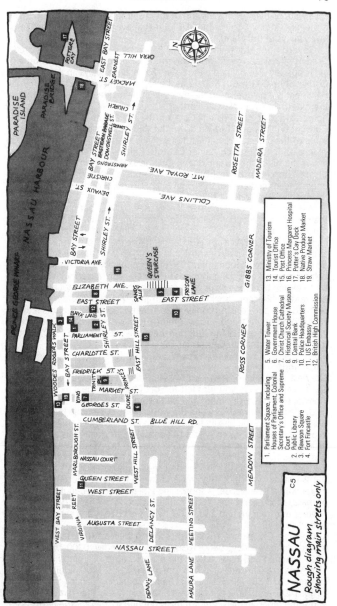

NASSAU

C5

Rough diagram
showing main streets only

1. Parliament Square, including
   Houses of Parliament, Colonial
   Secretary's Office and Supreme
   Court
2. Public Library
3. Rawson Square
4. Fort Fincastle
5. Water Tower
6. Government House
7. Christ Church Cathedral
8. Historical Society Museum
9. Central Bank
10. Police Headquarters
11. US Embassy
12. British High Commission
13. Ministry of Tourism
14. Tourist Office
15. Post Office
16. Princess Margaret Hospital
17. Potter's Cay Dock
18. Native Produce Market
19. Straw Market

(US$0.50) or the stairs to the top of the water tower to see its shape. This is the highest point on the island (216 feet above sea level) and gives some lovely views of the island.

Government House in traditional Bahamian pink (built 1801) is pretty. Gregory's Arch is an overpass to Government House. On Saturday mornings at 1000, the Royal Bahamian Police Force Band plays in front of the **Christopher Columbus Statue** at the top of the flight of stairs. On West Hill Street is a plaque set in the rock which claims the site as being that of the oldest church in Nassau. Further along the street you pass several old houses including the Postern Gate on the left and the Sisters of Charity Convent on the right. Turning down the steps to Queen Street you pass by some of the oldest and prettiest houses in Nassau (no 16 is said to be 200 years old). The **St Francis Xavier Catholic Cathedral** is on West Street and down the hill is the quaint **Greek Orthodox Church** in blue and white. **Christ Church Cathedral** (built 1837) stands on the corner of George's Street and immediately to the south is **Lex House**, thought to have housed the Spanish Garrison in 1782-83.

Vendue House on Bay Street is now used by BEC, but previously it was the site of slave auctions. Nearby is the renowned **Straw Market** with the offices of the Ministry of Tourism above. Almost all the straw work is imported from East Asia and is no longer native (better prices upstairs); they also sell carvings, jewellery and T-shirts. Bargain with the saleswomen but do not expect to get more than 15% off the originally stated price. Running behind the market is the enormous **Prince George Wharf** which can take up to eleven big cruise ships at once (peak time Saturday), where you can buy reasonable conch shells from fishermen. A duty free shopping area is planned here and construction work to increase facilities for visitors is under way. Continue east and you will return to Rawson Square. Free guided walking tours of old Nassau start from here, daily at 1000 and 1500, contact the Tourist Information Centre, Tel: 326 9772.

Excursions

Go west along Bay Street, past Nassau Street and continue to the Road Traffic Centre where you turn left to **Fort Charlotte**, built in 1787 out of limestone. It has a dry moat and battlements. Look down on the cricket field, the guns, Arawak Cay and the western end of Paradise Island. Guides will fill you in on the history for a small tip or just wander at leisure. **Coral World** (Tel: 328 1036, entry US$14 adults, US$10 children) is on the small reclaimed island, Arawak Cay. A US$3 bus runs from Cable Beach, a US$3 boat goes from the Prince George Wharf, or a US$3 bus and boat from Paradise Island. Highlights include descending the observatory tower to view the sea below, watching sting ray and sharks feed and selecting your own oyster with a pearl inside. A snorkelling trail has been added, US$7 for hire of mask, snorkel and fins, US$5 for life jacket. Allow half a day for a visit. There is a restaurant and also stands with sea biscuits and sand dollars for sale.

Going up Chippingham Road you come to the **Nassau Botanic Gardens** (open Monday-Friday, 0800-1630, Saturday-Sunday 0900-1600, adults US$1, children US$0.50), where there are 18 acres of tropical plants, and **The Ardastra Gardens and Zoo** (open daily, 0900-1700, adults US$7.50, children US$3.50, Tel: 323 5806). Trained, parading flamingoes march at 1100, 1400, and 1600, but can be a disappointment. There are also parrots and some other animals, but not really enough to warrant the term zoo.

Going west along the coast, Saunders Beach is bordered by casuarina trees and Brown's Point looks across to the *Carnival Crystal Palace* at **Cable Beach**, which at night is a multi-coloured sight when the dayglo lights are switched on, which is not always. Leaving Cable Beach you soon come to Delapoint Point and Sandy Port residential areas. Further on are some local bars (*Nesbits* is very popular in the evenings) where you can buy drinks and native conch salad before you get to some limestone caves. There is an inscription commemorating the first visit by the British Royal Family in 1841. Just beyond is Conference Corner where Macmillan, Kennedy and Diefenbaker planted trees in 1962. At this point Blake Road leads to the airport while West Bay Street continues past Orange Hill Beach and Gambier Village (*Travellers Rest*, bar and restaurant, very pleasant to watch sunset, excellent daiquiris, good meals US$12-25). Love Beach further on the right is probably one of the best beaches on New Providence. Park on the side of the road and walk down between the apartments.

Continuing as far west as you can go you reach Lyford Cay, a private residential area for the rich, protected by barriers. Turn left at the roundabout for Clifton, a stretch of rocky coast now being developed for a power station and industry. This road leads to South West Bay where you can turn right to visit the *Ramada* hotel and beach front (a good stop for a swim and a drink) before returning east. After two miles there is a signpost to Adelaide Village. This settlement is one of the oldest, founded when illegal slave traders were intercepted by the British Navy in the nineteenth century and the human cargo was taken to the Bahamas. The traditional houses are brightly painted, the beach is quite good, though the water is shallow, and the bars prepare fresh fish or conch salad. Continue east on Adelaide Road and you come to the Coral Harbour roundabout. To the right, the Bahamas Defence Force has its base. Join Carmichael Road and you will pass the Bacardi Company, open weekdays until 1600. Turn left to go along Blue Hill Road and join Independence Drive at the roundabout (with the cock on top). Here on the north side is the new Town Centre Shopping Mall.

Continue east on Independence until you come to traffic lights with another new mall. Eastern Road hugs the coast and has many impressive homes overlooking the sea. **Blackbeard's Tower**, an old lookout point, is now closed. **Fort Montagu** (and beach), constructed in 1741, is famous for having been captured briefly by Americans during the Revolution. It is a rather smelly area where conch is sold. If you turn left into Shirley Street and immediately left again into Village Road, you will come to **The Retreat** (opposite Queen's College), the headquarters of the Bahamas National Trust and an 11-acre botanical park. Guided tours (20 minutes) US$2, Tuesday-Thursday at 1150.

Returning to East Bay Street you will pass the now derelict *Montagu Hotel, Club Waterloo* and the *Nassau Yacht Club* before reaching the toll bridge which crosses over to **Paradise Island**. Scooters cross for US$0.50, taxis and hired cars are US$2, cars with local licence plates US$0.50, pedestrians US$0.25. You pay the toll when taking a taxi across. Stop at the **Versailles Gardens and Cloisters** on the way to the golf course. The gardens with various statues are not in very good shape, but walk down to the Ocean Club and look back to imagine how grand they once were. The cloisters were brought in pieces from France and date back to the 14th century. The gazebo looking across to Nassau is a favourite spot for weddings. Paradise has some lovely stretches of beach on the northern side, including Cabbage Beach and Victoria Beach to the east at the edge of the golf course. At

Britannia Towers there is a dolphin show daily at 1600 and some other pools with turtles etc.

Potters Cay, next to the Paradise Island toll bridge, has the main fish and produce market.

Island Information—New Providence

Airports Nassau International Airport, about 14 miles from Nassau. Taxi to Nassau US$10-12 and to Paradise Island US$16-18. Third and subsequent extra passengers should be charged US$2, but drivers sometimes try to charge everyone a separate full fare. This is illegal. Make sure meter is used. Paradise Island Airport is nearer to Nassau and receives flights from Miami and Fort Lauderdale. There is no public bus service to or from either airport, though some hotels have buses. For the return journey to Nassau Airport there is a bus from Nassau to Clifton (US$1.50); it leaves on the hour from Bay and Frederick Streets (Western Transportation Company) and will drop you 1½ miles from the airport, but this is not a recommended option.

The airport departure tax is US$15. During the day US immigration and customs formalities for those going to the USA are carried out at Nassau. Plenty of left luggage space is available.

Transport Taxis are abundant but expensive. You will be charged extra for additional passengers and for more than two pieces of luggage. To avoid overcharging, agree a price beforehand, or check that the meter is used. Taxi drivers in Nassau may "take you for a ride" otherwise. Tipping is not necessary. Buses called "jitneys", are good value at US$0.75, carrying from 9-44 people and going all over New Providence Island between 0600 and 1830. If you want to see some of the island catch any bus in town and it will bring you back about an hour later. They can be crowded and dirty but service is regular. Most buses run on one-way circular routes, which can be confusing. Route 10 goes out to Cable Beach along the coast road, route 16 goes along Eastern Road to Fox Hill and Western Transportation buses go to *Ramada* from Queen Street (US$1.75). A bus runs between hotels and the golf course on Paradise Island but no buses go over the bridge. To cross to Paradise Island from Woodes Rogers Walk take the Paradise Express boat for US$2, it leaves when full.

Car Hire A car can cost US$70 a day or US$400-450 a week. Prices depend on the model and features. Avis (Tel: 326 6380); Hertz (Tel: 327 6866); National (Tel: 325 3716) and Budget (Tel: 327 7406) have offices at the airport and at other locations but local firms can be cheaper. Large cash deposits can be required if you have no credit card. Scooters can be hired, Tel: 326 8329, 0900-1700, US$55 for two, US$40 for one (sometimes a US$25 deposit is required). Helmets are provided and it is recommended that you wear them. Traffic for such a small island is busy and roads are not well maintained. Take care.

Where To Stay The two main resort areas on New Providence are **Cable Beach**, which stretches three miles west of Nassau along the north coast, and **Paradise Island**, five minutes across Nassau harbour and reached by an ugly steel toll bridge. The benefit of staying at Cable Beach is that the jitney service into town is very easy to use, while from Paradise Island you need a taxi. Other hotels are in the town and suburbs. There is a great variety of accommodation, ranging from small guest houses, offering only rooms, to luxury hotels and sprawling resorts. Prices vary according to the season. Generally standards of hotels are disappointing considering the price paid and service is slow at reception desks. Watch out for room tolls (3%), resort levies (3%) and compulsory maid gratuities which are added to the basic price quoted. Up to date rates available at the Tourist Information Centres in Nassau, or write to the Tourist Offices listed under Information for Visitors. You can often pick up a cheaper package deal in the USA than by arranging a hotel on arrival. Summer 1992 rack rates are quoted here.

If you want a budget hotel try the *Diplomat Inn* (US$39), Delancey Street West (Tel: 325 2688), which like others in this price range is in a less salubrious area. On Paradise Island, *The Pink House* (US$80 inc breakfast) is a very small, smart, English-run hotel in the grounds of the *Club Med* (Tel: 363 3363, Fax: 393 1786). Away from it all the *Orange Hill Beach Inn* (US$71-90d), West Bay Street (Tel: 327 7157, Fax: 327-5186), offers peace and quiet and a lovely stretch of beach just across the road, 48 rooms, dive packages, pool, boat available for fishing or excursions. *Harbour Cove* (US$99-149d) on Paradise Island (Tel: 363 2561, Fax: 363 3803) and the *British Colonial* (US$89-139) in town, Bay and Marlborough Streets (Tel: 322 3301, Fax: 323 8248), now run by Best Western, offer good package deals year round. Ten minutes from a beach the *Parthenon* (US$44) on West Street (Tel: 322 2643), is clean and central. Off West Bay Street on St Alban's Drive is *Colony Club* (US$60) (Tel: 305 4824, Fax: 325 1240), extra beds in room for small charge, children under 10 free. Otherwise villas for up to 4 people can give value for money, weekly rates will work out cheaper than those quoted here: *Orange Creek* on Paradise Island (US$250 a night) (Tel: 323 6240) and *Henrea Carlette Hotel*, Cable Beach (US$90 a night for 1 bedroom or US$105 for 2 bedrooms) (Tel: 327 7801). *Club Land'Or* (Tel: 363 2400, Fax: 363 3403) is a good villa hotel on Paradise Island (US$205-225), smaller than the other hotel giants with good restaurant, and *Cable Beach Manor* (US$70-125d in summer, double that in winter) (Tel: 327 7785, Fax: 327 7782). There is much in the luxury range: *Ocean Club* on Paradise Island in 35 acres of well-landscaped grounds, is the most luxurious, with 9 clay tennis courts, golf, pool, beach, transport to the casino (US$195-445 for a room, US$770-875 for a suite) (Tel: 363 2501, Fax: 363 2424), *Coral World Villas*, Silver Cay, (US$245) (Tel: 328 1036, Fax: 323 3202) and of course the most expensive suite on the island in the *Carnival Crystal Palace*, Cable Beach at US$25,000 for one night (Tel: 327 6200). This 1,500-room hotel is usually lit up in shades of orange, yellow, purple and magenta at night and contains shopping malls, many bars and restaurants and a casino the size of a football pitch. At the opposite end of the spectrum the *Yoga Retreat* (US$60) (PO Box N-7550, Tel: 363 2902) charges US$25 for tent space, very strict, no onions, not allowed to skip meditation, guests cook and wash up. Guest houses include *Aliceanna's* (US$23-29) on Bay Street (Tel: 325 4974); *Mignon* (US$34) on Market Street (Tel: 322 4771); *Towne Hotel* on George Street is central (Tel: 322 8451, Fax: 328 1512, US$60-70); *Mitchell's Cottages* (US$38-40) on West Street (Tel: 322 4365); *Morris* (US$25-30) on Dan's Street (Tel: 325 0195) and *Olive's* (US$25) on Blue Hill Road (Tel: 323 5298).

Where To Eat Paradise Island offers two dining plans which can prove to be good value although they limit your choice (US$55 or US$39 daily, breakfast and dinner for those staying 3 nights minimum). A 15% gratuity will be added to every food and drink bill although service can be very slow and poor. Lunch is always cheaper than dinner and can be taken until 1700. For al fresco dining try *Ivory Coast* or the *Poop Deck* on East Bay, *Traveller's Rest* near Gambier Village, or *Captain Nemo's*, Deveaux Street on the waterfront (the last two specialize in good local food). Middle range tourist and expat places with bars and open air meals include *Coconuts* on Bay Street backing onto the harbour; *Tamarind Hill* on Village Road and *Pick-a-Dilly*, with small steel band, on Parliament Street. *Charley Charley's*, Delancey Street serves hearty German fare while *Café Delancey*, on same street is middle range, recommended. Cheap, cheerful and Bahamian are *The Shoal*, on Nassau Street, *Briteleys*, and *Three Queens* on Wulff Road. In the *Crystal Palace* there is a Chinese restaurant and in the *Riviera* there is a Mexican restaurant (US$18 main course). Both the *Blue Lagoon* on Paradise Island and the *Cellar* in town have music. *The Roselawn Café* on Bank Lane, off Parliament Square serves food after 2200. Most hotels have expensive and formal restaurants but they also have good value buffets (US$12-20): Sunday brunch at *Café Martinique* is excellent. For a special meal visitors are often encouraged to go to *Graycliff*, West Hill Street, in a colonial mansion (also a hotel, US$145-365, Tel: 633 7411), but service and food have declined, poor reports. *The Sun and...* and the *Blue Lagoon* in *Club Land'Or* (for fish) are recommended (over US$50 pp). Also expensive but good are *Ocean Club* on Paradise Island and *Buena Vista* on the street of the same name.

Night-life Some clubs have a cover charge or a two-drink minimum. *The Palace Theatre*, Cable Beach and *Le Cabaret Theatre*, Paradise Island offer a Las Vegas type musical show with dinner (US$38 or US$42) or without (US$25 or US$28). *Peanut Taylor's Drumbeat Club* has a native but not very authentic review (US$15, with dinner US$30) at 2030 and 2230 (Tel: 322 4233), West Bay Street, while *Trade Winds* on Paradise Island has a similar one at 2100 and some nights at 2200 or 2300 for US$15 including 2 drinks. Live bands can be heard at the *Waterloo*, East Bay, and the *Ritz*, Bay

Street (popular with Bahamians). *We Place*, Thompson Avenue, US$4, is full of Bahamians and very lively at weekends. *The Coliseum*, West Bay Street, Tuesday-Saturday, very smart, two restaurants and three separate rooms for jazz, calypso and US mainstream music, US$15. Discos can be found in most of the larger hotels. Dinner cruises in the harbour leave the *El Galleon Club*, Bay Street, nightly for US$35 (Tel: 393 7887). *The Village Lanes*, Village Road for bowling at US$2.50 a game (Tel: 393 2427). The *Dundas Centre for the Performing Arts*, Mackey Street, regularly has shows and plays by local groups (Tel: 322 2728).

Warning   There is a major 'crack' cocaine problem in New Providence. Partly for this reason armed robberies are frequent. Targets include pedestrians out after dark, supermarkets, bars, banks and casinos; customers will be asked to hand over their valuables. Guests have been held up (or raped) in hotel rooms and on their balconies and patios. Drivers have been made to hand over car keys at knife or gunpoint. The majority of tourists are not affected by these incidents and Nassau is no more dangerous than Kingston or Port of Spain. However visitors should be extremely careful, particularly at night or when venturing off the beaten track. Do not be lulled into a false sense of security.

Shopping   Shops are open 0900-1700, Monday-Saturday, but some close at 1200 on Thursday. As there is no sales tax and tariffs on luxury goods are very low, buying imported goods can save you about 20%, but shop around. *Bernard's* has some fine china, the *English Shops* and *Linen and Lace* have Irish linen. Look in the *Perfume Shop* for French perfume. Try *John Bull* for watches and cameras. For unusual gifts look in *Marlborough Antiques*, West Bay, *Coin of the Realm*, Charlotte Street, or *Best of the Bahamas*, east of the square. For clothing see the *Androsia* boutique in *Mademoiselle's*, batik fashions from Andros. There are also international names like *St Michael*, *The Body Shop*, *Benetton*, *Gucci* and *Greenfire Emeralds* from Colombia all in Nassau. In general, however, buy everything you could possibly need before you arrive as regular import duties are high. Most of the smarter, tourist-oriented shops are on (or just off) Bay Street. For everyday shopping most people use suburban centres, of which the most convenient is in the Mackey Street-Madeira Street area. Super Value supermarkets have good variety of breads and salad bar (sold by the pound). The best book shop is probably the book department of the Island Shop on Bay Street. Service in shops is often poor, be prepared to wait.

Film Developing   Try Foto Factory opposite the *British Colonial*, or Mr Photo chain on Palmdale, on Thompson Avenue, near Straw Market. Others have lost films.

Tourist Office   In the straw market. Ask for *What to Do* pamphlet and the *Tourist News*. Another, *Best-Buys*, is in your hotel or at the airport. There is also an information booth at the airport which will help you find accommodation. The Ministry of Tourism is at Market Plaza. The tourist office has a list of churches (and church services).

Tourist Agencies   Majestic Tours (Tel: 322 2606) and Happy Tours (Tel: 323 7900) arrange day trips to "deserted" islands or cays, US$30 including lunch although the Blue Lagoon trip (**see page 73**) is probably better value. The many organized excursions offer the visitor an easy way of getting about but you can sometimes do the same thing by yourself for a lot less. As well as drives to places of interest, tours include visits to beaches on the Family Islands and trips aboard a catamaran with stops for swimming and sunbathing.

Grand Bahama

The nearest to the USA and, with Great Abaco, the most northerly of the major Bahamas islands, is where the most spectacular development has taken place. Thanks to a fresh water table under the island it has no water problem. The pinewoods which this natural irrigation supports were, indirectly, the beginning of the present prosperity. Early in the 1940s, an American millionaire financier, Wallace Groves, bought a small timber company and developed it into an enterprise employing 2,000 people. In

1955, the Bahamas Government entered into an agreement with him as president of the Grand Bahama Port Authority Ltd, granting to the specific area, called **Freeport**, owned by the Port Authority, certain rights and privileges which apply to that area only and to no other section of the Colony. Most important, the area was to be free of taxes and with certain concessions on several imported goods. In return, Groves would pay for government services within the area, promote industry and dredge a deepwater harbour. By 1961 a large cement works was under construction and the harbour housed a thriving ship bunkering terminal. Seeing the potential for a tourist industry, Groves made a further agreement with the Government in 1960. He formed the Grand Bahama Development Company and purchased a large area of land which was to become **Lucaya**. He also built a luxury hotel and casino, the first of its kind in the Bahamas.

So successful was this that the population of the island grew from 9,500 in 1963 to 35,250 in 1967. In the same period, the total investment rose from US$150m to US$577m and the tonnage of cargo handled increased ten times to 1.25m tons. In 1969, however, the Government decided to introduce controls on the expansion of Freeport, and the vertiginous growth process has since slowed down. Official Bahamianization policies meant that many foreigners left or were forced to leave when their entry permits were not renewed. Today, Freeport's population consists mainly of Bahamians from the other islands who have been drawn there to find work.

Flora and Fauna
Grand Bahama is mostly covered in scrub or Caribbean pines. The Royal and Cabbage palms found on the island have been imported, the former coming originally from Cuba. In the north there are marsh and mangrove swamps. Much of the coast supports the attractive sea-grape tree and it is not unusual to see children collecting grapes from the trees. Common flowers and trees are the yellow elder, the national flower of the Bahamas, the lignum vitae, the national tree, hibiscus, bougainvillea, oleander, poinciana and poinsettia. Common fruit trees include avocado, lime, grapefruit, mango and custard apple. There is not a great deal of wildlife on Grand Bahama, although you may see racoons, snakes, lizards and frogs. Birds include pelicans, herons, egrets, owls, woodpeckers, magpies, humming birds (mostly Cuban Emeralds), cranes and ospreys. Watch out for Poison Wood which is found in the bush and pine copses around beaches and causes a very unpleasant rash over the body.

Diving and Marine Life
The paucity of wildlife on land is compensated by the richness of the marine life offshore. Rays often spring from the water in pairs, but be careful not to stand on them when snorkelling as they have a powerful whiplash sting. The spotted eagle rays are particularly beautiful when seen from above. Sea horses and moray eels are also common along the coral reef. It is illegal to break off coral or harvest starfish and there are fines for offenders. Shell collectors will find sand dollars and sea biscuits on the beaches. Conch usually has to be dived for but the beaches are often littered with empty shells. Scuba diving is popular, with attractions such as Treasure Reef, where more than US$1 million in sunken treasure was discovered in 1962, and Theo's Wreck, a deliberately sunk cement freighter. The Underwater Explorers Society (UNEXSO) in Port Lucaya (Tel: 373 1244) has a deep training tank and decompression chamber, and offers PADI and NAUI certification courses. A two-day resort course is US$79, a certification course is US$325

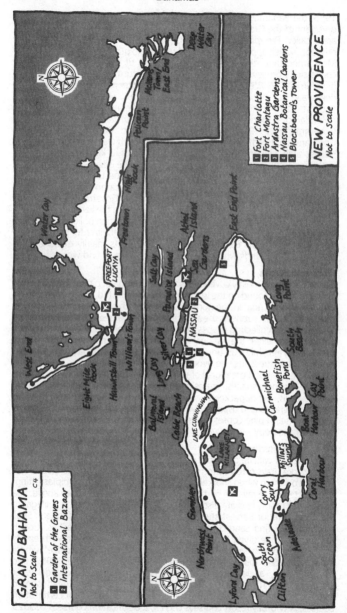

GRAND BAHAMA
Not to Scale
C4

1. Garden of the Groves
2. International Bazaar

NEW PROVIDENCE
Not to Scale

1. Fort Charlotte
2. Fort Montagu
3. Ardastra Gardens
4. Nassau Botanical Gardens
5. Blackbeard's Tower

all inclusive, each dive therafter is US$41 plus membership. They rent underwater photographic equipment. It also has a library and a museum of underwater treasures, wrecks and diving equipment dating from the 17th century (closed for renovations in 1990). The Dolphin Experience features swimming with dolphins and acoustic workshop (US$50), enrolling as a trainer for the day (US$95) and acoustic workshop (US$10). Despite opposition from animal rights groups because of the small size of the dolphins' pens, the programme is very popular and is usually booked well in advance. Sessions are at 1000, 1200, 1400 and 1600. There is also the Deep Water Cay Club at East End, with no certification courses available and Sun Odyssey Divers.

Beaches and Watersports

The island has several natural advantages over others in the group. It has miles of south-facing beaches sheltered from northerly winds and enjoys the full benefit of the Gulf Stream. Generally, beaches can be classed as tourist or local, the former having sports and refreshment facilities as well as security and regular cleaning. The more remote beaches, on the other hand, are usually completely empty, unspoiled by commercialism and very peaceful, their only drawback being that there is often considerable domestic waste and rubbish washed ashore, probably emanating from the garbage collection ships on their way to Florida.

Do exercise caution on the beaches as crime is common and most beaches have a security guard because of the high incidence of robbery and assault. Walking on beaches at night is definitely not a good idea and there is not necessarily safety in numbers. Also theft from parked cars is common so do not leave valuables in your car. Fortune Beach and the National Park Beach are both areas in which to be careful. Topless sunbathing is frowned upon by the Bahamians and skinny dipping is against the law.

Coral Beach, next to the hotel of the same name, is popular with windsurfers, cleaned regularly and has a small bar. Beach facilities are for hotel residents only and this policy is sporadically enforced with vigour. **Xanadu Beach** serves the *Princess Towers/Xanadu Hotel* and various watersports are available including jet skis, pedallos, catamarans, snorkelling equipment (there is a good reef here within easy reach) and parasailing. Use of jet skis and boats is limited to a cordoned area. Hair braiding is done on the beach by local children who have fixed prices according to the number of plaits and length of hair. Watch out for scalp burn afterwards. There is a straw market and a bar which has very loud live music on Sundays. Drinks or conch salad can be bought more cheaply if you walk just beyond the boundary fence where locals bring ice boxes of cold sodas. The *Glass Bottom Boat* operates from Xanadu Marina, tickets on sale on the beach. Make sure the sea is calm, it can be very rough outside the marina and then water visibility is poor and most passengers get seasick.

The **Lucayan Beach** area includes the beaches for the *Holiday Inn, Atlantik Beach Hotel* and the *Lucayan Beach Hotel and Casino*, which are clean, with bar and sports facilities. Windsurfers, hobie cats, Boston whalers, snorkelling equipment, water skis (about US$15 for two miles) and wave runners can all be hired here. At nearby Port Lucaya, Reef Tours operate the *Mermaid Kitty*, a glass bottomed boat which sails several times a day, US$12 for 1½ hours. They also have two-hour snorkelling trips, US$15 pp. Various booze cruises depart daily as well as a trimaran sunset trip. At West End, the beach at the *Jack Tar Holiday Village* (closed 1990) is rather small. There are good coral heads here, close enough to wade to.

One of the nicest beaches on the island with attractive palms and a few broken down old umbrellas is **Taino Beach**, which is over a mile long and has an excellent stretch of coral for snorkelling very close to the shore. The *Taino Beach Resort* on the first part of the beach has expensive condominiums which can be rented on a short term basis. Further along past the *Stone Crab Restaurant* is the *Surfside Bar/Restaurant*. **Fortune Beach** is sometimes used for tourist beach parties which are noisy and to be avoided. The main attraction of the beach is the restaurant *Blackbeards*. The beach is a bit rocky especially at low tide. Take care in this area, it is best to park near the restaurant as there have been many cars broken into in the rather lonely car park further along.

Of the less commercial beaches, **Gold Rock Beach** is probably the most beautiful on the island, about 20 miles east of Freeport and part of the Bahamas National Trust. En route to it you cross the Grand Lucayan Waterway, a canal built in the 1960s when development was booming. Barely used today, the canal bisects the island and the abandoned building sites are a reminder of what Freeport could have become had the planned development taken place. Once past the canal turn right and further along this road is a deserted, never-used film studio. If you take the left turn before the studio you come to a signposted road for the crossing to **Water Cay**. It is not always easy to get a boat across. If you take the left turn but carry on, the road becomes overgrown and pot holed, and the area is littered with small planes shot down by drug enforcement officers or abandoned by drug traffickers. Fat Albert, a barrage balloon full of radar equipment is supposed to have put a stop to aircraft landing on the road undetected. Another detour before reaching Gold Rock is to take the first turning after the film studio to Old Free Town, where there are blue holes and Mermaid's Lair, an opening to an underwater cave system. Further inland is a sink hole, the Owl Hole. Back on the road, turn off when you see the sign for the Lucayan National Park. There is a car park and a map. The park was set up by workers from Operation Raleigh and a subsequent expedition laid the foundations (but nothing more) for a visitors centre. The park contains the largest charted underwater cave system in the world. You can see two caves and climb to a lookout point. As well as bromeliads and orchids there are hundreds of bats in the first cave in the breeding season; also a rare water centipede found only in these waters. Across the road from the caves is a board walk through mangrove swamp which leads to Gold Rock Beach. The beach is best seen at low tide as the sea goes out a long way and there is not much room to sit when the tide is in. The beach stretches for over a mile and is usually deserted. There are dunes and a large rock sticks out of the water giving the beach its name. It is excellent for shell collecting, but horseflies are very persistent so bring insect repellent. The picnic area is often too strewn with rubbish to be pleasant. Occasionally the area is cleaned.

Peterson's Cay is the archetypal one tree desert island and because of this can be crowded. Some tour companies run day trips to snorkel and eat lunch here. You can hire a boat to get there from Port Lucaya (Reef Tours, US$75/3 hours with US$200 deposit), the approach is a bit tricky because of the reef. Directly opposite is **Barbary Beach**, pleasant and backed by a wide pine copse (good for hanging hammocks). An old church here called the Hermitage was built in 1901 by an ex-trappist monk. Another wide, beautiful beach is **Pelican Point**, backed by Royal Palms and a very pretty and colourful village. There are fishing boats on the beach and it is not uncommon to see people gutting or cooking fish here. Pelicans can be seen flopping by. At the south end of Beach Drive you will find **William's Town** and **Russell Town** beaches. The walk from William's Town to **Tyne Beach** is very pleasant, the vegetation being lush, mostly mangrove, sea grapes and tall grasses along the shore. The beach is used by Pinetree Riding Stables and occasionally local churches hold services here. Other beaches on the island include **Smith's Point** and **Mathers Town** just outside Freeport. Here you will find two popular bars: *Club Caribe* (Mathers Town) and the *White Wave Club* (Smith's Point). On the road to West End past Eight Mile Rock are two good beaches for shelling, **Bootle Bay** and **Shell Bay**.

Other Sports

There is no shortage of **golf courses** on Grand Bahama. At the *Bahama Princess Hotel and Golf Club* there are two championship courses, the 6,420-yard Emerald and the 6,450-yard Ruby, with 162 bunkers between them (also tennis courts). The sea views are recommended at the *Jack Tar Village* (closed in 1990), at the western tip of the island, where there is a 6,800-yard, 27-hole PGA-rated course (also 6 clay and 10 all-weather tennis courts and waterskiing). The *Bahama Reef Golf and Country Club* offers a 6,768-yard championship course (swimming pool), and the *Fortune Hill Golf and Country Club* a 3,453-yard, 18-hole scenic course. The oldest is the *Lucayan Golf and Country Club*, where there is an 18-hole, 6,488-yard PGA-rated championship course. You can play **tennis** at the *Holiday Inn* (US$25/hour), the *Silver Sands Sea Lodge*, guests free, the *Atlantik Beach* (guests US$1 per day, US$100 annual membership), the *Princess Country Club* (US$5/hour daytime, US$10/hour nightime), *Princess Tower* (same rates), *Lucayan Beach* and *Lucayan Marina* (guests free, no night play) and the *Xanadu Beach Hotel* (non-guests US$5/hour). The Grand Bahama Tennis and Squash Club (Tel: 373 4567) has courts available from 0930-2400 but you have to be a member. **Horse riding** is available at Pinetree Stables (Tel: 373 3600), $20 for 1½-hour trail ride, lessons can also be arranged. There is a Rugby and Hockey Club (Pioneers Way), which organizes various social events. The YMCA next to the Rugby Club can give information about watching local basketball and softball matches. Volleyball is a popular sport and many beaches and residential street corners have nets. Aerobics classes are available at most of the major hotels, check *Princess Towers* and *Holiday Inn* for times. There are several jogging routes but watch out for dogs. Bowling is available at Sea Surf Lanes, Queen's Highway. There is a Super-Cross Motor Cycle dash in the autumn and Vintage motor car races around Freeport take place in December. The Conchman Triathlon (swim/cycle/jog) is held in November and road running races of 10km and 5km in the spring. Contact Dave Warren, Tel: 373 7683. UNEXSO organizes a conch diving competition for locals at Port Lucaya. An annual speed boat race is held at West End.

Festivals

Junkanoo is held on 26 December in West End, and then on 1 January in Freeport. Beginning from the Ranfurly Roundabout, dancing outside *Bahama Princess Hotel* 0400 onwards with drums, cowbells, whistles, brass instruments and foghorns. Scrap gangs, impromptu groups, join in with the rushin'. Much smaller than Nassau's but worth seeing. Go to Ranfurly Roundabout early to see the participants flame heating their goat skin drums to stretch them. The **Goombay** Summer Festival consists of a series of events at the International Bazaar or in the Lucaya area. On 10 July, **Independence**

Day, a Junkanoo parade is held at 0400 in West End and also on the first Monday in August, which is a holiday to commemorate the emancipation of the slaves. A mini Junkanoo is held weekly as part of the Goombay Festival and many of the hotels include a small Junkanoo as part of their native show. Other events are also held during the festival, get a calendar of events from the Tourist Office in the Bazaar or behind the Library. On **Discovery Day,** 12 October, a fair is held at McLean's Town, including a conch-cracking competition started by a British couple in the 1940s. The aim is to see who can remove the most conch from their shell in ten minutes. The women's competition has many machete-wielding experts who bring a lot of partisan support. There is also a swimming race to a nearby islet and back, which attracts a lot of local competition. The plaiting of the Maypole is an interesting Caribbean version of the English tradition, with children dancing round the pole to the beat of Reggae songs. Although much of the road to McLean's Town has been paved, the road is very poor in parts. Minibuses run regularly from Ranfurly Roundabout (US$2). If you rent a car it is sometimes difficult to park. Look out for details of local fairs in the Freeport News and at the Ranfurly Roundabout.

Freeport
Freeporters have a reputation of being less friendly than other Bahamians, but this is often blamed on the design of the town and the lack of community spirit. Avenues are large and buildings are spaced far apart, there are few corner shops or neighbourhood bars and it is hard to go anywhere without a car. In downtown Freeport there are a few small shopping malls (see under Shopping). Many of the civic buildings have been moved to a recently completed large grey and white complex behind the Regency Building. If you take the main mall out of town towards the airport you will pass the Rand Memorial Hospital and the excellent Wallace Groves Library. The main Tourist Office is behind this building. Heading in the opposite direction on this road you pass a bright pink pseudo classical building which is the Port Authority Building. This road eventually takes you to the Ranfurly Roundabout (named after 1950s British Colonial Governor) and the **International Bazaar,** a 10-acre integrated shopping complex on East Mall and West Sunrise Highway, with streets built in various assorted national styles with the corresponding merchandise and food; the English street is a Tudor-style courtyard. There is also a straw market. Open Monday-Friday 0900-1600. To the rear of the International Bar, the other side of the street from Colombian Emeralds (where you can tour the factory) and the Straw Market, is a perfume factory in a replica of an old Bahamian mansion, which you can tour and even mix your own perfume, Tel: 352 9391, open Monday-Friday, 1000-1730. Just over a mile east of Ranfurly Roundabout you come to another roundabout. Turn right to get to the Lucaya area, where there is the **Port Lucaya** shopping and entertainment complex and a number of hotels. At the Market place there is another straw and crafts market and a marina. UNEXSO is based here. In the evenings live music is played at the bandstand by the waterwalk.

Excursions
The Hydroflora Gardens on East Beach Drive, five minutes drive from Ranfurly Circus adjacent to the Palace disco, contain four acres of tropical plants grown hydroponically. Although the garden is on pure oolite rock, growth of up to five feet a year is achieved by this method. Open Monday-Saturday 0900-1730, B$1 entry or B$2 guided tour, Tel: 352 6052.

The Garden of Groves is a 12-acre botanical garden of flowers, birds (the flamingoes have been killed by dogs), pools and waterfalls. The centrepiece is a stone replica of the original church built for the loggers on Pine Ridge, and is a popular place for weddings. The Grand Bahama Museum in the gardens contains displays of local history and geography, artefacts from the burial sites of the Lucayan Indians, marine life exhibits, a section on the treasure troves found off Grand Bahama in 1965 and 1972 and Junkanoo costumes with an explanation of their African origins. Museum and gardens located on Magellan Drive, eight miles out of Freeport, gardens open 1000-1700 except Wednesdays, free, museum open daily 1000-1600, adults B\$2, children under 15 B\$1. Closed holidays. Times subject to change according to how much voluntary help is available, Tel: 352 4045 for up to date information.

The Rand Memorial Nature Centre, East Settlers Way, two miles out of town, is a 100-acre bird sanctuary with lots of flamingoes, hummingbirds and the rare olive capped warbler. B\$2 entry, children under eight not allowed. Guided nature walks only, be there ½ hour before it begins, Monday-Friday 1030, 1400 and 1500, Sunday 1400 and 1500, Tel: 352 5438 or write to Ricardo A Lightbourn, PO Box F-2954, Freeport. Highly recommended for its explanation of the ecology of a Bahamian forest.

NB Be careful of wild dogs on the island and if out walking or jogging always carry a stick.

Away from Freeport are the villages of Seagrape, Pine Ridge and Water Cay. West of Freeport: **Eight Mile Rock** (eight miles from Freeport) is the name given to eight miles of rock stretching east and west of Hawksbill Creek. The name refers to the town west of the creek. The Rock, as locals call it, has a strong sense of community not found in Freeport. The coastal road is prettier than the road directly through EMR although if you pass through the town you can see the original wooden clapboard dwellings raised off the ground, some with verandahs where the inhabitants sit chillin' and rapping. Local bar, *The Ritz*, very friendly, but see below under **Bars**. Sample Mr Wildgoose's tequila. Along the coastal road is a boiling hole and the Catholic church in Hepburn Town with walls shaped like praying hands. East of Hawksbill Creek are the settlement areas of Pinders Point, Lewis Yard and Hunters. Off Pinders Point is a boiling hole called the Chimney, which causes a vortex. Below is a large cave system but you need to go with a very experienced cave diver to see it.

West End, 40 miles from Freeport, was supposedly the first settlement on Grand Bahama. It enjoyed prosperity as a haven for rum-runners during the American prohibition era. Today there is a huge resort complex there, the *Grand Bahama Hotel and Country Club*. The coastal road is pleasant with local fishermen hooking conch from their boats on one side and bars, shops and houses in pastel shades on the other. At the most westerly point is the *Jack Tar Hotel Village*, brainchild of Sir Billy Butlin (closed in 1990). On 1 August, there is a motor boat race in West End. Drug running boats with two or more powerful engines designed to outrun the coastguard are said to take part.

Driving east from Freeport, you can see evidence of the aborted development plans, with many half-built plots, now mostly covered by bush, and roads which lead to nowhere. 15 miles east of Freeport, towards High Rock, is the 40-acre Lucaya National Park, with about 250 plant species, caves, plus a path through a Mangrove swamp, built in March 1985 by volunteers from "Operation Raleigh". Continuing east you get to High Rock (20 miles) (*Ezekiel Pinder's Restaurant* has an ocean view—almost) and Pelican Point (10 miles further), excellent deserted beach. The road on to **McLean's Town** (see **Festivals**, above) and East End is poor, but passable. From McLean's Town you can get a boat across to Sweetings or Deep Water Cay. Neither has vehicular traffic. It is possible to rent cottages. There is a guest house on Deep Water Cay and the *Traveller's Rest Bar* on Sweetings Cay.

Island Information—Grand Bahama

Transport Getting to see most of Grand Bahama without a car is difficult. Cars can be rented at the airport or in Freeport on a daily (US$70 for a compact car, plus insurance of about US$12 a day) or weekly (US$420) basis, as can jeeps (US$90/day), mopeds (US$20/day) and bicycles. Five Wheels Car Hire, Tel: 352 7001; Hertz, Tel: 352 3297; National, Tel: 352 9308. Check the telephone yellow pages for many more. Taxi fares are fixed and cabs are metered (about US$6 for five miles), but expect additional charges for extra passengers and more than two pieces of luggage. Taxis are available at the airport; expect to share as they leave when full and they are big taxis. Fare to town about US$8. Minibuses run from Freeport to Lucaya and less frequently from Freeport to High Rock, Eight Mile Rock, West End and East End. Check for timetable details. Local bus journeys are a flat rate of US$0.75. Minibuses drive fast and recklessly. There are routed stops but usually drivers will stop wherever you leave "bus stop coming up" loud enough to be heard over the music. Buses do not generally leave the bazaar or centre until full. Many hotels have a complimentary bus service for guests to the beach or in to Freeport.

Where To Stay See note on Hotels under New Providence. Price lists can be obtained from the tourist office in the Bazaar, behind the Library or in Lucaya, summer 1992 rates quoted here. *Lucayan Beach Resort and Casino*, (US$130-180, Tel: 373 7777, Fax: 373 2826, PO Box F-336) lovely patio bar, overlooking garden and beach, arrangements can be made to visit lighthouse. *Xanadu Beach and Marina Resort*, Sunken Treasure Drive, (US$124-154, Tel: 352 6782, PO Box F-2438), Howard Hughes, the recluse, used to live on the top floor. There is a small study/library dedicated to him on the ground floor. *The Princess Tower* (US$120-700, Tel: 352 6721, Fax: 352 6842, PO Box F-207/2623), in mock Moorish style, ask for a room with a decent view. In West End, the *Harbour Hotel* (US$60-110, Tel: 346 6432, PO Box F-2670) caters for the quieter end of the market. Less expensive hotels are *The Freeport Inn*, on The Mall (US$39d-59 quad, double that in winter, Tel: 352 6648, PO Box F-200), *The New Victoria Inn* off Midshipman's Drive (US$65, Tel: 373 3040, Fax: 373 8374, PO Box F-1261) and *Castaways* off the Ranfurly Roundabout (US$70, Tel: 352 6682, Fax: 352 5087, PO Box F-2629), but none can be recommended for service. Self catering apartments are available at many resorts. *Tyne Beach Terrace* is recommended, tasteful, good beach, watersports, also *Taino Beach Condos*, pleasant location. *Windward Palms*, The Mall, is a fair walk from the beach US$55-65, Tel: 352 8821, Fax: 352 6229, PO Box F-2549); *Sun Club Resort*, East Mall and Settlers Way is friendly. To stay with a Bahamian family, write to the Ministry of Tourism, P O Box F251, Freeport, for details of the People To People Programme; see also under **Information for Visitors**. Vigilance is advised in Freeport. Never leave screen doors open at night, there have been a number of armed robberies and sexual assaults where intruders have just walked in through screen doors left open.

Where To Eat   The hotels have several expensive restaurants which serve native/international cuisine. Buffet brunches on Sundays are recommended, you can eat as much as you like at *Casino (Princess Towers), Xanadu Hotel* and *Lucayan Beach Hotel* (US$18 including as much champagne as you can drink). Many restaurants, particularly those in hotels, do Early Bird Specials from 1730-1830, the EBS for US$13 at *La Trattoria* in the *Princess Towers* is good value. Beach front restaurants: *Pier One*, at Freeport Harbour, and *The Stoned Crab* on Taino Beach are both expensive, romantic, with good views. *Surfside Restaurant* further down on Taino Beach is a wooden structure on stilts, popular with Bahamians, cheap special most evenings; *Blackbeard's* on Fortune Beach, friendly, reasonably priced menu, mosquitos and no see'ums can be troublesome if you eat outside; *The Buccaneer Club* at Deadman's Reef has a courtesy bus (call 348 3794) but if you use it you will be presented with a higher priced menu on arrival, about 40-minute drive from Freeport, Wednesday night specials, closed in October, interesting guest signature book. Other popular restaurants include: *Freddie's Native Restaurant* in Hunters Settlement, open 1100-2300 but phone in advance, food basic but freshly prepared, tasty and cheap with fish dishes for US$8; *The Traveller's Rest* in Williams Town has good cheap breakfasts, Johnny Cake and soused fish are popular; *The Outriggers* at the far end of Taino Beach, distinctly Bahamian flavour, phone to check menu; *The Native Lobster Hut*, Sergeant Major Drive, pea soup and steamed turtle; *Scorpios*, Explorers Way, reasonably priced native food, favourable reports. For Italian food, *Marcella's* on Pioneers Way is highly recommended for good food and excellent service, also *Silvano's* on Ranfurly Circus, *Luciano's* in Port Lucaya good, book a table outside to see fireworks over the square on Saturday evenings at 2030-2100, noisy music though. *Pisces*, near *Lucayan Towers*, popular for its pizzas and cocktails, run by Bahamian George and Scottish Rosie. For oriental dishes there is *Mai Tai* specializing in Polynesian food, overlooking Emerald Golf Course on Rum Cay Drive, and there are at least three Chinese restaurants in the International Bazaar. In Port Lucaya, the *Big Buddha* serves Japanese style food with meals cooked at the Hibachi table around which you sit, each table has own chef, generous portions, 3-course meal for US$13; *Granville's*, Unit 7, building 12, Tel: 373 3945, open for breakfast 0700, serving lunch and dinner until 2300, seafood specials. The *Phoenix (Silver Sands Hotel)* serves kebabs and curries and has an unusual bar. The *Ruby Swiss Restaurant* on West Sunrise (seafood) is expensive but service is good. *Fat Man's Nephew* in Port Lucaya is reasonably priced, good view of bandstand (*Fat Man* in Pinder's Point used to be popular but the owner—Fat Man—was gunned down by an armed robber). *The Bahama Beach Club*, just west of the *Xanadu Hotel*, has a superb view of the sea, usually only bar snacks available, but watch newspapers for specials, eg Fish Fry on Fridays, barbecue on Saturdays at 1900, nice local atmosphere; the *Brass Helmet*, upstairs at UNEXSO, a slightly different menu from normal, reasonable prices, good and popular with divers. Although some restaurants are efficient and friendly, be prepared for indifferent service and long waits in many. A poll showed that 51% of tourists were dissatisfied with service in local hotels and restaurants. Restaurants open and close with alarming speed, check the local newspapers for new ones or special offers. A cheap alternative is to go to one of the many cook outs, usually of a high standard. Often the proceeds go to a good cause, such as someone's hospital bills. Taino Beach hosts cook outs but best to look in local press for details.

Bars and Nightlife There are a large number of bars in Freeport, most have a Happy Hour between 1700-1900. Most of the restaurants mentioned above have bars. While Bahamians are usually very friendly towards visitors and local bars are interesting and rewarding if you meet the local characters, be alert for any violent incidents which may suddenly arise. The *Pub on the Mall*, *Britannia Pub* and the *Winston Churchill* are all English style pubs. The *Winston Churchill* sells draught Courage and hosts the Gong Show on Wednesdays (starts around 2330). *Pussers Pub* in Port Lucaya with an English style pub menu is in a very pleasant location overlooking the harbour and band stand where live calypso music is played most nights. Pussers Painkiller is recommended. *Sandpipers* on Coral Beach is a country and western style bar. Most hotels have native shows. The *Yellow Bird Club* close to the International Bazaar has limbo, fire dancing and a glass eater. The *Lucayan Beach Hotel* has a similar show with a mini Junkanoo and firework display, US$20 for buffet and show, you have to like very loud music to enjoy this, seating regimented. The casino at the *Princess Towers* has a glitzy Las Vegas style cabaret. At the *Xanadu Hotel* most weekends you can hear live jazz. Most of the Freeport bars sponsor darts teams. The league is taken seriously and on Tuesdays and Thursdays there are matches. Dominoes are also popular, particularly in the smaller bars. For cheaper drinks in a less touristy environment, *Outriggers*, *Surfside* and *The Traveller's Rest* are recommended. *The Ritz* in Eight Mile Rock has a number of hammocks outside which overlook the sea (rubbish spoils the view), there has been some night-time violence at the bar, better to go during the day. Others include *The Ruby Swiss* on East Sunrise Highway, lively 0100-0400 when casino workers gather there after their shift ends, *Café Valencia* in the International Bazaar, also known as a croupiers' hangout, does not get going until after midnight. *The Bahama Mama* bar in the eastern corner of the Port Lucaya complex is one of the most popular bars of the moment, attracting local, expatriate and tourist customers giving it a lively, cosmopolitan atmosphere, interesting music, busy from 2300 onwards, a good place to meet people.

Discos The croupiers and locals alternate between *Panache*, at *Holiday Inn*, B$10 entrance includes two free drinks and *Sultan's Tent*, *Princess Towers Hotel*, same price, Wednesday is ladies' night. Try the talent contest at the *Winston Churchill* pub, Wednesdays 2230. *Club Estée*, Port Lucaya market place, Tel: 373 2777, caters for the older crowd (aged 25-35), cover charge of US$12 includes two drinks, closed Tuesdays, smart clothes with jackets for men, Mondays, Wednesdays, Thursdays, disco party night with casual dress Friday-Sunday, free admission for women on Wednesday and for everyone 1900-2100 on Sunday. If you want to know which disco is "in", ask the English croupiers at the casinos as they closely monitor the night life. *Goombay Land* behind *The Palace* has roller skating and go-karts, very popular with local youth, entrance US$5.

Shopping Many items are tax exempt in the bonded area of Freeport/Lucaya and bargains include perfume, linens, sweaters, china, cameras, emeralds, watches, leather goods and alcoholic drinks. The two main shopping areas are the International Bazaar and Port Lucaya. The International Bazaar is off Ranfurly Roundabout. Built in 1967, the 10-acre complex was designed by a film special effects expert, with shops designed in national styles and selling corresponding food and goods, although the overall effect is very American. The entrance is a giant Torri gate, the Japanese symbol of welcome. Port Lucaya was the brainchild of Count Basie, who used to live on Grand Bahama. The atmosphere is usually friendly and there is live music most evenings. There are many different shops to buy souvenirs as well as a straw market. The Rastafarian Shop has some interesting souvenirs and there is a Bahamian Arts and Crafts stall in the centre of the complex, one row back from the central bandstand. In downtown Freeport there are a few small shopping malls; Churchills has a Marks & Spencers, there is also the Regency and the newly opened 17 Centre behind the main Post Office. Close by are a Winn Dixie and a Pantry Pride which have a virtual monopoly of the grocery supplies. Outside Pantry Pride is a fruit market which is colourful but expensive.

Tourist Office In Freeport, Bazaar, along the Mall, next to the library, as well as in any large hotel. The Tourist Information Centres in Freeport/Lucaya can give a brochure listing all licensed hotels in the Bahamas and their rates.

The Family Islands

The **Family Islands**, which used to be called the Out Islands, are very different in atmosphere from New Providence and Grand Bahama. The larger islands are up to a hundred miles long, but have only a few thousand inhabitants. Sea and sky come in every possible shade of blue; there are wild cliffs and miles of white sand beaches. Inland, pine forests grow in the northern islands, dry woodland in the central ones and sparse scrub vegetation in the south. Red-coloured salt ponds were once the basis of a thriving salt industry on the southern islands, but the land offered few other economic possibilities, though one other product was Cascarilla bark, used to flavour Vermouth and Campari. Before the drugs-and-tourism boom of the 1980s, most people earned their living from the sea. The villages have brightly painted, traditional-style houses and whitewashed churches. People are generally friendly and helpful and the way of life is much more Bahamian and less Americanized.

Thousands of yachts visit the islands, mainly during the winter season. The sea is clean and clear and ideal for swimming, snorkelling and scuba diving. Most of the islands have relatively few tourists, although Eleuthera and one or two others have big, resort-type hotels with marinas and sports facilities. Most islands have at least one Bahamasair flight a day and at least one mailboat a week. If you are travelling in a group, a small charter plane may be much more convenient and only a little more expensive. Some islands also have a direct flight from Miami or another US airport; this cuts out the need for an unreliable, time-consuming connection in Nassau. Travel is restricted to one main road per island, usually called the Queen's Highway.

Abaco

The Abaco islands (population 10,061), the boat-building centre of the Bahamas, are a chain of islands and cays covered in pine forests, stretching in a curve for 130 miles from **Walker's Cay** in the north to Hole in the Wall in the south. The New England Loyalists who settled here found wrecking to be a profitable pastime. Sponge, pineapple, sisal, sugar and lumber were later developed but nowadays the major agribusiness is citrus from two huge farms which export their crop to Florida. Abaco has developed its tourist industry more effectively than other Family Islands and has the highest employment rate. In the early 1970s some Abaco residents formed the Greater Abaco Council which was opposed to Bahamian independence. When independence became a reality in 1973, the Abaco Independence Movement tried to assert Abaco's independence from the rest of the Bahamas. This breakaway movement by white residents caused the islanders to split into two camps and there were bitter conflicts.

The main centre on Abaco is Marsh Harbour, which is the third largest town in the Bahamas. Its name reflects the swampy nature of much of Greater Abaco. The scrub and swamp give the island a rather desolate appearance, but like many islands, life revolves around the offshore cays and the coastal settlements. The area south of Marsh Harbour owes its development and particularly its roads to lumber companies. There are miles and miles of pine forests, secondary growth after the heavy logging earlier this century. Nobody lives south of Sandy Point although there is a lighthouse at Hole in the Wall.

Guy Fawkes Day is celebrated on 10 November with parades through the streets led by the Guy to a big bonfire in the evening (no fireworks).

Flora and Fauna
Like other northern Family Islands, Abaco is mostly covered by secondary growth stands of Caribbean pine, interspersed with hammocks or coppices of hardwoods such as mahogany and wild coffee. The Bahama parrot, extinct on all other islands bar Inagua, survives in these coppices, 42 breeding pairs have been counted. A captive breeding programme is now in progress and fledglings will be released back into these areas. Friends of the Environment, an environmental protection group, headquarters on Treasure Cay, Abaco, runs guided excursions to see the parrots (US$40 per person), and also has plenty of other, interesting information on the fauna of the Abacos, Tel: 367 2847.

Diving and Marine Life
Life revolves around the sea and Abaco is sometimes called the "sailing capital of the world", with good marina facilities at the *Treasure Cay Marina*, one of the largest tourist resorts in the Family Islands, the *Conch Inn Resort and Marina* and the *Green Turtle Yacht Club and Marina*. Marsh Harbour Regatta is 22 June to 4 July. The diving is superb, don't miss Pelican Cay National Park, which is an underwater wildlife sanctuary. Many areas are now officially protected and fish life is abundant, green turtles and porpoises

numerous in and around harbour areas. Fishing is strictly controlled in reef areas although the coral still shows signs of previous damage by bleaching and careless sailors. If you like exploring wrecks, the 110-year old *USS Adirondack* with her rusting cannon is worth a visit. Inland you can dive into Devil's Hole. Specialist dive operations include Dive Abaco at Marsh Harbour, Walker's Cay Dive Shop, Brendal's Dive Shop at Green Turtle Cay and Dave Gale's Island Marine Dive Shop (no courses) at Hope Town, who can offer introductory courses and a wide variety of facilities. Marsh Harbour lacks good beaches, but Mermaid's Cove on the road to the Point is a pretty little beach with excellent snorkelling. For offshore snorkelling, Captain Nick's Tours, from the *Jib Room* marina and restaurant, runs trips out to local reefs and beauty spots, including Pelican Cay. Snorkel gear is available for hire. Marsh Harbour is the starting place/drop off for many sailing charter companies. Charters can be arranged by the day or week, through numerous agencies, or more cheaply by private arrangement with boat owners. Ask at local marinas such as the *Jib Room*. Prices from $80 per day.

Other Sports

You can play tennis at *Bluff House* (guests free), *Great Abaco Beach Hotel* (guests free) or *Green Turtle Club* (US$5/hour). *Walker's Cay Hotel and Marina* (Tel: 305-522 1469), a 100-acre resort, has tennis courts (guests free) as well as a range of water activities, including windsurfing (US$15/hour). *Treasure Cay Beach Hotel and Villas* on a three-mile beach, has a 6,972-yard championship golf course, tennis, windsurfing (US$15/hour) and waterskiing (US$10/15 minutes). Other places where you can windsurf include *Abaco Inn* (US$30/day), at Hope Town, *Elbow Cay Club* (US$25/day), the *Green Turtle Yacht Club* (free), *Hope Town Harbour Lodge* (US$20/day), *Pinder's Cottages* (US$20/day) and *Romora Bay Club* (US$10/hour).

Excursions

Marsh Harbour straggles along the flat southern shore of a good and busy yachting harbour. It has the major airport about three miles from the town and is the commercial centre of Abaco. The town has a large white population, but at the last census 40% were found to be Haitian, most of whom live in the districts of Pigeon Pea and The Mud and work as domestic servants in the white suburbs. Shops are varied and well stocked and Barclays and CIBC banks are both represented. Places to stay include *Abaco Town By The Sea Resort*, two-bedroom villas (US$150-170 summer, US$170-180 winter EP, Tel: 367 2221, P O Box 486); *Conch Inn*, full marina facilities, well located but a bit run down (US$75 all year, Tel: 367 2800, P O Box 434); *Ambassador Inn*, slightly cheaper but not well located (US$65, Tel: 367 2022, P O Box 484); *Great Abaco Beach Hotel*, private beach, five minutes to the airport (US$165, Tel: 367 2158, Fax: 367 2819, P O Box 511), *Lofty Fig*, villas, nice looking (US$400/week, Tel: 367 2681). Restaurants include *Mangoes*, on the waterfront, excellent, pretty, food just right, about US$25 a head for dinner, *Wally's*, nearby is also attractive, but lunch only, both closed Sundays. *The Jib Room*, at Point on the north side of the harbour is open all week, less inspiring, but has a lively Sunday steak-out with band and dancing, US$12.

The picturesque and quaint village of **New Plymouth** on **Green Turtle Cay**, can be reached from Treasure Cay airport by a short taxi ride (US$20) and then a ferry from Treasure Cay Dock (US$5). The Albert Lowe Museum chronicles the British settlers who came in the 18th century and their shipbuilding skills. The Memorial Sculpture Garden is also worth a visit. The island has some lovely beaches, ideal for shelling, and boats are easily rented (US$50/day) for exploring other cays. On New Year's Day, the inhabitants celebrate the capture of Bunce, a legendary figure said to have lived in Abaco's pine forests. *Miss Emily's Blue Bee Bar* is worth a visit. Located in the centre of the settlement it is bursting with memorabilia of previous famous and infamous customers and serves unforgettable and very strong cocktails. *Green Turtle Club and Marina*, deluxe accommodation (US$105 summer, US$140 winter, Tel: 367 2572, Fax: 365 4272, P O Box 270). *New Plymouth Inn*, Green Turtle Cay, (US$100d MAP summer, US$110 winter, Tel: 365 4161, Fax: 365 4138, PO Box 462, New Plymouth). *Bluff House Club & Marina* (US$75-85, villas from US$135, Tel: 365 4247, Fax: 365 4247), a ferry ride to the north, has a marvellous view of the sea. *Coco Bay Cottages*, 4 cottages, US$500-800d/week, US$100/week per extra person, each with 2 bedrooms, comfortably furnished, in 5 acres of beach front property, fruit trees, snorkelling equipment available, in USA, Tel: (508) 443-4872. *Sea Star Beach Cottages* on beach from US$500/week (Tel: 365 4178, P O Box 282, Gilham Bay). To rent cottages sleeping up to 8 people per cottage, phone Sid's Grocery Store in New Plymouth, but take mosquito repellent in summer and autumn.

Man-O-War is a boat building centre with New England Loyalist origins, where, until recently, blacks were not allowed to stay overnight. It is very pretty, with a good beach on the east side and snorkelling at the north point. There is one little restaurant, *Arlene's*, no bars and no hotels. The CIBC bank is open Thursdays only. There are no cars, people use golf carts and scooters. Sundays are graveyard quiet.

Ferries run to **Great Guana** (with a 7-mile beach on the ocean side), where you can stay at the *Guana Beach Resort* (US$125d, Tel: 359 6194, P O Box 474, small, informal), and Little Harbour, which has many attractions. Randolf Johnston's art studio (open 1000-1600), featuring his unique bronze sculptures, is well worth a visit. *Pete's Pub*, down on the beach, serves island drinks and light snacks in an idyllic setting and Pete also makes and sells gold jewellery in his studio next door. A well marked path leads up to the abandoned lighthouse, offering good views over the island, and a pleasant beach is to be found, to the north of the dock. Also accessible by ferry across the bay is Elbow Cay and the settlement of **Hope Town**, marked by a striped lighthouse from the top of which you can get lovely views (open Monday-Friday 1000-1600). There are no cars allowed along the narrow streets edged by white picket fences and saltbox cottages. Half the houses are owned by non-Bahamians. Visit the Wyannie Malone Historical Museum which has a collection of old furniture from the town. Restaurants outside the town offer free transport. There are a number of rustic villages scattered throughout the 50 miles of mainland south of Marsh Harbour, with miles of shelling beaches and woodland preserved as a sanctuary for the Bahamian parrot. Cars, mopeds and bicycles can be hired easily. *Elbow Cay Beach Inn* (US$100, Tel: 367 2748), most watersports, secluded, Danish cuisine; *Hope Town Harbour Lodge* (US$65-80), 20 minutes from Marsh Harbour airport, good secluded beaches, sea views, most watersports, native food.

Albury's Ferry Service runs from Sandy Crossing, two miles east of Marsh Harbour to Hope Town and Man-O-War Cay, US$8 single, US$12 day return. Separate boats leave each island at 0800 and 1330, returning from the mainland at 1030 and 1600. Albury's boats can also be chartered to these two cays and to other islands. For five or more, a charter to Hope Town or Man-O-War works out at US$10pp each way. All day excursions to Treasure

Cay (US$25 Tuesdays), Guana Cay (US$15 Fridays) and Hope Town (US$12 Thursday), Man-O-War and Hope Town in one trip (US$15 Monday).

There are airstrips at Marsh Harbour, Treasure Cay and Walker's Cay. American Eagle, Gulfstream and Airways International fly daily from Miami. U S Air Express Airways International and Island Express fly from Fort Lauderdale daily. US Air Express flies from Orlando, Tampa and (along with Bahamasair and Airways International) West Palm Beach. Island Express flies also from Sanford, Florida. Bahamasair flies twice daily from Nassau and four days a week from Freeport to Marsh Harbour and Treasure Cay. Walker's Cay is served only by Walker's International from Fort Lauderdale. Look out for package deals to the various resorts with Bahamasair.

Andros

The Spanish called the island La Isla del Espíritu Santo, but its present name is said to come from the British commander Sir Edmund Andros. At 104 miles long and 40 miles wide, Andros (population 8,307) is the largest island in the Bahamas, with pine and mahogany forests, creeks and prolific birdlife. According to Indian legend, the forests house the "chickcharnie", a mythical, three fingered, three-toed, red eyed creature who hangs upside down and can cause good or bad luck. In fact, a large, three-toed, burrowing owl of this description did inhabit the forests until the early 16th century when it became extinct. More recent legend has it that the pirate, Sir Henry Morgan lit a beacon (bonfire) on the top of Morgan's Bluff, the highest point on the island at 67 feet. This lured passing ships on to the treacherous reef close by. Sir Henry and his pirates then ransacked the ships and hid their treasure in the caves below. Both the Bluff and the caves are now well signposted.

There are two separate islands, North and South Andros, with the central regions (middle bights) accessible from either direction. In the south there are wild bird reserves which allow hunting in the season (September-March). In central Andros near Fresh Creek, you can visit the Androsia clothing factory which makes batik fabrics in tropical colours and watch the whole process from the wax painting to the drying of the dyed cloth. Ask in the shop for a factory tour. South of Fresh Creek is the Atlantic Underwater Testing and Evaluation Center (Autec), a joint venture between the USA and the UK for underwater testing of weapons and consequently top secret. The main settlements in the north are **Nicholl's Town, Lowe Sound, Conch Sound, Red Bays, Mastic Point** and **Fresh Creek** (previously known as Andros Town and Coakley Town). **Mangrove Cay** is in central Andros, while in the south are Congo Town, **Deep Creek** and Prime Minister Sir Lynden Pindling's constituency at **Kemp's Bay**. Nicholl's Town has a lively Junkaroo on Christmas night and New Year's Eve, and Goombay Festival on every Thursday in July and August from 1900 onwards on Seaview Square. Red Bays is the only settlement on the west coast of the island. Long isolated and reached only by boat it is now connected by a good paved road cutting across the wild interior of the island. Originally a seminole Indian settlement many of the people have distinctly Indian features and a true out island life style. The village welcomes visitors. Locally caught sponges, hand made baskets and wood carvings can all be bought very cheaply. Mrs Marshall is the local bush granny and community celebrity. Usually found weaving in the centre of the village she will show how baskets are made, and explain local culture, politics and bush medicine to visitors. Mr Russell always has plenty of sponges for sale (and illegally caught turtle and iguanas, don't buy these). Henry Wallace is the local rastafarian wood carver, usually to be found chipping away to the beat of reggae music.

Fauna and Flora

Andros has an extensive creek system which is largely unexplored. In south Andros the 40-square-mile area beyond the ½ mile long ridge is also uninhabited and rarely visited. The large pine forests and mangrove swamps are home to a variety of birds and animals. Sightings of the Bahamian parrot have been reported in south Andros, while rare terns and whistling tree ducks, roseatte spoonbills and numerous different herons have been seen in the north and central areas. Green Cay, one of the many small islands off Andros (20 miles east of Deep Creek) has the world's second largest population of white crowned pigeons. These pigeons are prey to hunters from September to March each year (hunting season). The west side of Andros is undeveloped and other than Red Bays in the north west corner there are no settlements on this side, making it ideal for wildlife; large rock iguanas up to six feet long and hundreds of flamingos live here. During May to August the Andros land crabs migrate from the pine forests to the sea. These enormous crabs are to be found everywhere during this time. Many are caught and exported to Nassau.

Beaches and Watersports

In the north, Nicholl's Town has the best beach. A wide, golden beach runs the length of the northern coast, almost to Morgan's Bluff. It is ideal for swimming and excellent snorkelling spots are to be found directly off the beach. Windsurfers, snorkel equipment and paddlerafts are available from Andros Undersea Adventures, *Andros Beach Hotel*. Lowe Sound, Conch Sound and Mastic Point all have good beaches. A very pleasant, 2½-mile walk from Nicholl's Town to Morgan's Bluff along a leafy overgrown road (in fact the first road built on the island) leads to the caves at Morgan's Bluff and offers beautiful views of this part of the coast. Further south near Fresh Creek is Staniard Creek where there is an attractive palm-fringed beach with white sand and pleasant settlement close by. Sand bars, exposed at the mouth of Staniard Creek at low tide, are excellent shelling spots. Somerset beach is just south of Fresh Creek, signposted from the main highway. It is a spectacular spot, especially at low tide and another excellent shelling beach. At Victoria Point in central Andros there is a graveyard right on the water's edge. In some parts of Andros on Easter Monday at 0200-0600 there is a candlelight vigil by gravesites at which Easter hymns are sung. The east side of Mangrove Cay has spectacular beaches all lined with coconut groves. In south Andros along the 28-mile stretch from Mars Bay to Drigg's Hill are beautiful palm-lined beaches with occasional picturesque settlements.

Diving and Marine Life

Visitors mostly come for the unspoiled beaches, the diving on pristine reefs in 80°F water with excellent visibility and extraordinary bonefishing. Development has been concentrated on the east coast facing one of the world's largest underwater reefs. This huge barrier reef, the second largest in the Western Hemisphere, plunges 6,000 feet to the Tongue of the Ocean, an exciting drop-off dive. Wreck dive sites include the *Lady Gloria*, an old mailboat sunk recently off Morgan's Bluff, and the *Potomac*, a steel-hulled barge which sank just after the war and is now home to many huge, friendly grouper and parrot fish, as well as some impressive barracuda. Andros has 197 blue holes, of these 50 are oceanic, the rest inland. Formed by water erosion then flooded at the end of the last ice-age, the oceanic holes actually connect to the intricate inland underwater cave system. As tide rushes in and out ideal feeding grounds are created and consequently the oceanic blue holes harbour prolific and diverse marine life and are excellent dive sites at slack tide. The inland blue holes can be very deep (up to 350 feet) and contain a lens of freshwater 40-100 feet deep floating on seawater. Beautiful to swim in: Charlie's blue hole, near Nicholl's Town is clearly signposted as is Church's blue hole, just north of Fresh Creek. Marine life in the inland blue holes is limited, though the rare crustacean *Remepedidia* and the blind cave fish *Lucifuga* have been found. Earthwatch is currently conducting a detailed study on the mosquito fish, one of the few colonists of the blue holes on North Andros. On South Andros two popular blue holes are the "Giant Doughnut" near Deep Creek, south of Kemps Bay, and "Inland Blue Hole Lissy" near the Bluff, south Andros. Legends abound about blue holes, serpents known as Luka, originally a part of Seminole Indian legends are thought to drag unsuspecting swimmers and fishermen below. Caution should be exercised at some of the holes as they are extremely deep. The underwater cave system on Andros is considered to have some of the world's longest, deepest and most stunning caves. A 1991 expedition discovered remains of a Lucayan burial site in one of the blue holes of South Andros. Intact Lucayan skulls were recovered, as well as femurs and hip bones. Lowe Sound is considered by some to be the bonefishing capital of the world. Boat charters are available from most hotels. For ecological tours Forfar Field Station, north of Fresh Creek, runs guided diving, snorkelling and inland excursions, Tel: 329-6129 for details. Cheap accommodation may also be available. At the *Andros Beach Hotel* Neal Watson's Undersea Adventures organizes dive trips to the Tongue of the Ocean and dive wrecks. Windsurfing is also available. Diving and windsurfing also at *Small Hope Bay Lodge* near Fresh Creek, central Andros, diving and fishing at *Cargill Creek Fishing Lodge*, Andros Island bone fish resort next door is known locally as *Rupert's Place*, and bonefishing at *Charlie's Haven*. You can still see traditional Bahamian wooden sailboats here, made by local craftsman Ronald Young, although nowadays he makes mostly fishing boats. On Christmas Day, Columbus' Discovery Day and Easter Monday sailboat races, featuring locally-made Bahamian sloops, are held at Lowe Sound, Nicholl's Town and sometimes Conch Sound. Ask locals for details. Regattas also combine cook-outs, local music and dancing. On Independence Day there is a sailboats race in the Regatta.

Island Information—Andros

How To Get There Airports are at Andros Town (1½ miles from Fresh Creek), Mangrove Cay (both central), San Andros (north) and Congo Town (south). Boats can dock at Mastic Point (north), Fresh Creek (central) and Congo Town (south). Bahamasair has daily flights to Andros Town and San Andros from Nassau. Flights to Mangrove Cay four days a week from Nassau, twice via South Andros. Gulfstream International Airlines, a commuter air carrier, flies from Miami twice a day to San Andros and Andros Town. Airways International flies from Fort Lauderdale, Miami and West Palm Beach to Andros town. For mailboat schedules and fares see **Information for Visitors, Inter Island Travel**. Most settlements are linked by neatly paved roads. Taxis are available. Cars and scooters can be rented. In Kemps Bay Mr Rahming rents cars and also provides a charter service to any of the Family Islands (Tel: 329 2569). In Lowe Sound R & M Rentals (Tel: 320 2526), in Fresh Creek Berth Rent A Car (Tel: 368 2101) and at San Andros airport Cecil Gaitor has cars for hire. The *Donna Lee Motel & Store*, Nicholl's

Town, rents out bicycles, scooters and cars. It is often possible to hire cars for the day from private individuals, ask locally, taxi drivers have details. Bicycles also for hire from Andros Undersea Adventures, *Andros Beach Hotel*, Nicholl's Town; bicycles and scooters from the liquor store and fish market at Morgan's Bluff.

Where To Stay Five miles from Andros Town is the *Bannister's Cottages*, family run, US$75, cottages US$45 (Tel: 329 4188); on Lisbon Creek, Mangrove Cay, is *Longley's Guest House*, run by Bernard Longley US$50 (Tel: 325 1581); *Small Hope Bay Lodge*, Fresh Creek, US$130/night pp summer or US$140 pp winter, all inclusive, popular diving centre (Tel: 368 2014); *Trade Wind Villas*, US$65, run by Mrs Bowleg (Tel: 329 2040); *Chickcharnie Hotel* US$70 (Tel: 368 2025), has docking facilities, restaurant/bar and recommended for its freshly baked bread. Also in Fresh Creek, *Landmark Motel*, family-run by Skinny, the owner and Deno, his son, US$60 (Tel: 329 2024), comfortable rooms with sea view, recommended; *The Lighthouse Hotel*, government-run, opened 1991, docking facilities, dive shop, restaurant and swimming pool, US$110, good location. In Staniard Creek, Prince Munroe (Tel: 329 6044) has some rooms and *Riley's* is a family-run motel on the other side of the Creek, US$45 a/c, private bath all rooms. On the border of Congo Town and Long Bay, *Emerald Palms-By-The-Sea*, US$175 (Tel: 329 4661, PO Box 800) modern with balconies facing the sea, swimming pool, tennis court and boats for charter, patronized by Sir Lynden Pindling and his wife who comes from Congo Town; *Congo Beach Hotel*, US$35 (Tel: 329 4777), recently renovated, friendly, daily happy hour, recommended. At Kemps Bay Mr Rahming (Tel: 329 4608) who runs the local gas station and food store has rooms and beach houses to let, clean but the noise of slamming dominoes may keep you awake. He is a Seventh Day Adventist so the store is closed on Saturday and sells no pork or alcohol. He has cars to rent and also does a good, cheap haircut. In Nicholl's Town, *Villas of Andros Beach*, write to Mrs Bow, P O Box 4465, Nicholl's Town; *Andros Beach Hotel*, recommended, English style restaurant with red brick and wooden beams, on the ocean, US$75 (Tel: 329 2582); *Donna Lee Motel*, US$65, arranges boat trips with snorkelling and fishing, close to beach and town (Tel: 329 2194). *Conch Sound Resort Inn* (Tel: 329 2060), from US$80, swimming pool, restaurant, airport pick-up, a/c and TV in all rooms.

Where To Eat Andros has an exportable surplus of crabs, so crab dishes are very popular. May-July is the crab season. Try baked Andros crab, which uses the crab's own fat to cook it in, also Vetol's crab'n'rice and stewed crab cooked with conch. Although Andros is undergoing some commercialization, in the south it is relatively undeveloped and some restaurants may need advance warning. For a cheap meal look out for cook outs. In Congo Town, B Paul runs the *Jungle Club* and has barbecues frequently. Good, cheap conch fritters at the snack bar on Driggs Hill dock. Recommended restaurants include *Rupert's Fish Camp*, Cargill Creek, very good local game fish, candlelit verandah overlooks sea; the *Small Hope Bay Lodge* and *Chickcharnie Hotel* in Fresh Creek; *Skinnys Landmark* serves Bahamian meals and is very popular locally, lively disco at weekends, many American Servicemen from AUTEC, local politicians etc. among regular clientele; the *Bannister's Restaurant* with turtle pen in Lisbon Creek; the *Andros Beach Hotel* for its peas'n'rice and the *Picaroon Restaurant* for authentic Bahamian dishes in Nicholl's Town. Also in Nicholl's Town: *Rolle's* takeaway serves best local food on island, and *Daychelles* (known locally as *Lilly's*), excellent meals, including locally-caught dolphin fish, with lively disco and live rake'n'scrape band at weekends. Recommended bars include *Mr Sands'* in Little Creek, cheap and friendly; *Hole in the Wall*, in Mathers Town is good, as is Rev Henfield's *Beach Restaurant/Bar* in Nicholl's Town. *Rumours*, just outside Nicholl's Town, popular 'up beat' disco, some live bands at weekends. At Kemps Bay, *Dudley's Pink Pussy Cat Club* has a rake'n'scrape band and traditional stepping dancing with Rosita on saw and Ben on drums.

Berry Islands

There are 30 Berry Islands (population 500) which offer beautiful opportunities for divers and snorkellers. Most are the private homes of the wealthy or inhabited only by wildlife. **Bullock's Harbour** in **Great Harbour Cay** is the main settlement in the area, Great Harbour Cay is the largest cay in the Berry chain at just two miles across. First settled by ex-slaves in 1836, the cay proved difficult to farm. Tourism has not fared well either, a luxury resort with a golf course and sailing club is now derelict. Cruise ships drop anchor off Great Sturrup Cay and passengers can spend the day on the deserted beach there.

The only spot in the Berry Islands which caters for tourists is **Chub Cay**. The *Chub Cay Club* (US$85, Tel: 325 1490) has its own airstrip, tennis courts, restaurant, marina and extensive dive facilities offered by Chub Cay Undersea Adventures. There is a deep water canyon at Chub Cay where you can find a variety of colourful reef fish and open water marine life. Staghorn coral can be seen in the shallow waters near Mamma Rhoda Rock. Less natural, but still fascinating is the submarine deliberately sunk in 90 feet of water off Bond Cay, named after James himself.

Many of the cays do not welcome uninvited guests. Interesting wildlife can be found on Frozen and Alder Cay. Terns and pelicans can be seen here and although they are privately owned, sailors may anchor here to observe the birds. Hoffman's Cay, now deserted, was originally home to a thriving farming settlement. Ruins of houses, a church and a graveyard still stand. Paths also lead to a deep blue hole. A golden beach runs along the length of the eastern coast of the island. On Little Whale Cay, Wallace Groves, the founder of Freeport, has his own home and airstrip. Great Harbour Cay has its own airport served by Airways International from Miami and Fort Lauderdale.

Bimini

Once thought to be the site of the lost city of Atlantis, the Bimini chain of islands (population 1,411), only 50 miles from Florida, is divided into North and South Bimini and a series of cays. Ernest Hemingway lived on Bimini in 1931-37 at Blue Marlin Cottage and his novel *Islands in the Stream* was based on Bimini. A display of Hemingway memorabilia can be seen at the *Compleat Angler Hotel and Museum*. On South Bimini is the legendary site of the Fountain of Youth, sought by Ponce de León in 1512. The pool known as the Healing Hole is claimed to have some beneficial effects. There are more bars than shops on Bimini, service is minimal, telecommunications sporadic, car rental non-existent. It is not a glamorous resort, although there are plenty of luxury yachts moored there. The airplane wrecks at the edge of the airfield at **Alice Town** on North Bimini are mostly the results of unsuccessful drugs running attempts en route from Colombia to Miami. Bimini has been claimed as an important success in the fight against drug running to the US mainland; Gun Cay has become the centre for drug interdiction operations and is full of US DEA personnel.

Alice Town is the capital of Bimini although most people live in **Bailey Town** to the south along the King's Highway. Alice Town has a lot of bars and a straw market, if little else. Heading south from Alice Town you come to *The Anchorage*, a restaurant on the highest point on the island with good views of the sea. The beach in either direction is excellent with white sand and good surfing waves. Above the beach is a pathway which passes the picturesque Methodist Church (1858) and leads to Bailey Town.

Diving and Marine Life
Bimini is famous for big game fishing. Fishing is excellent all year round although 7 May-15 June is the tuna season (blue fin), June and July are best

for blue marlin, winter and spring for white marlin and championship fishing tournaments are held here from March to August. Blue marlin are the favourite target, averaging between 150 and 500 lbs, but which can exceed 1,000 lbs. The southern Biminis, Cat Cay and Gun Cay are the places to catch billfish and bluefin. *The Bimini Big Game Fishing Club* caters for most fishermen's needs and can arrange fishing trips with guides. It has 180 slips, charter/boat rental, all supplies and a large walk-in freezer for daily catches. Scuba diving is recommended, particularly over the Bimini Wall to see the black coral trees, or to the lovely reefs off Victory Cay. Bimini Undersea Adventures, run by Bill Keefe, has a comprehensive list of facilities and can also offer sailing, fishing and tennis.

Island Information—Bimini

How To Get There Bahamasair does not have flights to Bimini, but Chalk International has flights from Miami and from Nassau to Alice Town with sea planes which land in the harbour. Daily cruise ships are met by a tour bus. For mailboat details see **Information for Visitors, Inter Island Travel.**

Where To Stay *The Bimini Big Game Fishing Club* (US$139 EP all year, Tel: 347 2391, Fax: 347 2392, PO Box 699), owned by Bacardi, is the main hotel (cottages at US$164 recommended) and social centre (beware the Beastwhacker, a cocktail of champagne and Bacardi rum) and has swimming pool and tennis courts. *Bimini Blue Water Ltd* (Tel: 347 2166, Fax: 347 2293, PO Box 627), rooms US$90, three-bedroomed cottage US$285, suites US$190, private beach, swimming pool and marina; *Brown's Hotel and Marina* (Tel: 347 2227, PO Box 601), US$55, two-bedroomed cottage US$100, near beach; *Compleat Angler Hotel* (Tel: 347 2122, PO Box 601), US$70-80 in town, popular bar; *Admiral Hotel* (Tel: 347 2347), US$72-80 in Bailey Town; *Sea Crest*, US$75 (Tel: 347 2071, P O Box 654), Alice Town, managed by Alfred Sweeting.

Where To Eat After dark activities consist of drinking and dancing. *The End of the World Bar* in Alice Town has long opening hours and the back looks out to the harbour; *Yama's Bar*, run by former boxer Billy Yama Bahama Butler; *The Red Lion Pub* is recommended for its seafood, as is *Captain Bob Smith's* and *The Big Game Restaurant* on the sea front in Alice Town. The *Calypsonians* play weekly at *The Compleat Angler*, worth seeing, and *Glen Rolle and the Surgeons* provide musical entertainment at *Deandrias*. Other recommended nightspots are the *Hy Star Disco* and *Brown's Hotel Bar*, both in Alice Town.

Cat Island

Named after Arthur Catt, a British pirate who was in league with Henry Morgan and Edward Teach (Blackbeard), Cat Island (population 2,143) boasts Lucayan Indian caves near Port Howe, as well as the usual underwater sites of interest and beauty. Fifty miles long, it was once called San Salvador, and is a contender for the site of Columbus' first landfall. It has rolling hills and the highest point in the Bahamas, Mount Alvernia, 206 feet above sea level. The island is a centre for the practice of Obeah, a Bahamian voodoo incorporating both bush medicine and witchcraft, which is indicated by bottles and other small objects hanging from the branches of the trees.

Most development has taken place in the south. **New Bight** is the capital and shares an impressive bay with the quaint Old Bight, the site of an early 19th century attempt to establish a cotton plantation. You can see the ruins of Pigeon Bay Cottage, an old plantation house just outside Old Bight. New Bight has a few shops. The annual regatta is held here in August. Above the village you can climb Mount Alvernia and visit Father Jerome's Hermitage.

The Stations of the Cross are carved along a winding path leading to the Hermitage, built by Father Jerome, an Anglican priest who converted to Roman Catholicism and designed several churches on Cat Island and Long Island. Fernandez Bay, three miles north of New Bight and home to *The Fernandez Bay Village Resort*, has one of the island's best beaches, a secluded cove with excellent sands. On the most southerly tip of the island are two beaches with facilities: *The Cutlass Bay Club Beach* (tennis, waterskiing) has its own airstrip and a good restaurant. World famous bonefishing flats are within wading distance of the beach. Close by along the crumbling cliff tops are the impressive ruins of the Richman Hill plantation, with ruins of slave quarters, an overseer's house and a plantation house. The original plantation stretched from the ocean to the inland lake. Another interesting ruin is Colonel Andrew Deveaux' mansion at Port Howe. Granted land on Cat Island for delivering Nassau from the Spanish, he set up a briefly prosperous cotton plantation here. Early settlers in Port Howe lured ships on to the rocks in order to loot their cargoes. Today Port Howe is famous for its coconuts and pineapples, while the bread, cooked in Dutch or Rock wood-fuelled ovens, is said to be the Bahamas' tastiest. The Tabaluga Diving Centre at Port Howe offers scuba diving and fishing.

The main settlement in the north of the island is **Arthur's Town**, but other than an airstrip there is not much else; there are no restaurants and only one shop which does not sell much. Local people rely on the weekly mailboat from Nassau for groceries. There are bars but none serves food. Two miles inland is a small lake surrounded by mangrove thickets. Islanders refer to it as a blue hole and tell stories of its supernatural inhabitants. The beaches in the north are excellent. Northside Beach, reached by dirt road, stretches for 20 miles but has no facilities at all and has the ubiquitous debris. Orange Creek is an attractive inlet three miles north of Arthur's Town. Along the nearby shores are the "white sand farms" with small scale farming of beets, potatoes and carrots.

Flora and Fauna

Uninhabited **Conception Island** and its adjoining reefs, between Cat Island and Long Island, is a land and sea park visited by migrating birds and nesting turtles, protected by the Bahamas National Trust. Many great and little blue herons can be seen at Hawksnest Creek bird sanctuary. In inland ponds it is possible to find the Cat Island turtle (*pseudyms felis*). Unfortunately, the turtles are a source of very rich meat and their numbers have recently dwindled. Near the settlement of Gaitors you can visit large caves full of bats. There are more bat caves south of Gaitors, near Stephenson. Farming is mostly subsistence, using slash and burn to grow crops such as red corn, guinea corn, cassava, okra, peas, beans, sugarcane, watermelons, pineapples, coconuts and bananas. Pot hole farming uses small amounts of soil in deep limestone holes to cultivate plants like the banana tree.

Island Information—Cat Island

How To Get There Bahamasair has flights to Arthur's Town from Nassau four times a week, two of which go via San Salvador. Some hotels have their own airstrips. For details on mailboats see **Information for Visitors, Inter Island Travel**. Transport is difficult in the north as there are no taxis or buses and few cars for hitching lifts.

Where To Stay There is accommodation only in the south. *Fernandez Bay Village*, 1-3 bedroomed cottages (US$153-175), most watersports available, Fax: 809-354 5051, Tel: 305-792 1905, PO Box 2126, flights can be arranged through Tony Ambrister

(Tel: 305-764 6945); *Greenwood Inn*, at Port Howe on a private beach, US$80 (Tel: 354 5090); *The Bridge Inn*, New Bight, with disco, US$70-80, reasonable accommodation, good food, Tel: 354 5013; at Bennet's Harbour ask for Mrs Stracchan who lets rooms occasionally.

Where To Eat The Bahamas' biggest goat farm is near New Bight. Goat meat is used in a local dish called "souce stew", cooked with potatoes, onions and a lemon lookalike fruit called souce. The restaurant at the *Fernandez Bay Resort* is elegant and expensive. *Ambrister's Place*, Dumfries, is recommended. Bars in Arthur's Town: *Miss Nelly's* (pool table), the *Hard Rock Café* and *Mr Pratt's Bar* (dominoes); also *Lovers' Boulevard Disco and Satellite Lounge* is popular and has a good local band playing Rake'n'Scrape.

Crooked Island

Crooked Island (population 517), **Long Cay** and **Acklins** (population 616) comprise Crooked Island District, stretching three sides round the Bight of Acklins and bordered by 45 miles of treacherous barrier reef. At Crooked Island Passage, coral reefs can be found in very shallow water, falling sharply in walls housing sponges of every shape and colour. Although at 92 square miles, Crooked Island is larger than New Providence it is sparsely populated and the population is declining because of emigration. Tourism is not very developed and there is no electricity or running water in most of the settlements. Once as many as 40 plantations thrived here, but as in other islands, the crops failed because of poor soil and the industry declined. Nowadays, two valuable exports from the Crooked Island and Acklins District are aloe vera for use in skin preparations and the cascarilla bark which is sold to Italy for the production of Campari. Remains of the plantation era can be seen in Marine Farm and at Hope Great House in the north of the island. Bird Rock Lighthouse in the north is said to be the site of one of Columbus' original anchor spots on his first voyage. Close by is **Pittstown** where you can see the Bahamas' first General Post Office built in the era of William Pitt. It is now the restaurant of the hotel *Pittstown Point Landings* (US$85-95, Tel: 336 2507), which has its own airstrip, beaches, fishing, snorkelling, windsurfing and diving facilities. Gun Bluff, near the hotel was thought to have been a pirate's lookout, cannons have been found close by. In the surrounding area many North Americans have winter residences. Two miles away is **Landrail Point**, the main centre of the island, which has a hotel/restaurant and store. The people here are Seventh Day Adventists so no pork or alcohol is sold and everything closes on Saturdays. *Mrs Gibson's Lunch Room* is recommended for its freshly baked bread and simple Bahamian dishes.

Further south at Cabbage Hill are *T & S Guest Houses* run by the Rev Thompson, who also runs the *Crooked Island Beach Inn* (US$60, Tel: 336 2096, fishing available), near the beach and airport, and is the Bahamasair representative. The capital of Crooked Island is **Coloniel Hill**. There is a restaurant/baker's/guesthouse here run by Mrs Deleveaux, called *Sunny Lea*. Rooms have a good view of Major Cay Harbour. Close to the sheltered lagoon near Major Cay is a large cave; bromeliads can be seen at its entrance.

The airport is at Major Cay. The *Windward Express* mailboat docks at the harbour in Landrail Point once a week, see **Information for Visitors, Inter Island Travel**.

Acklins is a few miles from Crooked Island and a ferry operates between the two islands, docking at Lovely Bay twice a day. The island is approximately 150 square miles and was named La Isabella by Columbus before being known as Acklins Cay and then just Acklins. Archaeological evidence points to a large Indian community once existing between Jamaica Cay and Delectable Bay (possibly the largest in the Bahamas). Today, Acklins is not very developed; there are roads to the settlements, but they are not paved. Atwood Bay is recommended as one of the Family Islands' most beautiful curved bays.

The main settlement on Acklins is **Spring Point**, which has an airport and Bahamasair has scheduled flights twice a week from Nassau, one flight goes via Crooked Island. The *Airport Inn* run by Curtis Hanna is a popular meeting place, with rooms to rent and a restaurant/bar. At nearby Pompey Bay it is still possible to see rock walls which were plantation demarcation boundaries. Pompey was once prosperous and busy; today most of the town is deserted and a tall church on the coast is abandoned. There is also a guesthouse at Pinefield run by the Williams family.

To the south of Acklins is a group of uninhabited cays sometimes referred to as the Mira Por Vos Cays. The most southerly is called Castle Island and is distinguished easily from afar by its tall battery operated lighthouse. There is a large seabird population here. South, North Guana and Fish Cay are all noted as havens for wildlife. **Long Cay** is the largest of the cays in this area and is inhabited. Long Cay was once known as Fortune Island and enjoyed great prosperity in the 19th century as a clearing house for ships between Europe and the Americas. The advent of the steamship made the use of Long Cay port redundant. Today you can see reminders of its former prosperity in the large unused Catholic church, various civic buildings and the relics of a railway system. On the southern end of this island there is a large nesting ground for the West Indian flamingo.

Eleuthera

This was the first permanent settlement in the Bahamas when Eleutheran Adventurers came from Bermuda and American colonial loyalists fled the mainland during the American Revolution (see **History** above). Their descendants still live here, living in houses painted in pastel colours. The first black settlers were slaves and free Africans from Bermuda. Eleuthera (population 10,600) is only about one mile wide but 110 miles long, with lovely pink sand beaches, particularly on the Atlantic side, coves and cliffs. The main road which runs down the backbone of the island is called the Queen's Highway and makes exploring by car easy and direct.

Fauna and Flora
Eleuthera is visited by many migrant birds. At Hatchet Bay, a few miles south of the Glass Window (see below), there are ring necked pheasants. The Schooner and Kinley Cays in the Bight of Eleuthera are uninhabited but have large populations of white crowned pigeons. On Finlay Cay there are also sooty terns and noddy terns. The cays are protected by the Wild Bird Act. Local indigenous flowers include yellow elder, poincianas and hibiscus. Lizards, chicken snakes and feral goats and pigs are common. North of Hatchet Bay you can visit a bat cave where there are thousands of roosting leaf-nosed bats.

Diving and Marine Life
If you like exciting diving, try riding the Current Cut on the incoming tide, which propels you between islands at a speed of about seven knots. Surfing is also good here. A 300-year old shipwreck at Yankee Channel lies in only

ten feet of water, while on the shallow, sharp reefs to the north called the Devil's Backbone, there is the wreck of a train where a barge once sank with its cargo on its way to Cuba, and a 19th century passenger steamship. Four miles south of Royal Island is an old freighter, sunk by fire while loaded with a cargo of bat guano, now used as a landmark by sailors. The guano is an excellent fish food and the wreck is home to enormous fish, with Angel fish weighing up to 15 lbs and parrot fish of 20-30 lbs. A remarkable dive or snorkel site. Diving and other watersports can be arranged with Valentine's Dive Centre on Harbour Island (pronounced "Briland" by its residents), where there are nine hotels offering tennis, fishing and diving. Unfortunately, illegal bleach used by craw fishermen has spoiled many west side reefs. Sailing boats are recommended to use a local pilot along the notoriously dangerous stretch of coast between Harbour Island and Spanish Wells. Just north of Gregory Town is the Glass Window Bridge, where you can compare the blue Atlantic Ocean with the greenish water of the Caribbean on the other side, separated by a strip of rock just wide enough to drive a car across. Nearby are two small farming communities, Upper and Lower Bogue. The Bogue was once known as the bog because of its marshy ground. During the hurricane in 1965 the sea flooded the land and now there are salt water pools where you can find barracuda, grouper and snapper which were washed there by the tide. Also in the north is The Cave, which contains some impressive stalagmites and stalactites and the Preacher's Cave, where the Adventurers took shelter. The latter is reached by a rough unpaved track about 10 miles north of North Eleuthera; there is a pulpit carved out of rock from when the cave became a place of worship. Rock Sound Water Hole Park is an ocean or blue hole well stocked with grouper and yellowtail, while the walls are encrusted with flat oysters. Swimming is dangerous. Fishing is restricted. Bonefish and bonefishermen abound at Deep Creek in the south.

Beaches and Watersports
There are excellent beaches on the east side of South Eleuthera. The west coast, however, is a little rocky. Many of the easterly beaches are backed by coconut palms or rocky cliffs with cedars. Three miles north of Alice Town in North Eleuthera there is a bushy and bumpy road off the main road which leads to Surfers Beach. It has the best surfing waves in the Bahamas and is frequently visited by surfing enthusiasts. Harbour Island has a beautiful pink sand beach which is said to be one of the most photographed beaches in the world. Lighthouse Beach at Cape Eleuthera has three miles of good beach.

Other Sports
There is a 7,068-yard, championship golf course right by the sea at the *Cotton Bay Beach and Golf Club*, which also provides facilities for diving, snorkelling sailing and fishing. You can play tennis at the *Club Méditerranée* (also windsurfing etc, free for guests), the *Coral Sands Hotel*, the *Dunmore Beach Club*, *Pink Sands Lodge*, *Romora Bay Club* (diving, fishing, sailing, snorkelling), *Rainbow Bay Inn*, *Pineapple Cove* (Gregory Town), or *Spanish Wells Beach Resort* (the diving centre offers extensive watersports and diving courses).

Excursions
Spanish Wells, an island off the north of Eleuthera, gets its name from the use of the cay by Spanish ships as a water supply. 1¾ miles long and ½ mile wide, it is reputed to have the highest per capita income of the Bahamas islands, with the wealth coming from fishing the spiny Bahamian lobster

(known locally as bugs) as well as tourism. The population of about 1300 are descended from the original settlers, the Eleutheran Adventurers from Bermuda and the British Loyalists from the mainland, and are all white. A short ferry ride from northern Eleuthera, there are two hotels, *The Spanish Wells Beach Resort*, six cottages (US$135-150) and 21 rooms (US$110 in winter) directly on the beach, tennis and most watersports, reservations can be made in London (Tel: 071-491 4800) or direct (Tel: 333 4371, Fax: 333 4565) and *The Harbour Club*. Both novice and advanced scuba divers are particularly well catered for. A number of local fishermen can be hired as fishing guides off nearby Russell and Royal Islands (inhabited by a group of Haitians), payment by negotiation. Royal Island was once developed as a sheep farm by an estranged English dignitary. The old house still stands and paths weave through the overgrown grounds and gardens. Visitors can hire bicycles, but there are no cars.

The most desirable place to stay in North Eleuthera is **Harbour Island**. From the airport it is a quick taxi ride to the dock and from there water taxis wait to take passengers on a ten minute ride to the island (US$3 one way). **Dunmore Town**, named after Lord Dunmore, Governor 1786-1797, is a mixture of pastel coloured cottages, white picket fences and a number of small hotels and restaurants. The three mile pink sand beach is popular. Bicycles can be rented at the dock. Fishing trips are easily arranged (US$85/half day). *Pink Sands Lodge*, exclusive, US$275-325 including meals in winter, US$150 MAP summer, Tel: 333 2030, PO Box 86; *Coral Sands*, right on the beach (US$140d, winter, US$100d summer, meals an optional US$35), 33 rooms, closed November (Tel: 333 2350); *Romora Bay Club*, 37-room resort, US$148, pleasant garden, good watersports facilities (Tel: 333 2324, PO Box 146); *Runaway Hill Club* (US$160, Tel: 333 2150, PO Box 31), fresh water pool on the beach; *Valentine's Yacht Club*, US$100-120 (Tel: 333 2080, PO Box 1), tennis, specializes in diving and water sports. Cottages can be rented from Mrs Albury, Island Real Estate (4 bed house US$2,000/week). *Tingum Village*, US$65, Tel: 333 2161, PO Box 61.

Gregory Town is the only other main settlement in the north of the island and the home of pineapple rum. It is very well kept and has a beach with good surfing. It is 20 minutes drive from the airport. Locally-made stained glass can be seen and bought at the Simba studio gallery and shop. *Cambridge Villas*, in Gregory Town, US$45, two-bedroomed apartment US$50-80, (Tel: 332 0080, PO Box 5148), tennis, most watersports available, disco and bar are a popular meeting place; the resorts of *The Cove Eleuthera* (US$109, Tel: 332 0142, PO Box 5148) and *The Oleander Gardens* (US$95, Tel: 333 2058, PO Box 5165) are just outside the town within walking distance.

Governor's Harbour is one of the oldest settlements in the Bahamas with several interesting colonial period houses. The harbour is picturesque and is linked by a causeway to Cupid's Cay, the original settlement. A new cruise ship pier was built in 1991 but is unusable as no deep water channel was dredged. On 10 November a Guy Festival celebrates Guy Fawkes Day and parades are held, culminating in an evening bonfire. Tourism is dominated here by *Club Méditerranée* (Tel: 332 2270, PO Box 80), on the Atlantic beachfront, which also runs a watersports centre on the harbour side. *Rainbow Inn* (US$850/week for two including meals, or US$90 a night, three-bedroomed villa US$90, Tel: 332 0294, PO Box 53), has tennis, diving, fishing, swimming pool and a good restaurant but is 10 miles north of town; *The Cigatoo Inn* (US$52-82) (Tel: 332 2343, PO Box 86), six miles from the airport, sits on top of a hill with good views of the bay, be prepared for loud music; *Laughing Bird Apartments* (US$60 EP) (Tel: 332 2012, Fax: 332 2358, PO Box 76) a guest house in town managed by nurse Jean Davies.

In the south, **Windermere Island**, linked to the mainland by a small bridge, is an exclusive resort popular with the British Royal Family (US$125-230), offering tennis, watersports and fishing (Tel: 332 2538, PO Box 25, or 212-839 0222 in New York). **Tarpum Bay** is the home of MacMillan-Hughes' Art Gallery and Castle. It used to be a big pineapple centre and there are many examples of wooden colonial houses in good repair. *Hilton's Haven* (US$50) near beach and airport, recommended (Tel: 334 4231); *Cartwrights Ocean View* (US$70, cottage US$90-150) (Tel: 334 4215), recommended; *Ethel's Cottages*, on the waterfront (US$60), families welcomed, Mrs Ethel Knowles also rents out cars (Tel: 334 4233, PO Box 27). *Winding Bay Beach Resort* (US$280d summer, US$292d winter, all inclusive) on a secluded lagoon is a less formal resort (Tel: 334 4020, Fax: 334 4057, PO Box 93).

Further south is **Rock Sound**, the largest settlement on the island with a population of about 1,100. It was first known as New Portsmouth and then Wreck Sound. Rock Sound is surrounded by limey, bush covered hills. It has a large modern shopping centre, three churches and many bars. *Edwina's Place* (US$55), run by Edwina Burrows, modest accommodation but highly recommended, Tel: 334 2094, PO Box 30; *Cotton Bay Beach and Golf Club* (US$300 MAP), upmarket with its Robert Trent Jones 18-hole golf course designed by Arnold Palmer around the beach and ponds, and excellent tennis with four all-weather courts and pro-shop (a 'month of tennis' is planned for January 1993), croquet, snorkelling, most watersports are available here, including deep sea fishing, very good food, Tel: 334 6101, PO Box 28; *Palmetto Shores Vacation Villas* (US$70-80), at Palmetto Point, 12 miles south of the airport, Tel: 332 2305, PO Box 131.

A few farming villages exist in the extreme south with more stretches of beach and fishing. One such is **Bannerman Town**, once known as the Pearl of the South. In the 1930s it was a prosperous sponge fishing centre with 20 or more sponging schooners anchored off the west shore. Today the settlement is like a ghost town with large churches in ruins and few people. Those who have stayed eke out a living by farming goats and pineapples and catching land crabs to send to Nassau. At the most southerly point of the island, **Cape Eleuthera** and **Point Eleuthera** are sometimes likened to the opposite points on the tail of a fish. On Cape Eleuthera there is a lighthouse which was repaired by the Raleigh Expedition in 1988. At one time the keeper, Captain Finby, was also the local obeah man. Legend has it that he slept with a ghost called the White Lady, who visited him nightly. Lighthouse Beach is three miles long. *Cape Eleuthera Resort and Yacht Club*, recommended. At Eleuthera Point there is a good cliff top view of Cat Island and Little San Salvador. Be careful as the edges are badly eroded. From here you can also see nesting stacks of fairy terns, shark and barracuda channels and the spectacular blues, greens, yellows, reds and browns of fringing reefs. A lone tarpon known as Tommy cruises off this beach often in less than four feet of water.

Island Information—Eleuthera

How To Get There There are airports at Governor's Harbour (eight miles from the town, US$20 taxi fare), North Eleuthera and Rock Sound. Bahamasair have scheduled flights daily from Nassau. Airways International have flights from West Palm Beach, Miami and Fort Lauderdale to Eleuthera's three airports. US Air Express and Island Express fly from Fort Lauderdale to North Eleuthera and Governor's Harbour. Gulfstream International Airlines flies from Miami to all three. American Eagle flies from Miami to Governor's Harbour. Four mailboats call at Eleuthera. See **Information for Visitors, Inter Island Travel**, or ask the harbour master or shopkeepers about mailboat sailings. Car hire from all three airports and in town costs US$45-50/day, Ross Garage—U Drive It Cars (Harbour Island, Tel: 333 2122); ASA Rent-A-Car Service (Tel: 332 2575); Governor's Harbour Car Rental Service (Tel: 332 2575; also Ethel Knowles at *Ethel's Cottages*, at Tarpum Bay. You can also hire mopeds. There are some public buses.

Where To Eat The pineapples on Eleuthera are said to be the world's sweetest. In Gregory Town they produce a pineapple rum called "Gregory Town Special" which is highly recommended. There is a pineapple festival 7-10 July in Gregory Town. Pineapple upside down pudding is a common dish. Other local dishes include Cape Eleuthera's conch chowder, which is a substantial meal, the best is supposed to be from Mary Cambridge in Gregory Town. Hulled bonavas (a type of bean which tastes like split pea soup) or hulled corn soup with dumplings of rice. This is eaten traditionally after a special church service on Good Friday. On New Year's Eve traditional fare includes Benny Cake, pig or goat souse, or cassava/potato bread. In many of the smaller settlements such as James Cistern, outdoor or Dutch ovens are still used to bake bread. Most of the resorts have their own restaurants. Others which have been recommended are *Cambridge Villas*, in Gregory Town, good seafood, fairly expensive; in Governor's Harbour, *Blue Room* is a restaurant/bar/disco, as is *Ronnie's* in Cubitts Cay; there are plenty of Bahamian places to eat in Governor's Harbour, fairly smart are *Buccaneer* and *Sunset Inn* (on water), smarter is *Kohinoor; Lill Campbell's Restaurant* in the *Spanish Wells Beach Resort* serves good traditional Bahamian dishes, not cheap. Recommended restaurants in Dunmore Town are *Miss Mae's Tearoom, Harbour Lounge, Picaroon Landing* and *Ocean View. Angela's Starfish Restaurant* serves excellent local dishes and has a pleasant garden setting overlooking the harbour. On the main street, behind a huge banyan tree strung with Christmas lights, is an excellent cocktail bar, perfectly positioned for watching the spectacular sunsets. Goombay, on Thursday nights in July and August, takes place around the banyan tree. *Lady Blanche's Lifesaver Restaurant* in Upper Bogue serves the best cracked conch in the area, run by hospitable family, prices reasonable; for very cheap, tasty food try a takeaway meal of barbecue ribs or chicken for less than US$5 at roadside stands in James Cistern; *Big Sally's*, at Savannah Sound in far south; *Cush's Place* (between Gregory Town and Hatchet Bay) does cookouts Saturday and Sunday afternoons with music and dancing, US$10; Lida Scavella in Hatchet Bay does cheap food, her pastries are recommended; *Hatchet Bay Club* has good food, videos and music; outside Palmetto Point is *La Rastic*, a reasonably priced restaurant/bar with traditional fare; a popular bar in this area is *Mate and Jenny's*; in Rock Sound, *Edwina Burrows'* restaurant is highly recommended, good food reasonably priced, popular barbecue dishes; *Sammy's Place* is another recommended restaurant and bar. *The Islander* is a popular, friendly bar; several bars in Wemyss Bight and Green Castle sell spirits in half pint glasses very cheaply; recommended in Deep Creek are *Bab's Place* and *Mr Pratt's Bar; The Waterfront Bar* in Rock Sound is cheap, no food, while *The Ponderosa* and *The Dark Side* are bars and cheap fast food restaurants.

The Exumas

The chain of 365 Exuma cays and islands stretches for 90 miles although the majority of the 3,672 inhabitants live on **Great Exuma** and **Little Exuma** at the southern end. The island of Barre Terre (pronounced Barra Terry) can be reached from Great Exuma by a bridge. There is a ferry to Stocking Island from Great Exuma and another to Lee Stocking Island from Barre Terre. Great Exuma is long and narrow, covered with scrub and dry woodland. The soil is pitifully thin but there are aromatic shrubs, curly-tailed lizards and songbirds and a few wild peacocks. Around the villages are a few patches of what the Lands and Surveys map accurately calls 'casual cultivation'. The main industry is tourism, based on yachting and a few hundred winter visitors who own houses on the island.

The islands were virtually uninhabited until after the American Revolution, when Loyalists from the southern colonies were given land and brought their slaves to grow cotton. During the late 18th century the British Crown granted Denys Rolle, an Englishman, 7,000 acres of land and he set up cotton plantations at Rolletown, Rolleville, Mt Thompson, Steventon and Ramsey. Following the emancipation of the slaves and poor cotton harvests because of the exhaustion of the soil, it was believed that Rolle's son gave away his lands to his former slaves, who were also called Rolle as was customary at the time. However, no deeds have been found confirming transfer of title and longstanding squatter's rights provide an adequate title to the land for many. Today, half the population bears the surname Rolle and two of the largest settlements are Rolleville and Rolletown.

The Exuma cays are in general isolated communities which are difficult to get to (the exception being Staniel Cay). Their inaccessibility has attracted undesirable attention; Norman's Cay was for some time the drug smuggling centre of Carlos Lehder, the Colombian drug baron deported from the Bahamas in 1982 and now in prison in the USA. Recent attempts to control drug smuggling include mooring Fat Albert, an airship full of radar equipment, over Great Exuma, and low flying helicopters also monitor activity.

Diving and Marine Life

The Exuma Cays begin at Sail Rocks about 35 miles from Nassau. Much of the Exuma chain is encompassed in the Exuma Cays Land and Sea Park, an area of some 176 square miles set up by the Bahamas National Trust to conserve all underwater life and for boating, diving and observation of wildlife. There is a warden's residence on Waderick Wells Cay. On the northerly Allen Cays can be seen the protected Rock Iguanas which grow up to two feet long and are known as Bahamian Dragons, but they are extremely tame. The park stretches between Wax Cay and Conch Cut, 22 miles away and offers more delights for underwater explorers, with beautiful coral and limestone reefs, blue holes and shipwrecks. Worth visiting are the underwater valley at Ocean Rock, the huge caves filled with black coral called the Iron Curtain, or Thunderball Grotto at Staniel Cay, where part of the James Bond film and the Disney film *Splash*, were made. Watch out for dangerous currents. In 1992 all dive shops were closed.

Beaches and Watersports

Stocking Island is a long thin island about a mile from the mainland at Elizabeth Harbour, Georgetown. Its shape and position provide a natural protection for the harbour. It has good beaches and a burger bar and is famous for its Mysterious Cave, but this can only be reached by divers. A boat leaves the *Peace and Plenty Hotel* in Georgetown at 1000 and 1300, roundtrip US$5, free for guests, or boats can be hired from Minns Watersports (most watersports available) in Georgetown to visit the reefs off Stocking Island. **The Three Sisters Rocks** which rise out of the water some 100 feet from the shore, are situated between two very good beaches: Jimmy Hill, which is a long empty beach good for swimming, and the beautiful bay of Ocean Bight. Other recommended beaches are the Tropic of Cancer Beach, 15 miles east of Georgetown, Cocoplum Beach, 20 miles north of Georgetown, Goat Cay Beach, two miles west of Georgetown and Out Island Inn Beach, Georgetown.

The Visiting Yachts Regatta is held in early March and in mid-April the Family Island Regatta is held at Georgetown when working boats compete for the title of "Best in the Bahamas". During August there is a series of smaller regattas at Black Point, Barre Terre and Rolleville.

Excursions

The main town on **Great Exuma** is **Georgetown**, a pleasant little town built on a strip of land between a round lake and the sea. A narrow channel allows small boats to use the lake as a harbour but yachts moor offshore, often several hundred at a time in the peak winter months. The large and beautiful bay is called Elizabeth Harbour and is yet another contender for the site of Columbus' harbour that could "hold all the ships in Christendom." The main building is the Government Administration Building, pseudo colonial, pink and modelled on Nassau's Government House. Opposite is a large tree under which women plait straw and sell their wares. There are several pretty buildings, St Andrew's Church (Anglican), blue and white on the top of a little hill and the *Peace and Plenty Hotel* in an old warehouse. There is a good range of shops and the supermarket is well stocked. The Sandpiper shop has an interesting array of clothes and souvenirs.

To the south of Georgetown is **Rolletown**, a small village on a hill overlooking the sea. Many old houses are painted in bright blues, yellows and pinks. There is a small cemetery in which are buried settlers from the 18th century in three family tombs: husband, wife and small child of the Mackay family. **The Ferry** is a small settlement by the beautiful strait which separates Great and Little Exuma, but there is a bridge there now, not a ferry.

North of Georgetown there is a thin scatter of expatriate holiday houses and a few shops along the Queen's Highway. East of the road are several fine beaches, including Hoopers Bay and Tar Bay. The airport turning is north of Georgetown. Small villages are Moss Town, Mount Thompson, Steventon and Rolleville. Moss Town was once an important sponging centre. Close by you can see The Hermitage, brick tombs dating back to just after the American War of Independence, not to be confused with the Hermitage or Cotton House close to Williams Town on Little Exuma. Mt Thompson was once the farming centre of Exuma and is important for its onion packing house. Some of the cottages in **Rolleville**, 16 miles northwest of Georgetown, were originally slave quarters. The town overlooks a harbour and was the base of a group of rebellious slaves who attempted to escape and thereafter refused to work except in the mornings, until emancipation. Unfortunately, quite a large area of northern Exuma is disfigured by roads which were laid out as part of a huge speculative land development scheme in the 1960s. Almost all the lots are still empty, but Cocoplum Beach and the coastal scenery are unspoilt. At the north end of the island is a bridge to Barre Terre, with more fine scenery and places to eat lunch. At **Lee Stocking Island**, just offshore, the Caribbean Marine Research Centre is involved in research into the tilapia, a freshwater fish brought from Africa which can grow in salt water. This can be visited by prior appointment.

A bridge leads to **Little Exuma**, which is 12 miles long and one mile wide. An attractive cove is Pretty Molly Bay, next to the abandoned *Sand Dollar Hotel*. A mermaid story is based on Pretty Molly, a slave girl who sat on the rocks at night and gazed by the light of the moon towards Africa. Near Forbes Hill is the "Fort", built in 1892 and said to be haunted. On Good Friday a nearby tree is said to give off a substance the colour of blood. **Williams Town** is the most southerly of the settlements on Exuma. Salt used to be made in the lagoon. Perched on the cliff top here is a tall white obelisk which not only guided passing ships safely in the 19th century, but was an advertisement that salt and fresh water could be picked up here. The Cotton House, near Williams Town, is the only plantation owner's house still standing in the Exumas. It is at the end of a driveway marked by a pair of trees, but is tiny, not grand. Slave quarters can be seen close by.

The Cays Staniel Cay has excellent beaches with a half mile of sand dunes on the ocean side of the cay and good watersports facilities. On Staniel Cay during Bahamian Independence Day weekend on 10 July, there is a bonefishing festival, entrance fee US$20. The Staniel Cay Yacht Club provides free food in the evening and a rake'n'scrape band plays traditional music. The morning before the contest there is a sailing regatta for working Bahamian sailboats. A Bahamian sailboat regatta is held on New Year's Day. The Royal Entertainers Lounge serves food and drinks.

Farmer's Cay to the south of Staniel Cay has a lively annual festival called The Farmer's Cay First Friday in February Festival at which there are races, dancing games and the Bahamas' only Hermit Crab Race. Further south on **Darby Island** is an old mansion which is probably the remains of a large coconut plantation.

Forty miles off Staniel Cay on the edge of the Tongue of the Ocean is **Green Cay**, home to the world's second largest population of white crowned pigeons.

Island Information—Exuma

How To Get There There is an international airport at Moss Town. Island Express has daily scheduled flights from Fort Lauderdale. Airways International have three flights daily from Miami and Fort Lauderdale to Georgetown and three flights a day Wednesday-Sunday from West Palm Beach. Gulfstream also flies twice daily from Miami. Mr Harry Nixon runs a charter service, Nixon Aviation and Harken Air, based at Georgetown airport (PO Box 3, Airport, Georgetown, Tel: 336 2104). Bahamasair flights from Nassau through Georgetown to Long Island are once or twice daily, they are often booked up well in advance. For details on mailboat sailings, see **Information for Visitors, Inter Island Travel**.

Transport Taxis are expensive but plentiful. The fare from the airport to Georgetown is US$15. Hitching is easy. Cars can be rented from Georgetown, ask at *Peace and Plenty Hotel*. Buses run between Rolleville and Georgetown. Christine Rolle runs Island Tours from Georgetown, leaving at 1000 and 1400, including a native lunch, visits to various settlements and to Gloria, the "shark lady," on Little Exuma, who catches sharks and sells the teeth as souvenirs. Bicycles can be rented from *Two Turtles* shop.

Where To Stay *Two Turtles*, 200 yards from harbour in Georgetown, US$58-78, rooms large enough for four, barbecue on Friday nights (Tel: 336 2206); *Peace and Plenty Hotel*, Tel: 336 2551, 300 yards from harbour, the building was once the slave market and sponge warehouse, US$78-104. The hotel also has a *Beach Inn*, 16 rooms, US$84-114, one mile out of Georgetown; *Pirates Point* villas, private beach, just south of Georgetown, US$490/week (Tel: 336 2554); *Marshall's Guesthouse*, US$30 (Tel: 336 2571), John Marshall (grocery shop in Georgetown) has apartments to rent by week/month, so does Nancy Bottomley (near mailboat dock), rates negotiable; also apartments at Sea Watch, an isolated position 10 miles north of Georgetown on fine beach, Tel: 336 4031. *Staniel Cay Yacht Club*, has own private airstrip, accommodation for 16 guests in waterfront properties, US$ 180, boat rentals available (Tel: 355 2024).

Where To Eat The main hotels in Georgetown, *Peace and Plenty* (dance with local band Wed and Sat nights, you can charter boats from Clifford Dean, the singer), *Two Turtles* (barbecue Fri nights, very lively and good value but take your own cutlery if you want to cut up your steak, plastic only provided, happy hour 1700-2300, US$1.50 for spirit and mixer, frequented by visitors and ex-pats), have good restaurants. *Eddy's Edgewater* specializes in Bahamian food, fried conch is recommended; *Sam's Place*, run by Mr Sam Gray, manager of the marina (expensive); *La Shante*, Forbes Hill, good; *Silver Dollar*, Georgetown, traditional Bahamian cooking; *Gemelli Caffé e Pizzería*, Georgetown, pizzas at lunchtime, dish of the day in the evening, pasta and main course US$10-20; *Blue Hole*, spectacular location at the Ferry by bridge to Little Exuma, recommended. Others doing mainly peas'n'rice type dishes are *Iva Bowes* and *Three Sisters* in Mt Thompson, *Kermit Rolle's*, in Rolleville is by appointment only but he also has a good restaurant opposite the airport building; and *Fisherman's Inn*, Barre Terre, very good. Discos at *Paramount Club* (Moss Town), *Oasis* (Queen's Highway near Mt Thompson), *Flamingo Bay* (Georgetown, often closed because of fights), *Blue Hole*, special bus from Georgetown and back, disco very lively, Fridays only, also *Peace and Plenty* on Saturdays only.

Inagua

Inagua (Great and Little) is the most southerly of the Bahamas Islands and the third largest. Little Inagua is uninhabited now, but the 49-square mile island is reputed to hide the treasure of Henri Christophe, one-time ruler of Haiti. On a clear day, Great Inagua (population 939) is visible from both Cuba and Haiti. The highest points on the island are Salt Pond Hill at 102 feet and East Hill at 132 feet. Vegetation is sparse because of low rainfall, the buffetting trade winds and lack of fresh water, but this has granted ideal conditions for salt production leading to a development and prosperity not enjoyed by any of the surrounding islands. It is thought that the name Inagua comes from the Spanish *lleno* (full) and *agua* (water): *henagua*. This was apparently the name of the island when the first salt farmers settled there. In 1803 records show only one inhabitant, but the success of the salt industry meant that by 1871 the population had risen to 1,120. Although trade barriers in the USA caused the decline of the salt trade in Inagua for many years, the industry was revitalized in the 1930s with the establishment of the Morton Salt Company, which now utilizes 12,000 acres. Morton Bahamas Ltd installed a power plant which supplies electricity to all homes in **Matthew Town**. Inagua has the best telecommunications system in the Family Islands and nearly everyone has a telephone. For a while the island supported a cotton plantation; although a shortlived enterprise, wild cotton can still be found growing on Inagua today. Outside Matthew Town you can still see the ruins of the cotton mill and the narrow plantation roads, as well as the ruins of a prison from the days when the community was large enough to need one.

Flora and Fauna
The southeast side of the island is rocky and because of the effects of the sea and wind, the trees do not grow more than a foot tall. Further inland trees have a better chance of maturing. Many cactii are found in this rocky part of Inagua, in particular the dildo cactus and the woolly-nipple. On Little Inagua, although it is largely overgrown, it is possible to see some of the only natural palms in the Bahamas.

Inagua has a restricted access National Park which is home to a wide range of birds including the world's largest flamingo colony on Lake Windsor, a 12-mile stretch of marshy wildlife sanctuary. Almost half of Great Inagua is included in the 287-square-mile park. Visitors should contact the Bahamas National Trust in Nassau (PO Box N-4105, Tel: 393 1317). A basic but comfortable camp has been established on the western side, 23 long miles by jeep from Matthew Town. National Trust wardens will accompany you on tours of the area and it is possible to view the flamingoes close up. At certain times of the year they cannot be approached. Jimmy Nixon, one of the original wardens, is recommended as a guide. Early spring is the breeding season when large numbers of flamingoes congregate on the lake. At the Union Creek camp on the northwest side of the island is a breeding and research area for Green and Hawksbill turtles, called Turtle Sound. It is ideal for observing sea turtles at close quarters. On the eastern side of the island are mangrove swamps which are the nesting grounds for many birds including cormorants, pelicans and the rare reddish egret. Here you can also see the white tailed tropic bird and inland, the Bahamas parrot, the most northerly species of parrot in the world.

Beaches
Apart from the rocky southeastern side of the island, Inagua has many deserted and unspoiled beaches. Those which are used by locals include Cartwright's beach, with bar/restaurant, within easy reach of Matthew Town, Farquharson's Beach and Matthew Town Beach, which is pleasant and conveniently located.

Sports
It is possible to play tennis and basketball in Matthew Town, but the most popular pastime is hunting. You can arrange to go on a wild boar hunt with Herman Bowe (known as the Crocodile Dundee of the Bahamas, who prefers to hunt barefoot) or Jimmy Nixon (the excellent National Trust guide). On Emancipation Day (1 August) and other public holidays, wild boar is roasted on the beach and there are wild donkey races. Rodeos take place on an ad hoc basis.

Island Information—Inagua

How To Get There The airport is on Great Inagua. Bahamasair have scheduled flights from Nassau and Mayaguana. The mailboat takes two days from Nassau, see **Information for Visitors, Inter Island Travel**.

Transport A taxi from the airport to Matthew Town costs about US$4. There are no buses. The main road in Matthew Town, Bay Street, is paved but others are not. If you want to see the island properly you will need transport, particularly if you travel to the north side of the island. Jeeps for hire from Mr Burrows at Matthew Town Service Station, rates negotiable but expect to pay at least US$40/day. To get out to the camps arrange transport with the warden in Matthew Town (about US$10). To arrange fishing expeditions or trips around the island contact the local repair man, Cecil Fawkes (nicknamed the old Red Fox), whose boat is called "*The Foxy Lady*", or Mr Cartwright. There is no set rate, prices are negotiated. There is a marina and boats can moor here and refuel.

Where To Stay There are several guest houses in Matthew Town. The *Main House*, US$42, Tel: 267, has four rooms. There is also the *Ford's Inagua Inn*, Tel: 277, US$35, with six rooms and a few small private guesthouses (enquire locally for information). There are two camps, *Union Creek* in the northwest and *Flamingo Camp*, 23 miles from Matthew Town, with basic accommodation. Bunks cost about US$10 a night and reservations should be made with The Bahamas National Trust, PO Box N4105, Nassau (Tel: 323 1317 or 323 2848).

Where To Eat Eating out is cheaper than Nassau or Grand Bahama. For a typical Bahamian meal of macaroni, coleslaw, ribs or chicken and potato salad, expect to pay US$6-7. Local dishes include roast wild boar, baked box fish, crab meat 'n rice and roast pigeon and duck. A popular local drink is gin and coconut, which is made with fresh coconuts on special occasions. *Topps Restaurant and Bar*, run by the Palacious brothers is recommended for its seafood dishes, fresh boiled fish is served for breakfast; also recommended is *The Hide Out Club*, run by Mr Cox, which is a popular dance and drinking spot; *Pride*, run by Mr Moultry is very friendly. Nightlife revolves around the local bars, which periodically have live music and dancing.

Matthew Town has a Royal Bank of Canada, due to open daily in 1992, and six churches. For special meetings and the screening of films, the old Salt Theatre is used.

NB Mosquitoes can be a problem at some times of the year, avoid May. Credit cards are not generally accepted, take plenty of cash with you.

Long Island

Long Island (population 5,000) lies southeast of Little Exuma and is 57 miles long and four miles across at its widest. Columbus made a stop here and changed its name from the Arawak name Yuma to Fernandina, after Ferdinand, the King of Spain. The island has a variety of communities from different ethnic backgrounds, from Europe, Africa and North America. Most islanders live on the west side where the hills and dunes offer some protection from the sea. There are paths and dirt tracks to the east side, mostly used by fishermen. Villages to the south are rather neglected, with poor roads and no telephone service. The landscape is diverse, with tall white cliffs at Cape Santa Maria with caves below, old salt pans near Clarence Town, dense bush over much of the island and scattered areas of cactii. It has a rocky coastline on one side and lovely beaches and crystal clear water on the other, with the usual friendly fish and lots of convenient wrecks. One, a German freighter sunk in 1917, lies in 25 feet of water only 200 yards from the beach at Guana Cay, south of Salt Pond. Beaches in the south are good but rather hard to get to. Long Island is a major producer of vegetables and cattle and is known for its pot-hole farming which gives hearty supplies of tomatoes, bananas and onions. The *Stella Maris Resort Club* in the north is the biggest employer, but there are not enough jobs and most young people leave to work in Nassau or Grand Bahama.

The main settlements are **Deadman's Cay** in the north and **Clarence Town** further south. Most tourists stay at the *Stella Maris*, north of Deadman's Cay, which is supposed to have the best yachting marina in the southern Bahamas. From a lookout tower here it is possible to see right across the island and to see the nearby ruins of the Adderly Plantation House. The town of **Simms** is the home of the best straw work in the Bahamas, made by Ivy Simms and her workers. The mailboat calls here and there is a high school, magistrate's court and Commissioner's office. The settlement of Clarence Town in the centre of the island is very pretty and boasts two white, twin-spired churches built on opposite hilltops by Father Jerome (see under Cat Island). St Paul's is the Anglican church and St Peter's the Catholic. Both are still in use today. There are many caves to explore and ruins of old plantation houses: Adderly's near *Stella Maris* and the remains of a cotton gin and plantation gate posts at Dunmore. At Glinton's, north of *Stella Maris*, archaeologists have found the remains of an Arawak village, and at Hamilton, south of Deadman's Cay, caves have been discovered with Arawak drawings and carvings. The annual Long Island Regatta at Salt Pond is held in June. Locals compete for best seaman award, the fastest boat and the best kept boat over five years old. The Regatta is popular and accompanied by authentic Bahamian food and traditional rake'n'scrape music.

Island Information—Long Island

How To Get There There are two airports at Stella Maris and at Deadman's Cay. Island

Express flies once or twice daily from Fort Lauderdale to Stella Maris. There are six Bahamasair flights a week from Nassau to Stella Maris and six flights to Deadman's Cay. The drive from Deadman's Cay to Stella Maris is about two hours along a rough potholed road. Taxis are available and private cars often negotiate to carry passengers too. Taxis are generally expensive. If you are going to *Stella Maris* it is better to get a flight to the airport there if possible, from where it is only 20 minutes to the resort. The main road connecting all the main settlements on the island is the Queen's Highway, which is notoriously bad, particularly in the south where the potholes are said to be the size of a car in places. Avoid night driving.

Where To Stay The *Stella Maris Inn* (US$106 EP, add US$36 for MAP) is one of the top five resorts in the Caribbean (Tel: 336 2106, PO Box SM-105). It has 60 units in the inn itself and 12 marina units: 1-2 bedroom villas (US$106-270), some with kitchens. A shopping centre has a bank and post office. There are three pools and five beaches along with tennis, bicycles, diving, windsurfing (guests free) and waterskiing (US$25). Bicycles are free for guests; cars can be rented from US$50/day plus mileage. Glass bottom boat trips can be taken for US$20. Cave parties are held once a week and a Rum Punch party every Wednesday. 25 different diving areas offer a lot of variety for the experienced or the beginner and there is even a shark reef with tame shark feeding. Fishing trips can be arranged: during November and December huge shoals of grouper make fishing easy in the waters around Long Island. The blue hole close to the harbour at Clarence Town is good for line fishing. *Thompson Bay Inn* at Hardings near Salt Pond (US$45, Tel: 337 0000, PO Box 30123), recommended, small and friendly, eight rooms, pool, fishing, disco lounge, serves native food. There are also a few guest houses, *Knowles Cottages*, guest house in Clarence Town; *Hamilton's Guest House* in Hamilton; *Carroll's Guest House* (US$35) at Deadman's Cay; *O and S Guest House* at Simms.

Where To Eat Two island dishes to try are wild hog with onion and spices and grouper roe with liver. *Thompson Bay Inn* has a good restaurant and also a disco. *The Blue Chip Restaurant and Bar* in Simms is recommended. In Hard Bargain in the south the *Forget Me Not Club* has a popular bar and restaurant. In Mangrove Bush the Knowles family run the hillside tavern and bar. They also sell fresh fish at *Summer Seafood* close by.

Mayaguana

Mayaguana (an Arawak name), located 50 miles east of Acklins and 60 miles north of Inagua, is the least developed and most isolated of the Family Islands although there are now three Bahamasair flights a week (Tuesday, Thursday and Saturday) from Nassau, the Thursday and Saturday ones coming via Inagua. The main settlement is **Abraham's Bay**, a small town with a few shops and one bar/restaurant run by the Brown family who also own the guesthouse called *The Sheraton*. There are two other settlements, Betsy Bay and Pirate's Well, which are both very isolated. Several people will rent you a room in their homes for US$30-60; fresh water and food can sometimes be hard to come by, young coconuts are recommended if short of water. Take mosquito repellent. Most people earn their living from fishing or farming and many leave for Nassau and Freeport to look for work.

The island is on a direct route to the Caribbean and as such is sometimes visited by yachtsmen, although it is not a port of entry. There is a very large reef around the northwest side of the island. Twenty miles from Mayaguana are the Plana and Samana Cays, notable for their interesting wildlife, where you can see the Bahama hutia, thought to be extinct until the mid-1960s. A cross between a rat and a rabbit, this rodent's flesh is said to be similar to pork.

Rum Cay

Some 35 miles south of San Salvador, this small island is approximately 20 miles square. First known as Mamana by the Lucayan Indians, the cay was later renamed Santa María de la Concepción by Columbus. Spanish explorers once found a lone rum keg washed up on a shore and changed the name again to Rum Cay. In the north there is an interesting cave which has Lucayan drawings and carvings. Various artefacts from the Arawak period have been found by farmers in the fertile soil which the Indians enriched with bat guano. In common with other islands, Rum Cay has experienced a series of booms and busts. Pineapple, salt and sisal have all been important industries, but competition and natural disasters, such as the 1926 hurricane, have all taken their toll and today tourism is the main source of employment. Plantation boundaries known as "margins" can be seen all over the island, which date from the beginning of the 19th century when Loyalists settled here. Nearly everybody lives in **Port Nelson** where cottages can be rented. Settlements such as Port Boyd, Black Rock and Gin Hill are now deserted and overgrown.

This former pirates' haven is surrounded by deep reefs and drop-offs. There is staghorn coral at Summer Point Reef and good diving at Pinder's Point. At the Grand Canyon, huge 60-foot coral walls almost reach the surface.

San Salvador

Known as Guanahani by the original Lucayan inhabitants, this island claims to be the first place that Columbus landed in the New World and is cognisant of its history. Four sites vie for recognition as the first landing place and celebrations are being planned to mark the quincentennial anniversary in 1992. Three replica ships are to sail to San Salvador and each year about 500 Spanish speaking students retrace Columbus' route. One of the sites where Columbus may have come ashore is Long Bay. There is a bronze monument under the sea where he was supposed to have anchored and a white cross on the shore where he was said to have landed. Jewelry and pottery dating back to the Lucayan Indians have been found on the beach here. Close by is the Mexican Monument commemorating the handing over of the Olympic flame to the New World for the 1968 Olympics in Mexico. At Crab Cay in the east is the Chicago Herald Monument, erected in 1892 to commemorate the 400th anniversary of Columbus' landing. It is the oldest monument, but judging by the rocky setting it is the most unlikely of the putative landfall spots.

The island is about 12 miles long and six miles wide with a network of inland lakes (with names like Granny Lake and Old Granny Lake) which were once the main transport routes. For a good view, climb the lookout tower east of the airport on Mount Kerr, at 140 feet the highest point on the island. Until the 1920s San Salvador was known as Watling's Island after the legendary pirate John Watling, who was said to have built his castle on French Bay in the seventeenth century. Archaeologists have now proven that the ruins are the remains of a loyalist plantation. You can see the stone ruins including the master's house, slave quarters and a whipping post. Access to the ruins is via the hill to the west of the Queen's Highway near the bay. In the 1950s and 1960s, the US military leased land from the British Crown and built a submarine tracking station at **Graham's Harbour** in the north. Roads, an airport, a Pan American Base and a US Coast Guard Station were also built. The withdrawal of the military in the late 1960s led to unemployment and emigration. The building at Graham's Harbour is now occupied by the College of the Finger Lakes' Bahamian Field Station, a geological and historical research institute. Further development took place under the Columbus Landing Development Project, which built houses, condominiums, roads and a golf course around Sandy Point. The largest settlement is **Cockburn** in the northwest, once known as Riding Rock because of the tidal movement on rocks off the bay which give the impression that the rocks are moving up and down.

Flora and Fauna

San Salvador is famous for its reefs, beautiful bays, creeks and lakes. At Pigeon Creek in the southeast there is a large lagoon, edged by mangroves, which is a nursery for many different kinds of large fish, including sharks. White Cay and Green Cay, off Graham's Harbour, are designated land and sea parks. White Cay has tall white cliffs on one side where there are large numbers of Brown Boobies. They are docile and you can get very close (once making them easy prey for hunters). Green Cay also has a large bird population. Manhead Cay off the northeast is home to a rare species of iguana over one foot in length. There are large rock formations on the north side of the cay, access is possible from the south but is not easy, involving a climb up a rocky hill. Frigate birds can sometimes be seen here. Some subsistence farming using old slash and burn methods is still done on San Salvador.

Beaches and Watersports

French Bay is a popular beach with excellent shelling and snorkelling. There are large reefs of elk and staghorn coral in less than 50 feet of water, some of which are exposed at low tide. Overlooking French Bay are the ruins of Watling's Castle, now better known as the Sandy Point Estate. Going south following the Queen's Highway along the bay you come to the Government Dock and further on Sandy Point. Both spots are recommended for their privacy and good reefs for scuba divers and snorkellers. The entire eastern coastline, with the exception of the creek areas, is uninhabited and has fine beaches of white sand. East of Dixie Lighthouse past the sand dunes is East Beach, a mile-long stretch of excellent sands.

Diving and Marine Life

Fishing, diving and sailing are all popular. There are shallow reefs, walls, corals and several wrecks to interest scuba divers. Island Water Sports at *Riding Rock Inn* has a full range of watersports activities on offer, an eight slip marina and daily scuba excursions. There are facilities for taking and developing underwater colour photographs. On Discovery Day, 12 October, there is a dinghies race.

Excursions

North of Cockburn on the Queen's Highway is Dixon Hill Lighthouse, which was built in Birmingham in the 19th century and rebuilt in 1930. Mr Hannah, the keeper, gives tours of the lighthouse, which is run by candle power and clockwork and is one of the few remaining hand operated lighthouses. East of the lighthouse and past East Beach you get to Crab Cay and the Chicago Herald Monument (see above). At the small settlement of Victoria Hill is the New World Museum, owned by the local historian Ruth Wolper. There are interesting Lucayan artifacts, most of which came from the remains of an Indian settlement at Palmetto Grove, named after the silver top palmettos found there.

Island Information—San Salvador

How To Get There There are scheduled Bahamasair flights to Cockburn Town four times a week, two of which come via Arthur's Town. For details of mailboat sailings see **Information for Visitors, Inter Island Travel**. If you avoid the bush and water it is perfectly feasible to walk around San Salvador. The Queen's Highway encircles the island and there are no other main roads. You can hire cars, enquire in Cockburn Town. Mopeds are not available. There is a bus tour which visits the main points of interest, ask at *Riding Rock Inn*.

Where To Stay *Riding Rock Inn* (US$80), north of Cockburn Town, has 48 rooms, swimming pool and a restaurant overlooking the bay (Tel: 272 1492), write to 701 SW 48th Street, Fort Lauderdale, Florida for details. *Ocean View Villas*, for accommodation in cottages, US$80.

Where To Eat *Riding Rock Inn* is considered expensive at US$30, but it has a rake'n'scrape band once a week featuring Bernie the Band Leader (ask Bernie the airport manager). *Dixie Hotel and Restaurant*, Dixon Hill and *Ocean Cabin*, Cockburn Town, are both reasonable. *Harlem Square Rip Club* is recommended, friendly, Friday night disco. The local dish is crab'n'rice, made from the plentiful land crabs found on the island, average cost US$5-7.

Information for Visitors

Documents

US citizens do not need passports or visas but must carry some form of identification for stays of up to three weeks; for longer, a valid passport is required. Visitors may stay for up to eight months but must have sufficient funds for their stay and an onward or return ticket. Passports are required by all other nationalities, but visas are not needed by nationals of Commonwealth and West European countries, South Korea, Israel and Japan (length of permitted stay varies between 3 and 8 months), nor by most Latin American nationals if staying no longer than 14 days. Colombians without a US visa need a Bahamian visa. Nationals of Haiti, South Africa and communist countries need a visa. You will need a certificate of vaccination against yellow fever if you are coming from an infected area. To enter the Bahamas for business purposes the permission of the Immigration Department, Nassau, must be obtained. It is advisable to apply in writing to: Director of Immigration, Immigration Department, PO Box N3002, Nassau. No expatriate can be employed in a post for which a suitably qualified Bahamian is available, nor can a permit application be considered if the prospective employee is already in the country, having come in as a visitor.

Air Services

Most flights to the Bahamas originate in the USA although there are also flights from Montreal and Toronto in Canada with Air Canada. Connecting flights by Bahamasair go out from Nassau like spokes of a wheel to the Family Islands. **From the USA to Nassau**: American Airlines flies from New York and American Eagle from Miami; Bahamasair flies from Miami and West Palm Beach; Carnival Air Lines from Fort Lauderdale, Paradise Island Airways from Miami, Fort Lauderdale, Orlando and West Palm Beach to its own airport on Paradise Island (closer to Nassau than international airport); Chalk's International from Miami (also to Bimini); Delta from Atlanta, Dallas, Fort Lauderdale, Kansas City, Key West, Miami, New York (La Guardia and Newark), Oklahoma City, Orlando; USAIR from Baltimore, Charlotte, Las Vegas, Philadelphia, Pittsburgh and Providence, Rhode Island; Florida Air from Fort Lauderdale; Key Airlines from Atlanta and Savannah, Georgia. TCNA connects Cap Haitien, Grand Turk and Providenciales with Nassau, while Air Jamaica flies from Kingston. **From the USA to Freeport**: Key Airlines from Baltimore and Savannah; Delta from Birmingham, Fort Lauderdale, Orlando, Tallahassee and Tampa; American Eagle from Miami; Bahamasair from Miami and West Palm Beach. Air Canada flies from Montréal and Toronto, TCNA from the Turks and Caicos Islands. There are also several commuter airlines serving some of the Family Islands direct from airports in Florida including Airways International (Tel: 305-887 2794, Fax:

305-871 6522, tickets can be booked through computer systems but are normally purchased on the spot at the airport, routing and timing subject to last minute alteration depending on demand). Walker's International flies to Walker's Cay from Fort Lauderdale. Charter flights to Cuba with Bahatours (Tel: 328 7985), Mondays and Fridays, weekend package US$249-389 depending on hotel, including Havana city tour, Sunday-Friday 5-day package is US$369-649. Departure tax is US$15 except for children under the age of three.

Boats To USA

Sea Escape boat return trip to Miami, including meals and entertainment, costs about US$96. Journey is 8 hours one way; leaves from Freeport port area.

Inter Island Travel

Bahamasair operates scheduled **flights** between Nassau and the Family Islands. They are notoriously inefficient and unpunctual. Charter flights and excursions available through them and several private companies, see Prestel for details. Seaplanes fly to those islands which have no landing strip.

The Family Islands can also be reached by regular **ferry boat** services. The *Noel Roberts* sails from Nassau to Freeport at 1600 on Thursdays, leaving again at 1400 on Saturdays. The fare for the 15-16 hour trip is US$20 2nd class, or US$25 1st class (which includes a bunk). Tickets can be bought at City lumberyard on Bay Street. A colourful way of travelling between the islands is on the **mail boats**, which also carry passengers and merchandise. They leave from Potter's Cay Dock, just below the Paradise Island Bridge in Nassau, and Woodes Rogers Walk; their drawback is that they are slow and accommodation on board is very basic, but they do go everywhere. The Bahamas Family Islands Association has a helpful brochure listing fares and schedules, but do not expect the boats to leave according to the timetable. For the latest information listen to the radio on ZNS, which lists the daily schedule with last minute changes broadcast at lunchtime, or ask for information at the Dock Master's office on Potter's Cay.

The following 1992 timetable gives the name of the boat, its destination, departure time from Nassau (dep), arrival time back in Nassau (arr), travel time and fare: *Bahama Daybreak*, to North Eleuthera, Spanish Wells, Harbour Island, Bluff, dep Thurs 0600, arr Sun 1200, 5½ hrs, US$20; *Captain Moxey*, to South Andros, Kemp's Bay, Driggs Hill, Long Bay Cays, dep Mon 1100, arr Wed 2100, 7½ hrs, US$25; *Central Andros Express*, to Central Andros, Fresh Creek, Stafford Creek, Blanket Sound, Staniard Creek, dep Wed 0700, arr Sat 1200, 3¼ hrs, US$20; *Sea Hauler*, to Cat Island, Bluff, Bight, Smith's Bay, dep Tues 1500, arr Fri 0800, 9 hrs, US$30; *North Cat Island Special*, to North Cat Island, Arthur's Town, Bennet's Harbour, dep Tues 1400, arr Thurs 1000, 14 hrs, US$35; *Maxine*, to San Salvador, United Estates/Rum Cay, Cockburn Town, dep Tues 1200, arr Fri 1200, 17 hrs, US$35; *Grand Master*, to Exuma, George Town, Mt Thompson, dep Tues 1200, arr Fri 0800, 13 hrs, US$25-30; *Abilin*, to Long Island, Clarence Town, dep Tues 1200, arr Thurs 1330, 18 hrs, US$35; *Champion II*, to Abaco, Sandy Point, Moore Island, Bullock Harbour, dep Tues 1200, arr Thurs 1800, 11 hrs, US$20-30; *Lisa J II*, to North Andros, Nichol's Town, Mastic Point, Morgan Bluff, dep Wed 1600, arr Tues 1330, 5 hrs, US$20; *Lady Francis*, to Exuma Cays, Staniel Cay, Black Point, Farmer's Cay, Barraterre, dep Thurs 1200, arr Sat 0200, US$25; *Deborah K II*, Abaco, Marsh Harbour, Treasure Cay, Green Turtle Cay, dep Wed 0400, arr Mon 2100, 12 hrs, US$20; *Harley & Charley*, to Governor's Harbour, Hatchet Bay, dep Mon 1900, arr Tues 2000, 5½ hrs, US$20; *Mangrove Cay II* to Mangrove Cay, dep Thurs 2000, arr Tues 1600, 5½ hrs, US$24, *Betring Point* to Caragill Creek, dep Tues 1100, arr Sat/Sun, 5 hrs, US$20; *Current Pride* to Current Island, dep Thurs 1900, arr Tues 1200, 5 hrs, US$15; *Emmette and Cephas* to Ragged Island, dep Tues 1600, arr Thurs 1600, 21 hrs, US$40; *Bahamas Daybreak III*, to Rock Sound, Davis Harbour, South Eleuthera, dep Mon 1800, arr Tues 2000, 5½ hrs, US$20; *Nay Dean*, to North Long Island, Salt Pond, Deadman's Cay, Seymours, dep Mon (check time), 15 hrs, US$30-35; *Marcella III*, to Grand Bahama, Freeport, High Rock, Eight Mile Rock, West End, dep 1600, arr Sat 1900, 12 hrs, US$35; *Windward Express*, to Crooked Island, Acklins, Long Cay, Snug Corner, Spring Point (check time); *Bimini Mack*, to Bimini, Cat Cay, (check time), 12 hrs, US$25-30.

Yacht Charter

A pleasant way of seeing the islands is to charter your own yacht and several companies offer boats with or without crews. Abaco Bahamas Charters (ABC) is based in Hopetown. Bahamas Yachting Service (BYS) is based in Marsh Harbour, Abaco, Tel: 305-467 8644 or toll free 800-327 2276 in North America, prices start from about US$50 per person per day. Contact the Bahamas Reservation Service (see below) for the Bahamas Marina Guide, marina reservations, known as 'book-a-slip', with details of over 50 marinas in the Bahamas and confirmation of boat slip reservations down as far as Grand Turk. Most resort islands have boats to rent.

Vehicle Hire

Visitors are permitted to drive on a valid foreign licence or International Permit for up to 3 months. Beyond that they need a local licence issued by the Road Traffic Department in Nassau. Traffic keeps left, although most cars are left-hand drive. Strict speed limits: Nassau and Freeport 30 mph; elsewhere 40 mph. The roads are not in good condition and are congested in town; drivers pay scant attention to the laws.

On many of the Family Islands bicycles and mopeds are appropriate. These can be hired in Nassau, Freeport and in many other places through hotels; helmets should be worn. Approximate rates: bicycles US$8 per day, US$20 per week; mopeds: US$30 per day. Scooters and light motorcycles can also be hired. Remember, though, that rates for car and bike hire tend to vary, according to season. Minimum age for hiring in Exuma is 24.

Hotel Reservations

Nearly all the hotels in the Bahamas are represented by the Bahamas Reservation Service, toll free Tel: 800-327 0787 from anywhere in North America. The Bahamas Reservation Service Europe is at 306 Upper Richmond Road West, London SW14 7JG, Tel: 081 876 1296, Fax: 081 878 7854. Accommodation ranges from luxury hotels and resorts with every conceivable facility, to modest guest houses or self-catering apartments and villas.

People-to-People

The People-to-People programme is a recommended way to meet local Bahamians. Fill in a form from the Ministry of Tourism giving age, occupation and interests and you will be matched with a Bahamian. Each experience is different but it might lead to a meal in a Bahamian home, a tour of out of the way places or a trip to church. They also hold a tea party at Government House in January-August on the last Friday of each month and can arrange weddings. Tel: 322 7500 in Nassau or 325 8044 in Freeport, or ask at your hotel.

Food And Drink

Conch, crab, grouper, snapper, dolphin (not the Flipper variety) and other seafood are on all the menus. Conch is the staple diet of many Bahamians. It is considered an aphrodisiac and a source of virility, especially the small end part of the conch which is bitten off and eaten from the live conch for maximum effect. Conch is prepared in a variety of ways; conch fritters and cracked conch are both coated in batter and fried, while conch salad is made from raw, shredded conch, onion, lime, lettuce and tomatoes. It can be bought daily from vendors who let you choose your conch from their truck and will "jewk" it from the shell and prepare it for you in salad. Although delicious, conch has been linked to major outbreaks of food poisoning, so treat with caution. Bahamian cuisine is tasty, if a little predictable. The standard fare at most parties/cookouts is peas'n'rice, barbeque ribs and chicken wings, conch salad or fritters, potato salad, coleslaw and macaroni. Bahamian potato salad and macaroni are far richer than their English/Italian counterparts. The Bahamas have some good fruit: sapodilla, mango, breadfruit, sugar apple and pawpaw. Try soursop ice cream, coconut tarts and sugar bananas, which have an apple flavour. Guava duff is a popular sweet, a bit like jam roly poly pudding topped with guava sauce (often flavoured with rum). Tap water can be brackish; fresh water can be bought at the supermarket. The local beer brewed in Nassau, Kalik, is worth trying. The local rum is Bacardi; the Anejo variety is OK. Bahama Mammas, Yellowbirds and Island Woman are all popular rum-based cocktails.

Tipping

The usual tip is 15%, including for taxi drivers. Hotels and restaurants include a service charge on the bill.

Shopping

For those who want to pick up a bargain, prices of crystal, china and jewelry are cheaper than in the USA. You can find designer clothes and other goods from all over the world at the International Bazaar in Freeport. Local products include straw items, Androsia batik printed silk and cotton, shell jewelry and wood carvings. Bargaining is expected in the markets.

Banks

There are several hundred banks licensed to do banking or trust business in the Bahamas. Some of the largest commercial banks include: Royal Bank of Canada at Nassau, the airport, Abaco, Andros (Fresh Creek), Bimini, Grand Bahama, Harbour Island, Hatchet Bay (Eleuthera Island), Inagua, Long Island, Lyford Cay, and Spanish Wells; Lloyds Bank (Bahamas); Barclays Bank International, also at Grand Bahama, Eleuthera, Abaco; Scotiabank, also at Abaco, Grand Bahama, Exuma, Long Island; Canadian Imperial Bank of Commerce also at Grand Bahama, Andros (Nicholl's Town), Abaco; Chase Manhattan Trust Corp Ltd, Shirley and Charlotte Street, Nassau, Tel: 323 6811; Bank of America; Citibank.

Currency

The unit of currency is the Bahamian Dollar (B$) which is at par with the US dollar. Both currencies are accepted everywhere. There is no restriction on foreign currency taken in or out; Bahamian currency may be exported up to B$70 pp. Notes of B$ 100, 50, 20, 10, 5, 3, 1 and 50c; coins of B$5, 2, 1, 50c, 25c, 15c, 10c, 5c and 1c.

Credit Cards

All major credit cards are accepted on New Providence and Grand Bahama. Not all the hotels on the Family Islands take credit cards, although most take American Express, Mastercharge and Visa.

Climate

The sunshine and warm seas attract visitors throughout the year but winter, from December to April, is the high season. Temperatures are around 20°C (68°F). Summer temperatures average 30°C (86°F). Humidity is fairly high, particularly in the summer. The rainy season is May-October, when the showers are usually short but heavy. June-November is the official hurricane season, the last major one to hit the Bahamas being David in 1979.

Hours Of Business

Banks: in Nassau, Monday-Thursday 0930-1500, Friday 0930-1700; in Freeport, Monday-Friday 0900-1300 and Friday 1500-1700. Shops 0900-1700 Monday-Saturday. Government offices 0900-1730 Monday-Friday.

Public Holidays

New Year's Day, Good Friday, Easter Monday (very busy at the airport), Whit Monday, Labour Day (first Friday in June, a parade is organized by the trade unions), Independence Day (10 July), Emancipation Day (first Monday in August), Discovery Day (12 October), Christmas Day, Boxing Day.

Time Zone

Bahamas time is 5 hours behind GMT, except in summer when Eastern Daylight Time (GMT -4 hours) is adopted.

Diplomatic Representation

US Embassy, Mosmar Building, Queen St, Tel: 322 1181; *British High Commission* Bitco Building, East St, Tel: 325 7471; honorary consulates: **Canada**, Tel: 393 2123/4; **Belgium**, Tel: 323 8884; Denmark, Tel: 322 1340; **France**, Nassau Tel: 326 5061 (Freeport Tel: 373 2060); **West Germany**, Tel: 393 2156; **Israel**, Tel: 362 4421; **Italy**, Tel: 322 7586; Japan, Tel: 322 8560; **The Netherlands**, Tel: 393 3836; **Norway**, Tel: 323 1340; **Sweden**, Tel: 327 7785; **Switzerland**, Tel: 322 8345. There is a **Haitian** Embassy in Roberts Building, East and Bay Streets, Tel: 326 0325; consulate of the **Dominican Republic**, Tel: 325 5521.

Electric Current

120 volt/60 cycles.

Religion

There are about 20 denominations represented in the Bahamas, of which those with the largest congregations are the Baptists, Roman Catholics and Anglicans. There is a synagogue in Freeport and a Mosque in Nassau. The Tourist Office publishes a leaflet called *Bahamas Places of Worship*, with a full list of addresses and services.

Communications

Main post office is at East Hill Street, Nassau. Letters to North America and the Caribbean US$0.55, to Europe and South America US$0.60; to Africa, Asia and Australia US$0.70. All postcards US$0.40 Air mail to Europe takes four to eight days, surface mail takes a couple of months. There is no door to door mail delivery in the Bahamas, everything goes to a PO Box. Parcels must be opened at the Post Office with customs officials present. There is a public telephone, cable and telex exchange open 24 hours in the

Telecommunications Office on East Street, near the BITCO building. International calls can be made and faxes sent/received from Batelco office on East Street (24-hour service); also Shirley Street, Blue Hill Road and Fox Hill (0700-2000). Grand Bahama, New Providence and several of the other islands have automatic internal telephone systems. Direct dialling is available from New Providence all over the world. The code for the Bahamas is 809. International calls are expensive: US$4 a minute to the UK, US$2.50 to the Caribbean. Credit card facilities. Several Family Islands still have no telephone service (or electricity supply).

Media

There are three daily newspapers: the *Nassau Guardian* (circulation 12,500), *The Tribune*, published in the evening (12,500) and the *Freeport News* (4,000). The local commercial radio stations are ZNS1, owned by the Government and covering all the Bahamas, ZNS2 and ZNS3 covering New Providence and the northern Bahamas. The local commercial television station is ZNS TV 13. Transmissions from Florida can be picked up and satellite reception is common. There is one two-screen cinema in Freeport and a cinema in Governor's Harbour, Eleuthera.

Maps

The Lands and Surveys Department on East Bay Street, Nassau, PO Box 592, has an excellent stock of maps, including a marine chart of the whole archipelago for US$10 and 1:25,000 maps covering most of the islands for US$1 per sheet (several sheets per island). These are also available from Fairey Surveys, Maidenhead, Berks, UK. A good, up-to-date street map of New Providence is available from most Bahamian bookstores for US$2.95.

Tourist Office

The Bahamas Ministry of Tourism, PO Box N3701, Nassau, Bahamas, Tel: 322 7500. There are representatives of the Bahamas Tourist Office throughout the **USA**. In New York they are at 150 East 52nd Street, 28th floor N, NY 10022, Tel: 212-758 2777; also in other major US cities.

In the **UK** they are at 10 Chesterfield Street, London, W1X 8AH, Tel: 071-629 5238, Fax: 071-491 9311.

In **Canada**: 1255 Phillips Square, Montreal, Quebec, H3B 3G1, Tel: 514-861 6797, and 121 Bloor Street E, Toronto, Ontario, M4W 3M5, Tel: 416-363 4441.

In **France**: 7 Boulevard de la Madeleine, 75001 Paris, Tel: 1 42 61 60 20, Fax: 71 42 61 06 73.

In **Japan**: 4-9-17 Akasaka, Minato-Ku, Tokyo, Tel: 813-470 6162.

In **Germany**: Morfelder Landstrasse 45, D-6000 Frankfurt am Main, Tel: 069 62 60 51, Fax: 62 73 11.

In **Italy**: Foro Buonaparte 68, I-20121, Milano, Tel: 02-720 23003, Fax: 02-720 23123.

For help in the revision of this chapter we are most grateful to Rachel Cartwright (Andros) and Mark Wilson (Nassau).

CUBA

Introduction

THE ISLAND OF CUBA, 1,250 km long, 191 km at its widest point, is the largest of the Caribbean islands and only 145 km south of Florida. Gifted with a moderate climate, afflicted only occasionally by hurricanes, not cursed by frosts, blessed by an ample and well distributed rainfall and excellent soils for tropical crops, it has traditionally been one of the largest exporters of cane sugar in the world.

About a quarter of Cuba is fairly mountainous. To the west of Havana is the narrow Sierra de los Organos, rising to 750 metres and containing, in the extreme west, the strange scenery of the Guaniguánicos hill country. South of these Sierras, in a strip 145 km long and 16 km wide along the piedmont, is the Vuelta Abajo area which grows the finest of all Cuban tobaccos. Towards the centre of the island are the Escambray mountains, rising to 1,100 metres, and in the east, encircling the port of Santiago, are the most rugged mountains of all, the Sierra Maestra, in which Pico Turquino reaches 1,980 metres. In the rough and stony headland east of Guantánamo Bay are copper, manganese, chromium and iron mines. About a quarter of the land surface is covered with mountain forests of pine and mahogany. The coastline, with a remarkable number of fine ports and anchorages, is about 3,540 km long.

Some 66% of Cubans register themselves as whites: they are mostly the descendants of Spanish colonial settlers and immigrants; 12% are black, now living mostly along the coasts and in certain provinces, Oriente in particular; 21% are mulatto and about 1% are Chinese; the indigenous Indians disappeared long ago. Some 70% live in the towns, of which there are nine with over 50,000 inhabitants each. The population is estimated at 10.6 million, of which 13% live in Havana (the city and that part of the province within the city's limits). Infant mortality fell to 11.1 per 1,000 live births in 1989, compared with 19.6 in 1980. It is claimed that illiteracy has been wiped out.

History

Cuba was discovered by Columbus during his first voyage on 27 October 1492, and he paid a brief visit two years later on his way to the discovery of Jamaica. Columbus did not realize it was an island; it was first

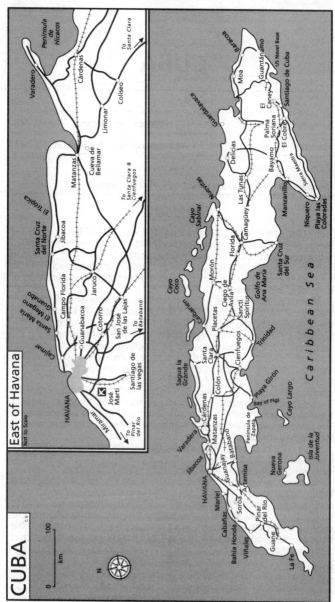

circumnavigated by Sebastián de Ocampo in 1508. Diego Velázquez conquered it in 1511 and founded several towns, including Havana. The first African slaves were imported in 1526. Sugar was introduced soon after but was not important until the last decade of the 16th century. When the British took Jamaica in 1655 a number of Spanish settlers fled to Cuba, already famous for its cigars, made a strict monopoly of Spain in 1717. The coffee plant was introduced in 1748. The British, under Lord Albemarle and Admiral Pocock, captured Havana and held the island in 1762-63, but it was returned to Spain in exchange for Florida.

The tobacco monopoly was abolished in 1816 and Cuba was given the right to trade with the world in 1818. Independence elsewhere, however, bred ambitions, and a strong movement for independence was quelled by Spain in 1823. By this time the blacks outnumbered the whites in the island; there were several slave rebellions and little by little the Créoles (or Spaniards born in Cuba) made common cause with them. A slave rising in 1837 was savagely repressed and the poet Gabriel de la Concepción Valdés was shot. There was a ten-year rebellion against Spain between 1868 and 1878, but it gained little save the effective abolition of slavery, which had been officially forbidden since 1847. From 1895 to 1898 rebellion flared up again under José Martí and Máximo Gómez. The United States was now in sympathy with the rebels, and when the US battleship *Maine* exploded in Havana harbour on 15 February 1898, this was made a pretext for declaring war on Spain. American forces (which included Colonel Theodore Roosevelt) were landed, a squadron blockaded Havana and defeated the Spanish fleet at Santiago de Cuba. In December peace was signed and US forces occupied the island. The Government of Cuba was handed over to its first president, Tomás Estrada Palma, on 20 May 1902. The USA retained naval bases at Río Hondo and Guantánamo Bay and reserved the right of intervention in Cuban domestic affairs, but granted the island a handsome import preference for its sugar. The USA chose to intervene several times, but relinquished this right in 1934.

From 1925 to 1933 the "strong man" Machado ruled Cuba as a dictator. His downfall was brought about by Fulgencio Batista, then a sergeant. Corrupt, ineffectual governments held office in the 1940s, until Batista, by then a self-promoted general, staged a military coup in 1952. His harshly repressive dictatorship was brought to an end by Fidel Castro in January 1959, after an extraordinary and heroic three years' campaign, mostly in the Sierra Maestra, with a guerrilla force reduced at one point to twelve men.

From 1960 onwards, in the face of increasing hostility from the USA, Castro led Cuba into communism. All farms of over 67 hectares have been taken over by the state. Rationing is still fierce, and there are still shortages of consumer goods. However, education, housing and health services have been greatly improved. Considerable emphasis is placed on combining productive agricultural work with study: there are over 400 schools and colleges in rural areas where the students divide their time between the plantations and the classroom. Education is compulsory up to the age of 17 and free.

Before the Revolution of 1959 the United States had investments in Cuba worth about US$1,000 million, covering nearly every activity from agriculture and mining to oil installations; it took 66% of Cuba's exports and supplied 70% of the imports in 1958. Today all American businesses, including banks, have been nationalized; the USA has cut off sugar imports from Cuba, placed an embargo on exports to Cuba, and broken off diplomatic relations. Promising moves to improve relations with the USA were given impetus in 1988 by the termination of Cuban military activities in Angola under agreement with the USA and South Africa. However, developments in Eastern Europe and the former USSR in 1989-90 provoked Castro to defend the Cuban system of government; the lack of political change delayed any further rapprochement with the USA.

In 1989 the country was shaken by the trials and executions of high-ranking officials for narcotics trafficking, abuse of power and corruption. President Castro pledged to fight against corruption and privilege and deepen the process of rectification begun in 1986. In an effort to broaden the people's power system of government introduced in 1976, the central committee of the Cuban Communist Party adopted resolutions in 1990 designed to strengthen the municipal and provincial assemblies and transform the National Assembly into a genuine parliament. Economic difficulties in the 1990s brought on by the changes in the former Soviet economy and Eastern Europe, together with higher oil prices because of the Gulf crisis, forced the Government to impose emergency measures and declare a special period in peace time. Rationing was increased, petrol became scarce, the bureaucracy was slashed and several hundred arrests were made in a drive against corruption. In the run-up to the US elections, President Bush increased pressure on Cuba in an attempt to force political change; the trade embargo was strengthened with a ban on foreign cruise and cargo ships from US ports if they also visited the island, while a new telecommunications deal was also stalled. Fidel Castro remained defiant, however, defending communism in Cuba.

Government

In 1976 a new constitution was approved by 97.7% of the voters, setting up municipal and provincial assemblies and a National Assembly of the People's Power, which has 510 members, elected by the members of the municipal assemblies. As a result of the decisions of the First Congress of the Communist Party of Cuba in December 1975, the number of provinces was increased from six to fourteen. Dr Fidel Castro was elected President of the Council of State by the National Assembly and his brother, Major Raúl Castro, was elected First Vice-President.

The Economy

Following the 1959 revolution, Cuba adopted a Marxist-Leninist system. Almost all sectors of the economy are state controlled and centrally planned, the only significant exception being agriculture where some 12% of arable land is still privately owned by 192,000 small farmers. Since October 1991, plumbers, carpenters, electricians and others have been authorized to work privately in the peso sector.

The Government has made diversification of the economy away from sugar the prime aim of economic policy. Some progress towards this has been made, but the overwhelming reliance on sugar remains and there is little expectation of achieving balanced and sustained growth in the foreseeable future. Aid from the USSR was traditionally estimated at about 25% of gnp. Apart from military aid, economic assistance took two forms: balance of payments support (about 84%), under which sugar and nickel exports were priced in excess of world levels and oil imports were indexed against world prices for the previous five years; and assistance for development projects. About 13m tonnes of oil were supplied a year, allowing 3m to be re-exported, providing a valuable source of foreign exchange earnings. There is, however, a trend towards more trade credits, which are repayable, rather than trade subsidies, and all trade agreements are being renegotiated over the next few years. From 1991, trade between Cuba and the former Soviet Union will be denominated in convertible currencies. The ex-USSR will continue to supply about 10m tonnes of oil, but at a price approximating the world market price, while it will buy 4m tonnes of sugar at 500 roubles per tonne (about US$0.14/lb) compared with the previously agreed price of 850 roubles. Other trade items will be priced in dollars. Two thirds of Cuba's exports go to the former USSR while over 70% of imports are sourced from there.

The sugar industry (70% of export earnings) has consistently failed to reach the targets set. Cuba's dream of a 10m tonne raw sugar harvest has never been reached and the 1991-92 crop was the worst for many years because of poor weather and shortages of oil and spare parts. Cuba is expected to remain the world's second-largest producer after Brazil and will probably retain its position as the world's leading exporter. Cuba became a member of the International Coffee Agreement in February 1985, and was allocated an export quota of 160,000 bags of 60 kg compared with production of 375,000 bags. Citrus has become the second-most important agricultural export. Production of food for domestic consumption has been encouraged as foreign exchange for imports has dwindled. Earnings from sugar exports are now devoted to purchasing oil, although shortages of fuel for electricity generating plants frequently lead to power cuts. Sugar mills now use bagasse as fuel, but the canefields use large quantities of oil for machinery to cut and transport the cane.

Construction and industry have been the main growth motors in recent years. A major construction project, initiated before the economic crisis, was the building of facilities for the 1991 Panamerican Games, five miles east of Havana, including a stadium seating 35,000 spectators, a swimming complex, a cycle racetrack and housing for 8,000 visitors. Tourism is set to expand considerably with the construction of 5,000 new hotel rooms. In 1991, about 500,000 tourists visited Cuba, mostly from Western countries, a record number and up from around 400,000 in 1990.

Commercial relations with market economies deteriorated in the late 1980s because of lack of progress in debt rescheduling negotiations. By the 1990s, however, a change in emphasis was noted following the moves towards greater political and economic liberalization in the Eastern bloc. Cuba could no longer rely on trade agreements with the USSR and Eastern Europe and began to concentrate on improving commercial relations with Western Europe, Latin America and the Caribbean, although progress was constrained by its serious lack of hard currency reserves and its US$7bn foreign currency debt, including substantial arrears to banks and suppliers. Trade agreements were also signed with China and Iran. The debt with the former USSR is a secret: estimates range from US$8.5bn (eq) to US$34bn (eq).

Culture
The Cuban Revolution has had a profound effect on culture both on the island itself and in a wider context. Domestically, its chief achievement has been to integrate popular expression into daily life, compared with the pre-revolutionary climate in which art was either the preserve of an elite or, in its popular forms, had to fight for acceptance. The encouragement of painting in people's studios and through a national art school, and the

support given by the state to musicians and film-makers has done much to foster a national cultural identity. This is not to say that the system has neither refrained from controlling what the people should be exposed to (eg much Western pop music was banned in the 1960s), nor that it has been without its domestic critics (either those who lived through the Revolution and took issue with it, or younger artists who now feel stifled by a cultural bureaucracy). Furthermore, while great steps have been made towards the goal of a fully-integrated society, there remain areas in which the unrestricted participation of blacks and women has yet to be achieved. Blacks predominate in sport and music (as in Brazil), but find it harder to gain recognition in the public media; women artists, novelists and composers have had to struggle for acceptance. Nevertheless, measures are being taken in the cultural, social and political spheres to rectify this.

The major characteristic of Cuban culture is its combination of the African and European. Because slavery was not abolished until 1886 in Cuba, black African traditions were kept intact much later than elsewhere in the Caribbean. They persist now, inevitably mingled with Hispanic influence, in religion: for instance *santería*, a cult which blends popular Catholicism with the Yoruba belief in the spirits which inhabit all plant life. This now has a greater hold than orthodox Catholicism, which lost much support in its initial opposition to the Revolution. Catholicism in Cuba today is in sympathy with the liberation theology professed elsewhere in Latin America.

Music is incredibly vibrant on the island. It is, again, a marriage of African rhythms, expressed in percussion instruments (batá drums, congas, claves, maracas, etc), and the Spanish guitar. Accompanying the music is an equally strong tradition of dance. A history of Cuban music is beyond the scope of this book, however there are certain styles which deserve mention. There are four basic elements out of which all others grow. The *rumba* (drumming, singing about social preoccupations and dancing) is one of the original black dance forms. By the turn of the century, it had been transferred from the plantations to the slums; now it is a collective expression, with Saturday evening competitions in which anyone can partake. Originating in eastern Cuba, *son* is the music out of which *salsa* was born. *Son* itself takes many different forms and it gained worldwide popularity after the 1920s when the National Septet of Ignacio Piñeiro made it fashionable. The more sophisticated *danzón*, ballroom dance music which was not accepted by the upper classes until the end of the last century, has also been very influential. It was the root for the *cha-cha-cha* (invented in 1948 by Enrique Jorrin). The fourth tradition is *trova*, the itinerant troubadour singing ballads, which has been transformed, post-Revolution, into the *nueva trova*, made famous by singers such as Pablo Milanés and Silvio Rodríguez. The new tradition adds politics and everyday concerns to the romantic themes.

There are many other styles, such as the *guajira*, the most famous example of which is the song "Guantanamera"; *tumba francesa* drumming and dancing; and Afro-Cuban jazz, performed by internationally renowned artists like Irakere and Arturo Sandoval. Apart from sampling the recordings of groups, put out by the state company Egrem, the National Folklore Company (Conjunto Folklórico Nacional) gives performances of the traditional music which it was set up to study and keep alive.

In Havana, a weekly guide (*Urbe*, US$1 from major hotels) appears every Thursday, with listing of concerts, theatre programmes, art exhibitions, etc. It also carries the names, addresses and programmes of the Casas de Cultura and Casas de la Trova, houses where traditional Cuban music can be heard for free, thoroughly recommended (in Havana: San Lázaro between Belascoaín and Gervasio).

In Vedado, the National Folklore Company, Calle 2 entre Calzada y 5ta, sometimes stage "Rumba Saturday" at 1500, 1 peso.

Festivals of dance (including ballet), theatre, jazz, cinema and other art forms are held frequently—tickets (in dollars) from lobbies of the major hotels. Outside Havana, ask in hotels for detailed information.

NB Last-minute changes and cancellations are common.

The Cuban Revolution had perhaps its widest cultural influence in the field of literature. Many now famous Latin American novelists (like Gabriel García Márquez, Mario Vargas Llosa and Julio Cortázar) visited Havana and worked with the Prensa Latina news agency or on the *Casa de las Américas* review. As Gordon Brotherston has said, "an undeniable factor in the rise of the novel in Latin America has been a reciprocal self-awareness among novelists in different countries and in which Cuba has been instrumental." (*The Emergence of the Latin American Novel*, Cambridge University Press, 1977, page 3.) Not all have maintained their allegiance, just as some Cuban writers have deserted the Revolution. One such Cuban is Guillermo Cabrera Infante, whose most celebrated novel is *Tres tristes tigres* (1967). Other established writers remained in Cuba after the Revolution: Alejo Carpentier, who invented the phrase "marvellous reality" to describe the different order of reality which he perceived in Latin America and the Caribbean and which now, often wrongly, is attributed to many other writers from the region (his novels include *El reino de este mundo, El siglo de las luces, Los pasos perdidos*, and many more); Jorge Lezama Lima (*Paradiso*, 1966); and Edmundo Desnoes (*Memorias del subdesarrollo*). Of post-revolutionary writers, the poet and novelist Miguel Barnet is worth reading, especially for the use of black oral history and traditions in his work. After 1959, Nicolás Guillén, a black, was adopted as the national poet; his poems of the 1930s (*Motivos de son, Sóngoro cosongo, West Indies Ltd*) are steeped in popular speech and musical rhythms. In tone they are close to the work of the *négritude* writers (see under Martinique), but they look more towards Latin America than Africa. The other poet-hero of the Revolution is the 19th-century writer and fighter for freedom from Spain, José Martí. Even though a US radio station beaming propaganda and pop music has usurped his name, Martí's importance to Cuba remains undimmed.

Flora and Fauna

The National Committee for the Protection and Conservation of National Treasures and the Environment was set up in 1978. There are six national parks, including three in Pinar del Río alone (in the Sierra de los Organos and on the Península de Guanahacabibes), the swamps of the Zapata Peninsula and the Gran Piedra near Santiago. The Soledad Botanical Gardens near Cienfuegos house many of Cuba's plants. The Royal Palm is the national tree. Other palms abound, as well as flowering trees, pines, oaks, cedars, etc. Original forest, however, is confined to some of the highest points in the southeastern mountains and the mangroves of the Zapata Peninsula.

There are, of course, a multitude of flowers and in the country even the smallest of houses has a flower garden in front. The orchidarium at Soroa has over 700 examples. To complement the wide variety of butterflies that can be found in Cuba, the buddleia, or butterfly bush, has been named the national flower. In fact, about 10,000 species of insect have been identified on the island.

Reptiles range from crocodiles (of which there is a farm on the Zapata Peninsula) to iguanas to tiny salamanders. Cuba claims the smallest of a number of animals, for instance the Cuban pygmy frog (one of some 30 small frogs), the almiqui (a shrew-like insectivore, the world's smallest mammal), the butterfly or moth bat and the bee hummingbird (called locally the *zunzuncito*). The latter is an endangered species, like the *carpintero real* woodpecker, the cariara (a hawk-like bird of the savannah), the pygmy owl, the Cuban green parrot and the *ferminia*. The national bird is the forest-dwelling Cuban trogon (the *tocororo*).

Also protected is the manatee (sea cow) which has been hunted almost to extinction. It lives in the marshes of the Zapata Peninsula. Also living in the mangrove forests is the large Cuban land crab. Many species of turtle can be found around the offshore cays.

Carnival

During July, carnivals are held in Havana and Santiago, reaching fever pitch with the 26 July festivities. Similar events are held in all Cuban cities and large towns at different times during the summer months. They generally last one-two weeks.

Havana

Havana, the capital, was before the Revolution the largest, the most beautiful and the most sumptuous city in the Caribbean. Today it is rather run-down, but thanks to the Government's policy of developing the countryside, it is not ringed with shantytowns like so many other Latin American capitals. With its suburbs it has 2.1 million people, half of whom live in housing officially regarded as sub-standard. Many buildings are shored up by wooden planks. Some of it is very old—the city was founded in 1515—but the ancient palaces, plazas, colonnades, churches and monasteries merge agreeably with the new. The old city is being substantially refurbished with Unesco's help, as part of the drive to attract tourists and has been declared a World Heritage Site by the United Nations.

The oldest part of the city, around the Plaza de Armas, is quite near the docks where you can see cargo ships from all over the world being unloaded. Here are the former palace of the Captains-General, the temple of El Templete, and La Fuerza, the oldest of all the forts. From Plaza de Armas run two narrow and picturesque streets, Calles Obispo and O'Reilly (several old-fashioned pharmacies on Obispo, traditional glass and ceramic medicine jars and decorative perfume bottles on display in shops gleaming with polished wood and mirrors). These two streets go west to the heart of the city: Parque Central, with its laurels, poincianas, almonds, palms, shrubs and gorgeous flowers. To the southwest rises the golden dome of the Capitol. From the northwest corner of Parque Central a wide, tree-shaded avenue, the Paseo del Prado, runs to the fortress of La Punta; at its northern sea-side end is the Malecón, a splendid highway along the coast to the western residential district of Vedado. The sea crashing along the seawall here is a spectacular sight when the wind blows from the north. On calmer days, fishermen lean over the parapet, lovers sit in the shade of the small pillars, and joggers sweat along the pavement. On the other side of the six-lane road, buildings which look stout and grand, with arcaded pavements, balconies, mouldings and large entrances, are salt-eroded, faded and sadly

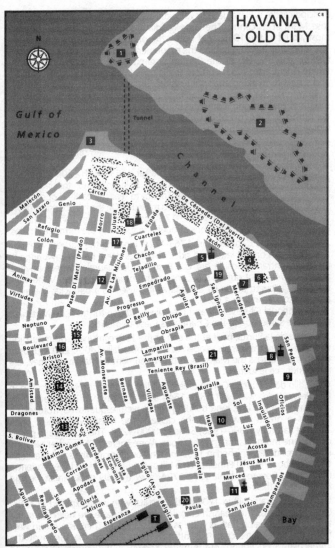

HAVANA - OLD CITY

decrepit inside.

Calle San Lázaro leads directly from the monument to General Antonio Maceo on the Malecón to the magnificent central stairway of Havana University. A monument to Julio Antonio Mella, founder of the Cuban Communist Party, stands across from the stairway. Further out, past El

Príncipe castle, is Plaza de la Revolución, with the impressive monument to José Martí at its centre. The large buildings surrounding the square were mostly built in the 1950s and house the principal government ministries. The long grey building behind the monument is the former Justice Ministry (1958), now the HQ of the Central Committee of the Communist Party, where Fidel Castro has his office. The Plaza is the scene of massive parades and speeches marking important events.

From near the fortress of La Punta a tunnel runs eastwards under the mouth of the harbour; it emerges in the rocky ground between the Castillo del Morro and the fort of La Cabaña, some 550 metres away, and a 5-km highway connects with the Havana-Matanzas road.

The street map of Havana is marked with numerals showing the places of most interest to visitors.

1. Castillo del Morro was built between 1589 and 1630, with a 20-metre moat, but has been much altered. It stands on a bold headland; the flash of its lighthouse, built in 1844, is visible 30 km out to sea. The castle is open to the public, Tuesday-Sunday, 1000-1800, as a museum. On the harbour side, down by the water, is the Battery of the 12 Apostles, each gun named after an Apostle. It can be reached by bus through the tunnel to the former toll gates.

2. Fortaleza de la Cabaña, built 1763-1774. Fronting the harbour is a high wall; the ditch on the landward side, 12 metres deep, has a drawbridge to the main entrance. Inside are Los Fosos de los Laureles where political prisoners were shot during the Cuban fight for independence. Visitors are no longer allowed inside La Cabaña as it is used as a barracks; there are plans to convert it into a hotel.

The National Observatory and the railway station for trains to Matanzas are on the same side of the Channel as these two forts.

3. Castillo de la Punta, built at the end of the 16th century, a squat building with 2½-metre thick walls, is open to the public, daily 1400-2200. Opposite the fortress, across the Malecón, is the monument to Máximo Gómez, the independence leader.

4. Castillo de la Fuerza, Cuba's oldest building and the second oldest fort in the New World, was built 1538-1544 after the city had been sacked by buccaneers. It is a low, long building with a picturesque tower from which there is a grand view. Inside the castle is the Museo de Armas, open Tuesday-Saturday, 1300-1900, Sunday, 0900-1200. The downstairs part is open in the mornings for art exhibitions. *Note*: There are two other old forts in Havana: Atarés, finished in 1763, on a hill overlooking the southwest end of the harbour; and El Príncipe, on a hill at the far end of Av Independencia (Av Rancho Boyeros), built 1774-1794, now the city gaol. Finest view in Havana from this hill.

5. The Cathedral, built in 1704 by the Jesuits, who were expelled in 1767. On either side of the Spanish colonial baroque façade are belltowers, the left one (west) being half as wide as the right (east). There is a grand view from the latter. The church is officially dedicated to the Virgin of the Immaculate Conception, but is better known as the church of Havana's patron saint, San Cristóbal, and as the Columbus cathedral. The bones of Christopher Columbus were sent to this cathedral when Santo Domingo was ceded by Spain to France in 1795; they now lie in Santo Domingo. The bones were in fact those of another Columbus. The Cathedral is open Monday-Friday 0900-1130 and Saturday 1530-1730.

6. Plaza de Armas, has been restored to very much what it once was. The statue in the centre is of Céspedes. In the northeast corner of the square is the church of El Templete; a column in front of it marks the spot where the first mass was said in 1519 under a ceiba tree. A sapling of the same tree, blown down by hurricane in 1753, was planted on the same spot, and under its branches the supposed bones of Columbus reposed in state before being taken to the cathedral. This tree was cut down in 1828, the present tree planted, and the Doric temple opened. There are paintings by Vermay, a pupil of David, inside.

7. On the west side of Plaza de Armas is the former palace of the Captains General, built in 1780, a charming example of colonial architecture. The Spanish Governors and the Presidents lived here until 1917, when it became the City Hall. It is now the Historical Museum of the city of Havana (open Tuesday-Saturday, 1430-2130; Sunday 0900-1230, Tel: 61-0722). The arcaded and balconied patio is well worth a visit (open in the morning). The former Supreme Court on the north side of the Plaza is another colonial building, with a large patio.

8. The church and convent of San Francisco, built 1608, reconstructed 1737; a massive, sombre edifice suggesting defence rather than worship. The three-storeyed tower was both a landmark for returning voyagers and a look-out for pirates. Having been restored to the Franciscan order, it is now open to the public on Sunday mornings or at other times immediately after services. Most of the treasures were removed by the government and some are in museums.

9. The Corinthian white marble building on Calle Oficinas south of the Post Office was once the legislative building, where the House of Representatives met before the Capitol was built.

10. The Santa Clara convent was built in 1635 for the Clarisan nuns. The quaint old patio has been carefully preserved; in it are the city's first slaughter house, first public fountain and public baths, and a house built by a sailor for his love-lorn daughter. You can still see the nuns' cemetery and their cells.

11. La Merced church, built in 1746, rebuilt 1792. It has a beautiful exterior and a redecorated lavish interior.

12. The Palacio de Bellas Artes now called the National Museum of Fine Arts (Tel: 61-2332). It also has a large collection of relics of the struggle for independence, sculptures, classical paintings (most of them copies), and a fine array of modern paintings by Cuban and other artists. It also has temporary exhibitions. Open Tuesday-Saturday 1000-1800, Sunday 0900-1300.

13. Parque Fraternidad, landscaped to show off the Capitol, north of it, to the best effect. At its centre is a ceiba tree growing in soil provided by each of the American republics. In the park also is a famous statue of the Indian woman who first welcomed the Spaniards: La Noble Habana, sculpted in 1837. From the southwest corner the handsome Avenida Allende runs due west to the high hill on which stands Príncipe Castle (now the city gaol). The Quinta de los Molinos, on this avenue, at the foot of the hill, once housed the School of Agronomy of Havana University. The main house now contains the Máximo Gómez museum (Dominican-born fighter for Cuban Independence). Also here is the headquarters of the young writers and artists (Asociación Hermanos Saiz). The gardens are a lovely place to stroll. North, along Calle Universidad, on a hill which gives a good view, is the University.

HAVANA
Orientation Map

1. Plaza de Armas
2. Parque Central
3. Plaza de la Revolución
4. Cathedral
5. El Principe Castle
6. Monument to General Antonio Maceo, & Torre San Lázaro
7. Napoleonic Museum
8. Decorative Arts Museum
9. Philatelic Museum & Ministry of Communications
10. University of Havana
11. Airline Offices
12. Habana Libre building
13. Hotel Capri
14. Hotel Nacional
15. Hotel Deauville
16. Hotel Caribbean

14. The Capitol, opened May 1929, has a large dome over a rotunda; it is a copy, on a smaller scale, of the US Capitol in Washington. At the centre of its floor is set a 24-carat diamond, zero for all distance measurements in Cuba. The interior has large halls and stately staircases, all most sumptuously decorated. Entrance for visitors is to the left of the stairway. The Capitol now houses the Museum of Natural Science, which is open Tuesday to Saturday 1400-2100, and Sunday 0900-1230.

15. Parque Central.

16. Gran Teatro de la Habana.

17. Presidential Palace (1922), a huge, ornate building topped by a dome, facing Av de las Misiones Park; now contains the Museum of the Revolution (Tel: 6-9210). Open Tuesday-Saturday 1300-2000, Sunday 1000-1300, 1400-2000, entry US$2, no cameras allowed either inside or in the adjoining park (allow several hours to see it all, explanations are all in Spanish). The history of Cuban political development is charted, from the slave uprisings to joint space missions with the ex-Soviet Union. The liveliest section displays the final battles against Batista's troops, with excellent photographs and some bizarre personal momentos, such as a revolutionary's knife, fork and spoon set and a plastic shower curtain worn in the Sierra Maestra campaigns. The yacht *Granma*, from which Dr Castro disembarked with his companions in 1956 to launch the Revolution, has been installed in the park facing the south entrance, surrounded by planes, tanks and other vehicles involved, as well as a fragment from a U.S. spy plane shot down in the 1970s.

18. The Church of El Santo Angel Custodio was built by the Jesuits in 1672 on the slight elevation of Peña Pobre hill. It has white, laced Gothic towers and 10 chapels, the best of which is behind the high altar.

19. Museo de Arte Colonial, Plaza de la Catedral (in the former Palacio de los Condes de Casa Bayona), Tuesday-Friday 1330-2030, Saturday 1500-2000, Sunday 0900-1245, contains colonial furniture and other items, plus a section on stained glass (Tel: 61-1367).

20. Birthplace of José Martí, opposite central railway station (Tuesday-Saturday 1315-2030, Sunday 0900-1230), Tel: 6-8852.

21. Carlos J Finlay Museum of Medicine, Calle Cuba 460 (Monday-Friday 0800-1200, 1300-1700, Tel:6-8006).

Other Museums
Museo de Alfabetización, Plaza de la Catedral, Tuesday-Saturday 1015-1300, 1415-1845, Sunday 0900-1300; **Napoleonic Museum**, Calle Ronda (Tuesday-Saturday 1330-2030; Sunday 0900-1300), houses paintings and other works of art, a specialized library and a collection of weaponry (Tel: 79-1412); **Decorative Arts Museum**, 17th and East Streets, Vedado (Monday-Saturday 1300-2100; Sunday 0900-1300 Tel: 32-1300); **Postal Museum**, Ministry of Communications, Plaza de la Revolución (Monday-Friday and alternate Saturdays 0900-1800, Tel: 70-5193; also **Numismatic Museum**, (Calle oficios 8 between Obispo and Obrapía, Tel: 63-2521, Tuesday-Saturday 1300-2100, Sunday 0900-1300). **Vintage Car Museum**, Oficios y Jústiz (just off Plaza de Armas; there are a great many museum pieces—pre-revolutionary US models—still on the road especially outside Havana, in among the Ladas, VWs and Nissans), **Arab Museum** (with restaurant) opposite, on Oficios between Obispo and Obrapía, open Tuesday-Saturday 1430-1630 and 1900-2145, Sunday 0900-1300; **Africa Museum**, on Obrapiá 157 between San Ignacio and Mercaderes, entry free (Tuesday-Saturday 1430-1830, 1900-2145, Sunday 0900-1300), small gallery of carved wooden artefacts and handmade costumes. **Music Museum**, corner of Tacón and Misiones, entry free; small and beautifully furnished old house; interesting collection of African drums and other instruments from around the world, showing history and development of Cuban *son* and *danzón* music. The *Hotel Ambos Mundos*, Calle Obispo 153, between San Ignacio and Mercaderes, has kept room 511 where Ernest

Hemingway lived, as a showpiece for visitors. Hemingway lived here for 10 years before moving to La Vigía in 1939. His room has some of the finest views over the old part of the city. Always check opening times in advance.

Suburbs

The western sections of the old city merge imperceptibly into Vedado. West of it, and reached by a tunnel under the Almendares river, lies Miramar, some 16 km west of the capital, and easily reached by bus. Miramar was where the wealthy lived before the Revolution; today there are several embassies and government buildings, and also many old, abandoned villas.

The Cuban pavilion, a large building on Calle 23, Vedado, is a combination of a tropical glade and a museum of social history. It tells the nation's story by a brilliant combination of objects, photography and the architectural manipulation of space.

The National Arts College, located in the grounds of the former Havana Country Club in Cubanacan, southwest of Miramar, houses schools for different arts and was designed by Ricardo Porro. Architects will be interested in this "new spatial sensation".

Pabexpo completed in January 1989, a sprawling new facility southwest of Havana, past Lenin Park, near the botanical gardens, features a score of pavilions showing Cuba's achievements in industry, science, agriculture and the arts and entertainment. Open weekdays Wednesday-Friday 1400-1600 and Saturday-Sunday 1000-1800 (times subject to change). Special trains leave from main terminal in Old Havana. Information on times (and special buses) from hotels.

South of the centre, in Cerro district, is the Estadio Latinoamericano, the best place to see baseball (the major league level, entrance free).

Beaches

The beaches in Havana, at Miramar and Playa de Marianao, reached by No 132 bus, are rocky and generally very crowded in summer (transport may also be difficult and time consuming). The beach clubs belong to trade unions and may not let non-members in. Those to the east, El Mégano, Santa María del Mar and Bacuranao, for example, are much better. Buses going along the Vía Blanca to these places leave from near the central railway station in the old city. To the west of Havana are Arena Blanca and Bahía Honda, which are good for diving and fishing but difficult to get to unless you have a car.

Local Information—Havana

Where To Stay (Payment for hotels used by tourists is in US$). Foreign tourists should obtain a reservation through an accredited Cubatur agent (see **Travel Agencies** at the end of this chapter). On arrival at José Martí International Airport, you must go straight to the Cubatur Individual Desk where pre-booked accommodation vouchers will be exchanged for Cubatur vouchers. If accommodation has not been pre-booked, it must be arranged (and paid for in US$) at the Cubatur desk before you are allowed through immigration and customs. Always tell the hotel each morning if you intend to stay on another day. Do not lose your "guest card" which shows your name, room number and meal arrangement. Tourist hotels are a/c, with "tourist" TV (US films, tourism promotion), restaurants with reasonable food, but standards are not comparable with Europe and plumbing is often faulty.

	Address	No of rooms	Tele-phone	Rates (US$) Single	Double
Capri	21 y N, Vedado	216	32-0511	56	75
Riviera	Paseo y Malecón, Vedado	360	30-5051	75	100
Nacional	21 y O, Vedado	480	7-8981	128	170
Habana Libre	L y 23, Vedado	568	30-5011	68	90
Victoria	19 y M, Vedado	32	32-6531	75	100
St John's	O, entre 23 y 25, Vedado	96	32-9531	32	43
Vedado	Calle O, No 244	185	32-6501	40	53
Colina	Calle 23	80		30	40
Deauville	Galiano y Malecón	150	61-6901	35	46

The Vedado hotels (the best) are away from the old centre; the others reasonably close to it. Prices at the *Habana Libre* depend on the floor number (approx. US$90), the hotel has an ugly exterior but most facilities are here, eg hotel reservations, excursions, Post Office, airlines nearby. The *Victoria* is small, quiet and pleasant, recommended. *Riviera*, comfortable, does a good breakfast. The *Hostal Valencia* in old Havana is a joint Spanish/Cuban venture modelled on the Spanish paradores. There are only 11 rooms, each named after a Valencian town, from US$86s to US$115d, tastefully restored building, nicely furnished, good restaurant; *Inglaterra*, next to Teatro Nacional, old style, beautifully restored, highly recommended, US$68s, US$76d with balcony overlooking Parque Central, helpful staff, several of whom speak English, restaurant serves nicely prepared, simple food at moderate prices, excellent buffet breakfast 0700-1000 in lovely, old tiled dining room, US$4, open to non-guests, also snacks available in pleasant inner courtyard, music at meal times, the bar often has late music. The *Colina* is popular with the airport Cubatur desk, small rooms, poor breakfast. Other "dollar" hotels are *Sevilla*, Trocadero y Zulueta, Tel: 6-9961, undergoing reconstruction in 1991, as was the *Nacional*; the *Comodoro* also, but was operating normally while adjoining cottages were built, US$50s, US$66d. The *Plaza* reopened in 1991 after refurbishment, very comfortable, excellent service, good buffet breakfast and dinner, recommended, US$90. *Lincoln*, in Central Havana on Italia, down from *Deauville*, US$30s, US$40d.

The cheaper hotels are usually hard to get into; often full. *Caribbean*, Paseo Martí 164 (bus 82 from Vedado), US$18s, US$23d, hot water (sporadic supply), fan and TV, popular with travellers, clean, old city, recommended, but avoid noisy rooms at front and lower floors at back over deafening water pump, and beware of petty theft from rooms, small cafe serves meals sandwiches and eggs at a low price. *Lido*, on Consulado near corner of Animas, good, although theft reported, choose a room away from the alley alongside, US$20s, US$26d, breakfast and some food available in coffee shop, running water all day, say staff, bar on roof terrace, sometimes live music, recommended. *Bruzón*, on Calle Bruzón near the Plaza de la Revolución, US$18s, US$20d, fan, TV in some rooms, staff from sleepy to helpful, aggressive lady in charge of breakfasts. *Ambos Mundos*, Obispo 153, between San Ignacio and Mercaderes, Tel: 614887, US$24d with air-conditioning, US$20d with fan, friendly, clean, old-fashioned charm, wonderful location with great view of old city from roof terrace restaurant, Hemingway's room is open to visitors (see **Museums** above), recommended. It is usually quite impossible for tourists to stay in "peso hotels" in Havana, but if you manage it, to pay in pesos at cheaper hotels involves presenting yourself in the morning to be listed at the hotel selected and then going back in the afternoon to collect a registration card. Some are reserved for Cuban tourists, most have two rates, one for nationals and another (higher) for foreigners.

If you have a car, the eastern beaches are good places to stay for visiting Havana. The hotels are usually booked up by package tours but you can rent an apartment on the beach away from the main tourist area for US$25. The office is at the end of the main road running along the beach nearest to Havana and furthest from the main hotel area.

Where To Eat Restaurants are not cheap. The choice of food is limited except in "dollar" restaurants, recognizable by the credit card stickers on the door, where meals are about US$10-15, paid only in US dollars. Check the bill carefully as overcharging is common in some Havana "dollar" restaurants, also the bill may not record what you actually ate. As a rule, in Havana, outside the hotels, the "dollar" places are the best bet. The pizzerías almost always have huge queues and the peso food situation in Havana is dire. **NB** Mealtimes in most cheap "peso" restaurants are limited 1130-1400 (the best dishes are gone by 1200) and from 1800-2030 (when the food runs out). For most peso restaurants you need a reservation and for that you may need connections or a Cuban 'guide'. The *Bodeguita del Medio*, Empedrado, near the Cathedral, made famous by Hemingway and worth a visit if only for a drink (*mojito*—rum, crushed ice and mint—is a must). Excellent food and wide range for vegetarians, about US$25 for two, drinks extra, colourful atmosphere and nice roof terrace. Book in advance or go early, very popular. *El Patio*, Plaza Catedral, nearby, is recommended for national dishes and *La Mina*, on Plaza de Armas, traditional Cuban food but both have uneven service, waits can be long and cooking gas shortages are common; nearby, *El Arabe*, Paseo Martí, upstairs in Arab Cultural Institute, cold a/c, very good hummus and lamb dishes; and *D'Giovanni*, Italian, Tacón between Empedrado and O'Reilly, lovely old building with patio and terrace, interesting tree growing through the wall, but food very bland. Handicrafts shop in doorway specializes in miniature ornaments. *Hostal Valencia* restaurant features paella, good food, charming; *El Tocororo* (national bird of Cuba), excellent food at US$30-35 a head, old colonial mansion with nice terrace, recommended as probably the best restaurant in town; *La Cecilia*, good international food, mostly in open air setting, recommended. *La Divina Pastora*, fish restaurant, not far from Castillo del Morro, dollars only, expensive, food praised; *Doce Apostolos*, nearby, fish and good criollo food (but not as good as the *Bodeguita del Medio*), good views of the Malecón. *El Pacífico*, Chinese restaurant, popular with Cubans. *Las Ruinas* in Parque Lenín, Cuba's most exclusive restaurant—and aptly named for its prices—is most easily reached by taxi; try to persuade the driver to come back and fetch you, as otherwise it is difficult to get back. Visit *Dulcería Doña Teresa* (end of Obispo) for the caramel pudding. Reasonable cafeteria-style meals are available at *Wakamba*, opposite *St John's* hotel; nearby is the *Pizzería Milán*; *Budapest*, near Parque Central, expensive but not recommended. In Vedado, *El Cochinito*, Calle 23 (national criollo dishes); *El Conejito*, Calle North, and *La Torre* (top of Edificio Fosca, poor food but good view), are quite expensive. *Lafayette* (Aguiar, entre O'Reilly y San Juan de Dios), recommended. *Daytona*, Calle Amistad off San Rafael, opens 1200 and 1900, is a good "peso" restaurant; also *Los Parados*, corner of Neptuno and Consulado. Good cheap restaurant, which accepts pesos from tourists, in Calle Trocadero near *Caribbean Hotel*. An Italian restaurant called *Prado 264*, near *El Arabe* on Paseo Martí, is one of the few remaining places that will let foreign tourists pay in pesos, basic and only two dishes on menu, spaghetti or tomato pizza, but very tasty, no drinks, tap water only. Must phone to reserve between 1800-2000 on previous day (Tel: 628427), but surprisingly not always a queue. Reports of other peso restaurants include *Potín*, Linca Paseo, *Carmelo*, Cazzada A, *7 Mares*, J with Calle 23, *Rancho Luna*, 17 with L, *Kamabali*, 25 with M and one at Brasil (Teniente Rey y Aguiar, be prepared for a 1½ hour queue. In the *Habana Libre Hotel*, try *El Barracón*, traditional Cuban with good fish and seafood at lobby level, open 1200-midnight, and *Sierra Maestra* restaurant and *Bar Turquino* on the 25th floor (spectacular views of Havana which makes the food acceptable). Also expensive, *"1830"* on Malecón. Along and near La Rampa there are some cheaper pizzerías and self-service restaurants. On Paseo Avenue and Calle 1, near the *Riviera*, there is a cafetería in the "Diploferretería" (dollar hardware store), open 1000-2200 every day for sandwiches (usual limited selection), beer and soft drinks, quicker and cheaper than hotel cafés. The cafetería at the Museo Nacional is OK, usually no queues, juice and sandwiches for 4 pesos, open about 1000-1200 for sandwiches. At Marianao beach there are also some cheaper bars and restaurants. Inside the hard currency shopping centre, 5ta and Calle 42 in Miramar, is an outdoor fast-foodery and an indoor restaurant, the latter with moderate dollar prices.

A visit to the *Coppelia* ice-cream parlour, 23 y L. Vedado, is recommended. It tends to be very crowded in the evenings as it and La Rampa are very popular with young people. To get an ice-cream (0.60-1.50 pesos), pay first, collect a dish and then the ice. This process can take more than an hour, but there are no queues at the dollar entrance. Alternatively, sample the Coppelia ice-cream in the tourist hotels and restaurants.

Rincón Criollo and the nearby *Tabernita* are just past Santiago de las Vegas, east of the airport (tourist taxi from *Habana Libre* US$15 one way). Both serve national dishes with uncertain menus, food sometimes limited to tinned meat. It is possible to take a bus to Santiago de las Vegas and take a taxi from there, but best to get there by rented car.

Bars Visitors often find that ordinary bars *not* on the tourist circuit will charge them in dollars. Unfortunately even if it is a local bar and the Cubans are all paying in pesos, you will almost certainly have to pay in US dollars. Even so, the prices in most places are not high by Caribbean standards.

The best bar in Old Havana is *La Bodeguita* (see above). *La Casa del Agua La Tinaja*, on southwest corner of the Plaza de Armas is a nice place selling drinking water for 5 cents (either type). Try a *mojito* in any bar. *El Floridito*, on the corner of Obispo next to the Parque Central, was another favourite haunt of Hemingway. It has had a recent face-lift and is now a very elegant bar and restaurant (US$5 for a daiquiri), reflected in the prices, but well worth a visit if only to see the sumptuous decor.

Shopping Local cigars and rum are excellent. Original lithographs and other works of art can be purchased directly from the artists at the Galería del Grabado, Plaza de la Catedral (Monday-Friday 1400-2100, Saturday 1400-1900). Just opposite this is the Galería de Arte (Monday-Friday 1030-1800, Saturday 1700-2200), where a variety of works of art are on sale. On Saturday afternoons there are handicraft stalls in the Plaza, very good value in pesos. There is a special boutique in the old mansion at Calle Cuba 64 where the largest selection of Cuban handicrafts is available; the artisans have their workshops in the back of the same building (open, Monday-Saturday 1230-1930), very expensive but it has things not available elsewhere. The "Intur-shops" in tourist hotels and elsewhere, which sell tourists' requisites and other luxury items, require payment in US$ (or credit cards: Mastercard, Visa) and will generally cash travellers' cheques and give change in US$ cash. Large diplomatic store at Miramar accepts all foreign currencies (no pesos) and has a variety of goods at prices way below the government Intur dollar shops. *La Maison* is a luxurious mansion on Calle 7 and 18 in Miramar, with dollar shops selling cigars, alcohol, handicrafts, jewelry and perfume. There is sometimes live music in the evening in lovely open-air patio, and fashion shows displaying imported clothes sold in their own boutique, free entry. The large department stores are along Galiano (Av Italia) near San Rafael and Neptuno. Rationed goods are distinguished by a small card bearing the code number and price but a great deal is now sold freely and these articles bear only the price. Most stores are open only in the afternoon. International bookstore at end of El Prado, near Parque Fraternidad and Capitol, English, French, German books but selection poor and payment has to be in dollars. Other good bookshops near Parque Central and La Moderna Poesía on Calle Obispo (books are very good value). Good art books (weighty) at the Maxim Gorky Soviet bookshop. Universal (San Rafael) and El Siglo de las Luces (Neptuno), both near Capitolio, are good places to buy *son*, *trova* and jazz (rock) records.

Cigar Factory Partagas on Calle Inglaterra behind the Capitolio, gives tours twice daily at 1000 and 1300, US$10 including drink and pack of small cigars. The tour lasts for about an hour and is very interesting. You are taken through the factory and shown the whole production process from storage and sorting of leaves, to packaging and labelling (explanation in Spanish only). Four different brand names are made here; Partagas, Cubana, Ramón Allones and Bolívar (special commission of 170,000 cigars made for the Seville Expo, Spain, 1992). These and other famous cigars can be bought at their shop here, and rum, at good prices. A box of 25 Davidoff No1 in April 1992 cost US$13 on the black market.

Night Club The *Tropicana* (closed Monday) is a must; book with Cubatur or through a tourist hotel, US$40-50, depending on seat, entry only, transport US$5 and drinks extra (2030-0200). Despite being toned down to cater for more sober post-revolutionary tastes, it is still a lively place with plenty of atmosphere, open-air (entry refunded if it rains). Drinks are expensive: minimum charge is 5 pesos a head; payment in dollars. Bringing your own bottle seems acceptable. Foreigners showing their exchange paper at the door may be admitted without booking if there is room. All the main hotels have their own cabarets, enquire at Cubatur and make a reservation. *Capri* is recommended, at US$15 and longer show than *Tropicana* but the drinks are expensive at US$40 for a bottle of best rum. Best to reserve through Cubatur.

Theatres *Teatro Mella*, Vedado, specializes in modern dance; more traditional programmes at *Gran Teatro de la Habana* on Parque Central next to *Hotel Inglaterra*. The Conjunto Folklórico Nacional dance company sometimes performs here, highly recommended, 2 pesos, (local currency accepted). Havana has some very lively theatre companies.

Casa De La Trova San Lázaro, entre Belascoán y Gervasio looked closed down in March 1992.

Jazz *Maxim Club*, Calle 10, Tel: 33981, free entry, music starts at 2100, worth arriving early, recommended but beware of 'friends' drinks appearing on your bill; *Coparrun*, *Hotel Riviera* (big names play there), jazz in the bar recommended.

Cinemas Best are *Yara* (opposite *Habana Libre* hotel); *América*, Galiano 253; *Payret*, Prado 505.

Zoo Av 26, Vedado (open Tuesday-Sunday 0900-1800).

El Bosque De La Habana Worth visiting. From the entrance to the Zoo, cross Calle 26 and walk a few blocks until you reach a bridge across the Almendares. Cross this, turn right at the end and keep going north, directly to the Bosque which is a jungle-like wood.

Aquaria National Aquarium, Calle 60 and Av 1, Miramar, specializes in salt-water fish and dolphins (open Tuesday-Friday 1300-1730, Saturday and Sunday 1000-1730) while the Parque Lenín aquarium has fresh-water fish on show.

Banks Banco Nacional and its branches. (See also under **Currency** below.)

Post Office There is a post and telegraph office in the *Hotel Habana Libre* building. For stamp collectors the Círculo Filatélico is on Calle San José 1172 between Infanta and Basarrata, open Monday-Friday, 1700-2000, and there is a shop on Obispo 518 with an excellent selection (Cuban stamps are very colourful and high quality, only available to foreign tourists with pesos if stamps franked).

Telephones A fire badly damaged the Havana central exchange in November 1988 and all telephones beginning with 6, 61 or 62 (including the British Embassy) were put out of service. Repairs were completed in 1990 when all the numbers listed were changed to new numbers. **Other cable offices** Calle Obispo 351, Tel: 6-9901/5; Telegraph in *Habana Libre* building. Ministerio de Comunicaciones, Plaza de la Revolución, Tel: 70-5581. The international telephone, telex and fax centre in the *Habana Libre* is open round the clock (also see **Travel Agents** below).

Travel Agents Gaviota Travel, Avenida 47 No. 2821. Tel: 294694/294528, claim to be the only private travel company in Cuba, recommended. *The Palacio del Turismo*, Obispo 252, on the corner of Cuba, is also recommended for arranging tours around the country (bearing in mind the warnings in **Information for Visitors, Excursions**). The office is part of a renovated colonial mansion which also houses souvenir shops, galleries and a telephone office (open daily 0900-2100, US$5.50 per minute to Europe).

Transport The economic crisis and shortage of fuel has led to severe transport problems. There is now very little local traffic, there are long queues at petrol stations and public transport has dwindled. Tourists are encouraged to use dollar transport, such as taxis or hired cars (when available), or not travel at all. Organized tours out of town are rarely more than day trips. Always check when booking that departure is definite, agencies will cancel through lack of passengers or fuel. A fleet of white **"Turistaxis"** has been introduced for tourists' use; payment in US$. **Panataxi** (Tel: 810153), 24 hrs., cheaper than most as they use Ladas instead of Nissans, and are not air-conditioned, US$1 call-out charge. If you ask your hotel to book a taxi for you they are more likely to call for the luxury variety (US$2 call-out charge). Some ordinary taxis are only allowed to operate in a restricted area (indicated by a sign in the window). If you want to go further afield look for one without a sign. The newer taxis have meters which should be set at No 1 during the daytime and at No 2 at night (2300-0700). In the older taxis there are no meters and there is normally a fixed charge between points in or near the city. The fare should be fixed before setting out on a journey. **Ordinary taxis** are not allowed to accept US dollars, so be sure to have pesos on you if they will take you (latest reports suggest that this is becoming increasingly difficult). Beware of unofficial taxis at the airport arrival gate who will overcharge.

Town buses are frequent and cheap (10 centavos flat rate fare), though crowded, and run hourly through the night as well. Destinations are sometimes indicated above or behind windshield. There are long queues for all buses; you must find out who is the last in the queue (*el último*).

The **out-of-town bus services** (reconfirm booking 30 minutes before departure) leave from the Terminal de Omnibus Interprovinciales, Av Rancho Boyeros (Independencia), buses Nos 67 and 84 go there from the hotel area, and No 47 from Prado and Animas near *Hotel Caribbean*. See **Information for Visitors** for advance booking addresses. **Trains** leave from the station in Av Monserrate (de Bélgica), Havana, to the larger cities. Trains for Pinar del Río leave from the West (Occidente) station. It is sometimes easier to get a seat on a train than on a bus (though there are waiting lists for buses), but all public transport out of Havana is heavily booked in advance and difficult to get on. Staff at the train station have been said to be unhelpful in providing information on departures, with little interest in helping you travel. The procedure and the prices change frequently. It might be easier to take a local bus to a nearby town, such as Santa Cruz, where buses can be caught to Matanzas. For details of services, **see below**.

The **peso taxi** base is beside the Interprovincial bus terminal (see also **Information for Visitors**).

Bicycle Hire from **Panataxi**, car-park in corner of O'Reilly and Cuba, Tel: 810153, US$1 per hour, US$12 per day. Check the bicycle carefully.

Airport José Martí, 18 km from Havana. No departure tax. Turistaxi to airport, US$13 (US$14 at night, US$11 Vedado-airport). The Cubatur desk will book a taxi for you from the airport, US$15 to old Havana. You can get from the airport to Vedado by taking bus No 76 (bus stop about 700 metres from terminal along road to your left and on other side), then changing at Ciudad Deportivo to No 84, or to the old part of Havana by staying on until the last stop and then changing to No 65. Each ride 10 centavos.

East from Havana

Short ferry rides across Havana Bay to Casablanca and Regla (10 centavos) are fun and a good way of looking at these "across the bay" villages and Havana itself from a different perspective. The best view of Havana is from Morro Castle.

An easy excursion is to Cojimar, the seaside village featured in Hemingway's *The Old Man and the Sea*. Take local bus (65 and others). The coastline is dirty because of effluent from tankers, but it is a quiet, pretty place to relax. *La Terraza* is a restaurant ("dollars") with a pleasant view, reasonably priced seafood meals.

Guanabacoa is 5 km to the east and is reached by a road turning off the Central Highway, or by No 29 bus or by launch from Muelle Luz (not far from No 9 on the map) to the suburb of Regla, then by bus direct to Guanabacoa. It is a well preserved small colonial town; sights include the old parish church which has a splendid altar: the monastery of San Francisco; the Carral theatre; and some attractive mansions. The Historical Museum of Guanabacoa, a former estate mansion, has an unusual voodoo collection in the former slave quarters at the back of the building, Calle Martí 108, between San Antonio and Versalles, Tel: 90-9117; take buses 5, 95 or 195. Open: Monday and Wednesday to Saturday 1330-2130, Sunday 0900-1300.

A delightful colonial town, ***Santa María del Rosario***, founded in 1732, is 16 km East of Havana. It is reached from Cotorro, on the Central Highway, or by 97 bus from Guanabacoa, and was carefully restored and preserved before the Revolution. The village church is particularly good. See the paintings, one by Veronese. There are curative springs nearby.

Hemingway fans may wish to visit the house in San Francisco de Paula, 11 km. from the centre, where he lived from 1939 to 1960 (called the Museo Hemingway, Tel: 082-2515). Bus 7 or 107 from park next to Capitolio, 10 cents (no change on bus), signpost opposite Post Office, leading up short driveway. Open Tuesday-Saturday, 0900-1700, Sunday 0900-1300 (closed on rainy days). Entry US$2. Visitors are not allowed inside the plain whitewashed house which has been lovingly preserved with all Hemingway's furniture and books, just as he left it. But you can walk all around the outside and look in through the windows and open doors, although vigilant staff prohibit any photographs. There is a small annex building with one room used for temporary exhibitions, and from the upper floors there are fine views over Havana. The garden is beautiful and tropical, with many shady palms. Next to the swimming pool (empty) are the gravestones of Hemingway's pet dogs, shaded by a flowering shrub. There is a bust of the author in the village of Cojimar.

Some 60 km east of Havana is *Jibacoa* beach, which is excellent for snorkelling as the reefs are close to the beach. To get there take bus 70 to Santa Cruz del Norte and from there either a 126 or "La Matancera"—be warned, though, that the journey takes some time. From the bus stop walk to the beach. Peso taxi Santa Cruz del Norte-Havana, 13 pesos. (*Camping de Jibacoa*, cabins for 4 or 2. Food is rather expensive: 1.40 pesos for breakfast, 5 for lunch, 5 for dinner.)

The old provincial town of *Matanzas* lies 104 km east of Havana along the Vía Blanca, which links the capital with Varadero beach, 34 km further east. There are frequent buses but the journey via the Hershey Railway is more memorable (four trains daily—3 hours, 1.03 pesos—from the Casablanca station, which is reached by public launch from near La Fuerza Castle, 0.50 peso). Those who wish to make it a day trip from Havana can do so, long queues for return tickets, best to get one as soon as you arrive. There are three peso hotels, always full, and nowhere for tourists to eat.

In Matanzas one should visit the Pharmaceutical Museum (Monday-Saturday 1400-1800, 1900-2100), the Matanzas Museum (Tuesday-Sunday 1500-1800, 1900-2200), and the cathedral, all near Parque La Libertad. There is a wonderful view of the surrounding countryside from the church of Montserrat. Bellamar Cave is only 5 km from Matanzas.

From Matanzas one can continue on to *Varadero*, 144 km from Havana, Cuba's chief beach resort with all facilities. It is undergoing large scale development of new hotels and cabins and joint ventures with foreign investors are being encouraged. 5,000 rooms had been built by 1991, with the aim of expanding to 30,000 rooms by the turn of the century. A Cuban-Spanish joint venture has opened two resort hotels managed by Sol Hotels of Spain: *Sol Pétalos* and *Sol Palmeras* (T 566110, US$100d, room only), while Jamaican investors have built the 160-room *Cactus* to be followed by a 250-room hotel later. Meliá, also of Spain, opened the *Meliá Gran Varadero* in 1991 (T 66220, US$150d, room only, 5 star). In Varadero all hotels, restaurants and excursions must be paid in US dollars; pesos only for local bus rides and the cinema. Book excursions at *Hotel Internacional*, Av Las Américas. Each November a festival is held in Varadero, lasting a week, which attracts some of the best artists in South America. Entrance US$2-10 per day. From Varadero it is possible to explore the interesting town of *Cárdenas*, where the present Cuban flag was raised for the first time in

1850. The sea here is polluted with oil and the air smells of phosphorous. Another excursion is to Neptune's Cave (thought a more appealing name than the old one, Cepero), which is south of the town of Carboneras, half-way between Matanzas and Varadero. It has an underground lagoon, stalagmites and stalactites, evidence of Indian occupation and was used as a clandestine hospital during the war of independence.

Where To Stay In Varadero (All prices high season, double, note that many hotels are changing names in 1992/93) *Paradiso*, US$140, attached to *Puntarenas*, also US$140, with all resort facilities, 3 pools, watersports, all shared by both hotels, good restaurants, fresh seafood, recommended. *Los Cactus*, US$78; *Kawama Inn*, US$64; *Internacional*, US$90-135d; *Oasis*, US$61; the *Siboney*, US$76; *Villa Punta Blanca*, made up of a number of former private residences with some new complexes; *Caribe*, US$42. *Pullman*, US$34, best value for the independent traveller; *Ledo*, Av Playa, US$30, not recommended; *Villa La Herradura*, Av Playa, US$37; *Los Delfines*, Av Playa, US$38. *Solymar Cabines* (adjacent to *Hotel Internacional*, whose facilities can be shared), US$52, recommended, pool, bar and shop but no restaurant; *Rincón Francés*, campsite 10 km from town, hourly 220 bus, *cabañas*, many mosquitoes.

Where to Eat Recommended restaurants, all between US$9-15, are *Mi Casita* (book in advance), *La Cabañita, Halong, La Esquinita, El Mesón del Quijote* (Spanish) and buffets at the restaurants of hotels *Kawama* and *Arenas Blancas*. *Albacora*, disappointing, all dishes except *pescado*, US$12-18, but if you want fish you may be told '*no hay*'; *Las Américas*, beautiful setting, food good one night, inedible the next; *Terrace* cafeteria at the *International* for the best lunches; *Bodegón Criollo*, pleasant atmosphere, popular, no vegetarian food. *Coppelia*, in town centre, ice cream US$0.90. It is now easier to buy food in Varadero because the new Aparthotels (*Varazul, La Herradura*) have a small food store.

Moped rental US$7.50 per hour, US$15 3 hours, US$24 for 24 hours, a good way to see the city.

A cheap, recommended method of getting to Varadero is to take the train to Matanzas (see above), then a taxi to Matanzas bus terminal (3 pesos) from where you catch a bus, 0.40 pesos, about 1 hour (state destination, take ticket, wait for bus and then your number to be called, and run for the bus). About 5½ hours in all.

Santa Clara, 300 km from Havana and 196 km from Varadero, is a pleasant university city in the centre of the island. It was the site of the last battle of the Cuban revolution before Castro entered Havana, and the Batista troop train captured by Che Guevara can be seen near the cathedral. There are two "dollar hotels", *Motel Los Caneyes* (outside the city), US$32 and *Santa Clara Libre* (central, on Plaza Vidal), US$24.

Cienfuegos, on the south coast, is an attractive seaport and industrial city 80 km from Trinidad and 70 km from Santa Clara. Interesting colonial buildings around the central Parque Martí. There are one "dollar hotel", *Jagua*, US$45, comfortable, palatial restaurant next door, gorgeous decor, live piano music, food basic; two "peso hotels", *Perla del Sur*, and *Ciervo del Oro*, Calle 29, No 5614 (entre 56 y 58), Tel: 5757, 11 pesos, both booked up three weeks in advance by the central booking agency. Many of the hotels are out of town or booked solid by Cubans. *Hotel Pasacaballo*, US$35 and *Rancho Luna*, US$31, are seaside complexes with cafeteria etc.

From Cienfuegos take a taxi to Playa Girón and the Bay of Pigs (26 pesos, 1½ hours). Ask the driver to wait while you visit the beach and tourist complex, and the site of national pilgrimage where, in 1961, the disastrous US-backed invasion of Cuba was attempted. Further west from Girón is the Zapata Peninsula, an area of swamps, mangroves, beaches and much bird and animal life. Access from Playa Larga or Guamá, inland. You can rent a cabin at Playa Girón (US$29) or Playa Larga (US$26). There is a crocodile farm at the Zapata Tourist Institute in Guamá, which can be visited. Varadero hotels organize day excursions for US$35 pp which includes lunch, English-speaking guide and a boat ride on the lagoon.

Trinidad, 133 km south of Santa Clara is a perfect relic of the early days of the Spanish colony: beautifully preserved streets and buildings with hardly a trace of the 20th century anywhere. It was founded in 1514 as a base for expeditions into the "New World"; Cortés set out from here for Mexico in 1518. The five main squares and four churches date from the 18th and 19th centuries; the whole city, with its fine palaces, cobbled streets and tiled roofs, is a national monument. The **Museo Romántico**, next to the church of Santíssima Trinidad on the main square, is excellent. It has a collection of romantic-style porcelain, glass, paintings and ornate furniture displayed in a colonial mansion, with beautiful views from the upper floor balconies. Admission free, no cameras allowed. **Museo de Historia Nacional** is on Calle Simón Bolívar, an attractive building but rather dull displays, admission free. The **Museo de Arte**, on the corner of Simón Bolívar and the main square, has a small collection of works by local artists, plus a few prints of old masterpieces, such as the Mona Lisa, admission free. One block from the church is the *Casa de la Trova*, open weekend lunchtimes and evenings, entry free. Excellent live Cuban music with a warm, lively atmosphere. "At lunchtime there was a range of drinks, sold to tourists with US$ only, but in the evening aguardiente was being served (from a plastic bucket), 10 cents a shot to all". There are mostly Cubans here, of all age groups, and it's a great place to watch, and join in with, the locals having a good time. Another venue for live music is *La Canchanchara*, Calle Real 44, Tel: 4345. Open 0900-1700, cocktails, no food. More touristy than *Casa de La Trova* (cigar and souvenir shop), but good traditional music at lunchtimes. Nearby are the excellent beaches of La Boca (8 km), a small fishing village, restaurant on beach, some buses or taxi. Inland from Trinidad are the beautiful, wooded Escambray mountains. There is no public transport but day trips are organized to Topes de Collantes by the *Hotel Ancón*, for US$43 pp. Their tour includes lunch, cocktail (at 1000) and visits coffee plantations, a crystal clear swimming pond and a pretty waterfall. Half-way up the mountainside, the paved road gives way to dirt track. Passengers transfer from air-conditioned mini-bus to Russian four-wheel drive lorry, an exhilarating experience! You can see hummingbirds and the tocororo, the national bird of Cuba. A great day out. There is also a huge hospital in the mountains, which offers special therapeutic treatments for patients from all over the world, and a hotel *Los Helechos*, US$26d—details about both places at the *Hotel Ancón*.

Where To Stay In Trinidad Hard to find, particularly in summer. *Motel Las Cuevas*, US$30d, on a hill 10 minutes' walk from town, chalets with balconies, very comfortable rooms with air-conditioning, TV, fridge, hot water, and very clean, two swimming pools, bar, discotheque (most rooms are far enough away not to be disturbed by noise), dollar shop, restaurant (about three waitresses per table but slow service and cold food), very good value, recommended. *Costa Sur*, good value, 10 km out of town, US$32, taxi fare approximately US$9. Pesos hotels are now closed down. Campsites at Ancón beach and La Boca (5-bed apartments for 10 pesos a night). Camping at Base Manacal in the mountains: tent or small hut for US$5 per day; take No 10 bus from Cienfuegos. The only restaurant seems to be (March 1992) the *Mesón del Regidor* on Calle Simón Bolívar, small menu but elegant setting. There are also a couple of dollar tiendas in the centre selling souvenirs, postcards and imported snacks.

Transport from Havana: a/c buses at 0335 (arrive 0905) and 1220 (arrive 1750), 8 pesos. Train from Estación 19 de Noviembre (on Tulipán) to Cienfuegos, number 1301 departs 2146 arrives 0440, number 1303 departs 0725 arrives 1420, 7 hours to travel 250 km; taxi to Cienfuegos, 20 pesos per person, from base beside Interprovincial bus terminal, then on to Trinidad. From Santa Clara to Cienfuegos there are about 10 buses daily; from Santa Clara to Trinidad only two. Transport to the east of Cuba is difficult from Trinidad as it is not on the Carretera Central. Best to go to Sancti Spiritus (see below) and bus from there, about 1½ hours through beautiful hilly scenery, 50 cents. As elsewhere, severe shortages and huge queues, trucks and tractors with trailers may be laid on as a back-up.

13 km. from Trinidad is Playa Ancón (not a town as such—just two resort hotels: *Costa Sur* and *Ancón*). The *Ancón*, Tel: 4011, is US$41d with air-conditioning, though they encourage you to take the daily package rate of US$100 including three meals, drinks and such extras as snorkels, bicycles and horse riding. Good restaurant, snack bar and many facilities, popular for families. The beach is lovely, pure white sand and clean turquoise water, highly recommended.

Sancti Spiritus, about 80 km from Trinidad and 90 km from Santa Clara, can be reached by bus from Cienfuegos, Santa Clara or Trinidad (2 hours over a mountain road through the Escambray). Daily train from Havana, 0645, 5.30 pesos, 6 hours (but may take 9 or more). The train seats are very comfortable, though the journey is hot and stuffy through flat countryside, endless fields of sugar cane and a few villages. Buffet car on board (serving tinned grapefruit juice, bread with oil, rice and beans), intriguing queueing system with cards, giving priority to pregnant mothers, the elderly, the disabled and children. It is one of Cuba's seven original Spanish towns and has a wealth of buildings from the colonial period. There are two peso hotels, the *Perla de Cuba* and the *Colonial*, both on the Parque Central. The former is a crumbling 19th century stuccoed building in splendid baroque decay, the latter is seedy and lacks the grandeur of the *Perla*. The nearest tourist hotel is the *Zaza*, US$32, 10 km outside the town on the Zaza artificial lake, rather run down but service and food praised by Cubans.

The Museo Ignacio Agramonte in the large city of ***Camagüey***, half-way between Santa Clara and Santiago, is one of the biggest and most impressive museums in the country. *Hotel Camagüey*, US$35, Carretera Central, Tel: 8834/6218; *Puerto Príncipe*, US$31, Av de los Mártires y Andrés Sánchez, La Vigía (in town), Tel: 7575/78; *Gran Hotel*, US$31, Maceo 67, Tel: 2093/4, and the *Plaza*, US$34, are the "dollar" hotels; "peso hotels": *Colón*, República 472, Tel: 2553 and *Isla de Cuba*, San Esteban y A. Popular, both 9 pesos.

Two tourist enclave developments have been built at Santa Lucía near Nuevitas, on the coast north of Camagüey, and at Marca del Portillo, on the coast south of Camagüey.

Holguín, a provincial capital in the east, near Santiago, has the *Hotel Pernik*, US$41; *Motel El Bosque* US$27, and *Motel Mirador de Mayabe*, US$24. From Holguín the Atlantic resort of Guardalavaca (*Hotel Guardalavaca*, pool, recommended, "dollar hotel", US$30), with good beach, can be reached by bus.

Santiago de Cuba, near the east end of the island, 970 km from Havana and 670 km from Santa Clara, is Cuba's second city and "capital moral de la Revolución Cubana". It is a pleasant colonial Caribbean city, with many balconies and *rejas* (grills). Of the several museums, the best is the Colonial Museum located in Diego de Velázquez' house (the oldest in Cuba), at the northwest corner of Parque Céspedes. It has been restored after its use as offices after the Revolution and is in two parts, one 16th century, one 18th century (each room shows a particular period; open Tuesday-Saturday 0800-2200, Sunday 0900-1300, Monday 0800-1200,

1400-1800, free). On the south side of Parque Céspedes is the Cathedral, and on the north side the Alcaldía. Two blocks east of the Parque, opposite the Palacio Provincial is the Museo Bacardí (exhibits from prehistory to the Revolution downstairs, paintings upstairs), open Monday 1400-1800, Tuesday-Saturday 0800-2145, Sunday 0900-1300. Also visit the Moncada barracks museum and the house of Frank País (General Bandera 226), leader of the armed uprising in Santiago on 30 November 1956, who was shot in July 1957. The national hero, José Martí, is buried in Santa Efigenia cemetery, just west of the city. Another historical site is the huge ceiba tree in the grounds of the *Leningrado* hotel, beneath which Spain and the USA signed the surrender of Santiago on 16 July 1898; at the Loma de San Juan nearby are more monuments of the Hispano-Cuban-American war (only worth visiting if staying at the *Leningrado*, or going to the zoo and amusement park behind the hotel).

The Festival de Caribe runs from 16 to 19 April, with traditional African dancing and beautiful costumes. There is daily live music and singing every weekend at the Casa de la Trova on Calle Heredia (but hope that there is no modern music at the Casa de Estudiantes Josué País García next door to drown out the real thing).

For stamp and coin collectors, the *círculo filatélico* and *numismático* is held every Sunday morning on the Plaza de la Catedral near the hotel reservations office.

Where To Stay In Santiago *Motel Versalles*, between airport and town, US$47; *Leningrado* (too far out of town, turistaxi US$3.95, a complex with cabins, pool, bar and several restaurants for which there are always queues, water shortages, being refurbished in April 1992, noisy from building work), US$30; *Las Américas*, US$35, not so far out of town, lively, recommended (turistaxi US$2.35); not far away is the new *Hotel Santiago*, Av Las Américas (10) y M, about US$100 a night, 5-star, swimming pool; and *Balcón del Caribe*, next to Castillo del Morro, US$32, overlooking the sea, quiet, pool, basic food, cold water in bungalows, pleasant but inconvenient for the town. *MES*, Calle L and 7 Terraza (about 5 blocks north of *Las Américas*), Tel: 4-2398, is the cheapest-dollar hotel at US$10 pp with colour TV and fan, two rooms share bath and fridge. The "peso hotels" are *Casa Granda* (where you will probably have to pay dollars, US$7s, US$9d, restricted water supply but great location and it's the best place to stay, consequently usually full, closed for refurbishment in April 1992), on Parque Céspedes, restaurant meals US$3-6 (book at the office 20 metres from corner of hotel, alongside cathedral, not at the Tourism Bureau at the corner of the same street); *Imperial*, José A Saco 261; *Libertad*, Aguilera 658; *Rex*, Av Garzón 10 (cheapest); *Venus*, San Félix 658, all 5-12 pesos. You can reserve beach accommodation in Santiago and pay in pesos, eg a Siboney apartment, two rooms, four people, 18 pesos, Mar Verde, crowded at weekends, a *cabaña*, basic, three people, 8 pesos.

Telephones For calls outside Santiago, Centro de Comunicaciones Nacional e Internacional, Heredia y Félix Pena, underneath the cathedral.

Train Santiago-Havana, 16.80 pesos, 12-20 hours; the day train takes longer than the night train.

Bus Terminal near Plaza de la Revolución for reservations.

For private/unofficial taxis, ask around the park at Av Victoriano Garzón and Plácido; you may be lucky.

Excursions

Excellent excursions can be made to the Gran Piedra (26 km inland—a viewpoint from which it is said you can see Haiti and Jamaica on a clear day, more likely their lights on a clear night "a must, but about 450 steps up to see the view, only for the fit") and along the Ruta Turística to the Castillo del Morro, a clifftop fort with a museum of the sea, piracy and local history (open all week, but only morning on Monday). Recommended, even if only for the view. Turistaxi to El Morro, US$5.50-6 round trip with wait. The road passes the ferry to the resorts of Cayo Granma and La Socapa in the estuary (5 cents each way). Also to Parque Bacanao, a wonderful amusement park in which you can visit La Granjita, El Valle Prehistórico (with lifesize replicas of dinosaurs), an old car and trailer museum (free, recommended) and the Daiquirí Beach and Hotel, basic facilities, quiet. There are buses Nos 14, 35 & 62 to the public beaches in the park. Siboney, the nearest beach to Santiago, is pleasant and unpretentious. Take bus 214 from Avenida Pujol (by junction with Av 10) or from near bus terminal. Make sure to catch a return bus before 1600; very crowded at weekends. Even nicer is Junagua beach, bus 207, along the same road; further development is projected in this area. Ten minutes from the centre of Santiago there is a rum factory, open to visitors, US$6 for a guided tour with English-speaking guide, including free sample.

From Santiago, it is possible to visit El Cobre (bus No 3) where the shrine of Cuba's patron saint, the Virgen de la Caridad del Cobre, is located (there is a hotel and reasonable restaurant). Interesting collection of personal offerings at foot of the statue, including a gold model of Fidel Castro.

Baracoa, 150 km east of Santiago, close to the most easterly point of the island, is an attractive place surrounded by a fruitful countryside. It is well worth the trip from Santiago (4 hrs drive) for the scenery of the last section of road, called La Farola, which winds through lush tropical mountains and then descends steeply to the coast. "Dollar hotel" *Castillo* remodelled in 1990, recommended, friendly staff, food OK, nice views, good swimming pool, US$42; "peso hotel" *Plaza*. The Cubana office is on Plaza Martí. The taxi base is in front of the hospital. Bus to Guantánamo takes 4 hours.

Guantánamo 80 km from Santiago on the Baracoa road, is close to the US base of the same name (which cannot be easily visited from Cuba). "Dollar hotel" *Guantánamo*, US$27; "peso hotel" *Brasil*.

Guardalavaca on the north coast is a lovely drive through the mountains from Santiago. Take a day driving to Frente II (eat at Rancho México), down to Sagua and across to Guardalavaca, which is beautiful and recommended. You can stay at Don Lino beach, which is small but pleasant, where there are comfortable huts (US$14) with refrigerator for cooling beer. Restaurant food is basic.

West from Santiago runs a wonderful coastal road along the Sierra Maestra with beautiful bays and beaches, completely deserted, some with black sand. It is only possible to visit by car. At La Plata, about 150 km from Santiago, is a little museum about the Cuban guerrillas' first successful battle. There is no curator so ask the local people to open it. En route you pass Las Coloradas, the beach where *Granma* landed. You can make a circular route back to Santiago via Manzanillo, Bayamo and Palma Soriano.

West from Havana

West from Havana a dual carriage highway has been completed almost to **Pinar del Río**, the major city west of Havana. At the eastern entrance to the city is the modern **Hotel Pinar del Río**, swimming pool, night club etc,

US$32; also the **Vuelta Abajo**, recommended, and the **Hotel Occidente**, Calle Gerardo Medina, clean but old, both under 20 pesos. For travel to Pinar del Río, train from Havana's West station, rather than bus, is recommended (leaves Havana 0512, leaves Pinar del Río 1702, arrives Havana 2206, 3.30 pesos each way); slow but comfortable.

If travelling by car on this route, you can make a detour to **Soroa** in the Sierra de Rosario, 81 km southwest of the capital. It is a spa and resort in luxuriant hills. As you drive into the area, a sign on the right indicates the Mirador de Venus and Baños Romanos. Past the baths is the *Bar Edén* (open till 1800), where you can park before walking up to the Mirador (25 minutes). From the top you get fine views of the southern plains, the palm-covered Sierra and the tourist complex itself; lots of birds, butterflies, dragonflies and lizards around the path; many flowers in season.

The road continues into the complex where there is an orchidarium with over 700 species (guided tours between 0830-1140, 1340-1555 daily, US$2) and the **Castillo de las Nubes** restaurant (1130-2200, entrees US$5-6), a mock castle. At the resort are cabins (US$32 high season), restaurant *El Centro* (quite good), disco, bar, olympic swimming pool, bike rental, riding nearby and handicrafts and dollar shops. Despite the ugly, gloomy cabins, it's a peaceful place and would be more so without the loud juke box.

Nearer Pinar del Río another detour north off the main road is to the spa of San Diego de los Baños, also in fine scenery in the Sierra de los Organos.

North of Pinar del Río, on a road which leads to the north coast and eventually back to Havana is **Viñales**, a delightful small town in a dramatic valley. Stands of palm and tobacco fields with their drying barns (*vegas*, steep, thatch-roofed buildings which you can enter and photograph with ease) lie amid sheer and rounded mountains reminiscent of a Chinese landscape, especially at dawn and dusk. These massifs were part of a cave system which collapsed millions of years ago and, on some, remnants of stalactites can still be seen.

6 km beyond Viñales is the Cueva del Indio which can be approached from two ends, neither far apart. Inside, though, you can travel the cave's length on foot and by boat (US$2 for foreigners), very beautiful. There is a restaurant at the cave (also at a smaller cave nearer Viñales).

Viñales itself is a pleasant town, with trees and wooden colonnades along the main street, red tiled roofs and a main square with a little-used cathedral and a Casa de Cultura with art gallery.

Where To Stay In Viñales *Motel Los Jazmines*, 3 km before the town, in a superb location overlooking the valley, US$31d, reasonable restaurant, bar with snacks available, shops, swimming pool, riding, easy transport, recommended; *La Ermita*, US$40d, 3 km from town with good view, pool (not always usable), reasonable food, but criticized for dingy rooms, arbitrary surcharges, unhelpful staff, no taxis; *Rancho San Vicente*, near Cueva del Indio, US$31, nice pool, pleasant. Book your hotel before you arrive as everywhere is often full.

Turistaxi from Havana to *Motel Los Jazmines* takes 2½ hours, but a bus back to the capital is easy to catch, 3½ hours, 2.70 pesos.

From Viñales to Havana along the coast road takes about 4 hours by car. It is an attractive drive through sugar and tobacco plantations, pines, the mountains inland, the coast occasionally visible. All the small houses have flower gardens in front. You pass through La Palma, Las Pozas (which has a ruined church with a boring new one beside it), Bahía Honda and Cabañas; many agricultural collectives along the way. After Cabañas the road deteriorates; either rejoin the motorway back to the capital, or take the old coast road through the port of Mariel to enter Havana on Av 5. Off this avenue is the Marina Hemingway tourist complex, with *El Viejo y El Mar*. Also in this area is *Hotel Tritón*, US$65 a Cubatur hotel operated by Cubanacán.

In the Gulf of Batabanó is the *Isla de la Juventud* (Isle of Youth), 97 km from the main island, reached by daily Cubana flights. At about 3,050 square kilometres, it is not much smaller than Trinidad, but its population is only 60,000. It gets its present name from the educational courses run there, particularly for overseas students. Columbus, who discovered it in 1494 called the island Evangelista and, until recently, it was called the Isla de Pinos. From the 19th century until the Revolution its main function was as a prison and both José Martí and Fidel Castro served time there. Today the main activities are citrus-growing, fishing and tourism. There are several beaches and ample opportunities for water sports. The capital is Nueva Gerona, with a museum in the old Model Prison (El Presidio) and four others. Main tourist hotel is *El Colony* (US$70 high season).

Cayo Largo, east of Isla de la Juventud, is a westernized island resort reached by air from Havana (US$45 return), or by light plane or boat from Juventud, or by charter plane from Grand Cayman. There are four hotels here at present, with all facilities shared and included in the package cost (prices quoted are high season per person and include 3 meals and free use of all water sports and other acitivites). *Cabañas* (Villa Capricho), US$110, *Isla del Sur*, US$105, *Pueblito* (Villa Coral) US$100, *Club* (Villa Iguana) US$95. The hotels and the thatched *cabañas* are low-lying and pleasantly spread out in gardens by the beach. Snorkelling and scuba-diving can be done at Playa Sirena, 10 minutes' boat ride away. Very tame iguanas can be spotted at another nearby cay, Cayo Rico (day-trips available for US$37 from Cayo Largo). Cayo Largo can also be visited for the day, from Havana or Vaaradevo, US$89 including return flight and lunch etc. (organized in Cuba by Turcimex, 5ta Avenida No 8203, Miramar, Havana, Tel: 228230). There are several restaurants attached to the hotels, including a highly recommended Italian place and a good pizzería. As with many Cuban resort hotels restaurants are run on a self-service buffet basis and food is reported to be plentiful and fresh. Hotel expansion is planned to cater for watersport tourism. Cayos Rosario and Avalos, between Juventud and Largo, have not yet been developed.

Information for Visitors

Documents

Visitors from the majority of countries need only a tourist card to enter Cuba, as long as they are going solely for tourist purposes. A tourist card may be obtained from Cuban embassies, consulates, or approved Cubatur agents (price in the UK £9-10, some other countries US$15). From some countries (eg Canada) tourist cards are handed out on the plane and checked by visa control at the airport; the first one is free but replacements cost US$10. Nationals of other countries

without visa-free agreement with Cuba, journalists and those visiting on other business must check what visa requirements pertain. US citizens wishing to visit Cuba should contact Marazul Tours, 250 West 57th Street, Suite 1311, New York City, 10107 New York, Tel: 212-582 9570, or Miami Tel: 305-232 8157 (information also from Havanatur, Calle 24 No 4314, La Sierra, Havana, Tel: 29-3555). In the USA, the Swiss Embassy in Washington, DC now represents the Cuban interests section and will process applications for visas. Visas can take several weeks to be granted, and are apparently difficult to obtain for people other than businessmen, guests of the Cuban Government or Embassy officials. When the applicant is too far from a Cuban consulate to be able to apply conveniently for a visa, he may apply direct to the Cuban Foreign Ministry for a visa waiver. The Cuban Consulate in Mexico refuses to issue visas unless you have pre-arranged accommodation and book through a travel agent; even then, only tourist visas are available. Visitors may stay in Cuba for 72 hours in transit without tourist card or visa.

Visitors travelling on a visa must go in person to Cubatur or the Immigration Office for registration the day after arrival. The office is on the corner of Calle 22 and Av 3, Miramar. (Bus 132 from the old city centre, get off at second stop after the tunnel; also bus 32 from La Rampa or *Coppelia* ice-cream parlour in Vedado, alight at same stop.) When you register you will be given an exit permit.

Travellers coming from or going through infected areas must have certificates of vaccination against cholera and yellow fever.

Some Latin American countries will not admit anyone carrying a passport stamped by the Cuban authorities but the Cubans will not insist on stamping your passport in and out if you ask them not to.

British business travellers should get "Hints to Exporters: Cuba", from DTI Export Publications, PO Box 55, Stratford-upon-Avon, Warwickshire, CV37 9GE. US citizens on business with Cuba should contact Foreign Assets Control, Federal Reserve Bank of New York, 33 Liberty St, NY 10045. Another useful leaflet "Tips For Travelers to Cuba" is available from the Passport Office, US Department of State, Washington DC 20524.

How To Get There

From Europe, Cubana flies from Berlin, Brussels, Lisbon and Paris, Iberia and Cubana from Madrid. There is a recently-introduced charter flight in conjunction with Thomson Holidays from Stansted to Varadero, via Gander in Canada, £349-369, weekly July to end-August, variable frequency at other times (Canadian visas required for the appropriate nationalities as this route involves customs clearance in transit. Price quoted by South American Experience).

Cubana and Aeroflot from Moscow. Aeroflot has one route via Luxembourg and one via Shannon (Eire). Some Aeroflot flights continue on to Lima. It is essential to check Aeroflot's flights to make sure there really is a plane going. Since Havana no longer enjoys the close relationship with Moscow that it used to have, these flights are now reported to be increasingly unreliable.

From the American mainland, Cubana from Montréal, Cubana and Mexicana de Aviación from Mexico City with some Mexicana flights via Mérida, Viasa and Aeropostal from Caracas, Cubana from Managua, Buenos Aires, Lima, Panama and Santiago de Chile. Within the Caribbean Cubana flies to Santo Domingo in the Dominican Republic (as does Iberia) and Kingston, Jamaica.

The frequency of these flights depends on the season, with twice weekly flights in the winter being reduced to once a week in the summer. Some of the longer haul flights, such as to Buenos Aires, are cut from once every two weeks in winter to once a month in summer. There are daily charters to Miami (US$157, but lots of restrictions on who can use this route) and twice a week to Cancún, Mexico, with ABC/Celimar, enquire at Havanatur. Weekly charter flights between Santiago de Cuba and Montego Bay, Jamaica. Regular charters between Cayo Largo and Grand Cayman. VASP has weekly charters from São Paulo, Brazil.

Mexicana de Aviación organizes package tours (see **Travel Agencies** below for ticket sellers). Unitours (Canada) run package tours to Cuba for all nationalities. Package tours also available from Venezuela. From the Bahamas, charter flights with Bahatours (Tel: 809 328 7985), Mondays and Fridays, weekend package tours, **see page 117**.

It is advisable to book your flight out of Cuba before actually going there as arranging it there can be time-consuming. Furthermore, it is essential to reconfirm onward flights as soon as you arrive in Cuba, otherwise you will lose your reservation.

No passenger ships call regularly.

Internal Air Services

Cubana de Aviación services between most of the main towns. From Havana to Camagüey (US$38), Cienfuegos, (US$20) Holguín ((US$44), Baracoa (US$58), Guantánamo (US$54), Manzanillo

(US$44), Moa (US$54), Nueva Gerona (US$12), Bayamo (US$44), Ciego de Avila (US$32), Tunas (US$42), Isla de Juventud (US$12) and Santiago (US$50) all have airports. Tourists must pay airfares in US$; it is advisable to prebook flights at home as demand is very heavy. It is difficult to book flights from one city to another when you are not at the point of departure, except from Havana, the computer is not able to cope. Airports are usually a long way from the towns, so extra transport costs will be necessary.

Airline Offices

All are situated in Havana, at the seaward end of Calle 23 (La Rampa), Vedado: eg Cubana, Calle 23 esq, Infanta, Tel: 7-4911; Aeroflot, Calle 23, No 64, Tel: 79-6138. Iberia, Tel: 72729; Mexicana, Tel: 792041, Viasa, Tel: 305011.

Customs

Personal baggage and articles for personal use are allowed in free of duty; so are 200 cigarettes, or 25 cigars, or 1 lb of tobacco, and 2 bottles of alcoholic drinks. Many things are scarce or unobtainable in Cuba: take in everything you are likely to need other than food (say razor blades, medicines and pills, tampons, reading and writing materials and photographic supplies). The X-ray scanners at customs reportedly do not affect the film in plastic containers but do affect film left in the camera.

Buses

The local word for bus is *guagua*. In 1991 it was very difficult to get on a bus, not many were running, because of the fuel shortages, some would take you a maximum of 60 km and others made it almost impossible for a foreigner to get on. Three days' wait in the station for a ticket was reported in 1991. From Varadero: to Havana 3 pesos (2 hours); to Santa Clara 2.50 pesos (4 hours). From Santa Clara to Santiago 13.20 pesos. From Holguín to Santiago 3.85 pesos (six departures daily, there are four to Havana). There are buses at 1330 and 0130 from Camagüey to Santiago. The 20-hour journey from Santiago to Havana costs 27.50 pesos, and leaves daily at 0500 and 1930. (It is best to travel on weekdays and at night.) From Havana to Santiago 1320 and 1930. Havana to Matanzas, 1.35 pesos, 2 hours; Havana-Cienfuegos, 6.50 pesos; Santa Clara to Cienfuegos, 0.60 peso, 2 hours; Cienfuegos to Trinidad, 1.20 pesos, 2

hours; Trinidad to Sancti Spiritus, 0.90 peso, 2 hours; Sancti Spiritus to Santiago, 13.20 pesos, 10 hours; Santiago—Guantánamo, 1.10 peso; Guantánamo-Baracoa, 2.30 pesos, 4 hours. The urban bus fare throughout Cuba is 10 centavos and you have to have the exact fare. In the rush hours they are filled to more than capacity, making it hard to get off if you have managed to get on. Cubans are very helpful if you are lost or have got on the wrong bus.

Bus Reservations

Tickets between towns must be purchased in advance from: Oficina Reservaciones Pasajes, Calle 21, esq 4, Vedado; Plazoleta de la Virgen del Camino, San Miguel del Padrón; Calzada 10 de Octubre y Carmen, Centro; Terminal de Omnibus Nacional, Boyeros y 19 de Mayo (all in Havana). However, the booking offices are often shut, increasing the difficulties of travelling around Cuba. In March 1992 Cubatur directed travellers to the office on the corner of Calles 21 and 4. This is the main booking office for buses and trains from Havana to anywhere in the country, one-way only. It is open Monday to Friday, 1200-1745, organized chaos. Bus tickets are sold up to 1 day in advance, train tickets up to 3 days, payable in pesos. Look for notices in the window for latest availabilities, find out who is last in the queues (separate queues for buses and trains, sometimes waiting numbers issued), and ask around for what is the best bet. Maximum 3 tickets sold per person, buses usually harder to get on than trains. If willing to pay in dollars, the Assistur office on Paso Martí, "somewhere between *Hotel Caribbean* and Parque José Martí", open 24 hours, will secure tickets without too much delay

Trains

Recommended whenever possible. Be at station at least 30 minutes before scheduled departure time, you have to queue to reconfirm your seat and have your ticket stamped. See above for latest booking procedure. Fares, payable in pesos, are very cheap, e.g. 5.30 pesos for the 6 hour journey to Sancti Spiritus (nearest station for Trinidad). See the text above for details. Bicycles can be carried as an express item only.

NB In major bus and train terminals, ask if there are special arrangements for tourists to buy tickets without queuing;

payment would then be in dollars. You can waste hours queuing and waiting for public transport. Travel between provinces is usually booked solid several days or weeks in advance. If you are on a short trip you may do better to go on a package tour with excursions. Trains and some buses are air-conditioned—you may need a warm jersey.

Taxis

For independent travellers who do not have the time to queue, **peso taxis** are an interesting way to travel although the fuel shortage in 1990/91 resulted in their virtual disappearance between towns, leaving them running on local routes only. In March 1992 foreigners were unable to pay for any taxi ride in pesos. The best you can do is avoid the most expensive tourist taxis. See **Transport** under Havana. However, if you can organize the fuel, eg with unused petrol coupons from a car hire, you may be able to organize rides to anywhere. They take as many passengers as can be crowded in; if you are travelling in a group, you can hire the taxi for yourselves, but this is only viable if you are using black market pesos. They are generally found in main squares; ask for Taxi Servicios Especiales and their base, where they can be booked in advance. Bear in mind that the taxi is liable to turn up at the agreed pick-up point up to two hours late if it arrives at all. Some examples of fares: Havana-Viñales, 60 pesos, 2½ hours, Havana- Varadera, 60 pesos, Havana-Santiago 240 pesos, four people; Trinidad-Santiago de Cuba, 149 pesos, 8 hours; Trinidad-Cienfuegos, 20 pesos, 1¼ hours; Santa Clara- Cienfuegos, 16.50 pesos, 1¼ hours; Santiago-Baracoa 60.80 pesos.

Second best is the *máquina particular* business and cars are usually to be found outside interprovincial bus terminals in the main cities. Six to ten people are packed into an old American car which leaves when full (a lengthy process for some destinations). Fuel shortages in 1992 meant these services were very hard to find.

Dollar tourist taxis can be hired for driving around; you pay for the distance, not for waiting time. Airport to Vedado US$13, to Playas del Este US$25, to old Havana US$14, to Varadero US$71; Havana to Varadero US$65; Varadero airport to Varadero hotels US$13; Santiago de Cuba airport to *Hotel Las Américas* US$8, to

Balcón del Caribe US$5.

Car Hire

Through Havanautos at a caravan in the car park of the International Airport, *Hotels Capri*, *Riviera* and *Triton* in Havana, at Varadero beach, *Hotels Marazul* and *Trópico* at the East Havana beaches, *Hotel Rancho Luna* in Cienfuegos and *Motel El Bosque* in Holguín; maximum four passengers allowed; vehicles can be returned to any depot but you will be charged extra. Minimum US$40 a day (or US$45 for a/c) plus US$0.90 each km after the first 100 km, and US$5 a day optional insurance. The overall cost may work out at around US$60-65 a day. In Veradera a car rises to US$105 a day. Buggies are available, mostly for use on the beach, at US$30 a day plus US$0.15 each km after the first 100 km. Visa and Mastercard accepted for the rental, or US$100-150 deposit; you must also present your passport and home driving licence. Petrol coupons must be purchased, in 20 litre amounts, when you rent the car, so work out how much you'll need; unused coupons are returnable or you can use them for securing other transport like peso taxis. Petrol, if you can find it, costs US$0.90 per litre. Recommended, in view of difficulties of getting seats on buses and trains and you can save a considerable amount of time but it is the most expensive form of travel. Breakdowns are not unknown, in which case you may be stuck with your rented car many kilometres from the nearest place that will accept dollars to help you. Be careful about picking up hitchhikers, although it can be an interesting and pleasant way of meeting Cubans.

Excursions

Cubatur, the national tourist office, offers day trips to Soroa, Viñales, Trinidad, Cienfuegos, Varadero (particularly recommended) and Guamá as well as tours of colonial and modern Havana. It is also possible to go on a "Vuelta a Cuba", 7-day round-trip of the island, travelling by bus to Santiago and returning by air. Details from the Cubatur office. A common complaint from individual tourists is that, when they sign up for day trips and other excursions (eg Cayo Largo), they are not told that actual departure depends on a minimum number of passengers. The situation was even worse by March 1992 as there are increasingly few tourists around, and most are on pre-arranged package tours. They are often subject to long waits on buses and at points of departure and are not informed of delays in departure times. Always ask the organizers when they will know if the trip is on or what the real departure time will be.

Hotel Reservations

It is advisable to book hotel rooms before visiting any of the provinces otherwise you may have to return to Havana. This can be done abroad through accredited Cubatur agencies, or through the Cubatur office, Calle 23, No 156, Vedado, La Habana 4; telex 511243; telephone 32-4521, or through Turismo Buró desks in main hotels. It is imperative to book the first night's hotel at the airport on arrival, if you have not done so beforehand (see under Havana **Where To Stay**). Cubana give a one-night hotel voucher to their passengers. Cubatur will inform you only about the main hotels, where you have to pay in dollars. On arrival in a town, check if there is a dollar hotel booking office for making reservations. You have to find the cheaper places, where you can pay in pesos, independently, but you may find it very difficult to get a room and some peso hotels have closed down altogether. "Peso hotels" may demand payment in dollars. It's also a good idea to book hotel rooms generally before noon. In the peak season, July and August (carnival time) and December to February, it is essential to book in advance. Prices given in the text are high season (December-April, July-August); low season prices (May-June, September-November) are about 17% lower. After 31 August many hotels go into hibernation and offer limited facilities, eg no restaurant, no swimming pool.

Camping

Official campsites are opening up all over the island, charging 5-8 pesos a night (in pesos); they are usually in nice surroundings and are good value. One such is El Abra International Campsite halfway between Havana and Varadero, which has extensive facilities (car hire, bicycles, mopeds, horses, watersports, tennis etc) and organizes excursions.

Note

Cuba is geared more to package tourism than to independent visitors and this has become more evident with the local petrol shortage. It is impossible to lodge with local families and camping out on the beach or in a field is forbidden. Because of rationing it is difficult to buy food in the shops. Do not take photographs near military zones. Also be prepared for long waits for everything: buses, cinemas, restaurants, shops etc. Service has improved somewhat in Havana tourist facilities with the passage of new legislation allowing employees to be sacked if they are not up to the job, but inefficiency is rife. Take care with unofficial guides or 'friends' you make; if they take you to a bar or nightclub or restaurant you will be expected to pay for them and pay in dollars.

This chapter catalogues a great many difficulties for the independent traveller, but if on a package, with a couple of days in Havana and a few days on the beach, the visitor should have no problems at all.

Eating Out

Visitors should remember that eating is often a problem and plan ahead. It is generally impossible to have an evening meal and go on to a concert or the theatre (performances start at 2030 or 2100 in Havana).

Breakfast can be particularly slow although this is overcome in the larger hotels who generally have buffets (breakfast US$3, lunch and dinner US$10-18). Look out for the *oferta especial* in small hotels which gives guests a 25% discount on buffet meals in larger hotels. Also, the "all-you-can-eat" vouchers for buffets in tourist hotels do not have to be used in the hotel where bought. Breakfast and one other meal may be sufficient if you fill in with street or "dollar shop" snacks.

In Havana the peso food situation is poor. Outside Havana, including Havana province, it is much worse according to a cyclist who found little or no food to buy. Likewise, in Trinidad, for example, our correspondents found just one shop selling bread, and another selling baby food but to ration-card holders only. Self-catering is extremely difficult as supermarkets are not accessible without ration cards and only occasionally do you find street vendors of fruit. Generally, although restaurants have improved in the last few years, the food in Cuba is not very exciting or enjoyable. There is little variety in the menu and menu items are frequently unavailable. Salads in restaurants are mixed vegetables which are slightly pickled and not to everyone's taste. Beer is cheap.

Tipping

Tipping customs have changed after a period when visitors were not allowed to tip in hotels and restaurants. It is now definitely recommended. Tip a small amount (not a percentage) in the same currency as you pay for the bill (typically US$1-2 on a US$25 meal, 1 peso on amount over 6-7 pesos). At times taxi drivers will expect (or demand) a tip. Turistaxis are not tipped. If you want to express gratitude, offer a packet of American cigarettes. Hotel staff are always happy to accept your left over pesos when you depart. Leaving basic items in your room, like toothpaste, deodorant, paper, pens, is also recommended.

Shopping

Essentials—rent and most food—are cheap; non-essentials are very expensive. Everything is very scarce, although imported toiletries and camera film (Kodak print only, from Mexico), is reasonably priced. Compared with much of Latin America, Cuba is expensive for the tourist (you can make it cheaper by using the black market–see below), but compared with many Caribbean islands it is not dear.

Language

Spanish, with local variants in pronounciation and vocabulary. Little English is spoken.

Currency

The monetary unit is the peso, US$1=0.76 peso. There are heavy penalties for Cubans caught exchanging money on the black market, though a tourist will frequently be approached, especially on the east side of La Rampa, in front of the *Hotel Caribbean*, in the Parque Central and along the Malecón in Havana (beware muggers). These "hasslers" can be extremely persistent and even charming—at first. However their conversation soon turns to money and, once you have shown them any sign of attention, they are very hard to shake off. Do not give them the name of your hotel. The best policy is to ignore them completely—rude but effective! Taxi drivers can be a good source of information. The extent of hustling for dollars depends on whether there is a government crackdown in operation. The going rate was 10 pesos = US$1 in March 1992, when it was still possible to change on the black market with caution, only

worth changing the absolute minimum as there is so little available to buy with pesos. Visitors on pre-paid package tours are best advised not to change any pesos at all. Bring US$ in small denominations for spending money, dollars are now universally preferred. Watch out for pre-1962 notes, no longer valid. There are notes for 3, 5, 10, and 20 pesos, and coins for 5, 20, and 40 centavos and 1 peso. You must have a supply of 5 centavo coins if you want to use the local town buses (10 centavos) or pay phones (very few work). The 20 centavo coin is called a *peseta*. US dollars are accepted in all tourist establishments. Credit cards acceptable in most places are Visa, Master, Access, Diners, Banamex (Mexican) and Carnet. No US credit cards accepted so a Visa card issued in the USA will not be accepted.

Currency Control

The visitor should be careful to retain the receipt every time money is changed officially; this will enable Cuban pesos remaining at the end of the stay to be changed back into foreign currency (to a maximum of US$10 equivalent).

Travellers' cheques expressed in US or Canadian dollars or sterling are valid in Cuba. Travellers' cheques issued on US bank paper are generally not accepted so it is best to take Thomas Cook. Don't enter the place or date when signing cheques, or they may be refused. You can occasionally get US dollars change when paying a hotel bill with travellers' cheques, but you can not cash travellers' cheques for US dollars, nor even for Cuban pesos. Instead you receive Dinero Cubatur (also known as Monopoly money or funny money) which can be used at any dollar store, including the Cubatur *tiendas*. Do not change money where there are groups of black marketeers or where you are outnumbered, you may be tricked. Avoid the Malecón changers.

There is a branch of the Banco Nacional at the 42nd Street 'diplomatic' shopping centre in Havana for changing money legally. It is useful for changing non-dollar currencies into dollars and also for changing travellers' cheques. Visitors have difficulties using torn or tatty US dollar notes.

Sale Of Possessions

Tourists willing to take risks can earn extra spending money by taking along consumer goods to sell to Cubans. It has been reported that you need to guard your clothes more closely than your camera and a T-shirt is greatly appreciated as a gift. Cubans are now rationed to one pair of new trousers a year. Any foreigner sitting in the Parque Central with a flight bag at his side is soon approached by buyers. One can usually get about three times what was paid for the articles. It's inadvisable to bring in too many of a single item or you may have trouble at Customs.

Security

Visitors should never lose sight of their luggage or leave valuables in hotel rooms (most hotels have safes). Do not leave your things on the beach when going swimming. Pickpocketing and pursesnatching on buses is quite common in Havana and Santiago. Visitors should remember that Cuba's dual (peso-dollar) economy means that the local population will often do anything to get hard currency, from simply asking for money or dollar-bought goods, to mugging. Take extra passport photos and keep them separate from your passport. You will waste a lot of time getting new photos if your passport is stolen.

Health

Sanitary reforms have transformed Cuba into a healthy country, though tap water is generally not safe to drink except in Havana; bottled and mineral water are recommended.

Medical service is no longer free for foreign visitors in Havana and Varadero, where there are clinics that charge in dollars. Visitors requiring medical attention will be sent to them. Emergencies are handled on an ad hoc basis. Check with your national health service or health insurance on coverage in Cuba. Charges are high, but reasonable and generally lower than those charged in western countries. According to latest reports, visitors are still treated free of charge in other parts of the country, with the exception of tourist enclaves with on-site medical services.

The Cira García Clinic in Havana (payment in dollars) sells prescription and patent drugs and medical supplies that are often unavailable in chemists.

Between May and October, the risk of sunburn is high—sun blocks are recommended when walking around the city as well as on the beach. In the cooler months, limit beach sessions to 2 hours.

NB The summers are unbearably hot and travel between Havana and Santiago is extremely difficult during Carnival (July) and also during the Christmas-New Year period.

Climate

Northeast trade winds temper the heat. Average summer shade temperatures rise to 30°C (86°F) in Havana, and higher elsewhere. In winter, day temperatures drop to 19°C (66°F). Average rainfall is from 860 mm in Oriente to 1,730 mm in Havana; it falls mostly in the summer and autumn, but there can be torrential rains at any time. Hurricanes come in June-October. The best time for a visit is during the cooler dry season (November to April). In Havana, there are a few cold days, 8°-10°C (45°-50°F), with a north wind. Walking is uncomfortable in summer but most offices, hotels, leading restaurants and cinemas are air-conditioned. Humidity varies between 75 and 95%.

Dress

Generally informal. Summer calls for the very lightest clothing, such as cotton or cotton-terylene mixture. Cuban men mostly wear the *guayabera* (a light pleated shirt worn outside the trousers). Men should not wear shorts except on or near the beach. Trousers are quite OK for women, if preferred. A jersey and light raincoat or umbrella are needed in the cooler months.

Hours Of Business

Government offices: 0830-1230 and 1330-1730 Monday to Friday. Some offices open on Saturday morning. Banks: 0830-1200, 1330-1500 Monday to Friday, 0830-1030 Saturday. The Banco Nacional de Cuba is the only bank in the country. Shops: 1230-1930 Monday to Saturday, although some open in the morning one day a week. Hotel tourist (hard currency) shops generally open 1000-2100.

Time Zone

Eastern Standard Time, 5 hours behind GMT; Daylight Saving Time, 4 hours behind GMT.

Holidays

Liberation Day (1 January), Victory of Armed Forces (2 January), Labour Day (1 May), Revolution Day (26 July), Beginning of War of Independence (10 October).

Weights And Measures

The metric system is compulsory, but exists side by side with American and old Spanish systems.

Electric Current

110-230 Volts. 3 phase 60 cycles, AC. Plugs are of the American type, an adaptor for European appliances can be bought at the Intur shop at the *Habana Libre*.

Post, Telecommunications

When possible correspondence should be addressed to post office boxes (Apartados), where delivery is more certain. Telegraphic services are adequate. You can send telegrams from all post offices in Havana. Telegrams to Britain cost 49 centavos a word. The night letter rate is 3.85 pesos for 22 words. Local telephone calls can be made from public telephones for 5 centavos. A telephone call to Britain costs US$15 for the first 3 minutes, US$5 a minute thereafter. The cost of phoning the USA is US$4.50 a minute from Havana, US$3 from Varadero. "Collect" calls are not permitted. Air mail rates to Britain are 31 centavos for half an ounce and 13 centavos to Canada. Postcards to North, Central America and Caribbean 20 centavos, to South America 25 centavos, Europe 30 centavos, USA, Asia, Africa 50 centavos. Stamps can be bought in pesos at Post Offices, in dollars at the *Habana Libre*. All postal services, national and international, have been described as appalling. Letters to Europe, for instance, take at least 4-5 weeks.

Newspapers

A shortage of newsprint has led to cuts in newspaper and magazine production. *Granma*, mornings except Sunday and Monday; *Trabajadores*, Trade Union weekly; and *Juventud Rebelde*, now also only weekly. *Granma* has a weekly English edition (also French and Portuguese editions available, International annual subscriptions US$40, main offices: Avenida General Suárez y Territorial, Plaza de la Revolución, La Habana 6, Tel: 708218, Telex: 0511 355). The Financial Times, Time, Newsweek and The International Herald Tribune are on sale at the telex centre in *Habana Libre* and in the *Riviera* (also telex centre, open 0800-2000). The previous day's paper is available during the week. Weekend editions on sale Tuesday. FT costs US$2, THT US$1.50.

Embassies and Consulates

Argentina, Calle 36 No 511 between 5 and 7, Tel: 22-5540, 22-5549; **Austria**, Calle 4 No 511, on the corner with 1st, Tel: 22-5825; **Belgium**, Av 5 No 7408 on the corner with 76, Tel: 29-6440; **Brazil**, Calle 16 No 503 between 5 and 7, Tel: 22-7476; **Canada**, Calle 30 No 518, on the corner with 7, Tel: 2-6421/3, 29-3393; **Germany**, Calle 28 No 313, between 3 and 5, Tel: 22-2560, 22-2569; **France**, Calle 14 No 312 between 3 and 5, Tel: 29-6048; **Mexico**, Calle 12 No 518 between 5 and 7, Tel: 2-8634, 22-1142; **Netherlands**, Calle 8 No 307 between 3 and 5, Tel: 2-6511/2; **Peru**, Calle 36 No 109 between 1 and 3, Tel: 29-4477; **Venezuela**, Calle 36A No 704 between 7 and 42, Tel: 22-1361, all these in Miramar. In Vedado, **The US Interests Section**, Calzada between L and M, Tel: 32-0551/9, 32-0543/6; **Italy**, Paseo No 606 between 25 and 27, Tel: 30-0378; **Japan**, Calle N No 62, on the corner with 15, Tel: 32-5554/5. In the old city, **UK**, Edificio Bolívar, 8th floor, Cárcel Nos 101 entre Morro y Prado, old Havana, Tel: 62-3071-5; **Spain**, Cárcel No 51 on the corner of Zulueta, Tel: 99-1515, 32-7710.

Travel Agents

In the UK, agents who sell holidays in Cuba include Regent Holidays, 15 John Street, Bristol BS1 2HR, Tel: 0272-211711, ABTA members, holding ATOL and IATA Licences; South American Experience Ltd, 47 Causton Street, Pimlico, London SW1P 4AT, Tel: 071-976 5511, Fax: 071-976 6908; Progressive Tours, 12 Porchester Place, Marble Arch, London W2 2BS, Tel: 071-262 1676, Fax: 071-724 6941, ABTA, ATOL, IATA. Festival Tours International Ltd, 96 Providence Lane, Long Ashton, Bristol BS18 9DN, T/Fax: 0275 392953, organizes packages to the Havana Film and Jazz Festivals. Recommended agents in Eire for assistance with Aeroflot flights are Cubatravel, Tel: Dublin 713422, Smurfit Travel, 38 Dane Street, Dublin 2, Tel: 774211, Fax: 01793436, and Concorde Travel, Tel: Dublin 763232. See above under **Documents** for Marazul Tours in the USA. If travelling from Mexico, many agencies in the Yucatan peninsula offer packages, very good value and popular with travellers wanting to avoid Mexico City. These include Havanatour, Calle 60 No. 448, Mérida (between Calles 49 and 51), Tel: 233597/239828/285729, Fax: 286943 (8-day package tours for US$325), Cuba-Mex SA (4- day package tours for US$269), Calle 63 No 500, Depto D, Edificio La Literaria, Mérida, Yucatán (Apartado Postal 508, CP 97000; Tel: 23-91-99/ 23-97-25, Fax: 24-91-91, Telex 753806 Cumeme), or Manzanillo No 123 D 104, esq

Baja California, Colonia Roma Sur, Mexico City, DF, Tel: 574-08-13/ 584-24-65, Fax: 584-68-14, CP 06760. Also Cubana Tours, Reforma 400C, local"B", Av Colón, Mérida, Tel: 25-79-91, Telex 75-36-22, or Baja California 255, Edit "B", Despacho 103, Col Hipódromo Condesa, México DF, Casilla Postal 06100, Tel: 574-7839/5208, Fax: 264-2865; Viñales Tours, Oaxaca 80, Col. Roma, 06700, Mexico City, DF, Tel: 208-99-00; Celeste Tours SA, Aguascalientes 191, Mexico City, and others. From Venezuela, Ideal Tours, Centro Capriles, Plaza Venezuela, have 4-day package tours for US$366, 8-day tours US$488, flight only US$295.

Tourist Information

The main Cubatur office is at Calle 23, No 156 between N and O, La Rampa, Vedado, Tel: 32-4521/3157 (open Monday-Friday 0800-1700, Saturday 0800-1200), and reservations for all Cuban hotels, restaurants, and night clubs can be made here. The Oficina de Turismo Individual is in the main Cubatur office on Calle 23; all problems with pre-booked accommodation, transport, etc should be dealt with here. Sr Justo Pérez handles British and Irish clients and is very helpful. Most tourist hotels have a Turismo Buró, which will arrange bookings, etc but some are inefficient (eg *Havana del Este*) and long waits are common.

Cubatur also has offices in: **Canada**, 440 Blvd René Levesque, Suite 1402, Montréal, Quebec H2Z 1V7, Tel: (514) 875-8004/5; 55 Queen St E, Suite 705, Toronto, M5C 1R5, Tel: (416) 362-0700/2, Fax: 362-6799; **Spain**, Paseo de la Habana No 28 4B, Tel: 411-3097; **France**, 24 rue du 4 Septembre, Paris 75002, Tel: 742-

5415; **Germany**, Steinweg 2, D-6000 Frankfurt am Main 1, Tel: (069) 288322; **UK** (Cuban Consulate, no tourist information), 15 Grape Street, London WC2H 8DR, Tel: 071-240 2488; **Mexico**, Insurgentes Sur 421 y Aguascalientes, Complejo Aristos, Edificio B, Local 310, México DF 06100, Tel: 574-9454; **Venezuela**, Av 3a with 2a in Campo Alegre, behind Clínica Sanatriz, open 0900-1300; **Argentina**, Paraguay 631, 2° piso A, Buenos Aires, Tel: 311-4198, 311-5820; **Italy**, Via General Fara 30, Terzo Piano, 20124 Milan, Tel: 66981463.

Maps

Mapa Turístico de la Habana, Mapa de la Habana Vieja, and similar maps of Santiago de Cuba, Trinidad, Camagüey and Varadero are helpful, but not always available.

Further Reading

Cuba Official Guide, by A Gerald Gravette (Macmillan Caribbean, 1988), a bit glossy, but contains lots of information and suggested routes; *Cuba*, Hildebrand's Travel guide, with map; *Cuba: The Test of Time*, Jean Stubbs (Latin America Bureau, London, 1989), an appraisal of the first 30 years of the Cuban Revolution.

We are most grateful to Huw Clough and Kate Hennessy for updating the chapter largely on the basis of a visit to Cuba in March 1992, and to Sofia Gomes, South American Experience, London, and Marjory Zimmerman (Havana) and travellers listed at the beginning of the book for their help in updating this chapter.

CAYMAN ISLANDS

Introduction

THE BRITISH CROWN COLONY of the Cayman Islands consists of Grand Cayman, Cayman Brac and Little Cayman, in the Caribbean Sea. **Grand Cayman**, the largest of the three islands, lies 150 miles south of Havana, Cuba, about 180 miles west northwest of Jamaica and 480 miles south of Miami. Grand Cayman is low-lying, 22 miles long and four miles wide, but of the total 76 square miles about half is swamp. A striking feature is the shallow, reef-protected lagoon, North Sound, 40 miles square and the largest area of inland mangrove in the Caribbean. However, dredging schemes and urban growth threaten the mangrove habitat and the reefs. **George Town**, the capital of the islands, is located on the west side of Grand Cayman. It is principally a business centre with many modern office blocks, but many of the older buildings are being restored.

Cayman Brac (Gaelic for "bluff") gets its name from the high limestone bluff rising from sea level in the west to a height of 140 feet in the east. The island lies about 89 miles east northeast of Grand Cayman. It is about 12 miles long and a little more than a mile wide. Here are beaches lapped by calm waters, ideal for swimming, sunning and diving. Those who find Grand Cayman a little too "citified" will enjoy lingering on Cayman Brac.

Little Cayman lies five miles west of Cayman Brac and is ten miles long and just over a mile wide with its highest point being only 40 feet above sea level. The oft-repeated legend that many Cayman Islanders have lived to the age of 115 or so can readily be accepted after a visit to Little Cayman. It is peaceful but not dull, and dedicated fishermen find it exhilarating.

Owen Island, an islet off the southwestern coast of Little Cayman, is uninhabited but visited by picnickers. None of the islands has any rivers, but vegetation is luxuriant, the main trees being coconut, thatch palm, seagrape and Australian pine.

The total population of mixed African and European descent was estimated at 27,980 in 1990, of which 94% live on Grand Cayman, most of them in George Town (12,972 in 1989), or the smaller towns of West Bay (5,646), Bodden Town (3,410), North Side (859) and East End (1,070). The population of Cayman Brac had fallen to 1,445 in 1989. Little Cayman is largely undeveloped with only about 33 residents and frequented by sports fishermen. The Caymans are very exclusive, with strict controls on who is allowed to settle there, although the proportion of Caymanians in the total population has fallen from 79% in 1980 to 66% by 1990. Consequently

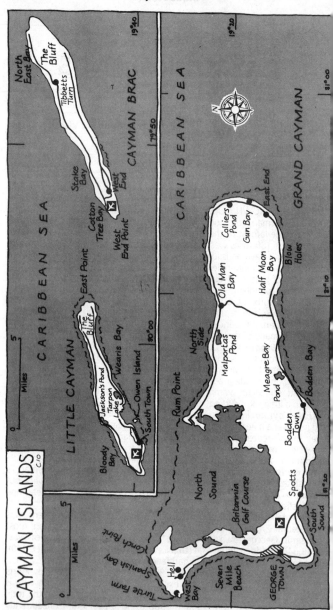

the cost of living is extremely high. On the other hand, petty crime is rare and the islands are well looked after (described as "a very clean sandbank"). Drug trafficking has increased though, and it is estimated that three quarters of all thefts and burglaries are drug-related.

History

The Cayman Islands were first sighted by Columbus in May 1503 when he was blown off course on his way to Hispaniola. He found two small islands (Cayman Brac and Little Cayman) which were full of turtles, and he therefore named the islands Las Tortugas. A 1523 map of the islands referred to them as Lagartos, meaning alligators or large lizards, but by 1530 they were known as the Caymanas after the Carib word for the marine crocodile which also lived there.

The first recorded English visitor was Sir Francis Drake in 1586, who reported that the *caymanas* were edible, but it was the turtles which attracted ships in search of fresh meat for their crews. Overfishing nearly extinguished the turtles from the local waters. The islands were ceded to the English Crown under the Treaty of Madrid in 1670, after the first settlers came from Jamaica in 1661-71 to Little Cayman and Cayman Brac. The first settlements were abandoned after attacks by Spanish privateers, but British privateers often used the Caymans as a base and in the eighteenth century they became an increasingly popular hideout for pirates, even after the end of legitimate privateering in 1713. In November 1788, a convoy of ten Jamaican merchantmen was wrecked on the reef in Gun Bay, on the east end of Grand Cayman, but with the help of the local settlers there was no loss of life. Legend has it that there was a member of the Royal Family on board and that in gratitude for their bravery, King George III decreed that Caymanians should never be conscripted for war service and Parliament legislated that they should never be taxed.

From 1670, the Cayman Islands were dependencies of Jamaica, although there was considerable self-government. In 1832, a legislative assembly was established, consisting of eight magistrates appointed by the Governor of Jamaica and ten (later increased to 27) elected representatives. In 1959 dependency ceased when Jamaica became a member of the Federation of the West Indies, although the Governor of Jamaica remained the Governor of the Cayman Islands. When Jamaica achieved independence in 1962 the Islands opted to become a direct dependency of the British Crown.

Government

A Governor appointed by the British Crown is the head of Government. The present Constitution came into effect in 1972 and provided for an Executive Council to advise the Governor on administration of the islands. The Council is made up of four (proposed to raise number to five) Elected Members and four Official Members. The former are elected from the 12 (proposed to raise number to 15) elected representatives in the Legislative Assembly and have a range of responsibilities allocated by the Governor, while the latter are the Chief Secretary, the Financial Secretary, the Attorney General and the Administrative Secretary. General elections were held in November 1988, and saw The Hon W Norman Bodden become the First Elected Member. The next elections are to be held on 18 November 1992. There have been no political parties since the mid-1960s although constitutional change could reintroduce party politics and at least one new party is in preparation. In 1991 a review of the 1972 constitution was concluded by two UK commissioners who recommended several constitutional changes to be debated by the Legislative Assembly. In 1992 the post of Chief Secretary was reinstated, after having been abolished in 1986. The Chief Secretary is the First Official Member of the Executive Council, leader of government business in the Legislative Assembly and acts as Deputy Governor in the absence of the Governor.

The Economy

The original settlers earned their living from the sea, either as turtle fishermen or as crew members on ships around the world. In 1906 more than a fifth of the population of 5,000 was estimated to be at sea, and even in the 1950s the government's annual report said that the main export was of seamen and their remittances the mainstay of the economy. Today the standard of living is high with the highest per capita income in the Caribbean. The islands' economy is based largely on offshore finance and banking, tourism, real estate and construction, a little local industry, and remittances of Caymanians working on ships abroad.

The Cayman Islands is the largest offshore centre in the world. In 1989 there were 503 licensed banks, 20,013 registered companies and 357 offshore insurance companies and the banking sector employs more than a tenth of the labour force. Tourism revenues have risen sharply in recent years; in 1990, 634,168 tourists visited the islands with a record 253,158 arrivals by air, an increase of 21% over 1989, and the rest cruise ship visitors. The slowdown in the US economy in 1991, however, brought a sharp drop in air arrivals as the US market makes up about 80% of total stopover visitors. Arrivals by air fell by 6.2% to 237,351 and hotel occupancy fell to 60% from 68% in 1990, although cruise ship visitors soared by 31% to 474,747, with the introduction of calls by the cruise liner *Ecstasy* which carries 2,500 passengers. Tourism provides about 35% of jobs and 70% of gross domestic product.

There has been a rapid rise in construction activity to meet demand and tourist accommodation has doubled in ten years. As a result, spectacular rates of economic growth were recorded: 15.6% in 1987, 15.2% in 1988, 10.6% in 1989, slowing to 8.0% in 1990. There is full employment and labour has to be imported to meet demand. Apart from a certain amount of meat, turtle, fish and a few local fruits and vegetables, almost all foodstuffs and other necessities are imported. The cost of living therefore rises in line with that of the main trading partners.

Fauna and Flora

There are over 180 species of birds, including the Antillean grackle, the smooth-billed ani, the green-backed heron, the yellow-crowned night heron and many other heron species, the snowy egret, the common ground dove, the bananaquit and the Cayman parrot. If you are interested in birdwatching, go to the mosquito control dykes on the West Bay peninsula of Grand Cayman, or walk to the Cistern at East End. There are booby nesting places on Little Cayman and a walk across Cayman Brac is rewarding. *Birds of the Cayman Islands*, published by Bradley, is a photographic record; it costs £22. Indigenous animals on the islands are few. The most common are the agouti, a few non-poisonous snakes, some iguana and other small lizards, freshwater turtle, the hickatee and two species of tree frogs. *Oncidium calochilum*, a rare orchid, indigenous to Grand Cayman with a small yellow flower about half an inch long, is found only in the rocky area off Frank Sound Drive. Several other orchid species have been recorded as endemic but are threatened by construction and orchid fanciers. There is protection under international and local laws for several indigenous species, including sea turtles, iguanas, Cayman parrots, orchids and marine life. For a full description of the islands' flora see George R Proctor, *Flora of the Cayman Islands*, Kew Bulletin Additional Series XI, HMSO (1984), 834 pp, which list 21 endemic plant taxa including some which are rare, endangered or possibly extinct.

There are two animal sanctuaries on Grand Cayman, at Colliers Pond and Meagre Bay Pond. On Little Cayman, the Rookery, and on Cayman Brac, the ponds near the airport are also sanctuaries.

Diving and Marine Life

The Cayman Islands are world-famous for their underwater scenery. There are tropical fish of all kinds in the waters surrounding the islands, especially in the coral reefs, and green turtles (*chelonia mydas*) are now increasing in numbers, having been deliberately restocked by excess hatchings at the Grand Cayman turtle farm. A project at the Turtle Farm to reintroduce the endangered Kemp's ridley species of turtle has shown initial success with some reproduction in captivity.

Since 1986, a Marine Parks plan has been implemented to preserve the beauty and marine life of the islands. Permanent moorings have been installed along the western coast of Grand Cayman where there is concentrated diving, and also outside the marine parks in order to encourage diving boats to disperse and lessen anchor damage to the reefs. These parks and protected areas are clearly marked and strictly enforced by a full-time Marine Conservation Officer who has the power to arrest offenders. Make sure you check all rules and regulations as there have been several prosecutions and convictions for offences such as taking conch or lobsters. The import of spearguns or speargun parts and their use without a licence is banned. Divers and snorkellers must use a flag attached to a buoy when outside safe swimming areas.

Many of the better reefs and several wrecks are found in water shallow enough to require only mask, snorkel and fins; the swimming is easy and the fish are friendly. *The Cayman Divers Guide* illustrates the major dive sites on all three islands with a fish index and photo review. Sting Ray City is a popular local phenomenon, where it is possible to swim with and observe large groups of extremely tame rays. Sting Ray City is better dived but half a mile away are the sand banks where sting rays also congregate, usually over 30 at a time. The water here is only 1-3 feet deep and crystal clear, so you hop out of your boat and the rays brush past you waiting to be fed. Their mouths are beneath their head and the rays, three feet across, swim into your arms to be fed on squid. The dive-tourism market is highly developed in the Cayman Islands and there is plenty of choice, but is frequently described as a cattle market with dive boats taking very large parties. Many companies with over 60 boats offer full services to certified divers as well as courses designed to introduce scuba diving to novices; there are several highly qualified instructor-guides. A complete selection of diving and fishing tackle, underwater cameras and video equipment is available for hire. The tourist office has a full price list for all operators. A morning departure two-tank boat dive costs from US$45-50 (Parrots Landing, Watersports Park Ltd, PO Box 1995 GT, Tel: 949 7884, Fax: 949 0294, Surfside Watersports, Tel: 949 7330) to US$60 (Peter Hughes Dive Tiara, Tel: 948 7553, Cayman Brac). Prices for the much-visited Sting Ray City range from US$20 for a snorkel trip to US$40 for a photo-dive, it is worth checking prices at different operators. There is also the liveaboard *Cayman Aggressor III*, which cruises around Grand Cayman and Little Cayman; six-day cruise in 1992 cost US$1,395. Contact Aggressor Fleet Limited, PO Drawer K, Morgan City, LA 70381, Tel: (504) 385 2416, Fax: (504) 384 0817.

Beaches and Watersports

The beaches of the Cayman Islands are said to be the best in the Caribbean. On Grand Cayman, West Bay Beach, now known as Seven Mile Beach, has dazzling white sand and is lined by hotels and tall Australian pines. Beaches on the east and north coasts are equally good, and are protected by an offshore barrier reef; the beaches around Rum Point are recommended for peace and quiet. Various companies offer glass-bottomed boats, sailing, snorkelling, windsurfing, water skiing, water tours and a host of other activities. You can hire wave runners, aqua trikes and paddlecats, take banana rides and go parasailing. When waterskiing, there must be a minimum of two people in the boat so that one person can look out for hazards. There is year-round deep sea game fishing for blue marlin, white marlin, wahoo, yellow fin tuna and smaller varieties, and shorefishing in all three islands. There are about 12 captains offering deep sea fishing or bone fishing from their boats, rates start from US$200 for a half day bone fishing, US$325 for deep sea fishing. For information about sailing fixtures phone Tim Ridley (Tel: 949 2081) of the Cayman Islands Yacht Club. The Cayman Islands Yacht Club, PO Box 1719, Grand Cayman, Tel: 947 4322, Fax: 947 4432, has docking facilities for 154 boats, nine-foot maximum draft. Kaibo, PO Box 50, North Side, Tel: 947 9064, has 12 slips, 40-foot maximum length, seven-foot maximum draft. Morgan's Harbour Marina and Restaurant, PO Box 815, Tel: 949 3099, Fax: 949 3822, also offers the usual facilities.

Other Sports

Jack Nicklaus has designed the Britannia **golf** course for the *Hyatt-Regency Grand Cayman* hotel, Tel: 949 8020 for starting times. There is a 9-hole Championship course, an 18-hole executive course and an 18-hole Cayman course played with a special short-distance Cayman ball, but it can only be laid out for one course at a time; the executive has 14 par 3s and four par 4s, so it is short, while the short-distance ball with local winds is a tourist gimmick. To play the executive course with hire of clubs and compulsory buggie will cost you about US$90. There are three **squash** courts at the Cayman Islands Squash Racquets Association at South Sound, also courts at Downtowner Squash Club in George Town. For information on matches contact John MacRury (Tel: 949 2269). Most of the larger hotels have their own **tennis** courts but the Cayman Islands Tennis Club next door to the squash courts at South Sound has six floodlit tennis courts and two club pros. Again, for match information contact John MacRury (Tel: 949 5164). For **soccer**, contact Tony Scott (Tel: 947 2511) of the Cayman Islands Football Association. **Cricket** matches are played at the Smith Road Oval near the airport, there are five teams in the Cayman Islands Cricket Association's league, details on matches from Joan Boaden (Tel: 949 4222) of the Cayman Islands Cricket Association. **Rugby** is played every Saturday between September and May at the Cayman Rugby Football Club at South Sound, for information phone John Law (Tel: 949 5688).

Excursions

Some of the many things of interest to visit in Grand Cayman include a tour round **Cayman Turtle Farm**, which houses over 12,000 green turtles. Located at North West Point, this is the only commercial turtle farm in the world. Most of the turtles are used for meat locally since the USA banned the import of turtle meat, but many thousands of hatchlings and year-old turtles are released into the wild each year to replenish native stocks. Those at the farm range in size from two-ounce hatchlings to breeding stock weighing around 400 pounds. Polished turtle shells are sold here for about US$100, but their import into the USA is prohibited. A new flora and fauna section of the farm includes three ten-foot crocodiles of the type which used to inhabit the islands and gave their name to the Caymans; there is also the Cayman green parrot, ground iguanas and agouti (known as the Cayman rabbit). Open daily 0830-1700, US$3.50 adults, US$2.50 children aged 6-12, Tel: 949 3893/4.

A trip to **Gun Bay** at the east end of the island will show you the scene of the famous "Wreck of the Ten Sails", which took place in 1788 (see above under **History**). On this trip you will pass the blow-holes: waterspouts that rise above the coral rock in unusual patterns as a result of water being funnelled along passages in the rock as the waves come rolling in. **Hell**, situated near West Bay, is an unusual rock formation worth visiting. Have your cards and letters postmarked at the sub-post office there. There are caves in Bodden Town, believed to have been used by pirates, where you can see bones and stocks, and a line of unmarked graves in an old cemetery on the shore opposite, said to be those of buccaneers. There are also caves on the other islands but these are not as accessible.

For a pleasurable day's outing, arrange a boat trip to North Sound for US$35 or so. This will include snorkelling, fishing and a good look at marine life on a barrier reef. Your guide will cook fish and lobster for you by wrapping them in foil and roasting them on hot coals. An additional refinement: Research Submersibles Ltd (now owned by Atlantis), PO Box 1719, Grand Cayman, Tel: 949 8296, Fax: 949 7421, operates a 20-foot research submarine, taking two passengers (fare US$265) to the 800-foot-deep Cayman Wall or to the wreck of the *Kirk Pride* at 780 feet. A larger submarine (50-foot) with room for 28 passengers is operated by Atlantis Submarine, PO Box 1043, Grand Cayman, Tel: 949 7700; fares are US$69 for a 1-hour day or night dive (children 4-12 half price), both to 150 feet along Cayman Wall. Atlantis brought into operation a new, 46-passenger submarine in 1992.

There is not much of historical interest to see on the islands, although the Government is now trying to promote museums and societies to complement beach and watersports tourism. The Cayman Islands National Museum, in the restored Old Courts Building in George Town, opened in 1990. Open Tuesday-Friday 0830-1630, Saturday 1000-1700, Sunday 1300-1700, Tel: 949 8368. Open 0930-1730 Monday-Friday, 0930-1330 Saturday, 1300-1700 first Sunday of each month, CI$4 adults, CI$2 children aged 6-18. The Cayman Maritime and Treasure Museum (Tel: 947 5033) on West Bay Road near the *Hyatt Regency*, has a collection of gold and silver relics from sunken Spanish ships, open Monday-Saturday 0900-1700, US$5 adults, US$3 children 6-12. An archaeological dig on the waterfront on the site of Fort George has been sponsored by the Cayman National Trust. The National Trust has designed a walking tour of George Town to include 28 sites of interest, such as Fort

George, built around 1790, the Legislative Assembly, the war and peace memorials and traditional Caymanian architecture. A brochure and map (free) is available from the National Trust or the Tourist Office. On Cayman Brac there is a museum at Stake Bay (Tel: 948 4222).

Festivals

Pirates' Week is the islands' national festival and takes place in the last week of October. Parades, regattas, fishing tournaments and treasure hunts are all part of the celebrations, which commemorate the days when the Caymans were the haunt of pirates and buccaneers. **Batabano** is Grand Cayman's costume carnival weekend, which takes place in the last week of April or beginning of May. Cayman Brac has a similar celebration, known as **Brachanal**, which takes place on the following Saturday. Everyone is invited to dress up and participate, and there are several competitions. At Easter there is a regatta with several sailing classes, power boat races and windsurfing. The **Queen's Birthday** is celebrated in mid-June with a full-dress uniform parade, marching bands and a 21-gun salute. **Million dollar month** during June is when fishermen from all over the world come to compete in this month-long tournament.

Information for Visitors

Documents

No passports are required for US, British or Canadian visitors. However, proof of citizenship such as voter registration or "British Visitor's Passport" is required, as well as an outward ticket. Married women using their husband's name should also show their marriage certificate. Passports but not visas are required for citizens of West European and Commonwealth countries, Israel, Japan and South Africa. If you are from any of these countries you may be admitted to the Cayman Islands for a period of up to six months providing you have proof of citizenship, sufficient resources to maintain yourself during your stay, and a return ticket to your country of origin or another country in which you will be accepted.

Visitors from other countries may enter without visa if staying only 14 days; this concession does not apply to nationals of communist countries. Luggage is inspected by customs officials on arrival; no attempt should be made to take drugs into the country.

How To Get There

Air communications are good and there are two international airports, the Owen Roberts International Airport on Grand Cayman and the Gerrard-Smith Airport on Cayman Brac. The national flag carrier, Cayman Airways, has regular services between the islands and Miami, New York, Houston, Atlanta, Baltimore and Tampa in the USA. With Air Jamaica it shares a service to Kingston. Grand Cayman is also served from Miami by American Airlines and Northwest Airlines, the latter additionally having flights from Lansing, Michigan, via Detroit and one from Knoxville and Memphis via Miami. American Airlines also flies from Dallas daily and from San Francisco daily except Sunday. Islena Airlines has charter rights to operate between Honduras and Grand Cayman about once a week. Regular charter flights also from Grand Cayman to Cayo Largo, Cuba, but you can not travel further to visit Cuba itself. Cayman Airways provides daily inter-island services from Grand Cayman to Cayman Brac and Little Cayman and return.

Owen Roberts International Airport is situated less than 2 miles from the centre of George Town and only ten minutes' drive from most of the hotels on Seven Mile Beach. There is a departure tax of US$7.50 for all visitors aged 12 and over payable either in Cayman or US currency when you leave the Islands.

The islands are not served by any scheduled passenger ships but there are cargo services between the islands and Miami and Tampa in the USA, Kingston in Jamaica and Costa Rica. The port at George Town comprises the south wharf, with a depth of 24 feet, and the west wharf, with a depth of 20 feet. The port at Creek, Cayman Brac, is equipped to handle the same class of vessels but Little

Cayman has only a small facility. There is a small jetty at Spotts, Grand Cayman, which caters for cruise ships when the weather is too bad to land at George Town.

Airlines

Cayman Airways, Tel: 949 8200. For information on flights to Cayman Brac, Tel: 948 7221. Air Jamaica, Tel: 949 2300. Northwest Airlines, Tel: 949 2955/6. Charter companies: Cayman Express, Tel: 947 4946; Executive Air Services, Tel: 949 7766.

Local Travel

There is a regular **bus** service between West Bay and George Town that stops at all the hotels on Seven Mile Beach. The fare from the hotels to town is about US$1 each way. **Taxis** are readily obtainable at hotels and restaurants. You can usually find taxis stationed at the *Holiday Inn* on West Bay Road. In George Town there are always lots of taxis at the dock when the cruise ships come in, otherwise hailing a taxi is most easily done in the vicinity of the Post Office. Fares are based on a fixed place-to-place tariff rather than a meter charge and vary according to how many people there are and how much luggage there is. For going a long distance (ie across the island) they are expensive. From the airport to George Town is US$6.25; to the *Holiday Inn*, US$10; to Governor's Harbour, US$12.50; to Silver Sands, US$14.25; to Mount Pleasant, US$17.50; to Spanish Cove and Bodden Town, US$20; to East End, US$31.25; to Rum Point and Water Cay, US$35. For **car hire**, Avis, National and Hertz are represented and there are a number of good local companies as well. Rental firms issue visitors with driving permits on production of a valid driving licence from the visitor's country of residence. Ace Hertz, PO Box 53, Tel: 949 2280, standard jeep CI$40.80 a day in winter, CI$38.40 in summer, automatic car CI$22.40-36.80; Andy's Rent A Car Ltd, PO Box 277 WB, West Bay, Tel: 949 8111, Fax: 949 1546, cheapest automatic car US$35 in winter, US$25 in summer, weekly rates US$210 or US$150; Cico Avis, PO Box 400, Tel: 949 2468, smallest standard car CI$28 winter/summer, jeeps, automatics and mini vans available, minimum 2-day rental, one day rental 25% extra, if paid in US dollars, add 25% for conversion; Coconut Car Rentals Ltd, PO Box 681, Tel: 949 4037, US$35/22 a day winter/summer or

US$210/132 a week, jeeps US$50/45, US$300/270; National Car, PO Box 1105, Tel: 949 4790, Fax: 949 4795, at airport, US$51/38 a day winter/summer automatic car, standards and vans available, seventh day free summer only. **Bicycles** (cheapest CI$10/day), mopeds and motorcycles (CI$20-27/day) can also be rented, from Honda Rentals Caribbean Motors, PO Box 697, Tel: 949 8878, Fax: 949 8502 or Cayman Cycle Rentals, PO Box 1299, Tel: 947 4021, at *Coconut Place*, *Hyatt Regency* and *Treasure Island*. Driving is on the left. Be careful of buses whose doors open into the centre of the road. Island tours can be arranged at about US$60 for a taxi, or US$10 pp on a bus with a minimum of 20 persons. Check with your hotel for full details.

Where To Stay

The winter season, running from 16 December to 15 April, is the peak tourist season. Visitors intending to come to the island during this period are advised to make hotel and travel arrangements well in advance. Accommodations are many and varied, ranging from resort hotels on the beach to small out-of-the-way family-run guest houses. There is also a wide variety of cottages, apartments (condominiums) and villas available for daily, weekly or monthly rental. Cottages, basic, may cost US$600-700 a week, and rates are usually by night, not per person. For longer stay visitors, a 2-bedroom, furnished house can be found away from the tourist areas in, say, Breakers or Bodden Town for US$600-1,000 a month.

There are over 40 hotels along **Seven Mile Beach**, ranging from US$115d at the *Windjammer Hotel*, Tel: 947 4608, Fax: 947 4391 to US$1,500 for the Royal Suite at the *Grand Pavilion* (closed January 1992 because of poor bookings), Tel: 947 4666, Fax: 947 4919, in high season. There are substantial reductions in May-November, with cut rates or even free accommodation for children under 12. Most hotels offer watersports, scuba diving and snorkelling, and many have tennis courts, swimming pools and other facilities.

Away from Seven Mile Beach, there are hotels on Grand Cayman at Spanish Bay, Conch Point, Rum Point, North Side, East End, Half Moon Bay and Bodden Bay. A recommended guest house is *Adam's Guest House*, PO Box 312G, on Melmac Ave, ¾ mile south of George Town, Tel:

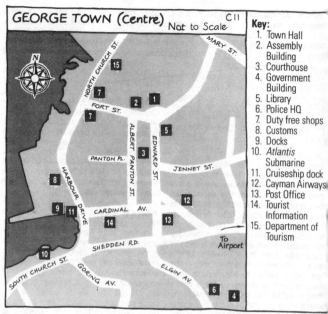

GEORGE TOWN (Centre) Not to Scale C 11

Key:
1. Town Hall
2. Assembly Building
3. Courthouse
4. Government Building
5. Library
6. Police HQ
7. Duty free shops
8. Customs
9. Docks
10. *Atlantis* Submarine
11. Cruiseship dock
12. Cayman Airways
13. Post Office
14. Tourist Information
15. Department of Tourism

949 2512, run by Tom and Olga Adams, excellent accommodation, 4 rooms, US$70d, US$10 additional person, a/c or fan, very helpful, about 300 yards from Parrots Landing dive shop, no credit cards. Two others in this prices range (no credit cards) include **Grama's Bed and Breakfast**, PO Box 198, Tel: 949 3798, north of Seven Mile Beach, US$60d including breakfast with fan, US$65 with a/c, pool and **Eldemire's Guest House**, PO Box 5387, Tel: 949 5387, US$70d EP in room, US$75d studio, US$90d apartment, one mile from town, ½ mile from beach.

On **Cayman Brac**, at West End Point there are the **Brac Reef Beach Resort** (PO Box 56, Tel: 948 7323, US$120d) and **Divi Tiara Beach Resort**, (Tel: 948 7553, US$140-200) both with full watersports and diving facilities, while there is also the **Brac Airport Inn**, Tel: 948 7323, US$99d, two miles from town, guests have full use of *Brac Reef* facilities.

On **Little Cayman** you can stay at **Sam McCoy's** (Tel: 948 4526, Fax: 949 6821, US$99 pp, diving US$47 pp, fishing US$300 pp full day, no credit cards), **Pirates Point** (Tel/Fax: 948 4210, 10 rooms,

US$180 all inclusive with diving, US$140 without, pp based on double occupancy, owned by a cordon bleu chef), **Dillon's Cottages**, **Suzy's Cottage** (US$777/ week) **Sefton's Cottages** (US$1,049/ week for a house, US$740/ week for an apartment) or **Southern Cross Club** (Tel: 948 3255, US$130 pp based on double occupancy, scuba, fishing, no credit cards, all in the west end of the island. Most offer full accommodation and diving and fishing facilities. A full list of tourist accommodation and prices, including hotels, cottages, apartments and villas, is available from Cayman Islands Department of Tourism at the addresses shown at the end of this section. The Cayman Islands Hotel Reservations Service represents 52 properties in the Caymans and can be contacted abroad through the Tourist Office; also in Italy, Gandin Associati Martinengo, Tel: (2) 48012068, Fax: (2) 463532; in Germany, Hans Regh Associates, Tel: (69) 70 40 13/15, Fax: (69) 70 40 43; Benelux, Tel: (20) 6261 197, Fax: (20) 6274 869.

A government tax of 6% is added to the room charge and most hotels also add a

15% service charge to the bill in lieu of tipping.

Where To Eat And Drink

There are dozens of restaurants on Grand Cayman ranging from gourmet standards where a jacket and tie is required, to smaller places serving native dishes. Fish, seafood and turtle meat are local specialities. In George Town, there are many restaurants catering for the lunchtime trade of the office workers and a number of fast-food places, takeaways and delicatessens. Prices obviously vary according to the standard of restaurant, but for dinner, main courses start at about US$10 and range upward to US$60 or more for a full meal including wine. Lunch prices can be around US$7-US$10 and breakfast from about US$5. During the high season it is advisable to reserve tables for dinner. People tend to eat early so if you reserve a table after 2000 you are likely to finish with the restaurant to yourself.

Good restaurants include: *The Wharf*, on the outskirts of George Town on the way to Seven Mile Beach, Tel: 949 2231, lunch Monday-Friday, 1200-1430, dinner daily 1800-2200, beautiful waterfront setting, quite a large restaurant, reservations advisable; *Crow's Nest*, about four miles south of George Town, Tel: 949 9366, open lunch Monday-Saturday, 1200-1430, dinner daily 1800-2200, a local's favourite, small, dining on the patio overlooking the sea or inside, moderate prices, reservations essential; *Pappagallo*, Barkers, West Bay, Italian cuisine, quite expensive, when it is windy tables are laid outside but otherwise not because of the mosquitoes, cover yourself with repellent and limit yourself to pre-dinner drinks outside and eat inside the haphazardly thatched building, excellent food but avoid the house red wine, reservations essential, Tel: 949 3479, open daily 1800-2300; *Cracked Conch*, Selkirk Plaza, West Bay Road, Tel: 949 5717; *Spanish Cove*, Barkers, West Bay, Tel: 949 3765; *Almond Tree*, North Church Street, Tel: 949 2893, outdoor dining, lobster specials Monday and Thursday, all you can eat for US$14 on Wednesday and Friday, open lunch and dinner; *Grand Old House*, South Church Street, Tel: 949 2020; *Lobster Pot*, North Church Street, Tel: 949 2736; *Welly's Cool Spot*, North Sound Road, Tel: 949 2541, has native food at reasonable prices. *Richard Fish* at the Seven Mile Shops,

deli-type restaurant serves breakfast through to 0200, inexpensive, own baked bread and local dishes. All of these restaurants are near George Town or on Seven Mile Beach on the west side of Grand Cayman. Good sandwiches from *Coconut Place Delicatessen*. Probably the best-value place to eat lunch on Grand Cayman is the *Wholesome Cafeteria* (closed Saturday and Sunday), located above the Wholesome Bakery on North Church Street. Others in the same price range include *Champion House*, *I* and *II*, both on Eastern Avenue, George Town, Tel: 949 2190 (*I*), 949 7882 (*II*), cheap, local food, recommended; *Dominique's*, Fort Street, Tel: 949 5747; *Island Taste*, South Church Street, Tel: 949 4945. Other bakeries are *Boulangerie Bakery*, Pleasant House, West Bay Road and *Caribbean Bakery and Pastry Shop*, West Bay.

For local colour visit *Farmers*, off Eastern Avenue near school. *Nelson Arms* on West Bay Road is fairly typical "pub", popular with expatriates. Open air bars are *Sunset House* and *Coconut Harbour* on South Church Street. In down town George Town, the *Shanghai Restaurant*, Tel: 949 5886, has a cocktail bar overlooking the harbour, jazz music; *Big Daddy's* in Seven Mile Shop, West Bay Road, Tel: 949 8511, and *Lone Star Bar and Grill*, next to the *Hyatt Hotel*, West Bay Road, Tel: 949 5575, are favourites with sports fans, showing international sporting events nightly.

On Cayman Brac there are a few restaurants; *Blackie's*, at the Youth Centre, South Side, Tel: 948 8232; *Bin's*, Watering Place, Tel: 948 8311; *Edd's Place*, West End, Tel: 948 7208; *La Esperanza*, Tel: 948 8531 and *Lagoon*, Tel: 948 7523, both at Stake Bay; *Sonia's*, White Bay, Tel: 948 7214; *Watering Place*, Tel: 948 8232.

Nightlife

Monkey Business nightclub, Cayman Falls on West Bay Road, Tel: 947 4024, popular Friday nights, dancing to disco and reggae. *Faces Nightclub* features local groups such as Cayman Edition, as well as rock, reggae and other Caribbean music, also on West Bay Road, Tel: 949 0528. Others include *Apollo II Club*, North Side, Tel: 947 9568; *McDoom's Club Inferno*, Hell, West Bay, Tel: 949 3263; *Rafaldos Club*, North East Bay on

Cayman Brac, Tel: 948 8323. Many hotels have their own nightclubs. The Cayman National Theatre Company, Tel: 949 5477, puts on plays and musicals at the Harquail Cultural Center on West Bay Road; the season runs from October to June. The Cayman Drama Society use the Prospect Play House, a small theatre on the road to Bodden Town.

Best Buys

As a free port, there is duty-free shopping and a range of British glass, china, woollens, perfumes and spirits are available. US citizens are entitled to a US$400 exemption after being away from the USA for 48 hours.

The day's fish catch can be bought from the fishermen most afternoons opposite the Tower Building just outside central George Town. Otto Watler makes and sells honey in Savannah, sign on the right just after the speed limit notice. Pure Art, on South Church Street (also at *Hyatt Regency*), sells the work of over 50 local artists and craftsmen and women; paintings, prints, sculptures, crafts, rugs, wallhangings etc, open Monday-Saturday 1000-1600.

Currency

The legal currency is the Cayman Islands dollar (CI$). The exchange rate is fixed at CI$1 to US$1.25, or CI$0.80 to US$1, although officially the exchange rate is CI$0.83 to US$1. US currency is readily accepted throughout the Islands, and Canadian and British currencies can be exchanged at all banks. There is no exchange control. Personal cheques are not generally welcome and credit cards are not accepted everywhere; do not assume that your hotel will accept them. Traveller's cheques are preferred.

Banks

Most of the major international banks are represented in George Town, Grand Cayman but not all are licensed to offer normal banking facilities. Those which are include Bank of Nova Scotia, Barclays Bank International, Canadian Imperial Bank of Commerce and Royal Bank of Canada. Commercial banking hours are 0900 to 1430 Monday to Thursday, and 0900 to 1300 and 1430 to 1600 on Friday. Barclays Bank and the Cayman National Bank have branches on Cayman Brac.

Warning

Care must be taken when walking on a highway, especially at night; highway shoulders are narrow and vehicles move fast.

Health

Medical Care on Grand Cayman is good and readily available. There is a 52-bed government hospital in George Town (Tel: 949 8600, out patients appointments Tel: 949 8601) and a 12-bed hospital in Cayman Brac. All hospital beds are in single rooms. Out-patients pay a fixed charge per visit. Primary care is provided through four district health centres in Grand Cayman. There is also a clinic on Little Cayman. Cayman Islands Divers, the local branch of the British Sub-Aqua Club, operates the only recompression chamber, behind Cayman Clinic, off Crew Road in George Town (Tel: 555).

Note

Although Grand Cayman is sprayed regularly, it is advisable to bring plenty of insect repellant to combat mosquitoes and sandflies, particularly when there is rain. Malaria does still occur occasionally although yellow fever and dengue fever appear to have been eradicated.

Climate

The Cayman Islands lie in the trade-wind belt and the prevailing northeast winds moderate the temperatures, making the climate delightful all year round. Average temperatures in winter are about 24°C and in summer are around 26°-29°C. Most rain falls between May and October, but even then it only takes the form of short showers.

National Holidays

New Year's Day, Ash Wednesday, Good Friday, Easter Monday, Discovery Day (third Monday in May), the Monday following the Queen's official birthday (June), Constitution Day (first Monday in July), the Monday after Remembrance Sunday (November), Christmas Day and Boxing Day.

Time Zone

Eastern Standard Time, 5 hours behind GMT, for the whole year.

Telecommunications

The Cayman Islands have a modern automatic telephone system operated by Cable and Wireless, which links them with the rest of the world by satellite and by submarine cable. International telephone, telex, telegram, data transmission and facsimile facilities are available and about 108 countries can be dialled directly. There is also a telephone route to the UK via Mercury. Public international telephone booths and a telegram counter are at the Cable and Wireless offices at Anderson Square, open from 0815-1700.

Postal Services
Airmail postal rates are divided into three groups. Group A: the Caribbean, USA, Canada, Central America and Venezuela, first class 25 cents, second class, post cards, airletters 10 cents. Group B: Europe, Scandinavia, West Africa, South America, first class 35 cents, others 15 cents. Group C: East Africa, the Arabian sub-continent, Asia and the Far East, first class 50 cents, others 25 cents.

Press
The *Daily Caymanian Compass* is published five days a week with a circulation of 25,000.

Maps
The Ordnance Survey produces a 1:50,000 scale map of the Cayman Islands with an inset map of George Town in its World Map Series. For information contact Ordnance Survey, Romsey Road, Maybush, Southampton SO9 4DH, Tel: 0703 792000, Fax: 0703 792404.

Tourist Information
Cable and Wireless, in conjunction with the Department of Tourism, provide a Tourist Hotline. By dialling 949 8989 you can find out this week's events and local information. Further information may be obtained from the Cayman Islands Department of Tourism at: PO Box 67, George Town, Grand

Cayman, BWI, Tel: (809) 949 0623.

USA: 250 Catalonia Avenue, Suite 401, Coral Gables, Florida 33134, Tel: (305) 444-6551; 980 North Michigan Avenue, Suite 1260, Chicago, Illinois 60611, Tel: (312) 944-5602; 420 Lexington Avenue, Suite 2733, New York, NY 10170, Tel: (212) 682 5582; 3440 Wilshire Boulevard, Suite 1202, Los Angeles, California 90010, Tel: (213) 738-1968. There are also offices in Atlanta, Tel: (404) 934-3959; Baltimore, Tel: (301) 625-4503; Boston, Tel: (617) 431-7771; Dallas, Tel: (214) 823-3838; Houston, Tel: (713) 461-1317; San Francisco, Tel: (415) 991-1836; and Tampa, Tel: (813) 934- 9078.

Canada c/o Earl B Smith, Travel Marketing Consultants, 234 Eglinton Avenue East, Suite 306, Toronto, Ontario, M4P IK5 Tel: (416) 485-1550.

UK Trevor House, 100 Brompton Road, London SW3 1EX, Tel: 071-581 9960, Fax: 071-584 4463.

Germany/Austria/Switzerland Hans Regh Associates, Postfach 930247, Ebinger Str 1, D-6000 Frankfurt/Main 90, Germany, Tel: 69-70 40 13/15.

Italy G & A Martinengo, Via Fratelli, Ruffini 9, 20123 Milano, Tel: 39 3 48 01 2068.

Belgium/Netherlands/Luxembourg Associated Travel Consultants, Leidsestraat 32, 1017 PB Amsterdam, Netherlands, Tel: 31 20 6261 197.

Japan International Travel Produce Inc., c/o Shuwa Dai-2, Tsukiji Residence 4-3-12, Tsukiji, Chuo-Ku, Tokyo 104, Tel: (03) 546-0760.

JAMAICA

Introduction

JAMAICA lies some 90 miles south of Cuba and a little over 100 miles west of Haiti. With an area of 4,411 square miles, it is the third largest island in the Greater Antilles. It is 146 miles from east to west and 51 miles from north to south at its widest, bounded by the Caribbean. Like other West Indian islands, it is an outcrop of a submerged mountain range. It is crossed by a range of mountains reaching 7,402 feet at the Blue Mountain Peak in the east and descending towards the west, with a series of spurs and forested gullies running north and south. Most of the best beaches are on the north and west coasts, though there are some good bathing places on the south coast too.

Jamaica has magnificent scenery and a tropical climate freshened by sea breezes. The easily accessible hill and mountain resorts provide a more temperate climate, sunny but invigorating. In fact, it would be hard to find, in so small an area, a greater variety of tropical natural beauty.

Over 90% of Jamaicans are of West African descent, the English settlers having followed the Spaniards in bringing in slaves from West Africa. Because of this, Ashanti words still figure very largely in the local dialect, which is known as Jamaica Talk. There are also Chinese, East Indians and Christian Arabs as well as British and other European minorities. The population is approximately 2.4 million. There is considerable poverty on the island, which has created social problems and some tension.

Jamaicans are naturally friendly, easy going and international in their outlook (more people of Jamaican origin live outside Jamaica than inside; compare the Irish). The Jamaicans have a "Meet the People" programme which enables visitors to meet Jamaicans on a one-to-one basis.

History
When Columbus discovered Jamaica in 1494 it was inhabited by peaceful Arawak Indians. Evidence collected by archaeologists suggests that the tribe

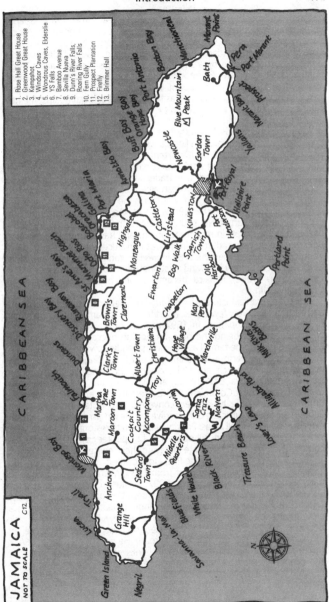

had not lived on the island much before the year 1000. Under Spanish occupation, which began in 1509, the race died out and gradually African slaves were brought in to provide the labour force. In 1655 an English expeditionary force landed at Passage Fort and met with little resistance other than that offered by a small group of Spanish settlers and a larger number of African slaves who took refuge in the mountains. The Spaniards abandoned the island after about five years, but the slaves and their descendants, who became known as Maroons, waged war against the new colonists for 140 years. The Cockpit Country, or "Look Behind Country," where the Maroons hid is still the home of some of their descendants.

After a short period of military rule, the colony was organized with an English-type constitution and a Legislative Council. The great sugar estates, which still today produce an important part of the island's wealth, were planted in the early days of English occupation when Jamaica also became the haunt of buccaneers and slave traders. In 1833 complete freedom was declared for slaves and modern Jamaica was born. The framework for Jamaica's modern political system was laid in the 1930s with the foundation of the Jamaica Labour Party (JLP) by Sir Alexander Bustamante, and the People's National Party (PNP) by his cousin, Norman W Manley. These two parties had their roots in rival trade unions and have dominated Jamaican politics since universal adult suffrage was introduced in 1944.

In 1958, Jamaica joined the West Indies Federation with nine other British territories but withdrew following a national referendum on the issue in 1961. On 6 August 1962, Jamaica became an independent member of the Commonwealth.

Most of the earlier historical landmarks have been destroyed by hurricanes and earthquakes. Very few traces, apart from place names, therefore remain of the Spanish occupation. In 1692 an earthquake destroyed Port Royal which, because of being the base for English buccaneers such as Henry Morgan, had become famed as the most splendid town in the West Indies. In 1907 another earthquake damaged much of Kingston. Some of the historic buildings which are still standing, including the 18th century churches at Port Royal, St Ann's Bay and Montego Bay, are now in the care of the National Trust Commission. The Great Houses are a reminder of the British settlers; some have been converted into hotels or museums. In September 1988, Hurricane Gilbert travelled the length of the island causing extensive damage in all areas. Priority was given to restoring tourist facilities, which were soon back in full operation, but poorer city districts and rural communities were less fortunate in having their services replaced promptly.

After 23 years as leader of the PNP, eight of them as Prime Minister in the 1970s and three as Prime Minister from 1989, Michael Manley, son of the party's founder, retired in March 1992 because of ill health. He was succeeded by the Party Chairman, former deputy Prime Minister and Finance Minister P J Patterson who overwhelmingly defeated his only rival in an election at a special party meeting. During Manley's first two terms in office between 1972 and 1980 he endorsed socialist policies at home and encouraged south-south relations abroad. He antagonized the USA by developing close economic and political links with Cuba. State control of the economy failed to produce the desired results and Mr Manley was rejected by the electorate. By 1989 however, his political thinking had changed dramatically and he was re-elected with policies advocating the free market. Before his retirement he oversaw the reduction in the size of the state, deregulation of the economy and close relations with the IMF. His successor promised to maintain these policies and deepen the restructuring of the economy.

Government

A Governor-General represents the British monarch, who is Head of State, and the Government is made up of a Prime Minister, who nominates the Cabinet, House of Representatives and Senate. All citizens over 18 are eligible for the vote. The judicial system is on British lines. There is a two-party system. Mr Michael Manley of the socialist People's National Party defeated Mr Edward Seaga's conservative Jamaica Labour Party in elections held in February 1989. In 1992 Mr Manley resigned because of ill health and was succeeded by Mr P J Patterson.

The Economy

Once one of the more prosperous islands in the West Indies, Jamaica went into recession in 1973 and output declined steadily throughout the 1970s and 1980s. Gdp per head fell considerably in real terms although by 1989-91 economic output was beginning to pick up and further improvement is expected in the 1990s. The average unemployment rate has improved to 16%. At the core of Jamaica's economic difficulties lay the collapse of the vital bauxite mining and alumina refining industries. Bauxite and alumina export earnings provided 46% of all foreign exchange receipts and 28% of gdp in 1980 but by 1984 these shares had fallen to 33% and 20% respectively. Nevertheless, Jamaica is the world's third largest producer of bauxite after Australia and Guinea, and higher output and prices have now improved the outlook for the industry. Figures for 1990 showed bauxite and alumina accounting for two thirds of merchandise exports, with mining output increasing by nearly 18%, although their share of gdp had fallen to 10%. In 1991 output of bauxite reached 11.5m tons, the highest level for ten years, while alumina production hit a record 3m tons, but export revenues fell because of lower prices. By comparison with mining, agriculture is a less important sector in terms of contribution to gdp, though it generates far more employment. Sugar is the main crop, and most important export item after bauxite and alumina. Other export crops include bananas, coffee, cocoa and citrus fruits.

Tourism is the second foreign exchange earner and Jamaica is the third most popular destination in the Caribbean after the Bahamas and the Netherlands Antilles. Stopover arrivals grew by an annual average of 8% and cruise visitors by 14% in the first half of the 1980s until, in 1987, combined stopover and cruise arrivals passed the million mark for the first time and in 1991 the country received 844,607 stopover visitors and 490,485 cruiseship passengers. In 1990, foreign exchange earnings from tourism were US$740m. The impact of tourism on a population of less than 2½ million is massive, both economically and socially. The Jamaicans are well aware of this and also of the fact that tourism is a very fragile industry. Bad publicity abroad (much of it unfair sensationalism) or a natural disaster, such as Hurricane Gilbert, can have a devastating effect.

The Government turned to the IMF for support in 1976 and has since been a regular customer. In compliance with IMF agreements, the Government had to reduce domestic demand commensurate with the fall in export earnings, by devaluing the currency and reducing the size of its fiscal deficits. Jamaica has rescheduled its debt to creditor governments and also to foreign commercial banks. Some debt forgiveness has also been granted. Debt to the IMF was US$360m in 1990, down from US$688m in 1986, although total official lending made up about three quarters of the total public foreign debt of around US$4.1 billion. Although the debt fell to US$3.8bn in 1991, its service absorbed nearly half of 1992 recurrent budget spending.

A 15-month SDR 82m standby credit facility was agreed with the IMF in January 1990 with targets to reduce the budget and current account deficits and eliminate payment arrears. Several tax increases were announced, together with the sale of hotels and other government assets and the ending of some unprofitable Air Jamaica routes. The Jamaican dollar was devalued (the foreign exchange market was deregulated in September 1991) and interest rates and credit ceilings were kept high to reduce consumption, close the trade gap and rebuild foreign reserves. A further standby agreement was negotiated in 1991, together with loans from the World Bank and the InterAmerican Development Bank, which aimed to cut the budget deficit still further. In 1992 talks began for an IMF three-year Extended Fund Facility when the Standby expired in June. The economy showed signs of growth but recovery was fragile. During the political leadership handover, uncertainties caused the currency to fall rapidly, but tighter monetary policies and private business sector support enabled it to recover soon afterwards. Plans to cut the civil service by 20% (8,000 jobs) in 1992 were met by strikes.

Culture

The predominant religion is Protestantism, but there is also a Roman Catholic community. There are followers of the Church of God, Baptists, Anglicans, Seventh Day Adventists, Pentecostals and Methodists. The Jewish, Moslem, Hindu and Bahai religions are also practised. It is said that Jamaica has more churches per square mile than anywhere else in the world. To a small degree, early adaptations of the Christian faith, Revival and Pocomania, survive, but the most obvious local minority sect is Rastafarianism. Followers of this cult are easily recognizable by their long dreadlocks; they are non-violent and do not eat pork. They believe in the divinity of the late Emperor of Ethiopia, Haile Selassie (Ras Tafari). Haile Selassie's call for the end of the superiority of one race over another has been incorporated into a faith which holds that God, Jah, will lead the blacks out of oppression (Babylon) back to Ethiopia (Zion, the Promised Land). The Rastas regard the ideologist, Marcus Garvey (born 1887, St Ann's Bay), as a prophet of the return to Africa (he is now a Jamaican national hero). In the early part of the twentieth century, Garvey founded the idea of black nationalism, with Africa as the home for blacks, be they living on the continent or not.

The music most strongly associated with Rastafarianism is reggae. According to O R Dathorne, "it is evident that the sound and words of Jamaican reggae have altered the life of the English-speaking Caribbean. The extent of this alteration is still unknown, but this new sound has touched, *more than any other single art medium*, the consciousness of the people of this region." (*Dark Ancestor*, page 229, Louisiana State University Press, 1981). The sound is a mixture of African percussion and up-to-the-minute electronics; the lyrics a blend of praise of Jah, political comment and criticism and the mundane. The late Bob Marley, the late Peter Tosh, Dennis Brown and Jimmy Cliff are among the world-famous reggae artists, and many, many more can be heard on the island. Closely related to reggae is dub poetry, a chanted verse form which combines the musical tradition, folk traditions and popular speech. Its first practitioner was Louise Bennett, in the 1970s, who has been followed by poets such as Linton Kwesi Johnson, Michael Smith, Oku Onora and Mutabaruka. Many of these poets work in the UK, but their links with Jamaica are strong.

Two novels which give a fascinating insight into Rasta culture (and, in the latter, Revival and other social events) are *Brother Man*, by Roger Mais, and *The Children of Sysiphus*, by H Orlando Patterson. These writers have also published other books which are worth investigating, as are the works of Olive Senior (eg *Summer Lightning*), the poets Mervyn Morris, Andrew Salkey and Dennis Scott (who is also involved in the theatre).

Kingston is the main cultural centre of Jamaica. There are two important institutes which can be visited: the African Caribbean Institute (ACIJ, on Little North Street) is involved in research into African traditions in Jamaica and the Caribbean; the Institute of Jamaica (East Street) has historical sections, including Arawak carvings, the National Library, science museum and occasional lectures and exhibitions. The National Gallery of Jamaica (Orange Street and Ocean Boulevard) has a large collection of Jamaican art; there are about a dozen other galleries in the city. The National Dance Theatre has an annual summer season; throughout the year plays and concerts are staged. The local press has full details of events in Kingston and other centres.

Flora and Fauna

Jamaica has been called the Island of Springs, and the luxuriance of the vegetation is striking (its Arawak name, Xaymaca, meant land of wood and water). There are reported to be about 3,000 species of flowering plants alone, 827 of which are not found anywhere else. There are over 550 varieties of fern, 300 of which can be found in Fern Gully (see below). The national flower is the dark blue bloom of the lignum vitae. There are many orchids, bougainvillea, hibiscus and other tropical flowers. Tropical hardwoods like cedar and mahogany, palms, balsa and many other trees, besides those that are cultivated, can be seen. Cultivation, however, is putting much of Jamaica's plant life at risk. Having been almost entirely forested, now an estimated 6% of the land is virgin forest. A great many species are now classified as endangered.

This is also a land of hummingbirds and butterflies; sea-cows and the Pedro seal are found in the island's waters. There are crocodiles, but no wild mammals apart from the hutia, or coney (a native of the island and now an endangered species), the mongoose (considered a pest since it has eliminated snakes and now eats chickens) and, in the mountains, wild pig. The Jamaican iguana (*Cyclura collei*), of the lizard family Iguonidae, subspecies Iguaninae, was thought to have died out in the 1960s, but in 1990 a small group was found to be surviving in the Hellshire Hills. Good sites for birdwatching are given in the text below. The national bird is the doctor bird hummingbird, with a tail much longer than its body, one of Jamaica's 24 endemic species. Many migratory birds stop on Jamaica on their journeys north or south. *Birds of Jamaica: a photographic field guide* by Audrey Downer and Robert Sutton with photos by Yves-Jacques Rey Millet, was published in 1990 by Cambridge University Press.

In 1989 the Government established two pilot national parks, the first in Jamaica, under the Protected Areas Resource Conservation (PARC) project. The Blue Mountain/John Crow Mountain National Park encompasses almost 200,000 acres of mountains, forests and rivers. Efforts are being made to stem soil erosion and restore woodland lost in Hurricane Gilbert, while developing the area for ecotourism and provide a livelihood for local people.

The other national park project is the Montego Bay Marine Park, which aims to protect the offshore reef from urban waste, over-fishing and hillside erosion leading to excessive soil deposition. A 15.3 km environmental protection zone is being established off Montego Bay, and watersports in the area will be strictly controlled.

Sport

Apart from the sports associated with the main resorts (tennis, riding, diving, and other water sports), **golf** is played at the Constant Sprint (18 holes, Tel: 924-1610) and Caymanas Clubs (18 holes, Tel: 923-7538) (Kingston), the Manchester Club (Mandeville, 9-hole, Tel: 962-2403), Upton (Ocho Rios, 18 holes, Tel: 974-2528), Runaway Bay Country Club (18 holes, Tel: 973-2561), Ironshore Country Club (18 holes, Tel 953-2381), Half Moon Club (18 holes, Tel: 953-2211) and Wyndham Rose Hall Golf Club (18 holes, Tel: 953-2650) (all east of Montego Bay) and Tryall Golf and Beach Club (between Montego Bay and Negril). The island's main spectator sport is **cricket**. Test matches are played in Kingston. **Polo** is played on Saturday afternoons at Drax Hall, near Ocho Rios, entrance free. International tournaments at Chukka Cove, Runaway Bay and Caymanas Polo Club, Kingston. **Riding** lessons and trail rides also available at Chukka Cove, Tel: 972-2506.

Festivals

Carnival has come only recently to Jamaica and is held around Easter time with floats, bands and mass dances, at various locations around the islands, attended by thousands. You can get very fit dancing for six hours a night for seven nights. The annual reggae festival, Sun Splash, is normally held in the middle of August, usually in Montego Bay, in the Bob Marley Centre. Also in August, the celebrations around Independence Day (1 August) last a week and are very colourful. The annual International Marlin Tournament at Port Antonio in October attracts anglers from all over the world and includes festivities other than fishing. The Tourist Board publishes a twice-yearly calendar of events which covers the whole spectrum of arts and sports festivals.

Kingston and its Surroundings

The capital since 1870 and the island's commercial centre, **Kingston** has a population of over 750,000 (part of St Andrew's Parish is included in the metropolitan area, which helps swell the figure). It has one of the largest and best natural harbours in the world. Following the earthquake of 1907 much of the lower part of the city was rebuilt in concrete. Since then efforts have been made to improve the area's appearance. But it still has some way to go before it can bear comparison for cleanliness with its rival New Kingston, some 2 miles away, where many hotels and restaurants are situated. On the waterfront there are some notable modern buildings including the Bank of Jamaica and the Jamaica Conference Centre which also houses the National Gallery.

Among older buildings of note in the downtown area are Gordon House (on Duke Street), which dates from the mid-18th century and houses the Jamaican legislature. Visitors are allowed into the Strangers' Gallery but must be suitably dressed (jackets for men and dresses for women). There is also the early 18th century parish church south of Parade, where Admiral Benbow is buried. Parade (Sir William Grant Park) is at the heart of the city centre; it is an open oasis amid the densely-packed surroundings. The name derives from the British soldiers' parades here during colonial rule. Now it is at the junction of the main east-west route through the downtown area (Windward Road/East Queen Street-West Queen Street/Spanish Town Road) and King Street/Orange Street which runs north to Cross Roads. At Cross Roads, the main route forks, left to Half Way Tree (recently renamed Nelson Mandela Park), straight on up Old Hope Road to Liguanea. These two roads encompass New Kingston.

The Parish Church at St Andrew at Half Way Tree dates from 1700. Half Way Tree, so called because it was a half-way stage on the road between the harbour and the hills, is a busy traffic junction which takes some negotiating in a car. Hope Road, on the northern edge of New Kingston, runs east from Half Way Tree. Just off it are Devon House, a former "great house" at the corner of Trafalgar and Hope Roads, now renovated as a museum, with craft shops and refreshment stalls (small admission fee to look inside the main house, but the shops and restaurants in the grounds are open to all and well worth a visit). Not far away is King's House, the official residence of the Governor-General and, nearby, Jamaica House, the Prime Minister's residence. About ten blocks east of Devon House, along Hope Road, is the Bob Marley Museum, entry US$1 including obligatory guided tour. The house where Marley used to live traces back to his childhood and family, with paintings, newspaper cuttings, posters and other memorabilia. He died tragically of brain cancer at the age of 36, having survived a controversial assassination attempt (the bullet-holes in the walls have been left as a reminder). There is a wax statue of Marley inside the recording studio, donated by Madame Tussauds, and an Egyptian restaurant in the garden serving some of his favourite vegetarian dishes. Further east, along Old Hope Road, are the Hope Botanical Gardens. The land was first acquired by Major Richard Hope in 1671 and 200 years later the Governor of Jamaica, Sir John Peter Grant, bought 200 acres and created a botanical gardens. In 1961 a zoo was opened alongside the gardens. After extensive damage in 1988 by Hurricane Gilbert, plans have been made to transform the small, traditional zoo into a showcase for the different natural habitats of Jamaica and its indigenous animals.

Local Information—Kingston

Airport The airport for Kingston is the Norman Manley (with restaurant, good tourist office, offering much information, maps and up-to-date hotel and guest house lists), 11 miles away, about 30 minutes' drive. There is an exchange desk in the arrivals lounge which will change cash or cheques (at a slightly lower rate than banks). You can also change back excess Jamaican dollars into US$ at the bank in the departure lounge, when you leave, as long as you show the exchange receipts. There are several reasonable shops in the departure lounge which will accept Jamaican currency (except for duty free goods). Bus No SR8 leaves West Parade for the airport, US$0.35, but the service is infrequent, so allow for waiting time. To get to New Kingston by bus involves a change of bus (to No. 27) downtown. Taxis generally charge US$11-13 for the same trip; best to bargain. The recognized service from town to airport is JUTA, taxi/minibus, which charges US$11 door-to-door (can be shared); between the airport and Port Royal (*Morgan's Harbour*) US$5.50.

Where To Stay A full list is available from Tourist Board: addresses in **Information for Visitors**. The only major hotel on the city waterfront is the *Oceana*, 2 King Street (PO Box 986, Tel: 922-0920, Fax: 922-3928), US$90 EP with conference centre and pool; *Morgan's Harbour* is conveniently close to the airport (see Port Royal); all the other main hotels are in or near New Kingston: *Jamaica Pegasus* (Trust House Forte), 81 Knutsford Boulevard (PO Box 333, Tel: 929-3691, Fax: 929-4062) US$172-189s/d EP;

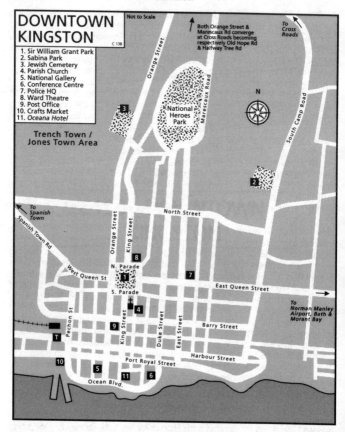

DOWNTOWN KINGSTON

C 138

Not to Scale

1. Sir William Grant Park
2. Sabina Park
3. Jewish Cemetery
4. Parish Church
5. National Gallery
6. Conference Centre
7. Police HQ
8. Ward Theatre
9. Post Office
10. Crafts Market
11. *Oceana Hotel*

Both Orange Street & Marescaux Rd converge at Cross Roads becoming respectively Old Hope Rd & Halfway Tree Rd

To Cross Roads

Orange Street

Marescaux Road

National Heroes Park

N

South Camp Road

Trench Town / Jones Town Area

To Spanish Town

Spanish Town Rd

North Street

Orange Street

King Street

8

N. Parade

1

S. Parade

West Queen St

To Norman Manley Airport, Bath & Morant Bay

East Queen Street

7

4

9

King Street

Duke Street

East Street

Barry Street

Pechon St

T

Harbour Street

10

5

11

6

Port Royal Street

Ocean Blvd.

Wyndham, 77 Knutsford Boulevard (Tel: 926-5430/9, Fax: 926-7439), US$125-145d EP; *Terra Nova*, 17 Waterloo Road (Tel: 926-2211, Fax: 929-4933), US$90-150s/d EP, popular with business travellers; *Mayfair*, 4 West King's House Close (adjoining the Governor General's residence), PO Box 163, Tel: 926-1610, Fax: 926-7741, US$50-60d EP; *Four Seasons*, 18 Ruthven Road, Tel: 929-7655, Fax: 929-5964, US$50-58d, EP, in a converted Edwardian house and gardens, good cooking, recommended; and a number of others. Among the cheaper hotels is *The Indies*, 5 Holborn Road (Tel: 926-2952), US$43-49 (television US$6 extra) EP, breakfast and lunch available, comfortable, pleasant patio garden. Next door is the popular *Johnson Holborn Manor* (ex Mrs Johnson's Guest House), 3, Holborn Rd, US$40d with breakfast and shower, fan, clean, safe and quiet, luggage storage available, friendly, new annex, recommended. *Sandhurst*, 70 Sandhurst Crescent, Kingston 6 (Tel: 927-7239), US$34-38s, US$42-46d EP. *Chelsea Guest House*, Chelsea Avenue, US$20d EP. About 25 minutes from Kingston is *Ivor Guest House* and restaurant, Jack's Hill, Kingston 6, high up in the hills overlooking Kingston and set in its own extensive grounds; three double bedrooms US$54s, US$76d CP; free transport to/from Kingston; charge for airport pickup; lunches US$12, dinners US$16 by reservation only, Helen Aitken, Tel: 927-1460, highly recommended. About 40 minutes from Kingston is *Pine*

NEW KINGSTON C 13A

Not to Scale

1. King's House
2. Jamaica House
3. Devon House
4. Bob Marley Museum
5. St Andrew's Church
6. Nelson Mandela Park
7. Tourist Board
8. British High Commission
9. US Embassy
10. British Airways / Air Jamaica
11. American Express
12. Western Union
13. New Kingston Mall
14. Village Mall
15. Springs Mall
16. Kings Mall
17. Jerk Pork Restaurant
18. Indies Pub
19. *Mayfair Hotel*
20. *Terra Nova*
21. *Johnson Holborn Manor*
22. *The Indies*
23. *Four Seasons*
24. *Chelsea Hotel*
25. *Wyndham Hotel*
26. *Pegasus*
27. *Sandhurst*

Grove, see under Eastern Jamaica and the Mountains. The YMCA, opposite Devon House on Hope Road, has a good swimming pool, many sports facilities and a cheaply priced restaurant.

Where To Eat A great many places to eat in downtown Kingston, New Kingston and the Half Way Tree area. There are plush establishments, inside and outside the hotels, and small places. The *Pegasus Hotel* does a good lunch and dinner special at US$5.50 and US$6.50 respectively. For the impecunious, meat patties may be had at US$0.25 each. Be warned that around the *Oceana* most places close at 1700. On Holborn Road, opposite the *Indies Hotel* is the *Indies Pub*, which is reasonable, and next door is the *Three Little Bears* with patisserie attached, cheap cakes and coffee, excellent lobster in the main restaurant for US$12 and quite palatable Jamaican wine. On Chelsea Avenue (in the same area) is *Jerk Pork*, popular with locals. Nearby are Mexican and Indian restaurants, both very good but not cheap. The *Lychee Restaurant* in the New Kingston Shopping Mall, on Dominica Drive, serves excellent Chinese food, moderately priced, several other eating places here, from takeaway pattie bakery to upmarket restaurant, popular lunch spot for office workers; *Hot Spot*, off New Kingston, serves good Jamaican food in a pleasant patio but you will never find it without asking for directions. Many outlets of international takeaway chains all over the city, *Burger King* and *Kentucky Fried Chicken*, etc, as well as Jamaica's own variation, *Mothers*, also widespread. At *Devon House* (**see page 177**), there is a plush expensive restaurant, a reasonably-priced snack bar and delicious ice-cream at "*I Scream*".

Entertainment Amusements in Kingston include cinemas (the Carib is the most luxurious), and concerts and plays at the Ward Theatre (North Parade) and Little Theatre (St Andrew) where the local Repertory Company performs regularly.

Night Life Most hotels have dancing at weekends, and there is a good discothèque, *Epiphany*, at Spanish Court, New Kingston. Tourists are strongly advised not to try, unless they have Jamaican friends, to probe deeply into real Jamaican night life, at least in towns. For genuine local dances and songs, see the advertisements in the local press.

Bathing The swimming at Kingston is not very good. The sea at Gunboat beach, near the airport, is dirty. Better at Port Royal (see below). "Hellshire", south of Port Henderson, is a locals' favourite, but is difficult to reach. At Port Henderson is the *Rodney Arms* restaurant.

Shopping In downtown Kingston, the Jamaica Crafts Market and many shops at west end of Port Royal Street have local crafts. Off West Queen Street is an interesting local market, selling fish, fruit and general produce. Reggae music shops can be found close together along Orange Street, just north of Parade. Bookland is a good bookshop on Knutsford Boulevard, with a wide range of US magazines and newspapers and also The Times. There are various duty-free concessions for visitors. There is a **laundry** in Chelsea Avenue.

Port Royal, the old naval base, lies across the harbour from Kingston, beyond the international airport, some 15 miles by excellent road. It can also be reached by boat from Victoria Pier; they leave every 2 hours, take 20 minutes and cost US$0.15. On 7 June 1692 an earthquake hit eastern Jamaica, coursing along the Port Royal fault line and bringing with it massive tidal waves. The port, commercial area and harbour front were cut away and slid down the slope of the bay to rest on the sea bed, while much of the rest of the town was flooded for weeks. About 3,000 people died and the naval, merchant and fishing fleets were wrecked. The town was gradually rebuilt as a naval and military post. Nelson served here as a post-captain from 1779 to 1780 and commanded Fort Charles, key battery in the island's fortifications. Part of the ramparts, known as Nelson's Quarterdeck, still stands. St Peter's Church, though the restoration is unfortunate, is of historic interest, as is the Historical Archaeological Museum (admission US$0.30). *Morgan's Harbour* at Port Royal is a favourite holiday centre (Tel: 924-8464, Fax: 924-8562), with water ski-ing, a salt water swimming pool, beach cabins (rates US$105d, EP), a good sea-food restaurant, and dancing, closest hotel to airport. Boats may be hired for picnic bathing lunches on the numerous nearby cays or at Port Henderson.

Spanish Town, the former capital, some 14 miles west of Kingston by road or rail, is historically the most interesting of Jamaica's towns. Bus S1 from Half Way Tree and S2 from Orange Street. Its English-style architecture dates from the 18th century. Well worth seeing are the Spanish Cathedral, the oldest in the anglophone West Indies; the fine Georgian main square with, of special note, the ruins of the King's House built in 1762; a colonnade and statue commemorating Rodney's victory at the Battle of the Saints (see under Guadeloupe and Dominica); the House of Assembly and the Court House. There is a museum with interesting relics of Jamaican history and accurate portrayal of life of the country people. Outside town, on the road to Kingston is the White Marl Arawak Museum. Restaurant: *Miami*, Cumberland Road, near the market area; food is delicious, especially the pumpkin soup.

Eastern Jamaica and the Mountains

Behind Kingston lie the **Blue Mountains** with Blue Mountain Peak rising to a height of 7,402 feet. This is undoubtedly one of the most spectacular and beautiful parts of Jamaica and an area which must be visited by keen bird watchers and botanists as also by those who like mountain walking. It is possible to explore some of the Blue Mountains by ordinary car from Kingston. Drive towards Papine and just before arriving there visit the Botanical Gardens at Hope with a splendid collection of orchids and tropical trees and plants. After leaving Papine and just after passing the *Blue Mountain Inn* (good restaurant and night club), turn left to Irish Town and thence to Newcastle, a Jamaica Defence Force training camp at 4,000 feet with magnificent views of Kingston and Port Royal. If energetic you may climb the road to Catherine's Peak directly behind the camp (about 1 hour for the moderately fit). Beyond Newcastle lies Hardwar Gap and Holywell National Park. This whole area is full of mountain trails with innumerable birds, some unique to Jamaica. The road then winds down to Buff Bay with a turning off to the right to Clydesdale and the Cinchona botanical garden. Unfortunately you are unlikely to be able to get an ordinary car past Clydesdale and perhaps not even to Clydesdale. From Clydesdale to Cinchona is about an hour's walk uphill but well worth it. If you wish to go towards Blue Mountain Peak, you drive straight on at Blue Mountain Inn (instead of turning left), through Gordon Town and on through Mavis Bank to Hagley Gap (if the Mahogany Vale ford is passable). Again, however, you will almost certainly not be able to get a car up to the starting point for the walk to the Peak. Public transport up the Blue Mountains is infrequent. There are supposed to be buses to Mavis Bank from Papine on the outskirts of Kingston, but probably none on Sundays. Taxis from here to Mavis Bank about US$7.50. 4 miles beyond Mavis Bank is the village of Hagley Gap, from where jeeps are available (ask for Errol) to go as far as Whitfield Hall (see below) for US$20. Only 4-wheel drive vehicles are advisable after Mavis Bank, and there are no petrol stations en route.

A much better solution is to stay at *Pine Grove Mountain Chalets* about half an hour's drive beyond Gordon Town. This consists of a series of cottages with central feeding and the atmosphere of a ski lodge. A double room with bathroom, kitchen area and couch costs about US$63 per night and meals about US$45 a day (breakfast, 2 main meals plus drinks). The proprietors, Barbara and Radwick, live there and are extremely welcoming and helpful. Apart from giving advice they will also provide 4-wheel drive vehicles at very moderate cost to take guests to Cinchona and the start of the trail to Blue Mountain Peak, etc. They will also pick up guests from the airport (US$50) or from Kingston (address: Pine Grove Mountain Chalets, c/o 62 Duke Street, Kingston, Tel: 922-8705, Fax: 922-5895)

Another possible solution for the young and active is to contact Peter Bentley of SENSE Adventures at Box 216, Kingston 7, who is also President of the Jamaican Alternative Tourism, Camping and Hiking Association (JATCHA). The office is at Maya Lodge and Hiking Centre, Juba Spring, Peter's Rock Road, Jack's Hill, Kingston, Tel: 927-2097. Buses from Kingston leave from Jack's Hill Road opposite Texaco station, get off at Foxy's Pub. Contact can also be made through Stuarts Travel Service, 40 Union Square, Kingston, Tel: 926-4291. SENSE Adventures specializes in hiking in the mountains, birdwatching, canoeing, rafting and camping, it lends out tents and other equipment and it is possible to stay or camp at Maya. Organized,

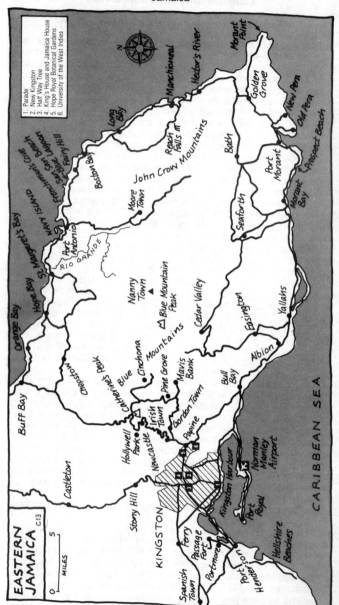

EASTERN JAMAICA C.13

1. Parade
2. New Kingston
3. Half Way Tree
4. King's House and Jamaica House
5. Hope Royal Botanical Gardens
6. University of the West Indies

MILES 0 5

island-wide trips range from ½ day to 9 days (recommended for good guides and very good food). It can also provide information about all sorts of other activities, itinerary planning and cheap places to stay island wide; assistance with planning and reservations for over 150 properties is offered for US$15 including all the camping areas. A room or cabin at Maya Lodge costs US$30d, hostal style US$20d, camping in own tent US$7.50 per person, tent rental US$3 extra, restaurant, 15 acres of land in jungle setting, many paths for hikes around area, highly recommended.

Finally there is John Algrove who can be contacted at 8 Almon Crescent, Kingston 6, Tel: 927-0986. He owns *Whitfield Hall Hostel* at the point where the Blue Mount Peak trail begins. It is a large wooden lodge with no electricity but gas for the kitchen and paraffin lamps, US$10 per person, capacity 40, some bunk beds, cold showers only. No meals but kitchen with stoves and crockery, etc, for guests' use. Very peaceful and homely with comfortable lounge, log fire and library (visitors' books dating back to the 1950's), highly recommended, staff very friendly and helpful. If the hostal is full, camping is permitted, US$5 per person. You can either take a bus to Mount Charles from where it is a steep 4-mile walk to Whitfield Hall, or ask Mr Allgrove to arrange transport from Mavis Bank, US$20 in a jeep for maximum 6 passengers, or US$40 all the way to/from Kingston. The hostal can also arrange mules and guide to the peak and to Cinchona, another mountain.

The walk to Blue Mountain Peak (6½ miles from Whitfield Hall) takes 3 to 4 hours up and 2 to 3 hours down. The first part is the steepest. Some start very early in the morning in the hope of watching the sunrise from the Peak. As often as not, though, the Peak is shrouded in cloud and rain in the early morning. The path winds through a fascinating variety of vegetation, coffee groves and banana plantations on the lower, southern slopes, to tree ferns and dwarf forest near the summit (with some explanatory and mileage signposts). The doctor bird (national bird of Jamaica) is quite common, a beautiful swallow-tailed hummingbird. Quite hard to spot at first but recognizable by its loud buzz, especially near the many flowering bushes. You must take your own food and torch, sweater and rainproof if you set out in the darkness. There are two huts on the Peak where one can overnight in some discomfort (empty concrete buildings with no door). There is a campsite with water and a shower at Portland Gap, about one hour up.

Bath at the eastern end of the island is another place from which one can make attractive trips into the **John Crow Mountains** (named after the ubiquitous turkey buzzards). There is a modest but cheap hotel (*Bath Spa*) dating from 1727 whose main attraction is that it contains natural hot water spring baths which are most relaxing at the end of a long day. There are two passes above Bath, called the Cuna Cuna Pass and the Cornpuss Gap, which lead down to the source of the Rio Grande River on the northern slopes of the mountain range. Both are tough going particularly the Cornpuss Gap. It is absolutely essential to take a local guide. The northern slopes of the mountain range are the home of the unique and extremely rare Jamaican butterfly, *papilio homerus*, a large black and yellow swallowtail. It can best be seen in May/June. Nearby, but not easily accessible, is the magnificent Pera beach between Port Morant and Morant Lighthouse. Near the lighthouse is another good beach but, like nearly all the beaches along the east coast round to Port Antonio, there is a dangerous undertow in certain spots. *Goldfinger's Guesthouse* in Morant Bay, US$100d, cars to rent, clean, friendly, good cooking. Just before reaching Manchioneal from Bath there is a road off to the left which leads to the Reach or Manchioneal Falls (about 3 miles). Well worth a visit if you have a car or are prepared to walk (45 minutes with views of rolling forested hills) from the main road. No facilities at the Falls, there may be an entry charge of US$0.50. Pretty tiers of smooth boulders, the highest fall about 15 feet, through a lush, green gorge. Buses from main road to Port Antonio infrequent, every 1-2 hours. Further northwest along the coast from Manchioneal are *Herman's Holiday Homes*, H Doswell, Long Bay, Portland, three minutes to the beach, US$15 pp, nice, clean, comfortable, helpful (also, 2 bedroom cottage, US$270 a week per couple). Several other cottages and guesthouses have been built on the beach at Long Bay, including *Rose Hill Cottage* (2 bedrooms, US$250 a week per couple), *Casa Pecaro, Seascape, Nirvana, Coconut Isle* and *Rolling Surf* (Tel: 0993 2856, Desmond Goldbourne in Port Antonio).

Once the major banana port where many of the island's first tourists arrived on banana boats, **Port Antonio** dates back to the 16th century. Its prosperity has for many years been in gentle decline, but it has an atmosphere unlike any other town in Jamaica with some superb old public buildings. The rainfall in this part of the island is very high and in consequence the vegetation very lush. Boston Bay, Fairy Hill Beach, San San Beach, the Blue Lagoon (also known as the Blue Hole) and Frenchman's Cave Beach are notable beauty spots to the east of the town. Boston Bay is renowned for its local jerk food pits; several unnamed places by the roadside serving hot spicy chicken, pork or fish, chopped up and wrapped in paper, cooked on planks over a pit of hot coals, very good and tasty. Also worth visiting is Nonsuch Cave, a few miles to the southeast, where there are fossils and evidence of Arawak occupation, Somerset Falls and Folly, an elaborate, turn-of-the-century mansion built in the style of Roman and Greek architecture, now in ruins (partly because the millionaire American's wife took an instant dislike to it). The Folly is about half an hour's walk around the bay from the town. Take a right fork off the path before going into a clump of trees on the peninsula (leading towards lighthouse inside military camp). It is a ghostly, crumbling old mansion in an open field with lovely views shared with grazing cows. A makeshift bar has been set up inside and it looks as though squatters have moved in. There is no public transport to Nonsuch Caves, return taxi fare US$10 including waiting time. Entry US$5, stalactites, gift shop and lunch area. For Somerset Falls, take a bus to Buff Bay (any westbound Kingston bus) and walk 5 minutes from there, entry US$1.

In the harbour it is possible to visit the 68-acre Navy Island, at one time owned by Errol Flynn, which has two beaches (one nudist) and a moderately expensive restaurant. Return boat fare US$2, from jetty on West Street near Musgrave Market, about every hour from 0900-1800. Accommodation US$100-180d EP in rooms or individual villas. Restaurant and bar open to non-guests, open view of bay. 'Errol Flynn Gallery' has display of movie stills and screenings of his golden oldies. There are three beaches on the island, all belonging to the resort but open to non-guests. Snorkelling available (at the nudist beach), US$2 for half-day hire, but there are strong currents and not many fish. Many other sports and other activities on offer, including a complete wedding ceremony in the resort chapel. Reservations, Tel: 993-2667, Fax: 993-2041. Flynn also saw the potential as a tourist attraction for the bamboo rafts which used to bring bananas down the Rio Grande River. Expert raftsmen now take tourists on these rafts down the river. One boatman is Keith Allen, with a registered licence, who can be contacted in Port Antonio at the Huntress Marina, but if you just turn up at Berrydale there are always rafters ready and willing to take you. Each raft (US$40 per trip) takes two passengers and the trip takes 1½-2 hours (depending on the river flow) through magnificent scenery and with an opportunity to stop en route. An unforgettable experience; a driver will take your car down from the point of embarkation to the point of arrival. This is known as Rafter's Rest and is on the main coastal road. Recommended as a place to have a moderately priced lunch or drink in pleasant surroundings even if you are not proposing to raft. The return taxi fare is US$10, there are also buses to Berrydale, the setting-off point, though infrequent. Returning from St Margaret's, downstream, is easier as there are plenty of buses passing between Annotto Bay and Port Antonio. The Rio Grande valley is also well worth exploring, including a trip to the Maroons (descendants of escaped slaves) at Moore Town, but the roads are rough and public transport minimal. Ask for Colonel Harris there who is the leader of the Maroons and is recommended for guided tours. No telephone contact and no accommodation, return taxi fare US$15. To the west of the Rio Grande lie the northern slopes of the Blue Mountains, many parts of which are still virtually unexplored. Nanny Town, the home of the Maroons, was destroyed by the British in 1734 and then "lost" until the 1960s.

Local Information—Port Antonio

Where To Stay Two upmarket hotels are *Trident Villas and Hotel*, US$250-320, Tel: 993-2602/2705, Fax: 993-2590, and *Jamaica Palace*, rates on request, Tel: 993-2020, Fax: 993-3459. On Titchfield Hill, five minutes walk from the town are *De Montevin Lodge*, 21 Fort George Street (PO Box 85, Tel: 993-2604), US$66d EP shared bath, US$74d EP private bath, charming and cosy old Victorian house, restaurant serves set meals, US$8-10, very good value, and *Ivanhoe* nearby US$10d EP shared bath, patio with bay view. Opposite the De Montevin also on Titchfield Hill is *Sunnyside Guest House*, US$10d EP shared bath, basic but quite clean and quiet, recommended and good views of the bay. Several nearby private houses also take guests. In the town centre are *Hope View Guest House*, 26 Harbour Street, Tel: 993-3040. US$10d EP with bath, small, friendly; *Triff's Inn*, 1 Bridge Street, Tel: 992-2162/2420, US$64d CP, modern, clean, pleasant lounge area; on top of a hill overlooking both bays is *Bonnie View*, set in its own working plantation, Tel: 993-2752/2862, US$63-82d EP (depending on room and season), charming rooms, many with excellent views, bar and restaurant, very good meals, probably the best place to stay in town, horse riding and other activities also available. *Frenchman's Cove* at San San, once one of the most luxurious and expensive hotels in the world, closed for refurbishment under new management in 1990, but there is still access to the beach costing about US$3.

Restaurants *Huntress Marina* on a jetty in the harbour, mainly a bar popular with yachting fraternity, but evening meals also served; *Coronation Bakery*, near Musgrave Market on West Street, good for cheap patties and spice buns; *Cream World*, good for ice-cream, cakes and cheap snacks; *Stop Group Jerk Centre* on the bay out of town towards the folly, bar and jerk pork, chicken and fish, also music and dance until late.

Post Office by the clock tower in town centre.

Tourist Office upstairs in shopping precinct on Harbour Street, quite helpful but not knowledgeable about local buses ("soon come"), which leave regularly when full, but at uncertain hours, from sea-front behind Texaco station.

Between Port Antonio and the **Buff Bay** area there are several roads into the interior from such places as Hope Bay and Orange Bay. It's worth a detour if you have a car, but well off the beaten track and public transport is minimal. However, just to the east of Buff Bay there is a new development called Crystal Springs with beautifully laid out gardens, a variety of fish in the clear waters of the streams, an aviary, a bird sanctuary and masses of orchids. There is a moderately priced restaurant, three cottages to rent (US$100 for 4 people maximum, more one-bedroom bungalows being built) and camping sites (tent can be rented). Take any bus between Port Antonio and Kingston (US$0.40, about 45 minutes from Port Antonio), signposted at a turn-off between Orange Bay and Buff Bay (marked Spring Garden on Discover Jamaica road map). About 1½ miles along flat paved road there is a small swimming pool surrounded by palms and flowering tropical plants. An idyllic spot, not busy during the week. Admission about US$1.3 including a complimentary drink of coconut water. Well worth a visit and a good base for exploring the foothills of the Blue Mountains. Contact Pauline Stuart of Stuarts Travel Service, 40 Union Square, Kingston, Tel: 926-4291 (or King's Plaza, Kingston 10, Tel: 929-4222), for up to date information. From Crystal Springs the road goes on to Chepstow and thence to Claverty Cottage and Thompson Gap; spectacular scenery, waterfalls in the valleys and very remote. It is possible to walk from Thompson Gap over the Blue Mountains via Morces Gap and down to Clydesdale, but this is a full day's trip and only to be undertaken with an experienced local guide and there is a problem of getting transport to meet you at Clydesdale. It is also possible to take a bus for part of the way up the Buff Bay valley and then walk on either to Clydesdale or over the Hardwar Gap to Newcastle. Both very long trips and only for the really fit.

The North Coast

The Kingston to Port Maria road (the Junction Road) passes through Castleton Gardens (in a very tranquil setting, well worth a visit by botanists, ask Roy Bennett to be your guide if available). The journey takes about two hours and there are plenty of minibuses. **Port Maria** itself is a sleepy and decaying old banana port but not without charm. East of Port Maria in Robin's Bay there is a camping and cottage resort, *Sonrise Retreat* (formerly Strawberry Fields), basic cabins and tent sites, bath house, Tel/Fax: 996-2351, two miles from village, transport essential. A few miles to the west of Port Maria lies the attractive looking *Casa Maria* hotel which has seen better days, US$80-100d EP. Close by the hotel is Firefly, Noel Coward's Jamaican home, now owned by the Jamaican National Trust. Worth a visit if only for the magnificent view (entrance fee about US$1). At Galina, about two miles further west, there is the prominently signposted *Blue Rock Estate Guest House* on the cliff edge. It was badly damaged by Hurricane Gilbert and is still pretty shambolic but it has a certain charm and a friendly Jamaican atmosphere. Recommended for young, low budget visitors, US$20d with shower, food prices to match, owner's wife is Canadian. Ten minutes further on by car lies Oracabessa, another old banana port with a half completed marina and Golden Eye, the house where Ian Fleming wrote all the James Bond books. To the west of Oracabessa is Boscobel, where the air strip for Ocho Rios is located. Opposite the air strip are numerous houses for rent.

On a bay sheltered by reefs and surrounded by coconut groves, sugar cane and fruit plantations, is **Ocho Rios**, which has become increasingly popular, with many cruise ships making a stop here. It is 64 miles east of Montego Bay, and claims one of the best beaches on the island. The beach in town is safe and well-organized with facilities, 200 metres from Main Street where most of the shops and vehicle hire companies can be found. The scenery of the surrounding area is an added attraction. Most spectacular are the beauty spots of Fern Gully, a marvel of unspoilt tropical vegetation, Roaring River Falls, which has been partially exploited for hydroelectric power, and Dunn's River Falls, tumbling into the Caribbean with invigorating salt and fresh water bathing at its foot.

Historical attractions in the area include Sevilla Nueva, some nine miles to the west, which was where the Spanish first settled in 1509. The ruins of the fort still remain. The site is being investigated by the University of California at Los Angeles and the Spanish Government and it was hoped to include it in the 1992 anniversary celebrations of Columbus' landing in the New World. Offshore, marine archaeologists, from the Institute of Nautical Archaeology at Texas A & M University, are investigating the St Ann's Bay area for sunken ships. Salvaged timbers are believed to have come from two disabled caravels, the *Capitana* and the *Santiago de Palos*, abandoned at Sevilla Nueva probably in 1503 during Columbus' last visit to Jamaica. There are numerous plantation tours available to tourists all along the north coast. Details are widely publicized. Probably the most attractive, informative and certainly most accessible, is the Prospect Plantation Tour (Tel: 974-2058), a short distance to the east of Ocho Rios nearly opposite the *Sans Souci Hotel*. Horseback riding also available there.

Beautifully sited, near Ocho Rios, is the *Upton Country Club*: golf links, tennis, riding and swimming. The *Lion's Den* is a friendly club frequented by Rastafarians; rooms available, good food, clean. West of Ocho Rios is Mammee beach, which is beautiful and less crowded than Ocho Rios, though there is no shade there. There is much fashionable night life in and around Ocho Rios.

Where To Stay The Tourist Board lists many hotels and resorts: *Jamaica Inn*, PO Box 1, Tel: 974-2514, Fax: 974-2449, US$350-400d FAP; *Plantation Inn*, PO Box 2, Tel: 974-5601, Fax: 974-5912, US$250-320d EP, watersports; and *Sans Souci Hotel*, PO Box 103, Tel: 974-2353, Fax: 974-2544, US$330-380d EP. Mid-price inns include *Hibiscus Lodge*, Main Street, PO Box 52 (Tel: 974-2676), US$62-68d EP, pool, jacuzzi, tennis. *Jeff's House*, 10 Main Street, Tel: 974-2664, owned by Jeffrey and Pearl McCoy, US$42-45d including tax, a/c, restaurant good, clean, cheap, kind and helpful, no credit cards. *Hunter's Inn*, 86 Main Street, Tel: 974-5627, Swedish proprietors, recommended as good and cheap. The *Hummingbird Haven*, 2 miles east of Ocho Rios Clock Tower on the main highway, near White River, PO Box 95, Ocho Rios, Tel: 974-5188, Fax: 974-2559, a lovely campsite (US$5d, 20 bare sites) with basic cabins (US$20, twin beds, fan, hot water) and a restaurant, very relaxed, friendly, excellent food, mosquito coils necessary, available on request.

Where To Eat On Main Street are *The Lobsterpot*, US$12-15 for lobster supper, and *Jerk Pork*, same price for barbecued pork, fish or chicken.

Watersports Scuba diving with Sea and Dive Jamaica, Tel: 972-2162; Fantasea, Tel: 974-2353; Sun Divers Watersport, Tel: 973-3509.

Continuing west along the coast is **Runaway Bay**, an attractive and friendly resort. It is named for the Spanish governor Ysasi, who left quickly for Cuba in a canoe when he saw the English coming. Only five miles away is Discovery Bay where Columbus made his first landing. From Runaway Bay, the

Runaway Caves can be visited with a boat ride on the underground lake in the Green Grotto. Among the hotels in this area is the *Runaway HEART Country Club* (PO Box 98, Tel: 973-2671, Fax: 973-2693), which is a hotel training centre (US$60d EP). The *Ambiance Hotel*, Tel: 973-2066, Fax: 973-2432, US$120-170d CP, has been described as adequate for fine weather but lacking in indoor facilities when it rains.

Falmouth is a charming small town about 20 miles east of Montego Bay. It has a fine colonial court house (restored inside), a church, some 18th century houses, and Antonio's, a famous place to buy beach shirts. There is good fishing (tarpon and kingfish) at the mouth of the Martha Brae, near Falmouth, and no licence is required. It is possible to go rafting from Martha Brae village. Expert rafters guide the craft for the 1-hour trip to the coast. Jamaica Swamp Safaris (a crocodile farm) has a bar and restaurant. Some 10 miles inland is the 18th century plantation guest house of Good Hope amongst coconut palms (Tel: 954-3289): de luxe accommodation in the superb setting of a working plantation, as well as day tours and horse riding—some of the best riding in Jamaica—and its own beach on the coast.

The Cockpit Country

This is a strange and virtually uninhabited area to the south of Falmouth and to the south west of Montego Bay. It consists of a seemingly endless succession of high bumps made of limestone rock. The tourist office and hotels in Montego Bay organize day trips to Maroon Town (no longer occupied by Maroons) and Accompong, the headquarters of the Maroons who live in the Cockpit Country area. Older locals can accurately describe what happened at the last battle between the Maroons and the British forces. Ask to see the "Wondrous Caves" at Elderslie near Accompong. If you have a car take the road on the eastern side of the Cockpit Country from Duncans (near Falmouth) to Clark's Town and thence to Barbecue Bottom and on to Albert town. Parts of the road are rough but negotiable with care in an ordinary car. The views from Barbecue Bottom are truly spectacular (the road is high above the Bottom) and this is wonderful birding country. If you wish to go on foot into the Cockpit Country make your way, either by car or on foot (no public transport), to the Windsor Caves due south of Falmouth. They are full of bats which make a spectacular mass exit from the caves at dusk. There are local guides to hand. The underground rivers in the caves (as elsewhere in much of Jamaica) run for miles, but are only for the experienced and properly equipped potholer. There is a locally published book called **Jamaica Underground** but the local caving club seems moribund at the time of writing. Mr Stephenson is a guide who has been recommended at the town of Quick Step; many caves and good walks in the area. It is possible to walk from the Windsor Caves across the middle of the Cockpit Country to Troy on the south side (about eight hours). It is essential to have a local guide and to make a preliminary trip to the Windsor Caves to engage him. Convince yourself that he really does know the way because these days this crossing is very rarely made even by the locals. It is also vastly preferable to be met with transport at Troy because you will still be in a pretty remote area.

Montego Bay and Western Jamaica

About 120 miles from Kingston by road or rail, situated on the northwest coast, is **Montego Bay**, Jamaica's principal tourist centre with all possible watersport amenities. It has superb natural features, sunshine most of the year round, a beautiful coastline with miles of white sand and deep blue water never too cold for bathing (20°- 26°C average temperature) and gentle winds which make sailing a favourite sport. There are underwater coral gardens in a sea so clear that they can be seen without effort from glass-bottomed boats at the Doctor's Cave, which is also the social centre of beach life (there is an admission charge). Scuba diving can be arranged through Seaworld, Tel: 953-2180; Poseidon Nemrod Club, Tel: 952-3624; Montego Bay Divers, Tel: 952-4874. A single dive costs about US$45, a snorkelling trip US$25. Montego Bay caters also for the rich and sophisticated. Visitors enjoy the same duty-free concessions as in Kingston. Gloucester Avenue, by Doctor's Cave, is one of the busiest streets for tourists, lined with duty-free shops, souvenir arcades and several restaurants and hotels. Constant importuning in the town's streets is a major problem.

Of interest to the sightseer are an old British fort (Fort Montego, landscaped gardens and crafts market) and the 18th century church of St James in Montego Bay (restored after earthquake damage in 1957). There are a few Georgian buildings, such as the *Town House Restaurant*, 16 Church Street, and the Georgian Court at the corner of Union and Orange Streets. The centre of town is Sam Sharpe Square, named after the slave who led a rebellion in 1831-2.

If you are staying in town, rather than at the hotel strip, there are beaches close by, either public ones with no services or a private beach (US$0.50 admission) with food, drinks, tennis, boat hire, snorkelling, shower, changing rooms etc. Walk from the traffic circle in the middle of town towards the hotels and the beach will be on your right.

Local Information—Montego Bay

Airport The Donald Sangster international airport is only 2 miles from the town centre. For those landing here who want to go to Kingston, there is a transfer service by Martins minibus which takes 5 hours. It is also possible to get to the Norman Manley airport, Kingston, by taking the minibus from the town centre to West Parade, Kingston, from where the airport buses leave; US$4.50, 3 hours. See **Information for Visitors** for the rail connection between Montego Bay and Kingston.

Transport There is no need to take the expensive tourist buses, except that the regular buses get crowded. The regular buses are fast, very frequent and cheap, about US$2 from Montego Bay to Negril with a 30-second transfer in Lucea. Buses from Kingston depart from Pechan Street, near the railway station, roughly every hour from 0600 to 1500, US$2.80. It is possible to get to Montego Bay from Port Antonio all along the north coast, a scenic journey involving changes in Annotto Bay (then shared taxi, US$0.60 per person, mad rush to squeeze into clapped-out Ladas, the locals give no quarter to slow tourists), Port Maria and Ocho Rios. **Bicycle** rentals through Western Bike Rentals and Sales Ltd, 27 Gloucester Avenue, Tel: 952-0185, US$8/24 hours, bikes a bit battered.

Where To Stay There are over 40 hotels, guest houses and apartment hotels listed by the Tourist Board, with prices ranging from US$40 to US$195d, without meals. The *Coral Cliff*, Gloucester Avenue, PO Box 253, Tel: 952-4130, Fax: 952-6532 (a US$7 cab ride from the airport) is recommended, with a beautiful veranda, restaurant and friendly service, winter rate US$60d, EP, not including 8% tax; also on Gloucester Avenue, *Harmomy House Hotel*, proprietor Mr Mack, US$40d, friendly, under construction, basic rooms, 5 minutes' walk from Doctor's Cave Beach and Duty Free shops; *Ocean View Guest House*, 26 Sunset Boulevard, PO Box 210 (Tel: 952-2662), 10 minutes' easy walk from the airport, US$45d (US$55 triple), many rooms overlook the bay, all clean, with bath, recommended (on arrival, ask tourist board to phone the hotel who will arrange free transport from the airport); *Ridgeway Guest House*, 34 Queen's Drive (Tel: 952-2709) 5 minutes' walk from airport, US$55d EP, with bath and fan, friendly, clean, family atmosphere (cheaper rates for longer stays). *The View Guest House*, Jarrett Terrace, Tel: 952-3175, US$30d, homely atmosphere, some rooms with excellent view over bay, very friendly staff, swimming pool, one of the cheapest, highly-recommended; *Mrs Craig's Guest House*, on Church Street, near Police Station, no sign, ask directions, noisy with uncomfortable mattresses and terrible showers but safe and cheap at US$25; *Pemco Hotel*, Union Street, on the way up to Brandon Hill, 20 minutes' walk from Doctor's Cave Beach, can arrange accommodation at good rates (Tel: 952-4000, Mr Samuel Clarke). *Mountainside Guest House*, Queen's Drive, near the airport, behind the *Cotton Tree Restaurant*, enquire at the restaurant, very pleasant, clean rooms, balcony, good views, private bathroom, mosquito coils provided, noisy in early evening because of restaurant, but quiet at night, US$30s, US$35d, friendly and helpful. There is a YMCA at Mount Salem with sports facilities available to members.

Where To Eat   On the way into town from the airport there are several reasonably-priced restaurants; recommended is the *Pork Pit* in pleasant open-air garden on Kent Avenue, near Cornwall Beach and the *Toby Inn*, very good for cheap barbecued chicken and pork, cheap drinks. *Cotton Tree*, Queen's Drive, near airport, free pick-up service, mainly seafood but very good vegetarian food on request, Tel: 952-5329 for reservation. *Orlan Caribe Vegetarian Restaurant*, 71 Barnett Street, tidy, comfortable, low prices, sole vegetarian restaurant. There are several restaurants along Gloucester Avenue, including *Shakey's*, for pizza and breakfasts (deliveries, Tel: 952-2665), not too good; *The Greenhouse*, opposite St James Place shopping arcade, good food and inexpensive; *Cascade*, in the Hotel Pelican, (Tel: 952-3171), seafood specialities at moderate prices; *Marguerite's*, on the sea-front, has two restaurants, one posh with air-conditioning and another simpler next door on a patio.

Night Clubs   *The Cave* (at *Seawinds Hotel*), at *Casa Montego Hotel*, *The Rum Barrel*, the *Cellar* and the *Reef Club*. Many others.

Excursions

Out of town, to the east, the great houses of Rose Hall and Greenwood may be visited. The latter was built by the forefathers of the poet, Elizabeth Barrett Browning, in 1780-1800. Rose Hall was started ten years earlier, in 1770, by John Palmer (a lively legend of witchcraft surrounds the wife of one of his descendants, Anne Palmer).

Inland, southeast of Montego Bay is the Arawak rock carving at Kempshot, while to the southwest is the bird sanctuary at Anchovy (Rocklands Feeding Station; open to visitors after 1530, but members of birdwatching societies will be admitted any time. Children under five are not admitted). Three miles to the west of Anchovy is Lethe, the starting point for rafting down the Great River. South of Anchovy, about 25 miles from Montego Bay, is Seaford Town, which was settled by Germans in the 1830s. Only about 200 of their descendants survive. Write to Francis Friesen, Lamb's River Post Office.

Lucea is a charming spot on the north coast where the *Tamarind Lodge* serves excellent Jamaican food. Visit the Rusea School, endowed by a refugee Frenchman in the 18th century, in a lovely location but badly damaged by Hurricane Gilbert. Between here and Montego Bay (bus, US$0.88) is Tryall, with one of the best golf courses on the island. The course is home to the Jamaica Classic, an LPGA Tour event and is set in a 2,200 acre resort complex. Tennis is also available and there is a clubhouse, beach bar and restaurant. Continuing around the island's western end, the road passes through Green Island before reaching Negril (29 miles from Lucea).

Negril, on a seven-mile stretch of pure white sand on the western end of the island, is far less formal than other tourist spots but is still a one-industry town. The town is at the south end of Long Bay; at the north is the smaller Bloody Bay, where whalers used to carve up their catch. The main part of the town has most of the resorts and all the beaches. There is no snorkelling here, however, and you have to take a boat. In the West End of the village are beautiful cliffs and many fine caves, with great snorkelling but no beaches. In between is an area with neither beaches nor cliffs. There is clothes optional bathing at certain hotels, which is still quite rare in non-French Caribbean islands. Watersports are a particular attraction and there are facilities for tennis and riding. There is a dive shop at *Hedonism II*, Tel: 957-4200, free for guests. Hawkers ('higglers') are annoying and reported to be worse than at Montego Bay. They will interrupt whatever you are doing to push their drugs, hair braiding, aloe etc. Politely decline whatever they are offering (if you do not want it), they do not want to be shrugged off or ignored, but neither do they want to hold a long conversation with you. Fruit is readily available although not ready to eat; ask the vendor to cut it up and put it in a bag for you. Behind the bay is the Great Morass, which is being drained for development.

Local Information—Negril

Transport The orange minibuses are the cheapest way to travel around the town. There are buses to Negril from both Savanna-la-Mar (about ¾ hour) and Montego Bay. From Montego Bay the fare is about US$2; there are also taxi and colectivo services. From the Donald Sangster airport minibuses run to Negril; you must bargain with the driver to get the fare to US$5-7.

Where To Stay Many Tourist Board listed establishments, ranging from the *Hedonism II* resort (Tel: 957-4200, Fax: 957-4289, PO Box 25) at US$1,200-1400 pp weekly double occupancy, all inclusive; *Grand Lido* at southern end of 2-mile sandy beach of Bloody Bay (P O Box 88, Tel: 957-4010, Fax: 957-4317), US$490-570d, all inclusive, clothes optional, pool and jacuzzi beside its nude beach area, guests can also use the facilities at *Hedonism II*, a short walk across Rutland Point, to several less expensive hotels on Norman Manley Boulevard (*Negril Gardens Hotel*, Tel: 957-4408, Fax: 957-4374, US$125-135, US$10 tax; *Negril Inn*, Tel: 957-4209, Fax: 957-4365, US$125-135d EP, *Foote Prints on the Sands*, PO Box 100, Tel: 957-4300, Fax: 957-4301, US$110-160d EP; *Poinciana Beach Hotel and Villas*, Tel: 957-4100/3, US$164d BP). *Charela Inn*, US$130-155d, US$12 tax, minimum stay 5 nights, on the beach (PO Box 33, Tel: 957-4277, Fax: 957-4414), is recommended. *Firefly Beach Cottages*, Norman Manley Blvd, on the beach and therefore not very private (PO Box 54, Tel: 925-5728), from a basic cabin for two, US$30-40, to studios, US$70-80, or 1-3 bedroomed cottages, US$100-250, or luxury villa, US$400 in winter, cabins fall to US$10-20 in summer, luxury villa to US$270, tax US$8 winter, US$4 summer, gymnasium, minimum 1 week rental in winter, 3 nights in summer. Hotels to the west of centre are about 10-20 minutes' walk, and are in a better area for mixing with the locals. *Rock Cliff*, West End, PO Box 67, Tel/Fax: 957-4331, US$115-140d EP, US$10 tax, on rocky promontory; *Ocean Edge Resort*, also on cliffs, PO Box 71, Tel: 957-4362, US$65-85 winter; *Addis Kobeb Guest House and Cottages* (PO Box 78, Tel: 957-4485) US$40 per room in house, entire house (6 rooms) US$240, cottages US$50, 20% less in summer, long term rates negotiable, wooden houses, hammocks outside, shady gardens, restaurant next door. *Negril Cabins* recommended by SENSE, only other accommodation on Bloody Bay, across the road from the beach, cabins on stilts, security guards keep away 'higglers'; *Captain Nemo's*, US$20, just across the street from Joe's Caves, an excellent snorkelling area. Accommodation is available at the Yacht Club, and rooms can also be rented at

Sunrise and other houses. *Lighthouse Park* on Negril's cliffs, campsite, cabins US$20-40 a night, tent site US$10, recommended. The East End is the more expensive part of town, but there are a few cheap cabins: *Roots Bamboo* is very neat, US$25 a night; *Coconut International*, on the beach, US$15d, basic cabin but clean and owners very friendly, excellent food at reasonable prices; *Mr Reynold's* (also known as *Mr Mack's*) is about US$30. This whole beach is lined with clubs and is noisy. *Mr Mack's* is at the edge of town after the craft market, and is one of the quieter places. None of the cabins has any services, nor do they provide blankets, but they are right on the beach. When choosing a cabin check to see whether it has a fan, whether there is a mesh or screen to keep out mosquitoes (if not, buy 'Destroyers', 8-hour incense to keep bugs away) and whether it looks safe (many get broken into). Locals living along the beach will often let you camp on their property.

Where To Eat For entertainment try the *White Swan*, where the locals go. *The Dolphin*, next to *New Providence Guest House*, is good. *The Yacht Club* and *Wharf Club* both have restaurants, the latter being cheaper. *Peewee's Restaurant*, in the West End of Negril, has excellent seafood and other dishes at reasonable prices. *Erica's* restaurant and *The Tigress*, both near West End; latter is cheaper than many and good. *The Hungry Lion*, on the West End road, vegetarian and fish dishes, excellent food and service, relaxing, moderately priced; *Rick's Café*, the "trendy" place to watch the sunset, but pricey with it. *Cool Runnings*, with a chef/owner, is also recommended. *The Office*, on the beach, open 24 hours, provides a good choice of Jamaican food, reasonably priced and friendly service, a good place to meet the locals. Eating cheaply is difficult but not impossible. The native restaurant-food stalls are good and relatively cheap; the local patties are delicious. Street hawkers will sell you jerk chicken for US$4-5, which is good but barely enough to whet your appetite. *The Bread Basket*, next to the banks at the mall in town is recommended, but even better is the *Fisherman's Club* supermarket, just off the beach in the main part of town near *Pete's Seafood*, which is a restaurant as well as a market and serves good local, filling meals for about US$4.

Entertainment Live reggae shows in outdoor venues most nights, featuring local and well known stars. Entrance is usually US$5-7, good fun, lively atmosphere, very popular. Nice bars are located along the beach, usually with music, unnamed bar next to *Coconut International* recommended, friendly service. For a pleasant drink in beautiful surroundings try the bar at the *Rock Cliff Hotel* on the West End Road, friendly barman who mixes great fruit punches and cocktails.

Banks Two banks (including National Commercial Bank) and *bureau de change* in the shopping centre in town.

About 18 miles east of Negril, on the coast, is *Savanna-la-Mar*, a busy, commercial town with shopping, banks etc, but no major attractions for tourists. It does not have a good beach, nor good quality restaurants and accommodation. Regular concerts are held at the remodelled St Joseph's Catholic Church (Tel: 955-2648). Talented local musicians play under the auspices of Father Sean Lavery, formerly a professor of music at Dublin University, recommended. It can easily be reached by minibus from Negril and there are hourly buses from Montego Bay (US$2). The Frome sugar refinery, five miles north of Savanna-la-Mar, will often allow visitors to tour their facilities during sugar cane season (generally November-June). Another interesting and unusual outing in this part of Jamaica is to the six-mile long Roaring River and the Ital Herbs and Spice Farm, two miles north of Petersfield, from where it is remarkably well signposted. The Farm, owned by an American, Ed Kritzler, employs organic methods. There is a cave at Roaring River and the Farm is about half a mile further on. It is a very scenic area with interesting walks and tumbling streams suitable for bathing. A good restaurant serves fish and vegetable dishes at the Farm, best to order lunch before exploring. Totally basic accommodation in a hut available, US$28, popular but it is suggested you look before you book.

The South Coast and Mandeville

Outside Savanna-la-Mar, the main south coast road (A2) passes by Paradise Plantation, a huge private estate with miles of frontage on Bluefields Bay, a wide protected anchorage with unspoiled reefs and wetlands teeming with birds. Just after Paradise, you come to Ferris Crossroads, where the A2 meets up with the B8 road, a well-maintained north-south connection and about 40 minutes drive to Montego Bay via Whithorn and Anchovy. For the next four miles the A2 hugs the coast along a beautiful stretch of road to *Bluefields*, where there is a lovely white sand beach mainly used by local Jamaicans and guests of the upmarket *Villas on Bluefields Bay*. This beach front resort offers exclusive, luxury, fully-staffed accommodation, US$750-2,000 per adult per week depending on season, children under 12 US$250, includes food, drinks, transfers, staff and sporting facilities, each villa has a secluded waterfront and pool. Information and bookings through the owners, Deborah and Braxton Moncure, 726 North Washington Street, Alexandria, Virginia 22314, USA (Tel: (202) 234-4010, Fax: (703) 549-6517). There is no mass tourism either in Bluefields or in the adjacent village of Belmont, where plenty of reggae is always playing at the numerous fishermen's bars, but there are a few expatriate homes which might sometimes be available for rent: *Oristano*, the oldest home in western Jamaica, dating back to the 1700s, owned by the Hon William Fielding, an Englishman who does beautiful drawings of the Jamaican greathouses, P O Box 1, Bluefields, Westmoreland Parish; *Two Pelicans*, built right on the side of the main road, this 1950s home is a waterfront cliffhanger with good views, contact the American owners, Steve and Linda Browne, Tel: (301) 924-3464; *Horizon*, a cottage in Belmont, owned by American Mary Gunst, Tel: (603) 942-7633. For accommodation with Jamaican families ask Mrs Monroe, opposite *KD's Keg Bar*.

The south coast is known as the best part of Jamaica for deep sea fishing and boat trips go out from Belmont to the reefs or to off-shore banks. Snorkelling is also good because the sea is almost always very calm in the morning. The Bluefields Great House, now privately owned, was the place where Philip Gosse lived in the 1830s when he wrote his famous book, *Birds of Jamaica*, and reportedly contains the first breadfruit tree planted in Jamaica by Captain Bligh after his expedition to the South Pacific. The next six miles of coast southeast of Bluefields is one of the most beautiful, unspoiled coasts in Jamaica, but see it now, there are plans to build a 300-room *Sandals South Coast* at Auchindown. Just beyond here, *Natania's*, a guest house and seafood restaurant at Little Culloden, White House, has been highly recommended. It is on the sea and has eight rooms (10 beds) at US$55 per room single, food extra but good and at reasonable prices. The owner is Peter Probst; address: Natania's, Little Culloden, White House PO, Westmoreland. Transport from Montego Bay can be arranged, as also local tours, deep sea fishing and water sports. A few miles further on, *South Sea View* guest house has eight bedrooms at US$38s, US$50d, food extra, British manager, John Ackerman, White House PO, Westmoreland, Tel: 965-2550.

The A2 road passes through Scotts Cove, where you leave Westmoreland and enter the parish of St Elizabeth. It proceeds to the town of Black River, travelling inland from there to Middle Quarters, YS Falls and Bamboo Avenue, after which it ascends to the old hill station of Mandeville.

Black River is one of the oldest towns in Jamaica. It had its heyday in the 18th century when it was the main exporting harbour for logwood dyes. The first car imported into Jamaica was landed here. Along the shore are some fine early 19th century mansions, some of which are being restored.

At Black River, Charles Swaby will take visitors by boat up the lower stretches of the Black River, the longest river in Jamaica (duration 1½-2 hours, US$12 pp, drinks included). You should see crocodiles (called alligators in Jamaica—most likely at midday when they bask on the river banks) and plenty of bird life in beautifully tranquil surroundings with a very knowledgeable guide (contact South Coast Safaris, Hotel Street, PO Box 129, Mandeville, Tel: 962-0220/3351). Charles Swaby will also arrange for you to visit the YS Falls.

Local Information—Black River

Transport To get to Black River from Mandeville by bus involves a change in Santa Cruz.

Where To Stay *Waterloo Guest House*, in a Georgian building (the first house in Jamaica with electric light), US$25 for the old rooms in the main house, to US$40 in the new annex, all with showers, very good restaurant (lobster for US$7 in season), recommended. *Hotel Pontio*, High Street (PO Box 35, Tel: 965-2255) US$29 a/c, US$19 without a/c, restaurant, recommended. Two miles east of Black River is the *Port of Call Hotel*, 136 Crane Road, Tel: 965-2360/2410, a bit spartan (about US$30) but on the sea. Also, *Bridge House Hotel*, on beach, US$25; *Kenchrismar Beach Cottage*, bedroom with private bath or dormitory, US$20 pp, each additional person US$8, children half price, run by Mr and Mrs Patrick Lee, Sweet Bakery, Apple Valley Farm, Maggotty, St Elizabeth (see below).

On the south coast past Black River is **Treasure Beach**, a wide dark sand beach with body surfing waves. It is largely used by local fishermen as it is the closest point to the Pedro Banks. There is one small grocery shop and a van comes to the village every day with fresh fruit and vegetables. Accommodation on the beach includes the *Treasure Beach Hotel*, Tel: 965-2305, Fax: 965-2544, US$70d EP, US$162d FAP; *Old Wharf Guest House* (apartments), *Four M's Cottage*, Fax: 965-2544, US$30d EP, and several houses you can rent: Sparkling Waters, Folichon, Caprice, and Siwind, with its own cove. *Ital Rest* is a wooden guesthouse, hard to find, known to locals and bus drivers, US$40d EP, verandah decks with mountain and sea views, very clean with helpful owners, kitchen available, highly recommended. Camping is possible in the grounds and "Ital Rest II" is due to open soon. This area is quite unlike any other part of Jamaica, still relatively unvisited by tourists and well worth a visit. To the east of Treasure Beach lies Lovers' Leap, a beauty spot named after the slave and his lover (his owner's daughter) who jumped off the cliff in despair, and Alligator Pond.

If you stay on the A2 instead of turning off at Black River, the road comes to Middle Quarters, on the edge of the Black River Morass (a large swamp); hot pepper shrimp are sold by the wayside, but insist that they are fresh (today's catch). Just after Middle Quarters is the left turn which takes you to the beautiful YS Falls (pronounced Why-Ess), an unspoiled spot in the middle of a large private plantation and well worth visiting. There is a 15-minute walk from where you park your car. You can bathe but there are no changing rooms or other facilities; plan a morning visit as there is no shelter in case of afternoon rain. Entrance fee about US$3. Further along the main road is the impressive 2½-mile long Bamboo Avenue (badly hit by

Gilbert but now recovering). The Jamaica Tourist Board is building a travellers' halt, which will have food and toilets. North of Bamboo Avenue is Maggotty, on the railway line from Montego Bay to Kingston and close to the Appleton Estate, where tours of the rum factory are offered. Opposite the Maggotty train depot is the Sweet Bakery, run by Mr and Mrs Lee, who also own the *Apple Valley Guest House*, US$30d with private bath, US$25d with shared bath, US$9 camping in own tent, US$12 in rented tent, very friendly and helpful, local trips organized, Mrs Lee is an excellent cook.

After Bamboo Avenue, the A2 road goes through Lacovia and Santa Cruz, an expanding town on the St Elizabeth Plain, and on up to **Mandeville**, a beautiful and peaceful upland town with perhaps the best climate in the island. It is very spread out, with building on all the surrounding hills and no slums (population 50,000). In recent years Mandeville has derived much of its prosperity from being one of the centres of the bauxite/alumina industry (though industrial activity is outside the city).

The town's centre is the village green, now called Cecil Charlton Park (after the ex-mayor, whose opulent mansion, Huntingdon Summit, can be visited with prior arrangement). The green looks a bit like New England; at its northeast side stands a Georgian courthouse and, on the southwest, St Mark's parish church (both 1820). By St Mark's is the market area (busiest days are Monday, Wednesday and Friday—the market is supposed to be moved elsewhere) and the area where buses congregate. West of the green, at the corner of Ward Avenue and Caledonia Road, is the Manchester Club (Tel: 962-2403), one of the oldest country clubs in the West Indies (1868) and the oldest in Jamaica. It has a nine-hole golf course (18 tee boxes, enabling you to play 18 holes) and tennis courts (you must be introduced by a member). Also, horse riding can be arranged, Tel: Ann Turner on 962-2527.

Local Information—Mandeville

Where To Stay Diana McIntyre-Pyke, the proprietress of the small, family run *Astra Hotel* (62 Ward Avenue, PO Box 60, Tel: 962-3265/3377, Fax: 962-1461) and her staff provide a highly efficient and cheerful information service about everything to be done in the area. Rooms are moderately priced (US$55-80 per room and food US$20-US$25 a day per person), the restaurant is good and service friendly, but the highly recommended hotel is some way from the town centre. Even if not staying at the *Astra*, you can seek information on the following there: community tourism (meeting the local community), tourism in central and south Jamaica, an island-wide bed and breakfast programme, villa rentals, staying with local families, and tours of Mandeville, free for guests.

In the centre is the *Mandeville Hotel*, 4 Hotel Street (PO Box 78, Tel: 962-2138, Fax: 962-0700), US$45-90 per room EP, TV, spacious, pool, restaurant, excursions arranged, good. Cheaper accommodation is available at *Rodan's Guest House*, 3 Wesley Avenue (Tel: 962-2552), US$28d with bath, basic, no fan, uncomfortable beds.

Where To Eat Technically a restaurant, but also recommended for its décor (of old cars and licence plates) and atmosphere is *Bill Laurie's Steak House*, 600 feet above the town, good for views, steaks, conversation (closed Sunday). *Pot Pourri*, on second floor of the Caledonia Mall, just north of the Manchester Club, clean and bright, good food and service; *International Chinese Restaurant*, Newport Road; *Hunger Hut*, 45 Manchester Road, cheap, excellent food and service (owner, Fay, grew up in England and likes a chat).

Shopping Westico Health Foods, by the West Indies College, run by Seventh Day Adventists; they also run a vegetarian restaurant behind the church in the town centre, opening hours erratic. Craft Centre, sponsored by the Women's Club of Manchester, on Manchester Road.

Banks Bank of Novia Scotia; National Commercial Bank.

Excursions

Although some way inland Mandeville is a good place from which to start exploring both the surrounding area and the south coast. (In fact, by car you can get to most of Jamaica's resorts, except those east of Ocho Rios or Kingston, in two hours or less.) Birdwatchers and those interested in seeing a beautiful "great house" in a cattle property should contact Robert Sutton at *Marshall's Pen* (Tel: 962-2260). Robert is the island's top ornithologist (23 of Jamaica's endemic bird species have been observed here). The *Astra Hotel* can arrange a visit. Also around the town you can visit the High Mountain Coffee and Pioneer Chocolate Factories, a factory making bammy (a delicacy from cassava root), the Alcan works, and local gardens.

There are interesting excursions north to Christiana (at about 2,800 feet, *Hotel Villa Bella*, 18 rooms and suites, restaurant, in six acres with orchard of ortaniques and bananas, nature walks, riding, special interest groups catered for, PO Box 473, Cristiana, Tel: 964-2243, Fax: 964-2762, US$50d, US$80 suite), southwest to the Santa Cruz mountains, and south to Alligator Pond on the coast. East of Alligator Pond is Gut River, where you can sometimes see alligators and manatees; cottages can be rented near the very picturesque river flowing into the sea (contact through *Astra Hotel*). Boat and fishing trips can be made to Pigeon Island, with a day on the island for swimming and snorkelling.

From Mandeville it is about 55 miles east to Kingston on the A2, bypassing May Pen, through Old Harbour then on to Spanish Town and Kingston. Before the May Pen bypass, a road branches south to **Milk River Bath**, the world's most radioactive spa. The baths are somewhat run down, but the medical properties of the water are among the best anywhere. About three miles from the baths is a marine conservation area, Alligator Hole, where manatees (sea cows) can sometimes be seen. Local boatmen will do their best to oblige.

Information for Visitors

Documents

Canadian and US citizens do not need passports or visas for a stay of up to six months, if they reside in their own countries and have some proof of citizenship (eg a birth certificate, certified by the issuing authority with an embossed seal, together with a voter's registration card). Residents of Commonwealth countries, Austria, Belgium, Denmark, Finland, Iceland, Eire, Israel, Italy, Luxembourg, Mexico, Netherlands, Norway, Spain, Sweden, Switzerland, Turkey and Germany, need a passport and an onward ticket for a stay not exceeding six months. Citizens of all other countries must have a visa, passport and onward ticket. Immigration may insist on your

having an address, prior to giving an entry stamp. Otherwise you will have to book a hotel room in the airport tourist office (friendly and helpful).

How To Get There By Air

Air Jamaica has services from Canada, UK, the Caribbean and USA (Atlanta, Baltimore, Miami, New York, Orlando, Philadelphia). British Airways and Air Jamaica fly direct, between London and Kingston and Montego Bay. LTU International Airways has a weekly flight to Montego Bay from Dusseldorf. Aeroflot has a weekly flight from Moscow via Shannon, Ireland, and on to Managua. Air Canada flies from Toronto to Jamaica. American Airlines flies from New York,

Dallas/Fort Worth and Miami daily to Montego Bay and Kingston, from Chicago and Raleigh to Montego Bay. American Trans Air to Montego Bay from Los Angeles, San Francisco and Orlando. Continental from New York, Key Airlines from Savannah, Georgia, and Northwest Airlines from Detroit, Kalamazoo and Tampa to Montego Bay and on to Grand Cayman in high season. Cayman Airways and Air Jamaica also connect the Caymans and Jamaica. BWIA and ALM serve the island from the southern and eastern Caribbean. There is a twice weekly Cubana flight to Havana from Kingston. Air Jamaica fly twice a week from Kingston to Nassau. Copa flies Panama City-Kingston twice a week. Enquire in Florida about cheap flights from Fort Lauderdale and Orlando.

Airport Information

Details of the two international airports are given under Kingston and Montego Bay.

There is an airport departure tax of J$100, payable in Jamaican or US dollars, for all those who have been in the island over 24 hours. There is no sales tax on air tickets purchased in Jamaica.

Airline Offices

Air Jamaica head office: The Towers, Dominica Drive, Kingston 5, Tel: 929-4661 (opens at 0830), offices in Montego Bay, Tel: 952-4300, Negril, Tel: 957-4210, Ocho Rios, Tel: 974-2566; British Airways is also in The Towers, Tel: 929-9020/5, 952-3771 (Montego Bay). BWIA, 19 Dominica Drive, Kingston 5, Tel: 929-3771/3, 924-8364 (airport), 952-4100 (Montego Bay). American Airlines, Tel: 924-8305 (Kingston), 952-5950 (Montego Bay).

It is extremely difficult to book a passage by ship to other Caribbean islands.

Local Transport

There are **internal flights** by Trans-Jamaica Airlines (Tel: 952-5401, Montego Bay) between Montego Bay, Kingston, Negril, Ocho Rios and Port Antonio. Charges are reasonable but using this method of travel is not very satisfactory unless you can arrange to be met at your destination. The Kingston airstrip is at Tinson Pen which is only 2 miles from the centre of town on Marcus Garvey Drive, but those at Ocho Rios and Port Antonio are a long way out of town.

There is a **train**, called "The Diesel",

between Kingston and Montego Bay through some spectacular scenery. Kingston to Montego Bay depart 0900, arrive 1400; Montego Bay to Kingston depart 0800, arrive 1300. 1st class US$3.50 (Saturdays and Sundays only), padded seats, not heavily booked up or crowded, 2nd class US$2, wooden seats. No buffet carriage, vendors come along with snacks. Beautiful hilly scenery for much of the journey, especially around the edge of the Cockpit Country. Kingston station is in a deserted, not very safe-looking area, no sign of buses, better to take a taxi. The line between Kingston and Port Antonio was damaged in a hurricane some years ago, and there are no plans to repair it. There is also a private train service from Montego Bay to the Appleton Estate where you can tour the rum factory, with stops along the way at Catadupa and the Ipswich Caves, open bar all day, free rum, contact Appleton Estate Express, Howard Cooke Highway, Montego Bay, Tel: 952-3692, Fax: 962-2762.

Public road transport is mostly by **minibus**. This is cheap but overcrowded and generally chaotic and only to be recommended for the young and fit ("Step Up!" shouted by the conductors means please move down the bus, there is plenty of room at the back!). Be prepared also for a certain amount of physical abuse from the bus company front men as they compete for your custom. Country buses are slow and sometimes dangerous; they run, for instance, to Irish Town, Mavis Bank, Gordon Town and Red Hills for US$0.40. Bus X20 goes from Victoria Square to Port Henderson. There are also minibuses which ply all the main routes and operate on a "colectivo" basis, leaving (only when full) from the Parade in Kingston. Colectivo to Ocho Rios costs US$2, and takes 2 hours. Crossroads and Half Way Tree are the other main bus stops. Other fares from Kingston are: US$1.40 to Mandeville, US$2.75 to Montego Bay, US$1.50 to Negril, US$1.25 to Ocho Rios, US$1.40 to Port Antonio. The buses are invaded by touts as they approach the bus station. Bus travel in Kingston costs between US$0.20 and US$0.30. A free map of Kingston bus routes is available from Jamaica Omnibus Services Ltd, 80 King Street. Travelling by bus is not safe after dark.

There are **taxis**, with red PP licence plates, in all the major resort areas and at the airports. Some have meters, some do not. But there are officially authorized charges to all destinations and you should insist on the taxi driver producing evidence to show that he is charging the correct fare. The tourist information centres should also be able to help in this respect. Some "non-tourist" taxis operate like minibuses, ie have a set route and can be flagged down. They will cram about six passengers into a small Lada, but if you do not want to share you can hire it all to yourself. Negotiate the fare in advance.

Undoubtedly a **rented car** is the most satisfactory, and most expensive, way of getting about. All the major car rental firms are represented both at the airports and in the major resort areas. There are also numerous local car rental firms which are mostly just as good and tend to be cheaper. The Tourist Board has a list of members of the Jamaica U-Drive Association. Be prepared to pay considerably more than in North America or Europe. Driving times and distances of major routes: Kingston to Montego Bay 117 miles, 3 hours, to Ocho Rios 55 miles, 2 hours, to Port Antonio 68 miles, 2 hours; Montego Bay to Negril 50 miles, 1½ hours, to Ocho Rios 67 miles, 2 hours; Ocho Rios to Port Antonio 67 miles, 2½ hours. Motor scooters are widely available for about US$24 a day. The speed limit is 30 mph in built up areas, 50 mph on highways.

Try to avoid driving outside towns at night. Roads, even on the coast, are twisty and in the mountains extremely so, add potholes and Jamaican drivers and you are an accident waiting to happen. Plan ahead because it gets dark early. Ask car hire firms or hotels for estimates of journey times but remember that distances stretch when overtaking is difficult.

Hotels And Restaurants

Because Jamaica is a major tourist destination there are a great many hotels and restaurants, particularly in the tourist areas. Full and up to date information is available at all tourist information centres. We only mention those which have recently been recommended for whatever reason. The brochure *Elegant Resorts* features most of the hotels in the top price-range which have reciprocal arrangements.

Visitors on a low budget should aim to arrive at Montego Bay rather than Kingston because the former is the island's tourism capital with more cheap accommodation. Get hold of the Tourist Board's list of Hotels and Guest Houses, which gives rates and addresses, and also a copy of *Jamaica Today* (both free). For bed and breakfast possibilities throughout Jamaica, contact the *Astra Hotel*, Mandeville (Tel: 962-3265/3377, telex 2426 Jamhotels, Diana McIntyre-Pike).

Information/reservations for self-catering villas and apartments can be done through the Jamaica Association of Villas and Apartments (JAVA), see below. Renting a villa may be an attractive option if you do not intend to do much travelling and there are 4/6 of you to share the costs (about US$1,000-1,500 per week for a really nice villa with private swimming pool and fully staffed). You will, however, probably have to rent a car (see **Local Transport** above) as you will have to take the cook shopping, etc.

Accommodation is subject to a tax, chargeable on a per day, per room basis. The tax varies from US$2 to US$12 per room, according to the season and to the type of establishment in which you are staying.

Larger hotels have introduced strict security to prevent guests being bothered by hustling.

Food

Local dishes, fragrant and spicy, are usually served with rice. There are many unusual and delicious vegetables and fruits such as sweetsop, soursop and sapodilla. National specialities include codfish ("stamp-and-go" are crisp pancakes made with salt cod) and ackee; curried goat; and jerked pork, highly spiced pork which has been cooked in the earth covered by wood and burning coals. Chicken is cooked in the same way and all along the roadsides are signs advertising jerk pork or jerk chicken. Patties, sold in specialist shops and bars, are seasoned meat or lobster in pastry; normally very good value.

Drink

Local rum, and the cocktails which combine it with local fruit juices; Tia Maria, the coffee liqueur; Red Stripe lager, with which, the locals say, no other Caribbean beer compares. Try the Irish Moss soft drink.

Tipping

Hotel staff, waiters at restaurants, barmen, taxi drivers, cloakroom attendants, hairdressers get 10-15% of the bill. In places where the bill already includes a service charge, it appears that personal tips are nonetheless expected.

Entertainment

Apart from the performance arts mentioned above, most large hotels and resorts have evening entertainment, usually including calypso bands, limbo dancers, fire eaters, etc.

Best Buys

In the craft markets and stores you can find items of wood (by Rastafarians and Maroons), straw, batik (from a number of good textile companies) and embroidery; jewellery from Blue Mountain Gems, near Rose Hall, Montego Bay area; Blue Mountain coffee is excellent (although the industry was badly affected by Hurricane Gilbert).

Please remember to check with legislation (and your conscience) before buying articles made from tortoiseshell, crocodile skin, and certain corals, shells and butterflies. Many such animals are protected and should not therefore be bought as souvenirs.

Currency

The Jamaican dollar (J$) is the only legal tender. The only legal exchange transactions are those carried out in commercial banks, or in official exchange bureaux in major hotels and the international airports. Inflation is high by Caribbean standards and the rate of exchange fluctuates, so change small amounts frequently if staying for long. Banks pay slightly more for US$ travellers cheques than for cash. Retain your receipt so you can convert Jamaican dollars at the end of your stay. Purchases in duty free shops must be in foreign currency.

Banks

The central bank is the Bank of Jamaica. National Commercial Bank of Jamaica, 77 King Street, Kingston and branches all over the island; the same applies to the Bank of Nova Scotia Jamaica Ltd (head office: Duke and Port Royal Streets, Kingston). Citibank, 63-67 Knutsford Boulevard, Kingston; and other local banks. It is difficult and time consuming to obtain money at banks using a credit card. Immediate money transfers can be made via the Western Union Bank, behind the National Commercial Bank at the top of Knutsford Boulevard, or through American Express, at Stuarts Travel Services, 9 Cecilio Avenue (Tel: 929-3077).

Security

The per capita crime rate is much lower than in most North American cities, despite occasional lurid publicity reports which suggest otherwise but there is much violent crime in Kingston. This is particularly concentrated in down town Kingston but you are advised not to walk any street in Kingston after dark. The motive is robbery so take sensible precautions with valuables. When in need of a taxi you are recommended to go into a shopping mall or hotel and have one ordered, rather than hail one in the street.

Beware of pickpockets in the main tourist areas and be firm but polite with touts. Do not wear jewellery. Do not go into the downtown areas of the towns especially at night. Observe the obvious precautions and you should have no problem. The vast majority of Jamaicans welcome tourists and want to be helpful. This is particularly true in the country districts. A sense of humour and courtesy reap rich dividends.

Drugs

Marijuana (ganja) is widely grown in remote areas and frequently offered to tourists. Cocaine (not indigenous to Jamaica) is also peddled on the north (tourist) coast. Possession of either drug is a criminal offence and on average well over 50 foreigners are serving prison sentences in Jamaica at any given moment for drug offences. The police may stop taxis, cars etc in random road checks and search you and your luggage. Airport security is being continually tightened (sniffer dogs, etc) to prevent drug exports. You have been warned.

Climate And Clothing

In the mountains, the temperature can fall to as low as 7°C during the winter season. Temperatures on the coast average 27°C, rising occasionally to 32° in July and August and never falling below 20°. The humidity is fairly high. The best months are December to April. Rain falls intermittently from about May, with daily short tropical showers in September, October and November.

Light summer clothing is needed all the year round, with a stole or sweater for cooler evenings. Some hotels expect casual evening wear in their dining rooms and nightclubs, but for the most part dress is informal. Bathing costumes, though, are only appropriate by the pool or on the beach.

Time Zone
Eastern Standard Time, 5 hours behind GMT.

Hours Of Business
Offices usually open from 0830 to 1630 Monday to Friday. **Shop** hours vary between 0900 and 0930 to 1600 and 1730, depending on area, Monday to Saturday; there is half-day closing (at 1300) on Wednesday in downtown Kingston, on Thursday in uptown Kingston and Montego Bay, and on Friday in Ocho Rios. **Banking hours** are 0900-1400 Monday to Thursday, 0900-1200, 1430-1700 on Friday (there may be some local variations).

Public Holidays
New Year's Day (1 January), Ash Wednesday, Good Friday and Easter Monday, Labour Day (25 May), Independence Day (first Monday in August), National Heroes Day (third Monday in October), Christmas and Boxing Day (25-26 December).

Electric Current
110 volts, 50 cycles AC; some hotels have 220 volts.

Telecommunications
International cable, telephone, fax and telex services are operated by Jamaica International Telecommunications Ltd. It has main offices in Kingston and Montego Bay, but calls can easily be made from hotels. "Time and charge" phone calls overseas cost the same in hotels as at the phone company, but there is a 10% tax and a J$2 service charge. The international telephone code for Jamaica is 809.

Post
There are post offices in all main towns. Post offices handle inland and overseas telegrams. Postcards and letters to the UK J$0.90.

Press
The daily paper with the largest circulation is *The Daily Gleaner*, which also publishes an evening paper, *The Star* and the *Sunday Gleaner*. The other daily is the *Jamaica Record*; also at weekends, *The Weekend Enquirer*.

Recommended Reading
Tour Jamaica by Margaret Morris is probably the best general guide to Jamaica for a traveller and widely available locally (US$7). The *Insight Guide to Jamaica*, besides being a general guide, delves more deeply into history, culture, etc, and is beautifully illustrated (US$14). Many other books about different aspects of Jamaica are also on sale, for example, *A to Z of Jamaican Heritage*, in the Heinemann Caribbean series. For ornithologists the standard work is *Birds of the Caribbean* by James Bond (after whom Ian Fleming named his James Bond).

Maps The *Discover Jamaica* road map, published by Travel Vision (1987), is available free from the tourist offices, very good and detailed. It has plans of Kingston, Montego Bay, Negril, Mandeville, Ocho Rios, Port Antonio and Spanish Town.

Consulates
British High Commission is at 26 Trafalgar Road, Kingston 5, Tel: 926-9050. Twenty six other countries represented. **The British Council** opened an office in 1991 in the First Life Building, 64 Knutsford Boulevard, PO Box 575, Kingston 5, Tel: 929-6915, 929-7049, Fax: 929-7090, with an information library, mainly on education, British newspapers available.

Jamaica Tourist Board
Circulates detailed hotel lists and plenty of other information. Head office at 21

Dominica Drive, Kingston 5, PO Box 360, Tel: 929-9200/19. Other offices in Jamaica: at the international airports; Cornwall Beach, Montego Bay, PO Box 67, Tel: 952-4425; Ocean Village Shopping Centre, Ocho Rios, PO Box 240, Tel: 974-2570; City Centre Plaza, Port Antonio, PO Box 151, Tel: 993-3051/2587; Shop No 9, Adrija Plaza, Negril PO, Westmoreland, Tel: 957-4243; 21 Ward Avenue (upstairs), Mandeville, Tel: 962-1072.

Overseas offices: **New York**: 866 Second Avenue, 10th Floor (2 Dag Hammarskjold Plaza), New York, NY 10017, Tel: (212) 688-7650; **Chicago**: Suite 1210, 36 South Wabash Avenue, Chicago, IL 60603, Tel: (312) 346-1546; **Miami**: Suite 1100, 1320 South Dixie Highway, Coral Gables, Fla 33146, Tel: (305) 665-0557; **Los Angeles**: 3440 Wilshire Boulevard, Suite 1207, Los Angeles, CA 90010, Tel: (213) 384-1123; **Dallas**: 8235 Douglas Ave., Suite 100, LB18, Dallas, TX 75225, Tel: (214) 361-8778; **Montréal**: Mezzanine Level, 1110 Sherbrooke Street West, Montréal, Québec H3A 1G9, Tel: (514) 849-6386/7; **Toronto**: 1 Eglinton Avenue East, Suite 616, Toronto, Ontario M4P 3A1, Tel: (416) 482-7850; **London**: 111 Gloucester Place, London W1H 3PH, Tel: (071) 224 0505, Fax: 224 0551; **Frankfurt**: Vogtstrasse 50 (1st floor), 6000 Frankfurt/Main 1, West Germany, Tel: (069) 597-5675.

The Jamaica Association of Villas and Apartments (JAVA), Pineapple Place, Ocho Rios, Box 298, Tel: 974-2508, Fax: 974-2967, has information on villas and apartments available for rent; also 1501 W. Fullerton, Chicago, IL60614, Tel: (312) 883-1020, Fax: (312) 883-5140 or toll free (800) 221-8830. In the UK, JAVA Jamaica, 21 Blandford Street, London W1H 3AD, Tel: 071-486 3560, Fax: 071-486 4108.

For their assistance in the research for and preparation of this chapter, we are extremely grateful to Huw Clough and Kate Hennessy. We would also like to thank Andrew Humphreys of Upholland, Lancashire for the base maps of New and Downtown Kingston.

TURKS AND CAICOS ISLANDS

Introduction

THE TURKS AND CAICOS ISLANDS lie some 575 miles southeast of Miami, Florida, directly east of Inagua at the southern tip of the Bahamas and north of Hispaniola. They comprise about forty low-lying islands and cays covering 193 square miles, surrounded by one of the longest coral reefs in the world. The Turks and the Caicos groups are separated by the Turks Island Passage, a 22-mile channel over 7,000 feet deep which connects the Atlantic and the Caribbean, contributing to the area's profusion of marine life. Generally, the windward sides of the islands are made up of limestone cliffs and sand dunes, while the leeward sides have more lush vegetation. The southern islands of Grand Turk, Salt Cay and South Caicos are very dry, having had their trees felled by salt rakers long ago to discourage rain. The other islands have slightly more rain but very little soil and most of the vegetation is scrub and cactus.

Only eight islands are inhabited. The main islands of the Turks group, Grand Turk and Salt Cay, shelter two fifths of the colony's 7,901 "belongers", as the islanders call themselves, but only a third of the total resident population of 11,465. The rest of the population is scattered among the larger Caicos group to the west: South Caicos, Middle (or Grand) Caicos, North Caicos, and Providenciales, the most populous, known locally as "Provo". Pine Cay and Parrot Cay are resort islands. East and West Caicos, inhabited from 1797 to the mid-19th century, are now the private domain of wild animals. East Caicos is home to swarms of mosquitoes and wild cattle, while West Caicos harbours land crabs, nesting pairs of ospreys and

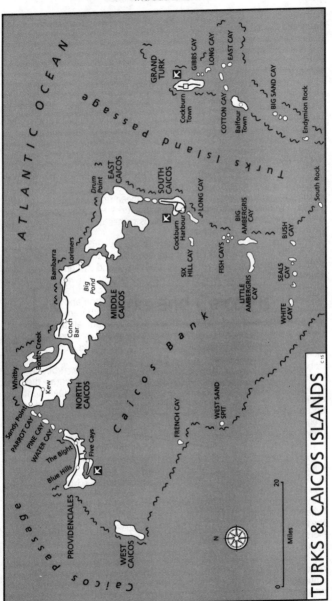

TURKS & CAICOS ISLANDS

flamingoes. Most of the smaller cays are uninhabited. The people of the Turks and Caicos are extremely welcoming and friendly; be prepared to say hello to anyone you pass on the road. The development of tourism on Provo has changed attitudes there, however, and friendliness is not universal.

History

The islands' first dwellers were probably the peaceful Tainos, who left behind some ancient utensils and little else. By the middle of the 16th century not one Lucayan, as Columbus named them, remained. Like the Lucayans in the Bahamas islands, they were kidnapped for use as slaves or pearl divers, while many others died of imported diseases. The discovery of the islands, whether by Columbus in 1492 or later by Ponce de León, is hotly disputed. There is a very convincing argument that Columbus' first landfall was on Grand Turk, not Watling Island in the Bahamas, now officially named San Salvador. The infamous Caicos Banks south of the Caicos group, where in the space of 1,000 yards the water depth changes from 6,000 to 30 feet, claimed many of the Spanish ships lost in the central Caribbean from the 16th to the 18th century. The islands were named after the Turk's Head 'fez' cactus found growing on the islands. The name Caicos comes from the Lucayan, *caya hico*, meaning string of islands.

The Bermudan traders who settled the islands of Grand Turk, Salt Cay, and South Caicos in the 17th century used slaves to rake salt for sale to British colonies on the American mainland, and fought pirates and buccaneers for over 200 years. During the American Revolution, British loyalists found refuge on the islands, setting up cotton and sisal plantations with the labour of imported slaves. For a while, cotton and sisal from the islands were sold in New York and London, solar salt became the staple of the economy, and the Turks and Caicos thrived, but all these products encountered overwhelming competition from elsewhere. The thin soil was an added disdvantage and a hurricane in 1813 marked the demise of cotton plantations.

Following an alternation of Spanish, French and British control, the group became part of the Bahamas colony in 1766. Attempts to integrate the Turks and Caicos failed, rule from Nassau was unpopular and inefficient and abandoned in 1848. Links with Jamaica were more developed, partly because London-Kingston boats visited frequently. The Turks and Caicos were annexed to Jamaica in 1874. After Jamaica's independence in 1962, they were loosely associated with the Bahamas for just over ten years until the latter became independent. At that point, the Turks and Caicos became a British Crown Colony. The Anglican Church maintained its links with the Bahamas, which is where the Bishop resides.

The main political parties are the People's Democratic Movement (PDM) and the Progressive National Party (PNP). The 1976 elections were won by the pro-independence PDM, which negotiated for independence from Britain if it won the next elections. However, when these were held in 1980 the PNP emerged victorious and talks were shelved. In 1984, the PNP, led by Norman Saunders, again won the elections and independence was not an issue.

The isolation of the Turks and Caicos and the benign neglect of the British government led to increasing use of the islands as refuelling posts by drug smugglers en route from South America to Florida until preventive action was taken in 1985. In that year the islands found themselves in the news headlines because of corruption and narcotics scandals. Norman Saunders and Stafford Missick, Minister for Development, were arrested in Miami on drugs charges and accused of accepting bribes to allow drugs planes to land and refuel. Saunders resigned as Chief Minister, was found guilty and imprisoned, although he has now returned to the islands and to politics. He was replaced by Nathaniel Francis, but the Blom-Cooper report in 1986 alleging arson and administrative malpractice, led to the resignations of Francis and two other ministers, while Oswald Skippings and two other members of the PDM were heavily criticized for incitement to commit acts of violence, although no criminal charges were ever brought. Constitutional government was suspended and direct rule from the UK was imposed while investigations continued into malpractice by other public officials.

In March 1988, general elections restored constitutional government. These were won by the PDM, and Oswald Skippings took office as Chief Minister. The PDM held 11 out of the 13 Legislative Council seats, the other two being held by the PNP, the pro-British NDA failing to win a single seat. The April 1991 elections, however, brought the PNP to power with eight seats (4,866 votes) while the PDM were reduced to five (4,542 votes). The Chief Minister is Washington Missick, who also has responsibility for Tourism, Planning and Private Sector Development.

Government
The Turks and Caicos are a British Dependent Territory. The British monarch is Head of State, represented by a Governor. The Executive Council chaired by the Governor is formed by five ministers, the Financial Secretary, the Attorney General and the Chief Secretary, the last two being British government appointments.

The Economy
The traditional economic activity, salt production, ceased in 1964, and for two decades there was little to generate legal income apart from fishing, government employment and some tourism. National resources are limited, even water has to be strictly conserved. Agriculture is almost non-existent and limited to subsistence farming of corn, pigeon peas, sweet potatoes and some livestock. Small scale fishing is important for job creation, and also for export. Sales abroad of lobster and conch generate about US$2m a year. Practically all consumer goods and most foodstuffs are imported. The lack of a manufacturing base and any major employment activities led in the 1960s and 1970s to thousands of local people emigrating to the nearby Bahamas or the USA to seek work. This trend has now been reversed as the economy has improved and the population is rising. Belongers have returned and unskilled labour, much of it illegal, comes from Haiti and the Dominican Republic.

One area of growth in the 1980s was that of offshore companies, over 9,000 of which were registered in the islands by 1990. There is no income tax, no company tax, no exchange control and no restriction on the nationality or residence of shareholders or directors. New legislation is designed to promote the growth of offshore finance and encourage banking, insurance and trust companies. Several international banks have requested offshore licences. A project to promote jurisdiction was started in the 1990s with several conferences to publicize the industry, which has a reputation for being well-administered and scandal-free.

Budgetary aid from the UK for recurrent expenditure was eliminated in fiscal year 1986/87 and the islands are aiming to be self-financing. Capital aid remains, augmented by financial assistance from the European

Community, the European Investment Bank and the Caribbean Development Bank. In 1992 the British Government approved a capital aid package of US$43m over three years, the largest ever awarded by the UK in the Western Hemisphere. The expansion of the airport terminal on Providenciales was the largest project on the list. Included in the aid was an award of US$2m for 'good government'.

The main area of economic growth and revenue for the islands is tourism. Investment has taken place in infrastructure, particularly airfields, hotels and marinas. The opening of a *Club Méditerranée* in 1984 doubled the number of visitors to the Turks and Caicos in two years. By 1991, the annual number of visitors reached 54,616, from 11,900 in 1980, of which about 65% came from the USA. New hotel, villa and condominium developments are planned and the Government aims to make the islands a high-quality, up-market destination.

Fauna and Flora

The islands support 175 resident and migrant species of birds, including flocks of greater flamingoes, frigate birds, ospreys, brown pelicans, the ruby throated humming bird, the belted kingfisher, white billed tropic birds, black-necked stilts, snowy plovers, peregrine falcons, red-tailed hawks, northern harriers, Baltimore orioles and scarlet tanagers and many others. There are lizards, a skink, iguanas, two species of snake, including a pygmy boa, and two species of bat. A system of National Parks, Nature Reserves and Sanctuaries has been set up; entrance to Sanctuaries is by permit only. A map, prepared by the National Parks Committee for the Ministry of Natural Resources is available at the Tourist Office. The southern parts of North, Middle and East Caicos have been designated a wetland of international importance under the Ramsar Convention to protect waterbirds, lobster, conch, flora and a fish nursery.

Diving and Marine Life

Marine life is varied and beautiful and can be enjoyed by snorkellers and sailors as well as scuba divers. Colourful fish and grouper can be seen on the coral and close to the shore you can find green turtles, loggerhead turtles and manta and spotted eagle rays. A bottle-nosed dolphin, known as Jojo, lives in the Marine Park along the north coast of Providenciales, although he is also found occasionally in other locations. He lives on his own and is attracted by boats and humans, apparently enjoying swimming and playing with people, while often coming in very close to the shore. If you are fortunate enough to swim with him, remember that he is a protected wild animal, do not stroke him or cover his eyes and ears. If you are nervous, get out of the water, as he can sense your anxiety. In January-March, hump back whales migrate through the deep Turks Island Passage on their way south to the Silver and Mouchoir Banks breeding grounds north of the Dominican Republic. Whale watching tours are organized. Beyond the reef are the game fish such as tuna, blue marlin, wahoo, snapper, bill fish and barracuda. Because there is a reef all round the islands, water visibility is excellent. Great care is being taken to conserve the reefs and the coral is in very good condition. The islands have become one of the most highly regarded diving locations in the region. Laws to conserve marine resources are strict. Do not take live coral, sea fans or other marine life. No spearguns are allowed.

There are now several dive operations on Provo, offering training programmes and dive packages. Flamingo Divers, PO Box 322, Providenciales, Tel/Fax: 946 4193, owned and operated by Jim Richardson and Larry McCain at Turtle Cove, is recommended for its professionalism, friendliness and flexibility. Small groups of experienced or novice divers are catered for and their two boats take a maximum of 12 divers each. A two-tank dive costs US$60, a night dive US$40, a snorkel trip US$25 and a 2-day resort course US$125. Provo Turtle Divers, PO Box 219, Tel: 946 4232/4845, Fax: 9415296, at Turtle Cove marina and run by the very knowledgeable and long-time resident, Art Pickering, is also recommended for small groups of experienced divers at similar prices. Other operators include Turtle Inn Divers, operating from the *Turtle Cove Inn*, a full-service dive centre with the *Caicos Cat*, accommodating 49 passengers, Tel: 946 4203, and Dive Provo, located at the *Ramada Turquoise Reef Resort* on Grace Bay, PO Box 350, Tel: 946 5029/5040, Fax: 946 5936. A two-tank dive ranges from US$55 to US$65, depending on the dive site. *Club Med* also has a dive boat. There is a recompression chamber at Menzies Medical Practice on Provo, DAN insurance is accepted. Some of the best diving is off Northwest Point, where there is an underwater cliff, and West Caicos, but there are also wrecks in other areas and a coral garden reef off the north coast.

On Grand Turk there are three dive organizers. Blue Water Divers Ltd is on Front Street, next to the museum, PO Box 124, Grand Turk, Tel/Fax: 946 2432. Mitch Rolling and Dave Warren offer a complete range of courses and special day trips with two small boats (no shade). Omega Divers, run by Cecil Ingham, next to the *Kittina Hotel*, Tel: 946 2232, is a larger operation with a range of watersports on offer. Up to 20 can be taken on the dive boat, US$55 for a two-tank dive. Off The Wall Divers, PO Box 177, Tel: 946 2159/2517, Fax: 946 1152 north of Cockburn Town at the *Guanahani Hotel*, uses a 42-foot customized boat taking up to 30 divers. The highlight of diving here is the wall off Cockburn Town, which drops suddenly from 40 feet to 7,000 feet only ¼ mile offshore. There are 25 moored sites along the wall where you can find coral arches, tunnels, canyons, caves and overhangs.

On Salt Cay, Porpoise Divers is based at the *Mount Pleasant Guest House*, run by Brian Sheedy, Tel: 946 6927 or 1-800-441 4419. The dive boat is an ex-landing craft and divers swim up the ramp, making it suitable for disabled divers. A two-tank dive is US$40, but most people stay at the guest house and take a five-day package for US$695 which includes three meals, transfers and unlimited day and night diving. There are seven moored dive sites and off Great Sand Cay there is an 18th century British shipwreck, still loaded with cannon.

On the western side of the Turks Island Passage the wall along the eastern shores of South Caicos and Long Cay also drops gradually or steeply from a depth of about 50 feet, with many types of coral and a variety of fish of all sizes. Grouper, barracuda, turtles, black durgeon, sharks and rays are all common. The disadvantage is that being on the windward side, the sea is often rough, making boat dives difficult. Snorkelling is rewarding with several shallow reefs close to the shore. At the southeastern tip of Long Cay, in about 60 feet of water, are the remains of a deliberately-sunk plane to explore. No dive operator is currently established on South Caicos.

There are four live-aboard boats for those who want to spend a week doing nothing else but diving. *Sea Dancer* (Tel: 800-367 3484) operates from the Provo shipyard, has accommodation for 18 people and offers five dives a day around French Cay, West Caicos and Northwest Point. Captain Bob Gascoine's *Aquanaut* (PO Box 101, Grand Turk, Tel: 946 2541) sleeps four to six experienced guests and has a resident marine biologist as cook/guide.

The *Ocean Outback* at Grace Bay, Provo, Tel: 941 5810, is a 70-foot liveaboard cruising mostly along the north reef and West Caicos. In 1992 *The Turks and Caicos Aggressor* was due to start operations; contact the Aggressor Fleet Limited, PO Drawer K, Morgan City, LA 70381, Tel: (504) 385 2416, 1-800-348 2628, Fax: (504) 384 0817.

All divers must have a valid certificate; there are plenty of training courses for novices. The best months for diving are April-November if there are no hurricanes. The sea is often rough in February-March. For detailed descriptive information consult the *Diving, Snorkelling, Visitor's Guide to the Turks and Caicos Islands*, by Captain Bob Gascoine.

Beaches and Watersports

There are 230 miles of white sand beaches round all the islands and each island naturally claims to have the loveliest spot with the clearest, azure water. Grace Bay on Provo is the longest stretch of sand and despite the hotels it is possible to find plenty of empty space. There is rarely any shade on the beaches. Most watersports can be arranged through the hotels. There are restrictions on motorized watersports in the marine park and jetskis have been banned. Windsurfing and sailing are offered by many hotels on Provo for around US$20/hour. You can parasail off Grace Bay beach; dry take-off and landing from the boat, no running required, suitable for the handicapped, reservations Tel: 941 5357, VHF Channel 16 'Parasail'. Daytime sailing excursions or sunset cruises are available. Contact *Tao* and *Two Fingers* Charters at PO Box 140, Provo. These two boats and the *Beluga* can be contacted through Dive Provo at the *Ramada*. The *Cristianna*, Tel: 946 5047, is a motor boat offering full or half day beach cruising; there is a cover on the boat for shade. In addition to running a ferry service, Caicos Express (Tel: 946 7111/7258, VHF Channel 16 'Caicos Express') also offers excursions from the Leeward Marina, eg to Middle Caicos with a tour of the caves; to North Caicos with a tour of the crab farm; to a deserted island for the day or whale watching.

Fishing is popular: Provo and Pine Cay have the best bonefishing but it is also possible at South Caicos, Middle Caicos, North Caicos and Salt Cay. May is the prime time. Bonefishing can be arranged through Captain Barr Gardiner, of Bonefish Unlimited, PO Box 241, Provo, Tel: 946 4874, VHF 'Light Tackle', full-day charters for US$250 for two people including swimming and snorkelling, all fuel, bait and tackle, or Bonefish Joe, on *Lights On*, Tel: 946 4126, Provo, VHF 'Hammerhead'. On South Caicos a bonefish specialist is Julius 'Goo the Guide' Jennings, US$20/hour, who can be contacted through Cornelius Basden at the *Club Caribe*, Tel: 946 3386/3360. Deep sea fishing is available at several Provo hotels. At the *Turtle Cove Yacht Club*, Provo, there is sport fishing aboard the *Sakitumi*, with Captain Bob Collins, Tel: 946 4203, VHF Channel 16 'Sakitumi'. On Middle Caicos all-inclusive sport fishing packages are available at *Eagle's Rest Villas*, contact R F Zeebo c/o Eagle Enterprises Ltd, 200 Foxbrook Drive, Landenberg, PA 19350, USA, Tel: 215-255 4640. A US$10 sport fishing licence is required from the Fisheries Department, Grand Turk, Tel: 946 2970, or South Caicos, Tel: 946 3306, or Provo, Tel: 946 4017. An international billfishing tournament is held annually coinciding with the full moon in July, Tel: 946 4307, Fax: 946 4771. Over US$1,000 in Calcutta money was distributed in 1991.

Other Sports

An 18-hole championship **golf** course is due to open late 1992. Owned by the water company, it is located inland from the *Club Med* and *Ocean Club*.

Most hotels on Provo are expected to offer golf as a sporting activity. There are **tennis** courts on Grand Turk at the *Coral Reef* and on Provo at *Turtle Cove Inn*, *Club Med*, *Erebus Inn* and the *Ramada*. There are also courts on Pine Cay, North Caicos at *The Prospect of Whitby* and Parrot Cay. **Cricket** is played from June to November.

Festivals

Most events are linked to the sea and land-based acitivities are tacked on to regattas or fishing tournaments. In Providenciales the billfishing tournament (see above) is a big event with lots of parties every night. Provo Day festivities follow Emancipation Day in August and a carnival procession starts in Blue Hills and ends Down Town, with floats, band and dancing. Wooden sloops compete in the sailing regatta the following day. On Grand Turk the Cactus Fest is held at the beginning of October, with competitions for sports, costumes, bands and gospel; there is a float parade, dancing and an art exhibition. On North Caicos, Festarama is in July; on Middle Caicos, Expo is in August; on South Caicos the Regatta with associated activities is in May.

Grand Turk

Grand Turk (population 3,691) is the seat of government and the second largest population centre, although it has an area of only seven square miles. The island was called Amuana by the Lucayans, Grand Saline by the French and Isla del Viejo by the Spanish. The east coast is often littered with tree trunks and other debris which have drifted across from Africa, lending credence to the claim that Columbus could have been carried here, rather than further north in the Bahamas chain. Grand Turk is not a resort island although there are hotels and dive operations which concentrate mostly on the wall just off the west coast. The vegetation is mostly scrub and cactus, among which you will find wild donkeys and horses roaming (there are plans to establish a donkey sanctuary with the aid of a British charity). Behind the town are old salt pans, with crumbling walls and ruined windmills, where pelicans and other waterbirds fish. More abandoned salt pans can be seen around the island, particularly towards the south.

Cockburn Town, the capital and financial centre, has some very attractive colonial buildings, mostly along Duke Street, or Front Street, as it is usually known. The government offices are in a nicely restored, small square with cannons facing the sea. The oldest church on Grand Turk is St Thomas' Anglican church, built by Bermudan settlers on Front Street overlooking the water. The Library is also an interesting Bermudan building, whitewashed, with shutters. Walking north along Front Street you come to the museum opened in 1991 in the beautifully renovated Guinep Lodge (entrance US$5 for non-residents, US$2 residents, US$0.50 students, open Monday-Friday 1000-1600, Saturday 1000-1300, depending on demand, ask next door in Blue Water Divers if it is shut, the administrator, Brian Riggs, may be there). The exhibition on the ground floor is of the early 16th century wreck of a Spanish caravel found on the Molasses Reef between West Caicos and French Cay in only 20 feet of water. The ship is believed to have been on an illegal slaving mission in the islands, as evidenced by locked leg irons found on the site. A guided tour is highly recommended although not essential. Upstairs there is an exhibition of local artifacts, photos, stamps, coins, a few Taino beads, figures and potsherds; expansion is planned, the museum is still growing. A local historian, Herbert Sadler, has compiled many

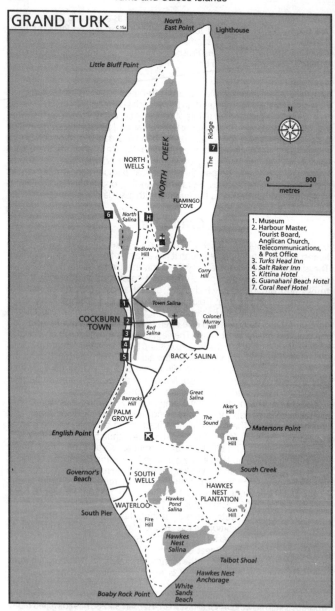

GRAND TURK C 15a

North East Point

Lighthouse

Little Bluff Point

NORTH WELLS

NORTH CREEK

The Ridge

7

N

0   800
metres

6 North Salina

FLAMINGO COVE

H

Bedlow's Hill

Corry Hill

Town Salina

1
COCKBURN TOWN
2
3
Red Salina
4
5

Colonel Murray Hill

BACK SALINA

1. Museum
2. Harbour Master,
   Tourist Board,
   Anglican Church,
   Telecommunications,
   & Post Office
3. Turks Head Inn
4. Salt Raker Inn
5. Kittina Hotel
6. Guanahani Beach Hotel
7. Coral Reef Hotel

Barracks Hill

PALM GROVE

English Point

Great Salina

Aker's Hill

The Sound

Matersons Point

Eves Hill

Governor's Beach

SOUTH WELLS

South Creek

HAWKES NEST PLANTATION

WATERLOO

South Pier

Hawkes Pond Salina

Fire Hill

Gun Hill

Hawkes Nest Salina

Talbot Shoal

Hawkes Nest Anchorage

Boaby Rock Point

White Sands Beach

volumes on the theory of Columbus' landfall and local history, some of which are on sale at the museum.

The Governor's residence, Waterloo, south of the airport, was built in 1815 as a private residence and acquired for the head of government in 1857. Successive governors and administrators have modified and extended it, prompted partly by hurricane damage in 1866 and 1945, and by the Queen's visit in 1966. Further south is an ex-USAF base, known as South Base, which is now used as government offices, and beyond there some pleasant beaches on the south coast, with good snorkelling at White Sands beach by the point. US Navy, NASA and Coast Guard bases were once important for the economy of Grand Turk; John Glenn, the first American to orbit the earth, splashed down off Grand Turk in the 1960s. North of Cockburn Town a paved road leads along The Ridge up the east side of the island to the lighthouse and another abandoned US base, from where there are good views out to sea. A channel at the north point gives access to North Creek, an excellent hurricane shelter for boats. The island's carnival takes place in late August.

Island Information—Grand Turk

How To Get There Airlines and schedules tend to change frequently. Cayman Airways flies once a week from Miami, via Providenciales, Carnival has two or three flights. Turquoise Airways flies daily. TCNA flies from Nassau and Freeport in the Bahamas, Cap Haitien in Haiti and Puerto Plata in the Dominican Republic. TCNA (Tel: 946 2082) and Charles Air operate frequent inter-island flights and it is often possible to turn up on the day you want to travel and catch the next flight. Reservations are recommended, however, particularly when going to Provo. There are no buses on Grand Turk and taxis are the only form of public transport (US$4 from the airport to the *Kittina Hotel*, the nearest). Jeeps or cars can be rented from Tropical Auto Leasing, Tel: 946 1000, or C J Car Rental, Tel: 946 2744. The *Kittina* rents bicycles, US$10/day.

Where To Stay Rates quoted are summer-winter. In an old Bermuda-style building on Duke Street facing the beach is the very friendly, relaxed and unpretentious *Salt Raker Inn*, run by Jenny Smith, 12 rooms, US$55-115, some basic, budget rooms, others redecorated in 1992, most with sea view, dive packages, PO Box 1, Tel: 946-2260, Fax: 946-2432; also recommended is the *Turks Head Inn* on Duke Street, built in 1869 by a Bermudan shipwright and once a guest house for the British Government, set back from the beach surrounded by tall trees, 6 rooms lovingly renovated in 1991/2 by the owner Xavier Tonneau (known as Mr X), with wooden floors, beds and balconies, US$80 including tax and breakfast, use of kitchen and fridge, dive packages with Blue Water Divers or Omega, PO Box 58, Tel: 946-2466; *Kittina*, 43 rooms either side of Duke Street, US$85-140, most face the beach or open directly onto the sand, but the cheaper rooms overlook the courtyard of the main building, suites available with kitchenette, comfortable but in need of redecoration, all watersports facilities arranged with Omega next door, small pool by the beach, PO Box 42, Tel: 946 2232, Fax: 946 2877; on Front Street, Angela and Douglas Gordon have a large guest suite with sea view, close to beach and restaurants, breakfast and afternoon tea included in year-round rate of US$65s, US$85d, Tel: 946 2470; *Coral Reef*, refurbished in 1991 with an extensive wooden deck running all round the hotel, on the east coast away from the town, lovely colours in the sea but debris washed up frequently, rather dark studios and one-bedroom apartments with kitchenette although all sea-facing, US$75-105, PO Box 156, Tel: 946 2055/7, Fax: 946 2911, pool, lit tennis court, fitness centre, dive packages arranged with Off The Wall Divers; *Guanahani Beach Hotel*, on the broad, sandy Pillory Beach on the west coast north of the town, 16 functional twin-bedded rooms, two apartments, all with sea view, balcony, TV, a/c, fan, US$75, dive packages with Off The Wall Divers next door, pool, PO Box 178, Tel: 946 2135, Fax: 946 1152.

Where To Eat The best restaurants and bars are at the hotels. The outdoor *Salt Raker*

Inn is recommended for good food and pleasant company, it is a popular meeting place and fills up on Wednesday and Sunday barbecue nights when Mitch and Dave, from Blue Water Divers, play the guitar and sing; the *Turks Head Inn* is also a gathering place with a friendly bar and good food; the *Guanahani* has a rather spartan restaurant but the fish is excellent; there is Chinese food at the *Coral Reef* and a beach bar for snacks, disco at weekends; *Discovery House* on Pond Street has pizza and Italian food; for local food and lunch specials try *Touch of Class* on the road south, a/c, TV, bar, filling, tasty portions; the *Poop Deck* is a tiny bar, set back from the road in the centre of town by the sea, local food and hamburgers at lunchtime, chicken and chips in the evenings; local food also at *Regal Beagle* on the road north of town on the west side of North Creek; the best conch fritters are at *Peanut's* snack bar on the waterfront, not to be missed. At weekends there is a discotheque at *The Lady* up by the lighthouse.

Salt Cay

Seven miles south of Grand Turk, Salt Cay (population 208) is out of the past, with windmills, salt sheds and other remnants of the old salt industry and little else. The island was first visited by the Bermudans in 1645; they started making salt here in 1673 and maintained a thriving salt industry until its collapse in the 1960s. Production ceased all together in 1971. The main village is **Balfour Town**, divided into North Side and South Side, noted for its Bermudan buildings and pretty cottages with stone walls around the gardens. The White House dominates the skyline; built in the 1830s of Bermudan stone brought in as ballast, by the Harriott family during the height of the salt industry. The Methodist Church nearby, one of several churches on the island, is over 125 years old. Look into some of the ruined houses and you will find salt still stored in the cellars. Plant life was curtailed during the salt raking days to prevent rainfall but there is an iguana, known as Iggie, who lives, apparently alone, alongside the road to *Windmills Plantation*. There are no mosquitoes as there is no fresh water. Snorkelling is good and diving is excellent; there are seven moored dive sites along the wall, with tunnels, caves and undercuts. In January-March you can often see the humpbacked whales migrating through the channel as they pass close to the west coast.

Island Information—Salt Cay

How To Get There There is a dirt airstrip for small aircraft, around which a fence has been erected to keep out the donkeys. The island is served by TCNA, with two five-minute flights a day from Grand Turk, US$12 one-way, one at 0700 and one at an indeterminate time in the afternoon, making a day trip possible. There is also a 45-minute daily ferry service, US$10, with no fixed schedule. The only public transport on the island is the taxi van run by Nathan Smith; there are very few vehicles of any sort.

Where To Stay The most expensive and exclusive hotel is the architect-designed and owned *Windmills Plantation* on a 2½-mile beach, which appeals to people who want to do nothing undisturbed, 8 suites, US$415 or US$550 including all food and drink, meals taken family style, local recipes, salt-water pool, no children, diving can be arranged with Porpoise Divers, reservations (minimum three nights) *The Windmills Plantation*, 440 32nd Street, West Palm Beach, FL 33407, Tel: 800-822 7715, Fax: 407 845 2982, on Salt Cay Tel: 946 6962; at the other end of the scale is the cheerful *Mount Pleasant Guest House*, owned by Brian Sheedy, who also runs Porpoise Divers, a salt raker's house built in 1830, can sleep 25 (but only take 12 on the dive boat) in four simple rooms in the main house, two with shared bath, and in a separate annex/guesthouse which has three basic rooms downstairs with kitchen and living room and a dormitory with 7 beds upstairs, daily rate US$85 room only but better value is the five-night dive package at US$695, nine nights US$895 including three meals, transfers and unlimited diving, processing facilities for dive photos, video/TV, library, bicycles, horses for riding or driving, outdoor restaurant/bar with the best food on the island, Tel: 946 6927, 1-800 441 4419; *The Brown House* was undergoing renovation in 1992 but was due to open by end-year, Tel: 946 6911; the *Castaways* villas along the beach north of *Windmill Plantation* are also available for rent. Leon Wilson, the Legislative Council PDM Representative for Salt Cay, runs a small, friendly bar, *One Down And One To Go*, with iced beer and Guinness stout, dominoes, pool table, table tennis.

South Caicos

The nearest Caicos island, 22 miles west of Grand Turk (population 1,198), South Caicos was once the most populous and the largest producer of salt, but is now the main fishing port, having the benefit of the most protected natural harbour. As a result, yachts frequently call here and there is a popular annual regatta held at the end of May. Excellent diving along the drop off to the south, snorkelling is best on the windward side going east and north. The beaches here are totally deserted and you can walk for miles beachcombing along the eastern shore. Boat trips can be organized with fishermen to the island reserves of Six Hill Cays and Long Cay. Further south are the two Ambergris Cays, Big and Little, where there are caves and the diving and fishing are good.

   Cockburn Harbour is the only settlement and is an attractive if rather run down little place with lots of old buildings, a pleasant waterfront with old salt warehouses and boats of all kinds in the harbour. The District Commissioner's house, currently unoccupied, stands atop a hill southeast of the village and can be recognized by its green roof. The School For Field Studies is in the 19th century *Admiral's Arm Inn*, and attracts US undergraduate students to the island, but otherwise there are very few visitors and most of those come by boat. Wild donkeys, cows and horses can be found roaming the island and several have made their home in an abandoned hotel construction site along the coast from the Residency. The old salinas dominate the central part of the island and there is a 'boiling hole', connected to the sea by a subterranean passage, which was used to supply the salt pans.

Island Information—South Caicos

How To Get There TCNA connects South Caicos with Providenciales (US$40 one-way, plus tax), North Caicos (US$27), Middle Caicos (US$20) and Grand Turk (US$20). There are a few taxis on the island, US$4 from the airport to *Club Carib* hotel.

Where To Stay The only hotel is the *Club Carib*, a two-storey, functional, adequate place to sleep, 24 rooms, US$60, with a lovely sea view across to the islets offshore, bonefishing can be arranged through the manager, Cornelius Basden, Tel/Fax: 946 3386/3360; a few people in the town rent out rooms.

Where To Eat *Muriel's* is in the front of an unprepossessing house one block from the *Club Carib*, filling native recipes, breakfast by prior arrangement, Tel: 946 3210; *Myrna Lisa*, also local food, has been recommended; *Love's* has local dishes; *Dora's Lobster Pot* at the airport, known for the lobster sandwich, not always a lot of choice; new places are opening which are often just the dining room in a private house.

East Caicos

Originally named Guana by the Lucayans, East Caicos has an area of 18 square miles, making it one of the largest islands and boasting the highest point in the Turks and Caicos, Flamingo Hill at 156 feet. A ridge runs all along the north coast, but the rest of the island is swamp, creeks, mangrove and mudflats. Jacksonville, in the northwest, used to be the centre of a 50,000 acre sisal plantation and there was also a cattle farm at the beginning of the 20th century, but the island is now uninhabited. There is an abandoned railway left over from the plantation days and feral donkeys have worn paths through the scrub and sisal. Caves near Jacksonville, which were once mined for bat guano, contain petroglyphs carved on the walls and there is evidence of several Lucayan settlements. Splendid beaches including a 17-mile beach on the north coast where turtles come to lay their eggs, but accommodation for mosquitoes only. Bring repellant. There is good snorkelling and diving around Lorimer's Cut, but the reefs and banks make access difficult. Off the north coast, opposite Jacksonville, is Guana Cay, home to the Caicos iguana.

Middle Caicos

Also known as Grand Caicos (population 272), this is the largest of the islands, with an area of 48 square miles. Its coastline is more dramatic than some of the other islands, characterized by limestone cliffs along the northern coast, interspersed with long sandy beaches shaded by casaurina pines or secluded coves. The southern part of the island is swamp and tidal flats. There are three settlements, **Conch Bar**, where there is an airstrip, a primary school and guesthouses, **Bambarra** and **Lorimers**, which are both very small with several abandoned homes of people who have emigrated to other islands to find work. The King's Road runs from the ferry dock in the west through to the east side, linking all the settlements and ending at Lorimers Creek where there is a small pier and a few old wooden boats. Visit the huge caves in the National Park at Conch Bar where there are bats, stalactites, stalagmites and underwater salt lakes, which link up with the sea. Ask in Conch Bar for a guide, around US$7. There are also caves between Bambarra and Lorimers, which were used by the Lucayan Indians and were later mined for guano. Archaeological excavations have uncovered a Lucayan ball court and a settlement near Armstrong Pond, due south of Bambarra, but these are not easily accessible. Bambarra beach is an empty, curving sweep of white sand, fringed with casaurina trees. Middle Caicos regatta is held here and there are small thatched huts which serve as restaurants for the very popular end-August Expo (some litter remains), but otherwise there are no facilities. A sand bar stretches out to Pelican Cay, half a mile out, which you can walk at low tide, popular with wading birds. The view from Conch Bar beach is marred by a rusting barge in shallow water, but there is afternoon shade at the west end under a cliff where the reef meets the land. A pretty cove, popular with day trippers, is Mudjeon Harbour, just west of Conch Bar, protected by a sand bar and with shade under a rocky overhang. The reef juts out from the land again here before branching out westwards along the rocky coastline which can be quite spectacular in the winter months with crashing waves. South of Middle Caicos there is a Nature Reserve comprising a frigatebird breeding colony and a marine sinkhole with turtles, bonefish and shark. The blue hole is surrounded by sandy banks and is difficult to get to, but it shows up on the satellite photo of the islands on display in the museum in Grand Turk.

Island Information—Middle Caicos

How To Get There TCNA flies from Grand Turk (US$31 one-way plus tax), South Caicos (US$20), North Caicos (US$12) and Providenciales (US$27). Private pilots will also stop off if flying to North Caicos, fare less than TCNA, or you can charter a plane. The Caicos Express also runs a ferry service from Providenciales via North Caicos, but this is usually combined with a day tour to the caves and Mudjeon Harbour for a picnic. Carlon Forbes runs a taxi service and fares are based on US$2 per mile for two people, eg Conch Bar to Bambarra US$14, to Lorimers US$20.

Where To Stay In Conch Bar: **Mrs Maria Taylor** has a pleasant, simple guesthouse with four bedrooms, kitchen and sitting/dining room, US$45 for twin-bedded room with private bathroom, US$40 with shared bath, US$60 for a triple room, fans, Tel: 946 3322; Annie Taylor runs her son's new *Sea View Guesthouse*, four double bedrooms, US$65, washing machine, carpets, plastic chair covers, bright colours; Stacia and Dolphus Arthur run *Arthur's Guesthouse* next to Arthur's Store, US$50, one double, one twin-bedded room, private bath, kitchen. At the west end of Bambarra Beach are *Eagle's Rest Villas*, two beach houses with two units each, TV/video, quiet, modern and comfortable, popular with sport fishermen, all-inclusive fishing packages available, contact Eagle Enterprises Ltd, 200 Foxbrook Drive, Landenberg, PA 19350, Tel: 215 255 4640 in the USA.

Where To Eat Most people are self-catering and buy their supplies from the few small stores in Conch Bar. Maria Taylor has milk and eggs and home made bread. Annie Taylor is known for her cooking and runs a restaurant on demand in her house, the conch stew at US$18 for two is recommended. Cardinal Arthur has a little of everything in his store and also arranges boat trips.

North Caicos

The lushest of the islands, North Caicos has taller trees than the other islands and attracts more rain. Like Middle and East Caicos, the southern part of the island is comprised of swamp and mangrove. There is one Nature Reserve at Dick Hill Creek and Bellefield Landing Pond, to protect the West Indian whistling duck and flamingoes, and another at Cottage Pond, a fresh/salt water sinkhole, about 170 feet deep, where there are grebes and West Indian whistling duck. Pumpkin Bluff Pond is a sanctuary for flamingoes, Bahamian pintail and various waders. Three Mary's Cays is a sanctuary for flamingoes and is an osprey nesting site. Flocks of flamingoes can also be seen on Flamingo Pond, but take binoculars. There is a viewing point at the side of the road, which is the only place from where you can see them and at low tide they can be a long way off. The beaches are good along the north coast where the hotels are, although the best is a seven-mile strip west of Pumpkin Bluff, where there has been no development so far. It can be reached via a footpath from *The Prospect of Whitby*. A cargo ship foundered on the reef in the 1980s, and is still stuck fast, making it of snorkelling interest. There is also good snorkelling at Three Mary's Cays and Sandy Point beach to the west is lovely. These beaches are best reached by boat. There is a rough road to Three Mary's Cays suitable for mopeds.

The population has declined to 1,275 inhabitants living at the settlements of Bottle Creek, Whitby, Sandy Point and Kew. **Kew**, in the centre, is a pretty, scruffy but happy little village with neat gardens and tall trees, many of them exotic fruit trees, to provide shade; there are three churches, a primary school, a shop and two bars. **Bottle Creek**, in the east, has a high school, clinic and churches; the paved road ends here and a rough road requiring four-wheel drive continues to Toby Rock. The backstreets of Bottle Creek run alongside the creek and here you can see the importance of water conservation, with people carrying buckets to and from the municipal water tap at the rain catchment area, while donkeys, goats and dogs roam around. The area is poor, but many people are building themselves bigger and better homes. **Whitby**, on the north coast, is rather spread out along the road, but this is where the few hotels are. Several expatriates have built their homes along Whitby Beach. **Sandy Point**, in the west, is a fishing community and the ferry landing. North Caicos is the centre of basket making in the islands and there are several women, including Clementine Mackintosh, Ann Missick and Cassandra Gardiner, who are expert in their craft. Prices do not vary much from those in the shops in Providenciales or locally. Wades Green Plantation, just to the west of Kew, is the best example of a Loyalist plantation in the islands, with many ruins, including a courtyard and a prison. Archaeologists from the University of California in Los Angeles carried out excavations in 1989. At Greenwich Creek in the northeast there is a crab farm, run by Kimberley Peyton and Kim Möller of West Indies Mariculture; Kimberley gives an excellent guided tour, US$11, children under 12 free, Tel: 946 7213. The King Crab will grow to 8 lbs, but is harvested at the soft shell stage when it is 7-9 months old, and sold to local restaurants. Whitby Drug and Variety Store sells T-shirts, crafts and non-prescription drugs at lower prices than on Provo.

Island Information—North Caicos

How To Get There TCNA flies from Provo (US$21 plus tax one way) and there are flights via Middle Caicos (US$12) and South Caicos (US$27) to Grand Turk (US$37). Charters can be arranged from Provo, or private pilots have three flights a day US$25 one way, popular. Caicos Express (Tel: 946 7111, 946 7258, VHF 16 'Caicos Express') runs a ferry boat service between Leeward Marina, Provo and Sandy Point, North Caicos via Pine Cay and Parrot Cay, US$15 one way, Monday-Thursday depart Sandy Point 0800 and 1500, depart Leeward 0900 and 1600; Friday depart Sandy Point 0800, 1200, 1500, depart Leeward 0900, 1330, 1600; Saturday depart Sandy Point 0800, 1200, 1600; depart Leeward 0900, 1330, 1630; Sunday depart Sandy Point 1530, depart Leeward 1630. Caicos Express also run tours to North Caicos from Provo with a nature tour and a visit to the crab farm. It can be a bumpy ride if the sea is rough, the boats are small but fast, ask for cushions if they are not distributed. You can take a bicycle on the boat for US$10-15 but you will have to hold it steady. You can rent a bicycle (motor bike or moped) from Whitby Plaza for the same price and less hassle. There are car hire facilities on North Caicos with Saunders Rent A Car, VHF Channel 16 'Sierra 7', or Gardiners Auto Service, US$35 for half day, US$70 for full day. A taxi costs US$10 from the airport to Whitby for one person, US$12 for two, US$15 for three. Taxi from Sandy Point to Whitby is US$20. A tour of the island by taxi costs US$80-100, the drivers are friendly and knowledgeable but some tend to run their own errands while working.

Where To Stay All accommodation is in the Whitby beach area on the north coast. *The Prospect of Whitby*, comfortable, popular with families but not as friendly as some places, managed by Raymond and Nadiane Hayon, Tel: 946 7119, Fax: 946 7114, US$80s in summer - US$170d for a suite in winter, pool, tennis, snorkelling equipment, bicycles, windsurfing, beach towels, two boats for excursions, often closes in summer; *Pelican Beach Hotel*, down a very poor road, friendly, relaxed, few facilities, 14 rooms, 2 suites, the older rooms face the beach, US$100-150 room, US$130-160 suite, run by Clifford Gardner, Tel: 946 7112, Fax: 946 7139; *Ocean Beach*, 10 luxury condominiums, Tel: 946 7113 or contact the Canadian office at PO Box 1152, Station B, Burlington, Canada, Tel: 416-336 8276, Fax: 416-336 1232; the only guesthouse, *Jo Anne's Bed and Breakfast*, belongs to Jo Anne James Selver, who also runs a tourist shop in Whitby, set back from the beach with purple sea fans outside, it is light and airy with a wonderful view, comfortable rooms, private bath, good breakfast included, US$65, Tel: 946 7184, Fax: 946 7301.

Where To Eat Good food at the *Pelican Beach Hotel*, average at the *Prospect of Whitby*. Simple local restaurants include *Club Titter's Restaurant and Bar*, near the airport, lobster US$15, ribs, recommended, and *Aquatic* restaurant and bar, open all day, lobster US$15, conch.

Parrot Cay

A luxury, 50-room hotel is due to open by end-1992 on this 1,300-acre private island, which will offer a health club and gym, tennis, watersports and conference facilities. There will be a gourmet restaurant with sea view, a beach club restaurant/bar and a swim-up bar in the pool. Golf carts will be available for getting around the island. Cotton used to be grown here and there are the remains of a plantation house. Despite the new hotel, the wetlands and mangroves are being preserved to protect wildlife. A second stage of development will be the construction of 37 villas, while later stages will bring a marina and more villas. Reservations can be made through Flagship Hotels & Resorts, Tel: 914-214 8771 or 800-777 2022, Fax: 914-214 6279.

Dellis Cay

Dellis Cay is uninhabited but frequently visited for its shells. A popular excursion is to be dropped off there for the day for shelling by the Caicos Express ferry service, no facilities.

Pine Cay

Pine Cay is an 800-acre private resort owned by a group of homeowners who also own the exclusive 12-room *Meridian Club*, US$380-US$545. No children under six allowed to stay in the hotel and lots of restrictions on where they are allowed if brought to a villa. The homes, which are very comfortable, with spectacular views, can be rented from US$2,000-3,400/week. A hurricane in 1969 left Pine Cay five feet under water for a while and since then the houses have been built slightly back from the beach and many of them are on stilts. There is a fairly well-stocked commissary or you can eat in the hotel; golf carts are used to get around the island. Note that the island is on the same time as Miami. Open 1 November-5 July, reservations can be made through Resorts Management Inc, The Carriage House at 201½ East 29th St, New York NY 10016, Tel: 800-331 9154, 212-696 4566, Fax: 212-689 1598. Non-motorized watersports and tennis are available and excursions to other cays can be arranged. May is a popular time for bonefishing. Day trippers are not encouraged although visitors may come for lunch at the restaurant by prior reservation as long as they do not use the facilities; the homeowners value their privacy and put a ban on visitors if they feel there have been too many. Pine Cay benefits from a few freshwater ponds and wells, so water is no problem here and the vegetation is more lush than on Provo. On the other hand mosquito control is a constant problem. Nature trails have been laid out around the ponds and through the trees. There is an airstrip, guests usually charter a flight with Charles Air, and a dock if they prefer to come in with the Caicos Express or the *Meridian Club's* shuttle boat.

Little Water Cay

Little Water Cay is a nature reserve and although classified as a separate island, is joined to Pine Cay by sand dunes created during the 1960 hurricane. Iguanas on the island are said to dance if you beat a rhythm outside their holes. Caicos Express will drop you off here for the day if you wish to spend time on a deserted island.

Providenciales

"Provo" (population 4,821) has a length of 25 miles and average width of three and is being vigorously developed for tourism although the north beach on which most hotels have been built is so long that they are rarely within 750 metres of one another. The Princess Alexandra Marine Park incorporates the reef offshore along 13 miles of beach. Development of the island only began in 1967 although it had been settled in the 18th century and there were three large plantations in the 19th century. The three original settlements, The Bight, Five Cays and Blue Hills, were very fragmented and have not grown into towns as the population has increased. Instead there have been efforts to build shopping malls at points along the Leeward Highway and create new villages. **Down Town** is where the government offices have been built and several office complexes, banks, supermarkets, church and a laundry have sprung up around Butterfield Square. **Turtle Cove** is the more interesting place for tourists, with a couple of hotels, a marina, dive operators, several restaurants, the Tourist Office and a few boutiques. On the south side of the island, South Dock is the island's commercial port and just to the west, Sapodilla Bay offers good protection for yachts. Chalk Sound, a National Park inland from Sapodilla Bay, is a shallow lagoon of marvellous turquoise colours, dotted with rocky islets. The Caicos Marina and Shipyard is also on the south coast further east, and is capable of major repairs. At the northeast end, a deep channel known as Leeward Going Through is another natural harbour and a marina has been built here. There is a conch farm at the Island Sea Centre at Leeward, open Monday-Saturday, 0800-1630, with daily tour (including the research facilities) at 1430 and 1530, US$6 adult, US$3 children. Despite all this development, North West Point, a marine park offshore, with a nature reserve at North West Point Pond for breeding and migrant waterfowl, still

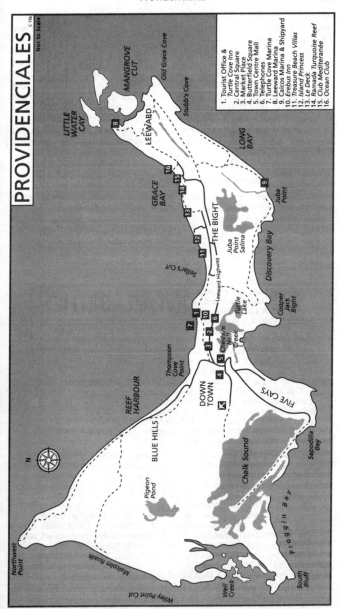

PROVIDENCIALES

Not to Scale

1. Tourist Office & Turtle Cove Inn
2. Centre Square
3. Market Place
4. Butterfield Square
5. Town Centre Mall
6. Telephones
7. Turtle Cove Marina
8. Leeward Marina
9. Caicos Marina & Shipyard
10. Treasure Beach Villas
11. Erebus Inn
12. Island Princess
13. Le Deck
14. Ramada Turquoise Reef
15. Club Mediterranée
16. Ocean Club

offers total seclusion, with good beaches, diving and snorkelling. Four-wheel drive is essential if driving, it is not accessible by conventional vehicle. Two other good places to snorkel are just to the east of Turtle Cove, where rays and turtles can be seen, and just west of *Treasure Beach Villas*, by the white house, where there is a variety of life, including grouper. Inland, along Seasage Hill Road, is The Hole, a collapsed limestone, water-filled sinkhole. A tunnel to the right hand side gives access to the main pool and has a rope tied to a tree if you are brave enough to descend, but it is slippery and dangerous, so take care. A small, handwritten, wooden sign on the side of the road marks the entrance. Ruins of Loyalist plantation houses can be seen at Cheshire Hall and Richmond Hill, while on the hill overlooking Sapodilla Bay a pole marks the location of stones engraved in the 18th century by sailors or wreckers.

Island Information—Providenciales

How To Get There Carnival Airlines, Cayman Airways and Turquoise Airways (a new service to start 1992) fly from Miami, Bahamasair and TCNA from Nassau, TCNA from Freeport, Bahamas, Cap Haitien, Haiti and Puerto Plata, Dominican Republic. TCNA and Charles Air operate internal flights within the Turks and Caicos islands, see above. Charter companies at Provo airport are TCNA, Tel: 946 4255; Charles Air Service, Tel: 946 4352; Blue Hills Aviation, Tel: 946 5226; Flamingo Air Services, Tel: 946 4933; Provo Air Charter, Tel: 946 4296. Caicos Express ferry to Leeward Marina, see details under North Caicos.

Transport Paved road out to The Bight, most roads still dirt. **Provo Rent A Car**, PO Box 137, Airport Road, Tel: 946 4404, VHF Channel 16, Fax: 946 4993, from US$44/day, CDW US$11.95, US$10 stamp duty, 60 miles free, at the airport only, free pick-up. **Highway Rent A Car**, Leeward Highway, Airport, Tel: 941 5262/3, Fax: 941 5264, smallest car US$39/day, Isuzu US$44, Ford Escort US$49. **Budget**, Down Town, Town Centre Mall, open Monday-Saturday, 0800-1700, Tel: 946 4709, at the *Ramada*, Grace Bay, 0900-1700, Tel: 946 5400, similar prices. **Scooter Rental**, Central Square, Leeward Highway, Tel: 946 4684 or VHF 'Scooter', open Monday-Saturday, 0900-1700, Sunday and holidays, 0900-1200, 24-hour rental starts at US$25, weekly rentals less, map supplied. A **public bus service** started in 1992, run by Executive Tours, with buses running from all the hotels along Grace Bay to Down Town every hour, starting from *Ocean Club* and *Club Med*, US$2, 0800-2100, Monday-Sunday, other fares are Down Town to Leeward, US$4, South Dock to the hotels, US$4, Tel: 946 4524, Fax: 941 5391, guided island tours for 8-22 people, US$10pp. Taxis charge US$2 per mile, a ride for one person from the airport to the *Ramada* is US$14 and a round trip to a restaurant can be US$40. Complaints have not lowered the rates. There are usually taxis at the large hotels, otherwise phone for one.

Where To Stay *Erebus Inn*, on hillside overlooking Turtle Cove, 30 rooms, larger than those in other hotels, US$85-170, popular with business travellers, a few basic chalets with wonderful view liked by divers, dive packages available, all watersports at the marina, gym and fitness centre on site, pool, tennis, two rooms fully equipped for ham radio operators, good restaurant, Tel: 946-4240, Fax: 946-4704; *Turtle Cove Inn (Yacht Club)*, US$85-150, poolside or ocean view, smallish rooms but comfortable, suite with kitchenette available, not on beach, docking facilities for guests, all watersports, at the marina, games room, two lit clay tennis courts, cable TV, two restaurants, Tel: 946-4203, Fax: 946-4141; along the north shore on the beach heading east are *Treasure Beach Villas*, 18 self-catering apartments, US$125-160 per night or US$540-960 per week, no restaurant, Tel: 946-4211, Fax: 946-4108; *Island Princess*, 72 rooms, US$70-120, rather run down, airless rooms, some on long term rental, Tel: 946-4460, Fax: 946-4666; *Le Deck Hotel and Beach Club*, 26 rooms, US$130-155 standard, US$175-200 junior suite, condos from US$260, all including breakfast, restaurant, lovely bougainvillea in the courtyard, no sports on site but can be arranged, Tel: 946-5547, Fax: 946-5770. *Ramada Turquoise Reef Resort*, 228 rooms and suites, squeaky clean, service has been criticized but is improving, US$170-410 winter, US$105-230 summer, several restaurants, tennis, diving, no motorized watersports, casino, conference facilities, tour desk, facilities for the disabled in a few rooms, condos next door under Ramada management, PO Box 205, Tel: 946-5555, Fax: 946-5522; *Club Méditerranée Turkoise*, Grace Bay, stays on same time as Miami, 298 rooms, no facilities for children, rooms stark but comfortable, keen young organizers, lots of watersports, communal dining. *Ocean Club at Grace Bay*, condos on the beach, US$150-450 winter, US$100-320 summer for studio with partial view to three bedroom ocean front apartment, very comfortable, well-equipped, balconies, good views the length of Grace Bay, daytime snack bar by the pool but no restaurant, PO Box 240, Tel: 946 5880. The only bed and breakfast on the island is run by Louise Fletcher, *Columbus Slept Here*, between *Ramada* and *Le Deck*, look out for the Canadian flag, one double room in house, two small self-catering apartments downstairs, US$65 October-April, US$55 May-September, weekly and monthly rates, 15% discount for residents, comfortable, lots of hot water, use of kitchen, very friendly, knowledgeable hostess, walking distance from sea, popular, Tel: 946 5878, PO Box 273. In the Sapodilla area there are self-catering villas: *Casaurina Cottages*, three houses, Tel: 946 4687, Fax: 946 4895; *Nautilus Villas*, 10 villas, Tel/Fax: 946 4069; *Neptune Villas*, 2 bedroom, 2 bath, short or long term rental, PO Box 380, Tel: 946 4859. Other 3-5 bedroomed rental villas with pools and luxury accommodation available through Elliot Holdings & Management, PO Box 235, Tel: 946 5355, Fax: 946 5176; Turks & Caicos Realty, PO Box 279, Tel: 946 4474, Fax: 946 4433; Prestigious Properties Ltd, PO Box 23, Tel: 946 4379, Fax: 946 4703; Alpha Omega, Tel: 946 4857, Fax: 941 5723; ASAP, Tel: 946 4080, Fax: 946 4081.

Where To Eat In the Turtle Cove area are *Alfred's Place*, Austrian owner, recommended, particularly if Alfred is cooking, although can be variable, Tel: 946 4679; *Banana Boat*, colourful, cheerful and fun, popular with locals and tourists, for a meal or a drink, fish, lobster or burgers, live music some evenings, Tel: 941 5706; *DJ's Tiki Hut*, open 0700-2300, food service until 2000, reasonable prices, music nightly, live band weekends and Wednesdays, Tel: 941 5575, and *Jimmy's Dinner House and Bar*, open 1700, pizza, pasta, ribs, steaks, early bird dinner 1730-1930, both behind the marina at Turtle Cove. *Dora's Restaurant and Bar*, east of Turtle Cove on Leeward Highway, open from 0730, local recipes, filling, eat in or take away, US$20pp for dinner from 1900 including transport to/from hotel, Monday-Thursday seafood buffet, Tel: 946 4558; *The Little House*, Leeward Highway, native and North American food, simple, immaculate, open from 1830, free transport, Tel: 941 5320; *Hey José*, Atlas House, The Centre, Leeward Highway, Mexican/American, tacos, huge pizza etc, lunch 1100-1500, dinner 1800-2200, closed Sunday, cheerful, friendly, good food, great margaritas, Tel: 946 4812; *Bonnie's Kitchen*, Market Place, owned by 'Bonnie' Arthur Williams, quiet, intimate garden setting, reasonable prices, friendly service, local specialities and seafood, lunch and dinner, eat in or take away, closed Sunday, Tel: 946 4072; *Hong Kong Restaurant*, within walking distance of *Ramada*, Chinese eat in, take away, or delivery, moderate prices, useful if you are vegetarian as they will cook good, special meals for you, Tel: 946 5678; *Gilley's at Leeward*, open 0800-2200, breakfast, lunch and dinner by the marina, a good place to wait for the ferry to North Caicos, recommended for a special night out, good lobster, quite expensive, free transport, Sunday barbecue, Tel: 946 5094; near the airport, *Where Its At* has Jamaican specialities, Tel: 946 2466; *Tasty Temptations*, next to the dry cleaners, Down Town, is a French bakery, with croissants and pastries, coffee, limited seating, Tel: 946 4049; *The Conch Bar* at the Island Sea Centre has cleaned conch for sale.

West Caicos

Rugged and uninhabited but worth visiting for its beautiful beach on the northwest coast and excellent diving offshore. The east shore is a marine park. Once frequented by pirates, there are many wrecks between here and Provo. Inland there is a salt water lake, Lake Catherine, which rises and falls with the tides and is a nature reserve, home to migrant nesting flamingoes, ducks and waders. The ruins of Yankee Town, its sisal press and railroad are a surface interval destination for scuba divers and sailors.

French Cay

An old pirate lair, now uninhabited, with exceptional marine life on the north side. It has been designated a sanctuary for frigate birds, osprey and nesting seabirds.

Information for Visitors

Documents

US and Canadian citizens need only proof of identity to enter Turks and Caicos. All others need a valid passport, although a visa is not necessary. Onward ticket officially required. Visitors are allowed to stay for 30 days, renewable once only.

How To Get There

Ports of entry for aircraft are Providenciales, South Caicos and Grand Turk, but the major international airport is on Providenciales. There are also airstrips on North Caicos, Middle Caicos, Pine Cay and Salt Cay. None of the runways is long enough to take long haul, large aircraft. Cayman Airways uses Boeing 737s from Miami to Provo. It is worth checking in early when returning to Miami, as "bumping" is not uncommon. If travelling in a small group it is worth considering a charter to Miami, Haiti and the Dominican Republic, Charles Air Service (Tel: 946 4352) has the newest planes and most reasonable prices, ask for the proprietor, Harold Charles. Bahamasair provides scheduled passenger service from the Bahamas to Provo and South Caicos once a week. Turks & Caicos National Airlines (TCNA) flies from Cap Haitien, Haiti (US$60), and Puerto Plata, Dominican Republic (US$84) and provides connecting flights between Grand Turk, Salt Cay, South Caicos, Middle Caicos, North Caicos and Providenciales. Flight time from Grand Turk to the furthest island (Provo) is 30 minutes (US$52), but TCNA delays are notorious. TCNA mainly uses 7-seater planes which are widely used by the islanders, rather like a bus service. Private charters are readily available within the island group and can easily be arranged by asking around at Grand Turk or Provo airport, as charter pilots wait to see if they can fill a plane in the mornings. **See page 220** for telephone numbers of charter companies. On other islands they are easily arranged by phone. Airport departure tax is US$10.

There is no scheduled shipping service and no port is deep enough to take cruise ships. See above for details of Caicos Express ferry service.

Internal Transport

On-island transport is restricted to expensive taxi service with a basic fare of US$2/mile, although drivers are not always consistent. Complaints are frequent. Taxis can be hired for island tours, agree the price before hand. Rental cars are available on Grand Turk, North and South Caicos and Provo. Bicycles and motor scooters can be rented from some hotels. Most roads are fairly basic and parts are accessible only with four-wheel drive. Driving is on the left. Maximum speed in urban areas is 20 mph and outside villages 40 mph, but driving is erratic. Local drivers do not dim their headlights at night. Watch out for donkeys on Grand Turk.

Where To Stay

There is a 10% service charge and 7% tax added to the bill. Do not expect miracles from the plumbing, even in new hotels. The hot and cold taps are frequently reversed, the toilets wobble. Hotels on Provo are aiming for North American standards and are expensive. Cheap accommodation is hard to find.

Camping

Camping is possible on beaches on most islands, but no facilities. If planning to stay on a deserted island take everything with you and leave nothing behind.

Where To Eat

Good but expensive in hotels. Restaurants and snack bars are generally of a good standard but not cheap. Seafood, mainly conch and lobster, is widely available and is an important export product, but nearly all food is imported and therefore costly. Fresh fruit and vegetables come from either the Dominican Republic or Florida. Vegetarians should order their meals in advance as there is rarely anything without meat or fish on the menu. There are no hamburger bars or fast food outlets.

Nightlife

Local bands play mostly calypso, reggae and the traditional island music with its Haitian and African influences. On "Provo", there are a couple of local bands which play in a different bar every night, *Erebus Inn*, *Banana Boat*, *Alfred's* on Provo, normally a great atmosphere. Dancing also at the *Banana Boat*. *Disco Elite* in Down Town, Provo, is a must for night hawks, good mix of Turks islanders and visitors, crowded, noisy. *Club Med* has nightly disco for guests and visitors who phone for reservations (which can include dinner/show). On Grand Turk: the *Lady* at the Old North Naval Base for dancing; the *Salt Raker Inn* for music on Wednesday and Sunday nights. There is no personal security problem on the islands and it is safe to walk around at night.

Launderette

On Provo there is a laundry/dry cleaners in Butterfield Square, Down Town, and a laundromat at *Treasure Beach Villas*.

Currency

The official currency is the US dollar, although some Turks and Caicos coins are in use, including a crown (US\$1) and a quarter crown. Most hotels, restaurants and taxi drivers will accept travellers' cheques, but personal cheques are not widely accepted. There are banks on Grand Turk and Providenciales. Barclays Bank is on Grand Turk, Tel: 946 2831, Fax: 946 2695, at Butterfield Square, PO Box 236, Provo, Tel: 946 4245, Fax: 946 4573, and an agency service is held on South Caicos on Thursdays, Tel: 946 3268. Scotiabank is at the Town Centre Mall, PO Box 15, Provo, Tel: 946 4750/2, Fax: 946 4755, and at Harbour House, PO Box 132, Grand Turk, Tel: 946 2506/7, Fax: 946 2667.

Health

There are no endemic tropical diseases and no malaria, no special vaccinations are required prior to arrival. On Provo, Menzies Medical Practice, Leeward Highway, between Suzie Turn and Down Town, open 0830-1700 Monday-Friday, 0830-1200 Saturday, two doctors and emergency service, dental care, pharmacy and recompression chamber, Tel: 946 4242. Provo Health Medical Centre, Down Town, open 0830-1700 Monday-Friday, 0830-1200 Saturday, two doctors providing primary care and emergency service as well as eye and dental clinic, Tel: 946 4201 for appointment, 946 4300 after hours. Dr Sam Slattery, Leeward Highway, Tel: 941 5252, is on call 24 hours. The government Blue Hills Clinic has a doctor and midwife on duty, Tel: 946 4228. Ambulance services available and emergency medical air charter with full life support can be arranged. On Grand Turk there is a hospital on the north side of town and a government clinic in town, open 0800-1230, 1400-1630. The other islands organize emergency air evacuation to Grand Turk hospital.

Climate

There is no recognized rainy season, and temperatures average 75°-85°F from November to May, reaching into the 90's from June to October, but constant tradewinds keep life comfortable. Average annual rainfall is 21 inches on Grand Turk and South Caicos but increases to 40 inches as you travel westwards through the Caicos Islands where more lush vegetation is found. Hurricane season is normally June-October. Hurricane Kate swept through the islands November 1985.

Clothing

Dress is informal and shorts are worn in town as well as on the beach. Topless sunbathing is accepted at *Club Med* but is frowned upon on public beaches, the islanders prefer women to cover up.

National Holidays

New Year's Day, Good Friday, Easter Monday, Commonwealth Day (last Monday in May), the Queen's birthday (second week in June), Emancipation Day (beginning of August), Columbus' Day and Human Rights Day (both in October), Christmas Day and Boxing Day.

Electric Current

110 volts, 60 cycles, the same as in the USA.

Communications

Grand Turk, Provo and South Caicos have a modern local and international telephone service, with Cable and Wireless offices in Grand Turk and Provo. Telephone services on the North and Middle Caicos and Salt City are limited but improving. There are a few public phones but it is often best to ask at a hotel or bar. The international code is 809. The small volume of international calls means that costs are high; a call to the UK costs US$3.30 a minute at peak time (US$2.70 off-peak). US 800 calls will be charged at the normal rate. The local phone book has a list of charges to anywhere in the world. There is also a 10% tax on calls. Phone cards are available from Cable and Wireless and from outlets near phone booths in US$5, US$10 and US$20 denominations, plus 10% tax. The Cable and Wireless Public Sales Office in Grand Turk and Provo has a public fax service, Fax: 946 4210.

Travel Agent

Marco Travel Services, Down Town and at Turtle Cove, Tel: 946 4393, Fax: 946 4048, for reconfirmation of tickets, emergency check cashing, travel services, traveller's cheque sales, Amex representative, but better to make flight arrangements from outside the islands. Provo Travel Ltd, run by Althea Ewing, opened in 1992 on Central Square, Leeward Highway, Tel: 946 4080, Fax: 946 4081, helpful. On Grand Turk; T & C Travel Ltd, at *Hotel Kittina*, Box 42, Tel: 946 2592, Fax: 946 2877, run by Daphne James, friendly, reliable.

Tourist Information

Ministry of Tourism & Development, Front Street, Grand Turk, Turks & Caicos Islands, Tel: 946-2300/2306/2321, Fax: 946-2733. On Provo the Tourist Office is at Turtle Cove, Tel: 946 4970.

USA: c/o The Keating Group, 425 Madison Avenue, New York, NY 10017, Tel: (212) 888 4110 or 1-800, 441 4419.

Thanks are due to Mr Clifford Hamilton, Director of Tourism, and Norma Outten, formerly of the Provo Tourist Office for greatly assisting Sarah Cameron during her 1992 visit to the islands. We are also most grateful to Louise Fletcher, *Columbus Slept Here*, Provo, for her hospitality and her help in improving and expanding this chapter; also to Jo Anne James Selver, *Jo Anne's Bed and Breakfast*, North Caicos, for her work and advice on North and Middle Caicos.

HISPANIOLA

Introduction

ONE MIGHT EXPECT that a relatively small island such as Hispaniola (from Spanish "Isla Española"—the Spanish island) lying in the heart of the Caribbean would be occupied by one nation, or at least that its people should demonstrate ethnic and cultural similarities. This is not so. Hispaniola, with an area of just over 75,800 square km, not much more than half the size of Cuba, is shared by two very different countries, the Dominican Republic and Haiti. The original indigenous name for the island, Quisqueya, is still used in the Dominican Republic as an "elegant variation". Hispaniola is mountainous and forested, with plains and plateaux. Haiti, with 27,400 square km, has a population of 6.6 million increasing at an annual rate of 1.9%. The Dominican Republic is much larger in area, 48,443 square km, including some offshore islands, but its population is not larger to the same degree at 7.3 million, growing at 2.3% a year. In the Dominican Republic, over 60% of the population is urban, yet only 30% in Haiti live in towns.

Columbus visited the north coast of Hispaniola, modern Haiti, on his first visit to the West Indies, leaving a few men there to make a settlement before he moved on to Cuba. Columbus traded with the native Arawaks for trinkets such as gold nose plugs, bracelets and other ornaments, which were to seal the Indians' fate when shown to the Spanish monarchs. A second voyage was ordered immediately. Columbus tried again to establish settlements, his first having been wiped out. His undisciplined men were soon at war with the native Tainos, who were hunted, taxed and enslaved. Hundreds were shipped to Spain, where they died. When Columbus had to return to Spain he left his brother, Bartolomé, in charge of the fever-ridden, starving colony. The latter sensibly moved the settlement to the healthier south coast and founded Santo Domingo, which became the capital of the Spanish Indies. The native inhabitants were gradually eliminated by European diseases, murder, suicide and slavery, while their crops were destroyed by newly introduced herds of cattle and pigs. Development was hindered by the labour shortage and the island became merely a base from which to provision further exploration, being a source of bacon, dried beef and cassava. Even the alluvial gold dwindled and could not compete with discoveries on the mainland. Sugar was introduced at the beginning of the sixteenth century and the need for labour soon brought African slaves to the island. In 1512 the Indians were declared free subjects of Spain, and missionary zeal ensured their conversion to Christianity.

The Haitians are almost wholly black, with a culture that is a unique mixture of African and French influences. Haiti was a French colony until 1804 when, fired by the example of the French Revolution, the black slaves revolted, massacred the French landowners and proclaimed the world's first black republic. Throughout the 19th century the Haitians reverted to a primitive way of life, indulging in a succession of bloody, almost tribal wars. Even today, nowhere else in the Caribbean do African cults, particularly voodoo, play such a part in everyday life. The standard of living is the lowest in the Caribbean and Americas.

The Dominicans are a mixture of black, Amerindian and white, with a far stronger European strain (but see **Introduction** to the Dominican Republic, below). Their culture and language are hispanic and their religion Roman Catholic. Economically, the country is much more developed, despite a stormy political past and unsavoury periods of dictatorship, particularly under Generalísimo Trujillo (1930-61). Nevertheless, in a material sense the country prospered during the Trujillo era and the standard of living is much higher than it is in Haiti.

The climate is tropical but tempered by sea breezes. The cooler months are between December and March.

HAITI

Introduction

THE REPUBLIC OF HAITI occupies the western third of the island. French and Créole are the official languages (and knowledge of either is virtually essential for the visitor), though the common speech of all classes is Créole. (It is not a patois, but a language.) Nine-tenths of the people are of African descent, and the remainder are mulattoes, the descendants of French settlers. Haiti means "high ground" and indeed it is the most mountainous country in the Caribbean. There are three mountain ranges, the main one stretching right across the northern peninsula. In this range the highest peaks are in the Dominican Republic, about 3,000 metres above sea-level (the highest being Pico Duarte). In Haiti, the highest is Pic Laselle, at 2,684 metres. The once luxuriant forest cover of Haiti's mountains is being rapidly destroyed for fuel and building.

History
In the seventeenth century the French invaded from their base on Tortuga and colonized what became known as Saint Domingue, its borders later being determined by the Treaty of Ryswick in 1697. The area was occupied by cattle hunting buccaneers and pirates, but Governor de Cussy, appointed in 1684, introduced legal trading and planting. By the eighteenth century it was regarded as the most valuable tropical colony of its size in the world and was the largest sugar producer in the West Indies. However, that wealth was based on slavery and the planters were aware of the dangers of rebellion. After the French Revolution, slavery came under attack in France and the planters defensively called for more freedom to run their colony as they wished. In 1791 France decreed that persons of colour born of free parents should be entitled to vote; the white inhabitants of Saint Domingue refused to implement the decree and mulattoes were up in arms demanding their rights. However, while the whites and mulattoes were absorbed in their dispute, slave unrest erupted in the north in 1791. Thousands of white inhabitants were murdered and the northern plain was devastated. Soon whites, mulattoes and negroes were all fighting with shifting alliances and mutual hatred.

Out of the chaos rose a new leader, an ex-slave called François-Dominique Toussaint, known as Toussaint Louverture, who became the leader of a marauding band after the 1791 uprising. When France and Spain went to war, he joined the Spanish forces as a mercenary and built up a troop of 4,000 negroes. However, when the English captured Port-au-Prince in 1794 he defected with his men to join the French against the English. After four years of war and disease, the English withdrew, by which time Toussaint was an unrivalled leader among the black population. He then turned against the mulattoes of the west and south, killing 10,000 in 1800. The same year, torrential rain broke the irrigation dams upon which the prosperity of the area depended. They were never repaired and the soil was gradually eroded to become a wilderness. By 1800 Toussaint was politically supreme. In 1801 he drew up a new constitution and proclaimed himself governor general for life. However, Napoleon had other plans, which included an alliance with Spain, complicated by Toussaint's successful invasion of Santo Domingo, and the reintroduction of the colonial system based on slavery. In 1802 a French army was sent to Saint Domingue which defeated Toussaint and shipped him to France where he died in prison. The news that slavery had been reintroduced in Guadeloupe, however, provoked another popular uprising which drove out the French, already weakened by fever.

This new revolt was led by an African-born ex-slave, Dessalines, who had risen to power in Toussaint's entourage and was his natural successor. In 1804 he proclaimed himself Emperor of the independent Haiti, changing the country's name to the Taino word for "mountainous". Dessalines died in 1806 and the country divided between his rival successors: the negro Christophe in the north, and the mulatto Pétion in the south. The former's rule was based on forced labour and he managed to keep the estates running until his death in 1820. (He called himself Roi Henri Christophe and built the Citadelle and Sans Souci near Milot—see below; for a fictionalized account of these events, read Alejo Carpentier's *El reino de este mundo—The Kingdom of This World*, arguably the first Latin American novel to employ the technique of "lo real maravilloso".) Pétion divided the land into peasant plots, which in time became the pattern all over Haiti and led to economic ruin with virtually no sugar production and little coffee. Revolution succeeded revolution as hatred between the blacks and the ruling mulattoes intensified; constitutional government rarely existed in the nineteenth century.

At the beginning of the twentieth century, the USA became financially and politically involved for geopolitical and strategic reasons. Intervention in 1915 was provoked by the murder and mutilation of a president, but occupation brought order and the reorganization of public finances. Provision of health services, water supply, sewerage and education did not prevent opposition to occupation erupting in an uprising in 1918-20 which left 2,000 Haitians dead. By the 1930s the strategic need for occupation had receded and the expense was unpopular in the USA. In 1934 the USA withdrew, leaving Haiti poor and overpopulated with few natural resources. Migrants commonly sought work on the sugar estates of the neighbouring Dominican Republic, although there was hatred between the two nations. In 1937 about 10,000 Haitian immigrants were rounded up and massacred in the Dominican Republic.

In 1957 François (Papa Doc) Duvalier, a black nationalist, was elected president and unlike previous autocrats he succeeded in holding on to power. He managed to break the mulattoes' grip on pol' ical power, even if not on the economy. In 1964 he became President-for-Life, a title which was inherited by his 19-year-old son, Jean-Claude (Baby Doc) in 1971. The Duvaliers' power rested on the use of an armed militia, the "Tontons Macoutes", to dominate the people. Tens of thousands of Haitians were murdered and thousands more fled the country. However, repression eased under Jean-Claude, and dissidence rose, encouraged partly by US policies on human rights. Internecine rivalry continued and the mulatto elite began to regain power, highlighted by the President's marriage to Michèle Bennett, the daughter of a mulatto businessman, in 1980. Discontent began to grow with the May 1984 riots in Gonaïves and Cap Haïtien, and resurfaced after the holding of a constitutional referendum on 22 July, 1985, which gave the Government 99.98% of the vote. Several months of unrest and rioting

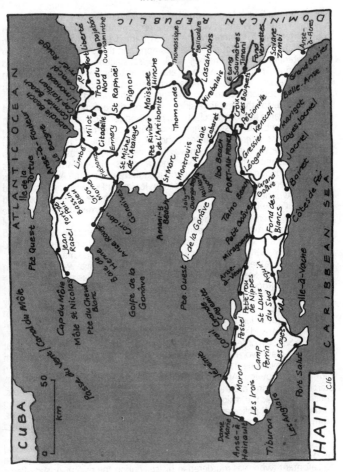

gradually built up into a tide of popular insistence on the removal of Duvalier, during the course of which several hundred people were killed by his henchmen. The dictatorship of the Duvaliers (father and son) was brought to a swift and unexpected end when the President-for-Life fled to France on 7 February 1986.

The removal of the Duvaliers has left Haitians hungry for radical change. The leader of the interim military-civilian Government, Lieutenant-General Henri Namphy, promised presidential elections for November 1987, but they were abandoned because of violence on polling day. New elections were held on 17 January 1988, and Professor Leslie Manigat of the centrist Rassemblement National des Démocrates Progressistes was elected president for a 5-year term. A number of leading contenders boycotted the election. Professor Manigat was ousted after 5 months in office by a military coup, after which General Namphy was named president. About seven months later, another coup deposed Namphy and the presidency was given to Lieutenant-General Prosper Avril. Dissatisfaction within the army resurfaced in April, 1989, when several coup attempts were staged within quick succession and lawlessness increased as armed gangs, including disaffected soldiers, terrorized the population. Nevertheless, the USA renewed aid, for the first time since 1987, on the grounds that Haiti was moving towards democratic elections, promised for 1990, and was making efforts to combat drug smuggling. Under General Namphy, cocaine worth US$700m passed through Haiti each month, with a 10% cut for senior army officers. However, Avril's position was insecure; he moved closer to hardline Duvalierists and arrests, beatings and murders of opposition activists increased. Foreign aid was again cut off in January 1990 when Avril imposed a state of siege and the holding of elections looked unlikely. Finally, in March, General Avril fled the country after a week of mass demonstrations and violence. Following his resignation, Haiti was governed by an interim President, Supreme Court judge, Ertha Pascal-Trouillot.

Despite poor relations between Mme Pascal-Trouillot and the 19-member Council of State appointed to assist her, successful elections were held on 16 December 1990. The presidential winner, by a landslide margin of 67% to 15%, was Father Jean-Bertrand Aristide; his nearest rival was the former finance minister Marc Bazin. The electoral campaign was marked by the candidacy of Roger Lafontant, a Duvalierist and former "security official" of Baby Doc. A warrant for his arrest did not prevent Lafontant running for the presidency; only the failure of his coup attempt against Mme Pascal-Trouillot in January 1991 brought him to justice.

President Aristide ("Titide"), a Roman Catholic priest who was expelled from the Salesian order in 1988 for "incitement to hatred, violence and class struggle", was sworn in on 7 February. His denunciations of corruption within the government, church and army over the previous decade had won him a vast following. Among his immediate steps on taking office were to start investigations into the conduct of Mme Pascal Trouillot and many other officials, to seek the resignation of six generals, to propose the separation of the army and police and to garner urgently-needed financial assistance from abroad for the new administration. Aristide's refusal to share power with other politicians, his attacks on the interests of the armed forces and the business elite and the actions of some of his militant supporters provoked his overthrow on 30 September 1991 by sections of the army sympathetic to Lafontant (who was murdered in his cell during the rising). Aristide fled into exile; a supreme court judge, Joseph Nerette, was made president, and Jean-Jacques Honorat, a fierce critic of Aristide and a former human rights activist was sworn in as prime minister. Harsh repression was imposed after the deposition of Aristide; at least 2,000 people were said to have died in the first six months, almost 600 during the coup itself. At the same time an estimated 22,000 Haitians fled the country in small boats, most heading for the United States' Guantánamo naval base on Cuba, but being returned to Haiti immediately.

International condemnation of the coup was swift, the Organization of American States, the EC, USA and Latin America all imposing trade and political embargos. The OAS tried to find a formula by which democracy could be restored, with no success. In June 1992, the army sacked President

Nerette and replaced Honorat with Marc Bazin as prime minister. At the time of writing, despite promises from Bazin, there were no signs of an end to repression, the restoration of press freedom or Aristide's return from exile.

Government
There is a 27-seat Senate and an 83-seat Chamber of Deputies.

The Economy
Haiti is the poorest country in the Western Hemisphere and is among the thirty poorest countries in the world. 75% of the population subsist below the absolute poverty level set by the World Bank and 47% are illiterate. It suffers from overpopulation, lack of communications, lack of cheap power and raw materials for industry, and mountainous terrain that cannot provide an adequate living for the farming population. Life expectancy at birth is only 55 years for males and 56 years for females, and the infant mortality rate 92 per 1,000 live births.

Haiti's recent economic problems have been caused by historical low productivity in the vital agricultural sector, compounded by the world recession which depressed commodity prices and therefore export earnings, and the continuing effects of hurricane damage. 1% of the population controls 40% of the country's wealth although the average farm size is less than one hectare. Only 33% of the land is arable, yet most of the people live in the country, using only the most rudimentary tools to grow maize, rice, sorghum and coffee. Deforestation has seriously damaged agriculture and watersheds, in the south in particular: some 70% of all fuel needs are met by charcoal, yet only 1.5% of the land is forested. Agriculture provides about a third of gdp and employs over half of the workforce. Coffee is the most important crop, providing 11% of total exports and a livelihood for 2m people. Production of sugar and sisal has been declining because population pressure has encouraged many farmers to plant subsistence crops.

The industrial and commercial sectors are small and are heavily concentrated in the Port-au-Prince area. There are assembly operations producing baseballs, electric and electronic parts and clothing for export to the USA, and domestic operations producing vegetable oils, footwear and metal products. Manufacturing wage rates average below US$3 a day and manufactured goods make up over two thirds of total exports. Tourism has declined in the 1980s, because of political uncertainties and a scare in the USA that Aids was endemic in Haiti. Several hotels have been forced to close and even cruise ship visits ceased altogether in 1992. The total number of arrivals has fallen sharply from nearly 150,000 in 1985; revenues were down to US$66m in 1990 and have fallen further since then. Between 1980 and 1989 the number of hotel rooms fell by half in Haiti and the country was excused from paying dues to the Caribbean Tourism Organization in 1989.

The suspension of bilateral aid by major foreign donors (principally the USA, France and Canada) in 1987 had severe repercussions on the economy. Restricted government spending led to declines in gross domestic product, while efforts to increase state revenues led to over or under invoicing, tax evasion and greater dollarization of the economy. In 1989 a standby credit agreement was signed with the IMF, but was never fully implemented because of the political upheaval. In 1990, as prospects of elections improved, several countries, including the USA, France and Japan, resumed aid. After Father Aristide's victory, USAID promised assistance worth US$82m and the European Community US$144m. International and local private sector funding was sought for social projects, a six-month emergency programme to create employment and assist agriculture was proposed and efforts were made to halt the black market in foodstuffs and lower the cost of living. An increase in the national minimum wage to 26 gourdes a day in the capital and 20 gourdes a day in the country was approved in August 1991. Any economic progress, in terms of renewed aid, improved fuel supplies, increases in government revenue and a reduction in inflation, was abruptly halted after the overthrow of President Aristide. The international trade embargo caused fuel supplies to be cut off, disrupting electricity and running water provision, US-owned manufacturing plants closed, prices soared and hundreds of workers were laid off. Some oil shipments escaped the embargo and smuggling from the Dominican Republic brought a little relief to the capital, but in rural areas deprivation was acute as food and transport costs soared and health care and other services collapsed.

Culture

Voodoo and Christianity exist side by side, each borrowing elements from the other. It is, however, voodoo which forms a large part of Haitian life and which attracts most attention (often, wrongly, to satisfy writers' and film-makers' more sensationalist urges). It is basically an African religion, involving elements of Catholicism which were designed to disguise it from the French slave owners. The complex rituals are to do with serving the *loas* (gods), and the ceremonies which maintain the harmony between them and the individual include dancing to drums until the believer is possessed by the spirits. Voodoo does place greater emphasis on magic than other African religions in black communities elsewhere in the Caribbean or Brazil, but it has as much potential for good as it does for evil. Visitors are not usually allowed to go to ceremonial centres (*péristyles*); you must be accompanied by a Haitian if you want to see a priest (*houngan*). The National Tourist Office used to publish a list of temples which may be visited, but tours are only a facsimile of the real thing. If you do consult a *houngan*, he will probably say that the god wants a large amount of dollars (say US$45, which may be bargained down).

Painting is the most obvious of the Haitian arts. It is noted for naive depictions of everyday activities and the surrealistic, voodoo-influenced school. Bright jungle scenes recalling a past land of origin are also popular. Work done by true artists run from a few hundred dollars to a few thousand. Representative work done by amateurs can be purchased for US$10 upwards. Many works are on display in the Musée d'Art Haitien du Collège St-Pierre in Port-au-Prince.

Haiti is very rich in its arts and crafts. You can find excellent examples of sewn, woven and embroidered textiles, mahogany ware, basketry, pottery, copper jewellery and cut-out metal wall hangings. Any would be a good buy. Many crafts are functional yet involve much inventiveness of design. For those who enjoy discovering the personality of a nation, negotiating with the street vendors and artists is quite an animated experience. There is, however, a lot of junk to go through before finding a special item. The Iron Market, the largest in Haiti, is situated in the filthy heart of Port-au-Prince. It is the place to get just about anything and witness a slice of Haitian life (it was damaged by fire in April 1991). For shops with the best choice of handicrafts, see **Art Centres** and **Shopping** sections below.

Haitian music is intimately related with everyday life, both religious and secular, while many of the dances stem from voodoo and, originally, Africa.

Foremost in local styles is the smooth, sophisticated *compás*. Another local style is *tamboo*. There has always been a close link between Haiti and New Orleans and while there is no shortage of good bands, many, like Tabou Combo, or Coupe Cloué, move to New York. A new generation of musicians, like Michel Martelly, is adopting Antillean Zouk, using synthesizers. Another new wave, led by Boukman Experience, is rejecting French and US influence, digging instead into Haitian voodoo and Créole roots.

There is also a wealth of Créole proverbs which express popular philosophy (the book *You can learn Créole*, from Caravelle bookshop, US$1.25, contains many). Twentieth-century Haitian writers have, as with others in the Caribbean, struggled to find a true identity, but within the island's specific constraints of the American occupation and the Duvalier regimes. Here, too, a preoccupation with Africa (not dissimilar to that seen in Jamaican reggae), the use of Créole and folk forms have played a part, together with some Marxist ideology. In the 1940s and 1950s, writers such as Jacques Roumain (particularly in his novel *Gouverneurs de la rosée—Masters of the Dew*) were concerned with the plight of the black Haitian peasant, but this has given way to a generation more critical of all aspects of Haitian society.

Le Théâtre National is the legitimate theatre group. A contemporary, covered, outdoor theatre was recently constructed for theatrical and cultural events. However, the unrest of the last few years has curtailed theatre activity. The Institute Français occasionally puts on minor performances acted by members. Folkloric and dance troupes, as well as commercial voodoo performances, are the closest to theatre spectacle available at the moment. Apart from popular dance and music, these arts are surprisingly undeveloped. Some performances occur in association with a hotel or in one of the larger cinemas. They are advertised in the papers or on the radio, or through the local cable channel that displays community announcements.

Flora and Fauna

Compared with its neighbour, Haiti is a very poor destination with regard to flora and fauna. Habitats have been destroyed on a large scale and only by hiking or riding into the few remnants of high forest is there much chance of finding less common birds or plants.

Festivals

Carnival in Haiti takes place on the three days before Ash Wednesday. It is not nearly as lavish as the Brazilian or Trinidadian carnivals. On Sunday afternoons before carnival there are practice parades in the main streets and the atmosphere is exuberant. Carnival used to attract many tourists. It is, nationally, a popular time, but recent political unrest has kept many tourists and expatriates living in Haiti off the streets now. For the adventurous, though, it can be fun either in the streets or on the floats. The crowds push and shove, so be prepared to defend yourself! Independence is celebrated on January 1-2.

Travel Hints

Haiti is especially fascinating for the tourist who is avid for out-of-the-way experience. In order that you may make the most of your visit, we offer the following hints. Although it is one of the poorest countries in the world, most of whose citizens suffer from one kind of oppression or another, Haiti is proud of having been the only nation to have carried out successfully a slave rebellion. Haitians at all levels are very sensitive to how they are treated by foreigners, commonly called "blanc". If you treat them with warmth and consideration, they will respond with enthusiasm and friendship. There is no hostility towards "blanc"; if you feel threatened it is probably the result of a misunderstanding.

Eye contact is very important; it is not avoided as in some other countries. Humour plays an important role in social interactions; Haitians survive by laughing at themselves and their situation. This, sadly, became a very difficult proposition during the events following the overthrow of President Aristide. Haitians are physical, touching and flirting a lot.

It is important to recognize the presence of each person in a social encounter, either with a handshake or a nod. When walking in the countryside, you usually wish "bon jour" (before 1100) or "bon soir" to anyone you meet. Coffee or cola are often offered by richer peasants to visitors (Haitian coffee is among the best in the world). Do not expect straight answers to questions about a peasant's wealth, property or income.

It is assumed that each "blanc" is wealthy and therefore it is legitimate to try to separate you from your riches. Such attempts should be treated with humour, indignation or consideration as appropriate.

Guides Young men and boys offer their services as guides at every turn and corner. It seems that it's worthwhile taking one (for about US$10-30 a day, depending where you go) just to prevent others pestering you. Most guides speak English and it is easier to get around with one than without. If you hire a guide you can also visit places off the beaten tourist track and avoid some of the frustrations of the public transport system. Max Church, a pastor who has been training English/French/Creole-speaking guides, can be called on 34-2622, Port-au-Prince. However, if you take guides you must realize that they expect you to buy them food if you stop to eat.

Secondly, and more important, the guides are often "on commission" with local shop- and stall-keepers, so that even if you ask them to bargain for you, you will not necessarily be getting a good price; nor will they necessarily go where you want to go. If you don't want a guide a firm but polite "non, merci" gets the message across. It is best to ignore altogether hustlers outside guesthouses, etc, as any contact makes them persist.

Note The political upheavals of 1991-92 have meant that it has been impossible to verify many of the services given in this chapter for the 1993 edition.

Port-au-Prince

Port-au-Prince, capital and chief port of Haiti, population more than 1 million, is set at the end of a beautiful deep horseshoe bay, with high mountains behind and a small island across the bay protecting it from high seas and tidal waves. The town, with its fascinating "gingerbread" houses, is built in the form of an amphitheatre. In the lower part, at sea-level, is concentrated the business section, with a palm-shaded sea-front known as the Exposition which unfortunately has become very dirty. On the heights are the private houses, generally surrounded by shady gardens. The heat is some degrees less at several summer resorts easily reached from the city. Port-au-Prince is very poor, apart from a few "swank" areas. The centre of the town is quite small and nearly everything of interest is within walking distance.

The Protestant Episcopal Cathedral of Sainte-Trinité has naive biblical

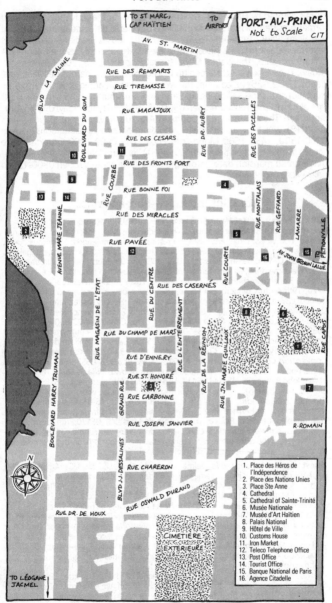

PORT-AU-PRINCE
Not to Scale CIT

1. Place des Héros de l'Indépendance
2. Place des Nations Unies
3. Place Ste Anne
4. Cathedral
5. Cathedral of Sainte-Trinité
6. Musée Nationale
7. Musée d'Art Haïtien
8. Palais National
9. Hôtel de Ville
10. Customs House
11. Iron Market
12. Teleco Telephone Office
13. Post Office
14. Tourist Office
15. Banque National de Paris
16. Agence Citadelle

murals painted by Haitian artists. The Musée du Panthéon National is in the former presidential mansion in the Place des Héros de l'Indépendence (213 Ave Jean Paul, Turgeau, Tel: 45-5647). It houses Haitian relics, early costumes, paintings and historic documents and also boasts the anchor of Columbus' ship, the *Santa María* (usually open 0830-1200 Monday to Friday). The Musée d'Art Haitien du Collège St-Pierre, Champs de Mars, rue Capois (Tel: 22-2510), contains the works of Haiti's leading artists. It also has exhibitions, a shop selling handicrafts and a restaurant with simple Asian fare at lunchtime (museum open 0900-1600 Monday to Friday, 0900-1400 Saturday). There is also the Centre d'Art, rue Roy, off rue Capois, Tel: 22-2018, which is an art gallery holding occasional exhibitions, open 0900-1300, 1430-1600 Monday to Friday and 0900-1200 Saturday. The Musée Defly, rue Légitime (Tel: 22-4081), is a restored and refurnished gingerbread mansion dating from the turn of the century (open 0900-1300 daily except Sunday).

Local Information—Port-au-Prince

Where To Stay *Castel Haiti*, St Gérard, Tel: 22-0393, most rooms air-conditioned, swimming pool, US$45 (bargaining possible, reductions available for longer stays), large rooms, good views, radio, a/c, clean, no restaurant, recommended; 5 minutes down hill is *Olofson*, Rue Capois, St Gérard, swimming pool, gardens, has rooms, bungalows and suites, US$49, 69 and 89 single, US$59,79 and 99 double, all include breakfast and a welcome drink, all with fan or a/c, all prices subject to tax and service as below and to a 3% energy charge, Tel: 23-4000/4101, Fax: 23-0919, Telex 2030471, PO Box 1720, 19th century gingerbread house, used as a model by Graham Greene for *The Comedians*, relaxed atmosphere, efficient, friendly, used by writers and journalists, shows Monday and Friday (dinner starts 1830, show 2130, entrance fee US$5), good restaurant, recommended; *Plaza Holiday Inn* 10 rue Capois, Tel: 23-9800/3722, Telex 2030356, Fax: 20822, US$98s, US$108d, including breakfast, energy charge US$6, all Holiday Inn facilities, good restaurant; *Park*, 25 rue Capois near Place des Héros, Tel: 22-4406; *Royal Haitian Club*, Carrefour, Tel: 34-0258. *Christopher Hotel Convention Center*, Bourdon, Tel: 45-6124/5, PO Box 962, US$38-55s, US$45-59d, all a/c, phone, balcony, swimming pool, good; just below is *Villa St-Louis*, 85 Bourdon et Ave John Brown, Tel: 45-6241/6417, US$44s, US$55d, apartments US$800/month, a/c, TV, radio, phone, views, excellent restaurant, popular with business travellers. Cheaper are *Splendid*, Rue N, off Jean Paul Deux, Tel: 45-0116, swimming pool, recommended, and *Prince*, Rue 3, Tel: 55-2764, small and friendly, rooms large and comfortable but dirty; *Palace*, rue Champ-de-Mars 55, US$20, run down, dirty, prostitutes, not recommended; *Central* rue du Centre 78, central, US$8s, US$16d, shower, fan, dirty, prostitutes, very basic; restaurant below is poor, but the new one opposite is cheap, clean and good (créole cuisine).

Guest Houses *Coconut Villa*, Delmas 19, Tel: 46-1691, US$35s, US$44d (plus 20%), CP; *Hillside*, Ave M L King; on same street *Le Triangle* is recommended, food available, possible to leave luggage; *L'Auberge Port-au-Prince*, 146 rue du Centre, Tel: 23-1059, near Iron Market, US$12s, US$18d, hot water US$1 extra, cold water US$0.60, basic but clean, cheap restaurant downstairs; *Hotel Acropolis*, 441 Blvd J J Dessalines, Tel: 22-1873, US$12-14d, electric fan, swimming pool; *Haiti Chérie*, near supermarket en route for airport, run by Haitian/American couple; *Villa Carmel*, Ave Jean Paul Deux 40, meals available, swimming pool. Other guest houses recommended as both cheap and good: *La Griffonne*, Rue Jean-Baptiste 21, Canapé Vert (Tel: 45-4095), US$16-25, breakfast and dinner available, in the hills above the main part of the town and so slightly cooler, yet within walking distance of the centre, and near to *publique* run to centre, swimming pool, clean, comfortable, friendly and recommended; *Sendral's*, 14 Bourdon, Ruelle Sendral, on the way to Pétionville just off Ave John Brown, Tel: 45-6052, US$25s, US$35d with breakfast, a/c, fan, very clean, friendly, swimming pool, fine views, taxi from airport about US$8, popular with Peace Corps and aid agencies, dinner available for US$8 (from Port-au-Prince take any *tap-tap* to Pétionville via Bourdon and get off when you see the sign or *Villa St-Louis*, which is nearby); *May's Villa*, 28 Debussy PO Box 160, over US$40 for air conditioned room, including taxes and 2 meals, clean, swimming pool and panoramic view of the city. *Idéal Villa*, 53 Delmas, Tel: 46-1123, US$20s, US$40d inclusive, CP; *Yaguana*, 2 Delmas 35, Tel: 46-2637, US$25d; *Villa Belle Soleil*, 102 Lafleur Ducheine, Tel: 22-2787, US$10s plus 10%, plus breakfast, US$34d inclusive.

Note Check all rooms in advance; service may leave something to be desired. There is a 10% service charge and 5-20% tax added to most hotel bills. Most hotels and guest houses do not have full air-conditioning, so aim for the upper range if you want something cool. Aim also for a hotel with its own generator since power shortages, especially at night, are common. Water is also rationed. In 1992 cheaper, central hotels lacked both running water and electricity. An energy charge of up to US$6 may be made and even a charge for swimming pool availability. Some hotels offer discounts if you pay in dollars instead of gourdes; practices vary with regard to credit cards, though.

Where To Eat There are some very good but very expensive eating places in Port-au-Prince. *Aux Cosaques*, 66 Chemin des Dalles, Tel: 45-4433, reasonable prices, excellent Haitian food; *La Table Ronde*, rue Capois near *Holiday Inn*, good, popular with business people and politicians; *Au Bec Fin*, 25 rue Miracles, Tel: 22-3065, open 0800-1600, reasonably priced; *Château Caprice*, at Mousseau (Continental and American food); *Chez Noelle*, rue Pavée; *Chez Tony*, 260 Route de Delmas, Tel: 46-0808, and downtown on rue Pavée, Tel: 22-2529, good, cheap meals (nearest thing to fast food). *Le Select* on rue Jean Paul Deux in a garden setting. *Yvone*, Blvd Harry Truman, near ACGH, créole, cheap, recommended. The terrace bars on the square between the Palais National and the *Hotel Palace* serve good, freshly-cooked chicken at a reasonable price. Good juices at *Red Star* bar next to *Palace Hotel*.

Clubs The Turgeau Club; society clubs such as the Bellevue and the Port-au-Princien; sports clubs. Pétionville Golf Club (Tel: 57-1437), also at Bourdon, 9-hole, clubs for rent.

Art Centres Commercial galleries include the Néhémy, Nader's (92 Place Geffrard) and Issa's (17 rue Chile), very good quality for buyers. Touche d'Art, rue Pétionville, an attractive gingerbread house selling paintings and other craftwork; also has a framing service. Local art can be seen at the Cathedral of Saint Trinité, the Airport, and Exposition buildings, and in the principal hotels. Olivier has a gallery near the *Hotel Oloffson* and is very knowledgeable about local artists. Also ask for Mr Thompson at the *Oloffson* for details on art galleries. There is a gallery at 29 rue Champs de Mars, run by Raoul Michel, which is one of the least expensive and has a good variety of work. In the stalls by the post office a selection of Haitian art is on sale at low prices, if you bargain.

Recommended **craft shops** include: Gingerbread, rue Lamartinière, antiques, voodoo-inspired craft, woven wall-hangings, etc (Taggart, of Cap Haitien—see below—exhibits here); Zin d'Art, Ave John Brown, wall-hangings, basket-ware, woven goods, tablecloths, painted trays, jewellery, and more; Pericles' Gallery, 46 rue Geffrard, Tel: 22-0059, for good copper jewellery.

Warning Watch out for pickpockets in the market, on buses and bus-station areas. Since the overthrow of President Aristide in 1991 and the imposition of international trade embargos, the city has become short of electricity and many other commodities; at the same time, violence has increased.

Taxis *Publiques*, shared taxis, charge US$0.40-0.80 a trip. They are identified by a red cloth or ribbon tied to the inside rear-view mirror. *Camionettes* (minibuses) charge US$0.25. *Tap-tap* (open-backed truck running on fixed routes) fares are US$0.20 anywhere in town; they are difficult to manage with luggage. Taxis charge per car, about US$1.50 within Port-au-Prince, but prices rise when going uphill and at night. They are scarce early in the morning, in the evening, and along the rue Dessalines. Good taxis, with meters, phone *Mick's Taxis*, Tel: 57-7777, Pétionville, new, a/c, yellow cars. Outside the capital, it costs US$25 for 1-4 people to Ibo Beach, US$38 for 1-2 people to beaches near St Marc. Taxis may also be hired, with driver, by the hour, half- or whole day: US$25 for 3 hours in the capital; US$40 for 3 hours to Kenscoff, etc.

Night Clubs In the Carrefour district, just south of Port-au-Prince, there are several places to dance (take a taxi, or *tap-taps* run past until about midnight), *Le Lambi* is the most reputable, good national food and music, open to the ocean; most are pick-up joints for prostitutes.

Cinemas Cheap and interesting: the best are *Imperial* (air conditioned), Delmas; *Capitol* (air conditioned), 53, rue Lamarre; *Paramount*, Champs de Mars. Popular foreign films (British, US, French) are shown; non-French films are dubbed into French.

Banks Banque Nationale de Paris, Ave John Brown, First National City Bank, route de Delmas, Bank of Nova Scotia; Banque de Boston, rue des Miracles, and others, including local banks. Banque d'Haiti (which has branches throughout the country) reported to have best rate for £ and Banque Populaire Haitienne best rates for travellers' cheques. Ask rates in banks before changing money. The black market is easily available, at the Iron Market, for instance; the *Holiday Inn* changes money at all times but at less than the black market rate. Good rates for US$ cash or travellers' cheques at *Express Market*, Ave John Brown, about 6 blocks down from *Villa St-Louis*, ask for M or Mme Handal.

Library Alliance Française open 0830-1200, 1430-1900 except Monday and Saturday afternoon.

Travel Agents *Agence Citadelle* (American Sightseeing of Haiti and American Express), PO Box 41, 36 place du Marron Inconnu, Tel: 22-5900; *Chatelain Tours* (Gray Lines Sightseeing of Haiti), rue Geffrard, Tel: 22-4469, PO Box 1056; *Continental Travel*, PO Box 1010, 105 rue Pavée, Tel: 22-0604; *Southerland Tours*, 30 Ave Marie Jeanne, PO Box 851, Tel: 22-1600; *Sans Souci*, 188 Ave John Brown (Lalue), Tel: 45-6980/6407. Tours offered by agencies or through hotels include to Kenscoff mountains (3 hours), city and shopping in Port-au-Prince (3 hours), beaches, voodoo (see above), Cap Haïtien (2 days) and Jacmel. Agencies can also handle travel documentation, car rental, travel and hotel reservations, cruises, etc.

Tourist Office was at Avenue Marie Jeanne, Cité de l'Exposition (Tel: 22-1729) but was reported closed in February 1992. It is worth checking bus and taxi fares to avoid being overcharged. Maps of Haiti available at US$1.50 from Carlos' shop opposite Tourist Office, and from bookshops. The Budget Rent a Car sketch map of the city contains a lot of useful information.

Internal Air Services Mission Air, known locally as MAF, run by Dan Rogers, has 2 flights daily to Cap Haïtien, US$84 return, and to Jérémie US$100 return, seats and passage must be reserved at office at the airport, Tel: 46-3993, tickets can be collected from office at 60 Delmas, Tel: 57-3086. Caribbe Inter, Tel: 46-0737, call Alix Cedras for reservations and for purchasing tickets at the airport, daily flights to Cap Haïtien; to Jérémie Tuesday, Thursday and Saturday. Planes can be rented for flights to specific destinations. Flights will not depart in bad weather.

Excursions from Port-au-Prince

A few km out in Port-au-Prince harbour is Sand Cay, said to be one of the most beautiful coral reefs in the world. No boats go there although Romi Roy (Tel: 57-4846), who owns a 16-foot catamaran, will take a large party if given sufficient notice. She will help with any enquiries if you phone her. She also owns a riding stable called Henfrasa Riding Club, Delmas 33 (same phone number), specializing in jumping and dressage to a high level of training and performance.

A paved road leads to (10 km) **Pétionville** . There is a track (45 minutes' walk) from near the Baptist church to the 19th century Fort Jacques, from where there is an excellent view across Port-au-Prince harbour (*publiques* from Pétionville turn round at the junction). At Bouteillier/Laboule, about 5 km outside Pétionville, visit the Jane Barbancourt (pseudo) Castle. One can sample an unlimited quantity of the company's 16 differently-flavoured rums, which include coffee, mango, coconut, orange. Rum is sold at US$6 a bottle. From the castle one can visit the bottlers and get an excellent view of Port-au-Prince (the sand quarry next door covers everything in a fine white dust, but it is still worth a visit). (Taxi from Port-au-Prince, US$16 for 1-2 people, US$3 for extra person.)

If you have time, a drive through the fertile Cul-de-Sac plain, about 30 km each way, is well worthwhile for those interested in agriculture and local life.

Local Information—Pétionville

Where To Stay Hotels include: *Montana*, rue Cardozo, between the capital and Pétionville (PO Box 523, Tel: 57-4030/4020/1920/1921), US$39s + 10%, US$48d + 10%, breakfast US$5 pp, prices change according to the view you have, US$14 for dinner, all rooms air conditioned, pool, tennis; *Villa Créole*, off Ave Panaméricaine (PO Box 126, Tel: 57-1570), from US$55s + 10% tax + 3% energy to US$70-75d, all meals extra, one of the only hotels whose generator will cope with air conditioning, also with pool, tennis, smart; *El Rancho*, elegant, "Mexican-style" hotel, same location and facilities as *Villa Créole*, good, US$60-75 EP, MAP supplement US$20, tax 15% (PO Box 71, Tel: 57-2080/1/2/3/4); *Kinam*, Place St Pierre (Tel: 57-0462), US$34s + 10% service + US$1.50 for energy, US$44d with US$2 for energy, air conditioning, restaurant, bar, pool, based on a gingerbread mansion; *Ibo Lélé*, on street of same name, same price range, recommended.

Guest houses: *Doux Séjour*, 10 rue Magny (Tel: 57-1560), US$25 with breakfast, shower, fan, clean, delightfully eccentric, 460 metres above sea-level; *Villa Kalewes*, 99 rue Gregoire (Tel: 57-0817), US$26s, US$40-42d including breakfast and all taxes, pool, nice, conveniently situated.

Where To Eat An excellent sea food restaurant is *Le Recif* in Route de Delmas; also good is *La Plantation*, Impasse Fouchard, Bois Moquette, Tel: 57-0979, highly recommended (French, US$35 per person for 3 course meal). Other French restaurants: *Le Chalet*, route de Kenscoff (US$25), *La Voile* (US$30); French/Créole: the moderately-priced *Belle Epoque*, and *Chez Gérard*. *Les Cascades*, rue Clerveaux and Ogé, charming surroundings, Tel: 57-6704, US$30 pp for meal, you can also simply have a drink in the bar. Caribbean cuisine at *Le Pote*, 43 rue Magny, Tel: 57-4141, US$30 a head. *Le Bolero* serves pasta/pizza and French food, US$15-20, popular; *Mama's Pizza*, 45 rue Faubert, Tel: 57-0600. Asian food at *Le Gregoire*, rue Gregoire, US$30, very good. *L'obsession*, 52 rue Faubert Tel: 57-0131 (French, dinner with wine costs US$15-20 per head). *Steak Inn*, rue Magny, Saturday and Sunday has live music, Haitian groups, expensive. Institut Français, 19 rue Lamarre, has excellent restaurant *Café des Arts*; several other good ones. Lots of informal pizza places in and around town, about US$15 a head.

Shopping There is a vegetable market here every Tuesday and Friday which is well worth a visit. Good quality local crafts can be purchased at the Baptist Church. Galérie Monin for Haitian art; Boutique Marassa, rue Lamarre, a variety of painted articles. Nader's (as in Port-au-Prince), rue Gregoire; Fleur de Canne, 34 rue Bis Gabart, Tel: 57-4266, charming little shop selling crafts. United Sculptors of Haiti, on the road to Kenscoff. Mountain Maid Shop Artisanal, Fermanthe, sells wooden plates and clothes at very reasonable prices (good snack bar attached).

Nightclubs Dancing is only possible at *Regis*, local live bands or taped music.

Transport *Publique* from Iron Market to Pétionville, US$0.25, two routes, either via avenue John Brown, or route Delmas.

A good paved 16 km road runs from Pétionville to the holiday resort of **Kenscoff**, 1,370 metres above sea-level, where the climate is excellent all the year round and the scenery splendid. (*Hotels Dereix, Florville; Restaurant Altitude 1300*, open Sunday only, local cuisine served out of doors, cool, very nice, US$15 per person; opposite Colette Latortue serves meals in her home on Sunday only, Tel: 45-3917 in advance to advise her of your arrival, Haitian and French cuisine; the Baptist Mission in Fermathe, a small town before Kenscoff, serves very American, fast food snacks and has the *Mountain Maid Shop* selling crafts at reasonable prices. *Publique* from Pétionville market, US$0.60.) Furcy is a mountain town nearby in a pleasant setting; worth a day's excursion for horse riding, or a picnic but the road is very bad.

South of Port-au-Prince

Take a Léogâne *tap-tap* west from Port-au-Prince, get off west of Gressier at the sign for Guilou beach (¼ km walk), clean and tidy with all amenities, entrance US$1. When available, food and drink on the beaches is expensive. Further to the southwest are Taino and Sun beaches, near Grand Goâve, while by Petit Goâve is the beautiful Cocoyer Beach. (*Le Relais de l'Empereur* hotel in Petit Goâve, PO Box 11399, Port-au-Prince, Tel: 22-9557, US$42 and up, CP, other meals US$15 each, has boat service to Cocoyer, US$9, including beach tariff; drinks on beach US$2, or US$3 for alcohol. The hotel itself was the residence of Emperor Faustin I, 1849-56.)

Jérémie , an attractive place with colonial buildings, can be reached from Port-au-Prince by bus (every other day, US$10, 8-10 hours), or *tap-tap*, or by weekly overnight boat (US$6 including bunk in bridge-house, no food, dirty and crowded). Mission Aviation (MAF) flies from the capital Monday, Wednesday and Friday, US$100 return. (Hotels: *La Cabane*, overlooking town, shady garden, US$50d including 2 meals, tax and service). Road to Les Cayes may be impassable after rain. One *tap-tap* a day goes to the fine beach of Anse d'Hainault (take plenty of food and drink), which can also be reached by boat from Port Salut, see below (arrange at *Bar-Restaurant Le Sable*).

Les Cayes is a pleasant town with several hotels including *Concorde* (PO Box 46, Gabions des Indigenes, US$45d plus 10% tax, excluding meals). In Cayes Bay is Vache Island (Henry Morgan's base for his 1670 attack on Panama), which can be visited by taking the boat leaving between 1600 and 1700 and spending the night there or by hiring a motorboat for a day (about US$30). There are several beaches on the island. Buses leave Port-au-Prince for Les Cayes every morning (US$3-5), but no buses from Jacmel. The road to Port-au-Prince is paved and very good.

About 1½ hours drive from Les Cayes (2 buses a day) is **Port Salut** , with beautiful beaches (eg Pointe Sable). There are 2 Swiss-owned hotels here: *Arada Inn*, known as *Deck's*, US$45, plus 10% tax, including 2 meals; basic rooms, at *Bar-Restaurant Le Sable*, 2 km outside town. The St Dominique and Althania bus companies go to Port Salut from Port-au-Prince.

A trip round this south-western corner of Haiti is recommended for the adventurous. From Les Cayes you can get transport to see Les Anglais and thence walk through the attractive town of Tiburon to Les Irois; alternatively it is possible to get on one of the sloops which sail from port to port round the coast. From Les Irois the road goes to Dame Marie (on Jérémie road, cheap hotel) and Jérémie, and from there a spectacular but rugged mountain route takes you back to Les Cayes. The round trip can take about 5-7 days; the missionaries in the larger villages sometimes have accommodation.

Jacmel, a port on the south coast, is 2-3 hours by *tap-tap* on a new road from Port-au-Prince, seat by driver US$3, in back US$2-2.20, they leave from behind the customs house on the corner of Rue du Quai and Rue des Césars, every hour. The road takes you through some spectacular scenery. The town itself is beautiful, with some interesting old architecture and many buildings are being restored. The town's Congo beach has black sand and although it is free, it is rather dirty. A new and expensive hotel has been built on the beach. Saturday is market day and at weekends local bands play on the beach in the evening.

Where To Stay The luxury *La Jacmélienne sur Plage*, 30 rooms, very expensive for what's offered, US$64s with 2 meals, US$52 without, US$98d with meals (may negotiate to US$80), US$74 without, plus 15% tax, Haitian cuisine (Tel: 22-4899); *Cyvadier*, 5 km east of Jacmel along a rough road, French-Canadian owned, US$35, pleasant rooms with fan and sea breeze, lovely grounds, swimming pool, excellent service, stairway to beach, good food, tends to be popular at weekends, recommended; *Guy's Guesthouse*, Ave François Duvalier 52 (Tel: 88-3421), unfriendly but clean, US$14-18; *Manoir Alexandra*, recommended, fairly basic, US$48, including 2 good meals, Tel: 88-2711; *Chez Madame Luc*, under US$10. Several discothèques, including *La Ruine*.

Shopping Art Centre, Les Créations Moro, rue de Commerce.

Near Jacmel, Raymond-les-Bains has a good beach and near the village of Cayes Jacmel is a beautiful white-sand beach (*tap-tap* from Jacmel, US$0.20). Cyvadier Cove has a small but protected white sand beach. It is best to take your own provisions with you to the beaches. A visit to the Bassin Bleu is well worthwhile. Horses are provided for the day's excursion; choose one that looks sound as part of the journey is steep and rocky. You have to walk the last kilometre and climb down a rope to the first waterfall. From there you can see a series of other cascades and enjoy the view out across the Bay of Jacmel. The cost is US$5 for the horse and US$2 per person for the guide.

North of Port-au-Prince

Beaches

To the north of Port-au-Prince is Ibo beach (very touristy, entrance fee US$3). Lee Sharon at Ibo (Tel: 46-1271) takes private deep-sea fishing trips. To get there, either go by boat (pay on board), or take the *tap-tap* from the Hachot factory to St Marc and tell the driver where you want to get off, US$1.40 (you will probably have a half-hour walk from the turnoff). The same *tap-tap* will take you to Kyona beach, about 1 hour from Port-au-Prince (entrance US$2.50, good diving) and Kaliko Beach Club, where you can hire scuba and snorkelling equipment, or take reef excursions (entrance US$5, US$2.50 for the beach, the remainder for a drink). Kaliko Dive Shop, PO Box 58, Tel: 22-8040 (in USA 800-223-9815), rents snorkelling and diving equipment, offers dive trips and lessons (4 days, 3 nights with two 2-tank dives, 1 guided shore night dive all accommodation, US$299 single; 7 days, 6 nights, five 2-tank boat dives, etc, US$490 single, reductions for doubles and triples, prices include breakfast, dinner, welcome drink, airport transfers, unlimited snorkelling but not 10% service). The *Kaliko Beach Club* has bungalows for US$75d MAP, US$60 CP, meals US$15, airport transfer US$40 (minimum 2 people), same phone numbers as dive club. The fare to Kaliko is US$1. Further on still are Ouanga bay, Wahoo Bay (formerly called Joly, entry US$2.50, rooms at the *Beach Club* are lovely, pool, horseriding, very popular, PO Box 15418, Pétionville, Tel: 22-9653), Moulin-sur-Mer (US$6, in beautiful surroundings among the restored ruins of a sugar mill, recommended), and

Amani-Y (very beautiful).

The highway from the capital to Cap Haïtien, from which all the above beaches can be reached, is fairly new, with some hair-raising bends, but also affording breathtaking views. 15 km north of Port-au-Prince, at Bon Repos, is the highly recommended *Roland Hotel*, owned by Roland Seide, rue Dr Acrouch, Livalois Bon Repos, Tel: 48-1515, a/c, good food, nice pool, helpful staff: "absolutely the best deal in Haiti". The road passes through Cabaret (Km 35), where there is a good beach, and the historic little port of St Marc (Km 98; *Belfort Hotel*, rue Louverture 166, US$10s, some rooms without window, fan, clean, snackbar). After St Marc, the road crosses the Artibonite valley and an area known as La Savane Désolée before climbing to **Gonaïves** (Km 152). Here General Dessalines proclaimed the independence of Haiti in 1804. There is a motel, *Chez Frantz*, with recommended restaurant, 3 km past the town; recommended is the *Pension Elias*, Rue L'Ouverture, clean, friendly and safe. The restaurant in town lets rooms above. Bus from Port-au-Prince, US$2.40, no fixed schedule. Most leave between 0700 and 1200. Buses from Gonaïves to Cap Haïtien also leave mornings only.

190 kilometres from the capital you cross Puylboreau hill and enter the greener northern region. At Plaisance (Km 204) there is a police checkpoint; at Limbé (Km 227) the hospital of Le Bon Samaritain (founded by an American missionary).

Cap Haïtien

Cap Haïtien on the north coast, 258 km from the capital, is the second city, locally known as Le Cap. Population 70,500. On entering the town, you have to register with the police at the checkpoint; keep an eye on your papers. The city is poor and scruffy, but with a good atmosphere and not without interest.

Beaches

There are many beautiful beaches near Le Cap but most are difficult to get to. The *Mont Joli* hotel has a beach at Rival (with glass-bottom boat trip daily at 0830) which is about 15 minutes' pleasant walk past the old fort, (good views of the city), from the public beach near the *Brise de Mer* hotel (both Rival and the public beach are dirty). **Cormier Beach** (admission US$2), 9 km from Le Cap (*Hotel Cormier*, T 26-1000, US$80-90 MAP, good food, popular Sunday buffet lunch at 1300, recommended, bungalows, boat trips with diving, friendly instructor, surfboards and snorkel equipment for hire, tennis) can be reached by the hotel bus (get your hotel to phone the *Hotel Cormier* to arrange transport) or, failing that, taxi (US$15-20). You may be able to get a lift back in the hotel minibus. At Cormier, where boats are built, you can buy freshly-caught lobster very cheaply and you can hire someone to row you to **Labadie**, a fine, deserted beach (except when the cruise ships are in port, usually Monday and Friday, but none in the first half of 1992), from where there is excellent snorkelling over coral reefs, or you can walk there from Cormier in 30 minutes. When cruise ships are in, *tap-taps* go to Labadie for US$2. The village of Labadie itself is worth a visit and bungalows can be rented there for about US$7. Coco Beach, close to Labadie, is a new resort utilized at times by cruise ships (admission US$3, US$20 if in use by cruise passengers). The road to Cormier and Labadie requires a 4WD vehicle. Fishermen on the beach near the *Brise de Mer* hotel can be hired to sail you to beaches further afield.

Labadie Pointe St Honoré is now a beautiful, US$5-million project belonging to Royal Caribbean Cruise Lines. The public may use all the facilities, such as watersports and restaurants, for a US$20 admission fee. On the days when no ship docks, the point is empty and facilities, except for one public lavatory, are locked. At these times, the premises may be entered for US$3. Nearest accommodation is at the villages of Labadie or Cormier Plage, each a few minutes away.

15 minutes beyond Cormier and Labadie is Belli Beach, small, with white sand and a basic hotel which charges US$8 a night. Meals are excellent (lobster, etc), but take your own ice box with ice and bread and butter (on cruise ship days, Belli is reported to be "the bordello for the crew", best avoided then). From here you can hire small boats, with or without outboard motor, for a nominal fee which must be arranged in advance. Beautiful secluded beaches can be discovered this way, and the locals are charming and helpful.

Local Information—Cap Haïtien

Where To Stay *Mont Joli*, north of town (PO Box 12, Tel: 62-0300/0326, Telex 2030 300), prices from US$45s/US$50d without meals to US$60/80 with 2 meals, panoramic views, superb service, air conditioning, pool, free tennis, bars (treat the rum punches with respect), excellent restaurant, night club, private beach 3 minutes from hotel, recommended; *Roi Christophe* (patronized by Pauline Bonaparte Leclerc while her own home was being built near Port-au-Prince), in town down hill from *Mont Joli*, rue 24B (PO Box 34, Tel: 509-62-0414, Telex 3490300), US$34-49, with breakfast, rooms with fan or a/c, pool, good, helpful, will give Amex cash advances for a small charge, very good restaurant, recommended; in the same area, *Pension Brise de Mer*, 4 Carrenage, Tel: 62-0821, not as expensive, 2 meals included, excellent food, private bathroom, pleasant atmosphere, but not very safe. *Beck*, a long way from centre, but has a good pool and attractive grounds and views, US$40-55s, US$45-65d including 2 meals, plus 10% tax, pricey bar, quite good, friendly German owner, may be amenable to bargaining (PO Box 48, Tel: 62-0001). In cheaper categories are: *Columbia*, rue 5, 3-K, US$10s, US$12d, fan, clean, safe, very helpful; *Le Gîte*, rue 7, US$10d, fan, dirty, daytime prostitution, restaurant attached; *Pension Colon*, on seafront opposite Post Office, without food (not recommended); *Dupuy*, very pleasant; *Bon Dieu Bon*, reasonably priced restaurant; *A à Z*, on main square opposite Cathedral, rambling, delightful colonial building with good views from the balcony, US$8, very clean but amenities and staff poor; *Universal*, rues D et 14, US$15-40d, unfriendly, good restaurant. Mme Manoir runs an unmarked *pension* in a rambling old colonial house on Ave E between rues 24 and 25, including 2 meals, rather run down.

Where To Eat *Sacade*, rues 18 et B, near *Pension Dupuy*; *San Raison*, near market, cheaper; *Universelle*, 2 blocks from *Sacade*, bakery with restaurant, friendly, cheap and good value. Unnamed restaurants on corner of 6 and I and on 11 between F and G, cheap meals. *Ti Paradis*, rues D et 15, good. Fresh and cold fruit juices served on Ave A, between rues 23 and 24.

Shopping Taggart Artilliers, Tel: 03-2-1931, make excellent Haitian crafts; run by Mme Ginette Taggart (she has built 2 houses on her property, which should be available for rent). Tourist market at the port with all kinds of Haitien crafts, including paintings, for sale; bargain hard. Art gallery at junction of Aves A and B, expensive but good, closed 1300-1500 (next door is *Cap 2000* bar which sells ice cream and sandwiches; opposite is restaurant with good pizza). Supermarket *Parisienne*, rue 8, is good, a/c; a new supermarket at the port, *Maritime*, sells American foods at high prices.

Exchange Banque Union Haïtien changes travellers' cheques, open until 1800.

Post Office Ave B at rue 17.

Travel Agent Cap Travel, 84 rue 23A, Tel: 62-0517.

Tourist Bureau Rue 24, Esplanade.

Rent-a-Bike Cap Rent-a-Bike at 11-D-D (Tel: 62-8831) rent bicycles and motorcycles. The cost is US$15-20 per day.

Transport *Tap-taps* and *camionettes* leave from the Mahogany Market, near the waterfront in Port-au-Prince, usually about 0630 (but waits until jam-packed). The journey to Le Cap can take as little as 4 hours but usually it is much longer, even as much as 10 hours. Fares vary as to whether you sit in the front or back. Public transport stops short of the town, at the police checkpoint, and from there it is an easy 15 minute walk. The official bus fare is US$7. Mission Aviation (MAF) have flights from the capital daily.

Excursions from Cap Haïtien

The **Citadelle** is a vast ruined fortress built for Roi Henri Christophe between 1804 and 1817 (see under **History**). 20,000 people were involved in its construction. With 4-metre thick walls, it covers 10,000 square metres on the summit of Pic La Ferrière. It was designed to protect the island from French invasion and its garrison of 5,000 soldiers (plus the royal family, their staff, etc) could have resisted siege for a year. Haitians claim that it is the eighth wonder of the world and it is indeed very impressive and has breathtaking views. Restoration work is being carried out. To get there take a *publique* or *tap-tap* from Le Cap to **Milot**, the fares being US$1 and US$0.30 respectively. (*Tap-taps* leave from outside the *Hotel Bon Dieu Bon* in the morning, hotel tour operators may charge US$60 pp round trip in a jeep, eg from the *Mont Joli*, guides' information is not necessarily correct.) From Milot it is an interesting two to three-hour walk on the steep road to the fortress. You can however hire a horse and with it two men—one to push and one to pull!—for about US$6.50 (in wet weather it is too dangerous for horses). Guides are also available. The men expect, if not a drink at each stage of the journey, then at least a tip. If you have your own transport you can drive 5-6 km along a very rough road from Milot to a parking area and thence have a much shorter walk up to the fortress. Admission to the Citadelle (including Sans-Souci) costs US$1.25. It is advisable to take refreshments with you: prices charged at the Citadelle are exorbitant. It is also essential to go protected against the sun and to wear stout shoes.

In Milot itself are the ruins of the **Sans Souci Palace** which was built in the early 19th century to rival Versailles. Even though it has been devastated by an earthquake (in 1842), it is well worth a visit. Admission is US$1.25. Try to avoid visiting the Citadelle and Sans Souci if cruise ships are in Le Cap. If intending to see both sites, you must arrive before 1300 as they close at 1700 and you will not have enough time. Also, there are no buses or *tap-taps* back to Le Cap after 1700.

Inland from Le Cap is Hinche with the nearby waterfall of Bassin Zin. Hinche can be reached from Port-au-Prince (by bus at least 6 hours; also by *tap-taps* for US$11 round trip) but from Le Cap the journey is more difficult: there are buses to Pignon (US$1.50) and from there you can take seats in a truck to Hinche. Trucks go from Hinche to Le Cap in 5 hours. In the rainy season cars cannot cross the river near St Raphaël (north of Pignon), but you can walk, locals will assist you for a small fee. The waterfall is a 3-hour walk from Hinche but it is also possible to hire horses. There is a guesthouse, *Centre d'Acceuil*, behind the church in the main square in Hinche, and *Hotel Prestige*, unmarked, 5 minutes from market hall, US$15s, shower, fan, clean, friendly. There is no accommodation in Pignon.

Information for Visitors

Documents

All visitors apart from North Americans need passports, and visas are required for all except nationals of Austria, Belgium, Denmark, Israel, Liechtenstein, Luxembourg, Netherlands, Switzerland, Germany and the UK (some airlines are unclear about this); US and Canadian visitors need only proof of citizenship. (It is however advisable to check this information.) Visas issued at the Haitian Embassy in New York (60 East 42nd Street 1365, New York, NY 10017) take 1 hour, 2 photos required, US$18, valid for 3 months. Visitors must have an onward ticket. All visitors, except cruise ship passengers, must complete an embarkation/disembarkation card on the plane; this is valid for 90 days, and may be extended. It is no longer necessary to have a *laissez-passer* before visiting the interior, but you must have some form of identification to satisfy the many police controls. It may also be wise to obtain a letter from the Tourist Office or police in Port-au-Prince confirming that you are a tourist.

Customs

Baggage inspection is thorough and drug-enforcement laws are strict. There is no restriction on foreign currency. You may bring in one quart of spirits, and 200 cigarettes or 50 cigars. There are no export limitations.

How To Get There

From USA: American Airlines fly from New York; American Airlines, Haiti TransAir and ALM all fly direct from Miami. There are direct flights from Miami to Cap Haïtien Monday to Friday with Gulfstream International. ALM also flies from Curaçao; Air France flies from Santo Domingo once a week. Air Canada flies direct from Montreal. Air France links Haiti with Paris and the French Caribbean: Fort de France in Martinique, Pointe-à-Pitre in Guadeloupe and Cayenne in French Guiana. Turks and Caicos National Airline (TCNA) flies from Cap Haïtien to Grand Turk for US$120. Travellers to Haiti report problems with flights, so check thoroughly. Note that flights from Miami are frequently overbooked. If you are not on a tight schedule, but have a confirmed seat, you may be asked to give your seat to a passenger with no confirmation in

return for credit vouchers to be used on another flight within 12 months. Your original ticket will still be valid for the next flight, or for transfer to a different flight.

Airport

13 km outside Port-au-Prince (administration Tel: 46-4105). Arrival can be pandemonium, especially if more than one flight is being accommodated at once. Knowledge of French helps; just get on with your affairs and try not to be distracted. The so-called "supervisors" at the airport are in fact taxi-drivers, touting for business. Porters charge US$0.50 per bag. Once through the squash inside you emerge into a squash outside, of taxi drivers and people awaiting friends. Taxi into town, US$10, or a seat in a *tap-tap* (open-backed truck), US$0.20, plus US$0.20 for large bag.

Tourist bureau at the airport is very helpful (when it is open), but the snackbar is expensive and service unfriendly. Upstairs are the duty free and handicraft shops. There are no exchange or bank facilities.

There is an airport departure tax of US$20, payable in dollars only. There is also a US$6 "security tax". If in transit (under 24 hours), you are exempt from this tax, but you must get a transit paper from immigration or the Information Office.

Airlines

American Airlines, Cité de l'Exposition, or at the airport (Tel: 22-4300 or 46-0100/2205); Air Canada, airport, Tel: 46-0441; Air France, Champ de Mars (Tel: 22-1700/1078, 46-2573/2086); Air Jamaica/BWIA, Madsen Import/Export (Tel: 22-3476), airport (Tel: 46-0949/7). Haiti TransAir, Tel: 23-4020/4010; ALM, Tel: 22-0900; Copa, Tel: 22-0900/0401, 46-0790/1090.

Shipping

Cruise traffic has fallen off because of travellers' reaction to the incessant begging, among other reasons.

Travel To The Dominican Republic

Regulations regarding travel to the Dominican Republic seem to change constantly. The best place for discovering the latest requirements is the Community Liaison Officer, American Embassy, J J Dessalines, Cité de l'Exposition, Port-au-Prince, Tel: 22-0200, ext 276 (open 0800-1630 Monday and Tuesday, 0800-1200 Wednesday, 1230-1630

Thursday). The Consulate of the Dominican Republic is at 84 rue Geffrard, Port-au-Prince, Tel: 22-9574 (the embassy is at 1 Imp José S Martin, Tel: 57-0383, Pétionville). The overland route involves a 3-4 truck-bus journey on an unmade road to the border at Jimaní (it is worth paying more to sit up front), then paying about US$1.50 for a moped to take you between immigration posts, then a minibus to Santo Domingo.

Internal Transport

Public transport services between towns are mainly operated by collective taxis known as *publiques* (they have a "P" on registration plate) and by open-backed pick-up trucks, known as *tap-taps*. *Camionettes* are a type of minibus (actually Peugeot station wagons) with fares similar to *publiques*. Timetables are normally ignored in the urge to fill up the conveyance with as many people as possible.

Chauffeurs-Guide

Used like regular taxis, or hired by the hour, half-day, day or for a tour, these vehicles are found around hotels and the airport. The drivers usually speak French and a little English. They can be booked through Association des Chauffeurs-Guide, 18 Blvd Harry Truman, Port-au-Prince, Tel: 22-0330.

Car Rental

There are numerous car rental firms, with all the major companies represented. Many have agencies at the airport. The hours there are 0800-2000 whereas offices in town tend to close earlier. The major firms offer air conditioned small cars, such as a Hyundai Pony, for about US$260/week. Hertz, Tel: 46-0700/2048, rents jeeps, cars and trucks (book well in advance). We have received mixed reports about some companies. Budget, Tel: 45-5813, rents cars at US$40/day plus US$19 insurance, 3-day minimum, unlimited mileage; Secom has been recommended by some, but not all, Tel: 57-1913; Avis Tel: 46-2696; and others. Paying by credit card does not attract as good a rate of exchange (7 gourdes = US$1) as paying in gourdes bought on the black market (see below). You have to pay for repairs. There is no car rental agency in Cap Haïtien, but there is in Pétionville.

Driving in Haiti is risky, with many hairpin bends to negotiate. Keep a pen and paper handy to take the number of other cars should an accident occur. Drivers don't often stop and, since in a rented vehicle you are liable for the first US$1,000, failure to get the relevant details could result in very expensive car hire. In 1992 it was not easy to get gasoline, diesel was less difficult. Gasoline is usually available outside Port-au-Prince only when there is electricity, normally 1730-1900 and for a short time in the morning. The capital's streets are very busy.

For driving to Jacmel and Cap Haïtien an ordinary car is fine, but for Jérémie or Port-de-Paix 4WD is necessary.

Foreigners may use a national driving licence for 3 months in Haiti, then a local permit is required.

Hitchhiking

Foreigners do not normally hitch. There are many young Haitian men who stick out a thumb asking for a "roue libre", especially from foreigners. Use your discretion.

Air Charter

See under Port-au-Prince for Mission Aviation's internal services. Plane rental and charter is limited to 2 private aircraft that are kept at General Aviation. The owners are willing to negotiate any arrangements. Documents for flight within Haiti are to be obtained from the Security Department at the International Airport.

Eating Out

Restaurants offer mostly Créole dishes which have a characteristic piquant sauce and/or French cuisine. There is a good selection of places which have great food and atmosphere.

Good local specialities are lobster, pepper steak, griot (deep fried pieces of pork), lambi (conch), tassot, rice and beans, rice with local djon-djon.

Barbancourt rum is excellent and is widely available in hotels and leisure spots; rum punch is a favourite drink. Prestige is the local beer and imported varieties are also available.

Haiti's wide range of micro-climates produces a large assortment of fruits and vegetables. It is popular to buy these in the regions where they grow and are freshest (prices can be bargained 40% below shop prices). The French influence is obvious in butcher shops where fine cuts of meat, cold cuts, paté and cheeses can be bought. The bakeries sell French croissants, together with Créole bread and meat pasties. American influence is felt in the supermarkets. Most common are US-brand foods along with smaller amounts of Haitian, French and Middle Eastern brands.

Camping

Camping in Haiti is an adventure. The dramatic scenery is very enticing but access to much of it is over rough terrain and there are no facilities, leaving exploring to the rugged. Campers have to take everything and create, or find their own shelter.

Peasant homes dot the countryside and it is almost impossible to find a spot where you will be spared curious and suspicious onlookers. It is best to set up camp or lodging before dark. To prevent misunderstanding, it is important to explain to the locals your intentions, or better yet, talk to the local elder and ask assistance or protection. Creating a relationship with the locals will usually ensure cooperation and more privacy.

Entertainment

Until the mid-1980s, Haiti used to be a very good place for night spots. With the drop in tourism and Haitians hesitating to be out late at night in uneasy times, many places have had to shut or curtail their level of entertainment. The few that survive offer a good evening's enjoyment and plenty of personality. Following French custom, entertaining starts late in the evening, about 2030-2100. Night clubbing starts around 2330 and continues into the small hours.

Tipping

Budget travellers, particularly outside Port-au-Prince, are a rarity. Expect to be the subject of much friendly curiosity, and keep a pocketful of small change to conform with the local custom of tipping on every conceivable occasion. Even cigarettes and sweets are accepted. Hotels generally add 10% service charge. Baggage porters at hotels usually get 50 cents per bag. Do not fail to reward good service since hotel and restaurant staff rely on tips to boost their meagre salaries. Nobody tips taxi, *publique*, *camionette* or *tap-tap* drivers, unless exceptional service has been given.

Shopping

There are many tourist shops in Port-au-Prince, but be warned that they charge high prices for items which can be bought for far less in the market. In the craft shops and stalls, many of the products are of high quality. Many good bargains still to be had at the Iron Market,

but it is said to be getting more and more touristy. People always ask for a discount in shops, except at food shops. All handicrafts can be bought at a discount. See above under **Culture** for best buys, and under towns for individual establishments.

Film processing services are the same as in the USA, but the price of film is high; transparency developing is considerably less.

Security

After the September 1991 coup and subsequent trade embargo, the level of health care has declined and the incidence of violence increased. Since few reports from tourists have reached us, it is unknown whether crime against foreigners now extends beyond petty theft in the Port-au-Prince area. Carry handbags securely and do not leave belongings in sight in a parked car. Some advise not going out alone in Port-au-Prince after 1830.

During any political unrest it is advisable to limit your movements in the daytime and not to go out at night. Streets are usually deserted by 2300. Foreigners are not normally targeted at such times, but seek local advice.

Currency

The unit is the gourde, divided into 100 centimes (kob); it is supposed to be exchangeable on demand and without charge at the fixed rate of 5 gourdes to the US dollar; in mid-1992 the banking rate was 9.50 gourdes to the US dollar. Coins in circulation are for 5, 10, 20 and 50 centimes, notes for 1, 2, 5, 10, 25, 50, 100, 250 and 500 gourdes. US coins co-circulate with local currency. Always double-check whether you are dealing in gourdes or dollars, especially since 5 gourdes are universally known as a "dollar". There is no exchange control. Travellers' cheques are widely accepted. The only credit card widely accepted is American Express (because businesses receive US dollars with Amex but gourdes with other cards).

See under towns above for **banks**. Note that a commission is charged on the exchange of currencies other than the US dollar. Prices given in the text are quoted at the 5 gourde = US$1 rate.

Health

Prophylaxis against malaria is essential. Tap water is not to be trusted (drink only filtered or treated water) and take care when choosing food. The local herb tea can help stomach troubles.

Good professional advice is available for the more common ailments. Ask friends, associates, or at the hotel desk for referrals to a doctor suited to your requirements. Office hours are usually 0730-1200, 1500-1800. A consultation costs about US$10-15.

Hospital care and comfort varies. Availability of medical supplies is not normally a problem in hospitals, clinics or at doctors' surgeries, but limited humanitarian aid after the September 1991 coup means that provision of health care is greatly curtailed. Pharmacies/chemists can fill out prescriptions and many prescription drugs may be bought over the counter.

Recommended hospitals (all in Port-au-Prince) are Canapé Vert, rue Canapé Vert (prefix 4 or 5, unknown, 5-1052/3/0984); Adventiste de Diquini, Carrefour Road (Tel: 34-2000/0521), Hospital Français de Haiti, rue du Centre (Tel: 22-2323); St Francois de Salles, rue de la Révolution (Tel: 22-2110/0232).

A note on prostitution: there are no laws in Haiti to suppress it. Activity seems to be evident only at night with the commonly known areas being along the main roads in Carrefour and street corners in Pétionville. After hours the women move into the dive-type joints, targeting foreigners. With regard to casual sex, there is a red alert in Haiti over Aids.

Climate

The climate is generally very warm but the cool on- and off-shore winds of morning and evening help to make it bearable. In coastal areas temperatures vary between 20° and 35° C, being slightly hotter in April-September. The driest months are December-March. In the hill resorts the temperature is cooler.

Clothing

As in most other countries in the Caribbean beachwear should not be worn away from the beach and poolside. Dress is casual but never sloppy; Haitians appreciate good manners and style. Above-the-knee hems for women are considered risqué but acceptable. Men always wear a shirt, but a tie is not necessary in the evening.

Hours Of Business

Government offices: 0700-1200, 1300-1600 (0800-1200, 1300-1800 October-April); banks: 0900-1300 Monday to Friday; shops and offices: 0700-1600 (an hour later October to April).

Public Holidays

New Year and Ancestors (1-2 January), Mardi Gras (the 3 days before Ash Wednesday), Americas Day (14 April), Good Friday, 1 May, Flag and University Day (18 May), Assumption (15 August), Deaths of Henri Christophe and Dessalines (8 and 17 October), United Nations Day (24 October), All Saints (1 November), Armed Forces Day (18 November), Discovery of Haiti (5 December), December 25. Corpus Christi and Ascension are also public holidays.

Time Zone

Eastern standard time, 5 hours behind GMT.

Embassies And Consulates

France, Place des Hèros de l'Indépendence (Tel: 22-3172); British Consulate, is now located at the Hotel Montana in Pétionville, PO Box 1302 (Tel: 57-1920, Telex RCA 32911, and ITT 349001), diplomatic representation is in Kingston, Jamaica; Netherlands, Rue des

F Forts (Tel: 22-0955); **Germany**, 41 Ave Marie Jeanne, Bldg-A Florida (Tel: 22-0903); **USA**, Embassy: Cité de l'Exposition, Tel: 22-0200, Consulate: rue O Durand, Tel: 22-1799; **Canadian Embassy**, c/o Bank of Nova Scotia, Route de Delmas, PO Box 826, Port-au-Prince, Tel: 22-2320.

Colombia, 41 rue Borno, Tel: 46-2599; **Dominican Republic**, see above; **Mexico**, Maison Percival Powell, Pétionville, Tel: 57-0308; **Panama**, 29A, rues Metellus et Chavannes, Tel: 57-3100; **Venezuela**, Cité de l'Exposition, Tel: 22-0971; **Bahamas Consulate**, 88 Ave J Brown, Tel: 22-3618; **Jamaican Consulate**, 141 rue Pavée, Tel: 22-1200; **Honduran Consulate**, 167 rue du Centre, Tel: 22-1581.

Weights And Measures

The metric system is used.

Electric Current

110 volt, 60 cycle AC.

Telephones

In 1990 all telephone numbers in Haiti changed; an extra digit was added to the prefix, thus: in Port-au-Prince 2- became 22-, 3=23, 4=34, 6=46, 7=57, 8=48, 9=49 and 5 became 45 (Turgeau), or 55 (Laboule). In Cap Haïtien 2- became 62-; Port de Paix 8=68; Gonaïves 4=74; Jérémie 4=84, Jacmel 8=88.

Media

There are radio broadcasts in English from 1100 to 1400 on 1,035 KHz, MW. 3 daily newspapers, and 3 main weeklies.

Tourist Office

Ave Marie Jeanne (on the corner of Rue Roux), Port-au-Prince, Tel: 2-3076/2-1729, gives information on hotels, guest-houses and transport, also has maps (very helpful); open Monday-Friday 0800-1400. It was closed in early 1992; it is not known if this is permanent. Hotel and Tourist Association, *Hotel Montana*, rue Cardozo, Pétionville, Tel: 57-1920, ext 483 (varying hours, best try in the morning).

In **New York**: Haiti Tourist Bureau, 18 East 41st Street, New York 10017, Tel: (212) 779-7177.

In other countries, go to the Haitian embassy or consulate.

DOMINICAN REPUBLIC

Introduction

THE DOMINICAN REPUBLIC occupies the eastern two-thirds of Hispaniola. The country is mountainous, but despite having the highest mountain on the island and in the Caribbean, Pico Duarte (3,175 metres), it is less mountainous than Haiti. Within a system of widespread food production are large sugar and fruit plantations.

The Republic is building up its tourist trade, and has much to offer in the way of natural beauty, old colonial architecture, attractive beaches, modern resorts and native friendliness. Its population (7.3 million in 1991) is mostly a mixture of black, white and mestizo, and is Spanish-speaking. These English terms should, however, be qualified: "blanco" (white) refers to anybody who is white, white/Indian mestizo, or substantially white with either or both Indian or African admixture; "indio claro" (tan) is anyone who is a white/black mixed mulatto, or a mestizo; "indio oscuro" (dark Indian) is anyone who is not 100% black (ie with some white or Indian admixture); "negro" is 100% African. "Negro" is not a derogatory term. There is a certain aspiration towards the Indian, especially after Trujillo's quest for national respectability; this can be seen not only in the use of the original name for the island, Quisqueya (and Quisqueyanos), but in place names (San Pedro de Macorís, from the Macorix tribe, the other Indian inhabitants being the Taino and the Ciguayo) and in given family names (Guainorex, Anacaona, etc). An introduction to the Indians of the region is given in the **Pre-Columbian Civilizations** chapter.

Population growth is 2.3% a year (1981-90). The birth rate is 31.3 per 1,000, death rate 6.8; infant mortality is 65 per 1,000 live births; life expectancy is 63.9 years for males, 68.1 years females (all 1985-90 statistics). 83.3% of the population over the age of 15 are literate.

History

For the general history of the island of Hispaniola after the arrival of the Spaniards, see the beginning of this chapter.

Although the Spanish launched much of their westward expansion from Santo Domingo, their efforts at colonizing the rest of the island were desultory. Drake sacked Santo Domingo in 1586, the French gained control of the western part of the island in 1697 and, by the mid-18th century, the number of Spaniards in the eastern part of the island was about one-third of a total of 6,000. Since there was little commercial activity or population of the interior, it was easy prey for Haitian invaders fired with the fervour of their rebellion at the turn of the 19th century. Between 1801 and 1805, followers of Toussaint L'Ouverture and Dessalines plundered the territory. Sovereignty was disputed for the next 17 years, then, in 1822, Haiti took control for a further 22 years.

After the declaration of the Dominican Republic's independence in 1844, by the writer Duarte, the lawyer Sánchez and the soldier Mella, the country underwent yet another period of instability, including more Haitian

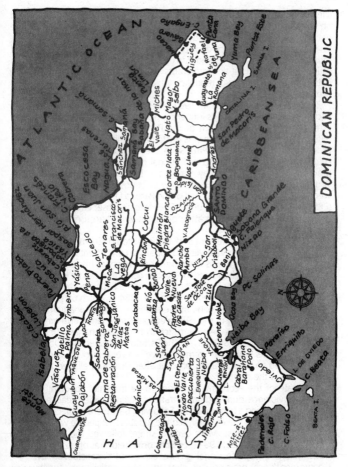

incursions and, in 1861, a four-year re-annexion with Spain. Independence was regained in the War of Restoration (la Restauración), but with no respite in factional fighting or economic disorder. Apart from the dictatorship of Ulises Heureux (1882-99), governments were short-lived. The country must be one of the very few where a Roman Catholic archbishop has served as head of state: Archbishop Meriño was President from 1880 to 1883.

In 1916, the USA occupied the Dominican Republic, having managed the country's customs affairs (on behalf of US and European creditors) since 1905. When the USA left in 1924, the Republic had a fully organized army, whose commander, Rafael Leonidas Trujillo Molina, became President in 1930. Thus began one of the most ruthless dictatorships ever seen in the Dominican Republic. With either himself or his surrogates at the helm

(Héctor Trujillo, 1947-60, and Joaquín Balaguer, 1960-62), Trujillo embarked on the expansion of industry and public works, the introduction of the national currency and the liquidation of the country's debts. Nevertheless, his methods of government denied any form of representation and included murder, torture, blackmail and corruption. During his reign, in 1937, an estimated 10,000 Haitian immigrants were slaughtered, prolonging the hatred between the two republics which had begun in the early 19th century.

Trujillo was assassinated in 1961. President Balaguer immediately set about eradicating his family's influence, but in 1962 Balaguer was defeated in elections by Dr Juan Bosch of the Partido Revolucionario Dominicano (PRD). After seven months he was ousted by a miltary coup led by Colonel Elías Wessin y Wessin. The PRD, with the support of a group of young colonels, tried to win back constitutional government in 1965, but were prevented from doing so by the army, backed by the USA and the Organization of American States. New elections were held in 1966; they were won by Balaguer, at the head of the Partido Reformista Social Cristiano (PRSC). He remained in office until 1978, forging closer links with the USA, but not without facing coup attempts, right-wing terrorism and left-wing guerrilla incursions.

A PRD President was returned in 1978, Antonio Guzmán, whose chief aims were to reduce army power and eliminate corruption. A month before leaving office in 1982, he discovered that members of his family, who had held office under him, had been involved in corruption, so he killed himself. His successor, Dr Salvador Jorge Blanco, also of the PRD, presided over severe economic difficulties which led to rioting in 1984 in which 60 people died. The party split over the handling of the economy, helping Joaquín Balaguer to win a narrow majority in the 1986 elections giving him a fifth presidential term. The 1990 elections were contested by two octogenarians, Dr Balaguer (83) and Dr Juan Bosch (80), now of the Partido de la Liberación Dominicana (PLD). Dr Balaguer won a sixth term of office by a very narrow majority, which was subjected to a verification process after Dr Bosch alleged fraud had taken place in the capital.

The state of the economy continues to be the chief concern; in 1987 there was violence during demonstrations against widespread economic hardship and during a general strike. Following Balaguer's re-election in May 1990, three general strikes paralyzed the republic; 12 people were killed by troops in that of August. More general strikes followed the signing of an IMF accord in July-August 1991 (See **Economy** below) as opposition parties, trade unions and professional groups expressed dissatisfaction over the Government's economic policies, shortages of essential items, and low pay.

Relations between the Dominican Republic and Haiti became very strained in 1991 after President Balaguer ordered the deportation of all illegal Haitian immigrants under the age of 16 and over 60. Many from outside these age groups left, putting pressure on the resources of President Aristide's government. Attitudes to the overthrow of Aristide were ambivalent because the Dominican Republic officially supported the Organization of American States' trade embargo while politicians vocally and traders in practice defied it. Aristide accused Haitian exiles in the Republic of funding the coup with drug money, but he did not, as reported at one stage, accuse the Dominican government of complicity.

For a study of contemporary Dominican politics and economics see *Dominican Republic:*

Beyond the Lighthouse, by James Ferguson (London: Latin America Bureau, 1992).

Government

The Dominican Republic is a representative democracy, with legislative power resting in a bicameral Congress: a 30-seat Senate and a 120-seat Chamber of Deputies. Senators and deputies are elected for a four-year term, as is the President, in whom is vested executive power. The three main parties are the Partido Reformista Social Cristiano (PRSC), the Partido Revolucionario Dominicano (PRD) and the Partido de la Liberación Dominicana (PLD).

The Economy

The land area is 4.8 million hectares, of which 13% is forest and woodland, 31% arable land and 43% pasture. Agriculture provides work for about 22% of the labour force, compared with 12% in manufacturing and 4% in construction. About 29% are unemployed. There are six main agricultural regions: the north, the Cibao valley in the north central area, Constanza and Tiero, the east, the San Juan valley, and the south. Cibao is the most fertile and largest region, while the eastern region is the main sugar-producing area. Sugar is the main crop. Until 1984, the US import quota system, of which the Dominican Republic was the largest beneficiary, provided a preferential market for over half the country's sugar exports as well as a cushion against the slump in world sugar prices. Major adjustments in US consumption patterns, particularly the switch by Coca Cola and Pepsi to High Fructose Corn Syrup, prompted the USA to cut quotas drastically. By 1988, the Dominican Republic's quota had been cut to 25% of previous levels. The Government is encouraging diversification of some cane lands to other crops, or converting them into tourist resorts.

Since 1975 gold and silver mining has been of considerable importance. The Pueblo Viejo mine's oxide ores are running out, but a transitional zone containing both oxide and sulphide ores was brought into operation in 1992. The country also produces ferronickel, which rivals sugar as the major commodity export earner. Reserves are estimated at 10% of total world deposits. Other sources of income are the 26 industrial free zones, where manufactured goods are assembled for the North American market, and remittances from Dominicans resident abroad.

The largest foreign exchange earner nowadays is, however, tourism, with annual receipts about US$750 million. New hotel projects brought the number of hotel rooms to 20,354 in 1990, compared with 11,400 in 1987 and this was expected to rise to 30,000 rooms in 1992. Tourist arrivals by air (excluding Dominicans resident overseas) in 1990 were 983,220, falling to 922,000 in 1991. The numbers were projected to rise to 1.3 million in 1992 on the strength of the Columbus Quinto Centenario celebrations.

In the first half of the 1980s, a combination of fiscal and external account problems brought about a sharp decline in the rate of gdp growth and led the Government to turn to the IMF for financial assistance. The Government agreed to reduce its fiscal deficit and take a number of other austerity measures, including a gradual devaluation of the peso. It failed to meet targets, so the programme was suspended in early 1984. Government measures to remove subsidies, as part of the austerity package agreed with the IMF, led to riots in Santo Domingo in April 1984 (see **History** above). Negotiations with the Fund were finally resumed and a one-year standby loan facility worth SDR78.5 million was approved in April 1985 but not renewed because of political opposition. The Government renegotiated its debts to foreign commercial banks, although persistent low world prices for its major export commodities made debt servicing commitments increasingly burdensome. Despite the widespread unpopularity of policies designed to satisfy IMF demands, President Balaguer in 1990-91 negotiated with the Fund for a new agreement. Having repaid debts worth US$81.6 million to the IMF, World Bank and other multilateral agencies, an IMF standby agreement was approved in August 1991. The Dominican Republic would receive US$53 million over 18 months, plus US$60 million compensatory financing for loss of export income and increased oil import costs in the previous financial year. The terms of the accord, which included the unification of the exchange rates, an end to price controls, balancing state corporation budgets and a commitment to pay outstanding foreign debt arrears, were greeted by a series of general strikes. Agreement with the IMF did, however, permit the rescheduling of US$926 million of debt with the Paris Club group of foreign governments in November 1991.

In 1990 the major problems confronting the Government were the high rate of inflation, unofficially estimated at 100% a year, and the disruptive electricity crisis, which had got steadily worse for several years. Inflation was pushed by heavy government spending on public works and increasing subsidies, while the state electricity company (CDE) could meet at best only 75% of demand (sometimes as little as 50%) because of poor maintenance, losses of about 35% on distribution lines and lack of funds to buy fuel. Some improvements were registered in 1991 as inflation was reduced to an estimated 4% as a result of a curtailment of spending, both in a refusal to increase public sector wages and after the completion of major public works. The introduction of a dual foreign exchange system (one rate for official transactions, and a free market rate for commercial banks) stabilized the exchange rate against the dollar. Against these bonuses had to be set a general downturn in economic activity owing to weak consumer demand, a lack of investment and the continuing shortfall in electricity supply. In October 1991 CDE signed a management contract with Unión Fenosa of Spain to rehabilitate the generating and distribution systems.

Culture

Music and Dance The most popular dance is the *merengue*, which dominates the musical life of the Dominican Republic; a great many orchestras have recorded *merengue* rhythms and are now world-famous. Other dances are the *mangulina*, the *salve*, the *bambulá* (from Samaná), the *ritmo guloya* (especially in San Pedro de Macorís), the *carabiné* (typical of the region around Barahona), and the *chenche matriculado*. The traditional *merengue* is played by a 3-man group called a *perico ripiao*, or *pri-prí*, which consists of a *tambora* (small drum), an accordion and a *güira* (a percussion instrument scraped by a metal rod, or, as originally used by Indians, a gourd scraped with a forked stick). There is a *merengue* festival in the last week of July and the first week of August, held on the Malecón in Santo Domingo. In the last week of December every year, the famous Jean Luis Guerra and his 4-40 hold a *merengue* concert in the Olympic Stadium as a kind of Christmas present to the people (capacity 50,000); there is also a firework display.

Puerto Plata holds it *merengue* festival in the first week of October and Sosúa has one the last week of September.

For details on theatres and other sites of cultural interest, see below under Santo Domingo, Puerto Plata and Sosúa.

Flora and Fauna

There are five major national parks in the Dominican Republic, all under the control of the Dirección Nacional de Parques (DNP, address below): **Armando Bermúdez** and **José del Carmen Ramírez**, both containing pine forests and mountains in the Cordillera Central are the only remaining areas of extensive forest in the republic; it is estimated that since the arrival of Columbus, two-thirds of the virgin forest has been destroyed. The reasons for the loss are fire and the establishment of smallholdings by landless peasants. By setting up these parks the gloomy prediction of 1973, that all the Dominican Republic's forest would vanish by 1990, has been avoided. The **Isla Cabritos** National Park in Lago Enriquillo is the smallest in the system; it is a unique environment, between 4 and 40 metres below sea level. Its original vegetation has been lost either to timber collection or to the goats and cattle which once grazed it. Now covered in secondary vegetation, 106 species of plant have been identified, including 10 types of cactus. The island has a large crocodile population, an endemic species of iguana, and other reptiles. 62 species of bird have been identified, 5 aquatic, 16 shore and 41 land birds; 45 are native to the island. Among the birds that can be seen (or heard) are the tiny manuelito (*myiarchus stolidus*) and the great hummingbird (*anthracothorax dominicus*), the querebebé (*chordeiles gundlachii*), best heard at dusk, and the cu-cú (*athene cunicularia*), which sings at night and dawn and excavates a hole in the desert for its nest.

Los Haitises, on the south coast of Samaná Bay (Bahía de San Lorenzo), is a protected coastal region, whose land and seascape of mangrove swamps, caves and strange rock formations emerging from the sea (*mogotes*) is unmatched in the republic. In Los Haitises you can visit the Cueva del Angel, cayes on which live many birds and humid tropical forest, as well as the mangroves. The **Parque Nacional del Este** is on the peninsula south of San Rafael del Yuma and includes the Isla Saona. It has remote beaches, examples of precolumbian art in a system of caves and is the habitat of the now scarce paloma coronita (crowned, or white-headed dove, *columba leucocephala*), the rhinoceros iguana and of various turtles. Also designated national parks are a number of panoramic roads, scientific reserves, botanical and zoological gardens (such as those in Santo Domingo, see below), aquaria and recreational parks. The National Parks Office (DNP) is at Avenida Independencia 539, Santo Domingo (Apartado Postal 2487, Tel: 682-7628). To visit the main forest reserves you must obtain a permit from the DNP for RD$50 (US$3.95).

A department of ecotourism has been set up to coordinate tours to the republic's protected areas. Various infrastructure works have been set up to allow visitors to stay overnight; the zones in question are Pico Duarte, Lago Enriquillo, Los Haitises, Isla Saona, Parque Submarino de la Caleta, Parque Armando Bermúdez and Parque del Este. Information from Departamento de Eco-Turismo (Ecoturisa), Parque Eugenio María de Hostos, Av George Washington (Tel: 221-4104), or from DNP.

The Jardín Botánico Nacional and the Museo de Historia Natural, Santo Domingo, have a full classification of the republic's flora. Of interest are the 67 types and 300 species of orchid found in this part of Hispaniola; there are a number of gardens which specialize in their cultivation. The most popular are *oncidium henekenii*, *polyradicium lindenii* and *leonchilus labiatus*. The national plant is the caoba (mahogany). There is a wide variety of palms, some of which grow only on Hispaniola.

The Dominican Republic is becoming a popular bird-watching destination. The national bird is the cotica parrot, which is green, very talkative and a popular pet. It is, however, protected. Among other birds that can be seen, apart from those mentioned above, are other parrots, hummingbirds, the guaraguao (a hawk), the barrancolí and the flautero.

Of the island's mammals, the hutia, an endemic rodent, is endangered. Hump-backed whales migrate from the Arctic yearly to the Banco de la Plata (Silver Banks) off the Samaná peninsula, where their young are born. The area has been declared a sanctuary. Trips are organized to see the whales, contact DNP or Tel: 535-0571. Also in Dominican waters manatee may be seen, but they are very shy. Trips to see manatees at Estero Hondo can be arranged by phoning Ecoturisa on 221-4104, cost is US$115.

Beaches and Watersports

According to Unesco, the Dominican Republic has some of the best beaches in the world: white sand, coconut palms and many with a profusion of green vegetation. The main ones are described in the text below. The beaches vary enormously in development, cleanliness, price of facilities, number of hawkers and so on. Boca Chica and Juan Dolio, for instance, are very touristy and not suitable for anyone seeking peace and quiet; for that, Bayahibe would be a much better bet. The best-known beaches are in the east of the republic, including: Boca Chica, Juan Dolio, Playa Caribe, Guayacanes and Villas del Mar in San Pedro de Macorís; Minitas (La Romana), Bayahibe, Macao, Bávaro, Puerto Escondido (Higüey); Anadel, Cayo Levantado, Las Terrenas, Playa Rincón and Portillo in Samaná and Sánchez; Playa el Bretón at Cabrera, Playa Grande in the Province of María Trinidad Sánchez and Laguna Gri-Gri at Río San Juan, where you can also visit the beaches of Puerto Escondido, Punta Preciosa in the Bahía Escocesa and Cabo Francés Viejo. Northeast of Puerto Plata, recommended, although in many cases fully developed, beaches include Cabarete, Ermita, Magante, Playa Grande and Sosúa. At Puerto Plata itself are Playa Dorada, Costámbar, Cofresí, Long Beach, Cabarete, Boca de Cangrejos, Caño Grande, Bergantín, Playa de Copello and Playa Mariposa. Towards the northwest and the Haitian border there are beaches at Bahía de Luperón, Playa de El Morro, Punta Rucia, Cayos los Siete Hermanos and Estero Hondo.

In the south the best beaches are Barahona, Saladilla, Monterrío, Palmar de Ocoa, Najayo, Nigua, Palenque and Nizao. The majority of beaches have hotels or lodgings, but those without are suitable for camping.

Watersports such as deep-sea fishing, diving and surfing can be arranged at the Náutico Clubs in Santo Domingo and at Boca Chica beach. Güibia Beach, on the Malecón, Santo Domingo, has good waves for **surfing**. Demar Beach Club, Andrés (Boca Chica, Tel: 523-4365) operates fishing, sailing, diving and water skiing charters, windsurfing, snorkelling and canoeing. Snorkelling and scuba-diving tours are operated by Mundo Submarino at Gustavo Mejía Ricart 99, Santo Domingo, Tel: 566-0340. All watersports can be arranged through Actividades Acuáticas, Tel: 688-5838, Fax: 688-5271, P O Box 1348, Santa Domingo. There is excellent **scuba diving** at the underwater park at La Caleta, the small beach near the turn-off to the airport, on the Autopista de las Américas; snorkelling and diving is good all along the south coast. Hotels on the north coast also offer diving and snorkelling facilities. For expert divers there are many sunken Spanish galleons on the reefs offshore. For full information on diving contact Buceo

Dominicano, Abraham Lincoln 960, Santo Domingo, Tel: 565-6116, or the Dirección Nacional de Parques, Tel: 682-7628. Cabarete, near Sosúa, is one of the best **windsurfing** places in the world, attracting international competitors to tournaments there. Other centres are Boca Chica and Puerto Plata; most beach hotels offer windsurfing facilities.

Several international **fishing** tournaments are held each year, the catch being blue marlin, bonito and dorado. There is an annual deep-sea fishing tournament at Boca de Yuma, east of La Romana, in June. For information about fishing contact Santo Domingo Club Náutico, Lope de Vega 55, Tel: 566-1684, or the Clubes Náuticos at Boca Chica and Cabeza de Toro. For renting boats and yachts, contact the Secretaría de Turismo. Parasailing is practised at the *Hotel Playa Dorada*, Puerto Plata, Tel: 586-3988 (same number for deep-sea fishing), and on Sosúa beach.

Other Sports

Golf The best course is at Los Cajuiles at the *Casa de Campo Hotel* in La Romana; the *Santo Domingo* and *Hispaniola* hotels in Santo Domingo can arrange guest passes. There are also golf courses at the Santo Domingo Country Club and at Playa Dorada, near Puerto Plata. Several more golf courses are being built at new resorts around the country. **Tennis** can also be played at the Santo Domingo Country Club and at the tennis centre which can be found by the Autopista 30 de Mayo. **Athletics** facilities can be found at the Centro Olímpico Juan Pablo Duarte in the heart of Santo Domingo. **Target shooting** at the Polígono de Tiro on Avenida Bolívar.

The national sport is **baseball**, which is played from October to January, with national and big league players participating. The best players are recruited by US and Canadian teams; about half of the 300 professional Dominican players in the USA come from San Pedro de Macorís. There are five professional stadia, including the Quisqueya. **Polo** matches are played at weekends at Sierra Prieta, 25 minutes from Santo Domingo (Tel: 565-9857). The **basketball** season is from June to August. **Boxing** matches take place frequently in Santo Domingo.

Festivals

In Santo Domingo, Carnival at the end of February, notable for the parade along the Malecón on 26 February; the *merengue* festival in July (see **Culture** above), including festivals of gastronomy, cocktails, and exhibitions of handicrafts and fruit. Puerto Plata has a similar, annual *merengue* festival at the beginning of October on the Malecón La Puntilla, as does Sosúa, in the last week of September, in the Parque Central, there are year-end celebrations from 22 December to 1 January. Carnival in Santiago de los Caballeros in February is very colourful; its central character is the piglet, which represents the devil. Each town's saint's day is celebrated with several days of festivities of which one of the most popular is the Santa Cruz de Mayo fiesta in El Seibo in May. Holy Week is the most important holiday time for Dominicans, when there are processions and festivities such as the *guloyas* in San Pedro de Macorís, the mystical-religious *ga-ga* in sugar cane villages and the *cachúas* in Cabral in the southwest.

The Quinto Centenario

Santo Domingo played a prominent role in the celebration of the five hundredth anniversary of Christopher Columbus' landfall in the Caribbean (1492-1992). Under the title of the **Quinto Centenario** a great many events were planned and a large restoration programme was set up for colonial sites in the capital and in the interior. Hispaniola was where Europe's first social and political activities in the Americas took place. Santo Domingo itself holds the title "first" for a variety of offices: first city, having the first Audiencia Real, cathedral, university, coinage, etc. In view of this, Unesco has designated Santo Domingo a World Cultural Heritage site (Patrimonio Cultural Mundial).

The capital was chosen as the host city of the majority of events surrounding the Quinto Centenario; the following list, by no means exhaustive, covers some of the major events due to be held after the publication date of this edition of the *Caribbean Islands Handbook*. The Comisión Permanente del Quinto Centenario, Calle Isabel La Católica esquina Conde, near the Cathedral, has information on all the historical sites related to the "Encounter of Two Worlds/Encuentro de Dos Mundos" and books on the subject. (Unless otherwise stated, events take place in Santo Domingo.) September 1992: 12, Inauguration of the Paseo de los Indios en América. October: 12 (the main event) Commemoration of the Quinto Centenario with the inauguration of the Columbus Lighthouse, the Faro a Colón, after the transfer of Columbus' remains to the lighthouse, a mass said by Pope John Paul II, and a *son et lumière*. The Faro a Colón has been built, at great cost (and not without controversy), in the Parque Mirador del Este, in the east of Santo Domingo. The building, in the shape of a cross, will project a crucifix of light onto the night sky. The rooms inside the lighthouse may be purchased by countries so that Columbus memorabilia may be placed inside (the USA bought a floor). Around the building gardens have been laid out. Entry to the Faro is US$3.85 (US$1.55 for Dominicans). Also in October is the Biennial Caribbean Art Exhibition (11) and the Puerto Plata *Merengue* festival (15-22). A series of commemorative coins in limited editions was struck, available from the Centro de Información Numismática, Casa del Quinto Centenario, Isabel la Católica 103, Tel: 682-0185, Fax: 530-9164, Santo Domingo.

To coincide with the Quinto Centenario, the Government undertook an extensive programme of public works, principally restoration work in the colonial city. For example, the Cathedral, the Capilla del Rosario, the Fuerte de la Concepción, the House of President Lilís, the Iglesia de San Antón and other buildings were restored. Some of the new developments are described below.

Santo Domingo

Santo Domingo, the capital and chief seaport, population now about 2 million, was founded in 1496 by Columbus' brother Bartolomé and hence was the first capital in Spanish America. For years the city was the base for the Spaniards' exploration and conquest of the continent: from it Ponce de León sailed to discover Puerto Rico, Hernán Cortés launched his attack on Mexico, Balboa discovered the Pacific and Diego de Velázquez set out to settle Cuba. In the old part of the city, on the west bank of the Río Ozama, there are many fine early 16th century buildings: some of them have been restored by the Government and others are in ruins (see above).

Buildings of the greatest interest are:
Catedral Basílica Menor de Santa María, Primada de América, Isabel La Católica esquina Nouel, the first cathedral to be founded in the New World. Its first stone was laid by Diego Columbus, son of Christopher, in

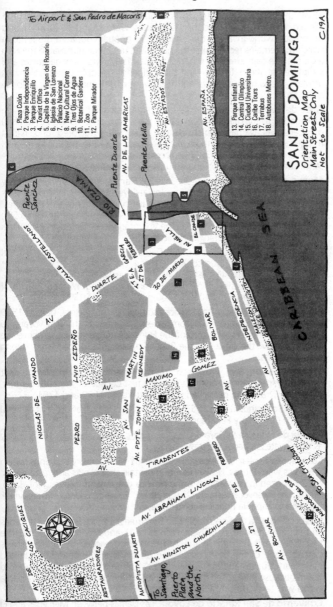

SANTO DOMINGO
Orientation Map
Main Streets Only
Not to Scale

C19A

1. Plaza Colón
2. Parque Independencia
3. Parque Enriquillo
4. Tourist Office
5. Capilla de la Virgen del Rosario
6. Iglesia de San Lorenzo
7. Palacio Nacional
8. New Cultural Centre
9. Tres Ojos de Agua
10. Botanical Gardens
11. Zoo
12. Parque Mirador

13. Parque Infantil
14. Central Olímpico
15. Ciudad Universitaria
16. Caribe Tours
17. Terrabus
18. Autobuses Metro.

To Airport & San Pedro de Macoris

AV. DE LAS AMERICAS

Puente Mella

AV. ESTADOS UNIDOS

AV. ESPAÑA

Puente Sancha

Puente Duarte

RIO OZAMA

CALLE CASTELLANOS

AV. NICOLAS DE OVANDO

AV. PEDRO LIVIO CEDEÑO

DUARTE

T.E.A. GARCIA

27 DE FEBRERO

30 DE MARZO

EL CONDE

AV. MELLA

BOLIVAR

CARIBBEAN SEA

AV. SAN MARTIN

PTE. JOHN F. KENNEDY

MAXIMO GOMEZ

INDEPENDENCIA

MALECON

AV. GEORGE WASHINGTON

TIRADENTES

AV. DE LOS CACIQUES

AUTOPISTA DUARTE

RESTAURADORES

AV. ABRAHAM LINCOLN

AV. 27 DE FEBRERO

AV. WINSTON CHURCHILL

AV. BOLIVAR

MIRADOR DEL SUR

To Santiago, Puerto Plata, and the North.

1514; the architect was Alonzo Rodríguez. It was finished in 1540. The alleged remains of Christopher Columbus were found in 1877 during restoration work. In 1892, the Government of Spain donated the tomb in which the remains rest, behind the high altar, until their removal to the Faro a Colón. The cathedral was fully restored for 1992, with new gargoyles and sculptures at the gates showing the indigenous people when Columbus arrived. The windows, altars and roof were all returned to their colonial splendour.

Torre del Homenaje inside Fortaleza Ozama, reached through the mansion of Rodrigo Bastidas (later the founder of the city of Santa Marta in Colombia) on Calle Las Damas, which is now completely restored and has a museum/gallery with temporary exhibitions. It is the oldest fortress in America, constructed 1503-07 by Nicolás de Ovando, whose house in the same street has been restored and turned into a splendid hotel.

Museo de las Casas Reales, on Calle Las Damas, in a reconstructed early 16th century building which was in colonial days the Palace of the Governors and Captains-General, and of the Real Audiencia and Chancery of the Indies. It is an excellent colonial museum (often has special exhibits, entry US$0.50); open 1000-1700; entry US$0.75. The Voluntariado de las Casas Reales has exhibitions of contemporary Dominican art.

Alcázar de Colón at the end of Las Damas and Emilio Tejera, constructed by Diego Colón (Columbus' son) in 1510-14. For six decades it was the seat of the Spanish Crown in the New World; it was sacked by Drake in 1586. Now completely restored, it houses the interesting **Museo Virreinal** (Viceregal Museum). Open 0900-1700 daily; entry US$0.75.

Casa del Cordón, Isabel La Católica esquina Emiliano Tejera, built in 1509 by Francisco de Garay, who accompanied Columbus on his first voyage to Hispaniola. Named for the cord of the Franciscan Order, sculpted above the entrance. Now the offices of the Banco Popular; free guided tours during working hours.

Monasterio de San Francisco (ruins), Hostos esquina E Tejera, first monastery in America, constructed in the first decade of the 16th century. Sacked by Drake and destroyed by earthquakes in 1673 and 1751.

Reloj de Sol (sundial) built 1753, near end of Las Damas, by order of General Francisco de Rubio y Peñaranda; by its side is

Capilla de Nuestra Señora de Los Remedios, built in the early 16th century as the private chapel of the Dávila family.

La Ataranza, near the Alcázar, a cluster of 16th century buildings which served as warehouses. Now restored to contain shops, bars and restaurants. Newly opened in La Ataranza is the **Museo del Jamón** (Museum of Ham), sponsored by several restaurants (*Catábrico, Reina de España, Tropic Snack Bar*) and Compañía Príncipe de Asturias, Tel: 685-9644.

Hospital-Iglesia de San Nicolás de Bari (ruins), Hostos between Mercedes and Luperón, begun in 1509 by Nicolás de Ovando, completed 1552, the first stone-built hospital in the Americas. Also sacked by Drake, it was probably one of the best constructed buildings of the period, it survived many earthquakes and hurricanes. In 1911 some of its walls were knocked down because they posed a hazard to passers-by; also the last of its valuable wood was taken. It is now full of pigeons.

Convento de San Ignacio de Loyola, Las Damas between Mercedes and El

Conde. Finished in 1743, it is now the National Pantheon. It was restored in 1955 and contains memorials to many of the country's heroes and patriots. It also contains an ornate tomb built before his death for the dictator Trujillo, the "Benefactor of the Fatherland", but his remains do not lie there.

Iglesia de Santa Bárbara, off Mella to the left near Calle J Parra, near the end of Isabel La Católica. Built in 1574, sacked by Drake in 1586, destroyed by a hurricane in 1591, reconstructed at the beginning of the 17th century. Behind the church are the ruins of its fort, where one can get good views.

Convento de los Dominicos, built in 1510. Here in 1538 the first university in the Americas was founded, named for St Thomas Aquinas; it now bears the title of the Universidad Autónoma de Santo Domingo. It has a unique ceiling which shows the medieval concept that identified the elements of the universe, the classical gods and the Christian icons in one system. The Sun is God, the four evangelists are the planetary symbols Mars, Mercury, Jupiter and Saturn. The University itself has moved to a site in the suburbs.

Iglesia de la Regina Angelorum, built 1537, contains a wall of silver near one of its altars.

Iglesia del Carmen, built around 1615 at side of Capilla de San Andrés, contains an interesting wooden sculpture of Christ.

Puerta del Conde (Baluarte de 27 de Febrero), at the end of El Conde (now a pedestrian street) in the Parque Independencia. Named for the Conde de Peñalva, who helped defend the city against William Penn in 1655. Restored in 1976, near it lie the remains of Sánchez, Mella and Duarte, the 1844 independence leaders.

Puerta de la Misericordia, Palo Hincado and Arzobispo Portes, so named because people fled under it for protection during earthquakes and hurricanes. It forms part of the wall that used to surround the colonial city, into which are now built many of the houses and shops of Ciudad Nueva. It was here on 27 February 1844 that Mella fired the first shot in the struggle for independence from Haiti.

Capilla de La Virgen del Rosario, on the other side of the Río Ozama, near the Molinos Dominicanos at the end of Avenida Olegario Vargas. It was the first church constructed in America, restored in 1943.

Museo De Duarte, Isabel La Católica 308, Tel: 689-0326. Contains items linked with the independence struggle and Duarte, the national hero, whose home it was (open 0900-1700, Monday-Friday, US$0.75).

Other old buildings are the Iglesia de las Mercedes, dating from 1555; the Puerta de San Diego, near the Alcázar; the Palacio de Borgella, Isabel la Católica, near Plaza Colón; the ruins of Fuerte de la Concepción, at the corner of Mella and Palo Hincado, built in 1543; the ruins of Fuerte de San Gil, Padre Billini, near the end of Calle Pina; and the ruins of Iglesia de San Antón, off Mella esquina Vicente Celestino Duarte.

At the mouth of the Río Ozama, the new Avenida del Puerto gives access to the Antigua Ceiba, where Columbus moored his caravelles, the Plaza de Armas, the city's original drainage system and the old city wall. Steps lead up to the Alcázar de Colón and the Fuerte Ozama, where a square has been established. The Avenida has in a short time become an open-air discothèque, more popular than the Malecón. Together with the inauguration of the Avenida del Puerto is a boat service on the Río Ozama

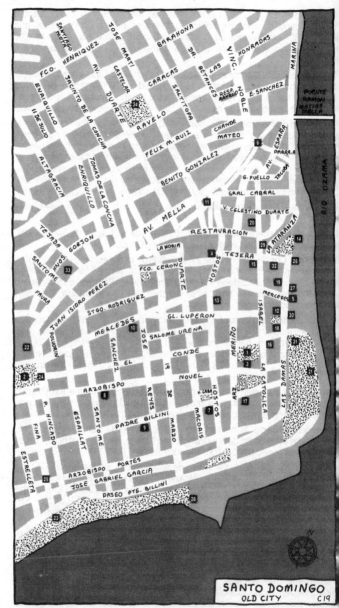

SANTO DOMINGO
OLD CITY
C 19

for sightseeing upstream; water sports and speed-boat races can also be seen.

The modern city is very spread out because, until recently, there was no high-rise building. The outer city has fine avenues, especially Avenida George Washington (also known as the Malecón) which runs parallel to the sea; it often becomes an open-air discothèque, where locals and foreigners dance the *merengue*. The annual *merengue* festival is held here. The spectacular monument to Fray Antón de Montesinos is at the eastern end of Avenida George Washington. The continuation (Prolongación) of Avenida México, which runs parallel to Avs Bolívar and 27 de Febrero, has many modern buildings, while Expreso Quinto Centenario, in the Villa Juana and Villa Francisca districts, is a new roadway which has rejuvenated these parts of the city. Other important avenues are Independencia, Bolívar, Abraham Lincoln, Winston Churchill, Núñez de Cáceres, 27 de Febrero, John F Kennedy, Juan Pablo Duarte, Ramón Matías Mella and General Gregorio Luperón.

Among the attractive parks are the Central Olímpico (see above) in the city centre, Parque Independencia (a peaceful haven amid all the traffic, with the Altar de la Patria, containing the remains of the country's founders, Juan Pablo Duarte, Francisco del Rosario Sánchez and Ramón Matías Mella), Parque Colón, Parque del Este (Autopista de las Américas, a 7 km-long *alameda*) and Parque Mirador (Paseo de las Indios at Mirador Sur, 7 km long, popular for walking, jogging, cycling, picnics). On Avenida José Contreras are many caves, some with lakes, in the southern cliff of Parque Mirador. Along this cliff the Avenida Cayetano Germosén has been built, giving access to a number of caves used at one time by Taino Indians. The road, lined with gardens, links Avenidas Luperon and Italia. The Jardín Botánico Nacional, Urbanización Los Ríos (open Tuesday-Sunday 0900-1700, admission US$0.80, children US$0.75) and the Parque Zoológico Nacional, Los Ríos (open Monday-Saturday 0900-1700, Sunday 0930-1800, US$0.75, small train US$0.15; for information Tel: 566-8151 or 565-2860. The Botanical Gardens are highly recommended (the Japanese Garden especially); horse-drawn carriages and a small train tour the grounds (US$0.80, children US$0.55). There is an Acuario Nacional, Avenida España, Tuesday-Sunday 0900-1700, US$0.35. Quisqueya Park, César Nicolás Penson, is a recreational park for children, entry US$0.40.

Gazcue is a quiet, attractive residential area with expensive homes built in the 1930s and 1940s, stretching west of the Zona Colonial as far as Avenida Máximo Gómez. The coral pink Palacio Nacional with a neo-classical central portico and cupola, built by Trujillo, is at the intersection of Doctor Delgado and Manuel María Castillo. It is used by the President, but guided tours of the richly decorated interior can be arranged, Tel: 686-4771 ext 340 or 360.

Key to Map of Santo Domingo

1. Plaza Colón; 2. Parque Independencia; 3. Cathedral; 4. Monasterio de San Francisco (ruins); 5. Capilla de Nuestra Señora de los Remedios; 6. Santa Bárbara (fort and church—ruins); 7. Convento de los Dominicos; 8. Iglesia del Carmen; 9. Iglesia de la Regina Angelorum; 10. Iglesia de las Mercedes; 11. Iglesia de San Antón (ruins); 12. Convento San Ignacio de Loyola/Panteón Nacional; 13. Hospital de San Nicolás de Bari (ruins); 14. Alcázar de Colón; 15. Casa del Cordón; 16. Palacio de Borgella; 17. Casa de Tostada/Museo de la Familia Dominicana; 18. Casa de Francia/Teatro Nacional; 19. Museo de las Casa Reales; 20. Museo de Duarte; 21. Torre del Homenaje y Fuerte Ozama; 22. Fuerte de la Concepción (ruins); 23. Fuerte de San Gil (ruins); 24. Puerta del Conde; 25. Puerta de la Misericordia; 26. Puerta de San Diego; 27. Sundial (Reloj del Sol); 28. Monument to Fray Antón de Montesinos; 29. La Ataranza; 30. Hostal de Nicolás Ovando; 31. Casa Bastidas; 32. Central Post Office; 33. Mercado Modelo; 34. Parque Enriquillo.

The new pink stone Capitolio Nacional is worth seeing; the government offices occupy a building known as El Huacal, on Avenida México esquina Leopoldo Navarro. The 1955/56 World's Fair (Feria de Confraternidad) buildings now house the Senate and Congress. The national museum collection, which includes a wonderful display of Taino artefacts, is in the **Museo del Hombre Dominicano** (US$0.75, 1000-1700, closed on Monday), which forms part of the Plaza de la Cultura, founded by Joaquín Balaguer on Avenida Máximo Gómez. It also includes the ultra-modern national theatre and national library; the **Galería de Arte Moderno** (open 1000-1700, US$0.75, closed Monday, Tel: 682-8280), the Cinemateca Nacional, the **Museo de Historia Natural** (Tel: 689-0106, US$0.75, open Tuesday-Sunday 1000-1700) and the **Museo de Historia y Geografía** (US$0.75). The **Museo de la Familia Dominicana** is housed in the Casa de Tostada (Calle Padre Billini esq Arzobispo Meriño), an early 16th century mansion (Monday-Friday, 1000-1700, US$0.80). The Banco Central has a **Museo Numismático y Filatélico**, open 0900-1700, free. On the Carretera Duarte (Km 4½) the Fundación García Arévalo has an exhibition of pre-hispanic art and civilization. For archaeologists there is the Instituto de Investigaciones Históricas, José Reyes 24.

Three bridges cross the Río Ozama: the nearest to the sea is Mella (nicknamed La Bicicleta because it is so narrow), next is Duarte, and further inland Sánchez. On the road to the airport are the Tres Ojos de Agua, two water-filled caves and a sunken lake which are worth a visit. To reach the last-named you must take the raft across the second cave; it is supposed to have two crocodiles in it, put there by the Botanical Gardens, but they didn't reproduce (no one bothered to check their sex). At the entrance to the airport is La Caleta Archaeological Museum (**Museo Ceremonial La Caleta**) with its display of Taino and Arawak artefacts, and a Taino cemetery (entry free).

Local Information—Santo Domingo

Where To Stay Hotels (prices are double, high season and include taxes)

	Address	Price US$	Telephone	Fax
Cervantes*†	Calle Cervantes 202	51	686-8161	686-5754
Comercial*	Calle El Conde esq Hostos	27	682-8161	
Comodoro†	Av Bólivar 193	50	687-7141	682-7166
Dominican Concorde†	Av Anacaona	104	562-8222	562-8938
El Nuevo Jaragua†	Av George Washington 367	142	686-2222	686-0528
Gran Hotel Lina*†	Av Máximo Gómez y 27 de Febrero	90	686-5000	686-5521
Hispaniola†	Av Independencia y Av Abraham Lincoln	96	535-4711	535-4050
Hostal Nicolás de Ovando*†	Calle Las Damas 53	65	687-3101	
Naco†	Av Tiradentes 22	70	541-6226	544-0957
Santo Domingo†	Av Independencia y Av Abraham Lincoln	130	535-1511	535-4050
Sheraton†	Av George Washington 365	140	221-6666	687-8150

*Convenient to centre † Swimming pool and fully air-conditioned.

The Domitel chain throughout the country has excellent, good value establishments: Isabel la Católica 165, Santo Domingo, Tel: 689-9191; prices vary through the year, and are more expensive for foreigners. Reservations can be made through Caribbean Reservation Centre (CRC), Alma Mater y Pedro Henríquez Ureña, 2nd floor, Edificio Banaco, Santo Domingo, Tel: 544-4700. *Hostal Nicolás de Ovando*, a restored 16th century mansion in the oldest part of the city, is warmly recommended for comfort, quiet and atmosphere but not for food nor food efficiency. *Gran Hotel Lina* is also highly recommended and has a good restaurant, and has recently been enlarged. The *Santo Domingo* is colonial style, plush and charming. The *Comodoro* is reasonable, with fridges in rooms. The *Comercial* is central, with big fans, TV, bath and a fair restaurant and an old bar, friendly, helpful, clean.

There are several apart-hotels: *Aladino*, H Pieter 34, Tel: 567-0677, US$27d, fan and a/c; *Plaza Colonial*, LO Pellerano y Julio Verne, Tel: 687-9111, Fax: 686-2877, US$38-75d; *Plaza Florida*, Tel: 541-4742, US$48d; *Delta*, Av Sarasota 53, Tel: 535-0800, US$42s, US$48d; *Plaza del Sol*, J Contreras 25-A, Tel: 687-1317, US$29d.

Other hotels include: on Av George Washington, *Napolitano*, Tel: 687-1131, Fax: 689-2714, US$47.50*†; *Royal*, Av Duarte y 27 de Febrero, Tel: 685-5400, US$30, fully a/c, small pool, good restaurant, *guaguas* leaving to north and west across the street. In the old city, *Hostal Nicolás Nader*, Duarte y General Luperón, Tel: 687-6674, US$53, small, friendly, personal service, pleasant. New is the *Casa Vapor*, Av Francia y Dr Delgado, US$46pp basic price, near Presidential Palace, in a house dating from Trujillo's time, in the shape of a ship, includes restaurant, *Café Francés, Terraza del Puerto, Sport Vapor* and *Cafetería La Proa*. Also new (but no details yet) is the *Quinto Centenario*, on the Malecón, 5 stars, central.

Cheaper hotels include: *Alameda*, Calle Cervantes opposite *Cervantes*, Tel: 685-5121, US$23, restaurant; *Aída*, El Conde and Espaillat, Tel: 685-7692, US$19 a/c (less without), fairly quiet (but record shop below may be noisy in day), mixed reports, emergency generator often out of action; *Independencia*, Estrella casi esquina Arzobispo Nouel, near Parque Independencia, US$12s, soap, towels etc provided, clean, convenient location, recommended, some rooms without windows, also has a club, bar, language school (across the street), a roof terrace and art exhibitions. *Señorial*, Vinicio Burgos 58, Tel: 687-4359, US$24, friendly, clean and informal, and famous for its "Hemingway" atmosphere. *Luna del Norte*, Benito González 89, Tel: 687-0124/2504, US$12, clean, friendly, recommended, restaurant. *Radiante*, Av Duarte between Av Mella and Benito González, US$8 with bath; *El Hidalgo*, Caracas 75, Tel: 683-3652/688-0097, US$12 with a/c and bath, small room, good location, but not recommended; *Benito*, Benito González near market, US$4 with bath, US$2.50 without; *Galán*, Benito González, near Av Duarte, US$6, basic, friendly, quiet, safe. On Mella, *Caribeño* (Tel: 688-2261, US$3, good value). There are dozens of cheap hotels, especially around the Mercado Modelo; have a good look round them before making any decision. For cheap rooms in hotels or *casas de pensión*, look in the classified section of daily paper, *Listín Diario*. Business travellers can often get cheaper rates than posted by requesting '*la tarifa comercial*'.

Where To Eat At main hotels, eg *Alcázar* at the *Santo Domingo*; the *Lina*; *La Piazzeta* at the *Hispaniola* (Italian specialities); *Le Gourmet* at the *Comodoro*. Many of the hotels have "buffets ejecutivos" at lunch time, costing US$10.

Recommended restaurants include *Le Jardin Français*, 3 Padre Billini, bar and restaurant, lovely patio; *El Bodegón*, Arzobispo Meriño y Padre Billini, Tel: 682-6864, excellent Spanish restaurant in colonial house; *Il Buco*, next door, Tel: 685-0884, for good Italian food; *América*, Arzobispo Nouel y Santome, Tel: 682-7194, unpretentious Spanish food; *Ché Bandoneón*, on El Conde between Damas y Parque Colón, Argentine owned, outdoor terrace, Argentine, criollo and French food, tangos, Tel: 689-2105; *Arleen*, next door, is also good, both stay open till after midnight. *Mesón de la Cava*, Parque Mirador, situated in a natural cave, good steaks, dancing, very popular so reserve in advance, Tel: 533-2818; *Lago Enriquillo*, also in Parque Mirador. *Jai-Alai*, Av Independencia 411, for excellent seafood and local specialities, Tel: 685-2409; *Fonda La Ataranza*, La Ataranza 5, Tel: 689-2900, popular for créole and international cuisine; *Lucky Seven*, Av Pasteur y Casimiro de Moya, good for seafood and steaks, popular haunt for baseball fans.

Also worth visiting are *Vesuvio I*, Av George Washington 521 and also *Vesuvio II*, Av Tiradentes 17, Italian and international cuisine; *Veneto Ice Cream* on Av Independencia; *Las Pirámides*, Rómulo Betancourt 351, and *Il Capo del Malecón*, Av George Washington 517 (other branches at Av Tiradentes and Jardines del Embajador), both good for pizzas. *Aubergine*, Av Alma Matar y Av México, German food; *La Esquina de Tejas* (Av 27 de Febrero) offers Spanish cuisine. For good Chinese food try *Marios*, Calle Mercedes 453, opposite Parque Independencia, very popular, or *La Gran Muralla*, Av 27 de Febrero. *Pacos Café*, El Conde, near Parque Independencia, local food at reasonable prices. For the local dish *mofongo* (see under **Food and Drink** below), *Palacio del Mofongo* Av George Washington 509, Tel: 688-8121, or *Casa del Mofongo*, 27 de Febrero y Calle 7 Eva Mo, Tel: 565-1778 (a long way from the centre).

Two good vegetarian restaurants are *Ananda*, Casimiro de Moya 7, Tel: 562-4465, and *Vegetariano*, Calle Luperón 9 (open 0800-1500). Also *El Terrenal*, Malecón y Estrelleta, Tel: 689-3161, some vegetarian dishes. *Vita Naturaleza*, Mercedes 255, sells health products (by small park at junction with Luperón).

The Village Pub, in Calle Hostos 350, opposite the ruins of Hospital San Nicolás de Bari, are good places for snacks and drinks in a pub-type atmosphere, in the colonial city; and so is *La Taberna* (classical music) at Padre Billini with Las Damas.

There are numerous pizzerias which are good value; also try a *chimichurri* (spiced sausage) from the stalls along the Malecón; throughout the city stalls sell sandwiches, *chimichurris*, hot dogs and hamburgers. Many fast food places offer dishes for about US$1.50, which would cost US$8 in a hotel restaurant. There are also take-away places where a meal costs about US$2.50. Cheapest are probably the Chinese restaurants, but in many cases the hygiene is dubious (the same applies to other basic restaurants).

Shopping   Duty-free at Centro de los Héroes, La Ataranza, shops in *Embajador, Sheraton* and *Santo Domingo* hotels; departure lounge at airport; all purchases must be in US dollars. The Mercado Modelo, on Avenida Mella esquina Santomé, includes gift shops and is the best place in the city for handicrafts (see **Best Buys** in Information for Visitors); you must bargain to get a good price. There are also "speciality shops" at Plaza Criolla, 27 de Febrero y Máximo Gómez. Calle El Conde, now reserved for pedestrians, is the oldest shopping sector in Santo Domingo; Avenida Mella at Duarte is a good spot for discount shopping and local colour. A flea market, Mercado de las Pulgas, operates on Sunday in the Centro de los Héroes and at the Mercado de Oportunidades, 27 de Febrero. In contrast are the modern complexes at Plaza Naco and the new US style shopping mall at the corner of Av 27 de Febrero and Av Abraham Lincoln; also Plaza Caribe, at 27 de Febrero y Leopoldo Navarro.

Buses   Public transport buses (Onatrate), commonly called *guaguas*, run throughout the city, fares are RD$1.50-2 (US$0.12-0.15), but the service is very limited, therefore crowded. Exact change is needed. Private companies (eg Caribe Tours) operate on some routes, charging RD$2.

Taxis   *Carros públicos*, or *conchos*, are shared taxis normally operating on fixed routes, 24 hours a day, basic fare RD$1 (US$0.08), though more on longer routes. *Públicos* can be hired by one person, if they are empty, and are then called *carreras*. They can be expensive (US$2.75, more on longer routes); settle price before getting in. Fares are higher at Christmas time. *Públicos* also run on long-distance routes; ask around to find the cheapest. Many private cars now operate as *públicos* as owners try to earn supplementary income. You can get to just about anywhere by bus or *público* from Parque Independencia, but you have to ask where to stand. Radio taxis charge between US$3 and US$4.60 on local journeys around Santo Domingo and are safer than street taxis, call about 20-30 minutes in advance: Apolo Taxi, Tel: 541-9595; Taxi Telex, Tel: 565-3033; Taxi Radio, Tel: 562-1313; Taxi La Paloma, Tel: 562-3660; Taxi Raffi, Tel: 689-2268; Taxi Enlace, Tel: 688-1974; Micromóvil, Tel: 689-6141. The 30-minute ride from Las Américas International airport to Santo Domingo should cost no more than US$14 in a radio taxi, about US$12.50 in a *carrera*. Most hotels have a taxi or limousine service with set fares throughout the city and to the airport. There are motorcyclists who offer a taxi service, known as *motoconchos*, RD$3 (US$0.25), they sometimes take up to three passengers on pillion; they raise the noise level (in most towns) very considerably.

Car Rentals   Many places at the airport, on the road to the airport and on Malecón. The prices given below are of May 1992 and are for the cheapest vehicle available at each agency. There are many more agencies than those listed: Thrifty (Tel: 1-800-367-2277), US$65/day, US$305/week, deposit US$540; National (Tel: 562-1444, airport Tel: 542-0162), US$62/day, US$280/week, deposit US$435; Budget (Tel: 567-0177), US$72/day, US$394/week; Nelly (Tel: 532-7346), US$58/day, US$359/week; Dollar (Tel: 689-5329), US$68/day, US$508/week; Patsy (Tel: 686-4333);

Hertz (Tel: 685-1216). See also under **Information for Visitors**.

Libraries Biblioteca Nacional, in the Plaza de la Cultura, has a fine collection and is a good place for a quiet read. Instituto Cultural Dominico-Americano, corner of Av Abraham Lincoln and Calle Antonio de la Maza; English and Spanish books. The National Congress has a good library, as do some of the universities: Pontificia Universidad Católica Madre y Maestra, the Instituto Tecnológico de Santo Domingo and the Universidad Autónoma de Santo Domingo.

Concerts Concerts and other cultural events are often held at the National Theatre, the Casa de Francia, corner of Las Damas and El Conde, where Cortés lived for a while (run by the French Embassy, also art gallery and library, open to non-members), and the Casa de Teatro (see below).

Theatres Teatro Nacional, Plaza de la Cultura, Av Máximo Gómez; Palace of Fine Arts, Av Independencia and Máximo Gómez; Casa de Teatro, small drama workshop, Calle Padre Billini and, in Barrio Don Bosco, Teatro Nuevo (performances all year).

Night Clubs *Salon La Fiesta* in the *Jaragua Hotel*; *El Yarey* in the *Sheraton*; *Embassy Club* in the *Hotel El Embajador*; *Napolitana*; *Maunaloa Night Club* and Casino; *Hotel San Gerónimo*, Independencia; *La Azotea* in *Hotel Concorde*; *Salón Rojo*, *Hotel Comodoro*, Av Bolívar; *Night Club Herminia*; *Las Vegas*, *Babilon*, *Fuego Fuego*, *Piano Bar Las Palmas* in *Hotel Santo Domingo*, *Piano Bar Intramuros*, *Primera Clase* and *Tablao Flamenco*.

Also *Instrumental Night Club* on Autopista Las Américas; *Exodus*, George Washington 511; *Le Petit Chateau*, Av George Washington Km 11½, nude shows.

Guácara Taína, Paseo de los Indios, between Avenida Cayetano Germosén and Parque Mirador, has shows of Taíno dancing in a deep cave with indigenous pictographs from 1700 (also Happy Hours and fashion shows).

To hear *pericos ripiaos*, go on Friday or Saturday night to the eating places (*colmados*) near the Malecón in Ciudad Nueva section of the city; the groups move from place to place.

Discothèques *Omni* in *Hotel Sheraton*, rock, merengue, salsa and ballads; *Hipocampo* in *Hotel El Embajador*; *Disco Piano* in *Hotel El Napolitano*; *Jet Set* and *Opus*, Av Independencia; *Shehara* and *Bella Blue* (next to *Vesuvio I*) on George Washington; *Punto Final*, Av Pasteur. *Tops* (*Hotel Plaza Naco*), *El Final*, *Magic Disco*, *Jet Set* and *Xappil*. *Club 60*, Máximo Gómez 60, rock, merengue and ballads; *Neon* in *Hotel Hispaniola*, upmarket, occasionally has live Latin jazz; *Sentimiento*, Hostos 99, down market with lots of merengue, very dark. For Cuban son music: *El Rincón Habanero*, Sánchez Valverde y Baltazar de los Reyes in Villa Consuelo, working class enthusiasts of Cuban son dance between tables to old records of 1940s and 1950s; *Secreto Musical Bar*, one block away, Baltazar de los Reyes and Pimentel, similar, headquarters of Club Nacional de los Soneros, rock, merengue, salsa and ballads; *La Vieja Habana*, in Villa Mella on the northern outskirts of town, called Generoso.

Casinos Hotels Dominican Concorde, Santo Domingo, San Gerónimo, Sheraton, El Embajador, Naco, Jaragua, Lina and Maunaloa Night Club, Centro de los Héroes.

Exchange Officially possible only in banks, many along Isabel La Católica, but check which banks accept which traveller's cheques. A list of commercial banks which will change dollars can be found in the **Information for Visitors**. Do not change money on the street; you will undoubtedly be cheated and you also run the risk of imprisonment.

Language School Escuela de Idiomas de la Universidad APEC, Av Máximo Gómez 72, Apartado Postal 59-2, Santo Domingo, Tel: 687-3181, offers Spanish courses, either 1 or 2 hours daily, Monday to Friday, for a term.

Post Office The head office is usually at Calle Emiliano Tejera, opposite the Alcázar de Colón, but in 1989 it moved to a provisional location on Isabel La Católica (and the entire service became chaotic). Open 0700-1800, Monday-Friday; also certain hours on Saturday. Lista de correo (poste restante) on 2nd floor keeps mail for two months. There are post offices on the 2nd floor of the government building El Huacal, tallest building in the city, on Av Padre Castellanos, near Av Duarte, and in *Hotel Embajador*.

To ensure the delivery of documents worldwide, use a courier service: American Airlines (Tel: 542-5151); DHL Dominicana (Tel: 541-7988), Servicio de Documentos y pequeños paquetes (Tel: 541-2119); Emery Worldwide (688-1855); Federal Express (Tel: 567-9547); Internacional Bonded Couriers (Tel: 542-5265).

Telephones International and long distance, also Telex and Fax: Codetel, Av 30 de Marzo 12, near Parque Independencia, and 11 others throughout the city (open 0800-2200). The Palacio de las Comunicaciones next to the Post Office (at Isabel La Católica y Emiliano Tejera) does not handle phone calls.

Episcopal Church Av Independencia 253, service in English, 0830 Sunday; also Iglesia Episcopal San Andrés, on Marcos Ruiz.

Health Clínica Abréu, Av Independencia and Beller, and adjacent Clínica Gómez Patiño are recommended for foreigners needing treatment or hospitalization. Fees are high but care is good. 24-hour emergency department. Other reputable clinics are Centro Médico UCE and Clínica Yunén on Av Máximo Gómez, and Clínica Abel González, Av Independencia.

Tours There are several tours of the city, taking in the duty-free shops, nightlife, etc. Recommended travel agents in Santo Domingo for sightseeing tours include: Halcón Travel (Tel: 566-6116), Gladys Tours (Tel: 688-1069), Metro Tours (Tel: 567-3138), Domitur (Tel: 567-5574), Portillo SA (Tel: 565-3027), Prieto Tours (Tel: 685-0102), Dimargo Tours (Tel: 582-3874), Merengue (Tel: 582-3373), Pebeco (567-8636), Viajes Barceló (Tel: 685- 8411), Dilia's Tours (Tel: 682-1068) and Viajes Internacional, El Conde 105. Companies that offer tours around the republic are given in **Information for Visitors. NB** See warnings at the end of this chapter about unofficial guides.

Airport Aeropuerto La Américas, 23 km out of town, Tel: 549-0450/80. Immediately on arrival there is a tourist office on your right, and just past that an office selling tourist cards (a blackboard indicates who needs a card, see **Documents** in **Information for Visitors**). You must check if you need a card, otherwise the long queue to get through immigration will be wasted. Just beyond immigration is a bank for exchanging dollars; it is open at night. In the departure area are lots of duty-free shops, one small café (dollars only) and limited seating. The X-ray machines are not safe for film.

The price of a taxi or minibus to town is given above (can be shared); it may be less if you bargain with drivers in the car park (though this is not easy) or telephone a radio taxi in advance (numbers given above). If arriving late at night it may be better to go to Boca Chica (see **East from Santo Domingo**), about 10 km from the airport, taxi US$9.50-11.50. Bus or *público* to town from *Restaurante La Caleta*; turn right out of airport compound along main road; cross over main highway; turn left to restaurant (about 25 minutes' walk). Buses pass every ½ hour, but are infrequent in evening, or walk down the airport road to the highway, Avenida de Las Américas, and flag down anything that passes! To get to the airport cheaply take a *público* at Av Duarte and París (to Savanna Larga). Get off before the car turns on to Savanna Larga, walk 50 metres and there are *carros* to the airport, US$4-7. Various tour agencies also run minibuses to the airport; check with your hotel. Herrera airport (Tel: 567-3900) for internal flights to Santiago, Puerto Plata, Barahona and La Romana (allow plenty of time).

North from Santo Domingo

To the north of Santo Domingo, along the Carretera Duarte, is **Bonao** (Hotels: *El Viejo Madrid*; *Yaraví Rooms*; *Elizabeth*, US$1.50 with bath, and other cheap hotels near the market such as *Mi Provincia*, US$3, and *San Juan*, US$1.50). Bonao is known as Villa de las Hortensias; as you come into town is the country's most famous bus stop: *Jacaranda* and *Don Raspadura*, where you can eat local dishes and sweets, or buy souvenirs.

Further north is **La Vega**, a quiet place in the beautiful valley of la Vega Real, in the heart of the Cibao. (Hotels: *América*, *Guaricano*, and, cheaper, *Royal*, *San Pedro*, and *Astral*. International artists appear at the *Astromundo* discothèque.) Further along the road from La Vega on the right is the turn for Santo Cerro, an old convent where the image of Virgen de las Mercedes is venerated. From there one can get a view of the valley of La Vega Real. If one continues along the road to the other side of the hill and into the valley the ruins of La Vega Vieja can be seen. It was founded by Columbus but destroyed by an earthquake in 1564; undergoing restoration (similarly La Vega's cathedral).

Continuing along the highway, on the left, is the turn for **Jarabacoa**. The road winds through some beautiful pine forests to the town itself, which is a popular summer hill resort with warm days and cool nights. *Público* from La Vega, US$1.20; bus from Santo Domingo, US$2.50 (Caribe Tours stop outside the *Pinar Dorado* hotel). There are several clubs offering golf, tennis and riding, and the good *balneario* (swimming hole) of La Confluencia, in the Río Jimenoa, is nearby (nice campsite, crowded at holiday times). The Jimenoa waterfalls are worth seeing, but you need to put your climbing skills into practice to reach them.

Where To Stay *Nacional*, US$15, friendly and clean; outside town, *La Montaña*, Tel: 682-8181, same price range, some km out, friendly, clean, highly recommended; and *Pinar Dorado*, US$28, which has cottages, good atmosphere and meals (Tel: 689-5105); *Pinos del Puerto*, a prestigious resort 14 km from town. *Lina*, US$7-8, dirty; unmarked hotel on corner of Independencia and El Carmen, US$7s without bath; *Continental* is short stay only; *Dormitorio*, basic, clean, friendly, with a good *comedor*, *Carmen*, nearby.

Where To Eat The town has several restaurants; try the *Rincón Montañés* on Calle El Carmen; *Basilia*, not as expensive as it looks, nice food; other good-value ones are run by shopkeepers.

Beyond Jarabacoa, on the same road, is **Constanza**, where the scenery is even better than in Jarabacoa, with rivers, forests and waterfalls. In winter, temperatures can fall to zero and there may be frosts. The valley is famous for food production, potatoes, garlic, strawberries, mushrooms and other vegetables, and for growing ornamental flowers. (Hotels: *Nueva Suiza*, built by Trujillo, run down, Tel: 539-2233, over US$20; *Hotel El Gran Restaurant*, US$4s, US$5.50d, without bath, good value, restaurant rather pricey; *Mi Cabaña*, US$4, good, Tel: 539-2472; *Nacional*, Tel: 574-2578; *Margarita* and *Casa de Huéspedes*, both on Calle Luperón, latter US$2.50 but poor; *Brisa del Valle*, US$1.25, simple, acceptable, meals available.) Constanza can be reached by taking a bus to Bonao from either Santo Domingo or Santiago, then two *públicos*, the last one making the rough 1½ hour trip to the town through the finest scenery in the Republic. *Público* from Jarabacoa, US$2.40; you will be told that the *público* goes only at 0700, but if you hang around something will turn up, eg a pick-up to El Río on the Bonao-Constanza route. You can get a *guagua* from there. Direct transport Constanza-Jarabacoa mornings only, otherwise you have to go via the main Santo Domingo-Santiago highway.

Steve Morris recommends a route from the west to Constanza by public transport, avoiding Santo Domingo, across country and more time consuming but much more exciting. He started in Neiba, near Lago Enriquillo (see below), took a *guagua* to Cruce de Ocoa, 2½ hours, US$1.50, and from there to San José de Ocoa (north east of Azua), 45 minutes, US$0.70. *(Hotel Marien*, on the main square, US$6.50d without bath, clean, good value.) He writes: 'Although what could hardly be called a road exists between San José de Ocoa and Constanza, there is no regular transport connecting the two towns. Apparently a gentleman named Pepe occasionally takes his jeep through the mountains to Constanza; the only hope is to get to La Isla gas station early in the morning and let everyone know that you want to get to Constanza. There is a regular bus service to Rancho Arriba and from there you can hire a motorcyclist to take you along a horrendous road to Piedra Blanca on the Santo Domingo-Santiago highway. Once on the highway it is very easy to get to Constanza.'

In the Cordillera Central near Jarabacoa and Constanza is **Pico Duarte**, at 3,175 metres the highest peak in the Caribbean. Before climbing it one must inform the army in Constanza; you must also purchase a permit from the Dirección Nacional de Parques at La Ciénaga de Manabao for US$3.95. (It is advisable to take a guide, who will tell you that mules are necessary for the ascent, but it can be done without them; the cost of guide and mules is US$15.75 a day. An organized climb with DNP, Nuevos Horizontes, Maritissant, Tel: 685-7887, costs about US$78, September and October.) The climb takes two days and the walk from the tropical rain forest of the National Park through pine woods is pleasant. There are two huts on the path, which is clearly marked; they are lacking in "facilities". Take adequate clothing with you; it can be cold (below 0°C) and wet. The last *carro* leaves Manabao for Jarabacoa at 1600, so aim to climb the peak well before lunch on the second day. The National Park itself is a 4 km walk from La Ciénaga, which is reached by a road passing through some magnificent scenery from Jarabacoa.

Santiago los Caballeros is the second largest city in the Republic (population 308,400) and chief town of the Cibao valley in the north-central part of the country. It is much quieter, cleaner, cooler and "slower" than Santo Domingo, from where it is easily reached by bus. The Río Yaque del Norte skirts the city with Avenida Circunvalación parallel to it. In 1494 Columbus ordered a fort to be built on the banks of the Río Yaque del Norte at a place called Jacagua; the resulting settlement was moved to its present site in 1563, but was destroyed by an earthquake. It is now a centre for tobacco and rum. On Parque Duarte are the Catedral de Santiago Apóstol, a neoclassical building (19th century) containing the tombs of the tyrant Ulises Heureux and of heroes of the Restauración de la República; the Museo del Tabaco (open 1000-1700, closed late 1991), the Centro de Recreo (one of the country's most exclusive private clubs) and the Palacio Conistorial. Part of the Centro de la Cultura is on Parque Duarte; theatrical performances and exhibitions are held here. Other places worth visiting are the Universidad Católica Madre y Maestra (founded 1962), the Museo Folklórico Tomás Morel, open 0900-1700 (free), and the Monumento a los Héroes de la Restauración, at the highest point in the city (panoramic views of the Cibao valley, remodelled in 1991 to include a *mirador* and museum). Calle El Sol is the main commercial street, selling fruit and handicrafts. A Plaza de Cultura, similar to that in the capital, is being built near the cathedral; inauguration was projected for 1992. There will be museums, a fine art school, a modern dance studio, all set in a park. The Instituto Superior de Agricultura is in the Herradura on the other side of the Río Yaque del Norte (km 6). A carriage ride around the city should not be missed (US$7, from the square opposite the cathedral) but choose your horse carefully; there have been international complaints about the poor state of carriage horses in the Dominican Republic.

Local Information—Santiago de Los Caballeros

Where To Stay Over US$30: *Camino Real*, Tel: 581-7000, Del Sol y Mella, has good restaurant and night club, no parking facilities; *Matum*, Av Monumental, Tel: 581-5454, has night club; *Don Diego*, Av Estrella Sadhalá, Tel: 587-4186, has restaurant and night club; under US$30: *Ambar*, also on Av Estrella Sadhalá, Tel: 583-1957; *Don Juan*, Av Salvador Cucurullo, Tel: 587-7563; *Santiago Plaza*, Colón 42, Tel: 581-7480; *Mercedes*, Calle 30 de Marzo 18, Tel: 583-1171, US$15, central so a bit noisy, tatty, but friendly, fast laundry (5 hrs). A recommended *pensión* is the *Diri*, Las Carreras and Juan Pablo Duarte, US$5. Many cheap hotels around Plaza Valerio.

Where To Eat The best are the *Pez Dorado*, El Sol 43, Tel: 582-2518 (Chinese and international); the restaurants of the *Hoteles Camino Real* and *Don Diego* are good; *Oriente*, Calle 30 de Marzo, good and cheap, and *El Dragón*, E Sadhalá, Tel: 582-0282 (Chinese). *Karen*, E Sadhalá, Tel: 587-4932; on El Sol, *El Pabellón*, *El Sol* (Tel: 583-0767) *Don Miguel*, Autopista Duarte opposite Universidad Católica, Tel: 583-3996, good local, Cuban and US food, popular. Others include *El Diamante*, Av Circunvalación, Tel: 583-9714; *Olimpic*, Imbert 162, Tel: 575-2007; *Rolly's*, 27 Febrero, Tel: 581-1555; *Las Antillas* (Parque Duarte), meals from US$4 upwards; *El Mexicano* (Ensanche El Ensueño); *Yaque* (Restauración), US$4 plus for a good meal; and *Olé*, Juan Pablo Duarte y Independencia, for light meals and pizzas. *Roma*, on Juan Pablo Duarte just past the Tobacco Institute, for Italian food, good pizza, salads etc (also in Puerto Plata). Try *chimi* stands, especially the *arepa* stand, on the road behind the monument, for a cheap dinner.

Discothèques *La Nuit*, in *Hotel Matum*, the only one in the country with lasers; *La Mansión*, Autopista Duarte, *La Antorcha*, 27 Febrero 58; *Tempo*, El Sol, and *Las Vegas*, Autopista Navarrete Km 9, all modern.

Shopping The market is located at Calle Del Sol and Avenida España.

Buses In Santiago RD$1.50/US$0.12 (very restricted service). *Carros de concho* also charge US$0.12 in the city; *carreras*, US$2.05. Taxi to Puerto Plata airport US$20, *carrera*, US$2.75. Transporte del Cibao, Restauración casi esquina J P Duarte, runs buses up to Dajabón in the northwest near the Haitian border, but no buses run to this area or to Monte Cristi between 1000 and 1700 (a taxi costs about US$35 after bargaining). *Público* to La Vega US$1.20; Caribe Tours bus to Puerto Plata US$1.60. For other services see **Information for Visitors**.

Tourist Information There is a Tourist Office in the basement of the Town Hall (Ayuntamiento), Av Juan Pablo Duarte; it has good maps and brochures.

An interesting day trip is to **Moca**, east of Santiago, which is a coffee and cacao centre and one of the richer regions of the country. The Iglesia Corazón de Jesús church has a magnificent organ, there is only one other like it in the Americas, in Brazil. Tourist information may be found at the Town Hall at the corner of Independencia and Antonio de la Maza. It is not recommended that you stay the night, there is only one hotel, *La Niza*, on JD Duarte towards Santiago, which does not charge by the hour. Outside Moca on the road towards the autopista Duarte, lies El Higüerito where they make faceless dolls. Every shack is a doll factory and you can bargain for better prices than in Santo Domingo or Puerto Plata. The road leading from Moca to Sabaneta on the coast is extremely beautiful, winding through lush green hills. At the crest of the hillside, about halfway between Moca and Sabeneta is a lovely restaurant called *El Molino*, "it has the most glorious chicken crêpes and a view to match, don't forget your camera". You can go from Moca to Sosúa by *guaguas*, changing at the Cruce de Veragua/Sabaneta. A very recommendable trip with a magnificent view from the summit just before you cross over the mountains, of Santiago, Moca and even La Vega.

To the southwest of Santiago is the pleasant, mountain town of **San José de las Matas** (Hotels, *Centro Vacacional La Mansión*, Tel: 221-2131/581-0393, Fax: 581-9085, fully-equipped cabins, US$43 full board, rising to US$90 in "villages", a/c, pool, very quiet; *Oasis* and *La Modenza*, both cheap). Nearby are the *balnearios* (bathing spots) and the Ríos Amina, Arroyo Hondo and Inoa; the climate is cool all year round. From Santiago take a *guagua* (US$1.60) or *público* (US$1.20) on Av Independencia.

To the northwest of Santiago a Highway runs through the Yaque del Norte valley to the Haitian border. The main route to Haiti turns south to Mao (Hotels *Cahoba*, about US$15, Tel: 572-3357, also *Céntrico*, Tel: 572-2122, *San Pedro*, Tel: 572-3134, *Marién*, Tel: 525-3558) and continues through Sabaneta to the border town of Dajabón. South of Dajabón is the *balneario* at Loma de Cabrera, recommended to visit if you are in the area. Instead of turning south to Mao, you can continue to **Monte Cristi**, a dusty little town at the western end of the republic's north coast. One can visit the house of Máximo Gómez, the Dominican patriot who played an important role in the struggle for Cuban independence and in the Dominican Restoration. Columbus rejected his original idea to make his first settlement here and the town was in fact founded in the 16th century, rebuilt in the 17th. In the 19th century it was a major port exporting agricultural produce. The town has an interesting old clock. Very near Monte Cristi is a peak named El Morro (a national park) which has a beach (very rocky) at the foot of its east side. There are mangroves and turtles which can be seen in the clear water. The Cayos Siete Hermanos, a sanctuary for tropical birds, with white beaches, are a good excursion. Hotels: *Chic*, Benito Monción 44, Tel: 579-2316; *Santa Clara*, Mayobanex 8, Tel: 579-2307; *Cabañas Las Carabelas*, J Bolaños, Tel: 579-2682. Restaurants: *La Taberna de Rafúa*, Duarte 84, Tel: 579-2291; *Heladería y Pizzería Kendy*, Duarte 92, Tel: 579-2386; *Mi Barrita*, Duarte 86, Tel: 579-2487.

At the town of Navarrete on the Santiago-Monte Cristi Highway, a road branches north, bifurcating at Imbert. The northeastern fork goes to Puerto Plata (see below), the northwestern road to the north coast at **Luperón**, which has fine beaches, suitable for water sports. *Hotel Luperón Beach Resort*, in Casa Marina Luperón. Tel: 581-4153, Fax: 581-6262, US$70-110pp (high season), and *Hotel Luperón*, Calle Independencia, Tel: 571-8125.

West of Luperón is **La Isabela**, the site of Columbus' first base on Hispaniola, his Fuerte de la Navidad. Here was founded the first European town in the Americas, with the first *ayuntamiento* and court, and here was said the first mass. The restoration and archaeological excavation of La Isabela by the Dirección Nacional de Parques is one of the principal works undertaken for the Quinto Centenario.

Between La Isabela and Monte Cristi are the beaches of Punta Rucia at Estero Hondo. Besides the beaches there are mangroves and interesting flora and fauna. Lodging at *Hotel Discovery Bay*, Tel: 685-0151/562-7475, Fax: 686-6741, US$139-170pp, all inclusive, no children under 16, watersports and other activities provided.

Puerto Plata, the chief town on the Atlantic coast (which is also known as the Amber Coast) was founded by Columbus in 1502 and has some fine colonial architecture. It is 235 km from the capital. The older scenic road from Santiago to Puerto Plata is now in poor condition. A visit to the colonial San Felipe fortress, the oldest in the New World, at the end of the Malecón is recommended. Just 1,000 metres past Puerto Plata, you can catch a *teleférico* (cable car) to the summit of Loma Isabel de Torres, an elevation of 779 metres. There is a statue of Christ that looks out over all of Puerto Plata; it also houses craft shops, a café and there are botanical gardens with a lovely view of the coast and mountains. The fare is US$0.80, daily except Wednesday; or you can take your chances with horses, bikes or even a car, but be prepared, the road is impassable at some points. The Museum of Dominican Amber, Duarte 61, houses a collection of rare amber; open Monday-Saturday 0900-1700, Tel: 586-2848. The mountains behind Puerto Plata contain the world's richest deposits of amber, which is a fossilized tree resin. The cathedral is worth a visit, as are the ruins of the Vieja Logia and the Parque Central. The town is a stop for cruise ships, thus attracting hordes of beggars and overly persistent small boys. If you are led into a shop by a local boy, tour guide or taxi driver, you will more than likely be paying a hidden commission on the price of your purchase, even after you bargain. If you want a guide, call the Association of Official Tour Guides, on 586-2866. Fishing: contact Santiago Camps (Tel: 586-2632) for equipment and boat hire.

To the west is the new Costambar resort area (hotels, cottages, sports facilities, in all about 500 rooms available, eg *Costambar Beach Resort*, Tel: 586-3828) and Cofresí beach (several hotels, cabins, US$30 pp and more at weekends). At the east end of town is Long Beach, 2 km from the centre, US$0.15 by bus, but it is crowded at weekends, rather dirty, and it is best to be on your guard (*Hotel Balneario Colón*, Tel: 586-2551). Just east of Puerto Plata, 4 km from the airport, is the beach resort of **Playa Dorada** with an exceptional golf course, and other sporting facilities. The Playa Dorada Resort is an umbrella name for a complex of 10 large hotels. Already the resort has 2,450 rooms and there are plans to build many more. Montellano, to the east of Playa Dorada, about half way to Sosúa, is the town in which all the processing of sugar cane is done for the north coast. It is undeveloped as a tourist town, but there are tours of the cane processing plant. For those who are adventurous, it has a great discothèque called *Las Brisas*, on the river, that all the locals visit, especially on Sunday afternoons. A bottle of rum, bucket of ice and 2 colas will cost about US$4. The town is a bit primitive, but the disco is not; guaranteed to have a great time, dancing merengue, salsa and some American music.

Local Information—Puerto Plata and Playa Dorada

Where To Stay At Puerto Plata *Puerto Plata Beach Resort and Casino*, the sort of place found in package tour brochures and so difficult to get in to, Tel: 562-7475/685-0151, Fax: 686-6741, US$95d without meals, US$39 pp basic low season price. *Montemar*, short walk to seafront, PO Box 382, Tel: 586-2800, Fax: 586-2009, US55-90, all facilities, taxi from centre US$4.80; *Hostal Jimessón*, John F Kennedy 41, Tel: 586-5131/364-2024, close to Parque Central, old colonial building, US$35s or d high season, US$25 low season, lobby furnished with antiques, clean, a/c, pleasant, no restaurant; *Castilla*, US$12d with shower and fan, on José del Carmen Ariza in centre of town, Tel: 586-2559, splendid atmosphere, good restaurant, but toilets not recommended; *El Condado*, Av Circunvalación Sur, Tel: 586-3255; *Caracol*, on sea front, modern, Tel: 586-2588. *Swedish Guest House*, Av Circunvalación Sur 15, Tel: 586-5086, Krystyna Danielsson, 9 rooms with toilet and shower, s and d, nice garden, cheap, backpackers welcome, rooms can be rented for long periods. At Plaza Anaconda, 30 de Marzo 94-100, are *Hotel Arawak*, under US$20, with fan, clean; *Restaurant Indio*, good breakfast and fish, expensive, Mexican music on Saturdays; a patio with native plants, palm trees and hummingbirds; and a Red Cross emergency station. Ask for Pedro Brunschwiler (who speaks German, English and Spanish) if you want to go scuba diving, horse riding or on adventure trips. Plaza Anaconda's owner, Wolfgang Wirth (who also speaks German, English and Spanish) is very helpful; he is the founder of the Dominican Red Cross.

Lira, Calle Villa Nueva, Tel: 586-2337, good food, US$6; *Alfa*, US$8s with shower, pleasant but watch out for mosquitoes, friendly, safe, clean, Tel: 586-2684; *Andy's Guest House*, US$10, recommended, one of many of similar price range, breakfast US$1 extra; some houses also available from US$22 a week. Ask in the *Wienerwald* restaurant, Long Beach, about cheap rooms.

At Playa Dorada *Jack Tar Village* hotel, from US$66 pp basic price to US$200, all inclusive, PO Box 368, Tel: 586-3800/530-5817, Fax: 586-4161, US style and US prices, casino; *Heavens*, from US$36 pp basic to US$150d full board, PO Box 576, Playa Dorada, Tel: 685-0151/530-5817, Fax: 686-6741; *Playa Dorada* (formerly *Holiday Inn*), PO Box 272, Tel: 586-3988, from US$66 pp, casino; *Eurotel*, touted as the most beautiful of the Playa Dorada hotels, Tel 586-3636/3663, 530-5817, Fax: 586-4858, from US$65 pp (US$35 low season), also has a casino; *Dorado Naco*, PO Box 162, US$35 pp basic low season price, Tel: 586-2019; *Villas Doradas Resort Hotel* 207 rooms, or 5 individual houses with kitchenettes, Tel: 586-3000, Fax: 586-4790, from US$60 (low) to 120 (high season); *Villas Caraibe, Playa Dorada Princess* (Tel: 530-5871, US$50 pp low season), *Flamenco, Puerto Plata Village* (Tel: 586-4012, Fax: 586-5113), and many others. Many establishments in Playa Dorada offer all inclusive accommodation; the average price for a room is over US$100. Contact the Asociación de Proprietarios de Hoteles y Condominios de Playa Dorada, Tel: 586-3132, telex ITT 346-0360, Fax: 586-5301.

Where To Eat The food is superb at all the main hotels. *Los Pinos*, international cuisine, Tel: 586-3222; *De Armando*, in city centre, near Parque Central, very good; *Jimmy's*, French and Italian cuisine in restored gingerbread house with verandah, three blocks west of Parque Central on corner of Beller and Villanueva, Tel: 586-4325; *Pizzería Portofino*, Hermanas Mirabel and *Pizzería Roma*, Tel: 586-3904; *Costa Brava*, Spanish, pleasant, guitarists; *La Carreta*, Calle Separación; *Oceánico* on sea front; *El Canario*, 12 de Julio; all have good food at relatively low prices. *Valter*, on Hermanas Mirabel, in a gingerbread house, seafood and Italian specialities, good food and service, US$10 pp (Tel: 586-2329). *D'Amico*, Luis Ginebra 150; *El Sombrero*, Playa Cofresí, Autopista Santiago-Puerto Plata; *Terraza La Carpa*, Av John F Kennedy; also on this avenue *Palacio*, bar and restaurant, good value. Opposite the stadium are *Internacional* and *Thursday's Fondu*. *Madrid*, very good value; *Cafetería Los Bonilla*, La Javilla, highly recommended, *merengue* players visit it most evenings. *La Canasta*, 2 blocks north of main square, good for lunches; *Pollo al Carbón*, for inexpensive and delicious roast chicken, on Calle Circunvalación. *Pepe Postre* bakery chain in Puerto Plata/Montellano area, good breads, yoghurt, etc. Also recommended are *Café Terminus* (where you can get information on horseback safaris), *El Cable, La Paella, Wienerwald, Infratur* and the *Beach Club Restaurant*, all at Long Beach.

Discothèques *Andromeda* in *Heavens Hotel, Charlie's* in *Jack Tar Village Casino* and *Crazy Moon* in *Eurotel*; all three are popular (although *Charlie's* is the most popular) and offer a mix of *merengue, salsa* and international pop music. All have cover charges, about US$2.

Casinos There are four casinos on the north coast. *Jack Tar Village, Playa Dorada Hotel, Eurotel* and *The Puerto Plata Beach Resort*. Only the last named is right in Puerto Plata, the other three are in the Playa Dorada complex. The casinos feature black jack, craps, roulette and poker. There are slot machines but these can be played **only** in US dollars. If you play other games in US dollars, you win in US dollars, if you play in pesos, you win in pesos. Do not change your foreign money to pesos in the casino, the rate given is very unfavourable. *Jack Tar Village Casino* offers novices a one hour lesson in black jack or craps at 2130 nightly, free of charge. Two other casinos are being built, at Playa Chiquita in Sosúa (which will be ready for the 92/93 season), and Tierra del Sol near Cabarete.

Motorcycle Rental US$20-25 a day, from any rental agency. Make sure to lock your motorcycle or scooter, as bike theft is big business in the area and there is no theft insurance on motorbikes.

Useful Phone Numbers Police, 586-2331; Centro Médico Antera Mota, 586-2342; Codetel (telephone office) 586-3311; association of tourist guides, 586-2866; US consular agency, 586-3676.

Tourist Information There is a tourist office on the Malecón (No 20) which has plenty of useful information.

Local Transport *Públicos* in the city RD$1.50/US$0.12; *guaguas* RD$2/US$0.15; *carreras* US$3.15; *motoconchos*, US$0.55. *Carreras* from Puerto Plata to Playa Dorada, US$12 (tourists); US$3.85 (Dominicans); to Sosúa, US$19.75; from the airport to Playa Dorada US$11. Bus to Nagua, US$4, 3½ hours. *Conchos* from Puerto Plata to Playa Dorada, US$0.07, *motoconchos* between US$0.27-0.70.

A *carro público* to/from the capital costs US$4.75, but is not the most comfortable way to travel. Metrobus (Tel: 586-6063) and Caribe Tours (Tel: 586-4544) run a/c coaches to/from Santo Domingo, 4 hours (for fares see **Information for Visitors**).

Airport Puerto Plata international airport, Tel: 586-0219 serves the entire north coast. It is 20 minutes from Puerto Plata, 7 minutes from Sosúa and 15 from Cabarete. Taxi from airport to Puerto Plata or Cabarete US$10, to Sosúa US$7. Do not panic at the airport when approached by Dominicans in overalls attempting to take your bag. They are baggage handlers trying to make a living. Proper tipping is about US$2 per bag.

28 km east of Puerto Plata is **Sosúa**, a quaint little town that has a beautiful and lively 1 km beach, perfect for diving and water sports. A *público* from Puerto Plata costs US$3.15, a taxi will cost about US$12 and is far more comfortable. The town is popular with Europeans, Americans and Canadians. The main street (correctly named Calle Pedro Clisante, but only ever referred to as Main Street, or Calle Principal in Spanish) is lined with all variety of shops, restaurants and bars. The unusual European atmosphere stems from the fact that the El Batey side of town (the side that houses most of the hotels and restaurants) was founded by German Jewish refugees who settled here in 1941. A synagogue and memorial building are open to the public. Although many of the original settlers have moved away, services are still held, and in 1991 a 50th year anniversary party brought settlers and their relatives from all over the world for a reunion. The western end of the town is referred to as Los Charamicos (the two ends are separated by the beach); this is the older side of town, where the Dominicans themselves generally live, shop and party.

Note Sosúa, although crowded with tourist spots, is a small town. Little or no attention is paid to street names or numbers.

Where To Stay *Casa Marina Beach Club*, Tel: 571-3690/530-5817, US$70d, high season (US$42 low), but special offers may be available, located on the Little Beach, pool, restaurant, excellent value. *Sosúa-by-the-Sea*, Tel: 571-3720, owned and operated by German-Canadians on Little Beach, immaculate, beautiful a/c rooms, good restaurant, pool, bar, US$77d high season; *Playa Chiquita Beach Resort*, Tel: 571-2800, US$45d, slightly out of the way, located on own private beach, good restaurant, accommodation and service, casino to open for 92/93 season, has shuttle to town and beach. *Corallillos*, unpretentious, perched on a cliff with breathtaking view of beach, US$55d in winter, US$30d in summer, Tel: 571-2645; *Auberge du Village*, family-run guest house five minutes walk from beach, US$35d in winter, Tel: 571-2569. *One Ocean Place*, El Batey, Tel: 571-3131, US$60, restaurant, pool, 10-minute walk to beach; *Hotel Sosúa*, Tel: 571-2683, Fax: 586-2442, in town centre, 3 minutes from main beach, restaurant, pool, quiet; *Sandcastles Beach Resort*, Tel: 530-5817/571-2420, Fax: 571-2000, just outside Sosúa, private beach, restaurants, self-contained, shuttle buses into Sosúa, US$120d, high season (US$45 low). *Charlie's Cabañas*, 27 cabins, quiet, tropical, ocean front pool, on a cliff overlooking the sea, 5 minutes to beach, US$45d, special rates for groups, Tel: 571-2670; *El Oasis*, Tel: 571-3606, for the budget-minded. *Chévere*, near Ciné and Los Charamicos, US$8s, with bath, fan, clean. There are many other hotels, guest houses and villas for rent, ask around locally. If you are looking for a place to stay for longer than the average charter flight, or would like to get a group together to stay in a house, or have any questions regarding rentals in the Sosúa/Cabarete area, call *Sosúa Central Rental*, Tel: 571-2103.

Where To Eat *On the Waterfront*, excellent food and a spectacular view overlooking the sea, pleasant entertainment nightly in *Charlie's Cabañas Hotel*, on the lookout point, down from the Codetel offices, tel: 571-3024; *Sonya's*, for fine dining in Sosúa, atmosphere and food of a small French restaurant, lovely food and service, two sittings a night, reservations needed, in *Hotel Yaroa*, Tel: 571-2651; *PJ's International*, for fast food and a good view of the main street's comings and goings. *El Oasis*, for basic food at a reasonable price (it is the oldest existing restaurant in El Batey, as a plaque at the front will tell you), on the corner of Main Street and Calle Dr Rosen; *Café Mamajuana*, owned by Canadians, run by Swiss, frequented by all, in the centre of main street Sosúa, good German food; *Pavillion*, slightly out of the way on a side street, great European food, steaks and an ice cream crêpe, worth the walk, located on Calle García, follow the signs for it all over town. *Charlie's Restaurant*, in the *North Shore Hotel* on the main street, good food, try his Wiener Schnitzel. *Marco Polo Bar & Restaurant*, panoramic view of Sosúa Bay, international menu from ribs to seafood, open 1000 to midnight, in El Batey, on Calle Alejo Martínez. *Garden of Eden*, Tel: 571-3720, the newest restaurant in town, located on top of *Hotel Sosúa-by-the-Sea*, an elegant rooftop restaurant, delicious food and entertainment nightly. *La Macia*, same street as city hall with clock tower, and *El Carey*, E Kunhart 22, 2nd floor, near *Hotel Chévere*, both excellent. For delicious baked products go to the *German Bakery*, in Villas Ana María, just off Main Street.

Bars and nightclubs *Tree Top Lounge*, good atmosphere for conversation, has lots of games (backgammon, cards, scrabble, etc). *Casa del Sol*, a/c discothèque seating about 500, mix of music, cover charge; *Casablanca*, on main street, hottest night spot in Sosúa, the place for late night dancing and partying. *Rumours*, Plaza del Fuente, owned and operated by former British tour rep, pub atmosphere, fun; *Barock*, 4th floor, lively bar, young clientèle; *Sully's Sports Bar*, Main Street, televized sporting events, popular.

Services For organized tours by plane to Haiti, Samaná, Turks and Caicos, Santo Domingo, contact Columbus Air, Tel: 571-2711 or 586-6991. Car and bike rentals are everywhere, shop around for prices, and once again be cautioned as to theft. The most popular form of transportation within Sosúa is *motoconcho* (motorcycle taxi), pay 3 pesos during the daylight hours and 5 pesos at night, per person, to anywhere in town, not a penny more, no matter how much the driver asks. Sosúa Business Services, for all typing, faxing, phoning, photocopying needs, on Main Street, upstairs from *Casablanca Bar*, Tel: 571-3452.

Police Tel: 571-2293.

12 km east of Sosúa is **Cabarete**, nowadays the windsurf capital of the world, having hosted the World Windsurf Championship. International competitions are held annually in June. The 2 km curving bay has a strip of guest houses catering for windsurfers' needs and the *Punta Goleta Beach Resort* for package tours (PO Box 272, Puerto Plata, Tel: 535-4941, basic price US$50 pp). Another development is *Camino del Sol*, Tel: 571-2858. Other hotels and apartment/hotels include *Casa Laguna*, Tel: 571-0724, *Cita del Sol*, Tel: 571-0720, *Cabarete Windsurf Club*, Tel: 571-0710. All are on Cabarete beach. There are many more hotels and rooms for rent, just ask around when you arrive. Conditions vary according to season: in summer there are constant trade winds but few waves, in winter there are days with no wind, but when it comes the waves are tremendous. November and December are the worst months. Boards rent for US$40/day, US$165/week. The headquarters of the championship organizers is the *Hosteriá del Rey*, the biggest guesthouse, US$30d, no a/c, Tel: 576-0770. Cabarete has many restaurants on Main Street, most specializing in fast food and with views of

the beach. There are many kilometres of white sand beach lined with coconut palms and a lagoon with many waterbirds, and waterskiing.

On the northeast coast, **Río San Juan**, is a friendly town with a lagoon called Gri-Grí (*guagua* from Puerto Plata US$2.40). Boats take visitors through the mangrove forests and to see caves and rocks, and to the natural swimming pool called the Cueva de las Golondrinas (US$16, up to 10 people). Also worth visiting from the town is Puerto Escondido beach. Best hotel is *Río San Juan*, on main street, US$20, which also has a good restaurant and there is a good pizzería opposite (the hotel offers boat trips on the lagoon, US$16 for up to 20 people, if more US$0.80 pp, recommended), *San José* and *Santa Clara*, smaller. Cheaper hotels: *San Martín* and *Caridad*. Further to the east is **Playa Grande**, 60 km from Puerto Plata, another beautiful new resort which is being developed, in conjunction with Playa Dorada, at a cost of many millions of dollars.

Between Río San Juan and Samaná, the coast road runs through Cabrera to **Nagua**, a dirty fishing village on the shores of the Bahía Escocesa (several small and medium-sized hotels; *Hotel San Carlos*, US$6.50s with shower; *Hotel Corazón de Jesús*, under US$5; *Hotel Carib Caban*, 8 km south of Nagua, US$30 in studio (less in smaller room), pleasant, directly on beach, restaurant with Austrian food (hire a motorcycle to get there, US$2, Tel: 584-3145). Puerto Plata-Nagua, three buses, 3½ hours, US$4; Nagua-Santo Domingo, 3½ hours, US$2.25; Río San Juan-Nagua, US$1.60, Nagua-Samaná also US$1.60. The scenery along the northern coast from Sosúa to Samaná is exceptionally beautiful. The road has been repaved all the way from Sosúa to Samaná, with the exception of the area around the town of Gaspar Hernández. **Sánchez** is a pleasant, unspoilt little place with some basic accommodation. Much of the architecture is 19th century. It was at one time a prosperous sea port and had the only railway in the country, which ran to San Francisco de Macorís and La Vega.

The Samaná Peninsula

On the peninsula of **Samaná** is the city of the same name. Columbus arrived here on 12 January 1493, but was so fiercely repelled by the Ciguayo Indians that he called the bay the Golfo de las Flechas (the Gulf of Arrows). Samaná Bay, as it is now called, is very picturesque, fringed with coconut palms and studded with islets. The present town of Santa Bárbara de Samaná was founded in 1756 by families expressly brought from the Canary Islands. The city, reconstructed after being devastated by fire in 1946, shows no evidence of this past, with its modern Catholic church, broad streets, new restaurants and hotels, and noisy motorcycle taxis. In contrast to the Catholic church, and overlooking it, is a more traditional Protestant church, white with red corrugated-iron roofing, nicknamed locally "La Churcha". Traditional dances, such as *bambulá* and the *chivo florete* can be seen at local festivals (4 December, the patron saint's day; 24 October, St Raphael). An airport for the peninsula is at Arroyo Barril (8 km from town, good road, but only 25 minutes' flying time from Santo Domingo, US$30). Many Caribbean-cruising yachts anchor at Samaná, taking advantage of the calm waters.

Local Information—Samaná

Where To Stay *Gran Bahía*, large US-owned luxury resort on coast road, 8 km east of town, US$58 pp, small beach, good food, tennis, water sports, shuttle service to Cayo Levantado. *Cayacoa* (formerly *Bahia Beach Resort*), Tel: 538-2218/530-5817, US$45 pp, on a hill overlooking the bay, is undergoing major renovations (will be open for 92/93 season). *Tropical Lodge*, on east exit along Malecón, Tel: 538-2480, US$36, 8 rooms; *Nilka*, Santa Bárbara y Colón, Tel: 538-2244, 10 rooms, US$11 with a/c (less without downstairs), all with bath, popular; *Guest House Alcide*, Tel: 538-2512; *Casa de Huéspedes Tete de Casado*, Duarte 4, very friendly, good value (owner is a teacher). *Cotubanamá*, Tel: 538-2557, basic, but excellent, US$14. *Cico*, US$11d, small but clean rooms, recommended; *Coco Loco*, near rotunda, helpful German owner, who is also a guide to the National Park, good barbecue. There are other hotels, eg *King*, Tel: 538-2404, *Casa de Huéspedes Irene*, *Fortuna*, *Ursula*, *Paco's Bar*, the cheaper ones near the market.

Where To Eat   Going east along the Malecón: *Típico El Coco*, *L'Hacienda*, Tel: 538-2383, grill and bar; *Le Café de Paris*, pizzeria, crêperie, cocktails; *La Mata Rosada*, *Camilo* (on corner of Parque), local and not-so-local food, reasonable (takes credit cards), some are closed out of season. *La France* on Malecón, Tel: 538-2257, French owned, excellent. Chinese restaurant on the hill. At the dock, *El Marino* and *La Serena*. Between the Malecón and market: *Quioli*, *Le Belge*; *Salt and Pepper*.

The local cuisine is highly regarded, especially the fish and coconut dishes.

Other Services   Petrol station at the dock, open 0700-2200. Banco Hispano Dominicano on Malecón. Post Office behind *Camilo*, just off Parque; Codetel, Calle Santa Bárbara, 0800-2200 daily. Tourist information at Richard Tours at *Samaná Sam* sandwich bar and Samaná Information Service, Tel: 538-2451; both on Malecón, and closed out of season; alternatively, Tel: 538-2219, or 538-2206 (Ayuntamiento), or 538-2210 (provincial government).

Transport   From the capital either by bus direct, 4½ hours via San Francisco de Macorís (10-minute stop by a park with trees whose trunks are painted red, white and blue, *Hotel Joya*, near Plaza Mayor, US$4.80, quiet, clean, friendly), Nagua and Sánchez (return bus to capital, Caribe Tours on Malecón, 0630, 0900, 1400, US$4.75), or by bus or *público* to San Pedro de Macorís, then another to *Sabana la Mar* (*Hotel Villa Suiza*, US$16, pool, run down; *Hotel Brisas de la Bahía*, US$7-10 range), and cross by boat (3 return trips a day, US$1.50 one way) from Sabana to Samaná at 0900, 1100, 1700; boats to Sabana from Samaná at 0700, 1000 and 1500 (safety conditions leave something to be desired). The road from Sabana la Mar to Hato Mayor is fair, the scenery beautiful, but from Hato Mayor to San Pedro de Macorís (see below) it is excellent.

Excursions from Samaná

There are several beautiful offshore islands. Cayo Levantado is a popular picnic place, especially at weekends when the beach is littered. The white sand beach is nice, though, and there are good views of the bay and the peninsulas on either side. The hotel on the island is shut; drinks and fish lunches (not worth it) are for sale. Public boats go there from the beach in Samaná (US$0.80); alternatively, take a *público* or *motoconcho* 8 km out of town to Los Cacaos (US$0.50) to where two companies, Transportes José and Simi Báez, run boats to the island and will pick you up later for US$10-15 (the latter company also does fishing and whale-spotting trips). At the eastern end of the peninsula is Playa Galeras, 26 km, worth a visit. The 1 km beach is framed by the dark rock cliffs and forested mountains of Cape Samaná and Cape Cabrón. No electricity, no telephone. One small French-owned hotel, the *Marea Beach*, two restaurants. The area will soon be dominated by the *Cala Blanca* resort development; only 40 time share apartments so far, but there are plans for more with golf courses, sports centres etc. 20 minutes away by boat, or 40 minutes by jeep along a very rough track is the deserted Playa Rincón, dominated by the cliffs of 600-metre high Cape Cabrón. The whole peninsula is beautiful, but many beaches are accessible only by boat (and the Samaná boatmen charge the earth). Others are reached by a dirt road, negotiable by ordinary cars.

Visits to the Parque Nacional de Haitises, across the bay, can be arranged by launch for US$60, US$15 from Samaná, eg *Hotel Cayacoa* or from Sabana la Mar, or ask at Samaná Tourist Information; various companies organize tours to Los Haitises and to caves in the area (eg Ecoturisa, Parque Eugenio María de Hostos, on the Malecón, Santo Domingo, Tel: 221-4104, US$107 for two days; Crisol organizes one-day trips, US$31, Tel: 687-2423; Delia's Tours, Tel: 682-1068, runs trips to Los Haitises, Cayo Levantado and Playa Grande from Santo Domingo, all bus and boat transport, meals, bar, beach parties, etc, included for US$115, in Semana Santa only). The DNP, from whom permits must be obtained, also organizes tours; see above, **Flora and Fauna**.

On the north coast of the peninsula is ***Las Terrenas***, with some of the finest beaches in the country, from which, at low tide, you can walk out to coral reefs to see abundant sea life. The region is frequently visited by divers, drawn by its excellent reefs, sponges and underwater caves. Insect repellent is necessary at dawn and dusk to combat the sandflies. Many people go there by private plane, but it is reachable by a newly-paved 17 km road from Sánchez which zig-zags steeply up to a height of 450 metres with wonderful views before dropping down to the north coast. No petrol beyond Sánchez, but houses sell it in gallon jugs for US$0.80. Hotels in Las Terrenas: *Playa Bonita*, US$60, clean, good view, but very touristy; *Atlantis*, US$75d, run down, overpriced in 1991, restaurant serves "continental", but no typical food; *Acaya*, US$40d, nice atmosphere, good breakfast and restaurant, recommended; *Trópico Banana*, one of the larger guesthouses, popular bar, US$50d, Tel: 566-5941 and ask for M-40 (the hotel's radio code); *Cacao Beach*, 190 rooms, biggest hotel, Tel: 530-5817, prices from US$35 (low season); cheaper are *Las Palmas*, US$11.50; *Dinny*, on the beach, with restaurant and dancing; bungalows to right of *Dinny* as you face the sea are only a little more expensive (French-owned). Small hotels or guesthouses include *Espinal*, *La Selva*, *Habitaciones*, *Louisiane*, there are several others. Ask for Doña Nina, turn right for 800 metres along the beach in Las Terrenas, basic cabins US$2.50, very friendly. *El 28* Spanish restaurant on the beach near the start of the road to *El Portillo*, run by chef Manuel, from Coruña, and wife Txoni, fish for US$5, great paella for US$8pp; *La Salsa*, thatched roof restaurant on the beach near *Trópico Banana*, French-owned; *Chez Mammy*, on the main road, créole food, cheap, recommended. There is no mains electricity or telephone in Las Terrenas. Most guest-houses have their own generators which run from dusk to 2200, and use radio to link with the Santo Domingo telephone system.

Where the road reaches the shore, at Las Terrenas village, a left turn takes you along a sandy track that winds between coconut palms alongside the white sand beach for about 4 km, past a dozen French and Italian-run guest-houses and restaurants. At the end of the beach, walk behind a rocky promontory to reach Playa Bonita, with three more guest-houses. Beyond the western tip of this beach is the deserted Playa Cosón, a magnificent 6 km arc of white sand and coconut groves ending in steep wooded cliffs. A right turn at Las Terrenas takes you along a potholed road about 4 km to the largest hotel in the area, *El Portillo*, Tel: 685-0821, cabins (US$50d), no a/c, secluded, used by Spanish package holidays, own airstrip. 10 km further on is El Limón, a farming village on the road across the peninsula to Samaná. From El Limón you can hike for an hour into the hills to a 50-metre high waterfall and swim in a pool of green water at its foot. Behind the falls is a small cave. The landscape between the village and the falls is beautiful, with many different fruits growing in the woods. If taking a guide to the falls, fix the price in advance. *Motoconcho* Las Terrenas—El Limón US$2, but they will try to charge US$5-10. Motorcycles can be hired in Las Terrenas for US$15-20/day, also bicycles, but they have no brakes.

East from Santo Domingo

About 25 km east of Santo Domingo is the beach of **Boca Chica**, the principal resort for the capital. It is a reef-protected shallow lagoon, with many kilometres of white sand. Offshore are the islands of La Matica and Pinos. Tourist development has been intensive and, at weekends, the place is invaded by the citizens of Santo Domingo (and by attendant hawkers and prostitutes). There are a great many hotels, apartahotels and restaurants. It is worth considering staying here if arriving at the airport late at night, rather than looking for a hotel in the capital. Hotels include: *Boca Chica Beach Resort*, Tel: 567-9575, US$42d; *Sun Set*, Tel: 523-4580, Fax: 523-4975, US$32d; the new, 5-star *Hotel Hamaca*; *Sancoussi*, US$30d, clean, beautiful; *Las Brisas*, US$16d, helpful owner but not clean, very noisy, disco next door; *Caney*, US$8d (no singles). Restaurants: *L'Horizon* is excellent and *Buxeda* is recommended for seafood, especially *centolla*—crab; on the beach *fritureras* sell typical dishes, among them the famous *yaniqueques*—Johnny cakes. For cheaper meals go to Andrés, the next village, 2 km away. At the western end of the beach is the marina of the Santo Domingo Club Náutico (see above, **Beaches and Watersports**). Taxi Santo Domingo-Boca Chica US$15.40-17.30.

A few kilometres southwest of Boca Chica is La Caleta, with a small, often rough beach. It is right by the airport. Here is the only Taino burial on public display; the bones can be seen in the tombs in which they were found. Stone reproductions of Taino artefacts are on sale.

The Guayacanes and Embassy beaches, east of Boca Chica, are also popular, especially at weekends. Guayacanes is being developed. Further east again is Juan Dolio, one of the most vigorous resort developments in the country. Latest reports (1992) indicate that Juan Dolio is dirty, littered, expensive and has murky water; there are also masses of hawkers. Here too are plenty of hotels: *Metro Hotel y Marina*, Tel: 544-4580/526-1706, Fax: 526-1808, from US$73; *Marena Beach Resort* and *Tamarindo Sun Club*, for both Tel: 567-9575, prices from US$30-35d; *Punta Garza* bungalows, Tel: 529-8331, *Hotel Playacanes*, Tel: 529-8516; and many others; casino at the *Hotel Decámeron* (from US$47s to US$135d all inclusive, Tel: 530-5817) and at *Tropics* (US$115d all inclusive), reservations for both through AMHSA, Av México 66, Santo Domingo, Tel: 685-0151, Fax: 686-6741, and restaurants (eg *Oasis*, *BBQ*, *Quisqueya*, etc). *Hotel Playa Real* has Sunday buffets with dancing, use of pool and beach for US$9.25 pp (US$2.50 pool and beach only). Buses going along the south coast will drop you, and pick you up again, at the turn-off to the beaches.

Inland from this stretch of coast, if you want a change from sea bathing, there is the recommended *balneario* at Bayaguana, some 45 km from the capital.

San Pedro de Macorís (population 86,950), on the Río Higuamo, is a quiet sea port whose economy is heavily dependent on the sugar estates which surround it. Tourist development is also under way here. Facing the river is the cathedral, by which is the bus terminus. In the city is the Universidad Central del Este and a baseball stadium. There is a marked cultural influence from immigrants from the Leeward and Windward Islands, especially in the dances called *guloyas*. Another name is *momise*, which derives from the English mummer tradition; dance-dramas known as *la danza salvaje* (the wild dance), *la danza del padre invierno* (the dance of Father Winter, which imitates the St George and the Dragon legend) and *la danza de El Codril* take place on 29 June, St Peter, and other festivals. For further information Tel: 529-3600 (Ayuntamiento) or 529-3309 (provincial government). (Hotel: *Macorix*, Tel: 596-3950, US$15-20.)

East of San Pedro is **La Romana**, population 101,350). (Hotels: *Frano*, 21 rooms, US$16 with a/c, less without, inconveniently located away from main plaza and restaurants; *Condado*, 24 rooms; *Cabañas Tío Tom*; *San Santiago*, Calle Hernández, US$10s with bath; *Pensión de Aza*, Ramón Bergés y A Miranda, at plaza, US$5.65s without bath, basic; *dormitorio*, US$2, dark, basic, but ok, from southeast corner of market go 2½ blocks west and it's on the right. Good restaurant, *De América*). La Romana can be reached by air (international airport) and by bus or *público* from Santo Domingo (US$3.55 and US$3.95 respectively). *Casa de Campo*, near La Romana, is the premier tourist centre in the republic, P O Box 140, Tel: 523-3333/221-1511, Fax: 523-8548: hotel, villas, bars, restaurants and country club with many sporting facilities (on land and sea) in 7,000 acres, prices start at US$96, low season, rising to US$230-890, high season. The Playa Minitas beach is within the complex. An international artists' village in mock-Italian style has been established at Altos de Chavón, near La Romana, in a spectacular hilltop setting; there is a free bus every 15 minutes from *Casa de Campo*. Taxi from La Romana US$4. There are a hotel here, two restaurants, a Museo Arqueológico Regional, open 0900-1700 (free) and an amphitheatre which was inaugurated with a show by Frank Sinatra (many international stars perform there, as well as the best Dominican performers).

Off La Romana is the Isla Catalina, to which Costa Lines run excursions for the day, US$30 including lunch, supper and drinks; Tel: 685-7910, Maritissant, for details. Costa is to build a cruise ship terminal on the island.

Although inland the south eastern part of the island is dry, flat and monotonous, the beaches have fine, white sand with some of the best bathing in waters protected by reefs and excellent diving. The area is being heavily developed and by 1992 there should be about 9,000 hotel beds available. Following the coastal road east, you come to **Bayahibe**, a fishing village on a small bay (*Hotel Bayahibe*, US$16s with bath, new, very clean; *Bahía* restaurant right on the sea, excellent lobster for US$12) and just round the point there is an excellent, 1.5 km curving white sand beach with no hotels and just a couple of restaurants. A coral reef with sponges is popular with divers. About 10 km southeast is *Dominicus*, an Italian-run tourist complex with its own beach, Tel: 530-5817/686-5638 (prices start at US$54 pp). Sandflies can be a nuisance.

Further east is **Boca de Yuma**, an interesting fishing village which is the scene of a deep-sea fishing tournament every June. A recently repaved road runs from Boca de Yuma inland to Higüey; along this, about 2 km north of San Rafael de Yuma, is the restored residence of Ponce de León (1505-1508).

Higüey has the Basílica de Nuestra Señora de la Altagracia (patroness of the Republic), a very impressive modern building to which every year there is a pilgrimage on 21 January; the old 16th century church is still standing. (Plenty of cheap hotels on Calle Colón; also *Brisas del Este*. Buses from Santo Domingo cost US$3.55, *públicos* US$3.95; bus from La Romana US$2.40.) Due east from Higüey, on the coast again, is **Punta Cana** which has some beautiful beaches and good diving; there is a *Club Méditerranée* (Tel: 567-5228, Fax: 565-2558, P O Box 106, Higüey, US$400 low season, US$750d high per week), a new *Meliá* hotel (Tel: 530-5817, US$72d) and an international airport five minutes away. Accommodation at the *Punta Cana Beach Resort* (Tel: 541-2714/530-5817, Fax: 541-2286, P O Box 1083) costs US$85 pp (55 low season), or US$152d MAP (99 low season), beautiful beach, good diving, but sparse public transport. Most people staying there arrive by plane and only leave the resort on a tour bus; a taxi to Higüey costs US$6, *Club Med's* bus to Higüey US$6.40, and there is transport provided for employees. The *Punta Cana Yacht Club* has villas and one-bedroom apartments, golf course under construction, Tel: 565-3077. Continuing round the coast, there are many other beaches to be visited, with white sand and reef-sheltered water. Another resort on the eastern tip, *Bavaro-Beach* and *Bavaro Gardens* has the largest hotel in the country with 1,000 rooms on a 2 km beach, Tel: 530-5817/682-2162, Fax: 682-2169, P O Box 1, Higüey, to which charter flights go. Hotel rates US$122-177 in high season, (from US$43 low season) half board. Take a taxi from Higüey. If exploring the eastern tip, Spanish is essential. A road runs west from Higüey to Hato Mayor, via El Seibo; its first 30 km to the El Pintado junction with the road from La Romana is dusty and in poor condition (unpaved). From here to **El Seibo** (16 km) is good. (Bus San Pedro de Macorís-Hato Mayor, US$0.80). El Seibo is a quiet little town with painted houses (*Hotel Las Mercedes*, US$4.50, is clean, quiet, pleasant, no generator; the town's water supply depends on the electricity supply). A *guagua* can be taken to El Llano (US$0.50), from where you can either return to El Seibo, or continue on foot to Miches on the coast (two days, lovely scenery).

West from Santo Domingo

The far southwest of the Republic is a dry zone with typical dry-forest vegetation. A new highway has been built from the capital, cutting journey times to half what they used to be. Tourist development is proceeding apace and by the mid-1990s a number of resorts should be operating. For the time being, exploring by car is the best way to enjoy this relatively untouched area.

To the west of Santo Domingo is Haina, the country's main port and an industrial zone. It has a teachers' vacation centre (with accommodation at US$1.60 a day) and a country club with swimming pool.

Further west one can visit **San Cristóbal** in the interior, 25 km from the capital, the birthplace of the dictator Rafael Leonidas Trujillo. Trujillo's home, the Casa de Caoba (now rapidly disintegrating, but open 0900-1700) may be reached by *público* from behind the market (US$4.75), or by motorcycle taxi (US$0.25), though you may have to walk the last kilometre, uphill. You can also visit El Palacio del Cerro, the luxury residence which he built but never lived in. Both buildings are being restored. Also due for restoration are the Iglesia Parroquial and the Ingenio Diego Caballero, a colonial sugar mill at Boca de Nigua. Other attractions are the Palacio del Ayuntamiento in which the republic's first constitution was signed, the Iglesia de Piedras Vivas, the caves at El Pomier (with Taino petroglyphs) and the Santa María caves, where African-influenced stick and drum festivals are held. The local saint's day festival is from 6-10 June. Nearby are La Toma natural pools, for scenery and swimming, and the beaches at Palenque, Nigua and Najayo. At the last named are the ruins of Trujillo's beach house. Hotels: *San Cristóbal*, *Constitución*, cheaper, former has a disco, and there are others in town. A famous local dish is *pasteles en hojas*, made from plátano, minced meat and other ingredients. Minibus Santo Domingo-San Cristóbal from the Malecón, US$0.65, *público* US$1; radio taxi US$10.75-16.15; La Covancha company organizes group transport (27 passengers) to San Cristóbal, La Toma and Palenque Beach.

From San Cristóbal the road runs west to **Baní**, birthplace of Máximo Gómez, 19th century fighter for the liberation of Cuba. The town is a major producer of sugar cane, coffee, vegetables, bananas and salt. The parish church is Nuestra Señora de Regla (festival, 21 November). *Hotel Brisas del Sur* (Tel: 522-3548); cheaper hotels to be found near the market on Máximo Gómez; minibus from Santo Domingo, US$1.60. The local goats' milk sweets from Paya are renowned throughout the country. Don't bother with the beach (although at Los Almendros a tourist development is being built), better to carry on to Las Salinas. Las Tablas, a village nearby, was one of the last places to conserve indigenous ways of life. On the Bahía de Calderas are salt marshes, a military base and sand dunes unique to this part of the country. The fishing village of Palmar de Ocoa hosts a fishing tournament each year and a number of summer houses have been built there. The main road, in excellent condition, carries on from Baní through Azua to Barahona. **Azua** de Compostela was founded in 1504 on the orders of Fray Nicolás de Ovando; at one time Puerto Viejo was an alternative port to Santo Domingo. An important victory by Dominican troops against the Haitian army took place here on 19 March 1844. The main beach is Monte Río. Hotels: *Altagracia*, Tel: 521-3813, *Brisas del Mar*, Tel: 521-3813 also; *El Familiar*, Tel: 521-3656; *Hotel Restaurant San Ramón*, Tel: 521-3529 (none is of high quality). Restaurants: *El Gran Segovia*, *José Segundo*, *Mi Bosquecito Bar*, *Patio Español*. Santo Domingo-Azua is 2 hours by *guagua*, US$2.35, *público* US$2.75, and Azua has good bus connections for Barahona, under 2 hours, US$1.80, San Juan and Padre Las Casas.

At **Barahona** *Hotel Guarocuya* is particularly recommended, being cheap, clean and on the beach at Saladilla (the dawns here are spectacular), US$11.60 for double room with fan, more with a/c; also *Hotel Barahona* on Calle Jaime Mora, *Cacique*, slightly cheaper, nice, and *Fenicia*, *Palace* and *Victoria*, US$8s; adequate *Hotel Caribe*, same range as *Cacique*, basic, with an excellent open-air restaurant (*La Rocca*) next door. Journey time from the capital is 2½ hours. Minibus fare is US$2.35, *público* US$3.15, Caribe Tours runs buses (group transport also available with Metro Tours, La Covacha and Taxi Raffi). The province of Barahona produces coffee (excursions can be made to Platón or Santa Elena), sugar, grapes, salt, bananas and other fruits.

Be careful when swimming at the small, public beach at Barahona, as there are frequently stinging jelly fish. Those with a car can visit other, more remote beaches from Barahona (public transport is limited to *públicos*). A new road has been built south of Barahona, running down the coast through some of the most beautiful scenery in the republic, mountains on one side, the sea on the other, leading to Pedernales on the Haitian border (146 km). All along the southern coast are many white sand beaches which offer the best snorkelling and scuba diving in the Republic. One such is San Rafael (about 40 minutes from Barahona) where there is a fresh-water swimming hole in the river at the end of the beach. There is a small, pleasant restaurant on the beach and it is possible to camp. At weekends it gets very crowded. There are cool, fresh-water lagoons behind several of the other beaches on this stretch of coast. Limón lagoon is a flamingo reserve. At the village of Enriquillo, 54 km south of Barahona, a new dock has been constructed (*Hotel Dajtra*, on main road, US$2, basic; the only place with light at night is a disco where half the village hangs out, its prices are "normal"). One must explore for oneself: the area is not developed for tourism, yet. It is scheduled for development when Punta Cana is finished.

William E Rainey, of Berkeley, California, writes: "South from Barahona between Baoruco and Enriquillo there is wet tropical forest with rushing mountain streams and fruit stands in little roadside settlements. At Enriquillo you enter the Barahona Peninsula lowlands and the terrain grows markedly drier. Continuing west from Oviedo to Pedernales the road is in good condition and the surrounding habitat, particularly near Pedernales, is tropical thorn scrub with abundant cacti growing on karstic limestone.

"The entire country is dotted with checkpoints adjacent to roadside military installations; at most of these the traffic is simply waved through. At the checkpoint in Pedernales (perhaps because gringos were an anomaly there) there were brief interrogations each time we passed (with automatic weapons pointed at us by uniformed teenagers). The last time we passed this point, one of them initiated a detailed search of our gear. Fortunately, this entertainment was cut short by a senior officer who apologized. It was, on balance, a minor aggravation, but one likely to be experienced by travellers near the Haitian border."

Pedernales is the most westerly town of the republic, on the Haitian border. Beautiful beaches include Cabo Rojo and Bahía de las Aguilas, where there is abundant fishing. Here is the Parque Nacional Jaragua in which are the islands Beata and Alto Velo; many iguanas.

Inland from Barahona, near the Haitian border, is **Lago Enriquillo**, whose waters, 30 metres below sea level, are three times saltier than the sea. It has a wealth of wild life including crocodiles (best seen in the morning), iguanas and flamingoes. The iguanas can, however, only be seen on the largest of the three islands in the lake, which make up the Cabritos National Park (see **Flora and Fauna** above) which is also where the crocodiles lay their eggs and spend their nights. A large colony of flamingoes overwinters at the lake. You need to purchase a Dirección Nacional de Parques (DNP) permit (US$3.95) to visit the island and only groups with a guide are permitted to go there. The two smaller islands are Barbarita and La Islita. To visit the lake it is best to stay in Barahona at the *Hotel Guarocuya* and go by car, though it is possible to get there by bus from Santo Domingo to Jimaní (US$5, La Experiencia and Riviera companies; the journey takes 8 hours) and getting off either at Los Ríos or at La Descubierta. From these places walk or hitch a lift to the lake. At Jimaní at least one of the hotels has closed but here is accommodation in basic, low cost *dormitorios*. It is possible to take a tour to this region from the capital with Ecoturisa (Tel: 221-4104), Maritissant (see **Tourist Travel** in **Information for Visitors**) and Grupo Nuevos Horizontes (Tel: 682-1068), US$40 staying overnight in tents. The DNP also runs tours; group travel is also possible with Taxi Raffi, Compañia Nacional de Autobuses or Metro Tours, and others.

For drivers, the road around the lake has been completely reconstructed. *La*

Descubierta, at the northwest end, is larger than Jimaní, has several *dormitorios* (unmarked dormitorio on the corner opposite the disco on the central square, US$4, very basic), a disco, and a celebrated *balneario* (swimming hole, highly recommended). It is the best place on the lake to stay. There are two routes from Barahona: via Neiba and Villa Jaragua (Barahona-Neiba, 1½ hours, US$1, and from there Neiba-La Descubierta, there appear to be *guaguas*, US$0.70 if you are lucky), or via Davergé and Jimaní. From these routes the *balnearios* at Las Marías and Las Barías (very cold) can be visited. Between Barahona and Neiba is Las Caritas where Taíno petroglyphs have been preserved. To get to the Isla Cabritos National Park, drive 4 km southeast of the town to La Zofrada. Below the road on a curve is a building where arrangements can be made (US$15 for 4 people). Bathe in the sulphur springs, La Azufrada, while you wait, or on the way back; many people take their medicinal waters.

San Juan de la Maguana is on the main road to the Haitian border at Comendador. Soldiers frequently patrol this route. Visit the Corral de Los Indios, an ancient Indian meeting ground several km north of the San Juan. (Hotels: *Tamarindo*, Tel: 541-2211; *Maguana*, Tel: 557-2244, US$15 or so.)

Information for Visitors

Documents

Citizens of the following countries do not need a tourist card to enter the Dominican Republic: Argentina, Austria, Denmark, Ecuador, Finland, Greece, Ireland, Israel, Italy, Japan, Liechtenstein, Norway, South Korea, Spain, Sweden, Switzerland, UK, Uruguay. All others need a tourist card, which costs US$10, purchased from consulates, tourist offices or at the airport on arrival. Immigration officers usually leave the time limit blank, but if necessary extensions are obtainable from Immigration, Huacal Building, Santo Domingo (Tel: 685-2505/2535). Check all entry requirements in advance if possible.

All visitors should have an outward ticket (not always asked for).

Customs

The airport police are on the lookout for illegal drugs. It is also illegal to bring firearms into the country.

Duty-free import of 200 cigarettes or one box of cigars, plus one litre of alcoholic liquor and gift articles to the value of US$100, is permitted. Military-type clothing and food products will be confiscated on arrival. Currency in excess of US$5,000 may not be taken out of the country without special permission.

How To Get There By Air

American and Dominicana fly from Miami and New York. Continental also from New York. Dominicana, Copa and American fly from San Juan. Iberia flies from Madrid several times a week and has connecting flights from most European and Spanish cities, eg Amsterdam, Barcelona, Bilbao, Brussels, Frankfurt, Lisbon, London, Milan, Rome. Iberia also flies from Guatemala City. Air France from Paris (via Martinique or Guadeloupe), with a Santo Domingo – Port-au-Prince flight once a week. Alitalia flies from Rome and TAP from Lisbon, each once a week. Air Aruba has flights from Aruba, ALM from Curaçao and both from Sint Maarten. Aeropostal from Curaçao; Copa from Panama City. Flights from South America: Avianca and Iberia fly Bogotá-Santo Domingo; Viasa, Dominicana and Aeropostal fly from Caracas; other capital cities are connected through Miami.

To the international airport at Puerto Plata there are flights from Miami, New York, Nashville, Washington and Puerto Rico by American, also from New York, Continental, Hispaniola Airways and Dominicana; from Miami, Dominicana and Hispaniola Airways; from Amsterdam, Martinair; from Dusseldorf, LTU International, from Grand Turk and Providenciales, TCNA.

Airport Information

There is a departure tax of US$10. Details of airports are given in the text above.

Airline Offices

In Santo Domingo: Aeropostal, Abraham Lincoln, Tel: 541-4232; Air Canada, Kennedy y Lope de Vega, Tel: 567-2236;

Air France, Av George Washington 101, Tel: 686- 8419; ALM, L Navarro 28, Tel: 687-4569; American, Edificio IN TEMPO, Tel: 542-5151; Avianca, R Pastoriza 401, Tel: 562-1797; Continental, Edificio IN TEMPO, Tel: 562-6688; Copa, Tiradentes 10, Tel: 562-5824; Dominicana, Av Jiménez Moya, Tel: 532-1146; Iberia, El Conde 401, Tel: 685-7171; Lufthansa, George Washington 353, Tel: 689-9625; Viasa, L Navarro 28, Tel: 687-2688.

By Sea

There are cargo and passenger shipping services with New York, New Orleans, Miami and South American countries. Many cruise lines from USA, Canada and Europe call at the Dominican Republic on itineraries to various ports on Caribbean islands or the mainland. Agencies which handle cruises are Emely (Tel: 682-2744, for Festival, Holidays, Jubilee, Sur Viking), Vimenca (Tel: 532-7381, for Costa, Norwegian Cruise Lines, Carnival, Royal Caribbean), Caribe International (Tel: 541-5151).

Travel To Haiti

No special permit is needed, just a passport or visa (check if you need one, US$12, takes a day). Haitian Embassy, Juan Sánchez Ramírez 33, Tel: 686-5778, Santo Domingo. By plane to Port-au-Prince takes ½ hour, US$50 approximately; by bus US$40 about twice a week from *Hotel San Tomé*, Calle Santomé, beside Mercado Modelo, Santo Domingo (Tel: 688-5100, ask for Alejandro). Also try Línea Sur, Tel: 682-7682. Alternatively, take a minibus to Jimaní from near the bridge over the Río Seco in the centre of Santo Domingo, about 6 hours; get a lift up to the Haitian border and then get overcharged by Haitian youths on mopeds who take you across 3 km of no-man's-land for US$3. From Haitian immigration take a lorry-bus to Port-au-Prince, 3-4 hours, very dusty. If driving to Haiti you must get a vehicle permit at the Foreign Ministry (Tel: 533-1424). The drive from Santo Domingo to Port-au-Prince takes about six hours.

To Cuba

Emely Tours in Santo Domingo (Tel: 682-2744) run weekly excursions to Cuba, US$500. Many Dominicans used to take advantage of Cuba's medical facilities, but since the increase in Cuban medical fees it is not known how popular the flights are, nor their cost, nor their availability to foreigners.

Internal Travel

Agencia Portillo (Tel: 565-0832) offers air taxi services to Puerto Plata and Punta Cana, US$32 including transfers and a meal, Herrera airport. Other domestic flights are operated by Servicio Aéreo Dominicano, Tel: 541-2667, Aeronaves Dominicanas, Tel: 567-7195 and others. Dorado Air flies between Santo Domingo and Puerto Plata three times a day on Friday, Saturday and Sunday. Flights go to Santiago, Puerto Plata, Barahona, Portillo and La Romana daily.

Hitchhiking is perfectly possible, though bus (*guagua*) services between most towns are efficient and inexpensive. In rural areas it can be easy to find a *guagua* (mini bus or pickup) but they are often filled to the point where you can not move your legs.

There are usually fixed *público* rates (see under Santo Domingo) between cities, so inquire first. Average rates in 1992 from Santo Domingo were: Puerto Plata, US$4.75; Santiago, US$2.05 and US$2.75; Barahona, US$3.15; Boca Chica, US$2.05; La Romana, US$3.95; Río San Juan, US$6.85; San Juan de la Maguana, US$4.80. Many drivers pack a truly incredible number of passengers in their cars, so the ride is often not that comfortable. If travelling by private taxi, bargaining is very important.

Motorcyclists (*motoconchos*) also offer a taxi service and take several passengers on pillion. In some towns eg Samaná, motoconchos pull 4-seater covered rickshaws. Negotiate fare first. If negotiating transport by boat, a *canuco* is a small dugout, a *yola* is a medium-sized rowing boat taking up to 10 passengers, a *bote* takes 20 or more.

Buses

Services from Santo Domingo: Autobuses Metro (Tel: 566-7126) operate from Av Winston Churchill and Hatuey, near 27 de Febrero and have buses to La Vega (US$2.70), Santiago (US$3.95), Puerto Plata (US$5.40), Nagua, Azua, San Juan, San Pedro de Macorís and other points. Caribe Tours, (Tel: 687-3171/6) operates from Av 27 de Febrero at Leopoldo Navarro (and Av Sadhalá in Santiago); most of their services (cheaper than Metro) are in air-conditioned buses, recommended (eg US$4.25 to Puerto Plata, US$3 to Santiago, US$2.30 to La

Vega and Jarabacoa); they run to all parts except east of Santo Domingo. Transporte del Cibao, opposite Parque Enriquillo, to Puerto Plata, US$2.95. Also to Santiago, Terrabús, US$3.95, and El Expreso, US$1.30. La Covacha buses leave from Parque Enriquillo (Av Duarte and Ravelo) for the east: Higüey (US$3.55), Nagua, San Pedro de Macorís, Miches, etc. Expresos Moto Saad, Av Independencia near Parque Independencia runs 12 daily buses to Bonao and La Vega (US$2). Línea Sur (Tel: 682-7682) runs to San Juan, Barahona, Azua and Haiti. Guaguas for Azua, 2 hours US$2.35, depart from Av Bolívar near Parque Independencia; easy connections in Azua for Barahona, San Juan and Padre las Casas. In Puerto Plata, Metro, Tel: 586-6063; Caribe, Tel: 586-4544.

Tourist Travel

A number of companies hire vehicles for group travel, which is fairly economical as long as you have a large enough number of friends. For instance Transporte Turístico Tanya, Tel: 565-5691, 24-seat buses to Puerto Plata, US$195; Autobuses Metro, Tel: 566-7126, 54-seaters to Puerto Plata, US$578; Compañia Nacional de Autobuses, Tel: 565-6681, 25, 45 and 60 seaters, US$272, US$315, US$317 respectively to Puerto Plata. Other destinations also served. LC Tours and La Covacha run 30-seat minibus trips to the east of the country, including Samaná. Taxi companies (eg Apolo, Raffi, addresses under Santo Domingo) run trips to towns in the republic, again as an example, US$100-120 to Puerto Plata.

Maritissant, Tel: 685-7910, has tours to the national parks, also group travel, some with overnight stops in a hotel: Lago Enriquillo, 27 people, US$27 pp (including drinks and lunch), Parque del Este, US$78, Isla Saona, US$31 (one day), US$55 (overnight); plus tours to La Isabela, US$95, Boca Chica, US$55, and Santo Domingo City Tours US$24. Many other companies operate tours (some are mentioned in the text above).

The Museo de Historia y Geografía in Santo Domingo organizes archaeological and historical tours in the east of the country, visiting the Casa de Ponce de León, San Rafael del Yuma, the colonial church in Higüey, the Basílica Nuestra Señora de la Altagracia and Altos de Chavón (La Romana). The tour is by bus; Tel: 686-6668.

Driving

A valid driving licence from your country of origin or an international licence is accepted. Dominicans drive on the right. The main road from Santo Domingo to Puerto Plata, the Carreterra Duarte, is very good, but most other roads are in poor condition with lots of potholes, so avoid night driving. The main exception is in the southwest, where new roads have been built. The speed limit for city driving is 40 kph, for suburban areas 60 kph and on main roads 80 kph. Service stations generally close at 1800, although there are now some offering 24-hour service (petrol/gasoline costs just under US$1 per gallon). Cars driven by tourists can expect to be stopped by the police at the entrance to and exit from towns (normally brief and courteous); most police or military posts have "sleeping policemen", speed humps, usually unmarked, outside them. Local drivers can be erratic; be on the alert. Beware motorcyclists in towns. There are tolls on all principal roads out of the capital: US$0.08 going east, US$0.04 going west. Road signs are very poor: a detailed map is essential, plus a knowledge of Spanish for asking directions.

If renting a car, avoid the cheapest companies because their vehicles are not usually trustworthy; it is better to pay more with a well-known agency. Car rental is expensive because of high import tariffs on vehicles (rates are given under **Car Rentals** in Santo Domingo). Credit cards are widely accepted; the cash deposit is normally twice the sum of the contract. The minimum age for hiring a car is 25; maximum period for driving is 90 days.

Mopeds and motorcycles are everywhere and are very noisy. Most beach resorts hire motorcycles for between US$15 and 25 a day.

Accommodation

Hotels are given under the towns in which they are situated. Note that 5-star hotels charge an average of US$140, plus 23% tax. In apartahotels, the average price is US$130 for two. In more modest guest houses, a weekly or monthly rate, with discount, can be arranged. All hotels charge the 23% tax; the VAT component is 8%.

The better hotels have a high occupancy rate and it is best to book in advance, particularly at holiday times. Standards in the five-star hotels are not equivalent to those, say, in the Bahamas. You will frequently hear 'No problem, no problem' from the staff when something does not work, a refrain which has become so common that T-shirts are now sold with the words 'No Problem' printed on them.

Food and Drink

Local dishes include *sancocho* or *salcocho prieto* (a type of stew made of six local meats and vegetables, often including *plátanos*, *ñame* and *yautia*), *mondongo* (a tripe stew), *mofongo*, ground *plátano* with garlic and *chicharrón de cerdo* (pork crackling), usually served with a soup, a side dish of meat and avocado (very filling), *chicharrón de pollo* is small pieces of chicken prepared with lime and oregano, *locrio de cerdo* or *pollo* (meat and rice), *cocido* (a soup of chickpeas, meat and vegetables), *asopao de pollo* or *de camarones*, *chivo* (goat). Also try *pipián*, goats' offal served as a stew. Fish and seafood are good; lobster can be found for as little as US$12. Fish cooked with coconut (eg *pescado con coco*) is popular around Samaná. The salads are often good; another good side dish is *tostones* (fried and flattened *plátanos*), *fritos verdes* are the same thing. *Plátano* mashed with oil is called *mangú*, often served with rice and beans. Sweet bananas are often called *guineo*. *Quipes* (made of flour and meat) and *pastelitos* (fried dough with meat or cheese inside) can be bought from street vendors; can be risky. *Casabe* is a cassava bread, flat and round, best toasted. *Catibias* are cassava flour fritters with meat. The most common dish is called *bandera dominicana*, white rice, beans, meat/chicken, *plátano* or *yuca* and, in season, avocado. The traveller should be warned that Dominican food is rather on the greasy side; most of the dishes are fried. Local food can often be obtained from private houses, which act as *comedores*. Basic prices, US$3-6.

Juices, or *jugos*, are good; orange is usually called *china*, papaya is *lechosa*, passion fruit is *chinola*. *Agua de coco* is coconut milk, often served cold, straight from the coconut, chilled in an ice box. Local beers, Presidente, Bohemia, Quisqueya and Heineken, are excellent. There are also many good rums (the most popular brands are Barceló, Brugal, Bermúdez, Macorix and Carta Vieja). Light rum (*blanco*) is the driest and has the highest proof, usually mixed with fruit

juice or other soft drink (*refresco*). Amber (*amarillo*) is aged at least a year in an oak barrel and has a lower proof and more flavour, while dark rum (*añejo*) is aged for several years and is smooth enough, like a brandy, to be drunk neat or with ice and lime. Brugal allows visitors to tour its factory in Puerto Plata, on Colón between Duarte and Beller, and offers free daiquiris. In a discothèque, *un servicio* is a 1/3 litre bottle of rum with a bucket of ice and *refrescos*. In rural areas this costs US$3-4, but in cities rises to US$15. Imported drinks are very expensive. Many of the main hotels have a 'Happy Hour' from 1800-2000, on a 'two for one' basis, ie two drinks for the price of one with free snacks.

Tipping

In addition to the 16% service and 8% VAT charge in restaurants, it is customary to give an extra tip of about 10% in restaurants, depending on service. Porters receive US$0.50 per bag; taxi drivers, *público* drivers and garage attendants are not usually tipped.

Best Buys

The native amber is sold throughout the country. Larimar, a sea-blue stone, and red and black coral are also available (remember that black coral is protected). Other items which make good souvenirs are leather goods, basketware, weavings and onyx jewellery. The *muñeca sin rostro* (faceless doll) has become a sort of symbol of the Dominican Republic, at least, as something to take home. There are excellent cigars at very reasonable prices.

Note

There are well-trained guides who speak two or more languages, usually congregated around the Cathedral in Santo Domingo, who are courteous and do not push themselves on you. However, in Santo Domingo, on the beaches and at other tourist attractions, visitors will be approached by unofficial English-speaking guides, sellers of rum, women or black market pesos. The last three are undoubtedly a rip-off and probably the only value in taking an unofficial guide is to deter others from pestering you (similarly, hiring a lounger chair on the beach). Beware of drug-pushers on the Malecón in Santo Domingo and near the Cathedral in Puerto Plata. It has been reported to us that these unofficial guides refuse to give prices in advance and then at the end, if they are not happy with the tip, they make a scene and threaten to tell the police that the customer had approached them to deal in drugs etc. Guides also collaborate with street money changers to cheat the tourist. Single men have complained of the massive presence of pimps and prostitutes. Be prepared to say "no" a lot.

It must be stressed that these problems do not occur in rural areas and small towns, where travellers have been impressed with the open and welcoming nature of the Dominicans.

Violent crime against tourists is rare but be careful about thieving and watch your money and valuables. The streets of Santo Domingo are not considered safe after 2300. Purse snatchers on motorcycles operate in cities.

Banks

The Central Bank determines monetary policy. Among the commercial banks in the Republic are Scotiabank (Santo Domingo, Santiago, and Puerto Plata), Chase Manhattan (Santo Domingo and Santiago), Citibank (Santo Domingo and Santiago – does not change travellers' cheques), Banco de Reservas, Banco Popular, Banco Metropolitano, Banco Central, Bancrédito, Intercontinental, Banco Dominicano Hispano, Banco Mercantil and others.

Currency

The Dominican peso (RD$) is the only legal tender. The peso is divided into 100 centavos. There are coins in circulation of 1, 5, 10, 25 and 50 centavos, and notes of 1, 5, 10, 20, 50, 100, 500 and 1,000 pesos. In 1991, new legislation outlawed all exchange transactions except those in branches of the major banks. You will be given a receipt and, with this, you can change remaining pesos back into dollars at the end of your visit. Do not rely on the airport bank being open. Most European currencies can be changed at the Banco de Reservas (and some other banks). The black market usually offers rates higher than the official rate; illegal money changers on the street approach foreigners (do *not* use them, sometimes they work with a policeman who will demand a large bribe not to imprison you).

Health

It is not advisable to drink tap water. All hotels have bottled water. The supply of drinking water in Santo Domingo was

improved in 1992. The local greasy food, if served in places with dubious hygiene, may cause stomach problems. Hepatitis is common. It is also advisable to avoid the midday sun.

Climate

The climate is tropical. The rainy months are May, June, August, September and November. The temperature shows little seasonal change, and varies between 18° and 32°C. Only in December does the temperature fall, averaging about 20°C. Humidity can be high, particularly in coastal areas, making physical activity difficult.

Clothing

Light clothing, preferably cotton, is best all year round. It is recommended to take one formal outfit since some hotels and nightclubs do not permit casual dress.

Business Hours

Offices: 0830-1230, 1430-1830; some offices and shops work 0930-1730 Monday-Friday, 0800-1300 Saturday. Banks: 0830-1730 Monday-Friday. Government offices 0730-1430. Shop hours are normally 0800-1900, some open all day Saturday and mornings on Sunday and holidays.

Public Holidays

New Year's Day (1 January), Epiphany (6 January), Our Lady of Altagracia (21 January), Duarte Day (26 January), Independence Day (27 February), Good Friday, Labour Day (1 May), Corpus Christi (60 days after Good Friday), Restoration Day (16 August), Our Lady of Las Mercedes (24 September), Christmas (25 December).

Time Zone

Atlantic Standard Time, 4 hours behind GMT, 1 hour ahead of EST.

Useful Addresses

US Embassy and Consulate, César Nicolás Penson, Tel: (embassy) 541-2171, (consulate) 689-2111; **Canada**, Máximo Gómez 30, Tel: 689-0002; **UK**, Independencia 506, Tel: 682-3128 (Honorary Consul, Maureen Tejada, St George School, Abraham Lincoln 552, Tel: 562-5010); **Germany**, J T Majía y Calle 37, Tel: 565-8811; **France**, George Washington 353, Tel: 689-2161; **Netherlands**, John F Kennedy 12, Tel: 565-5240; **Spain**, Independencia 1205, Tel: 533-1424; **Switzerland**, Tel: 689-4131; **Venezuela**, Bolívar 832, Tel:

687-5066; **Israel**, P. Henríquez Ureña 8, Tel: 687-7888; **Jamaica**, J. Contreras 98, Tel: 532-1079; **Japan**, Torre BHD, Tel: 567-3365.

Churches
Roman Catholicism is the predominant religion. There are also Episcopalian, Baptist, Seventh Day Adventist, Presbyterian and Methodist churches in the main towns. There is a synagogue on Avenida Sarasota, Santo Domingo; call the Israeli Embassy (533-7359) for details of services. Voodoo, technically illegal, is tolerated and practised mostly in the western provinces.

Electric Current
110 volts, 60 cycles AC current. American-type, flat-pin plugs are used. There are frequent power cuts, often for several hours, so take a torch with you when you go out at night. Many establishments have their own (often noisy) generators. There was improvement to the capital's supply in 1992.

Weights And Measures
Officially the metric system is used but business is often done on a pound/yard/US gallon basis. Land areas in cities are measured by square metres, but in the countryside by the *tarea*, one of which equals 624 square metres.

Postal Services
Don't use post boxes, they are unreliable. For each 10 grams, or fraction thereof, the cost to Europe is 1 peso; to North America, Venezuela, Central America and the Caribbean, 50 centavos; to elsewhere in the Americas and Spain, 70 centavos; to Africa, Australia, Asia and Oceania, RD$1.50. It is recommended to use *entrega especial* (special delivery, with separate window at post offices), for 2 pesos extra, on overseas mail, or better still a courier service (see under Santo Domingo).

Telephones
Operated by the Compañía Dominicana de Teléfonos (Codetel), a subsidiary of GTE. All local calls and overseas calls to the Caribbean, European Community, US and Canada may be dialled directly from Santo Domingo. For phone boxes you need two 5-centavo coins or one 10-centavo coin. Phone calls to the USA cost US$7.85, to Europe US$8.50, to Australia US$9.60 and Argentina US$14.80 (3 mins). AT &T's USA-Direct is available on 1-800-872-2881, US$1.45 for the first minute, US$1.06 additional and US$2.50 service charge. Codetel publishes a bilingual Spanish/English business telephone directory for tourism (a sort of tourist's yellow pages), called the *Dominican Republic Tourist Guide/Guía Turística de la República Dominicana*, which contains a lot of information as well as telephone numbers. Emergency number: 711.

Newspapers
There are 10 daily papers in all, seven in the morning, three in the afternoon. *Listín Diario* has the widest circulation; among the other morning papers are *El Caribe*, *Hoy*, *El Siglo* and *El Nuevo Diario*. In the afternoon, *Ultima Hora*, *El Nacional* and *La Noticia* are published. The English-language *Santo Domingo News*, published every Wednesday, is available at hotels. *La Información*, published in Santiago, carries international news in English on its front page.

Broadcasting
There are over 170 local radio stations and 7 television stations. Also 1 cable TV

station broadcasting in English.

Maps

Publicaciones Triunfo has a map of the Dominican Republic, with plans of Santo Domingo, Santiago, Puerto Plata and Sosúa. Texaco also produce a good (Rand McNally) map of the country, capital and Santiago. A set of five (US$11) covering the whole country can be got at Instituto Geográfico Universitario, El Conde with Las Damas.

Tourist Information

The head office of the Secretaría de Estado de Turismo is in the Edificio de Oficinas Gubernamentales, Avenida México esquina Calle Dr Delgado, Ala "D", near the Palacio Nacional (PO Box 497, Tel: 682-8181, 1-800-752-1151, Fax: 682-3806); it publishes a tourism guide called La Cotica. There are also offices at Las Américas International Airport, La Unión Airport at Puerto Plata, in Puerto Plata (Malecón 20, Tel: 586-3676), in Santiago (Ayuntamiento, Tel: 582-5885), Jimaní, Samaná and Boca Chica.

Outside the Dominican Republic, there are tourist offices in the **USA**: 485 Madison Avenue, 2nd Floor, New York, NY 10022,

Tel: (212) 826-0750, or Tel: 800-752-1151 (toll free), and 2 other New York locations; 2 East Fayette Street, 11th floor, Baltimore, Maryland 21202, Tel: (301) 576-2050, Fax: 576-2066; Woot Street, P O Box 75202, Dallas, Texas, Tel: (214) 670-9800, Fax: 670-9782; 2355 Salzedo Street, Suite 305, Coral Gables, Miami, Florida 33134, Tel: 444-4592/3, Fax: 444-4845, and 5 other Miami locations; in **Canada**: 24 Bellair Street, Toronto, Ontario, M5R 2C7, Tel: (416) 928-9188; 1464 Crescent Street, Montréal, Québec, H3A 2B6, Tel: (514) 845-6525; in **Puerto Rico**: Edificio Miramar Plaza, Ponce de León 954, San Juan, Tel: (809) 725-4774; in **Venezuela**: Oficentro Rovica, piso 3, oficina 3, Boulevard Sabana Grande, Caracas, Tel: 71-77-67; in **Spain**: Núñez de Balboa 37, 4° Izquierda, Madrid 1, Tel: (01) 431-5354; in **Germany**, Voelckerstrasse 24, D-6000 Frankfurt am Main 1, Tel: (49-69) 597-0330, Fax: 590982.

For their help in updating this chapter, we are most grateful to Dania Goris, resident in Santo Domingo and Dianne Erdos (Sosúa).

PUERTO RICO

Introduction

THE COMMONWEALTH OF PUERTO RICO, the smallest and most easterly island of the Greater Antilles, is the first Overseas Commonwealth Territory (defined as a "free and associated State") of the USA. Spanish is the first language but the citizenship is US and English is widely spoken (as is "Spanglish"). Since 4 March 1991, Spanish is the official language. *Puerto Rico* lies about 1,600 km southeast of Miami between the island of Hispaniola and the Virgin Islands, which give it some shelter from the open Atlantic, and is between longitudes 66° and 67° west and at latitude 18°30 north.

Almost rectangular in shape, slightly smaller than Jamaica, it measures 153 km in length (east to west), 58 km in width, and has a total land area of some 8,768 square km.

Old volcanic mountains, long inactive, occupy a large part of the interior of the island, with the highest peak, Cerro de Punta, at 1,338 metres in the Cordillera Central. North of the Cordillera is the karst country where the limestone has been acted upon by water to produce a series of small steep hills (*mogotes*) and deep holes, both conical in shape. The mountains are surrounded by a coastal plain with the Atlantic shore beaches cooled all the year round by trade winds, which make the temperatures of 28-30°C bearable in the summer. Temperatures in the winter drop to the range 21-26°C and the climate all the year round is very agreeable. Rain falls mainly from May to October, with most precipitation from July to October.

The population is 3.5 million, over two thirds of them live in urban areas. An estimated 2 million Puerto Ricans live in the USA. The country is a strange mixture of very new and very old, exhibiting the open American way of life yet retaining the more formal Spanish influences. This is reflected in the architecture, not just the contrast between the colonial and the modern but also in the countryside, where older buildings sit side by side with concrete schools and dwellings. It is also found in the cuisine, a plethora of fast food restaurants together with local cuisine which has its roots in the same hybrid culture of all the Caribbean. However, if you do not stray beyond the tourist areas around San Juan, you will not experience the real Puerto Rico. Puerto Ricans are sometimes referred to as Boricuas after the Indian name of the island (see below). Second generation Puerto Ricans who were born in New York, but who have returned to the island, are called Nuyoricans. The people are very friendly and hospitable but there is crime, probably because of economic difficulties and unemployment.

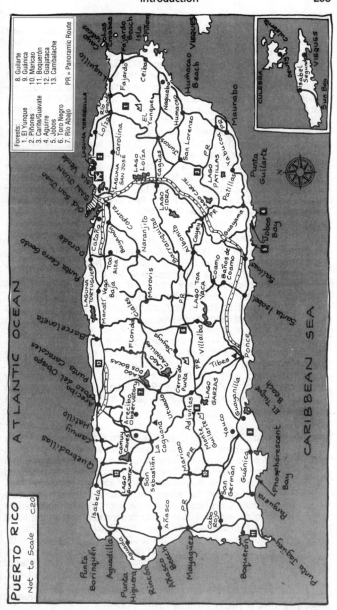

PUERTO RICO
Not to Scale   C20

ATLANTIC OCEAN

Forests:
1. El Yunque
2. Piñones
3. Carite/Guavate
4. Aguirre
5. Jobos
6. Toro Negro
7. Río Abajo
8. Guilarte
9. Guánica
10. Maricao
11. Boquerón
12. Guajataca
13. Cambalache

PR = Panoramic Route

CARIBBEAN SEA

History

Columbus, accompanied by a young nobleman, Juan Ponce de León, arrived in Puerto Rico on 19 November 1493. Attracted by tales of gold, Ponce obtained permission to colonize Borinquén, as it was called by the natives. In 1508 he established the first settlement at Caparra, a small village not far from the harbour of San Juan. A year later the Spanish Crown appointed him the first Governor. In 1521, however, the settlement was moved to the present site of Old San Juan as the former site was declared unhealthy. In that year Ponce de León was mortally wounded in the conquest of Florida.

Because of Puerto Rico's excellent location at the gateway to Latin America, it played an important part in defending the Spanish empire against attacks from French, English and Dutch invaders. After the Spanish-American war, Spain ceded the island to the United States in 1898. The inhabitants became US citizens in 1917, with their own Senate and House of Delegates, and in 1948, for the first time, they elected their own Governor, who is authorized to appoint his Cabinet and members of the island's Supreme Court. In 1952 Puerto Rico became a Commonwealth voluntarily associated with the United States.

Government

The Governor (1988-92) is Sr Rafael Hernández Colón of the Popular Democratic Party, which favours enhancement of the island's existing Commonwealth status. The other main party is the New Progressive Party, which favours Puerto Rico's full accession to the USA as the 51st state. Pro-independence groups receive little overt support. A small guerrilla group, the Macheteros, demands that all US presence be removed from the island. A referendum on Puerto Rico's future status was held in 1991, but voters rejected the administration's proposals to guarantee that they remain citizens of the USA regardless of any change in Puerto Rico's political status. A plebiscite is also proposed for the electorate to decide whether to retain the current commonwealth status or become a state of the union or move towards independence. The 1991 vote was seen as a rejection of the policies of the governing party and Governor Hernández Colón subsequently decided not to seek re-election in the 1992 elections. Puerto Ricans do not vote in US federal elections, nor do they pay federal taxes, when resident on the island.

The Economy

Income per head is high at over US$8,000. Life expectancy is now 71 years (males), 78 (females) and illiteracy has been reduced to about 10%. Great social and economic progress has been made in the past thirty years, as a result of the "Operation Bootstrap" industrialization programme supported by the US and Puerto Rican governments, which was begun in 1948. Accordingly manufacturing for export has become the most important sector of the economy, in place of agriculture. Until 1976, US Corporations were given tax incentives to set up in Puerto Rico and their profits were taxed only if repatriated. Industrial parks were built based on labour intensive industries to take advantage of Puerto Rico's low wages. In the mid-1970s, however, the strategy changed to attract capital intensive companies with the aim of avoiding the low wage trap. Nowadays about 70% of manufacturing income is repatriated; manufacturing produces about 40% of total output, but only 20% if remittances are excluded, about the same as in the 1950s. Investment has also fallen recently to 17% of gdp, having risen from 15% in 1950 to 30% in 1970.

The principal manufactures are textiles, clothing, electrical and electronic equipment and pharmaceuticals. Dairy and livestock production is one of the leading agricultural activities; others are the cultivation of sugar, tobacco, coffee, pineapples and coconut. Tourism is another key element in the economy. In 1991, 635,567 visitors stayed on the island (down nearly 7% from 1990), of whom 81% came from the USA, while cruise ship arrivals were 994,905 (up 19%).

Despite the progress made to industrialize the country, the economy has suffered from US budget cuts. Some 30% of all spending on gnp originates in Washington and high unemployment is possible because of food stamps and other US transfers. Migration is a safety valve, and there are more Puerto Ricans living in New York than San Juan. The issue of whether to seek full statehood will be determined principally on economic considerations. The economy depends heavily on the tax incentives given to US mainland companies and on federal transfers, which could be reduced if the island became a state. Puerto Rico is also used to channel loans to other Caribbean and Central American countries under the Caribbean Basin Initiative (CBI). It is unlikely that lending commitments of US$100m per year would be continued under statehood.

Culture Puerto Rico may be part of the United States, but its **music and dance**, and indeed its soul, are wholly Latin American. A visitor who sticks to the hotels and beaches will be largely subjected to rock music and salsa and to hear the real Puerto Rican music he should head for the countryside and especially to the hilly interior, the "Montaña". The island was Spanish until 1898 and the oldest musical tradition is that of the nineteenth century Danza, associated particularly with the name of Juan Morel Campos and his phenomenal output of 549 compositions. This is European-derived salon music for ballroom dancing, slow, romantic and sentimental. The peasants of the interior, the Jíbaros, sing and dance the Seis, of Spanish origin, in its many varied forms, such as the Seis Chorreao, Seis Zapateao, Seis Corrido and Seis Bombeao. Other variants are named after places, like the Seis Cagueño and Seis Fajardeño. Favoured instruments are the *cuatro* and other varieties of the guitar, the *bordonúa*, *tiple*, *tres* and *quintillo*, backed by *güiro* (scraper), *maracas*, *pandereta* (tambourine) and *bomba* (drum) to provide rhythm. One uniquely Puerto Rican phenomenon is the singer's "La-Le-Lo-Lai" introduction to the verses, which are in Spanish ten-line *décimas*. The beautiful Aguinaldos are sung at Christmastime, while the words of the Mapeyé express the Jíbaro's somewhat tragic view of life. Many artists have recorded the mountain music, notably El Gallito de Manatí, Ramito, Chuito el de Bayamón, Baltazar Carrero and El Jibarito de Lares.

Puerto Rico's best-known musical genre is the Plena, ironically developed by a black couple from Barbados, John Clark and Catherine George, known as "Los Ingleses", who lived in the La Joya del Castillo neighbourhood of Ponce during the years of the First World War. With a four-line stanza and refrain in call-and-response between the "Inspirador" (soloist) and chorus, the rhythm is distinctly African and the words embody calypso-style commentaries on social affairs and true-life incidents. Accompanying instruments were originally tambourines, then accordions and *güiros*, but nowadays include guitars, trumpets and clarinets. The Plena's most celebrated composer and performer was Manuel A Jiménez, known as "Canario".

There are relatively few black people in Puerto Rico and the only specifically black music is the Bomba, sung by the "Cantaor" and chorus, accompanied by the drums called *buleadores* and *subidores* and naturally also danced. The Bomba can be seen and heard at its best in the island's only black town of Loiza Aldea at the Feast of Santiago in late July. Rafael Cepeda and his family are the best known exponents.

For a modern interpretation of traditional music, recordings by the singer/composer Tony Croatto are highly recommended, while Rafael Cortijo and his Combo have taken the Plena beyond the confines of the island into the wider world of Caribbean salsa.

The Jíbaro, mentioned above, is a common figure in Puerto Rican literature. The origin of the name is unknown, but it refers to the "campesino del interior", a sort of Puerto Rican equivalent to the gaucho, native, but with predominantly hispanic features. The Jíbaro, as a literary figure, first appeared in the 19th century, with Manuel Alonso Pacheco's *El gíbaro* emerging as a cornerstone of the island's literature. In 29 "scenes", Alonso attempted both to describe and to interpret Puerto Rican life; he showed a form of rural life about to disappear in the face of bourgeois progress. The book also appeared at a time (1849) when romanticism was gaining popularity. Prior to this period, there had been a definite gulf between the educated letters, chronicles and memoires of the 16th to 18th centuries and the oral traditions of the people. These included "coplas", "décimas", "aguinaldas" (see above) and folk tales. The Jíbaro has survived the various literary fashions, from 19th century romanticism and "realismo costumbrista" (writing about manners and customs), through the change from Spanish to US influence, well into the 20th century.

One reason for this tenacity is the continual search for a Puerto Rican identity. When, in 1898, Spain relinquished power to the USA, many Puerto Ricans sought full independence. Among the writers of this time were José de Diego and Manuel Zeno Gandía. The latter's series of four novels, *Crónicas de un mundo enfermo* (*Garduña* – 1896, *La charca* – 1898, *El negocio* – 1922, *Redentores* – 1925), contain a strong element of social protest. As the series progresses, a new theme is added to that of local economic misery, emigration to New York, which booms after 1945. For a variety of domestic reasons, many fled the island to seek adventures, happiness, material wealth in the United States. While some writers and artists in the 1930s and 1940s, eg Luis Lloréns Torres, tried to build a kind of nationalism around a mythical, rural past, others still favoured a complete separation from the colonialism which had characterized Puerto Rico's history. For a while, the former trend dominated, but by the 1960s the emigré culture had created a different set of themes to set against the search for the Puerto Rican secure in his/her national identity. These included, on the one hand, the social problems of the islander in New York, shown, for example, in some of the novels of Enrique A Laguerre, *Trópico en Manhattan* by Guillermo Cotto Thorner, stories such as "Spiks" by Pedro Juan Soto, or plays like René Marqués' *La carreta*. On the other there is the americanization of the island, the figure of the "piti-yanqui" (the native Puerto Rican who admires and flatters his North American neighbour) and the subordination of the agricultural to a US-based, industrial economy. Writers after 1965 who have documented this change include Rosario Ferré and the novelist and playwright, Luis Rafael Sánchez. The latter's *La guaracha del Macho Camacho* (1976), an alliterative, humorous novel, revolves around a traffic jam in a San Juan taken over by a vastly popular song, "La vida es una cosa fenomenal", a far cry from the Jíbaro's world.

Flora and Fauna

Although less than 1% of the island is virgin forest, there are several forest reserves designed to protect plants and wildlife. In El Yunque Tropical Rain Forest (called The Caribbean National Forest) there are an estimated 240 types of tree (26 indigenous), and many other plants, such as tiny wild orchids, bamboo trees, giant ferns, and trumpet trees. The forest falls into four overlapping types: at the lowest level the rain forest, then thicket, palm forest and, at the highest altitudes, dwarf forest. The total area is 28,000 acres. Several marked paths, recreational areas and information areas have been set up, but note that Route 191, which some maps show traversing the forest, is closed beyond the Sierra Palma Visitors' Centre. Hurricane Hugo in 1989 did a great deal of damage to the forest; some say it will be 15 years before El Yunque is back to normal. It is also home to the Puerto Rican parrot, which has been saved from extinction. The whole forest is a bird sanctuary. Other forest areas, some of which are mentioned in the text below are Guajataca in the northwest; Río Abajo, between Arecibo and Utuado; Maricao, Guilarte, Toro Negro and Carite (Guavate), all on the transinsular Panoramic Route. Mangroves are protected in Aguirre Forest, on the south coast near Salinas, at the Jobos Bay National Estuarine Research Reserve, at the western end of Jobos Bay from Aguirre, and at Piñones Forest, east of San Juan (also hit by Hurricane Hugo). Unlike the north coast mangroves, those on the south coast tend to die behind the outer fringe because not enough water is received to wash away the salt. This leaves areas of mud and skeletal trees which, at times of spring tide, flood and are home to many birds. In winter, many ducks stop on their migration routes at Jobos. Also at Jobos Bay, manatees and turtles can be seen. A short boardwalk runs into the mangroves at Jobos, while at Aguirre a man runs catamaran trips to the offshore cays (US$4-6), and there are some good fish restaurants; take Route 7710. For Jobos Bay take Route 703, to Las Mareas de Salinas (marked Mar Negro on some maps). Before going to Jobos, contact the office at Jobos, Box 1170, Guayama, Puerto Rico 00655, Tel: 864-0105, or 724-8774 in San Juan.

The largest number of bird species can be found at Guánica Forest, west of Ponce, which is home to several unique and endangered species. (*Las aves de Puerto Rico*, by Virgilio Biaggi, University of Puerto Rico, 1983, US$12.95, is available in San Juan, eg the bookshop in Fort San Cristóbal.) Guánica's dry forest vegetation is unique and the Forest has been declared an International Biosphere Reserve by UNESCO. Most of the trails through these and other forests are now marked, but it may be advisable to contact the wardens for directions before wandering off. One of the most notable creatures on Puerto Rico is the inch-long tree frog called a *coquí*, after the two-tone noise it makes.

Puerto Rico also has some of the most important caves in the western hemisphere. The Río Camuy runs underground for part of its course, forming the third largest subterranean river in the world. Near Lares, on Route 129, Km 9.8, the Río Camuy Cave Park has been established by the Administración de Terrenos (PO Box 3767, San Juan, Tel: 893-3100), where visitors are guided through one cave and two sinkholes, open Wednesday to Sunday, and holidays 0800-1600, last trip 1545, US$2 for adults, US$1 for children, highly recommended, but entry is limited. There are fine examples of stalactites, stalagmites and, of course, plenty of bats. Nearby is the privately-owned Cueva de Camuy, Route 486, Km 11; much smaller, with guided tours, the area also has a swimming pool and waterslide, amusements, café, ponies, go-karts, entertainments, entry US$1, children US$0.50, open daily 0900-1700 (till 2100

Sunday). Nearby is Cueva del Infierno, to which 2-3 hour tours can be arranged by phoning 898-2723. About 2,000 caves have been discovered; in them live 13 species of bat (but not in every cave), the *coquí*, crickets, an arachnid called the *guavá*, and other species. For full details contact the Speleological Society of Puerto Rico (Sepri).

Beaches and Watersports

Swimming from most beaches is safe; the best beaches near San Juan are those at Isla Verde in front of the main hotels; Luquillo to the east of San Juan is less crowded and has a fine-sand beach from where there are good views of El Yunque. The north coast Atlantic sea is rougher than the southern waters, particularly in winter; some beaches are semi-deserted. There are 13 *balneario* beaches round the island where lockers, showers and parking places are provided for a small fee. *Balnearios* are open Tuesday-Sunday 0900-1700 in winter and 0800-1700 in summer.

The shallow waters are good for snorkelling and while a boat is needed to reach deeper water for most scuba diving, divers can walk in at Isabela. There are many companies offering equipment rental and diving instruction, including Coral Head Divers, Marina de Palmas, *Palmas del Mar Resort*, Humacao (Tel: 850-7208 US$50-75), Cueva Submarina Training Centre, Galerías, 19 Estación, Isabela, on the north coast (Tel: 872-3903), Mundo Submarino, Laguna Gardens, Isla Verde (Tel: 791-5764), also in San Juan, Caribbean School of Aquatics, *La Concha Hotel*, Ashford Avenue, Condado (Tel: 723-4740) and Caribe Aquatic Adventures, San Juan Bay Marina, Miramar (Tel: 724-1882); at Fajardo, in the Villa Marina Shopping Centre, Scuba Shoppe (Tel: 863-8465). Dive packages start at about US$50. Diving also at some of the larger hotels. *Qué Pasa* lists all the operators approved by the Tourism Company.

The most popular beaches for surfing are the Pine Beach Grove in Isla Verde (San Juan), Jobos (near Isabela in the northwest, not the south coast bay), Surfer and Wilderness beaches in the former Ramey Field air base at Punta Borinquén, north of Aguadilla and Punta Higuero, Route 413 between Aguadilla and Rincón on the west coast. Several international surfing competitions have been held at Surfer and Wilderness. The Condado lagoon is popular for windsurfing (there is a windsurfing school in Santurce, Lisa Penfield, 2A Rambla del Almirante, Tel: 726-7274, with rentals at US$25 per hour and lessons starting at US$45 for 1½ hrs), as is Boquerón Bay and Ocean Park beach.

Puerto Rico's coastline is protected in many places by coral reefs and cays which are fun to visit and explore. Sloops can be hired at US$60 a day, with crew, and hold six passengers (eg Captain Jayne at Fajardo, Tel: 791-5174).

There are three marinas at Fajardo, the Club Náutico at Miramar and another at Boca de Cangrejos in Isla Verde (both in San Juan) and one at the *Palmas del Mar Resort* near Humacao. There is a marina for fishing motor launches at Arecibo. The first phase of an ambitious marina project at Puerto del Rey, Fajardo, opened late 1988 and is awaiting expansion following damage from Hurricane Hugo.

Deep-sea fishing is popular and more than 30 world records have been broken in Puerto Rican waters, where blue and white marlin, sailfish, wahoo, dolphin, mackerel and tarpon, to mention a few, are a challenge to the angler. Fishing boat charters are available: eg Mike Benítez Marine Services, Inc, at the Club Náutico de San Juan, PO Box 5141, Puerta de Tierra, San Juan, PR 00906, Tel: 723-2292 (till 2100), 724-6265 (till 1700), prices from

US$650. You can also fish in the many lakes out on the island. Contact the Department of Natural Resources (Tel: 722-5938) for details.

Other Sports

Golf There are 14 golf courses around the island. The *Cerromar* and *Dorado Beach* hotels in Dorado have excellent 36-hole championship golf courses; among the 18-hole courses, Berwind Country Club accepts non-members on Tuesday, Thursday and Friday, Palmas del Mar (Humacao), Club Riomar (Río Grande), and Punta Borinquén (Aguadilla) all have golf pros and are open to the public. **Tennis** Over 100 tennis courts are available, mostly in the larger hotels. There are also 16 public courts in San Juan's Central Park, open daily. The Dorado del Mar Country Club has 6 courts and the Palmas del Mar resort, at Humacao, has 20 courts. **Cockfighting** The season is from 1 November to 31 August. This sport is held at the new, air-conditioned Coliseo Gallístico in Isla Verde, near the Holiday Inn (Route 37, Km 1.5). Saturday 1300-1900, Tel: 791-1557/6005 for times. Admission from US$4 to US$10. **Horse Racing** El Comandante, Route 3, Km 5.5, Canóvanas, is one of the hemisphere's most beautiful race courses. Races are held all the year round (Wednesday, Friday, Sunday and holidays). First race is at 1430. Wednesday is ladies' day. Children under 12 not admitted at any time. **Riding** On mountain trails or beaches, riding is a good way to see the island. Puerto Rico also prides itself on its paso fino horses. At Palmas del Mar, Humacao, there is an equestrian centre which offers beach rides and riding and jumping lessons. Hacienda Carabalí (Tel: 795-6351), offers beach or hill riding and has paso fino horses.

Popular spectator sports are boxing and baseball (at professional level, also a winter league at San Juan stadium, US$4 for a general seat, US$5 box seat, Tuesday is Ladies' Night), basketball, volleyball and beach volleyball. Running, competitive and non-competitive, is also popular. Puerto Rico is a member of the Olympic Committee, and it is likely that even if the island becomes a US state it will retain its independence in this respect.

San Juan

Founded in 1510, **San Juan**, the capital (population about 1 million) spreads several km along the north coast and also inland. The nucleus is Old San Juan, the old walled city on a tongue of land between the Atlantic and San Juan bay. It has a great deal of charm and character, a living museum; the Institute of Culture restores and renovates old buildings, museum and places of particular beauty. The narrow streets of Old San Juan, some paved with small grey-blue blocks which were cast from the residues of iron furnaces in Spain and brought over as ships' ballast, are lined with colonial churches, houses and mansions, in a very good state of repair and all painted different pastel colours. Electric trolley buses, and small yellow buses run around the old city all day, free, *paradas* (stops) are marked.

Some of the restored and interesting buildings to visit include La Fortaleza, the Governor's Palace, built between 1533 and 1540 as a fortress against Carib attacks but greatly expanded in the 19th century (open 0900-1600 Monday-Friday; guided tours in English every hour, in Spanish every half hour, tours of second floor 0930, 1000, 1030 and 1050, Tel: 721-7000 ext 2211; the Cathedral, built in the 16th century but extensively restored in the 19th and 20th, in which the body of Juan Ponce de León rests in a marble tomb (open daily 0630-1700); the tiny Cristo Chapel with its silver altar, built

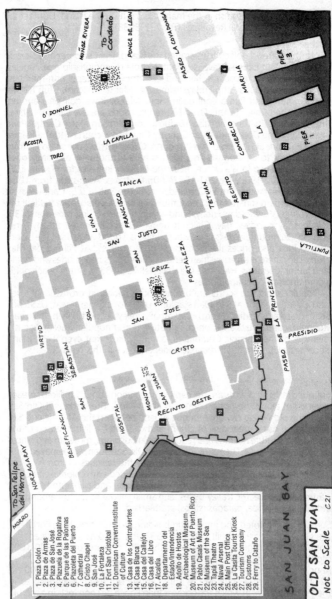

1. Plaza Colón
2. Plaza de Armas
3. Plaza de San José
4. Plazuela de la Rogativa
5. Parque de las Palomas
6. Plazoleta del Puerto
7. Cathedral
8. Cristo Chapel
9. San José
10. La Fortaleza
11. Fort San Cristóbal
12. Dominican Convent/Institute of Culture
13. Casa de los Contrafuertes
14. Casa Blanca
15. Casa del Callejón
16. Casa del Libro
17. Alcaldía
18. Departamento del Estado/Intendencia
19. Adolfo de Hostos Archaeological Museum
20. Museum of Art of Puerto Rico
21. Pablo Casals Museum
22. Museum of the Sea
23. Tapiá Theatre
24. Naval Arsenal
25. Main Post Office
26. La Casita Tourist Kiosk
27. Tourism Company
28. Customs
29. Ferry to Cataño

OLD SAN JUAN
Not to Scale   C21

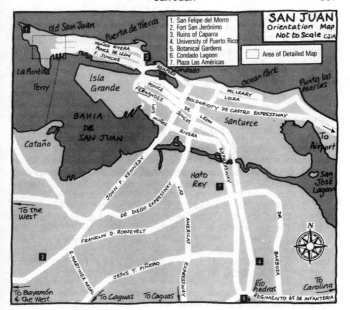

after a young man competing in 1753 in a horse-race during the San Juan
festival celebrations plunged with his horse over the precipice at that very
spot (open Tuesdays 1000-1600), next to it is the aptly-named Parque de
las Palomas, where the birds perch on your hand to be fed; San Felipe del
Morro, built in 1591 to defend the entrance to the harbour, and the
11-hectare Fort San Cristóbal, completed in 1772 to support El Morro and
to defend the landward side of the city, with its five independent units
connected—good views of the city (both open daily 0800-1800, admission free);
the Dominican Convent built in the early 16th century, later used as a
headquarters by the US Army and now the office of the Institute of Culture,
with a good art gallery (Chapel museum open Wednesday-Sunday,
0900-1200, 1300-1630; cultural events are sometimes held in the patio, art
exhibitions in the galleries, Tel: 724-0700); the 16th-century San José church,
the second oldest church in the Western Hemisphere and once the family
church of Ponce de León's descendants, Ponce was buried here until moved
to the Cathedral in the 20th century (open Monday-Saturday 0830-1600,
Sunday mass at 1200); the early 18th century Casa de los Contrafuertes
believed to be the oldest private residence in the old city, now has periodic
art exhibitions on the second floor and a small pharmacy museum with 19th
century exhibits on the ground floor (open Wednesday-Sunday, 0900-1630,
Tel: 724-5949); the Casa Blanca, built in 1523 by the family of Ponce de
León, who lived in it for 250 years until it became the residence of the
Spanish and then the US military commander-in-chief, and is now a historical
museum which is well worth a visit (open daily 0900-1200, 1300-1630,

guided tours Monday-Friday by appointment, Tel: 724-4102); the Alcaldía, or City Hall, built 1604-1789 (open Monday-Friday 0800-1600 except holidays, Tel: 724-7171 ext 2391); the Intendencia, formerly the Spanish colonial exchequer, a fine example of 19th century Puerto Rican architecture, now houses Puerto Rico's State Department (open Monday-Friday 0800-1200, 1300-1630, Tel: 722-2121); the naval arsenal was the last place in Puerto Rico to be evacuated by the Spanish in 1898, exhibitions are held in three galleries (open Wednesday-Sunday, 0900-1200, 1300-1630, Tel: 724-5949); and the Casa del Callejón, a restored 18th-century house containing two colonial museums, the architectural and the Puerto Rican Family (both closed for restoration in 1992, Tel: 725-5250).

Museums
Apart from those in historic buildings listed above, there are the Pablo Casals Museum beside San José church, with Casals' cello and other memorabilia (Tuesday-Saturday 0930-1730, Sunday 1300-1700, Tel: 723-9185); the San Juan Museum of Art and History, Norzagaray y MacArthur, built in 1855 as a marketplace (closed for repairs in 1992); the Casa del Libro is an 18th century house on Calle Cristo, has a collection of rare books, including some over 400 years old (Tuesday-Saturday, except holidays, 1100-1630, Tel: 723-0354); and the Museum of the Sea on Pier One, with a collection of maritime instruments and models (open when the pier is open for cruise ships, Tel: 725-2532). Another museum in the old city is a military museum at Fort San Jerónimo (open Wednesday-Sunday, 0930-1200, 1300-1630, Tel: 724-5949).

The metropolitan area of San Juan includes the more modern areas of Santurce, Hato Rey, and Río Piedras. Río Piedras was founded in 1714 but became incorporated into San Juan in 1951. On the edge of Río Piedras, the gardens and library of the former governor, Luis Muñoz Marín, are open to the public, Tuesday-Saturday 0900-1300 (Tel: 755-7979), with a museum showing his letters, photos and speeches.

The University of Puerto Rico at Río Piedras is in a lovely area. The University Museum (open Monday-Friday, 0900-2100, weekends 0900-1500, Tel: 764-0000, ext 2452) has archaeological and historical exhibitions, and also monthly art exhibitions. The Botanical Garden at the Agricultural Experiment Station has over 200 species of tropical and sub-tropical plants, a bamboo promenade, an orchid garden, and a lotus lagoon (open Tuesday-Sunday, 0900-1630, Tel: 766-0740).

Hato Rey is the financial district of San Juan nicknamed "the Golden Mile". The Sacred Heart University with the Museum of Contemporary Puerto Rican Art (Tuesday-Saturday 0900-1600, Sunday 1100-1700, Tel: 268-0049) is in Santurce, as is the modern Fine Arts Center, opened in 1981, which has theatres and halls at the corner of De Diego and Ponce de León (Tel: 724-4751). The residential area Miramar has several moderately priced hotels as well as some expensive ones. Miramar is separated from the Atlantic coast by the Condado lagoon and the Condado beach area, where the luxury hotels, casinos, night clubs and restaurants are concentrated. From Condado the beach front is built up eastwards through Ocean Park, Santa Teresita, Punta Las Marías and Isla Verde. Building is expanding along the narrow strip beyond Isla Verde, between the sea and the airport. Along this road, Avenida Boca de Cangrejos, there are lots of food trucks selling barbecued specialities.

Directions
Up until the 1950s tramcars ran between Río Piedras and Old San Juan along

Avs Ponce de León and Fernández Juncos. To this day directions are given by Paradas, or tram stops, so you have to find out where each one is.

Excursions
A ferry, Old San Juan (Pier Two) – Hato Rey, Cataño, crosses every half hour, 0600-2100, Tel: 788-1155, US$0.50, to Cataño where you can catch a *público* (US$1 pp), or bus to the Bacardi rum distillery. There are free conducted tours around the plant Monday-Saturday, 0930-1530, travelling from one building to the next by a little open motor train, Tel: 788-1500.

On Route 2, shortly before Bayamón, is the island's earliest settlement, Caparra, established by Ponce de León in 1508. Ruins of the fort can still be seen and there is a Museum of the Conquest and Colonization of Puerto Rico (open daily 0900-1600, Tel: 781-4795).

The Interior

Out of the metropolitan area "on the island" are a variety of excursions; as it is a small island it is possible to see forested mountains and desert-like areas in only a short time. However, because the public transport system is rather limited, it is difficult if not impossible to visit some places without a rented car. This is a highly recommended way of exploring the island. The cool climate in the mountains has caused resort hotels to be built in several towns inland.

An interesting round trip through the eastern half of the island, starting east from San Juan, is as follows: San Juan-Río Piedras (there are *públicos* between these two places, US$1.85) El Yunque-Luquillo-Fajardo-Vieques-Culebra-Humacao-Yabucoa-Guayama (you can get from Humacao to Guayama by a series of *públicos*, the whole journey costing about US$3.50)-Cayey-Aibonito-Barranquitas-Bayamón-San Juan. A variant between San Juan and El Yunque takes you on Route 187 from Isla Verde, outside San Juan, to Loíza along a stretch of the North coast, which includes the Piñones State Forest, sand blown and palm-lined road and much evidence of Hurricane Hugo's passing. Some parts are unspoilt, some parts pass through apartment blocks on the outskirts of towns, and the road is a popular rush-hour route. The bay at Vacía Talega is beautifully calm. The section which joins the coast to Route 3 at Río Grande is also tree-lined and attractive.

El Yunque (see also **Flora and Fauna** above) is a tropical forest and bird sanctuary. Trails (very stony) to the various peaks: El Yunque (The Anvil) itself, Mount Britton, Los Picachos. In view of the heavy rainfall, another name for the forest is Rain Forest. Visitors need not worry unduly, as storms are usually brief and plenty of shelter is provided. (No buses through the national forests, unfortunately; El Yunque is reached via Route 3 from San Juan towards Fajardo, and then right on Route 191.)

At Luquillo there is a beach in town and a *balneario* (see **Beaches and Watersports**); just by the latter is a row of restaurants on the slip road off the dual carriageway (Route 3). Fajardo is a boating centre with several marinas and a public beach at Seven Seas; beyond Seven Seas is Las Croabas beach. Offshore is an uninhabited, but much visited, coral island, Icacos. You can camp at Seven Seas Beach, but Tel: 722-1551 first. (Bus San Juan-Fajardo US$6.)

The quiet, unspoilt offshore islands of **Vieques** and **Culebra** can be reached daily by air from Isla Grande airport, San Juan, ½ hour, US$20 and 25 one way respectively: to Vieques, Vieques Air Link, Tel: 863-3020/722-3736;

Sunaire (Tel: 800-595-9501) and Lapsa (Tel: 723-4144); to Culebra, Flamenco, from Fajado or Isla Grande, Tel: 863-3366, 725-7707 on Culebra; Flamenco flies between Vieques and Culebra (tickets from the airport only). There are also frequent flights between Vieques and St Croix (Vieques Air Link and Sunaire) and daily to St Thomas (Lapsa). From Fajardo Vieques Air Link and Sunaire fly to Vieques, Flamenco to Culebra, or by launch from Fajardo Playa (a dock, not a beach), 1¼ hours, US$2.25 one way (Tel: 863-0705/0852) reservations needed for cars but not passengers. Vieques-Fajardo: Monday-Friday 0700 and 1500, Saturday and Sunday 0700, 1300 and 1630, Fajardo-Vieques 0930 and 1630 in the week, 0900, 1500 and 1800 weekends. Fajardo-Culebra, Monday-Friday 1600, Saturday, 0900 and 1600, Sunday 0800 and 1430; Culebra-Fajardo, 0700 weekdays, Fridays also 1400, 1800, Saturday, 0700, 1400 and 1730, Sunday 1300 and 1630. Fajardo ticket and information office is open 0800-1100, 1300-1500. (It is best to arrive in Fajardo in time for the last ferry if you are going to the islands; there is little to do in the town and it is not a cheap place.)

On Vieques the main settlement is Isabel Segunda, with an attractive square and the last fort built by Spain in the Americas. There are fine beaches, but much of the island is US Navy property. The public beach of Sun Bay has picnic and camping areas. Blue Beach on the south coast is good for snorkelling. Motorcycles can be hired.

Culebra's main village, Dewey (called Pueblo by the locals) is attractively set between two lagoons, with *Culebra Island Villas* and others (see **Where To Stay**), and houses to let; bicycles can be hired at US$2 a day from Jody's (Tel: 742-3266) and Posada Hamaca (742-3516); cars and jeeps from George's (742-3112), Prestige (742-3141) and Stanley's (742-3575); scuba equipment, Paradise Divers (742-3569) and Gene Thomas (742-3555); snorkel rental from Kathy's (742-3112) or Jody's. There are also good beaches, particularly Flamenco. A visitor's information centre is in the City Hall. Prices rise steeply at weekends. The Culebra National Wildlife Refuge protects large colonies of sea birds, particularly terns and boobies. Both Vieques and Culebra were heavily damaged by Hurricane Hugo.

One of the prettiest parts of Puerto Rico, which should be visited, lies south of Humacao, between Yabucoa and Guayama. Here are the villages of Patillas (*público* from Guayama) and Maunabo (*público* from Patillas, and from Yabucoa), where you can camp on the beach. There are a number of restaurants in this area, especially on the coast, which sell good, cheap food. Yabucoa is the eastern starting point of the Panoramic Route which runs the length of the island. There is an extension to the Route around the Cerro La Pandura and the Puntas Quebrada Honda, Yaguas and Toro; this affords lovely views of the Caribbean coast and Vieques island. Guayama, the cleanest town in Puerto Rico, it claims, has a delightful square, on which are the church and the Casa Cautiño, built in 1887, now a museum and cultural centre. Route 3, the coastal road around the eastern part continues from Guayama to Salinas (see below), where it joins Route 1 for Ponce.

A round trip through the western half of the island would take in Ponce, the second city (reached by motorway from San Juan via Caguas), Guánica, Parguera, San Germán, Boquerón, Mayagüez (the third city), Aguadilla, Quebradillas and Arecibo, with side trips to the Maricao State Forest and fish hatchery, the Río Abajo State Forest and Lake Dos Bocas, the precolumbian ceremonial ball-park near Utuado, and the Arecibo observatory (open for tours Tuesday to Friday at 1400, Tel: 878-2612 for groups, and on Sunday pm, no tour, but there is no public transport, so you have to hitchhike from Arecibo).

Off the motorway which runs from San Juan to Ponce is Baños de Coamo, which was the island's most fashionable resort from 1847 to 1958; legend has it that the spring was the fountain of youth which Juan Ponce de León was seeking. (Take Route 153 from the motorway and then 546.) It has been redeveloped by Paradores Puertorriqueños and still has a thermal bath (see under **Where To Stay**). About 45 minutes southeast of Coamo is Salinas, a fishing and farming centre. There are several good seafood restaurants on the waterfront.

Ponce has a very fine art museum, donated by a foundation established by Luis A Ferré (industrialist, art historian and Governor 1968-72) in a modern building with a beautiful staircase, now famous. It contains a representative collection of European and American art from the third century BC to the present day. As well as an extensive Baroque collection and fine examples of pre-Raphaelite painting, there is a small collection of precolumbian ceramics and two cases of beautiful Art Nouveau glass. There are three gardens, one Spanish, one American and one Puerto Rican. (Open 0900-1600, Monday and Wednesday-Friday, 1000-1600 Saturday, 1000-1700 Sunday and holidays, closed Tuesday; entry US$2.50 for adults, US$1.50 for children under 12.) The cathedral is also worth a look, and so is the black and red fire-station, built for a fair in 1883. Both buildings stand back to back in the main square, Plaza Las Delicias, which has fountains and many neatly-trimmed trees. Also on the plaza is the Casa Armstrong-Poventud (or Casa de las Cariatides), facing the Cathedral, with the Instituto de Cultura Puertorriqueño (Región Sur) and tourist information centre (Monday-Friday 0800-1200, 1300-1630; the Instituto is open 0900-1200, 1300-1600 Tuesday to Sunday). East of the plaza is the Teatro La Perla, painted cream, white and gold, the city's cultural centre (19th century), restored in 1990, as was the Alcaldía on the Plaza. Much renovation is going on in the heart of the city; the Casas Villaronga and Salazar-Zapater are being restored (the latter to accommodate the Museo de Historia de Ponce), other houses are being repainted in pastel shades, streets are being made into pedestrian areas (eg the Paseo Peotonal Atocha and Callejón Amor), and the large, air-conditioned market on Vives and Atocho (north of the plaza) has been remodelled. Two new museums have opened, the Museo de la Música Puertorriqueña, Calle Cristina 70, Tel: 844-9722, open Tuesday to Sunday 0900-1200 and 1300-1600, catalogue US$3, and the Museo Castillo Serrallés, on El Vigía hill (Tel: 259-1774), open Wednesday to Sunday 1000-1700, US$3, children US$1.50, groups must reserve in advance. This fine, 1930s mansion has been restored by the Municipio. Also on El Vigía is the Observation Tower (open Tuesday-Wednesday, 0900-1730, Thursday-Sunday 1000-2200, US$0.50). The walkway next to the Yacht and Fishing Club is a good place to be at the weekend: good atmosphere. Most *carros públicos* leave from the intersection of Victoria and Unión, 3 blocks north of the plaza (fare to San Juan US$6-7; to Guayama, either direct or via Santa Isabel, US$3).

A short drive away on Route 503, in the outskirts of the city, is the Tibes Indian Ceremonial Center. This is an Igneri (300 AD) and pre-Taino (700 AD) burial ground, with seven ball courts (*bateyes*) and two plazas, one in the form of a star, a replica of a Taino village and a good museum, open Tuesday-Sunday 0900-1600. The site was discovered in 1975 after heavy rain uncovered some of the stone margins of the ball courts. Under the Zemi Batey, the longest in the Caribbean (approximately 100 by 20 metres), evidence of human sacrifice has been found. Underneath a stone in the Main Plaza, which is almost square (55 by 50 metres), the bodies of children were found, buried ceremonially in earthenware pots. In all, 130 skeletons have been uncovered near the Main Plaza, out of a total on site of 187. All the ball courts and plazas are said to line up with solstices or equinoxes. The park is filled with trees (all named), the most predominant being the higuera, whose fruit is used, among other things, for making maracas (it's forbidden to pick them up though). Admission US$2 for adults, US$1 for children; bilingual guides give an informative description of the site and a documentary is shown.

Two other recommended excursions are: to Hacienda Buena Vista, at Km 16.8 on Route 10, north of the city. Built in 1833, converted into a coffee plantation and corn mill in 1845 and in operation till 1937, this estate has been restored by Fideicomiso de Conservación de Puerto Rico. All the machinery works (the metal parts are original), operated by water channelled from the 360-metre Vives waterfall; the hydraulic turbine which turns the corn mill is unique. Reservations are necessary for the 2-hour tour (in Spanish or English), Tel: 722-5882 (information and at weekends 848-7020), open Friday-Sunday, tours at 0830, 1030, 1330 and 1530; groups of 20 or more admitted Wednesday to Friday; US$4 adults, US$1 children under 12. At weekends trips can be made to the beach at Caja de Muerto, Coffin Island, the ferry leaves Ponce at 0900, returns 1600, Tel: 848-4575, US$5.50 return, children US$3.50.

Going West from Ponce is **Guánica**, the place where American troops first landed in the Spanish-American war. It has an old fort from which there are excellent views. Although Guánica has a history stretching back to Ponce de León's landing in 1508, the first of many colonist landings in the bay, the town was not actually founded here until 1914. Outside Guánica is a *balneario* with a large hotel alongside, *Copamarina*. For details on the Guánica Forest, see **Flora and Fauna**. Further west is La Parguera, originally a fishing village and now a popular resort with two *paradores*, guest houses, fish restaurants, fast food outlets. Noisy on holiday weekends. Nearby is Phosphorescent Bay, an area of phosphorescent water, occurring through a permanent population of minescent dinoflagellates, a tiny form of marine life, which produce sparks of chemical light when disturbed. One hour boat trips round the bay depart between 1930 and 0030, hourly departures, the experience is said to be rather disappointing, however.

Inland from La Parguera, off the main Route 2, **San Germán** has much traditional charm; it was the second town to be founded on the island and has preserved its colonial atmosphere. It is an excellent base from which to explore the mountains and villages of south west Puerto Rico. The beautiful little Porta Coeli chapel on the plaza contains a small, rather sparse museum of religious art. (Open Wednesday-Sunday, 0830-1200, 1300-1630.) A university town: it can be difficult to get cheap accommodation in term time.

On the southern side of the west coast is **Boquerón**, in Cabo Rojo district, which has an excellent beach for swimming. It is very wide and long, admission US$1, parking for hundreds of cars, camping, changing rooms, beach and first 30 yards of sea packed with bodies on holiday weekends. About a mile away across the bay is a beautiful, deserted beach, but there is no road to it. The small village is pleasant, with typical bars, restaurants and street vendors serving the local speciality, oysters. This is one of the cheapest spots on the island because it is a centre for the Department of Recreation and Sports to provide holiday accommodation for Puerto Rican families. Fully self-contained apartments, with barbecues, front the beach, and at US$20 a night they are a bargain. Foreigners are welcomed, but not at public holidays or long weekends. There are other hotels and a *parador* (see **Where To Stay** in **Information for Visitors**). South of the town is Boquerón Lagoon, a wildfowl sanctuary; also the Cabo Rojo Wildlife Refuge, with a visitors' centre and birdwatching trails. The Cabo Rojo lighthouse (Faro), at the island's southwest tip is the most southerly point on the island with a breathtaking view; the exposed coral rocks have marine fossils and, closer inshore, shallow salt pools where crystals collect. Popular beaches in this area are El Combate (miles of white sand, undeveloped, but now a favourite with university students), south of Boquerón, and Joyuda (small island just offshore offers good snorkelling and swimming, but beach itself not spectacular) and Buye (camping US$8 a night) to the north.

Mayagüez has fine botanical gardens, at the Tropical Agricultural Research Station, near the University of Puerto Rico: well worth visiting, free admission, open Monday-Friday, 0730-1630. The city also has an interesting zoo; open Tuesday-Sunday, 0900-1630, adults US$1, children US$0.50. *Públicos* leave from a modern terminal in Calle Peral. The tourist office is in the Municipalidad on Plaza Colón. *Mona Island*, 50 miles west of Mayagüez, is fascinating for historians and nature lovers, but can only be reached by chartered boat or plane. Originally inhabited by Taino Indians and then by pirates and privateers, it is now deserted except for its wildlife. Here you can see three-foot iguanas, colonies of sea birds and bats in the caves. 200-foot high cliffs are dotted with caves, ascending to a flat table top covered with dry forest. The island is managed by the Department of National Resources (Tel: 722-1726), who have cabins to rent with prior permission. Camping is allowed at Sardinera Beach, US$1 per night. There are no restaurants or facilities. Take all your food and water with you and bring back all your rubbish.

Going north from Mayagüez, you come to *Rincón*, on the westernmost point of the island. Here the mountains run down to the sea, and the scenery is spectacular. The town itself is unremarkable, but the nearby beaches are beautiful and the surfing is a major attraction. The beaches are called Steps, Dome (named after the nearby nuclear storage dome) and the recent Public Beach, with lifeguard. *Tamboo I*, on the beach, rents snorkelling equipment and surfboards (US$15 a day), low-key entertainment in evening; *Tamboo II*, also on the beach, has live reggae bands (see also **Where To Stay** in **Information for Visitors**). Humpback whales visit in winter. There are cottages to rent and there is also accommodation in Rincón and the neighbouring village of Puntas (see below). There are also some small bars and restaurants, including *Danny's Café* in Rincón, a health food restaurant in Puntas and a pizzeria just north of Puntas. Rincón can be reached by *público* from Mayagüez or (less frequent) from Aguadillas. Public transport is scarce at weekends.

Route 2, the main road in the north, is built up to some extent from Arecibo and completely from Manatí to San Juan. If you have the time it is much nicer to drive along the coast. Take Route 681 out of Arecibo, with an immediate detour to the Poza del Obispo beach, by Arecibo lighthouse. Here a pool has been formed inside some rocks, but the breakers on the rocks themselves send up magnificent jets of spray. The bay, with fine surf, stretches round to another headland, Punta Caracoles, on which is the Cueva del Indio (small car park on Route 681, US$1 charge if anyone is around). A short walk through private land leads to the cave, a sea-eroded hole and funnel in the cliff; watch out for holes in the ground when walking around. There are drawings in the cave, but whether they are precolumbian, or contemporary modern graffiti is not made clear. *Públicos* run along Route 681 from Arecibo. Rejoin Route 2 through Barceloneta. The State Forest of Cambalache is between Arecibo and Barceloneta.

The coast road is not continuous; where it does go beside the sea, there are beaches, seafood restaurants and some good views. Route 165, another coastal stretch which can be reached either through Dorado on the 693, or through Toa Baja, enters metropolitan San Juan at Cataño.

Heading east from Mayagüez is the Panoramic Route which runs the whole length of Puerto Rico, through some of the island's most stunning scenery. It passes through the Cordillera Central, with large areas of forest, and there are several excursions to various countryside resorts. Despite the fact that you are never far from buildings, schools or farms, the landscape is always fascinating. In the evening the panoramas are lovely and you can hear the song of the *coquí*. No trip to the interior should miss at least some part of the Panoramic Route, but if you want to travel all of it, allow three days. The roads which are used are narrow, with many bends, so take care at corners. The Maricao State Forest (Monte del Estado) is the most westerly forest on the Route; its visitors' areas are open from 0600 to 1800. It is a beautiful forest with magnificent views. As it approaches Adjuntas and the transinsular Route 10, the Panoramic Route goes through the Bosque de Guilarte, again with fine views, flowering trees, bougainvillaea, banks of impatiens (busy lizzie, miramelinda in Spanish), and bird song (if you stop to listen). After Adjuntas, the road enters the Toro Negro Forest Reserve, which includes the highest point on the island, Cerro de Punta (1,338 metres). The Recreation Areas in Toro Negro are open from 0800-1700. After this high, lush forest with its marvellous vistas, the road continues to Aibonito, around which the views and scenery are more open (mainly as a result of deforestation). Thence to Cayey and, beyond, another forest, Carite (also known as Guavate). Finally the road descends into the rich, green valley which leads to Yabucoa.

From various points on the Panoramic Route you can head north or south; eg Route 10 goes south from Adjuntas to Ponce, or north to Utuado and then on to Río Abajo State Forest (open 0600-1800) where there are a swimming pool and various picnic spots. It is approached through splendid views of the karst hills and the Dos Bocas Lake. Free launch trips are offered on this lake at 0700, 1000, 1400 and 1700; they last two hours and are provided by the Public Works Department. Route 10 reaches the north coast at Arecibo.

The Caguana Indian Ceremonial Park, west of Utuado, dates from about 1100 AD, and contains ten Taino ball courts, each named after a Taino *cacique* (chieftain). The courts vary in size, the longest being about 85 metres by 20 (Guarionex), the largest 65 by 50 (Agueybana). These two have monoliths in the stones that line the level "pitch", and on those of Agueybana there are petroglyphs, some quite faint. None of the monoliths is taller than a man. A path leads down to the Río Tanamá. The setting, amid limestone hills, is very impressive. It is believed to be a site of some religious significance and has been restored with a small museum in the landscaped park. It is on On Route 111 to Lares, Km 12.3, open 0900-1700 (gate to the river closes at 1630), admission free. Further west of Utuado, Lares is a hilltop town (*públicos* go from one block from church) from where you can either carry on to the west coast at Aguadilla, or head north on one of the many routes to the Atlantic coast. Route 453 passes Lago de Guajataca, continuing as Route 113 to Quebradillas (see *Paradores* under **Where To Stay**, below). Route 455 branches west off the 453, leading via a short stretch of the 119 to the 457 and 446 (good view at the junction of these two). Route 446 traverses, as a single track, the Bosque de Guajataca, which has several paths into the forest (25 miles in all) and three recreational areas (open 0900-1800). Permission to camp must be obtained from the Departamento de Recursos Naturales, office in the Bosque open Monday-Friday 0700-1530 (in theory). Route 129 goes to Arecibo, passing the Río Camuy Cave Park, with side trips to the Cueva de Camuy and the Arecibo Observatory (see above for all these). Driving on the country roads in the area between the Panoramic Route and the north coast is twisty but pleasant, passing conical limestone hills (*mogotes*) and farms set among patches of lush forest.

Information for Visitors

Documents

All non-US residents need a US visa, or a US visa waiver for participating countries.

How To Get There

International: from Europe, British Airways from London Gatwick (Tel: 725-1575 or 800-247-9297), American Airlines from Heathrow or Brussels or Paris or Manchester via New York JFK, all via Miami with immediate connection to San Juan (Tel: 721-1747); Lufthansa from Frankfurt via Antigua (Tel: 723-9553); Iberia from Madrid (Tel: 721-5630). Most South and Central American countries are connected via Miami but there are also direct flights from Caracas (Avianca Airlines, Aeropostal, Tel: 721-2166, and Lacsa, Tel: 724-3330), Lima (American Airlines), Mexico City (Mexicana de Aviación, Tel: 721-2323), Panama City (Lacsa and Copa) and San José (Iberia and Lacsa). From Canada, US Air flies from Montreal. From other Caribbean Islands: Anguilla, Antigua, Aruba, Barbados, Dominica, Fort-de-France, Grenada, Kingston, La Romana, Montego Bay, Pointe-à-Pitre, Port of Spain, Puerto Plata, Punta Cana, St Barts, St Croix, St John, St Kitts, St Lucia, St Maarten, St Thomas, Santiago (Dominican Republic), Santo Domingo, Tortola and Virgin Gorda, with BWIA, Liat (Tel: 791-3838), American Airlines, American Eagle, Air Guadeloupe, Air St Barthélémy, Virgin Air, Virgin Island Seaplane Shuttle, Sunaire, Lapsa, Dominair, Dominicana de Aviación (Tel: 724-7100). **Domestic**: A great many US cities are served by American Airlines and American Eagle; Delta (Tel: 800-221-1212); Carnival, Tower Air, TWA (Tel: 728-9400), US Air and United Airlines. A number of airlines have offices at Miramar Plaza Center, Av Ponce de León 954: British Airways and Delta (9th floor), Dominicana, Mexicana, Aeropostal, Lufthansa, Lacsa, US Air; others can be found at Ashford 1022, Condado: American, BWIA, ALM, Air France, Viasa (Tel: 721-3340), Liat (best to use their office at the airport for reconfirmation). Several local airlines operate services within Puerto Rico, including American Eagle, Flamenco, Sunaire, Lapsa and Vieques Air Link, and they have offices either at the Luis Muñoz Marín International Airport, or the Isla Grande airport (eg Flamenco and Vieques Air Link). There are cheap American Airlines night flights between New York and San Juan, and three daily American Eagle flights between San Juan and Ponce. Carnival Airlines flies to Ponce and Aguadilla from New York, and Virgin Island Seaplane flies to Ponce from St Croix. Some charter or inter-island flights leave from the Isla Grande airport.

Airport Tax

None is payable, although Liat demands a "security tax" of US$5.

Shipping

From Fajardo Beach to St Thomas, the *Happy Hooker* sails Thursday to Sunday if demand is sufficient, US$45 return, Tel: 860-8830, or enquire at Blue Water Maritime Inc, Fajardo Playa. There are no boats to other Caribbean destinations, apart from cruise ships, which call at San Juan and Ponce.

Airport

There are airport limousines to a number of hotels. There is also a bus service (T1), US$0.25 to and from Plaza Colón and the airport; note that people take precedence over luggage if the bus is full (it rarely is). The bus departs from the upper deck near the Departures area, the furthest corner from Arrivals. The taxi fare to old San Juan is US$10-12, to Condado US$6 (make sure the taxi meter is used; note that drivers prefer not to go to old San Juan, the beach areas are much more popular with them).

Car Hire

There are 13 car rental agencies, including Hertz (Tel: 791-0840), Isla Verde International Airport; National (Tel: 791-1805), 1102 Magdalena Ave; Charlie, Box 41302, Tel: 728-6555/2420/2418, office in Isla Verde, on Av Isla Verde opposite Marbella del Caribe, provides pick-up service to airport. Budget (Tel: 791-3685) have a bus service from the airport to their office. Target (Tel: 783-6592/782-6381), not at airport, among the cheapest, will negotiate rates. A small car may be hired for as little as US$28 (not including collision damage waiver, US$12.50) for 24 hours, unlimited mileage (national driving licence preferred to international licence), but rates vary according to company and demand. The Rand McNally road map is recommended (US$1.85); the Gousha road map costs US$1.50 at Texaco stations. A good map is essential because there are few signs to places, but frequent indications of Route numbers and intersections. Avoid driving in the San Juan metropolitan area as traffic can be very heavy.

Taxis

Lease Division Caribe Motors, 519 Fernández Juncos; Metro Taxicabs, Km 3.3, Route 3, Isla Verde; Metropolitan Taxi Cabs, 165 Quisquella. University Taxi, Río Piedras. All taxis are metered, charge US$1 for initial charge and US$0.10 for every additional $^{1}/_{10}$ mile; US$0.50 for each suitcase; US$1 is charged for a taxi called from home or business. Approximate fares: San Juan to Condado, US$4; Condado to Isla Verde, US$4.50-5. Taxis may be hired at US$12 an hour unmetered. Taxi drivers sometimes try to ask more from tourists, so beware, insist

that the meter is used, and avoid picking up a taxi anywhere near a cruise ship.

There are also shared taxis, usually Ford minibuses (carros públicos) which have yellow number plates with the letters P or PD at the end and run to all parts of the island. Most of them leave from Río Piedras in San Juan, although some leave from the main post office and others collect at the airport; elsewhere, ask around for the terminal. They do not usually operate after about 1900. Público to Caguas costs US$1.25, from south side of Plaza Colón; to Ponce takes 7 hours (US$6-7). A service referred to as linea will pick up and drop off passengers where they wish. They operate between San Juan, and most towns and cities at a fixed rate. They can be found in the phone book under Líneas de Carros.

Buses

San Juan: There is a city bus (guagua) service with a fixed charge of US$0.25. (No change given; make sure you have right money.) They have special routes—sometimes against the normal direction of traffic, in which case the bus lanes are marked by yellow and white lines. Bus stops are marked by white and orange signs or yellow and black notices on lampposts marked "Parada". From the terminal at Plaza Colón in old San Juan, T1 goes along Av Ponce de León, through Miramar, past the Fine Arts Center in Santurce, to Isla Verde (Route 37) and the International Airport; No 2 goes to Río Piedras via Condado, Av Muñoz Rivera and the University; No 46 goes to Bayamón along Av Roosevelt; A7 goes to Piñones, through Condado and Isla Verde (Av Ashford to Route 37). From behind Pier 2, No 8 goes to Puerto Nuevo and Río Piedras, No 12 to Río Piedras, and No 14 to Río Piedras via Av Ponce de León, Santurce, Hato Rey and the University. City buses are not very frequent, however; they run to a 30-, or 45-minute schedule and many do not operate after 2200.

Hitchhiking is possible, but slow.

Where To Stay

Most of the large San Juan hotels are in **Condado or Isla Verde** and overlook the sea, with swimming pools, night clubs, restaurants, shops and bars. The summer season runs from 16 April to 14 December and is somewhat cheaper than the winter season, for which we give rates where possible. A 7% tax is payable on rooms costing more than US$5 a day. A full list is given in the monthly tourist guide, Qué

Pasa, published by the Puerto Rican Tourism Company, but listed below is a selection. To get value for money, it may be advisable to avoid the luxury hotels on the sea front. There is plenty of cheaper accommodation within walking distance of the beaches. Condado: *Ambassador Plaza*, 1369 Ashford, Tel: 721-7300, US$170-270d, or US$300-385 for a suite, 233 rooms, casino; *Caribe Hilton*, Ocean Front, Puerta de Tierra, on the old city side of Condado bridge, Tel: 721-0303, US$275-385d, or US$470-970 suites, 733 rooms, casino, set in 17 acres of gardens, many sporting facilities. On the Condado side of the bridge is the *Condado Plaza*, Tel: 721-1000, US$245-360d, or suites US$315-1,045, 587 rooms, casino, with *Tony Roma's* restaurant, small beach, etc; *Condado Beach*, Ashford, next to the Convention Center, Tel: 721-6888, US$183-250d, suites US$420, 245 rooms. Cheaper: *Mirabel Condado Lagoon*, 6 Clemenceau, Tel: 721-0170, US$95d, 44 rooms, good, with good restaurant on the premises, *Ajili-Mojili*; *Dutch Inn*, 55 Condado Av, Condado, Tel: 721-0810, US$110d, 144 rooms, casino; good value are *El Canario by the Sea*, 4 Condado Av, Tel: 722-8640, US$80-95, including continental breakfast, 25 rooms, close to beach, comfortable, and *El Canario Inn*, 1317 Ashford, Tel: 722-3861, US$80d, breakfast included, 1 block from the beach, good, clean, safe.

Hostería del Mar, 1 Tapia Street, Ocean Park, Tel: 727-3302, US$60d minimum up to US$145, on the beach; a recommended guest house in Ocean Park is *Numero Uno on the Beach*, 1 Santa Ana, Tel: 727-9687, US$47-75d, with pool.

Isla Verde: *Sands*, on Route 37 (the main road through Isla Verde), Tel: 791-6100 (US$235 upwards) and *El San Juan*, Ocean Front, Tel: 791-1000 (from US$285) are the two poshest hotels in Isla Verde; there is also a *Travel Lodge*, on Route 37, Tel: 728-1300, US$135. *Holiday Inn Crowne Plaza*, Tel: 841-5381, Fax: 841-8085, Km 1.5 on Highway 187, resort, golf, tennis, US$220-270d. Recommended is *Carib Inn*, Route 187 (Tel: 791-3535), from US$100, clean, pool, 2 restaurants, near airport. *La Casa Mathieson*, Uno 14, Villamar, Isla Verde and *Green Isle Inn*, 36 Calle Uno, are jointly owned, Tel: 726-8662 or 4330, *Mathieson* charges US$37-60, *Green Isle* US$64-69, both near airport, and have

swimming pools, cooking facilities, friendly, free transport to and from airport; between the two is *The Mango Inn*, Calle Uno 20, Villamar, Tel: 726-5546, US$70-85, pool; *El Patio*, Tres Oeste 87, Bloque D-8, Villamar, Tel: 726-6298, swimming pool, use of kitchen, US$50d all year, recommended; *Casa de Playa Guest House*, Av Isla Verde 86, Tel: 728-9779, on beach, US$70-90d (high season) including continental breakfast, TV, bath, a/c, pleasant, restaurant and bar under construction; *Borinquen Royal*, Av Isla Verde 58, Tel: 728-8400, US$60, also on beach.

In **Old San Juan**, *El Convento* (Ramada), a converted Carmelite nunnery at Cristo 100, is a charming hotel with a Spanish atmosphere and the dining room is in the former chapel, US$150-200, but cheaper rates available, pricey, swimming pool, nice garden in which to have a drink, Tel: 723-9020. Guest houses on Calle San Francisco, information from Joyería Sol, Tanca 207, fan, cooking and washing facilities, friendly and helpful, but absolutely filthy and like cells. Also in Old San Juan are *Central*, Plaza de Armas, Tel: 722-2751, pleasant, satisfactory, US$30d with shower, ask for a room with fan away from a/c units. *Enrique Castro Guest House*, Tacna 205, Tel: 722-5436, at Relojería Suiza Mecánico Cuarzo, 2nd floor (Box 947), difficult to find, US$100d per week. *Buena Vista Guesthouse by the Sea*, Gral Valle 2218, Sta Teresita, English, French spoken, with kitchen, near beach, airport pickup for US$1.

In **Miramar**, *Excelsior*, 801 Ponce de León, Tel: 721-7400, US$124-148d, restaurant, bar, pool; *Miramar*, 606 Av Ponce de León, Tel: 722-6239, "not chic", but clean and friendly, longer stays possible, US$42-50; *El Toro*, 605 Miramar, Tel: 725-5150, US$38-48d, good value, pleasant, close to bus shop, there is an airport limousine to *El Toro*.

In **Santurce**, *Pierre* (Best Western), 105 De Diego, Tel: 721-1200, Fax: 721-3118, from US$113d to US$134.

In **Ponce**, *Hotel Meliá* US$65-70d can be recommended, friendly, roof top and garden terraces (2 Cristina, just off main plaza, PO Box 1431, Tel: 842-0260, Fax: 841-3602), also the *Ponce Holiday Inn*, Route 2, west of the city, Tel: 844-1200, Fax: 841-8085, US$134-170d all year, where there are tennis courts, pools, and golf arrangements made; to the east of the city, on Route 1 near the junction with the autopista is *Days Inn*, Tel: 841-1000, US$120-147. Cheaper hotel near main square; *Hotel Bélgica*, 122 Villa St, Tel: 844-3255, US$25 upwards, some with a/c but not necessarily with windows, hot water but basic. There are about 5 other guesthouses. To the west of Ponce, at Guánica, *Cycle Center Youth Hostel*, cooking facilities.

On Vieques, *La Casa del Francés*, near Esperanza, Tel: 741-3751, US$80d winter, US$55d summer, 18 rooms, casino; *Ocean View Guesthouse*, US-type motel, Tel: 741-3696, US$50d, balconies on seafront; *Sea Gate Guesthouse*, Barriada Fuerte, Tel: 741-4661, US$35-50s or d, pool, tennis and other sports; *New Dawn's Caribbean Retreat*, P O Box 1512, Tel: 741-0495, on hillside 3 miles from Sun Bay, 2-storey wooded house with large deck and hammocks, room upstairs US$35s, US$45d, bed in dormitory US$15, tent space (no tents provided) US$10, kitchen facilities, breakfast and dinner US$15 on request, simple but comfortable accommodation, lots of peace and quiet, community suppers on Thursdays, recommended.

On Culebra, *Bay View Villas*, P O Box 775, Tel: 742-3392/765-5711, two 2-bedroomed villas, US$1,200/week or US$1,000/week, well-equipped, good views overlooking Ensenada Honda, walking distance of Dewey; *Culebra Island Villas*, Tel: 742-3112, or in USA 52 Marlowe Ave, Bricktown, NJ 08724, Tel: (201) 458-5591, 10 units all with kitchen, daily rates (2 days min) from US$65-95 in a studio, US$100-150 in 2-room villa, weekly rates US$395-475, 650-775 respectively; *Posada La Hamaca*, 68 Castelar, Tel: 742-3516, US$45d, well kept.

On the **east coast**, *Las Delicias*, Fajardo Playa, on the dock, across street from post office and customs building, Tel: 863-1818, US$55-60d, bar; in Fajardo try *Guez House de Express*, near ferry dock, 388 Union, small, clean, US$35d, Tel: 863-1362. *Palmas del Mar Hotel*, Humacao, Tel: 852-6000, US$230 and up, hotel rooms or villa resort, 7 restaurants, 18-hole golf course, swimming pools and other sports. On the southeast coast, near Patillas, Km 112, Route 3, is *Caribe Playa*, US$70d winter, US$59 summer, right on the Caribbean, comfortable, restaurant (order dinner in advance), sea bathing and snorkelling in a small, safe area, very

friendly and helpful (owner Esther Geller, manager Minerva Moreno), recommended, Tel: 839-6339 (USA 212-988-1801), Box 8490, Guardarraya, Patillas, PR 00723. At Salinas is a cheap motel.

At Arecibo, *El Cid*, about cheapest of all the hotels and guesthouses which are situated around the main square.

At Mayagüez, *Hilton*, casino, pool, Tel: 831-7575, US$166-196d; *Palma*, on Méndez Vigo, Tel: 834-3800, US$45-55d; *RUM Hotel* (hotel of the Recinto University of Mayagüez), US$9s, US$12d, central, safe, pool, library, Tel: 832-4040 (similar prices at other branches of the University); *Las Américas*, cheap but adequate, on road from *público* terminal to main square; *Colón*, Plaza Colón, no bath, ask for a quiet room. *Hospedaje San Vicente*, Calle San Vicente, very basic.

At Rincón, *La Primavera*, excellent, in US$200 range. *Villa Cofresí* (US$70d) and, alongside it, *Villa Antonio*, see *Paradores* below. Tamboo Resorts has 2 types of accommodation at Rincón: *Beside the Pointe* beach-front hotel on Sandy Beach, US$45-75 high season, US$35-75 low, children welcome, bar, café, water sports (11 rooms, 5 with ocean view, kitchens, ceiling fans); and *Rincón Surf and Board*, ¼ mile from *Beside the Pointe*, in the foothills, US$25-65 high season, US$15-50 low, access to all amenities at *Beside the Pointe*, in either case Tel: 823-8550 (address H-Col 4433, Rincón, PR 00743-9709), or USA (301) 523-9508, reservations advised. *The Lazy Parrot*, P O Box 430, Carrera 413, km 4.1, Barrio Puntas, Tel: 823-5654, rooms sleep 4 in bunk beds, US$20s, US$30d, US$35 triple, US$40 quad, including breakfast Tuesday – Sunday. (At Puntas, Carmen's grocery store has rooms, basic, cooking facilities.)

At Utuado, *Riverside*, bargain with the manager.

There are 16 *Paradores Puertorriqueños* to put you up while touring, some old, most new, with prices starting at US$50d: the majority are to the west of San Juan; for reservations Tel: 721-2884, or 137-800-462-7575. On the north coast, near Quebradillas are *El Guajataca* (Tel: 895-3070), US$75-83, beautifully located on a beach (dangerous swimming), pool, entertainment, restaurant, bars; on the other side of the road, Route 2, and higher up the hill is *Vistamar*, US$58-80, Tel: 895-2065, also with pool, restaurant and bar. On the west coast, near Rincón, *Villa Antonio*, US$60-90 (Tel: 823-2645) pool, beach, tennis courts.

In Mayagüez, *Sol*, Tel: 834-0303, US$50-65, 9 S R Palmer Este; south of Mayagüez are *Boquemar*, at Boquerón, Tel: 851-2158 and *Perichi's*, Playa Joyuda, Tel. 851-3131 (both US$60-65d, latter is well-run, with good restaurant), *Villa Parguera* and *Porlamar* at La Parguera (US$70-80 and US$55 respectively, Tel: 899-3975 and 899-4015, the latter has a/c, kitchen facilities), *Oasis* at San Germán, Tel: 892-1175, not as close to the beach as it claims, but is ideal for the hills, good food and service, pool, jacuzzi, gym, sauna, a/c, US$58-60d.

Another is at **Baños de Coamo** where there are thermal water springs (maximum 15 minutes) and an ordinary pool (spend as long as you like), US$60, Tel: 825-2186, PO Box 540, Coamo, Puerto Rico 00640, recommended; the *Hacienda Gripiñas*, an old coffee plantation house, US$70d, which lies in the mountains near Jayuya, north of Ponce, east of Utuado (Tel: 828-1717); in the same area is *Casa Grande*, Barrio Caonillas, Route 612, Tel: 894-3939, US$65. The only paradores on the east side are *Martorell* at Luquillo, 6A Ocean Drive, close to beach, modern, US$58-60d winter (cheaper with private bath), Tel: 889-2710, advisable to reserve in advance here at any time; *Familia*, on Route 987, Fajardo, US$52-65d, Tel: 863-1193.

Tourism Marketing Group, Tel: 721-8793, arranges Fly-Drive packages, with car hire and accommodation at paradores; rates depend on which paradores you choose, but 3 days, 2 nights, starts at US$165 pp in a double room, 6 days, 5 nights US$350 pp.

See above in the main text under Boquerón for details of Dept of Recreation and Sports family accommodation; there are 3 other such centres at Punta Santiago on the east coast, Punta Guilarte near Patillas and Monte de Estado in the Maricao Forest.

Where To Eat

All major hotels. In **old San Juan**: *Fortaleza*, Fortaleza 252; for Puerto Rican cuisine, *La Tasca del Callejón*, Fortaleza 317; *La Mallorquina*, San Justo 207, the oldest restaurant in the Caribbean, recommended; also on San Justo: *Café de Paris*, No 256; *Szechuan*, Chinese, No

257, and other cafés and *Taco Maker*, No 255. There are several Mexican places in the city, eg *Parián* on Fortaleza; *Taza de Oro*, Luna 254, near San Justo. *La Zaragozana*, San Francisco 356, some Spanish specialities, highly recommended; *Bodegón de La Fortaleza*, Fortaleza 312; *La Danza*, corner of Cristo and Fortaleza; *La Bombonera*, San Francisco 259, restaurant and pastry shop. *4 Seasons Café*, in *Hotel Central*, Plaza de Armas, for good value local lunches; *Tropical Blend*, juice bar in La Calle alley on Fortaleza; *El Batey* bar, Cristo 101; *Manolin Café*, US$5 for just about anything, Puerto Rican food, lunch specials daily. *Nono's*, San Sebastián y Cristo, bar, burgers, salads, steaks, sandwiches, and nearby on San Sebastián (all on Plaza San José), *Patio de Sam* very good for local drinks (happy hour 1600-1900), and *Tasca El Boquerón*. On Av Ponce de León, *El Miramar*, good, but not cheap. *La Buena Mesa*, 605 Ponce de León, good, small, middle price range. Several bars and cafés on Plaza Colón in Old San Juan. There is a huge selection of restaurants in Condado, from the posh to all the fast food chain restaurants. Similarly, Isla Verde is well-served by the fast food fraternity; on the beach at Isla Verde is *The Hungry Sailor* bar and grill, sandwiches, tapas, burgers, with a snack bar next door. *Cecilia's Place*, Rosa St, Isla Verde.

For breakfast or lunch seek out the fondas, not advertised as restaurants but usually part of a private home, or a family-run eating place serving criollo meals which are filling and good value. Recommended in San Juan are: *Macumba*, 2000 Loíza; *Lydia's Place*, 38 Calle Sol, old San Juan, at corner of Escalera de Las Monjas, room for 20 on a rooftop terrace (pork chops, chicken, steak and daily local specialis); *Casa Juanita*, 242 Av Roosevelt, Hato Rey (try chicken asopao or pork chops con mangu); *Cafetería del Parking*, 757 José de Diego, interior, Cayey (specialities include mondongo, and boronia de apio y bacalao – cod and celery root); *D'Arcos*, 605 Miramar, Santurce, speciality is roast veal with stuffed peppers and white bean sauce, also try pega'o (crunchy rice).

Outside San Juan a network of 42 restaurants, called *Mesones Gastronómicos*, has been set up. These places serve Puerto Rican dishes at reasonable prices. Most of the *Parador* restaurants are included; a full list is available for tourist offices. *Qué Pasa* magazine gives a full list of restaurants on the island.

In **Ponce**, the restaurant of the *Meliá Hotel* is good (look out for the "Breaded Lion" on the menu), there is a vegetarian restaurant in the Plaza del Mercado shopping centre, Calle Mayor, 4 blocks northeast from the main plaza. Fast food places on main plaza.

In **Mayagüez** the *Vegetarian Restaurant*, Calle José de Diego, open 1100-1400; *Fuente Tropical*, same street, run by Colombians, good fruit shakes and hamburgers; *Recomeni*, Calle Vigo, good inexpensive food, open all hours, eat in or take away. The area known as Joyuda, just outside the city limits, is famous for seafood restaurants on the beach; inexpensive food, good quality, nice atmosphere, whole, grilled fish is a must, especially snapper (*chillo*).

Camping

Camping is permitted in the Forest Reserves; you have to get a permit (free) from the visitor centres. Camping is also allowed on some of the public beaches, contact the Recreation and Sports Department (Tel: 722-1551 or 721-2800 ext 225). There are tent sites at Añasco, Cerro Gordo, Luquillo, Sombé, near Lake Guajataca and Punta Guilarte, cabins at Boquerón, Punta Guilarte and Punta Santiago, tent and trailer site at Seven Seas. Since Hurricane Hugo, many beach camping facilities have been closed; phone ahead to check.

Food And Drink

Good local dishes are the mixed stew (chicken, seafood, etc), *asopao*; *mofongo*, mashed plantain with garlic served instead of rice, very filling; *mofongo relleno* is the *mofongo* used as a crust around a seafood stew. *Sacocho* is a beef stew with various root vegetables, starchy but tasty. *Empanadillas* are similar to South American *empanadas* but with a thinner dough and filled with fish or meat. *Pastillas* are yucca, peas, meat, usually pork, wrapped in a banana leaf and boiled. *Tostones* are fried banana slices. Rice is served with many dishes; *arroz con habichuelas* (rice with red kidney beans) is a standard side dish. Sometimes a local restaurant will ask if you want *provisiones*; these are root vegetables and are worth trying. *Comida criolla* means "food of the island", *criollo* refers to anything "native" Some local fruit names: *china* is orange, *parcha* passionfruit, *guanábana* soursop, *toronja* grapefruit; juices are made of all these, as well as guava, tamarind and mixtures. *Papaya* in a restaurant may not be fresh fruit, but *dulce de papaya* (candied), served with cheese, a good combination. Guava is served in a similar manner. Local beers are Medalla (a light beer), Gold Label (a premium beer, very good but hard to find) and Indio (a dark beer); a number of US brands and Heineken are brewed under licence. Rums: Don Q is the local favourite, also Palo Viejo, Ron Llave and the world-famous Bacardi (not so highly regarded by puertorriqueños); Ron Barrilito, a small distillery, has a very good reputation. Many restaurants pride themselves on their *piñas coladas*. *Maví* is a drink fermented from the bark of a tree and sold in many snack-bars. Home-grown Puerto Rican coffee is very good.

As most food is imported, the tourist, picknicker, or anyone economizing can eat as cheaply in a restaurant as by buying food in a grocery store.

Tipping

Service is usually included in the bill, but where no fixed service charge is included, it is recommended that 15-20% is given to waiters, taxi drivers, etc.

Nightclubs

Jazz at The Place, Calle Fortaleza 154 in old San Juan, no admission charge, drinks about US$2. *Shannons Irish Pub*, Condado, T1 bus from airport passes it, live music (rock and roll), beer US$2.50.

Sports

All the major hotels provide instruction and equipment for water skiing, snorkelling, boating and day trips to areas of aquatic interest. At Puerta de Tierra, near the *Caribe Hilton*, is the sports complex built for the 1979 Pan-American Games.

Shopping

Puerto Rico is a large producer of rum, with many different types ranging from light rums for mixing with soft drinks to dark brandy-type rums (see above). Hand made cigars can still be found in Old San Juan and Puerta de Tierra. The largest shopping mall in the Caribbean is Plaza las Américas in Hato Rey, others include Plaza Carolina in Carolina, Río Hondo in Levittown, Plaza del Carmen in Caguas and Mayagüez Mall in Mayagüez. There are more traditional shops, but also many souvenir shops in Old San Juan. Imported goods from all over the world are available. Local artesanías include wooden carvings, musical instruments, lace, ceramics (especially model house fronts, eg from La Casa de Las Casitas, Cristo 250), hammocks, masks and basketwork. There are several shops in San Juan, but it is more interesting to visit the workshops around Puerto Rico. Contact the Centro de Artes Populares (Tel: 724-6250) or the Tourism Artisan Office (Tel: 721-2400 ext 248) for details. Many of the tourist shops in the old city sell Andean goods.

There are a number of bookshops in the metropolitan area: The Bookstore, in Old San Juan, has an excellent selection of English and Spanish titles. The Instituto de Cultura Puertorriqueña, Plaza de San José, has a good book and record shop with stock of all the best known Puerto Rican writers (all in Spanish). Another record shop near here is Saravá, Cristo at the corner of Sol 101, local, Caribbean, jazz and "world music".

Banks

Banco Popular; Banco de San Juan; Banco Mercantil de Puerto Rico; and branches of US and foreign banks.

Currency

United States dollar. Locally, a dollar may be called a *peso*, 25 cents a *peseta*, 5 cents a *bellón* (but in Ponce a *bellón* is 10 cents and a *ficha* is 5 cents). Most international and US credit cards are accepted.

Warning

Female tourists should avoid the Condado beach areas at night if alone. Take precautions against theft from your person and your car, wherever you are on the island.

Health

"La monga" is a common, flue-like illness, nothing serious, it goes away after a few days. Avoid swimming in rivers: bilharzia may be present.

Medical Services

Government and private hospitals. Ambulance, Tel: 343-2500.

Public Holidays

New Year's Day, Three Kings' Day (6 January), De Hostos' Birthday (11 January), Washington's Birthday (22 February), Emancipation Day (22 March), Good Friday, José de Diego's Birthday (16 April), Memorial Day (30 May), St John the Baptist (24 June), Independence Day (4 July), Muñoz Rivera's Birthday (17 July), Constitution Day (25 July), Dr José Celso Barbosa's Birthday (27 July), Labour Day (1 September), Columbus Day (12 October), Veterans' Day (11 November), Discovery of Puerto Rico (19 November), Thanksgiving Day (25 November), Christmas Day.

Everything is closed on public holidays. One of the most important is 24 June, though in fact the capital grinds to a halt the previous afternoon and everyone heads for the beach. Here there is loud *salsa* music and barbecues until midnight when everyone walks backwards into the sea to greet the Baptist and ensure good fortune.

Places Of Worship

Roman Catholic, Episcopal, Baptist, Seventh Day Adventist, Presbyterian, Lutheran, Christian Science and Union Church. There is also a Jewish community. At the Anglican-Episcopal cathedral in San Juan there are services in both Spanish and English.

Postal Service

Inside the new Post Office building in Hato Rey, on Av Roosevelt, there is a separate counter for sales of special tourist stamps. In Old San Juan, the Post Office is in an attractive old rococo-style building, at the corner of San Justo and Recinto Sur. *Poste restante* is called General Delivery, letters are held for 9 days.

Telephone

Operated by Puerto Rico Telephone Co, state-owned. Local calls from coin-operated booths cost US$0.10, but from one city to another on the island costs more (eg US$1.25 Ponce-San Juan). Local calls from hotel rooms cost US$2.60 and often a charge is made even if there is no connection. The area code is 809; 800 numbers can be used. Overseas calls can be made from the AT&T office at Parada 11, Av Ponce de León 850, Miramar (opposite *Hotel Excelsior*, bus T1 passes outside, a chaotic place), from an office next to the Museo del Mar on Pier One, and from the airport. Three minutes to New York, US$2.35 and to the UK, US$14. The blue pages in the telephone book are a tourist section in English, divided by subject.

Broadcasting

Two radio stations have English programmes.

Newspapers

San Juan Star is the only daily English paper. There are three Spanish daily papers of note, *El Mundo, El Vocero* and *El Nuevo Día*.

Tourist Information

The Puerto Rico Tourist Bureau, PO Box 4435, San Juan 00905, with offices also at the international airport (Tel: 791-1014), Convention Center Condado (Tel: 723-3135), Ashford 1106, Condado; the Puerto Rico Tourism Company, in the old jail on Princesa, below the city walls in old San Juan (the building was built in 1837, tours may be given if you ask), Tel: (800) 866-5829 for information about Puerto Rico in the USA or Tel: 721-2400, La Casita, near the piers, for cruise ship visitors (serves free rum drinks Wednesday, Thursday and Saturday from midday onwards), and an office on the Plaza de Armas. There are also offices in Chicago (Tel: 312-861-0049), New York (Tel: 800-223-6530), Los Angeles (Tel: 213-874-5991), Miami (Tel: 305-381-8915), London (67-69 Whitfield Street, London W1P 5RL, Tel: 071-636-6558, Fax: 255-2131), Paris (10 rue de l'Isly, 75008 Paris, Tel: 429-30-012), Madrid (Calle Capitán Haya 23, 1-7-4, 28020 Madrid, Tel: 34-1-555-6811, Fax: 555-6851), Mexico City (Calle Xola 535, Piso 15, Colonia del Valle, Mexico DF 03100, Tel: 525-523-9905), Milan (Via Le Maino 35, 21022 Milan, Tel: 02-792966), Stockholm (Sergat Scandinavia, Kamma Kargatan 41, S-111 24 Stockholm, Tel: 468 115495) and Toronto (Tel: 416-969-9025). The Caribbean Travel Service, Av Ashford 1300, Condado, is happy to help. Out in the country, tourist information can be obtained from the town halls, usually found on the main plaza; in Ponce the office is in the Casa Armstrong-Poventud, Plaza las Delicias, Tel: 840-5695. In Aguadilla, Tel: 890-3315 and in the west of island, Tel: 831-5220. Hours are usually Monday-Friday, 0800-1200, 1300-1430.

Qué Pasa, a monthly guide for tourists published by the Tourism Company, can be obtained free from the tourist office. It is very helpful.

The Puerto Rico Tourist Zone Police are at Vieques Street, Condado (Tel: 722-0738 and 724-5210).

Two books which may be useful to visitors are *The Other Puerto Rico*, by Kathryn Robinson (Permanent Press, 1987), US$11.95, and *The Adventure Guide to Puerto Rico*, by Harry S Pariser (Hunter, 1989), US$13.95, they give more detail on the out of the way places than we have space for.

There is a Dominican Republic Tourist Office at Av Ponce de León 954.

US VIRGIN ISLANDS

Introduction

THE VIRGIN ISLANDS are a group of about 107 small islands situated between Puerto Rico and the Leeward Islands; the total population is about 122,000. Politically they are divided into two groups: the larger western group, with a population of 105,000 (1990 est), was purchased from Denmark by the USA in 1917 and remains a US Territory; the smaller eastern group constitutes a British Crown Colony, with a population of only 16,750. Apart from their historical background, having been discovered by Columbus on the same voyage and named by him after Ursula and her 1,000 virgin warriors, the islands have little in common. The two groups share the same language, currency and cost of living, but the US group is very much more developed than the British, and tourism has been a prime source of income for much longer.

THE US VIRGIN ISLANDS (USVI), in which the legacies of Danish ownership are very apparent, contain three main islands: St Thomas, St John and St Croix, lying about 40 miles east of Puerto Rico. There are 68 islands in all, although most of them are uninhabited. They have long been developed as holiday centres for US citizens and because of that are distinct from the British Virgin Islands, which have only recently started to develop their tourist potential. The population, mainly black, has always been English-speaking, despite the long period of Danish control, although some Spanish is in use, particularly on St Croix. The West Indian dialect is mostly English, with inflections from Dutch, Danish, French, Spanish, African languages and Créole.

History
The islands were "discovered" by Columbus on his second voyage in 1493 and, partly because of their number, he named them "Las Once Mil Vírgenes" (the 11,000 virgins) in honour of the legend of St Ursula and her 11,000 martyred virgins. There were Indian settlements in all the major

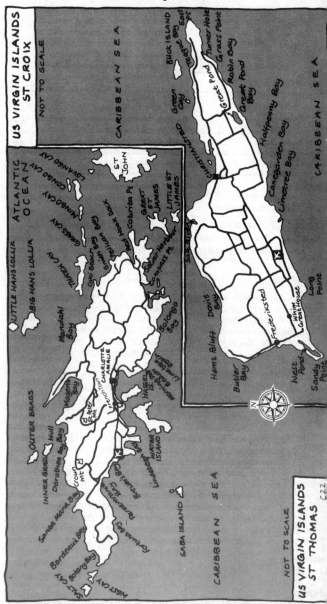

US VIRGIN ISLANDS
ST CROIX

NOT TO SCALE

CARIBBEAN SEA

BUCK ISLAND

Green Cay

Teague Bay

East Pt

Turner Hole

Grass Point

Robin Bay

Great Pond

Great Pond Bay

Halfpenny Bay

Canegarden Bay

Limetree Bay

CARIBBEAN SEA

CHRISTIANSTED

SOUTH RIVER

Harn's Bluff

Davi's Bay

Frederiksted

Whim Great House

Butler Bay

West Pond

Long Point

Sandy Point

N

US VIRGIN ISLANDS
ST THOMAS

NOT TO SCALE

C22

ATLANTIC OCEAN

LITTLE HANS LOLLIK

BIG HANS LOLLIK

LOVANGO CAY

CONGO CAY

MINGO CAY

GRASS CAY

THATCH CAY

ST JOHN

Sib Reef Bay

Hull Bay

Red Hook Dock

Cabrita Pt

GREAT ST JAMES

LITTLE ST JAMES

OUTER BRASS

INNER BRASS

Santa Maria Bay

Magens Bay

Mandahl Bay

Dorothea Bay

St Peter Mt

CHARLOTTE AMALIE

French Town

HASSEL IS

Water Bay

Compass Pt

Sugar Bay

Crown Mt

Lindberg Bay

HATHA ISLAND

Brewers Bay

Fortuna Bay

Bordeaux Bay

Bohang Bay

SALT CAY

WEST CAY

SABA ISLAND

CARIBBEAN SEA

islands of the group and the first hostile action with the Caribs took place during Columbus' visit. Spain asserted its exclusive right to settle the islands but did not colonize them, being more interested in the larger and more lucrative Greater Antilles. European settlement did not begin until the 17th century, when few Indians were to be found. St Croix (Santa Cruz) was settled by the Dutch and the English around 1625, and later by the French. In 1645 the Dutch abandoned the island and went to St Eustatius and St Maarten. In 1650 the Spanish repossessed the island and drove off the English, but the French, under Philippe de Loinvilliers de Poincy of the Knights of Malta, persuaded the Spanish to sail for Puerto Rico. Three years later de Poincy formally deeded his islands to the Knights of Malta although the King of France retained sovereignty. St Croix prospered and planters gradually converted their coffee, ginger, indigo and tobacco plantations to the more profitable sugar, and African slavery was introduced. Wars, illegal trading, privateering, piracy and religious conflicts finally persuaded the French Crown that a colony on St Croix was not militarily or economically feasible and in 1695/6 the colony was evacuated to St Domingue.

A plan for colonizing St Thomas was approved by Frederik III of Denmark in 1665 but the first settlement failed. The Danes asserted authority over uninhabited St John in 1684, but the hostility of the English in Tortola prevented them from settling until 1717. In 1733 France sold St Croix to the Danish West India & Guinea Company and in 1754 the Danish West Indies became a royal colony. This was the most prosperous period for the Danish islands. After the end of Company rule and its trading monopoly, St Thomas turned increasingly toward commerce while in St Croix plantation agriculture flourished. St Thomas became an important shipping centre with heavy reliance on the slave trade. Denmark was the first European nation to end its participation in the slave trade in 1802. Illegal trade continued, however, and British occupation of the Virgin Islands between 1801 and 1802 and again between 1807 and 1815 prevented enforcement of the ban.

The Danish Virgin Islands reached a peak population of 43,178 in 1835, but thereafter fell to 27,086 by 1911. Sailing ships were replaced by steamships which found it less necessary to transship in St Thomas. Prosperity declined with a fall in sugar prices, a heavy debt burden, soil exhaustion, development of sugar beet in Europe, hurricanes and droughts and the abolition of slavery. In 1847 a Royal decree provided that all slaves would be free after 1859 but the slaves of St Croix were unwilling to wait and rebelled in July 1848. By the late 19th century economic decline became pronounced. The sugar factory on St Croix was inefficient and in the 20th century the First World War meant less shipping for St Thomas, more inflation, unemployment and labour unrest. The Virgin Islands became a liability for Denmark and the economic benefits of colonialism no longer existed. Negotiations with the USA had taken place intermittently ever since the 1860s for cession of the Virgin Islands to the USA. The USA wanted a Caribbean naval base for security reasons and after the 1914 opening of the Panama Canal was particularly concerned to guard against German acquisition of Caribbean territory. In 1917, the islands were sold for US$25m but no political, social or economic progress was made for several years. The islands were under naval rule during and after the War and it was not until 1932 that US citizenship was granted to all natives of the Virgin Islands.

A devastating hurricane in 1928, followed by the stock market crash of 1929, brought US awareness of the need for economic and political modernization. Several years of drought, the financial collapse of the sugar refineries, high unemployment, low wages and very high infant mortality characterized these years. In 1931 naval rule was replaced by a civil government. In 1934, the Virgin Islands Company (VICO) was set up as a long term development "partnership programme". The sugar and rum industry benefited from increased demand in the Second World War. VICO improved housing, land and social conditions, particularly in rural areas, but the end of the wartime construction boom, wartime demand for rum and the closing of the submarine base, brought further economic recession. However, the severance of diplomatic relations between the USA and Cuba shifted tourism towards the islands. Construction boomed and there was even a labour shortage. With immigrant labour, the population increased and by 1970 per capita income reached US$2,400, five times that of the Caribbean region as a whole, with about half of the labour force engaged in tourist activities and tourism providing about 60% of the islands' revenues. With the shift from agriculture to tourism, VICO was officially disbanded in 1966, along with the production of sugarcane. Various tax incentives, however, promoted the arrival of heavy industry, and during the 1960s the Harvey Alumina Company and the Hess Oil Company began operating on St Croix. By 1970, the economy was dominated by mainland investment and marked by white-owned and managed enterprises based on cheap imported labour from other Caribbean islands.

On 17 September 1989, Hurricane Hugo ripped across St Croix causing damage or destruction to 90% of the buildings and leaving 22,500 people homeless. The disaster was followed by civil unrest, with rioting and looting, and US army troops were sent in to restore order. The territorial government, located on St Thomas, had been slow to react to the disaster on St Croix and was strongly criticized. Subsequently, a referendum endorsed the establishment of some sort of municipal government on each island which would be more responsive to that island's needs. Work on constitutional reform was expected to take some time.

Government

In 1936 the Organic Act of the Virgin Islands of the United States provided for two municipal councils and a Legislative Assembly in the islands. Suffrage was extended to all residents of twenty one and over who could read and write English. Discrimination on the grounds of race, colour, sex or religious belief was forbidden and a bill of rights was included. Real political parties now emerged, based on popular support. In 1946, the first black governor was appointed to the Virgin Islands and in 1950 the first native governor was appointed. In 1968 the Elective Governor Act was passed, to become effective in 1970 when, for the first time, Virgin Islanders would elect their own governor and lieutenant governor. The Act also abolished the presidential veto of territorial legislation and authorized the legislature to override the governor's veto by a two-thirds majority vote. The USVI is an unincorporated Territory under the US Department of Interior with a non-voting Delegate in the House of Representatives. The Governor is elected every four years; there are 15 Senators; judicial power is vested in local courts. All persons born in the USVI are citizens of the United States, but do not vote in presidential elections while resident on the islands. The present Governor is Mr Alexander Farrelly.

The Economy

USVI residents enjoy a comparatively high standard of living (the cost of living is the highest in the USA), unemployment is low, at around 4%, but the working population is young and there is constant pressure for new jobs. The islands used to rely on the Martin Marietta alumina plant, and the Hess oil refinery, operating well below capacity, for employment and income, but nowadays the major economic activity is tourism. About 1.9m visitors come every year, of which over 35% arrive by air and about 64% are cruise ship passengers. Earnings from tourism average US$600-700m, about 70% of non-oil revenues. The number of hotel rooms is now around 5,000, generating jobs for two thirds of the labour force.

Industry is better developed than in many Caribbean islands and exports of manufactured goods include watches, textiles, electronics, pharmaceuticals and rum. The Hess Oil refinery operates at less than 400,000 barrels a day nowadays, compared with its previous peak capacity of 728,000 b/d, but investment of US$550m is being made in a fluid catalytic cracking unit to produce unleaded gasoline. Industrial incentives and tax concessions equivalent to those enjoyed by Puerto Rico, are designed to attract new investors with US markets to the islands. Over 30 large US corporations have set up manufacturing operations in the USVI and industrial parks are being built.

Agriculture has declined in importance since sugar production ended, and the poor soil prevents much commercial farming. Emphasis is placed on growing food crops for the domestic market and fruit, vegetables and sorghum for animal feed have been introduced. Fishing in the USVI waters is mostly for game rather than for commercial purposes. The islands' lack of natural resources makes them heavily dependent on imports, both for domestic consumption and for later re-exports, such as oil and manufactured goods. The trade account is traditionally in deficit, but is offset by tourist revenues and by US transfers.

Damage from Hurricane Hugo, principally on St Croix which was declared a major disaster area, was estimated at US$1.25 bn, equivalent to annual gnp. The islands were destined to receive US$600m in federal assistance. Reconstruction led to improvements in infrastructure and most houses were upgraded.

Flora and Fauna
The Virgin Islands' national bird is the yellow breast (*Coereba flaveola*); the national flower is the yellow cedar (*Tecoma Stans*). Most of St John is a national park (see below). Also a park is Hassel Island, off Charlotte Amalie. The National Parks Service headquarters is at Red Hook, St Thomas. In Red Hook too is the Island Resources Foundation (Tel: 775-6225, PO Box 33, USVI 00802; US office, 1718 P Street NW, Suite T4, Washington DC 20036, Tel: 265-9712). This non-governmental office which is also a consulting firm, but non-profit-making, is open to serious researchers and investigators seeking information on wildlife, tourism and the environment; it has an extensive library. It may also be used as a contact base for those seeking specialist information on other islands. The Audubon Society is represented on St John by Peg Fisher at the At Your Service Travel Agency. *Virgin Islands Birdlife*, published by the USVI Cooperative Extension Service, with the US National Park Service, is available for birdwatchers.

On St Croix, the National Parks Service office is in the old customs building on the waterfront. Buck Island (see below) is a national marine park. In Christiansted, contact the Environmental Association, PO Box 3839, Tel: 773-1989, office in Apothecary Hall Courtyard, Company Street. The Association runs hikes, boat trips and walks, and in March-May, in conjunction with Earthwatch and the US

Fish and Wildlife Department, takes visitors to see the leatherback turtles at Sandy Point (Tel: 773-7545 for information on trips). The association plans to make Salt River (**see page 332**) a natural park for wildlife, reef and mangroves. There are books, leaflets, etc, available at the association's office. *Exploring St Croix* by Shirley Imsand and Richard Philibosian costs US$10 and is very detailed on out of the way places and how to get to them.

The mongoose was brought to the islands during the plantation days to kill rats that ate the crops. Unfortunately rats are nocturnal and mongooses are not and they succeeded only in eliminating most of the parrots. Now you see them all over the islands, especially near the rubbish dumps. There are many small lizards and some iguanas of up to four feet long. The iguanas sleep in the trees and you can see them and feed them (favourite food hibiscus flowers) at the Limetree beach. St John has a large population of wild donkeys which are pests; they bite, steal picnic lunches and ruin gardens. On all three islands, chickens, pigs, goats and cows have the right of way on the roads.

St Thomas

St Thomas lies about 75 miles east of Puerto Rico at 18°N, 40 miles north of St Croix. Thirteen miles long and less than three miles wide, with an area of 32 square miles and population of 51,000, St Thomas rises out of the sea to a range of hills that runs down its spine. The highest peak, Crown Mountain, is 1,550 feet, but on St Peter Mountain, 1,500 feet, is a viewpoint at Mountain Top. Various scenic roads can be driven, such as Skyline Drive (Route 40), from which both sides of the island can be seen simultaneously. This road continues west as St Peter Mountain Road, with a detour to Hull Bay on the north coast. Route 35, Mafolie Road, leaves the capital, Charlotte Amalie, heading north to cross the Skyline Drive and becomes Magens Bay Road, descending to the beautiful bay described below. It should be said that much of the island has been built upon, especially on its eastern half.

Beaches and Watersports

There are 44 beaches of which Magens Bay on the north coast is considered to be the finest on the island and wonderfully safe for small children. There are changing facilities and you can rent snorkelling equipment (but the snorkelling is not the best on the island) and loungers. Other good beaches are at Lindberg Bay (southwest, close to the airport runway, good for plane spotters, also several constuction sites in the area), Morningstar Bay (south coast near *Frenchman's Reef Hotel*, beach and watersports equipment for hire), Bolongo Bay, Sapphire Bay (east coast, good snorkelling, beach gear for rent) and Brewer's Bay (can be reached by bus from Charlotte Amalie, get off just beyond the airport). Hull Bay on the north coast is good for surfing and snorkelling. At Coki Beach (northeast, showers, lockers, water skiing, jet skiing), a US$6.50 taxi ride from St Thomas, is the Coral World underwater observatory (US$12 entrance). On the beach snorkelling equipment can be rented for US$6, snorkelling is good just off the beach. Windsurfing lessons and rentals at Morningstar, Magens Bay, Sapphire Beach, Secret Harbour and the *Stouffer Grand*. Snorkelling gear can be rented at all major hotels and the dive shops. Sunfish sailboats for rent at Morningstar, Magens Bay and the *Stouffer Grand*. Waterskiing and jet skiing at Mad Max Watersports at Lindberg Bay. There are few deserted beaches left on St Thomas, although out of season they are less crowded. The most inaccessible, and therefore more likely to be empty, are those along the northwest coast, which need four-wheel drive to get there.

Otherwise for solitude take a boat to one of the uninhabited islets offshore and discover your own beaches.

Diving and Marine Life

There is deep sea fishing with the next world record in every class lurking just under the boat. The open Atlantic Blue Marlin tournament is held in August every year; other game fish include white marlin, kingfish, sailfish, tarpon, Alison tuna and wahoo. No fishing license is required for shoreline fishing; government pamphlets list 100 good spots (Tel: 775-6762). Deep sea boats include *Fish Hawk* (Tel: 775-9058), *Prowler* (Tel: 779-2515), which offers a discount if you fail to catch a fish, *Boobie Hatch* (Tel: 775-0685), specializes in tuna, marlin, wahoo at the 100 fathom drop, *The Naked Turtle* (Tel: 774-9873). For inshore light tackle fishing, *Ocean Quest* (Tel: 776-5176). Sailing of all types and cruises are available. Half day sails from US$40, full day from US$65 and sunset cruises from US$30 are offered by many boats, including *Coconuts* (Tel: 775-5959), a 51-foot trimaran; *Independence* (Tel: 775-1405), a 44-foot ketch; *Naked Turtle Too* (Tel: 774-9873), a 53-foot catamaran; *Ann-Marie II* (Tel: 771-1858), a 40-foot yacht, maximum four guests; *The Alexander Hamilton* (Tel: 775-6500), a 65-foot traditional schooner; and *Spirit of St Christopher*, a 70-foot catamaran claiming to be the fastest sailboat in the Caribbean, lovely sailing, especially at sunset, half day US$45, sunset cruise US$30, Tel: 774-7169. Power boats offering day trips are *Stormy Petrol* (Tel: 775-7990) and *Limnos II* (Tel: 776-4410). Rafting Adventures (Tel: 779-2032) offers very fast, hard bottom inflatables for tours to St John and the BVI. You can explore on your own by renting a small power boat from Nauti Nymph (Tel: 775 5066), 21-foot runabouts; See An Ski (Tel: 775-6265), 21-foot makos; or Calypso (Tel: 775-2628), 22-foot, six passengers, US$150/day, 27-foot, eight passengers, US$185/day, including fuel, boats equipped with VHF radios, ice chest, stereo, fish finder, snorkelling gear, very helpful with planning a route, also scuba, waterskiing and fishing gear can be provided. Charter yachts available in a wide variety of luxury and size, with or without crew, cost about the same as a good hotel; Virgin Island Charter Yacht League, Tel: 774-3944 or (800) 524-2061. Note that if you plan to sail in both the US and British Virgin Islands it is cheaper to charter your boat in the BVI. To get on a yacht as crew, either for passage or paid charter jobs, try 'Captains and Crew', at *Yacht Haven* in Charlotte Amalie, a placement service which charges US$15/year and a portion of your first pay cheque.

The waters around the islands are so clear that snorkelling is extremely popular. Spearfishing is not allowed and you may not remove any living things from underwater such as coral, live shells or sea fans. For divers, there are over 200 dive sites, caves, coral reefs, drop offs and lots of colourful fish to see, although be careful of short sighted barracuda if you swim into murky water. There are several wrecks of ships and even a wrecked plane to explore. Many of the resorts offer diving packages or courses and there are several dive companies. Equipment and instruction for underwater photography are available. A one-tank dive costs around US$40 while a two-tank dive starts from US$55. Coki Beach Dive Club, Tel: 775-5620 offers an introductory dive for US$25, cruise ships bring their guests here. Chris Sawyer Diving Centre, Tel: 775-7320, specializes in quality service to small groups, great all day wreck of the *Rhone* trip once a week. Joe Vogel Diving Co, Tel: 775-7610, in business since 1960, excellent night dives. Sea Horse, Tel: 776-1987, will provide ground transport, offers lobster dives for experienced divers. The Atlantis Submarine dives to 150 feet for those who can not scuba dive but want to see the exotic fish, coral sponges and other underwater life. Located at Building VI, Bay L, Havensight Mall, St Thomas Tel: 776-5650 for reservations, or 776-0288 for information (also kiosk on waterfront, usually 6 dives daily). You have to take a four-mile launch ride on the *Yukon III* to join the submarine at Buck Island. One-hour day dives US$58, night dives US$66, children 4-12 half price.

Sports

There are a few public tennis courts (two at Long Bay and two at Sub Base) which operate on a first come first served basis, but the hotel courts at *Bluebeard's Castle, Frenchman's Reef, Lime Tree Tennis Center, Mahogany Run Sapphire Beach* and *Stouffer Grand* are mostly lit for night time play and open for non-residents if you phone in advance to book. Rates range around US$10 for 45 minutes. There is an 18-hole, 6,300-yard golf course with lovely views at Mahogany Run, green fee US$60 pp, cheaper after 1400. A miniature golf course is at Smith Bay, lots of fun, $4 for 18 holes. Horse riding can be arranged. Horse racing is a popular spectator sport.

Festivals

Carnival 21-26 April. Most spectacular. Dating back to the arrival of African slaves who danced bamboulas based on ritual worship of the gods of Dahomey the festivities have since been redirected towards Christianity. Parades with costumed bands include the J'Ouvert Morning Tramp, the Children's Parade Mocko Jumbis on stilts and steel bands (for information on Mocko Jumb dancing, contact Willard S John, see below under St Croix **festivals**).

The Capital

The harbour at **Charlotte Amalie**, capital of St Thomas and also of the entire USVI, still bustles with colour and excitement, although the harbour area can be a startling contrast for the visitor arriving by sea from the British Virgin Islands. As the Fort Christian Museum (see below) puts it, "Oversized architecturally inappropriate buildings have marred the scenic beauty of the harbour. Harbour congestion has become a major problem." One could add that the streets are congested, too. But as the museum also says, there are still a number of historical buildings. The town was built by the Danes, who named it after their King's consort, but to most visitors it remains "St Thomas". Beautiful old Danish houses painted in a variety of pastel colours are a reminder of the island's history. There are also picturesque churches one of the oldest synagogues in the Western Hemisphere (1833) is on Crystal Gade, an airy, domed building, with a sand floor and hurricane-proof walls it has books for sale in the office, iced spring water and visitors are given a 10-minute introduction, free, worth a visit. The Dutch Reformed Church is the oldest established church, having had a congregation since 1660 although the present building dates from 1846. The Frederick Lutheran Church dates from 1820 and its parish hall was once the residence of Jacob H S Lind (1806-27). There are several old fortifications to see: Bluebeard's Castle Tower and Blackbeard's Castle, the latter built in 1679, now an inn and restaurant. The Virgin Islands Museum, in the former dungeon at Fort Christian (1666-80), is open Monday-Friday, 0830-1630, Saturday 0930-1600, free, but donations welcome as much restoration work remains to be done; there are historical and natural history sections and an art gallery. In contrast to the red-painted fort is the green Legislative Building, originally the Danish police barracks (1874). Government House, off Kongens Gade

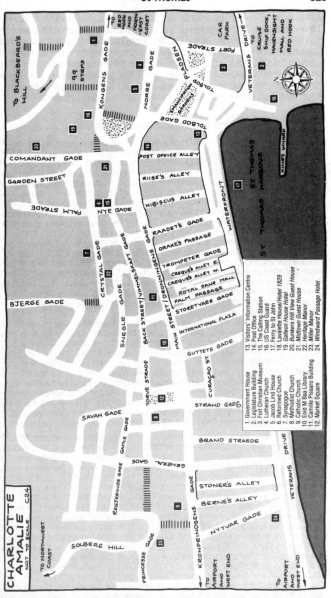

CHARLOTTE AMALIE
NOT TO SCALE
C24

1. Government House
2. Legislature Building
3. Fort Christian Museum
4. Lutheran Church
5. Jacob Lind House
6. Reformed Church
7. Synagogue
8. Methodist Church
9. Catholic Church
10. Enid M Baa Library
11. Camille Pissaro Building
12. Market Square
13. Visitors' Information Centre
14. Post Office
15. The Calling Station
16. US Coast Guard
17. Ferry to St John/Red Hook
18. Lavalette House Hotel 1829
19. Galleon House Hotel
20. Bunkers Hill View Guest House
21. Midtown Guest House
22. Heritage Manor
23. Miller Manor
24. Windward Passage Hotel

was built in 1865-87. The Enid M Baa Library and Archive is on Main Street, it is another early 19th century edifice. Two historical buildings which cannot be visited are the Danish Consulate, on Denmark Hill, whose red and white flag can be clearly seen above the town, and the house of the French painter, Camille Pissaro, on Main Street. The Dockside Bookshop in Havensight Mall (at the Cruise Ship Dock) has books and other publications on the Virgin Islands and the Caribbean in general. The Old Mill, up Crown Mountain Road from Sub Base traffic light is an old sugar mill open to the public.

Island Information—St Thomas

Transport Harry S Truman international airport; the taxi stand is at the far left end of the new terminal, a long way from the commuter flights from Puerto Rico and other islands. Taxi to town US$4.50 (US$4 if more than one passenger). There are public buses every 20 minutes 0600-1900 from the terminal to the town, US$1, and hourly open-air taxi-buses which charge US$3 for the trip from Red Hook to Market Square. Bus services (US$0.75 city fare, US$1 country fare, exact change) with a new fleet of buses, run from town to the university, to Four Winds Plaza and to Red Hook (every hour); new routes are being added, contact Mannassah bus liners (Tel: 774-5678). Cabs are not metered but a list of fares is published in St Thomas This Week and Here's How; fares list must be carried by each driver. Rates quoted are for one passenger and additional passengers are charged extra; drivers are notorious for trying to charge each passenger the single passenger rate. Airport to Red Hook is US$10 for one, US$6.00 each for multiple passengers, town to Magens Bay is US$6.50 for one, US$4 each for multiple. When travelling on routes not covered by the official list, it is advisable to agree the fare in advance. VI taxi Radio Despatch, Tel: 774-4550, Indpendent Taxi, Tel: 776-1006, 24-hour Radio Dispatch Taxi Service, Tel: 776-0496. Gypsy cabs, unlicensed taxis, operate outside Charlotte Amalie; they are cheaper but if you use one make sure you agree fare and route before you get in.

All types of wheels are available with rental firms plentiful. Car hire is about US$35/day, or from Budget US$42 with second day free and coupons for entry into local attractions. There are also group tours by surrey, bus or taxi. Island tours cost US$12 pp, many leave from Main Street at about 1200; complete tours only are sold. Road works in Charlotte Amalie were started in mid-1992 and construction time were estimated at 1-2 years, causing terrible traffic jams. Try to avoid driving in town.

There are a number of ferry boats to various destinations, including one from Red Hook to nearby St John (every hour from 0800 to 2400 plus 0630 and 0730 Monday to Friday, takes 20 minutes, US$3 each way). Charlotte Amalie to St John, US$7, 45 minutes; there is also a ferry from downtown to Frenchman's Reef Hotel and Morningstar beach, US$3 each way, leaving every hour 0900-1700, 15 minutes, a nice way to go to the beach.

Where To Stay There are many hotels on St Thomas and it is possible to find somewhere to stay for US$40d a night in town or up in the hills. If you can afford it, the newer, chain hotels are comfortable, but their rates start from US$90d. Summer rates are about 33% cheaper. There is a Hotel Association counter at the airport which can help you with reservations. Please note that non-inclusion does not imply non-recommendation. Resorts, apartments and condominiums are clustered around the east end, such as the *Stouffer Grand Beach* on Water Bay (PO Box 8267, Tel: 775-1510), hill or beachside suites ranging from US$295 to US$415, well-appointed, 2 pools, restaurants, bars, complimentary watersports, sailing can be arranged, lovely views over the resort's own beach to St John and the British Virgins; next to *Stouffer* is *Point Pleasant Resort*, US$240-350d, Tel: 775-7200. On the south coast is *Bolongo Bay Beach* US$200-215 (PO Box 7337, Tel: 775-1800), among others, and overlooking the entrance to Charlotte Amalie harbour and above Morningstar Beach, the huge *Frenchman's Reef* (a *Holiday Inn*, PO Box 7100, Tel: 776-8500), all facilities, US$250-295d. West of Charlotte Amalie are Emerald Beach Resort, opened in 1991, pool, bar, restaurant, 'The Palms' rooms have ocean and airport view and *Island Beachcomber* (PO Box 2579, Tel: 774-5250, US$125-140, poor plumbing but pleasant), both on Lindberg Bay, sheltered beach at end of airport runway. *Magens Point Resort Hotel*, Tel: 775-5500,

Fax: 776-5524, half a mile from the sea overlooking Magens Bay, 3 miles from Charlotte Amalie, pool, tennis, adjacent to Mahogany Run Golf Course, sailing, fishing, diving packages available, 32 rooms and 23 suites, US$160-300, *Pavilions and Pools*, Tel: 775-6110, on Sapphire Beach, offers suites and kitchens and your own private pool, very romantic, recommended, US$230-255, CP. Two new luxury hotels with all facilities were due to open in summer 1992: *The Grand Palazzo* on Great Bay and *Sugar Bay*, part of the *Holiday Inn* chain, near the *Stouffer Grand*.

In Charlotte Amalie, winter rates: *Bluebeard's Castle*, Tel: 774-1600, US$180-230, 150 rooms, sports, pool; *Blackbeard's Castle*, on Blackbeard's Hill, Tel: 776-1234, US$170-190d, restaurant. On the waterfront, Veterans' Drive heading towards the airport, is *Windward Passage* (PO Box 640, Tel: 774-5200), US$135-230, with pool, restaurant, entertainment in modern block. In the centre, on Government Hill is *Hotel 1829*, another historical building, with pool, restaurant, very comfortable (PO Box 1576, Tel: 776-1829), US$80-280; next door, behind *The Fiddle Leaf Restaurant*, is *Galleon House*, US$65-115 (PO Box 6577, Tel: 774-6952), swimming pool, verandah, gourmet breakfast, recommended. *Heritage Manor* Snegle Gade (just off Back Street), Tel: 774-3003, US$70 (shared bath) to US$180 (suite), breakfast included in winter season only, small pool (in old baker's oven), honour bar, clean, comfortable, helpful, each room different, recommended; *Bunkers' Hill View Guest House*, 9 Commandant Gade, Tel: 776-8056, from US$80, 2 sections, kitchens, TV, etc, good value; in same area but closer to centre, *Midtown Guest House* (PO Box 521, Tel: 774-6677), US$45-75, cash or travellers' cheques only; *Domini Hus*, US$35d, friendly, often full, but reported to be dirty; *Miller Manor* (PO Box 1570, Tel: 774-1535), on the hill behind the Catholic Cathedral, clean, very friendly, a/c, from US$48-50 (no credit cards), recommended; up Solberg Hill, going up from *Miller Manor*, is *Danish Chalet*, Tel: 774-5764, US$65-85, seventh day free, helpful, honour bar, pool, short walk to town, pleasant; *Beverley Hill Guesthouse*, US$35-60, Tel: 774-2693, on road to airport, basic but clean. The *Ramada Yacht Haven*, Tel: 774-9700, US$130-180, pool, restaurant, next to marina; also at the marina, check the bulletin board for boats providing overnight accommodation for US$15-30 pp.

Where To Eat There are many very good restaurants on the island, most of which are listed in *Here's How* and *St Thomas This Week*, or you can get details in your hotel. The large hotels all have their own restaurants, you will not be short of places to eat. *Hotel 1829*, on Government Hill, superb food and service; *Café Normandie* in Frenchtown for great French cuisine, or *Entre Nous* at Bluebeard's Castle. *Virgilio's*, between Main and Back streets, up from Store Tvaer Gade, Italian, good food and service; *Little Bopeep*, 7 Back Street, Creole specialities and pasta etc, reasonable; *Luigi's*, Back Street on corner with Snegle Gade, pizzas, Italian and bar; opposite is *Coconuts* bar and restaurant, and on same alley, *Rosie O'Grady's*; *Eat Street* on Back Street has breakfast all day plus sandwiches, pizza; *Island Reef* on Garden Street specializes in Jamaican jerk chicken for lunch, or dinner, also all you can eat spaghetti on Wednesdays. *Zorba's*, Greek, next to *The Fiddle Leaf*, both across park from Post Office; *Arby's Upstairs*, on the waterfront, good, inexpensive breakfast, lunch and dinner, sometimes live music; *Hard Rock Café*, was due to open summer 1992 next to *The Green House*, on harbour front, Veterans Drive, Tel: 774-7998, excellent restaurant at reasonable prices, attracts younger crowd, serves drinks, happy hour 1630, in season has a band, and dancing at 2100, cover charge US$4 if no dinner ordered, ladies' night Wednesday, open 0700-0230 for breakfast, lunch and dinner; as does *Drake's Inn*, restaurant and bar, Drake's Passage and Trompeter Gade (good value breakfast special—best 0630 to 0900 but doesn't open that early on Sunday); breakfast also at *Burger King*; there are also *Kentucky Fried Chicken*, *Baskin-Robbins* ice cream, etc. *Upper Crust Bakery* behind *The Green House*. There is a *Wendy's* hamburger restaurant on Veterans Drive by the cruise ship docks, with a small Heineken bar above. The area west of the Market Square is more local, with restaurants and bars, including *Long Look* vegetarian restaurant, on General Gade. *Bavarian Restaurant and Pub* on Raphune Hill offers German cuisine and beer, live music Wednesday-Saturday, Tel: 775-3615; *Paradise Point* on the hill overlooking Charlotte Amalie, US$10 all you can eat buffet, happy hour 1600-1900 half price drinks, excellent view, great place to watch the sunset; *For the Birds* (Tel: 775-6431) is a Tex-Mex style restaurant and bar outside town on the road to Red Hook, on Scotts beach, good view of Cays, Friday free buffet and happy hour 1600-1900, half price drinks, live band Thursdays, free drinks for ladies Thursday and Sunday, Sunday is the big night, especially crowded during American colleges' spring break (March-early May). At Red Hook, inexpensive breakfast and lunch at *The Three Virgins*; waiting for the ferry is easy at *Piccola Marina Café-Bar*, lunch and dinner, right on the water. The *Fish Shack*, a seafood retailer, also serves lunch and dinner, Tel: 776-7190; the *East Coast Bar and Grill* is the locals' pub with food, drinks, and conversation. At *Yacht Haven*, the *Gourmet Gallery* has excellent deli sandwiches on homemade bread to eat outside in the courtyard, also a great selection of domestic and international wines at reasonable prices (for the USVI). Award winning ribs from the *Texas Pit BBQ*, a mobile truck that shows up on the waterfront Tuesday-Thursday 1830-2000. The *Squirrel Cage*, on Norre Gade next to World Wide Travel, cheap food, breakfast, lunch and dinner. *Wok on Water* in Frenchtown, Tel: 777-8886 for excellent Vietnamese, Thai and Chinese food, right at the water's edge.

Nightlife St Thomas offers the greatest variety of nightlife to be found in the Virgin Islands. Bands and combos play nightly at most hotels. Several of the hotels offer limbo dancing three or four nights a week and the ubiquitous steel bands remain a great favourite with both visitors and inhabitants. At any time you will hear plenty of bass booming from the smart cars cruising the town's streets. Nightclubs include *Club Z*, *Famous*, *JP's Steak House* (also known as the *Old Mill* bar, has a progressive music night on Thursdays, popular), *The Green House*, live rock and roll bands Monday-Saturday, *Barnacle Bill's*, Frenchtown, live bands every night, some comedy, poetry reading, Monday is talent night, very popular with locals and yacht crews, *The Limetree* has three nightclubs, a disco, a club with West Indian bands and *Iggie's*, a bistro with pool tables, darts and a sing along video machine, your chance to be a star.

Unfortunately, because of the increase in crime, you are not recommended to walk around downtown Charlotte Amalie at night, take a taxi. Between downtown and Havensight the police have put up signs advising you not to walk along the water front path.

Shopping Charlotte Amalie is packed with duty free shops of all description, and is also packed with shoppers. Local produce can be bought in the Market Square (most produce brought in by farmers on Saturday 0530) and there are some small supermarkets and grocery stores. Solberg Supermart on Solberg Hill has a launderette (US$2 a load). Large supermarkets: Pueblo Grand Union, Woolworths, east end of town. Check the prices in supermarkets; what you see on the shelf and what you are charged are not always identical.

Phone Office The Calling Station, Bakery Square Mall, Nye Gade, for local and international calls, Monday-Thursday 0730-1930, Friday-Saturday until 2130, Sunday 1000-1600; also video rentals. Red Hook Mail Services, upstairs at Red Hook Plaza.

St John

Only 16 miles square, **St John** is about 5 miles east of St Thomas and 35 miles north of St Croix. The population is only 3,500, mainly concentrated in the little town of Cruz Bay and the village of Coral Bay. The population of St John fell to less than a thousand people in 1950 when 85% of the land had reverted to bush and second growth tropical forest. In the 1950s Laurence Rockefeller bought about half of the island but later donated his holdings to establish a national park which was to take up about two thirds of the predominantly mountainous island. The Virgin Islands National Park was opened in 1956 and is covered by an extensive network of trails (some land in the park is still privately owned and not open to visitors). Several times a week a Park ranger leads the Reef Bay hike, which passes through a variety of vegetation zones, visits an old sugar mill and some unexplained petroglyphs and ends with a ferry ride back to Cruz Bay. The trail can be hiked without the ranger, but the National Park trip provides a boat at the bottom of the trail so you do not need to walk back up the three-mile hill. You should reserve a place on the guided hike at the Park Service Visitors' Centre, Cruz Bay (on north side of harbour) open daily 0800-1630, Tel: 776-6201; information on all aspects of the park can be obtained here, there are informative displays, topographical and hiking trail maps, books on shells, birds, fish, plants, flowers and local history, sign up here for activities. There are 22 hikes in all, 14 on the north shore, 8 on the south shore. The trails are well-maintained and clearly signed with interpretive information along the way. Insect repellent is essential. A seashore walk in shallow water, using a glass bottomed bucket to discover sea life, is recommended. There is a snorkel trip round St John in which the boat takes you to five-six reefs not accessible by land (and therefore less damaged), a good way to see the island even if you do not snorkel. An informative, historical bus tour goes to the remote East End. There are evening programmes at Cinnamon Bay and Maho Bay camps, where rangers show slides and movies and hold informal talks.

Beaches and Watersports
Off Trunk Bay, the island's best beach, there is an underwater snorkelling trail maintained by the National Parks Service. Not surprisingly, the beach tends to get rather crowded (especially when tour groups come in); lockers for hire, US$2 (deposit US$5), snorkelling equipment US$4 (deposit US$40) return by 1600. Other good beaches include Hawk's Nest Bay, Caneel Bay, Cinnamon Bay (there is a small museum of historical photographs and pictures here), Salt Pond (excellent beach with good snorkelling and a spectacular hike to Ram's Head), Lameshur Bay (difficult road but worth it), Maho Bay (beach is five feet from the road, lots of turtles, sometimes tarpon, nice and calm) and Solomon Bay (unofficial nudist beach about half an hour's walk from the road). Reef Bay has excellent snorkelling. In the National Park there are snack bars at Cinnamon Bay and Trunk Bay only. Bring water and lunch if you are hiking or going to other beaches which will not be so crowded.

Windsurfers can be rented at Cinnamon Bay and Maho Camps, sunfishes at Maho Camp. For parasailing, contact Ken at Low Key Watersports, Tel: 776-7048, for sea kayaking contact Big Planet, Tel: 776-6638 or Low Key for half or full day trips. Coral Bay Watersports, Tel: 776-6850, next to *The Still*, rents sail and power boats, waterskiing, sport fishing and tackle. The Coral Bay Sailing School, Tel: 776-6922/776-6665, offers J-boat and laser rentals and group or private sailing lessons. Half and full day sails and fishing trips can be arranged by Connections, Tel: 776-6922. Power boat *Ocean Diver*, booked through Connections, offers excellent trips to Jost Van Dyke, snorkel round St John, sunset cruises, night snorkelling trips and full moon cruises. For one and two tank scuba dives, wreck dives and night dives: Low Key Watersports at Wharfside Village, specializes in small groups, maximum six people, Jimbo is a recommended guide; Cruz Bay Watersports, Tel: 776-6234, across from *Joe's Diner*, offers a free snorkel map; St John Watersports, Tel: 776-6256, at Mongoose Junction.

Carnival
St John's carnival is in the week of 4 July.

Island Information—St John

Transport There are only three roads on St John although the government map shows more roads that are barely passable four-wheel drive dirt tracks. The island is covered with steep hills and it is hot. Mountain bicycles and long distance backpacking are not recommended ways of getting around. The road from Cruz Bay to Coral Bay is only seven miles but it takes about 40 minutes to drive it. There are no buses on St John, you have to use taxis or jeeps. Official taxi rates can be obtained from St John Police Department. A two-hour island tour costs US$30 for one or two passengers, or US$12 per person if there are three or more. Taxi from Cruz Bay to Trunk Bay, US$3; to Cinnamon Bay US$4. Vehicles may be rented, see **Information for Visitors** below. Scooters can be rented but are very dangerous, especially when it rains. Hitchhiking is easy. It is almost impossible to persuade a taxi to take you to Coral Bay, so hitchhike by waiting with everyone else at the intersection by the supermarket deli. There are two service stations, open 0800-1900, both in Cruz Bay, may be closed on holidays.

Ferry to St Thomas: hourly 0700 to 2200 and 2315 to Red Hook, every two hours 0715 to 1315, 1545 and 1715 to Charlotte Amalie (fares and length of journey under St Thomas). The Sea Air Shuttle flies sea planes from St John to St Croix and Puerto Rico.

Where To Stay *Caneel Bay Plantation*, US$325-535 (PO Box 720, Tel: 776-6111); *Hyatt Regency*, US$295-475, Tel: 776-7171; *Gallows Point*, US$225-275 (PO Box 58, Tel: 776-6434). Within walking distance of town are *Villa Caribe* and *Battery Hill*, both under new management in 1992 with studios, one and two-bedroom apartments with kitchens, pools, personal service, attentive management, US$110-138d in summer, US$ 185-195d in winter. Cheaper places: *Cruz Inn*, Tel: 776-7688 (PO Box 566), US$50-85, CP, West Indian style inn, helpful advice on what to do and see, great sunsets from the Bamboo Bar, music and movies some nights, book swap; *The Inn at Tamarind Court*, Tel: 776-6378 (PO Box 170), US$48-88, inexpensive breakfast and dinner, bar, music and movies some nights, both are in Cruz Bay; *Raintree Inn*, also in Cruz Bay, Tel: 776-7449, US$70-95 (PO Box 566 also). At Cinnamon Bay (frequent taxibuses from Cruz Bay) there is a campground and chalet site run by the National Park Service, usually full so book in advance, maximum stay two weeks; space and tents, US$59d, chalets US$75, bare site US$13, a few shared showers, food expensive in both the cafeteria and grocery store. Write to Cinnamon Bay Camp, Box 720, St John, USVI, 00830-0720, Tel: 776 6330; or to Rockresorts Reservations, 30 Rockefeller Plaza, Suite 5400, New York City, NY 10122, Tel: 800-223-7637. At Maho Bay (8 miles fron Cruz Bay, regular bus service) there is a privately run campground, write to Maho Bay Camp, Cruz Bay, St John, USVI 00830, Tel: 776 6226. "Tent cottages" are available from US$75d a night. Tents are connected by a raised boardwalk to protect the environment, lots of steps, magnificent view from restaurant, lots of planned activities, guests come back year after year. There is a restaurant; also facilities for scuba diving and snorkelling and evening lectures on diving, sailing etc. It is possible to stay in private homes; contact Havens with Ambiance, PO Box 635, Cruz Bay. Virgin Island Bed and Breakfast Homestays (PO Box 191) Tel: 779-4094/776-7836, also arrange rooms in private houses, US$85 and up. *Serendip Apartments*, PO Box 273, Tel: 776-6646, fully equipped apartments, US$80-100. To rent a villa contact Vacation Vistas, run by Lisa Durgin, PO Box 476, about a dozen houses to rent all round the island, some with pools, nearly all over US$1,000 a week for two, 25-50% less in summer, honeymoon specials. *Caribbean Villas and Resorts*, Tel: 776-6152, offers 1 and 2 bedroom apartments with pools for as low as US$100/day double, off season, US$135/day in season.

Where To Eat In Cruz Bay, *Fred's* and *Hercules* serve inexpensive, filling, delicious West Indian food. Opposite the Post Office is the *Chicken B-B-Q*. For sandwiches and light meals, *Joe's Diner*, *Jumby's*, *Dockside Pub*, *Wendy's* and *Luscious Lick's* (also has ice cream). At the *Lime Inn* restaurant, seafood, steak, lobster and pasta, all you can eat shrimp night on Wednesday, very popular with locals and visitors; *The Barracuda Bistro* at Wharfside Village is a bakery, a deli, and a "home cooking" type restaurant for breakfast, lunch and dinner; *The Old Gallery*, West Indian and American food; *Paradiso*, Italian; *Mongoose Restaurant*, American, also serves breakfast; *Ellington's* at Gallow's Point, continental and seafood; *Café Roma*, Italian food and good pizza; *Beni Iguana's*, sushi, stir fry; *Fish Trap*, seafood, pasta and steak; *JJ's Texas Café*, on the park, very good Tex-Mex food, hearty meat and potato type specials. Breakfast is served at *Mongoose Restaurant, Wendy's, Ellington's* and *Jumby's*. In

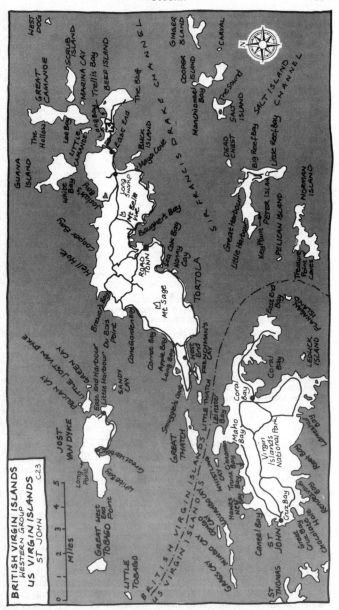

Coral Bay, *Skinny Legs* has inexpensive grilled hotdogs, hamburgers, chicken, etc, plus horse shoes and darts to play with; *Shipwreck Landing*, continental cuisine; *The Still*, continental and seafood; *Sea Breeze*, different menu every night, popular with locals, inexpensive; *Lucy's*, West Indian and continental. *Caneel Bay* and *The Hyatt* have several restaurants and entertainment. *The Hyatt Regency* is recommended for brunch, US$25, a treat, you will not need to eat for weeks after, very lush and exquisite, super service.

Nightlife Up to date information on events is posted on the trees around town or on the bulletin board in front of Connections. In Coral Bay, *Shipwreck Landing* has jazz on Sunday, a two-day music festival in April; *Skinny Legs* has live music some nights, horse shoes, darts, and lots of special events. In Cruz Bay, the place to go and dance is *Fred's*, calypso and reggae Wednesdays and Fridays; guitar and vocals at *Pusser's* and at *JJ's*; band and crab races on Fridays at *Beni Iguana's* on the beach. Popular places to 'lime' (relax) are *JJ's*, the *Rock Lobster Bar*, *The Backyard*, *Beni Iguana's* and sitting in Cruz Bay Park, watching the world go by.

Shopping Scattered around Cruz Bay and concentrated in Wharfside Village and Mongoose Junction are shops selling souvenirs, arts and crafts and jewelry. Right in the Park is Sparkey's, selling newspapers, paperbacks, film, cold drinks, gifts. The St John Pharmacy is next to the Supermarket Deli, open seven days a week. Small markets sell groceries, Pine Peace Market, Oscar's, the Supermarket Deli, Supernatural Foods and Marina Market. Joe's Discount Liquor has food and liquor. Food is expensive (rum is cheaper than water) and the selection is limited. If you are camping for a week, shopping at the big supermarkets on St Thomas is a good idea. Fresh produce is available at Nature's Nook, also fish and produce is sold from boats a couple of times a week at the freight dock. Love City Videos at the Boulon Centre, rents videos and VCRs, stop in and say hello to Jay, who is also the person to talk to if you want to get married, St John Weddings, P O Box 9, St John, USVI 00831, Tel: 776-8329.

Bank Chase Manhattan in Cruz Bay is the only bank, open 0900-1500, cashes US$ travellers' cheques but will not exchange currency or process cash advances on credit cards, you must go to the St Thomas banks for that.

Telecommunications Connections (Tel: 776-6922), as well as arranging sailing trips and villa rentals, is the place for business services, local and international telephone calls, faxes, Western Union money transfers, photocopying, wordprocessing, notary, VHF radio calls and tourist information (they know everything that is happening).

Newspaper The St John newspaper, *Tradewinds*, is published bi-weekly, US$0.50. The funny, informative, free, St John Guidebook and map is available in shops and also at the ticket booth at the ferry dock.

St Croix

With 84 square miles, **St Croix** is the largest of the group (population 55,000), lying some 75 miles east of Puerto Rico and 40 miles south of St Thomas. The name is pronounced to rhyme with "boy". People born on the island are called Cruzans, while North Americans who move there are known as Continentals. The east of the island is rocky, arid terrain, the west end is higher, wetter and forested. Columbus thought that St Croix looked like a lush garden when he first saw it during his second voyage in 1493. He landed at Salt River on the north coast, which has now been approved as a National Park encompassing the landing site as well as the rich underwater Salt River drop off and canyon. It had been cultivated by the Carib Indians, who called it Ay-Ay, and the land still lies green and fertile between the rolling hills. Agriculture was long the staple of the economy, cattle and sugar the main activities, and today there are the ruins of numerous sugar plantations with their Great Houses and windmills. Whim Estate is restored to the way it was under Danish rule in the 1700s and is well worth a visit; it is a beautiful oblong building housing a museum of the period, and in the grounds are many of the factory buildings and implements (open Monday-Saturday 0930-1600, US$4). There is a gift shop. St George Botanical Garden, just off Centreline Road (Queen Mary Highway), in an old estate, has a theatre as well as gardens amid the ruined buildings. Judith's Fancy, from the time of the French, is now surrounded by building developments and has less to see than the other two. Today agriculture has been surpassed by tourism and industry, including the huge Hess oil refinery on the south coast. Note that St Croix was badly hit by Hurricane Hugo, the effects of which were still somewhat visible in town and countryside in May 1992. 90% of the buildings were damaged, but much rebuilding has been, and continues to be done; the cruise ship pier at Frederiksted has been reopened and hotels, restaurants and most shops are fully operational.

Beaches and Watersports

St Croix has it all: swimming, sailing, fishing, and above all, diving. Good beaches can be found at Davis Bay, Protestant Cay, Buccaneer, the Reef, Cane Bay, Grapetree Beach and Cormorant Beach. Cramer Park on the east shore and Frederiksted beach to the north of the town, both have changing facilities and showers. All beaches are open to the public, but on those where there is a hotel (*Buccaneer*) which maintains the beach, you may have to pay for the use of facilities. Generally the north coast is best for surfing because there are no reefs to protect the beaches. On the northwest coast, the stretch from Northside Beach to Ham's Bay is easily accessible for shell collecting; the road is alongside the beach. The road ends at the General Offshore Sonorbuoy Area (a naval installation at Ham's Bluff), which is a good place to see booby birds and frigate birds leaving at dawn and coming home to roost at dusk. Shells can also be found on Sprat Hall beach (ask Judy or Jill at *Sprat Hall Plantation* for details). Water skiing, jet skiing, windsurfing and parasailing are all on offer. Paradise Parasailing, Tel: 773-7060, has windsurfing, aqua bikes, waterskiing, sea kayaking, sailing, snorkelling and parasailing. The *Elinor*, a 3-masted schooner, sails between Christiansted and Frederiksted daily, from US$35 for a sunset cruise to US$60 for a day sail (PO Box 1198, Frederiksted, Tel: 772-0919/773-7171).

Diving and Marine Life

At Buck Island there are guided tours on underwater snorkelling trails, the two main ones being Turtle Bay Trail and East End Trail. The fish are superb, but much of the coral is dead; it is hoped that it will come back. The reef is an underwater national park covering over 850 acres, including the island. Half-day tours to Buck Island, including 1¼ hours' snorkelling and ½ hour at the beach, cost between US$25 and US$35 and can be arranged through hotels or boat owners on the waterfront at Christiansted. (Mile Mark Charters, in *King Christian Hotel* complex, Tel: 773-2628; Big Beard's, Tel: 773-3307; Capt Heinz, Tel: 773-3161, Llewellyn, the Calypso King, takes 6 passengers, as does Clydie; all trips, and these are, must be approved by the National Parks Service.) Another attraction is the Salt River coral canyon. Scuba diving is good around St Croix, with forests of elkhorn coral, black coral, brain coral, sea fans, a multitude of tropical fish, drop offs, reefs and wrecks. Diving trips are arranged by several companies, many of which also charter boats out and offer sailing lessons. VI Divers, Tel: 773-6045, are located in the Pan Am Pavilion in Christiansted, they offer introductory or certification courses, equipment rentals and a full diving service. Other dive companies include: Dive St Croix, in *King Christian Hotel* complex,

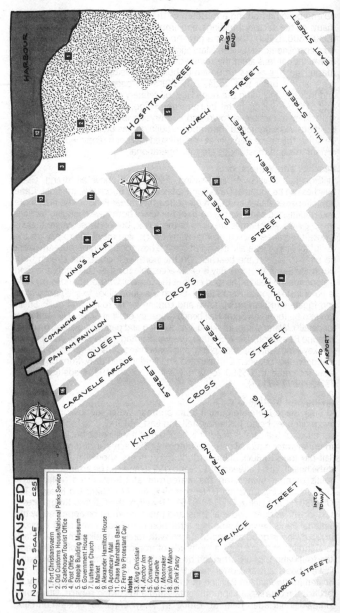

CHRISTIANSTAED
NOT TO SCALE   c25

1. Fort Christiansværn
2. Old Customs House/National Parks Service
3. Scalehouse/Tourist Office
4. Post Office
5. Steeple Building Museum
6. Government House
7. Lutheran Church
8. Market
9. Alexander Hamilton House
10. Apothecary Hall
11. Chase Manhattan Bank
12. Ferry to Protestant Cay

Hotels
13. King Christian
14. Anchor Inn
15. Comanche
16. Caravelle
17. Moonraker
18. Danish Manor
19. Pink Fancy

Christiansted, Tel: 773-3434; Dive Experience, Christiansted, Tel: 773-3307; Cruzan Divers, 12 Strand St, Frederiksted, Tel: 772-3701 (open 1200-1600, closed Tuesday and Thursday). Average rates start at US$35 for a pier dive, to US$45 for a two-tank boat dive, to US$205 for a 10-dive package. February, March and April are the months when you are likely to see hump backed whales near the islands. Boats sometimes go out to watch them.

Other Sports

Most of the large hotels have **tennis** courts for residents, but you can also play at the *Buccaneer Hotel* (8 courts, US$5 per person for non-guests), the *Hotel on the Cay* (3 courts, US$5 per person), Chenay Bay, Club St Croix, The Reef Club (2 courts, US$5/hour) and others, and there are four public courts at Canegata Park in Christiansted and two public courts near the fort in Frederiksted. Two 18-hole **golf** courses, one at the *Carambola* (Tel: 778-0747), summer green fees US$20, and the other at the *Buccaneer Hotel* (Tel: 773-2100), non-guest green fees US$20. There is also a 9-hole course at The Reef (Tel: 773-9200), green fee US$9. **Horse riding**: Jill's Equestrian Stables (Tel: 772-2880 or 772-2627), at Sprat Hall Plantation, 1½ miles north of Frederiksted, on Route 63, reserve one day in advance if possible for rides through the rain forest, past Danish ruins, for all levels of ability, US$50 for 2 hours, no credit cards.

In April/May a Sports Festival Week is held, with at least three events open to all, followed the next week by the American Paradise Triathlon which attracts over 600 participants. Phone VI Pace Runners on 773-7171 for details of running courses and tours. For the Virgin Islands Track and Field Federation, contact Wallace Williams (secretary), PO Box 2720, Christiansted, Tel: 773-5715. For swimmers, the Finmen have open water swim meetings, Tel: Bill Cleveland 773-2153, or look in the local papers. VI Cycling organize regular monthly rides and races, Tel: John Harper 773-0079.

Festivals

St Croix's Festival lasts from Christmas week to 6 January. There is another festival on the Saturday nearest to 17 March, St Patrick's Day, when there is a splendid parade. Mocko Jumbi dancing (on stilts) takes place at festivals and on other occasions; for information on Mocko Jumbi, contact Willard S John, PO Box 3162, Frederiksted, St Croix, USVI 00840, Tel: 773-8909 (day), 772-0225 (evening).

The Towns

The old town square and waterfront area of **Christiansted**, the old Danish capital, still retain the colourful character of the early days. Overhanging second-floor balconies designed by the Danes to shade the streets serve as cool arcades for shoppers. Red-roofed pastel houses built by early settlers climb the hills overlooking Kings Wharf and there is an old outdoor market. Old Christiansted is compact and easy to stroll. The best place to start is the Visitors' Bureau, housed in a building near the Wharf which served a century ago as the Customs Scale House. Here you can pick up brochures.

Across the way is Fort Christiansvaern, which the Danes built in 1774 on the foundations of a French fort dating from 1645. Admission is free (open 0800-1645). See the punishment cells, dungeons, barracks room, officers' kitchen, powder magazine, an exhibit of how to fire a cannon, and the battery, the best vantage point for photographing the old town and harbour. The Fort and the surrounding historic buildings are run by the National Parks

Service. In front of the Fort is the old customs house, now the National Parks Service office.

The Steeple Building is a minute's walk away. Built as a church by the Danes in 1734, then converted into a military bakery, storehouse and later a hospital, it is now a museum of the island's early history. Open 0930-1200, 1300-1530.

The area here is a treasury of old Danish architecture, and many of the original buildings are still in use. The West India and Guinea Co, which bought St Croix from the French and settled the island, built a warehouse on the corner of Church and Company Streets in 1749 which now serves as a post office.

Across the way from Government House on King St is the building where the young Alexander Hamilton, who was to become one of the founding fathers of the USA, worked as a clerk in Nicolas Cruger's countinghouse. Today the building houses the Little Switzerland shop.

Government House has all the hallmarks of the elegant and luxurious life of the merchants and planters in the days when "sugar was king". The centre section, built in 1747 as a merchant's residence, was bought by the Secret Council of St Croix in 1771 to serve as a government office. It was later joined to another merchant's town house on the corner of Queen Cross St and a handsome ballroom was added. Visitors are welcome to view the ballroom, stroll through the gardens and watch the proceedings in the Court of Justice. Across Queen Cross Street from Government House is the Dutch Reformed Church.

Queen Cross St leads into Strand and the fascinating maze of arcades and alleys lined with boutiques, handicrafts and jewellery shops. Along the waterfront there are bars, restaurant pavilions and a boardwalk, rebuilt after the Hurricane destroyed the original. Just offshore is Protestant Cay (just called The Cay), reached by ferry for US$3 return for the beach, and the *Hotel on the Cay* and restaurants, pool, tennis, watersports (Tel: 773-2035, room rates US$198).

Frederiksted, 17 miles from Christiansted, is the only other town on St Croix and although quiet, its gingerbread architecture has its own charm. Public taxis link the two towns and there are taxis from the airport to Frederiksted. Hurricane damage is still evident here (May 1991). Historic buildings such as Victoria House, 7-8 Straid Street, and the Customs House, have been repaired. Fort Frederik (1752) is a museum; it was here that the first official foreign salute to the 13 US States was made in 1776 (see also **Sint Eustatius**). Also here was read the proclamation freeing all Danish slaves in 1848. The rain forest to the north of town is worth a visit; although Hurricane Hugo caused much damage to the forest, it is recuperating. Two roads, the paved Mahogany Road (Route 76) and the unpaved Creque Dam Road (Road 58) traverse it.

Island Information—St Croix

Where To Stay The best resorts are: *Buccaneer*, US$184-325, Tel: 773-2100, on Gallows Bay north coast, 3 beaches, sports (see above), several restaurants, and closer to Christiansted are: *Cormorant Beach* (hotel) and *Cormorant Cove* (condominium), US$260-385, first class, Tel: 778-8920. *Chenay Bay*, Box 24600, Tel: 773-2918, one-room cottages with kitchenettes on nice north coast beach, US$175, tennis, pool, snorkelling, windsurfing; *St Croix by the Sea*, north coast, 3 miles west of Christiansted, Tel: 778-8600, US$149-169, pool, beach, etc, families welcome, restaurants and bars.

In Christiansted: *King Christian*, 59 King's Wharf, Tel: 773-2285, Fax: 773-9411 (PO Box 3619), with superior and minimum rooms, US$90-125, honeymoon and dive packages, pool; *Caravelle*, Queen Cross St, Tel: 773-1556, US$95-125, also good, pool, diving; *The Breakfast Club*, 18 Queen Cross Street, near the Lutheran Church, Tel: 773-7383, newly remodelled, rooms with bath and kitchenette, US$55d/day, US$290/week, gourmet breakfasts, nice view, manager is skillful golf player, highly recommended; *Comanche* Comanche Walk (Strand St, Tel: 773-0210, older style, no two rooms alike, US$70-129; *King's Alley*, on waterfront, Tel: 773-0103, US$84-140; *Anchor Inn*, also on waterfront with watersports, fishing charters and scuba diving available on hotel broadwalk, 58 King St, Tel: 773-4000, Fax: 773-4408, restaurant, pool, cable TV, refrigerator, a/c, etc, US$141-156, EP, scuba diving packages available. Slightly cheaper are *Moonraker*, Queen Cross Street, Tel: 773-1535, US$70, small breakfast, fair but friendly; *Danish Manor*, 2 Company St, Tel: 773-1377, US$59-135, pool in old courtyard, renovated rooms. *Pink Fancy*, 27 Prince Street, Tel: 773-8460, 5 minutes from shopping centre and waterfront, US$125-150, bar, pool, in 18th century townhouse.

In Frederiksted: *The Frederiksted*, 20 Strand St, Tel: 772-0500, modern, pool, restaurant, bar, good, US$115-130; ½ mile from town, *King Frederik*, on beach, pool, US$105-180, Tel: 772-1205; *Prince Street Inn*, 402 Prince Street, Tel: 772-9550, another historic building, small, US$44-85, charming, each room unique, recommended.

North of Frederiksted: *Sprat Hall* (PO Box 695, Tel: 772-0305), a former Great House, dating from the French Occupation, has antique furnishings, strictly non-smoking rooms in the old building, also has modern units, efficiency suites and a 2-bedroom cottage, double rates from US$80-140 in summer to US$110-240 in winter, excellent restaurant, beach bar serving lunch till 1530, highly recommended, also has riding stables (see *Jill's* above) and can organize diving and fishing trips. On the north coast, *Cane Bay Reef Club*, Box 1407, Kingshill, Tel: 778-2966, rebuilt after the hurricane, nine suites with balconies over the sea, pool, restaurant, bar, rough sea but short walk to beach, US$110-150d winter, US$70-95d summer, weekly rates cheaper, US$15 extra person; *Waves At Cane Bay*, Tel: 778-1805, oceanfront efficiencies with balconies and cable TV, natural grotto pool, beach, good snorkelling and scuba from property, US$115-175. South of Frederiksted is *Cottages by the Sea*, Tel: 772-0495, good beach, recently extended, good. *Ackie's Guesthouse*, US$50d, basic, kitchen facilities, in peaceful, rural location, though rather difficult to get to and from: it is a 15 minute walk to the main road whence shared taxis run to Christiansted or Frederiksted, US$0.50, double after 1800. In the east, *Villa Madeleine* is a villa development, each one/two bedroomed villa has its own pool and terrace, US$320-420 EP, PO Box 24190, Gallows Bay, Tel: 773 8141, Fax: 773 7518.

Where To Eat Restaurant life on St Croix includes charcoal-broiled steaks and lobsters, West Indian créole dishes and Danish and French specialities. Do not miss the open-air Crucian picnics. *Club Commanche*, Strand Street, Tel: 773-2665, popular and good for lunches and dinners; *Chart House*, on the wharf, steaks, seafood, very good salad bar; *Lunchería*, Mexican food, cheap margaritas on Company Street; also on Company Street are *Harvey's Bar and Restaurant*, local cuisine, *The Captain's Table* seafood restaurant and *The Three Dolphins*; *The Smoothie Shop*, health food sandwich shop; *Stixx Hurricane Bar and Restaurant*, Pan Am Pavilion, breakfast, lunch, dinner, steaks, pizzas, burgers, etc, popular bar; also *Hondo's The Backyard*, Queen Cross St and *Kings Alley Café*; *Ship's Galley*, deli and food store, Strand St, good. There are many other restaurants and fast food places in Christiansted. In Frederiksted, *Star of the West* (Mrs Mary Pennyfeather), Strand Street, for Créole food (Blinky and the Road Masters play local music here each Sunday), *Le Crocodile* French restaurant at *The Royal Dane Hotel*. For seafood and native dishes plus music, the *Blue Moon* or the *Motown Bar and Restaurant*, both on Strand Street. The out of town resorts have restaurants too.

Food Local dishes include stewed or roast goat, red pea soup (a sweet soup of kidney beans and pork), callalou (dasheen soup); snacks, Johnny cakes (unleavened fried bread) and pate (pastry filled with spiced beef, chicken or salt fish); drinks, ginger beer, *mavi* (from the bark of a tree).

Nightlife Most hotels provide evening entertainment on a rotating basis, the custom of many of the Caribbean islands, so it is sometimes best to stay put and let the world of West Indian music and dance come to you. Some restaurants also provide entertainment, eg *The Captain's Table*, *Tivoli Gardens* (Queen Cross and Strand Streets), *Calabash* (Strand Street) and *The Galleon* (Green Cay Marina, piano bar). *The Wreck Bar*, Hospital Street, has crab races on Friday, folk guitar on Wednesday, Green Flash rock Thursday-Saturday. *The Blue Moon*, 17 Strand Street, has live jazz every Friday and on full moons. *Two plus Two Disco*, Northside Road, west of Christiansted (closed Monday), live entertainment Friday and Saturday, US$5 cover charge; snack bar from 1200 till 1800. Most cultural events take place at the Island Centre, a 600-seat theatre with an open air amphitheatre seating another 1,600, where drama, dance and music are performed.

Transport Alexander Hamilton international airport. Boat, cycle, plane or car, the scenery is consistently beautiful (less so since Hurricane Hugo) and all methods of getting to see it are easy to arrange. Taxi airport-Christiansted US$5; airport-Frederiksted, US$4, taxi dispatcher's booth at airport exit. A taxi tour costs US$20 pp, less for groups; contact St Croix Taxi and Tours Association, Alexander Hamilton Airport, Tel: 778-1088, PO Box 1106, Christiansted, Fax: 778-6887. Taxi vans run between Christiansted and Frederiksted. The major car rental agencies are represented at the airport, in hotels and in both cities. For scooter rental, A and B, 26 Friendensthal, Christiansted, Tel: 778-8567. There is a distinct lack of road signs on St Croix, so if you use a car, take a good map with you.

Shopping *St Croix Leap* (Life and Environmental Arts Project), on Route 76, the Paved Rain Forest Road, is a woodworking centre, from which the artefacts may be bought direct. *Many Hands*, Pan Am Pavilion, sells only arts and crafts from the Virgin Islands. The market in Christiansted is on Company Street, and has been on the site since 1735. Bookshops (all Christiansted): *Collage*, Apothecary Hall Upper Courtyard, bookshop, café and gallery, open Monday-Saturday 1000-1800 (later Wed-Sat pm); *Jeltrup's* 51 ABC Company Street (on King Cross Street), both have good selection; *The Writer's Block*, King's Alley, for novels.

People to People Programme. If you wish to contact someone in a similar profession to your own, contact Geri Simpson, PO Box 943, Kingshill, St Croix, USVI 00851, Tel: 778-8007.

Information for Visitors

Documents
US citizens do not of course require passports for visits to the US Virgin Islands. British visitors to the US islands need passport and US visa (or waiver). Visitors of other nationalities will need passports, visas (or waiver for participating countries) and return/onward tickets.

How To Get There By Air
From the USA there are flights to St Croix and/or St Thomas with American Airlines (Baltimore, Chicago, Hartford Ct, Miami, New York, Orlando, Raleigh/Durham), Delta (Atlanta, Orlando,) and Continental (New York). From Europe there are no direct flights, but there are good connections from Puerto Rico and Antigua. British Airways to San Juan (Wednesday or Saturday) from Gatwick, with a connection on one of the many Sunair Express or American Eagle flights, will get you to St Croix the same day. Airlines operating on the St Croix/St Thomas-Puerto Rico (San Juan, Ponce,

Vieques or Fajardo) route include American Airlines, American Eagle, LAPSA, Sunair Express, Virgin Air, Virgin Islands Seaplane Shuttle (Tel: 778-7711), Vieques Air Link and Flamenco Airways. Regional airlines link the USVI with other Caribbean islands and there are flights to Anguilla, Antigua, Dominica, Guadeloupe, Jamaica, St Barthélémy, St Kitts, Nevis, St Maarten, St Lucia, Trinidad and Tobago and the BVI. St Thomas, St Croix and St John are linked by the Virgin Islands Seaplane Shuttle and Sunair. St Thomas-St Croix costs US$88 round trip. No departure tax at the airport. The runways at St Croix airport and St Thomas airport are being lengthened to take transcontinental aircraft.

How To Get There By Sea
Ocean going ships can be accommodated at Charlotte Amalie in St Thomas and Frederiksted and the South Shore cargo port in St Croix. There are regular services between the USVI and the BVI (Tortola and

Virgin Gorda). Inter-Island Boat Services, *Sundance II*, between Cruz Bay, St John, and West End, Tortola, twice a day; also Water Taxi available, Tel: 776-6282. *Native Son*, *Oriole* and *Voyager Eagle* between St Thomas and Road Town or West End, Tortola, several daily, Tel: 54617 (Tortola). *Speedy's Fantasy* and *Speedy's Delight* on the routes Virgin Gorda-Road Town-St Thomas and Virgin Gorda-Road Town-St John, Tel: 774-8685. *Mona Queen* (Tel: 776-6282) runs between Red Hook, St John and Jost Van Dyke, three trips per day on Friday and Sunday. To St John: ferries run hourly from Red Hook or about every two hours from the Charlotte Amalie Waterfront. Varlack Ventures between Cruz Bay, St John and West End, Tortola, daily ferry boat, Tel: 776-6412. For information on chartering your own boat, write to the Executive Director of the VI Charteryacht League, Homeport, St Thomas, USVI 00802.

Car Hire

In St Thomas rental agencies include Budget (Tel: 776-5774), Cowpet (775-7376), Avis (Tel: 774-1468), Sun Island (774-3333), Discount (776-4858), VI Auto Rental (776-3616, Sub Base), Gassett (776-4600); most have an office by the airport. Rates range from US$40 to US$80 a day, unlimited mileage, vehicles from small cars to jeeps. Honda scooters, from A1's, Tel: 774-2010, for example, range from US$25 to US$40 a day. Driving in Charlotte Amalie during business hours is a slow business. It is best to park and walk (municipal car park beside Fort Christian). Country speed limits are 35 miles an hour, in towns, 20 miles an hour, although the traffic is so heavy you will be lucky if you can go that fast. On St. John: Hertz, Tel: 776-6695; Delbert Hill's Jeep Rental, Tel: 776-6637; Budget, Tel: 776-7575; Avis, Tel: 776-6374; Cool Breeze, Tel: 776-6588, St John Car Rental, Tel: 776-6103; Scooter Rental at *Joe's Diner*. On St John the speed limit is 20 mph everywhere. In St Croix: Avis, at the airport, Tel: 778-9355/9365. Budget at the airport, Tel: 778-9636, or Christiansted (*King Christian Hotel* 773-2285), also Hertz, Tel: 778-1402, or *Buccaneer Hotel*, Tel: 773-2100 Ext 737; Caribbean Jeep and Car Rental, 6 Hospital Street, Christiansted, Tel: 773-4399; Green Cay Jeep and Car Rental, Tel: 773-7227; Berton, 1 mile west of Christiansted, Tel: 773-1516.

NB Driving is on the left, even though the cars are lefthand drive. Donkeys, goats, chickens and cows have the right of way. There is a new seatbelt law that the police enforce with a vengeance (US$50 fine).

Hotels

There is a 7½% tax on all forms of accommodation in the US Virgin Islands. Hotels may also charge a US$1/night Hotel Association charge and/or a 2½-3% energy tax.

Tipping

As in the mainland USA, tipping is usually 15% and hotels often add 10-15%.

Shopping

The USVI are a free port and tourist related items are duty-free. Shops are usually shut on Sundays unless there is a cruise ship in harbour. There are several local rums in white or gold: Cruzan (guided tours of the distillery, on St Croix, Monday-Friday 0830-1115, 1300-1615, but phone in advance, Tel: 772-0799), Old St Croix and Brugal.

Banks

US banking legislation applies. Bank of America, Citibank, Chase Manhattan, and First Pennsylvania Bank (Virgin Islands National Bank) are all represented and have several branches. Also Barclays Bank, Bank of Nova Scotia, Banco Popular de Puerto Rico, First Federal Savings and Loan of Puerto Rico.

Currency

The US dollar. Credit cards are widely accepted.

Warning

Take the usual precautions against crime, lock your car, leave valuable jewellery at home and be careful walking around at night. The Tourist Office recommends that you do not go to deserted beaches on your own, but always in a group.

Health

St Thomas has a 250-bed hospital, Tel: 776-8311, St John has a 7-bed clinic and St Croix has a 250-bed hospital, Tel: 778-6311. All three have 24-hour emergency services. Mobile medical units provide health services to outlying areas.

Emergency

Telephone numbers: Police 915; Fire 921; Ambulance 922; Air Ambulance 778-9177 (day), 772-1629 (night); decompression chamber 776-2686.

Climate

The climate in the Virgin Islands is very pleasant, with the trade winds keeping the humidity down. The average temperature varies little between winter (25°C or 77°F) and summer (28°C or 82°F). Average annual rainfall is 40 inches.

Clothing

Bathing suites are considered offensive when worn away from the beach, so cover up. There is even a law against it, you can get a fine for having your belly showing.

Hours Of Business

Banks open Monday-Thursday, 0900-1430, Friday 0900-1400, 1530-1700. Government offices open Monday-Thursday, 0900-1700.

National Holidays

New Year's Day, Three Kings Day (6 January), Martin Luther King Day (15 January), Presidents' Day (19 February), Holy Thursday, Good Friday, Easter Monday, Transfer Day (31 March), Memorial Day (28 May), Organic Act Day (18 June), Emancipation Day (3 July), Independence Day (4 July), Hurricane Supplication Day (23 July), Labour Day (beginning of September), Puerto Rico/Virgin Islands Friendship Day (mid-October), Hurricane Thanksgiving Day (mid-October), Liberty Day (1 November), Veterans' Day (11 November), Thanksgiving Day (mid-November), Christmas Day, 26 December.

Time Zone

Atlantic Standard Time, 4 hours behind GMT, 1 ahead of EST.

Electric Current

120 volts 60 cycles.

Consulates

On St Thomas: Danish, Tel: 774-1780; Dominican Republic, Tel: 775-2640; Finnish, Tel: 776-6666; French, Tel: 774-4663; Norwegian, Tel: 776-1780; Swedish, Tel: 776-1900. On St Croix: Dutch, Tel: 773-7100; Norwegian, Tel: 773-7100.

Religion

On St Croix: Apostolic, Baptist, Christian Scientist, Church of God, Episcopalian, Hindu, Jehovah's Witnesses, Jewish, Lutheran, Methodist, Moravian, Moslem, Presbyterian, Roman Catholic, Seventh Day Adventist. On St John: Baptist, Christian Scientist, Episcopalian, Jehovah's Witnesses, Jewish, Lutheran, Methodist, Moravian, Moslem, Presbyterian, Roman Catholic, Salvation Army, Seventh Day Adventist. On St Thomas: Apostolic, Baha'i, Baptist, Christian Scientist, Episcopalian, Jehovah's Witnesses, Jewish, Lutheran, Methodist, Moravian, Moslem, Presbyterian, Roman Catholic, Salvation Army, Seventh Day Adventist.

It is a simple procedure to get married in the USVI and you do not need to employ wedding consultants if you do not want them. You can obtain the relevant papers from any USVI Tourist Office, send them off about three weeks before your visit, then pick up the marriage licence at the Territorial Court on arrival. A recommended church in which to be married is the Frederick Lutheran Church in Charlotte Amalie, contact Pastor Coleman, PO Box 58, St Thomas, USVI 00804, Tel:776-1315/774-9524.

Newspaper

The Daily News is published daily, US$0.50, and on Friday it includes the weekend section, a complete listing of restaurants, night clubs, music and special events for the week, for all three islands.

Telecommunications

Local telephone calls within the USVI from coin-operated phones are US$0.25 for each 5 minutes. Long distance calls are operated mainly by AT&T. The area code is 809. Most 800 numbers can be used. Cable, Telex, Fax, data and other business services are all available.

Tourist Information

On St Thomas, the Tourist Information Centre at the airport is open daily 0900-1900. Offices at the town waterfront and at the West Indian Company dock are open 0800-1700 Monday-Friday (PO Box 6400, Charlotte Amalie, USVI 00804, Tel: 774-8784, Fax: 774-4390). On St Croix, there is a Tourism Booth at the airport in the baggage claim area and next to it the First Stop Information Booth. In Christiansted there is a Visitor's Bureau by the wharf in the Old Customs Scalehouse (PO Box 4538, Christiansted, USVI 00822, Tel: 773-0495, Fax: 778-9259), and in Frederiksted the Visitors' Centre is opposite the pier (Tel: 772-0357). There is also an office in Cruz Bay, St John (PO Box 200, Cruz Bay, USVI 00830, Tel: 724-3816). The publications, St Croix This Week and St Thomas This Week have regularly updated tourist information, including shopping news, ferry schedules, taxi fares, restaurants, nightlife and other tourist news. The Government offers a free road map (available at Tourist Information Offices) but considerable optimism was used in showing road classifications, especially on the St John map. Some of the 'paved highways' are really bad, unpaved roads which require hard, four-wheel drive.

There are offices of the USVI Division of Tourism in the **USA** at: 122 South Michigan Ave, Suite 1270, Chicago, 60603, Tel: (312) 461-0180; 2655 Le Jeune Rd, Suite 907, Miami 33134, Tel: (305) 442-7200; 1270 Av of the Americas, New York, NY 10020, Tel: (212) 582-4520; 900 17th Street NW, Suite 500, Washington DC, 20006, Tel: (202) 293-3707; 225 Peachtree St, Suite 760, Atlanta, GA 30303, Tel: (404) 688-0906.

In the **UK**: 2 Cinnamon Row, Plantation Wharf, York Place, London SW11 3TW, Tel: 071-978-5262, Fax: 071-924-3171.

In **Germany**: Postfach 10-02-44, D-6050 Offenbach, Tel: (069) 892008, Fax: 898892.

In **Puerto Rico**: 1300 Ashford Ave, Condado, Puerto Rico 00907, Tel: (809) 724-3816.

Hotel and restaurant lists, weekly guides and descriptive leaflets available. Texaco issues a map of the US islands, as does Phillip A Schneider, Dept of Geography, University of Illinois at Urbana-Champaign, price US$3.95.

A useful book is *The Settlers' Handbook for the US Virgin Islands*, Megnin Publishing (PO Box 5161, Sunny Isle, St Croix, USVI 00823-5161), US$7.95.

The editors are grateful to Pamela Gaffin, St John, USVI, for a comprehensive updating of the three islands.

BRITISH VIRGIN ISLANDS

Introduction

THE BRITISH VIRGIN ISLANDS (BVI), grouped around Sir Francis Drake Channel, are much less developed than the US group, and number some 60 islands, islets, rocks, and cays, of which only 16 or so are inhabited. They are all of volcanic origin except one, Anegada, which is coral and limestone. Most of the land was cleared years ago for its timber or to grow crops, and it is now largely covered by secondary forest and scrub. In the areas with greatest rainfall there are mangoes and palm trees, but generally the islands can look brown and parched, or green and lush just after rain. Mangrove and sea grape can be found in some areas along the shore. The two major islands, Tortola and Virgin Gorda, along with the groups of Anegada and Jost Van Dyke, contain most of the total population of about 16,750, which is mainly of African descent. The resident population was only 11,205 in 1980 and most of the increase has come from inward migration of workers for the construction and tourist industries. Everyone speaks English. While there are some large resorts in the BVI, there are no high-rise hotels, nightclubs and casinos, as found in some of the other islands which depend heavily on tourism. In fact, there is very little to do at all on land and nearly everything happens in the beautiful water which surrounds the islands. If you are keen on watersports and sailing and have adequate finance (the Virgin Islands are not cheap), you will enjoy island hopping.

History

Although discovered by the Spanish in 1493, the islands were first settled by Dutch planters before falling into British hands in 1666. In 1672 the Governor of the Leeward Islands annexed Tortola and in 1680 planters from Anguilla moved into Anegada and Virgin Gorda. Civil government was introduced in 1773 with an elected House of Assembly and a part-elected and part-nominated Legislative Council. Between 1872 and 1956 the islands were part of the Leeward Islands Federation (a British Colony), but then became a separately administered entity, building up economic links with the US Virgin Islands rather than joining the West Indies Federation of British territories. In 1960 direct responsibility was assumed by an appointed Administrator, later to become Governor. The Constitution became effective in 1967 but was later amended in 1977 to allow the islands greater autonomy in domestic affairs. Mr H Lavity Stoutt, of the Virgin Islands Party (VIP), became Chief Minister in 1967. After an interlude in the 1970s, he regained office in 1979 and has retained power in subsequent elections.

Government

A nearly self-contained community, the islands are a Crown Colony with a Governor appointed by London, although to a large extent they are internally self-governing. The Governor presides over the Executive Council, made up of the Chief Minister, the Attorney-General and three other ministers. A 12-member Legislative Council comprises nine members elected by universal adult suffrage, one member appointed by the Governor, a

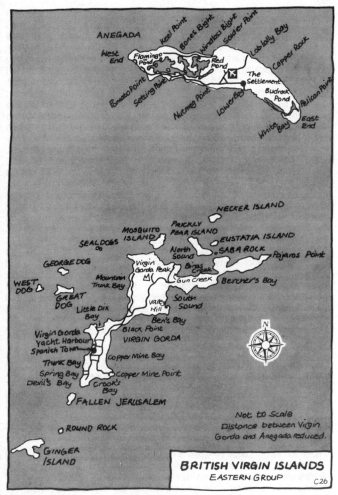

Speaker elected from outside by members of the Council, and the Attorney-General as an ex-officio member. At the most recent general election, in November 1990, Mr Lavity Stoutt, of the Virgin Islands Party, became Chief Minister for the fourth consecutive time, with six seats, against one for the Independent People's Movement (IPM, formed in 1989) and two Independents.

The Economy
The economy is based predominantly on tourism; the islands offer up-market

tourism in quiet, unspoiled surroundings and earnings are around US$125m a year. Of the 136,443 visitors who stayed on the islands in 1991, more than half stayed on more than 330 charter boats; there are approximately 1,043 hotel rooms, half of which are on Tortola and a third on Virgin Gorda, the rest being scattered around the other islands. A further 78,851 cruise ship passengers, yachtsmen and women and other excursionists visited the BVI in 1991. Tourism in the BVI has been hit badly by the recession and in 1991 stopover arrivals were down by nearly 17% while cruise ship passengers declined by almost 19%, with the fall being registered in all markets. The yacht charter business saw several closures in 1991/92 because of declining demand, higher air fares and tax changes in the USA and France, which brought greater competition from the French Caribbean.

A growth industry of the last few years is the offshore company business, which has benefited from uncertainty in Hong Kong and Panama. International Business Company legislation passed in 1984 allows locally-registered foreign companies tax exemptions with little currency risk as the US dollar is the national currency. By 1991, 16,000 companies were registered as IBCs and fees from new licences generated substantial revenues. Doubts over the structure and financial base of the 1,500 registered insurance companies led to the suspension of new licenses pending new legislation to regulate their operation. Industry on the islands is limited to small scale operations such as rum, sand or gravel, and desalination plants are being built. Farming is limited to some fruit and vegetables which are shipped to the USVI. Fishing is expanding both for export, sport and domestic consumption. However, nearly all the islands' needs are imported. Although current revenues are healthy, the Government is still dependent for capital sources on British assistance, as well as funding from the EEC, the Caribbean Development Bank and the Commonwealth Development Corporation. Loans have also been raised from commercial banks.

Damage caused by Hurricane Hugo in September 1989 was estimated at US$120m, split almost equally between the residential sector, roads and sea walls, and business. Loans and aid funds were promised by the Caribbean Development Bank, the British Government and the European Community. Reconstruction work proceeded swiftly and the winter tourist season began normally, with only the Peter Island Resort temporarily closed because of storm damage.

Beaches and Watersports

There are lovely sandy beaches on all the islands and many of them are remote, empty and accessible only from the sea. The clean, crystal-clear waters around the islands provide excellent snorkelling, diving, cruising and fishing. A local permit is required for fishing, call the Fisheries Division for information, Tel: 494-3429; spearfishing is not allowed, hunting on land is also banned and no firearms are allowed. Most of the hotels offer a wide variety of watersports, including windsurfing, sunfish, scuba, snorkelling and small boats.

Most hotels offer dive packages, or you can hire equipment and dive on a daily basis. Liveaboard boats, *Cuan Law, Lammer Law* or *Misty Law* (operated by Trimarine Boat Company, Road Town, Tortola, Tel: 494-2490), travel around the islands picking the best spots for day or night diving. Many companies offer diving for novices and others, instruction courses are available. A one-tank dive costs from US$45 and night dives are from US$65.

The dive shops also offer snorkelling or tours in glass-bottomed boats, underwater photography and video equipment rental. On Tortola, Baskin In The Sun is based at *Prospect Reef Hotel* but has other dive shops at *Long Bay Hotel* and Sopers Hole, West End, with a wide range of courses on offer, daily collection from your hotel. On Virgin Gorda, Kilbrides at *Bitter End Yacht Club* has two fully-equipped dive boats.

"Bareboating" (self-hire yacht chartering) is extremely popular, or you can charter a boat complete with crew. Navigation is not difficult, the weather is good so you can always see where you are going. Aerial photographs are usually provided to illustrate the island approaches. Be careful at all north shore anchorages, where a swell can often prevent overnight anchoring. Charter companies are too numerous to list here (although the recession and greater competition has led to some closures), there are many on Tortola and several more on Virgin Gorda. Contact the Tourist Office for a list with prices. Marinas are plentiful with several on Tortola and Virgin Gorda and another on Peter Island. Sailing and boardsailing schools offer 3-hour to one-week courses. The annual spring Regatta is held in Sir Francis Drake's Channel, considered one of the best sailing venues in the world. The best centres for fishing are Anegada, Salt Island, Peter Island, Jost Van Dyke and West End, Tortola. There are several charter companies for fishing boats and equipment. A cruising permit is required by everyone cruising in the BVI: 1 December-30 April, all recorded charter boats US$2 pp/day, all non-recorded charter boats US$4 pp/day; 1 May-30 November, US$0.75 and US$4 respectively.

Other Sports

There is a tennis club on Tortola and many hotels have their own courts. Golf has not been developed although a couple of the hotels have small practice courses. Horse riding can be arranged through the hotels. Walking and birdwatching are quite popular and trails have been laid out in some places. Spectator sports include cricket, soft ball and horse racing.

Tortola

The main island, with a population of 13,568, or 81% of the total population of the BVI. Mount Sage, the highest point in the archipelago, rises to 1,780 feet, and traces of a primeval rain forest can still be found on its slopes. Walking trails have been marked through Mount Sage National Park. The southern part of the island is mountainous and rocky, covered with scrub, frangipani and ginger thomas. The north has groves of bananas, mangoes and palm trees, and long sandy beaches. ***Road Town***, on the south shore, is the capital and business centre of the territory. There are also communities at East End and West End (reached by bus from Road Town or hitch hike). Cruise ships now call frequently at Road Town harbour and there are more gift shops, hotels and restaurants being built to cater for the tourist market. There is a pretty botanical garden near the Police Station in Road Town (free admission) with a good selection of tropical and subtropical plants such as palm trees, succulents, ferns and orchids.

The best beaches are along the north coast. Smugglers Cove and Apple Bay, West End, have fine sandy beaches. If you have no transport, Smugglers Cove is an hour's walk on a dirt road over a steep hill from West End. There is an old hotel with a bar which is often self-service; the beach is usually deserted. Cane Garden Bay is the best beach and has excellent facilities for yachts. There are two reefs with a marked gap in between. Brewers Bay is a long curving bay with plenty of shade and a small campsite in the trees by the beach. Josiah's Bay and Long Bay, East End, are also pleasant beaches. Apple Bay is popular with surfers from November for a few months, as is the eastern end of Cane Garden Bay and Josiah's Bay.

Tortola is superb, but the full flavour of the BVI can only be discovered by cruising round the other islands. A day's sailing excursion to Norman and Salt Islands can be arranged from Tortola. In and around Tortola there is a number of yachting marinas, where boats can be hired, including those at Wickham's Cay, Maya Cove, Nanny Cay, Marina Cay, Prospect Reef, Baughers Bay and Trellis Bay.

Island Information—Tortola

Where To Stay There is a 7% hotel tax and a 10% service charge in the BVI. Rates apply to double rooms, EP, winter/summer. **Road Town**: *Fort Burt*, converted from the old fort which protected the entrance to harbour, pool, sports club, harbour facilities, boat to private beach, 7 rooms, US$80-90, overpriced, no breakfast on Sunday, ants in rooms, Tel: 494-2587; *Admiralty Estate Resort Hotel*, 30 rooms, restaurant, beach trips, US$150-270/105-189, Tel: 494-0014; *Treasure Isle*, overlooking Sir Francis Drake Channel, pool, tennis, marina, watersports, tours, free transport to a different beach every day, US$120-135/80-90, children under 12 free, Tel: 494-2501; *Hotel Castle Maria*, friendly, pool, US$65-120/48-98, triple and quad rooms too, kitchenettes, Tel: 494-2553; *Maria's Inn By The Sea*, family run, 11 rooms, US$75-95/60-70, Tel: 494-2595; *Wayside Inn*, small, basic, sometimes dirty, no window screens so bring insect repellent, US$120, restaurant; *Jenny's* self-catering apartments nearby, US$375-575d winter, US$310-450d summer per week, brochures at the tourist office; *Prospect Reef Resort*, 131 rooms, sea and freshwater pools, 7 tennis courts, watersports, US$130-220/66-118, children under 12 free, Tel: 494-3311; *Moorings-Mariner Inn*, tennis, pool, watersports, US$120-170/70-130, Tel: 494-2332; *CSY Yacht Club*, US$65-75 all year, Tel: 494-2741, charter business closed 1992; *Village Cay Resort Marina*, under new owners and taken out of receivership, 18 rooms, dive shop, marina facilities, food store, US$110-150/70-90, Tel: 494-2771; *Sea View Hotel*, a few minutes walk from centre, US$40-160/35-160, 12 rooms, 8 studios, pool, self-catering facilities, recommended, Tel: 494-2483; *New Happy Lion Apartments*, Tel: 494-2574, US$40 all year; *Nanny Cay Resort and Marina*, in the hands of the receivers, just outside Road Town, 41 rooms, TV and VCR, tennis, diving, sailing, marina, US$150-170/90-110, Tel: (800) 786-4753 in USA.

West End: *Frenchman's Cay*, on the south coast overlooking Sir Francis Drake's Channel, villas or rooms, US$170-270/112-178, *Smith's Villa* at Frenchman's Cay, Tel: 495-4312, US$35-55/25-40; *Smugglers Cove*, beach, 4 rooms, US$88-98/63-73, Tel: 495-4234; *The Villas At Fort Recovery Estate*, Tel:495-4467, Fax: 495-4036, 10 villas on beach, built around 17th century Dutch fort, commissary, yoga, massage, US$130-500/90-388; *The Jolly Roger Inn*, Tel: 495-4559, 6 rooms, restaurant, dinghy dock, windsurfing, US$49-59/40-50; *BVI Aquatic Hotel*, US$20-35 winter, Tel: 495-4541; *The Towers*, Tel: 495-4725, 2-bedroomed apartments, US$65-85/45-65. **On the north coast**, *Long Bay Hotel*, in a 50-acre estate with a mile-long beach, pool, tennis, 9-hole golf, studios, cabins, cottages available, rooms US$175-305/65-195 MAP, Tel: 495-4252; *Turtle Dove Lodge*, Long Bay Hill, Tel: 495-4430, 12 beds, cabins, beach, kitchenettes, US$40-80d winter, 15% less in summer. *Sebastian's on the Beach*, Apple Bay, pleasant, beach bar, watersports and indoor games, popular with surfers, US$90-170/55-95, Tel: 495-4466; *Sugar Mill West Estate*, a restored West Indian cottage and new buildings, Apple Bay, gardens, pool, beach, US$125-200/100-135, suites for families but no children under 10 in winter, Tel: 495-4355; *Cane Garden Bay Beach Hotel*, sometimes known as *Rhymers Hotel*, Tel: 495-4639, on beautiful beach, 27 rooms, games room, watersports, laundromat, general store (the bakery behind the grocery is ridiculously expensive), US$65-70/35-45; *The Elm*, Cane Garden Bay, Tel: 495-4376, five one-bedroomed apartments, US$135-150 in winter, 40% less in summer; *Harbour View Guest House*, Cane Garden Bay, Tel: 495-4549, 15 rooms, US$120-420/100-340 a week; *Ole Works Inn*, 8 rooms, fridge, a/c, US$70-95/50-85, Tel: 495-4837; *Tamarind Country Club Hotel*, Josiah's Bay, 10 rooms, pool, live entertainment, tours, horseriding, US$70/50, also villas, US$600-1000/400-800 a week, Tel: 495-2477; *Maya Cove*, on south coast, rooms with cooking facilities, restaurant, good value, depending on season; *Brewers Bay* campsite on north coast, Tel: 494-3463 bare site US$7, tent hire US$20 for two people, babysitters available, beach bar and simple restaurant, 3 buses a day along a bad road (US$5, Scato's bus service). *Seabreeze Yacht Charter*, East End, near the airport, 9 rooms, boat charters, US$80-130/60-100, Tel: 495-1560. There is lots of self-catering accommodation in what are variously known as houses, villas, apartments, guest houses, "efficiencies" or "housekeeping units". Prices are usually set on a weekly basis according to size and standard of luxury, and there is often a 30%-40% discount in the summer. Contact the Tourist Office for a full list.

Where To Eat Restaurants serving West Indian specialities in Road Town include: *Aries Club*, Tel: 494-3329, by the Old Ball Field, Baughers Bay; *Beach Club Terrace*, Tel: 494-2272, at Baughers Bay, open 0800-2200; *Butterfly Bar and Restaurant*, Main Street, open 0700-2200 except Sunday; *Midtown*, Tel 494-2764, Main Street, open Mon-Sat 0700-2300; *Roti Palace*, Tel: 494-4196, Russel Hill, East Indian specialities from Trinidad and Guyana; *Scatliffe's Tavern*, Tel: 494-2797, near the high school, open 0730-2100. Recommended restaurants include *The Struggling Man*, Tel: 494-4163, Sea Cows Bay, between Road Town and Nanny Cay, and *Mr Fish*, Tel: 494-3626, at the Columbus Centre, behind Village Cay Marina, open 1100-2215, reservations recommended, seafood. *Tavern in the Town*, Road Town, traditional English pub food and atmosphere, garden looks out across harbour, Tel: 494-2790; *Virgin Queen*, Road Town, Tel: 494-2310, homemade pizza plus West Indian and European food, live music on Fridays; *Chopsticks* across from Wickham's Cay, Tel: 494-3616, Szechuan, Chinese, Japanese, Asian food, eat on the verandah or take away; *Bing's Drop Inn Bar and Restaurant*, at Fat Hog's Bay, East End, Tel: 495-2627, home cooked dinners, excellent conch fritters, known as an after hours dance spot, late night menu; *Pusser's Co Store & Pub* on Main Street, Road Town, yachties' meeting place, good pub atmosphere, open 1100-2200, on ground floor bar store and restaurant for simple dishes such as English pies and New York deli sandwiches, first floor restaurant superior but not overpriced, reservations recommended, cheap drink specials Monday and Thursday nights. *Mrs Scatliffe's*, Tel: 495-4556, Carrot Bay, upstairs in a yellow and white building opposite the Primary School, local cuisine, home grown fruit and vegetables, family fungi performance after dinner, lunch Mon-Fri 1200-1400, dinner daily 1900-2030, reservations essential. There is also *Pusser Landing*, at West End and many more excellent restaurants in the hotels and yacht clubs. At Cane Garden Bay you can "Jump Up" (Caribbean music), almost every night at *Stanleys* or *Rhymers* (serves breakfast, lunch and dinner; folk music at *Quito's Gazebo*, Tel: 495-4639, open daily 0800-2130, restaurant and beach bar at north end of Cane Garden, buffets of fish, lobster and conch four nights a week and a US$8 fish fry on Fridays). There are a number of small restaurants serving excellent food along the road going towards the rum distillery ruins; check in the late afternoon to make reservations and find out what the menu will be. Ten minutes' drive from Road Town or Cane Garden Bay is the *Skyworld Restaurant*, with a panoramic view of all the Virgin Islands, good food and reasonably priced.

Fish dishes are excellent, try snapper, dolphin (not the mammal), grouper, tuna and swordfish. If you are self-catering, you can get reasonably priced food from the "Rite Way" supermarket just east of Road Town, although most things are imported and will cost the same as in Florida. Try local produce which is cheaper; yams and sweet potatoes rather than potatoes, for example. There is a local market just outside Road Town by the Police Station. Once the centre of rum production for the Royal Navy "Pussers" (Pursers), rum is still available from Callwoods Grocery Store/Rum Distillery in Road Town, or at the *Pusser Landing* restaurant at West End.

Nightlife In Road Town, *Bobby's Disco* on Wickham Cay; *Mariners Inn*, Wednesday is movie night, bands on Thursday; *Paradise Pub*, entertainment Monday-Saturday; *Treasure Isle Hotel*, steel band on Saturday; *Pusser's Landing* at Frenchman's Cay has steel bands, fungi bands, fire eaters, limbo dancers, reggae and calypso bands Tuesday-Sunday; *Bomba Shack*, on the beach is Apple Bay has music Wednesdays and Sunday, famous full moon party every month, sleep before you go, the party goes on all night.

Laundry   Sylvia's Laundromat, on Flemming Street, Road Town, Tel: 494-2230.

Beef Island

This island was famed as a hunting ground for beef cattle during the buccaneering days. The island is linked to Tortola by the Queen Elizabeth bridge (US$0.50 toll one way eastwards). The main airport of the BVI is here. (Taxi to Road Town, US$12) Long Bay beach is on the northern shore. Also Trellis Bay which has an excellent harbour and bars. *The Last Resort*, run by Englishman Tony Snell, based on Bellamy Cay, provides a lavish buffet menu US$20 plus one-man show cabaret, entrance for cabaret only is US$2, happy hour 1730-1830, dinner 1930, cabaret 2130, ferry service available, reservations required, Tel: 495-2520 or channel 16. *De Loose Mongoose*, Trellis Bay, burgers etc, good and reasonable desserts, plus cheap drinks during happy hour, 1700-1800. Also Boardsailing BVI, the *Conch Shell Point Restaurant* and a painting and jewellery shop. *Beef Island Guest House* has four rooms on the beach, US$100/65, Tel: 495-2303.

Marina Cay

This tiny private island of six acres just north of Beef Island was where Robb White wrote his book *Our Virgin Isle*, which was made into a film starring Sidney Poitier and John Cassavetes. A charming cottage hotel, *Marina Cay Hotel*, comprises most of the island, which is encircled by a reef, offering some of the best snorkelling in the BVI. Marina facilities, laundry, showers, diving, sailing, snorkelling etc, there are 12 rooms available only in winter, US$250, includes breakfast and dinner, Tel: 494-2174 or VHF channel 16. Bar, restaurant, beach barbecue on Fridays, champagne brunch on Sundays. Ferry service from Trellis Bay jetty. If sailing, enter from the north, moorings available for US$10.

Guana Islands

North of Tortola, Guana Island is an 850-acre private island and wildlife sanctuary as well as having a hotel, *The Guana Island Club*, 15 rooms, tennis, restaurants, watersports, US$285-485/120-240, Tel: 494-2354. The island is available for rent.

The Dogs

Northeast of Tortola are The Dogs, small uninhabited islands. West Dog is a National Park. On Great Dog you can see frigate birds nesting. The islands are often used as a stopping off point when sailing from North Sound to Jost Van Dyke, and are popular with divers. The best anchorages are on George Dog to the west of Kitchen Point and on the south side of Great Dog.

Virgin Gorda

Over a century ago, Virgin Gorda was the centre of population and commerce. It is now better known as the site of the geological curiosity called The Baths, where enormous boulders form a natural swimming pool and underwater caves. The snorkelling is spectacular, especially going left from the beach. Climbing over and around the boulders is difficult and not rewarding, exploring in the water is the recommended way to do it. The island is seven miles long and has a population of about 2,500. The northern half is mountainous, with a peak 1,370 feet high, while the southern half is relatively flat. There are some 20 secluded beaches; the most frequented are Devil's Bay, Spring Bay, and Trunk Bay on the west coast. North of the island is North Sound, formed to the south and east by Virgin Gorda, to the north by Prickly Pear Island, and to the west by Mosquito Island. On the southeast tip is Copper Mine Point, where the Spaniards mined copper, gold and silver some 400 years ago; the remains of the mine can be seen. The rocky façade here is reminiscent of the Cornish coast of England. The amateur geologist will find stones such as malachite and crystals embedded in quartz. All land on Virgin Gorda over 1,000 feet high is now a National Park, where trails have been blazed for walking. Just off the southwestern tip of the island is Fallen Jerusalem, an islet which is now a National Park. There is a 3,000-foot airstrip near the main settlement, Spanish Town. Bitter End and Biras Creek are good anchorages and both have a hotel and restaurant.

Island Information—Virgin Gorda

Where To Stay *Little Dix Bay*, Rockefeller's Rockresort 102-roomed hotel, pool, beach, watersports, tennis, horseriding, US$565/360 FAP, Tel: 495-5555; under same management is the *Virgin Gorda Yacht Harbour*, a large marina at St Thomas Bay offering convenient facilities. *Biras Creek Estate*, at North Sound, luxurious and exclusive, with Scandinavian architecture, pool, tennis, US$415-595, FAP, winter, special package rates on request, Tel: 494-3555. *Ocean View Hotel*, only 12 rooms, opposite Virgin Gorda Yacht Marina, US$70-80/50-60, Tel: 495-5230. *Guavaberry Spring Bay*, well-equipped rooms or cottages, beautiful, friendly, beach, babysitting, US$120-185/80-130 EP, highly recommended, Tel: 495-5227. *Bitter End Yacht Club*, at North Sound, rooms, beach villas and live-aboard yachts, watersports, US$195-450/195-350 AP, Tel: 494-2746. *Fischer's Cove Beach Hotel*, 125-150/85-90, or cottages US$140-250/100-195 at St Thomas Bay, Tel: 495-5252. *Olde Yard Inn*, The Valley, US$110-355/75-85 EP, 14 rooms, restaurant, Tel: 495-5544. *Leverick Bay Hotel* Tel: 495-5644, rooms, villas or studios, US$100-125 a day or US$595-744 weekly, watersports, pool, tennis, beaches, marine facilities, Tel: 495-7421. *Diamond Beach Club*, Tel: 495-5452, 14 rooms, villas, beaches, US$144-230/98-155; *Mango Bay Resort*, Tel: 495-5672, 21 rooms, villas or studios, beach, snorkelling, US$135-735/86-565 EP. *Bay View Vacation Apartments*, The Valley, Tel: 495-5329, two-bedroomed apartments, US$130/95; *Taddy Bay*, The Valley, Tel: 495-5618, two-bedroom house US$850/750 a week, or room with bath US$45 a day all year; *Paradise Beach Resort*, Mahoe Bay, 1, 2, or 3 bedrooms with kitchens, 170-680/115-470, cooks, maids and babysitters available.

Where To Eat For upmarket, elegant dining try *Biras Creek*, five-course dinner for US$35, 1930-2100, dress smartly; *Bitter End Yacht Club* for the sailing fraternity, champagne breakfast US$10, buffet lunch US$15, dinner US$25; *Olde Yard Inn*, international food, library, classical music, art gallery/boutique for local artists; *Chez Michelle*, Tel: 495-5510, international cuisine; restaurants serving West Indian recipes include *Fischer's Cove Beach Hotel*, *The Wheelhouse*, Tel: 495-5230, *Teacher Ilma's*, in the Valley at Princess Quarters, dinner only, reservations after 1600; also *Crab

Hole, South Valley, locals eat here, inexpensive West Indian food, entertainment on Friday; *Lobster Pot*, at *Andy's Chateau de Pirate*, Tel: 495-5252, beach pig roast on Monday, seafood buffet on Thursday, barbecue on Saturday; *The Bath and Turtle*, Virgin Gorda Yacht Harbour, standard pub fare, open 0730-2130 daily, good place to wait for the ferry; *Pusser's* Leverick Bay, Tel: 495-7369, newly opened; *Mad Dog*, next to the parking lot at The Baths, drinks, sandwiches and friendly conversation, open 1000-1900; there is also a bar on the beach at The Baths, not always open, be sure to bring a bottle of water just in case.

Nightlife Live music at *The Bath and Turtle* and *Little Dix Bay*, live music and/or DJ at *Pirate's Pub* and *Bitter End*. Check the bulletin board at the Virgin Gorda Yacht Harbour for special events and concerts.

Necker Island

This 74-acre, private island northeast of Virgin Gorda is owned by Richard Branson, who wanted a Virgin island to add to his Virgin enterprise. It is available for rent, contact Ruth Kemp in London, Tel: 071-938 3618. The house, in Balinese style, sleeps 20, and in winter costs US$8,250 a day, or US$6,050, if there are only ten of you, falling to US$5,500 in summer. Lovely beaches, protected by a coral reef, all water sports provided, private.

Cooper Island

In the chain of islands running southwest from Virgin Gorda is Cooper Island, which has a beautiful beach and harbour with palm trees, crystal waters, coral reefs and a beach restaurant (Thursday night barbecue and disco). A lovely beach is that at Manchioneel Bay.

Salt Island

The two salt ponds attract tourists during the gathering season (April-May). A bag of salt is still sent to the British monarch every year. There is a small settlement on the north side as well as a reef-protected lagoon on the east shore. The population numbers about 20. The British mail ship *Rhone*, a 310-foot steamer, sank off Salt Island in a hurricane in 1867 and the site was used in the film *The Deep*. The wreck is still almost intact in 20-80 feet of water and is very impressive. There are moorings provided at Lee Bay, just north of the *Rhone*, for those diving the wreck, to minimize anchor damage.

Dead Chest

A tiny island in Salt Island Passage, between Salt Island and Peter Island, this is reputedly the island where the pirate Blackbeard abandoned sailors: "15 men on a Dead Man's Chest—Yo Ho Ho and a bottle of rum!"

Peter Island

This 1,000-acre island has a tiny population and offers isolated, palm-fringed beaches, good anchorage and picnic spots. The *Peter Island Hotel and Yacht Club* is built on reclaimed land jutting out into Sir Francis Drake Channel, forming a sheltered harbour with marine facilities. Built by Norwegians, there are chalet-type cottages, harbour rooms, or beach rooms US$350-625/250-525, full board, a pool, tennis, horseriding, watersports, Tel: 494-2561. Nine daily ferry departures from Tortola.

Norman Island

The island is uninhabited (apart from the converted 1910 Baltic Trader floating bar/restaurant *William Thornton*, Tel: 494-2564, anchored in the Bight of Norman to the north of the island; launch service from Fort Burt Marina, Road Town, daily at 1715), but reputed to be the "Treasure Island" of Robert Louis Stevenson fame. On its rocky west coast are caves where treasure is said to have been discovered many years ago. These can be reached by small boats. There is excellent snorkelling around the caves and the reef in front slopes downward to a depth of 40 feet. Be careful with the wild cattle: their tempers are unpredictable.

Jost Van Dyke

Lying to the west of Tortola, the island was named after a Dutch pirate. It is mountainous, with beaches at White Bay and Great Harbour Bay on the south coast. Great Harbour looks like the fantasy tropical island, a long horseshoe shaped, white sandy beach, fringed with palm trees and dotted with beach bar/restaurants. Population about 300, very friendly with lots of stories to tell. Jost Van Dyke is a point of entry and has a Customs House. In January 1991, the island was provided with electricity for the first time and a paved road. It is surrounded by some smaller islands, one of which is **Little Jost Van Dyke**, the birthplace of Dr John Lettsome, the founder of the British Medical Society. *Sandcastle*, at White Bay, owned by Darryl Sanderson, four wooden cottages, basic amenities but great for total relaxation, hammocks between palm trees on the beach, restaurant, snorkelling, windsurfing, US$225-295/175-235 AP, Tel: 496-0496 or (USA) 803-237 8999, there is also an answering service on Tel: 775 5262, *The Soggy Dollar Bar* is popular at weekends, most people arrive by boat and swim or wade ashore; *Rudy's Mariner Inn*, Great Harbour, 3 rooms, beach bar and restaurant, kitchenettes, grocery, water taxi, US$75-220/55-180 AP, Tel: (USVI) 809-775 3558. *Harris' Place*, Tel: (809) 774-0774 (USVI) or call VHF channel 16, two rooms, beach bar, restaurant, grocery, water taxi, live music, Harris calls his place the friendliest spot in the BVIs, US$50-65/40-55; *Sandy Ground*, Tel: 494-3391, 8 luxury villas, provisioning, free water taxi from/to Tortola, US$1,150/750 a week. **Camping**: *Tula's N and N Campground*, Little Harbour, Tel: (USVI) 809-774 0774 8' X 10' US$25 per day, 9' X 12' US$35 (per couple), US$15 bare site (3 people), winter rate, US$10 per day per person in summer, US$4 per person bare site, restaurant, snack bar, beach, grocery, recommended. Restaurants in Little Harbour: *Harris' Place*, open daily, breakfast, lunch and dinner, happy hour 1100-1500, pig roasts with live music Tuesdays and Thursdays, lobster night on Mondays, ferries from Tortola and St Thomas/St John arranged for these feasts; *Sidney's Peace and Love*; *Abe's By The Sea*, pig roast on Wednesdays, call VHF channel 16 for reservations. In Great Harbour: *Ali Baba's*, run by Baba Hatchett, west of the Customs House, breakfast, lunch and dinner, happy hour 1600-1800; *Rudy's Mariner's Rendezvous*, open for dinner until 0100, US$9-20, reservations at Customs House or channel 16; *Foxy's Tamarind Bar*, friendly and cheap, occasional singer with guitar, big parties on New Year's Eve and other holidays, wooden boat regatta on Labour Day draws hundreds of boats from all over the Caribbean for a three-day beach party, very easy to get invited on board to watch or race, special ferry service to USVI and Tortola; *Happy Laury's*, very good value for breakfast, happy hour is 1500-1700, try the Happy Laury Pain Killer. There is a pig roast on Jost Van Dyke every Friday. For details of ferries see **Information for Visitors**.

Sandy Cay

This small uninhabited islet just east of Jost Van Dyke is owned by Lawrence Rockefeller. It is covered with scrub but there is a pleasant trail set out around the whole island, which makes a good walk. Bright white beaches surround the island and provide excellent swimming. Offshore is a coral reef and exquisite ferns.

Anegada

Unique among this group of islands because of its coral and limestone formation, the highest point is only 28 feet above sea level. There are still a few large iguanas, which are indigenous to the island. The waters abound with fish and lobster, and the extensive reefs are popular with snorkellers and scuba divers who also explore wrecks of ships which foundered in years past. Some were said to hold treasure, but to date only a few doubloons have been discovered. Anegada has excellent fishing and is one of the top bone fishing spots in the world. There are beaches on the north and west ends. From the wharf on the south shore, all the way round to the west end, across the entire north shore (about 11 miles) is perfect, uninterrupted, white sandy beach. Have a taxi drop you off somewhere, then walk back to Jack Bay or the *Anegada Reef Hotel* where there are beach bars and rides back to town (The Settlement). Bring water and sun screen. The population numbers about 290. There is an airstrip 2,500 feet long and 60 feet wide, which can handle light aircraft. *Anegada Reef Hotel*, 12 rooms, where there is an anchorage, fishing and dive packages, snorkelling, dive shop, beach bar, restaurant, great service, famous lobster barbecue, good value, recommended, no credit cards, 155-215/130-205 AP, Tel: 495-8002, or by VHF Radio Channel 16; *Wheatley Guest House*, sometimes is and sometimes is not in business, no phone. *Beach Cottage* at Pomato Point, a modern, 1-bedroom cottage on beach, full kitchen, US$250/weekend, US$400/week, US$1,200/month, Tel: 495-9236. *Anegada Beach Campground*, Tel: 495-8038, 8'x10' tents US$20d, US$12s, 10'x12' tents US$30d, bare site US$5 a day, plus 10% service, no credit cards, beach bar, restaurant, snorkelling, windsurfing. Restaurants: *Pomato Point Beach Restaurant*, Tel: 495-8038, champagne breakfasts from 0800, lunch and dinner, seafood; *Neptune's Treasure*, breakfast US$5, lunch from US$2, dinner US$8-20, daily; *Del's Restaurant and Bar*, in The Settlement, Tel: 495-8014, West Indian food, breakfast, lunch and dinner. Recommended to make dinner reservations before 1600 at all restaurants.

Information for Visitors

Documents

An authenticated birth or citizenship certificate or voter's registration may suffice for US or Canadian citizens. All other nationalities need a valid passport and a return or onward ticket. Visitors from some countries, such as Guyana, require a visa. The Chief Immigration Officer is in Road Town, Tel: 494-3701.

How To Get There By Air

There are international airports on Tortola and Virgin Gorda, but no direct flights from Europe or from the USA. British

Airways from London has same day connecting flights via Puerto Rico and Antigua with Liat; Lufthansa also flies to Puerto Rico from Frankfurt with same day connections to the BVI. From the USA: connecting flights can be arranged through Puerto Rico or the USVI; Virgin Air, Virgin Islands Seaplane Shuttle, Sunair Express, American Eagle and Liat fly from the former, Virgin Islands Seaplane Shuttle and Sunair Express, Virgin Islands Seaplane Shuttle, Virgin Air and Liat fly from St Croix and St Thomas. Liat flies to Tortola from Antigua, Barbados, St Kitts, St Maarten, Puerto Rico. Within the BVI there are flights: Anegada/Tortola, Anegada/Virgin Gorda, Virgin Gorda/Tortola with Virgin Air and Sunair. Pack light, there is limited luggage space on the small aircraft. In 1991 Air BVI, a commuter carrier, ceased operations, but may start flying again in 1992/93.

How To Get There By Sea

Port Purcell at Road Town is the principal port of entry with an 800-foot, deep water berth for cruise ships; Government Jetty, Road Town, is also used. There are others at West End, Tortola; St Thomas Bay, Virgin Gorda; and Great Harbour, Jost Van Dyke. There are frequent connections with the USVI and within the BVI. Inter-Island Boat Services, *Sundance II* between Cruz Bay, St John, and West End, Tortola, three times a day Monday-Thursday, four times on Friday, three times on Saturday and Sunday, US$14 one way, US$25 return; also Water Taxi available, Tel: 776-6597. *Native Son Inc*, between St Thomas and Road Town (US$27 return) via West End, or between Red Hook, St Thomas and St John to West End, several daily, or St Thomas to Virgin Gorda Wednesdays and Sundays, Tel: 495-4617. Transportation Services, Tel: 776-6282, runs from red Hook to St John then to Virgin Gorda, Thursday and Sunday, US$30 return with free rum punch. Smiths Ferry Services, *M/V Daphne Elise* and *M/V Marie Elise*, from St Thomas to West End and the Government Jetty, Road Town and on to The Valley, Virgin Gorda, several daily, Tel: 494-4430. *Speedy's Fantasy* and *Speedy's Delight* on the routes Virgin Gorda-Road Town-St Thomas, Virgin Gorda-Road Town-St John and Virgin Gorda-Road Town-Anegada, Tel: 495-5240 Virgin Gorda, or 774-8685 St Thomas. The North Sound Express has four daily crossings Beef Island-North Sound (Bitter End), 30 mins, with a bus

service to and from Road Town waterfront and Beef Island ferry dock, Tel: 494-2746. Peter Island Boat Schedule has 9 daily crossings from the Caribbean Sailing Yachts Dock, (CSY charters ceased operations in 1992), Tortola, to Peter Island. Reel World, Tel: 494-3450, three times a day between West End and Jost Van Dyke, also Jost Van Dyke Ferry Service, Tel: 495-2775, four crossings a day Monday-Friday, three on Saturday, two on Sunday.

There is a departure tax of US$5 if you leave by air or by sea. Metal detectors are to be introduced at all entry points following several shootings at policemen in 1992.

Local Transport

BVI Taxi Association, Tel: 494-2875, island tours for US$12 pp. Taxi stands: in Road Town, Tel: 494-2322; on Beef Island, Tel: 495-2378. Taxis are easy to come by on Tortola but ask for a quote first. Rates are fixed, based on number of passengers and route, and published by the Tourist Office. The fare from Beef Island Airport to Road Town, Tortola is US$12. There is a local bus service which is cheap if a bit erratic, rates US$1, US$2, US$3. It is possible to hitch-hike on the island.

Self-Drive Cars

There are only about 50 miles of roads suitable for cars. Drive on the left. Maximum speed limit 30 miles per hour, in residential areas 10-15 mph. Minimokes and jeeps can be hired on Tortola and Virgin Gorda. Jeeps may be more useful for exploring secluded beach areas. Car rental offices (or the Police Headquarters) provide the necessary temporary BVI driving licence (US$10) but you must also have a valid licence from your home country. It is advisable to book in advance in the peak season. Rates range from US$25 a day in summer to US$40 a day in winter for a small car. **Tortola**: Airways Car Rentals, Inner Harbour Marina, Tel: 494-4502, or Airport, Tel: 495-2161, jeeps for US$35-65/day. Alphonso Car Rentals, Fish Bay, Tel: 494-3137, US$35-65/day; Budget, Wickhams Cay, Tel: 494-2639; International Car Rentals, Road Town, Tel: 494-2516, US$43-53/day; Avis Car Rentals, opposite Police Station, Road Town, Tel: 494-2193, US$35-50/day; Caribbean Car Rental, *Maria's Inn*, Wickhams Cay, Tel: 494-2595, US$45-49/day; National Car Rental, Duffs

Bottom, Road Town, Tel: 494-3197, US$37-45/day; Anytime Car Rental, Wayside Inn Guest House, Road Town, Tel: 494-2875, rates average US$30/day; Island Suzuki Rentals, Palestina Estate, near Nanny Cay, Tel: 494-3666, US$29-50/day; Roy's Car Rental, East End, US$40 winter, US$35 summer, free pick up and delivery. **Virgin Gorda**: Speedy's Car Rentals, The Valley, Tel: 495-5235, US$35-50/day; L & S Jeep Rentals, South Valley, Tel: 495-5297, small or large jeeps, US$35-50/day, US$210-315/week; Mahogany Car Rentals, The Valley, Tel: 495-5542, US$42-68 includes insurance, no credit cards; Patters Car Rentals, The Valley, Tel: 495-5329, US$40-45 winter, US$35-45 summer, no deposit.

Also on Tortola: Hero's Bicycle Rental, Main Street, Road Town, for bicycles (US$3/hour, US$10/day), tandems (US$5/hour, US$15/day) and scooters (US$11/hour, US$26/day) by the hour/day/week, Tel: 494-5071. DJ's Scooters, MacNamara, Tortola, Tel: 494-5071; Honda Scooter Rental, The Valley, Virgin Gorda, Tel: 495-5212, from US$8/hour, US$25/day, deposit required, minimum age 23. All bicycles must be registered at the Traffic Licencing Office in Road Town and the licence plate must be fixed to the bicycle, cost: US$5.

Camping
Allowed only on authorized sites.

Shopping
The BVI is not duty-free. There are gift shops and boutiques in Road Town, Tortola and in Spanish Town, Virgin Gorda. The BVI Philatelic Bureau or Post Offices sell stamps for collectors. You can also buy BVI coins, but they are not used as a currency.

Banks
Barclays Bank, Road Town, Tel: 494-2171, with agencies in The Valley and Virgin Gorda; Bank of Nova Scotia, Road Town, Tel: 494-2526; Chase Manhattan Bank, Road Town, Tel: 494-2662; First Pennsylvania Bank, Road Town, Tel: 494-2117; Development Bank of the Virgin Islands, Tel: 494-3737.

Currency
The US dollar is the legal tender. There are no exchange control restrictions. Try to avoid large denominated traveller's cheques. Credit cards are all right for most hotels and the larger restaurants, but not for the majority of the bar/restaurants. Cheques accepted rarely, cash is king. There is a 10% stamp duty on all cheques and travellers' cheques.

Health
There is a public hospital, twelve doctors on Tortola and one on Virgin Gorda, two dentists and a small private hospital. Vaccinations certificates for yellow fever and cholera are required if you are arriving from an infected area. Be careful in the sun, always use a sunscreen.

Climate
The temperature averages 84°F in summer and 80°F in winter. At night temperatures may drop about ten degrees. Average annual rainfall is 40 inches.

Clothing
Island dress is casual and only the most exclusive restaurants require formal clothes. However, bathing suits are for the beach only, it is very offensive to locals to see bare chests and bellies, so cover up.

Business Hours
Banks open Monday-Thursday, 0900-1400, Friday 0900-1400, 1600-1730. Shops open Monday-Friday, 0900-1700. Government offices open Monday-Friday, 0830-1630.

National Holidays

New Year's Day, Commonwealth Day (2nd Monday in March), Good Friday, Easter Monday, Whit Monday in May, Queen's Birthday (2nd Monday in June), Territory Day (1 July), Festival beginning of August, St Ursula's Day (21 October), Prince Charles' Birthday (14 November), Christmas Day, Boxing Day.

Religion

Methodist, Anglican (Episcopal), Roman Catholic, Seventh Day Adventist, Baptist, Church of God, Church of Christ, Jehovah's Witness and Pentecostal Churches.

Time Zone

Atlantic Standard Time, 4 hours behind GMT, 1 ahead of EST.

Electric Current

100 volts, 60 cycles.

Telecommunications

Direct dialling is available locally and worldwide. The code for the BVI is 809-49 followed by a 5-digit number. All telecommunications are operated by Cable & Wireless. Telephone, telex, facsimile transmission, data transmission and telegraph facilities are all available. Phone cards are available, discount rates in evenings at weekends. To make a credit card call, dial 111 and quote your Visa or Mastercard number. Cable & Wireless is at the centre of Road Town. They also operate Tortola Marine Radio, call on VHF channel 16, talk on 27 or 84. The CCT Boatphone company in Road Town offers cellular telephone services throughout the Virgin Islands for yachts, Tel: 494-3825. There is a General Post Office in Road Town, branches in Tortola and Virgin Gorda and sub-branches in other islands.

Press

The Island Sun is published on Wednesdays and Saturdays, while the BVI Beacon comes out on Thursdays. The Limin' Times, printed weekly, is a free magazine giving entertainment news: nightlife, sports, music etc.

Radio

Radio ZBVI broadcasts on medium wave 780 KHZ. Weather reports for sailors are broadcast hourly from 0730 to 1830 every day. There are three FM stations: Z Wave, Z Gold and Z Hit.

Maps

The Ordanance Survey publishes a map of the BVI in its World Maps series, with inset maps of Road Town and East End, Tortola, tourist information and some text; Ordnance Survey, Romsey Road, Southampton, SO9 4DH, Tel: 0703 792792.

Tourist Office

The BVI Tourist Board Office in Tortola: PO Box 134, Road Town, Tel: 494-3134; some offices overseas can help with reservations. In the **USA**: 370 Lexington Avenue, Suite 511, New York, NY 10017, Tel: (212) 696-0400 or (800) 835-8530. BVI Information Offices: 1686 Union Street, San Francisco, CA 94123, Tel: (415) 775 0344 or (800) 232-7770; in the **UK**: BVI Tourist Office, c/o Intermarketing UK, 82 Baker Street, London W1M 2AE, Tel: 071 935 6726, Fax: 071 224 6540; in **Germany**: Lomerstrasse 28, Hamburg 70, Tel: (4940) 695 8846.

We are grateful to Pamela Gaffin, St John, for updating the BVI chapter.

LEEWARD ISLANDS

ANTIGUA AND BARBUDA

Introduction

ANTIGUA, with about 108 square miles, is the largest of the Leewards, and also the most popular and the most developed. The island is low-lying and composed of volcanic rock, coral and limestone. Boggy Peak, its highest elevation, rises 1,330 feet (399 metres). There is nothing spectacular about its landscape, although its rolling hills and flowering trees are picturesque, but its coast line, curving into coves and graceful harbours, with 365 soft white sand beaches fringed with palm trees, is among the most attractive in the West Indies. It had a population of around 63,880 in 1991, most of them of African origin although some are of English, Portuguese, Lebanese and Syrian descent.

History
Antigua (pronounced Anteega) was first inhabited by the Siboney (stone people), whose settlements date back to at least 2400 BC. The Arawaks lived on the island between about AD 35 and 1100. Columbus discovered it on his second voyage in 1493 and named the island Santa María de la Antigua. Spanish and French colonists attempted to settle there but were discouraged by the absence of fresh water springs and attacks by the Caribs.

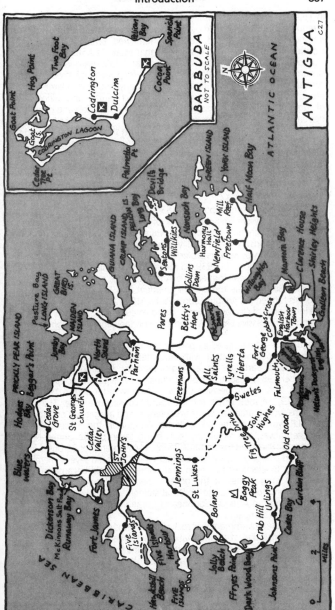

BARBUDA
NOT TO SCALE

Two Foot Bay
Hog Point
Goat Point
Goat Is.
Cedar Tree Pt.
Codrington
CODRINGTON LAGOON
Dulcina
Palmetto Pt.
Cocoa Point
Spanish Point
Palaster Bay

ANTIGUA
C27

N

ATLANTIC OCEAN

Prickly Pear Island
Hodges Bay
Beggar's Point
Pasture Bay
Long Island
Maiden Island
Jumby Bay
North Sound
Great Bird Is.
Guiana Island
Crab Island
Pelican Is.
Long Bay
Devil's Bridge
Indian Town
Seatons
Willikies
Nonsuch Bay
Green Island
York Island
Half Moon Bay
Mill Reef
Freetown
Newfield
Harmony Hall
Collins Dam
Betty's Hope
Pares
Parham
Willoughby Bay
Mamora Bay
Clarence House
Shirley Heights
Galleon Beach
English Harbour Town
Falmouth
Cobbs Cross
Fort George
Liberta
Tyrells
All Saints
Freemans
Swetes
John Hughes
Figtree Drive
Old Road
Nelsons Dockyard
Blue Waters
Dickenson Bay
McKinnons Salt Pond
Runaway Bay
Cedar Grove
St Georges Church
Cedar Valley
ST. JOHN'S
Jennings
St Lukes
Bolans
Boggy Peak
Crab Hill
Urlings
Cades Bay
Curtain Bluff
Johnsons Point
Fort James
Five Islands
Five Harbour
Hawksbill Beach
Jolly Beach
FFryes Beach
Dark Wood Beach
Five Islands

CARIBBEAN SEA

0 2
miles

In 1632 the English successfully colonized the island and, apart from a brief interlude in 1666 when held by the French, the island and its dependencies, Barbuda and uninhabited Redonda, remained British. Sir Christopher Codrington established the first large sugar estate in Antigua in 1674 and leased Barbuda to raise provisions for his plantations. Barbuda's only village is named after him. Forests were cleared for sugarcane production and African slave labour was imported. Today, many Antiguans blame frequent droughts on the island's lack of trees to attract rainfall, and ruined towers of sugar plantations stand as testament to the destruction and consequent barrenness of the landscape. In the 17th and 18th centuries, Antigua was important for its natural harbours where British ships could be refitted safe from hurricanes and from attack. The Dockyard and the many fortifications date from this period. *Shirley Heights, The Story of the Red Coats in Antigua*, by Charles W E Jane, published by the Reference Library of Nelson's Dockyard National Park Foundation at English Harbour, Antigua, in 1982, gives a detailed account of the military history of the island and the building of the fortifications, price US$4.

The slaves were emancipated in 1834 but economic opportunities for the freed labourers were limited by a lack of surplus farming land, no access to credit, and an economy built on agriculture rather than manufacturing. Poor labour conditions persisted and violence erupted in the first part of the twentieth century as workers protested against low wages, food shortages and poor living conditions. In 1939, to alleviate the seething discontent, the first labour movement was formed: the Antigua Trades and Labour Union. Vere Cornwall Bird became the union's president in 1943 and with other trade unionists formed the Antigua Labour Party (ALP). In 1946 the ALP won the first of a long series of electoral victories, being voted out of office only in 1971-76 when the Progressive Labour Movement won the general election.

Antigua was administered as part of the Leeward Islands until 1959 and attained associated status, with full internal self-government in 1967. Antigua and Barbuda, as a single territory, became independent in November 1981, despite a strong campaign for separate independence by Barbuda. Vere C Bird became the first Prime Minister and in 1989, at the age of 79, he took office for the fourth consecutive time. The general elections were marked by some irregularities and allegations of bribery, but the ALP won 15 of the 16 seats for Antigua in the 17-seat House of Representatives, the remaining seats being taken by the United National Democratic Party and the Barbuda People's Movement, for Barbuda. Mr Bird appointed a largely unchanged cabinet which included several members of his family. By-elections for seven seats were later held because of a court ruling on irregularities at the general elections. However, the ALP was returned unopposed, as the UNDP abstained in the absence of electoral reforms, and the Antigua Caribbean Liberation Movement (ACLM) could not finance a campaign.

In 1990 the Government was rocked by an arms smuggling scandal which exposed corruption at an international level when allegations were made that Antigua had been used as a transit point for shipments of arms from Israel to the Medellín cocaine cartel in Colombia. Communications and Works Minister, Vere Bird Jr, became the subject of a judicial inquiry, following a complaint from the Colombian Government, for having signed authorization documents. His Cabinet appointment was revoked although he remained an MP. The Blom-Cooper report recommended no prosecutions although it undermined the credibility of the Government and highlighted the rivalry between the two Bird sons, Vere Jr and Lester. Repeated calls for the resignation of 82-year-old Prime Minister Vere Bird were ignored although several cabinet reshuffles became necessary as ministers resigned from his Government. Demonstrations were organized in 1992 by the newly-formed three-party United Opposition Front, seeking the resignation of the Prime Minister amid allegations of his theft and corruption. Scotland Yard assistance was sought in investigating a number of fire bombs and arson attacks.

Government

Antigua and Barbuda is a constitutional monarchy within the Commonwealth and the British Crown is represented by a Governor General. The head of government is the Prime Minister. There are two legislative houses: a directly elected 17-member House of Representatives and a 17-member Upper House, or Senate, appointed by the Governor General, mainly on the advice of the Prime Minister and the Leader of the Opposition. Antigua is divided into six parishes: St George, St John's, St Mary, St Paul, St Peter and St Phillip. Community councils on Antigua and the local government council on Barbuda are the organs of local government.

The Economy

The economy was long dominated by the cultivation of sugar, which was the major export earner until 1960, when prices fell dramatically and crippled the industry. By 1972 sugar had largely disappeared and farming had shifted towards fruit, vegetables, cotton and livestock. The economy is now based on services, principally tourism and offshore banking. Hotels and restaurants contribute over 15% of gross domestic product and employ about one quarter of the work force. Tourism receipts make up about 60% of total foreign exchange earnings. There is some light industry which has been encouraged by tax and other incentives, but export-orientated manufacturing is hampered by high wage and energy costs. A major expansion of tourist infrastructure has taken place, with development of harbour, airport, road and hotel facilities. Nearly half a million tourists visit the island by air or by sea each year, of whom over half are cruise ship passengers. Nearly 40% of the tourists who arrive by air are from the USA, but numbers from the UK and other European countries, particularly Germany, have risen to over 30% of the total. This investment has not yet touched the bulk of the population and in rural areas small wooden shacks still constitute the most common form of dwelling, often alongside resorts and villa developments. Economic growth slowed in the 1990s; political instability and corruption discouraged private sector investment, while government finances were weakened by high levels of debt, wages and tax evasion.

Many visitors regard Antigua as the ideal Caribbean holiday destination. The role of tourism in Antigua today is, however, one of the objects of a vehement attack in Jamaica Kincaid's book *A Small Place* (1988). Addressed to the foreign visitor, the essay proposes to reveal the realities underneath the island's surface. What follows is a passionate indictment of much of Antiguan government, society, the colonists who laid its foundations and the modern tourist. It is a profoundly negative book, designed to inspire the visitor to think beyond the beach and the hotel on this, or any other, island. Jamaica Kincaid was brought up on Antigua (she now lives in the USA), and memories and images from her childhood figure strongly in her two other books to date, the prize-winning collection of dream-like stories, *At The Bottom Of The River* (1983) and the novel *Annie John* (1985). A new novel *Lucy* was published in 1991. An account of an Antiguan working man's life can be found in *To Shoot Hard Labour* by Keithlyn B Smitt and Fernando C Smitt (Karia Press, London 1989).

Fauna and Flora

Around 150 different birds have been observed in Antigua and Barbuda, of which a third are year-round residents and the rest seasonal or migrants. Good spots for birdwatching include McKinnons salt pond, north of St John's, where thousands of sandpipers and other water birds can be seen. Yellow crowned night-herons breed here. Potworks Dam is noted for the great blue heron in spring and many water fowl. Great Bird Island is home to the red-billed tropic bird and on Man of War Island, Barbuda, frigate birds breed. At Pasture Bay, on Long Island, the hawksbill turtle lays its eggs from late May to December. The Wide Caribbean Sea Turtle Conservation Network (Widecast) organizes turtle watches.

Beaches and Watersports

Tourist brochures will never tire of telling you that there are 365 beaches on Antigua, one for every day of the year, some of which are deserted. The nearest beach to St John's is Fort James which is sometimes rough and has a milky appearance, lots of weed and not good for swimming. It is rather secluded, do not go alone, drugs-users confrontations have been recorded there. Further but better is Dickenson Bay. Also good is Deep Bay which, like most beaches, can only be reached by taxi or car. Near English Harbour is Galleon Beach, which is splendid, but again can only be reached by taxi or car. It has an excellent restaurant. Dark Wood Beach, on the road from St John's to Old Road round the south west coast, is very nice, quiet, with a bar and restaurant at the southern end, reasonable food but not cheap. Half Moon Bay, in the east, has a resort at one end, but there is plenty of room; the waves can be rough in the centre of the bay, but the water is calm at the northern end.

Antigua offers sailing (sailing week at end-April, beginning of May, is a major yacht-racing event, with lots of noisy nightlife), water-skiing, snorkelling and deep-sea fishing. "Cocktail" and "barbecue" cruises are reasonably priced. From Shorty's Watersports at Dickenson Bay, glass-bottomed boats take people out to the coral reefs; there are also excursions to Bird Island, food and drink provided. Trips round the island with stops at smaller islands can be arranged on the catamarans *Siboney* (Tel: 462 4101), *Falcon* (Tel: 462 4792) or *Cariba* (Tel: 462 2269), or you can charter a yacht from English Harbour or Sun Yacht Charters at Parham. *Servabo* is a Brixham fishing trawler now used for excursions and beach parties, children under six free, 6-12 half price, Tel: 462 1581 for information and current rates. *Galleon Girl* can be chartered for fishing trips (Tel: 462 2064) for a maximum of six people. *Missa Ferdie*, a fast and well-equipped sports fishing boat, available for half (US$440) or full day (US$780) charters, can be hired for picnics and excursions too, maximum six people, contact Captain Pello, Catamaran Marina, Tel: 460 1503 or David Shoul, PO Box 974, St John's, Tel: 462 1440/4357, Fax: 462 1788. There is also, of course, the *Jolly Roger* (Tel: 462 2064), a wooden sailing ship used for entertaining would-be pirates, with Wednesday lunchtime cruises from Jolly Beach, Thursday cocktail cruises from the *Royal Antiguan*, and Saturday night barbecue and dancing cruise, helped along with plentiful rum punch.

Dickenson Bay is the only beach with public hire of watersports equipment but some hotels will hire to the public especially out of season, eg the *Jolly Beach* hotel near Bolan's Village (bus from West End bus station). At EC$13.50 per hour, windsurfing is only half as expensive as at Dickenson Bay. The *Sandals* all-inclusive resort on Dickenson Bay will admit outsiders, at EC$450 per couple 1000-1800 or EC$250 for the evening, giving you the use of all sports facilities, meals, bar etc. Windsurfing Antigua at the *Lord Nelson Beach Hotel* north of the airport (no frills accommodation and food), offers package holidays for beginners or keen windsurfers (Tel: 461 2691).

Diving and Marine Life
There are barrier reefs around most of Antigua which are host to lots of colourful fish and underwater plant life. Diving is mostly shallow, up to 60 feet, except below Shirley Heights, where dives are up to 110 feet, or Sunken Rock, with a depth of 122 feet where the cleft rock formation gives the impression of a cave dive. Popular sites are Cades Reef, which runs for 2½ miles along the leeward side of the island and is an underwater park; Sandy Island Reef, covered with several types of coral and only 30-50 feet deep; Horseshoe Reef, Barracuda Alley and Little Bird Island. There are also plenty of wrecks to explore, including the *Andes*, in 20 feet of water in Deep Bay, the *Harbour of St John's* and the *Unknown Barge*, also in Deep Bay. Diving off Barbuda is more difficult unless you are on a boat with full gear and a compressor, as facilities are very limited. The water is fairly shallow, though, so snorkelling can be enjoyable. There is little information on the island about conservation and few warnings on the dangers of touching living coral.

Dive shops are located nearly all round the island and include: Aquanaut Diving Centre, at *St James's Club*, Tel: 460 5000 or *Royal Antiguan*, Tel: 4621801, or *Galleon Beach Club*, Tel: 463 1024; Dive Runaway, *Runaway Beach Club*, Tel: 462 2626, training sessions, PADI certification courses, equipment rental; Dive Antigua, *Halcyon Cove Hotel*, Tel: 462 0256; Jolly Dive, *Jolly Beach Hotel*, Tel: 462 0061; Curtain Bluff Dive Shop, *Curtain Bluff Hotel*, Tel: 462 8400 (certified hotel guests only); Long Bay Dive Shop, *Long Bay Hotel*, Tel: 460 2005 (certified hotel guests only).

Other Sports
There are **golf** courses, including the professional 18-hole one at Cedar Valley, near St John's, Tel: 462 0161, and a 9-hole course open to visitors at *Half Moon Bay Hotel*, Tel: 463 2101.

Many of the large hotels have **tennis** courts, the most prestigious of which are probably at *Half Moon Bay Hotel*, which hosts several professional competitions during the year, Tel: 463-2101. Also courts at the *Royal Antiguan Hotel*, Tel: 462 3733, Deep Bay; *Hodges Bay Club*, Tel: 462 2300; Temo Sports, Tel: 463 1536. *St James's Club* has floodlit courts, Tel: 463 1113. There is a new tennis and squash club open to the public next to the *Falmouth Harbour Beach Apartments*.

Riding is available through the hotels. The Antigua Riding Academy has accompanied riding tours. Wadadli Riding Stables at Gambles Bluff, Tel: 462 2721. *St James's Club* also arranges horseriding, Tel: 463 1430.

Cricket is the national sport and Test Matches are played at the Recreation Ground. There are matches between Antiguan teams and against teams from neighbouring islands.

Horse racing takes place on public holidays at Cassada Park.

There is a sports complex overlooking Falmouth Harbour, next to the Yacht Club, which has synthetic grass tennis courts and squash courts (Tel: 463 1781), and a Fitness Club in Hodges Bay, which offers aerobic classes, weight training rooms and other facilities (Tel: 462 1540).

Festivals

Antigua's carnival is at the end of July and lasts until the first Tuesday in August. The main event is "J'ouvert", or "Juvé" morning when from 0400 people come into town dancing behind steel and brass bands. Hotels and airlines tend to be booked up well in advance. For information contact the Carnival Committee, High Street, St John's, Tel: 462 0194. Barbuda has a smaller carnival in June, known as "Caribana".

St John's

Built around the largest of the natural harbours is **St John's**, the capital, with an estimated population of about 30,000. It is rather quiet and a little run-down but parts are rapidly being developed for tourism and the town is a mixture of the old and the new. Although parts of the town are rather tatty, it is generally safe to walk around even late at night. New boutiques, duty-free shops and restaurants are vying for custom. Redcliffe Quay is a picturesque area of restored historical buildings now full of souvenir shops and the only toy shop in town. Heritage Quay, opened in 1988, is a duty free shopping complex strategically placed to catch cruise ship visitors. It has a casino and a big screen satellite TV, a cool, pleasant place to have a drink. Most activity now takes place around these two quay developments, especially when there is a cruise ship in dock.

However, St John's does have interesting historical associations. Nelson served in Antigua as a young man for almost three years, and visited it again in 1805, during his long chase of Villeneuve which was to end with the Battle of Trafalgar. Some of the old buildings in St John's, including the Anglican Cathedral, have been damaged several times by earthquakes, the last one in 1974. A cathedral in St John's was first built in 1683, but replaced in 1745 and then again in 1843 after an earthquake, at which time it was built of stone. Its twin towers can be seen from all over St John's. It has a wonderfully cool interior lined with Pitchpine timber. Donations requested.

The Museum and Archives at the former Court House in Long Street are worth a visit, both to see the exhibition of pre-Columbian and colonial archaeology and anthropology of Antigua and for the Court House building itself, first built in 1747, damaged by earthquakes in 1843 and 1974 but now restored. There is also Viv Richard's cricket bat, with which he scored the fastest century, various 'hands on' items and games. Entrance free, although donations requested; gift shop. Open Monday-Friday 1000-1500, Saturdays 1000-1300. (Tel: 463 1060). You can also visit Viv Richard's childhood home on Viv Richard's Street. The Museum of Marine and Living Art, Gambles Terrace, opposite Princess Margaret School, Tel: 462 1228, Fax: 462 1187, exhibits of sea shells, shipwrecks and pre-Columbian history. Recommended weekly lectures, Thursday 1000, on the evolution of the earth and the formation of the continents and civilizations.

A short drive west of St John's are the ruins of Fort Barrington on a promontory at Goat Hill overlooking Deep Bay and the entrance to St John's Harbour. These fortifications were erected by Governor Burt, who gave up

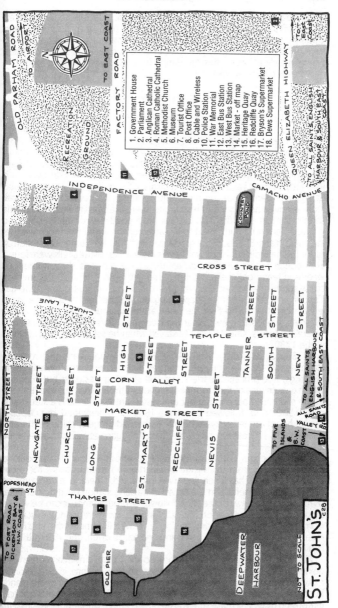

St. John's

1. Government House
2. Parliament
3. Anglican Cathedral
4. Roman Catholic Cathedral
5. Methodist Church
6. Museum
7. Tourist Office
8. Post Office
9. Cable and Wireless
10. Police Station
11. War Memorial
12. East Bus Station
13. West Bus Station
14. Market - off map
15. Market
16. Heritage Quay
17. Bryson's Supermarket
18. Dews Supermarket

OLD PARHAM ROAD
TO EAST COAST
TO AIRPORT
FACTORY ROAD
QUEEN ELIZABETH HIGHWAY
TO EAST COAST
RECREATION GROUND
INDEPENDENCE AVENUE
CAMACHO AVENUE
COUNTRY POND
TO ALL SAINTS, ENGLISH HARBOUR & SOUTH EAST COAST
CROSS STREET
CHURCH LANE
STREET
TANNER STREET
STREET
NEW STREET
HIGH STREET
TEMPLE STREET
SOUTH STREET
STREET
CORN ALLEY
MARKET STREET
NEWGATE STREET
CHURCH STREET
LONG STREET
ST MARY'S STREET
REDCLIFFE STREET
NEVIS STREET
NORTH STREET
TO ALL SAINTS, ENGLISH HARBOUR & SOUTH EAST COAST
ALL SAINTS ROAD
VALLEY RD
TO FIVE ISLANDS & S.W. COAST
POPESHEAD ST.
THAMES STREET
TO FORT ROAD DICKENSON BAY & N.W. COAST
OLD PIER
DEEPWATER HARBOUR
NOT TO SCALE
ST. JOHN'S c.26

active duty in 1780 suffering from psychiatric disorders; a stone he placed in one of the walls at the Fort describes him grandly as 'Imperator and Gubernator' of the Carib Islands. At the other side of the harbour are the ruins of Fort James, from where you can get a good view of St John's. There was originally a fort on this site dating from 1675, but most of what can now be seen dates from 1749.

Excursions

On the other side of the island is **English Harbour**, which has become one of the world's most attractive yachting centres. Here "Nelson's Dockyard" has been restored and is one of the most interesting historical monuments in the West Indies. It was designated a National Park in 1985 (Parks Commissioner, Tel: 463-1379). Entrance US$1.60, children under 12 free. Souvenirs and T-shirts are on sale at the entrance. See *Admiral's Inn*, with its boat and mast yard, slipway and pillars still standing but which suffered earthquake damage in the nineteenth century. The *Lumber and Copper Store* is now a hotel bar and restaurant. There is a small museum, with gift shop in the same building. *Limey's Bar* has a good view of the harbour and is a nice place for a drink. Next to it is an art centre with work by local artists including Katie Shears, who specializes in flora and fauna. The Ralph A Aldridge shell collection in a wall case is fascinating, all the shells were found in Antiguan waters. On the quay are three large capstans, showing signs of wear and tear. Boat charters can be arranged from here; also a 20-minute cruise round the historic Dockyard for US$5 on *Horatio*, from outside the *Copper and Lumber Store*, depending on seasonal demand. A footpath leads round the bay to **Fort Berkeley** at the harbour mouth, well grazed by goats, wonderful views. Near the Dockyard, Clarence House still stands where the future King, William IV stayed when he served as a midshipman in the 1780s.

At **Shirley Heights**, overlooking English Harbour, are the ruins of fortifications built in the 18th century with a wonderful view. Some buildings, like officers' quarters, are still standing, restored but roofless, which give an idea of their former grandeur. At the lookout point, or Battery, at the southernmost end is a bar and restaurant. On Sundays a steel band plays 1500-1800, followed by reggae 1800-2200, very loud and popular, can be heard at the dockyard below. Barbecued burgers, chicken, ribs and salad US$6-11. Great fun, recommended. Antiguans as well as tourists enjoy it.

Great George Fort, on Monk's Hill, above Falmouth Harbour (a 30-minute walk from the village of Liberta, and from Cobb's Cross near English Harbour) has been less well preserved. There is a museum of pre-Columbian artefacts in the Dow Hill tracking station building (formerly used in connection with the US Apollo space programme). It can be visited by prior arrangement, or on Thursday afternoons there are tours, starting from Nelson's Dockyard and taking in Dow Hill (check the details at Nicholson's travel agency). If advance notice is given, the Antigua Rum Distillery welcomes visitors.

Fig Tree Drive between Old Road and the Catholic church on the road going north from Liberta, is a steep, winding, bumpy road, through mountainous rainforest. It is greener and more scenic than most of the island, but the rainforest is scanty and can not be compared with islands like Dominica. If travelling by bicycle make sure you go *down* Fig Tree Drive from the All Saints to Liberta road, heading towards Old Road, the hill is very steep.

Boggy Peak, in the southwest, is the highest point on the island and from the top you can get wonderful views over to Guadelupe, St Kitts, Nevis and Montserrat. It is a good walk up, or you can take a car. From Urlings walk (or take minibus) about ½-¾ mile in the direction of Old Town. Take the second major path to the left (the first goes to a ruined house visible from the road) which runs very straight then ascends quite steeply. When you get to the top, walk round the fence surrounding the Cable and Wireless buildings to get a good view in all directions.

A recommended excursion to the east coast, if you have a car, is to take the road out to the airport from St John's. Do not enter the airport but take the right fork which runs alongside it. After about 1½ miles take a right turn down a small road to St George's Church, on Fitches Creek Bay, built in 1687 in a beautiful location, interesting gravestones. From there, follow the rough road round the coast to **Parham**, which is interesting for being the first British settlement on the island and for having an unusual octagonal church, St Peter's, which dates from the 1840s. Lovely flamboyant trees surround the church and enhance its attractiveness. From Parham take the road due south and then east at the petrol station through Pares to Willikies. On this road, just past Pares Village, is a sign to **Betty's Hope**, a ruined sugar estate built in 1650 and once owned by the Codrington family. Restoration was started by the Antigua Museum in St John's but abandoned. The ruins are now becoming overgrown again, but there are plans for further restoration and a building has been erected for a visitors' centre. It is an extensive site with two towers, a still house and other ruined buildings, fascinating to explore, but wear stout shoes and trousers, there are long, sharp thorns. For a guided tour contact the Antigua Museum, Tel:462 3946 ext 14/16, or Mr Hubert Mack, of Parham Town. After Willikies the road is signed to the Pineapple Beach Club at Long Bay, but before you get there, take a right turn down a small road, which deteriorates to a bumpy track, to **Devil's Bridge** at Indian Town Point. The area on the Atlantic coast is a national park where rough waves have carved out the bridge and made blowholes, not easily visible at first, but quite impressive when the spray breaks through. Good view of Long Bay and the headland.

Returning through Willikies to Glanvilles, take a left turn shortly after St Stephen's Church down a small road south past Collins Dam. When you meet up with the main road (petrol station) turn left and then right towards St Phillips. The scenery after this village is quite attractive, there are several ruined sugar mills dotting the landscape. The road continues on to Half Moon Bay and tracks lead up the coast to Mill Reef and many small beaches and jetties. Alternatively, take a left turn through Freetown to visit **Harmony Hall** (Tel: 460 4120), Brown's Bay Mill, at Nonsuch Bay, a restored Great House and mill which has been converted into a Caribbean art and craft exhibition centre. Open daily 1000-1800. There is a shop, bar and restaurant (Sunday barbecue, dinner by reservation only), and a jetty for those arriving by sea. Moorings also available for anchoring in the bay. Harmony Hall broadcasts a daily weather service at 0900 on VHF Channel 68. There are two villas for rent with use of swimming pool. Twice a week the catamaran *Wizard* leaves from the jetty at 1000 for a snorkelling and sightseeing cruise.

Warning

Finding your way around is not easy: street names are rarely in evidence. The Ordnance Survey map, US$7.50, is recommended if you are exploring the island. It is a little dated, but there is nothing better. A map hand drawn by Brian Dyde is available from several locations and is adequate for driving around.

Barbuda

Some 30 miles to the north is Barbuda, a flat coral island some 68 miles square, one of the two island dependencies of Antigua. The population i about 1,500 and most of them live in the only village on the island Codrington, which stands on the edge of the lagoon. The people of Barbuda are unusually tall, descended from the Corramante tribe in Africa and used by Codrington in his experiments in slave breeding. Barbuda has some excellent beaches and its seas are rich with all types of crustaceans and tropical fish. Palaster Reef is a marine reserve to protect the reef and the shipwrecks (there are around 60 ships documented). You can swim from the beach to the reef. This is one of the few islands in the area where there is still much wild life, although much of it introduced by man: duck, guinea fowl, plover, pigeon, wild deer and wild pig. There is an impressive frigate bird colony in the mangroves in Codrington Lagoon, particularly on Man o War Island where hundreds of birds mate and breed in August-December Local fishermen will take you out there; you can get quite close for photography or just to watch. Wild donkeys also roam the island.

Barbuda is being developed as a tourist resort with attractions for snorkellers and skin-divers such as exploring old wrecks. The elkhorn coral and staghorn coral formations are very impressive. Take your own scuba equipment or join one of the dive boats from Antigua. Snorkelling equipment is available but is more expensive than on Antigua. There are two hotels, two villas and a few guesthouses, although more are planned *Cocoa Point Lodge*, which charges US$400 per night to include all meals and drinks, is quiet and exclusive, islanders and non-guests are not admitted The *K-Club*, opened in 1991 is even more expensive, with its own golf course as well as water sports, welcomes islanders and non-residents. The *Sunset View Resort* is just south of the Codrington airport, US$75d, dining room Tel: 460 0016/0078. Do not expect any "mod cons" on Barbuda. The local night spot is *Jam City*, with beer cheaper than Antigua. Paradise Tours, run by Lynton Thomas, is highly recommended, as is his guest house, *Thomas Guest House*, in Codrington, north of the airport, Tel: 460 0135. The island has a Martello Tower and fort. The tower is 56 feet high and once had nine guns to defend the southwestern approach. From Codrington, River Road runs three miles to Palmetto Point (with beautiful pink sand beaches), pass Cocoa Point and on to Spanish Point, a half-mile finger of land that divides the Atlantic from the Caribbean Sea. There is a small ruin of a lookout post here and the most important Arawak settlements found in Barbuda.

Excellent 1:25,000 maps are available from the Codrington post office or from the map shop in Jardine Court, St Mary's, St John's (good 1:50,000 maps of Antigua as well). It is possible to hire jeeps or horses in Codrington otherwise everywhere is a long hot walk, so take liquid refreshment with you. Easily reached by air (taking 10 minutes), or (with some difficulty and at a high price) by boat from St John's. There are two airports. The main one is just south of Codrington, to which Liat has regular flights, US$36 return while Four Island Airways or Carib Aviation will arrange charters and day trips. The second airport is near Cocoa Point and principally serves the two hotels nearby: *Cocoa Point* and *K-Club*.

Redonda

Antigua's second dependency, 35 miles to the south west and at half a mile square, little more than a rocky volcanic islet, is uninhabited. According to the Antigua and Barbuda Tourist Office, "In 1865, the island was claimed by Matthew Shiell as a kingdom for his son Philippe. Philippe's successor, the poet John Gawsworth, appointed many leading literary figures of his day as dukes and duchesses of his kingdom; the lucky peers included J B Priestley, Dylan Thomas and Rebecca West. The current king lives in Sussex, and his subjects are not likely to produce any great works of fiction as they are all either goats, lizards or sea-birds. Since the decline of the mining industry (guano and phosphates), this fairly harmless brand of English eccentricity has been Redonda's main claim to fame, although for bird-watchers, the island is well-known for its burrowing owl, now extinct on Antigua".

Information for Visitors

Documents
A valid onward ticket is necessary. American, Canadian and British nationals need only proof of citizenship. Passports but not visas are required by nationals of other Commonwealth countries and British Dependent Territories, if their stay does not exceed six months. The following countries need valid passports but not visas: Argentina, Austria, Belgium, Brazil, Denmark, Germany, Finland, Greece, Ireland, Italy, Japan, Liechtenstein, Luxembourg, Malta, Mexico, Monaco, Netherlands, Norway, Portugal, Spain, Suriname, Sweden, Switzerland, Turkey and Venezuela. Nationals of all other countries require visas, unless they are in transit for less than 24 hours. Visitors must satisfy immigration officials that they have enough money for their stay. You will not be allowed through Immigration without somewhere to stay. The Tourist Office can help you and you can always change your mind later. If you arrive at English Harbour by boat you must clear Customs at the Police Station.

How To Get There
V C Bird airport, some 4½ miles from St John's, is the centre for air traffic in the area and is served by British Airways (four direct flights a week from Gatwick, connections with Barbados and Grenada, Tel: 462 0876/9), Lufthansa (two flights a week direct from Frankfurt, Tel: 462 3142, represented by Liat), American Airlines (from Baltimore, Washington DC, New York, Puerto Rico, St Maarten, Tel: 462 0950), BWIA (from Barbados, Jamaica, New York, Trinidad, St Croix, St Kitts, Puerto Rico, Miami, St Maarten) and Air Canada (and BWIA from Toronto, Tel: 462 1147).

There is an airport departure tax of EC$25.

Inter Island Transport
There are frequent air services to neighbouring islands (Anguilla, Barbados, Barbuda, Dominica, Martinique, Grenada, Jamaica, Montserrat, Nevis, Guadeloupe, Trinidad, St Croix, St Eustatius, St Kitts, St Lucia, St Maarten, St Thomas, St Vincent, Puerto Rico, Tortola) operated by Liat (Tel: 462 3142/3), BWIA (Tel: 462 0262/3) and American Airlines. Carib Aviation arranges charters to neighbouring islands in planes carrying 5, 6 or 9 passengers and can often work out cheaper and more convenient than using Liat. The office is at the airport, Tel: 462 3147 0800-1700, after office hours Tel: 461 1650. They will meet incoming flights if you are transferring to another island, and make sure you make your return connection. Also day tours. The flight to Montserrat takes 18 minutes.

Occasional boat services to St Kitts and Dominica; see boat captains at Fisherman's Wharf. There is a cargo boat to Dominica once a week and you can arrange a passage for EC$102 including departure tax through Vernon Edwards Shipping Company on Thames Street; very basic facilities, no toilet.

Local Travel
Minivans (shared taxis) go to some parts of the island from the West End bus terminal by the market in St John's. Buses, which are banned from the tourist area (north of the line from the airport to St John's), run frequently between St John's and English Harbour, EC$2 There are also buses from the east terminal by the war memorial to Willikies, whence a 20 minute

walk to Long Bay beach. There are no buses to the airport and very few to beaches though two good swimming beaches on the way to Old Road can be reached by bus. Bus frequency can be variable, and there are very few buses after dark or on Sundays. Buses to Old Road are half-hourly on average, though more frequent around 0800 and 1600. There are no publicly displayed timetables, you'll have to ask for one. Buses usually go when they are full; ask the driver where he is going. **Taxis** have H registration plates. In St John's there is a taxi rank on St Mary Street, or outside Dew's or Bryson's supermarkets. They are not metered and frequently try to overcharge, so agree a price first, they should have a EC$ price list so ask to see it. There is a list of government approved taxi rates published in *It's Happening, You're Welcome*; the list is also posted in EC$ and US$ at the airport just after customs. From St John's to Runaway Bay, 10 minutes, is US$6; to the airport, US$7 or EC$20 per car, from the airport to town EC$20 per person. If going to the airport early in the morning, book a taxi the night before as there are not many around. For excursions a knowledgeable and recommended taxi driver is Mr Graham at the *Barrymore Hotel*. A day tour normally costs about US$55. Taxi: excursions advertised in the hotels are generally overpriced. Hitchhiking is easy in daylight but at night you might fall prey to a taxi driver.

Car Hire

All in St John's and some at airport, most will pick you up: Antigua Car Rentals (*Barrymore Hotel*); Carib Car Rentals (*Michael's Mount Hotel*); Lapp's Rent-a-Car (Long and Cross Streets); Alexander Parris (St Mary's Street); Prince's Rent-a-Car (Fort Road); Capital Rental (High Street); Dollar Rental (Nevis Street); E J Wolfe Ltd (Long Street); National and, cheaper, Hustler Hires at The Toy Shop (Long Street). Sunshine Car Rental (Tel: 461 2426) recommended, good value compared with agencies at the airport who push up the extras (although Jacob's at the airport is reported friendly and reliable). Rates are from US$40 a day, US$225 a week (no mileage charge), including insurance charges, in summer, more in winter.

A local driving licence, US$12, valid for three months, must be purchased on presentation of a foreign licence.

Renting a car or motorcycle is probably the best way to see the island's sights if you have only a short time to spend, as the bus service is inadequate. Ivor's at English Harbour has a monopoly on renting motorcycles at US$20/day (plus US$12 driving licence), bikes not in good condition. Bicycle hire from House of Vitamins, US$10/day, US$100 deposit.

Remember to drive on the left. There is a 24-hour petrol station on Old Parham Road outside St John's. Traffic lights were installed in St John's in 1989, but these are the only ones on the island. Be careful with one way streets in St John's. In rural areas watch out for potholes; the roads are very narrow in places. At night people do not always dim their headlights, beware also of cows straying across the road in the dark. Petrol costs US$2.15/gallon everywhere.

Where To Stay

There are hotels, resorts and apartments all round the island and more are being built all the time. The greatest concentration of developments is in the area around St John's, along the coast to the west and also to the north in a clockwise direction to the airport. A second cluster of places to stay is around English Harbour and Falmouth Harbour in the southeast of the island. Many may be closed September-October in preparation for the winter season. A full list of hotels, apartments and guesthouses should be available from the Tourist Office at the airport, although it is not always easy to get hold of. The Tourist Office will book you a hotel room on arrival if you have not already done so. There are lots of self-catering apartments available all round the island but a common complaint is that sufficient provisions are not available locally and you have to go into St John's for shopping.

In **St John's**: *Spanish Main Inn*, on Independence Drive opposite the cricket oval, originally the house of the American Consul, English-style pub with clean rooms above, US$35-50, cold shower intermittent water supply, good, cheap food, roast beef Sunday lunch, EC$30 good meeting place, recommended, but a bit noisy at night; *Main Road Guest House*, near the market, EC$25-40, about the cheapest but no fan, noisy, mice visit at night. *Miami*, near market on Main Road, US$25-30d with bath, Chinese restaurant. *Montgomery Hotel*, Tindale

Road, usually plenty of room except during carnival and cricket matches, central but not a very nice part of town, noisy roosters across the street, scruffy and basic, shared bath, rats in downstairs rooms, no water after midnight, cable TV, US$30d, Tel: 462 1164; *Palm View Guest House*, 57 St Mary's Street, no sign, around the corner from *Spanish Main Inn*, friendly, basic, good, EC$40; *Murphy's Apartments*, PO Box 491, All Saints Road, Tel: 461 1183, run by Elaine Murphy, US$35 with breakfast; *Cortsland*, Upper Gambles, PO Box 403, overpriced at US$75-90d, Tel: 462 1395. *Pigottsville Guest House*, at Clare Hall, very basic, in need of repairs, but cheap, no signs, about two miles from the airport and within easy walking distance of St John's, 20 rooms, US$20-30d, Tel: 462 0592; *Barrymore*, US$75-85d winter rate, US$60-70 summer, on Fort Road, on the outskirts of the town, transport and use of facilities at the *Barrymore Beach Club* on Runaway Bay, 2 miles from St John's, which has rooms and apartments, recommended, clean, comfortable, Tel: 462 4101, US$115-275 winter rate, US$75-130 summer, on 1½ miles of white sand beach; *Runaway Beach Club*, on Runaway Bay, friendly, beachfront cabins, rooms or villas, US$70-275, 110V electricity, excellent beach restaurant, *The Lobster Pit*, Tel:462 2650-2, Fax: 462 4172; *Siboney Beach Club*, good, small, US$200 winter, US$110 summer, Tel:462 0806, Fax: 462 3356; *Coral Sands* beach front cottages at Runaway Bay, US$200/night for 2-bedroomed or $250 for 3-bedroomed in winter, reservations through Mrs Sonia King, PO Box 34, St John's, Tel: 461 0925. The *Ramada Rennaissance Royal Antiguan*, three miles from St John's, depressing drive

through tatty suburbs, 270 rooms, high rise, comfortable, good facilities, quiet in summer, casino, pool, tennis etc, US$175-750d winter, US$135-550d summer, Tel: 462 3733, Fax: 462 3732. Further round the coast *Hawksbill Beach Resort*, four miles from St John's, lovely beaches, good food, pleasant rooms, friendly staff, PO Box 108, Tel/Fax:1515, tennis, table tennis, pool, watersports, 88 rooms, US$280-365.

At Dickenson Bay: *Antigua Village* has villas with free watersports from US$95-275 summer rate to US$170-470 winter rate for a studio or beach front 2-bedroomed villa, there is a small store for provisions, nothing exciting, Tel: 462 2930, Fax: 462 0375, PO Box 649, St John's. *Divi Anchorage*, US$265-325, winter rate, PO Box 147, Tel: 462 0267, has 99 rooms, 3 tennis courts and all watersports, but is closed July/August. *Halcyon Cove Beach Resort and Casino*, US$220-370 winter rate, US$101-259 summer EP, on the beach with full watersports facilities and tennis. On the north coast, *Blue Waters*, Tel: 462 0290, Fax: 462 0293, P O Box 256, US$315-355, winter, US$135-165, summer, excellent but expensive when tax and service is added to everything, taxis from hotel nearly always try to overcharge; at Crosbies Estate, is the *Sandpiper* (PO Box 569, St John's, Telex 2168-AK), which is on a nice beach with reef, is very friendly, 24 airy rooms, quiet, US$330-380d winter, US$90-130d summer EP/MAP, food not recommended.

In the southwest: *Jolly Beach*, US$150-270d winter, US$140-210d MAP summer rate, a/c, very large package hotel with plenty of activities, service and tax added to MAP but not to drinks, snacks etc, buses to St John's; *Golden Rock Studios*, at Johnson's Point are comfortable self-catering apartments on a pleasant beach, but facilities for buying provisions are poor, US$250/week summer, US$300/ week winter for one bedroom, double for two bedrooms, Tel: 462-8218.

At **English Harbour**: *Admiral's Inn*, US$96-116d winter rate, US$66-82d summer rate, PO Box 713, Tel: 460 1027, (from abroad), 460 1534 (in Antigua), Fax: 460 1534, 14 rooms in restored 17th century building, transport to the beach, excellent location, good food, mixed reports regarding service, but ask for Ethelyn Philip, the manageress, she is keen to help. *Copper and Lumber Store* (restored dockyard building) PO Box 184, Tel: 463 1058, studios and suites available, US$80-140 summer rate, US$160-280 winter, boat transport to nearby beaches. *The Inn*, set in 10 acres with lovely white sand beach, watersports provided, tennis and golf nearby, US$325-400d winter rate, US$100-155d summer, PO Box 187, St John's, Tel: 463 1014.

At **Falmouth Harbour**: *Catamaran Hotel and Marina*, on narrow beach, friendly, US$65-100d winter rate, Tel: 463 1036. *Falmouth Harbour Beach Apartments* (same management as *Admiral's Inn*) good value, 28 studio apartments on or near private beach, US$78-84d per day in summer or US$110-120d in winter, excluding tax, very clean, friendly staff, including use of boats and other watersports equipment, all apartments have lovely view of harbour, PO Box 713, St John's, Tel: 463 1027/1094, Fax: 460 1534.

In the **east**: *Half Moon Bay Hotel*, good setting, not obtrusive, 9-hole golf, tennis with pro, watersports, pool etc, closed September-October, US$300-375d winter, US$180-225 summer MAP, no children under five in winter, PO Box 144, St John's, Tel: 460 4300.

On **Long Island**: *Jumby Bay Resort*, secluded, luxurious and incredibly expensive at US$895d all inclusive winter rate, US$525d summer, PO Box 243, St John's, Tel: 462 6000, US reservations: Tel: 800 437 0049 or (212) 819 9490. The resort does not accept credit cards.

If you are changing planes and have to stop over, take a taxi into St John's where the accommodation is much better than near the airport. *Antigua (Sugar) Mill*, near the airport, Tel: 462 3044, Fax: 462 1500, P O Box 319, US$80-100d winter, US$60-80d summer.

Camping is illegal.

There is a 10% service charge and 7% government tax at all hotels.

Where To Eat

If you are planning to eat out in hotels, you need to allow at least US$300 pp per week, but it is possible to eat much more cheaply in the local restaurants in St John's. Restaurants tend to move, close down or change names frequently. In St John's, *18 carat* Lower Church Street, local food, light lunches and salads, popular, Tel: 462 0016, open 1000-2200, closed Sundays. *Pizzas on the Quay* (Big Banana Holding Co), at Redcliffe Quay, very popular at lunch time, recommended, Tel: 462 2621, open Mon-Sat 0830-2200, Sun 1630-2200; *La Dolce Vita* makes own pasta, 4-course dinner EC$110, service and wine extra; *Redcliffe Tavern*, good lunch, EC$17-35, evening main course EC$25-40; *Ginger House*, also Redcliffe Quay, EC$45-75 main course, lunch EC$25, salad bar EC$30; *Lemon Tree*, on Long Street, also recommended but management reported to be rude, Tel: 462 1969, closed Sundays; *Brother B's*, opposite the Museum, for drinks and meals, live band at lunch time, slow service, local cuisine, pleasant atmosphere; *Talk of the Town*, lively but place for a cheap filling lunch, EC$15-20; *Calypso Café*, Redcliffe Street, West Indian, seafood, EC$20-30; *Smoking Joe's*, opposite the cricket ground, for barbecued ribs, chicken, etc, Joe is a local calypsonian; *The Ridley Arms*, Newgate Street, local dishes, US$6-7; *Nature's Way*, Market Street, upstairs verandah, Indian style meals, also for vegetarians, good rotis and salads. For a full English breakfast go to the *Spanish Main*, EC$15. For cheap (EC$8), good set meals, go to the restaurant by the fishing boat harbour. *Dubarry's Restaurant (Barrymore Hotel)* is recommended. At Dickenson Bay, *Buccaneer Cove* has barbecue suppers on the beach, caters for mini-cruises, very quiet in summer. Other recommended restaurants in the area are the *Lobster Pit*, *French Quarter* and *Siboney*. In the Hodges Bay area, near the airport, *Le Bistro*, excellent French food, dinner only, closed Mondays (Tel: 462 3881). At English Harbour, there is a restaurant and bar on Shirley Heights, steel band and barbecue every Sunday fternoon (See **Excursions**). *Admiral's on*, Nelson's Dockyard, breakfast (slow ervice but good value, recommended), anch and dinner (limited selection but ood, slightly overpriced) every day, achtsman's dinner EC$40, (Tel: 463 027). *The Copper and Lumber Store* is verpriced, you pay for the 'atmosphere', vhich is not to everybody's taste and the ortions are small although the food is xcellent. On Galleon Beach, *Colombo's* alian restaurant, recommended for good ood but expensive (Tel: 463 1452). etween English and Falmouth Harbours, e *Cap Horn*, pizzeria, great food, for oth lunch snacks and full evening meal, easonably priced; *La Perruche*, French vith regional flavour, expensive at about C$200 each but well worth it, friendly ervice, tasteful decor, recommended. At almouth Harbour the Antigua Yacht Club rovides a moderately priced dinner on nost nights of the week, though it is velier at weekends, barbecued burgers, C$20. If you are stuck at the airport, nere is a restaurant which serves simple neals but gets very full when planes are everely delayed.

ood

n addition to a wide selection of imported delicacies served in the larger hotels, local pecialities, found in smaller restaurants in t John's, often very reasonable, should ever be missed: saltfish, pepper-pot with ungi (a kind of cornmeal dumpling), goat vater (hot goat stew), shellfish (in reality he local name for munk fish), and the ocal staple, chicken and rice. Oranges are green, while the native pineapple is black. ocally made Sunshine ice cream, American style, is available in most supermarkets. Imported wines and spirits are reasonably priced but local drinks (fruit and sugar cane juice, coconut milk, and Antiguan rum punches and swizzles, ice cold) must be experienced. The local Cavalier rum is a light golden colour, usually used for mixes. Beer costs US$1.25-2.00 in bars. There are no icensing restrictions. Tap water is safe all over the island. Most luxury hotels provide rain water.

Tipping

Tips for taxi drivers are usually 10% of the fare. Porters expect EC$1 per bag.

Nightlife

The largest hotels provide dancing, calypso, steel bands, limbo dancers and moonlight barbecues. There are cinemas, nightclubs, discothèques and casinos. *Colombo's Night Club*, English Harbour; also local dances where Burning Flames and other Antiguan musicians play, usually advertised by poster in St John's, or ask around. In St John's, *Tropix*, in Reddiffe Quay is the best disco and night club. There is also a seedy casino in the King's Building at Heritage Quay. Casinos at *Flamingo, Royal Antiguan* and *St James's Club* hotels. A free newspaper, *It's Happening, You're Welcome*, contains lots of information on forthcoming events.

Shopping

Market day in St John's is Saturday. The market building is at the south end of Market Street but there are goods on sale all around. Avoid the middle of the day when it is very hot. In season, there is a good supply of fruit and vegetables, which are easy to obtain on the island. The Epicurean Supermarket, on Old Parham Road outside St John's on the way to the airport, sells cheese and fresh milk, imported from the USA on Thursdays, stock soon sells out although the local people prefer powdered milk. The two main supermarkets in St John's are Dew's and Bryson's, on Long Street, not much to choose between them, imported items mostly, fresh fruit and vegetables limited and poor quality. Hutchinson's is a drive-in supermarket on Old Parham Road beyond the roundabout. Most grocery stores open 0800-1600, although many close at 1300 on Thursdays. You can buy fish from the fishing boats at the back of the Casino. Heritage Quay (has public toilets) and Reddiffe Quay are shopping complexes with expensive duty-free shops in the former, and boutiques. There are several shops on St Mary Street and others nearby, which stock clothing, crafts and other items from neighbouring islands, eg Caribelle Batik and Co Co shop (recommended). Some tourist shops offer 10% reductions to locals: they compensate by overcharging tourists.

Banks

Scotia Bank, Barclays Bank, Royal Bank of Canada, Fidelity Trust Bank, Antigua and Barbuda Development Bank, Antigua Commercial Bank. The Swiss American Bank of Antigua is the only bank at English Harbour, accepts Visa and Mastercard for cash and is open on Saturday morning (also a branch in St John's). Barclays are reported to charge EC$5 to cash travellers cheques while Scotia Bank charges 10 cents per cheque. American Express is at Antours near Heritage Quay, staff helpful and friendly.

Currency

Eastern Caribbean dollars are used, at a rate of EC$2.70 = US$1. It is advisable to change some currency at the airport on arrival. The airport bank is open 0900-1500, Mon-Thurs, closes at 1330 on Friday just as Lufthansa and American Airlines come in, closed when BA flight comes in at 1800. US dollars are accepted in most places, but no one will know the exchange rate of other currencies. The conventional rate of exchange if you want to pay in US dollars is EC$2.50=US$1, so it is worth changing money in a bank. Credit cards are accepted, especially Visa and American Express, but small restaurants will take only cash or travellers' cheques.

Health Warnings

Tiny sandflies, known locally as "Noseeums" often appear on the beaches in the late afternoon and can give nasty stings. Keep a good supply of repellent and make sure you wash off all sand to avoid taking them with you from the beach.

Do not eat the little green apples of the manchineel tree, as they are poisonous, and don't sit under the tree in the rain as the dripping oil from the leaves causes blisters.

Some beaches, particularly those on the west coast, get jelly fish at certain times of the year, eg July/August.

Climate

Antigua is a dry island with average rainfall of about 45 inches a year and although September-November is considered the rainy season, the showers are usually short. Temperatures range from 73 (23°C) to 85°F (30°C) between winter ar summer and the trade winds blo constantly.

Hours Of Business

Banks: 0800-1400 Monday-Wednesda 0800-1300 Thursday; 1500-1700 Frida Bank of Antigua opens Saturda 0800-1200. Shops: 0800-120 1300-1600 Monday-Saturday. Thursday early closing day for most non-touri shops. On Sundays everything close except churches and Kings Casin although *Kentucky Fried Chicken* opens the afternoon.

National Holidays

New Year's Day, Good Friday, East Monday, Labour Day (first Monday in May Whit Monday (end-May), Queen's Birthda (second Saturday in June), Carnival (fir Monday and Tuesday in August Independence Day (1 November Christmas Day and Boxing Day.

Time Zone

Atlantic standard time, 4 hours behin GMT, 1 ahead of EST.

Electric Current

220 volts usually, but 110v in some areas check before using your own appliance Many hotels have transformers.

Post Office

At the end of Long Street, St John's opposite the supermarkets, ope Monday-Thursday, 0815-120C 1300-1600, until 1700 on Friday; also Post Office at the airport. Federal Expres is on Church Street. DHL is in the Verno Edwards building on Thames Street.

Telecommunications

Cable and Wireless Ltd, 42-44 St Mary Street, St John's, and at English Harbour.

Tourist Office

Antigua Tourist Office on Thames Street, between Long Street and High Street. Postal address: PO Box 363, St John's, Antigua, W Indies. Tel: 462 0480, Fax: 462 2483. Open 0830-1600 (Monday-Friday) and 0830-1200 (Saturday). Gives list of official taxi charges and hotel information. Also has an office at airport, very helpful, will help book accommodation.

USA: Antigua and Barbuda Department of Tourism, 610 Fifth Avenue, Suite 311, New York, N Y 10020, Tel: (212) 541-4117, Fax: 757 1607; 121 SE 1st Street, Suite 1001, Miami, Florida 33131, Tel: (305) 381 6762, Fax: 381 7908.

Canada: Antigua and Barbuda Department of Tourism, 60 St Clair Avenue East, Suite 205, Toronto, Ontario, M4T 1N5, Tel: (416) 961-3085, Fax: 961 7218.

UK: Antigua and Barbuda Tourist Office, Antigua House, 15 Thayer Street, London W1M 5LD, Tel: 071-486 7073/5, Fax: 071-486 9970.

Germany: Antigua and Barbuda German Office, Postfach 1331, Minnholzweg 2, 6242 Kronberg 1, Tel: 06173/5011, Fax 49-6173 7299.

We are grateful to Lars Karlsson for his help in updating this chapter.

ST KITTS–NEVIS

Introduction

THE ISLANDS OF ST KITTS (officially named St Christopher) and NEVIS are in the northern part of the Leeward Islands in the Eastern Caribbean. St Kitts has an area of 68 square miles, made up of three groups of rugged volcanic peaks split by deep ravines, and a low lying peninsula in the southeast where there are salt ponds and fine beaches. Nevis, separated by a two-mile channel to the south, has an area of 36 square miles. It is almost circular, rising to a peak of 3,232 feet and surrounded by beaches of coral sand. Each island is fully aware of its heritage and cares for its historical buildings; owing to the early colonization, many are of stone and are in interesting contrast with those of wood. Of the total population, estimated at 44,100 in 1990, 78% live on St. Kitts and 22% on Nevis; 86% are black, 11% mixed, 2% white and 1% Indo-Pakistani.

History
Before the islands were discovered by Columbus in 1493, there were Amerindians living there, whose relics can still be seen in some areas. As in most of the other islands, however, they were slaughtered by European immigrants, although the Caribs fought off the British and the French for many years and their battle scenes are celebrated locally. St Kitts became the first British settlement in the West Indies in 1623 and soon became an important colony for its sugar industry, with the importation of large numbers of African slaves. For a time it was shared by France and England; partition was ended by the Peace of Utrecht in 1713 and it finally became a British colony in 1783. From 1816, St Christopher, Nevis, Anguilla and the British Virgin Islands were administered as a single colony until the Leeward Islands Federation was formed in 1871. From 1958-62, St Kitts-Nevis and Anguilla belonged to the West Indies Federation, until St Kitts-Nevis gained Associated Statehood. The Federation of St Christopher and Nevis finally became independent in September 1983.

Government
St Christopher and Nevis is a constitutional monarchy within the Commonwealth. The British monarch is Head of State and is represented locally by a Governor General. The Prime Minister is Dr Kennedy Simmonds, who was elected for a third consecutive term in March 1989. His party, the People's Action Movement (PAM), holds six of the eleven directly elected National Assembly seats. The PAM's coalition partner, the Nevis Reformation Party (NRP), holds two of the three Nevis seats, while the St Kitts Labour Party has two seats and the Concerned Citizens Movement (CCM) one Nevis seat. There are also three nominated Senators. Under the Federal system, Nevis also has a separate legislature and may secede from the Government of the Federation. In 1992 Mr Simeon Daniel, the Premier of Nevis for 21 years, lost his assembly seat in elections which saw Mr Vance Amory become the new leader. Mr Daniel had been in favour of secession for Nevis but his party won only two of the five seats.

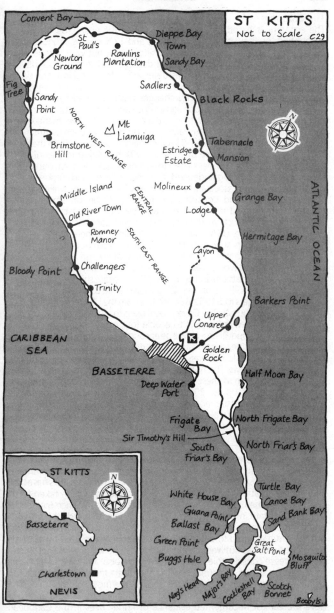

ST KITTS
Not to Scale C29

Convent Bay
St Paul's
Newton Ground
Rawlins Plantation
Dieppe Bay Town
Sandy Bay
Fig Tree
Sandy Point
Sadlers
Black Rocks
NORTH WEST RANGE
Mt Liamuiga
Brimstone Hill
Estridge Estate
Tabernacle
Mansion
Middle Island
CENTRAL RANGE
Molineux
Grange Bay
Old River Town
Lodge
ATLANTIC OCEAN
Romney Manor
SOUTH EAST RANGE
Hermitage Bay
Bloody Point
Challengers
Cayon
Trinity
Barkers Point
CARIBBEAN SEA
Upper Conaree
BASSETERRE
Golden Rock
Half Moon Bay
Deep Water Port
Frigate Bay
North Frigate Bay
Sir Timothy's Hill
South Friar's Bay
North Friar's Bay
White House Bay
Turtle Bay
Guana Point
Canoe Bay
Ballast Bay
Sand Bank Bay
Green Point
Great Salt Pond
Mosquito Bluff
Buggs Hole
Nags Head
Major's Bay
Cockleshell Bay
Scotch Bonnet
Booby Is.

ST KITTS
Basseterre
Charlestown
NEVIS

The Economy

The economy is based on agriculture. Sugar is the main crop on St Kitts, accounting for about a quarter of exports and 12% of jobs. Production has been in the hands of the Government since 1975, but with low prices for sugar in the world markets, hurricane damage and recent droughts, the industry runs at a loss. Low wages deter locals from seeking jobs on the plantations and labour is imported from St Vincent and Guyana. The Government is considering policy changes recommended by World Bank consultants, which would include allowing private investment in the industry and production incentives for cane cutters. In the meantime, management of the state-owned Sugar Manufacturing Company has been contracted to Booker Tate, of the UK, for 1991-93, with financial assistance from the World Bank. Sugar production rose by 28% in 1991 to 19,500 tonnes of which exports were 19,100 tonnes. The Government has been encouraged to diversify away from sugar dependence and reduce food imports. More vegetables, sweet potatoes and yams are now being grown, while on Nevis, Sea Island cotton and coconuts are more common on smallholdings. Livestock farming and manufacturing are developing industries. There are enclave industries, such as data processing and garment manufacturing, which export to the USA and Caricom trading partners, while sales of sugar-based products such as pure cane spirit go mainly outside the region.

Tourism is becoming an increasingly important foreign exchange earner, while remittances of workers abroad also provide a steady source of income. In 1988 69,608 tourists arriving by air and 53,645 cruise ship passengers spent nearly US$54m. By 1991, stopover visitors had risen to 83,903 while yacht and cruise ship passengers rose to 52,834. Visitors from the USA make up just under half of all stopover guests. The Government plans to increase cruise ship arrivals with a port improvement project to enable four cruise liners to berth at the same time, while stopover arrivals will be encouraged by the huge development projects on the southeast peninsula of St Kitts, a 275-room *Sandals Resort* in the Banana Bay/Cockleshell area, and the already completed 196-room *Four Seasons* hotel on Nevis. The number of hotel beds in St Kitts-Nevis is forecast to rise to 2,200 when all these resorts are open, giving the islands a potential annual capacity of up to 200,000 visitors. Damage caused to housing infrastructure, agriculture and fishing by Hurricane Hugo in 1989 was estimated at US$43m but all except two hotels reopened for the winter season. The Frigate Bay area was untouched by the hurricane.

Fauna and Flora

Both islands are home to the green vervet monkey, introduced by the French some 300 years ago, now dwelling on the forested areas in the mountains. They can be seen sometimes on Hurricane Hill. American scientists have been studying these attractive little creatures and some have been taken to the USA for experiments; a Sunday visit to the Behavioural Science Foundation at Estridge Estate in St Kitts gives visitors a chance to watch the research, and the monkeys, in action. The monkey is the same animal as on Barbados but the Kittitians used to eat them. Another animal imported by colonists, the mongoose, has outlived its original purpose (to kill now-extinct snakes) but survives in considerable numbers. There are also some wild deer on the southeast peninsula. In common with other West Indian islands, there are highly vocal frogs, lots of lizards (the anole is the most common), assorted bats and butterflies, although nothing particularly rare. St Kitts and Nevis have the earliest documented evidence of honey bees in the Caribbean.

Birds are typical of the region, with lots of sea fowl like brown pelicans and frigate birds to be seen, as well as three species of hummingbirds. Fish abound in local waters (rays, barracuda, king fish and brilliantly-coloured smaller species) and the increasingly rare black coral tree can be sighted in the reef of the same name.

The rainforests on the sister islands are restricted in scale but provide a habitat for wild orchids, buttress trees, candlewoods and exotic vines. Fruits and flowers, both wild and cultivated, are in abundance, particularly in the gorgeous gardens of Nevis. Trees include several varieties of the stately royal palm, the spiny-trunked sandbox tree, silk cotton, and the turpentine or gum tree. Visitors can explore the rainforests with guides on foot, horseback or by jeep, but gentle hikes through trails and estates reap many rewards in terms of plant-gazing. Several trails are clear and do not need a guide, such as Old Road to Philips, the old British military road, which connected the British settlements on the northeast and southwest coasts of St Kitts without going through French territory when the island was partitioned. There are also trails from Belmont to the crater of Mount Liamuiga, from Sadlers to Peak, from Lamberts to Dos d'Ane lake. St Kitts is a small island, yet it has a wide variety of habitats, with rainforest, dry woodland, grassland and a salt pond.

Beaches and Watersports

St Kitts Most of the beaches are of black, volcanic sand but the beaches known as Frigate Bay and Salt Pond fringing the southern peninsula have white sand. The southeast peninsula itself also has white sand beaches. Swimming is very good in the Frigate Bay area where all water sports are available. There is also very good snorkelling and scuba diving. There is black coral, coral caves, reefs and wrecks with abundant fish and other sea creatures of all sizes and colours. Much of the diving is suitable for novices. Kenneth's Dive Centre based in Basseterre (Bay Road, Newtown, Tel: 465 2670; Kenneth Samuel is a PADI-certified Dive Master and he uses a catamaran, *Lady Peggy*, or a 32-foot motor launch, *Lady Majesta*). The Pelican Cove Marina at the *Ocean Terrace Inn*, Tel: 465 2754/2380, operates Dive St Kitts (US$30 for one-tank dive, US$50 two tanks), offering water-skiing, fishing, hobiecat rental, windsurfer rental (US$10/hour) and boat cruises. Pro-Divers gives PADI instruction, at Fisherman's Wharf and Turtle Beach, Tel: 465 3223, Fax: 465 1057, dive gear available for rent, dive packages available, single tank dive US$30, two tank dive US$50, resort course US$60, snorkel pack US$10. Leeward Island Charters' *Caona*, a 47' catamaran or *Spirit of St Kitts*, a 70' catamaran (owned by Tim and Allison Leypoldt, Tel: 465 7474, sometimes operates in the waters around the US Virgin Islands), take visitors on a sail and beach barbecue. Sailing is becoming increasingly popular. There are local and international regattas and even a local catamaran boatyard, Brooke's Boats. Deep sea fishing can be arranged. In summer there is a race for windsurfers and sunfish to Nevis.

Nevis has superb white sandy beaches, particularly on the leeward and northern coasts. The beautiful four mile Pinney's beach is only a few minutes' walk from Charlestown and is never crowded. However, the entire middle stretch of Pinney's Beach has been given over to a 196-room *Four Seasons Hotel*. Watersports facilities are available at *Oualie Beach Club*. Snorkelling off Oualie Beach is excellent (round the rocks to the right) and at least as rewarding, if not more than, scuba diving. Scuba Safaris, run by Ellis Chaderton, is based there, Tel: 469 9518: diving (US$45 for a single tank dive, US$80 for two tanks), instruction, equipment rental and glass-bottomed boat tours. Watersports also at Newcastle Bay Marina, Tel: 469 9373, Fax: 469 9375, where there is the HIFLY windsurfing school. On the Atlantic side of Nevis, the beaches tend to be rocky and the swimming treacherous; there is, though, an excellent beach at White Bay in the southwest.

Other Sports

Horse riding (Trinity Stables, Tel: 465 3226), mountain climbing, tennis and golf are available. There is an 18-hole international championship golf course at Frigate Bay and a 9-hole golf course at Golden Rock, St Kitts. On Nevis, the *Four Seasons* has an 18-hole golf course. Races are held on the small, stoney race track at Black Bay, St Kitts (near White Bay beach), four times a year: Whit Monday, August Bank holiday, Independence Day and Boxing Day.

Festivals

St Kitts and Nevis are very proud of their masquerade traditions. The liveliest time to visit **St Kitts** is for the carnival held over Christmas and the New Year. It gets bigger and better every year with parades, calypso competitions and street dancing. For details, contact the Carnival Office, Church Street, Basseterre, Tel: 465 4151.

On **Nevis**, the annual equivalent is Culturama, held in end-July and August, finishing on the first Monday in August. The Nevis Tourist Office has full details.

St Kitts

The dormant volcano, Mount Liamuiga (3,792 feet, pronounced Lie-a-mee-ga) occupies the central part of St Kitts. The mountain was previously named Mount Misery by the British, but has now reverted to its Carib name, meaning "fertile land". The foothills of the mountains, particularly in the north, are covered with sugar cane plantations and grassland, while the uncultivated lowland slopes are covered with forest and fruit trees.

The small port of **Basseterre** is the capital and largest town, with a population of about 15,000. By West Indian standards, it is quite big and as such as has a quite different feel from its close neighbour, Charlestown. It was founded some 70 years later in 1727. Earthquakes, hurricanes and finally a disasterous fire in 1867 destroyed the town. Consequently its buildings are comparatively modern. There is a complete mishmash of architectural styles from elegant Georgian buildings with arcades, verandahs and jalousies, mostly in good condition, to hideous twentieth century concrete block houses. In recent years, the development of tourism has meant a certain amount of redevelopment in the centre. An old warehouse on the waterfront has been converted into the Pelican duty-free shopping and recreational complex. It also houses the tourist office and a lounge for guests of the *Four Seasons Hotel* in Nevis awaiting transport. A new pier for ships of less than 20 feet draught is to be built in front of Pelican Mall, starting in 1992.

The Circus, styled after London's Piccadilly Circus (but looking nothing like it), is the centre of the town. The clock tower is a memorial to Thomas Berkely, former president of the General Legislative Council. South down Fort Street is the imposing façade of the Treasury Building with its dome covering an arched gateway leading directly to the sea front (it is equally impressive from the bay). Next door is the Post Office (open Monday-Saturday 0800-1500, 0800-1100 on Thursdays). Head north up Fort Street, cross the main thoroughfare (Cayon Street) and you will come

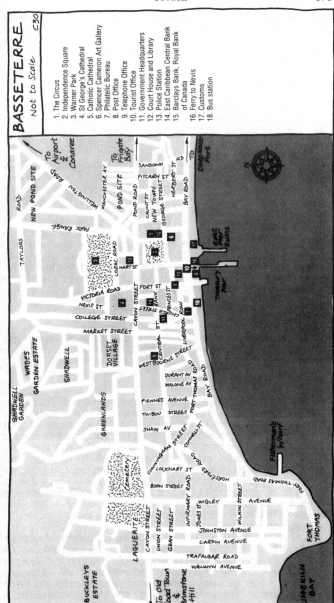

BASSETERRE
Not to Scale   C30

1. The Circus
2. Independence Square
3. Warner Park
4. St George's Cathedral
5. Catholic Cathedral
6. Spencer Cameron Art Gallery
7. Philatelic Bureau
8. Post Office
9. Telephone Office
10. Tourist Office
11. Government Headquarters
12. Court House and Library
13. Police Station
14. East Caribbean Central Bank
15. Barclays Bank, Royal Bank of Canada
16. Ferry to Nevis
17. Customs
18. Bus station

to St George's Cathedral, set in its own large garden, with a massive, square buttressed tower. The site was originally a Jesuit church, Notre Dame, which was raised to the ground by the English in 1706. Rebuilt four years later and renamed St George's, it suffered damage from hurricanes and earthquakes on several occasions. It too was a victim of the 1867 fire. It was rebuilt in 1856-69 and contains some nice stained glass windows. There is a fine view of the town from the tower.

Independence Square was built in 1790 and is surrounded now by a low white fence; eight gates let paths converge on a fountain in the middle of the square (it looks like the Union Jack when seen from the air). Unfortunately the gaily painted muses on top of the fountain seem not to work at present. Originally designed for slave auctions and council meetings, it now contains many plants, spacious lawns and lovely old trees. It is surrounded by 18th-century houses and at its east end, the Roman Catholic cathedral with its twin towers. Built in 1927, the Immaculate Conception is surprisingly plain inside. At 50 Independence Square you can visit the very attractive building housing The *Spencer Cameron Art Gallery*. See Rosie Cameron-Smith's paintings, prints and leisurewear of West Indian scenes. The Royal Bank of Canada is housing some interesting paintings of Brimstone Hill by Lt Lees of the Royal Engineers, circa 1783, pending the building of a museum as a permanent home: St Christopher Heritage Society, Bank Street and West Independence Square, PO Box 338, Basseterre. They are also doing a lot to preserve wildlife and are grateful for donations. Heading back towards the Circus there are lots of nice restaurants and cafés. Basseterre is very quiet on Sundays and many of the restaurants are closed.

Excursions

A clockwise route round the island will enable you to see most of the historical sites. A cheap way of touring the island is to take a minibus from Basseterre bus station in Bay Road to Dieppe Bay Town, then walk to Sadlers (there might be a minibus if you are lucky) where you can get another minibus back to Basseterre along the Atlantic coast.

The island is dominated by the south east range of mountains (1,159 feet) and the higher north west range which contains Mount Verchilds (2,931 feet) and the crater of Mount Laimuiga (3,792 feet). There are several good island tours, including excellent hiking tours to the volcano and through the rain forest with Kriss Tours (US$40, Tel: 465 4042) and Greg's Tours, recommended, pleasant and informative, (Tel: 465 4121). To climb Mt Liamuiga, arrange for transport from Belmont or Harris Estate. At 2,600 feet is the crater into which you can climb down, holding on to vines and roots; on the steady climb from the end of the road note the wild orchids in the forest. A full day is required for this climb. You can reach the attractive, but secluded, Dos D'Anse pond near Mount Verchilds from the Molyneux estate, a guide is recommended.

Evidence of sugar cane is everywhere on the comparatively flat, fertile coastal plain. You will drive through large fields of cane and particularly on the west coast glimpse the little railway which is now used to transport it from the fields. Disused sugar mills are also often seen. Here are situated the Great Houses: Fairview, Romney Manor, Golden Lemon, the White House, Rawlins and perhaps most famous for its colonial splendour, Ottley's. They have nearly all been converted into hotels and have excellent restaurants.

The west coast in particular is historically important. It is guarded by no less than nine forts and the magnificent Brimstone Hill Fortress. Taking the road out of Basseterre, you will pass the sites of seven of them: Fort Thomas, Palmetto Point Fort, Stone Fort, Fort Charles, Charles Fort, Sandy Point Fort and Fig Tree Fort. The remaining two are to the south of Basseterre: Fort Smith and Fort Tyson. Little now remains of any of them. Sir Thomas Warner landed at Old Road Bay in 1623 and was joined in 1625 by the crew of a French ship badly mauled by the Spanish. Initially befriended by the local Carib chief Tegreman, as many as 3,000 Caribs, alarmed at the rapid colonization of the island, tried to mount an attack in 1626. 2,000 of them were massacred by the combined French and English forces in the deep ravine at **Bloody Point** (the site of Stone Fort). This is the first point of interest and is just before Old Road Town. An amicable settlement meant that the English held the central portion of the island roughly in line from Sandy Point to Saddlers in the north to Bloody Point across to Cayon in the south. French names can be traced in both of their areas of influence (Dieppe Bay Town in the north, the Parishes are called Capisterre and Basseterre in the south). The south east peninsula was neutral. This rapprochement did not last many years as following the colonization of Martinique and Guadeloupe, the French wished to increase their sphere of influence. St Kitts became an obvious target and in 1664 they squeezed the English from the island. For nearly two hundred years the coast was defended by troops from one nation or another.

At **Old Road Town** you turn right to visit **Romney Manor**, one of the great houses. You drive through a deserted sugar mill and the edge of rain forest. The manor is set in beautiful gardens with pleasant views over the coast and a giant 350-year old saman tree. It is now home to Caribelle Batik, open Monday-Friday, 0830-1600, Tel: 465 6253. Apart from a well-stocked shop you can watch the artists producing the highly colourful and attractive material. A guide will explain the process. Also near here the remains of the island's Amerindian civilization can be seen on large stones with drawings and pictographs at **Wingfield Manor Estate**.

After a further 1½ miles, at the village of **Middle Island**, you will see on your right and slightly up the hill, the church of St Thomas at the head of an avenue of royal palms. Here is buried Sir Thomas Warner who died on 10 March 1648. The raised tomb under a canopy is inscribed "General of y Caribee". There is also a bronze plaque with a copy of the inscription inside the church. Other early tombs are of Captain John Pogson (1656) and Sir Charles Payne, "Major General of Leeward Carribee Islands" who was buried in 1744. The tower, built in 1880, has been severely damaged.

Turn right off the coastal road just before *J's Place* (a good place for a drink and local food, open 1100-2000, watch the caged green vervet monkeys: they are very aggressive) for the **Citadel of Brimstone Hill**, one of the "Gibraltars of the West Indies" (a title it shares with Les Saintes, off Guadeloupe). Sprawled over 38 acres on the slopes of a mountain 800 feet above the sea, it commands an incredible view for 70 miles around, of St Kitts and on clear days, Montserrat (40 miles), Saba (20 miles), St Eustatius (5 miles), St-Barts (40 miles) and St-Martin (45 miles) can be seen. The English mounted the first cannon on Brimstone Hill in 1690 in an attempt to force the French from Fort Charles below. It has been constructed entirely out of local volcanic stones and was designed along classic defensive lines. The five bastions overlook each other and also guard the only road as it zig zags up to the parade ground. The entrance is at the Barrier Redan where payment is made. Pass the Magazine Bastion but stop at the Orillion Bastion which contains the massive ordnance store (165 feet long with walls at least six feet thick). The hospital was located here and under the south wall is a small cemetery. You come next to the Prince of Wales Bastion (note the name of J Sutherland, 93rd Highlanders 24 October 1822 carved in the wall next to one of the cannons) from where there are good views over to the parade ground. Park at the parade ground, there is a snack bar and shop in the warrant officer's quarters with barrels of pork outside it. A narrow and quite steep path leads to Fort George, the Citadel and the highest defensive position. Restoration is continuing and several areas have been converted to form a most interesting museum. Barrack rooms now hold well-presented and informative displays (pre-colombian, American, English, French and Garrison). Guides are on hand to give more detailed explanations of the fortifications. The Fortress was eventually abandoned in 1852 but was inaugurated as a National Park by the Queen in October 1985. Open 0930-1730 daily, entrance EC$13 or US$5 for foreigners, EC$2 for nationals, it is highly recommended both for adults and children (half price). Allow up to two hours.

The remainder of the drive through the cane fields is less interesting. There is a a black sand beach at Dieppe Bay. Otherwise pass through Saddlers and stop at the **Black Rocks**. Here lava has flowed into the sea providing interesting rock formations. The road continues past Ottley Plantation, through Cayon back to Basseterre via the Golden Rock Airport. With advance notice, you can tour the sugar factory near the airport, very interesting and informative. Tours are only during harvest season, February-August.

To visit the southeast pensinsula, turn south at the end of Wellington Road (just after the Texaco filling station). This leads to the narrow spit of land sandwiched between North and South Frigate Bays. This area is being heavily developed, the natural lagoons providing an additional attraction. A number of establishments, including a casino, tennis courts and an 18-hole golf course, which are international in style, but lacking in character or greenery, have been built. The new six-mile Dr Kennedy A Simmonds Highway runs from Frigate Bay to Major's Bay. After Frigate Bay the peninsula is almost deserted and quite different from the north of the island. The road climbs along the backbone of the peninsula and overlooks North and South Friar Bays where you may see green vervet monkeys before descending to White House Bay (an abandoned jetty and wreck provides good snorkelling). Skirt the Great Salt Pond. Half way round turn left to reach Cockleshell Bay, the site of the new five star *Casablanca* luxury resort (due to open late-1992) and beyond it the more secluded Turtle Beach (good for watersports and stunning views across to Nevis). The other branch leads to Major's bay where another large development is planned. At the moment however most of the peninsula is isolated and extremely attractive. Despite the road the majority of beaches are difficult to reach. Try to obtain local knowledge if you want to visit them.

Island Information—St Kitts

Where To Stay There is a wide variety of accommodation ranging from first class hotels to rented cottages, but it is advisable to book well in advance. *Ocean Terrace Inn* (*OTI*, Box 65, Tel: 465 2754, Fax: 465-1057) in summer, US$83-135d, EP, in winter, US$105-204d EP, apartments also available, and *Fort Thomas Hotel* (Box 407, Tel: 465 2695, Fax: 465 7518), winter rates, US$85-95d, EP, summer rates, US$50-55, EP, are a few minutes walk from Basseterre and have pools, beach shuttles and restaurants. *OTI* also organizes tours and other activities, evening shows and has a fairly expensive but nice restaurant with views over Basseterre harbour; good service throughout. The *Fairview Inn* close to Basseterre is situated around an eighteenth century great house (double rates range from US$70-140 depending on season and type of room, EP, MAP supplement US$30, reductions for children, pool, Box 212, Tel: 465 2472, Fax: 465 1056). The highly recommended *Rawlins Plantation*, 16 miles from Basseterre in the northwest of the island, is pricey, but beautiful, tranquil and offers grass tennis, horse riding and croquet, no credit cards accepted (ten cottages, rates US225d, in summer, US$375d, in winter, MAP only, laundry service and afternoon tea and wine with dinner included, Box 340, Tel: 465 6221, Fax: 465 4954). *The White House*, British-run, PO Box 436, Tel: 465 8162, Fax: 465 8275, 10 rooms in the carriage house and other buildings of a plantation great house, grass tennis court, swimming pool, courtesy transport to beach 15 minutes away, winter rates US$350d, US$250s, MAP plus afternoon tea and laundry service, US$300d and US200s in summer, elegant and quiet; *Bird Rock Beach Hotel*, Tel: 465 8914, Fax: 465 1675, 24 rooms/cottages, US$95-250 EP in winter, US$65-170 EP, in summer, up on the cliffs overlooking the tiny black sand beach and industrial estate, inconvenient suburban location, taxi to Basseterre US$6, pool, tennis, watersports; 520' above sea level in 35 acres, is the *Ottleys Plantation Inn*, PO Box 345, Tel: 465 7234, Fax: 465 4760, rooms in the 1832 great house or cottages, winter rate, US$140-260d, EP, US$180-300d, MAP, US$110-170d EP in summer. Other hotels have expanded their capacity: *The Golden Lemon*, Dieppe Bay, Tel: 465 7260, Fax: 465 4019, now has 36 rooms, having built some beachfront cottages next to the original great house building dating from 1610, US$225-825d, MAP, winter rate, US$150-630 in summer, pool, tennis, watersports. The *Windsor Guest House* is one of the cheapest at US$28 but not recommended, beds uncomfortable, stuffy, shared toilets (Box 122, Tel: 465 2894). Alternatives to this are the *Parkview* (Box 64, Tel: 465 2100), good, and *On the Square*, 14 Independence Square (Box 81, Tel: 465 2485), US$32d, very clean, tastefully decorated, a/c, private bathroom, also single rooms available and 2 larger rooms with kitchenette to sleep 3 with verandah overlooking square, prices include tax, recommended. *Rosie's Guest House* New Pond Site, Tel: 465 4651, is clean and friendly, US$20 (plus tax and service); *Canne à Sucre* on Church Street, EC$40, central, good value, opposite *Chef's Place*; *Glimbaro Guest House*, Cayon Street, Tel: 465 2935, almost opposite *Windsor Guest House*, very basic but cheap at US$15 without bath, US$25 for small room with bath, extra person US$5. There is a 7% occupancy tax.

Where To Eat The hotels have gourmet restaurants, usually serving local specialities, with set meals of around EC$90 or à la carte entrées from EC$65. There are also many places offering snacks, light meals, ice creams and drinks in Basseterre and in the Frigate Bay area. West Indian and continental cuisine can be sampled in the elegant dining rooms of the *The OTI* (see above) and *Fisherman's Wharf* (Tel: 465 2472) beside it offers barbecued seafood and a spicy conch sauce. The latter is lively, on the quay, open daily for dinner only from 1900, go early. OTI also runs a beach bar/restaurant at Turtle Beach, excellent barbecue lunch, very friendly, watersports, good snorkelling if you can ignore the seaweed, open late on Saturdays with disco after 2200. Other good restaurants include the *Ballahoo* in town (opposite the Treasury) which is very reasonable and has a nice gallery, open Monday-Saturday 0800-2300, Tel: 465 4197; also in Basseterre and in original buildings, *The Georgian House*, southeast corner of Independence Square, good, indoor or outdoor dining, open Tuesday-Saturday, 1100-2100, Sunday 1800-2100, reservations Tel: 465 4049. *Chef's Place*, Church Street, Tel: 465 6176, excellent lunchtime and evening food at reasonable price, Kittitian with a few added touches, usually choice of one fish dish and one other, all fresh ingredients, about the only non-tourist place open after 2000, no credit cards. *Coconut Café* in Frigate Bay serves local and seafood, open daily, 0730-2300, good. The *Golf View Restaurant*, Frigate Bay, Tel: 465 1118, open from 0700, West Indian and vegetarian dishes.

Entertainment There is live music in the evening at *Fisherman's Wharf* at weekends, and the *OTI* has lively evenings in the week (see above). *J's Place* is a disco at the foot of Brimstone HIll; *Reflections*, above Flex Fitness Centre, open Thursday-Sunday from 2100, cover charge US$4, strict dress code, on Frigate Bay Road, Tel: 465 7616; *Cotton

House in Canada Estate also fairly smart. *Jack Tar Village* in the modern Frigate Bay development now offers a EC$50 night pass which covers all drinks, a light buffet and entertainment. A more local place with free admission is on Monkey Hill on Sunday nights. There is also a casino. On Sundays everything closes down in Basseterre, including the restaurants.

Nevis

Across the two-mile Narrows Channel from St Kitts is the beautiful little island of Nevis, with a population of only 9,000. The central peak of the island is usually shrouded in white clouds and mist, which reminded Columbus of Spanish snow-capped mountains and is why he called the island "Las Nieves". (It reminds others, in the wet, of the English Lake District, as does St Kitts.) For the Caribs, it was Oualie, the land of beautiful water. Smaller than St Kitts it is also quieter. The atmosphere is civilized, but low-key and easy-going; all the same, it is an expensive island. Less fertile than St Kitts, the principal crop is cotton. Nevis was badly effected by Hurricane Hugo but despite considerable damage, nobody was killed.

The main town is **Charlestown**, one of the best preserved old towns in the Caribbean. Situated on Gallows Bay and guarded by Fort Charles to the south and the long sweep of Pinney's Beach to the North, it is a small town with a compact centre. At first sight it would be easy to be disappointed. However there are several interesting buildings dating from the eighteenth century and an excellent, but small, museum.

Whether travelling from Newcastle airport or by sea on the *Caribbe Queen* from St Kitts, you will arrive in D R Walwyn's Plaza. This is dominated by the balconied Customs House built in 1837 on a much older site, it now houses the Customs and Agricultural Ministry. Immediately to the north is the Post Office. Opposite it on the other side of the square is the Tourist Office. Apart from much useful information, it contains a plaque commemorating the landing of Captain John Smith and 143 English on 24th March 1607 – the original Virginia settlers. Memorial Square is larger and more impressive than D R Walwyn's Plaza, the War Memorial in the small garden has a German machine gun pointing at it. Inscribed on it is "In Memory The World War 1914-18 Captured from the Germans". Explore the small arcade with several shops including *Caribelle Batik* before seeing the Courthouse and library above it (open Monday-Friday 0900-1800, Saturday 0900-1700). It was built in 1825 and used as the Nevis Government Headquarters but largely destroyed by fire in 1873. The curious little square tower was erected in 1909-10. It contains a clock which keeps accurate time with an elaborate pulley and chain system. Visit the library and you can see them together with the weights among the elaborate roof trusses. The courthouse, is not open to the public, look in through the open windows. Along Government Road is the well-preserved Jewish Cemetery dating back to 1679, but also closed to the public. At the small market a wide range of island produce, including avocados, ginger root, yams and sweet potatoes, is on sale but go early if you want to catch the bustle. Markets are held on Tuesday, Thursday and Saturday mornings. Market Street to the right houses the philatelic bureau, airconditioned and open from 0800-1600 Monday-Friday. The Cotton Ginnery is still in use during the cotton picking season (February onwards). On Chapel Street the Wesleyan Holiness Manse built in 1812 is one of the oldest stone buildings surviving on the island while the Methodist Manse (next to the prominent Church) has the oldest wooden structure, the second floor being built in 1802.

Call home.

AT&T USADirect® Service
Your Express Connection to AT&T Service.

Calling the States from overseas is fast and easy
with AT&T USADirect® Service.
- Available from over 100 countries worldwide
- Use your AT&T Card or call collect
- Save with AT&T international rates

When in the Caribbean, dial the number shown
below from any phone in that country.

ANGUILLA	1-800-872-2881	DOMINICA	1-800-872-2881
ANTIGUA (Boatphone Marine)	872	DOM. REP.††	1-800-872-2881
(Public Card Phones)	#1	GRENADA†	872
	800-1011	HAITI†	001-800-872-2881
ARUBA	1-800-872-2881	JAMAICA††	0-800-872-2881
BAHAMAS	1-800-872-2881	MONTSERRAT†	1-800-872-2881
BERMUDA†	001-800-872-2881	SABA	001-800-872-2881
BONAIRE	1-800-872-2881	ST. EUSTATIUS	001-800-872-2881
BRITISH V.I.	1-800-872-2881	ST. KITTS/NEVIS	1-800-872-2881
CAYMAN ISLANDS	1-800-872-2881	ST. MAARTEN	001-800-872-2881
CURACAO	001-800-872-2881		

†May not be available from every phone.
††Collect calling only.

DESIGNATED TELEPHONE CARIBBEAN COUNTRIES
Look for specially marked telephones in major airports,
hotels, cruise ports, telephone centers and on U.S.
military bases and fleet centers in these countries and
in many of the "Dial Access" countries: Barbados,
St. Lucia, Trinidad & Tobago, Turks & Caicos.

T **USADirect**® Service
ou dial directly to the States.
dditional information, or to receive a
wallet card, call toll-free in the U.S.
) 874-4000, ext. 332, or when overseas
ollect 412-553-7458, ext. 932.

ADirect® Service is offered in conjunction with local telephone administrations.

GULF OF

MEXICO

Tampa
St. Petersburg ⊙ ⊙Lakeland
Tampa
Ft. Myers ⊙
Lake Okeechobee
The Everglades
C. Romano
C. Sable
Key West
Florida Keys
U.S.A.
West Palm Beach
Freeport
Ft. Lauderdale
Miami
Great Abac
Grand Bahama I.
New Providence
Nassau
Ele
Straits of Florida

25°

Tropic of Cancer

Yucatan Channel
C. San Antonio
Havana (La Habana)
Matanzas
Marianao ⊙
Pinar del Rio
Guane
Golfo de Batabano
Nueva Gerona
Isla de la Juventud
Cardenas
Guines
Sagua la Grande
Cienfuegos
Santa Clara
Trinidad
Sancti Spiritus
Jardines de la Reina
Caibarien
Moron
Ciego de Avila
Camaguey
Andros I.
Exuma I.
Gt. Exum
Sabana
Archo. de Camaguey
Nuevitas
Victoria de las Tunas
Turquino 1971
Bayam
Sa
C. Cruz

20°

Progreso
Merida
Campeche
Tizimin
Puerto Juarez
C. Catoche
I. Mujeres
Cancun
Cozumel I.
CUBA

Yucatan Peninsula
Terminos Lagoon
Chetumal
Chetumal Bay
Corozal
Ambergris Cay
Belize
Turneffe Is.
Belmopan
Maya Mts.
BELIZE
Gulf of Honduras
Bay Is.
C. Camaron
Swan Is. (Honduras)

Grand Cayman
Little Cayman
Cayman Brac
Cayman Islands (U.K.)
Georgetown

C A R I B

Montego Bay
St. Ann's B
Black River
JAMAICA Kingst

G r e a t

GUATEMALA
Guatemala City
Coban
Flores
Puerto Barrios
Pto. Cortes
Tela
La Ceiba
San Pedro Sula
Quezaltenango
Antigua
Zacapa
Chiquimula
Copan
Santa Ana
HONDURAS
Comayagua
Tegucigalpa
Juticalpa
Danli
Caratasca Lagoon
Mosquitia Plain
C. Gracias a Dios
Pto. Cabezas

Escuintla
San Jose
San Salvador
La Libertad
San Miguel
EL SALVADOR
San Vicente
G. of Fonseca
Choluteca
Chinandega
Corinto
Amapala
Esteli
Jinotega
Matagalpa
NICARAGUA
Rio Grande
Isabela
Puerto Cabezas
Prinzapolca
Rio Coco
Mosquito Coast
I. de Providencia (Colombia)
Is. del Maiz (Nicaragua & U.S.A.)
I. de San Andres (Colombia)

Managua
Granada
Lake Nicaragua
Jinotepe
Rivas
Rama
Rio Escondido
Bluefields

C. Sta. Elena
Liberia
Nicoya
Nicoya Peninsula
Puntarenas
C. Blanco
Rio San Juan
San Juan del Norte
Irazu
Puerto Limon
Cartago
COSTA RICA

PACIFIC

OCEAN

Pto. Quepos
Pta. S. Pedro
Osa Pen.
Pto. Armuelles
Pta. Burica
Coiba I.
Golfito
David
Chiriqui
Chiriqui Lagoon
Gulf of Mosquitos
Santiago
Azuero Peninsula
Penonome
Colon
Gatun
PANAMA
Balboa Panama City
Gulf of Panama
Archo. de las Perlas
San Blas
San Miguelito
Is. de San Blas
Gulf of Darien
Mon
El Real
Riosucio
Gulf of Uraba
Jurbo
Atra

10°

90°   85°

©Collins-Longman

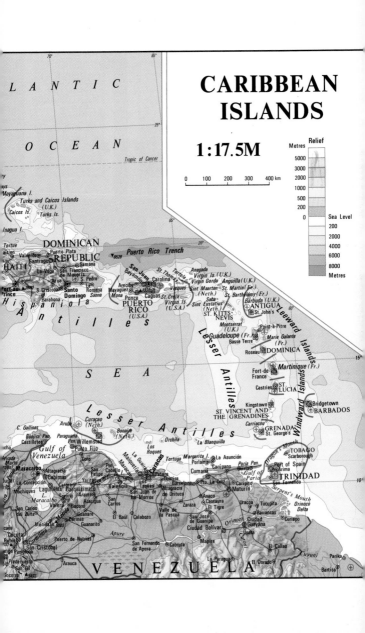

CARIBBEAN ISLANDS

1:17.5M

Relief

Metres	
5000	
3000	
2000	
1000	
500	
200	
0	Sea Level
	200
	2000
	4000
	6000
	8000
	Metres

0   100   200   300   400 km

L A N T I C

O C E A N

Tropic of Cancer

Mayaguana I.
Turks and Caicos Islands
(U.K.)
Caicos Is.   Turks Is.
Inagua I.

Tortue
aitien   Valverde   Puerto Plata   **DOMINICAN**
HAITI   Santiago   **REPUBLIC**   Puerto Rico Trench
La Vega   San Francisco de Macoris   8529
rt-au-   S. Cristobal   S. Pedro   Bayamon   San Juan   St Thomas   Anegada
rince   Santo   Romana   Arecibo   Carolina   Tortola   Virgin Is. (U.K.)   Anguilla (U.K.)
Barahona   **Domingo**   Saona   Mayaguez   1330   Vieques   Virgin Gorda   Sint Maarten   St Martin (Fr.)
Hispaniola   Mona   Ponce   Caguas   St Croix   Saba   St Barthélémy (Fr.)
A   *n*   *t*   *i*   **PUERTO**   Virgin Is.   Sint Eustatius   St Kitts
l   *l*   *e*   *s*   **RICO**   (U.S.A.)   (Neth.)   **NEVIS**   Barbuda (U.K.)
(U.S.A.)   (U.S.A.)   **ANTIGUA**
St John's
Montserrat   Point-à-Pitre
(U.K.)   **Guadeloupe** (Fr.)   Marie Galante
Basse Terre   (Fr.)
S   *E*   *A*   Roseau   **DOMINICA**

Lesser

Antilles   Fort-de-   **Martinique** (Fr.)
France
Castries   **ST.**
LUCIA

Kingstown   **ST. VINCENT AND**   Bridgetown
THE GRENADINES   **BARBADOS**
Lesser   Carriacou
Curaçao   **GRENADA**   Scarborough
Aruba   (Neth.)   St. George's   **TOBAGO**
C. Gallinas   *Antilles*   Orchila   Port of Spain
Guajira Pen.   Bonaire   La Blanquilla   Arima
Paraguaná   (Neth.)   **TRINIDAD**
Castilletes   Pen. Paraguaná   Los   San Fernando
cha   *Gulf of*   Punta Fijo   Roques   Tortuga   Margarita I.   La Asunción
Maracaibo   *Venezuela*   Coro   La Guaira   Porlamar   Tarúpano   Paria Pen.   Serpent's Mouth
ta   Altagracia   Maiquetía   Cumaná   *Gulf of*   Orinoco
Marta   Cabimas   Pto. Cabello   Caracas   Barcelona   Pto. La Cruz   Carúpano   *Paria*   Delta
La Concepción   Yaritagua   Turmero   Altagracia de Orituco   Anaco   Maturín   Curiapo
Machiques   Lagunillas   Valencia   San Juan de   Zaraza   Cantaura   Uracoa   Tucupita
Trujillo   Barquisimeto   Araure   los Morros   El Tigre   Barrancas   Orinoco
San Carlos   Acarigua   San   Valle de   Ciudad   Delta
del Zulia   Valera   Bocono   Carlos   la Pascua   Guayana
Mérida   Guanare   Guanarito   El Baúl   Calabozo   Ciudad Bolívar   Upata   Curiapo
5002   Barinas   Apure   El Callao
Cúcuta   Puerto de Nutrias   San Fernando   Cabruta   Mapire   Uyuní   Parika
Bucar   de Apure   Orinoco   Ciudad   Bartica
S. Cristóbal   La Paragua   El Dorado
nga Pamplona   Arauca   **V E N E Z U E L A**
Piedecuesta   5493
Socorro   S. Gil

O C E A N

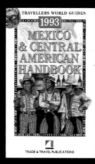

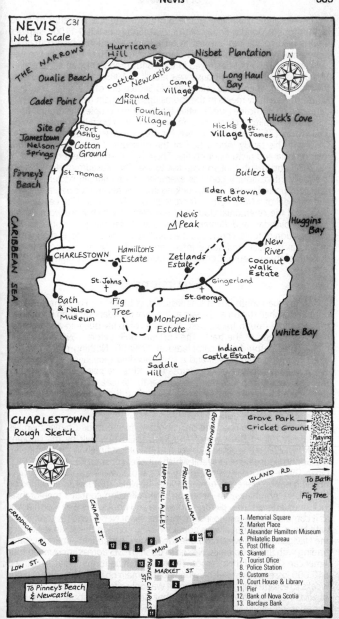

NEVIS C31
Not to Scale

THE NARROWS

Oualie Beach

Cades Point

Hurricane Hill

cottle Newcastle

Nisbet Plantation

Long Haul Bay

Camp Village

Round Hill

Fountain Village

Hick's Village

Hick's Cove

St. James

Site of Jamestown
Nelson Springs

Fort Ashby

Cotton Ground

St. Thomas

Pinney's Beach

CARIBBEAN SEA

Butlers

Eden Brown Estate

Nevis Peak

CHARLESTOWN

Hamilton's Estate

Zetlands Estate

Gingerland

Huggins Bay

New River

Coconut Walk Estate

St. Johns

Fig Tree

Montpelier Estate

St. George

White Bay

Bath & Nelson Museum

Saddle Hill

Indian Castle Estate

CHARLESTOWN
Rough Sketch

Grove Park Cricket Ground

Playing Field

GOVERNMENT RD.

ISLAND RD.

To Bath & Fig Tree

CRADDOCK RD.

CHAPEL ST.

HAPPY HILL ALLEY

PRINCE WILLIAM ST.

LOW ST.

PRINCE CHARLES ST.

MAIN ST.

MARKET ST.

To Pinney's Beach & Newcastle

1. Memorial Square
2. Market Place
3. Alexander Hamilton Museum
4. Philatelic Bureau
5. Post Office
6. Skantel
7. Tourist Office
8. Police Station
9. Customs
10. Court House & Library
11. Pier
12. Bank of Nova Scotia
13. Barclays Bank

The Alexander Hamilton House Birthplace and the Museum of Nevis History (open Monday-Friday 0800-1600, Saturday 1000-1200, entrance free) is next to the sea and set in an attractive garden which contains a representative collection of Nevis plants and trees. The original house was built around 1680 but destroyed in the 1840s probably by an earthquake . This attractive two-storey house was rebuilt in 1983 and dedicated during the Islands' Independence celebration in September of that year. The Nevis House of Assembly meets in the rooms upstairs (again restored after being damaged by Hurricane Hugo), while the museum occupies the ground floor. Alexander Hamilton, Nevis' most famous son, was born in Charlestown on 11 January 1757. He lived on Nevis for only five years before leaving for St Croix with his family. About half of the museum is given over to various memorabilia and pictures of his life. There is also an excellent collection of historical documents that you can ask to see. The Museum of Nevis History is equally interesting. It contains examples of Amerindian pottery, African culture imported by the slaves, cooking implements and recipes, a rum still, and a model of a Nevis lighter. There is also a collection of 17th century clay pipes and the ceremonial clothes of the Warden which were worn on the Queen's birthday and Remembrance Day. A section is devoted to the conservation of reefs, conch and the rain forest. There is a small shop which sells local produce and some interesting books. All proceeds go to the upkeep of the museum. Concerts are held here on Sunday nights at 1800.

Excursions

Taking the road south out of Charlestown, you can visit **Fort Charles**. Fork right at the Shell station and again at the mini roundabout, keep right along the sea shore (rough track), past the wine company building and through gates at the end of the track. The Fort was built before 1690 and altered many times before being completed in 1783-90. Nothing much remains apart from the circular well and a small building (possibly the magazine). The gun emplacments looking across to St Kitts are being badly eroded by the sea, eight cannon point haphazardly to sea. The Nevis Council surrendered to the French here in 1782 during the seige of Brimstone Hill on St Kitts. A hotel is being built close to the site so there is a possibility that some of it may be restored.

Back on the main road and only about ½ mile outside Charlestown lies the largely ruined **Bath Hotel** and **Spring House**. Built by the Huggins family in 1778, it is reputed to be one of the oldest hotels in the Caribbean. The Spring House lies over a fault which supplies constant hot water at 108°F. Open 0900-1600 daily, small charge for those wishing to bathe. A new building has been erected here to house the **Nelson Museum**. Founded by Mr Robert Abrahams, an American, the collection contains memorabilia including letters, china, pictures, furniture and books. It is well worth a visit as it contains an interesting insight into the life of Nelson and his connection with Nevis. He was not always popular having come to the island to enforce the Navigation Acts which forbade the newly independent American states trading with British Colonies. Nelson in his ship *HMS Boreas* impounded four American ships and their cargos. The Nevis merchants immediately claimed £40,000 losses against Nelson who had to remain on board his ship for eight weeks to escape being put into gaol. It was only after Prince William, captain of *HMS Pegasus*, arrived in Antigua that Nelson gained social acceptability and married Fanny Nisbet (reputedly for her uncle's money: this proved a disappointment as her uncle left the island and spent his wealth in London).

More evidence of the Nelson connection is found at the **St John's Fig Tree Anglican Church** about two miles on from the Bath House. Originally built in 1680, the church was rebuilt in 1838 and again in 1895. The marriage certificate of Nelson and Fanny Nisbet is displayed here. There are interesting memorials to Fanny's father William Woodward and also to her first husband Dr Josiah Nisbet. Many died of the fever during this period and taxi drivers will delight in lifting the red carpet in the central aisles for you to see old tomb stones, many connected with the then leading family, the Herberts. The graveyard has many examples of tombstones in family groups dating from the 1780s.

Slightly off the main road to the south lies **Montpelier Great House** where the marriage of Nelson and Nesbit actually took place; a plaque is set in the gatepost. The house is now a hotel with pleasant gardens. Enormous toads live in the lilly ponds formed out of old sugar pans. A very pleasant place for lunch or a drink. Beyond the house lies **Saddle Hill** (1,820 feet). It has the remains of a small fort and it is reputedly where Nelson would look out for illegal shipping. You can follow several goat trails on the hill, giant aloes abound, a track starts at Clay Ghaut. The *Hermitage* (another of the Great Houses) is signposted left just after the sign for the Montpelier.

The small village of **Gingerland** is reached after about three miles. Its rich soils make it the centre of the islands ginger root production (also cinnamon and nutmeg) but it is noteworthy for the very unusual octagon Methodist Church built in 1830. You turn right here along Hanleys Road to reach **White Bay Beach**. Go all the way down to the bottom and turn left at the Indian Castle experimental farm, avoiding Dark Bay (the site of St George's Port, little remains), past the race course (on Black Bay) and Red Cliff. There is a small shelter but no general shade. Beware, this is the Atlantic coast, the sea can be very rough and dangerous. On quieter days, the surf is fun and provides a welcome change from the quiet Leeward coast at Pinney's. There is a reef further out which is good for fishing (several fishing boats in the bay, one may take you out). There are good views across to Montserrat. On the way back beware of the deep (and hidden) storm drain crossing the road near the church.

After Gingerland the land becomes more barren. Several sugar mills were built here because of the wind, notably **Coconut Walk Estate, New River Estate** (fairly intact) and the **Eden Brown Estate**. Built around 1740, a duel took place between the groom and best man at the wedding of Julia Huggins. Both men were killed, Julia became a recluse and the great house was abandoned. It has the reputation of being haunted. Although government owned and open to the public, the ruins are in a poor condition and care should be taken.

The island road continues north through Butlers, past St James church (Hick's village), Long Haul and Newcastle Bays (with the *Nisbet Plantation Inn*) to the small fishing community of **Newcastle**. You can visit the Newcastle pottery where distinctive red clay is used to make among other things the traditional Nevis cooking pot. The **Newcastle Redoubt** can be seen from the road. Built in the early 17th century, it was used as a refuge from Carib attack and may have been the site of a Carib attack in 1656. The airport is situated here.

The road continues through an increasingly fertile landscape and there are fine views across the Narrows to south east peninsula of St Kitts, looking for all the world like the west coast of Scotland. Note **Booby Island** in the middle of the channel, it is mostly inhabited by pelicans (all birds are referred to as boobies by the local population). It offers good diving. The road between here and Charlestown often passes gardens which are a riot of colour. The small hill on your left is **Round Hill** (1,041 feet). It can be reached on the road between Cardes Bay and Camps Village (there is supposed to be a soufrière along this road). Turn off the road at Fountain Village by the methodist church. There are good views from the radio station at the top over Charlestown, across to St Kitts and beyond to Antigua. Do not expect to see much wildlife however. There is a small beach at **Mosquito Bay** and some good snorkelling can be had under the cliffs of Hurricane Hill. The *Oualie Beach hotel* offers a range of watersport facilities including scuba diving and snorkelling equipment.

Under Round Hill lies **Cottle chapel** (1824). It was the first Anglican place on Nevis where slaves could be taught and worship with their master. Ruined now, its beautiful little font can be seen in the Alexander Hamilton museum. Nearby, just off the island road, lies Fort Ashby. Nothing remains of the Fort (it is now a restaurant on Cardes Bay). It protected Jamestown, the original settlement and former capital, which was detroyed by an earthquake and tidal wave in 1680. Drive past the Nelson springs (where the barrels from *HMS Boreas* were filled) and **St Thomas' church** (built in 1643, one of the oldest surviving in the Caribbean) to Pinney's Beach. There are many tracks leading down to the beach often with a small hut or beach bar (eg *Golden Rock Beach Bar* and *Mariners*) at the end of them. The *Four Seasons hotel* lies in the middle of the beach. However the beach is so large that the hotel has had little impact on its undoubted beauty. More intrusive is the golf course which straddles the island road together with the electric cars which transport the guests from the hotel to the first tee. The manicured fairways and greens are in marked contrast with the quiet beauty of the rest of the island but the hotel's considerable efforts at landscaping will undoubtedly lessen its impact. There is much evidence of the power of Hurricane Hugo here, snapped off palm trees and wrecked buildings.

There are several interesting walks over old sugar plantations and through the rain forest on Mount Nevis. *Sunrise Tours* arranges trips to Nevis Peak, Saddle Hill or Water Source for US$45 pp. David Rollinson of the *Nevis Academy* (Tel: 2091) offers "eco rambles" over the eighteenth century Coconut Walk and New River Estates on Sundays, Mondays, Tuesdays and Wednesdays, US$10 pp.

Island Information—Nevis

Where To Stay Accommodation on Nevis tends to be up-market, in reconstructions of old plantation Great Houses, tastefully decorated in an English style (collectively called *The Inns of Nevis*). By agreement with the management, MAP guests can dine elsewhere and get at least a partial refund on the price of dinner. They are well worth a visit. They include the *Golden Rock Estate*, St George's Parish, PO Box 493, Tel: 469 3346, Fax: 469 2113, US$175d, EP, US$235d, MAP, winter rate, US$110d EP, US$175d MAP in summer, pool, tennis, beach shuttle, specialist interest tours, principally of ecological content; *Hermitage Plantation*, St John's Parish, Tel: 469 3477, Fax: 469 2481, US$100-180, EP, in summer, US$195-295, EP, in winter, very friendly, beautiful cottages, pool, stunning setting, many guests extend their stay; *Montpelier Plantation Inn*, also St John's, PO Box 474, Tel: 469 3462, Fax: 469 2932, a favourite with British tourists, delightful, friendly and helpful, pool, tennis, beach shuttle, US$175-230d, MAP, in summer, US$350d, MAP, in winter, child reductions, seven cottages (16 rooms, no credit cards). The *Nisbet Plantation Inn* 38 rooms in cottages/suites with tennis, swimming pool, a beach bar and pavilion,

US$190-290, MAP in summer, US$298-398d MAP, winter. *Pinney's Beach Hotel* PO Box 61, Tel: 469 5207, 48 rooms, 7 cottages, pool, watersports, horse riding, US$90d EP, summer, US$140d EP, winter, on the beach, dining room has no view, food and service reported poor off season. New hotels and resorts are being built all the time. A 196-room *Four Seasons Hotel* has opened on Pinney's Beach, PO Box 565, Tel: 469 1111, Fax: 469 1040, US$225-275 summer, US$400-450 winter, has Robert Trent Jones golf course and all entertainment; the *Mount Nevis Hotel*, PO Box 494, Tel: 469 9373, Fax: 469 9375, modern, rooms and studios, a/c, pool, watersports, US$120-150d EP in summer, US$170-210d EP in winter; *Croney's Old Manor* has 14 rooms including a cottage, beach shuttle, pool, minimum stay 3 nights, not recommended for children under 12, US$115d EP summer, US$175d EP winter, PO Box 70, Tel: 469 3445, Fax: 469 3388; *Oualie Beach Hotel*, on the beach, informal, comfortable, diving and other watersports, expanding to 18 rooms, US$85d summer, US$115d winter EP, 1-2 bedroom studios US$100-200 summer, US$140-290 winter, Tel: 469 9735, Fax: 469 9176.

There are also many guest houses, apartments and cottages including *Hurricane Cove Bungalows*, Tel/Fax: 469 9462, on hillside with wonderful sea view, well-equipped wooden bungalows of Finnish design, swimming pool, path down to stoney beach, good snorkelling, helpful manageress, Brenda, highly recommended, sports facilities nearby, US$115 for one bedroom, US$175 for two, US$350 for three-bedroomed villa with private pool, 3 night minimum stay in winter, long term discounts; *Donna's Self-Catering Apartments*, PO Box 503, Tel: 469 5464, and *Sea Spawn Guest House*, PO Box 233, Tel: 469 5239, in Charlestown, highly recommended, US$30-40 double, 1 minute from town, 2 from Pinney's Beach, has two fishing boats, car rental and kitchen and dining facilities.

Where To Eat The best restaurants are in the hotels and it is usually necessary to reserve a table. The above hotels provide exceptional cuisine as well as barbecues and entertainment on certain nights of the week. There are very few eating places in Charlestown, but *Unellas* on the waterfront offers local dishes at very reasonable prices (open 0900-0400 in season, shuts at 2200 out of season). The *Oualie Beach Club* does local lunches and dinners. Most restaurants only open in the evenings in the off season or even shut completely, the exception is *Caribbean Confections* opposite the Tourist Office, open for breakfast from 0730, good for ice cream and snacks, on Saturday night a special dinner is held in *The Courtyard* at the back, recommended, the owner Peggy Lyman is a fountain of information, they also make excellent birthday cakes to take away. There is a Pizza delivery service from Newcastle Marina, Tel: 469 9395.

Information for Visitors

Documents
US and Canadian visitors do not require passports but need only produce proof of citizenship to stay up to six months. Other nationalities need passports and a return ticket but for up to six months visas are not required for Commonwealth and EEC countries, Finland, Iceland, Liechtenstein, Norway, San Marino, Sweden, Switzerland, Turkey, Uruguay, Venezuela and nationals of other member countries of the OAS, with the exception of the Dominican Republic and Haiti. There are no resident ambassadors or high commissioners.

How To Get There
The main airport is at Golden Rock, St Kitts, two miles from Basseterre (the facilities for passengers are limited; there is no duty free shop). There are direct flights from Miami and New York on BWIA. Connections to North America and Europe can be made through San Juan (American Eagle and LIAT) and Antigua (BWIA and LIAT). In 1992 BWIA was to start flights from London twice a week and from Zurich and Frankfurt once a week. There are good connections with other Caribbean Islands (Anguilla, Saba, St Croix, St Eustatius, St Lucia, St Maarten, St Thomas, Tortola) and Trinidad with BWIA, LIAT and Windward Islands Airways (Winair). There is an airport departure tax of EC$20. It is possible to get a bus to the airport and walk the last five minutes from the main road; some buses go up to the terminal.

There is also an airport on Nevis, at Newcastle airfield, 7 miles from Charlestown, served by LIAT, Winair, Coastal Air Transport and light charter aircraft from St Kitts, Anguilla, Antigua,

St-Barthélémy, St Croix, St Eustatius, Saba and St Maarten. Expect to have your baggage searched on your way in to the island and likewise expect chaotic scenes on departure. The grander hotels on Nevis will arrange chartered air transfers from Antigua or St Kitts for their guests (for instance, Carib Aviation, US$55 pp from Antigua), this is highly recommended to avoid the crush.

A number of cruise lines, including Cunard, make stops in St Kitts. Basseterre has a deep water port.

Airlines

LIAT, TDC Airline Services, PO Box 142, Basseterre, Tel: 465 2511/2286, and Evelyn's Travel, on Main Street, general sales agent for BWIA, LIAT, American Airlines and British Airways, PO Box 211, Charlestown, Tel: 469 5302/5238; BWIA, Tel: 465 2286 on St Kitts, 469 5238 on Nevis; American Eagle, Tel: 465 8490 (St Kitts); Winair, Tel: 465 2186 on St Kitts, 469 5583 on Nevis; Carib Aviation, Tel: 465 3055 (St Kitts), Fax: 465 3168, Tel: 469 5295 (Nevis). Air St Kitts Nevis, PO Box 529, Basseterre, Tel: 465 8571, 469 9241, Fax: 469 9018, a charter company specializing in day excursions to neighbouring islands eg Saba, Dominica, Les Saintes, St-Barths.

Inter-Island Transport

A passenger ferry, the *Caribe Queen*, operates on a regular schedule between St Kitts and Nevis. The crossing takes about 45 minutes and costs EC$20 round trip. Charlestown to Basseterre early morning and afternoon/evening crossing daily except Thursday and Sunday. Basseterre to Charlestown early morning and afternoon crossing Monday, Friday and Saturday, afternoon only on Tuesday, three crossings on Wednesday making it a good day for a day trip, no service Thursday and Sunday. *The Spirit of Mount Nevis* runs daily except Wednesday, but was out of commission in 1992, check schedules. The ferry is preferable to the LIAT flight, which is always overbooked. Island tours operate from St Kitts and there is also a water taxi service between the two islands (US$25 return, minimum 4 passengers, only 20 minutes, operated by Kenneth's Dive Centre, Tel: 465 2670 in advance).

Road Transport

There are good main roads on St Kitts but do not expect high quality on Nevis, where storm ditches frequently cross the paved road; drive slowly and carefully. Cars,

jeeps, mini mokes can be hired from a variety of agencies on both islands, eg TDC Rentals, West Independence Square, Basseterre, Tel: 465 2991, or Main Street, Charlestown, Tel: 469 5690; Caines Rent-A-Car, Princes Street, Basseterre, Tel: 465 2366; Sunshine Car Rental, Cayon Street, Basseterre, Tel: 465 2193. If you are arriving in St Kitts from Nevis, there are several car hire companies on Independence Square, some three minutes walk from the ferry pier. The most convenient is *Holiday Car Rentals* (US$33 per day for a Nissan automatic and efficient). Nisbett's Car Rental, 100 yards from Newcastle airport, Minimoke US$40/day, collision damage waiver US$8/day, recommended, particularly if you are flying in/out of Nevis. A local driving licence must be obtained from the Post Office or any Police Station on production of your normal driving licence (EC$30). Companies insist on you having collision damage waiver, which adds another US$5-10 to quoted rates. There is a 5% tax on car rentals. Fuel is US$4.50 per gallon. **Minibuses** do not run on a scheduled basis but follow a set route (more or less), EC$1-2.50 on most routes, EC$3 from Basseterre to the north of the island, frequent service from market area. There are no minibuses to Frigate Bay. Maximum **taxi** fares are set, for example: on St Kitts, from Golden Rock Airport to Basseterre EC$13-16 (depending on area of town), to the Deep Water Port, EC$22, to Frigate Bay, EC$25, to Old Road, EC$27, to Middle Island, EC$30. From Basseterre to Old Road, EC$24, to Frigate Bay, EC$18, to Middle Island, EC$26, to Sandy Point, EC$30. Taxis within Basseterre cost EC$8, with additional charges for waiting or for more than one piece of luggage. Between 2300-0600 prices rise by 25%. **On Nevis** a taxi from the airport to Charlestown costs EC$30, to *Pinney's Beach Hotel*, EC$30, to *Oualie Beach*, EC$20, to the *Montpelier Inn*, EC$45, to *Hermitage Inn*, EC$40 and to *Nisbet Plantation Inn*, EC$17. Fares from Charlestown are EC$10, EC$23, EC$26, EC$26 and EC$36 respectively. A 50% extra charge is made on Nevis between 2200 and 0600. An island tour of Nevis costs US$50 for about 3 hours. Complaints have been received that taxis do not stick to the regulated fares and are extremely expensive. There is no need to tip.

Food And Drink

Food on the whole is good. Apart from almost every kind of imported food and drink, there is a wide variety of fresh seafood (red snapper, lobster, king fish, blue parrot), and local vegetables. The excellent local spirit is CSR—Cane Spirit Rothschild—produced in St Kitts by Baron de Rothschild. It is drunk neat, with ice or water, or with "Ting", the local grapefruit soft drink (also recommended).

Tipping
A 10% service charge is added to hotel bills. In restaurants about 10%-15% is expected.

Shopping
The shopper has plenty of choice and is not swamped by US or British merchandise. Shops are well stocked. Local Sea Island cotton wear and cane and basketwork are attractive and reasonable. Shop opening hours 0800-1200, 1300-1600, Monday-Saturday. Early closing on Thursdays. Pharmacies open through lunch. Walls De Luxe Record and Bookshop on Fort Street has a good selection of music and Caribbean books.

The Island Hopper Boutique at the Circus, underneath the *Ballahoo* restaurant, stocks the Caribelle Batik range of cotton fashions but also carries clothes from Trinidad, St Lucia, Barbados and Haiti; open 0800-1600 Monday-Friday, 0800-1200 Saturday, Tel: 465 1640.

Supermarkets in Basseterre include B & K Superfood on the south side of Independence Square and George Street, and Rams on Bay Road. On Nevis, there are well-stocked supermarkets: Nisbets in Newcastle and Superfood, Parkville Plaza, Charlestown. Several local craft shops in Charlestown. On the road to the *Four Seasons Hotel* is an industrial estate with shops selling crafts and a toy shop.

There are **philatelic bureaux** on both St Kitts and Nevis which are famous (the latter more so) for their first day covers of the islands' fauna and flora, undersea life, history and carnival. The St. Kitts bureau is in the new development for cruise ship arrivals on the wharf.

Laundry
Warners, Main Street, Charlestown, including dry cleaning.

Banks
The Eastern Caribbean Central Bank (ECCB) is based in Basseterre, and is responsible for the issue of currency in Antigua and Barbuda, Dominica, Grenada, Montserrat, St Kitts and Nevis,

St Lucia and St Vincent and the Grenadines. There are two local banks on St Kitts: St Kitts-Nevis National Bank and Development Bank of St Kitts-Nevis. In addition, on Nevis, there is the Nevis Co-operative Bank and the Bank of Nevis. Foreign banks on St Kitts: Barclays Bank International, Royal Bank of Canada, Bank of Nova Scotia; on Nevis, Barclays and Bank of Nova Scotia. Open 0800-1500 Monday-Thursday, Fridays until 1700. St Kitts-Nevis National Bank opens on Saturdays 0830-1100. If you are in a hurry, choose a foreign bank as their queues are often shorter.

Currency
East Caribbean dollar: EC2.70=US$1. US dollars accepted. When prices are quoted in both currencies, eg for departure tax, taxi fares, a notional rate of EC$2.50 = US$1 is used. There are no restrictions on the amount of foreign currency that can be imported or exported, but the amount of local currency exported is limited to the amount you imported and declared. Check which credit cards are accepted, Visa is the most widely used, Access/Mastercard and Diners Club are not so popular.

Health
Mains water is chlorinated, but bottled water is available if preferred for drinking, particularly outside the main towns. Dairy produce, meat, poultry, seafood, fruit and vegetables are generally considered safe. A yellow fever or cholera vaccination certificate is required if you are arriving from an infected area.

Security
Note that the penalties for possession of narcotics are very severe and no mercy is shown towards tourists.

Climate
The weather is pleasant all year round but the best time to visit is during the dry months from November to May. Locals insist that, with changing weather patterns, May to early August can be preferable. The temperature varies between 17°C and 33°C, tempered by sea winds and with an average annual rainfall of 55 inches on St Kitts and 48 inches on Nevis.

Public Holidays
New Year's Day (1 January), Good Friday, Easter Monday, May Day (first Monday in May), Whit Monday (end of May), the Queen's birthday (June), August Bank

Holiday Monday (beginning of the month), Independence Day (19 September), Christmas Day (25 December).

Time Zone
Atlantic Standard Time, 4 hours behind GMT, 1 ahead of EST.

Electric Current
230 volts AC/60 cycles (some hotels have 110V).

Communications
The telephone company, Skantel, has installed new digital telecommunications systems for the two islands and international direct dialling is available. USA direct public phones available at Skantel office. Coin boxes take the older, round EC$1 coins, not the multisided ones. Codes: 809-465 (St Kitts), 809-469 (Nevis). Call charges are EC$4.50 (EC$3.60 reduced rate) to the USA or the UK. The Boat Phone Company on the Frigate Bay Road offers cellular phone service for yachts. Telex and telegram facilities in the main hotels.

Post office in Basseterre is on Bay Road; in Charlestown on Main Street. Airmail letters to the UK take up to two weeks.

Media
Newspapers come out weekly (*The Democrat*) or twice weekly (*The Labour Spokesman*). There are 3 radio stations, 1 TV station and cable TV. AM/FM ZIZ Radio is on medium wave 555 kHz and FM 96 mHz and Radio Paradise on St Kitts. VON Radio in Nevis is on 895 kHz medium wave.

Tourist Office
The St Kitts Tourist Board produces very good information (Pelican Mall, PO Box 132, Basseterre, Tel: 465 2620/4040, Fax:

465 8794). The Nevis Tourist Board is in D R Walwyn Plaza, Charlestown (Tel: 469 5521, ext 2049/2037); it is extremely helpful, with plenty of information available.

There are tourist offices in
USA: at 414 East 75th Street, New York NY 10021, Tel: 212-535 1234, Fax: 212-879 4789/1464 Whippoorwill Way, Mountainside, NJ 07092, Tel: 908-2326701.

Canada: 11 Yorkville Ave, Suite 508, Toronto M4W 1L3, Tel: 416-921 7717, Fax: 416-921 7997.

UK: c/o the High Commission for Eastern Caribbean States, 10 Kensington Court, London W8 5DL, Tel: 071-376 0881, Fax: 071-937 3611.

The St Kitts/Nevis Hotel Association can be reached at PO Box 65, Basseterre, St Kitts, Tel: 465 5304.

Useful publications are *The Official St Kitts and Nevis Tourist Guide* (annual, published by the Tourist Board) and *The Traveller* (biannual, published in association with the Tourist Board by Pentaal Ltd, PO Box 535, Basseterre); *A Motoring Guide to Nevis* by Janet Cotner and Sunny Northrup (Heidelberg Press, Burlington NJ); the Nevis Historical and Conservation Society's *Walking and Riding Tour of Nevis* pamphlet (available from Alexander Hamilton House, Charlestown).

We are grateful to Patrick Dawson, of Trade and Travel Publications, for a comprehensive revision of this chapter who would like to thank Bob and Althea Turner of the *Hurricane Cove Bungalows* and their manageress Brenda for their help and hospitality.

ANGUILLA

Introduction

ANGUILLA is a small island, only about 35 miles square, the most northerly of the Leeward Islands, five miles north of St Martin and 70 miles northwest of St Kitts. The island is low lying, the highest point being Crocus Hill at 213 feet above sea level. Unlike its larger sisters it is not volcanic but of coral formation. It is arid, covered with low scrub and has few natural resources. However, it has excellent beaches and superb diving and snorkelling, protected by the coral reefs. The island's name is the Spanish word *anguilla* (eel), a reference to its long, narrow shape. Its Carib name was Malliouhana. The population numbers about 10,496, predominantly of African descent but with some traces of Irish blood. The administrative centre is **The Valley**, the largest community on the island with a population of 500. The people of Anguilla are very friendly and helpful and it is one of the safest islands in the Caribbean.

To the northwest is the uninhabited Dog Island which is excellent for swimming, and beyond that is Sombrero Island, where there is an important lighthouse. Other islets include Scrub Island at the northeast tip of Anguilla, Little Scrub Island next to it, Anguillita Island and Blowing Rock at the southwestern tip and the Prickly Pear Cays and Sail Island to the northwest on the way to Dog Island.

History

The earliest known Amerindian site on Anguilla is at the northeastern tip of the island, where tools and artefacts made from conch shells have been recovered and dated at around 1300 BC. Saladoid Amerindians settled on the island in the fourth century AD and brought their knowledge of agriculture, ceramics and their religious culture based on the god of cassava (**see page 51**). By the mid-sixth century large villages had been built at Rendezvous Bay and Sandy Ground, with smaller ones at Shoal Bay and Island Harbour. Post Saladoid Amerindians from the Greater Antilles arrived in the tenth century, building new villages and setting up a chiefdom with a religious hierarchy. Several ceremonial items have been found and debris related to the manufacture of the three-pointed zemis, or spirit stones, associated with fertility rites. By the 17th century, Amerindians had disappeared from Anguilla: wiped out by enslavement and European diseases.

Anguilla was first mentioned in 1564 when a French expedition passed en route from Dominica to Florida, but it was not until 1650 that it was first colonized by the British. Despite several attempted invasions, by Caribs in 1656 and by the French in 1745 and 1796, it remained a British colony. From 1825 it became more closely associated with St Kitts for administrative purposes and ultimately incorporated in the colony. In 1967 St Kitts-Nevis-Anguilla became a State in Association with the UK and gained internal independence. However, Anguilla opposed this development and almost immediately repudiated government from St Kitts. A breakaway movement was led by Ronald Webster of the People's Progressive Party (PPP).

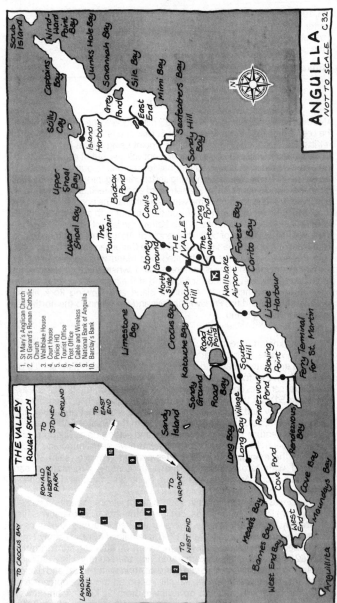

ANGUILLA C 32
NOT TO SCALE

THE VALLEY ROUGH SKETCH

1. St Mary's Anglican Church
2. St Gerard's Roman Catholic Church
3. Wallblake House
4. Court House
5. Police HQ
6. Tourist Office
7. Post Office
8. Cable and Wireless
9. National Bank of Anguilla
10. Barclay's Bank

In 1969 British forces invaded the island to install a British Commissioner after negotiations had broken down. The episode is remembered locally for the unusual presence of the London Metropolitan Police, who remained on the island until 1972 when the Anguilla Police Force was established.

Government
In 1980, Anguilla formally separated from the State and became a British Dependent Territory with a Governor to represent the Crown. A new constitution was introduced in 1982, providing for a Governor, an Executive Council comprising four elected Ministers and two ex-officio members, and an 11-member legislative House of Assembly presided over by a Speaker. The post of Chief Minister has alternated for two decades between the rival politicians, Ronald Webster and Emile Gumbs, the latter being re-elected in 1989 and currently also holding the portfolios of Home Affairs, Tourism and Economic Development. In 1990 the constitution was amended to give the Governor responsibility for international financial affairs. A new post of Deputy Governor was created, to replace the Permanent Secretary for Finance as a member of the Executive Council and House of Assembly.

The Economy
The main economic activities used to be livestock raising, lobster fishing, salt production and boat building, but tourism is increasingly important as a generator of foreign exchange and employment. In 1991, 90,544 foreign tourists visited or stayed on the island, a small rise over the previous year. In 1991 there were 740 rooms available in guest houses, villas and apartments and hotels, although the number is steadily rising. Economic growth averaged 9.5% a year in 1988-89, led by tourism and construction, but slowed to an average of 7.4% in 1990-91. There is also some offshore banking and the Government aims to establish a reputable offshore financial services industry. Thirty out of 43 offshore banks, who pay an annual licence fee to the Government, had their licences cancelled in 1990 following a review of the sector. At end-1991 the House of Assembly approved legislation to tighten control of offshore finance, giving the Governor complete and final authority over the granting of licences.

Previously, high levels of unemployment led to migration to other Caribbean islands and further afield, but the unemployment rate has fallen from 26% in 1985 to almost nil and shortages of labour have delayed expansion programmes, as well as putting pressure on prices and wages. Work permits have been granted to more than 1,000 non-Anguillans, but many people have two jobs. Workers' remittances are crucial, particularly since the 1984 suspension of budgetary support in the form of UK grants-in-aid, although the British Government does still provide aid for the development programme, along with other donors such as the EEC and the Caribbean Development Bank. There is no income tax and the Government gets its revenues from customs duties, bank licences, property and stamps.

Diving and Marine Life
The reefs and Prickly Pear Island are well worth exploring. Scuba diving can be arranged through Tamariain Watersports Ltd, PO Box 247, Sandy Ground, Tel: 2020. Owned and run by qualified PADI instructors, Iain Grummit and Thomas Peabody, training courses are available. Retail shop open daily 0800-1600, equipment for sale or rent. There are good dives just off the coast, particularly for novices or for night dives, while the others are generally in a line due west of Sandy Island, northwest of Sandy Ground, and along

the reef formed by Prickly Pear Cays and Sail Island. Off Sandy Island, there are lots of soft corals and sea-fans, while at Sandy Deep there is a wall which falls from 15 to 60 feet. There are also a few wrecks.

Further west, Paintcan Reef at a depth of 80 feet contains several acres of coral and you can sometimes find large turtles there. Nearby, Authors Deep, at 110 feet has black coral, turtles and a host of small fish, but this dive is more for the experienced diver. On the north side of the Prickly Pear Cays you can find a beautiful underwater canyon with ledges and caves where nurse sharks often go to rest. Marine life is under conservation and nothing may be removed. Most of the reefs around Anguilla have some red coral; be careful not to touch it as it burns.

Beaches and Watersports

There are twelve miles or 45 beaches with white coral sand and crystal clear water. Most of them are protected by a ring of coral reefs and offshore islands. The beaches are clean, and many of them are relatively unpopulated, but nude (or topless for women) swimming or sunbathing is not allowed. Shoal Bay is the most popular beach and claims to be one of the most beautiful in the Eastern Caribbean. There are snack bars for lunch, although only one has a toilet. The snorkelling is good, with the closest of two reefs only 10 yards from the shore and you can rent snorkelling equipment. Mead's Bay is also popular with more expensive bars and watersports. Road Bay/Sandy Ground has most nightlife and restaurants and is the starting point for most day trips, dive tours and a popular anchorage for visiting yachts. Watersports equipment rentals can be organized here. Sundays are recommended when there is live music at *Johnno's Beach Bar*. Scilly Cay is a small cay off Island Harbour with good snorkelling. A free ferry takes you to the bar on a palm-clad beach. Live music on Sundays. Captain's Bay is rougher but the scenery is dramatic and not many people go there. The dirt road is full of potholes and goats and may be impassable with a low car. At Crocus Bay the rocks on both sides have nice coral and underwater scenery. There is a bar/restaurant and toilets. At the end of Limestone Bay is a small beach with excellent snorkelling, but be careful, the sea can be rough here. Little Bay is more difficult to reach but eagle rays and turtles can be seen; turn right in front of the hospital in the Valley, after about half a mile there are some trails leading down to the water, fishermen have put up a net for the last bit.

Windsurfing and sailing are readily available and some of the hotels offer water skiing, paddle boats, snorkelling, fishing and sunfish sailing. Sport fishing is available at Sandy Island Enterprises, Tel: 6395. Yacht or motorboat charters can be organized through Sandy Island Enterprises, Suntastic Yacht Services, Tel: 3400/3699, or Enchanted Island Cruises, Road Bay, Tel: 3111, which has a 50-foot catamaran, *Wild Cat*. Ocean Charters have half or full day charters to beaches, US$50 pp per day, open bar, also ½ day fishing trips, US$45/hour, Tel: 3394 or *Ripples Restaurant*, Tel: 3380. Boat racing is the national sport, the boats being a special class of wooden sloop made in Anguilla. There are frequent races, but the most important are on Anguilla Day (30 May) and during Carnival Week in August.

Other Sports

Several hotels have tennis courts. The *Malliouhana* has four championship courts; *Cinnamon Reef* has two at a cost of US$20 per hour for non-residents.

Festivals

Carnival is at the beginning of August (the Friday before the first Monday), when the island comes to life with street dancing, Calypso competitions, the Carnival Queen Coronation, the Prince and Princess Show, nightly entertainment in The Valley and beach barbecues.

Excursions

Near The Valley, Wallblake House is a restored, eighteenth-century plantation house where the priest from St Gerard's Roman Catholic Church lives. The Church itself is worth a visit to see the unusual ventilation. Several resident artists exhibit their work on Saturday mornings during the winter season in the grounds of Wallblake House. At Sandy Ground Village, you can see the salt pond, around Great Road Pond, although it is not currently in operation. Northeast of The Valley, by Shoal Village, is The Fountain national park. Its focus is in fact a cave which has a source of constant fresh water and a series of Amerindian petroglyphs. Artefacts have been found and it is hoped they will be housed in a museum at the site, but in 1992 the national park was closed while archaeologists considered policy alternatives and was likely to remain so for a few years. Anguilla awaits detailed archaeological investigation, but it is thought that the island had several settlements and a social structure of some importance, judging by the ceremonial items which have been found. Contact the Anguilla Archaeological and Historical Society for more information; the Society is involved in setting up a national museum and in several publications including a Review (PO Box 252). Local deposits of clay have been found and pottery is now made on the island; the work of Barbadian potter and sculptor, Courtney Devonish, and his students, is on display at the Devonish Gallery in the Old Factory Plaza.

Day trips can be arranged to some of the neighbouring islands or to the offshore islands and cays. Sandy Island is only 15 minutes from Sandy Ground harbour and is a pleasant desert island-type place to swim, snorkel and spend half a day or so. Motorboats or sailboats cross over hourly from 1000. Lunch or drinks available from a beach bar under coconut palms. There are trips to Prickly Pear, six miles from Road Bay, which is well worth a visit, where you can snorkel if you are not a scuba diver, or to some of the other cays where you can fish or just have a picnic. Enchanted Island Cruises have a boat that goes to Prickly Pear daily (except Thursday) leaving 1000 and returning 1600, US$70 including drinks, barbecue lunch and snorkelling equipment. Scrub Island, two miles long and one mile wide, off the northeast tip of Anguilla, is an interesting mix of coral, scrub and other vegetation and is worth a visit. It is uninhabited, except by goats, and can only be reached by boat. There is a lovely sandy beach on the west side and ruins of an abandoned tourist resort and airstrip. There can be quite a swell in the anchorage, so anchor well. Chartered yachts and motorboats leave from Road Bay or Island Harbour.

Information for Visitors

Documents

All visitors need an onward ticket. All must also have a valid passport, except US citizens who need only show proof of identity with a photograph. Visas are not required by anyone.

How To Get There By Air

Wallblake airport is just outside The Valley. International access points for Anguilla are Antigua, St Maarten or San Juan, Puerto Rico. LIAT has daily flights from Antigua; some flights connect with British Airways from London. Alternatively, Carib Aviation, will meet any incoming BA flight and fly you to Anguilla without you having to clear customs in Antigua. LIAT also connects Anguilla with St Kitts and Nevis, St Maarten, St Thomas and Tortola (the LIAT office is at Gumbs Travel Agency, Tel: 2238 and also at Tel: 2748). American Eagle (Tel: 3500) has a twice daily air link with Puerto Rico. Winair (Tel: 2238/2748) provides several daily flights from St Maarten (5 minutes, about US$15). Coastal Air Transport flies from St Croix, USVI, while Winair flies from St Thomas, USVI. Air Anguilla (mainly charters, Tel: 2643) and Tyden Air (Tel: 2719) operate air taxi services to the British and US Virgin Islands, St Maarten and St Kitts.

There is a departure tax of EC$15/ US$6.

How To Get There By Sea:

The principal port is Sandy Ground, which is being improved. Ferry between Blowing Point (departure tax EC$3/US$1.15) and Marigot, Saint-Martin takes at least 20 minutes and costs US$9, one way. The service starts at about 0730 and continues every 30-40 minutes until 1700; (there are also two evening ferries in high season at 1900 and 2300 (Marigot to Anguilla) and 1815 and 2215 (Anguilla to Marigot). Visiting yachts anchor at Sandy Ground, Crocus Bay and Mead's Bay on the north coast, and Blowing Point or Rendezvous Bay on the south coast. Periodic boats from St Kitts and Nevis, the British and US Virgin Islands and Puerto Rico. Immigration and customs formalities for boats are at Blowing Point. At Road Bay the customs office is at the big wharf close to the *Riviera*, the Immigration office is at the Police station behind *Johnno's*.

Taxis

Expensive and the driver usually quotes in US dollars, not EC dollars: from Wallblake airport to The Valley costs about US$5; from The Valley to Blowing Point (ferry) US$10. Fares are fixed by the Government. To hire a taxi for a tour of the island works out at about US$40 for two people, US$5 for additional passengers.

Car Rental

There are several car hire companies, including Apex, The Quarter, Tel: 2642; H and R, The Valley, Tel: 2656/2606; Bennie's (Avis, requires US$100 deposit one month in advance for lowest price), Blowing Point, Tel: 2788/2360/6221; Budget, The

Quarter, Tel: 2217, free pick up and delivery (to get their low price of US$167/week, reservations must be made direct to Anguilla, not through their US or European offices); Connors, South Hill, Tel 6433; Island Car Rentals, Tel: 3733, and many others. Rates are from US$25/day off season, US$35/day high season.

Driving is on the left. Speed limit 30 miles an hour. A local driving permit i issued on presentation of a valid driver's licence from your home country and car be bought at car rental offices; US$6 for three months. Hitchhiking is very easy.

Where To Stay

Anguilla has the reputation of catering for upmarket, independent travellers. This i reflected in the number of relatively small but expensive hotels and beach clubs. The following have flexible accommodation in rooms, suites, studios or villas, winte 1991/92 prices quoted. *Cap Juluca* a Maundays Bay (Tel: 6666/6779, Fax 6617), 98 rooms, every facility here, with two beaches, pool, watersports, tennis where winter rates are US$390-600d US$875-1,800 suites, CP, but a third les in summer; *The Mariners*, Sandy Ground Tel: 2671/2815, Fax: 2901, 50 rooms US$210-490d, EP, in high season (US$150-370 in summer, suites and cottages available, on beach, watersports pool, tennis); *Malliouhana Hotel* Mead's Bay, Tel: 6111, Fax: 6011, 6 rooms, US$480d, EP (US$240 out of season, suites up to US$1,080, on beach watersports, tennis, pool); *Anguilla Great House*, Rendezvous Bay, Te 6061/6621, Fax: 6019, 25 rooms US$200d, falling to US$115 in summer suites up to US$475, EP, beach, poo *Coccoloba Plantation*, Barnes Bay, Te 6871, Fax: 6332, 51 rooms, US$360-460 including full breakfast, beach, poo tennis; *Fountain Beach*, Shoal Bay Tel/Fax: 3491, 6 units, US$225 for a studio US$340 for 2-bedroom suite, EP, beach *Cinnamon Reef*, Little Harbour, Tel: 2727 Fax: 3727, 22 rooms, US$250-550 E beach, pool, tennis; *La Sirena*, Meads Bay Tel: 6827, Fax: 6829, US$180-215d, villa up to US$340, beach nearby, poo *Masara Resort*, Katouche Bay, Tel: 3200 Fax: 3223, 11 rooms, US$175-250, beac nearby, tennis; *Rendezvous Bay Hotel* Tel: 6549, Fax: 6026, 20 rooms US$170-200, villas up to US$725, beach tennis; *Shoal Bay Villas*, Tel: 2051, Fax 3631, 9 units, US$210-360, beach, pool

Cove Castles Villa Resort, Shoal Bay West, Tel: 6801, Fax: 6051, PO Box 248, futuristic architecture, 4 3-bedroom villas, 8 2-bedroom beach houses, US$490-890 EP, beach, tennis, sunfish, bicycles included, watersports available.

There are also villas and apartments to rent, among the cheapest being *Sydan's Apartments*, Sandy Ground, Tel: 3180, one-bedroom apartments at US$75 day, Mexican restaurant; *Sea View*, Sandy Ground, Tel: 2427, US$45-90, ceiling fans, kitchen facilities, beach nearby; *Viewfort Cottage*, Viewfort, Tel: 2537, US$60, kitchen, TV; *La Palma*, Sandy Ground, Tel: 3260, Fax: 5381, US$55-60, on beach, restaurant, ceiling fans.

Travellers on a lower budget can find accommodation in one of about ten guesthouses. These include *Casa Nadine*, The Valley (Tel: 2358), 11 rooms, US$25d, EP, with shower, kitchen facilities, basic but very friendly; *Florencia's*, The Valley (Tel: 2319), 5 rooms, US$50, MAP, basic, little privacy; *Yellow Banana*, Stoney Ground (Tel: 2626), 12 rooms, US$30-40d, EP, simple, clean, small lounge, but not very friendly; at Lower South Hill, *Inter Island*, Tel: 6259, Fax: 5381, 14 rooms, US$60, fans, kitchen facilities, restaurant; at North Side, *Norman B*, Tel: 2242, 11 rooms, US$40d EP; and others.

The Anguilla Department of Tourism has a list of all types of accommodation. In London there is a free reservation service on 071-937 7725. In North America, call (800) 553 4939, c/o Medhurst and Associates Inc, 271 Main Street, Northport, NY 11768.

Where To Eat

Apart from hotel restaurants, where a dinner can cost US$50 and above in a 4-5 star restaurant you can find local cuisine (*Lucy's Harbour View*, Back Street, South Hill, medium prices, Tel: 6253; *Ship's Galley*, breakfast, lunch and dinner, closed Wednesdays, Tel: 2040, Sandy Ground); French (*Dockside Grill*, Sandy Ground, medium prices, dinner only, Tel: 3380; *Le Bistro*, Corito Bay); and seafood specialities (*Ripples at Dockside*, Sandy Ground, run by Jacquie Ruan and friends, indoors or terrace, seafood, daily specials, reasonable prices, Tel: 3380; *Barrel Stay*, Sandy Ground, Tel: 2831, overpriced because of all the charter boat tourists). Also, *The Old House*, George Hill, for breakfast, lunch or dinner, Tel: 2228. *Le Fish Trap*, Island Harbour, is expensive but

one of the best for seafood, Tel: 4488; *Koalkeel*, The Valley, also expensive, in a restored 18th century Great House with 100-year old rock oven, Euro-Caribbean style, Tel: 2930; *La Sirena*, in the hotel, breakfast, lunch and dinner, Sunday buffet brunch with live music, fondue specialities, medium priced, Tel: 6827; *Roy's Place*, Crocus Bay, moderate prices, seafood lunch and famous Sunday brunch, Tel: 2470, closed Mondays; *Johnno's*, Sandy Ground, mostly barbecue, especially lively evenings are Saturday and Sunday, with live music, Tel: 2728; *Qué Pasa*?, Sandy Ground, Mexican and vegetarian specialities, also take away or delivery, Tel: 3171, lunch 1200-1430, dinner 1900-2130; *La Palma*, Sandy Ground, local food, inexpensive, Tel: 3260; *Cora's Pepper Pot*, The Valley, inexpensive local food, Tel: 2328; *Oriental Restaurant*, The Quarter/The Valley, Chinese, usual low prices and plenty of food for your money, Tel: 2763. Most of the restaurants are small and reservations are needed, particularly in high season. For those who are self-catering, *Fat Cat*, Main Road, George Hill, Tel: 2307, has meals to go from the freezer, picnic meals, pies and cakes. Vista Food Market, South Hill Roundabout, Tel: 2804, good selection, cheeses, meats, pâtés, wines, beer etc, open Monday-Saturday 0800-1800.

Nightlife

Out of season there is not much to do during the week; *Johnno's* and *Lucy's Palm Palm* are normally the liveliest bars/restaurants. On Friday the whole island changes, several bars have live music, check the local papers, try *Lucy's Palm Palm*, Sandy Grand, or *Round Rock*, Shoal Bay. On Saturday go to *Johnno's Place*, Sandy Ground; on Sunday to brunch at *Roy's Place*, Crocus Bay, draft beer, then around 1500 at *Johnno's Place* for a beach party. When the music dies people go to the neighbouring bar, *Ship's Galley* for the night shift. At the weekend the *Dragon Disco* opens around midnight. In high season the resort hotels have live music, steel bands etc, check in the tourist *Anguilla Life* magazine.

Bookshop

National Bookstore, above Lynette's Bakery, The Valley, Tel: 3009, open Monday-Saturday 0800-1700, wide selection of novels, magazines, non-fiction, children's books, tourist guides, Caribbean history and literature, managed by Mrs Kelly.

Banks
In The Valley, Barclays Bank International, Tel: 2301; Caribbean Commercial Bank (Anguilla), Tel: 2571; National Bank of Anguilla, Tel: 2101.

Currency
The East Caribbean dollar. Scotia Bank, US dollars always accepted.

Climate
The climate is sub-tropical with an average temperature of 27°C (80°F) and a mean annual rainfall of 914 milimetres (36 inches), falling mostly between September and December.

Clothing
Bathing costumes are not worn in public places. Nude bathing or sunbathing is not allowed.

Hours Of Business
0800-1200, 1300-1600 Monday to Friday; banks 0800-1500 Monday to Thursday, 0800-1700 on Friday. Gas stations are open in The Valley, Monday to Saturday 0700-2100, Sunday 0900-1300, and at Blowing Point, Monday to Sunday 0700-2400.

National Holidays
New Year's Day, Good Friday, Easter Monday, Whit Monday, 30 May (Anguilla Day), the Queen's official birthday in June, the first Monday (August Monday) and the first Thursday (August Thursday) and Friday (Constitution Day) in August, 19 December (Separation Day), Christmas Day, Boxing Day.

Time Zone
GMT minus 4 hours; EST plus 1 hour.

Weights And Measures
Metric, but some imperial weights and measures are still used.

Electric Current
110 volts AC, 60 cycles.

Telecommunications
Cable and Wireless operates internal and external telephone links (IDD available), telex and fax services. There are two AT&T USA direct telephones by Cable and Wireless office in the Valley and by the airport. The international code is 809-497, followed by a four-digit number. **Main Post Office** is in The Valley, opposite Webster Park, open Monday-Friday 0800-1200, 1300-1530.

Radio
Radio Anguilla is on medium wave 1505 kHz and ZJF on FM 105 MHz.

Travel Agents
Malliouhana Travel and Tours, The Quarter, Tel: 2431/2348, has been recommended; Bennie's Travel Tours (address under **Car Rental**, above); Travel and Tours, Inc, The Valley, Tel: 2788/2360.

Tourist Office
Anguilla Department of Tourism, The Valley, Tel: 2759/2451, Fax: 2751, open weekdays 0800-1200, 1300-1600.
    UK: 3 Epirus Road, London, SW6, 7UJ, Tel: 071-937 7725, Fax: 071-938 4793.
    USA: Medhurst and Associates, 271 Main Street, Northport, NY 11768, Tel: (800) 553-4939, Fax: (516) 261-9606.

MONTSERRAT

Introduction

MONTSERRAT, known as "the Emerald Isle", is pear-shaped and has a land area of 39 square miles. About 11 miles long and 7 miles wide, its nearest neighbours are Nevis, Guadeloupe and, 27 miles to the northeast, Antigua, from where frequent short-hop flights connect Montserrat with longer-haul aircraft. Three mountain ranges dominate this green-clad island, the highest, the Soufrière Hills, rising to 3,002 feet above sea level at the summit of Mount Chance. Volcanic in origin, the island has active fumaroles and hot mineral springs. Villages, linked by good roads, mostly lie on the west coast of the island at the foot of the hills. The capital, Plymouth, has the best harbour. The second largest town on the island is Harris, which is on the east side, near the airport.

The population of 11,000 has not increased throughout this century, because of emigration and birth control. The vast majority of the people are of African descent, but recent years has seen the influx of white Americans, Canadians and Britons who have purchased retirement homes on the island. In consequence, local amenities like the excellent museum and many of the cultural activities are run by expatriate volunteers with money and time to spare. Montserratians are notable for their easy friendliness to visitors, speaking English flavoured by dialect and the odd Irish expression (see History). The island is quiet all year round but visitors in search of revels should aim for the festive Christmas season, although accommodation rates peak then. The high season, in common with much of the region, is from 15 December to mid-April.

In 1989, Montserrat was devastated by Hurricane Hugo, the first hurricane to strike the island for 61 years. No part of the island was untouched by the 150 mph winds as 400-year-old trees were uprooted, 95% of the housing stock was damaged or destroyed, agriculture was reduced to below subsistence level and even the 180-foot jetty at Plymouth harbour completely disappeared, causing problems for relief supplies. However, within a few months, all public utilities were restored to service and the remaining standing or injured trees were in leaf again. Much has still to be done, but for the visitor the island is back in working order, with restaurants, hotels and cafés open and sand back on the beaches. In December 1991 a Best Kept Village competition was fiercely fought, resulting in a splendid clean-up of all the villages. This is to be continued on a quarterly basis.

History

Columbus sighted Montserrat on 11 November 1493, naming it after an abbey of the same name in Spain, where the founder of the Jesuits, Ignacio de Loyola, experienced the vision which led to his forming that famous order of monks. At that time, a few Carib Indians lived on the island but by the middle of the seventeenth century they had disappeared. The Caribs named the island Alliouagana, which means "land of the prickly bush". Montserrat was eventually settled by the British Thomas Warner, who brought English

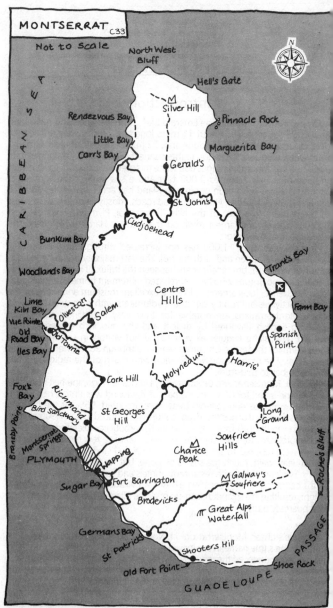

MONTSERRAT C33

Not to scale

and Irish Catholics from their uneasy base in the Protestant island of St Kitts. Once established as an Irish-Catholic colony, the only one in the Caribbean, Catholic refugees fled there from persecution in Virginia and, following his victory at Drogheda in 1649, Cromwell sent some of his Irish political prisoners to Montserrat. An Irishman brought some of the first slaves to the island in 1651 and the economy became based on sugar. Slaves quickly outnumbered the original British indentured servants. A slave rebellion in 1768, appropriately enough on St Patrick's Day, led to all the rebels being executed and today they are celebrated as freedom fighters. Montserrat was invaded several times by the French during the seventeenth and eighteenth centuries, sometimes with assistance from the resident Irish, but the island returned to British control under the Treaty of Versailles (1783) and has remained a colony to this day.

The elections held in 1991 resulted in a resounding defeat for the Chief Minister, John Osborne. He failed to hold his seat and only one of the candidates of his People's Liberation Movement was elected and he won by only two votes. The National Development Party, previously considered the main Opposition Party also fared badly with only one candidate elected. One independent also won a seat. Success went to a new party founded by Reuben Theodore Meade called the National Progressive Party, which won four seats. Mr Meade became Chief Minister on 10 October amid general optimism that a new, young and dynamic team would secure improvements for the island.

Government

A British dependent territory, Montserrat has a representative government with a ministerial system. Queen Elizabeth II is Head of State and is represented by a resident Governor. The Government consists of a Legislative and an Executive Council, with elections being held every five years for membership in the former. The head of Government is called the Chief Minister; a Speaker presides over the seven-member Council of Representatives. As executive authority and head of the civil service, the Governor is responsible for defence, internal security and external affairs. A constitutional reform in 1989 added financial services to the Governor's powers and recognized Montserrat's right to self-determination. Montserratians continually discuss the pros and cons of opting for independence, but the official position is that economic independence must precede political independence, so colonial status may remain for many years to come.

The Economy

Tourism is the largest supplier of foreign exchange and the Government actively encourages investment in tourism projects. The influx of foreign residents in the 1980s saw a sharp rise in real estate deals and building construction with a parallel dependence on imports of capital and consumer goods. Gross domestic product grew rapidly at the end of the 1980s, expanding by 12.8% in 1988, although a slower rate was recorded in 1989 because of the devastation wreaked by Hurricane Hugo. 95% of the housing stock was totally or partially destroyed and overall damage was estimated at US$260m. Production and exports were disrupted, infrastructure severely damaged and the public sector's finances were hit by reduced income and greater expenditure demands. Tourist arrivals had been rising at an annual rate of about 7.5%, with earnings by nearly twice that rate, but even after strenuous efforts at rehabilitation only half the island's hotel capacity was available at the beginning of the 1989/90 winter season. Inflation rose because of shortages of all supplies, as stocks had been wiped out and food crops destroyed, while 100-150 people lost their jobs because of the temporary closure of the offshore American Medical School (now reopened on a smaller scale), hotels and retail businesses. However, the need for skilled construction workers forced a relaxation of work permit restrictions and contractors were brought in from Dominica and other islands.

The economy is still based on agriculture, although much of this is subsistence farming. Small scale commercial farming is being encouraged. An integrated cotton industry had been developing before the hurricane but the looms used for processing the fine Sea Island cotton were very badly damaged by Hugo. There is a small manufacturing sector (primarily electric and electronic components). In 1978 an offshore banking sector was set up, initially attracting little interest, but by 1987-88 showing rapid growth with the granting of 347 banking licences. However, no bank supervision was introduced and applicants were attracted mainly by the low cost of licences, the speed with which they were granted and the relatively few checks on ownership or accounts. Evidence of fraud on a large scale was investigated by Scotland Yard and the FBI in 1989; most banks were examined and all had their licences revoked after it became clear that they had been used for money laundering and fraud. The Government has now reorganised the banking industry and introduced new legislation for the sector to avoid a repetition of previous problems, providing for higher fees and greater supervision to generate foreign confidence.

Culture
The Irish influence can still be seen in national emblems. On arrival your passport is stamped with a green shamrock, the island's flag and crest show a woman, Erin of Irish legend, complete with her harp, and a carved shamrock adorns the gable of Government House. There are many Irish names, of both people and places, and the national dish, goat water stew, is supposedly based on a traditional Irish recipe. A popular local folk dance, the Bam-chick-lay resembles Irish step dances and musical bands may include a fife and a drum similar to the Irish bodhran.

The African heritage dominates, however, whether it be in Caribbean musical forms like calypso (the Montserratian Arrow is now an international superstar), steel bands or the costumed masqueraders who parade during the Christmas season. Another element in the African cultural heritage are the Jumbie Dancers, who combine dancing and healing. Only those who are intimate with the island and its inhabitants will be able to witness their ceremonies, though. Local choirs, like the long-established Emerald Isle Community Singers, mix calypso with traditional folk songs and spirituals in their repertoire, and the String Bands of the island play the African shak-shak made from a calabash gourd, as well as the imported Hawaiian ukelele.

There are drama and dance groups in Montserrat, which perform occasionally, and a single cinema, The Shamrock, in Plymouth. At the University Centre (the local education wing of the University of Continuing Studies) poetry readings and writing workshops are held. Paintings by local artists can be seen at the Montserrat Museum (National Trust), a restored sugar mill tower on Richmond Hill (open Wednesday and Sunday 1430-1700, entrance is free but donations accepted). The museum houses permanent exhibitions on three floors of Arawak and Carib artefacts found on the island, a complete collection of the attractive Montserratian stamps, newspaper cuttings, maps and prints. Lots of bits and pieces of geological, anthropological and historical interest. Worth a visit. George Martin's famed recording studios, the Air Studios, used to attract rock megastars such as Elton John, the Rolling Stones and Sting to the island, but the studios were closed after Hurricane Hugo.

Note: On Montserrat a Maroon is not a runaway slave but the local equivalent of "barn-raising", when everyone helps to build a house, lay a garden, etc.

Flora and Fauna

The island is lushly green, with natural vegetation confined mostly to the summits of hills, where elfin woodlands occur. At lower levels, fern groves are plentiful and lower still, cacti, sage bush and acacias. Flowers and fruit are typical of the Caribbean with many bay trees, from which bay oil (or rum) is distilled, the national tree, the mango and the national flower, the heliconia caribaea (known locally as "lobster claw"). Montserrat cannot boast many wild animals, although it shares the terrestrial frog, known as the mountain chicken, only with Dominica. Some thirty species of land birds breed on the island. At sunset many can be seen in the Fox's Bay Bird Sanctuary (see Excursions). Unique to Montserrat is the icterus oberi, a black and gold oriole named the national bird. Agoutis, bats and lizards. Including iguanas which can grow to over four feet in length, can all be found and tree frogs contribute to the island's "night-music".

Beaches and Watersports

Montserrat's beaches are volcanic "black" sand, which in reality means the sand may be a silvery grey or dark golden brown colour. The single white coral beach is at Rendezvous Bay in the north of the island, most easily reached by a boat from Old Road bay. The best beaches are Woodlands (with simple beach hut facilities) where you can safely swim through caves, Fox's Bay (nice beach but pebbly and rocky just offshore, snorkelling worthwhile at north end, shower provided in a tree in the car park), Emerald Isle (near the *Montserrat Springs Hotel*), Old Road (by the *Vue Pointe Hotel*) and Little Bay in the north. Two fledgling scuba dive operations are Dive Montserrat, Box 223, Plymouth, Tel/Fax: 8812, and Sea Wolf Diving School, Box 400, Plymouth, Tel: 6859. There are no dive shops and arrangements can be made by telephone only; they are as yet unproven and not so far endorsed by discriminating divers. If the dive boat is not operational you will have to persevere to get a dive. Yachting can be organized through the small Yacht Club at Wapping, outside Plymouth (temporary membership available), Sunfish racing every Sunday morning, or at *Vue Pointe*, which also has facilities for snorkelling and windsurfing. Danny's Watersports on Old Road beach, run by Danny Sweeney, offers boat trips (see also below, Rendezvous Bay), fishing trips (US$40/hour, maximum 3 fishermen), waterskiing (US$10), windsurfing (US$10/hour), snorkelling (EC$20/day), pedalos (US$10/hour) etc., Tel: 5645. For yacht charters on a trimaran, the *John Willie*, Captain Martin Haxby can be contacted through the *Vue Pointe Hotel* (US$45 pp with open bar), which can also provide picnics if ordered the previous night. The *Montserrat Springs Hotel* can also arrange yacht charters. There are two whirlpool baths, one with hot mineral spring water, at the *Montserrat Springs Hotel*, just north of Plymouth (Tel: 2481).

Other Sports

The Belham River Valley golf course (Tel: 5220) covers an area of nearly 100 acres and has eleven holes that can be played as two nine-hole courses. Beautiful location edged by flowering trees. Hazards include iguanas who sometimes take the balls mistaking them for eggs. Rates are EC$50/day, EC$250/week, full equipment rental EC$7.50. Well-maintained **tennis** courts exist at the *Vue Pointe Hotel*, Tel: 5211, where they are floodlit for night play, and at the *Montserrat Springs Hotel*, Tel: 2481. The Golf Club has two tennis courts which can be rented for EC$20. An enormously popular Annual Open Tournament is held in early March; entries open in October. **Cricket** is the national sport and played between February and July while football or soccer dominates sporting events during the last half of the year, both at Sturge Park. Basketball is becoming increasingly popular; so, too, volleyball, both played at Shamrock car park.

Festivals

Not surprisingly in the "Emerald Isle", St Patrick's Day (a national holiday) is celebrated on 17 March with a fund-raising dinner at St Patrick's Roman Catholic Cathedral in Plymouth, cricket matches are held, and concerts, dances and feasting at St Patrick's village. Another national knees-up is August Monday, connected to Emancipation Day on 1 August, but the island's main festival is the Christmas season, which starts around 12 December and continues through New Year's Day. Costumed masqueraders parade around the island in small bands, culminating in a Boxing Day competition in Plymouth's Sturges Park, where the finals of the calypso competition are also held. There is a queen show, a whole series of concerts (choirs and bands) and all the night clubs are in full swing. It's very small-scale and low-key compared with a carnival like Trinidad's, but great fun and visitors are made to feel welcome.

Plymouth

In the capital of **Plymouth** (population 2,500) there are a lot of very attractive old wooden buildings in a variety of ornate styles and colours. Luckily the older buildings suffered less damage during Hurricane Hugo than the newer ones, many of which were totally destroyed. You can tour the grounds of the Victorian Government House (week days, except Wednesdays, 1030-1200) but not the mansion itself, now closed to visitors, which houses a painting collection, antique furniture etc, on a green hill above Wapping Village. The older part of the house was all right after Hurricane Hugo, but the newer part was badly damaged. The gardens were back to their former glory in 1990. St Anthony's Anglican Church is white-walled, airy, with a wooden interior. On Parliament Street is the Lands and Surveys Department, with, upstairs, the National Trust. Here you can buy the Ordnance Survey map of Montserrat (1983, EC$15), which is recommended. Also on Parliament Street, in the Empire Building, is the Lloyds Shipping Agency (Llewellyn Wall), which has a notice up of shipping sailings, cargo only. The arrival of supplies is very important in Montserrat, where so much is imported. The town is well-kept and bustling, by a quiet harbour, and with an adequate range of restaurants, bars and gift shops. The local market is at its liveliest on Friday and Saturday. Outside festive seasons like Christmas there is little nightlife in Plymouth, most of the action is in the larger hotels or discos outside town.

Excursions

Montserrat is easy to explore as distances are short, roads good, and trails well-maintained. Ask at the tourist office about expeditions organized by the local hiking group (visitors welcome). House and garden tours are organized by the Rotary Club, in season contact the Rotary Club direct, but out of season call Gary Swanston, Tel: 2998 (home) or 2075 (work).

Little remains of the **Old Fort** on **St George's Hill** except some cannons and a recently restored powder magazine, but the site offers a commanding view over Plymouth and environs and it is very pleasant. More cannons and the ruins of a small fort are located at the **Bransby Point Fortification**, from where there are lovely views across the sea to Plymouth in one direction and Old Road Bay in the other (below the Point are two sandy beaches where the sea is a bit rough). The **Fox's Bay Bird Sanctuary** on the southwest coast is best visited after 1800, when egrets and other birds return to roost at sunset. This fifteen-acre mangrove swamp and woodland lies next to an excellent beach, so a full day can happily be spent in the area. Trails are marked.

Popular excursions and hikes south of Plymouth include Chances Peak, Galway's Plantation, Galway's Soufrière and the Great Alps Waterfall. From St Patrick's onwards, you will be pestered by guides offering their services and insisting that you will get lost without them. They are difficult to shake off. If you have a decent map, such as the Ordnance Survey map, you will be fine on your own. However, if you have children with you it may be worth hiring a surefooted, adult guide, who can assist them over gulleys and rivers, particularly at Galway's Soufrière and the Great Alps Waterfall. If you can be at the turn-off for **Chances Peak** by 0830, the Cable and Wireless engineers, who make the ascent twice a week, will probably take you half way up or you can drive up to where the track starts. It's a steep, hard, hot climb, with ropes along the way to pull you up; one to two hours from the end of the road to the top, go on a clear day for brilliant views all the way up. Legend has it that a mermaid lives in the shallow lake (more like a swamp) on top of the mountain. Take plenty of drinking water with you. The ruins of **Galway's Plantation** can be reached via a paved road south out of Plymouth, which turns east at St Patrick's. This 18th-century sugar estate is the subject of an ambitious archaeological project which has identified the various stone buildings like the Great House on one side of the road, the tower mill and the boiling house on the other (entrance free). The ruins are in quite a good state of repair and are in a lovely location with the peaks above and sea views below. If you continue up the road you reach **Galway's Soufrière**. From a lookout point where you get a general view, a path leads steeply down to the bubbling, sulphurous, steaming, stinking vents and springs. The path is not difficult, although it can be a bit of a scramble in places, but if you want, a guide will take you for EC$20. Guides will also take you to the Bamboo Forest in the southern mountains, a 1½ hour walk from the car park at Galway's Soufrière, EC$100 for two people. Another soufrière, Gages, is no longer accessible; visitors have been prohibited since the path was destroyed in an earthquake. On the other side of the island, a trail to the ruins of Roche's Estate has been reopened but this hike involves negotiating Mefraimie Ghaut and should be attempted only by the reasonably fit. Joemac of Long Ground (Tel: 4468) is very responsible and will advise on the state of the trail and provide a guide if required.

The **Great Alps Waterfall** is seventy feet high and reached by a woodland trail that takes about forty-five minutes to walk. From St Patrick's, drive along the coast to the White River. Just before the bridge over the river turn left towards a small hut (which sells drinks when open) and a small car park by a tree where guides congregate. Continue on foot on the track out of the car park. Cross the stream, pass a big cashew tree and a little further on is a path going left through thorn scrub, goats etc. It is an easy path to follow, crossing and recrossing the White River (a misnomer, it is yellow ochre from the sulphur in the mountains from which it springs). After a short while you get into a more enclosed, wooded ascent up the river which is cooler and more green and tropical. The waterfall drops down a sheer cliff into a small pool. Take a sulphurous shower, have a picnic, take your litter home. Guide rates are EC$15 for one person, EC$10 pp for two, less for more.

A drive along the dramatic cliffs of the north coast is a must. Going northwards from Plymouth along the west side you come to **Carr's Bay** (bus from Plymouth EC$3), from where there is a little road which goes on to **Little Bay**, but it is in very bad condition and it is best to walk round Potato Hill from Carr's Bay. There are plans for a large tourist resort to be built at Little Bay, where there is a nice beach, but at the moment it is completely empty. From Little Bay you can follow a track through a gate at the end of the beach for a stiff hike along a very steep mountainous trail (not suitable for children) to the white sands of **Rendezvous Bay**. Take food and water, it is a long, hot walk. Alternatively, take a boat. Murphy's at the junction in Carr's Bay, offers boat rides to Rendezvous Bay for EC$50 for two people, while Danny's at Old Road Bay by the *Vue Pointe Hotel* charges US$20 pp in a Boston Whaler, returning to pick you up whenever you wish. Two-hour sails are also on offer, but you will not get as far as Rendezvous Bay and back. Rendezvous Bay is the only white sand beach on the island and it is worth making the effort to go there. There is little shade, so take precautions. Also watch out for the spiney sea urchins among the rocks at the north end and avoid the poisonous manchineel trees.

Driving round the north of the island is twisty and steep in places but the road is good on the main route. From the Carr's Bay area you can see Redonda and beyond to Nevis; from the northeast you can see Antigua and from the east Guadeloupe is just visible. There is a good view of the airport as you come round the northeast coast and you can watch the small planes landing below you. Turning off the road before you get to Harris and continuing south you come to Tuitt's, where Mr Green has a monument which is a nice place to visit for a picnic. Tel: 2494 and ask for Mistress Green for opening hours. Just the other side of Harris is Farrell's Estate, which used to be the main rum producer and made a 150° proof rum called 'Plastic'. However, the estate was bought some time ago by a US missionary who stopped sugar production and instead reared cattle.

Day excursions are offered by Montserrat Airways (Tel: 2713/4 or UK Tel: 0279 680144) who do charters on request (see below). Charters can also be arranged by Carib Aviation from Antigua throughout the Caribbean Tel: Antigua 3147, Fax: 3125.

The sites of Montserrat can be explored in two or three days, but such speed would force visitors to neglect the gentle charms of the island which can best be appreciated by leisurely strolls and unhurried meals, swimming, and encounters with the delightful local people.

Information for Visitors

Documents

A valid passport is required except for US visitors, who must only show proof of citizenship for stays of up to six months. Those without an onward or return ticket may be required to deposit a sum of money adequate for repatriation.

How To Get There

By air Blackburne Airport, on the east

coast some eleven miles from Plymouth, has recently been expanded and has night landing facilities. LIAT provides several flights daily from Antigua (an 18-minute hop), where there are direct connections with international carriers like British Airways, BWIA, Air Canada and various American airlines. LIAT also has a daily flight from St Thomas, via Sint Maarten and St Kitts. There are connections with other islands via LIAT, the charter companies, Carib Aviation (see above) or Montserrat Airways (Tel: 2713 at Carib World Travel or UK Tel: 0279 680144, Fax: 0279 680356), who have 9-seater planes with prices ranging from US$275 to Antigua (15 minutes) or Nevis (20 minutes) to US$2,595 to Trinidad (3 hours). A day trip to Montserrat from Antigua costs from EC$100 return.

By sea The Atlantic Lines, Harrison Line and Nedlloyd provide regular services to the port at Plymouth. If you enquire at a shipping agent in Plymouth you may be able to arrange passage on the cargo boat which goes to Guadeloupe, but this is difficult. Arriving yachtsmen have criticized Customs at the harbour for being very unfriendly and high-handed. The jetty was washed away in the 1989 hurricane and a barge moored offshore is being used for offloading supplies etc, for the moment while a decision is made over what to do.

There is a departure tax of EC$15/US$6 for all aged 12 and over.

Internal Travel

Driving is on the left. Roads are fairly good, but narrow. Drivers travel fast, passing on blind corners with much use of their horns. There are several **car hire** companies (the cars are mostly Japanese). Car hire rates are similar in all agencies: Montserrat Enterprises in Marine Drive, Tel: 2431, hires out small cars for US$45/day or US$210/week, US$230/week with air conditioning, jeeps for US$50/day or US$40 for 2-6 days; NBA car rentals in Lime Court Building, Parliament Street, Tel: 2070; Jefferson's Car Rental, Dagenham, Tel: 2126; Ethelyne's Car Rentals, Weekes Road, Tel: 2855; Pauline's Car Rental, Amersham, Tel: 2345; Budget Rent a Car, Lovers Lane, Tel: 6065. You have to pay for half a tank of petrol and usually accept liability up to EC$2,000. With a valid driving licence, you can obtain a local three-month licence (EC$30) at the airport immigration desk or the police traffic office in Plymouth (open from 0900-1200 on

Wednesday, otherwise weekdays from 0900-1300). The standard fare in **minibuses** is EC$2-3. Some mini-buses to villages in the north leave from Papa's Supermarket on Church Road, those to the east go from the end of Evergreen Road and those to the south depart from opposite the Royal Bank of Canada on George Street. As a general rule, buses run into town in the morning with an immediate return to source, doing the trip about four times a day. Outside the fixed times and routes they operate as taxis and journeys can be arranged with drivers for an extra fee. **Taxis** are usually small buses, which can be shared and there is a taxi stand by the Clock Tower War Memorial at the harbour. Fares are set—the tariff list can be obtained from the tourist office (see address below), eg airport to Plymouth EC$29, Plymouth to *Vue Pointe Hotel* EC$13; a sightseeing tour is EC$39 per hour. Drivers are usually knowledgeable about historical sites and are happy to wait while passengers hike to beauty spots, or return at an appointed time. Fares from Plymouth to the Great Alps Waterfall EC$60 return, to Galways Soufrière EC$60 return, to St George's Hill EC$21, including waiting and return. John Ryner is recommended, Tel: 2190.

For the fit, hire a mountain bike from Island Bikes of Harney Street, Plymouth, Tel: 4696, prices start at EC$280 per week, EC$54 per day or EC$11 per hour.

Hitching is safe and easy because the local people are so friendly. Similarly, don't be afraid to pick them up when you are driving. Out-of-town hotels like the *Vue Pointe* provide a free bus service into the capital for their staff, phone Carol Osborne at the hotel to see if there is space.

Where To Stay

There are only a couple of large hotels and a handful of guesthouses. Most tourism is accommodated in villas and apartments and resort developments have not yet arrived on the island. By far the most welcoming of the large hotels and the centre of social activities for the island is the *Vue Pointe* (PO Box 65; Tel: 5210/5711, Fax: 4813) which charges from US$126 for a double, EP, to US$166 for a rondavel (small cottage), falling to US$70d and US$95d (children under 12 sharing with two adults free) in summer, 10 rooms have a/c, conference facilities, swimming pool, tennis courts, free transport to Plymouth, UK representative Kathy and Brian Coombes, Garway Mill, Garway, Herefordshire, HR2 8RL, Tel: 060 084683, Fax: 060 084470. *Montserrat Springs Hotel* (PO Box 259, Tel: 2481, Fax: 4070), the other large hotel, was completely refurbished after Hurricane Hugo with 46 a/c rooms to a high standard, US$140-160d winter, one-bedroomed efficiency suites US$200-210 winter, six two-bedroomed suites US$310-325 winter, 20-30% cheaper in summer. *Oriole Plaza Hotel*, PO Box 250, Parliament Street, Tel: 6982/6985, Fax: 6690, almost opposite the Land Survey Department, constructed and extended from the old *Wade Inn*, US$65-85d winter, US$50-65 summer, EP, TV, fans; *Flora Fountain* (PO Box 373, Tel: 6092/3, Fax: 2568) on Lower Dagenham Road, 18 rooms, a/c, private bathrooms and balconies, US$85d winter, US$70 summer, EP. In Kinsale, *Niggy's Bistro* offers simple accommodation from US$15 single and US$20 double, small, spartan rooms, two on either side of bar, shared bathrooms, pleasant, friendly, but no peace and quiet, run by Anglo Americans Tony and Niggy Overman, Tel: 7489/2690, Fax: 3257; *Marie's Guesthouse*, run by Marie and Austin Bramble, Tel: 2745, close to the road and downwind of the power plant but any noise drowned by frogs at night, EC$30d, double or single beds, bathroom, lots of towels, large, shared kitchen with starter food pack, friendly, welcoming, highly recommended.

The Department of Tourism has a complete list of other smaller establishments, apartments and rooms to let, with some nine agencies renting and selling apartments and villas. Montserrat Enterprises, PO Box 58, Plymouth, Tel: 2431, Fax: 3257, has an extensive list of pleasant villas to rent, average price for one or two-bedroomed villa with pool, US$350-400 low season, but the same property rents for US$450-550 in winter. Jacquie Ryan Enterprises Ltd, PO Box 425, Plymouth, Tel: 2055, Fax: 3257, villas available at similar rates. Neville Bradshaw Agencies, PO Box 270, Plymouth, Tel: 5270, Fax: 5069 has two-bedroomed properties from US$325 in summer. Villas of Montserrat, PO Box 421, Plymouth, Tel: 5513, have some very grand properties at US$1,650 in summer and US$1,950 in winter for six people or less, including private charter from Antigua. Of two

residential developments in Montserrat Wood Realtors, Woodville, Tel: 5119, Fa 5230, offer one-three-bedroome properties to purchase from US$75,00 and also rentals on a weekly or month basis. The other residential developme Isles Bay Plantation offers rental of two its properties to give potential purchase a taste of elegant living; prices to purchas start at US$245,000 and rentals US$1,50 low season and US$2,000 high season p week. They all have 40-foot pools, Te 4842, Fax: 4843, UK: 071 482 1418, Fa 071 482 1071. Agencies usually includ maid service most days. For cheape self-catering accommodation withou maid service, *Lime Court Apartments* Plymouth, PO Box 250, Tel: 3656, a sometimes vacant, one an two-bedroomed apartments with balcor overlooking the sea, rather noisy, roo dark but clean, about US$30 a day plus ta or US$150-225 a week with monthly c long term rates available.

There is a 7% Government tax on MA rates, regardless of which meal plan chosen, and a 10% service charge usually added.

Where To Eat

A large frog called mountain chicke indigenous here and in Dominica, is th local delicacy; that and goat water ste are the most commonly found local item on the menu; most other things, like stea and sole are imported. The *Belham Valle* (PO Box 420, Tel: 5553), which also ha four apartments to rent, quite elegan reservations required, lunch 1200-140(Tuesday-Friday, dinner from 183(Tuesday-Sunday. On Wednesday night the place to go is the *Vue Pointe Hote* Tel: 5210, for a barbecue and steel banc food served from 1930, EC$66 set pric includes all the salad and sweets you ca eat, EC$33 for children if they eat chicke drinks extra, food good, band from 210 less impressive. A Sunday lunchtim barbecue is US$35 in summer an US$38.50 in winter, half price for childre under 10. *The Nest* at Old Road Bay, fo sandwiches from EC$8, roti: EC$8.5(Caesar salad EC$11, excellent menu quiet, pleasant, 1030-2000 every da except Monday, Tel: 5834. Local cuisin can be found in several Plymout restaurants: the *Emerald Café*, a meal fo two with wine US$52, pleasan reasonable; the *Evergreen*, Tel: 3514, fa food and pastries; the *Attic*. In nearb

Wapping the *Yacht Club*, Tel: 2237, open Tuesday-Friday for lunch and dinner for non-members, music Fridays from 2200, EC$3 cover charge; the *Oasis*, Tel: 2528, Wapping Road, open daily 1000-2400, British-run, meal for two with wine EC$100, basic food; the *Iguana*, meal for two with wine EC$140, very good, also pizzas, recommended; *The Casuarina*, bar and restaurant, continental and Chinese food, very popular Friday evenings with students from medical school. Also in Wapping are bars such as *The Inn on Sugar Bay*, a restaurant/bay/nightclub with live music twice a week. A must is *Annie Morgan's* at St John's for goat water, open Friday and Saturday at lunchtime, other days by arrangement if you can arrange a party of ten or so, Tel: 5419. *Niggy's Bistro* in Kinsale, Tel: 7489, bar indoors, restaurant seating on the porch, steak or pasta and salad from EC$15, wine from EC$25 a bottle, food and service highly recommended, recorded jazz and blues music drowned out on Friday and Saturday by Champion Sound down the road. *Andy's Village Place*, Tel: 5202, in the pretty hamlet of Salem is famous for its chicken, prepared in gregarious proprietor Andy's special sauce. A night club with food is the *Nepcoden* in Weekes, which serves excellent rotis.

Tipping
10% service charge is usually added to bills. Taxi drivers happily accept a tip but there is no pressure to offer one.

Shopping
Wednesday is half day closing. Sea Island cotton or goods manufactured from this pricey but soft, comfortable fabric; tapestries and wall hangings by local artists; glass and ceramics produced at a studio in Olveston; leather goods from locally-tanned leather; small but delightful range of post cards of naive paintings. The Sea Island Cotton shop has very little in stock, one loom has been repaired following Hugo damage to make table cloths, mats, shawls etc. Montserrat Tapestries sells hand woven items. Montserrat Shirts has masses of T-shirts in attractive designs for all ages. Montserrat's beautiful stamps can be bought at the Post Office or at the Philatelic Bureau (sold from the basement of the building by Fort Ghaut, which was damaged by Hugo). Ram's Supermarket in Plymouth on the road to the airport, probably the best stocked and good for currency exchange. Supermarkets stock a variety of expensive imported food and drink to cater for the

demands of the growing expat population, but the choice is fairly limited. Shamrock supermarket on Marine Drive is open on Wednesdays when others are not. Captain Weekes supermarket on the road out of town going south has a good supply of drink but poor stocks of provisions. Peter & Christina's, a 24-hour bakery on George Street, beyond the Catholic Church on the way to the airport, sells excellent and varied breads and pasties, recommended. Just before you get there, on the outskirts of town, a green painted house on your left sells home made ice cream in tropical fruit flavours. The local ginger beer is delicious.

Cost Of Living
Middle to upmarket prices, generally speaking, so it is not an island for back-packers and impecunious young people, although cheap accommodation can be found in private homes and guest houses and eating out can be reasonably priced if you stick to local foods and drink. It's cheap and easy to get around on local minibuses or by hitching.

Currency
The currency is the East Caribbean dollar (EC$). The exchange rate varies from EC$2.53 = US$1 to a high of EC$2.67 at Royal Bank of Canada.

Health
With its bracing climate and clean, plentiful water, Montserrat is a healthy island. Glendon Hospital in Plymouth, with 68 beds, also offers a range of services but for specialist treatment patients are sent to larger centres in the region. There is a government health service and also private practitioners. During the rainy season there are mosquitoes and "no-see-um's", but a good anti-bug repellent should suffice. Rooms that lack air-conditioning often provide mosquito nets for beds. No poisonous snakes or insects.

Climate
Although tropical, the humidity in Montserrat is low and there is often rain overnight which clears the atmosphere. The average temperature is 26-27°C with little variation from one season to another. The wettest months, according to official statistics, are April and May plus July through September, although weather patterns are changing here, as elsewhere.

Clothing
The island is not a formal place, but skimpy clothing on the streets of Plymouth and

nude or topless bathing are frowned upon. Informal, lightweight clothes are suitable for virtually every occasion but evenings can be cool and require jackets, wraps or sweaters. There is a laundromat with dry cleaning facilities on Church Road.

Banks

There are two international banks: The Royal Bank of Canada on Parliament Street (open Monday-Thursday 0800-1500, Friday 0800-1700), and Barclays Bank on Church Road. The Bank of Montserrat on Parliament Street is open Monday, Tuesday, Thursday 0800-1500, Wednesday 0800-1300, Friday 0800-1700, avoid Saturday 0930-1230.

Hours Of Business

Government: 0800-1200; 1300-1600 (Monday-Friday); Business 0800-1200; 1300-1600 except Wednesday, 0800-1300, Saturday 0800-1200, 1300-1530 (or 0800-1300).

National Holidays

New Year's Day, St Patrick's Day (17 March), Good Friday, Easter Monday, Labour Day (2 May), Whit Monday (seventh Monday after Easter), first Monday in August, Christmas Day, Boxing Day (26 December) and Festival Day (31 December).

Time Zone

Atlantic Standard Time, 4 hours behind GMT, 1 ahead of EST.

Electric Current

Electric current is 220 volts, 60 cycles but newer buildings also carry 110 volts.

Postal Services

The main Post Office is in Plymouth (open 0815-1555 Monday, Tuesday, Thursday, Friday, but 0815-1125 on Wednesday and Saturday) and there is a Philatelic Bureau, also in the capital, selling the attractive Montserrat stamps to collectors.

Telecommunications

Cable and Wireless (West Indies) Ltd operates an excellent telecommunication system with a new digital telephone system, international dialling, telegraph, telex, facsimile and data facilities. The international code for Montserrat is 809-491, followed by a four-digit number.

Media

Antilles TV is not yet operational after Hugo although they hope to recommence sometime. Satellite TV Cable is operational in most areas, and stations broadcasting from nearby islands can be received. Radio Montserrat ZJB (government owned) provides daily broadcasting services, and does GEM Radio, the exclusive outlet for the Associated Press. Radio Antilles was expected to re-start in 1992 in conjunction with the BBC, who have a management contract. There is one weekly newspaper, the *Montserrat Reporter*.

Tourist Office

Montserrat Tourist Office, PO Box 7, Plymouth, Tel: 2230, Fax: 7430, on Church Road in the Government Headquarters building, helpful plenty of information. The Montserrat Chamber of Commerce complements the Tourist Office and offers a business directory, PO Box 384, Tel: 3640, Fax: 4660.

In the Macmillan series, *Montserrat Emerald Isle of the Caribbean*, by Howard A Fergus, has been recommended; also *Alliouagana Folk*, by J A George Irish (Jagpa, 1985), as an introduction to Montserratian language, proverbs and traditions.

We are grateful to Kathy Coombes, UK representitive for the *Vue Point Hotel* for her continued assistance with updating this chapter, and to Louis Fletcher (Providenciales) for additional information.

NETHERLAND ANTILLES
The 3 S's

Introduction

THE "3 S's", Saba, Sint Eustatius (Statia) and Sint Maarten lie 880 km north of the rest of the Netherlands Antilles group lying off the coast of Venezuela, and known as the ABC islands (Aruba, Bonaire and Curaçao). Each has a distinct character and flavour, Statia being the poorest, Saba the smallest and Sint Maarten the most developed and richest. Lacking in natural resources, they each depend to a greater or lesser degree on tourism for their foreign exchange revenues, but are developing their potential in different ways. Saba's strength is the richness of the underwater world surrounding the island and is noted for its pristine diving locations. Sint Maarten has the best beaches and resorts, while St Eustatius is promoting its historical associations.

   Although the "3 S's" precede the ABC islands in this Handbook, the introduction to the Netherlands Antilles group and much of the general Information for Visitors is contained in the ABC chapter.

SABA

SABA, pronounced "Say-bah", is the smallest of this group of islands. Only five miles square, it lies 28 miles south of St Maarten and 17 miles northwest of St Eustatius. The island is an extinct volcano which seems to shoot out of the sea, green with lush vegetation but without beaches. In fact there is only one inlet amidst the sheer cliffs where boats can come in to dock. The highest peak of this rugged island is the 870-metre Mount Scenery, also known as "the Mountain", and because of the difficult terrain there were no roads on Saba until 1943, only hand-carved steps in the volcanic rock.

Although the island was once inhabited by Caribs, relics of whom have been found, there is no trace of their ancestry in the local inhabitants. The population numbers about 1,100, half of them white (descendants of Dutch, English and Scots settlers) and half black. Their physical isolation and the difficult terrain has caused them to develop their ingenuity to enable them to live harmoniously with their environment. Originally farmers and seafarers, the construction in 1963 of the Juancho E Yrausquin Airport on the only flat part of the island, and the serpentine road which connects it tenuously to the rest of the island, brought a new and more lucrative source of income: tourism. However, the island's geographical limitations have meant that tourism has evolved in a small, intimate way. About 25,000 tourists visit each year, most of whom are day trippers. Those who stay are few enough to get to know the friendliness and hospitality of their hosts, who all speak English, even though Dutch is the official language. Development is small scale; the island still merits its unofficial title, "the Unspoiled Queen".

History

Saba was first discovered by Columbus on his second voyage in 1493 but not colonized. Sir Francis Drake sighted it in 1595, as did the Dutchmen Pieter Schouten in 1624 and Piet Heyn in 1626. Some shipwrecked Englishmen landed in 1632, finding it uninhabited. In 1635 the French claimed it but in the 1640s the Dutch settled it, building communities at Tent Bay and The Bottom. However, it was not until 1816 that the island became definitively Dutch, the interregnum being marked by 12 changes in sovereignty, with the English, Dutch, French and Spanish all claiming possession.

Diving and Marine Life

The waters around Saba became a Marine Park in 1987 and 36 permanent mooring buoys have been provided for dive boats. Spearfishing is prohibited, as is the removal of coral or shells. Diving tourism has increased rapidly; scuba divers and snorkellers visit the Marine Park which is noted for its "virginity". Saba has no beaches so diving and snorkelling is from boats, mostly along the calmer southern and west coasts. The west coast from Tent Bay to Ladder Bay, together with Man of War shoals, Diamond Rock and the sea offshore comprise the main dive sites, where line, trap, and spearfishing are prohibited. From Ladder Bay to Torrens Point is an all-purpose recreational zone which includes Saba's only beach, a pebbly stretch of coast with shallow water for swimming and areas for diving, fishing, and boat anchorage. Another anchorage is west of Fort Bay. East of Fort Bay along the south, east and north coast to Torrens Point is a multiple use zone where fishing and diving are permitted. Some of the most visited dive sites are Third Encounter, Outer Limits, Diamond Rock and Man of War. Ladder Labyrinth is a dive site which is good for snorkelling. Seven dive operators have been granted permits and they collect the mandatory visitor fees to help maintain the Park. A guide to the dive sites by Tom Van't Hof went to press in 1991. Saba now has a four-person recompression chamber, donated by the Royal Netherlands Navy, which is administered through the Marine Park but operated by volunteers. Summer visibility is 75-100 feet with water temperatures of about 86°F, while winter visibility increases to 125 feet and water temperatures fall to 75°F. Saba's rugged, volcanic terrain is replicated underwater where there are mountains, caves, lava flows, overhangs, reefs, walls, pinnacles and elkhorn coral forests.

Not much fishing is done in these waters, so there is a wide range of sizes

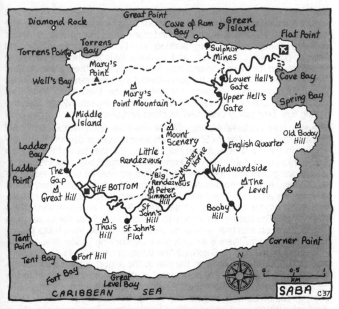

and varieties of fish to be seen. Tarpon and barracuda of up to eight feet are common, as are giant sea turtles. From February to April humpback whales pass by on their migration south, while in the winter dive boats are often accompanied by schools of porpoises. Smaller, tropical fish are not in short supply and together with bright red, orange, yellow and purple giant tube sponges and different coloured coral, are a photographer's delight.

There are three dive shops on Saba. Saba Deep at Fort bay, near the pier, run by Adrienne Gonia and Mike Myers Tel/Fax: 63347, has NAUI and PADI instructors and offers a resort course with instruction in the swimming pool at *Captain's Quarters*. They have three 25-foot boats but take out no more than eight in a group. A two-tank dive costs US$60. Saba Deep also offers a sunset cruise round the island, which takes about an hour, and full day excursions to nearby islands. Sea Saba Dive Centre at Windwardside, Tel: 62246, Fax: 62237, has two boats, one which can take groups of 14 and one which carries only eight. A two-tank dive costs US$65. Run by Joan and Louis Bourque, who are both PADI instructors, they also offer introductory and five-day certification courses, fishing and other non-diving excursions. They have a 40-foot cabin boat for 15 divers or a 36-foot boat for 10 divers. Wilson's Dive Shop at Fort Bay Pier has three boats taking a maximum of five divers each, US$60 including all equipment, even skins, for a two-tank dive. There are also two live-aboard boats: the *Sea Dancer* (Peter Hughes Diving), Tel: 800-367-3484 and the *Caribbean Explorer*, Tel: 800-322-3577, which offer week-long trips for serious divers, usually starting in St Maarten and spending much of their time in Saban waters.

Walking

Before the road was built people got about Saba by donkey or on foot and there are still numerous steep trails and stone steps linking villages which make strenuous, yet satisfying, walking. The Conservation Foundation of Saba is preserving, upgrading and marking trails for those who like a challenge and for those who prefer a gentle stroll. All of them are accessible from the road and many can be done without a guide. Named trails include: Tent Point, Booby Hill, The Level, The Boiling House, The Sulphur Mine, The Ladder, Giles Quarter, Rendezvous, Crispeen, Bottom Hill, Mount Scenery, Spring Bay, Troy, Sandy Cruz, Middle Island and Mary's Point.

The most spectacular hike is probably the one from Windwardside up 1,064 steps to the crest of Mount Scenery, best done on a clear day otherwise you end up in the clouds. It is a hard slog, but a road goes part of the way up and drinks are available where it ends. The summit is a disappointment, it is very overgrown and needs clearing before you will be able to see down to Windwardside. Take a sweater and waterproof jacket, it can be very rough and slippery after rain. There are lots of birds and the botanical changes are noticeable as you climb. You can get out of the rain in several shelters on the way up. The Ladder is a long path of stone steps from the shore up to The Bottom, up which all provisions used to be hauled from boats before the road was built. There is a picnic place overlooking Ladder Bay. A guide is recommended for the Sulphur Mine track; at Lower Hell's Gate, about halfway up the sharp bends on the way to the airport, a track north of the road leads to the cliffs of the north coast, with splendid scenery, and to the remains of the old sulphur mines. A very nice lookout point is from Bobby Hills, up the 66 terraced steps to the Bobby Hill Peak. If you want a guide, Bernard Johnson, who works in the *Chinese Family Restaurant* at night, is knowledgeable. A botanical tour can be arranged with Anna Keene, of Saba Botanico at Weaver's Cottage, Under the Hill in Windwardside, who can help you find orchids, philodendron, heliconias, ferns, begonias and other plants native to tropical rainforests or dry bushlands; highly recommended, she can also be reached through the Saba Tourist Office.

Other Sports

There is a **tennis** court (concrete) at the Sunny Valley Youth Centre in The Bottom which is open to the public. Basket ball and volley ball matches are held, contact the Tourist Office for a schedule.

Excursions

There are four picture book villages on Saba, connected by a single spectacular 6½ mile road which begins at the airport and ends at the pier. The road itself is a feat of engineering, designed and built by Josephus Lambert Hassell in the 1940s, who studied road construction by correspondence course after Dutch engineers said it was impossible to build a road on Saba. From the airport, the road rises to **Hell's Gate** and then on through banana plantations to **Windwardside**, a walk of 20-30 minutes, where most of the hotels and shops are situated. There is a small museum, a bank, post office and the Tourist Office is here. On the first Sunday in each month, a 'happening' is held in the grounds of the Harry L Johnson Museum. Everyone dresses in white (including visitors), plays croquet and drinks mimosas. The museum was a sea captain's house and dates from the 1890's. It is filled with antique furniture and family memorabilia. Open 1000-1200

1300-1530, Monday-Friday. The road goes on past Kate's Hill, Peter Simon's Hill and Big Rendezvous to **St John's**, which has a wonderful view of St Eustatius, then climbs over the mountain and drops sharply down to **The Bottom**, the island's seat of government, with a population of 350. The Bottom is on a plateau 800 feet above the sea, and gets its name from the Dutch words "*de botte*", meaning "the bowl". Leaving The Bottom, the road makes its final descent to **Fort Bay**, where small cruise ships, yachts and the ferry from St Maarten arrive at the 277-foot pier. Most of the houses on the island are painted white with red roofs and some have green shutters. There are watercolour workshops for those who find the scenery picturesque.

Information for Visitors

Documents
See main Netherlands Antilles section under Curaçao Information for Visitors. Saba is a free port so there are no customs formalities.

How To Get There
The landing strip is only 1,312 feet long, so large aircraft cannot yet be accommodated although there are plans to build a longer runway. Planes do not land in bad weather in case they skid off the end. Winair (Tel: 62255) has up to five daily 20-seater flights from St Maarten (20 minutes/US$50 return) and one or two from St Eustatius. It is essential to reconfirm your return flight. Saba can also be reached by boat, *Style* (50 passengers), from St Maarten, three times a week in 1992 but schedules change, 90 minutes, US$50 round trip, plus departure tax, details from Great Bay Marina, St Maarten, Tel: 22167. A deep water pier at Fort Bay allows cruise ships to call. Airport departure tax is US$1 to Netherlands Antilles, US$5 elsewhere.

Local Transport
There are no buses. There are taxis at the airport and a few others on the island. Airport to Hell's Gate, US$4; to Windwardside, US$6; to The Bottom, US$9; Hell's Gate to Windwardside, US$4. Taxis can be hired for tours round the island (US$30-35) and the drivers are knowledgeable guides. Some are also fishermen or hotel owners, so they can be valuable contacts. You can hire a jeep or car from Avis, Windwardside, for about US$30-35 a day, Tel: 2279. Drive on the right. Hitchhiking is safe, very easy and a common means of getting about.

Where To Stay
There are no resort hotels on Saba and even the most expensive are small and friendly. There is a 5% room tax and usually a 10%-15% service charge.
Windwardside: *Captain's Quarters*,

US$125d winter, US$95d summer, CP, Tel: 62201, Fax: 62377, best known and largest with 10 rooms, is a handsomely decorated restored sea captain's house, with a pool; *Juliana's Apartments*, US$95d winter, US$75d summer, for room with bath, or US$100d winter, US$80d summer for Flossie's cottage, or US$100 winter, US$75 summer for 2½ room apartment, Tel: 62269, Fax: 62389, the facilities of *Captain's Quarters* are available for guests; *Scout's Place*, US$65-85d, with breakfast, Tel: 62205, Fax: 62388, former government guest house, simple, relaxed, service has been criticized.
The Bottom: *Cranston's Antique Inn*, US$57.50 all year, Tel: 63218, 130-year old inn, some four poster beds, restaurant; *Caribe Guesthouse*, clean comfortable, no frills, five rooms, kitchen available, US$45 all year, Tel: 63261.
Hells Gate: *Sharon's Ocean View*, US$55d, two rooms with bath and balcony, Tel: 62238, overlooking airport, pool, owner has taxi and Colombian wife, very helpful, recommended.

The Tourist Office has a list of one-two bedroom cottages and apartments for rent from US$40-1,000 a night, which can be let on a weekly or monthly basis, and can also provide hotel rates. Saba Real Estate, PO Box 17, Saba, Tel/Fax: 62299, manages property rentals, from one bedroom apartments to luxury four bedroom villa.

Where To Eat
At *Scout's Place*, dinner is at 1930, reservations needed, slow service; the *Saba Chinese Restaurant* (open 1100-2200, closed Monday) and the *Chinese Family Restaurant* serve Cantonese food, both in Windwardside, the one higher up the hill has good food, and *Cranston's Antique Inn* has Chinese and native dishes; *Guido's Italian Restaurant*, for pizzas and burgers;

Captain's Quarters for more elegant dining, food average, reservations recommended. In Hells Gate: *Sharon's Ocean View Bar*, good view, fresh fish, reservations needed. In The Bottom: native specialities at *Lime Time* and *Queenie's Serving Spoon*.

Nightlife
Most of the nightlife takes place at the restaurants. At weekends there are sometimes barbecues, steel bands and dances. Weekend movies are held at the Royal Theatre. Generally, though, the island is quiet at night.

Shopping
Shops open 0900-1200, 1400-1800. Local crafts have been developed by the Saba Artisan Foundation in The Bottom and include dolls, books and silk-screened textiles and clothing. The typical local, drawn-thread work "Saba Lace" (also known as "Spanish Work" because it was learned by a Saban woman in a Spanish convent in Venezuela at the end of the last century) is sold at several shops on the island. Each artisan has his or her own style. Taxi drivers may make unofficial stops at the houses where Saba lace, dolls, pillows etc are made. Saba Spice is the local rum, very strong (150° proof) and mixed with spices, sugar and orange peel.

Banks
Barclays Bank, Windwardside, Tel: 62216, open 0830-1230, Monday-Friday. The florin or guilder is the local currency, but US dollars are accepted everywhere. Hotels and dive shops accept credit cards, but no one else does.

Climate
The average temperature is 78°-82°F during the day but at night it can fall to the low 60's. The higher up you get, the cooler it will be; so take a jersey, if hiking up the mountain. Average annual rainfall is 42 inches.

National Holidays
New Year's Day, Good Friday, Easter Monday, Queen's Birthday (30 April), Labour Day (1 May), Ascension Day, Saba Day (7-8 December), Christmas Day, Boxing Day. Carnival is a week in July and is celebrated with jump-ups, music and costumed dancing shows, games and contests including the Saba Hill Climb. The first weekend in December is Saba Day, when donkey races are held, with dancing and other festivities.

Time Zone
Atlantic Standard Time, 4 hours behind GMT, 1 ahead of EST.

Electric Current
110 volts AC, 60 cycles.

Communications
Most hotels have direct dialling worldwide, otherwise overseas calls can be made from The Bottom. The international code for Saba is 599-4 followed by a five digit number.

Churches
There are four churches: Anglican, Roman Catholic, Wesleyan Holiness and Seventh Day Adventist.

Tourist Office
The Saba Tourist Board is in Windwardside, Tel: 62231. In the USA, Saba Tourist Information Office, c/o Medhurst & Associates Inc, 271 Main Street, Northport, NY 11768, Tel: (800) 344-4606 or (516) 261-7474.

SINT EUSTATIUS

Introduction

ST EUSTATIUS, or STATIA, 35 miles south of St Maarten and 17 miles southeast of Saba, was originally settled by Caribs and evidence of their occupation dates back to AD300. The name Statia comes from St Anastasia, as it was named by Columbus, but the Dutch later changed it to Sint Eustatius. The island is dominated by the long-extinct volcano called "The Quill" at the southern end, inside which is a lush rainforest where the locals hunt land crabs at night. Visitors are advised, however, to go there only during the day. The northern part of the island is hilly and uninhabited; most people live in the central plain which surrounds the airport.

Statia is quiet and friendly and the poorest of the three Windward Islands, with only 1,800 people living on the eight square mile island. A variety of nationalities are represented, the island having changed hands 22 times in the past. Everybody speaks English, although Dutch is the official language and is taught in schools. The traditional economic activities of fishing, farming and trading have been augmented by an oil storage and refuelling facility, but the major hope for prosperity is tourism. Although over half of the 17,600 visitors in 1988 were cruiseship passengers, the number of longer stay arrivals is increasing steadily. Investment in airport expansion and a cruiseship pier is designed to increase capacity. Nevertheless, it remains the sort of place where you will be greeted by passers by and there is no crime.

History

Statia was sighted by Columbus on his second voyage but never settled by the Spanish. The Dutch first colonized it in 1636 and built Fort Oranje, but the island changed flag 22 times before finally remaining Dutch in 1816. The island reached a peak of prosperity in the 18th century, when the development of commerce brought about 8,000 people to the tiny island, over half of whom were slaves, and the number of ships visiting the port was around 3,500 a year. Trading in sugar, tobacco and cotton proved more profitable than trying to grow them and the slave trade was particularly lucrative, gaining the island the nickname of "The Golden Rock".

The island still celebrates 16 November 1776 when the cannons of Fort Oranje unknowingly fired the first official salute by a foreign nation to the American colours. At that time, Statia was a major trans-shipment point for arms and supplies to George Washington's troops, which were stored in the yellow ballast brick warehouses built all along the Bay and then taken by blockade runners to Boston, New York and Charleston. However, the salute brought retaliatory action from the English and in 1781 the port was taken without a shot being fired by troops under Admiral George Brydges Rodney, who captured 150 merchant ships and £5 million of booty before being expelled by the French the following year.

With continuing transfers of power, the economy never recovered, many merchants were banished and the population began a steady decline. The emancipation of slaves in 1863 brought an end to any surviving plantation

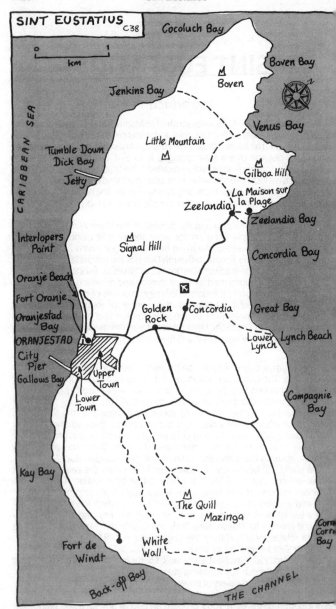

agriculture and the remaining inhabitants were reduced to subsistence farming and dependency upon remittances from relatives abroad. Prosperity has returned only recently with the advent of tourism and the island is still relatively underdeveloped.

Diving and Marine Life

Statia's waters offer a wonderful combination of coral reefs, marine life and historic shipwrecks, of which there are about 200 to explore. Water visibility is over 100 feet and snorkelling is also very good. There are 16 charted dive sites, at a depth of 20-80 feet. The Supermarket, half a mile off the coast from Lower Town at a depth of 60 feet, has two shipwrecks 150 feet apart with beautiful coral, red and purple sponges, shoals of fish, sea turtles and the rare flying gurnard. The Garden is another very beautiful reef with hundreds of fish of all kinds from the smallest wrass to large barracudas and extremely tame angel fish.

There are two dive shops on the island: Golden Rock Dive Centre, Tel: 82319, and Dive Statia, nearby, run by Judy and Mike Brown, Tel: 82435. Seven-night diving packages are arranged with the hotels, and it is possible to combine Saba and Statia for a diving, or non-diving package. In the USA, Tel: 800-468 1708.

Beaches and Watersports

Oranje Beach stretches for a mile along the coast away from Lower Town. The length and width of the beach varies according to the season and the weather, but being on the Leeward side it is safe for swimming and other watersports. Following Hurricane Hugo in 1989 much of the beach disappeared and only half a mile of black sand remained, running east from the hotels to the shipwreck in a rather inconsistent manner. On the Windward side are two fine beaches but there is a strong undertow and they are not considered safe for swimming. Zeelandia Beach is two miles of off-white sand with heavy surf and interesting beachcombing, particularly after a storm. It is safe to wade and splash about in the surf but not to swim. There is a short dirt road down to the beach just before you get to *Maison Sur La Plage*; do not drive too close to the beach or you will get stuck in the sand. Avoid the rocks at the end of the beach as they are very dangerous. The other beach on the Windward side is Lynch Beach, which is small and a bit safer for swimming as long as you do not go out very far and pay attention to the undertow. Drive past the airport terminal entrance for about 75 yards and turn right on to a dirt road. Go past the Agricultural Experiment Station, keeping right at intersections but staying on the dirt road. Park just beyond the small white house on the left and walk for six minutes, not to the beach you can see, which is unsafe for swimming, but down a steep gully and then down a stony path to the smaller beach. It is often empty during the week. Take your litter home with you.

Other Sports

There is little to offer on Statia for the sporting enthusiast. At the Community Centre on Rosemary Lane: tennis (US$5), basketball, softball and volleyball; changing rooms are available. There is also a children's playground.

Oranjestad

Oranjestad is the capital, situated on a cliff overlooking the long beach below and divided between Upper Town and Lower Town. The town used to be defended by Fort Oranje (pronounced Orahn'ya) perched on a rocky bluff. Built in 1636, the ruins of the fort have been preserved and large black cannons still point out to sea. The administrative buildings of the island's Government are

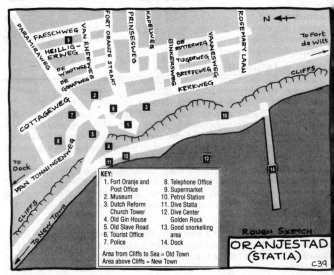

KEY:
1. Fort Oranje and Post Office
2. Museum
3. Dutch Reform Church Tower
4. Old Gin House
5. Old Slave Road
6. Tourist Office
7. Police
8. Telephone Office
9. Supermarket
10. Petrol Station
11. Dive Statia
12. Dive Center Golden Rock
13. Good snorkelling area
14. Dock

Area from Cliffs to Sea = Old Town
Area above Cliffs = New Town

ROUGH SKETCH.
ORANJESTAD
(STATIA)
C39

here. The fort was partly destroyed by a fire in 1990, but rebuilding work has started. Other places of historical interest include the ruins of the Honen Dalim Synagogue built in 1738 and the nearby cemetery. Statia once had a flourishing Jewish community and was a refuge for Sephardic and Ashkenazic Jews, but with the economic decline after the sacking of Oranjestad by Admiral Rodney, most of the Jewish congregation left. The Dutch Reformed Church, built in 1774, suffered a similar fate when its congregation joined the exodus. The square tower has been restored but the walls are open to the elements. The surrounding graveyard has some interesting tombs. Legend has it that it was here that Admiral Rodney found most of his booty after noticing that there were a surprising number of funerals for such a small population. A coffin, which he ordered to be opened, was found to be full of valuables and further digging revealed much more.

On Wilheminaweg in the centre, the 18th century Doncker/De Graaff House, once a private merchant's house and also where Admiral Rodney lived, has been restored by the St Eustatius Historical Foundation and is now a museum. There is a pre-columbian section which includes an Arawak skeleton and a reconstruction of 18th century rooms at the height of Statia's prosperity. Open 0900-1600, Monday-Friday, admission US$1 or US$0.50 for children, the curator normally shows you around, explaining the history of the exhibits.

It is possible to walk round the village and see the sights in a morning. The museum or Tourist Office will provide you with a Walking Tour brochure listing the historical sites and other walking tours. In its heyday Lower Town stretched for two miles along the bay, with warehouses, taverns and slave markets attracting commercial traffic. Parts are now being restored as hotels or restaurants. If you like beach combing, blue, five-sided slave beads over 200 years old can be found along the shore at Oranjestad.

Excursions

Twelve hiking trails using old donkey or farm tracks are marked and numbered. The Tourist Office has a guide book of the trails. There are several paths to the rainforest crater at the top of The Quill, which is remarkable for its contrast with the dry scrub of the rest of the island. The plant life includes mahogany and breadfruit trees, arums, bromeliads, lianas and orchids. The walk to the top is of course steep, but once there you can walk down a path to the centre. The vegetation in the crater is very dense and a local guide is recommended. The highest point, called Mazinga, affords a magnificent view. The Quill was damaged by Hurricane Hugo in 1989 and it is now not possible to walk round the rim. The crater is the breeding ground for land crabs, which Statians catch at night by blinding them with a flashlight.

A road, and then a track, leads round the lower slopes of The Quill to the White Wall, a massive slab of limestone which was once pushed out of the sea by volcanic forces and is now clearly visible from miles away across the sea. You can also see it from Fort de Windt, built in 1753, the ruins of which are open to the public, at the end of the road south from Lower Town. St Kitts can also be seen clearly from here. About 14 forts or batteries were built around the island by the end of the 18th century but the ruins of few of them are accessible or even visible nowadays. Another track affording panoramic views is that up Gilboa Hill. If you start from the Venus Bay track, turn east at post 11; you can see all across Statia.

Information for Visitors

Documents

See main Netherlands Antilles section under Curaçao Information for Visitors. There are no customs regulations as Statia is a free port.

How To Get There

Winair has several daily 20-minute flights from St Maarten (US$50) connecting with flights from the USA, Europe and other islands. It is possible to get to Statia in a day from New York. There are other connecting flights from St Kitts, with either Winair or Liat, which take only 15 minutes. Winair also flies to Saba (10 minutes) and Nevis (35 minutes). Liat flies once a week from Antigua via St Kitts or Nevis. All flights are in small planes, although the airport has been extended to 4,290 feet to allow larger jets to land. You get an impressive view of The Quill when you come in to land. Airport departure tax is US$4. Liat, Tel: 82398. Windward Islands Airways (Winair) Tel: 82362/82381.

Cruise ships come in at Gallows Bay, where there is a deep-water pier. Boat charters are available in the larger nearby islands. A boat, Ted, leaves Marigot, St-Martin every Thursday for Statia and sometimes takes passengers for US$15-20 one way.

Local Transport

There are several taxi drivers who are well-informed guides and can arrange excursions, although most places are within walking distance if you are energetic. A round island tour costs US$35. To hire a car you need a driving licence from your own country or an international driver's licence. (Because of difficulties in arranging driving tests in the Netherlands, some Dutch come to Statia to take their tests; the licence is valid in the Netherlands). Avis at the airport rents elderly baby Daihatsus for US$36/day, cars are well-maintained, credit cards accepted. Mopeds are also available. The speed limit in the country is 50 km (31 miles) an hour and in residential areas it is 30 km (19 miles) an hour. Driving is on the right, but some roads are so narrow you have to pass where you can. Cows, donkeys, goats and sheep are a traffic hazard as they roam about freely, but if you drive slowly and carefully they will soon get out of your way.

Where To Stay

The Old Gin House, Lower Town, Tel: 82319, a reconstructed 18th century cotton gin building, using old ballast bricks, 20 rooms, the most expensive and luxurious of all the hotels, US$140d summer, US$180d winter, EP, no children under ten accepted, all children pay full adult rate, closed September/October; *La Maison Sur La Plage*, at Zeelandia Bay, US$75d summer, Tel: 82256, beautiful location, pool, boules, particularly noted for its French cuisine, closed September; *Golden Era Hotel*, Lower Town, Tel: 82345, on the beach, modern, 20 rooms, US$88d EP in winter. *Talk of the Town*, on road to airport a little way out of Oranjestad, eight rooms, a/c, US$61 double, including breakfast.

There are several guest houses and apartments for rent which are much cheaper: *Henriquez Apartments*, Tel: 82299, two places, one near the airport, US$35, and also in Oranjestad on Prinsesweg, near the hospital, US$30 winter, US$20 summer; also near the airport, *Alvin Courtar Apartments*, Tel: 82218; and *Lens Apartments*, Tel: 82226, no children; off the road towards The Quill, *Daniel's Guest House*, Tel: 82358, De Ruyterweg 20; *Richardson Guest House*, Tel: 82378, Union Estate 3; *Sugar Hill Apartments*, Tel: 82305, upper end of Rosemary Lane. On the northern side of The Quill, *Harry's Efficiency*, PO Box 82, no phone, good view.

Guest houses, villas and apartments are in the US$30-50 price range, double occupancy. Expect a 7% government tax, 15% service charge and sometimes a 5% surcharge. The Tourist Office also has a list of home rentals, Tel: 82209 or 82213, ext 117.

Where To Eat

The best restaurants are in the three hotels. *The Old Gin House* menu caters for the US market, while *La Maison Sur La Plage* serves a high standard of simple French cuisine with excellent French wine. Reservations recommended for both. Cheaper meals at *Chinese Restaurant*, Prinsesweg 9, Tel: 82389, shut Sundays; *L'Etoile*, Heillegerweg, Tel: 82299, same ownership as *Henriquez Apartments*, local style cooking, spicey pastechis recommended, open from 1200-2200 Monday-Saturday, closes at 1800 on Sundays; *Statia Bar & Restaurant*, Paramiraweg 43, Tel: 82280, Chinese and Caribbean dishes, closed Mondays; *Stone Oven*, Faeschweg, Tel: 82247, West Indian food, the liveliest place, on Fridays open from 2100 until any time; *Talk of the Town*, Golden Rock, Tel: 82236, varied menu, also sandwiches and cakes; you can order their specialities, lobster stew, eggplant soufflé, spiced crab backs in the morning or at lunchtime for dinner, the bar is a good meeting place. If you are self-catering and want to buy fresh fish, you have to deal direct with the fishermen as there is no fish shop.

They usually come in somewhere alone the shore road in Lower Town. Fresh bread is baked daily in outdoor charcoal-fired stone ovens and best bought straight from the oven at "fresh bread time", which varies according to who makes it. Listings of fresh bread times are available.

Entertainment

Statians like partying and every weekend something is always going on. Quite often you will hear a 'road block' from far away, cars stopped with huge stereos blaring and everyone jumping up in the street. Ask anybody what is going on next weekend, or just wait for the music to start in the evening.

Shopping

Lots of shops or businesses are in people's homes with no visible sign of the trade from the outside, but if you ask for help it will be willingly given and you will find the right place. The Handcraft Shop is on Van Tonningenweg, next to the school, and sells gifts, clothing and furniture. Open Monday-Friday, 0800-1200, 1400-1700. Hole in the Wall, close to the telephone office, sells hand-painted T-shirts; Green and White Boutique also for clothes. Mazinga Gift Shop sells local books and a wide range of gifts. Duty free shops catering for cruise ship visitors open when there is a demand.

Bank

Barclays Bank, Wilhelminaweg, Tel: 82392, open 0830-1300, Monday-Friday, and 1600-1700 on Fridays. The currency is the Netherlands Antilles florin or guilder, but US dollars are accepted everywhere. Credit cards are not widely used, although some shops do now accept them. Check beforehand at hotels and restaurants.

Health

There is a hospital on Prinsesweg, Tel: 82371 for an ambulance, or 82211 for a doctor. Outpatient hours are 0800-1100, Monday, Tuesday, Thursday and Friday, or by appointment. A dentist comes only once a month, the nearest is on St Kitts or St Maarten.

Climate

Average temperature is around 82°F with cooling trade winds from the east. Average rainfall is 45 inches a year. Average water temperature in the sea is 79°F.

National Holidays

New Year's Day, Good Friday, Easter Monday, Queen's Birthday (30 April), Labour Day (1 May), Ascension Day, Statia Day (16 November), Kingdom Day (15 December), Christmas Day, Boxing Day.

Carnival is in July and is celebrated with steel bands, picnics, sports and contests.

Time Zone
Atlantic Standard Time, 4 hours behind GMT, 1 ahead of EST, all year.

Electric Current
110 volts A/C 60 cycles.

Communications
Public telephones, telex and cablegrams at Landsradio, Van Tonningenweg, Open Monday-Friday, 0800-1200, 1400-1700, 1800-1830. The telephone code number for Statia is 599-3. New exchanges have been introduced and some phone numbers may have changed. The **Post Office** is in Fort Oranje, open Monday-Friday, 0730-1200, 1330-1700. Mail departure 0800. There are special stamp issues and First Day Covers for collectors.

Churches
Anglican, Apostolic Faith, Methodist, Roman Catholic and Seventh Day Adventist.

Tourist Office
There are three on Statia: at the airport; in Lower Town opposite Roro Pier, operated by St Eustatius Historical society; and in the village centre, Tel: 82433. In the **USA**: St Eustatius Tourist Information Office, c/o Medhurst & Associates Inc, 271 Main Street, Northport, NY 11768, Tel: (800) 344-4606 or (516) 261-7474. In **Canada**: 243 Ellerslie Ave, Willowdale, Ontario, Tel: 416-223 3501. In **Venezuela**: Edificio EXA, Oficina 804, Avda Libertador, Caracas, Tel: 313832.

SINT MAARTEN

Introduction

SINT MAARTEN (Dutch) or St-Martin (French—see under French Antilles section) lies 260 km north of Guadeloupe and 310 km east of Puerto Rico, in a cluster of islands on the Anguilla Bank. The island is amicably shared by the Dutch, who have 37 square km and the French, who have 52 square km. The population of at least 50,000 (27,000 in St Maarten and 23,000 in St-Martin) has mushroomed with the tourist boom: the 1950 St Maarten census gave the total population at 1,484. While many of the residents were formerly ex-patriates who returned to their island, there is a large proportion who have come from other Caribbean islands to seek work. Few people speak Dutch, the official language, although Papiamento has increased with the migration of people from the ABC Dutch islands. Nearly everybody speaks English and there is a large Spanish-speaking contingent of guest workers from the Dominican Republic.

The Dutch side of the island has the main airport and seaport and most of the tourists. The French side is noticeably Gallic and few people speak English. There are no border formalities between the two parts: only a modest monument erected in 1948, which commemorates the division of the island three centuries earlier. The Dutch side occupies the southern part of the roughly triangular island. The western part is low-lying and mostly taken up by the Simpson Bay Lagoon, which provides a safe anchorage for small craft. The lagoon is separated from the sea by a narrow strip of land on which the airport has been built. The rest of the Dutch part is hilly and dry and covered with scrub, although it can quickly turn green and lush after rain. The coastline is indented with sandy bays, while just inland are several salt ponds, which were what attracted the first settlers to the island.

History

The Amerindians who originally settled on the island named it Sualouiga, meaning land of salt. The belief that Columbus discovered the island on his second voyage in 1493 is disputed, with historians now claiming it was Nevis he named St Martin of Tours, and that later Spanish explorers misinterpreted his maps. Nevertheless, the Spanish were not interested in settling the island and it was not until 1629 that some French colonists arrived in the north, and then in 1631 the Dutch were attracted to the southern part by the salt ponds. By this time, there were no Caribs left on the island and the two nationalities lived amicably enough together. Spain reconsidered and occupied St Maarten from 1633 to 1648, fending off an attack by Peter Stuyvesant in 1644 which cost him his leg.

When the Spanish left, the Dutch and French settlers returned and after a few territorial skirmishes, they divided the island between them with the signing of the 23 March 1648 Treaty of Mount Concordia. Popular legend has it that the division was settled with a race starting from Oyster Pond. The Frenchman went north and the Dutchman went south, but the Frenchman walked faster because he drank only wine while the Dutchman's

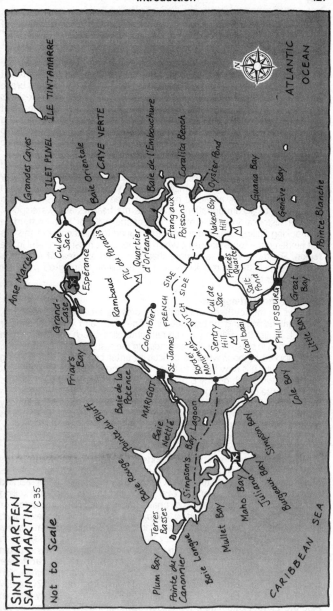

SINT MAARTEN
SAINT-MARTIN C35

Not to Scale

penchant for Genever (a drink similar to gin) slowed him down. Since 1648, however, St Maarten has changed hands 16 times, including brief occupations by the British, but the Dutch-French accord has been peaceably honoured at least since it was last revised in 1839.

At the height of its colonial period, sugar cane and livestock were the main agricultural activities, although the poor soil and lack of rain meant they were not very profitable. The emancipation of slavery in 1863 broke up the plantation system and the population began to decline as ex-slaves left to look for work elsewhere. Most of the salt produced from the Great Salt Pond behind Philipsburg was exported to the USA and neighbouring islands, but by 1949 this industry had also ended and a further exodus to other islands took place. The remaining population survived on subsistence farming, fishing and remittances from relatives abroad.

However, in 40 years the island has become unrecognizable, hotels and resorts, villas and guest houses now line the shore and there is no bay untouched by tourism. Over 1 million tourists visit St Maarten (and French St Martin) every year, attracted by the duty-free shopping, the casinos and a wide range of accommodation, as well as the beaches and watersports. Little of historical interest remains, except the walls of Fort Amsterdam overlooking Philipsburg, and a few other ruined fortifications, but this has not hindered the tourist industry, which is among the most successful in the region. For those who want more than sun, sand and sea, St Maarten's well-developed transport links make it an excellent jumping-off place for visiting other islands.

Beaches and Watersports
The bays on the southern and western shores are excellent for swimming, diving and fishing, and the beaches are of fine white sand. The most popular beach is Mullet Bay, where you can rent umbrellas, beach chairs etc. It can get crowded in season and all weekends. On the eastern side is Oyster Pond, a land-locked harbour which is difficult to enter because of the outlying reefs, but which is now home to a yacht club and is a centre for bare boat charter. Dawn Beach nearby is popular with body surfers and snorkelling is good because of the reefs just offshore; Guana Bay, next to Dawn Beach, is the bodysurfers best beach. Maho Beach, by the airport, has regular Sunday beach parties with live music competitions; don't forget to duck when planes arrive. The most western beach on the Dutch side of the island is Cupecoy, where rugged sandstone cliffs lead down to a narrow sandy beach, providing morning shade and a natural windbreak.

Every conceivable form of watersports is available and the resort hotels offer all facilities. Surfing is possible all year round, from different beaches depending on the time of the year. Water visibility is usually 75-125 feet and the water temperature averages over 70°F, which makes good snorkelling and scuba diving, from beaches or boats. Training with NAUI instructors or just equipment rental is offered by Maho Watersports, at *Mullet Bay Resort*, Beach Bums and Ocean Explorers at Simpson Bay, Red Ensign Watersports at *Dawn Beach Hotel*, and Little Bay Watersports at *The Little Bay Beach Hotel*. They also have water skiing, jet skiing, windsurfing, para sailing, pedal boats, sunfish sailing and glass-bottomed boat trips. There are boat charter companies with sailing boats and motor boats, with or without a crew. You find most of them around *Bobby's Marina*, Philipsburg, from US$200 a day for bare boat. The *Eagle* and *Falcon* sail to St-Barts from Great Bay Marina. Also the 75-foot catamaran, *White Octopus*, departs 0930, returns 1700, from *Bobby's Marina*, Tel: 22366. *El Tigre*, a 60-foot catamaran, makes day trips to St Barts and Anguilla from *Pelican Resort*, leaving 0930, returning 1730. The trip to St Barts is normally quite rough on the way there but more pleasant on the return journey. Check the weather, the swell and the waves can be up to 12 feet even on a nice day. *Gandalf* at Pelican Watersports goes to Anguilla (US$70) and has dinner and sunset cruises. *Style* goes from *Pelican Marina* to Saba, three times a week, scuba equipment offered. Most boats offer some snacks, sodas and rum punch. Trips cost from US$40-70, plus departure tax. There are around 40 boats offering different trips around the islands, some just going out for snorkelling on the reefs or taking cruise ship passengers around. Some of the time share resorts offer free boat trips with snorkelling, lunch, taxis, (you pay departure tax), if you participate in one of their sales drives. For fishing there are numerous boats available for a whole or half day from *Bobby's Marina* or *Great Bay Marina*. Arrangements can be made through the hotels. Marlin, barracuda, dolphin (not the mammal) and tuna are the best catches. Game fishing tournaments are held all year round. The largest annual regatta takes place each February and lasts for three days with a round the island race on the Sunday. A race to Nevis and back is held in mid-June with a day for resting/parties. Other regattas held are for catamarans, match racing with charter boats, windsurfing etc. For more information check with St Martin Yacht Club or ask Robbie Ferron at Budget Marina in Philipsburg. A half day excursion is match racing on *Canada II* or *True North*, two boats from the Americas Cup, US$40, races held when cruise ships are in port. In February 1993, St Marten will be visited by maxiboats (Whitbread round the world racers) for a race to France.

Other Sports

All the large hotels have **tennis** courts, many of which are lit for night play. There is an 18-hole championship **golf** course for guests at *Mullet Bay Resort* or *Caravanserai* at *Mullet Bay Resort & Casino*, which stretches along the shores of Mullet Pond and Simpson Bay Lagoon. **Running** is organized by the Road Runners Club, St Maarten, with a fun run of 5-10 km every Wednesday at 1730 and Sunday at 1830, starting from the *Pelican Resort & Casino* car park. On Sundays at 0700 there are 2-20 km runs. There are monthly races with prizes and an annual relay race around the island to relive the legendary race between the Dutch and the French when they divided the island. Contact Dr Fritz Bus at the Back Street Clinic or Malcolm Maidwell of *El Tigre*. Crazy Acres Riding Centre takes groups **horseriding** every weekday morning at 0900 from the Wathey Estate, Cole Bay, to Cay Bay, where horses and riders can swim, Tel: 22061. Make reservations two days in advance.

Carnival

Carnival starts in mid-April and lasts for three weeks, culminating in the burning of King Mouí-Mouí. It is one of the biggest in the area, with up to 100,000 people taking part. Most events are held at the Carnival Village, next to the University.

Philipsburg

Philipsburg, the capital of Dutch St Maarten, is built on a narrow strip of sandy land between the sea and a shallow lake which was once a salt pond. It has two main streets, Front and Back, and a ringroad built on land reclaimed from the salt pond, which all run parallel to Great Bay Beach,

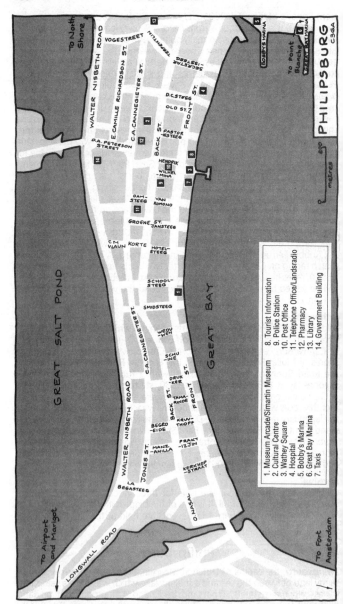

PHILIPSBURG C3GA

GREAT SALT POND

GREAT BAY

WALTER NISBETH ROAD

VOGESTREET

E. CAMILLE RICHARDSON ST.

C.A. CANNEGIETER ST.

TERRENTIJN

SECRETARISSTEEG

D.C. STEEG

OLD ST.

FRONT ST.

BACK ST.

PASTOR HESTEEG

D.A. PETERSON STREET

HENDRIK WILNEL MINA

VAN ROMONO

DAM-STEEG

GROENE ST. JANSTEEG

C.M. VLAUN KORTE

HOTEL-STEEG

SCHOOL-STEEG

SMIDSTEEG

C.A. CANNEGIETER ST.

WEDU-WEN

SCHU-INE

DRUK-KER

BACK ST.

TAMA-RINDE

FRONT ST.

BEGRO-EIDE

KRUY-THIOFF

PRAKT-IZJIN

MANZ-ANILLA

JONES ST.

LA BEGASTEEG

KERKHOP-STRAAT

O. NASAL

WALTER NISBETH ROAD

LONGWALL ROAD

To Airport and Marigot

To Fort Amsterdam

To North Shore

To Point Blanche

LOTEN'S MARINA

GREAT BAY MARINA

metres

1. Museum Arcade/Simartin Museum
2. Cultural Centre
3. Wathey Square
4. Hospital
5. Bobby's Marina
6. Great Bay Marina
7. Taxis
8. Tourist Information
9. Police Station
10. Post Office
11. Telephone Office/Landsradio
12. Pharmacy
13. Library
14. Government Building

perhaps the safest and cleanest city beach anywhere. Front Street is full of shops offering duty-free goods. The Simartin Museum at Museum Arcade on Front Street is open 1000-1700, closed Sundays. Back Street contains low cost clothes shops and low budget Chinese restaurants. The historic Townhouse (court-house and post office) dating from 1793, on De Ruyterplein, better known as Wathey Square, faces the pier. The harbour is frequented by cruise ships and a host of smaller craft and the town gets very crowded when up to eight cruise ships are in port. For information on outdoor concerts, choirs, theatre and art exhibitions, ask at the Cultural Center of Philipsburg on Back Street (Tel: 22056). There is a zoo, opened 1991, in Madam Estate, close to New Amsterdam shopping centre, with a small exhibition of the fauna and flora from the islands, open weekdays 0900-1700, weekends 1000-1800, entrance US$4, children US$2.

Excursions

You can take a day trip round the island, visiting the ruined Fort Amsterdam overlooking Philipsburg and the French part of the island. It is well worth having lunch in one of the many French restaurants in Grand Case or the other French villages. Generally, however, there is not much of either historical or natural interest to see on the island, and most excursions are day trips to neighbouring islands: Anguilla, St-Barthélémy, Saba, St Eustatius, St Kitts or Nevis, either by boat or by plane.

Information for Visitors

Documents
See main Netherlands Antilles section, under Curaçao Information for Visitors. The local immigration officials are particularly concerned that you fill in your tourist card with a hotel address, even if you do not know whether you will be staying there.

How To Get There
From Europe: Air France three times a week from Paris, KLM twice a week from Amsterdam and Lufthansa once a week from Frankfurt. From the USA: Direct flights from New York (American Airlines, Continental), Los Angeles via Dallas (American Airlines), Washington (American Airlines), Boston (Continental) and Miami (American Airlines, BWIA and Air Guadeloupe) with connecting flights from several other US cities. There are lots of flights from other Caribbean Islands: Anguilla, Antigua, Aruba, Barbados, Curaçao, Dominica, Martinique, Montserrat, Nevis, Guadeloupe, Trinidad and Tobago, Saba, St Barthélémy, USVI (St Croix and St Thomas), St Eustatius, St Kitts, Puerto Rico, St Lucia, Haiti, Dominican Republic and the British Virgin Islands (Tortola), with a variety of regional and international carriers. Air Guadeloupe also

flies from Cayenne, in French Guiana.

Departure tax US$5 when leaving for the Netherlands Antilles, US$10 for other destinations at Juliana Airport except for French visitors returning to Guadeloupe or France. Travel agents ask for US$3 to confirm flights.

Airport Information
Airline offices at the airport: ALM/Winair, Tel: 44230; Air Guadeloupe, Tel: 44212; KLM, Tel: 44244; Liat, Tel: 44203; American Airlines/Lufthansa, Tel: 42040.
Airport flight information, Tel: 42161.

Local Transport
There are plenty of taxis, which are not metered so check the fare first, which is fixed according to your destination. Trips to other beaches or tours of the island can be arranged with taxi drivers. 1991 rates: island tour US$35 plus US$2 for each additional passenger; hourly rate US$10 plus US$2.50 each additional 15 minutes. From Philipsburg to Juliana airport US$8, Dawn Beach US$10, Marigot US$7, Mullet Bay US$8, Pelican Resort US$7, all for two passengers, additional passengers US$1 each. Night tariffs are an extra 25% 2200-2400, an extra 50% 0001-0600. Pick up taxi at the square in Philipsburg

(Tel: 22359) or Juliana airport (Tel: 54317). Mini-vans or tour **buses** also offer tours and are generally cheaper than taxis. Island tours from US$15; for more information ask at the Tourist Office on the square. There is a fairly regular bus service from 0600 until 2000 to Marigot, French Quarters and St Peters, and from Marigot to Grand Case on the French side. After 2000 there are few buses. The best place to catch a bus is the Police Station bus stop on Back Street. Buses run along Back Street and Pondfill and only stop at bus stops. Outside towns, however, just wave to stop a bus. Fare price is usually US$0.80 in town, US$1 for short trips, US$1.50 for long trips. There is no regular bus service between Philipsburg and the airport although the route to *Mullet Bay Resort* passes the airport. Buses on this route run mostly at the beginning and the end of the working day (although there are a few during the day) and drivers may refuse to take you, or charge extra, if you have a lot of luggage. **Hitchhiking** is possible but allow half an hour waiting time; it is not recommended for women, there have been several rapes.

Car Hire

There can be a shortage of cars or jeeps for hire in high season, although there are now 15 rental companies, and it is advisable to request one from your hotel when you book the room. Many have offices in the hotels; free pick up and delivery are standard and you can leave the car at the airport on departure. Car hire companies include: Risdon's Car Rentals, Front Street, Tel: 23578; Avis, Cole Bay, Tel: 42322; Hertz, Juliana Airport, Tel: 44314; Budget, Philipsburg, Tel: 44038, Cannegie Car Rental, Front Street, Tel: 22397; Opel Car Rental, Airport, Tel: 44324; Speedy Car Rental, Airport, Tel: 23893. Two-wheeled transport hire from Super Honda, Bush Road Cul-de-Sac, Tel: 25712; Moped Cruising, Front Street, Tel: 22330; OK Scooter Rental, at *Maho Beach Hotel* and *Cupecoy Resort*, Tel: 42115, 44334. Foreign and international driver's licences are accepted. Drive on the right. The roads on both sides of the island are very busy and full of pot holes, making them rather unsafe for mopeds or walking, particularly at night.

Where To Stay

There is a 5% Government tax on all hotel bills and a 10-15% service charge. Some add an energy surcharge. Prices are high, winter rates quoted here, summer rates can be half price in the resorts. The largest resort hotels are *Mullet Bay Resort & Casino*, beach, watersports, pools, tennis, golf, casino, Tel: 52801, Fax: 54281, US$225-580, 600 rooms-suites; *Great Bay Beach Hotel & Casino*, convenient for Philipsburg, all resort facilities, Tel: 22446, Fax: 23859, US$170-290, 285 rooms-suites; *Cupecoy* perched on a cliff above Cupecoy beach, pool, tennis, casino, Tel: 52309 Fax: 52312, US$250-1,050, rooms-suites; *Dawn Beach* on Dawn Beach at Oyster Pond, watersports, tennis, pool, Tel: 22929, Fax: 24421, US$190-320, 155 rooms-suites with kitchenette, terrace, a/c, TV; *Maho Beach Hotel & Casino*, all facilities, Tel: 52115, Fax: 53018, US$180-505, 247 rooms-suites; *La Plage at Royal Islander Club*, on Maho Bay, 126 apartments, pool, tennis, watersports, casino, Tel: 52388, Fax: 53495, US$240-650, one and two bedroom apartments; *Pelican Resort & Casino*, pool, tennis etc, Tel: 42503, Fax: 42133, on Simpson Bay, huge, 654 units, US$205-780; *Divi Little Bay Beach Resort & Casino*, tennis, pool, watersports, Tel: 22333, Fax: 23911, 220 rooms, US$225-815; *The Towers At Mullet Bay*, watersports, disco, casino, close to airport, 5 miles from Philipsburg, Tel: 53069, Fax: 52147, 81 units, a/c, kitchenettes, TV, VCR etc., US$235-990.

Middle-sized hotels and resorts include *The Caravanserai*, near the airport, pool, tennis, Tel: 52510, Fax: 53483, on beach at Maho Bay, US$135-450, children under 18 free; *Bel Air Beach Hotel*, at Little Bay, Tel: 23366, Fax: 25295, US$225-590, suites; *La Vista*, near *Pelican*, suites and cottages, tennis, pool, horse riding, Tel: 43005, Fax: 43010, US$125-215; *Seaview Beach Hotel*, on Great Bay Beach, Philipsburg, casino, a/c, TV, children under 12 free, Tel: 22323, Fax: 24356, US$80-150; *Port de Plaisance*, on Simpson Bay, unlimited watersports, tennis, pool, fitness centre, night clubs etc, Tel: 45222, Fax: 42428, US$275-500. *Oyster Pond Hotel*, near Dawn Beach, marina, fishing and water sports, tennis, pool, beach, Tel: 22206, Fax: 25695, US$170-310, no children under 10.

Small hotels incude *Pasanggrahan*, in Philipsburg, recommended, formerly the Governor's home, the oldest inn, Tel: 23588, Fax: 22885, no children under 12, no credit cards, US$115-165; *Bute*, Illidge Road 2, Philipsburg, on Great Bay Pond, 13 rooms, a/c available, US$35-50 (Tel:

22400); **Mary's Boon**, on Simpson Bay beach, 12 studios with kitchenettes, no children under 16, no credit cards, US$150, Tel: 44235.

Guesthouses on Front Street: **Marcus**, 7 rooms, US$28-35 (Tel: 22419), **Seaside**, 5 rooms, US$25, PO Box 72; on Back Street: **Lucy's**, US$30-60, 9 rooms, no children under 6, PO Box 171, (Tel: 22995) **Bico's**, US$30-60, extra person US$15, children welcome, no credit cards, (Tel: 22294), PO Box 298, **Jose's**, US$22-40, US$10 extra person, 11 rooms, (Tel: 22231); **Joshua Rose**, Secretarissteeg 4, 14 rooms, US$50-110, extra person US$15 (Tel: 24317); at Simpson Bay: **The Horny Toad**, 8 studios, no children under 7, no credit cards, Tel: 54323, Fax: 53316, US$180-260, extra person US$30, **Calypso**, US$69-115, 8 efficiency apartments, Simpson Bay, PO Box 65 (Tel: 44233); at Pointe Blanche, **Great Bay Marina**, 10 rooms, fridge, a/c, TV, grocery, pier facilities, US$70-90, PO Box 277, (Tel: 22167), **Tamarind** 50 apartments with kitchenettes, swimming pool, US$67-155 daily, US$408-792 a week, Tel: 24359, Fax: 25391, **Rama**, 16 rooms, US$50-100, pool, kitchenettes, clean, friendly, recommended, (Tel: 22582); at Cole Bay: **Ernest**, 9 rooms in Cay Hill, 16 on Bush Road, swimming pool, a/c, TV, US$50 (Tel: 22003), **George's**, 10 rooms in Cole Bay, 10 rooms in Philipsburg, a/c, kitchen, US$30-75, US$10 extra person (Tel: 45363 or 22126).

The Tourist Office has a list of apartments, villas and houses to rent weekly or monthly. The best way of finding an apartment is to look in the free newspaper, *St Martin's Week*. There are several apartments for rent on Back Street, look for signs on the houses. A studio will cost about US$450-550/week in a good location.

Camping is safe but you must seek permission from the landowner.

Where To Eat

All the major hotels have restaurants with international cuisine. Pick up a free tourist guide to choose from the myriad restaurants now open on St Maarten with food from all over the world. In Mullet Bay: **The Frigate**, serves excellent charcoal-broiled steaks and lobster; **Bamboo Garden** offers some of the best Chinese dining. In Philipsburg: **Le Bec Fin**, French, highly recommended, favoured by the Dutch Royal Family and winner of the

awards. Front Street is full of good restaurants and even a **Burger King**. **San Marco**, is a very good Italian restaurant, **Carrí Pizza** on Pondfill Road serves good pizza. **Callaloo**, a pleasant bar/restaurant, steaks, hamburgers and pizzas are served at reasonable prices, very popular. Indonesian rijsttafel at the hotels. Pizzas at **Portofino**. For the budget minded try Back Street where you mostly find Chinese and *roti* places such as **Hong Kong**, **ABC Restaurant** and **Kings Fastfood** where you can eat for US$5. Also good value, **Harbour Lights Bar and Restaurant** on road to Pointe Blanche, delicious West Indian and Créole dishes. Americanized French at **L'Escargot**, Front Street. In the Simpson Bay area: **Turtle Pier Bar and Restaurant** is reasonably priced at US$10-15 pp for dinner with an interesting setting in a mini zoo with parrots, monkeys, turtles etc, live music two or three times a week; **Lynette's** is a local restaurant with good seafood and upstairs is **Clayton's** sport bar, where you can see most major sporting events on a big screen TV; **Don Carlos**, tasty Mexican food, US$10-15 pp for dinner, Tel: 53112; **The Greenhouse Bar and Restaurant**, next to Bobby's Marina at Great Bay, view over yachts, menu includes hamburgers, steak and local fish, disc jockey, dancing, Tel: 22941; **Doc Charlie's**, bar and restaurant, popular, in a former mine sweeper from World War II, live music a few nights; **J & J**, some of the best seafood on the island, pool room/bar next door; **Rembrandt Café** at New Amsterdam shopping centre, a Dutch coffee shop/café, very popular for late drinks, best after 2100-2200. The most popular bars with nice sunsets are **Greenhouse** and **Chesterfield**, where you can find yachtsmen if you want to hitchhike by boat.

Drink

The traditional local liqueur is *guavaberry*, made from rum and the local berries, whose botanical name is *Eugenia Floribunda*. They are not related to guavas. The berries are found on the hills and ripen just before Christmas. Used nowadays mostly in cocktails.

Entertainment

Nearly all the resorts have casinos, which are a major attraction, the most popular being *Pelican Casino* (Pelican Resort) and *Casino Royale* (Maho/Mullet Bay). The *Studio 7* discotheque at Grand Casino,

Mullet Bay, is the most visited, entrance US$10 including one drink, can be higher if they have a special show, all drinks US$5, the disco starts late, recommended to pass the time in *Cherry's* bar, a 5-minute walk away, when people leave there most head for the disco. *Coconut Comedy Club* have stand up comedians Tuesday-Sunday, 2130 and 2330, US$10 cover charge, most comedians from HBO or Carsons, well worth the price. *L'Horoscope* at Simpson Bay, opens 0100, starts to come alive only after 0200. *Caribbean Revue*, at *Mullet Bay Resort*, has a Caribbean show with Calypsonians and Limbo dancers, keep an eye open for King Bo Bo, the King of Calypso. Most resorts have live entertainment, such as limbo dancing, fire eating or live music, both local and international. In Philipsburg, *The Movies*, on Pondfill, has newly released films, US$5.

Shopping

Duty-free shopping is a tourist attraction, but it helps if you have an idea of prices at home to compare, and shop around as prices vary. Check your duty-free allowance when returning home. Most of the shops are along Front Street. Open 0800-1200, 1400-1800.

Banks

Bank of Nova Scotia, Back Street, Tel: 22262; Windward Islands Bank, Tel: 23485; Bardays Bank, 19 Front Street, Tel: 22491; Chase Manhattan Bank, Mullet Bay, Tel: 44204; Algemene Bank Nederland, main office at Front Street, Tel: 23505; Citco Bank Antilles, 16 Front Street, Tel: 23471, three other offices on the island as well; Nederlandse Credietbank, Tel: 22933. Open 0830-1500, Monday-Thursday, 0830-1500, 1600-1700, Friday. Credit cards widely accepted.

Currency

Netherlands Antilles guilders or florins are the official currency, but the most common currency is the US dollar, which one need never change at all. You will get a poor exchange rate for French francs. It is often difficult to get change from payments in any currency other than US dollars.

Warning Crime has increased on St Maarten and there have been armed robberies on the roads in the Lowland area.

Health

St Rose Hospital, Philipsburg, Tel: 22300. Ambulance, Tel: 22111. Drinking water in the hotels is purified. Be careful of the sun. A helicopter airlift to Puerto Rico is available for extreme medical emergencies.

Climate

Average temperature is 80°F and average annual rainfall is 45 inches.

National Holidays

New Year's Day, Carnival Monday (April), Good Friday, Easter Monday, 30 April, Labour Day (1 May), Ascension Day, St Maarten Day (11 November), Christmas Day, Boxing Day.

Time Zone

Atlantic Standard Time, 4 hours behind GMT, 1 ahead of EST.

Electric Current

110 volts AC. Note that it is 220 volts on the French side.

Telephones

At Landsradio telecommunications office in Back Street, open until midnight. This is where you can buy telephone cards for the Dutch side of the island, open from 0700. You can also buy telephone cards at

Landsradio's offices at Simpson Bay, Cole Bay and St Peter's. There are USA-Direct (AT&T) phone booths at the pier in front of Wathey's Square and at Bobbie's Marina. The international dialling code for St Maarten is 5995, followed by a 5-digit local number. To call the French side, dial 06 before the number.

Mail

Two safe places for holding mail are *Bobby's Marina*, PO Box 383, Philipsburg and *Island Underwater World*, PO Box 234, Cole Bay. It is not possible to send a parcel by sea, only airmail which is expensive.

Churches

Many denominations are represented. Seventh Day Adventist, Anglican, Baptist, Jehovah's Witness, Methodist, Roman Catholic, Church of Christ, Baha'i, The New Testament Church of God.

Newspapers

Local events are noted in the free weekly newspaper, *St Martin's Week*, published in French and English every Thursday afternoon on the French side and Friday morning on the Dutch side. *The Chronicle* and *The Guardian* come out six times a week and *Newsday* twice a week. After 1500 in the shops on Front Street or at the airport you can find US newspapers (*New York Times*, *Miami Herald* and *San Juan Star*). American magazines (30%-40% more expensive than the USA) are especially good at Paiper Garden, Front Street.

Radio

PJD2 Radio is on medium wave 1300 kHz and FM 102.7 mHz.

International Clubs

The Lions, Rotary, Kiwanis, Jaycees and YMCC meet on both sides of the island.

Tourist Office

De Ruyterplein, at the Little Pier, Tel: 22337, Fax: 24884. Well supplied with brochures and guides to St Maarten, and the monthly *St Maarten Holiday*. Sightseeing tours available by bus or by car.

In the **USA**: St Maarten Tourist Office, 275 Seventh Avenue, 19th floor, New York, NY 10001, Tel: 212-989 0000, Fax: 212-242 0001.

In **Canada**: 243 Ellerslie Ave, Willowdale, Toronto, Ontario, M2N 1Y5 Tel: 416-223 3501, Fax: 416-223 6887.

In **Venezuela**: Edificio EXA, oficina 804, Avda Libertador, Caracas, Tel: 31 38 32, Fax: 416-223 6887.

The editors would like to thank Lars Karlsson of St Maarten for his help in updating St Maarten, Statia and Saba.

FRENCH ANTILLES

Introduction

WHILE AWARE OF THE FACT that we are breaking the geographical sequence of the book, we shall deal with the French Antilles as a single entity. The French Caribbean islands form two Départements d'Outremer: one comprises Martinique, and the other Guadeloupe with its offshore group, Marie-Galante, Les Saintes, La Désirade, and two more distant islands: Saint-Barthélémy and the French part of Saint-Martin (shared with the Dutch).

Geographically, the main islands form the north group of the Windward Islands, with the ex-British island of Dominica in the centre of them. Saint-Barthélémy and Saint-Martin are in the Leeward group.

As the islands are politically Departments of France they have the same status as any Department in European France. Each Department sends two senators and three deputies to the National Assembly in Paris. The inhabitants are French citizens. The currency is the French franc (F). The connection with France confers many benefits on the islands, which enjoy French standards of social legislation etc, but it also drives up the cost of living, which is rather higher than elsewhere in the Caribbean. There is an independence movement, whose more extremist members have been responsible for violent protests against high unemployment.

Both the main islands were sighted by Columbus on his second voyage in 1493, but no colonies were established by the Spanish because the islands were inhabited by the Caribs (who are now virtually extinct); it was not until 1635 that French settlers arrived.

Because of their wealth from sugar, the islands became a bone of contention between Britain and France; other French islands, Dominica, St Lucia, Tobago, were lost by France in the Napoleonic wars. The important dates in the later history of the islands are 1848, when the slaves were freed under the influence of the French "Wilberforce", Victor Schoelcher; 1946, when the islands ceased to be colonies and became Departments; and 1974, when they became Regions.

Culture

The cultural, social and educational systems of France are used and the official language is French. However, Créole is widely spoken on Guadeloupe and Martinique; it has West African grammatical structures and uses a mainly French-derived vocabulary. Although still not officially recognized, it is the everyday language of the Guadeloupean and Martiniquan people. English is not widely spoken, not even by hotel staff. A knowledge of French is therefore a great advantage.

Another feature common to the two main islands is the pre-Lenten Carnival, said to be more spontaneous and less touristy than most. There are also picturesque Ash Wednesday ceremonies (especially in Martinique), when the population dresses in black and white, and processions take place that combine the seriousness of the first day of the Christian Lent with the funeral of the Carnival King (Vaval).

Also shared are the African dances: the *calinda, laghia, bel-air, haut-taille, gragé* and others, still performed in remote villages. The famous biguine is a more sophisticated dance from these islands, and the mazurka can also be heard. French Antillean music is, like most other Caribbean styles, hybrid, a mixture of African (particularly percussion), European, Latin and, latterly, US and other Caribbean musical forms. Currently very popular, on the islands and in mainland France, is zouk, a hi-tech music which overlays electronics on more traditional rhythms.

Traditional costume is commonly seen in the form of brightly-coloured, chequered Madras cotton made into elegant Parisian-style outfits. It is the mixture of French and Créole language and culture that gives Martinique and Guadeloupe an ambience quite different from that of the rest of the Caribbean. An extra dimension is added by the Hindu traditions and festivals celebrated by the descendants of the 19th century indentured labourers.

The spectacles of cockfighting and mongoose versus snake are popular throughout the French Islands. Betting shops are full of atmosphere (they are usually attached to a bar). Horseracing is held on Martinique, but not Guadeloupe, but on both islands gambling on all types of mainland France track events is very keen.

The dominance of French educational and social regimes on its colonial possessions led, in the 1930s and 1940s, to a literary movement which had a profound influence on black writing the world over. This was *négritude*, which grew up in Paris among black students from the Caribbean and Africa. Drawing particularly on Haitian nationalism (1915-30), the *négritude* writers sought to restore black pride which had been completely denied by French education. The leaders in the field were Aimé Césaire of Martinique, Léopold Senghor of Senegal and Léon Damas of Guyane. Césaire's first affirmation of this ideology was *Cahier d'un retour au pays natal* (1939); in subsequent works and in political life (he was mayor of Fort-de-France) he maintained his attack on the "white man's superiority complex" and worked, in common with another Martiniquan writer, Frantz Fanon, towards "the creation of a new system of essentially humane values" (Mazisi Kunene in his introduction to the Penguin edition of *Return to My Native Land*, 1969).

Cuisine is also quite distinctive and the description given under **Food** and **Drink** in the Martinique section can equally apply to Guadeloupe (although note that the brands of rum are different; note also on Guadeloupe that beer is four times as expensive in a bar as it is in a supermarket).

Information for Visitors

Documents
In most cases the only document required for entry is a passport, the exceptions being citizens of Australia, South Africa, Bolivia, Cuba, Haiti, Honduras, El Salvador, Dominican Republic, Turkey, and the English-speaking Caribbean islands, when a visa is required. However, any non-EEC citizen planning to stay longer than three months will need an extended visa. Citizens of the United States and Canada intending a stay of less than ten days will not need a passport, although some form of identification is required. An onward ticket is necessary but not always asked for.

How To Get There
Transport to each island is given separately. Note: as said above, French Saint-Martin has only a small airport; the international flights arrive and depart from Juliana International Airport on the Dutch side. Contact Continental Shipping and Travel, 179 Piccadilly, London W1V 9DB, Tel: 071-491 4968, for help in arranging passage from France to the French Antilles.

Accommodation And Restaurants
Addresses for the local *gîtes* associations are also under the individual islands. In France, contact Gîtes de France, 35 Rue Godot de Mauroy, 75009 Paris, Tel: 4742 2543. **Food** and **Drink** is described under Martinique.

Tipping
Check if your bill says "Service Compris", in which case no tip is necessary.

Time Zone
4 hours behind GMT, 1 ahead of EST in all cases.

Holidays
New Year's Day; Carnival at the beginning of February; 8 March Victory Day; Good Friday; Easter Monday; Labour Day on 1 May; Ascension Day at the beginning of May; Whit Monday in May; National Day on 14 July; Schoelcher Day on 21 July; Assumption Day in August; All Saints Day on 1 November; Armistice Day on 11 November and Christmas Day.

Currency Exchange
Banking hours are given under the various islands, as are the names of banks. There are money-changing offices in the big hotels and at airports. The French franc is the legal tender, but it seems US$ are preferred in Saint-Martin and are widely accepted elsewhere. There is no limit to travellers' cheques and letters of credit being imported, but a declaration of foreign banknotes in excess of 3,500F must be made. 500F in French banknotes may be exported and 3,500F in foreign banknotes.

Tourist Information
Les Antilles, produced by Nouvelles Frontières (Les Éditions JA, 2nd edition, Paris, 1987), contains both practical information and very interesting background information on geography, local customs and architecture, and the French Antilles' place in the Caribbean and in relation to France.

Addresses of the French Tourist Offices on the individual islands are given separately.

Tourist Offices
Office Inter-Régional du Tourisme des Antilles et de la Guyane Françaises, 12 Rue Auber, 75009 Paris, Tel: 42 68 1107. Nearest Métro: Opéra; open 0930-1800.

Service Official Français du Tourisme:
UK: 178 Piccadilly, London, Tel:

071-491 7622.

USA: 610 Fifth Avenue, New York, NY 10020, Tel: 212 757 1125; 645 North Michigan Ave, Suite 630, Chicago, Illinois 60611, Tel: 337 6301.

Canada: 1981 Ave MacGill College, Suite 490, Montréal PQH 3A 2W9, Tel: 288 4264; 1 Dundas Street West, Suite 2405, Ontario NS 1-2-3, Tel: 593 6427.

Germany: Westendstrasse 47, Postfach 2927, D-600 Frankfurt/M, Tel: 597 52029.

Italy: 5 Via San Andrea 20121, Milan, Tel: 2 700268.

Belgium: 21 Ave de la Toison d'Or, 1060 Brussels, Tel: 2512 9790.

Switzerland: 84 Rue du Rhône, 1204 Geneva, Tel: 02221 2749; Bahnofstrasse 16—CH 8022, Zurich, Tel: 123 3350.

Spain: Administration: Gran Via, 59-28013 Madrid, Tel: 241 8808.

We are grateful to Lars Karlsson, St Maarten, for updating the French Antilles.

GUADELOUPE

Introduction

GUADELOUPE is surrounded by the small islands La Désirade, Marie Galante and Les Saintes, all of which can easily be visited from the main island, with each one offering something different. Including the two more distant islands of Saint-Barthélémy and Saint-Martin in the Leewards, the total area of the Department is 1,780 square km. Population in 1990 was 386,600.

Guadeloupe (1,510 square km) is really two small islands, separated by the narrow bridged strait of the Rivière Salée. To the west is mountainous egg-shaped Basse-Terre, with the volcano Grande Soufrière (1,484 metres) at its centre. It has an area of 777 square km, a total of 150,000 inhabitants, and the administrative capital of the same name on its southwest coast. The commercial capital of Guadeloupe is Pointe-à-Pitre, situated in the flat half of the island, Grande-Terre. Grande-Terre, triangular in shape and slightly smaller than Basse-Terre, has a total population of 190,000. The names of the two parts shows a most un-Gallic disregard of logic as Basse-Terre is the higher and Grande-Terre is the smaller; possibly they were named by sailors, who found the winds lower on the Basse-Terre and greater on the Grande-Terre side.

Guadeloupe was badly hit by Hurricane Hugo in 1989. Much of the structural damage has been repaired or replaced with aid from the French Government, but the island's flora will take much longer to recuperate. For instance, there were few coconut palms left standing.

History

Christopher Columbus discovered Guadeloupe in 1493 and named it after the Virgin of Guadalupe, of Extremadura, Spain. The Caribs, who had inhabited the island, called it Karukera, meaning "island of beautiful waters". As in most of the Caribbean, the Spanish never settled, and Guadeloupe's history closely resembles that of Martinique, beginning with French colonization in 1635. The first slaves had been brought to the island by 1650. In the first half of the seventeenth century, Guadeloupe did not enjoy the same levels of prosperity, defence or peace as Martinique. After four years of English occupation, Louis XV in 1763 handed over Canada to Britain to secure his hold on these West Indian islands with the Treaty of Paris. The French Revolution brought a period of uncertainty, including a brief reign of terror under Victor Hugues. Those landowners who were not guillotined fled; slavery was abolished, only to be restored in 1802. Up to 1848, when the slaves were finally freed by Victor Schoelcher, the island's economy was inhibited by sugar crises and imperial wars (French and English). After 1848, the sugar plantations suffered from a lack of manpower, although indentured labour was brought in from East India.

Despite having equal status with Martinique, first as a Department then as a Region, Guadeloupe's image as the less-sophisticated, poor relation persists. In common with Martinique, though, its main political voice is radical (unlike the more conservative Saint-Barthélémy and Saint-Martin), often marked by a more violent pro-independence movement.

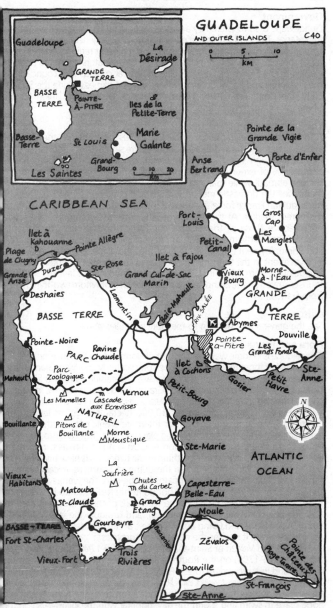

GUADELOUPE
AND OUTER ISLANDS C40

Government

Guadeloupe is administered by a prefect, appointed by the French Ministry of the Interior. The local legislature consists of a 42-seat general council, elected by popular vote, which sits for six years, and a 41-seat regional council made up of the locally-elected councillors and the two senators and three deputies elected to the French parliament. Guadeloupe also sends two councillors to the Economic and Social Council in Paris. Political parties include the Socialist Party, the Communist Party, Union for French Democracy, Union for the Liberation of Guadeloupe and Rally for the Republic.

The Economy

Agriculture and, increasingly since the 1970s, tourism are the principal activities. Bananas have displaced sugar as the single most important export earner, although sugar and its by-products (rum and molasses) generate about 35% of exports. Melons and tropical flowers have been promoted for sale abroad, while many other fruits, vegetables and coffee are grown mainly for the domestic market. Wages and conditions similar to those in metropolitan France force the price of local products to levels viable only on the parent market. At the same time, the high rate of imports raises local prices above those of the island's non-French neighbours. Consequently there has been little move towards industrialization to satisfy a wider market and unemployment is high, at 24% of the labour force at end-1989.

Investment in the tourism industry raised the number of hotel rooms on Guadeloupe from 3,037 in 1980 to an estimated 4,500. In 1991 132,003 tourists arrived on the island and its dependencies, of whom two-thirds came from France.

Culture

See the general introduction to the French Antilles above.

Flora and Fauna

Guadeloupe is in some ways reminiscent of Normandy or Poitou, especially the farms, built in those regional styles. The comparatively low-lying Grande-Terre is mainly given over to sugar cane and livestock-raising. Mostly a limestone plateau, it does have a hilly region, Les Grands-Fonds, and a marshy, mangrove coast extending as far north as Port-Louis on its western flank.

The island's Natural Park covers 30,000 hectares of forest land in the centre of Basse-Terre, which is by far the more scenic part. As the island is volcanic there are a number of related places to visit. The Park has no gates, no opening hours and no admission fee. Do not pick flowers, fish, hunt, drop litter, play music or wash anything in the rivers. Trails have been marked out all over the Park, including to the dome of Soufrière volcano with its fumaroles, cauldrons and sulphur fields (see below). The waters after which the Caribs named the island come hot (as at the Ravine Chaude springs on the Rivière à Goyaves), tumbling (the waterfalls of the Carbet river and the Cascade aux Écrevisses on the Corossol), and tranquil (the lakes of Grand Étang, As de Pique and Étang Zombi). One traveller has described the island as "idyllic—were it not for the noise of motorcycles".

A Maison du Volcan at Saint-Claude (open 0900-1700) and a Maison de la Fôret (0915-1700) on the Route de la Traversée give information on the volcano and its surrounding forest. From the Maison de la Forêt there are 10, 20 and 60-minute forest walks which will take you deep among the towering trees. The Cascade des Ecrevisses is about 2 km from the Maison and is a good place to swim and spend the day; popular with the locals. Also on the

Route de la Traversée is the Parc Zoologique above Mahaut, which allows you to see many of the species which exist in the Natural Park. It is worth a visit for the fine panoramic views from the café and the restaurant is simple but excellent.

The Natural Park's emblem is the racoon (*raton laveur*) which, although protected, is very rare. You are much more likely to see birds and insects in the Natural Park. On La Désirade a few agoutis survive, as well as iguana, which can also be found on Les Saintes. Much of the island's indigenous wildlife has vanished.

The vegetation of Basse-Terre ranges from tropical forest (40% of the land is forested: trees such as the mahogany and gommier, climbing plants, wild orchids) to the cultivated coasts: sugar cane on the windward side, bananas in the south and coffee and vanilla on the leeward. As well as sugar cane on Grande-Terre, there is an abundance of fruit trees (mango, coconut, papaya, guava, etc). On both parts the flowers are a delight, especially the anthuriums and hibiscus.

Beaches

Guadeloupe has excellent beaches for swimming, mostly between Gosier and St-François on Grande Terre. The best is Ste-Anne where the fine white sand and crystal clear water of a constant depth of 1.5 metres far from shore make idyllic bathing. Further east are good beaches at St-François while at the tip of the peninsula is Plage Tarare, the island's only nude bathing beach (part of *Club Méditerranée*). A much quieter beach can be found at Petit Havre where two small bays, each inside a promontory, lie 1 km off the road some 11 km before Ste-Anne (coming from Pointe-à-Pitre). Here are mostly fishermen and locals and a small shed selling fish meals and beer. More deserted beaches can be found on the northeast of Grande Terre. On the leeward coast of Basse-Terre are some good beaches. South of Pointe Noire on the west coast is Plage Caraïbe, which is clean, calm and beautiful, with picnic facilities, toilets and a shower. A small, black sand beach, La Grand Anse, just west of Trois Rivières, has a barbecue and drinks on the beach and a shower and toilets. In the northwest, La Grande Anse at Deshaies is superb and undeveloped with no hotels. Camping sites in the area and a beach restaurant at the southern end with charcoal-grilled chicken and rice.

Marine Life and Watersports

On the Leeward Coast (Côte-Sous-le-Vent, or the Golden Corniche), is the Underwater Reserve developed by Jacques Cousteau. Diving trips can be arranged at Les Heures Saines (Tel: 98 86 63) or Chez Guy (Tel: 98 81 72, friendly, recommended for beginners' confidence, 140F for one dive, everything included), both at Pigeon, Bouillante. Both also offer fishing trips as do Fishing Club Antilles, Tel: 84 15 00, Le Rocher de Malendure, Tel: 98 73 25, and Nautilus Club near Bouillante, all around 4,000-4,500 F per boat for a full day. *Papyrus*, Marina Bas-du-Fort, Pointe-à-Pitre, Tel: 90 92 98, is a glass-bottom boat which runs excursions through the Rivière Salée to l'Îlet Caret and coral reef off the northeast coast of Basse-Terre. *Nautilus*, from Malendure beach, Tel:98 89 08, is a glass-bottom boat which takes you round the marine park, departs 1030, 1200, 1430 and 1630, 80F adults, 40F children 5-12 years. Most of the hotels on the seaboard offer windsurfing for guests and visitors, and some arrange water skiing and diving courses. Windsurfers gather at the UCPA Hotel Club in Saint François.

Sailing boats can be chartered for any length of time from Captain

Lemaire, Carénage A, Route du Gosier, 97110 Pointe-à-Pitre. With a crew of 3 the cost works out at about US$75-100 pp per day, excluding food, or US$250-300 per boat. There are two marinas between Pointe-à-Pitre and Gosier, and good, shallow-draught anchorage at Gosier.

Other Sports
Hiking in the Natural Park (contact the Organisation des Guides de Montagne de la Caraïbe (OGMC), Maison Forestière, 97120 Matouba, Tel: 80 05 79, a guided hike to La Soufrière will cost around 300 F, make sure the guide speaks a language you understand, approximate hiking times, mileage and description of terrain and flora are included in the booklet *Promenades et Randonnées*); **horseriding** (Le Criolo, Saint-Félix, 97190 Gosier, Tel: 84 38 90, or Le Relais du Moulin, Châteaubrun, 97180 Sainte-Anne, Tel: 88 23 96); **tennis**, with lighting for night games, at several hotels, including *Auberge de la Vieille Tour*, *PLM Arawak*, *Salako*, *Creole Beach*, *Novotel*, and *Village Viva* (also squash), all at Gosier, *Méridien*, *Hamak*, *Trois-Mâts* at Saint-François, and *Les Alizés* at Le Moule. There is one 18-hole, municipal **golf course** at Saint-François (Tel: 88 41 87). The *Hotel Golf Marine Club* at Saint-François, Tel: 88 60 60, has an 18-hole course designed by Robert Trent Jones, green fees 220F/day or 1,000F/week.

Festivals
Carnival starts on Epiphany and runs through Ash Wednesday with different events each Sunday, the main ones on the last weekend. The Festival of the Sea is in mid-August with beach parties, boat races, crab races, etc. La Fête des Cuisinières (Cooks' Festival) in early August is a lot of fun with parades in créole costumes and music.

Grande-Terre

Pointe-à-Pitre, on Grande-Terre at the south end of the Rivière Salée, is the chief commercial centre, near the airport of Le Raizet and the port of entry for shipping (population is 80,000). It is a functional city, variously described as characterless, or colourful and bustling. Its early colonial buildings were largely destroyed by an earthquake in 1845; nowadays it is an odd mixture of parts which could have been transplanted from provincial France and parts which are Caribbean, surrounded by low-cost housing blocks. The tree-shaded Place de la Victoire was once the site of a guillotine, and the streets adjacent to it contain the oldest buildings. Having been refurbished in 1989 it lost several of its large trees in Hurricane Hugo. The colourful central market place (between rues Peynier, Fréboult, St-John Perse and Schoelcher) is indeed bustling, with the nearest thing to local hustlers, women who try to sell you spices, fruit, vegetables or hats. There are other markets on the dockside in Place de la Victoire, between Blvd Chanzy and the docks and between Blvd Légitimus and the cemetery. Local handicrafts, particularly Madras cotton (from which the traditional costumes of the *doudous*, or local women, are made), are good buys. Such items are in great contrast to the French fashions, wines and perfumes available at normal French domestic prices in the shops.

There are two museums: Musée Schoelcher, 24 rue Peynier, which celebrates the liberator of the slaves (open Monday-Tuesday 0900-1230, 1400-1730, Thursday-Friday 0900-1230, 1400-1830, Saturday 0900-1230, entry 10 F), and Musée Saint-John Perse, in a lovely colonial-style house, rues Nozières et A R Boisneuf, dedicated to the poet and diplomat who was

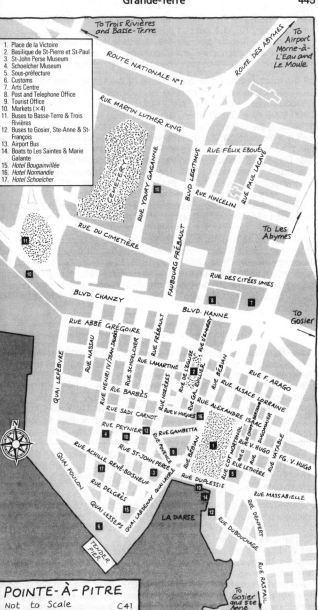

1. Place de la Victoire
2. Basilique de St-Pierre et St-Paul
3. St-John Perse Museum
4. Schoelcher Museum
5. Sous-préfecture
6. Customs
7. Arts Centre
8. Post and Telephone Office
9. Tourist Office
10. Markets (×4)
11. Buses to Basse-Terre & Trois Rivières
12. Buses to Gosier, Ste-Anne & St-François
13. Airport Bus
14. Boats to Les Saintes & Marie Galante
15. *Hotel Bougainvillée*
16. *Hotel Normandie*
17. Hotel Schoelcher

To Trois Rivières and Basse-Terre

To Airport Morne-à-L'Eau and Le Moule

ROUTE NATIONALE N°1

ROUTE DES ABYMES

RUE MARTIN LUTHER KING

RUE FÉLIX EBOUÉ

BLVD LEGITIMUS

RUE PAUL LACAVE

RUE YOURY GAGANNE

RUE HINCELIN

CEMETERY

RUE DU CIMETIÈRE

To Les Abymes

FAUBOURG FRÉBAULT

RUE DES CITÉES UNIES

BLVD. CHANZY

BLVD. HANNE

To Gosier

RUE ABBÉ GRÉGOIRE

RUE FRÉBAULT

RUE NASSAU

RUE HENRI IV / JEAN JAURÈS

RUE SCHOELCHER

RUE LAMARTINE

RUE DE L'ÉGLISE

RUE BÉBIAN

RUE F. ARAGO

RUE GA... OUILLIER

RUE BARBÈS

RUE NOZIÈRES

RUE GA... DEBIEN

RUE ALEXANDRE ISAAC

RUE ALSACE LORRAINE

RUE SADI CARNOT

RUE V. HUGUES

RUE CDT MORTENOL

RUE DUGOMMIER

RUE PEYNIER

RUE GAMBETTA

RUE COMMANDANT

RUE V. HUGO

RUE VATABLE

RUE ACHILLE RENÉ-BOISNEUF

RUE ST-JOHN PERSE

RUE PROVENCE

RUE BÉBIAN

RUE FG. V. HUGO

QUAI LEFÈBVRE

RUE LETHIÈRE

RUE DELGRÈS

RUE DUPLESSIS

RUE MASSABIELLE

QUAI FOULON

QUAI LESSEPS

QUAI LARDENAY

QUAI LATING

RUE DENFERT

RUE DUBOUCHAGE

LA DARSE

RUE RASPAIL

N

TENDER PIER

POINTE-À-PITRE
Not to Scale   C41

To Gosier and Ste Anne

awarded the Nobel Prize for literature in 1960 (open 0900-1700, closed Sundays, entry 10F, children half price).

La Darse, the harbour on which the Place de la Victoire stands, is where the inter-island vessels, schooners and pleasure craft tie up. You should be able to see the peaks of Basse-Terre across the water, if they are not shrouded in cloud

Off the main road to Gosier are the ruins of the 18th-century fortress, Fort Fleur d'Epée (open daily 0900-1800, free). Gosier itself is the holiday centre of Guadeloupe, with hotels, restaurants, night clubs, and an aquarium (0900-1900 daily, 30F, children half price). There has been lots of building in this area, even up into the hills above the coast road. Nevertheless, Gosier itself is a pleasant place with a marvellous picnic spot overlooking a small island and lighthouse. Sainte-Anne, further east has lovely beaches; Saint-François, the next town on the coast, is well-developed with a marina, golf courses, watersports etc. The rugged Pointe-de-Châteaux is the easternmost tip of the island; on its northern shore is Plage Tarare. From the point there is a good view of the flat island of Désirade.

Between Saint-François and Le Moule, a colonial mansion at Zévalos can be visited. Le Moule was the original capital of Guadeloupe. A precolumbian Arawak village, called Morel, has recently been uncovered on the beautiful sandy beaches north of the town; the Musée d'Archéologie Précolombienne Edgar Clerc is at La Rosette (open Monday-Tuesday 0900-1230, 1400-1700, Thursday-Saturday 0900-1230, 1400-1800, free). From Le Moule you can either return to Point-à-Pitre through Les Grands Fonds, or continue up the rugged, rough Atlantic coast to Pointe de la Grande Vigie in the extreme north. Grande-Terre's leeward coast has beaches at Port-Louis and Petit-Canal.

Basse-Terre

Basse-Terre, on the other wing of the island, is the administrative capital of Guadeloupe and the entire Department, with a population of 20,000. There can be found in the city some very pretty and authentic old buildings of the colonial period. It is a charming port town of narrow streets and well-laid-out squares with palm and tamarind trees, in a lovely setting between the sea and the great volcano La Soufrière. There is an interesting 17th-century cathedral, and nearby are the ruins of Fort Saint-Charles (original building 1650, considerably enlarged in the 17th and 18th centuries; open daily 0900-1200, 1400-1700, free).

Saint-Claude, a wealthy suburb and summer resort 8 km into the hills, is surrounded by coffee trees and tropical gardens. Matouba, above Saint-Claude, is an East Indian village in lovely surroundings (waterfall and springs) with a good restaurant.

On Basse-Terre island one of the main sights is the volcano La Soufrière, reached through a primeval rain forest. A narrow road leads up from Basse-Terre town to a car park at Savane à Mulets (1,142 m) from where the crater is a 300 metre climb up the Chemin des Dames, a fascinating trail with changing flora. (The best clothing for the climb is the least; anoraks or coats worn against the dampness merely compound the problem; but take a sweater, it can get quite chilly. Leave some spare clothes in the car.) From the top there is a spectacular view (if you are not enveloped in clouds, which is usually the case, but less likely to be so at mid-day and slightly after), above the lush jungle foliage and sulphurous fumes spurting over yellow and orange rock. It is possible to come down on the Trace Micael, along a forest path, to the Chutes de Carbet waterfalls where the water becomes cool and clear. Carry on down, past more waterfalls, until you get to a car park. If starting from the bottom, take a bus from Capesterre to Routhiers, 10F, then walk along the D3 road until it ends. Follow a trail and within 50 minutes you will reach the third waterfall of 20 metres. Go back 100 metres and follow the trail upwards again for 1½ hours until you reach the 110-metre, second waterfall, 711 metres above sea level. From here you can continue climbing to the first waterfall, or turn southeast to the picnic place, Aire d'Arrivée, 15 minutes, where there is a barbecue (good chicken). The D4 road starts here and descends to St-Sauveur. La Citerne, a neighbouring volcano, has a completely round crater. There is a trail but part requires climbing ladders straight up the wall. There are more leisurely trails to other craters, fumaroles and lakes. Also on this side are Grand Étang and Étang Zombi. You can drive, hitchhike or walk down the D4 road from the Chutes de Carbet to the edge of Grand Étang and walk around it, about one hour through lush vegetation. Do not swim in the lake because of bilharzia. Walk down to St-Sauveur for fine views over banana plantations, the coast and Les Saintes. Allow at least five hours to walk from Capesterre to St-Sauveur via the waterfalls and Grand Étang and wear good hiking shoes. You can walk the Trace Victor Hugues, along the main ridge of Basse-Terre (a 29-km hike), and a number of other Traces. Other features of the Natural Park are described under **Flora and Fauna**, above.

Besides the Maisons du Volcan and de la Fôret (see above), there are on Basse-Terre Maisons du Café at Grande Rivière, Vieux Habitants (closed for renovations in 1992, due to reopen in 1993), du Bois at Bourg, Pointe Noire (a cabinet-making and woodworking centre with a permanent exhibition of furniture and other things made of wood, daily hours 0915-1700, 5F) and a Centre de Broderie, Fort l'Olive, Vieux-Fort (daily 0900-1800). Vieux-Fort is on the island's southwest tip, on the other side of the Monts Caraïbes from the main Basse-Terre to Pointe-à-Pitre road.

A good hike is the Trace des Contrebandiers, three hours, from the Maison du Bois, Pointe Noire. A long but beautiful road takes you to the Trace. When you leave the trail on the other side you need to hitch-hike because there are no buses.

Also visit the ancient Carib rock carvings near Trois Rivières, on Basse-Terre's south coast; the most important is a drawing of the head of a Carib chief inside a cave where he is presumably buried. The site is now in a garden setting, with wardens (it's a good idea to consult the leaflet which comes with the 4F entry fee because some of the engravings on the stones are hard to decipher; the pamphlet also explains the garden's trees). The Parc is a ten-minute walk down from the church in Trois Rivières. Five minutes further down the hill is the boat dock for Les Saintes (paying car park). Back towards Pointe-à-Pitre, see Sainte-Marie, where a statue commemorates the site of Columbus' landing in 1493.

Between Basse-Terre town and the Route de la Traversée are Vieux-Habitants, with a restored 17th-century church and the underwater reserve (see **Marine Life** above). North of the Traversée, on the Côte-Sous-Le-Vent are the calm, clean beaches at Ferry and Grand-Anse and the rougher ones at Deshaies. Round the north of Basse-Terre is the town of Sainte-Rose; the road continues south to Lamentin (visit the Grosse-Montagne distillery for guided tours and tastings) and the hot springs at Ravine Chaude.

Outer Islands of Guadeloupe

The outer islands of Guadeloupe are among the least visited of the West Indian islands; they can easily be reached by air or boat from Guadeloupe. One can still get on a trading schooner between the islands if patient.

Les Saintes

On *Les Saintes* (a string of small islands named Los Santos by Columbus: only Terre-de-Haut and Terre-de-Bas are inhabited) the people are descendants of Breton fisherfolk who have survived among themselves with little intermarriage with the dominant West Indian races. Some still wear the same round hats that Breton fisherfolk used to wear, and fishing is still the main occupation on the islands. They are a popular excursion from Guadeloupe now, but are not too spoilt. Nevertheless, to get a better idea of the islanders' traditional way of life, staying overnight is recommended so that you can appreciate it once the day trippers leave at 1600.

Terre-de-Haut is the main island: there are some excellent beaches including that of Pont Pierre (admission 1F) where camping is possible, Marigot, L'Anse du Figuier, L'Anse Crawen (nudist) and Grand'Anse (white sand, rougher waters, swimming not allowed). Snorkelling is good at Plage de Pompierre. Boats and diving equipment can be rented at the landing stage. Walking on the islands is good, either from the town to the beaches, or to the top of Le Chameau on Terre-de-Haut's western end (spectacular views of Les Saintes, Marie Galante, Guadeloupe and Dominica). An easy trail, Trace des Crétes, starts at Terre-de-Haut. Turn right at the pier, follow the main street about 100 metres, turn left at the chapel and follow the road up to Le Marigot and on to the beach of Baie de Pont Pierre, a lovely golden beach with rocks, Roches Percées, in the bay. At the end of the beach the trail leads up the hill where you have a good view of the islands, if you keep left, one branch of the trail leads to Grand'Anse beach. The 'white' cemetery, worth visiting, is close to the beach and from here you can walk back to Terre-de-Haut, about 1½ hours in total. There are beautiful views also from Fort Napoléon, which is being restored, open 0900-1200 only (10F to enter, children 6 to 12 half price). The views demonstrate the strategic importance of Les Saintes (the Gibraltar of the Caribbean), and the museum in Fort Napoléon gives the French view of the decisive sea battle of Les Saintes (1782—the English Admiral Rodney defeated and scattered the fleet of France's Commander de Grasse, who was preparing to attack Jamaica). If not historically-minded, just sit and watch the weather. There are exhibits also of local fishing and crafts, a bookshop and drinks on sale. On the Ilet à Cabrit are the ruins of Fort Joséphine.

Island Information—Les Saintes

How To Get There There are daily boats from Trois Rivières (Guadeloupe) to Terre-de-Haut via Terre-de-Bas (40F one way, 30 minutes, 70F return: depart Trois Rivières between 0800 and 0900, and 1500 and 1645, different each day; depart Terre-de-Haut 0545-0630, 1500-1615, Tel: 92 90 30/99 53 79) and from Pointe-à-Pitre (80F one way, 160F return, about 1 hour, daily 0800, return 1600, Trans Antilles Express from La Darse, Tel: 83 12 45). Boat from Basse-Terre Monday, Wednesday, Thursday and Saturday 1230, 45 minutes. It can be a rough crossing, not suitable for those prone to seasickness. Daily flight except Sunday from Pointe-à-Pitre, 15 minutes, Air Guadeloupe (address above); or Air Sport, Le Raizet, Tel: 82 25 80.

Island Transport Minibuses take day trippers all over Terre-de-Haut; tour of the island 52F, bus up to Fort Napoléon, 10F (or 25 minutes' walk). No transport after dark. Scooter rental, 200F/day, also bicycles, several central locations, 80F/day.

Where To Stay On Terre-de-Haut: *Bois Joli*, 620-1,100F, MAP, reached by 10-minute boat ride from town, rather inconvenient at the end of the island, 21 rooms, 5 bungalows, Tel: 99 50 38; *Kanaoa*, Pointe Coquelot, Tel: 99 51 36, 480F, CP, a/c, but rather basic, beautiful waterfront setting 10 minutes' walk from landing jetty, very quiet; *Le Village Créole*, Pointe Coquelot, Tel: 99 53 83, 40 rooms, 22 duplex, yacht charter, boats to rent, private beach, 640-900F; *La Saintoise*, Tel: 99 52 69, in town (closed in November), 350F CP, *Auberge des Anacardiers*, Tel: 99 50 99, attractive, intimate, clean, pool, good restaurant, recommended and *Jeanne d'Arc*, good, Tel: 99 50 41, at Fond de Curé village on south coast 290F, CP (closed in November), all with 10 rooms. On both Terre-de-Haut and Terre-de-Bas there are rooms and houses to rent; tourist office has list of phone numbers. Recommended are Mme Bonbon, Tel: 90 50 51, on the road to the airfield, and Mme Maisonneuve, Tel: 99 53 38, on the same road as the *Mairie*. Reservations are generally recommended in peak season, especially Christmas and New Year. The Mairie and the Gendarmerie are reported as very unhelpful regarding accommodation and will not tell you where the hotels are situated. The telephone at the jetty only takes phone cards. Not good for first impressions but otherwise idyllic. There is a shortage of water on the island.

Plenty of **restaurants** around the island, specializing in seafood, but try the *tourment d'amour* coconut sweet. Home made coconut rum punches are also recommended, particularly in the little bar on the right hand side of the *gendarmerie* in front of the jetty. *Le Mouillage* restaurant has been recommended.

Marie-Galante

Marie-Galante, a small round island of 153 square km, is simple and old-fashioned but surprisingly sophisticated when it comes to food and drink. It was named by Christopher Columbus after his own ship, the *Santa María La Galante*, and has three settlements. The largest is Grand-Bourg in the southwest with a population of around 8,000; Capesterre is in the southeast and Saint-Louis in the northwest. The beaches, so far almost completely untouched by the tourist flood, are superb. By Capesterre, the Plage de la Feuillère has fine sand beaches and is protected by the coral reef offshore. The Trou à Diable is a massive cave which runs deep into the earth. To visit it, it is essential to have strong shoes, a torch with extra batteries, and a guide. It is very remote spot and there is no organized tourism. The descent requires ropes and should not be attempted unassisted. The walk from the road through the forest is striking. In the nineteenth century the island boasted over 100 sugar mills; a few have been restored and may be visited: Basses, Grand-Pierre, Agapit and Murat. Some are still operating. The former plantation houses of Château Murat (museum open Monday to Thursday 0900-1300, 1500-1800, Saturday and Sunday 0900-1200, free) and Brûle are interesting. There is a cinema in Grand-Bourg, El Rancho, which has movies dubbed into French.

Island Information—Marie-Galante

How To Get There To get to the island there are regular flights (20 minutes) from Pointe-à-Pitre, which is only 43 km away (Air Guadeloupe, as above). There are also ferries between Pointe-à-Pitre and Grand-Bourg (85F one way, 160F return, 1-1½ hours, times are posted on the booth at the dockside): *Tropic* and *Regina* sail at least three times a day (Tel: 90 04 48), Trans Antilles Express twice a day except three times on Monday and once on Sunday. The latter also runs a service from Saint-François to Saint-Louis, (depart Wednesday and Saturday 0800). *Amanda Galante*, a car ferry, crosses from Pointe-à-Pitre to Saint-Louis in 1½ hours, 560F car and driver return, 50F for each passenger, takes 22 cars and 156 passengers. Trans Antilles offer full and half-day tours to Marie-Galante from Pointe-à-Pitre, including boat trip, visits to beaches, the towns, sugar factories, rum distillery (plus tasting) and other sites (0800-1630 daily, except 0730 weekends, 230F, or 180F for half day, meals 75F extra). The *Mistral* also does a Thursday tour to Marie-Galante from Saint-François (210F, 0800-1600, Tel: 88 48 74 or 88 48 63).

Inland Transport On the island there are buses and taxis. Self-drive cars can be hired from the airport or in the towns, eg M Seytor, rue Beaurenom, Grand-Bourg. Rates for a full day 240F, for part of a day 190F (2,000F deposit); scooters 200F (1,000F deposit).

Where To Stay There are no deluxe hotels on Marie-Galante: at Grand-Bourg there are the *Soledad*, 200-250F, EP (Tel: 97 75 45), and *L'Auberge de l'Arbre à Pain* (Tel: 97 73 69); *Le Salut* (clean) is south of the pier at St-Louis, Tel: 97 02 67 (150-300F, EP breakfast 30F, dinner 80F); *Hajo* at Capesterre, Tel: 97 32 76. *Touloulou*, 2 km from Capesterre on the Grand Bourg road, clean, well-equipped bungalows backing directly on to the sea, discotheque and restaurant nearby, 22F, EP, recommended. There are rooms to let (enquire at the tourist board), about 100F a day, and gîtes (175F a night, 1,250F a week). For accommodation, 24-hour advance booking is necessary.

La Désirade

La Désirade is an attractive but rather arid island with 1,600 inhabitants, who occupy themselves in fishing, sheep-rearing and cultivating cotton and maize. A road 10 km long runs along the south coast to the east end of the island, where a giant cactus plantation can be seen. Also at the east end of the island is Pointe du Mombin where there is an outstanding view of the coastline. There are excellent beaches, such as at Souffleur. Perhaps the nicest is in the east at a village called Baie-Mahault, enhanced by a good restaurant/bar, *Chez Céce*, where you can sample dozens of different rum punches.

Island Information—La Désirade

How To Get There There are air services from Guadeloupe 4 times a week (Air Guadeloupe) and boat services from St-François, Guadeloupe (depart 0800, return 1600, 2 hours), to La Désirade, on which is found the *Hôtel L'Oasis du Désert*, Tel: 20 02 12, 6 rooms, 160F, EP reservations advisable. The *Mistral* (as above) runs excursions from Saint-François to La Désirade daily, except Tuesday and Thursday, 0830-1530 (1630 Saturday, 1600 Sunday), including minibus tour of the island and lunch, 180F. Minibuses normally meet incoming flights and boats. There are bicycles and scooters for hire.

Information for Visitors—Guadeloupe

How To Get There

By Air Like Martinique, Guadeloupe is on Air France's direct route from Paris (about 8 hours) with other flights from Cayenne, Miami, Paramaribo, Port-au-Prince and Santo Domingo; for more details, see under Martinique for Air France's services from France and elsewhere. Other services to Pointe-à-Pitre: Air Canada has direct flights from Toronto via Montréal; American Eagle has flights from San Juan, with connections from the USA. Liat offers inter-Caribbean connections to Dominica, Antigua, and Barbados via St Lucia. Air Guadeloupe connects Pointe-à-Pitre with Cayenne, Dominica, Fort-de-France, La Désirade, Marie-Galante, Miami, Paris, Port-au-Prince, St Barts, St Lucia, St Maarten, St Thomas, San Juan and Terre-de-Haut. Other airlines with services to Guadeloupe include Minerve (from Paris), Linea Aeropostal Venezolana (Caracas), Air Martinique (Martinique), Air St-Barthélémy (from Sint Maarten and St-Barts).

Numerous cruise lines sail from US and French ports.

Airline Offices

Air France, Blvd Légitimus, Pointe-à-Pitre,

el: 82 50 00/82 30 00, or Le Raizet airport, Tel: 82 30 20; all others are at Le Raizet: American, Tel: 83 62 62; Air Canada, Tel: 83 62 49; Liat, Tel: 82 12 26/82 00 84. Nouvelles Frontières for charter flights, Tel: 90 36 36, Pointe-à-Pitre. Air Guadeloupe, Le Raizet, Tel: 82 28 35, or 10 rue Sadi Carnot, Pointe-à-Pitre, Tel: 90 12 25.

Inter-Island Transport

You can get a small motor-sail vessel to Dominica from Pointe-à-Pitre for 240F (not much less than the flight). The boat leaves at 1300, 3 days a week, takes 2 hours, is not very comfortable and sea sickness is a distinct possibility.

Transport On Guadeloupe

In Pointe-à-Pitre there are three main bus terminals: from La Darse (by Place de la Victoire), buses run to Gosier (4F), Sainte-Anne (11F), Saint-François (11F); for northern Grande-Terre destinations, buses leave from the Mortenol station. From Blvd Chanzy (near the cemetery) they go to Trois Rivières (20F) and Basse-Terre (22F, 2 hours). Pointe-à-Pitre to La Grande Anse, 15F, 1 hour 45 minutes. Basse-Terre to Trois Rivières, 20 minutes. The terminal in Basse-Terre is on Blvd Général de Gaulle, between the market and the sea. Buses run between 0530 and 1800, leaving for the main destinations every 15 minutes or so, or when full. The airport bus leaves from 0800 from rue Peynier, near the market, 4F. It is possible to cover the whole island by bus in a day—cheap, interesting and easy. You can just stop the bus at the side of the road or wait at the bus stations in the villages. Buses are crowded and play loca music at top volume (exhilarating or deafening, depending on your mood); have your money ready when you get off.

Taxis are rather expensive; some are metered; some routes have fixed fares. All fares double at night. Taxi from the airport to Place de la Victoire costs about 30F it may be only 45F to the airport from Place de la Victoire.

Organized bus tours and boat excursions are available. Check with Tourist Office, Petrelluzzi Travel Agency (American Express Agents), 2 rue Henri IV, Pointe-à-Pitre, and other agencies.

Hitch hiking is no problem and if you speak French it is a recommended way of meeting local people, who are very friendly. However, a bus will often come before you have been waiting long.

Vehicle Rental

Self-drive hire cars are available mainly at the airport, which is inconvenient for those not arriving by air. A small, old Peugeot will cost about US$70 per day. In Pointe-à-Pitre, there is a small office above an icecream parlour on Av V Hugues, just off Place de la Victoire, which has a small selection. Rental can also be arranged through the major hotels. International and local agencies are represented. At Trois Rivières, Rosan Martin, Location de voitures, is close to the dock, Tel: 92 94 24, 262F a day, unlimited mileage, for a Renault B571, deposit 3,000F or credit card. There are also mopeds for hire in Pointe-à-Pitre, Gosier, Saint-François, or through hotels. Mokes and scooters can be rented at Sainte-Anne. Bicycle rental from Velo-Vert, Pointe-à-Pitre, Tel: 831574, Le Relais du Moulin, near Sainte-Anne, Tel: 882396, Rent-a-Bike, Meridien Hotel Saint-François, Tel: 845100, around 50F a day. If you don't have a credit card you normally have to deposit up to 5,000F for a car; 2,000F for a scooter; and 1,000F for moped or bicycle.

Where To Stay

On Grande-Terre: At Pointe-à-Pitre: top of the range is *La Bougainvillée*, 9 rue Frébault, Tel: 82 07 56, 510-545F, EP, which is comfortable, a/c, but at that price the plumbing could be better, good expensive restaurant; *Normandie*, 14 Place de la Victoire, Tel: 82 37 15, 300F with shower and a/c, cheaper without bath, CP, popular, best to book in advance, restaurant is good; even better, however, is the new hotel next door, *La Maison de la Marie Galante*, much the same price; next best is *Schoelcher*, rue Schoelcher, 190-250F, EP, not very clean, but good, reasonably-priced restaurant; *Relais des Antilles*, corner of rue Massabielle and rue Vatable, just off the Place de la Victoire, basic, noisy but friendly and cheap, 250F, EP, with toilet; *Karukera*, 15 rue Alsace-Lorraine, 200F with bath, no fan, EP, not good.

There are a great many hotels in the Bas du Fort Bay/Gosier tourist area; the Tourist Board publishes full descriptions and price lists for the majority. We include a small selection: *Auberge de la Vieille Tour*, Montauban, 97190 Gosier, Tel: 84 23 23, named after an 18th-century sugar tower incorporated into the main building, is on a bluff over the sea, beach, pool, tennis, refurbished in 1990, 3 2-room bungalows and 8 rooms in French colonial style, gourmet restaurant, US$120-160d (summer) including tax and service, breakfast US$12, like a number of others this is a member of PLM-Azur group; another is *Marissol*, 15 minutes from Pointe-à-Pitre, 200 rooms and bungalows, restaurants, discothèque, tennis, beach with watersports and a spa/gym with instructors and physiotherapist, US$75-95d EP including tax and service (summer rate); *Residence de la Pergola*, on the beach, reasonably priced, 350-420F, EP, but unfriendly; better is *Chez Rosette Restaurant/Hotel*, 300F, EP, basic but clean, on other side of main road. *Arawak*, Tel: 84 24 24, nice beach, pool, 890-1,130F, CP, 425-600Fd EP in low season, a/c, buses 400 m away; *Callinago* is slightly smaller, beach, pool, 782-914F, Tel: 84 25 25, also apartments at *Callinago Village*, from US$62d for a studio EP summer rates, larger apartments up to US$125-200; *Serge's Guest House*, on seafront, Tel: 84 10 25, 296F, CP, poor reports, very basic, not very clean, convenient for buses and beach, has nice garden and swimming pool. In the same area, *Les Flamboyants*, is clean, a/c, same price, pool, sea view, some kitchenettes, friendly. A smaller establishment is the *Hotel Corossol*, Mathurin, 97190 Gosier, Tel: 84 39 89, 125F pp, CP, friendly, good meals, easy walking to Gosier. Many places advertise rooms to let.

At **Sainte-Anne** are *Relais du Moulin*, 40 a/c bungalows, 590-685F, CP and 893-985F, MAP (Tel: 88 23 96); *Motel Sainte-Anne*, Tel: 88 22 40, ten rooms, a/c, 450F EP, 510F, CP, 690F, MAP, *Auberge du Grand Large*, neither grand nor large, but friendly and with good restaurant on the beach, Tel: 88 20 06, 600F, CP; and *Mini Beach*, 1 km from town, also on the beach, relaxed, good location, many restaurants nearby, Tel: 88 21 13, 500-750F, CP, can fall to half price in summer, good restaurant, meals from 100F, excellent fish soup 15F, a meal in itself. Between Gosier and Sainte-Anne, at La Marie-Gaillarde, is *Marie-Gaillarde*, Tel: 85 84 29, overlooking Les Grands Fonds, 2 km from Petit Havre beach, with restaurant and bar, 310F EP, 360F CP. At Saint-François, *Méridien*, Air France's modern and conventional seaside complex, beach, pool, golf, tennis, flying school, dock, discothèque, and casino,

1800-2900F, CP; among other luxury places: *Hamak*, 1,500-2,730F, CP, and **VVFG**. *Chez Honoré*, Place du Marché, clean, simple, friendly, noisy because of the disco next door but still one of the cheapest in the French West Indies at 275F CP. At **Le Moule**: *Les Alizés* Canadian-owned, good horseshoe-shaped beach, pool, golf, 225-450F, Tel 23 17 80.

Club Méditerranée has a hotel-village on the island (membership is required): *La Caravelle* at Sainte-Anne is on a spectacular white sand beach, perhaps the best on Guadeloupe, surrounded by a 13-hectare reserve; atmosphere strictly informal (nude bathing), all sports equipment available, gourmet dining unlimited, non-members seem to be able to get in. Apply to your local representative for rates. Bus from Pointe-à-Pitre 7F.

On **Basse-Terre**: accommodation i neither plentiful nor high class in **Basse-Terre** city: Hotel *Basse-Terre-Charlery*, 52 rue Maurice Marie Claire, Tel: 81 19 78, central, basic, clean and cheap, 125F, breakfast 16F good oriental restaurant next door; also central is *Le Drouant*, 26 rue Dr Cabre 200F; *Le Relais d'Orléans*, rue Lardenoy *Hotel Higuera*, 225F, on main square opposite Hotel de Ville, Tel: 81 11 92. A **Saint-Claude**: *Relais de la Grand Soufrière*, an elegant but rather poorly-converted old plantation mansion a/c, attractive surroundings, old wooden furniture, friendly staff, Tel: 80 01 27 400-500F, EP, regular bus service to Basse-Terre, including Sundays. For *Royal* at Deshaies, Tel: 28 41 10, is slightly run-down old luxurious hotel which used to belong to *Club Med* dramatically situated on a promontor between two beautiful but rather rough beaches, 650-800F CP. At **Trois Rivière** are *Le Joyeux*, a 3F bus ride from the centre of the town (bus stop right outside or short walk, in Le Faubourg, 100m above the sea, Tel: 92 71 24, 220-260F, CP, simple rooms, kitchenettes, Créol restaurant, bar, disco, closed Monday except for reservations, recommended good views to Les Saintes, very friendly Monsieur will drive you to the boat dock for nothing, the family also run a small supermarket and the Serie Bleu maps are sold there; *Grand'Anse*, Tel: 92 90 47 bungalows, also has Créole restaurant and views 400F, CP; *Les Gîtes de l'habitation*

Cardonnet, Tel: 92 70 55, 5 self-contained cottages.

The Tourist Board has current price lists (they run an information desk at Raizet airport).

Gîtes

Throughout the island there are a large number of gîtes for rent on a daily, weekly or monthly basis. Weekly rates range from 700F to 3,000F, but most are in the 1,000-1,500F bracket. The tourist offices in both Pointe-à-Pitre and Basse-Terre have lists of the properties available and should be consulted in the first instance. Gîtes are arranged by the local Syndicats d'Initiative who have an office next to the Tourist Office on rue Provence. For example, the Syndicat d'Initiative de Deshaies, Tel: 28 49 70, lists 14 local people who let gîtes. Some gîtes are quite isolated, so choose one that is conveniently located. The Syndicats charge a 5% rental fee.

The tourist offices also have lists of villas for rent (there are a number in Saint-François, for instance); prices vary between 1,500F and 4,500F depending on number of occupants, size of villa and season.

Camping

Compared with metropolitan France, camping is not well organized and the Tourist Office does not have much information. A small but highly recommended campsite is Sable d'Or, near Deshaies, Basse-Terre, Tel: 81 39 10. The charge is approximately 69F per tent for 2 people. Also small bungalows, 80-150F, cooking facilities, helpful owner, the only problem being his small daughter who likes to rummage through the tents when the family is there at weekends. There are buses from Pointe-à-Pitre. VVF Guadeloupe hotel at Saint-François has a camping ground with all amenities (Tel: 88 41 27). Camping Traversée is near Mahait on Basse Terre. Otherwise ask mayors if you may camp on municipal land, or owners on private property. Camper vans can be arranged through Découverts et Loisirs Créoles in Abymes, Tel: 20 55 65, from 700F.

Where To Eat

Apart from the hotel restaurants mentioned above, there are a large number of restaurants, cafés and patisseries to choose from. Many are closed in the evening. In **Pointe-à-Pitre**: *Oasis*, rues Nozières et A R Boisneuf (French); *Relais des Antilles* (cheaper, but good Créole cooking); near the *Auberge Henri IV*, in a private house, good, cheap meals (ask Valentin at the *Auberge* for directions); *Krishna*, 47 rue A R Boisneuf, Indian. At Le Raizet airport: *Oiseau des Iles* (French), and *Godire*, self-service. On the Grande-Terre holiday coast: *La Case Créole*, Route de la Rivièra; *Chez Rosette*, Av Général de Gaulle, both Créole at Gosier; *Chez Gina*, in a little village caféière, 2½ km inland from Les Sables d'Or campsite, up the hill, excellent food, order in advance in the morning for an evening meal, 60F pp for 4 courses and apéritif, served in a sort of garage with flowers, friendly, don't be put off by the untidy surroundings; *Côté Jardin*, at Bas du Fort marina, French; *La Plantation*, same location, same cuisine. In Sainte-Anne, *Chez Yvette* is budget-priced; and in Saint-François, *Madame Jerco* has good food in a small creaking house. On Basse-Terre, *Chez Paul* in Matouba has been recommended for Créole and East Indian cuisine. The *Relais de la Grande Soufrière*, at Saint-Claude offers two menus for lunch, highly recommended créole meals at reasonable prices, 120F for the menu.

Shopping

An unusual fruit, the *carambole*, can be bought in Pointe-à-Pitre. The location of the markets is given above. Good Mamouth Supermarket near Le Raizet airport 3.50F by bus from Pointe-à-Pitre.

Climate

The temperature on the coasts varies between 22° and 30° C, but is about 3° lower in the interior. January to April is the dry season (called *carême*), July to November the wet season (*l'hivernage*), with most rain falling from September to November. Trade winds moderate temperatures the year round.

Business Hours

0800-1200, 1430-1700 weekdays, morning only on Saturday; government offices open 0730-1300, 1500-1630 Monday and Friday, 0730-1300 Tuesday-Thursday. Banking hours: 0800-1200, 1400-1600 Monday to Friday.

Banks

Banque Nationale de Paris (good for Visa cash advances), Banque Française Commerciale, Banque des Antilles Françaises, BRED, Crédit Agricole all have branches throughout the island. Banks

454 Guadeloupe

charge 1% commission and 4% *dessier* (filing fee). Exchange is handled up to midday so go early to avoid the late morning pandemonium. American Express is at Petreluzzi Travel, 2 rue Henri IV, English spoken, helpful.

Exchange
Hotels give the worst rates, then banks (but their rates vary so shop around), post offices change dollars (but not all makes of travellers' cheque, slow service), and the best rates can be found in Edouard Saingolet, Bureau de Change, rues Nozières et Barbès, Pointe-à-Pitre (Tel: 90 34 63), open daily (am only Saturday and Sunday). There is one exchange facility at the airport and it is closed all day Monday.

Post And Telecommunications
Post office and telephones building in Pointe-à-Pitre is on Blvd Hanne, crowded, sweltering. For local calls you must buy phone cards; to call abroad, you must hand over identification at the desk (calls to the USA 12.85F/minute, Europe 18.50F/minute, Australia 23.10F/minute; hotels charge twice as much). Post and phones in Basse-Terre is on rue Dr Pitat, between Dumanoir and Ciceron, smaller but a bit more comfortable than the Pointe-à-Pitre office. Parcel post is a problem and you can usually send parcels of up to 2 kg only. In Pointe-à-Pitre there is an office near the stadium where you can mail parcels of up to 7 kg by air but it is unreliable; one correspondent sent a tent but received a cake wrapped in the same paper.

Useful Addresses
Police assistance: Tel: 82 00 05 i Pointe-à-Pitre, 81 11 55 in Basse-Terre nautical assistance, Tel: 82 91 08; medica centre, Tel: 82 98 80/82 88 88. Mo diplomatic representation in the Frenc Antilles is in Martinique; however, th Netherlands has a consulate at 5 rue o Nozières, Pointe-à-Pitre, Tel: 82 01 16 and the Dominican Republic at rue St-John Perse et Frébault, Pointe-à-Pitre Tel: 82 01 87.

Tourist Information
Tourist offices in Guadeloupe: 5 Square d la Banque, Pointe-à-Pitre, Tel: 82 09 3 (very unhelpful, unlike the Gîtes office nex door); Maison du Port, Cours Nolivos Basse-Terre, Tel: 81 24 83 (very helpful); A de l'Europe, Saint-François, Tel: 88 48 74 The tourist office publishes a bookle called *Bonjour Guadeloupe*, whic contains descriptive and practica information, and a broadsheet, *Pratique* which gives details on concerts an exhibitions, flights, shipping, emergenc numbers and all-night chemists an doctors. The Serie Bleu maps (1:25,000) maps of Guadeloupe, No 4601G-4607G issued by the Institut Geógraphiqu National, Paris, which include all hikin trails, are available at the bigger boo stores in the rue Frébault in Pointe-à-Pitre and at *Le Joyeux* hotel in Trois Rivières/L Faubourg for 52F. National Park: Par National de la Guadeloupe, Habitatio Beausoleil, Montéran, BP13-97120 Saint-Claude, Tel: 80 24 25, Fax: 80 05 46

SAINT-MARTIN

SAINT-MARTIN, the largest of Guadeloupe's outer islands, is divided between France and the Netherlands. See Netherlands Antilles section for general description, map and information. The French part used to be a sleepy place, but has become very Americanized since the building of the yacht marina.

Government and Economy
The French side is a sub-prefecture of Guadeloupe, with the sub-prefect appointed in Paris. There is an elected town council, led by a mayor. The economy is entirely dependent upon tourism, with the twin attractions of duty-free shopping and the sea (for bathers and sailors).

Marigot

Marigot, the capital of French Saint-Martin, lies between Simpson's Bay Lagoon and the Caribbean sea. ("Marigot" is a French West Indian word meaning a spot from which rain water does not drain off, and forms marshy pools.) Shopping is good. Boutiques offer French *prêt-à-porter* fashions and St Barts batiks, and gift shops sell liqueurs, perfumes, and cosmetics at better duty-free prices than the Dutch side. At the *Marina Port La Royale* complex there are chic shops, cafés and bistros where you can sit and watch the boats. Rue de la République and Rue de la Liberté also have good shopping with fashion names at prices well below those of Europe or the USA. A fruit market is held every morning in the market place next to Marigot harbour. It is best on Wednesdays and Saturdays. On the right hand side of the market place is the Tourist Office and taxi rank; also the only public toilet on the French side (1F or US$0.25). From here it is a ten minute walk to Fort St Louis overlooking Marigot Bay and Marigot. Follow the signs from the Tourist Office. On the waterfront the historical and archaeological Museum "On the trails of the Arawaks" open 0900-1300, 1500-1830, Monday-Saturday. May open longer during high season, has a well-presented exhibition from the first settlers of Saint-Martin around 3500 BC to 1960. Entrance US$5 (US$3 children). Carnival is held pre-Lent and most of the events are on the waterfront in Marigot. It is not as big and grandiose as on the Dutch side, where carnival is held a few weeks later, but there are calypso and beauty contests and a Grand Parade. Bastille Day (14th July) has live music, jump-ups and boat races; the celebrations move to Grand Case the weekend after (more fun). In Grand Case on New Year's Day there is a small parade with live music, while at Easter another parade is held with a lot of dancing.

Excursions

Grand Case, 13 km from the capital, is anything but grand: a quaint town between an old salt pond (which has been partially filled in to provide the Espérance airstrip) and a long sandy and secluded beach. At the far northeast end is another beach, Petite Plage, delightfully *petite* in a calm bay. Every other Saturday all year round there are sailing races of old fishing boats

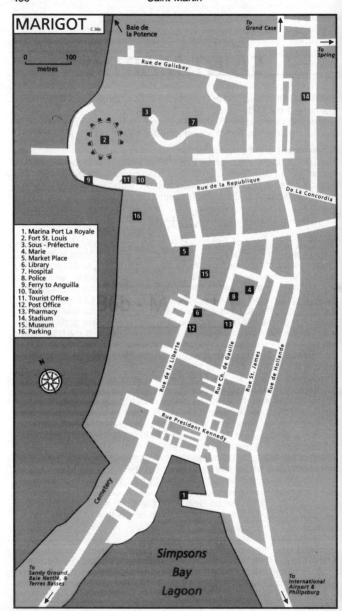

MARIGOT C 36b

0   100
metres

To Grand Case
To Spring

Baie de la Potence

Rue de Galisbay

Rue de la Republique

De La Concordia

1. Marina Port La Royale
2. Fort St. Louis
3. Sous - Préfecture
4. Marie
5. Market Place
6. Library
7. Hospital
8. Police
9. Ferry to Anguilla
10. Taxis
11. Tourist Office
12. Post Office
13. Pharmacy
14. Stadium
15. Museum
16. Parking

N

Rue de la Liberte

Rue Ch. de Gaulle

Rue St. James

Rue de Hollande

Rue President Kennedy

Cemetery

Simpsons
Bay
Lagoon

To Sandy Ground, Baie Nettlé, à Terres Basses

To International Airport & Philipsburg

between Anguilla and St-Martin, mostly to Grand Case. Ask for information at the *Ranch Bar* at the beach (live music every Sunday). Anse Marcel, north of Grand Case, is a shallow beach, ideal for small children. Inland, Pic Paradise (424m) is a good lookout point from where, on a fine day, you can see Anguilla, Saba, St Eustatius, St Kitts, Nevis and St-Barts. By car, take a turn off at Rambaud on the Marigot-Grand Case road. There are also footpaths from Colombier (1½ km) and Orleans (1 km). Colombier is a small, sleepy village with some wonderful gardens, well worth a visit. In Orleans you can visit Roland Richardson, the only well-known native artist on St-Martin, whose home is open 1000-1800 on Thursdays. On the Atlantic, Cul-de-Sac, is a traditional village, from where you may be able to hitch a ride on a fishing boat to the Île de Tintamarre. The sea here is calm and there are boat trips to Pinel Island just offshore. Baie Orientale is beautiful but rough (beware of its undertow); it's also nudist. There are several new developments along the beach and the naturist area is often overrun with day visitors and shrinking. From here you can find boats to Caye Verte, just offshore. Further south, snorkelling is good at Coconut Grove. Topless bathing is accepted at all beaches on the French side, but not on the Dutch.

From Marigot to Anguilla by ferry boat (20 minutes) US$18 round trip plus 10F departure tax, or with one of the many boats operating from the French side; they tend to do it for only one tourist season, so names change quickly. Boat charter companies, with or without crew, are around *Marina Port La Royale*, about US$200/day. There are two squash courts at Le Privilège (Tel: 87 37 37). Horse riding at Caid and Isa, 131 Boulevard de Grand Case, Grand Case, Tel: 87 32 92, daily rides at 0900 and 1500 if there is enough demand, US$45, reservations one day in advance. Helicopter excursions with Heli-Inter Caraibes, Tel: 87 34 47 or 87 37 37. A glass bottom boat, *Carib 1*, leaves from Marigot daily for a tour of the reef, also night excursions on Saturdays, US$45-60.

Information for Visitors—Saint-Martin

How To Get There
International **flights** arrive at the Juliana airport on the Dutch side. On the French side is the Espérance airport which can only take light planes. Air Guadeloupe (address under Guadeloupe above) has daily scheduled services to Saint-Martin from Guadeloupe and Saint-Barthélémy. There is a US$5 departure tax on Saint-Martin, payable only at Juliana airport.

Connections with the French side by **sea**, besides the excursions to Anguilla (see above), can be made with Saint-Barthélémy; St Barts Express, twice daily except Sunday and holidays, departs Gustavia 0815, Philipsburg 0900 and arrives Marigot 0930, returns from Marigot 1530, Philipsburg 1600, arrives Gustavia 1700. On Thursdays a boat, *Ted*, leaves Marigot for Sint Eustatius, may take passengers, US$15-20 one way. Ask at the tourist office, travel agencies or in the Marigot marina. Try putting a notice up at the Capiteneri Marina Port La Royale for hitching a lift to other islands.

Island Transport
Buses run from Grand Case to Marigot (US$1.50) and from Marigot, French Quarters and St Peters to Philipsburg, normally until 2030, US$1.50. Inside town or short trip US$0.75-1. At night time fares rise by US$0.50. There are plenty of taxis, with controlled fares. You find them next to the Tourist Office in Marigot, Tel: 87 56 54. From Marigot to Philipsburg about US$7, add 25% 2200-2400 and 50% 2400-0600. It is easy to hitchhike.

Car rental from several agencies, eg L C Fleming, Marigot, Tel: 87 50 01 (also travel agency); Sunrise, St-James, Marigot, Tel: 87 51 91, Saint-Martin Auto, Grand Case, Tel: 87 50 86, or Marigot Tel: 87 54 72; Avis, Port La-Royale, Marigot, Tel: 87 54 36; many others.

Where To Stay There are a number of luxury resorts, lesser establishments and guest houses and a building boom has raised the total number of hotel rooms to 3,000. The tourist office lists only those in the upper range. *La Sammana*, Baie Longue, Tel: 87 51 22, Fax: 87 87 86, one of the most exclusive resorts in the Caribbean, US$500-720d (2 and 3 bedroomed villas also available, up to US$1,400, tennis, water skiing, windsurfing, sunfish sailing). *Le Galion Beach Hotel et Club* offers a private beach at Quartier d'Orléans on the northeast side of the island near Baie Orientale, 510F to 960F without meals, it also has good water sport facilities (Tel: 87 31 77); *Le Grand Saint-Martin*, 177 rooms, US$300-420d all inclusive, winter, with discothèque, Tel: 87 57 91/2, Fax: 87 80 34; *Le Pirate*, Marigot, a favourite with island-hoppers, studio 750-1,060F, duplex 950-1,280F, CP, Tel: 87 78 37; *Beauséjour*, Tel: 87 52 18, Rue de la République in centre of Marigot, US$45-50 with breakfast. *Royal Beach*, a Pullman Hotel on Nettle Bay, modern, a/c, beachfront but not all rooms have sea view, pool, bar, restaurant, watersports nearby, US$66-104d EP (winter) including tax and service, Tel/Fax: 87 89 89, in the USA call (800) 223-9862 or (212) 719-9363; in Canada (800) 638-9699. At Grand Case: *Tackling's Beach Apartments*; *Hodge's Guest House*; *Goetz Guest House*, apartments about US$250-335 weekly; *Bertines*, Savana, US$75-100 inc breakfast, Tel: 87 58 39; *Hévèa*, from 58-100F, EP, Tel: 87 56 85, Fax: 87 83 88, small colonial-style hotel, gourmet restaurant, beach across the street; *Mme Huckleman*, double apartments US$35-55, Tel: 87 52 21; *Les Alizés*, seven rooms with kitchenettes US$50-100, Tel: 87 95 38; *Cagan's Guest House* and *Le Fish Pot* have a few reasonably-priced rooms; *Petite Plage* (Tel: 87 77 83), housekeeping units on beach at US$120-150 a week, not open all year. Other hotels include the *Grand Case Beach Club*, 76 rooms, and apartments, watersports, tennis, on the beach, Tel: 87 51 87, Fax: 87 59 93; *Coralita Beach Hotel* (Quartier d'Orléans), 24 rooms, 600F EP, Tel: 87 31 81 and *Chez Martine*, Tel: 87 51 59, Fax: 87 87 30, 7 rooms, 1 suite, restaurant, overlooks Grand Case Bay, US$80-96d, winter, EP. *Club Orient* (naturist), is 10 miles from the airport, tennis, volleyball, watersports, massage, US$175d EP, chalets for 3-4 people US$300-405, Tel: 87 33 85, Fax: 87 33 76.

Where To Eat

French cuisine in all hotel restaurants on the French side is quite good but expensive. Picturesque gourmet dining places on the seashore are the islanders' favourites. The likelihood of finding a cheap meal is rare. In Marigot: the *Mini-Club* with its bar and dining arbour, serves a Caribbean buffet Wednesday and Saturday, closed August and September, and *Le Boucanier* for seafood species. Very popular for its Créole specialities is *Cas Anny*. Traditional French in centre of Marigot is *La Calanque*. *David's Pub and Restaurant*, near the Post Office, good food, not expensive, fun bar, recommended. For travellers on a small budget try the snackbars and cafés on Rue de Hollande. *La Maison sur le Port*, *L'Aventure* and *Le Poisson d'Or* offer excellent seafood. *La Fiesta*, cocktail bar/restaurant, the place to be seen at night time, live music every night except Monday; *Le Bar de la Mer*, serves lunch and dinner, good place to go before a disco; *San Remo*, not too expensive Italian, good pizza, pasta and home made ice cream; many bars on the water front next to the tourist office serving barbecue lunch and dinner. *Jamaica* serves low budget lunch and dinner, around US$5. A Vietnamese restaurant is *Santal Thai Garden* in Sandy Ground, next to the French bridge. *Chez René* at the Lagoon Bridge, Sandy Ground, promises really gourmet fare but overpriced. *La Coupole* is French fare in 1930s ambience. Grand Case has a reputation of having more restaurants than inhabitants. Most are on the street next to the beach. *Fish Pot*, overlooking the sea, exquisite sea food. Across the street is *Rosemary's* for Créole cooking. *Chá Chá Chá*, a block away, has Brazilian food, OK but too expensive. *Coralita* offers French/Créole fare. At the small snackbars near the little pier you can find barbecue fish, ribs and lobster as well as other local snacks, very popular at weekends and holidays, recommended. At weekends there is usually live music in one of the bars/restaurants along the beach.

Entertainment

L'Atmosphere is a disco for 'chic' French people, at Marina Port La Royale, very little English spoken, drinks US$5. *Le bar de la mer* at the waterfront is a popular meeting place for French-speaking young travellers, with live music once a week. Grand Case normally has live music Fridays-Sundays in high season with beach party style entertainment in one of the many bars. *Surf Club South*, Grand Case, a New Jersey-type bar, has beach parties every other Sunday, all food and drinks US$1, with mainly 60s and 70s music, great fun. *Circus* bar in Nettle Bay in the newly built resort area is a popular night bar, live music once in a while. *Le Privilège Disco* at Anse Marcel US$10 entrance, one drink included, is one of the favourite night clubs. Every full moon there is a beach party at Friar's Bay starting around 2100-2200.

Hours Of Business

Shops open around 0900 and close between 1800-1900 with normally a two-hour lunch break between 1200-1500, depending on the shop. Banks open 0800-1300; both slightly different from the Dutch side.

Currency

The US dollar is as widely used as the franc, but watch the rate. It is sometimes difficult to get change from payments in francs. Dollars are preferred. The best place for exchange is the Post Office in Marigot where they will change all currencies and traveller's cheques, but normally only into francs. There are several exchange houses for changing from francs to dollars, one in Rue du Kennedy and one in the *Marina Royale* complex. Two banks, both on rue de la République, Marigot, Banque des Antilles Françaises and Banque Française Commerciale.

Electricity

220 volts, 60 cycles (compared with 110 volts on the Dutch side).

Telecommunications

There are several telephone booths on the French side but they only take telephone cards, (supposed to be interchangeable with the Dutch telephone cards). 120 units for 81F, sold at the Post Office and at the bookshop opposite. There are eight telephones on the square in Marigot and two in Grand Case in front of the little pier. To call the Dutch side use the code 599-5. All Dutch side numbers have 5 digits while French side numbers have 6. The international code for St-Martin is 590. The Post Office will hold mail, but only for two weeks. Letters sent c/o Capiteneri Marina Port La Royale, Marigot, will be kept 4-6 weeks.

Newspapers

Le Monde, *France Soir* and *Le Figaro* from France are available 1-3 days after publication. *France Antilles*, same day. A few German and Italian magazines are sold at Maison de la Presse (opposite Post Office) and other locations.

Telephone Numbers

Hospital Tel: 87 50 07, Ambulance Tel: 87 54 14, Gendarmerie Tel: 87 50 10.

Tourist Office

Port de Marigot, Tel: 87 53 26.

SAINT-BARTHÉLÉMY

SAINT-BARTHÉLÉMY (St Barts or St Barth's), also in the Leewards, is 230 km north of Guadeloupe, 240 km east of the Virgin Islands, and 35 km southeast of Saint-Martin. Its 21 square km are inhabited by a population of 3,500, mostly people of Breton, Norman, and Poitevin descent who live in quiet harmony with the small percentage of blacks. Thirty-two splendid white sandy beaches, most of which are protected by both cliff and reef, are surrounded by lush volcanic hillsides. The Norman dialect is still largely spoken while most of the islanders also speak English. A few elderly women still wear traditional costumes (with their characteristic starched white bonnets called *kichnottes*); they cultivate sweet potato patches and weave palm fronds into hats and purses which they sell in the village of Corossol. The men traditionally smuggled rum among neighbouring islands and now import liqueurs and perfumes, raise cattle, and fish for lobsters offshore. The people are generally known for their courtesy and honesty. Although the Rockefellers, Fords, and Rothschilds own property on the island, there is little glitter or noise.

History
Named after Christopher Columbus' brother, Saint-Barthélémy was first settled by French colonists from Dieppe in 1645. After a brief possession by the Order of the Knights of Malta, and ravaging by the Caribs, it was bought by the Compagnie des Iles and added to the French royal domain in 1672. In 1784, France ceded the island to Sweden in exchange for trading rights in the port of Göteborg. In 1801, St Barts was attacked by the British, but for most of this period it was peaceful and commercially successful. The island was handed back to France after a referendum in 1878.

Government and Economy
St Barts is administered by the sub-prefect in Saint-Martin and is a dependency of Guadeloupe. The island has its own elected mayor, who holds office for seven years. Much the same as Saint-Martin, St Barts relies on its free port status and its anchorages and beaches for the bulk of its revenue. It is popular with both French and North American visitors and, despite the limitations of its airstrip, it is claimed that twice as many tourists as the island's population pass through each month.

Watersports and Beaches
St Barts is a popular mid-way staging post on the yachting route between Antigua and the Virgin Islands. Boat charters are available, also courses in, or facilities for, windsurfing (Toiny is the windsurfers' favourite beach), diving (in Gustavia), snorkelling (very good, particularly at Marigot), water-skiing, deep-sea fishing and sailing. Surfboard rental (not windsurfing) at Hookipa, Tel: 27 71 31. Game fishing at La Maison de la Mer, Tel: 27 81 00, Fax: 27 67 29, or Marine Service, Tel: 27 70 34, Fax: 27 70 36 the latter also does day charters to Colombier, waterskiing, scuba rentals, speedboat rentals etc. There is excellent diving all round St Barts, especially out round the offshore rocks, like the Groupers, and islands like Ile Fourche. Dive shops are Plongée

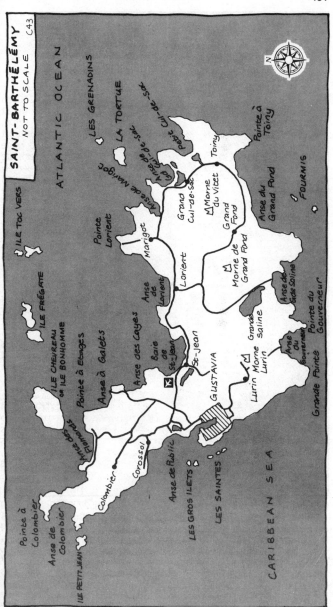

SAINT-BARTHÉLÉMY
NOT TO SCALE
C43

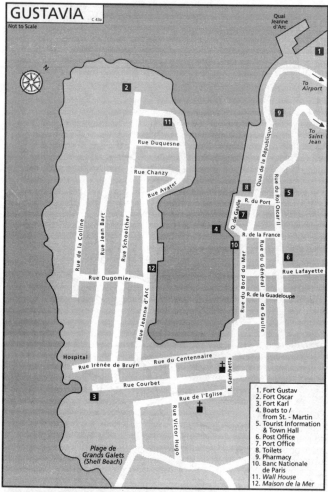

GUSTAVIA C 43a
Not to Scale

Quai Jeanne d'Arc

To Airport

To Saint Jean

Rue Duquesne

Rue Chanzy

Rue Avater

Rue de la Colline

Rue Jean Bart

Rue Schoelcher

Rue Dugomier

Rue Jeanne d'Arc

Quai de la République

Rue du Roi Oscar II

R. du Port

Q. de Gaulle

R. de la France

Rue du Général de Gaulle

R. de la Guadeloupe

Rue du Bord du Mer

Rue Lafayette

Hospital

Rue Irénée de Bruyn

Rue du Centenaire

Rue Courbet

Rue de l'Eglise

Rue Victor Hugo

R. Gambetta

Plage de Grands Galets (Shell Beach)

1. Fort Gustav
2. Fort Oscar
3. Fort Karl
4. Boats to / from St. - Martin
5. Tourist Information & Town Hall
6. Post Office
7. Port Office
8. Toilets
9. Pharmacy
10. Banc Nationale de Paris
11. Wall House
12. Maison de la Mer

La Bulle, Tel: 27 68 93 and Daniel (PADI instructor), Tel: 27 64 78.

Some beaches are more accessible than others, most uncrowded. The main resort area is Baie de Saint-Jean, which is two beaches divided by Eden Rock, the most visited beach with several bars and restaurants open for lunch or a snack, watersports, small boats, snorkelling rentals, ideal for families, good windsurfing, safe swimming, some snorkelling. Others are Lorient, Marigot, Grand Cul-de-Sac on the north coast, Grande Saline, Gouverneur on the south, and Colombier and Flamands at the northwest tip, to name but a few. To get to Gouverneur from Gustavia take the road to Lurin. A sign will direct you to the dirt road leading down to the beach, lovely panoramic view over to the neighbouring islands, where there is white sand with palm trees for shade. A legend says that the 17th century pirate, Montbars the Exterminator, hid his treasures in a cove here and they have never been found. Also a very good spot for snorkelling. Colombier is the most beautiful beach on St Barts. It can not be reached by car but is well worth the 20-30 minute walk during which you have majestic views of the island. Park the car at Colombier, there are several trails going down to the beach. There are also several day tours by boat from Gustavia. Flamands beach is of very clean white sand, bordered with Latania palm trees. The surf can be rough, watersports available. Sometimes in May the migrating sperm whales pass close by. From April to August female sea turtles come to Colombier, Flamands and Corossol to lay their eggs. In Corossol is the Inter Oceans Museum, a private collection of sea shells open for visitors daily 1000-1600. Petite Anse de Galet, in Gustavia, 3-5 minute walk from Fort Karl, is also known as Shell beach because it is covered in shells, not sand. Trees give shade and swimming is safe, shelling is of course extremely good.

Other Sports
Tennis at several hotels. Some opportunities for hiking. Horse riding at Flamands, Laure Nicolas, Tel: 27 80 72. A new golf course has been built at Gouverneur, Tel: 27 62 49.

Festivals
Carnival is held before Lent, on Mardi Gras and Ash Wednesday; the patron saint's day is 24 August, with celebrations on the weekends before and after.

The St Barts regatta in February is the main event for sailors. Other regattas should be checked at Lou Lou's Marina, Gustavia, because none is fixed annually.

A music festival is held annually in January with ten days of classical, folk, jazz music and ballet performed by both local school children and guest artistes and musicians from abroad.

Gustavia

In **Gustavia**, the capital, there are branches of several well-known French shops (such as Cartier). The small crowd of *habitués* is mostly young, chic, and French. The food, wine, and aromas are equally Gallic. The harbour of Carénage was renamed Gustavia after the eighteenth-century Swedish king, Gustavus III, and became a free port, marking the beginning of the island's greatest prosperity. In 1852 a fire severely damaged the capital, although the Swedish influence is still evidenced in the city hall, the belfries, the Forts (Karl, Oscar and Gustave), the streetnames and the trim stone houses which line the harbour. St Barts ECO Museum with an exhibition of the history, traditions and local crafts of the island, is at La Pointe, near the *Wall House*, open Monday, Tuesday, Thursday and Friday, 0830-1130, 1500-1900, Wednesday 0830-1100, Saturday 1500-1900.

From Gustavia, you can head north to the fishing village of Corossol (see above), continuing to Colombier and the northwestern beaches; south over Les Castelets and the hills of Morne Lurin to Anse du Gouverneur; or to Saint-Jean and beaches and settlements on the eastern end. A hired car can manage all the roads.

Information for Visitors—St Barts

How To Get There

Scheduled flights from St Maarten with Air Guadeloupe, Air St-Barthélémy and Winair; from Guadeloupe with Air Guadeloupe and Air St-Barthélémy; from St Thomas with Air Guadeloupe and Virgin Air (some flights via Virgin Gorda). San Juan, Puerto Rico, is served by these two and Air St-Barthélémy, Saint Croix by Coastal Air Transport, Anguilla by Winair and Coastal Air Transport, Saba by Winair, and Dominica (Canefield) by Air Guadeloupe 6 times a week. Charters available locally (Air St-Barthélémy, Tel: 87 61 20, St Barts, or 82 25 80, Pointe-à-Pitre).

Enquire locally for boat services between St Barts and the French and Dutch sides of Saint-Martin/Sint Maarten. St Barts Express goes to St Martin and several catamarans go to Sint Maarten, but you leave in the afternoon and return in the morning so a day trip is not possible. There are no other regular boats to other islands. Full docking facilities are available at the Yacht Club in Gustavia, and anchor-place for yachts up to 10 foot draft at Saint-Jean Bay.

Island Transport

Minibuses (and ordinary taxis) do island tours, US$10, dropping you off at Baie de Saint-Jean and collecting you later for the boat if you are on a day trip. Or hire a car from one of the many agencies at the airport. It is not easy to hire a car for only one day: ask your hotel to obtain a car if required.

Where To Stay

At Saint-Jean beach: *Village St-Jean*, modern bungalows, with kitchen facilities from US$68-195 (Tel: 27 61 39, Fax: 27 77 96), reasonable lunches in *Le Beach Club* restaurant, watersports facilities; *Emeraude Plage*, similar, from 600-800F, EP (Tel: 27 64 78, Fax: 27 83 08); others: *PLM Azur Jean Bart*, *Tropical*, 20 units, US$100-130, EP (Tel: 27 64 87, Fax: 27 81 74) and *Filao Beach*, 30 units, US$165-315 (Tel: 27 64 84, Fax: 27 62 24), all 2-, and 3-star.

At Anse des Cayes: the luxury, 4-star *Manapany Cottages*, Tel: 27 66 55, Fax: 27 75 28, US$200-260, CP, 32 cottages on hillside overlooking sea, two gourmet restaurants, can be booked through Mondotels in New York, Tel: 212-719 5750 or 800-847 4249 or in Canada

800-255 3393. A few hundred yards from Lorient beach is *La Banane*, owned by Jean-Marie Rivière, who owns two nightclubs in Paris, pastel painted bungalows, no two the same, beautifully furnished and decorated, two pools, lots of bananas, 1,150F CP, including breakfast, tax and airport transfers, highly recommended if you can afford it, fine dining, Tel: 27 68 25, Fax: 27 68 44.

At Flamands beach: *Hotel Baie des Flamands*, modern, near Anse Rockefeller, US$115-140, CP, Tel: 27 64 85, Fax: 27 83 98, and *Auberge de la Petite Anse*, Tel: 27 64 60, Fax: 27 72 30, US$80 EP. At Colombier, overlooking Flamands beach is *François Plantation*, elegant plantation style hotel with 12 bungalows, pool, good restaurant, a/c, fan, telephone, satellite TV, Tel: 27 78 82, Fax: 27 61 26, US$200-220, CP. *Les Castelets*, high in the hills, under US management, Tel: 27 78 80, *Club Estimanet* restaurant (overpriced). Least expensive: *La Presqu'île*, in Gustavia, 350 F, Tel: 27 64 60, Fax: 27 72 30, restaurant specializes in French and Créole cooking (closed September- October). At Anse de Grand Cul-de-Sac: *St Barths Beach Hotel*, Tel: 27 62 73, Fax: 27 75 57, and *El Sereno*, bungalows, US$135-170 EP, a/c, TV, telephone, fridge, large pool, superb restaurant in winter, *La Toque Lyonnaise*, Tel: 27 64 80, Fax: 27 75 74. The above is just a selection. Apartments and villas may also be rented.

Where To Eat

Several good ones on Saint-Jean beach; the hotel restaurants are generally good (some are mentioned above). *La New Vieille France*, beachside with dancing at Corossol. In Gustavia: *Wall House*, Tel: 27 71 83 for reservations, for exquisite French cuisine on the waterfront with harbour view; *Au Port* also offers fine dining overlooking the harbour, Tel: 27 62 36 for reservations, one of the most expensive restaurants on the island; there is a good restaurant on the first floor of the *Yacht Club*, overlooking the harbour, offers few but well-prepared French dishes (also has a few rooms to let); *Auberge du Fort Oscar* specializes in Créole cooking, reserve first with Mme Jacque; *La Taverne* occupies an old warehouse and is open quite late; *Côté Jardin* (Tel: 27 70 47) for Italian food and ice creams. *Bar Le Select* is a central meeting spot, an informal bar for lunch with hamburger menu, but also one of the most popular night-time bars and sort of general store, with a few tables in a small garden. *L'Escale*, across the harbour, a pizza, pasta place with low prices for St Bart's but still expensive, Tel: 27 81 06. For breakfast try *Tasted Unlimited* in Gustavia, for their delicious croissants and Danish pastries.

Nightlife

Most of the nightlife starts around the bars at Bay Saint Jean. In Gustavia at *Bar Le Select* (closed Sundays). The night club *Autour Du Rocher* in Lorient opens 2200-0230, entrance US$10, one drink included, very crowded at weekends. In Saint Jean try *Pearl's Club* or *Club La Banane*.

Hours Of Business

0800-1200, 1430-1700, morning only on Saturday.

Banks

Only two: Banque Nationale de Paris (0815-1200, 1400-1600) and Banque Française Commerciale (0800-1200, 1400-1530), both in Gustavia.

Currency

As on Saint-Martin, dollars are widely accepted.

Telephone Numbers

Gendarmerie Tel: 27 60 12; Police Tel: 27 66 66; Fire Tel: 27 62 31; Sub Prefect Tel: 27 63 28; Radio St Barts Tel: 27 74 74, broadcasting on FM 98 mHz; Hospital Tel: 27 60 85; Doctor On Call Tel: 27 76 03. The SiBarth agency on General de Gaulle in Gustavia, Tel: 27 62 38, has a fax service and a mail holding service.

Tourist Office

Rue Auguste Nyman, Tel: 27 60 08. Open Monday-Friday until 1200.

MARTINIQUE

Introduction

THE ISLAND OF MARTINIQUE is 65 km long and 31 km wide. It lies at 14°40' North and 61° West and belongs to the Lesser Antilles. The Caribbean Sea is to the west, the Atlantic Ocean to the east. Martinique's neighbouring islands are Dominica to the north and St Lucia to the south, both separated from it by channels of approximately 40 km.

Martinique is volcanic in origin and one active volcano still exists, Mount Pelée (1,397m), situated to the northwest, which had its last major eruption in 1902. The rest of the island is also very mountainous; the Pitons de Carbet (1,207m) are in the centre of the island and Montagne du Vauclin is in the south. Small hills or *mornes* link these mountains and there is a central plain, Lamentin, where the airport is situated. An extensive tropical rainforest covers parts of the north of the island, as well as pineapple and banana plantations, with the rest of the island mainly used for the cultivation of sugar cane. The coastline is varied: steep cliffs and volcanic, black sand coves in the north and on the rugged Atlantic coast, and calmer seas with large white or grey sand beaches in the south and on the Caribbean coast.

The population of the island is about 359,600 of which half live in the capital, Fort-de-France. This is the main settlement located on the Baie des Flamands on the west coast, with the burgeoning town of Lamentin, slightly inland, the second largest. The rest of Martinique is fairly evenly scattered with the small towns or *communes*.

History

When Christopher Columbus discovered Martinique either in 1493 or in 1502 (the date is disputed), it was inhabited by the Carib Indians who had exterminated the Arawaks, the previous settlers of the Lesser Antilles. Columbus named the island Martinica in honour of St Martin; the Caribs called it Madinina, or island of flowers.

The Spanish abandoned the island for richer pickings in Peru and Mexico and because of their constant troubles with the Caribs. In 1635 Martinique was settled by the French under the leadership of Pierre Belain d'Esnambuc. The cultivation of sugar cane and the importation of slaves from West Africa commenced. Fierce battles continued between the Caribs and the French until 1660 when a treaty was signed under which the Caribs agreed to occupy only the Atlantic side of the island. Peace was shortlived, however, and the Indians were soon completely exterminated.

During the seventeenth and eighteenth centuries England and France fought over their colonial possessions and in 1762 England occupied Martinique, only to return it to the French in exchange for Canada, Senegal, the Grenadines, St Vincent, and Tobago. France was content to retain Martinique and Guadeloupe because of the importance of the sugar cane trade at the time.

More unrest followed in the French Caribbean colonies when in 1789 the French Revolution encouraged slaves to fight for their emancipation.

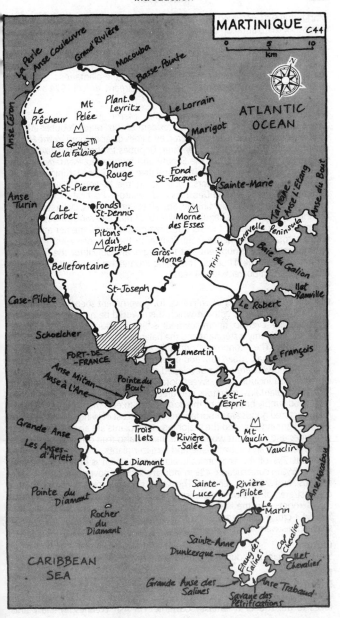

MARTINIQUE C44

ATLANTIC OCEAN

CARIBBEAN SEA

La Perle
Anse Couleuvre
Grand Rivière
Macouba
Basse-Pointe
Anse Céron
Le Prêcheur
Mt Pelée
Plant. Leyritz
Le Lorrain
Marigot
Les Gorges de la Falaise
Morne Rouge
Fond St-Jacques
Sainte-Marie
Anse L'Etang
Tartane
Anse du Bout
Anse Turin
St-Pierre
Fonds St-Dennis
Le Carbet
Morne des Esses
Caravelle Peninsula
Baie du Galion
Pitons du Carbet
Gros-Morne
La Trinité
Ilet Ramville
Bellefontaine
Case-Pilote
St-Joseph
Le Robert
Schoelcher
FORT-DE-FRANCE
Lamentin
Le François
Anse Mitam
Anse à L'Ane
Pointe du Bout
Ducos
Le St-Esprit
Grande Anse
Les Anses-d'Arlets
Trois Ilets
Rivière-Salée
Mt Vauclin
Vauclin
Le Diamant
Sainte-Luce
Rivière-Pilote
Anse Macabou
Pointe du Diamant
Rocher du Diamant
Sainte-Anne
Dunkerque
Le Marin
Etang des Salines
Cap Chevalier
Ilet Chevalier
Grande Anse des Salines
Savane des Pétrifications
Anse Trabaud

Martinique was occupied by the English again from 1794 to 1802, at the request of the plantation owners of the island who wanted to preserve the status quo and avoid slave revolts.

Slavery was finally abolished in 1848 by the French and in the late nineteenth century tens of thousands of immigrant workers from India came to Martinique to replace the slave workforce on the plantations.

In 1946 Martinique became a French Department, and in 1974 a Region.

Government

Martiniquans are French citizens and Martinique is officially and administratively part of France. The President of the French Republic is Head of State and the island is administered by a Prefect, appointed by the French Government. It is represented by three Deputies to the National Assembly in Paris, by two Senators in the Senate and by one representative on the Economic and Social Council. The Legislative Council of Martinique has 36 members elected for six years, who sit on the Regional Council which includes the locally elected Deputies and Senators. Political parties include the Progressive Party of Martinique, Socialists Communists, Union for French Democracy, Rally for the Republic and several small left-wing parties. A small independence movement exists but most people prefer greater autonomy without total independence from France. In the October 1990 elections, pro-independence groups entered the Regional Council for the first time, winning nine of the 41 seats. The ruling Progressive Party lost its majority but remained in power with 14 seats.

The Economy

Martinique is dependent upon France for government spending equivalent to about 70% of gnp, without which there would be no public services or social welfare. Even so, unemployment is high at about 32% of the labour force, the economy is stagnant and the balance of payments deficit expands continuously. The economy is primarily agricultural and the main export crops are bananas, sugar, rum and pineapples, while aubergines, avocados, limes and flowers are being developed. Crops grown mainly for domestic consumption include yams, sweet potatoes, Caribbean cabbages, manioc, breadfruit, plantains, tomatoes and green beans. Fishing contributes to the local food supply but most of the domestic market is met by imports. Most manufactured goods are imported, making the cost of living very high. There is some light industry and the major industrial plants are an oil refinery, rum distilleries and a cement works, while there is also fruit canning, soft drinks manufacturing and polyethylene and fertilizer plants.

About 7% of the economically active population is in agriculture and fishing, 5% in construction, 4% in industry, 23% in government and public services, and 26% in services. The latter includes tourism, which is the greatest area of economic expansion. In 1988 hotel and villa capacity was 3,274 rooms and the island received 280,000 visitors arriving by air and 385,513 cruise ship visitors, all of whom spent US$230m. In 1991 cruise ship arrivals were 417,043 while stopover tourists rose to 315,131.

Culture

See the general introduction to the French Antilles.

Festivals

Martinique has more than its fair share of festivals. The main carnival, Mardi Gras, takes place at the beginning of February when the whole of Martinique takes to the streets in fantastic costume. On Ash Wednesday, black and white clad "devils" parade the streets lamenting loudly over the death of Vaval. At Eastertime, the children fly coloured kites which once had razors attached to their tails for kite fights in the wind. At *Toussaint* in November, the towns are lit by candlelight processions making their way to the cemeteries to sit with the dead.

Watersports

Sailing and windsurfing at Club de Voile de Fort-de-France, Pointe-Simon, Tel: 70 26 63; Club Nautique de Marin, Tel: 74 92 48; Circle Nautique de Schoelcher, Anse Madame, Tel: 61 15 21. Diving is especially good along the coral reef between St-Pierre and Precheur. A medical certificate is required. Sub Diamant Rock, *Hôtel Novotel*, Diamant, Tel: 76 42 42; Tropicasub, La Guinguette, St-Pierre, Tel: 77 15 02; Planète Bleue, La Marina, Pointe du Bout, Tel: 66 08 79. Aquascope: a glass bottom boat, *Sedan Explorer*, leaves from marina Pointe du Bout (Trois-Ilets), at 1030, 1130, 1430 and 1530 in season, 150 F, for a trip round Trois-Ilets, one hour, Tel: 68 36 09. Many hotels like Bambou, La Dunette, Diamant-les-Bains organize fishing trips with local fishermen and their guests. Deep sea fishing can be arranged at Bathy's Club (*Meridien*), Tel: 66 00 00 or Rayon Vert, Tel: 78 80 56, for around 4,000F per boat.

Gommier races (huge rectangular sailing boats with coloured sails and teams of oarsmen) are an amazing sight at festivals all over the island from July to January. In Fort-de-France races take place in November and December from the little beach next to Desnambuc quay.

Sports

Tennis: courts are at many large hotels; *Bakoua*; *Club Méditerranée*; *Plantation Leyritz*; *PLM Azur Carayou*; *Novotel*; *Meridien* and *Hôtel Casino la Batelière* where visitors can play at night as well as during the day by obtaining temporary membership. For more information contact *La Ligue Regional de Tennis*, Petit Manoir, Lamentin, Tel: 51 08 00.

Golf: At Trois-Ilets is a magnificent, eighteen-hole golf course with various facilities including shops, snackbar, lessons and equipment hire. Contact *Golf Départemental de Trois-Ilets*, Tel: 76 32 81.

Riding is a good way to see Martinique's superb countryside; Ranch Jack, Anse d'Arlets, Galochas, Tel: 68 63 97; Black Horse, La Pagerie, Trois-Ilets, Tel: 66 00 04; La Caval, Diamant, Tel: 76 20 23; Ranch Val d'Or, Ste-Anne, Tel: 76 70 58. At *Plantation Leyritz* there are two horses for guests' use.

Cycling. Touring the island by bike is one of the activities offered by the Parc Naturel Régional. For information Tel: 73 19 30.

Spectator Sports: Mongoose and snake fights and cockfights are widespread from December to the beginning of August at Pitt Ducos, Quartier Bac, Tel: 56 05 60; Pitt Marceny (the most popular), Le Lamentin, Tel: 51 28 47, and many others. Horse racing is at the Carère racetrack at Lamentin, Tel: 51 25 09.

Fort-de-France

Fort-de-France was originally built around the Fort St Louis in the seventeenth century. It became the capital of the island in 1902 when the former capital, St-Pierre, was completely obliterated by the eruption of Mount Pelée. The city of today consists of a bustling, crowded centre bordered by the waterfront and the sprawling suburbs which extend into the surrounding hills and plateaux. The bars, restaurants, and shops give a French atmosphere quite unlike that of other Caribbean cities. The port of

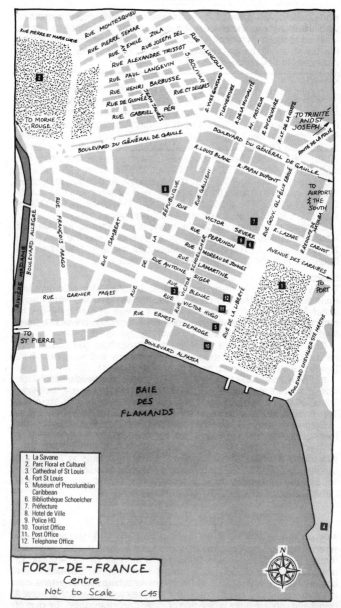

1. La Savane
2. Parc Floral et Culturel
3. Cathedral of St Louis
4. Fort St Louis
5. Museum of Precolumbian Caribbean
6. Bibliothèque Schoelcher
7. Préfecture
8. Hotel de Ville
9. Police HQ
10. Tourist Office
11. Post Office
12. Telephone Office

FORT-DE-FRANCE
Centre
Not to Scale   C45

Fort-de-France is situated to the east of the town centre, where cargo ships and luxury cruise liners are moored side by side.

The impressive Fort St-Louis still functions as a military base. Built in Vauban style, it dominates the waterfront. It is sometimes open to the public for exhibitions but once inside beware the low ceiling arches said to have been designed to foil the invading English who were generally taller than the French at that time. Adjacent to the fort is La Savane, a park of five hectares planted with palms, tamarinds, and other tropical trees and shrubs. The park contains statues of two famous figures from the island's past: a bronze statue of Pierre Belain d'Esnambuc, the leader of the first French settlers on Martinique; and a white marble statue of the Empress Josephine, first wife of Napoléon Bonaparte, who was born on the island.

The Bibliothèque Schoelcher is situated on the corner of Rue Victor Sévère and Rue de la Liberté, just across the road from the Savane. This magnificent baroque library was constructed out of iron in 1889 in Paris by Henri Pick, also the architect of the Eiffel Tower. The following year it was dismantled, shipped and reassembled in Fort-de-France where it received the extensive collections of books donated by Victor Schoelcher (responsible for the abolition of slavery in Martinique). Today it still functions as a library and regularly holds exhibitions.

Just along the Rue de la Liberté towards the seafront is the Musée Départemental de la Martinique. It contains relics of the Arawak and Carib Indians: pottery, statuettes, bones, reconstructions of villages, maps, etc. Open 0900-1300 and 1400-1700 Monday-Friday, 0900-1200 Saturday, Tel: 71 57 05. Price of admission 7F. Worth a visit.

In the centre of town, in the Square of Père Labat there is a second chance to see the baroque architecture of Henri Pick with the Cathedral of St Louis which towers above the Fort-de-France skyline. The interior is very beautiful and has stained glass windows depicting the life of St Louis.

The Parc Floral et Culturel is a shady park containing two galleries, one of which concentrates on the geology of the island, the other on the flora. Almost 2,800 species of plants have been identified in Martinique and the Parc Floral has a very good selection. Open Monday to Saturday, 0900-1200 and 1500-1800, Tel: 70 68 41. Admission 5F.

Next to the Parc Floral are a feature of Fort-de-France not to be missed, the markets. The fishmarket is by the Madame river, where the fishermen unload from their small boats or *gommiers*. Close by is one of several markets selling fruit, vegetables and flowers as well as exotic spices. The markets are always bustling with activity from 0500 to sunset, but are best on Friday and Saturday. A fresh green coconut picked from a huge pile by the seller and hacked open with a machete, makes a refreshing drink for about 4F.

North Martinique and the East Coast

The coastal road heading north from Fort-de-France passes through several fishing villages and is flanked by beaches that gradually become blacker with volcanic sand. At the popular beach of Anse Turin just north of **Carbet**, is the small Gauguin Museum. The artist stayed at Anse Turin during 1887 before he went to Tahiti. Open 1000-1700 every day. Admission 10F. The museum has letters, sketches and some reproductions of the artist's work as well as some pieces by local artists and examples of traditional costume.

Carbet also has a small zoo containing seventy species of animal including monkeys, lions, and ocelots, mainly from the Amazon region. Open every day 0900-1800. Admission 15F.

To the north of Carbet is the famous *St-Pierre*. The modern village is built on the ruins of the former capital of Martinique, which was destroyed by a cloud of molten volcanic ash when Mount Pelée erupted in May 1902. As the cultural and economic capital, the town was known as the "Petit Paris" of the West Indies. Out of 26,000 inhabitants there was only one survivor, named Cylbaris, a drunkard who had been thrown into a cell for the night. Today his small cell is one of the ruins that visitors can still see. It is hidden away behind the remains of the once splendid and celebrated theatre of St-Pierre. The ruined church, originally built in the Fort of St- Pierre, also survives. In the Volcanological Museum (open every day 0900-1230 and 1500-1700, Tel: 77 15 16, admission 7F) is an interesting collection of remains from the disaster: household metal and glass objects charred and deformed by the extreme heat, photographs and volcanology displays. Guided tours of the Museum are available. The town of St-Pierre is well worth a visit and is an eerie reminder of destructive natural forces that dominate life in the Caribbean. For a guided tour in English or French ask at *La Guinguette* restaurant between 0900 and 1200 weekdays, tours around 15F per person.

The next village on the coastal road is the picturesque fishing village of **Le Prêcheur**. The road then continues towards the spectacular beach of Anse Ceron where the sand seems to be at its blackest. A rock called the Pearl juts out from the sea which is roughish on this beach but safe for swimming. It is a wild and beautiful beach, a pleasant change from the calm, white sand tourist beaches in the south. The coastal road ends a mile or two further on at another beach, Anse Couleuvre.

At the extreme north of the island is another small fishing village, **Grande Rivière**. There is no direct road linking Grande Rivière and Le Prêcheur but there is a coastal track through the rain forest which is a lovely six-hour walk crossing several rivers (see **Tourist Agencies**, Island Information). The first 20 minutes on a concrete road are discouraging, but once in the forest the path is cooler and the views beautiful. Grande Rivière itself is set in breathtaking scenery characteristic of this part of the island; plunging cliffs covered with the lush vegetation of the rainforest. The island of Dominica faces the village from across the sea. Winding roads lead through the mountains to the next village, Macouba, perched on top of a cliff.

Inland, heading towards the area of **Basse-Pointe**, is the pineapple cultivation area of the island, where huge fields of spikey pineapple tops cover the easternmost flanks of Mount Pelée. In this area is Plantation Leyritz, one of several former plantation houses (mostly in ruin). The restored eighteenth century building is now a hotel and restaurant (recommended) and anyone can stroll around the extensive grounds. There is a small exhibition of dolls made from plants and vegetables, exploiting the colours and textures of tropical leaves, which is open every day from 0800-1800.

From the road along the north-east coast of the island tempting beaches with crashing waves are visible, but the Atlantic Coast is too dangerous for swimming. However, there is a safe beach at Anse Azérot, just south of **Ste-Marie**. To the north is the ancient monastery of Fond St-Jacques, built in 1658, where a restored chapel, a mill and aqueduct can be seen.

The Père Labat Museum in Ste-Marie presents the life story of the famous Dominican friar who lived in Martinique at the turn of the eighteenth century. Also, the history of the island is interestingly summarized using documents and photographs. Open 0900-1800 every day. Admission 10F.

Nearby, in the St James Distillery, is the Rum Museum. The free guided tour includes an explanation of the process of rum production and its history, and rum tasting. There is a collection of engraved spoons. The grounds are also very attractive. Rum is sold here but it is cheaper at the airport at the duty free shops. Open Monday to Friday, 0900-1800 and Saturday and Sunday 0900-1300, Tel: 69 30 02. A little inland is **Morne-des-Esses** which has a good view of Trinité and the Caravelle peninsula. There is an exhibition of Carib-style handicrafts: pottery, baskets, rugs and bags; and artisans can be seen at work.

The bustling sea front at **Trinité** looks out onto the Caravelle Peninsula, where the vegetation is scrubby but the scenery is gently interesting. The peninsula has beaches at Tartane (the only village on the Caravelle), Anse l'Etang (the best) and Anse du Bout. It is an area protected by the Parc Naturel of Martinique; several well-marked paths criss-cross the peninsula so that visitors can enjoy the varied flora and fauna. It is also possible to visit the historic ruins of the various buildings that belonged to a Monsieur Dubuc, a smuggler and pirate who lived in the area. Open every day, 0830-1230 and 1430-1730, Sundays 0800-1200.

The southernmost village on the Atlantic Coast is **Vauclin** where the main activity is fishing. Pointe Faula is a very safe beach here, with dazzling white sand and shallow water. To the south of Vauclin a road leads to Anse Macabou, a group of impressive white sand beaches.

The Tropical Rainforest and Mount Pelée

La Route de la Trace winds through the tropical rainforest from Fort-de-France to Morne Rouge, Ajoupa-Bouillon and Mount Pelée. The forest itself is truly magnificent, covering the sides of the steep, inland mountains (Les Pitons de Carbet and Pelée) with a bewildering array of lush, green vegetation that stretches for miles. Giant bamboo, mountain palms, chestnut and mahogany trees, over a thousand species of fern and many climbing and hanging parasitic plants and orchids are examples of rainforest vegetation. The forest is protected as part of Martinique's Parc Naturel and makes interesting walking country (see **Tourist Agencies**).

At **Balata**, not far from the capital along the Route de la Trace is the bizarre building of Sacré Coeur, a close replica of the Parisian Cathedral, perched high up in the forest. A little further along the road is the Botanical Garden of Balata with superb views across to the capital. The gardens have a marvellous setting, though are slightly disappointing, depending on the season, when compared with the pictures in the official brochure. They are normally good in November-December. However, the gardens are well planted and the display of anthuriums, ranging from dark maroon, crimson and pink to white, is impressive. Look out for the numerous hummingbirds and brilliant green lizards. Umbrellas are provided if it is raining and the foliage gleams impressively when wet. Open 0900-1800 every day (last ticket sold at 1700). Admission 30F. All signs are in French. A No. 7 bus goes from the rue A Aliker near the fish market, 6F each way.

As the Route de la Trace winds its way through the rainforest, the flanks of the surrounding mountains are clearly visible, covered with cultivated tropical flowers such as anthuriums and ginger lillies. The MacIntosh plantation, a 5 km steep climb from Morne Rouge, has a tourist route through its extensive fields of waxy blooms.

Mount Pelée is reached via a track branching off the Route de la Trace, between Morne Rouge and Ajoupa-Bouillon. From the car park at the foot of the volcano there is a view of the Atlantic Coast, Morne Rouge and the bay of St-Pierre. The mountain air is deliciously fresh and cool even at the foot of the volcano. Not far away are Les Gorges de la Falaise, the dramatic waterfalls of the Falaise river, wonderful for swimming in, accessible only by following the course of the river on foot.

South Martinique

The small village of **Trois-Ilets** across the bay from Fort-de-France has a charming main square and is surrounded by tourist attractions. At the Museum of La Pagerie, where Empress Josephine was born, it is possible to walk among the ruins of the old plantation house and the sugar processing plant. There is a collection of furniture, letters, and portraits which belonged to the Empress. Also on display are local works of art both contemporary and dating from the precolumbian era. Open every day except Monday, 0900-1730, entrance 15F, children 3F, Tel: 68 34 55. Close by is the sugar cane museum (Musée de la Canne) which uses documents, machinery and superb models of sugar processing plant to illustrate the history of the Martiniquan sugar industry. Guided tours are available. Open 0900-1730 every day except Monday, entrance 15F, Tel: 68 32 04. The pottery at Trois-Ilets has an exhibition room where traditional pottery is on sale.

A short bus ride from Trois-Ilets is the tourist complex of **Pointe du Bout**, directly opposite Fort-de-France, and linked by regular ferries. There is a marina, shops, discothèques, cafés, restaurants, sport facilities and a conglomeration of luxury hotels. The first beach after stepping off the ferry is a crowded strip of sand in front of the *Hotel Meridien*, almost completely covered with deckchairs for hire. Perhaps preferable is the beach at Anse Mitan, a five-minute walk away, where there are numerous reasonably priced restaurants and bars. There is a direct ferry from the capital to Anse Mitan, a little way along the coast to the west. This beach is quieter than Anse Mitan and Pointe du Bout and has a pleasant atmosphere. Nearby, in the Musée de Coquillave (seashell museum), local scenes are depicted using seashells. Open 0900-1200 and 1500-1700 every day except Tuesday. Admission 10F.

At Grande Anse is a magnificent beach, less frequented by tourists than the beaches at Pointe du Bout, although it does get more crowded at weekends. The pretty village of Anse d'Arlets is nearby.

Just south of Anse d'Arlets and around the **Pointe de Diamant** is Diamant beach. This is an idyllic beach stretching for two and a half miles along the south coast and dominated by the famous Rocher du Diamant (Diamond Rock). This huge rock, of volcanic origin, is about a mile out to sea and was occupied by the English at the beginning of the eighteenth century. They stationed cannons and about two hundred soldiers there before the French reconquered it a year and a half later in 1605. British ships passing it still salute "Her Majesty's Ship Diamond Rock". The beach itself is secluded and bordered by groves of coconut palms and almond trees. The area is pleasantly unspoiled by the tourist industry. The sand is splendid but there are strong currents and it is advisable not to swim out too far, or indeed at all in rough conditions.

Inland and to the west of Diamant is the town of **Rivière-Pilote**, the largest settlement in the south of the island. The Mauny Rum distillery is located here, where free guided tours are available. The famous Cléry cock-fighting pit stages the only regular mongoose-snake fights in Martinique. These take place on Sunday afternoon. From the town of Marin, southwards are long white sand beaches lined with palm groves, and calm clear sea which epitomize the classic image of the Caribbean. Marin itself boasts a very fine eighteenth century Jesuit church.

At **Ste-Anne** is the extensive Club Méditerrannée complex. It has its own private beach adjacent to the long public beach, which has a spectacular view along the south-west coast, including Rocher du Diamant. Ste-Anne beach is picturesque and shady with trees that overhang the sea in some places. There is a wide selection of lively bars and restaurants.

The road heading eastward from Marin leads to the beach at Cap Chevalier, a popular family beach at weekends. Among others along the barrier reef, the islet of Chevalier is visible from here.

At the southernmost tip of the island is the famous Grande Anse de Salines and the beaches of Dunkerque, Baham and Anse Trabaud, all of which are remarkably attractive. Inland from Anse Trabaud lies the salt marsh and the forest petrified by former lava flow. The forest is now sadly diminished thanks to the efforts of museums and souvenir hunters.

Information for Visitors—Martinique

How To Get There

Scheduled direct flights from Europe are with Air France, which has flights from Bordeaux, Lyons, Marseilles, Nantes, Paris and Toulouse. Air France also has direct flights to Cayenne, Miami , Pointe-à-Pitre, Port-au-Prince and Santo Domingo. Ask Air France for youth fares if you are under 26, or for seasonal prices, as they vary. Nouvelle Frontiers has charter flights from France. American Eagle flies from San Juan, with connections from the USA. Linea Aeropostal Venezolana flies from Caracas. Local airlines include Air Martinique, which flies to Barbados, Canouan, Cayenne, Guadeloupe, Mustique, Paris, St Lucia, Sint Maarten, St Vincent and Union Island, Air Guadeloupe, which flies to Cayenne, Miami, Paris, Pointe-à-Pitre, Port-au-Prince, St Maarten and San Juan, while Liat flies to Antigua, Barbados, Dominica, Paris, St Lucia, St Vincent and Union Island. There are connecting flights from the UK via Antigua or Barbados, and from the USA via Miami, linked with most major North and South American airports.

Airport

Lamentin Airport, Tel: 51 51 51. To get to the airport at Lamentin, either take a taxi, which presents no difficulties but is expensive, or take a bus marked "Ste-Anne" and ask to be set down on the highway near the airport. It is then a 100 metres' walk. The fare is 10F and the buses take reasonable-sized luggage.

Inter-Island Transport

Martinique is on the route of most Caribbean cruises. Information on travelling by cargo boat can be obtained from the travel agency next door to the CGM office at the harbour, but if going to South America it is cheaper to fly.

Yachting

The facilities are among the best in the Caribbean. The marina at Pointe du Bout is very safe, but congested and hot.

For those looking to hitch on a boat, consult the noticeboards at the Yacht Clubs, especially the bar at the Public Jetty and refuelling at the western end of Boulevard Alfassa on the Baie des Flamands.

Tourist Agencies

Guided tours of the island by bus, trips on sailing boats and cruise ships around Martinique and to neighbouring islands, and excursions on glass-bottom boats are organized by the following companies: *STT Voyages*, 23 Rue Blénac, Fort-de-France, Tel: 71 68 12; *Jet Tours*, Marina, Pointe du Bout, Tel: 66 02 56; *Madinina Tours*, Rue Schoelcher, Fort-de-France, Tel: 73 35 35.

Touring on foot: contact the *Parc Naturel Régional*, 9 Boulevard Général-de-Gaulle, Tel: 73 19 30, for well-organized walks in the island's beauty spots such as the rainforest and the Caravelle Peninsula. The charge is 60-80F per person and includes the coach fare to the walk's starting point. Guides can be found through the tourist office, or at Morne Rouge for climbing Mount Pelée and at Ajoupa-Bouillon for the Gorge de la Falaise walk.

Buses

There are plenty of buses running between Fort-de-France and the suburbs which can be caught at Pointe-Simon on the seafront and from Boulevard Général-de-Gaulle. The buses are all privately owned and leave when they're full and not before. Short journeys cost around 5F and the buses run from 0500-2000 approximately. From Fort-de- France to St-Pierre is 20F one way; to Ste-Anne 25F one way. To request a stop shout "arrêt"!

Taxis

To go further afield the *taxi collectif* (estate cars or minibuses) are the best bet. "Taxicos", or TCs, run until about 1800 and leave Pointe Simon for all the communes; Ste-Anne 25F, Diamant 15F, St-Pierre 13F, airport 7.50F. It is worth noting that there are no buses to the airport, and a private taxi is the only way of getting into town from the airport, around 70F. There is a 40% surcharge on taxi fares between 2000 and 0600 and on Sundays. Private taxi stands are at the Savane, along Boulevard Général-de-Gaulle and Place Clemenceau.

Ferries

There are ferries running between Desnambuc quay on the sea front and Pointe du Bout, Anse Mitan and Anse à l'Ane, 17F return. These run until about 2300 and apart from a few taxis are about the only form of transport on a Sunday or after 2000. The 20-minute ferry from Fort de France to Trois-îlets costs 18F return, is punctual, pleasurable and saves a 45-minute drive by road. To the *Méridien* there is only one boat each hour (don't believe boatmen who say they go near, they drop you at Anse à l'Ane which is a long hot walk away). For information about ferry timetables call 73 05 53 for Somatour and 63 06 46 for Madinina.

Car Hire

There are numerous car hire firms at the airport and around town; *Europcar International*, Zone Industrielle, Le Lamentin, Tel: 51 20 33 and Pointe du Bout, Tel: 66 05 44; *Hertz*, 24 Rue Ernest-Deproge, Fort-de-France, Tel: 60 64 64. Airport, Tel: 51 28 22; *InterRent*, 46 Rue Ernest-Deproge, Fort-de-France, Tel: 60 00 77; *Avis*, 4 Rue Ernest-Deproge, Fort-de-France, Tel: 70 11 60. Airport, Tel: 51 26 86. Prices start from a minimum of 225F a day for a Fiat Uno. It will normally be cheaper to have unlimited mileage. You can get a discount if you book your car from abroad at least 48 hours in advance. An international driver's licence is required for those staying over twenty days.

One look at Fort-de-France's congested streets will tell you it's well worth avoiding driving in the city centre. Parking in central Fort-de-France is only legal with a season ticket and the capital's traffic wardens are very efficient; cars may be towed away.

Mopeds can be hired at *TS Auto*, 38 Route de Ste-Thérèse, Fort-de-France, Tel: 63 33 05 and at Rue de Caritan, Ste-Anne, Tel: 76 92 16. Other agencies include Funny, in Fort-de-France, Tel: 63 33 05 and Sainte-Anne, Tel: 76 92 16; Scootonnerre, Le Diamant, Tel: 76 41 12; Discount, Trois Ilets, Tel: 66 04 37; and Marquis-Moto, Sainte-Luce, opposite the church. Motorcycles of 80cc and over need a licence, those of 50cc do not. Rental for all is about 170F/day. A bicycle can be hired for 50F/day, 250F/week, 350F/fortnight, from Funny, Tel: 63 33 05; Discount, Tel: 66 33 05; TS Location Sarl, Tel: 63 42 82, all in Fort-de-France.

Hitching is a common way of getting around, and very easy, recommended.

Where To Stay

Martinique offers a wide range of accommodation from the modest family-run *auberges* scattered over the remote and spectacular north, to the huge five star complexes of Pointe du Bout and Trois Ilets, the main tourist area, in the south. *Gîtes*, furnished holiday apartments and bungalows are widely available, some connected to hotels. Ste-Anne, with its attractive white sand beaches typical of the south-west coast, boasts a *Club Méditerranée* and one of the island's three main campsites. Information and reservations can be made through Centrale de Réservation, BP823-97208 Fort de France Cédex, Tel: 71 56 11, Fax: 73 66 93. Generally, prices are high and some hotels add 10% service charge and/or 5% government tax to the bill. (Prices quoted here are for a double room).

De luxe hotels. Pointe du Bout is the main tourist centre, well equipped with shops, night clubs, casinos, a marina, facilities for golf, watersports and tennis as well as several beaches. The two main hotels here are *Meridien*, 97229 Trois-Ilets, Tel: 66 00 00, Fax: 66 00 74, where the staff show a lack of interest at this huge modern complex with 295 rooms and traditional bungalows in landscaped grounds, the swimming is superb and it is fun to walk through the marina village (take a picnic lunch because food and drink is expensive), 1,680-2,500F, CP, and *Bakoua* (named after traditional Martiniquan straw hats) with apartments and rooms, Tel: 66 02 02, Fax: 66 00 41, 200-250F, CP. At Schoelcher, on the outskirts of Fort-de-France, is *La Batelière* with pool, tennis courts and casino, Tel: 61 49 49, Fax: 61 62 29, 1,300-1,600F, EP.

Medium to low priced hotels in Fort-de-France include *Le Palais Créole*, 26 Rue Perrinon, 480F d, 380F s, but negotiable, rooms comfortable, attractive, several with balconies, all with a/c, TV, phone and bar, some suites available, very good restaurant, friendly staff, excellent value, recommended; *Impératrice*, Tel: 63 06 82, Fax: 72 66 30, 420-510F, CP, 1950s décor and architecture, apparently unchanged since it was built in 1957, friendly, and *La Malmaison*, good and clean, but some rooms smell of cigarettes, Tel: 63 90 85, 290-380F, EP, more during Carnival, both in Rue de la Liberté opposite the Savane and both with lively bars and restaurants frequented by a young crowd; the *Balisier* on Rue Victor Hugo is also very centrally located with a view over the port, Tel: 71 46 54, 330-380F, EP. On Rue Lazare Carnot are *Un Coin de Paris*, Tel: 70 08 52, 250-300F CP and *Le Rêve Bleu*, Tel: 73 02 95, 180F EP, both small, friendly and cheap. Close by is *Les Hibiscus*, 11 rue Redoute de Matouba, Tel: 60 29 59, 170-200F. The *Blenac*, 3 Rue Blenac has small, hot, smelly rooms but is conveniently located, cheap and has a helpful proprietor, best rooms are nos 8 and 9, Tel: 70 18 41, 180-200F, EP. *Le Gommier*, 3 Rue Jacques Cazotte, Tel: 71 88 55, highly recommended, has clean spacious rooms and good continental breakfasts, friendly management, 255-340F, EP. Slightly away from the crowded tourist centre of the capital, yet still centrally located near the canal are the *Palasia*, Tel: 60 32 60, 350F, EP, 410F, CP, and the *Bristol*, Tel: 63 66 76, which was closed for renovation in 1991-92. In the elegant suburbs of Didier is the *Victoria*,

Tel: 60 56 78, Fax: 60 00 24, buses into town every few minutes, pool, EP, 450-520F.

At Trois-Ilets, benefiting from the facilities of Pointe du Bout and the pleasant beaches of Anse Mitan and Anse à l'Ane, a twenty minute ferry ride from Fort-de-France are *Hôtel la Pagerie, PLM Azur*, pool, Tel: 66 05 30, Fax: 66 00 99, 614-690F, EP; *Auberge de l'Anse Mitan*, Tel: 66 01 12, a friendly, family-run hotel with apartments and rooms, 420F, CP, 550F, MAP; *Le Calalou*, Tel: 68 31 67, 750F, CP; *Le Nid Tropical*, rents studios and has a lively beach bar and restaurant, Tel: 68 31 30, 250F, EP, also camping, see below. *La Bonne Auberge Chez André*, Tel: 66 01 55, Fax: 66 04 50, again basic but clean, offering underwater fishing and watersports, 400F, CP, 550F, MAP.

The hotels at **Diamant** on the south coast benefit from miles of superb, uncrowded beach with magnificent views of coastal mountains and, of course, Diamant Rock. *Novotel* has excellent facilities but cockroaches in the bar and restaurant, lovely pool, tennis courts, watersports, disco and it rents apartments and rooms, Tel: 76 42 42, Fax: 76 22 87, 1,070-1,690F CP. *Diamant les Bains*, recommended, fine views over swimming pool and sea, 500-600F, CP, Tel: 76 40 14, Fax: 76 27 00, and *Le Village*, Tel: 76 41 89, Fax: 63 53 32, 480-500F, EP, has 25 basic, beachside bungalows for rent.

At **Ste-Anne** where the most popular beaches are found are *Le Manoir de Beauregard*, Tel: 76 73 40, an elegant eighteenth century hotel was closed in 1991-92 for renovation; *La Belle Martinique* which has double rooms only, EP, 230-300F. Nearby at Ste-Luce *Aux Delices de la Mer* offers fishing amongst other activities, Tel: 62 50 12, 300F, CP, 450F, MAP; and at Marin *The Last Resort* is cheap and popular, Tel: 74 83 88, 200F, EP.

On the rugged **south Atlantic coast**, *Chez Julot*, Tel: 74 40 93, a modest but pleasant hotel, one street back from foreshore road, a/c, recommended, restaurant, 285F, CP, 465F, MAP, rue Gabriel Perí, Vauclin. *Les Brisants*, Tel: 54 32 57, Fax: 54 69 13, at François provides good Créole cuisine, 380F, CP, 520F, MAP. On the old NI, near Trinité, within easy reach of the Caravelle peninsula, *St Aubin* is a magnificent colonial-style hotel, splendid location, views and exterior, but interior badly damaged by 1960s refubishment, 540F, CP, Tel: 69 34 77, Fax: 69 41 04, and *Le Village de Tartane* is near the pretty fishing village of Tartane, Tel: 58 46 33, Fax: 63 53 32, 490F, EP. In Tartane, *Madras*, hotel and restaurant, on the beach, good views, spotless rooms, sea view 450F, CP, road view 350F, CP, summer rates.

Moving northwards through dramatic scenery to **Lorrain**, the *Gibsy Hotel* is very comfortable with only six rooms and facilities for horse riding nearby, Tel: 53 73 46, 350-450F CP; and at Basse Pointe, rather difficult to find, *Plantation de Leyritz*, Tel: 78 53 92, Fax: 78 92 44, is a former plantation house set in beautiful grounds with a lot of insects because of all the fruit trees and water, excellent restaurant serving local specialities, pool, tennis courts, health spa, discotheque, 680F, CP. In the remote, northern- most commune, Grand-Rivière, a small fishing village surrounded by rainforest and close to several idyllic black sand coves, *Chanteur Vacances* (formerly *Les Abeilles*) is a simple, clean hotel with only seven rooms, shared facilities, restaurant, Tel: 55 73 73, 195F, CP. In same price range is *Chez Tante Arlette*, only two rooms, book in advance.

One of the few hotels within easy reach of the ruined town of **St-Pierre** is *La Nouvelle Vague*, five rooms only (doubles), Tel: 78 14 34, 200F, EP, run down rooms over bar, overlooks beach, poor value. Moving inland to the foot of the volcano that destroyed St-Pierre *Auberge de la Montagne Pelée*, Tel: 52 32 09, Fax: 73 20 75, 8 rooms, 305F, EP, at Morne Rouge, good, an ideal base for keen walkers to explore the volcano and the surrounding countryside. There are bungalows for rent and hot water, a necessary luxury because of the cool mountain air. Book well in advance.

Also benefiting from beautiful countryside and fresh mountain air, *Chez Cecilia* at Morne Vert offers agreeable accommodation, Tel: 55 52 83, Fax: 75 10 74, 400F, MAP, 400-500F, AP.

On **Carbet's** enormous black sand beach are *Le Cristophe Colomb*, good value, Tel: 78 05 38, 275F, EP, and the more upmarket *Marouba Club* which has apartments and bungalows, pool, disco, Tel: 78 00 21, 600-700F, MAP, 800-900F, AP. Further down the Caribbean coast, *Auberge du Vare* at Case-Pilote, Tel: 78 80 56, was closed for renovation in 1991-92.

Finally, convenient for the airport at Ducos in the plain of Lamentin, *Le Bourbon Motel*, Tel: 56 14 10, 300-380F, EP and *Airport Hotel*, Tel: 56 01 83, 300F, EP, both offer adequate accommodation.

Other accommodation includes *Bungalows de la Palmerie* at Ste-Anne, Tel: 76 78 41; *Studios La Caravelle* at Tartane, Tel: 58 37 32; *Immeuble Plaisance* at Anse à l'Ane, Trois-Ilets, 5 apartments for two and three people, 1,560F for one week (2 people); *Aurore No 1 et 2* at Quartier Dizac, Diamant, 1,670F for one week (2 people).

A fuller list of hotels and other accommodation available on Martinique can be obtained from the Office Departmental du Tourism, BP 520, 97206, Fort-de-France Cédex. Tel: 63 79 60. The tourist office at the airport is helpful and will telephone round the hotels to get you a room for your first night if you have not booked beforehand.

Gîtes

To rent a gîte contact Gîtes de France Martinique, Maison du Tourisme Vert, 9 Bd du Général-de-Gaulle, BP 1122, 97248 Fort-de-France Cédex, Tel: 73 67 92, or Centrale de Réservation Martinique, BP 823, 97208 Fort-de-France Cédex, Tel: 71 56 11. They rent rooms in private houses, apartments, houses, in all price ranges with weekly or monthly tariffs (weekly rates between 1,500-3,000F). For information about the *Club Méditerranée* hotel village at Ste-Anne, contact Club Méditerranée, 516 Fifth Ave, New York, NY 10036 or 5 South Molton St, London W1.

Camping

The most convenient campsite for Fort-de-France is at Anse à l'Ane where the *Courbaril Campsite* is situated, with kitchenette and washing facilities. They also have small bungalows to rent, 112-230F, Tel: 68 32 30. Right next to it is *Le Nid Tropical* campsite, 70F for two people if you have your own tent, 100F, if you rent one. A small bakery/restaurant on the beach serves cheap meals, bread and pastries. On the south coast, Ste-Luce has a good campsite with adequate facilities in the *VVF Hotel*, but the beach is not nice. There are no tents for hire. Tel: 62 52 84. *Camping Municipal* at Ste-Anne is a popular campsite with a pleasant situation in a shady grove right on the beach. Next to the *Club Med*, it is on the cleanest and nicest beach and was fully renovated in 1989. You can rent tents from Chanteur Vacances, 65 rue Perrinun,

Fort-de-France, Tel: 71 66 19, around 35F/day.

Where To Eat

Sampling the French and Créole cuisine is one of the great pleasures of visiting Martinique. There is an abundance of restaurants, cafés, and snack bars to be found everywhere. The quality is generally very high so it is worth being adventurous and trying the various dishes and eating places. The main meal of the day is at midday and many restaurants and cafés offer very reasonable fixed price *menus du jour* ranging from 35-45F. Some favourites worth seeking out are as follows:

A popular yachtsman's haunt is *l'Abricotier*, situated on the waterfront at Pointe Simon in Fort-de-France, serves French and Créole dishes but run down and dirty now with uncaring staff. For an Italian atmosphere try *Pizza Savane* on Avenue des Caraïbes, where authentic pizza and pasta dishes are served. There are a few restaurants serving Vietnamese and Chinese food, of which the *Mandarin*, 13 rue Garnier-Pages, Tel: 71 62 80, in the centre of Fort-de-France, is recommended. For traditional French cuisine try *Chez Gérard* on Rue Victor Sevère or *l'Europe*, a quiet hotel-restaurant just off the Savane. *La Case Créole* near Pointe Simon is a stylish place to eat out.

Amongst the many restaurants across the Baie des Flammands at Anse Mitan is the charming *L'Amphore* where the fresh lobster is delicious. *Bambou* is a little further along the beach, specializes in fresh fish and offers an excellent *menu du jour*. *Chez Jojos* on the beach at Anse à l'Ane has a varied seafood menu as does *l'Ecrevisse*. At Diamant, *Hotel Diamant Les Bains* has a reasonable and well-situated restaurant. There are several other restaurants in the town which front directly on to the beach.

At Carbet the *Grain d'Or*, a spacious airy restaurant, is another good spot to sample Martinique's seafood specialities, and *La Guinguette* on the beach near St-Pierre is also recommended. On the coast, north of St-Pierre is *Chez Ginette*, superb.

The restaurant at *Plantation Leyritz* near Basse Pointe is in the restored plantation house and has waterfalls trickling down the walls giving a cool, peaceful feel to the place. At Grand' Rivière, *Chez Tante Arlette* serves excellent créole food in cool, pleasant surroundings, finished off with home made liqueurs.

At Ste-Anne, dine in style at the *Manoir de Beauregard* or at *Aux Filets Bleus*, right on the beach and lighter on the pocket. At Cap Chevalier, *Gracieuse* is a good créole restaurant, choose the terrace and order the catch of the day, not too expensive.

For travellers on a smaller budget wishing to eat out in the capital there are plenty of good snackbars and cafés serving various substantial sandwiches and *menus du jour*. The area around Place Clemenceau has lots of scope; *Le Clemenceau* is very good value and extremely friendly—try the *accras* or a fresh *crudité* salad; *Le Lem* on Boulevard Général-de-Gaulle has superior fast food at low prices and a young crowd. It also stays open later than many restaurants that close in the evenings and on Sundays. Behind the Parc Floral on Rue de Royan is the *Kowossol*, a tiny vegetarian café which serves a cheap and healthy *menu du jour*. The pizzas are recommended and the fruit juice is especially delicious—try *gingembre* (ginger) or *ananas* (pineapple). On François Arago *Los Amigos* and *Le Coq d'Or* are particularly good for substantial sandwiches for around 12F. Try *poisson* (steak fish) or *poulet* (chicken). *Le Renouveau* on Boulevard Allegre offers delicious, filling *menus du jour* for 40F, again with a warm welcome.

The place to head for in the evening when all of these eateries close (except *Le Lem* which stays open until 2100), is the Boulevard Chevalier de Ste-Marthe next to the Savane. Here every evening until late, vans and caravans serve delicious meals to take away, or to eat at tables under canvas awnings accompanied by loud Zouk music. The scene is bustling and lively, in contrast to the rest of the city at nighttime, and the air is filled with wonderful aromas. Try *lambis* (conch) in a sandwich (15F) or on a *brochette* (like a kebab) with rice and salad (30F). Paella and *Colombo* are good buys (40F) and the crêpes whether sweet or savoury are delicious.

Food

A delightful blend of French, African, and Indian influences is found in Créole dishes, making it easy to see why Martiniquans are so proud of their cuisine. Basic traditional French and African recipes using fresh local ingredients; seafood, tropical fruits and vegetables are combined with exotic seasonings to give original results rich in colour and flavour. Here are a few local specialties not to be missed:

Ti-boudin, a soft well-seasoned sausage; *court bouillon de poisson* or *blaff* is conch (*lambis*), red snapper or sea urchin cooked with lime, white wine and onions; *ragout*, a spicy stew often made with squid (*chatrous*), or conch, or with meat; *colombo*, a recipe introduced by Hindu immigrants in the last century, is goat, chicken, pork or lamb in a thick curry sauce; *poulet au coco*, chicken prepared with onions, hot peppers (*piment*) and coconut; chunks of steakfish (usually tuna, salmon, or red snapper) marinaded and grilled; *morue* (salt cod) made into sauces and *accras* (hot fishy fritters from Africa) or grilled (*chiquetaille*), or used in *feroce d'avocat*, a pulp of avocados, peppers and manioc flour; lobster, crab and crayfish are often fricaséed, grilled or barbequed with hot pepper sauce.

Main dishes are usually accompanied by white rice, breadfruit, yams or sweet potatoes (*patate douce*) with plantains and red beans or lentils. *Christophine au gratin*; a large knobbly pear-shaped vegetable grilled with grated cheese and breadcrumbs, or a plate of fresh *crudités* are delicious, lighter side dishes.

Exotic fresh fruit often ends the meal; pineapples, papayas, soursops and bananas can be found all year round and mangos, mandarin oranges, guavas and sugar apples in season.

Drink

As in other Caribbean islands the main alcoholic drink is rum. Martiniquan rum has a distinctive flavour and is famous for its strength. There are two main types: white rum (*blanc*) and dark rum (*vieux*) which has been aged in oak vats and is usually more expensive. *Ti punch* is rum mixed with cane syrup or sugar and a slice of lime and is a popular drink at any time of the day. *Shrub* is a delicious Christmas liqueur made from rum and orange peel. *Planteur* is a rum and fruit juice punch. There is a huge choice of Martiniquan rum, recommended brands being Trois Rivières, Mauny, Neisson and St Clément. French wines are available in Martinique, although even red wine is usually served as a cool drink with ice. The local beer is Lorraine, a clean-tasting beer which claims to be 'brewed for the tropics'. Corsaire, made in Guadeloupe, is bitter tasting and insipid. Locally-brewed Guinness, at 7% alcohol, stronger than its Irish counterpart, is thick and rich. Malta, a non-alcoholic beverage similar to malt beer, is produced by most breweries and said to be full of minerals and vitamins. Thirst quenching non-alcoholic drinks to look out for are the fresh fruit juices served in most snackbars and cafés. Guava, soursop, passionfruit, mandarin, and sugar cane juice are commonly seen. Tap water is drinkable all over Martinique.

Entertainment

For those whose visit does not coincide with any festivals, there is plenty of other entertainment. The *Ballet Martiniquais* (Tel: 63 43 88) is one of the world's most prestigious traditional ballet companies. Representing everyday scenes in their dance, they wear colourful local costume and are accompanied by traditional rhythms. Information about performances and venues, usually one of the large hotels, can be obtained from the tourist office. Every year in July, SERMAC (Parc Floral et Culturel, Tel: 73 60 25) organizes an arts festival in Fort-de-France with local and foreign artistes performing plays and dance. CMAC (Centre Martiniquais d'Action Culturelle, Avenue Franz Fanon, Fort-de-France, Tel: 61 76 76) organizes plays, concerts, and the showing of films and documentaries all year round.

There are several comfortable, air-conditioned cinemas in Fort-de-France and the various communes. No film is in English; tickets cost 30F. The two main theatres are the *Théâtre Municipal* in the lovely old Hôtel de Ville building and *Théâtre de la Soif Nouvelle* in the Place Clemenceau. Night Clubs abound and tend to be very expensive (70F to get in and the same price for a drink, whether orange juice or a large whisky). Night clubs include *Le New Hippo*, 24 Blvd Allegre, Fort-de-France, *La Vesou Carayou* at *PLM Azur*, *Zipp's Dupe Club*. At *Coco Lobo*, next to the Tourist Office in Fort-de-France, regular jazz sessions are held. Most large hotels lay on Caribbean-style evening entertainment for tourists; limbo dancers, steelbands, etc. Hôtel Meridien has the island's main casino 2300-0300, proof of identity is required for entry. *Choubouloute*, the local entertainments guide, is sold in most newsagents, priced 5F.

Shopping

Fort-de-France has ample scope for shoppers, with an abundance of boutiques selling the latest Paris fashions, as well as items by local designers, and numerous street markets where local handicrafts are on sale. Seekers of clothing and perfume should head for Rue Victor Hugo and its two *galleries* (malls). Jewellery shops are mostly in Rue Isambert and Rue Lamartine, selling crystal, china and silverware, and unique gold jewellery. At markets in the Savane and near the cathedral bamboo goods, wickerwork, shells, leather goods, T-shirts, silk scarves and the like are sold. Wines and spirits imported from France and local liqueurs made from exotic fruits are readily available, and Martiniquan rum is an excellent buy. There are large shopping centres at Cluny, Dillon, and Bellevue. American and Canadian dollars are accepted nearly everywhere and many tourist shops offer a 20% discount on goods bought with a credit card or foreign traveller's cheques.

Cost Of Living

Remember that the standard of living is high and expect to pay French prices or higher, which means expensive. Small beers or cokes cost around 15F, petrol 52F/litre, a nice meal at a medium priced restaurant will be at least 350F for two.

Banks And Exchange

Change Caraïbe, Airport, open 0800-2000, Monday-Friday, 0800-1800, Saturday, Tel: 51 57 91, Gallerie des Filibustiers, Fort-de-France, Tel: 60 24 40; Banque National de Paris, Avenue des Caraïbes, Tel: 63 66 67 (the best for cash advances on Visa, no commission). Banks and exchange houses charge 5% commission on travellers' cheques. Not all banks accept US dollar travellers' cheques. Always go to the bank early; by mid-morning they are very crowded. Do not change US dollars at the Post Office in Fort-de-France, you lose about 15% because of the poor exchange rate and commission. American Express at Roger Albert Voyages, 10 rue Victor Hugo, upstairs, efficient.

Laundry

There are several launderettes in Fort-de-France; Laverie Automatique, Galerie des Filibustiers, rue E Deproge; Lavexpress, 61 rue Jules-Monnerot; Laverie Self- Service, Lavematic, 85 rue Jules-Monnerot, Terres Sainville, Tel: 63 70 43.

Climate

The lushness of Martinique's vegetation is evidence that it has a far higher rainfall than many of the islands, due to its mountainous relief. The wet season lasts from June to late November and the frequency of sudden heavy showers make an umbrella or raincoat an essential piece of equipment. The cooler dry season lasts from December to May and the year round average temperature is 26°C although the highlands and Mount Pelée are quite cool.

Hours Of Business

Shops are open from 0900-1800 (banks from around 0730) and until 1300 on Saturdays. Nearly everything closes from 1200-1500 and on Sundays.

Useful Addresses

American Consulate: 14 Rue Blénac, Fort-de-France, Tel: 63 13 03, no visas. France has responsibilty for diplomatic representation; other countries with a consular service in Fort-de-France are: Belgium, Denmark, Haiti, Italy, Netherlands, Norway, Spain, Sweden, Switzerland, UK, Venezuela and Germany.

Weights And Measures

The metric system is in use.

Electricity

The electric current is 220 volts AC.

Post And Telephones

Nearly all public telephones are cardphones except a few in bars and hotels which take coins. At the PTT office in Rue Antoine Siger, just off the Savane, there are numerous card and coin phones and *Télécartes* (phone cards) are sold. These can also be bought in most newsagents, cafés, and some shops for 36.50F upwards. Don't get caught out on arrival at the airport where there are only cardphones. Try the tourist office where they are very helpful and will phone round endless hotels to find the unprepared new arrival a room.

Post offices are open from 0700-1800 and Saturday mornings. The main post office is on Rue de la Liberté and always has long queues.

Tourist Offices

Lamentin Airport, Tel: 51 28 55; Bord de la Mer, Fort-de-France, Tel: 63 79 60, Fax: 73 66 93. Postal address: Office Départemental du Tourisme de la Martinique, BP 520, 97206 Fort-de-France Cédex.

WINDWARD ISLANDS

DOMINICA

Introduction

DOMINICA (pronounced Domineeca) is the largest and most mountainous of the anglophone Windward Islands. The official title, Commonwealth of Dominica, should always be used in addresses to avoid confusion with the Dominican Republic. It is 29 miles long and 16 miles wide, with an area of 290 square miles. The highest peak, Mount Diablotin, rises to 4,747 feet and is often covered in mist.

Materially, it is one of the poorest islands in the Caribbean, but the people are some of the friendliest; many of them are small farmers: the island's mountainous terrain discourages the creation of large estates. In Dominica, over 2,000 descendants of the original inhabitants of the Caribbean, the once warlike Caribs, live in the Carib Territory, a 3,700-acre "reservation" established in 1903 in the northeast, near Melville Hall airport. There are no surviving speakers of the Carib language on the island. The total population, which is otherwise almost entirely of African descent, is around 71,800, of whom about 29% live in and around Roseau, the capital, on the Caribbean

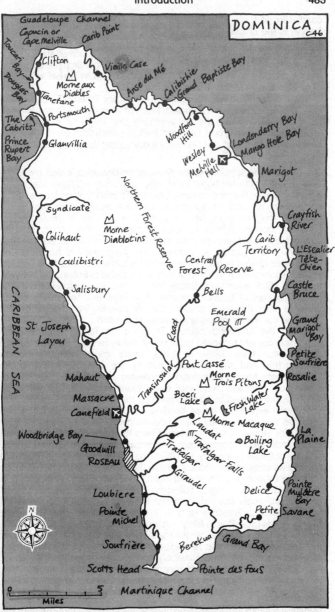

DOMINICA
C46

Guadeloupe Channel
Capucin or Cape Melville
Carib Point
Toucari Bay
Douglas Bay
Clifton
Vieille Case
Anse du Mé
Calibishie
Grand Baptiste Bay
Morne aux Diables
Tanetane
Portsmouth
The Cabrits
Prince Rupert Bay
Glanvillia
Woodford Hill
Wesley
Melville Hall
Londonderry Bay
Mango Hole Bay
Marigot
Syndicate
Morne Diablotins
Northern Forest Reserve
Colihaut
Coulibistri
Central Forest Reserve
Carib Territory
Crayfish River
L'Escalier Tête-Chien
Salisbury
Bells
Castle Bruce
Emerald Pool
St Joseph
Layou
Road
Pont Cassé
Grand Marigot Bay
Petite Soufrière
CARIBBEAN SEA
Mahaut
Massacre
Canefield
Transinsular
Morne Trois Pitons
Boeri Lake
Fresh Water Lake
Rosalie
Woodbridge Bay
Goodwill
ROSEAU
Laudat
Morne Macaque
Trafalgar Falls
Trafalgar
Boiling Lake
La Plaine
Giraudel
Delice
Pointe Mulâtre Bay
Loubiere
Pointe Michel
Petite Savane
Soufrière
Berekua
Grand Bay
Scotts Head
Pointe des fous
Martinique Channel

N

0   5
Miles

coast. Like St Lucia, Dominica was once a French possession; although English is the official tongue, most of the inhabitants also speak creole French (French-based patois). In the Marigot/Wesley area a type of English called "cocoy" is used; the original settlers of the area, freed slaves, came from Antigua and are mostly Methodists. The Catholic church predominates, though there are some Protestant denominations and an increasing number of fundamentalist sects, imported from the USA.

In 1979 the island was devastated by Hurricane David, 37 people were killed and 60,000 were left homeless. Much of what David left standing was felled by Hurricane Allen the next year. Since then major reconstruction has taken place, a new airport has been built at Canefield, new roads made, new hotels established and Dominica is developing its tourist trade.

History

The Caribs, who supplanted the Arawaks on Dominica, called the island Waitukubuli ("tall is her body"). Columbus sighted it on 3 November, 1493, a Sunday (hence the modern name), but the Spanish took no interest in the island. It was not until 1805 that possession was finally settled. Until then it had been fought over by the French, British and Caribs. In 1660, the two European powers agreed to leave Dominica to the Caribs, but the arrangement lasted very few years; in 1686, the island was declared neutral, again with little success. As France and England renewed hostilities, the Caribs were divided between the opposed forces and suffered the heaviest losses in consequence. In 1763, Dominica was ceded to Britain, and between then and 1805, it remained British. Nevertheless, its position between the French colonies of Guadeloupe and Martinique, and the strong French presence over the years ensured that despite English institutions and language the French influence was never eliminated.

During the nineteenth century, Dominica was largely neglected and underdevelopment provoked social unrest. Henry Hesketh Bell, the colonial administrator from 1899 to 1905, made great improvements to infrastructure and the economy, but by the late 1930s the British Government's Moyne Commission discovered a return to a high level of poverty on the island. Assistance to the island was increased with some emphasis put on road building to open up the interior. This, together with agricultural expansion, house building and use of the abundant hydro resources for power, contributed to development in the 1950s and 1960s.

In 1939, Dominica was transferred from the Leeward to the Windward Islands Federation; it gained separate status and a new constitution in 1960, and full internal autonomy in 1967. The Commonwealth of Dominica became an independent republic within the Commonwealth in 1978. The Dominica Labour Party dominated island politics after 1961, ushering in all the constitutional changes. Following independence, however, internal divisions and public dissatisfaction with the administration led to its defeat by the Dominica Freedom Party in the 1980 elections. The DFP Prime Minister, Miss (now Dame) Mary Eugenia Charles, adopted a pro-business, pro-United States line to lessen the island's dependence on limited crops and markets. Miss Charles was re-elected in 1985 and again in 1990, having survived an earlier attempted invasion by supporters of former DLP premier, Patrick John. (For a thorough history of the island, see *The Dominica Story*, by Lennox Honychurch, The Dominica Institute, 1984.)

Government

Dominica is a fully independent member of the British Commonwealth. The single chamber House of Assembly has 31 members: 21 elected by the constituencies, 9 Senators who are appointed by the President on the advice of the Prime Minister and Leader of the Opposition, and the Attorney-General. The Prime Minister and Leader of the Opposition also nominate the President, currently Sir Clarence Seignoret, who holds office for five years. In the general election of 1990 the Dominica Freedom Party (DFP) retained its majority by a single seat, winning 11 of the 21 seats. The official opposition is the recently-formed (1988) United Workers Party (UWP) led by Edison James, with six seats, while the former official opposition party, the Dominica Labour Party (DLP) holds four seats.

The Economy

Owing to the difficulty of the terrain, only about a quarter of the island is cultivated. Nevertheless, it is self-sufficient in fruit and vegetables and agriculture contributes about 27% to gross domestic product. The main products are bananas (the principal export), coconuts (most of which are used in soap and cooking oil production), grapefruit, limes and other citrus fruits. Bananas were badly hit by Hurricane Hugo in 1989 and over 70% of the crop was damaged, but output has since recovered. Other crops are under development, such as coffee, cocoa and rice; some, like passionfruit and aloes, are being promoted to diversify away from bananas. There is a successful aqua culture project, prawn farming. Potential areas for expansion are the exploitation of the island's timber reserves, and ornamental flowers for export. Manufacturing industry is small, but can take advantage of locally-generated hydroelectricity. Labour intensive electronic assembly plants and clothing manufacturing are being encouraged for their foreign exchange earnings potential, while data processing is also growing.

Tourism is also being promoted. Arrivals in 1991 were 46,312, a rise of only 2.7% over 1990, although tourist spending increased much faster. The authorities claim they do not wish to jeopardize the "Nature Island" image, but concern has been expressed by conservationists that mooted projects like a motorboat marina on the serene Indian River could damage the island's greatest asset, its environment. Meanwhile, the island's hotel capacity continues to expand while more hotels are planned; construction of a 250-room *Shangrila Hotel*, with Taiwanese investment, has begun opposite the *Layou River Hotel*, now also owned by Taiwanese. A new jetty for cruise ships, with related facilities, has been built at Prince Rupert Bay. Controversy arose in 1992 over the Government's decision to grant economic citizenship to investors; up to 1,200 economic citizens, plus their dependents, are to be accepted and the first to be granted passports all came from Taiwan.

Culture

The best known of Dominica's writers are the novelists Jean Rhys and Phyllis Shand Allfrey. Rhys (1894-1979), who spent much of her life in Europe, wrote mainly about that continent; only flashback scenes in *Voyage in the Dark* (1934), her superb last novel, *Wide Sargasso Sea* (1966), her uncompleted autobiography, *Smile Please* and resonances in some of her short stories draw on her West Indian experiences. Allfrey published only one novel, *The Orchid House* (1953); *In the Cabinet* was left unfinished at her death in 1986. Allfrey was one of the founder members of the Dominica Labour Party, became a cabinet minister in the short-lived West Indian Federation, and was later editor of the *Dominica Herald* and *Dominica Star* newspapers. *The Orchid House* was filmed by Channel 4 (UK) in 1990 for international transmission as a 4-part series.

Popular culture reflects the mixture of native and immigrant peoples. While most places on Dominica have a Carib, a French or an English name, the indigenous Carib traditions and way of life have been localized in the northeast, giving way to a dominant amalgam of Creole (French and African) tradition. Dominicans are proud of their local language, which is increasingly being used in print. A dictionary was published in 1991 by the Konmité pou Etid Kwéyol (Committee for Creole Studies). Many of the costumes, dances and songs, even the Masquerade (Dominica's carnival), are being lost to more modern Caribbean influences (in Masquerade's case, to Trinidadian-style Carnival). For more detail on these, and other areas, see *Our Island Culture*, by Lennox Honychurch (Dominican National Cultural Council, 1988). Examples of arts and crafts can be seen at the Old Mill Cultural Centre, Canefield ("Lavi Domnik"), an old sugar mill converted into a museum (donations welcome), with a nearby wood carving studio run by Haïtian emigré Louis Desiré (open to the public) and a new studio building for the Dominican School of Dance (director Daryl Phillip).

Flora and Fauna

Dominica is rightly known as the Nature Island of the Caribbean. Much of the southern part of the island has been designated the Morne Trois Pitons National Park. Its principal attractions include the Boiling Lake (92° celsius), the second largest of its kind in the world and reached after a six-mile, three or four-hour challenging climb. An experienced guide is recommended as the trail can be treacherous, but it is easy to follow once you are on it (guides charge about EC$80 per couple, EC$150 for two couples; Benjamín has been recommended, Tel: 88575, young, friendly but experienced, also Lambert Charles, Tel: 83365, strong and knowledgeable). In the valley below the Boiling Lake is a region known as the Valley of Desolation, where the forest has been destroyed by sulphuric emissions. At the beginning of the trail to the Boiling Lake is the Titou Gorge, now considerably damaged by rock fall from the hydroelectric development in the area, where a hot and a cold stream mingle. Also in the Park is the Freshwater Lake; it is to the east of Morne Macaque at 2,500 feet above sea level, and can be reached by road (2 miles from Laudat). Do not swim here, it is the drinking water reservoir for Roseau. A trail leads in ¾ of an hour on foot (follow the road where the river joins the lake about ½ mile to the pipeline, take the path to the left through the dense forest) to the highest lake in the island, Boeri, situated between Morne Macaque and Morne Trois Pitons. Work on a hydroelectric project in this area was completed in 1991. There will be lasting consequences for both the Trafalgar Falls (a diminished flow of water) and the Freshwater Lake (a raised water level).

The National Park Service has built a series of paths, the Middleham Trails, through the rain forest on the northwest border of the Park. The Trails are accessible from Sylvania and Cochrane on the Laudat road. About 1½-2 hours walk from Cochrane are the Middleham Falls, about 150 metres high, falling into a beautiful blue pool in the middle of the forest (take the road out of Cochrane, which becomes a path, then fork right at the sign).

North of the Transinsular road are the Central and Northern Forest Reserves. In the latter is Morne Diablotin; if you wish to climb it, you must take a guide. At the highest levels on the island is elfin woodland, characterized by dense vegetation and low-growing plants. Elfin woodland and high montane thicket give way to rainforest at altitudes between 1,000 and 2,500 feet, extending over about 60% of the island. Despite the large area of forest, its protection is essential, against cutting for farm land and other economic pressures, as a water source, and as a unique facility for scientific research. It is hoped, moreover, that tourism can coexist with conservation, since any losses, for whatever reason, would be irreversible.

The Cabrits Peninsula in the northwest is also a National Park of 260 hectares, its twin hills covered by dry forest, separated from the island proper by marshland (under threat from a marina development, a pier and cruise ship reception centre have been built and shops and restaurants are opening) which is a nesting place for herons, doves and hosts a variety of migrant bird species. A walk through the woods and around the buildings of Fort Shirley (abandoned in 1854) will reveal much flora and wildlife (easiest to see are the scuttling hermit- or soldier- and black crabs, ground lizard—abòlò—and tree lizard).

The Emerald Pool is a small, but pretty waterfall in a grotto in the forest, fifteen minutes by path from the Pont Cassé-Castle Bruce road. Unfortunately, visitors walking alone or in couples to the pool have been mugged and cameras have been stolen from parked cars; also avoid the area on days when cruise ships have docked, as hundreds of passengers are taken to visit the Pool, with resulting damage to its delicate ecology. The Trafalgar waterfalls are in the Roseau Valley, five miles from the capital. Hot and cold water flows in two spectacular cascades in the forest, but the volume of the hot fall has been sharply diminished by a hydroelectric scheme higher up. The path to the falls is easy to follow. Trying to cross over the falls at the top is very hazardous; bathing should be confined to pools in the river beneath the falls. The Trafalgar Falls are crowded because they are close to the road (bus EC$3 from Roseau) and children pester to be your guide. There is a one-hour trail from the Sulphur springs of the tiny settlement of Wotten Waven through forest and banana plantations across the Trois Pitons River up to the Trafalgar Falls.

Dominica is a botanist's paradise. In addition to the huge variety of trees, many of which flower in March and April, there are orchids and wild gardens of strange plant life in the valleys. It is a birdwatcher's paradise, too. Indigenous to the island are the imperial parrot, or sisserou, which is critically endangered, and its marginally less threatened relative, the red-necked parrot, or jacquot. They can be seen in the Syndicate area in the north west which is now a protected reserve and the site of a future information and research centre for visitors and scientists. The parrots are most evident during their courting season, in April and early May. While there are other bird species, such as the forest thrush and the blue-headed hummingbird, there are a great many others which are easily spotted (the purple-throated carib and antillean-crested hummingbirds, for instance), or heard (the siffleur montagne). Waterfowl can be seen on the lakes, waders on the coastal wetlands (many are migrants).

There are fewer species of mammal (agouti, manicou -opossum, wild pig and bats), but there is a wealth of insect life (for example, over 53 species of butterfly) and reptiles. Besides those mentioned above, there is the rare iguana, the crapaud (a large frog, eaten under the name of mountain chicken), and five snakes, none poisonous (including the boa constrictor, or tête-chien). Certain parts of the coast are used as nesting grounds by sea turtles (hawksbill, leatherback and green).

The National Parks Office at the Forestry Division in the Botanic Gardens, Roseau, has a wide range of publications, posters and leaflets (some free) on Dominica's wildlife and National Parks, Tel: 448 2733/2401.

Diving and Marine Life

Dominica is highly regarded as a diving destination. Features include wall dives, drop-offs, reefs, hot, freshwater springs under the sea, sponges, black coral, pinnacles and wrecks, all in unpolluted water. Visibility is excellent, at up to 150' and milkiness is seldom encountered, even after heavy rain. Many drop-offs are close to the beaches, making boats unnecessary. There is a marine park conservation area in Tacouri Bay and part of Douglas Bay, north of the Cabrits where an underwater trail for snorkellers is marked by white buoys, but the most popular scuba sites are south of Roseau, at Point Guignard, Soufrière Bay and Scott's Head. Note that the taking of conch, coral, lobster, sponge, turtle eggs etc is forbidden and you may not put down anchor in coral and on reefs; use the designated moorings. Scuba diving is permitted only through one of the island's registered dive operators or with written permission from the Fisheries Division. Dive Dominica Ltd, at the *Castle Comfort Guest House* (P O Box 63, Roseau, Tel: 82188, Fax: 86088), offers full diving and accommodation packages, courses, single or multiple day dives, night dives and equipment rental. Owned by Derek Perryman who has two fast, well-equipped dive boats, this company has been recommended for its professional service. Dive Dominica is represented in the UK by Traveller's Tree (see under Tours section). The *Anchorage*, *Castaways Beach Hotel*, *Picard Beach Cottage Resort* and *Portsmouth Beach* hotels also have scuba diving facilities.

Beaches and Watersports

Compared with other Caribbean islands, Dominica has few good beaches, but does have excellent river bathing. The best beaches on the west coast are immediately south of Prince Rupert Bay in the Picard area. Other beaches on the Caribbean coast, such as at Mero, where the *Castaways Hotel* is located, are of "black" (really a silver-grey) sand. Although there are no beaches near Roseau, Scott's Head can be reached in about 20 minutes by bus, EC\$3, excellent snorkelling and a few small stretches of sandy beach. There are smaller, mostly white sand beaches on the northeast coast, suitable for bathing and snorkelling, for example at Woodford Hill (near Melville Hall airport, the best beach on the island but entirely lacking facilities) and Hampstead. Beware of strong undercurrents on the Atlantic Coast. Pointe Baptiste (see under **Where To Stay**, has a fine golden beach featured in the TV series "The Orchid House".

The Waitikubuli Dive Centres at the *Anchorage*, *Portsmouth Beach* and *Picard Cottage Resort* and *Castaways Hotel* offer sailing and the *Anchorage* has deep-sea fishing. They also offer water-skiing and windsurfing, as does James Water World at *The Shipwreck* in Canefield, Tel: 91059.

The best harbour for yachts is Portsmouth (Prince Rupert Bay), but there are no facilities and yachtsmen have complained about the hostile attitudes of some locals. This may change with the opening of the new cruise ship jetty, but guard your possessions. Stealing from yachts is quite common. Both the *Sisserou* and *Anchorage* Hotels have moorings and a pier, and yachtsmen and women are invited to use the hotels' facilities.

Other Sports

Football and cricket are among the most popular national sports; watch cricket in the beautiful setting of the Botanical Gardens. Basketball and netball are also enthusiastically played. There are hard tennis courts at the privately-owned Dominica Club, *Reigate Hall* and *Castaways*. *Anchorage Hotel* has squash courts. Cycling is growing in popularity and the island's roads, although twisty, are good. Hiking in the mountains is excellent, and hotels and tour companies arrange this type of excursion. Mountain climbing can be organized through the Forestry Division in the Botanical Gardens, Roseau. Guides are necessary for any forays into the mountains or forests, some areas of which are still uncharted.

Festivals

The main one is Carnival, on the Monday and Tuesday before Ash Wednesday; it is not as commercialized as many in the Americas (see above, under **Culture**). During Carnival, laws of libel and slander are suspended. Independence celebrations (3/4 November) feature local folk dances, music and crafts. On Creole Day, the last Friday in October, the vast majority of girls and women wear the national dress, 'la wobe douillete' to work and school and most shop, bank clerks etc speak only creole to the public. Domfesta, The Festival of the Arts, takes place during July and August and includes exhibitions by local artists (notably Kelo Royer, Earl Etienne, Arnold Toulon), concerts and theatre performances, (see local paper, *The New Chronicle*, for details or ask at hotel.)

Roseau

Roseau is small, ramshackle and friendly, with a surprising number of pretty old buildings still intact. The Old Market Plaza has been made into a pedestrian area, with a tourist kiosk and shops in the middle. Between the Plaza and the sea is the Post Office, painted cream and green, contrasting with the wood and corrugated iron of most of the other buildings. The new market, at the north end of Bay Street, is a fascinating sight on Saturday mornings from about 0600-1000; it is also lively on Friday morning, closed Sundays. In 1992 development of the sea wall in Roseau was noisily under way, due for completion in June 1993. The project involves constructing a new sea wall 20 metres seaward of the existing one and extensive land reclamation as far south as the *Fort Young Hotel*. Most of the Bay Front is now sealed off, with narrow passageways to the Post Office and the Royal Bank of Canada. The seaward section of Roseau market is also closed for the duration and venders have been squashed into the far side. New facilities promised include new restaurants and shops and another cruise ship berth. An aviary is planned for 1992. The 40-acre Botanic Gardens are principally an arboretum, although seriously damaged by Hurricane David in 1979; it has a collection of plant species, including an orchid house. In honour of its centenary in 1990, trees and plants lost in the hurricane were replaced. An aviary is planned for 1992. The town has no deep-water harbour; this is at Woodbridge Bay, over a mile away, where most of the island's commercial shipping is handled, and tourist vessels are accommodated.

Excursions

South of Roseau are the villages of Soufrière and Scott's Head. There are plenty of buses (EC$3) to Scott's Head, over the mountain with excellent views all the way to Martinique. Ask around the fishing huts if you are hungry, and you will be directed to various buildings without signs where you can eat chicken pilau for EC$6 and watch draughts being played. There is a new, clean and friendly café on the main road just across from the most active fishing area (this boasts the only lavatories for the use of visitors). On

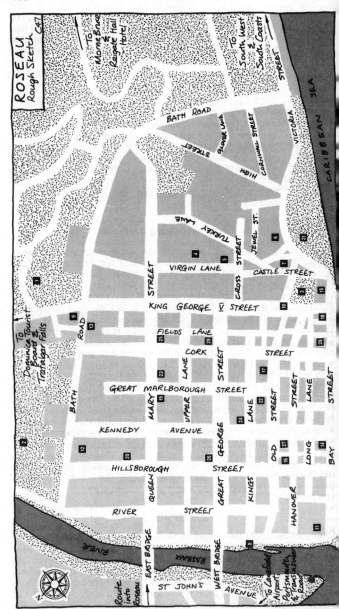

ROSEAU
Rough Sketch
C47

To
Morne Bruce
Regate Hall
hotel

To
South West
&
South Coasts

CARIBBEAN SEA

BATH ROAD

GLOVER LANE

CORNWALL STREET

HIGH STREET

VICTORIA STREET

TURKEY LANE

JEWEL ST.

CROSS STREET

STREET

VIRGIN LANE

CASTLE STREET

KING GEORGE V STREET

To
Dominica Tourist
Board &
Trafalgar Falls

BATH ROAD

FIELDS LANE

CORK STREET

STREET

GREAT MARLBOROUGH STREET

MARY LANE

UPPER LANE

LANE

STREET

STREET

STREET

LANE

BAY STREET

KENNEDY AVENUE

GREAT GEORGE STREET

OLD STREET

LONG LANE

HILLSBOROUGH STREET

QUEEN STREET

KINGS LANE

HANOVER STREET

RIVER STREET

ROSEAU RIVER

EAST BRIDGE

WEST BRIDGE

Route
into
Roseau

ST JOHN'S AVENUE

To Canefield
Airport,
Portsmouth &
Trans insular Road

the south coast is Grand Bay, where there is a large beach (dangerous for swimming), the ten-foot high Belle Croix and the Geneva Estate, founded in the 18th century by the Martinican Jesuit, Father Antoine La Valette. From Grand Bay, it is a two-hour walk over the hill, past Sulphur Spring to Soufrière.

The Leeward coastal road, north from Roseau, comes first to **Canefield**, where are the new airport, the Old Mill Cultural Centre, and the junction with the Transinsular Road. The coast road passes through Massacre, reputed to be the settlement where eighty Caribs were killed by British troops in 1672. Among those who died was Indian Warner, Deputy Governor of Dominica, illegitimate son of Sir Thomas Warner (Governor of St Kitts) and half-brother of the commander of the British troops, Colonel Philip Warner. From the church perched above the village there are good views of the coast.

The road continues to **Portsmouth**, the second town. Nearby are the ruins of the 18th-century Fort Shirley on the Cabrits, which has a museum in one of the restored buildings (entry free). Clearly marked paths lead to the Commander's Quarters, Douglas Battery and other outlying areas. The colonial fortifications, apart from the main buildings which have been cleared, are strangled by ficus roots, and cannon which used to point out to sea now aim at the forest. From the bridge just south of Portsmouth, boats make regular, one-hourly trips up the Indian River (about EC$20 pp), a peaceful trip. Negotiate with the local boatmen about price and insist they use oars rather than a motor, so as not to disturb the birds and crabs. Sometimes there is a tiny bar open at the final landing place on this lovely river. In 1991 a development agreement was signed for the construction of a tourist and residental project, including a large hotel and sports complex near Portsmouth at the 700-acre Pointe Ronde Estate. From Portsmouth, one road carries on to the island's northern tip at Cape Melville; another heads east, winding up and down to the bays and extensive coconut palm plantations of the northeastern coast, Calibishie, Melville Hall airport and Marigot.

The shortest route from Roseau to Marigot and Melville Hall is via the Transinsular Road, which climbs steeply and with many bends from Canefield. At Pont Cassé, the road divides three ways at the island's only roundabout. One branch turns left, down the Layou Valley, to join the Leeward coast at Layou; the Transinsular Road goes straight on, through Bells, to Marigot; the third branch goes east, either to Rosalie and La Plaine on the southeastern Windward coast, or to Castle Bruce and the Carib Territory.

The Atlantic coast is much more rugged than the Caribbean, with sandy or pebbly bays, palms and dramatic cliffs. After Castle Bruce the road enters the Carib Territory, although there is nothing to indicate this. At the northern end there is a sign, but it would still be easy to drive through the Territory without seeing anything of note. In fact, there is much to see; to appreciate

---

Key to Map of Roseau

1. Botanical Gardens; 2. Windsor Park; 3. Old Market Plaza and Tourist Office; 4. Roman Catholic Cathedral; 5. Methodist Church; 6. Anglican Church; 7. LIAT; 8. Northbound buses; 9. Buses to Trafalgar and Laudat; 10. Southbound buses; 11. New market; 12. Government Headquarters; 13. Police Headquarters; 14. Customs; 15. Post Office; 16. Cable and Wireless; 17. Barclays Bank; 18. Royal Bank of Canada; 19. Banque Française Commerciale; 20. National Commercial Bank; 21. Fort Young Hotel; 22. Kent Anthony's Guesthouse; 23. Continental Inn; 24. Cherry Lodge; 25. Vena's Guesthouse and The World of Food; 26. Scotiabank; 27. Whitchurch Travel; 28. Paperbacks; 29. Cee-Bee's Bookshop.

it fully, a guide is essential. Horseback Ridge affords views of the sea, mountains, the Concord Valley and Bataka village. At Crayfish River, a waterfall tumbles directly into the sea by a beach of large stones. The Save the Children Fund has assisted the Waitukubuli Karifuna Development Committee to construct two traditional buildings near Salybia: a large oval *carbet* (the nucleus of the extended Carib family group), and an A-frame *mouina*. The former is a community centre, the latter a library and office of the elected chief, Irvince Auguiste. The dilapidated Church of the Immaculate Conception at Salybia is being restored as a Carib Museum (due to open November 1992; it has been replaced by the new church of St Marie of the Caribs, which opened in May 1991), its design is based on the traditional *mouina* and has a canoe for its altar, murals about Carib history both inside and out. Outside is a cemetery and a three-stone monument to the first three Carib chiefs after colonization: Jolly John, Auguiste and Courriett. L'Escalier Tête-Chien, at Jenny Point, is a line of rock climbing out of the sea and up the headland. It is most obvious in the sea and shore, but on the point each rock bears the imprint of a scale, circle or line, like the markings on a snake. It is said that the Caribs used to follow the snake staircase (which was made by the Master Tête Chien) up to its head in the mountains, thus gaining special powers. However, there are more prosaic, geological explanations.

Taking the road from Pont Cassé to the southeastern part of the island, you come to Rosalie. Cross the River Rosalie and go south to Pointe Daniel and Delices. You can see the Victoria Falls from the road. The Forestry Division plans to improve the rugged trail to the Falls. Be sure to take an experienced guide if you attempt the steep hike to these Falls and avoid it in the rainy season. The White River falls in the Atlantic at Savane Mahaut, reached by a steep road from Victoria Laroche down to the sea. There are delightful places to picnic, rest or swim in the river. At the weekend local families picnic and wash their cars here. If it has not rained much the previous day you can follow the river up, jumping from one to another of the big stones in the river bed. Be wary of flash floods and do not attempt to cross the river if there has been heavy rainfall as you might not be able to get back. Sea bathing here is very dangerous.

Information for Visitors

Documents

All visitors entering Dominica must be in possession of an outward ticket and a valid passport. Proof of citizenship only is required for US and Canadian citizens. Visas are required by nationals of communist countries: they can be obtained from the Ministry of Home Affairs, Government Headquarters, Roseau.

Warning

The police are strict in their enforcement of anti-narcotic laws. The present Government takes a strong stand on "moral" issues.

How To Get There

Dominica has two airports, the older

Melville Hall (DOM), which handles larger planes, and **Canefield (DCF)**, which can only take small aircraft. Check which your flight will be using. Melville Hall, in the northeast is 36 miles from Roseau; taxis cost EC$42 on the Transinsular Road, but they can go via the East Coast Road or the West Coast Road and charge more. From Melville Hall to Portsmouth by taxi is EC$22. These rates are per seat; find someone to share with, or it will be assumed you want the vehicle to yourself, which is much more expensive. Canefield is only a ten-minute drive from Roseau; taxi fare to town is EC$20, per car. Minibus (public transport) fare from Canefield to Roseau is EC$1.50. (You must flag one down on the highway passing the airport.)

There are no direct flights from Europe
r North America to Dominica.
onnections must be made in Barbados,
ntigua, St Lucia or the French Leewards.
AT flies from Antigua, Barbados,
lartinique, Guadeloupe, St Lucia, St
laarten and St Vincent; Air Guadeloupe
om Guadeloupe, St-Barts, St Lucia, St
homas and San Juan, Puerto Rico; Air
araibes from Barbados, St Lucia and St
laarten and short connecting hops
etween Dominica's two airports.

There is a departure tax of EC$25
JS$7.40) and a security service charge of
C$5 (US$2).

irlines

AT, 8 Fort Lane, Roseau, Tel: 82421.
gent for Air Guadeloupe is Whitchurch
ravel, Old Street, Roseau, Tel: 82181, or
anefield Airport, Tel: 91060. Air
araibes, Canefield, Tel: 91416/ 92998,
ax: 92999.

ternal Transport

linibuses run from point to point. Those
om Roseau to the northwest and
ortheast leave from between the East
nd West bridges near the modern
arket; to Trafalgar and Laudat from
alley Road, near the Police Headquarters;
or the south and Petite Savane from Old
larket Plaza. They are difficult to get on
the early morning. Apart from the
oufrière/ Scott's Head route, it is difficult
o get anywhere on the island by public
ansport, and return to Roseau, on one
ay. This is because buses leave Marigot,
herever, to arrive in Roseau around 0700,
en return at about 1300. It is just
ossible to get to Portsmouth and return
one day, the first bus is at 1000,
eturning at 1600. Many buses pass the
otels south of Roseau (eg *Anchorage*).
ares are fixed by the Government.

Hitchhiking rides in the back of the
biquitous pick-up trucks is possible. It is
ften difficult at weekends.

axis

sightseeing tour by taxi will cost EC$35
er hour, per car (4 people), but it is wise
use experienced local tour operators for
ghtseeing, particularly if hiking is
volved. Fares on set routes are fixed by
e Government (see above for rates to the
rports). Ask at your hotel for a taxi; in
oseau, Mally's Taxi Service, 64 Cork
treet, Tel: 83360/ 83114, Eddie, 8
llsborough St, Tel: 86003, and others.

Car Rental

Rates are about US$35 per day for a small
Hyundai, plus US$8 for collision damage
waiver; unlimited mileage for hiring for 3
days or more. It may be preferable to rent a
car or jeep as the taxi service is expensive and
buses take a lot of planning. Jeep rental is
about US$45-55 a day including collision
insurance of US$600-700. Failing that, get
a bicycle from Den's, 21 Winston Lane, Tel:
85095. On either hand, Dominicans drive
fast in the middle of the road and many
visitors prefer to take a taxi so that they can
enjoy the views. Companies: Anselm's, 3
Great Marlborough St, Tel: 82730; Budget,
Canefield Industrial Estate, Tel: 92080,
recommended as cheaper, more reliable and
informative than some other companies,
cars in good condition; Wide Range Car
Rentals, 81 Bath Road, rents out old Lada
cars for US$30 a day, not recommended for
smaller roads, also Suzuki jeeps, US$60 a
day including 80 miles and collision
protection free; Valley, PO Box 3, Tel: 82279,
on Goodwill Road, next to Dominican
Banana Marketing Corporation, or in
Portsmouth, Tel: 55252, free delivery to
Canefield and within 2 miles of Roseau or
Portsmouth offices, cars in need of
maintenance but in the cheaper category;
also on Goodwill Road, S T L, PO Box 21, Tel:
82340, free deliveries as for Valley, but only
in Roseau area; Shillingford, 10 Winston
Lane, Tel: 83151; C N C, 37 Kennedy Ave,
Tel: 85888; Wide Range, 79 Bath Road, Tel:
82198. No car rental at the airports. It is
extremely difficult to hire a vehicle between
Christmas and New Year without prior
reservation.

Driving is on the left. The steering wheel
may be on either side. You must purchase a
local driving permit, valid for one month, for
EC$20, for which a valid international or
home driving licence is required; the permit
may be bought from the police at airports,
or at the Traffic Dept, High Street, Roseau
(Monday to Friday). Main roads are good;
the Portsmouth-Marigot road built in 1987
is excellent, but in towns and south of
Roseau, roads are very narrow and in poor
condition. There are no road signs, but with
a good map finding your way is not
difficult. The Tourism Office in the Old
Market, Roseau, sells Ordnance Survey
maps.

Where To Stay

There are a number of small, informal
hotels, guest houses and apartment
facilities on the island. 1991/92 rates are

quoted here and are therefore subject to change. The only large hotel in **Roseau** is the *Fort Young Hotel*, within the old fort (P O Box 519, Tel: 85000, Fax: 85006), which has been attractively renovated, good food and been service, international-type atmosphere. Weekdays it is occupied by businessmen and visiting politicians, the atmosphere is more relaxed on weekends, special events like concerts and barbecues and a popular Happy Hour every Friday, 1800-1900, expensive, US$110d, EP. Otherwise, lodging in town is in guesthouses: *Continental Inn*, 37 Queen Mary Street, Tel: 82214/ 5, US$34-42, EP, used by travelling salesmen and visiting sailors, adequate, good food but very slow service; *Kent Anthony Guesthouse*, 3 Great Marlborough Street, Tel: 82730, US$24-25d, EP, with fan and bath, cheaper rooms without, good food, rooms of varying standard, brusque but friendly landlady, mice and cockroaches; *Vena's Guesthouse*, US$25d, EP, prices higher during carnival, 48 Cork Street, Tel: 83286, Jean Rhys' birth place, interesting, rooms small and grim, rooms without bath more spacious and comfortable but noisy as on the corner of the two main streets, *The World of Food* restaurant is next door; *Wykies Guesthouse*, 51 Old Street, EC$35d including small breakfast, clean, rats and cockroaches but not in the rooms, basic, friendly, recommended, good bar but noisy at night so do not plan an early night. *Cherry Lodge Guesthouse*, 20 Kennedy Ave, Tel: 82366, historic and quaint, US$16-34d, some rooms with bath, good value meals available to order (EC$15 for 3-course meal). Apartments are available to rent in and around Roseau, check at the Tourist Office, look in the New Chronicle or ask a taxi driver. The *Honeychurch apartment*, 5 Cross Street, Tel:83346, US$60/day, US$360/week.

Outside Roseau, up a steep and windy hill (King's Hill), is *Reigate Hall*, with a splendid location but laid back management Tel: 84031/2/3 (Fax: 84034), US$70-140 double, service in restaurant sloppy and slow, diving, bar, swimming pool, tennis courts. A short distance south of Roseau, at Castle Comfort on the way to Soufrière, are: *Anchorage*, on seafront, Tel: 82638/9 (Fax: 85680), US$80-100d EP, US$110-130 MAP, restaurant and some rooms rather tatty, bar, swimming pool and diving facilities, good squash court, as well as facilities mentioned above; friendlier and a delightful place to stay, with good

restaurant is *Evergreen*, P O Box 309, Te 83288/ 83276, Fax: 86800, US$90 MA *Sisserou*, P O Box 134, Tel: 83111/3, Fa 83500, US$65-70d EP, pool, restauran recently refurbished; *Castle Comfo Guesthouse*, highly recommended, ve friendly, professional, excellent food, goo service, P O Box 63, Tel: 82188, Fax: 8608 US$80-85d MAP, a 7-night 10-dive packa costs US$756 pp double occupancy, (se above under **Diving and Marine Life**).

Also close to Roseau is *Excelsior*, with walking distance of Canefield airport, P O B 413, Tel: 91501/2, from US$55d EP to US$9 MAP, reasonable restaurant, comfortabl but can be noisy, good for business visitor *The Hummingbird Inn*, Morne Daniel, P Box 20, Roseau, Tel: 91042, Fax: 85778, fro US$30, run by Mrs Finucane who is ve knowledgeable on Dominica, simpl comfortable, good food, stunning vie down the hill over the sea, five minutes nor of Roseau. *Itassi Cottages*, self-catering, Morne Bruce, spectacular view of sou coast, one studio, two cottages, attractive furnished, phone, TV, US$35-80, less f longer stays, contact Mrs U Harris, PO B 319, Tel: 84313, who also has a cottage rent in Lydiaville, Scott's Head, on the mo southerly part of the island, US$25/da US$150/week; on the road to Trafalgar ar Papillotte, the Honychurch family rents a on bedroom apartment on their lovely estat *D'Auchamps*, US$35/day, US$210/wee Tel: 83346, this and *Itassi* can be booke through Travellers Tree in the UK, see **Tou** below. Near the Trafalgar Falls (15 minute walk) is *Papillotte Wilderness Retreat*, P Box 67, Tel: 82287, Fax: 82285, US$50-6(EP, US$110-120d MAP, seve complimentary reports, in beautiful garde with hot mineral pool, good terra restaurant (unforgettable lunch 1000-160 except Sunday, avoid days when cruise sh passengers invade, reservations require recommended if you want to get away fro it all but not for those who are afraid insects, no window screens in chalet-typ rooms. Bad road from the nearby village Trafalgar because of heavy traffic f hydroelectric scheme and heavy rains, b being improved, spectacular setting. *Ro Mountain Lodge* in Laudat, US$22-30 good breakfast and hearty supper US$ extra, basic rooms, good beds, hot shower management and staff reported rude ar off-hand, convenient for visiting Boilin Lake, Boeri Lake, Middleham Fal Trafalgar Falls and Freshwater Lake, within walking distance, guides arranged if required, transport into Roseau 0700 except Sunday, returning 1615, EC$3. *Springfield Plantation*, in the interior but only 6 miles north from Roseau, Tel: 91401, has a magnificent setting 1,200 feet above sea level, overlooking a lush valley, lovely rooms, apartments, suites, cottages, modernised and enlarged plantation house, but now also an agricultural research centre so periodically overrun by students, erratic management, but food can be good, US$55-80d EP.

Castaways, Mero, P O Box 5, Tel: 96244/5, Fax: 96246 conveniently located, just north of St Joseph, for visiting all parts of the island, on large, black sand beach, US$80 (summer), US$100d (winter) EP, restaurant, good food, staff slow but friendly, reasonable rooms all with balcony and sea view but over-priced, watch out for lots of extra taxes, get a receipt for safety box deposits, watersports and dive shop attached, German spoken. *Lauro Club*, opened 1992, self-contained bungalows sleep 1-4, half-way between Roseau and Portsmouth, Swiss owners, pool, bowls, small shops and snack bar in central building, US$58 pp. **Near Prince Rupert Bay**, *Portsmouth Beach Hotel* is primarily used by students at the nearby Ross Medical Institute (P O Box 34, Tel: 55142, Fax: 55599), US$50s EP, US$60d, US$70 triple, there is a pool, restaurant. On the beach is a sister establishment, *Picard Cottage Resort* (also PO Box 34, Tel: 55130) which has an attractive open-sided restaurant and bar, self-catering cottages which, at a pinch, can sleep 4 (US$100-US$180, MAP US$35 op), good sea bathing. *Coconut Beach* has apartments for US$65 double, bungalows for US$90, US$800 a week, bar, restaurant, beach, car hire, tours arranged, P O Box 37, Tel: 55393, Fax: 55693 (expensive, reported chaotic but improvements are now underway). In **Portsmouth** are *Casa Ropa*, on Bay Street, Tel: 55492, rooms for rent for US$35d with bath, single downstairs US$20, friendly, clean, recommended, and *Purple Turtle* guesthouse, US$21 CP, Tel: 55296; *Douglas Guest House*, Bay Street, Tel: 55253, US$10-16s, US$20-32d EP, no fan, clean, next to noisy disco and cinema; *Mamie's On The Beach*, Prince Rupert's Bay, Tel: 55997 has pleasant, modern rooms, fans, bathroom, adjoining restaurant, US$30d EP, thefts reported; *Sunshine Village*, north of Portsmouth,

Tel: 55066, US$49 EP, on beach, is referred to by locals as 'the concentration camp'. Enough said. There has been a change of management, which might upgrade the accommodation and grounds. Very near the new cruise ship jetty, so there will be a big increase in passing traffic. Ask around for low budget rooms/huts to let.

On the north coast near the charming fishing village of Calibishie, *Pointe Baptiste* estate rents out the Main House, sleeping 6, US$150-160 a night including cook and maid, stay a week and pay for 6 nights, spectacular view from the airy verandah, house built in 1932, wooden, perfect for children, cot, welcoming staff, very popular, also smaller house sleeping 3, self-catering, US$50-55 a night, reduced weekly rates, book locally through the housekeeper Geraldine Edwards, Tel: 57322, or in the UK through Traveller's Tree, Tel: 071-935-2291. Next door are three new self-catering villas *Red Rock Haven*, Tel: 83031, Fax: 86007, tastefully decorated, expensive, share beach with guests from *Pointe Baptiste*. *Atlantic Inn* at Wesley, Tel: 57800, only two miles to Melville airport, US$28d, breakfast US$2.50, dinner US$6, good value. In Marigot, *Thomas's Guest House*, west end of main street, Tel: 57264, US$12 EP, clean, basic, near Melville Hall airport (check in advance if it is open).

Away from the Leeward Coast: *Layou River*, P O Box 8, Tel: 96281, Fax: 96713 US$40s, US$50d, US$60 triple EP, US$60s, add US$20 pp MAP, nice location, pool, restaurant, bar, river bathing, may be noisy because of construction of neighbouring hotel; *Layou Valley Inn*, 5 rooms, very comfortable, excellent cuisine, high in the hills with superb views, need a car to get there, US$60d EP, add US$27.50 pp MAP, Tel: 96203, Fax: 85212, PO Box 196. *Emerald Bush Hotel*, about 1 mile from Emerald Pool, 6 A-frame cottages without electricity, a few small rooms, simple bar and restaurant, suitable for the fit and adventurous, accommodation very basic, US$10 to stay in the bush 'camp', US$34d for room, Tel: 86900/84545, Fax: 87954, P O Box 277. *Floral Gardens*, Concorde Village, at the edge of the Carib Territory, Tel/Fax: 57636, owned by ex-prime minister Oliver Seraphin and his wife Lily, comfortable rooms, US$35s, US$45d, with breakfast, 10% discount for stays of 5 days and over, dinner, good food but expensive and service very slow, lovely gardens by the Pagwa River where you can swim, 15 minutes away from beaches of Woodford Hill, electrics basic, ask for a mosquito coil for your room, many minibuses in the morning, easy to get a pick-up, bus to Roseau EC$9, 1 hour, bus to airport and Woodford Hill Beach, lovely walks in the area, either into the Carib territory or around Atkinson further north, recommended. Charles Williams and his wife, Margaret, run the **Carib Territory Guest House**, Crayfish River, Tel: 57256, US$38-44 EP, US$60-66 MAP, she cooks if meals are ordered in advance but there are no restaurants nearby as an alternative and you may go hungry, water intermittent, several complaints, he also does island-wide tours but is better on his own patch. About a mile away, **Olive's Guest House** at Atkinson has been recommended, bamboo huts, comfortable, friendly, EC$18, meals extra, Tel: 57521.

There are a 10% service charge and 5% government tax on hotel bills. A sales tax of 3% may be added to meal charges.

Camping is not encouraged and, in the National Parks, it is forbidden. Designated sites may be introduced in the future.

Where To Eat

(Not including hotels.) In Roseau, perhaps the best is **La Robe Créole**, Victoria Street, créole and European, but expensive; with same ownership is the **Mouse-Hole Café**, underneath, which is excellent for little pies and local pasties; **The World of Food**, next to Vena's Guesthouse, local dishes including lobster and "mountain chicken", good, breakfast about EC$10, lunch and dinners EC$20-30, drink your beer under a huge mango tree which belonged to writer Jean Rhys's family garden. **Guiyave**, 15 Cork Street, for midday snacks and juices, patisserie and salad bar, popular, crowded after 1300. **Cartwheel Café**, Bay Street (next to Royal Bank of Canada), clean, on waterfront, good place to stop for a coffee, and **Green Parrot**, same street, small, family-run, good value creole food, daily specials for US$4-5, may be closed because of sea wall construction; **Orchard**, corner of Great George and King George V Streets (slow service, but food OK). Lots of "snackettes", eg **Hope Café**, 17 Steber St, good local dishes and snacks, lively, open till late. **Cathy's Pizzeria**, opposite the Old Market Plaza; **Erick's Bakery** has opened a small patisserie on Old Street for

'tasty island treats'. **Wykie's**, 51 Old Street, caters for serious drinkers; the **Pina Colada Bar**, 30 Bath Road, is lively, popular with the young crowd, light meals. On weekdays in the capital the lunch hour begins at 1300 and places fill up quickly. Dominicans eat their main meal at lunch time and it is often hard to get anything other than takeaways after 1600 or on Sundays except at hotels.

Near Canefield, The **Shipwreck** offers simple barbecue meals, occasional live music, a seafront bar and Sunday beach party (see under Entertainment). **La Flambeau Restaurant** at Picard Cottage near Portsmouth, is comfortable, has an attractive beachside setting and a good varied menu. The **Almond Tree** at Calibishie on the north coast has been recommended.

Food

There is little in the way of international or fast food on the island, but plenty of local fruit and vegetables, fish and "mountain chicken" (crapaud, or frog) in season. Try the seedless golden grapefruit, US$1 for six in the market. The term 'provisions' on a menu refers to root vegetables: yams, sweet potatoes, tannia, pumpkins, etc. To buy fresh fish listen for the fishermen blowing their conch shells in the street, there is no fish shop or fish market.

Entertainment

Mid-week entertainment at Anchorage and Sisserou hotels. Weekends at Fort Young Hotel. Discos at Canefield Warehouse on Saturday; Aqua Cade on Friday; The Shipwreck, restaurant, bar, live entertainment at weekends before you get to the airfield, turn left after the bottling plant and twin bridges; turn left at end of road. **Good Times**, an old house next to the Warehouse Disco in Checkhall offers a good barbecue and loud music from Wed-Sun, opening at 1830, convivial proprietor, Ian Georges.

Shopping

Straw goods are among the best and cheapest in the Caribbean; they can be bought in the Carib Territory and in Roseau. Best shops for crafts in Roseau are the Caribana, 31 Cork St and, for the famous vetiver-grass mats, Tropicrafts, Queen Mary Street. Other good buys are local Bay rum (aftershave and body rub) and candles. Cee-Bee's Bookshop, 20 Cork Street and Paperbacks at 6 Cork Street, for Caribbean and other English books and magazines.

Banks

Royal Bank of Canada, Bay Street, Roseau, Tel: 82771; Barclays Bank Plc, 2 Old Street, Tel: 82571 (branch in Portsmouth); National Commercial Bank of Dominica, 64 Hillsborough Street, Tel: 84401 (opens lunchtime, branch at Portsmouth); Banque Française Commerciale, Queen Mary Street, Tel: 84040; Credit Union, Great Marlborough Street and island-wide; Scotia Bank, 28 Hillsborough Street, Tel: 85800. American Express agent is Whitchurch Travel, efficient and helpful for emergency cheque cashing. Visa and Mastercard well accepted with cash advances from all banks.

Currency

East Caribbean dollar.

Climate And Clothing

Daytime temperatures average between 70° F and 85° F, though the nights are much cooler, especially in the mountains. The rainy season is from July to October though showers occur all through the year. (Note that the mountains are much wetter and cooler than the coast, Roseau receives about 85 inches of rain a year, while the mountains get over 340 inches.) Clothing is informal, though swimsuits are not worn on the streets. A sweater is recommended for the evenings. When hiking take a raincoat and/or a pullover; a dry T-shirt is also a good idea. Take good walking shoes.

Hours Of Business

Government offices: Monday, 0800-1300, 1400-1700, Tuesday to Friday, close one hour earlier in the afternoon; the only government offices open on Saturday are the tourist kiosk in Old Market Plaza, and the tourist office at Canefield airport (open daily 0615-1115, 1415-1730—or last flight); the Melville Hall tourist office is only open at flight arrival times. Shops: 0800-1300, 1400-1600, Monday-Friday, 0800-1300 Saturday. Some of the larger supermarkets in Roseau stay open until 2000 and tiny, local shops may still be open at 2200 even on Sundays. Banks: 0800-1200 Monday-Friday, plus 1500-1700 Friday.

National Holidays

1 January; Carnival; Good Friday and Easter Monday; 1st Monday in May; Whit Monday; 3/4 November (Independence); Christmas Day and Boxing Day. 2 January is a merchant's holiday, when all shops and restaurants are closed, although banks and hotels remain open; Government offices will in most cases not be open.

Time Zone

Atlantic Standard Time, 4 hours behind GMT, 1 ahead of EST.

Electric Current

220/240 volts AC, 50 cycles. There is electricity throughout the island, but many places lack running water, especially in the villages between Marigot and La Plaine.

Post Office

Castle Street and Bay Street, Roseau, 0830-1300, 1430-1700 Monday, to 1600 Tuesday to Friday; has a list of other stamp sellers around the island. Temporary entrance through a passage, because of seawall construction project in 1992. Stamps can also be purchased in Roseau at the Tourist Kiosk in the Old Market, Paperbacks on Cork St and other stationers or gift shops. A postcard to Europe costs EC$0.35. Parcels go airmail only.

Telecommunications

Telephone, fax and telex services at Cable and Wireless, Mercury House, Hanover

Street, Roseau, open 0700-2000, Monday-Saturday. The international telephone code for Dominica is 809-44 followed by a five-digit number.

Radio

DBS broadcasts on medium wave 595 kHz and FM 88.1 MHz. There are two religious radio stations (one Protestant and one Catholic) as well as a repeater for St Lucian Radio Caribbean International on FM 98.1 MHz.

Tours

Island tours can be arranged through many of the hotels, for instance Dominica Tours at the *Anchorage Hotel* (an 8-day, 7 night package including accommodation, all meals, transfers, plus a photo safari, scuba, hiking, birdwatching, boating and sailing, costs US$560 double per person). The most knowledgeable operators are Antours (Anison's Tour and Taxi Service), Woodstone Shopping Mall, Roseau. Tel:86460, Fax: 86780, Ken's Hinterland Adventure and Taxi Service, 62 Hillsborough, St Roseau, Tel: 84850 and Lambert Charles, strong on conservation and hiking, no office but Tel: 83365. Other operators include Paradise Tours, 4 Steber Street, Pottersville, Roseau, Tel: 85999/ 84712 and Ivor Rolle's Rainbow River Tours, Tel: 88650. In the UK, Traveller's Tree specializes in holidays in Dominica, highly recommended, 116 Crawford Street, London W1H 1AG, Tel: 071-935 2291, 0703 671312, Fax: 071-486 2587. BA Holidays and Caribbean Connection

organize individual, personalized tour through La Robe Creole Tours and Travel PO Box 270, Tel: 448 4436/2896, Fax: 448 5212, who can also offer tours, excursions transfers, hotel reservations and ca rentals.

Maps

The Ordnance Survey, Romsey Road Southampton, SO9 49H, UK, Tel: 070: 792792, publishes a 1:50,000 colourfu map of Dominica, with a 1:10,000 stree map insert of Roseau, including roads footpaths, contours, forests, reserves ane National Parks. This can be bought at the Old Market tourist office in Roseau.

Tourist Information

The Dominica Division of Tourism has it headquarters in the Industrial Developmen Office, Valley Road, Roseau (PO Box 73, Te 82045). Travellers should visit the kiosk in Old Market Plaza or at the airport. Staff changes are frequent. A useful brochure i *Discover Dominica*. **USA**: In New Yor information can be obtained from the Caribbean Tourism Association, 20 East 46th St, New York, NY 10164, Tel: 212-682 0435 **UK**: The Dominica Tourist Office for the Ul and Europe is at 1 Collingham Gardens, Earl Court, London SW5 0HW, Tel: 071-37: 8751, Fax: 071-373 8743.

For her assistance in the preparation of thi chapter, we should like to thank Jan Murra of Traveller's Tree for a thorough revision o the text.

ST LUCIA

Introduction

LUCIA is the second largest of the Windwards, lying between St Vincent
d Martinique. Its total population is around 151,000, and the area is about
8 square miles. St Lucia (pronounced "Loosha") has become a popular
urist destination, with sporting facilities, splendid beaches, a clear, warm
a and sunshine. (The island was the scene of the films *Dr Doolittle, Water,*
d *Superman Two*.) It also has some of the finest mountain scenery in the
est Indies. The highest peak is Morne Gimie (3,145 feet); the most
ectacular are the Gros Piton (2,619 feet) and the Petit Piton (2,461 feet)
nich are old volcanic forest-clad plugs rising sheer out of the sea near the
wn of Soufrière on the west coast. A few miles away is one of the world's
ost accessible volcanoes. Here you can see *soufrières*: vents in the volcano
nich exude hydrogen sulphide, steam and other gases and deposit sulphur
d other compounds. There are also pools of boiling water. The mountains
e intersected by numerous short rivers; in places, these rivers debouch into
oad, fertile and well-cultivated valleys. If you are staying in one of these
lleys on the west coast (eg Marigot Bay) expect to be hot, they are
ll-sheltered from the breeze. The scenery is of outstanding beauty, and
the neigbourhood of the Pitons it has an element of grandeur. Evidence
volcanic upheaval can be found in the layers of limestone and even sea
ells in the perpendicular cliffs on the west coast and which occur at about
0 to 150 feet just north of Petit Piton above Malgretout and in other areas.
n uplift of from 50-100 feet is supposed to have occurred comparatively
cently and is thought to explain the flat plain of Vieux Fort district in the
uth and the raised beaches of the northern Gros Islet district.

story

en though some St Lucians claim that their island was discovered by
olumbus on St Lucy's day (13 December, the national holiday) in 1502,
ither the date of discovery nor the discoverer are in fact known, for
cording to the evidence of Columbus' log, he appears to have missed the
and and was not even in the area on St Lucy's Day. A Vatican globe of
20 marks the island as Santa Lucía, suggesting that it was at least claimed
Spain. In 1605, 67 Englishmen en route to Guiana touched at St Lucia
d made an unsuccessful effort to settle though a Dutch expedition may
ve discovered the island first. The island at the time was peopled by Caribs.
ere are Amerindian sites and artefacts on the island, some of which are
Arawak origin, suggesting that the Caribs had already driven them out
the time the Europeans arrived, as no trace of the Arawaks was found
them. The Indians called their island Iouanalao, which may have meant:
here the iguana is found. The name was later changed to Hiwanarau and
en evolved to Hewanorra. In 1638 the first recorded settlement was made
English from Bermuda and St Kitts, but the colonists were killed by the
aribs about three years later.

In 1642 the King of France, claiming sovereignty over the island, ceded

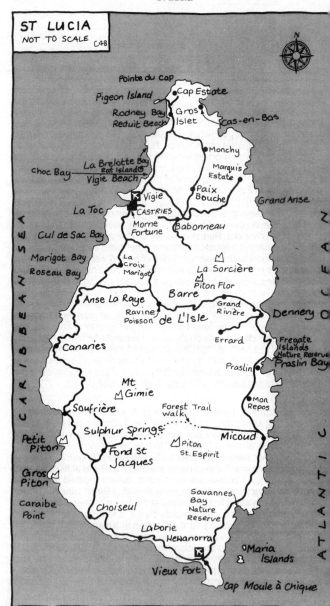

ST LUCIA
NOT TO SCALE C48

N

Pointe du Cap
Pigeon Island
Cap Estate
Rodney Bay
Gros
Reduit Beach
Islet
Cas-en-Bas
Monchy
Marquis
Estate
Choc Bay
La Brelotte Bay
Rat Island
Vigie Beach
Vigie
Paix
Bouche
Grand Anse
La Toc
CASTRIES
Cul de Sac Bay
Morne
Fortune
Babonneau
Marigot Bay
Roseau Bay
La
Croix
Marigot
La Sorcière
Piton Flor
Anse La Raye
Barre
Ravine
Poisson
de L'Isle
Grand
Rivière
Dennery
Canaries
Errard
Fregate
Islands
Nature Reserve
Praslin Bay
Praslin
Mt
Gimie
Mon
Repos
Soufrière
Forest Trail
Walk
Petit
Piton
Sulphur Springs
Micoud
Gros
Piton
Fond St
Jacques
Piton
St. Espirit
Caraibe
Point
Savannes
Bay
Nature
Reserve
Choiseul
Laborie
Hewanorra
Maria
Islands
Vieux Fort
Cap Moule à Chique

CARIBBEAN SEA

ATLANTIC OCEAN

it to the French West India Company, who in 1650 sold it to MM Houel and Du Parquet. There were repeated attempts by the Caribs to expel the French and several governors were murdered. From 1660, the British began to renew their claim to the island and fighting for possession began in earnest. The settlers were mostly French, who developed a plantation economy based on slave labour. In all, St Lucia changed hands fourteen times before it became a British Crown Colony in 1814 by the Treaty of Paris (more historical details can be found in the text below).

From 1838, the island was included in a Windward Islands Government, with a Governor resident first in Barbados and then Grenada. Universal adult suffrage was introduced in 1951. The St Lucia Labour Party (SLP) won the elections in that year and retained power until 1964. The United Workers' Party (UWP) then governed from 1964-79. In 1967, St Lucia gained full internal self-government, becoming a State in voluntary association with Britain, and in 1979 it gained full independence.

Government

St Lucia is an independent member of the Commonwealth and the British monarch is the Head of State, represented by a Governor General. The Government is led by Mr John Compton, of the UWP, who held power in 1964-79 and who has since won elections in 1982, 1987 and 1992. The UWP holds an 11-6 seat majority in the 17-member House of Assembly. The third political party, the left wing Progressive Labour Party (PLP), has failed to win any seats since 1987. The 11 members of the Senate are appointed by the Governor General, six on the advice of the Prime Minister, three on the advice of the Leader of the Opposition and two of his own choice.

The Economy

St Lucia's economy has historically been based on agriculture, originally sugar, but since the 1920s particularly on bananas and also cocoa and coconuts. It has the largest banana crop in the Windward Islands, bananas are 70% of total exports and the Geest boats call weekly to take them to the UK. Greater competition in the UK banana market, particularly after EC unification in 1992, is leading to diversification away from bananas; dairy farming and fisheries are being encouraged. There is also some industry, with data processing and a diversified manufacturing sector producing clothing, toys, sportswear and diving gear, and 20% of the workforce is now engaged in manufacturing. The island is promoted as a location for industrial development within the US Caribbean Basin Initiative. An oil transshipment terminal has been built and the Government has set up several industrial estates. Public sector investment in large scale infrastructure projects includes electricity expansion and road construction.

Tourism is now a major foreign exchange earner, and in 1991 322,371 people visited the island, of which 162,781 were cruise ship passengers and other day trippers. Air arrivals from Europe rose by over a third to become the largest market with over 36% of the total. In 1991 there were 2,000 hotel rooms and another 975 rooms in apartments, villas and guest houses. Further expansion is taking place with new hotels being built in the north of the island. The Atlantic Rally for Cruisers was changed from Barbados, its normal venue, to St Lucia in 1990-92 and this brought revenue of up to US$2m to the tourist industry. Tourists are estimated to have spent over US$174m in the island in 1991.

Culture

There is still a good deal of French influence: most of the islanders, who are predominantly of African descent (though a few black Caribs are still to be found in certain areas), speak a French patois, and in rural areas many people have great difficulty with English. There is still a French provincial style of architecture; about 85% of the population are Roman Catholics. The French Caribbean also has an influence on music, you can hear zouk and cadance played as much as calypso and reggae. One of the Caribbean's most renowned poets and playwrights in the English language, Derek Walcott was born in St Lucia in 1930. He has published many collections of poems, an autobiography in verse (*Another Life*), critical works, and plays such as *Dream on Monkey Mountain*. Walcott uses English poetic traditions, with a close understanding of the inner magic of the language (Robert Graves), to expose the historical and cultural facets of the Caribbean. His books are highly recommended, including his latest, award-winning work, the narrative poem *Omeros*. A quotation from one of his poems may be found on the title page of this *Handbook*. Another St Lucian writer worth reading is the novelist Garth St Omer (for instance *The Lights on the Hill*).

Fauna and Flora

The fauna and flora of St Lucia is very similar to that on Dominica, the Windwards chain of islands having been colonized by plants and animals originally from South and Central America, with endemic species such as sisserou and jacquot. Rainforest would have covered most of the island prior to European colonization but the most dramatic loss has been in the last twenty years. Much of the remaining forest is protected, mainly for water supply, but also specifically for wildlife in places. There are many orchids and anthurium growing wild in the rain forests, while tropical flowers and flowering trees are found everywhere. There are several endemic reptile species including St Lucia tree lizard, pygmy gecko, Maria Island ground lizard and Maria Island grass snake. The only snake which is dangerous is the Fer de Lance which is restricted to dry scrub woodland on the east coast near Grande Anse and Louvet and also near Anse La Raye and Canaries in the west. The agouti and the manicou are present throughout the island but rarely seen. The national bird is the colourful St Lucian parrot (*Amazona versicolor*), which is most frequently seen in the dense rain forest around Quillesse. A successful conservation programme established in 1978 probably saved the species from extinction and has allowed numbers to rise from 150 birds in 1978 to over 400 today. Other endemic birds are the St Lucia oriole, Semper's warbler and the St Lucia black finch. Several other species such as the white breasted thrasher are rare and endangered. Measures are being taken to protect these birds and their habitats.

In the north of the island, Pigeon Island, Pointe du Cap and Cap Hard are worth visiting for their landscapes, seabird colonies and interesting xerophytic vegetation, including cactus, thorn scrub etc. Union is the site of the Forestry Department headquarters, where there is a nature trail, open to the public, a medicinal garden and a small, well-organized zoo (free, but donations welcome). The Forestry Department also organizes a strenuous seven-mile trek across the island (franchized to several local tour operators and booked only through them, US$35, Mondays and Wednesdays, with pickup from your hotel) through rainforest and mature mahogany, Caribbean pine and blue mahoe plantations which will give you the best chance of seeing the St Lucia parrot, as well as other rain forest birds.

thrashers, vireos, hummingbirds, flycatchers etc. Wear good shoes and expect to get wet and muddy. The isolated east coast beaches are rarely visited and have exceptional wildlife. Leather backs and other turtles nest at Grand Anse and Anse Louvet and the Fisheries Department/Naturalists Society organize nocturnal vigils to count nesting females and discourage poachers. This area is also the main stronghold of the white-breasted thrasher and St Lucia wren; there are also iguanas (although you will be lucky to see one) and unfortunately the fer de lance snake, although attacks are extremely rare. The bite is not always fatal but requires hospitalization (it is extremely painful). Avoid walking through the bush, especially at night, and wear shoes or boots and long trousers. La Sorcière and Piton Flor are densely forested mountains in the north with excellent rainforest vegetation. Piton Flor can be walked up in 40 minutes although it is a strenuous climb and you will need to ask how to get to the top, from where there are spectacular views. It is the last recorded location of Sempers warbler, an endemic bird now probably extinct.

In the south, Cap Moule à Chique has spectacular views and good bird populations. The Maria Islands, just offshore, are home to two endemic reptiles, a colourful lizard and small, harmless snake. The National Trust (Tel: 450 5005/ 453 1495) and Eastern Caribbean Natural Areas Management Programme (ECNAMP) run day trips with a licensed guide. Interpretive facilities are on the mainland at Anse de Sables, where you can arrange boat transport. Unauthorized access is not allowed. Good beach, excellent snorkelling. From 15 May to 31 July public access is not permitted while the birds are nesting. However, you can visit the Fregate Islands Nature Reserve, handed over to the National Trust by the Government in 1989. Frigate birds nest here and the dry forest also harbours the trembler, the St Lucian oriole and the ramier. There is a major southeast coast conservation programme being coordinated by ECNAMP.

Some of these areas are very isolated and you are recommended to get in touch with the relevant organizations before attempting to visit them.

The St Lucia Naturalists Society meets every month at the Castries Library and often has interesting talks and slide shows on St Lucia. Visitors welcomed. Details in local press or from Library.

Diving and Marine Life

There is some very good diving off the west coast, although this is somewhat dependent on the weather, as heavy rain tends to create high sediment loads in the rivers and sea. Diving on the east coast is not so good and can be risky unless you are a competent diver. Several companies offer scuba diving with professional instructors, catering for the experienced or the novice diver. One of the best beach entry dives in the Caribbean is directly off Anse Chastenet, where an underwater shelf drops off from about 10 feet down to about 60 feet and there is a good dive over Turtle Reef in the bay. Below the Petit Piton are impressive sponge and coral communities on a drop to 200 feet of spectacular wall. There are gorgonians, black coral trees, huge barrel sponges and plenty of other beautiful reef life. Other popular dive sites include Anse L'Ivrogne, Anse La Raye Point and the Pinnacles, not forgetting the wrecks, such as the *Volga* (north of Castries harbour, well broken up, subject to swell, requires caution), the *Waiwinette* (several miles south of Vieux Fort, strong currents, competent drivers only), and the *Lesleen M* (deliberately sunk in 1986 off Anse Cochon Bay in shallow water). Scuba St Lucia operates from Anse Chastanet, P O Box 216, Soufrière, Tel: 459

7354/5, five dive boats, photographic hire and film processing, day and night dives, resort courses and full PADI certification; Buddies Scuba at Vigie Marina, Tel: 450 5288/450 7044, two tank day dives, one tank night dives, camera rental, open water certification or resort course, dive packages available; Moorings Scuba Centre at *Club Mariner*, Marigot Bay, Tel: 453 4357, day and night dives, equipment rental, certification courses and underwater camera hire. Peter Jackson Diving and Photographic Services takes a maximum of six people, full PADI certification, PO Box 274, Soufriére, Tel: 459 7269. The St Lucia Tourist Board can give help and advice on sites and the dive companies. The Fisheries Department is pursuing an active marine protection programme; divers should avoid taking any coral or undersized shellfish. Corals and sponges should not even be touched. It is also illegal to buy or sell coral products on St Lucia.

Beaches and Watersports

All the west coast beaches have good swimming but they are dominated by resort hotels. Exceptions are Vigie (lots of shade) and Rodney Bay (very little). The Atlantic east coast has heavy surf and is dangerous but very spectacular with beaches at Grande Anse, Anse Louvet, Anse Lapins and others, which are isolated (difficult to get to without local knowledge or the Ordnance Survey map and four wheel drive) and make a pleasant change from the west coast. Many are important habitats and nesting places for the island's wildlife (see **Fauna and Flora**, above). Of the beaches on the west coast Vigie (1½ miles from Castries) and Reduit are both beautiful, but heavily populated. The best are La Brelotte and Rodney Bay on the northwest shore, where people can use bar and sports hire facilities at the *St Lucian Hotel*. The trade winds blow in to the southern shore and the sandy beach of Anse de Sable near Vieux Fort offers ideal windsurfing. Many hotels hire out hobbycats, dinghies, jet bikes and small speedboats. At Marigot Bay and Rodney Bay you can hire any size of craft, the larger ones coming complete with crew if you want. Bareboat yacht charter costs around US$575 a week while a captained yacht including cook, food and drink will be about US$1,000 per person per week. Many of these yachts sail down to the Grenadines. Rodney Bay has been developed to accommodate 1,000 yachts and hosted the 1990-92 Atlantic Rally for Cruisers race, with over 150 yachts arriving there in December. Charters can be arranged to sail to neighbouring islands. *Nananan* does day sails to Martinique, 2-3 hours, Tel: 452 3763. There is a yacht basin at Gros Islet. Soufrière has a good anchorage, but as the water is deep it is necessary to anchor close in. There is a pier for short term tie-ups. Fishing trips for barracuda, mackerel, king fish and other varieties can also be arranged (eg with Captain Mike Hackshaw, Vigie Marina, Tel: 450 0216/450 7044, for fishing and lunch cruises). Several other fishing boats sail from Rodney Bay Marina. As some of the best views are from the sea, it is recommended to take at least one boat trip. There are several boats which sail down the west coast to Soufrière, where you stop to visit the volcano, Diamond Falls and the Botanical Gardens, followed by lunch and return sail with a stop somewhere for swimming and snorkelling. The price usually includes all transport, lunch, drinks and snorkelling gear; the *Unicorn*, a 140-foot replica of a 19th century brig (used in the filming of *Roots*), sails on Tuesday, Thursday and Friday in low season, more often in high season, and has been recommended, US$65 pp, can only be booked through a travel agent. Other excursions on catamarans and private yachts can be booked in travel agencies in Castries or through the hotels. At the swimming stop on the return journey local divers may try to sell you coral. Don't buy it, a reef dies if you do and what is more, it is illegal.

Other Sports

There are two nine-hole golf courses, at Cap Estate (green fee US$30, Tel: 450 8523) and at La Toc (green fee US$25, Tel: 450 3081). The larger hotels usually have tennis courts, or there is the St Lucia Tennis Club. Horses for hire at Trim's Stables, Cas-en-Bas (PO Box 1159, Castries, Tel: 450 8273), riding for beginners or advanced; also offers lessons and picnic trips. There are fitness centres at *Hotel La Toc*, aerobics classes, equipment, open 0700-1900, Tel: 450 3081 ext 6095; Fitness Palace, on Vigie Peninsula, aerobics on Monday, Wednesday, Thursday at 1800, general workouts, bodybuilding equipment open Monday-Saturday 0500-2030, Tel: 453 1688, no credit cards; Laborde's Gym, Old La Toc Road, exercise equipment and body building, open Monday-Friday 0600-2000, Tel: 452 2788, no credit cards. *Hotel Le Sport* specializes in health and fitness, with tennis, cycling, weight training, volley ball etc, all inclusive packages. Jogging is organized by The Roadbusters, who meet outside JQ's Supermarket, La Clery, on Tuesdays and Thursdays at 1700 and on Sundays at 0800. Cricket and football are the main spectator sports.

Festivals

Carnival is held in the days leading up to Shrove Tuesday and Ash Wednesday (although in 1991 it was rescheduled to July) and is a high point in the island's cultural activities, when colourful bands and costumed revellers make up processions through the streets. 22 February is Independence Day. At Whit weekend, usually end-May or beginning of June, there is an Aqua Action watersports festival at Rodney Bay, which includes all the usual watersports events and a few more unusual ones as well. On 29 June St Peter's Day is celebrated as the Fisherman's Feast, in which all the fishing boats are decorated. Street parades are held for the Feast of the Rose of Lima (La Rose), on 30 August, and for the Feast of St Margaret Mary Alacoque (La Marguerite), on 17 October, which are big rival flower festivals. 22 November is St Cecilia's Day, also known as Musician's Day. The most important day, however, is 13 December, St Lucy's Day, or the national day, on which cultural and sporting activities are held throughout the island.

Castries

The capital, **Castries**, (population 60,000) is splendidly set on a natural harbour against a background of mountains. The town was originally situated by Vigie and known as Carenage (the dock to the west of Pointe Seraphine is still referred to as Petit Carenage). An area of disease and defensively vulnerable, it was moved in 1768 and renamed Castries after the Minister of the French Navy and the Colonies, Marechal de Castries. It was guarded by the great fortress of Morne Fortune (Fort Charlotte and Derrière Fort). There is a spectacular view from the road just below Morne Fortune where the town appears as a kaleidoscope of red, blues, white and green: it promises much. However it can be a disappointment as, close to, the town is thoroughly modern but this is more than compensated by the bustle of its safe streets. Castries is twinned with Taipei who have provided all of the town's litter bins.

Largely rebuilt after being destroyed by four major fires, the last in 1948, the commercial centre and government offices are built of concrete. Only

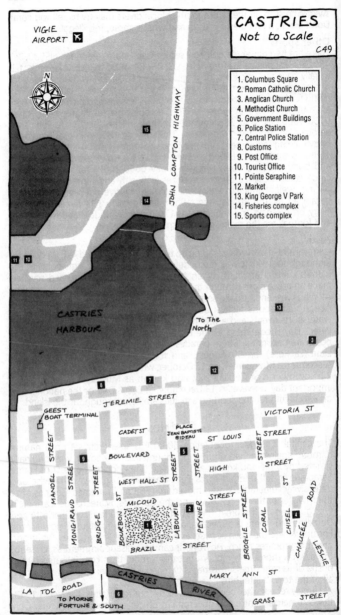

CASTRIES
Not to Scale
C49

1. Columbus Square
2. Roman Catholic Church
3. Anglican Church
4. Methodist Church
5. Government Buildings
6. Police Station
7. Central Police Station
8. Customs
9. Post Office
10. Tourist Office
11. Pointe Seraphine
12. Market
13. King George V Park
14. Fisheries complex
15. Sports complex

VIGIE AIRPORT

JOHN COMPTON HIGHWAY

CASTRIES HARBOUR

To The North

GEEST BOAT TERMINAL

JEREMIE STREET

CADET ST

PLACE Jean Baptiste BIDEAU

VICTORIA ST

BOULEVARD

ST LOUIS STREET

STREET

HIGH STREET

MANOEL STREET

MONGIRAUD STREET

BRIDGE STREET

WEST HALL ST

MICOUD

BOURBON ST

LABOURIE STREET

PEYNIER STREET

BROGLIE STREET

CORAL ST

CHISEL ST

CHAUSSÉE ROAD

LESLIE

BRAZIL STREET

CASTRIES RIVER

MARY ANN ST

GRASS STREET

LA TOC ROAD

To Morne FORTUNE & SOUTH

the buildings to the south of Columbus Square along Brazil Street were saved. Here you will see late nineteenth and early twentieth century wooden buildings built in French style with three stories, their gingerbread fretwork balconies overhanging the pavement. *The Rain* restaurant, 1885, is a fine example as is Marshalls pharmacy further along the street. The other area which survived was the market on the north side of Jeremie Street. Built entirely of iron in 1894, it was conceived by Mr Augier, member of the Town Board, to enhance the appearance of the town and also provide a sheltered place where fruit and produce could be sold hygienically. Covered with rather flaky red paint, the fine old clock seems to be permanently stuck at 0915. Not much fruit is sold here now but basketwork and T-shirts are cheap to buy. The foodstalls sell cold drinks and bottled Guinness. Other items include leeches, spices and hot pepper sauce. A new market has been built next door to house the many fruit sellers.

Columbus Square was the site of the Place D'Armes in 1768 when the town transferred from Vigie. Renamed Promenade Square, it finally became Columbus Square in 1893. It was the original site of the Courthouse and the market. The library is on its west side. The giant Saman tree is about 400 years old. On its east side lies the Cathedral which, though sombre outside, bursts into colour inside. Suffused with yellow light, the side altars are often covered with flowers while votive candles placed in red, green and yellow jars give an almost fairy tale effect. The ceiling, supported by delicate iron arches and braces is decorated with large panelled portraits of the apostles. Above the central altar with its four carved screens, the apse ceiling has paintings of five female saints with St Lucy in the centre. The walls have murals of the work of the church around the island painted by Dunstan St Omer, probably the most famous of St Lucia's artists.

As you wander around the town, note the Place Jean Bapiste Bideau (a sea captain who dedicated his life to freedom and heroically saved the life of Simón Bolívar) and the mural on Manoel Street behind the Dennery bus stand. It was painted in 1991 by one of Dunstan St Omer's sons and depicts scenes of St Lucian life: banana boats, tourism, 18th century sea battles, the king and queen of the flower festivals and Carib indians.

On the outskirts of Castries is **Pointe Seraphine**, a duty-free complex (see below, **Shopping**), near the port. From Castries take the John Compton Highway north towards Vigie airport and branch off just past the new fish market. All of the goods are priced in US dollars and it consists largely of chic boutiques. The tourist office here is only fully operational when cruise ships are tied up alongside (it is not particularly useful, try the one at Vigie airport instead). **NB** There are plenty of people who will "mind your car" here. Ignore them. The rather curious pyramid-shaped building is the Alliance Française, the French cultural centre built in conjunction with the St Lucia Ministry of Education. If you continue on the John Compton Highway past the sports complex and at the traffic lights turn left to go to the airport, you are sandwiched between the runway on your left and the beautiful Vigie beach on your right. There is a small war cemetery here mostly commemorating those from the British West Indies regiment who lost their lives. You can drive around Vigie point, there is much evidence of the colonial past. The St Lucia National Trust has its headquarters here in an old barrack.

Just south of Castries you can walk (unfortunately only on the main road, allow about one hour each way) or drive to the Governor's Mansion with its curious metalwork crown, at the top of Mount Morne. From here carry on to **Fort Charlotte**, the old Morne Fortune fortress (now Sir Arthur Community College). You will pass the Apostles' battery (1888) and Provost's redoubt (1782). Each has spectacular views, but the best is from the Inniskilling Monument at the far side of the college (the old Combermere barracks) where you get an excellent view of the town, coast, mountains and Martinique. It was here in 1796 that General Moore launched an attack on the French. The steep slopes give some idea of how fierce the two days of fighting must have been. As a rare honour, the 27th Inniskillings Regiment were allowed to fly their regimental flag for one hour after they took the fortress before the Union Jack was raised. The college is in good condition having been carefully restored in 1968. On returning to Castries, branch left at the Governor's mansion to visit La Toc point with its luxury Cunard hotel. Take the road to the hotel through its beautiful gardens and take the path to the the right of the security gate if you want to visit the beach. Further on is the road leading to Bagshaws studio. Down a long leafy drive, you can buy attractive prints and visit the printshop to watch the screen printing process. Max, a blue green Guyanese Macau, has been in residence for 15 years. Open Monday-Friday 0830-1600, Saturday 0830-1200.

North to Pointe du Cap

The part of the island to the north of Castries is the principal resort area, it contains the best beaches and the hotels are largely self contained. It is the driest part of the island with little evidence of the banana plantations or rain forest. The John Compton highway leaves Castries past Vigie airport and follows the curves of Vigie Beach and Choc Bay. Hotels here will arrange a picnic on Rat Island in the bay. Where the road leaves the bay and crosses the Choc river, a right turn to Babonneau will take you past the **Union Agricultural station** (about 1 mile) where there is a nature trail and interpretive centre. A mini zoo boasts a pair of St Lucian parrots. The trail goes through a nursery and herbal garden before going through Caribbean pine trees, latanier palms and cinnamon and bay trees. It takes about 20 minutes.

Back on the main highway, the road passes the turning to **Labrellotte Bay** (dominated by the *Windjammer Hotel*) before reaching Rodney Bay and the town of Gros Islet. Here is the site of the US Naval Air Station of **Reduit**. Built in February 1941, the swamps were reclaimed and the bay dredged. It was the first of a chain of bases established to protect the Panama Canal. Acting as a communications centre (code name "Peter Item"), it supported a squadron of sea planes. The base was eventually closed in 1947. The whole area now supports a mass of tourist facilities including the *St Lucian* and *Royal St Lucian* hotels, restaurants and sport facilities. You pass through the entrance gates of the old Naval Air Station on the road to the hotels. If you drive past them all to the end of the road there is good access to the beach. **Rodney Bay** is an excellent base for watersports; it is ideal for windsurfing. At the back of the development is a 1,000-boat marina. Development is still taking place and at Rodney Heights a huge area has been set aside for condominiums. **Gros Islet** holds a popular jump-up in the street each Friday night, from 2200, music, dancing, bars, cheap food, rather touristy but still recommended for night owls. Try the grilled conch from one of the booths selling local dishes.

About ¾ mile after Elliot's Shell filling station on the outskirts of Gros Islet, turn left to **Pigeon Island** national park (see also above, **Fauna and Flora**), once an island, now joined to the mainland by causeway. The park was opened by Princess Alexandra on 23 February 1979 as part of St Lucia's Independence celebrations. It has two peaks which are joined by a saddle. The higher rises to a height of about 360 feet. Owned and managed by the National Trust, the island is of considerable archaeological and historical interest. Amerindian remains have been found, the French pirate François Leclerc (known as Jamb de Bois for his wooden leg) used the large cave on the north shore and the Duke of Montagu tried to colonize it in 1722 (but abandoned it after one afternoon). From here, Admiral Rodney set sail in 1782 to meet the French navy at the Battle of Les Saintes (see under Guadeloupe). It was captured by the Brigands (French slaves freed by the leaders of the French revolution) in 1795 but retaken in 1798 by the English. Used as a quarantine centre from 1842 it was abandoned in 1904 but became an US observation post during World War II. The island finally became the home of Josset Agnes Huchinson, a member of the D'Oyly Carte Theatre who leased the island from 1937 to 1976. The bay became a busy yacht haven and "Joss" held large parties to entertain the crews. Her abandoned house can still be seen on the south shore of the island. On the lower of the two peaks lies Fort Rodney. There is a steep climb but well worth it for the 360° panorama. The museum (located in the Officers' Mess) contains an interesting display of the work of the National Trust. There is a small entrance fee (EC$3, open every day 0900-1800; museum closed Sundays). The park also contains *Les Pigeones* restaurant which is recommended for snacks and a cool drink (open 0900-1600, closed Saturdays). You can swim off the small beach, although sandy, it has a lot of broken coral. The park is a good place for watching sea birds. Offshore are the remains of the Castries telephone exchange, donated to the Fisheries Department by Cable and Wireless to make an artificial reef. You can walk to Pigeon Island along Rodney Bay. Take plenty of sun creams and protective clothing as there is no shade on the walk.

The road north passes through the Cap estate (golf course and the *Club St Lucia* and *Cariblue* hotels) to **Pointe de Cap**, a viewpoint some 470 feet high with a splendid panorama along the coast. If you wish to explore further the north part of the island contact Safari Adventures Ltd (Tel: 452 8778) who run all terrain vehicles to Cas-en-Bas beach. The road to Monchy from Gros Islet is a pleasant drive inland through several small villages. You gradually leave the dry northern part of the island and climb into forest. The ridge between Mount Monier and Mount Chaubourg gives particularly impressive views over the east coast. You will also pass through Paix Bouche where it is thought that Napoleon's empress Josephine was born. There are no road signs. Watch out for the names on schools and if in doubt at junctions bear west. At the larger village of Babonneau, you can turn right to follow the river down to the coast at Choc Bay or go straight on to Fond Cacao where a west turn will take you back to Castries. The road to Forestière is the access point for the climb to Piton Flor (1,871 feet).

East Coast to Vieux Fort

The transinsular highway from Castries to Vieux Fort has been completely repaved for most of the 33 miles to the south. Leaving Castries, one gets an increasingly good view of the town and harbour as the road climbs to the "top of the morne", over a thousand feet. The road goes through extensive banana plantations with the occasional packaging plant through the village of Ravine Poisson before climbing steeply over the **Barre de l'Isle**, the mountain barrier that divides the island. There is a short, self-guided trail at the high point on the road between Castries and Dennery, which takes about 10 minutes and affords good views of the rainforest and down the Rouseau valley. There is a small picnic shelter. It is neglected and can be slippery after rain. The experience is rather spoilt by the noise of traffic. A longer walk to Mount La Combe can also be undertaken from this point although it is overgrown and easy to get lost. The Forestry Department may provide guides for the day for a fee. Unfortunately there have been incidents of tourists being robbed here, so caution is advised.

The road descends through Grande Rivière to **Dennery** where the vegetation is mostly xerophytic scrub. Dennery is set in a sheltered bay with Dennery Island guarding its entrance and dominated by the Roman Catholic church. Here you can see the distinctive St Lucia fishing boats pulled up on the beach. Carved out of single tree trunks, the bows are straight and pointed rather than curved and are all named with phrases such as "God help me". There are lots of small bars but no other facilities. You can follow the Dennery River inland towards Mount Beaujolais. At Errard there is a photogenic waterfall. Permission should be obtained from the estate office before attempting this trip.

Fregate Island Nature Reserve, on the north side of Praslin Bay has a small but interesting visitor centre. The two small islands provide nesting sites for the frigate bird and the northern promentory of Praslin bay gives a good vantage point. The reserve is closed from May-July during the breeding season. At other times Tel: 452 5005 for a guide. The area is also of some historical interest as there was an Amerindian lookout point in the reserve. It was also the site of a battle between the English and the Brigands. It used to be known as Trois Islet and the nearby Praslin River is still marked as Trois Islet river on maps today.

Praslin is noted as a fishing community with traditional boat building. The road leaves the coast here and goes through banana plantations and the villages of Mon Repos and Patience. Mon Repos is a good area to witness the flower festivals of La Rose and La Marguerite. The coast is regained at **Micoud**. There are one or two restaurants (including *Palm*, simple and clean), a department store, post office and a branch of Barclays bank. Between here and Savannes is the proposed site of Ivan Lendl's tennis camp, the *Jeaumassee Resort Hotel*. It is also the centre of St Lucia's wine industry: banana, guava, pineapple and sugar cane brewed and bottled under "Helen Brand".

Mangrove swamps can be seen at **Savannes Bay Nature Reserve**. The bay is protected by a living reef and is a very active fishing area. The shallow bay is excellent for the cultivation of sea moss, an ideal breeding ground for conch and sea eggs. Scorpion island lies in the bay and to the north are more archaeological sites on Saltibus Point and Pointe de Caille (the latter excavated by the University of Vienna in 1983 and 1988).

After about three miles you reach **Vieux Fort** (population 14,000), the island's industrial centre, where the Hewanorra international airport is situated. It is a bustling town with a good Saturday market, a lot of traditional housing and gaily-painted trucks for transport, although they are gradually being replaced by the ubiquitous Toyota vans. The area is markedly less sophisticated than the north of the island. The town boasts lots of supermarkets. The post office is on Theodore Street which with the police station is right in the middle of the town. Fishing boats are pulled up on the small beach but there is no proper beach here. On Clarke Street you will pass the square with a war memorial and band stand. The bus terminal is being relocated to a site at the end of Clarke Street near the airport. Vieux Fort makes a good base for exploring the south of the island.

The perimeter road skirts Anse de Sables beach (no shade), the base for *Club Med* watersports and looks across to the **Maria Islands**. The interpretive centre on the beach is not always open. If you want to visit **Cape Moule à Chique**, turn left at the T junction and follow the road to the banana loading jetty (you will pass truck after truck waiting to be weighed). Bear left and go up a badly maintained track. Finally go left again through the Cable and Wireless site up to the lighthouse. The duty officer will be glad to point out the views including the Pitons, Mount Gomier (1,028 ft) with Mount Grand Magazin (2,022 ft) behind it. Unfortunately Mount Gimie ((3,118 feet) is largely obscured. Further to east is Piton St Esprit (1,919 ft) and Mount Durocher (1,055 ft) near Praslin. The lighthouse itself is 730 feet above sea level and also has good views over the Maria islands and south west to St Vincent.

The west coast to Soufrière and the Pitons

Take the transinsular highway out of Castries and instead of branching left at Cul de Sac bay carry straight on. The road quickly rises to La Croix Marigot where you get good views of the Roseau banana plantation. On reaching the Roseau valley take the signposted road to Marigot Bay (plenty of "guides" waiting to pounce). A good place to stop for a drink, the Marigot bay resort dominates both sides of the valley. In between is a beautiful inlet which is a natural harbour and provided the setting for *Dr Doolittle* . It supports a large marina and not surprisingly a large number of yachts in transit berth here to restock with supplies from the supermarket and chandler. You will notice a small strip of land jutting out into the bay. This has a small beach (not particularly good for swimming) and can be reached by the *gingerbread express* (a small water taxi) either from the hotel or the customs post. It is a good place for arranging watersports and the staff of the resort are most helpful. There is a police station and immigration post here. High above the bay are *JJ's* and *Albert's* bars, popular alternatives to Gros Islet on Friday nights. You can also eat well at *JJ's*, a much cheaper alternative to the expensive restaurants at Marigot Bay. The road continues to Soufrière and passes through the fishing villages of **Anse La Raye** and **Canaries** (no facilities).

Note that this road is spectacular with lots of bends, panoramic views of the Pitons and the coast and many ups and downs through lush valleys. In 1992 it was being completely reconstructed and was closed beyond Anse La Raye. The work was expected to take at least a year. Check with the tourist authorities to make sure that it is open.

After Canaries the road goes inland and skirts Mount Tabac (2,224 ft) before descending into **Soufrière** (population 9,000). This is the most picturesque and interesting part of the island, with marvellous old wooden buildings at the foot of the spectacular Pitons, surrounded by thick vegetation and towering rock formations looming out of the sea. Note that Petit Piton is dangerous to climb (several people have fallen off in recent years) and also that it is restricted Crown Lands. This does not stop local guides offering to show visitors up, though. Because of its location, the town is a must for tourists and consequently there have been many reports of harassment. It can help to have an hotel guide or dayboat skipper with you. In any event it is not cheap, expect to be charged for everything (see warnings under **Information for Visitors**). A stay in this town within view of the majestic Pitons is well worth while. Indeed, it is essential if you have no transport of your own and want to see the volcano and the Pitons, as there are no buses back to Castries after midday unless you make a roundabout journey via Vieux Fort. To do this, leave Castries at 0800, the ride can take two hours. After visiting Soufrière, wait at the corner opposite the church and ask as many people as possible if they know of anyone going to Vieux Fort; you will get a lift before you get a bus. It is important to get off at Vieux Fort 'crossroads', where there are many buses returning to Castries by another route, 1¼ hours. Buses to Castries leave from the market area. If you arrive by boat head for the north end of the bay, you will find plenty of help to tie up your yacht (EC\$5) and taxis will appear from nowhere. It is a much cheaper alternative to tying up at the jetty.

Soufrière is a charming old West Indian town dating back to 1713 when Louis XIV of France granted the lands around Soufrière to the Devaux family. The estate subsequently produced cotton, tobacco, coffee and cocoa. During the French Revolution, the guillotine was raised in the square by the Brigands but the Devaux family were protected by loyal slaves and escaped. It is situated on a very picturesque bay totally dominated by the pitons. The water here is extremely deep and reaches 200 feet only a few yards from the shore, which is why boats moor close in. To reach Anse Chastanet from here take the rough track at the north end of the beach (past the yacht club) about one mile. This is an absolute must if you enjoy snorkelling (the south end near the jetty is superb but keep within the roped off area). The hotel has a good and inexpensive restaurant and the dive shop is extremely helpful, they will hire out equipment by the hour. The *Unicorn* and day boats often stop here for a brief swim in the afternoon on their return to Castries.

Most visitors come to the town to see the Diamond Gardens and Waterfall and the Sulphur springs. There are no road signs in Soufrière and locating these two places can be difficult (or expensive if forced to ask). From the square take the road east to reach the **Diamond Gardens**. These were developed in 1784 after Baron de Laborie sent samples taken from the Diamond river (fed from the sulphur springs) to Paris for analysis. They found minerals present which were equivalent to those found in the spa town of Aix-la-Chapelle and were said to be effective against rheumatism and other complaints. The French King ordered baths to be built. Despite being destroyed in the French Revolution, they were eventually rebuilt and can be used by members of the public for about EC\$6. The gardens are well maintained and many native plants can be seen. It was here that Superman collected the orchid for Lois Lane in *Superman II*. Only official guides are allowed in, do not accept offers from those at the gates. Entrance EC\$4.50 (children EC\$2.25), open 1000-1700.

To get to the **Sulphur Springs** take the Vieux Fort road between wooden houses about half way along the south side of Soufrière square. Originally a huge volcano about eight miles in diameter, it collapsed some 40,000 years ago leaving the west part of the rim empty (where you drive in). The sulphur spring is the only one still active, although there are seven cones within the old crater as well as the pitons which are thought to be volcanic plugs.

Tradition has it that the Arawak deity *Yokahu* slept here and it was therefore the site of human sacrifices. The Caribs were less superstitious but still named it *Qualibou*, the place of death. Water is heated to 180°F and in some springs to 275°F. It quickly cools to about 87°F below the bridge at the entrance. There has been much geothermal research here since 1974. From the main viewing platform, you can see over a moonscape of bubbling, mineral rich, grey mud. It is extremely dangerous to stray onto the grey area. The most famous "crater" was formed a few years ago when a local person fell into a mud pocket. He received third degree burns. There are good, informative guides (apparently compulsory) on the site but you must be prepared to walk over uneven ground. Allow approximately ½ hour. Entrance EC$3, open every day 0900-1700. South of Soufrière, in the valley between Petit Piton and Gros Piton, a luxury all-inclusive resort, *Jalousie Plantation*, has been built despite complaints from ecological groups and evidence from archaeologists that it is located on a major Amerindian site. An important burial ground is believed to be under the tennis courts and there have been many finds of petroglyphs and pottery.

The road from Soufrière to Vieux Fort takes about 40 minutes by car. The branch of the road through Fond St Jacques runs through lush rain forest and a track takes you to the western end of the rain forest trail. In a few kilometres the road rapidly descends from Victoria Junction (1,200 feet) to the coastal plain at Choiseul. Choiseul is a quaint old West Indian village – there is a fish market and church on the beach. You can visit Caraibe Point from here: the last place on St Lucia where Caribs still survive, living in simple thatched houses. On the south side of Choiseul is the Art and Craft development centre sponsored by China. Experts from Taiwan are teaching St Lucians skills in bamboo handicrafts and you can buy pottery and carvings, as well as baskets. Bigger pieces of furniture are made from mahogany in the workshops at the back of the complex. There is a snack bar.

Information for Visitors

Documents

Citizens of the UK, USA and Canada may enter with adequate proof of identity, as long as they do not intend to stay longer than six months. A British Visitors Passport is valid. Citizens of the Organization of Eastern Caribbean States (OECS) may enter with only a driving licence or identity card. Visas are not required by nationals of all Commonwealth countries, all EEC countries except Eire and Portugal, all Scandinavian countries, Switzerland, Liechtenstein, Turkey, Tunisia, Uruguay and Venezuela. Anyone else needs a visa; check requirements, duration of validity, cost, etc. at an embassy or high commission. Without exception, visitors need a return ticket.

The immigration office at the central police station in Castries is very bureaucratic about extending visas: ask for plenty of time when you first arrive at the island.

How To Get There

The only direct scheduled services from Europe are with BWIA or British Airways from London, or BWIA once a week from Frankfurt, Cologne/Bonn, Munich and Zurich. From the USA, BWIA has direct flights from New York or Miami. American Airlines flies from Tampa/St Petersburg and connects other US cities through San Juan, Puerto Rico, from where there are daily flights. Air Canada and BWIA fly from Toronto and Liat flies from Caracas. There are excellent connections with other Caribbean islands: from Antigua (Liat, BWIA and British Airways), Barbados (Liat, BWIA), Canouan (Air Martinique), Carriacou (Liat), Dominica (Liat, Air Guadeloupe), Grenada (Liat), Guadeloupe (Air Guadeloupe and Liat), Jamaica via St Croix (BWIA), Martinique (Liat, Air Martinique), Mustique (Air Martinique), St Kitts (BWIA), St Maarten (BWIA), St Vincent (Liat, Air Martinique), Trinidad and

Tobago (BWIA and Liat) and Union Island (Liat, Air Martinique). Aerotuy flies small planes from Vigie to Caracas on Mondays and Thursdays and offers charter services to the Angel Falls and other sites in Venezuela, Tel: 452 23131 or Air Martinique at Vigie Airport.

St Lucia has two airports: Vigie Airport, for inter-island flights only (2 miles from Castries, taxi for EC$10, no exchange facilities), and Hewanorra International Airport in the Vieux Fort district, where international flights land; there is an air shuttle to Vigie. Alternatively a taxi to Castries costs EC$117 (though, out of season, you can negotiate a cheaper rate) and it will take you 1½-2 hours to reach the resorts north of Castries. If you are travelling light you can walk to the main road and catch the minibus for US$5. No baggage storage yet available at Hewanorra. Try to arrange it with one of the Vieux Fort hotels. Porters expect a tip of EC$0.50 at Vigie and EC$0.75 at Hewanorra.

At both airports there is a departure tax of EC$27.

Airline Offices

The following airlines have offices on Brazil Street, Castries: LIAT Tel: 452 3051, or at Hewanorra airport Tel: 454 6341, or Vigie airport Tel: 452 2348, Air Canada (Tel: 452 2550 on Columbus Square, at Hewanorra Tel: 454 6249, reservations Tel: 452 3051) and BWIA (Tel: 452 3778/9 and at Hewanorra Tel: 454 6249, Fax: 454 5223); British Airways is at Cox and Co Building, William Peter Boulevard (Tel: 452 3951 and at Hewanorra Tel: 454 6172); Air Martinique, Vigie Airport (Tel: 452 2463); American Airlines, Micoud Street, Tel: 453 2970 and Hewanorra Airport (Tel: 454 6777, 454 6779, 454 6795). American Eagle, at Vigie Airport, Tel: 452 1820. Eagle Air Services, at Vigie, Tel: 452 1900. Helenair, at Vigie, Tel: 452 7196, Fax: 452 7112.

Shipping

The island is served by several shipping lines, including Geest Industries: cargo and passenger vessels; Harrison Lines: cargo vessels only; West Indies Shipping Corporation; also local trading schooners. The *Stella S-2* does a Barbados-St Lucia-Dominica-Barbados trip every two weeks, primarily cargo but takes passengers: St Lucia-Barbados, EC$110 one way, EC$224 return (cheaper Barbados-St Lucia: EC$90 and EC$176

respectively); Dominica-St Lucia, EC$135 one way, EC$245 return; agency: Delice Joseph Shipping, Jeremie Street, Castries. Windward Lines Ltd operate a weekly passenger and cargo ferry service linking Venezuela, Trinidad, Grenada, St Vincent, Barbados and St Lucia, arriving St Lucia 0700 Saturday, departing 0700 Sunday, fare St Lucia-Port of Spain TT$271 one way, TT$407 return, cabin TT$43 per berth per night, child reductions. For information contact United Caribbean Shipping Agency, Suite 106, Furness Building, 86B Independence Square, Port of Spain, Trinidad, Tel: 625 6328, Fax: 624 6865. Many cruise lines call.

Car Hire

Cars and Suzuki jeeps can be rented. They are more expensive than on some islands because of all the extras which are included. Car hire starts at about US$40 a day, jeep rental is US$53 a day, US$318 a week; if you hire for 8 days you will be charged for one week and one day. Collision Damage Waiver is US$15/day, personal accident insurance US$2-2.10 a day, deposit US$100. A 5% tax is added to everything. Car rental agencies include Avis, Vide Bouteille (Tel: 452 2202/452 2700); Hertz, 36 Chaussee Road (Tel: 452 2878/452 4777/452 2780); National, Gros Islet Highway (Tel: 452 8721/452 8028); Royal (Tel: 452 8833/452 0117); Carib Touring Auto Rentals, Laborie Street (Tel: 452 2689/452 3184); Budget (Tel: 452 0233/452 8021, Fax: 452 9362. Most have offices at the hotels, airports and in Castries. If dropping off a car at Vigie airport you can sometimes leave the keys with the Tourist desk if there is no office for your car hire company. If you have an international driving licence a temporary licence can be obtained for free; if you only have a national permit, a temporary licence costs EC$30. If arriving at Vigie airport, get your international licence endorsed at the tourist information desk before going through Customs. Car hire companies can usually arrange a licence. Drive on the left. Although there are about 500 miles of roads on the island only half are paved so be prepared for some rough driving. Filling stations are open Monday-Saturday 0630-2000, Sundays and holidays 1400-1800. Leaded fuel costs EC$6, unleaded EC$6.50.

Water taxis and speedboats can be rented. Bicycles for hire from *Hotel La Toc*; G I Ryan's Cycles, Rodney Bay, Tel: 450

8489 and *Couples* at the end of the Vigie runway.

Taxi

Fares are supposedly set by the Government, but the EC$90 Castries-Soufrière fare doubles as unlucky tourists discover that there are no buses for the return journey. *Club St Lucia*, in the extreme north, to Castries, about 10 miles away, costs EC$40 one way. Fare to or from Gros Islet (for Friday evening street party), EC$30; to Pigeon Island National Park, EC$35 one way; to Vigie airport, EC$10; to Hewannora airport, EC$117. If in doubt about the amount charged, check with the tourist office or hotel reception. You can pick up a list of the fixed fares at the airport. A trip round the island by taxi, about US$20 per hour for 1-4 people, can be arranged. Many agencies operate tours of the island. Coach tours are cheaper and are usually daily in high season, falling to once or twice a week off season, ask in hotels. Coach tours of the south of the island can be frightening, however, as the roads are narrow and extremely bad. Alternatives are to go by boat or by helicopter (recommended for a spectacular view of the sulphur springs). From Pointe Seraphine a north island helicopter tour costs US$35, ten minutes, south island US$70, twenty minutes, St Lucia Helicopters, PO Box 1742, Castries, Tel: 453 6950.

Buses

It is much cheaper to go by bus, but the service has been described as tiresome. St Lucia's buses are usually privately-owned minibuses and have no fixed timetable. There are several bus stands in Castries: those going to Gros Islet and Rodney Bay leave from behind the market on Trinity Church Road; to Dennery from the Customs shed on Jeremie Street; to Jacmal, Marigot, Bois D'Inde and Roseau Valley from Mongiroud Street (between Bridge and Micoud Streets); to Vieux Fort from lower Micoud Street. From Castries to Vieux Fort, EC$5; to Choc Beach, EC$1; to Soufrière, EC$5; to Dennery EC$2.25; to Gros Islet EC$1.50; to Morne Fortune EC$0.75.

Hitching is considered fairly safe, though some drivers might expect a tip. With increasing crime directed often at tourists, it is advisable to travel by bus if you want cheap transport.

Where To Stay

Most of the hotels are resorts, providing everything their guests need. Apart from those around Rodney Bay they are remote and you will have to arrange car hire or expensive taxis to get around the island or go to restaurants. Hotels include (all prices EP, except where stated): *Club St Lucia*, Tel: 450 0551, Fax: 450 0281, was damaged by fire in 1990 but reopened in 1991 with 312 rooms, making it the island's largest hotel, rooms and family suites US$210-330 including taxes and all activities and entertainment; *Hurricane Hole*, where much of the *Dr Doolittle* film was made, and nearby *Marigot Inn* comprise the *Marigot Bay Resort* (Tel: 453 4357/453 4246, Fax: 453 4353), from US$140d, studios-2 bedroomed villas in winter, US$80-120d in summer (MAP add US$41 per person), children under 12 free, rats, there is a pleasant beach 300 yards away by ferry, also by ferry you can get to *Doolittle's bar and restaurant*, excellent but expensive, the swimming pool and bar (happy hour 1730-1830) overlook the marina; *Green Parrot Inn*, The Morne (Tel: 452 3399/452 3167, Fax: 453 0022), US$80d in summer, US$100d in winter, business rates on request (add US$30 for MAP); *East Winds Inn* (La Brelotte, Tel: 450 8212, Fax: 450 5434), 10 hexagonal bungalow rooms, US$195 pp, all inclusive, recommended; *La Toc* (a Cunard hotel, Tel: 452 3081/9, Fax: 452 1012) luxuriously appointed, US$200-265d, in hotel, winter rates, US$375-550 in cottages, MAP supplement US$44, tennis courts, golf course, watersports; *St Lucian* (Reduit Beach, Tel: 450 8351, Fax: 450 9639), on the beach, 222 a/c rooms, 6 miles from Castries, watersports, tennis, discotheque, restaurants, US$135-175d, US$85d in summer, MAP supplement US$40; the *Royal St Lucian*, its sister property, opened next door in December 1990, Tel: 450 9999, Fax: 450 9639, 98 luxury suites, interconnecting pools, swim up bar and waterfalls, restaurants, watersports, all facilities, very elegant, US$260-360d winter rate; *Couples* (Vigie Beach, Tel: 452 4211, Fax: 452 7419), couples only, prices from US$2,185 to US$2,895 per couple per week, all inclusive, has some self-catering cottages, many facilities, recommended despite the noise of aircraft landing and taking off, but overbooking reported and many couples get put in the inferior *Le Sport*, try making a fuss and demanding compensation if it happens to you, it is no way to start a honeymoon; *Le Sport*, Tel: 452 8551, is for health and fitness lovers, lots of sporting facilities, US$260-450 pp winter, US$190-350 pp summer, hotel in need of redecoration; *New Vigie Beach Hotel*, Vigie Beach (PO Box 395, Tel: 452 5211, Fax: 452 5434), US$100d, recommended, pool, garden, good restaurants (West Indian business lunch is excellent), 5 minutes walk from airport; *Halcyon Beach Club* (Choc Beach, Tel: 452 5331, Fax: 452 5434), pools, watersports, tennis, 180 a/c cabin and chalet-style rooms, US$140-165d in winter, US$118-148d in summer, MAP supplement US$39; *Bois d'Orange Village*, 4½ miles north of Castries, Tel: 452 8213, Fax: 452 0021, PO Box 1741, Castries, US$55d in studio, US$120d in 2-bedroom cottage, weekly rates on request, a/c, restaurant, bar, pool, sports facilities can be arranged; *Windjammer Landing*, Labrelotte Bay, (Tel: 452 0311, Fax: 452 0907), probably the best villa complex with hotel facilities, 1-bedroomed suites clustered together, 2/3-bedroomed villas more spread out with own plunge pool, luxury resort, tennis and all watersports available, US$260-500d winter, US$180-375d summer, honeymoon, family, diving packages available, recommended; *Jalousie Plantation*, Soufrière Tel: 459 7232, Fax: 459 7288, US$400-500d all inclusive, 115-room luxury resort built in 1991 amid much controversy over its location and its detrimental effect on the ecology and an important Amerindian archaeological site as well as on the scenery; *Anse Chastenet Hotel* (Soufrière, Tel: 459 7000, Fax: 459 7700), from US$260-400d, in winter, US$120-260d in summer, scuba diving, watersports, tennis, frogs in rooms, plumbing unreliable, avoid the hotel laundry; *Dasheene Ladera* (Soufrière, Tel: 459 7323), in spectacular setting between Gros Piton and Petit Piton, 2-3 bedroomed villas, some with pool, fully staffed, US$70-320 in winter, used to film *Superman II*, good restaurant. *Kimatrai Hotel* (Vieux Fort, 5 minutes from Hewanorra, Tel: 454 6328), US$40d, also has self-catering apartments, US$45d, winter rates; *Cloud's Nest Hotel* (Vieux Fort, Tel: 454 6711), US$45-90 for 1-3 bedroom apartments. *Top of the Morne Apartments*, Morne Fortune, Tel: 452 3603, Fax: 453 1433, US$88-110d in summer, US$120-170d in winter, no credit

cards, discounts given on car rental; *Harmony Apartel* (Rodney Bay Lagoon, Reduit, Tel: 450 8756, Fax: 450 8677), US$93-145d, winter, US$58-92 summer, studios, apartments, MAP supplement US$29; *Villa Beach Cottage* (Choc Beach, Tel: 452 2884/452 2691, Fax: 25416), US$55d in summer, US$65d in winter, no credit cards. There is also a *Club Méditerranée* at Vieux Fort, Tel: 454 6547, several other apartment hotels and villas for rent. Full details from tourist offices.

Guesthouses Castries: *Lee's*, Chaussee Road, no water in the evenings, noisy and no fan, US$9.50 pp EP with bath, although sometimes US$12.25; *Chateau Blanc*, on Morne du Don Road 300 metres away, US$14 pp EP, food available, Tel: 452 1851; *Thelma's Guesthouse*, near Courts Store on Morne du Don Road, Tel: 452 7313 US$20, pay cash in advance, fan, TV in rooms, private bathroom, kitchen, laundry, popular, clean and central, hot and noisy, recognizable by its bright red awnings; *Dubois Guesthouse*, Morne Fortune, Tel: 452 2201, US$12d EP, US$15d CP, a long way from anything; *Twin Palm Inn*, Morne Fortune, Tel: 452 2438; *Tropical Haven*, La Toc, 10 minutes by car from town, Tel: 452 3505, Fax: 452 7967, US$50d, 10 rooms and 2 apartments (negotiable), no credit cards, more than adequate, excellent food. *Hotel Bon Appetit*, on the Morne, Tel: 452 2757, beautiful view, clean, friendly, US$38-45d including breakfast. *Sunset Lodge Guesthouse*, near Vigie Airport (Tel: 452 4120), John Compton Highway, US$40-55d, MAP supplement US$18, convenient, dirty kitchen, ask for a room away from the road. *Summersdale Hideaway*, 20 minutes walk north of Vigie airport, Tel: 452 1142 for directions, US$22d EP. In the hills at **Marisule**, a 15 minute walk from La Brelotte Bay, the Zephirin family has cottages to let, self-catering, highly recommended. *Vide Bouteille* (just outside Castries): *Créole Inn*, Tel: 452 1295, US$23-30d EP, with bath, clean and simple; *Modern Inn*, on the main road north of Castries, 3 km from the centre, Tel: 452 4001, US$26-40, friendly, good rooms, clean and pleasant. At **Gros Islet**: *La Panache*, PO Box 2074, Tel: 450 0765, on Cas-en-Bas Road, run by Henry Augustin, helpful and friendly, US$20s, US$30d, US$35 triple, 6-10 rooms, clean, fans, good meals, highly recommended. Others include *B&B Guesthouse*, US$20s; *Scott's Café/Bar*, EC$25, friendly but noisy location; *Daphil's*, US$25s. Soufrière: *Soufrière Sailing Club Guest House*, Tel: 459 7194, 4 rooms, US$30 room only, US$35 with breakfast, US$45 with dinner too, no credit cards; *Home Guesthouse*, US$30d, Tel: 459 7318, on the main square, recommended; *Tropical Palm Inn*, US$35d, it is possible to bargain cheaper rates for longer stays, friendly, basic, helpful, Tel: 459 7489. Mrs Mathurin, 18 Church Street, Soufrière, has rooms to rent, EC$40 for bed and cooking facilities, reduction for long stay. There is an apartment to rent on the edge of Soufrière, new, basic but good, rates negotiable but competitive, PO Box 274, Tel: 459 7269. Vieux Fort: *St Martin*, on main street, clean, friendly, cooking and washing facilities, recommended. Until 1989, the National Research and Development Foundation had a recommended hostel which has had to close; write to the NRDF at P O Box 1097, Castries, or Tel: 452 4253/452 6535, to see what facilities are now available.

There is a 10-15% service charge and a 8% government tax on all hotel bills.

St Lucia is a budget traveller's nightmare and very expensive for what is available.

Where To Eat

Flamingo Restaurant, at *St Lucian Hotel*, Tel: 450 8351 ext 403 for reservations, gourmet food, live music some nights, open daily 1900-2145, prices from EC$29-80; *The Lime*, near the hotel, offers a good meal at reasonable prices, open 0900-0100, Tel: 450 0761; *Rain* in a lovely old building on Columbus Square, staff wear traditional clothes, pleasant, expensive, open Monday-Saturday 0900-2300, Tel: 452 3022; *Green Parrot*, highly recommended, buffet lunch EC$20, good value, excellent food, open daily from 0700, Saturday night specials, Tel: 452 3399; *Kimlan's*, top floor, on the park in Columbus Square, family-run restaurant and bar with nice verandah from which to watch the action, food excellent, meals of the day US$5, rotis US$3, open 0700-2300, no credit cards, Tel: 452 1136, recommended. *Cannelle*, Brazil Street, Tel: 452 3842, small, cheap and good, suitable for vegetarians; any of the roti houses on Chaussee Road, especially at the southern end, are recommended;

Dubois fish restaurant on the Morne, for cheap/mid-price food; *San Antoine*, Morne Fortune (Castries), old plantation house, English-owned, lovely gardens, very good but expensive (EC$45-100) open Monday-Friday 1130-1430, Monday-Saturday 1830-2230, reservations required, Tel: 452 4660. *Bon Appetit*, Morne Fortune, Tel: 452 2757, recommended, about EC$75. *Banana Split*, quite good, in Gros Islet, live music or disco most evenings, open 0900-0100, happy hour 1300-1400, lunch specials EC$12, no credit cards; *Ginger Lily*, Rodney Bay, Chinese food, recommended, open 1130-1430, 1830-2330, closed Monday, takeaway service, Tel: 452 8303; recommended is the *D's* restaurant at Vide Bouteille. Créole dishes are served at the *Pelican* and local cuisine is the main feature of *The Still* (Soufrière) open from 0830, dinner by reservation only, Tel: 459 7224, no credit cards; *The Humming Bird* (Soufrière) is a good place to eat and take a swim, French, Créole and seafood, daily specials, open from 0700, Tel: 459 7232; *Dasheene* (Soufrière) good food, EC$20-65, recommended. *Pisces* (Choc Bay), créole cooking; *Vigie Beach Bar*, beside *Couples* tourist complex, good rotis, beer inexpensive and cold; *Jimmie's Restaurant*, near Vigie airport, fantastic food and great views of the harbour at sunset, seafood and local specialities, open Monday-Saturday 1100-2400, Sunday 1800-2400, main courses EC$10-55, Tel: 452 5142, regularly wins 'small restaurant of the year' award, highly recommended; *Jammer's* at *Windjammer Landing*, Labrellotte Bay, reservations Tel: 452 0912, open 0700-2200, Sunday brunch recommended, EC$60, all you can eat; *Le Bambou* has a discothèque (admission EC$8 at weekends) as well as a restaurant and pizza parlour. *Behind The Wall Club*, in Gros Islet, has live steel band Friday nights (see page 508).

Camping

Allowed on most beaches.

Shopping

Pointe Seraphine, next to the main port in Castries, is a designer-built, duty-free shopping centre, with many tourist-oriented outlets, restaurants, entertainment and tour operators. Goods bought here can be delivered directly to the airport. It even has a London bus to take visitors to and from Castries. Cruise ships can tie up at the complex's own berths. Batik fabrics and cotton clothing (Bagshaw's silk screening workshops at La Toc, Tel: 452 2139, are very popular, studio open Monday-Friday 0830-1630, Saturday 0830-1200, also shops at *Marigot* and *Windjammer*); souvenirs from Noah's Arkade, Jeremie Street, Castries, and other branches at Rodney Bay, Pointe Seraphine and Soufrière; local crafts and clothing from Artsibit, corner of Brazil and Mongiraud Streets, open Monday-Friday 0900-1700, Saturday 0930-1300. Perfume from Caribbean Perfumes, by *Green Parrot*, Tel: 453 7249. Sunshine Bookshop, Brazil Street, Columbus Square, Castries, books, foreign newspapers and magazines, open Monday-Friday 0830-1630, Saturday half day, no credit cards at either bookshop; Book Salon, Jeremie Street on corner of Laborie Street, good selection of paperbacks, several books on St Lucia, also stationery. Market day in Castries is Saturday, very picturesque (much quieter on other days, speakers of Patois pay less than those who do not). Although there is a new Fisherman's Cooperative Market on the John Compton Highway at the entrance to Pointe Seraphine, most fishermen still sell their catch wherever they can. JQ's supermarket at the traffic lights at the end of the Vigie runway, open Monday-Friday 0800-1900, Saturday 0800-1600, bank next door, fair range of goods. JD Charles supermarket on Jeremie Street opposite the Fire Station. Wholesale meat from Chicken Galore behind shell station on Manoel Street. A shopping mall, Gablewoods, opened in 1992 in the northern part of Castries. In Castries cold drinks are sold on street corners, EC$1 for a coke, drink it and return the bottle. Snokone ice cream vendors roam the beach and streets, a cup of ice cream should cost EC$1.

Banks

Bank of Nova Scotia, Royal Bank of Canada, Canadian Imperial Bank of Commerce, all on William Peter Boulevard, Castries; Barclays Bank, National Commercial Bank and the St Lucia Cooperative Bank, all on Bridge Street, Castries. All have branches in Vieux Fort, and Barclays in Soufrière; Barclays and Royal Bank of Canada at Rodney Bay marina. It is better to change currency at a bank than in a hotel where you can get 5-10% less on the exchange. There is no rate quoted for many currencies, such as

Deutsch Marks; if you insist, Canadian banks will convert them first into Canadian dollars and then into EC dollars, but you get a poor rate. The Thomas Cook representative is on Brazil Street.

Currency

East Caribbean dollar.

Warnings

Roads to the waterfalls and sulphur springs on Soufrière lack signposts, and "guides" might expect large payments for their services. Be prepared to say no firmly, they are persistent and bothersome. We have received more reports from St Lucia of harassment and hostility towards tourists than from any other island in the Lesser Antilles (especially on the West Road between Marigot Bay and Soufrière, on the Soufrière beaches and in other remote areas). Attacks on tourists are often drugs related. We should point out, though, that this is not every visitor's experience. People staying at well-protected resorts and using organized tours generally have no problem. Be careful taking photographs, although everybody seems to be accustomed to cameras in the market.

Health

Drinking water is safe in most towns and villages. Many rivers, however, cannot be described as clean and it is not recommended that you swim or paddle in them unless you are far upstream. There is bilharzia. There is a doctor's surgery on Manoel Street, Castries, Monday-Thursday 0800-1330, 1715-1815, Friday 0800-1330. Most villages have health centres.

Climate

There is a dry season roughly from January to April, and a rainy season starting in May, lasting almost to the end of the year. The island lies in latitudes where the northeast trade winds are an almost constant influence. The mean annual temperature is about 26°C. Rainfall varies (according to altitude) in different parts of the island from 60 to 138 inches.

Clothing

Lightweight clothing all year; a summer sweater may be needed on cooler evenings. Short shorts and swimming costumes are not worn in town. An umbrella or light mac may be handy in the wet season.

Business Hours

Shops: 0800-1230, 1330-1700 Monday-Friday (shops close at 1200 on Saturday); banks: 0800-1300 Monday-Thursday, plus 1500-1700 on Friday; government offices: 0830-1230, 1330-1600 Monday-Friday.

National Holidays

New Year's Day, Carnival, Independence Day on 22 February, Good Friday, Easter Monday, Labour Day on 1 May, Whit Monday, Corpus Christi, Emancipation Day on 7 August, Thanksgiving Day, National Day on 13 December, Christmas Day and Boxing Day.

Time Zone

Atlantic Standard Time, 4 hours behind GMT, 1 ahead of EST.

Electric Current

220v, 50 cycles.

Communications

The island has an adequate telephone system, with international direct dialling, operated by Cable and Wireless, Bridge Street, Castries. There is a sub-office on New Dock Road, Vieux Fort. Telex and Fax facilities at both offices. Hotels do not generally allow direct dialling, you will have to go through the operator, which can be slow and costly. Intra-island calls are EC$0.27, no limit if on the same exchange, EC$0.27 for 90 seconds to another exchange. Pay phones use EC$0.25 and EC$1 coins. Cable and Wireless phone cards are sold for EC$10 or EC$40; with these you can phone abroad, EC$1.25/5minutes to Europe or EC$1.45/7 minutes to the USA. There is a credit card phone at Vigie airport operated via the boat phone network, open daily 0800-2200. In 1992 telephone numbers were changed from five to seven digits. In most cases prefix the old number by 45 except in Cap Estate, where 28273 becomes 450 8273, and in Soufrière, where 47194 becomes 459 7194. Main Post Office is on Bridge Street, Castries, open Monday-Friday, 0800-1200, 1300-1630, poste restante at the rear. The DHL office is on Bridge Street.

Media

The Voice is a thrice-weekly paper (Monday, Wednesday and Saturday), and *The Crusader* and *The Star* appear weekly. There is a commercial radio station, Radio Caribbean, which broadcasts daily in French and English, and a government-owned station, Radio St Lucia. A commercial television service operates in English only. There is lots of cable TV.

Tours

Most hotels will arrange tours to the island's principal attractions either by road, boat or helicopter. Tours can also be arranged to coconut oil and other craft shops, fabric manufacturers, and so on. Local tour operators offer plantation tours; Errard, Marquis and Balembouche offer fascinating insights into colonial history and local environments.

Maps

Maps of the island may be obtained from the Land Registry building on Jeremie Street. Ordnance Survey, Romsey Road, Southampton, UK (Tel: 0703 792792), produce a map of St Lucia in their World Maps series which includes tourist information such as hotels, beaches, climbing and climate. The Tourist Board map is expensive at EC$20.

Diplomatic Representation

UK: British High Commission, 24 Micoud Street, Castries, Tel: 452 2484, open Monday-Friday 0830-1230. **Venezuelan** Embassy, Casa Vigie, PO Box 494, Castries, Tel: 452 4033. **French** Embassy, Vigie, Tel: 452 2462, open Monday-Friday 0800-1230, 1330-1600. **German** Consul, 6 Manoel Street, PO Box 195, Tel: 452 2511, open Monday-Friday 0800-1230, 1330-1630. **Italian** Vice Consul, 15-17 Brazil Street, PO Box 832, Tel: 452 6319, Monday-Friday 1300-1600. **Danish** Consul, Halcyon Beach, Tel: 452 5331, Monday-Friday 0900-1700. **Netherlands** Consul, M & C Building, Bridge Street, PO

Box 1020, Tel: 452 2811, Monday-Friday 0800-1630.

Tourist Information

St Lucia Tourist Board, Pointe Seraphine, P O Box 221, Castries, St Lucia, Tel: 453 0053, Telex 6380 LC, Fax: (809) 453 1121. There are Tourist Board offices at the Pointe Seraphine Duty Free Complex, Tel: 452 7577; Vigie Airport (the most helpful), Tel: 452 2596; Hewanorra Airport (only open when flights are due or leave), Tel: 454 6644 and Soufrière, Tel: 459 7419. *The Tropical Traveller* is distributed free to hotels every month and contains some quite useful information.

USA: 9th Floor, 820 2nd Avenue, New York, NY 10017, Tel: (212) 867-2950, Telex 023-666762, Fax: (212) 370-7867.

Canada: 151 Bloor Street West (Suite 425), Toronto, Ontario M5S 1S4, Tel: (416) 961-5606, Telex 021-06217775, Fax: (416) 961-4317.

UK: 10 Kensington Court, London W8 5DL, Tel: (071) 937 1969, Fax: (071) 937 3611.

Germany: Postfach 2304, 6380 Bad Homberg 1, Tel: (06172) 30-44-31, Telex 041-411806, Fax: (06172) 30-50-72.

France: ANI, 53 Rue François Ler, 7th floor, Paris 75008, Tel: 47-20-3966, Fax: 47-23-0965.

The editors are most grateful to Patrick Dawson, of Trade and Travel Publications, and family for new material on St Lucia.

ST VINCENT

Introduction

ST VINCENT, and its 32 sister islands and cays which make up the Grenadines, were, until fairly recently, almost unknown to tourists except yachtsmen and divers, and are still uncrowded. St Vincent is very picturesque, with its fishing villages, coconut groves, banana plantations and fields of arrowroot, of which the island is the world's largest producer. It is a green and fertile volcanic island, with lush valleys, rugged cliffs on the leeward and windward coasts and beaches of both golden and black volcanic sand. The highest peak on the island is La Soufrière, an active volcano in the north rising to about 4,000 feet. It last erupted in 1979, but careful monitoring enabled successful evacuation before it blew. The steep mountain range of Morne Garu rises to 3,500 feet and runs southward with spurs to the east and west coasts. Most of the central mountain range and the steep hills are forested. St Vincent is roughly 18 miles long and 11 miles wide and has an area of 133 square miles, while the Grenadines contribute another 17 square miles all together.

According to preliminary results of the 1991 census, the population numbers 107,598, an increase of 9.1% over 1980, with 53,977 males and 53,621 females. About a quarter of the people live in the capital, **Kingstown** and its suburbs. 66% of the population is classed as black and 19% as mulatto, while 2% are Amerindian/black, 6% East Indian, 4% white and the remainder are 'others'. The main religious affiliation is Protestant, including Anglicans, Methodists, Seventh Day Adventists, Plymouth Brethren and others, while about a fifth of the people are Roman Catholic.

History

By the time Columbus discovered St Vincent on his third voyage in 1498, the Caribs were occupying the island, which they called Hairoun. They had overpowered the Arawaks, killing the men but interbreeding with the women. The Caribs aggressively prevented European settlement until the eighteenth century but were more welcoming to Africans. In 1675 a passing Dutch ship laden with settlers and their slaves was shipwrecked between St Vincent and Bequia. Only the slaves survived and these settled and mixed with the native population and their descendants still live in Sandy Bay and a few places in the northwest. Escaped slaves from St Lucia and Grenada later also sought refuge on St Vincent and interbred with the Caribs. As they multiplied they became known as "Black Caribs". There was tension between the Caribs and the Black Caribs and in 1700 there was civil war.

In 1722 the British attempted to colonize St Vincent but French settlers had already arrived and were living peaceably with the Caribs growing tobacco, indigo, cotton and sugar. Possession was hotly disputed until 1763 when it was ceded to Britain. It was lost to the French again in 1778 but regained under the Treaty of Versailles in 1783. However, this did not bring peace with the Black Caribs, who repeatedly tried to oust the British in what became known as the Carib Wars. A treaty with them in 1773 was soon violated by both sides. Peace came only at the end of the century when in

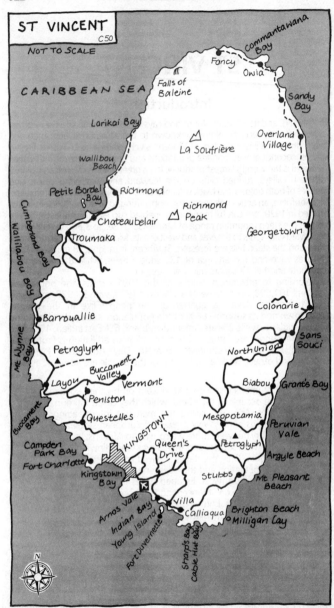

ST VINCENT
C50
NOT TO SCALE

CARIBBEAN SEA

Commantawana Bay
Fancy
Owia
Sandy Bay
Falls of Baleine
Larikai Bay
Overland Village
La Soufrière
Wallibou Beach
Petit Bordel Bay
Richmond
Richmond Peak
Chateaubelair
Georgetown
Troumaka
Cumberland Bay
Wallilabou Bay
Colonarie
Barrouallie
Sans Souci
Mt Wynne Bay
Petroglyph
North Union
Buccament Valley
Vermont
Biabou
Grant's Bay
Layou
Peniston
Mesopotamia
Peruvian Vale
Buccament Bay
Questelles
KINGSTOWN
Petroglyph
Campden Park Bay
Queen's Drive
Argyle Beach
Fort Charlotte
Stubbs
Mt Pleasant Beach
Kingstown Bay
Arnos Vale
Villa
Indian Bay
Calliaqua
Brighton Beach
Young Island
Milligan Cay
Fort Duvernette
Sharp's Bay
Cable Hut Bay

N

1796 General Abercrombie crushed a revolt fomented the previous year by the French radical Victor Hugues. In 1797, over 5,000 Black Caribs were deported to Roatán, an island at that time in British hands off the coast of Honduras. The violence ceased although racial tension took much longer to eradicate. In the late nineteenth century, a St Vincentian poet, Horatio Nelson Huggins wrote an epic poem about the 1795 Carib revolt and deportation to Roatán, called *Hiroona*, which was published in the 1930s. Nelcia Robinson, above Cyrus Tailor shop on Grenville Street, is an authority on Black Caribs/Garifuna and is the coordinator of the Caribbean Organization of Indigenous People on St Vincent.

In the nineteenth century labour shortages on the plantations brought Portuguese immigrants in the 1840s and East Indians in the 1860s, and the population today is largely a mixture of these and the African slaves. Slavery was abolished in 1832 but social and economic conditions remained harsh for the majority non-white population. In 1902, La Soufrière erupted, killing 2,000 people, just two days before Mont Pelée erupted on Martinique, killing 30,000. Much of the farming land was seriously damaged and economic conditions deteriorated further. In 1925 a Legislative Council was inaugurated but it was not until 1951 that universal adult suffrage was introduced.

St Vincent and the Grenadines belonged to the Windward Islands Federation until 1959 and the West Indies Federation between 1958 and 1962. In 1969 the country became a British Associated State with complete internal self-government. Government during the 1970s was mostly coalition government between the St Vincent Labour Party and the People's Political Party. In 1979 St Vincent and the Grenadines gained full independence, but the year was also remembered for the eruption of La Soufrière on Good Friday, 13 April. Fortunately no one was killed as thousands were evacuated, but there was considerable agricultural damage. In 1980 Hurricane Allen caused further devastation to the plantations and it has taken years for production of crops such as coconuts and bananas to recover. Hurricane Emily destroyed an estimated 70% of the banana crop in 1987.

Government

St Vincent and the Grenadines is a constitutional monarchy within the Commonwealth. The Queen is represented by a Governor General. The elections in 1989 were won again by the centrist New Democratic Party, formed in 1975 and led by the founder, James F Mitchell, who was re-elected Prime Minister, Minister of Foreign Affairs and Finance. There is a House of Assembly with 15 elected representatives and six senators. The New Democratic Party holds all of the elected seats. The main opposition party is the St Vincent Labour Party (SVLP), two smaller parties are the Movement for National Unity (MNU) and the United People's Movement (UPM).

The Economy

The St Vincent economy is largely based on agriculture and tourism, with a small manufacturing industry which is mostly for export. Unemployment is high at 25-30% of the labour force. The main export is bananas, the fortunes of which fluctuate according to the severity of the hurricane season; in 1990 the volume rose to 79,586 tonnes, the highest ever, but the 1991 output was reduced because of drought. Nevertheless, the Government is encouraging farmers to diversify and reduce dependence on bananas with incentives and land reform. About 7,000 acres of state-owned land is being split up into 1,500 small holdings. Arrowroot starch is the second largest export crop, of which St Vincent is the world's largest producer; the

Government plans to increase production by raising the area sown from 140 acres in 1990 to 1,200 acres by 1996. Arrowroot is now used as a fine dressing for computer paper as well as the traditional use as a thickening agent in cooking. Other exports include coconuts and coconut oil, copra, sweet potatoes, tannias and eddoes. Over half of all exports are sold to the UK. Healthy economic growth was recorded in the 1980s: government receipts grew faster than spending, investment in infrastructural development was promoted and social development projects such as schools and hospitals received foreign concessionary financing. St Vincent emerged as the largest flag of convenience in the Caribbean, with 521 ships on its register in 1990. In 1991 about 100 more were added as a direct result of the Yugoslav conflict, most of which came from Croatia and Slovenia. Tourism has grown steadily in St Vincent and the Grenadines and is important as a major employer and source of foreign exchange. Expansion is limited by the size of the airport. In 1991 stopover tourists declined by 4% to 51,629 although day excursionists arriving by air rose by 40% to 29,413, cruise ship passengers increased by 11% to 87,591 and arrivals by yacht were up by 15% to 4,659. Tourist accommodation expanded rapidly in the 1980s, reaching 1,157 rooms in hotels, villas, apartments or guest houses in 1988. Visitor expenditure was estimated at US$53m in 1991.

Fauna and Flora

St Vincent has a wide variety of tropical plants, most of which can be seen in the botanical gardens, where conservation of rare species has been practised since they were founded in 1765. There you can see the mangosteen fruit tree and one of the few examples of *spachea perforata*, a tree once thought to be found only in St Vincent but now found in other parts of the world, as well as the famous third generation sucker of the original breadfruit tree brought by Captain Bligh of the *Bounty* in 1793 from Tahiti. Other conservation work taking place in the gardens involves the endangered St Vincent parrot, *Amazona guildingii*, which has been adopted as the national bird. An aviary, originally containing birds confiscated from illegal captors, now holds 12 parrots. In 1988 the first parrot was hatched in captivity and it was hoped that this was the first step towards increasing the number on the island, estimated at down to only 500. This mostly golden brown parrot with a green, violet, blue and yellow-flecked tail, spectacular in flight, is found in the humid forests in the lower and middle hills on the island. The main colonies are around Buccament, Cumberland-Wallilabou, Linley-Richmond and Locust Valley-Colonaire Valley. Their main enemy is man, who has encroached into the forest for new farming land and exploited the bird's rarity in the illegal pet trade, but they have also suffered severely from hurricanes and volcanic eruptions such as in 1979. They are protected now by the Wildlife Protection Act, which covers the majority of the island's birds, animals and reptiles and carries stiff penalties for infringements. A parrot reserve is being established in the upper Buccament Valley.

Another protected bird unique to St Vincent is the whistling warbler, and this, as well as the black hawk, the cocoa thrush, the crested hummingbird, the red-capped green tanager, green heron and other species can be seen, or at least heard, in the Buccament Valley. There are nature trails starting near the top of the Valley, passing through tropical forest, and it is possible to picnic. The Vermont Nature Trail can be reached by bus, from the market square in Kingstown to the road junction in Peniston near the *Emerald Valley Hotel and Casino*; the sign for the trail is clearly marked. If travelling by car, look for the Vermont Nature Trail sign about one mile past Questelles. The car park, at 975 feet, is close to the Vermont Nature Centre. There is a rest stop on the trail, at 1,350 feet, and a Parrot Lookout Platform at 1,450 feet. It is a beautiful trail, through thick forest and is probably the best place to see the St Vincent parrot. Be prepared for rain, mosquitoes and chiggars, use insect repellant. Anyone interested in nature trails should visit the Forestry Department (in the same building as the Land and Survey Department), who have prepared official trail plans, published in conjunction with the Tourism Department. A pamphlet details the Vermont Nature Trails, Wallilabou Falls, Richmond Beach, Trinity Falls, Falls of Baleine, Owia Salt Pond and La Soufrière Volcano Trails.

Diving and Marine Life

The underwater wildlife around St Vincent and the Grenadines is varied and beautiful, with a riot of fish of all shapes and sizes. There are many types and colours of coral, including the black coral at a depth of only 30 feet in places. On the New Guinea Reef you can find all three types of black coral in six different colours. The coral is protected so do not remove any. Bequia has a leeward wall which is a designated marine park where no spearfishing, traps, nets or anchors are allowed. There are ten marine protected areas scattered throughout St Vincent and the Grenadines, of which the Tobago Cays are the most visited.

There are facilities for scuba diving, snorkelling, deep sea fishing, windsurfing and water ski-ing, with experienced scuba diving instructors for novices. The St Vincent reefs are fairly deep, at between 55 to 90 feet, and there is a great deal of colourful marine life to see, so scuba diving is more rewarding than snorkelling. Bequia is also considered an excellent dive site. Snorkellers will prefer the Tobago Cays and Palm Island. No licence is needed for gamefishing, but spearfishing is illegal. Contact the Fisheries Department for more information on rules and regulations, Tel: 62738. As well as the specialist companies, many of the hotels offer equipment and services for their guests and others.

There is a network of dive shops: Dive St Vincent (Bill Tewes) at Young Island Dock, P O Box 864, Tel: 74714/74928, Fax: 74948, links up with other dive operators in Wallilabou Bay, Bequia and Union Island to offer a ten-dive package throughout the area; also on St. Vincent are Dive Beachcomber, Tel: 84283, Caribe Divers, Tel: 87270, and there is diving at Petit Byahaut Bay organized by the hotel there. On the other islands are: Dive Bequia, at the *Sunny Caribbee* complex, near Port Elizabeth, P O Box 16, Bequia, Tel: 83504, Fax: 83612; the *Frangipani Hotel* on Bequia has diving (Sunsports), windsurfing and sailing (Tel: 83255). Dive Paradise, Friendship Bay, Bequia, Tel: 83563, Fax: 83689; Dive Anchorage on Union Island, Tel: 88221; Grenadines Dive (Glenroy Adams), Clifton, Union Island, Tel: 88138/88122, Fax: 88398; Canouan Diving Club on Canouan, Tel: 88888. Also offering scuba diving, wind surfing, water skiing, ocean taxis and yacht charters is Mariners Watersports and Yacht Charters (opposite Young Island, Susan Halbich), P O Box 639, Tel: 84228.

Beaches and Watersports

St Vincent has splendid, safe beaches on the leeward side, most of which have volcanic black sand. The windward coast is more rocky with rolling surf and strong currents. All beaches are public. Some are difficult to reach by road, but boat trips can be arranged to the inaccessible beauty spots. Sea urchins are a hazard, as in many other islands, especially among rocks on the less frequented beaches.

Sailing is excellent, indeed it was yachtsmen who first popularized the Grenadines; St Vincent has a good yacht marina and boats can be chartered from several companies on St Vincent, Young Island, Bequia or Union Island. Yacht races include the Bequia Easter Regatta, in which there are races for all sizes and types of craft, even fishing boats. There are other contests on shore. The centre of activities is the *Frangipani Hotel*, which fronts directly on to Admiralty Bay. The Canouan Yacht Race is in August and the CSY Skippers' Regatta in September.

CSY Hotel, Blue Lagoon, has yacht charters (P O Box 133, Tel: 84308), as does the *Anchorage Yacht Club* on Union Island (Tel: 88244). There are a number of other yacht charterers.

Other Sports

Many of the more expensive hotels have tennis courts but there are others at the Kingstown Tennis Club and the Prospect Racquet Club. Squash courts can be found at the Cecil Cyrus Squash Complex, the *Grand View Beach Hotel* and the Prospect Racquet Club. Horse riding can be arranged at the *Cotton House Hotel*, Mustique. Spectator sports include cricket (Test Match cricket ground at Arnos Vale, near the airport), soccer, netball, volleyball and basketball. Cricket is played throughout the Grenadines on any scrap of ground or on the beach. In Bequia, instead of the usual three stumps at the crease, there are four, while furthermore bowlers are permitted to bend their elbows and hurl fearsome deliveries at the batsmen. This clearly favours the fielding side but batsmen are brought up to face this pace attack from an early age and cope with the bowling with complete nonchalance. Matches are held regularly, usually on Sundays, and sometimes internationals are staged. In Lower Bay v England, which Lower Bay usually wins, the visitors' team is recruited from cricket lovers staying in the area. Ask at *De Reef*; it is best to bat at number 10 or 11. Pick up games of basket ball are played on St Vincent after 1700, or after the heat has subsided, at the Sports Complex behind the Arnos Vale airport. Everyone is welcome, although it can get very crowded and there is only one court, arrive early. There is also a court in Calliaqua (same times), but it is right on the street. Players beware, fouls are rarely called, although travelling violations are. No one is deliberately rough but overall the game is unpolished, unschooled but spirited.

Festivals

St Vincent's carnival, called Vincy Mas, is held in the last week of June and the first week of July. Mas is short for masquerade, and the three main elements of the carnival are the costume bands, the steel bands and the calypso. Thousands of visitors come to take part, many of whom come from Trinidad. From 16 December, for nine mornings, people parade through Kingstown and dances are held from 0100. At Easter on Union Island there are sports, cultural shows and a calypso competition. Also on Union Island, in May, is the Big Drum Festival, an event which marks the end of the dry season, culminating in the Big Drum Dance.

Kingstown

The capital, **Kingstown**, stands on a sheltered bay where scores of craft laden with fruit and vegetables add their touch of colour and noisy gaiety to the town. However, much land has been reclaimed and continuing dock works shield the small craft from sight, except at the northern end of the bay.

KINGSTOWN
ROUGH SKETCH
Not to Scale

1. Botanical Gardens
2. Victoria Park
3. Bentinck Square
4. Market Square
5. Anglican Cathedral of St George
6. Catholic Cathedral of St Mary
7. Methodist Church
8. Archaeological Museum
9. LIAT Office
10. Grenadines Boat Dock
11. Port Area
12. Customs
13. Police HQ
14. Tourism Department
15. Post Office
16. Cable and Wireless
17. Public Library
18. Court House
19. *Heron Hotel*
20. *Cobblestone Inn*
21. *Kingstown Park Guest House*
22. *Bellavista Guest House*
23. Hospital
24. Little Tokyo Fish Market

TO LAYOU AND LEENARD COAST

TO CRAFTSMEN'S CENTRE, AIRPORT, INDIAN BAY AND WINDWARD COAST

KINGSTOWN BAY

RECLAIMED LAND

DEEP WATER WHARF

The market square in front of the Court House is the hub of activity. Market day is Friday and Saturday and very colourful with all the produce spread out on sacks or on makeshift tables. The shopping and business area is no more than two blocks wide, running between Upper Bay Street and Halifax Street/Lower Bay Street and Grenville Street. There are quite a lot of new buildings, none of them tall. A new Fish Market, built with Japanese aid, was opened in 1990 near the Police Headquarters. This new complex, known as Little Tokyo, has car parking facilities and is the new point of departure for minibuses to all parts of the island. Looking inland from the bay, the city is surrounded on all sides by steep, green hills, with houses perched all the way up.

Kingstown has two cathedrals, St George's (Anglican) and St Mary's (Catholic). St George's, parts of which date from 1820, has an airy nave and a pale blue gallery running around the north, west and south sides. There is an interesting floor plaque in the nave, commemorating a general who died fighting the Caribs. St Mary's is of far less sober construction, with different syles, all in dark grey stone, crowded together on the church, presbytery and school. Building was carried out throughout the nineteenth century, with renovation in the 1940s. The exterior of the church is highly decorated but the interior is dull in comparison. The Methodist church, dating from 1841, also has a fine interior, with a circular balcony.

At the jetty where the boats for the Grenadines berth, you can see island schooners loading and unloading, all of which is done by hand. The men throw crates from one to the other in a human chain; the whole business is accompanied by much shouting and laughter. When the Geest boat is in dock, the farmers queue in their pick-ups to unload their boxes of bananas, and the food and drink stalls on the road to the Reception Depot do good business.

In Kingstown the Botanical Gardens just below Government House and the Prime Minister's residence are well worth a visit (for a description see above under **Fauna and Flora**). Established in 1765, they are the oldest in Western Hemisphere. In the Gardens, there is a very interesting Archaeological Museum of Amerindian artefacts, some of which date from about 4,000 BC. Outside is a collection of shrubs which may have been planted in a Carib garden. Anyone interested in St Vincent history, flora or fauna should talk to Dr Earle Kirby (Doc) at the museum; he is very knowledgeable and friendly. Unfortunately, the museum is only open Wednesday morning 0900-1200 and Saturday afternoon 1500-1800. The Gardens themselves are open 0600-1800 daily. They are about a 20-minute walk from the market square: go along Grenville Street, past the cathedrals, turn right into Bentinck Square, right again and continue uphill to the gate. You will be approached by guides who can explain which plant is which. There are notices specifying the official tour rates (in US$), so make sure you agree a price beforehand. Some guides can be persistent and bothersome, and have been known to get aggressive and demand payment for unrendered services.

Fort Charlotte (completed 1805) is on the promontory on the north side of Kingstown Bay, 636 feet above sea level, 15 minutes' drive out of town. The views of Kingstown and surroundings are spectacular, and on a clear day the Grenadines and even Grenada are visible. Although the fort was designed to fend off attacks from the sea, the main threat was the Black Caribs and many of its 34 guns (some of which are still in place) therefore faced inland. In the old barrack rooms, a series of paintings shows the early history of St Vincent. There is also a coast guard lookout which controls the comings and goings of ships entering the port. Below, the ruins of a military hospital can be seen, as well as a bathing pool at sea level on the end of the point, used when the fort housed people suffering from yaws. The National Trust and the Caribbean Conservation Association (CCA) are proposing to develop Fort Charlotte as part of an Eastern Caribbean plan for historic military sites, with an Interpretive Centre, gift shop and museum. The National Trust of St Vincent and the Grenadines, PO Box 752, Tel: 62591, has further information.

Excursions

The highest peak on the island, the Soufrière volcano, rises to about 4,000 feet. In 1970 an island reared itself up out of the lake in the crater: it smokes and the water round it is very warm. Hiking to the volcano is very popular, but you must leave very early in the morning and allow a full day for the trip. About two miles north of Georgetown on the Windward side you cross the Dry River, then take a left fork and drive through banana plantations to where the trail begins. A local guide is recommended, always useful for carrying food and water as well as ensuring you do not get lost. It takes about three hours to reach the crater edge and it is a strenuous hike, the first three miles are through the Rabacca plantation, then up, along Bamboo Ridge and all the way to the crater's magnificent edge; the top can be cloudy, windy, cold and rainy, take adequate clothing and footwear. There is an alternative, unmarked and even more challenging route from the Leeward side starting from the end of the road after Richmond, but you will need a guide. After crossing a river delta, turn right into a ravine and climb; it will take about four hours. Guided tours usually on Tuesdays and Thursdays, about US$20-35, guides provide and carry drinks. Leave an extra set of clothes in the van in case you get wet through. Take water and insect repellent.

There are few good roads, but cars, including self-drive, can be hired and most of the beauty spots are accessible by road (but see below under **Car Rental**). The Leeward Highway is a dramatic drive, passing through Questelles and Layou. Much of this road is in very poor condition north of Barrouallie. This drive along the west coast towards La Soufrière should not be missed; it has been described as a "tropical corniche". There are lush valleys and magnificent sea views. On the Leeward coast 14 miles north of Kingstown and two miles north of Barrouallie, are the Wallilabou Falls, 15-20 feet high with a pool at the bottom which you can bathe in. There are changing rooms, toilets and a picnic site. On the opposite side of the road is a nutmeg plantation. You can get there by car or by bus from Little Tokyo Fish Market to Barrouallie and walk from there. Another set of falls, also on the Leeward side, is 20 miles north of Kingstown; Petit Wallibou Falls are a double waterfall in a very remote region and you can bathe at the bottom of the second waterfall. To get there, go through Richmond and turn right up the side road beside the Richmond Vale Academy; follow this road for one mile, it then turns into a track for two miles. At the river the top of the waterfall is on your left. There is a steep climb on the left hand side of the waterfall to reach the pool where you can swim.

The Queens Drive takes you into the hills east of Kingstown and gives splendid views all around. The Marriaqua Valley with its numerous streams is particularly beautiful. In the Valley, beyond Mesopotamia, the lush, tropical gardens of Montreal are worth a visit; anthuriums are grown commercially there. The drive along the Windward coast to Georgetown offers good views of rocks, black sand beaches and rolling breakers. The road to Sandy Bay (beyond Georgetown), where St Vincent's remaining Black Caribs live, is now good, however you have to cross the Dry River, which sometimes is not dry and therefore not passable. Sandy Bay is poor but beyond it is an even poorer village along a rough dirt road, Owia. Here is Salt Pond, a natural area of tidal pools filled with small marine life. The rough Atlantic crashes around the huge boulders and lava formations and is very picturesque. The villagers have planted flowers and made steps down to the Salt Pond area. There is also an arrowroot processing factory which can be visited. Past Owia is Fancy, the poorest village on the island, also Black Carib and very isolated, reached by a rough jeep track which makes a pleasant walk. Baleine Falls (see below) are a two-mile hike from here around the tip of the island, rugged and not recommended for the unadventurous. Fishing boats can be hired in Fancy to collect you (do not pay in advance).

A boat trip to the falls of Baleine (on the northwest coast) is recommended. Wading ashore and for a few minutes up a river which originates on Soufrière, you come to the falls. At their base are natural swimming pools. It is possible to reach the falls on foot, but the easiest way is to take an excursion by motor boat (eg with Dive St Vincent, or Grenadine Tours), which includes a stop for snorkelling, and a picnic lunch, for US$35-40. Sea Breeze Boat Service uses a 36-foot auxillary sloop, not recommended if you get seasick, otherwise nice, includes snorkelling stop, rum punch but no lunch, for EC$50 pp, Captain Al is an authority on the bottle-nosed dolphin and will probably find a school of them to watch, recommended, Tel: 84969.

There are some interesting petroglyphs and rock carvings dating back to the Siboney, Arawak and Carib eras. The best known are just north of Layou.

The Grenadines

THE GRENADINES, divided politically between St Vincent and Grenada, are a string of 100 tiny, rocky islands and cays stretching across some 35 miles of sea between the two. They are still very much off the beaten track as far as tourists are concerned, but are popular with yachtsmen and the "international set".

Young Island

A tiny, privately-owned islet, 200 yards off St Vincent. Pick up the phone at the crossing to see if you will be allowed over. Fort Duvernette, on a 195-foot high rock just off Young Island, was built at the beginning of the 19th century to defend Calliaqua Bay. To visit it, arrangements must be made with the hotel or ask around the dock for a boat to take you out: approximately EC$20 to be dropped off there and picked up later; wonderful view, inspires imagination, recommended. There is a lovely lagoon swimming pool, surrounded by tropical flowers. *Young Island Resort*, P O Box 211, Tel: 84826, Fax: 74567; all accommodation in cottages, double-occupancy rates (MAP) range from US$240-380 a day in summer to US$410-550 in winter.

Bequia

Named the island of the clouds by the Caribs, (pronounced Bek-*way*) this

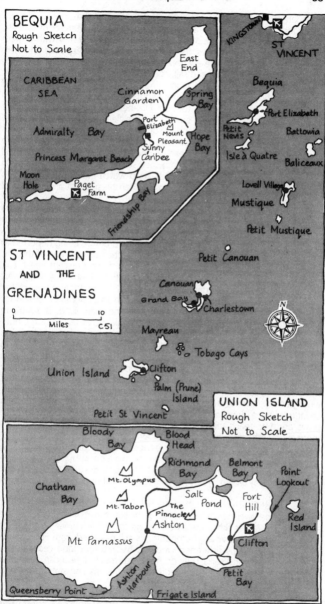

is the largest of the St Vincent dependencies. Nine miles south of St Vincent and about seven miles square, Bequia attracts quite a number of tourists, chiefly yachtsmen. The island is quite hilly and well-forested with a great variety of fruit and nut trees. Its main village is **Port Elizabeth** and here Admiralty Bay offers a safe anchorage. Boat building and repair work are the main industry. Experienced sailors can sometimes get a job crewing on boats sailing on from here to Panama and other destinations. For maps and charts (and books) go to Iain Gale's Bequia Bookshop, which is very well stocked. The nearest beach to Port Elizabeth is the pleasant Princess Margaret beach which shelves quickly into the clear sea. There are no beach bars to spoil this tree-lined stretch of soft sand. At its southern end there is a small headland, around which you can snorkel to Lower Bay, where swimming is excellent and the beach is one of the best on the island. Local boys race their homemade, finely finished sailing yachts round the bay. In the village is *Kennedy's Bar*, a good place to watch the sunset with a rum punch. Further along is *De Reef*, whose bar and restaurant are the hub of much local activity.

Away from Port Elizabeth the beaches are empty. Take a taxi through coconut groves past an old sugar mill to Industry Bay, a nice beach surrounded by palms with a brilliant view across to Bullet Island, Battowia and Balliceaux where the Black Caribs were held before being deported to Roatán. Some luxury homes have been built at the northern end of the bay. Food and drink available at the somewhat run down *Crescent Beach Inn*, Tel: 83400, which has a taxi to get you back to Port Elizabeth. A short walk along the track leads to Spring Bay, to the south, where there is a beach bar (may be closed). Both beaches are narrow with shallow bays and a lot of weed, making them less good for swimming and snorkelling. The walk up Mount Pleasant from Port Elizabeth is worthwhile (go by taxi if it is too hot), the shady road is overhung with fruit trees and the view of Admiralty Bay is ever more spectacular. There is a settlement of airy homes at the top, from where you can see most of the Grenadines. By following the road downhill and east of the viewpoint you can get to Hope Bay, an isolated and usually deserted sweep of white sand and one of the best beaches. At the last house (where you can arrange for a taxi to meet you afterwards), the road becomes a rough track, after ½ mile turn off right down an ill-defined path through cedar trees to an open field, cross the fence on the left, go through a coconut grove and you reach the beach. The sea is usually gentle but sometimes there is powerful surf, a strong undertow and offshore current, take care. Friendship Bay is particularly pleasant, there is some coral but also quite a lot of weed, a taxi costs EC$12, or you can take a dollar bus (infrequent) in the direction of Paget Farm, get out at Mr Stowe's Store (EC$1.50) and walk down to the bay (you may have to ring for a taxi at one of the hotels to get back, though).

The Tourist Office by the jetty (very helpful) can help you arrange a visit to the cliffside dwellings of Moon Hole at the south end of the island, where a rocky arch frames the stone dwelling and the water comes up the front yard. At Paget Farm, whale harpooning is still practised from February to May by a few elderly fishermen who use two 26-foot long cedar boats, powered by oars and sails. They do not catch much. If you can arrange a trip to **Petit Nevis**, to the south, you can see the whaling station and find out more about Bequia's whaling tradition.

For about $30, you can take a taxi around the island. You can also rent Honda scooters (and bicycles) from an agency between the bookstore and the National Commercial Bank for US$10/hour or US$30/day, but you need to get the police to verify your licence. Water taxis scoot about in Admiralty Bay for the benefit of the many yachts and people on the beach, whistle or wave to attract their attention, fare EC$10 per trip.

There are good restaurants on Bequia and good craft-type shops, most of which face on to Admiralty Bay in Port Elizabeth. There are two supermarkets in Port Elizabeth (limited choice of meat), fish is sometimes on sale in the centre by the jetty although a new fish market is being built, fruit and vegetable stalls by the jetty daily, frozen food and homemade bread from Doris's, also Daphne's for homemade bread.

An airport named the J F Mitchell Airport, after the Prime Minister, has been built on reclaimed land with a 3,200-foot runway, a terminal and night landing facilities, at the island's southwestern tip. Residents view it as a mixed blessing, some not wanting the island's peace and tranquility disturbed by an influx of visitors. The island's infrastructure and hotel accommodation is inadequate to handle greater numbers of tourists.

Mustique

Lying 18 miles south of St Vincent, Mustique is three miles long and less than two miles wide. In the 1960s, Mustique was acquired by a single proprietor who developed the island as his private resort where he could entertain the rich and famous. It is a beautiful island, with fertile valleys, steep hills and twelve miles of white sandy beach, but described by some as "manicured". It is no longer owned by one person and is more accessible to tourists, although privacy and quiet is prized by those who can afford to live there. There is no intention to commercialize the island; it has no supermarkets and only one petrol pump for the few cars (people use mopeds or golf carts to get around). House building will be limited to thirty. All house rentals are handled by the Mustique Company (Jeanette Cadet), which organizes activities such as picnics and sports, especially at Easter and Christmas. Radio is the principal means of communication, and the airstrip, being in the centre of the island is clearly visible, so check-in time is five minutes before take off (ie after you've seen your plane land).

There is sailing, diving, snorkelling, and good swimming (very little water-skiing), while riding can also be arranged or you can hire a moped to tour the island. Take a picnic lunch to Macaroni Beach on the Atlantic side. This gorgeous, white sand beach is lined with small palm-thatched pavilions and a well-kept park/picnic area. It is isolated and wonderful. *Basil's Bar and Restaurant* is *the* congregating spot for yachtsmen and the jet set. From it there is a well-beaten path to the *Cotton House Hotel*, which is the other congregating point.

Since the island has no fresh water, it is shipped in on Mustique Boats *Robert Junior* (Tel: 71918) and the *Geronimo*. Both take passengers and excursions on Sunday (EC$10, 2 hours trip).

Union Island

40 miles from St Vincent and the most southern of the islands, it is three miles long and one mile wide with two dramatic peaks, Mount Olympus and Mount Parnassus, the latter being 900 feet high. Arrival by air is spectacular as the planes fly over the hill and descend steeply to the landing strip. A walk around the interior of the island (about two hours Clifton-Ashton-Richmond

Bay-Clifton) is worth the effort, with fine views of the sea, neighbouring islands, pelicans and Union itself. It has two settlements, Clifton and Ashton (minibus between the two, EC$2), and the former serves as the southern point of entry clearance for yachts. The immigration office is opposite the harbour, but they may send you to the airport to get your passport stamped and your bags checked. The *Anchorage Yacht Club* seems to be full of French people. The barmen are slow and sometimes rude. You can make phone calls from here (there are no pay phones) but expect a charge of about EC$17 per minute to the UK compared with a pay phone price of EC$5. A good reason to visit Union Island is to arrange day trips to other islands or to find a ride on a yacht to Venezuela towards the end of the season (May-June). Day trip boats leave around 1000 and are all about the same price, EC$100, including lunch. Ask at the *Anchorage Yacht Club* or Park East, across the airport runway, about boats going to the **Tobago Cays** (see below), you may be able to join a group quite cheaply. A large catamaran, *Typhoon*, runs a charter service, well worth while. An old sailing vessel, *Scaramouch*, also sails to the Tobago Cays, stopping additionally at Mayreau and Palm Island. The *Clifton Beach Hotel* arranges tours of Palm Island, Petit St Vincent and other small islands. The beach at Chatham Bay is beautiful and deserted (very good mangoes grow there), but not particularly good for swimming as there is a coral ledge just off the beach. An area at the north end of the bay has been cleared for a hotel development and a road has been cut over the mountain from Ashton to Chatham Bay.

Canouan

A quiet, peaceful, crescent-shaped island 25 miles south of St Vincent, with very few tourists and excellent reef-protected beaches. The beach at the *Canouan Beach Hotel* is splendid with white sand and views of numerous islands to the south. There are no restaurants outside the hotels and only basic shops. The main anchorage is Grand Bay, although anchorages exist all round the island. A recommended day trip is to the Tobago Cays, Mayreau or Petit St Vincent, depending on the weather and conditions, on the *Canouan Beach Hotel* 35-foot catamaran, EC$100 with lunch and drinks, non-hotel guests are permitted to make up numbers if the boat is not fully booked. There is an airstrip and Air Martinique provides a scheduled service. A Swiss company, Canouan Resorts Development Ltd, has leased 1,200 of the island's 1,866 acres in a US$100m development plan. In the first stage a hotel training school was to open in 1992 as part of a US$1.5m villa hotel project.

Mayreau

A small privately-owned island with deserted beaches and only one hotel, *Salt Whistle Bay* (contact by radio, VHF Ch 16; rates on request), and one guest house, *Dennis' Hideaway*, 6 rooms, US$60d winter, US$50d summer, EP, Tel: 88594, though there is a plan to develop tourism. You can reach it only by boat. Once a week, however, the island springs to life with the arrival of a cruise ship which anchors in the bay and sends its passengers ashore for a barbecue and sunburn. In preparation for this, local women sweep the beach and the manchineel trees (poisonous) are banded with red. Good food and drinks at reasonable prices can be found at *Dennis' Hideaway*. The **Tobago Cays** are a small collection of islets just off Mayreau, protected by a horseshoe reef and surrounded by beautifully clear water and colourful fish, making them ideal for snorkelling. The beaches are some of the most beautiful in the Caribbean. There are day charters out of St Vincent and Union Island.

Petit St Vincent

Locally referred to as PSV, this is a beautiful, privately-owned island with one of the Caribbean's best resorts, the *Petit St Vincent* (rates vary during the year from US$325s to US$650d, FAP, closed September/October). Accommodation is in 22 secluded cottages, and a wide range of watersports is available, Tel: 84828. US reservations: PSV, PO Box 12506, Cincinnatti, Ohio 45212; Tel: (513) 242-1333. The island can be reached by launch from Union Island.

Palm Island

Also known as **Prune Island**, is another privately-owned resort, about 400 yards from Union Island, with coral reefs on three sides. There are four beaches, of which the one on the west coast, Casuarina, is the most beautiful. *Palm Island Beach Club*, individual bungalows, Tel: 84824, Fax: 88804 (US$210-320d full board, depending on season, no credit cards). Sailing, windsurfing, scuba diving, snorkelling, fishing, tennis, healthclub all available. There is a 10-minute launch service from Union Island. Shared charter flights can be arranged on Mustique Airways from Barbados to Union Island, where you will be met.

Information for Visitors

Documents

All visitors must have a passport and an onward, or return, ticket. Nationals of the UK, USA and Canada may enter for up to six months on proof of citizenship only. As well as the three countries already mentioned, citizens of the following countries do not need a visa: all Commonwealth countries, all the EC countries (except Eire and Portugal), Chile, Finland, Iceland, Liechtenstein, Norway, Switzerland, Sweden, Turkey, Uruguay, Venezuela. You will be asked where you will be staying on the island and will need a reservation, which can be done through the Tourist Office at the airport, before going through immigration.

How To Get There

By air, there are no direct services out of the Caribbean but same day connecting flights with BWIA, British Airways, Air France, Air Canada, American Airlines are available through Barbados, St Lucia, Martinique, Puerto Rico, Trinidad and Grenada. The only carriers with scheduled services are LIAT, which connects **St Vincent** with Antigua, Barbados, Carriacou, Dominica, Puerto Rico, Guadeloupe, St Maarten, Martinique, BVI,

Trinidad, St Lucia and Grenada, and Air Martinique, with flights to St Lucia and Martinique (linking with Air France to Paris). **Mustique** has scheduled service connections with Canouan, Grenada, St Vincent and Union Island, using Liat and/or Air Martinique. Air Martinique flies to **Canouan** from Fort de France, St Lucia, St Vincent and Union Island. **Union Island** is reached by Liat and/or Air Martinique from Canouan, Carriacou, Fort de France, Grenada, Mustique, St Lucia and St Vincent. Inter island charters are also operated by SVGAIR, Mustique Airways and Aero Services.

Flights within the Grenadines are cheap but prices rise if travelling to or from another country, eg Carriacou or St Lucia. If economizing it is worth considering a boat to travel internationally, eg from Union Island to Carriacou. Inter-island flights operated by Air Martinique are erratic and sometimes leave early, while Liat often fails to appear at all, but do not expect the ferry to be any different. Check in for flights a good hour before departure.

Windward Lines Ltd operates a passenger

and cargo ferry service on the MV Windward from Trinidad on Thursday 1600, arriving St Vincent Friday 0700, departing 1000 for Barbados-St Lucia-Barbados arriving back in St Vincent Monday 0700 and leaving for Trinidad at 1700 with a following service to Venezuela. For information contact United Caribbean Shipping Agencies, Suite 106, 86 B Independence Square, Port of Spain, Trinidad. The Geest Line calls weekly at St Vincent en route from and to Wales (passengers are taken; Tel: 61718 in St Vincent, (0446) 700 333 in UK). Several flour ships ply between St Vincent and St Kitts via Montserrat, and it is possible to hitch a lift on these, Tel: 71918. There is a regular boat service to Grenada and the Grenadines (see below).

Airlines
LIAT, Halifax Street, Kingstown, Tel: 71821 for reservations, airport office Tel: 84841, on Union Island Tel: 88230; Air Martinique Tel: 84528/64711 or 88328 on Union Island; Mustique Airways, P O Box 1232, Tel: 84380; SVGAIR, PO Box 39, Blue Lagoon, St Vincent, Tel: 69246, Fax: 69238; British Airways, Tel: 84841.

Airport
Arnos Vale, 2 miles from Kingstown. Taxi fare to town EC$15 (with other fares ranging from EC$10-35 for nearer or more distant hotels set by government); minibus to Kingstown EC$1.50, 10 minutes. On Union Island there is an airport fee of EC$6 on both arrival and departure as it is private property. Check in is at the Anchorage by the gate to the airfield, no signs, you have to carry your own luggage over to the airport building.

There is a departure tax of EC$15.

Customs
200 cigarettes, or 50 cigars, or 250 grams of tobacco, and 40 fluid ounces of alcoholic beverage may be imported duty free.

Boat Services
From Kingstown to Bequia, MV Admiral 1 sails at 0900 and 1900 Sun-Fri, returning 0730 and 1700; 0700 returning 1700 on Saturday, 1 hour; MV Admiral II (passengers and cars) sails at 1030 and 1630 Mon-Fri (1230 on Sat), returning 0630 and 1400 (0630 on Sat), 1 hour journey (both vessels run by Admiralty Transport Co Ltd, Tel: 83348 for information); if you travel under sail, be prepared to get wet from the spray as the crossing is often rough, Friendship Rose and Maxann O (island schooners) sail

at 1230, returning 0630 Mon-Fri, 1¼ hours.

MV Snapper sails on Monday and Thursday from Bequia (0600) for Kingstown, then returns (1030) to Bequia, continuing (1145) to Canouan, Mayreau, arriving in Union Island at 1545; on Tuesday and Friday she returns to St Vincent via Mayreau, Canouan and Bequia, leaving Union Island at 0530, arriving St Vincent 1200. On Saturday she departs St Vincent at 1030 for Canouan, arriving 1400, then sails via Mayreau to Union Island, returning to St Vincent at 2230. There are 3-4 cabins, two of which are used by the crew but you can negotiate for one quite cheaply if you need it. The Snapper is the islands' main regular transport and carries everything, families and their goods, goats and generators; she rolls through the sea and is very cheap, eg Bequia-Union EC$15, Union-Canouan EC$12, Canouan-Mayreau EC$8; the trip can be highly entertaining but note that the timetable is highly unreliable.

MV Obedient sails twice a week (Monday and Thursday) between Union Island, departs 0745 approximately, and Carriacou, arriving 1300. Two fishing boats sail Carriacou-Union Island from Hillsborough Pier, Monday 1300, 1 hour, EC$10. Frequent boat trips are organized, ask at hotels, take your passport even though not strictly necessary. For other services, check at the Grenadines dock in Kingstown. There are often excursions from Kingstown to Bequia and Mustique on Sundays. Fares from Kingstown to Bequia EC$10, EC$12 at night and weekends, Canouan EC$13, Mayreau EC$15 and Union Island EC$20. From Bequia you can take a boat trip to Mustique for US$40 pp by speedboat from Friendship Bay or by catamaran from Port Elizabeth, ask at Sunsports at Gingerbread. Throughout the Grenadines local power boats can be arranged to take small groups of passengers almost any distance. If possible try to ensure that the boat is operated by someone known to you or your hotel to ensure reliability. Prices are flexible. Do not expect a dry or comfortable ride if the sea is rough.

For possibilities of crewing on yachts, check the notice board at the Frangipani Yacht Services, Bequia.

For an exit stamp, go to the airport customs and immigration one day before departure.

Buses
Minibuses from Kingstown leave from the new Little Tokyo Fish Market terminal to all parts of the island, including a frequent

service to Indian Bay, the main hotel area; they stop on demand rather than at bus stops. They are a popular means of transport because they are inexpensive and give an opportunity to see local life. No service on Sundays or holidays. Fares start at EC\$1, rising to EC\$2 (Layou), EC\$4 (Georgetown on the Windward coast), to EC\$5 to the Black Carib settlement at Sandy Bay in the northeast (this is a difficult route, though, because buses leave Sandy Bay early in the morning for Kingstown, and return in the afternoon). It is worthwhile to make a day trip to Mesopotamia (Mespo) by bus (EC\$2.50). On Bequia, buses leave from the jetty at Port Elizabeth and will stop anywhere to pick you up, a cheap and reliable service.

Car Rental

If you do want to travel round St Vincent, it is better to rent a car, or hire a taxi with driver for EC\$30 per hour. Note that the use of cars on the island is limited, so that only jeeps may be used to go right up Soufrière or beyond Georgetown on the east coast. Charges at Kim's (Tel: 61884) for example are: EC\$100/day for a car, with restrictions on where you drive in the north, EC\$125 for a jeep, 60 miles free a day, EC\$1/mile thereafter, weekly rental gives one day free, EC\$1,000 excess deposit in advance, delivery or collection anywhere on the island, at a charge, credit cards accepted. Among other agencies (all offering similar rates and terms) are Avis (Tel: 69334/84945), Davids (Tel: 71116), Star Garage (Hertz, Tel: 71169), Johnsons (Tel: 84864), and others. Scooter rentals from J G Agencies (Tel: 61409). Bicycles and scooters from Sailors Cycle Centre, Tel: 71712.

Driving is on the left. A local driving licence, costing EC\$10, must be purchased at the airport, the police station in Bay Street, or the Licensing Authority on Halifax Street, on presentation of your home licence. There are limited road signs on St Vincent.

Taxis

Kingstown to Airport EC\$15, Indian Bay EC\$20, Mesopotamia EC\$35, Layou EC\$35, Orange Hill EC\$75, Blue Lagoon EC\$30. Hourly hire EC\$35 per hour. Taxi fares are fixed by the Government. On Bequia, taxis are pick-up trucks with benches in the back, brightly coloured with names like 'Messenjah', call them by phone or VHF radio.

Where To Stay

There are first-class hotels and more modest guest houses; St Vincent is regarded as one of the cheaper islands to visit. All prices are for a double room, MAP, unless otherwise stated. There is a government tax of 5% on hotel rooms, and most add a 10% service charge. Air conditioning is not generally available. If there is no fan in your room, it is often worth asking for one.

In **Kingstown**: on Upper Bay Street, *Cobblestone Inn* (P O Box 867, Tel: 61937), upstairs in a building which used to be a sugar and arrowroot warehouse, US\$62d, CP, including tax, a/c, very quiet, rooms good; nearby, at junction with South River Road, is *Heron* (P O Box 226, Tel: 71631), also once above a warehouse (now above a screenprinting shop and bookshop), popular with business visitors, good, set-menu food in restaurant, a/c, TV lounge, recommended, US\$53-57d CP, the place for a well-earned bacon and egg breakfast after crossing from Bequia on the early boat; *Haddon*, Grenville Street (P O Box 144, Tel: 61897, Fax: 62726) good food, helpful, US\$35d EP, US\$77d MAP, air conditioning, tennis courts, car hire available. Two guest houses close to each other are *Kingstown Park* (P O Box 41, Tel: 61532), the oldest guest house on the island (originally the governor-general's residence), US\$17 pp without bath, US\$19 pp with bath, EP, also modern flats, clean, basic, very helpful and friendly staff, haphazard management, breakfast at EC\$12 overpriced, but dinner at EC\$24 good value, bar in basement, and *Bella Vista* (Tel: 72757), smaller, more modern, US\$14-21d EP, good location and recommended except for bed bugs.

At **Villa Point and Beach**, and **Indian Bay**, 3 miles from town, *Grand View Beach*, Villa Point (P O Box 173, Tel: 84811, Fax: 74174), 20 rooms, first class, pool, tennis, squash, fully-equipped gym, snorkelling, excursions arranged, restaurant, US\$210d winter, US\$120d summer EP; *Villa Lodge*, Villa Point (P O Box 1191, Tel: 84641, Fax: 74468) US\$95-105d EP, US\$175d MAP, 5 minutes from airport, recommended; *Mariner's Inn*, Villa Beach (P O Box 868, Tel: 84287) US\$70-75d winter, US\$50-55d summer, EP, US\$25 for MAP, attractive old colonial house with own beach and good restaurant, being refurbished in 1992; *Umbrella Beach* (P O Box 530, Tel: 84651), US\$48 for double room with kitchen, bath, balcony, nice, simple. Also at Villa Beach is *Sunset Shores*, PO Box 849, Tel: 84411, Fax: 74800, US$115-130d winter; *Tranquility Beach Apartment Hotel*, Indian Bay (P O Box 71, Tel/Fax: 84021), US$50 EP, 2 minutes from beach, clean, friendly and highly recommended, delicious meals if given a few hours' notice; *Indian Bay Beach Apartments* (P O Box 538, Tel: 84001, Fax: 74777) hotel on beach, nice verandah, good snorkelling just outside the hotel, US$55d EP. The *CSY Hotel* is at Blue Lagoon (P O Box 133, Tel: 84308, Fax: 72432) US$85d EP. Other guest houses: *Sea Breeze Guest House*, Arnos Vale, near airport (Tel: 84969), EC$60d EP, cooking facilities, noisy, friendly, helpful, bus to town from the door; *The Moon*, Arnos Vale (Tel: 84656) EC$60d EP.

On the Leeward coast, *Petit Byahaut*, set in a 50-acre valley, 10 x 13-foot tents with floors, queen-sized bed, shower and hammock in each tent, US$45 per person double occupancy first night, US$40 each night thereafter, packages available, Tel/Fax: 77008, VHF 68, transport by boat, diving and snorkelling good in the bay, boats for rent, tours arranged.

Bequia hotels include: *The Old Fort*, on Mount Pleasant, a 17th century French built fortified farmhouse, probably oldest building on Bequia, magnificent views, idyllic restaurant (dinner only, must book), animals in spacious grounds including donkeys, kittens, peacocks, talking parrot, 4 apartments and a cottage, US$120d EP winter, US$90 summer, Tel: 83440, Fax: 83824, excursions, diving, boat trips available, highly recommended, German run; *Friendship Bay* (PO Box 9, Tel: 83222, Fax: 83840), US$95-160d winter, US$70-125d summer, CP, lovely location, boat excursions, water and other sports facilities, friendly, refurbished in 1991/92; *Blue Tropic Apartments*, Friendship Bay, Tel: 83573, US$80d winter, US$60d summer, EP; *Bequia Beach Club*, Friendship Bay, Tel: 83248, Fax: 83689, new, clean apartments, US$140d MAP; *Spring on Bequia* (Tel: 83414), on a bay to the northeast of Port Elizabeth, US$110-165d EP in winter. In Port Elizabeth itself, *Frangipani* (PO Box 1, Tel: 83255, Fax: 83824), US$40-65d EP in summer, US$50-100d EP in winter, on beach, pleasant, bar, terrible sandflies and mosquitoes in wet season, mosquito net provided; *Gingerbread* apartments, PO Box 1, Tel: 83800, Fax: 83907,

one-bedroomed with kitchen and bathroom, no children, US$65/day, US$400/week in summer, US$80 and US$500 in winter, also restaurant and bar upstairs, café downstairs, dive shop, tennis, water skiing, international phone calls 0700-1900 in upstairs office of restaurant, attractive, friendly, recommended, run by Mrs Mitchell, Canadian, ex-wife of Prime Minister; *Mitchells*, overlooking harbour (above Bookshop, go round the back and seek out the owner), EC$50d, including morning coffee, but 10% more if you are staying only one night, cooking facilities available, good, cheap, basic; *Isola and Julie's Guest House*, opposite the jetty (Tel: 83304), mosquito nets in rooms, US$45d MAP year round, recommended. *'Sunny Caribbee' Plantation House Hotel*, rebuilt after 1988 fire, on beach at Admiralty Bay, cottages or hotel rooms, tennis, swimming pool, watersports, Dive Bequia dive shop, US$295d cabana in winter, US$240d rooms, US$160-170 in summer, all MAP, PO Box 16, Tel: 83425, Fax: 83612, entertainment at weekends; *The Old Fig Tree*, by *Sunny Caribbee*, Tel: 83201, restaurant with basic rooms at US$12, meals extra (good), friendly, on extremely narrow beach. *The Village Apartments* in Belmont, overlooking Admiralty Bay above *Sunny Caribbee Hotel*, studio, one or two-bedroomed apartments US$240-675 a week in winter, US$140-525 summer, Tel: 62960, Fax: 62344, PO Box 1621, Kingstown. *Keegan's Guesthouse* (Tel: 83254), US$49d MAP, lovely position, and *Lower Bay Guest House* at Lower Bay (Tel: 83675) EC$60d EP; There are also apartments to rent at Lower Bay: *De Reef Apartments*, Tel: 83447, US$280/week for a cottage or US$500-525/week for an apartment, good, beach bar and restaurant next door is popular; *Kingsville Apartments*, PO Box 41, Tel: 83404, US$400 a week in summer, US$500 in winter for a 2-bedroomed bungalow, excellent, modern, friendly, helpful owners.

Mustique hotels: *Cotton House*, a refurbished cotton plantation house built of rock and coral, is the only hotel and is outrageously expensive (US$260-550d in summer, winter US$475-730d, FAP), Tel: 64777; smaller, less expensive *Firefly House*, Tel: 84621 (all rooms with view overlooking the bay), bed and breakfast in US$70-85 range. Many of the private residences are available for rent, with staff, at exorbitant rates. Contact the Mustique Company, Tel: 84621/2, Fax: 72551.

Union Island hotels: *Anchorage Yacht Club*, Clifton, with French restaurant, US$90/ room, US$200/ apartment, US$220/bungalow, in winter, Tel: 88244/88221; *Clifton Beach Hotel and Guest House* (Tel: 88235), US$29-33d EP, US$60-70d MAP, a bit run down; *Sunny Grenadines* (Tel: 88327, Fax: 88398), US$55d CP, reductions sometimes offered if business is slack, 5 minutes walk from airport, adequate rooms, bar quite lively, food very good; cheaper is *Seaview*, Tel: 88206, US$25d EP, but not recommended, mosquitoes, mice, slow service, noisy and a long walk to everywhere, but good food and a good view; *Alexander's*, EC$45, filthy rooms, overpriced, not recommended despite being the cheapest.

Canouan: *Crystal Sands* (Tel: 88015), Grand Bay, rather run down, US$140-160d MAP US$110-125d EP, no credit cards; *Canouan Beach Hotel* has developed the southern part of the island with de luxe bungalows as well as the main building, nudist beach, US$1,159-1,568/week in winter, US$927-1,253/week in summer, all-inclusive (Tel: 88888, Fax: 88875); *Villa la Bijou* (Mme Michelle de Roche, Tel: 88025), US$75 pp MAP, on hill overlooking town, superb views, friendly, helpful; George and Yvonne at the *Anchor Inn Guest House* in Grand Bay, Tel: 88568, offer clean and basic accommodation, for double rooms, US$60 EP, breakfast, dinner and packed lunches available; also possible to rent houses. You are recommended to phone in advance to book rooms as there is so little accommodation on the island.

Camping

Camping is not encouraged and there are no organized camp sites. Exceptions are made for groups such as Boy Scouts or Girl Guides.

Where To Eat

At the *Bounty Café*, Halifax Street, Kingstown, where local artists' paintings are exhibited, you can have a good light meal. The *Reigate Bar and Restaurant*, also on Halifax Street has good, cheap food. There are a number of other eating places in the town, such as *J Bee's* on Grenville Street; *Vee-Jay's* restaurant on Lower Bay Street is friendly and offers local food; *Juliette's*, Middle Street, good local

food, inexpensive. *Basil's Bar and Restaurant* (see below) has a branch underneath the *Cobblestone Inn*, in Upper Bay Street, recommended buffet 1200-1400 for hungry people, open from 1000, Tel: 72713. *The Roof Bar*, belonging to the *Cobblestone Inn*, is a good place for breakfast, as is the *Heron Hotel* (see above). In the Villa area, *The French Restaurant*, Tel: 84972, VHF Channel 68, open daily for lunch and dinner, very good food, recommended, but do not order conch. The *Lime'n' Pub* on the waterfront at Villa has a casual menu and a dinner menu, reasonable prices; *The Beachcomber* on Villa Beach has light fare and drinks, very casual; The *Coconut Beach Inn* on Indian Bay has a good restaurant and rooms to let at reasonable prices. *Village Lodge Hotel* is a good place to eat, not cheap but wonderful piña colada. For entertainment there is *Basil's Too*, Villa Beach, good restaurant, disco, live music at weekends, Tel: 72713. At the bus station (Little Tokyo) you can buy freshly grilled chicken and corn cobs, good value and tasty. On market days fruit is plentiful and cheap, great bananas. On **Young Island** the Thursday noon buffet for US$12 is highly recommended.

On **Bequia**, apart from hotel restaurants, *Mac's Pizza* is recommended, very popular, get there early or reserve in advance, even in low season, also takeaways, Tel: 83474; *Le Petit Jardin*; *Daphne's*, just off the main street, cooks excellent créole meals to eat in or take away; *Dawn's Creole Tea Garden*, Lower Bay, at the far end, good home cooked food, fairly expensive, must book, Tel: 83154; the *Gingerbread House* has sandwiches and snacks all day; *De Reef*, Lower Bay, lovely position, popular with yachties, set meals and bar snacks, the place for Sunday lunch; the *Frangipani* has sandwiches and snacks all day, Thursday night barbecue and jump up with steel band is well-organized, with excellent food, recommended. There is something going on most nights either at Admiralty Bay or Friendship Bay, check locally. Bands play reggae music in the gardens of several hotels, popular with residents and tourists.

On **Mustique**, *Basil's Bar and The Raft*, for seafood and night life, Tel: 84621 for reservations. Locals' night on Monday with buffet for EC$35 excluding drinks and dancing, Wednesdays are good, on

Saturdays go to the *Cotton House*. Up the hill from *Basil's* is the local *Piccadilly* pub, where rotis and beer are sold, and pool is played; foreigners are welcome, but is best to go in a group and girls should not go on their own.

On *Union*, food is expensive; *Clifton Beach* and *Sunny Grenadines* hotels both have good restaurants and bars. The *Anchorage* restaurant has been criticized for serving bland, overpriced food and is unfriendly, the occupants of the shark pool are given food rejected by customers.

The national dish is fried jackfish and breadfruit. The island's rum is called Captain Bligh, and the local beers are Hairoun and EKU.

Tipping
10% of the bill if not already included.

Banks
Barclays Bank plc, Scotia Bank, Canadian Imperial Bank of Commerce, National Commercial Bank of St Vincent, all on Halifax Street, Caribbean Banking Corporation, on South River Road, Kingstown. Barclays Bank has a branch on Bequia; National Commercial Bank has branches at Arnos Vale airport, on Bequia and Union Island. There is no bank on Canouan, but the National Commercial Bank at Grand Bay opens every alternate Wednesday from 1000-1400. When you cash traveller's cheques you can take half in US dollars and half in EC dollars if you wish.

Currency
The East Caribbean dollar, EC$.

Shopping
The St Vincent Philatelic Society on Bay Street, between Higginson Street and River Road, sells stamps in every colour, size and amount for the novice and collector alike. Service is helpful but slow in this second floor warehouse, complete with guard. The St Vincent Craftsmen's Centre is on a road to the right off James Street, heading towards the airport; all local handicraft items are on display here. For handicrafts and books, Noah's Arkade, Blue Caribbean Building, Kingstown (Tel: 71513, Fax: 69305), and at the *Frangipani* and *Plantation House* Boutique on Bequia. Other bookshops: Wayfarer, beneath the Heron Hotel, and the Bequia Bookshop in Port Elizabeth, run by Iain Gale, who keeps an excellent stock of books, maps and charts. A map of St Vincent, 1:50,000 (and Kingstown, 1:10,000), EC$15, is available

from the Ministry of Agriculture, Lands and Surveyors Department, Murray Road (on the road to Indian Bay, or if walking, go through the alleyway at the General Post Office and turn right at the Grammar School). In 1992 the Ordnance Survey (Southampton, UK) brought out a new tourist map of St Vincent, 1:50,000, with insert of Kingstown, 1:10,000, double sided with Grenadines on the reverse, with text panels giving information, walks etc.

Climate And Clothing
Temperatures the year round average between 77°F and 81°F (25-7°C), moderated by the trade winds; average rainfall is 60 inches on the coast, 150 inches in the interior, with the wettest months May to November. Best months to visit are therefore December to May. You can expect a shower most days, though. Low season is June to mid-December.

Wear light, informal clothes, but do not wear bathing costumes or short shorts in shops or on Kingstown's streets.

Hours Of Business
Shops: 0800-1200, 1300-1600 Monday-Friday (0800-1200 only, Saturday); government offices: 0800-1200, 1300-1615 Monday-Friday; banks: 0800-1200 or 1300 Monday-Friday, plus 1400/ 1500-1700 on Friday. The bank at the Airport is open Monday-Saturday 0700- 1700.

Public Holidays
1 January, St Vincent and the Grenadines Day (22 January), Good Friday and Easter Monday, Whit Monday, Caricom Day and Carnival Tuesday (first Monday and Tuesday in July), first Monday in August, Independence Day (27 October), Christmas Day and Boxing Day.

Time Zone
Atlantic Standard Time, 4 hours behind GMT, 1 hour ahead of EST.

Electric Current
220/240 v, 50 cycles.

Post Office
Halifax Street, open 0830-1500 (0830-1130 on Saturday, closed Sunday). St Vincent Philatelic Services Ltd, General Post Office, Tel: 71911, Fax: 62383; for old and new issues, World of Stamps, Bay 43 Building, Lower Bay Street, Kingstown..

Telecommunications
are operated by Cable and Wireless, also on Halifax Street; there is a 5% tax on international phone calls. Portable phones can be rented through Boatphone or you

can register your own cellular phone with them upon arrival, Tel: 62800.

Radio

NBC Radio is on 705 kHz.

Press

Two newspapers, *The Vincentian* and *The News*, are both published every Friday.

Tour Agency

Paradise Tours organize day tours for US$30 pp including lunch to the Botanic Gardens, Fort Charlotte, Vermont Valley Nature Trail, Layou Petroglyphs and Mount Wynne beach on Sundays and Thursdays, and to La Soufrière Volcano on Tuesdays, Tel: 84001/71502.

Tourist Offices

St Vincent and the Grenadines Department of Tourism, Finance Complex, Bay Street, P O Box 834, Kingstown, Tel: 71502, Fax: 62610 open Monday-Friday 0800-1200, 1300-1615; helpful desk at Arnos Vale airport, Tel: 84685, hotel reservation EC$1; on Bequia (at the landward end of the jetty), Tel: 83286, open Sunday-Friday 0900-1230, 1330-1600, Saturday morning only; on Union Island, Tel: 88350, open daily 0800-1200, 1300-1600.

There is a desk in the arrivals hall at the Grantley Adams airport on Barbados, open daily from 1300 until 2000 or the last flight to St Vincent (Tel: 428-0961). This is useful for transfers to LIAT after an international flight.

UK: 10 Kensington Court, London W8 5DL, Tel: 071-937 6570, Fax: 071-937 3611. **USA**: 801 2nd Avenue, 21st floor, New York, NY 10017, Tel: (212) 687-4981, Fax: (212) 949-5946 and 6505 Cove Creek Place, Dallas, Texas, 75240, Tel: (214) 239 6451, Fax: (214) 239 1002. **Canada**: Suite 504, 100 University Avenue, Toronto, Ontario M5J 1V6, Tel: (416) 971-9666, Fax: (416) 971-9667. **Germany**: Karibuk Pur, Wurmberg Str 26, D-7032, Sindelfingen, Tel: 49-7031 806260, Fax: 49-7031 805012.

We are grateful to Karen Mills of the St Vincent and the Grenadines Tourism Office, London for revisions to this chapter.

GRENADA

Introduction

GRENADA, the most southerly of the Windwards, is described as a spice island, for it produces large quantities of cloves and mace and about a third of the world's nutmeg. It also grows cacao, sugar, bananas and a wide variety of other fruit and vegetables. Some of its beaches, specially Grand Anse, a dazzling two-mile stretch of white sand, are very fine. The majority of the tourist facilities are on the island's southwest tip, but the rest of the island is beautiful, rising from a generally rugged coast to a mountainous interior. The highest point is Mount St Catherine, at 2,757 feet. The island seems to tilt on a northeast-southwest axis: if a line is drawn through ancient craters of Lake Antoine in the northeast, the Grand Étang in the central mountains and the Lagoon at St George's, it will be straight. Northwest of that line, the land rises and the coast is high; southeast it descends to a low coastline of rias (drowned valleys). The island is green, well forested and cultivated and is blessed with plenty of rain in the wet season.

Grenada (pronounced "Grenayda") has two dependencies in the Grenadines chain, Carriacou and Petit Martinique. They, and a number of smaller islets, lie north of the main island. The group's total area is 133 square miles. Grenada itself is 21 miles long and 12 miles wide.

The population of some 91,000 (of which 5,253 live on Carriacou and Petit Martinique) is largely of African descent. In contrast to other Windward Islands which have had a similar history of disputed ownership between the French and English, the French cultural influence in Grenada has completely died out. Nevertheless, it is a predominantly Catholic island, though there are Protestant churches of various denominations, and a Baha'i Centre. Many people who emigrated from Grenada to the UK are returning to the island and are building smart houses for their retirement which are in stark contrast to the tiny, corrugated iron shacks which are home to many of their countrymen.

History

When Columbus discovered the island on his third voyage in 1498, it was inhabited by Caribs, who had migrated from the South American mainland, killing or enslaving the peaceful Arawaks who were already living there. The Amerindians called their island Camerhogue, but Columbus renamed it Concepción, a name which was not to last long, for shortly afterwards it was referred to as Mayo on maps and later Spaniards called it Granada, after the Spanish city. The French then called it La Grenade and by the eighteenth century it was known as Grenada. Aggressive defence of the island by the Caribs prevented settlement by Europeans until the seventeenth century. In 1609 some Englishmen tried and failed, followed by a group of Frenchmen in 1638, but it was not until 1650 that a French expedition from Martinique landed and made initial friendly contact with the inhabitants. When relations soured, the French brought reinforcements and exterminated the Amerindian population. Sauteurs, or Morne des Sauteurs, on the north coast, is named after this episode when numerous Caribs apparently jumped to their death in the sea rather than surrender to the French.

GRENADA

0 1 2 3
miles
C53

Southwest Tip

The island remained French for about one hundred years, although possession was disputed by Britain, and it was a period of economic expansion and population growth, as colonists and slaves arrived to grow tobacco and sugar at first, followed by cotton, cocoa and coffee. It was during the Seven Years' War in the eighteenth century that Grenada fell into British hands and was ceded by France to Britain as part of a land settlement in the 1763 Treaty of Paris. Although the French regained control in 1779, their occupation was brief and the island was returned to Britain in 1783 under the Treaty of Versailles. The British introduced nutmeg in the 1780s, after natural disasters wiped out the sugar industry. Nutmeg and cocoa became the main crops and encouraged the development of smaller land holdings. A major slave revolt took place in 1795, led by a free coloured Grenadian called Fedon, but slavery was not abolished until 1834, as in the rest of the British Empire.

In 1833, Grenada was incorporated into the Windward Islands Administration which survived until 1958 when it was dissolved and Grenada joined the Federation of the West Indies. The Federation collapsed in 1962 and in 1967 Grenada became an associated state, with full autonomy over internal affairs, but with Britain retaining responsibility for defence and foreign relations. Grenada was the first of the associated states to seek full independence, which was granted in 1974. Political leadership since the 1950s had alternated between Eric (later Sir Eric) Gairy's Grenada United Labour Party (GULP) and Herbert Blaize's Grenada National Party. At the time of independence, Sir Eric Gairy was Prime Minister, but his style of government was widely viewed as authoritarian and corrupt, becoming increasingly resented by a large proportion of the population. In 1979 he was ousted in a bloodless coup by the Marxist-Leninist New Jewel (Joint Endeavour for Welfare, Education and Liberation) Movement, founded in 1973, which formed a government headed by Prime Minister Maurice Bishop. Reforms were introduced and the country moved closer to Cuba and other Communist countries, who provided aid and technical assistance. In 1983, a power struggle within the government led to Bishop being deposed and he and many of his followers were murdered by a rival faction shortly afterwards. In the chaos that followed a joint US-Caribbean force invaded the island to restore order. They imprisoned Bishop's murderers and expelled Cubans and other socialist nationalities who had been engaged in building a new airport and other development projects. An interim government was set up until elections could be held in 1984, which were won by the coalition New National Party, headed by Herbert Blaize. Since the intervention, Grenada has moved closer to the USA which maintains a large embassy near the airport. Further reading on this era of Grenada's history includes: *Grenada: Whose Freedom*? by Fitzroy Ambursley and James Dunkerley, Latin America Bureau, London, 1984; *Grenada Revolution in Reverse* by James Ferguson, Latin America Bureau, London, 1990; *Grenada: Revolution, Invasion and Aftermath* by Hugh O'Shaughessy, Sphere Books, London, 1984; *Grenada: Revolution and Invasion* by Anthony Payne, Paul Sutton and Tony Thorndike, London, Croom Helm, 1984; *Grenada: Politics, Economics and Society*, by Tony Thorndike, Frances Pinter, London 1984, and many others.

After the New National Party (NNP) coalition's victory at the polls, with an overwhelming majority, Herbert Blaize became Prime Minister. The NNP won 14 of the 15 seats in the legislature while GULP, led by Sir Eric Gairy, won one. In 1987, the formation of a new opposition party, the National Democratic Congress, led to parliamentary changes. Defections reduced the NNP's representation to nine seats while the NDC gained six. Further divisions within the NNP preceded Mr Blaize's death in December 1989; his faction, led by Ben Jones, became the National Party, while the New National Party name was retained by Keith Mitchell's faction. In general elections held on 13 March 1990, each of these parties won two seats while the NDC, led by Nicholas Brathwaite (formerly head of the interim administration), won seven. The GULP gained four seats, but one of its members joined the Government of Mr Brathwaite in a gesture of solidarity after the fire on the Carenage in April 1990 (see below, under **St George's**), another subsequently joined the NDC and a third left GULP to become an Independent. The fourth was expelled from the party in 1992. By mid-1991 the NDC Government could count on the support of 10 of the 15 MPs. Another opposition party, the left wing Maurice Bishop Patriotic Movement (MBPM), led by Terry Marryshow, failed to win a seat in the elections.

In 1991 the Government decided to commute to life imprisonment the death sentences on 14 people convicted of murdering Maurice Bishop after world wide appeals for clemency. The decision set an important precedent in the region, where the death penalty is still practised. Soon afterwards, Grenada was readmitted to the OECS court system, which it had left in 1979, and which allows for final recourse to the Privy Council.

Government
Grenada is an independent state within the Commonwealth, with the British monarch as Head of State represented by a Governor General. There are two legislative houses, the House of Representatives with 15 members. and the Senate with 13 members. The Government is elected for a five year term.

The Economy
Agriculture accounts for about 20% of gdp and employs about 6,000 people. The major export crops are nutmeg, bananas and cocoa; nutmeg and mace together account for about 40% of all exports and Grenada is a leading world producer of this spice. However, prices have tumbled following the collapse of the minimum price agreement with Indonesia. Banana exports have been falling because of labour shortages, disease and higher land prices, while cocoa exports have risen, thanks to a five-year sales agreement with a US company. There is also some cotton grown on Carriacou and limes are grown on both Carriacou and Grenada. Sugar cane is grown in the south of Grenada but efficiency is not high. Most of the rest of farming land is devoted to fruit and vegetables for domestic consumption, such as yams, eddoe, sweet potatoes, tannia, pumpkin, cassava, pigeon peas and maize. Manufacturing is also mostly processing of agricultural produce, making items such as chocolate, sugar, rum, jams, coconut oil, honey and lime juice. There is also a large brewery and a rice mill. There are 10,000 acres of forest, of which three-quarters are owned by the Government which is undertaking a reafforestation programme to repair hurricane damage. Fishing is a growing industry, involving about 1,500 people, and there are plans for new fisheries complexes at Halifax Harbour, Gouyave and Grenville.

The economy suffered from the uncertainties surrounding the Bishop murder and the US invasion, but confidence has gradually returned and investment has picked up. The main area of expansion has been tourism, which has benefited from the airport expansion started with Cuban assistance by the Bishop administration. In 1991 Grenada received 92,947 tourists by air (a rise of nearly 13% over 1990, a much better performance than many of its Caribbean neighbours). The greatest increase, however, has been in cruise ship visitors, although they are low spending and do not generate so much foreign exchange. In 1984 only 65 cruise ships called, but have now risen to over 300, with the number of passengers rising from 34,166 in 1984 to 196,144 in 1991. The Government elected in 1990 announced an arrival tax of US$1 per cruise ship passenger, to raise EC$350,000 per year for improving tourist facilities. The number of hotel rooms is to rise from 1,105 in 1991 to around 2,000 in 1994, with projects at Point Salines, Grand Anse and a new marina. The number of yachts calling is now well over 3,000 a year.

Despite bouyant tourism, Grenada has considerable financial imbalances and unemployment is estimated at 30% of the labour force. Imports are three times the value of exports and tourism revenues are insufficient to cover the trade deficit. Total debt was EC$285.5m at the end of March 1990, of which EC$152.5m was external debt, most of which was contracted on concessionary terms to finance infrastructure and other development projects. The need to repay the IMF loans contracted in 1979-83 and reduce the growing budget deficit led the Government to increase levies and fees in the 1991 budget. Income tax was abolished in 1985/86 but there have been problems in collecting the value added tax which replaced it; a 10% levy introduced on higher incomes to help service the debt was criticized as reintroducing a form of income tax. A five-year economic programme announced in 1991, called for fiscal balance to be achieved in 1993. It envisaged selective debt rescheduling, a reduction in the number of public employees, the sale of certain state assets and an overhaul of the tax system. IMF approval was sought for a structural adjustment programme to allow Grenada to seek credits from other multilateral agencies.

Flora and Fauna

A system of national parks and protected areas is being developed. Information is available from the Forestry Department, Ministry of Agriculture, Archibald Avenue, St George's. To date, the focal point of the system is the **Grand Étang National Park**, eight miles from the capital in the central mountain range. It is right on the transinsular road from St George's to Grenville. The Grand Étang is a crater lake surrounded by lush tropical forest. A series of trails has been blazed which are well worth the effort, but can be muddy and slippery after rain; the Morne Labaye nature trail is only 15 minutes' long, return same route, but there are longer hikes to waterfalls (such as Annandale, a Natural Landmark) and mountain peaks (Mount Qua Qua, for instance). It is also possible to walk back to St George's. An interpretation centre overlooking the lake has videos, exhibitions and explanations of the medicinal plants in the forest. There is a bar, a shop and some amusing monkeys and parrots. The Park is open 0830-1600, entrance US$2. There is overnight accommodation at Lake House, Tel: 442-7425 or enquire at forest centre, also for camping.

The high forest receives over 150 inches of rain a year. Epiphytes and mosses cling to the tree trunks and many species of fern and grasses provide a thick undergrowth. The trees include the gommier, bois canot, Caribbean pine and blue mahoe. At the summit, the vegetation is an example of elfin woodland, the trees stunted by the wind, the leaves adapted with drip tips to cope with the excess moisture. Apart from the highest areas, the island is heavily cultivated. Of interest to the visitor is the variety of spices harvested, many of which can be seen (and samples purchased) at the Dougaldston Estate (see below): nutmeg and its secondary product, mace, cloves, cinammon, allspice, bay, tumeric and ginger. In addition there are calabash gourds, cocoa and more common crops, bananas and coconuts.

In the northeast, the area around **Levera Pond** is now designated for inclusion into the parks system (not all the infrastructure is in place yet). As well as having a bird sanctuary, Levera is one of the island's largest mangrove swamps; the coastal region has coconut palms, cactus and scrub, providing habitat for iguana and land crabs. There are white beaches where turtles lay their eggs and, offshore, coral reefs and the Sugar Loaf, Green and Sandy islands (boat trip to the last named on Sunday, see **Inter-Island Transport**). South of Levera is Lake Antoine, another crater lake, but sunken to only about 20 feet above sea level; it has been designated a Natural Landmark.

On the south coast is **La Sagesse Protected Seascape**, a peaceful refuge which includes beaches, a mangrove estuary, a salt pond and coral reefs. In the coastal woodland are remains of sugar milling and rum distilleries. Accommodation, restaurant, shopping and watersport facilities have been set up at the plantation house (see **Where To Stay** below). To get there turn south off the main road opposite an old sugar mill, then take the left fork of a dirt road through a banana plantation. Close to the pink plantation house, a few feet from a superb sandy beach, is *La Sagesse* bar and restaurant, good food, nutmeg shells on the ground outside. Walk to the other end of the beach to where a path leads around a mangrove pond to another beach, usually deserted apart from the occasional angler, fringed with palms, good snorkelling and swimming, reef just offshore.

Marquis Island, off the east coast, can be visited; at one time it was part of the mainland and now has eel grass marine environments and coral reefs. Nearby is La Baye Rock, which is a nesting ground for brown boobies, habitat for large iguanas and has dry thorn scrub forest. It too is surrounded by coral reefs.

To see a good selection of Grenada's flowers and trees, visit the Bay Gardens at Morne Delice (turn off the Eastern Main Road at St Paul's police station, the gardens are on your left as you go down). It's a pleasant place with a friendly owner; the paths are made of nutmeg shells. In the capital are the Botanic Gardens.

Grenada is quite good for birdwatching. The only endemic bird is the Grenada Dove, which inhabits scrubby woodland in some western areas. In the rainforest you can see the emerald-throated hummingbird, yellow-billed cuckoo, red-necked pigeon, ruddy quail-dove, cocoa thrush and other species, while wading and shore birds can be spotted at both Levera and in the south and southwest. Watch also for the chicken hawk. Yellow-breasted bananaquits are very common. There is little remarkable animal life: frogs and lizards, of course, and iguana, armadillo (tatoo) and manicou (possum), all of these are hunted for the pot. One oddity, though, is a troop of Mona monkeys, imported from Africa over 300 years ago, which lives in the treetops in the vicinity of the Grand Étang. Another import is the mongoose.

Diving and Marine Life

Some of the reefs around Grenada have been mentioned above; they and other reefs provide excellent sites for **diving**. A popular dive is to the wreck of the Italian cruise liner, *Bianca C* which went down in 1961. A number of diving companies operate from Grand Anse, eg Underwater Discovery of Grenada, Tel: 444-4371 ext 638; also HMC Diving Centre at the *Ramada Renaissance*, Tel: 444-4371 ext 638, evenings Tel: 440-5875, Fax: 444-4800. A basic two-hour scuba dive costs about US$40 pp, a two-tank dive is US$60, resort course US$50, snorkelling trips US$16; dive packages and open water certification are available. **Snorkelling** equipment hire costs about US$12 for 3 hours, sometimes for a day; again, there are plenty of opportunities for this. Glass-bottomed boats make tours of the reefs.

Beaches and Watersports

There are 45 beaches on Grenada. The best are in the southwest, particularly Grand Anse; a lovely stretch of white sand which looks north to St George's. It can get crowded with cruise passengers, but there's usually plenty of room for everyone. Watch your bags, petty theft has been reported. There are other nice, smaller beaches around Lance aux Épines. The beaches at Levera and Bathway in the northeast are also good, and since the construction of a new road are much easier to get to.

Windsurfing, water-skiing and parasailing all take place off Grand Anse beach. Windsurf board rental about US$7 for half an hour, waterskiing, US$15 per run, parasailing US$25. The Moorings' Club Mariner Watersports Centre at *Secret Harbour*, Tel: 444-4439, Fax: 444-4819, has small sail boats, sunfish, windsurfing, waterskiing, speedboat trips to Hog Island including snorkelling.

Sailing in the waters around Grenada and through the Grenadines, via Carriacou, is very good; sheltered harbours, such as Halifax Bay on the Leeward coast, can be found and there are two marinas: Grenada Yacht Services in St George's harbour (Tel: 440-2508) and Spice Island Marina in Prickly Bay (Lance aux Épines, Tel: 444-4257/4342). There are no port dues or fees for visiting yachts. Grenada Yacht Services, Lagoon Road, St George's, Tel: 440-2508/2883, Go Vacations, Tel: 444-4924, and Stevens Yachts, Lance aux Épines, Tel: 444-4257/4342, charter boats for cruises. *Starwind Enterprise*, skippered by Mosden Cumberbatch, Tel: 440-3678 or at Grenada Yacht Services, US$50 pp day sail, snorkelling included, US$15 sunset cruise. The Moorings Club Mariner Watersports Centre at *Secret Harbour* has a 43-foot yacht for charter with skipper only at US$25 pp half day, US$40 pp whole day, minimum four people, Tel: 444-4548/9. On the first weekend in August the Carriacou Regatta is held, which has developed into a full-scale festival, with land as well as watersports and jump-ups at night. On Grenada yacht races are held at New Year and Easter (another big regatta). Inshore sailing on sunfish, sailfish and hobiecats is offered by Grand Anse and Lance aux Épines hotels and operators; try HMC at the *Ramada Renaissance*. Rates are about US$10 for ½ hour for sunfish rental. If you want someone else to do all the work, take a booze cruise on the *Rhum Runner* (Tel: 440-2189/3422), daytime or evening.

Deep-sea fishing can be arranged through Grenada Yacht Services. At the end of January each year, Grenada hosts a game-fishing tournament.

Other Sports

Cricket, the island's main land sport, is played from January to June. There is a large stadium at Queen's Park, just outside St George's, but the locals play on any piece of fairly flat ground or on the beaches. Soccer is also played. Hotels have tennis courts and the Richmond Hills and Tanteen Clubs welcome guests to use their courts. A recommended tennis pro is Richard Hughes, an ex-Davis Cup player who teaches at Richmond Hills and goes round the hotels giving basic tuition and advanced level sessions, contact him through the *Ramada*, Tel: 444-4371. There is a nine-hole golf course at the Grenada Golf and Country Club, Woodlands, above Grand Anse; the club is open daily 0800 to sunset, but only till 1200 on Sunday (green fee EC$15, club hire EC$5, Tel: 444-4128). Hiking is possible in the Grand Étang National Park (see above). An annual triathlon is held in January, with a 1½ km swim along the Grand Anse beach to the *Ramada Renaissance*, a 25-km bicycle race to the aiport, St George's and back to the hotel, then a 5-km run to the Carib brewery and back. For information, contact Paul Slinger, PO Box 44, St. George's, Tel: 444-3343.

Festivals

Carnival takes place over the second weekend in August, although some preliminary events and competitions are held from the last week in July, with calypsos, steelbands, dancing, competitions, shows and plenty of drink. The Sunday night celebrations continue into Monday, J'Ouvert; Djab Djab Molassi, who represent devils, smear themselves and anyone else (especially the smartly dressed) with black grease. On Monday a carnival pageant is held on the stage at Queen's Park and on Tuesday the bands parade through the streets of St George's to the Market Square and a giant party ensues. Also in August, over the first weekend, are the Carriacou Regatta (see above) and the Rainbow City cultural festival in Grenville. Carriacou celebrates its carnival at the traditional Lenten time, unlike Grenada. It is not spectacular but it is fun and there is a good atmosphere.

Throughout the island, but especially in Gouyave, the Fisherman's Birthday is celebrated at the end of June (the feast of Saints Peter and Paul); it involves the blessing of nets and boats, followed by dancing, feasting and boat races. Independence Day is 7 February.

During Carnival it is difficult to find anywhere to stay and impossible to hire a car unless booked well in advance.

St George's

The island's capital, **St George's**, with its terraces of pale, colour-washed houses and cheerful red roofs, was established in 1705 by French settlers, who called it Fort Royal. Much of its present-day charm comes from the blend of two colonial cultures: typical 18th century French provincial houses intermingle with fine examples of English Georgian architecture. Unlike many Caribbean ports, which are built around bays on coastal plains, St George's straddles a promontory. It therefore has steep hills with long flights of steps and sharp bends, with police on point duty to prevent chaos at the blind junctions. At every turn is a different view or angle of the town, the harbour or the coast.

The town stands on an almost landlocked sparkling blue harbour against a background of green and hazy blue hills. The Carenage runs around the inner harbour, connected to the Esplanade on the seaward side of Fort George Point by the Sendal Tunnel. There is always plenty of dockside activity on the Carenage, with food, drinks and other goods being loaded and unloaded from wooden schooners. It is planned to redevelop St George's harbour, moving the cruise liner dock from the mouth of the Carenage to a point further down the southwest coast. The Carenage would then be left to small shipping and all the shopping would be duty-free. So far, a small promenade and shelter have been built.

The small National Museum, in the cells of a former barracks, in the centre of town (corner of Young and Monckton Streets) is worth a visit; it includes some items from West Africa, exhibits from the sugar and spice industries and of local shells and fauna (entry EC$1). The museum is to be moved to a new historical centre in Forts Frederick and Matthew (see below), with lectures and slides and other features; due open in 1992. Fort George on the headland is now the police headquarters, but public viewpoints have been erected from which to see the coast and harbour. Some old cannons are still in their positions; tremendous views all round. Just down from the Fort is St Andrew's Presbyterian Kirk (1830). On Church Street are a number of important buildings: St George's Anglican Church (1825), the Roman Catholic Cathedral (tower 1818, church 1884) and the Supreme Court and Parliament buildings (late 18th, early 19th century). St George's oldest religious building is the Methodist Church on Green Street. The Post Office and the Public Library are examples of old government buildings on the Carenage (the Library has been renovated and is being stocked with foreign assistance). In this part of the city are many brick and stone warehouses, roofed with red, fish tail tiles brought from Europe as ballast. A serious fire on 27 April 1990 damaged six government buildings on the Carenage, including the Treasury, the Government Printery, the Storeroom and the Post Office. They are still not repaired. Also on the Carenage is a monument to the Christi Degli Abbissi, moved from the entrance to the harbour, which commemorates "the hospitality extended to the crew and passengers of the ill-fated liner", *Bianca C* (see **Diving and Marine Life** above). It stands on the walkway beside Wharf Road. The Market Square, off Halifax Street (one of the main streets, one steep block from the Esplanade), is always busy. It is the terminus for many minibus routes and on Saturday holds the weekly market.

Just north of the city is Queen's Park, which is used for all the main sporting activities, carnival shows and political events. It is surrounded by a turquoise palisade. From Richmond Hill there are good views of both St George's and the mountains of the interior. On the hill are Forts Matthew, Frederick and Adolphus (built in a higher position than Fort George to house new batteries of more powerful, longer range cannon), and the prison in which are held those convicted of murdering Maurice Bishop.

The Southwest

From the Carenage, you can take a road which goes round the Lagoon, another sunken volcanic crater, now a yacht anchorage. It is overlooked by the ruins of the *Santa Maria Hotel*, which was taken over by the revolutionary government and subsequently destroyed in the intervention. Several plans have been submitted for the rehabilitation of the hotel. Carrying on to the southwestern tip you come to **Grand Anse**, Grenada's most famous beach. Along its length are many hotels, but none dominates the scene since, by law, no development may be taller than a coconut palm. A side road leads round to the very pleasant bay and beach at Morne Rouge, which is away from the glitz of Grande Anse. There is a good view across Grande Anse to St George's from the little headland of Quarantine Point. From Grand Anse the road crosses the peninsula to the new Point Salines airport and the Lance aux Épines headland. The road to Portici and Parc à Boeuf beaches leads to the right, off the airport road; follow the signs to *Groomes* beach bar on Parc à Boeuf (food and drink available). Portici beach is virtually deserted, with good swimming despite a steeply shelving beach and excellent snorkelling around Petit Cabrits point at its northeast end. On Prickly Bay (the west side of Lance aux Épines) are hotels, the Spice Island Marina and other yachting and watersports facilities. Luxury homes take up much of Lance aux Épines down to Prickly Point. There is a glorious stretch of fine

---

Key to Map of St George's

1. St George's Anglican Church; 2. St Andrew's Presbyterian Kirk; 3. Roman Catholic Cathedral; 4 Fort George; 5. National Museum; 6. Public Library; 7. Parliament; 8. Queen's Park; 9. Botanical Gardens; 10. Market Square and bus terminal; 11. LIAT; 12. Cruise ship dock; 13. Grenada Yacht Services; 14. Grenada Yacht Club; 15. Department of Tourism; 16. Tourist Bureau; 17. Post Office; 18. Cable and Wireless/Telephone office; 19. Barclays Bank; 20. National Commercial Bank; 21. Scotia Bank; 22. Police HQ; 23. *St James Hotel*; 24. *St Ann's Guest House*; 25. *Delicious Landing*; 26. *The Nutmeg*; 27. *Esplanade*.

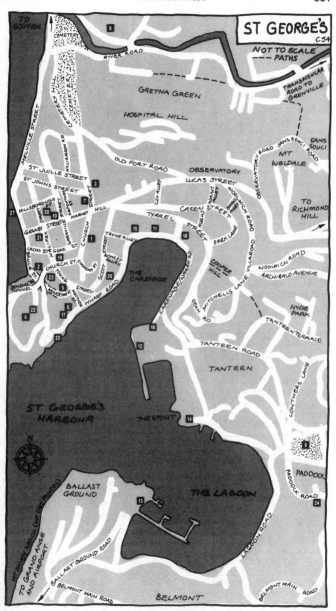

ST GEORGE'S
C54

NOT TO SCALE
--- PATHS

white sand, the lawns of the *Calabash Hotel* run down to the beach, very nice bar and restaurant open to non-residents, steel bands often play there.

From the Point Salines/Lance aux Épines crossroads you can head east along a road which snakes around the south coast. At Lower Woburn, a small fishing community, you can see vast piles of conch shells in the sea, forming jetties and islets where they have been discarded by generations of lambie divers. Any number of turn-offs, tracks and paths, go inland to join the Eastern Main Road, or run along the rias and headlands, such as Calivigny (which is being developed, together with neighbouring Calivigny and Hog Islands, into a resort), Fort Jeudy, Westerhall Point or La Sagesse with its nature reserve (see above). Many of Grenada's most interesting and isolated bays are in the southeast, accessible only by jeep or on foot; taxi drivers can drop you off at the start of a path and you can arrange to be picked up later.

Around the Island

The west coast road from St George's is being rebuilt with funds from the government, the Caribbean Development Bank, the EEC and USAID; the entire island network will eventually be completed in 1992 (a plan originally undertaken by the revolutionary government with Cuban assistance). The western section is behind schedule, partly because of the difficulties of construction on narrow ledges between cliff and sea. It is good only just beyond Beauséjour, then there are a few reasonable (but short) stretches all the way round the north and east coasts to Grenville, from where it is good, but twisty, on the transinsular road back to the capital.

Beauséjour Estate, once the island's largest, is now in ruins (except for the estate Great House). On its land are a Cuban-built radio station, a half-completed stadium and squatters; the owners and the government cannot agree on the estate's future. Beyond Beauséjour is Halifax Bay, a beautiful, sheltered harbour.

At Concord, a road runs up the valley to the First Concord Falls, where you can pay US$1 to go to a balcony above the small cascade. The Second Concord Falls are a 45-minute walk (each way), with seven rivers to cross; a guide will charge EC$20. The Tourist Board intends to build bridges and make a proper route. Three hours further uphill is Fedon's Camp, at 2,509 feet, where Julian Fedon (see **History** above) fortified a hilltop in 1795 to await reinforcements from Martinique to assist his rebellion against the British. After bloody fighting, the camp was captured; today it is a Historical Landmark. It is possible to hike from Concord to Grand Étang in five hours.

North of Concord, just before Gouyave, is a turn-off to Dougaldston Estate. Before the revolution 200 people were employed here in cultivating spices and other crops. Now there are only about 20 workers, the place is run down, the buildings in disrepair, the vehicles wrecked. Still, you can go into a shed where bats fly overhead and someone will explain all the spices to you. Samples cost EC$3 for a bag of cinammon or cloves, EC$2 for nutmeg, or there are mixed bags; give the guide a tip.

Gouyave, "the town that never sleeps", is a fishing port, nutmeg collecting point and capital of St John's parish. At the Nutmeg Processing Station, you can see all the stages of drying, grading, separating the nutmeg and mace and packing (give a tip here too). The husks are used for fuel or mulch and the fruit is made into nutmeg jelly (a good alternative to breakfast marmalade). The Station is a great wooden building by the sea, with a very powerful smell. Gouyave is the principal place to go to for the Fisherman's Birthday festival (see above).

Just outside Victoria, another fishing port and capital of St Mark's Parish, is a rock in the sea with Amerindian petroglyphs on it (best to know where to look over the parapet). The road continues around the northwest coast, turning inland before returning to the sea at *Sauteurs*, the capital of St Patrick's parish, on the north coast. The town is renowned as the site of the mass suicide of Grenada's last 40 Caribs, who jumped off a cliff rather than surrender to the French (see **History** above). Behind Sauteurs is McDonald College from whose gate there are marvellous views out to sea, with the Grenadines beyond the town's two church towers, and inland to cloud-covered mountains.

From Sauteurs a road approaches Levera Bay (see above) from its west side. Turn left at *Chez Norah's* bar, a two-storey, green, corrugated iron building (snacks available); the track rapidly becomes quite rough and the final descent to Levera is very steep, suitable only for 4-wheel drive. A better way to Levera approaches from the south. The road forks left about two miles south of Morne Fendue, passes through River Sallee and past Bathway Beach. Swimming is good at the beautiful Levera Beach and there is surf in certain conditions. Do not swim far out as there is a current in the narrows between the beach and the privately-owned Sugar Loaf Island. Further out are Green and Sandy Islands; you may be able to arrange a trip there with a fisherman who keeps his boat on Levera Beach.

Morne Fendue plantation house offers accommodation (four rooms, US$35s, US$40-75d including meals), and serves lunch for EC$40, including drinks; good local food and all you can drink, Tel: 440-9330, reservations essential. The house, owned by Betty Mascoll MBE, is full of atmosphere (although some of the plaster and stucco work is in poor shape), and the driveway ends in a flowerbed full of poinsettias. St Patrick's is an agricultural region, comparatively poor and marginal.

On the eastern side of the island, Amerindian remains can be seen on rock carvings near Hermitage (look for a sign on the road) and at an archaeological dig near the old Pearls airport. Apparently it's so unprotected that lots of artefacts have been stolen. An excursion can be made to Lake Antoine (see above) with, nearby, the River Antoine Rum Distillery, driven by a water mill.

Grenville is the main town on the east coast and capital of St Andrew's Parish. It is a collection point for bananas, nutmeg and cocoa, and also a fishing port. South of Grenville is Marquis village, which was the capital of St Andrew's in the 17th and 18th centuries. Nowadays it is the centre of the wild pine handicraft industry. Historical sites nearby are Battle Hill and Fort Royal. From here boats go to Marquis Island (see above).

The transinsular, or hill road, from Grenville to St George's used to be the route from the Pearls airport to the capital, which all new arrivals had to take. Now it is well-surfaced, but twisty and narrow. The minibus drivers on it are generally regarded as "maniacs". To give an idea of the conditions, one bend is called "Hit Me Easy". The road rises up to the rain forest, often entering the clouds. If driving yourself, allow up to 1½ hours from Levera to St George's and avoid the mountain roads around Grand Étang in the dark, although the night time sounds of the dense jungle are fascinating. Shortly before reaching the Grand Étang (full details above), there is a side road to the St Margaret, or Seven Sisters Falls. They are only a half-hour walk from the main road, but a guide is essential. After Grand Étang, there is a viewpoint at 1,910 feet overlooking St George's. A bit further down the hill is a detour to the Annandale Falls which plunge about 40 feet into a pool where the locals dive and swim. The road enters the capital on River Road.

Note that away from the southwest peninsula, some of the young Grenadians adopt an aggressive attitude to tourists.

Carriacou

Carriacou (pronounced *Carr*-yacoo) is an attractive island of green hills descending to sandy beaches. It is much less mountainous than Grenada, which means that any cloudy or rainy weather clears much quicker. With an area of 13 square miles, it is the largest of the Grenadines. It lies 23 miles northeast of Grenada; 2½ miles further northeast is Petit Martinique, which is separated by a narrow channel from Petit St Vincent, the southernmost of St Vincent's Grenadine dependencies. Efforts are being made by the Government to curb contraband and drug smuggling in Carriacou. An opposition proposal has been put forward to make the island a free trade zone, or to allow it to secede from Grenada.

Carriacou's population is under 5,000, less than 600 of whom live in the capital, **Hillsborough**. On the one hand, the islanders display a strong adherence to their African origins in that the annual Big Drum Dances, which take place around Easter, are almost purely West African. The Tombstone Feasts are unique. On the other hand, French traditions are still evident at L'Esterre and there is a vigorous Scottish heritage, especially at **Windward**, in the craft of hand-built schooners. Begun by a shipbuilder from Glasgow, the techniques are unchanged, but the white cedar used for the vessels now has to be imported from Grenada or elsewhere. The sturdy sailing vessels are built and repaired without the use of power tools in the shade of the coconut palms at the edge of the sea. The people of Windward are much lighter skinned than elsewhere on the island as a result of their Scottish forebears. To demonstrate the qualities of these local boats, the Carriacou Regatta was initiated in 1965. It has grown into the major festival described above. The local painter, Canute Calliste, has his studio at L'Esterre. His naive style captures the scenes of Carriacou (kite flying, launching schooners, festivals); a collection of his paintings have been published in a book by MacMillan, he is also an accomplished violinist and performs the quadrille, a dance which is part of the island's cultural heritage. The Carriacou Museum in Hillsborough has exhibits from Amerindian settlements in the island and from later periods in its history; the woman who runs it is the daughter of Canute Calliste, and can tell you about the Arawak ruins on the island, open Monday-Friday, 0930-1430. There are also ruined plantations. On Hospital Hill, Belair, northeast of Hillsborough, there is an overgrown old sugar Mill, stunning views. There is good walking on the back roads and the woods are teeming with wildlife such as iguanas.

Off the island are interesting underwater reefs and sandy islets with a few palms on them, ideal for snorkelling and picnicking. Sandy Island is a tiny, low-lying atoll in Hillsborough Bay off Lauriston Point, with a few palm trees for shade, safe and excellent swimming and snorkelling, take food, drink and plenty of suntan lotion. Boat from Hillsborough EC$60, 30 minutes each way, pick a day when the islet is not swamped with boat loads of cruise ship visitors. Alternatively try White Island, a similar islet in Manchineel Bay off the south coast, ask for boats at *Cassada Bay Hotel*. Visitors should see the oyster beds at Tyrrel Bay where "tree-oysters" grow on mangrove roots. Tyrrel Bay is a favourite anchorage for the many yachts which visit the island.

A recommended beautiful beach is Anse La Roche, which faces west and has a spectacular view across the strait to the mountains of rugged Union Island. Walk from Bogles along the dirt road heading northwards, past the *Caribbee Inn* and Honey Hill House; after about 30 minutes the road starts to rise, turn left at the large tree which overhangs the track and follow a narrow path through the woods to a ruined farmhouse. The path leads to the right, through bushes; keep to the downhill side of the open slope, bear right down a steep slope leading through more trees to the beach. Take food and drink, there are no facilities and few people, about 45 minutes' walk each way. Very peaceful, watch the yachts rounding the headland on their way to anchorage; at night turtles swim ashore to lay their eggs. If instead of turning off the track to Anse La Roche, you carry on walking northwards, the well-shaded, grassy road rounds Gun Point with lovely views of the Grenadines. A path leads down (opposite a mauve-painted house) to the beach at Petit Carenage Bay, which has coarse, coral sand, good swimming and modest surf in some conditions. Returning to the road, Windward is a few minutes walk further on, a few shops and local bars.

Buses go from Hillsborough to Bogles, Windward (EC$1.50) and to Tyrrel Bay. The normally excellent service goes to pieces if it is wet. There are also plenty of taxis, or you can hire a car. Alternatively, just walk around. Fishing and sailing trips from Hillsborough pier or ask at hotels. Out of season the island is quiet, and not all the hotels are open.

Barclays Bank and National Commercial Bank have branches on Carriacou. These, the government and customs offices, post office and the commercial centre are around the pier in Hillsborough. The market is here too; it comes alive on Monday when the produce is brought in. Food is limited in variety, especially fresh vegetables. "Jack Iron" rum (180° proof) is a local hazard, it is so strong that ice sinks in it. It is distilled in Barbados but bottled in Carriacou; it costs around EC$10 per bottle and is liberally dispensed on all high days and holidays (fairly liberally on other days too).

It is advisable to use insect repellent on the beaches, especially in the rainy season. At night it is best to use a mosquito net.

Petit Martinique

Petit Martinique is the only offshore island from Carriacou on which people live (about 600 of them). Its area is 486 acres, rising to a pointed peak. The principal occupations are boatbuilding and fishing. There are no hotels.

Information for Visitors

Documents
Citizens of the UK, USA and Canada need only provide proof of identity (with photograph) and an onward ticket (but note that if you go to Grenada via Trinidad, a passport *has* to be presented in Trinidad). For all others a passport and onward ticket are essential, though a ticket from Barbados to the USA (for example) is accepted. Departure by boat is not accepted by the immigration authorities. Citizens of certain other countries (not the Commonwealth, France, Germany) must obtain a visa to visit Grenada. Check before leaving home. When you arrive in Grenada expect to have your luggage examined very thoroughly. It may take you at least 45 minutes to get through passport control and customs. You must be able to give an accommodation address when you arrive.

Airport Tax
For stays of over 24 hours, departure tax is EC$25 (EC$12.50 for children aged 10 to 16). There is a EC$5 tax on airline tickets purchased in Grenada. No tax payable on flights from Grenada to Carriacou.

How To Get There By Air
Scheduled flights from London, Gatwick, once a week with British Airways, or connections via Antigua with Liat; from

the USA, BWIA flies daily from New York and Miami. American Airlines fly from the USA via San Juan, Puerto Rico.

Within the Caribbean BWIA connects Grenada with Trinidad and Barbados. Liat flies to Grenada from Antigua, Barbados, Mustique, Trinidad, St Lucia, St Maarten, St Vincent, Tobago, Tortola (BVI) and Union Island. Liat connects Grenada with Carriacou, flying seven times a day from 0640 to 1715. (The airline is sometimes forgetful where luggage is concerned, so make sure yours is loaded on and off the plane. Also be sure to reconfirm your flights.)

Several companies operate charters to Grenada from the Caribbean and North America. Aereotuy flies Mondays and Fridays to Isla Margarita, departs 0745, returns 1830, Tel: 444-1656.

Airport

The Point Salines airport is 5 miles from St George's: taxis only, EC$30 to St George's, 15 minutes; EC$25 to Grand Anse and Lance aux Épines. Journeys within a one-mile radius of the airport EC$7. Add EC$10 to fares between 1800 and 0600. Returning to the airport you can take a bus from St George's market to Calliste (EC$1.50) then walk, 20 minutes downhill. Another route is by bus to the 'Sugarman', EC$1, then catch another minibus or collective taxi to the airport, EC$5. Alternatively, when reconfirming your ticket with Liat ask about taxis, they offer a reliable taxi service for EC$20 if paid in advance. There are no exchange facilities at the airport.

Carriacou's airport is Lauriston, a EC$10 taxi ride from Hillsborough, EC$15- 20 from Windward. Disconcertingly, the main road goes straight across the runway. A nice new fire engine drives out from Hillsborough to meet incoming flights, bringing the Immigration Officer, who clings to a platform at the back in Keystone Kops fashion.

Airline Offices

Liat, The Carenage, St George's, Tel: 440-2796/7 (444-4121/2 Point Salines, 443-7362 Carriacou); same number in St George's for British Airways and ALM; BWIA, The Carenage, St George's, Tel: 440-3818/9 (same number as above at airport); American Airlines, Tel: 444-2222; Aeropostal, Tel: 444-4732/6.

How To Get There By Sea

A large number of North American cruise lines call, including Chandris American Line and Royal Caribbean Cruise Line. Geest Line stops at the island on its Barry, South Wales/Windward Islands run. Tel: Isaac

Joseph, St Andrew's 7512, for information about sailing on the *Fazeela* to Trinidad. The *Eastward* sails about once a month to Isla de Margarita, Venezuela, US$60 one way but you have to buy a return to satisfy Venezuelan entry requirements (the captain will refund your return fare, less 10%, on arrival).

Inter-Island Transport

Every day Liat flies between Grenada and Carriacou: US$62 return, half that one way (flying time is 12 minutes).

On Wednesday and Saturday at 1000 the trading schooners *Alexia II* and *Adelaide B* sail from The Carenage, St George's to Carriacou (4 hours, EC$20 one way, EC$30 return), returning on Thursday and Monday. The *MV Edna David* sails on Sunday 0700, arriving Carriacou 1030, returning 1700, arriving in St George's 2030. Times are subject to change and you must check. There are also unscheduled schooner services between these islands; by asking around you might be able to get a passage on one. *Eagle Quest* sails from Grenada to Sandy Island and back on Sunday, departing 0930, return 1700.

Carriacou is one hour by schooner from Union Island; scheduled service by MV *Obedient* twice a week, EC$10. Two small fishing boats sail Monday 1300 from Hillsborough pier, one hour, EC$10.

Local Transport

Buses run to all parts of the island from the Market Square and the Esplanade in St George's; on the Esplanade look for the signs, in the Square, ask around. The public transport system has new, white and blue Mitsubishi buses and there are also privately-run minibuses (which are more expensive). Fares are EC$0.50-1 within St George's, EC$2-3 to Grand Étang, and EC$4 to Grenville and Sauteurs. The last buses tend to be in mid-afternoon and there are very few on Sundays.

Taxi fares are set by the Tourist Board. Fares from the airports are given above. On Grenada, taxis charge EC$4 for the first 10 miles outside St George's, then EC$3 per mile thereafter (an additional charge is made after 1800, EC$10 per journey). Island tours of Carriacou cost between EC$100 and EC$140 by taxi.

Taxis and buses are heavily 'personalized' by the drivers with brightly coloured decorations and names like 'Rusher with Love' or 'Danny Boy', while large speakers blast out steel bands or reggae music; taxi drivers will adjust the volume on request. A water taxi service 'uns from in front of the *Nutmeg* restaurant, St George's to the Grand Anse beach. Hitchhiking is quite easy though the roads are not very good.

Car Rental

Cars can be rented from a number of companies for about US$55 or EC$150 a day, plus US$2,500 excess liability and 5% tax (payable by credit card). You must purchase a local permit, on presentation of your national driving licence, for EC$30/US$12; a local permit is not required if you hold an international driving licence. Driving is on the left. When driving, be prepared for no road signs, no indication which way the traffic flow goes (just watch the other cars), and few street names. Maps are often not accurate, so navigation becomes particularly difficult. Also be careful of the deep storm drains along the edges of the narrow roads.

Companies in St George's include Spice Island Rentals (Avis), Paddock and Lagoon Road, Tel: 444-4022; David's, Archibald Avenue, Tel: 440-2399 (has an office at the airport); McIntyre, Lagoon Road, Tel: 440-2044; Maitland's (who also rent motorcycles), Market Hill, Tel: 440-4022; Romain's, Paddock Street, Tel: 440-1553; C Thomas and Sons, cars, minibuses, jeeps, *True Blue*, near airport, Tel: 440-7329, 444-4384, mixed reports. We have received reports that daily rates quoted over the phone are not always honoured when you pick up the car; check that the company does not operate a three-day minimum hire if you want a rate for one day only. On Carriacou: Barba Gabriel, Tel: 443-7454; Leo Cromwell, Tel: 443-7333; Martin Bullen, Tel: 443-7204; *Silver Beach Resort*, Tel: 443-7337.

Where To Stay

Hotel rooms are subject to a 10% service charge and an 8% tax. Note also that meals are subject to 20% VAT. The majority of hotels are in the Grand Anse area, with several around Lance aux Épines. In St George's there are more guesthouses than hotels.

Hotels St George's: *Balisier*, Richmond Hill, PO Box 335, Tel: 440-2346, Fax: 440-6604, out of town, double rooms in season US$90-104 including breakfast, excellent views, restaurant, swimming pool, recommended; ask here about 1-day walking tours to plantations and other areas of interest.

On Grand Anse: *Coyaba*, PO Box 336, St George's, Tel: 444-4129, Fax: 444-4808, popular with package tours, but very comfortable, lots of facilities, double rooms US$95 to US$165 depending on season; *Ramada Renaissance*, PO Box 141, St George's, Tel: 444-4371, Fax: 444-4800, 184 rooms and suites, a/c, US$100-300 in summer to US$158-300 in winter, many facilities, restaurant pricey, open 0700-2300; *Spice Island Inn*, PO Box 6, St George's, Tel: 444-4258, Fax: 444-4807, US$320-450 or US$430-560 all inclusive for suites in season (US$235-295 or US$345-405 all inclusive off season, quality and service have been sharply criticized); *Hibiscus*, PO Box 779, St George's, Tel: 444-4233, Fax: 444-4655, cottages US$80-90, two-bedroomed suites US$115 in season, recommended, car hire available; *Blue Horizons Cottage Hotel*, PO Box 41, St George's, Tel: 444-4316, Fax: 444-2815, US$120-145 in season (US$90-105 off season), its *La Belle Créole* restaurant is one of the island's best. *South Winds Holiday Cottages and Apartments*, Grand Anse, PO Box 118, St George's, Tel: 444-4310, Fax: 444-4847, from US$50 to US$80 per day, monthly rates on request, 5-10 minute walk from beach, good view, recommended (also car hire).

At **Morne Rouge**: *Gem Holiday Beach Resort*, Tel: 444-4224, Fax: 440-4847, US$45-65d summer to US$60-95d winter, depending on quality, two-bedroomed apartments US$85-110, lovely beach, good position but poorly equipped and hot, restaurant limited. *True Blue Inn*, P O Box 308, St George's, Tel: 444-2000, Fax: 444-1247, between Grand Anse and Point Salines airport, owner-managed cottages and apartments, kitchenettes, pool, US$110-165 winter, US$70-100 summer, dock facilities, boat charter available, restaurant and bar.

Lance aux Épines: *Calabash*, PO Box 382, St George's, Tel: 444-4334, Fax: 444-4804, winner of a prestigious Golden Fork award for quality of food and hospitality, probably the poshest hotel on Grenada, expensive (US$150-240 BP, US$205-295 MAP double off season, US$295-465 in season, MAP), on beach, nice grounds, pool suites, tennis, games room; *Secret Harbour*, PO Box 11, St George's, Tel: 444-4548, Fax: 444-4819, 20 luxury rooms, US$125d EP in summer, US$208 EP in winter, pool, friendly, steel band at times, no children under 12 accepted; *Horse Shoe Beach*, PO Box 174, St George's, Tel: 444-4244, Fax:

444-4844, self-catering cottages US$110, suites US$130 in season (US$85-95 off season), children under 18 US$10; *Holiday Haven*, above a cove on Prickly Point, 2-3 bedroomed villas US$600-700/week in winter, US$500-600/week in summer, 1-2 bedroomed apartments also available, contact Dr John Watts, Tel: 440-2606. **On the south coast:** *La Sagesse Nature Center* (see **Flora and Fauna** above), PO Box 44, St David's, Grenada, Tel: 444-6458, Fax: 444-4847, rooms in winter cost US$70 double, in summer US$60, small, excellent, perfect setting, an old plantation house on a secluded, sandy bay (the sea may be polluted in the rainy season, seek the hotel's advice), good restaurant, excursions, highly recommended. **On the east coast:** near Grenville, *St Martins Catholic Retreat Centre*, Mount St Ervans, PO Box 11, Grenville, Tel: 442-7348, spectacular views, lovely surroundings, good spot for lunch, open to non-residents.

Carriacou: *Silver Beach Resort*, from US$70-85d off season to US$95-115 in season, depending on room or apartment, though for a longer stay a cheaper rate can be negotiated with the owner, Tel: 443-7337, Fax: 443-7165; *Cassada Bay Resort*, 9 cabins, 14 double rooms, use of private island, fitness room, use of watersports equipment, mini-cinema room, US$120d EP winter, US$90d summer, Tel: 443-7494; *Caribbee Inn*, Prospect, Tel: 443-7380, Fax: 443-7999, lovely setting, pricey US$100-130d for small room, expensive food, snorkelling off stoney beach, 40 minute walk to excellent beach, out of town.

Guesthouses (all prices year round) **St George's:** *Mitchell's Guest House*, Tyrrel Street, Tel: 440-2803, US$35d, noisy, loud music, stray dogs, preachers; *Simeons* (formerly *Plantation Inn*), Green Street (no sign), Tel: 440-2537, 9 rooms, US$35d including breakfast, central, clean, friendly, recommended, view over Carenage; *St Ann's Guest House*, Paddock, beyond Botanic Gardens (some distance from centre), Tel: 440-2717, US$31d, excellent breakfast included, very clean and friendly, entrance forbidden to "prostitutes and natty dreds", recommended, meals (communal), EC$20, good value, a bit difficult to sleep because of dogs and roosters, take ear plugs; *Yacht's View*, Lagoon Road, Tel: 440-3607,

US$20d, friendly and helpful, kitchen facilities, recommended; *Mamma's Lodge*, P O Box 248, Lagoon Road, Tel: 440-1459, Fax: 440-1623, good value, six double, four single rooms, pleasant, US$25 single, US$35 double, including breakfast, no credit cards; *Lakeside*, at the end of Lagoon Road going towards Grand Anse, Tel: 440-2365 (Mrs Ruth Haynes), view over yacht marina, helpful, cooking facilities, US$10pp without meals, drinks available, mixed reports. *Skyline*, Belmont, between St George's and Grand Anse Beach, Tel: 444-4461, US$25, mixed reports. At **Grand Anse:** *Roydon's*, Tel: 444-4476, US$40-50d EP, US$70-85 MAP, helpful staff, fans, very nice, recommended, restaurant, 10 minutes walk from beach, access through *Ramada Renaissance*; *Windward Sands Inn*, PO Box 199, Tel: 444-4238, US$60d CP winter, US$55 summer, apartments US$275-340/week, friendly, helpful, tours arranged, nice place, good cooking. **Grenville:** *Rainbow Inn*, Tel: 440-7714, US$45.

Carriacou *Peace Haven Cottages*, south of pier, Main Street, Hillsborough, Tel: 443-7475, family and bachelor units from US$19-30, basic rooms, share small kitchen and bathroom, contact Lucille Atkins, very friendly and helpful, on the sea front a few hundred yards south of the jetty, rooms rather small, sometimes water shortages; other guest houses, *Ade's Dream*, Tel: 443-7317, north of pier, Main Street, Hillsborough, US$20d, 7 rooms share large kitchen, very clean, run by hard-working and friendly Mrs Mills (good reports); *Sand's*, Tel: 443-7100, between Hillsborough and the airport, quiet, basic but clean, across the road is a nice beach, 6 rooms, US$25d with shared kitchen and bathroom; *Scraper's*, Tyrrel Bay, Tel: 443-7403, local restaurant and rooms EC$60d, two-bedroomed cottages EC$120/day, close to bay, cheaper for locals; *Constant Spring*, Tel: 443-7396, overlooks Tyrrel Bay, three double rooms with shared bathroom and kitchen, comfortable, attractive, EC$120/room.

There are also many furnished villas and apartments available for rent from various agents, with prices for daily or weekly rental. Daily rates start at US$35 off season, rising to US$115 in season. On Carriacou, there are many fully equipped houses to rent, costing about US$100 a month. See Mr Emmons or Mrs Joseph, or ask at the tourist office on the quay.

Where To Eat

There is quite a wide choice of restaurants, apart from the hotels mentioned above, and you are recommended to eat the local dishes, which are very good. Service of 10% is usually added to the bill. Unless stated otherwise, restaurants below are in St George's. *Nutmeg*, on the Carenage (Tel: 440-2241), delicious local dishes and its own famous rum punch, very popular; *Rudolph's*, also on the Carenage, (Tel: 440-2241), expensive, but good, local and international food, excellent rum punch; *Sand Pebble*, the Carenage too, cheap and clean, good rotis EC$5, take away or eat in, bar snacks only; *Delicious Landing* at the Post Office end of the Carenage, local and international, recommended but very slow service; *Tropicana*, in the Lagoon, Chinese and local food, good, meals from EC$6, barbecues, Fridays and Saturdays, closed Sundays; *Mamma's Bar*, Lagoon Road, try multifarious local foods (famous for wild meat dishes), good value, need to book, quite commercialized now; also *Snug Corner* and *Pitch Pine Bar* near the Market Square.

At the St George's end of Grand Anse is *The French Restaurant*, Tel: 444-4644, with excellent food and fruit juices and punches. *The Bird's Nest* at Grand Anse has good Chinese food, very reasonable, opposite *Ramada Renaissance*, Tel: 444-4264; *Southwinds*, Grand Anse, about 20 minutes' walk from *Ramada*, is recommended as probably the best seafood restaurant on the island, on top of a hill with magnificent view, friendly and expertly-trained staff. Tel: 444-4310; *Canboulay*, Morne Rouge, Tel: 444-4401, recommended, upmarket and very good but not cheap. *The Green Parrot*, recommended but take plenty of insect repellent, you eat on little islands connected by walkways, lots of croaking frogs and mosquitoes at night. *Aquarium Beach Club and Restaurant*, Tel: 444-1410, Balls Beach, run by Ollie and Rebecca, recommended, bar open from 1030, kitchen 1200-2200, Saturday volleyball, Sunday barbeque, showers toilets, snorkelling offshore, good food, lobster, fish, steak, sandwiches, closed Monday.

See above for *Morne Fendue* plantation house restaurant, said to serve the best Caribbean food on the island and the best rum punch in the Caribbean.

On **Carriacou**, there are some basic local bar/restaurants but they often run out of food quite early or close in the evenings, check during the day if they will be open; finding meals is particularly difficult at weekends. *Barba's Oyster Bar*, at Tyrrel Bay above a supermarket, is new and clean but has slow service; *L'Aquilone*, above Tyrrel Bay, 15 minutes' walk from bus stop, Tel: 443-7197, marvellous view, small restaurant serving good Italian food at moderate prices, is also coastguard station with radio contact and has takeaway/delivery service to boats; *Constant Spring*, Tyrrel Bay, does takeaway chicken; *Love Knott*, Tyrrel Bay, French food, moderate prices; *Roof Garden*, misleading name, near Market Hall, Hillsborough, clean and friendly but limited choice; *Hillsborough Bar*, Main Street, attractive place for a drink, meals can be ordered the day before; *Callaloo*, Hillsborough, EC$30 for dinner, plenty of choice, recommended; *Talk of the Town*, in Hillsborough, cheap and good; *Turtle Dove* snack bar in Hermitage, Tel: 443-7194.

Food And Drink

To repeat, Grenada's West Indian cooking is generally very good. Lambi (conch) is very popular, as is callaloo soup (made with dasheen leaves), soue (a sauce made from pig's feet), pepper pot and pumpkin pie. There is a wide choice of seafood, and of vegetables. Goat and wild meat (armadillo, iguana, manicou) can be sampled. Nutmeg features in many local dishes, try nutmeg jelly for breakfast, ground nutmeg comes on top of rum punches. Of the many fruits and fruit dishes, try stewed golden apple, or soursop ice cream. There is limited food or choice on Carriacou.

Rum punches are excellent, and be sure to try the local sea-moss drink (a mixture of vanilla, algae and milk). There are two makes of rum, whose superiority is disputed by the islanders, Clarke's Court and River Antoine. The term "grog", for rum, is supposed to originate in Grenada: taking the first letters of "Georgius Rex Old Grenada", which was stamped on the casks of rum sent back to England. Grenada Breweries brew Carib Lager, Guinness and non-alcoholic malt beers.

Entertainment

The resort hotels provide evening entertainment, including dancing, steelband and calypso music, limbo, etc. There are not a great many discothèques and night clubs outside the hotels; *La*

Sucrier, Panache, Fantazia 2001 and Club Paradise at Lance aux Épines are some examples. On Carriacou there is a good jump-up every Friday after mass at Liz' Refreshment, Tyrrel Bay, with excellent DJ.

Shopping

The Yellow Poui Art Gallery sells Grenadian paintings and is worth a visit, above Noah's Arkade souvenir shop on Cross Street. Spice Island Perfumes on the Carenage sells perfumes and pots pourris made from the island's spices, as well as batiks, T-shirts, etc (it has a branch at the Spice Island Inn, Grand Anse). Arawak Island factory and retail outlet on the Upper Belmont Road between Grand Anse and St George's, Tel: 440-4577, open Monday-Friday 0830-1630, perfumes, body oils, spices, syrups, cocoa bars etc. Grencraft on the Esplanade; Blind People's Work Shop at Delicious Landing, and others. You can purchase straw and palm wares, and items in wood. There is duty-free shopping at the airport and on the Carenage for cruise ship passengers.

St George's Bookshop is on Halifax Street; The Sea Change Book and Gift Shop is on the Carenage, beneath the Nutmeg bar. Good supermarkets include one opposite the Ramada Renaissance and one also on Lagoon at Belmont end.

Currency

The currency is the East Caribbean dollar: EC$2.70 = US$1.

Banks

Barclays Bank (branches in St George's-Halifax Street, Grenville and Carriacou), Tel: 440-3232; National Commercial Bank of Grenada, (Halifax Street, St George's, Grenville, Gouyave, St David's, Carriacou), Tel: 440-3566; Scotiabank (Halifax Street, St George's), Tel: 440-3274; Grenada Bank of Commerce (Halifax and Cross St, St George's, and Grand Anse), Tel: 440-3521; Grenada Co-operative Bank (Church St, St George's, Grenville and Sauteurs), Tel: 440-2111. They do not exchange European currencies other than sterling.

Climate

The average temperature is 26°C. The weather is sunny and hot from December to May. The rainy season runs from June to November.

Clothing

Dress is casual, with lightweight summer clothes suitable all year. Bathing costumes are not accepted in hotel dining rooms, shops or on the streets.

High Season

Winter (high) season prices come into effect from 16 December to 15 April. The tourist season is at its height between January and March.

Business Hours

Banks: 0800-1200 or 1400 Monday-Thursday; 0800-1200 or 1300, 1430-1700 Friday. Shops: 0800-1145, 1300-1545 Monday-Friday, 0800-1145 Saturday; government offices the same, but closed all day Saturday.

Holidays

New Year's Day (1 January), Independence Day (7 February), Good Friday and Easter Monday, Labour Day (1 May), Whit Monday (in May/June), Corpus Christi (June), August holidays (first Monday and Tuesday in August) and Carnival (second weekend in August), Thanksgiving (25 October), 25 and 26 December.

Time Zone

Atlantic Standard Time, 4 hours behind GMT, 1 ahead of EST.

Venezuelan Embassy

Archibald Avenue, St George's, Tel: 440-1721/2

Electric Current

220/240 volts, 50 cycles AC.

Postal Services

The General Post Office in St George's is on the Carenage, open 0800-1530 Monday to Thursday, and 1630 on Friday (operating from a temporary building after the fire of May 1990). Villages have sub-post offices.

Telecommunications

Cable and Wireless Ltd, the Carenage, St George's (open 0700-1900 Monday-Saturday; 1600-1800 Sunday), operates fax and telex services; Grenada Telephone Company (Grentel, a joint venture with Cable and Wireless), Tel: 440-1000, with offices behind Cable and Wireless, operates telephone services, including "USA Direct" and calls to USA on Visa card, etc, at a fee, facsimile, telex, telegraph and cellular phones. If you dail 872 at any public phone (no coin required), you get through to AT and T. A call to the UK costs approximately EC$37.50 for 5 minutes.

Newspapers

There are no daily papers, only weeklies, including *Grenadian Voice*, *Indies Times*, *Grenada Guardian*, *The National*, and *The Informer*. There is a state-run radio station (Radio Grenada) and one television station.

Religion

Roman Catholic, Anglican, Presbyterian, Methodist, Scots Kirk, Seventh Day Adventist, Jehovah's Witnesses, Islam, Salvation Army, First Church of Christian Scientists, Church of Christ and Baha'i.

Travel Agents

All in St George's: Grenada International Travel Service, of Church Street (American Express representative), Tel: 440-2945; Huggins Travel Service, the Carenage, Tel: 440-2514; McIntyre Brothers, Lagoon Road, Tel: 440-2901; Grenada Tours and Travel, the Carenage, Tel: 440-3316 (PO Box 46, operates a people-to-people scheme in which visitors may meet locals with similar interest or professions). Otway's, also on the Carenage, Tel: 440-2558; and many others. Edwin Frank, from the Tourism Department, Tel: 443-5143, does guided tours at weekends, US$20 pp island tour, very knowledgeable on history, politics, geography, people, fauna, hiking etc, recommended and much better than an untrained taxi driver. Henry, of Henry's Travel (Tel: 443-5313) conducts tours of the island and is very well informed on all aspects of Grenada. Arnold's Tours, Grenville Street, Tel: 440-1781/2213, Fax: 440-4118, offers similar services to Henry's, also recommended, but in German as well. Q and K Sunsation Tours is very knowledgeable and recommended, bilingual guides are available for half or full day tours, P O Box 856, St George's, Tel: 444-1656, 444-1594, Fax: 444-4819. In the UK, Canada and Carriacou Travel Service, 81 Askew Road, London W12, organizes trips, Tel: (71) 743 4518, ask for Mr Harroo, helpful.

Hiking

For guided hikes contact Telfer Bedeau in the village of Soubise on the east coast; you must ask around for him (or see if the Tourism Department can put you in touch). The Overseas Surveys Directorate, Ordnance Survey map of Grenada, published for the Grenada Government in 1985, scale 1:50,000, is available from the Tourist Office, from the Lands and Surveys Department in the Ministry of Agriculture (at the Botanic Gardens) and from shops for EC$10.50-15 (it is not wholly accurate). Also available from Ordnance Survey, Southampton, are two separate sheets, North (1979) and South (1988) at 1:25,000 scale. A tourist style map of Grenada is planned for 1993.

Tourist Information

Grenada Tourism Department, the Carenage, St George's (PO Box 293), Tel: 440-2279/2001, Fax: 440-6637. Its hours are 0800-1600 and it is very helpful. There is also a tourist office at the airport, helpful, hotel reservation service.

In the USA: Grenada Tourist Office, 820 2nd Avenue, Suite 900D, New York, NY 10017, Tel: (212) 687-9554, (800) 927 9554, Fax: (212) 573 9731; in Canada: Grenada Tourist Office, Suite 820, 439 University Avenue, Toronto, Ontario M5G 1Y8, Tel: (416) 595-1339, Fax: (416) 595 8278; in the UK: 1 Collingham Gardens, London SW5 0HW, Tel: (071) 370 5164/5, Fax: (071) 370 7040.

BARBADOS

Introduction

BARBADOS is 21 miles long and 14 miles wide, lying east of the main chain of the Leeward and Windward islands. It is flatter, drier, and more prosperous and tourists who come here looking for the "untouched" Caribbean are in for a disappointment. There are no volcanoes or rain forests, and hardly any rivers, but there are plenty of white sand beaches and lots of pleasantly rolling countryside with fields of sugar cane, brightly painted villages, flowering trees and open pastures. The island is probably better equipped with infrastructure and reliable tourist services than anywhere else to the south of Miami on this side of the Atlantic.

Barbados has a population of 257,000. This is more than any of the Windwards or Leewards, and is considered enough to make the island one of the "big four" in the Caribbean Community. With population density of 1,548 per square mile in 1990, Barbados is one of the most crowded countries in the world.

History
There were Amerindians on Barbados for upwards of a thousand years. The first Europeans to find the island were the Portuguese, who named it "Os Barbados" after the Bearded Fig trees which grew on the beaches, and left behind some wild pigs. These bred successfully and provided meat for the first English settlers, who arrived in 1627 and found an island which was otherwise uninhabited. It is not clear why the Amerindians abandoned the island, although several theories exist. King Charles I gave the Earl of Carlisle permission to colonize the island and it was his appointed Governor, Henry Hawley, who in 1639 founded the House of Assembly. Within a few years, there were upwards of 40,000 white settlers, mostly small farmers, and equivalent in number to about 1% of the total population of England at this period. After the "sugar revolution" of the 1650s most of the white population left. For the rest of the colonial period sugar was king, and the

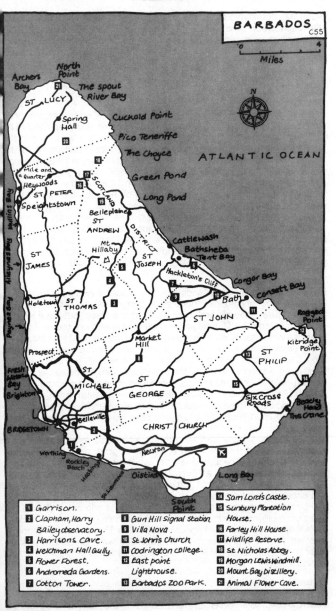

BARBADOS
C55

0 Miles 4

Archers Bay
North Point
The Spout
River Bay
ST LUCY
Spring Hall
Cuckold Point
Pico Teneriffe
The Choyce
Green Pond
Long Pond
ATLANTIC OCEAN
N
Mile and a Quarter
Heywoods
SCOTLAND
ST PETER
Speightstown
Belleplaine
ST ANDREW
Mt Hillaby
DISTRICT
ST JOSEPH
Cattlewash
Bathsheba
Tent Bay
Hackleton's Cliff
Congor Bay
Consett Bay
Bath
ST JOHN
Ragged Point
Kitridge Point
ST JAMES
Holetown
ST THOMAS
Prospect
Market Hill
Mullins Bay
Alleynes Bay
Payne's Bay
Fresh Water Bay
Brighton
ST MICHAEL
Belleville
ST GEORGE
ST PHILIP
Sam Lord's Castle
Six Cross Roads
Beachy Head
The Crane
BRIDGETOWN
CHRIST CHURCH
Newton
Worthing
Rockley Beach
Hastings
St Lawrence
Oistins
South Point
Long Bay

1 Garrison.
2 Clapham, Harry Bailey observatory.
3 Harrison's Cave.
4 Welchman Hall Gully.
5 Flower Forest.
6 Andromeda Gardens.
7 Cotton Tower.
8 Gun Hill Signal station.
9 Villa Nova.
10 St John's Church.
11 Codrington College.
12 East point Lighthouse.
13 Barbados Zoo Park.
14 Sam Lord's Castle.
15 Sunbury Plantation House.
16 Farley Hill House.
17 Wildlife Reserve.
18 St Nicholas Abbey.
19 Morgan Lewis Windmill.
20 Mount Gay Distillery.
21 Animal Flower Cave.

island was dominated by a small group of whites who owned the estates, the "plantocracy". The majority of the population today is descended from African slaves who were brought in to work on the plantations; but there is a substantial mixed-race population, and there has always been a small number of poor whites, particularly in the eastern part of the island. Many of these are descended from 100 prisoners transported in 1686 after the failed Monmouth rebellion and Judge Jeffrey's "Bloody Assizes".

Government
Barbados has been an independent member of the Commonwealth since November 1966. The British Monarch is the Head of State, represented by a Governor General. There is a strong parliamentary and democratic tradition. The House of Assembly is the third oldest parliament in the Western Hemisphere and celebrated its 350th anniversary in 1989, although voting was limited to property owners until 1950. There are 21 senators appointed by the Governor General, of whom 12 are on the advice of the Prime Minister, 2 on the advice of the Leader of the Opposition and 7 at his own discretion to reflect religious, economic and social interests. 28 single-member constituencies elect the House of Assembly. The two principal political parties are the Barbados Labour Party (BLP) and the Democratic Labour Party (DLP). The Democratic Labour Party has been in office since 1986, and was re-elected in 1991, when it won 18 seats in a general election. The Prime Minister is Mr Erskine Sandiford.

The Economy
Barbados is now officially a "middle income" country, with a per capita gnp higher than that of European countries like Portugal, Malta, or Greece. There are few natural resources and sugar is still the main crop, but there is some export-oriented manufacturing and an expanding offshore financial sector. There is a well-established service sector, and a wide range of light industries which produce mainly for the local, regional, and North American markets. More than half the households own a car, and almost all have a piped water supply and a telephone. By far the main foreign exchange earner is now tourism. In 1991, 394,242 tourists, over a third of whom came from Europe, stayed in Barbados and 372,140 cruise ship passengers also visited, spending about US$500m. There are about 6,650 rooms available in hotels, guest houses and apartments but occupancy rates fell in 1991 to slightly over 50%.

The slowdown in the USA and other industrialized countries has had a negative affect on the Barbadian economy. Stopover arrivals declined by over 7% in 1990 and nearly 9% in 1991, while construction and agriculture also declined, leading to an overall gdp contraction. The Government's budget deficit rose to 8.9% of gdp in 1990, while foreign reserves declined and unemployment rose to 14.7%. The 1991 budget sought to close the gap by raising taxes and the deficit fell to 2.9% of gdp but at the cost of rising unemployment with 20% of the labour force out of work. In 1992 the IMF approved a loan package of US$65m over 15 months and economic forecasts for the year were more positive. Gdp was expected to pick up slightly, the fiscal deficit to fall to 1% of gdp, inflation to be around 5% and foreign reserves to rise.

Culture
Because Barbados lies upwind from the main island arc, it was hard to attack from the sea, so it never changed hands in the colonial wars of the

seventeenth and eighteenth centuries. There is no French, Dutch, or Spanish influence to speak of in the language, cooking or culture. People from other islands have often referred to Barbados as Little England, and have not always intended a compliment. Today, the more obvious outside influences on the Barbadian way of life are North American. Most contemporary Barbadians stress their Afro-Caribbean heritage and aspects of the culture which are distinctively "Bajan". There are extremes of poverty and wealth, but these are not nearly so noticeable as elsewhere in the Caribbean. This makes the social atmosphere relatively relaxed. However, there is a history of deep racial division. Although there is a very substantial black middle class and the social situation has changed radically since the 1940s and 50s, there is still more racial intolerance on all sides than is apparent at first glance.

Two Barbadian writers whose work has had great influence throughout the Caribbean are the novelist George Lamming and the poet Edward Kamau Brathwaite. Lamming's first novel, *In The Castle Of My Skin* (1953), a part-autobiographical story of growing up in colonial Barbados, deals with one of the major concerns of anglophone writers: how to define one's values within a system and ideology imposed by someone else. Lamming's treatment of the boy's changing awareness in a time of change in the West Indies is both poetic and highly imaginative. His other books include *Natives Of My Person*, *Season Of Adventure* and *The Pleasures Of Exile*.

Brathwaite too is sensitive to the colonial influence on black West Indian culture. Like Derek Walcott (see under St Lucia) and others he is also keenly aware of the African traditions at the heart of that culture. The questions addressed by all these writers are: who is Caribbean man, and what are his faiths, his language, his ancestors? The experience of teaching in Ghana for some time helped to clarify Brathwaite's response. African religions, motifs and songs mix with West Indian speech rhythms in a style which is often strident, frequently using very short verses. His collections include *Islands*, *Masks* and *Rights Of Passage*. Heinemann Caribbean publish the *A to Z of Barbadian Heritage* which is worth reading. Macmillan publish *Treasures of Barbados*, an attractive guide to Barbadian architecture.

Beaches

There are beaches along most of the south and west coasts. Although some hotels make it hard to cross their property to reach the sand, there are no private beaches in Barbados. The west coast beaches are very calm, and quite narrow, beach erosion is a serious worry and hoteliers are investing heavily to try and sort it out. A swell can wash up lots of broken coral making it unpleasant underfoot. The south coast can be quite choppy. The southeast, between the airport and East Point, has steep limestone cliffs with a series of small sandy coves with coconut trees, and waves which are big enough for surfing. Be careful on the east side of the island, currents and undertow are strong in places. Don't swim where there are warning signs, or where there are no other bathers. Some hotels sell day passes, eg *Hilton*, US$10 pp, for the use of their facilities: pool, showers, deck chairs, etc.

There are large numbers of "beach bums" on the south and west coasts. They generally carry a briefcase full of imported coral jewellery; this provides a conversation-starter to facilitate the sale of other goods and services.

Watersports

There are a large number of motor and sailing boats available for charter by the day or for shorter periods. These include *Irish Mist*, Tel: 436 9201, *Station*

Break, Tel: 436 9502, *Tiami*, Tel: 436 5725, *La Paloma*, Tel: 427 5588, *Cap'n Jack*, Tel: 427 5800, *Calypso Charters*, Tel: 426 7166, *Secret Love*, Tel: 432 1972, *Jolly Jumper*, Tel: 432 7090. Others are moored in the Careenage in Bridgetown, with a telephone number displayed. Most are equipped for fishing and snorkeling, and will serve a good meal on board. Rates and services offered vary widely.

Glass-bottomed boats can be hired from several private operators along the west coast. In December, the Mount Gay International Christmas Regatta for yachts is held.

The south coast is good for windsurfing and the International Funboard Challenge is held in March. Club Mistral at the Barbados Windsurfing Club Hotel, Maxwell, Christ Church, Tel: 428 9095, and at *Silver Sands Hotel*, Tel: 428 6001, ext 4227, rent equipment at US$13 an hour, US$40 a day, US$165 a week. Lessons are extra. Easy windsurfing for beginners with private operators near *Sandy Beach Hotel*. There is also windsurfing at *Hilton Hotel*, Tel: 427 4350. Skyranger Parasail, Holetown, Tel: 432 2323 or 424 5687 for parasailing. The best surfing is on the east coast and the Barbados International Surfing Championship is held at the Soup Bowl, Bathsheba, in early November.

Scuba diving to the reefs or the wrecks around the coast can be arranged with Jolly Roger Watersports at Sunset Crest, St James, Tel: 432 7090 and at Colony Club, St James, Tel: 422 2335; Dive Boat Safari, *Hilton Hotel*, Needham's Point, Tel: 427 4350; Underwater Barbados, *Sand Acres Hotel*, Maxwell, Tel: 428 9739; Exploresub, St Lawrence Gap, Tel: 435 6542; Willie's Watersports, Black Rock, St Michael, Tel: 425 1060; Shades of Blue at Coral Reef, St James, Tel: 422 3215; Blue Reef Watersports, *Royal Pavilion Hotel*, St James, Tel: 432 7090; The Dive Shop, Tel: 426 9947. These companies also offer diving courses, equipment rental and other facilities such as snorkelling. The first two also offer waterskiing, as do several other west coast operators. There is a recompression chamber at St Anne's Fort, Tel: 427 8819, or tell the operator if there is an emergency. For those who want to see the underwater world without getting wet, the Atlantis Submarine near the Careenage in Bridgetown (1st floor, Horizon House, McGregor Street), Tel: 436 8929, has day and night dives at US$58, children aged 4-12 half price. The tour starts with a short video and then you go by bus to the deep water port or join the launch at the Careenage. The boat takes about ten minutes to get to the submarine, sit at the back to be first on the sub, an advantage as then you can see out of the driver's window as well as out of your own porthole. Booking is necessary, check in half an hour before dive time, whole tour takes 1½ hours.

Sports

Cricket Lots of village cricket all over the island at weekends. A match here is nothing if not a social occasion. For information about the bigger matches at Kensington Oval phone the Barbados Cricket Association, Tel: 436 1397.

Horseracing At the Garrison on Saturdays for most of the year. Again, this is something of a social occasion. The Cockspur Gold Cup Race, held in March, features horses from neighbouring islands. For information on race meetings phone Barbados Turf Club, Tel: 426 3980.

Golf There are three courses, the best and most prestigious of which is Sandy Lane, 18 holes, Tel: 432 2946/432 1311/432 1145. *Rockley* has no clubhouse and is not highly rated, 9 holes, Tel: 435 7880. *Heywoods*, 9 holes, Tel: 422 4900. The Barbados Open Golf Championship is held in December.

Polo Barbados Polo Club near Holetown, St James, Tel: 432 1802.

Squash *Rockley Resort* has two courts, Tel: 435 7880, Barbados Squash Club, Tel: 427 7193, *Casuarina Hotel*, Tel: 428 3600, *Marine House* has three courts. **Tennis** The best courts are at *Paradise Beach Hotel*; they are also good at *Royal Pavilion* and *Glitter Bay*. *Paragon*, Tel: 427 2054, *Hilton*, Tel: 426 0200, *Rockley Resort*, Tel: 435 7880, *Sam Lord's*, Tel: 423 7350, *Crane Hotel*, Tel: 432 6220.

Motor racing on the circuit in St Philip. **Riding** Congo Road Riding Stables, Tel: 423 6180, one hour ride including lift to and from hotel is US$25, beginners or advanced; also Brighton Stables on west coast, Tel: 425 9381.

Running The Run Barbados Series is held in December and is comprised of a 10 km race and a marathon.

Walking The most beautiful part of the islands is the Scotland District on the east coast. There is also some fine country along the St Lucy coast in the north and on the southeast coast. Walking is straightforward. There is a good 1:50,000 map available from the Public Buildings in Bridgetown, from the museum, in the airport and from some bookstores in town. The Ordnance Survey, Southampton, UK, produces a map of Barbados in its tourist map series, 1:50,000 scale with 1:10,000 inset of Bridgetown. There is a particularly good route along the old railway track, from Bath to Bathsheba and on to Cattlewash. The National Trust, Tel: 426 2421, organizes walks at 0600 on a Sunday morning and sometimes at 1530 on Sunday afternoon. Details are usually printed in the *Visitor* magazine.

Festivals

Cropover is the main festival, with parades and calypso competitions over the weekend leading up to Kadooment Day (the first Monday in August), and calypso "tents" (mostly indoors though) for several weeks beforehand. The bands and costumes are a pale imitation of what Trinidad has to offer but even Trinidadians now take Barbadian calypso seriously. Some related activities take place in July.

The Holetown Festival in February, commemorating the first settlers' landing in February 1627, and the Oistins Fish Festival at Easter, celebrating the signing of the Charter of Barbados and the history of this fishing town, are much less elaborate. There are competitions and a big street party with music goes on until late at night. Many villages will also hold a "street fair" from time to time.

NIFCA, the National Independence Festival of Creative Arts, is a more serious affair, with plays, concerts and exhibitions in the weeks before Independence on 30 November.

Bridgetown

The capital, **Bridgetown**, is on the southwest corner of the island. The city itself covers a fairly small area. It is busy, and full of life. There are no really large buildings except the central bank. The suburbs sprawl most of the way along the south and west coasts, and quite a long way inland. It is houses and hotels almost all the way along the coastal strip between Speightstown in the north and the airport in the southeast, but many of the suburban areas are very pleasant, full of flowering trees and nineteenth century coral stone gingerbread villas. There are two interesting areas, downtown Bridgetown with Trafalgar Square on the north side of the Careenage and the historic area at Garrison.

Trafalgar Square has a statue of Lord Nelson, sculpted by Sir William Westmacott and predating its London equivalant by 27 years. It has recently

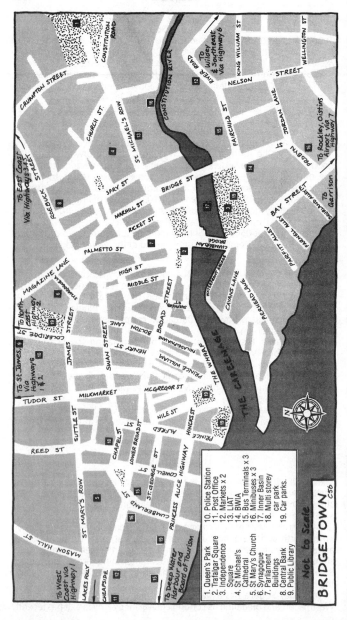

BRIDGETOWN C56

Not to Scale

1. Queen's Park
2. Trafalgar Square
3. Independence Square
4. St Michaels Cathedral
5. St Mary's Church
6. Synagogue
7. Parliament Buildings
8. Central Bank
9. Public Library
10. Police Station
11. Post Office
12. Markets x 2
13. LIAT
14. BWIA
15. Bus Terminals x 3
16. Minibuses x 3
17. Inner Basin
18. Multi storey car park
19. Car parks.

been the subject of some controversy as it was thought to link Barbados too closely with its colonial past. There were plans to remove it but instead Nelson was turned through 180° and now no longer looks down Broad Street, the main shopping area. There is a memorial to the West Indian Regiment and the fountain commemorates the piping of water to Bridgetown in 1861. To the north is the Parliament Building. Built in 1872, the legislature is an imposing grey building with red roof and green shutters. Built in gothic style, the clock tower is more reminiscent of a church. You can walk between the buildings (providing you are correctly dressed). Take the northeast exit out of Trafalgar Square along St Michaels Row to reach the eighteenth century **St Michael's Cathedral**. It has a fine set of inscriptions and a single-hand clock. The first building was consecrated in 1665 but destroyed by a hurricane in 1780. The present cathedral is long and broad, with a balcony. It has a fine vaulted ceiling and some tombs (1675) have been built into the porch. Completed in 1789, it suffered hurricane damage in 1831. If you contine west, you reach Queen's Park, a pleasant, restful park just outside the city centre. **Queen's Park House** is now a small theatre and art gallery. There is a small restaurant and bar, which does a good lunch and a buffet on Fridays.

The **Synagogue** is an early nineteenth century building on the site of a seventeenth century one, one of the two earliest in the western hemisphere. Built in the late 1660s by Jews fleeing Recife, Brazil, who heard that Oliver Cromwell had granted freedom of worship for Jews and gained permission to settle in Barbados. The tomb of Benjamin Massiah, the famous circumciser of 1782 lies on the left hand side of the graveyard, just inside the entrance. The original synagogue was destroyed in 1831, the present one was dedicated in 1838. Recently painstakingly restored, it is now used for religious services again although some work still needs to be done on the ceiling and cemetery. It is supported by only 16 families now.

The area south of James Street is good for street markets. A whole range of goods can be bought along Swan Street and Boulton Lane, good fruit and vegetables as well as leather goods. Street music is sometimes performed. This is in marked contrast to the large shopping malls and department stores on Broad Street. Here you will find a whole range of sophisticated shops catering for tourists (see **Shopping** below). More developments are planned along by the Careenage where old warehouses are being converted.

Further out, to the south of the Constitution river is **Ronald Tree House** on Tenth Avenue, Belleville (Tel: 426 2421), the headquarters of the Barbados National Trust. Nineteenth century suburban house with furniture, photographs and objets d'art. Useful source of information on historical and natural sites. The National Trust runs an Open House programme of visits to interesting private houses on Wednesday afternoons from January to April every year (entry US$5). National Trust properties admit children under 12 for half price and children under 6 free. The Duke of Edinburgh Award Scheme (Bridge House, Cavans Lane, Bridgetown, Tel: 436 9763) also arranges early Sunday morning walks to places of historical and natural interest.

The **Harry Bailey Observatory** in Clapham (Tel: 426 1317/422 2394) is open Friday nights 2030-2230. It is just south of the main airport road before the Barletts roundabout. A chance for northern visitors to look at the southern hemisphere stars.

The Garrison area

Cross the Careenage by the Charles Duncan O'Neale Bridge (one of the bus terminals and market area are just to the west) and follow Bay Street around the curve of Carlisle Bay. You will pass St Patrick's Cathedral (Roman Catholic), the main government offices with St Michael's Hospital behind it before reaching the historic Garrison area. From here you can visit **Fort Charles** on Needham Point (turn right at the Coca Cola plant). The Fort was the largest of the many which guarded the south and west coasts. It now forms part of the gardens of the *Hilton Hotel*. Only the ramparts remain but there are a number of 24 pounder cannons dating from 1824. There is a military cemetery here and the Mobil oil refinery was the site of the naval dockyard. Built in 1805, it was subsequently moved to English Harbour, Antigua. The buildings were then used as barracks before being destroyed in the 1831 hurricane.

Carry on up the hill to the **Garrison Historical Area**, which contains many interesting nineteenth century military buildings, grouped around the Garrison Savannah. There are numerous buildings surrounding the parade ground, now the 6 furlong race course. These were built out of brick brought as ballast on ships from England. They are built on traditional colonial lines, the design can be seen throughout the Caribbean but also in India. Painted red and white they now contain government offices. There are several memorials around the oval shaped race course, for instance in the southwest corner, the "awful" hurricane which killed 14 men and 1 married woman and caused the destruction of the barracks and hospital on 18 August 1831 and outside the Barbados Museum in the northeast corner to the men of the Royal York Rangers who fell in action against the French in Martinique, Les Saintes and Guadeloupe in the 1809/10 campaign. Across the road is St Anne's fort which is still used by the Barbados defence force. You cannot enter but look for the crenellated signal tower with its flag pole on top. It formed the high command of a chain of signal posts, the most complete of which is at Gun Hill (see below). The long, thin building is the old drill hall. **The Main Guard**, overlooking the savannah, has a nice old clock tower and a fine wide verandah. It has been turned into an information centre and houses exhibits about the West Indian Regiment. The Garrison Secretary of the Regiment is here. Outside is the **National Cannon Collection**, an impressive array of about 30 cannon, some are mounted on metal "garrison" gun carriages (replaced with wooden ones during action as they were prone to shatter). There are also a number of newer howitzers, dating from 1878.

The **Barbados Museum** (Tel: 427 0201/436 1956; Monday-Saturday 0900-1800, US$4) is housed in the old military prison on the northeast corner of the savannah. Based on a collection left by Rev N B Watson (late rector of St Lucy Parish), it is well set out through a series of 10 galleries. It displays natural history, local history (in search of *Bim*), a fine map gallery including the earliest map of Barbados by Richard Ligon (1657), colonial furniture (Plantation House Rooms), military history (including a reconstruction of a prisoners cell), prints and paintings which depict social life in the West Indies, decorative and domestic arts (17-19th century glass, china and silver), African artefacts, a children's gallery and one to house temporary exhibits. The museum shop has a good selection of craft items, books, prints, and cards. Library available for research purposes. The *Cafe Musée* under the trees in the museum courtyard is a delightful place for a drink or for lunch. The popular review *1627 and all that* takes place here in the evenings. Allow at least 1 hour.

Nearby there are stables for the race course. The Barbados Turf Club holds meetings on Saturdays during three seasons (January to March, May to October and November to December). The biggest one being the Cockspur Gold cup held in March. Races go clockwise. A good place to watch is from the Main Guard. At other times, it is used as a jogging course for people on weekday evenings.

Excursions

Being the most easterly island and extremely difficult to attack, there are no defensive forts on Barbados. Instead the great houses of the sugar growing plantocracy give the island its historic perspective and most of its tourist attractions. The island is not large but it is easy to get lost when driving. Rivers have carved deep gullies through the limestone base of the island. These are often full of wildlife and plants but make travelling around very confusing. It sometimes helps to remember that the island is divided into eleven parishes named after eleven saints. A good map is essential. The bus service is cheap and efficient and recommended even for families with small children.

The West Coast

The mass development of the west coast was carried out only recently. The beaches are easily eroded and can be covered with broken coral after storms. Pre-war, the area was regarded by the local Bajans as unhealthy. They preferred to go for their holidays to the east coast. Nowadays, the road north of Bridgetown on Highway 1 is wall to wall hotels. Highway 2a runs parallel inland and goes through the sugar cane heartland, with small villages and pleasant views.

Holetown today is a thoroughly modern town but was the place where the earliest settlers landed on 17 February 1627. The Holetown monument commemorates Captain John Powell claiming the island for England. Initially named Jamestown, it was renamed Holetown because of a tidal hole near the beach. It was quite heavily defended until after the Napoleonic Wars. Little trace of the forts can be seen now. Well worth visiting is **St James Church**. Originally built of wood in 1628, it was replaced by a stone structure in 1680. This building was extended 20 feet westward in 1874 when columns and arches were added and the nave roof raised. You can see the original baptismal font (1684) under the belfry and in the northern porch is the original bell of 1696. Many of the original settlers are buried here (although the oldest tombstone of William Balston who died in 1659 is in the Barbados Museum). Church documents dating to 1693 have been removed to the Department of Archives. It was beautifully restored between 1983-86.

On the beach at the back of the church is the post office and also the **Folkestone Marine Museum** and **Underwater Park**. Here you can snorkel in a large area enclosed by buoys. The reef is not in very good condition but there are some fish. The small museum is open Monday-Friday 1000-1700. Slide shows are held about every hour. Entrance B$1. Snorkelling equipment (eg mask and snorkel B$5) for hire as are glass bottomed boats which will take you over the reef to two small wrecks further down the coast opposite the *Gold Palm Hotel*. A diving platform about 100 yards offshore allows you to snorkel over the wrecks. Expect to pay B$20 pp (children B$10) but be prepared to bargain. There are toilets and a shower here.

The **Portvale Sugar Factory** (best in the crop season, February to May) and Sugar Machinery Museum inland has an exhibition on the story of sugar and its products. Open usually 0900-1600, Monday-Friday, Tel: 432 1100 to check.

Follow the coast road and glimpse the sea at Gibbes and Mullins Bays to reach **Speightstown**. An important trading port in the early days, when it was known as Little Bristol. Speightstown (pronounced Spikestong) is now the main shopping centre for the north of the island. There are several interesting old buildings and many two-storey shops with Georgian balconies and overhanging galleries (although sadly many have been knocked down by passing lorries). The Lions Club is in a seventeenth century structure, built very much on the lines of an English late mediaeval town house. In 1989, the Barbados National Trust launched an appeal for funds to help restore the town.

St Lucy

The road north of Speightstown is mercifully free of buildings and there is a good sandy beach on Six Men's Bay. Go through Littlegood Harbour and notice the boat building on the beach. The jetty you can see is at Harrison Point. You are now entering the almost unspoilt parish of St Lucy. Almost any of the roads off Highway 1b will take you to the North coast, at first green and lush around Stroud Point but becoming more desolate as you approach North Point. The northwest coast, being slightly sheltered from the Atlantic swells, has many sandy coves (for example Archers Bay). The cliffs are quiet and easy to walk. You may spot turtles swimming in the sea.

The **Animal Flower Cave** at **North Point** is a series of caverns at sea level which have been eroded by the sea. The animals are sea anemones. There are various "shapes" in the rock which are pointed out to you. The main cave can be closed due to dangerous seas, so Tel: 439-8797 around 0930 to enquire. Entrance B$3 (B$2 if you cannot see full cave). The floor of the cave is very stony and can be slippery. Following the rocky coast, turn into the semi-abandoned *North Point Surf Resort* (park outside the wall to avoid being charged for parking) where you can walk around the Spout, which has lots of blow holes and a small, rather dangerous beach. Good walks along the cliffs can be enjoyed, for instance from River Bay to Little Bay along the Antilles Flat, but beware as there is no shade and there are shooting parties during the season. If driving, several back roads go through the attractive communities of Spring Garden and St Clements. At Pie Corner you can rejoin the coast and visit Little Bay. This is particularly impressive during the winter months with the swell breaking over the coral outcrops; lots of blowholes. Note the completely circular hole on the northern edge of the Bay. At Paul's Point is a popular picnic area. If the ground looks wet park at the millwall by the Cove Stud Farm as it is easy to get bogged down. You will get at good view of Gay's Cove with its shingle beach (safe to swim in the pools at low tide) and beyond it the 240-feet high Pico Teneriffe, a large rock (almost in the shape of Barbados) on top of a steeply sloping cliff. The white cliffs are Oceanic rocks consisting of myriad tiny white shells. The whole of the coast to Bathsheba is visible and it is easy to see the erosion taking place in Corben's Bay. Indeed you get an excellent impression of the Scotland District, where the coral limestone has been eroded. The whole of this coast between North and Ragged Points has been zoned, no further development will be allowed along the seafront.

The Mount Gay Rum Distillery is reached off the road between the St Lucy church junction and Alexandra. There are tours Monday-Friday at 1100 and 1400. This makes an alternative to Cockspur's West Indian Rum Refinery (see **Entertainment**, page 583).

The Scotland District

Heading south, you get excellent views from Cherry Tree Hill. Just to the northwest is **St Nicholas Abbey** which is approached down a long and impressive avenue of mahogany trees. Dating from around 1660, it is almost certainly the oldest surviving house in Barbados and one of the oldest domestic buildings in the English-speaking Americas. Three storied, it has a façade with three ogee-shaped gables. It was never an abbey, some have supposed that the "St" and "Abbey" were added to impress, there being lots of "Halls" in the south of the island. Visitors are given an interesting tour of the ground floor and a fascinating film show in the stables behind the 400-year-old sand box tree. Narrated by Stephen Cave, the present owner and son of the film maker, its shows life on a sugar plantation in the 1930s. You will see the millwall in action and the many skilled workers from wheel wrights to coopers who made the plantation work. The importance of wind is emphasized. If the millwall stopped the whole plantation came to a halt as the cane would quickly dry out. The waste was used to fuel the boilers. There is a collection of toy buses and lorries in the stables.

Going back down the steep Cherry Tree Hill you come to the National Trust-owned **Morgan Lewis Mill**, a restored millwall with original machinery. You can climb to the top of it. Note the 100-foot tail, this enabled the operators to position the mill to maximize the effect of the wind. It is on a working farm. Open Monday-Friday 0800-1600, entrance B$2. On the flat savannah at the bottom of the hill is a cricket pitch, a pleasant place to watch the game at weekends.

The **Barbados Wildlife Reserve**, established with Canadian help in 1985, is set in four acres of mature mahogany off Highway 2. It is an excellent place to see lots of Barbados green monkeys close up. Most of the animals are not caged, you are warned to be careful as you wander around the shady paths as the monkeys can bite. They have a collection of the large red-footed Barbados tortoise. Also (non-Barbadian) toucans, parrots and tropical birds, hares, otters, opossums, agoutis, wallabies, porcupines, and iguanas. You can observe pelicans and there is a spectacled caiman (alligator) in the pond. The primate research centre helps to provide farmers with advice on how to control the green monkeys who are regarded as a pest. The animals are fed near it at about 1600. Café and shop. Open daily 1000-1700. Admission B$10, children half price. Tel: 422-8826. Can be reached by bus from Bridgetown, Holetown, Speightstown or Bathsheba. The centre has also developed a nature trail in the neighbouring Grenade Hall Forest, ask for further details.

Farley Hill House, St Peter (Tel: 422 3555), is a 19th century fire-damaged plantation house; a spectacular ruin on the other side of the road from the Wildlife Reserve, set in a pleasant park with views over the

Scotland District. There is a large number of imported and native tree species planted over 30 acres of woodland. Open daily 0830-1800. US$1 per vehicle.

The Atlantic Parishes

The five-mile East Coast Road, opened by Queen Elizabeth on 15 February 1966 affords fine views. From Bellepleine, where the railway ended, it skirts Walker's Savannah to the coast at Long Pond and heads southeast to Benab, where there is the Barclays Park, a good place to stop for a picnic under the shady casaurina trees. It continues through Cattlewash, so named because Bajans brought their animals here to wash them in the sea, to Bathsheba.

Bathsheba has an excellent surfing beach. Guarded by two rows of giant boulders, the bay seems to be almost white as the surf trails out behind the Atlantic rollers. Surfing championships are often held here. A railway was built before the war between Bridgetown and Bathsheba. Originally conceived as going to Speightstown, it actually went up the east coast to St Andrews. The railway suffered from mismanagment and underfunding so that the 37 miles of track was in places in very bad condition. The crew would sprinkle sand on the track, the first class passengers remained seated, the second class walked and the third class pushed. Above the bay at Hillcrest (excellent view) are the **Andromeda Gardens**. Owned by the Barbados National Trust, the gardens contain plants from all over Barbados as well as species from other parts of the world. There are many varieties of orchid, hibiscus and flowering trees. Open every day. Admission B$8. The *Atlantis Hotel* is a good place for lunch especially on Sunday (1300 sharp) when an excellent buffet meal containing several Bajan dishes is served. Almost an institution and extremely popular with Bajans, so book ahead.

From Bathsheba you can head inland to **Cotton Tower signal station** (also National Trust owned but not so interesting as Gun Hill). Then head south to Wilson Hill where you find Mount Tabor Church and **Villa Nova**, another plantation Great House (1834), which has furniture made of Barbadian mahogany and beautiful gardens. It is worth a visit not least as it was owned by the former British Prime Minister, Sir Anthony Eden (open Monday-Friday, 0900-1600, entrance B$6, children B$3). You can continue from here via Hotersal along the scenic Hackleton's Cliffs (allegedly named after Hackleton who committed suicide by riding his horse at full gallop over the cliff) to Pothouse, where **St John's Church** stands with excellent views over Scotland. Built in 1660 it was another victim of the great hurricane of 1835. There is an interesting pulpit made from six different kinds of wood. You will also find the curious grave of Fernando Paleologus "descendant of ye imperial line of ye last Christian emperors of Greece". The full story is in Leigh Fermor's *The Traveller's Tree*.

At the satellite tracking station turn off to **Bath**. Here you will find a safe beach, popular with Barbadians and a recreation park for children. It makes a good spot for a beach barbecue and a swim.

Codrington College is one of the most famous landmarks on the island and can be seen from Highway 4b down an avenue of Cabbage Palm trees. It is steeped in history as the first Codrington landed in Barbados in 1628. His son acted as Governor for three years but was dismissed for liberal views. Instead he stood for parliament and was elected speaker for nine years. He was involved in several wars against the French and became probably the wealthiest man in the West Indies. The third Codrington succeeded his father as Governor-General of the Leeward islands, attempted to stamp out the considerable corruption of the time and distinguished himself in campaigns (especially in taking St Kitts). He died in 1710, a batchelor aged 42, and left his Barbadian properties to the Society for the Propagation of the Gospel in Foreign Parts. It was not until 1830 that Codrington College, where candidates could study for the Anglican priesthood, was established. From 1875 to 1955 it was associated with Durham University, England. Apart from its beautiful grounds with a fine avenue of Royal Palms, a huge lily pond (flowers close up in the middle of the day) and impressive façade, there is a chapel containing a plaque to Sir Christopher Codrington and a library. There are plans to develop it as a conference centre. You can follow the track which drops down 360 feet to the sea at the beautiful Consett Bay. You can take the Sargeant Street bus as far as Codrington College, then walk 7 miles back along the Atlantic Coast to Bathsheba.

At **Ragged Point** is the automatic East Point lighthouse standing among the ruined houses of the former lighthouse keepers. There are good views north towards Consett Point, the small Culpepper island, and the south coast. Note the erosion to the 80-foot cliffs caused by the Atlantic sweeping into the coves.

The Centre

Northeast of Holetown and reached from St Simon's Church are **Turners Hall Woods**, a good vantage point. Some think that the wood would have been very similar to the one covering the island before the English arrived. You can walk over the steep paths here and see many species, ranging from the sandbox tree to Jack-in-the-box and the 100-foot locust trees supported by massive buttresses.

On Highway 2, take the Melvin Hill road just after the agricultural station and follow the signs to the **Flower Forest**, a 50-acre, landscaped plantation, opened in 1983 with beautifully laid out gardens. Dropping downhill, the well-maintained paths afford excellent views over the valley to the east coast. To the west you can see Mount Hillaby, at 1,116 feet the island's highest point. It too contains species not only from Barbados but also from all over the world, they are beautifully arranged with plenty of colour all year round. There is a *Best of Barbados* shop, cafeteria and toilets. Good information sheet. Open daily 0900-1700, entrance B$10, Tel: 433 8152.

Close by and to the south on Highway 2 is **Welchman Hall Gully**, a fascinating walk through one of the deep ravines so characteristic of this part of Barbados. You are in the middle of the limestone cap which covers much of the centre of the island at a depth of about 300 feet. There is a small car park opposite the entrance (despite the sign to the contrary). Maintained by the National Trust, a good path leads for about half a mile through six sections, each with a slightly different theme. The first section has a devil tree, a stand of bamboo and a judas tree. Next you will go through jungle, lots of creepers, the "pop-a-gun" tree and bearded fig clinging to the cliff (note the stalactites and stalagmites); a section devoted to palms and ferns: golden, silver, macarthur and cohune palms, nutmegs and wild chestnuts; to open areas with tall leafy mahogany trees, rock balsam and mango trees. At the end of the walk are ponds with lots of frogs and toads. Best of all though is the wonderful view to the coast. On the left are some steps leading to a gazebo, at the same level as the tops of the cabbage palms. Open daily, 0900-1700, B$5, children B$2.50.

Harrison Cave nearby has an impressive visitor's centre which has a restaurant (fair), shop and a small display of local geology and Amerindian artefacts. You are taken into the cave on an electric "train". The visit takes about twenty minutes and you will see some superbly-lit stalactites and stalagmites, waterfalls and large underground lakes. There is a guide to point out the interesting formations and two stops for photo-opportunities. Interesting as it is, it is all rather overdone, you even have to wear hard hats and serviettes on your head despite claims that the caves are totally stable. Open daily 0900-1600, admission B$15, children half price, Tel: 438 6640.

If you take Highway 2 heading to Bridgetown you will pass Jack-in-the-Box gully, part of the same complex of Welchman Hall Gully and Harrison Cave. Coles Cave (an "undeveloped" cave nearby, which can easily be explored with a waterproof torch or flashlight) lies at its north end.

At **Gun Hill** is a fully restored signal tower. The approach is by Fusilier road and you will pass the Lion carved by British soldiers in 1868. The road was built by Royal Scot Fusiliers between September 1862 and February 1863 when they were stationed at Gun Hill to avoid yellow fever. The signal station itself had its origins in the slave uprising of 1816. It was decided that a military presence would be maintained outside Bridgetown in case of further slave uprisings. The chain of six signal stations was intended to give very rapid communications with the rest of the island. The hexagonal tower had two small barrack rooms attached and would have been surrounded by a pallisade. They quickly lost importance as military installations but provided useful information about shipping movements. Informative guides will explain the workings of the signal station and point out interesting features of the surrounding countryside. Entrance B$5 (children B$2.50), guide book B$2.

The South Coast

The area around Six Cross Roads was where the Easter Rebellion of 1816 took place, an uprising by slaves led by Washington Franklin who thought (incorrectly) that William Wilberforce had introduced a bill in the English parliament granting slaves their freedom. It was thought by the slaves that the Barbados plantation owners were denying them this freedom. Despite destroying a large acreage of cane fields, no owners or their families were killed and the uprising was quickly crushed. You can visit two of the great houses. Turn north at Six Cross Roads for **Sunbury Plantation**. Some three hundred years old, the house is elegantly furnished in Georgian style, much of it with mahogany furniture, and you can roam all over it as, unusually, there is access to the upstairs private rooms. In the cellars, you can see the domestic quarters. There is a good collection of carriages. Open 1030-1630 every day. There is a restaurant in the courtyard.

Take the road to Harrow and Bushy Park to reach **Oughterson Plantation House** and the **Barbados Zoo Park**. Although not as extensive as Sunbury, the entrance to the Wildlife Park takes you through the ground floor of the house which is quite interesting. There is a self-guided nature trail. The zoo is very small but has expanded from a bird garden and more animals have slowly been added. Vikki, a small monkey, is a great favourite with children as she will stroke their hands. You are given bread and encouraged to feed the ducks.

Sam Lord's Castle on the southeast coast is the site of the *Marriott Hotel*.

It is high on the list of tourist attractions because of the reputation of Sam Lord who reputedly lured ships onto to Cobbler's Reef where they were shipwrecked. There is supposed to be a tunnel from the beach to the castle's cellars to facilitate his operation. The proceeds made him a wealthy man although the castle was supposed to have been financed from his marriage to a wealthy heiress. The castle is not particularly old or castle-like, being in fact a regency building. Unfortunately the rooms are poorly lit making it difficult to appreciate the fine mahogany furniture or the paintings. Note the superb staircase, you are not allowed upstairs. Wander down to the cove where there is a good example of a turtlecrawl, a salt water pond enclosed by a wall. Here turtles were kept alive until wanted for the kitchen. Today the *Marriott hotel*, in conjunction with the Barbados Wildlife park, keeps a few hawksbill turtles, a shark and a congor eel. There is a B$7 entrance charge (children free) even though the hotel reception forms part of the two rooms open to the public.

Crane Bay, southwest of Sam Lord's Castle, is worth a detour. It is a pleasant cove overlooked by 80-foot cliffs.

Information for Visitors

Documents
Visitors from North America, Western Europe, Venezuela, Colombia, and Brazil need a passport but no visas. Visitors from most other countries are usually granted a short stay on arrival, but holders of passports of East European countries, India, Pakistan, and South Africa should be particularly careful to obtain a Barbados visa in advance. Officially, you must have a ticket back to your country of origin as well as an onward ticket to be allowed in.

State the maximum period you intend to stay on arrival. Overstaying is not recommended if you wish to re-enter Barbados at a later date. Extending the period of stay is possible at the Immigration Office on the Wharf in Bridgetown but costs US$12.50 and is fairly time consuming. When visiting the Immigration Office, which is open from 0830-1630, you will need to take your passport and return ticket.

You will need an accommodation address on arrival, they do not check your reservation but if you say you do not know where you will be staying, you will be sent to the back of the queue and 'helped' to select a hotel (which may be more expensive than you wanted) at least for one night.

Work permits are extremely difficult to obtain and the regulations are strictly enforced.

How To Get There
By Air From North America BWIA and American Airlines fly from New York and Miami daily; BWIA and Air Canada fly from Toronto and Air Canada from Montreal. From Europe British Airways and BWIA have several flights a week from London and BWIA has once-weekly flights from Cologne/Bonn, Frankfurt, Munich, Stockholm and Zurich. From South America Liat and Aeropostal fly from Caracas and Liat daily from Georgetown, Guyana. Connections with Caribbean islands are good, from Antigua (Liat, British Airways, BWIA), Dominica (Liat), Fort-de-France, Martinique (Liat, Air Martinique), Grenada (BWIA, Liat), Kingston and Montego Bay, Jamaica (BWIA), Pointe-à-Pitre, Guadeloupe (Liat), Port of Spain, Trinidad (BWIA, Liat, British Airways), St Croix, USVI (BWIA), St Lucia (BWIA, Liat, British Airways), St Maarten (Liat), St Vincent (Liat), San Juan, Puerto Rico (Liat, BWIA, American Airlines), Tobago (Liat) and Tortola, BVI (Liat). Air tickets bought in Barbados, and tickets bought elsewhere for journeys starting in Barbados, have a 20% tax added. It is usually worth organizing ticketing at the start of your journey so that Barbados appears as a stopover rather than as the origin for any side trips you make. Note that flights to Barbados are heavily booked at Christmas and for Cropover.

There is a departure tax of B$25, not payable if your stay is for less than 24 hours.

By Sea Barbados is not well served by

small inter-island schooners. But the *Stella S 2* which travels to St Lucia and Dominica every two weeks takes passengers. Information and tickets from the shipping agents, Eric Hassell & Son, 2nd floor, Citibank building, Bridgetown (Tel: 436 6102). The fare is rather less than the air fare. The departure tax from the port is US$2. If you buy a one-way ticket, you will need to show passport and onward ticket when paying for your passage. The trip to St Lucia is overnight (leaving Sunday afternoon) and is quite dramatic, especially when there is a moon. Passengers sleeping on deck will have an excellent view of the sun rising behind the Pitons. You may be able to get a passage to another island on a yacht, ask at the harbour or at the *Boatyard*.

Windward Lines Limited based in Trinidad, run a weekly passenger/car/cargo ferry service: Trinidad - Venezuela - St Vincent - Barbados - St Lucia - Barbados - St Vincent - Trinidad. Arriving Friday 1900 from Tinidad, departing 2300, coming back from St Lucia on Sunday at 1900, departing 2200. Information from United Caribbean Shipping Agencies, Suite 106, 86B Independence Square, Port of Spain, Trinidad, Tel: 625-6328, Fax: 624-6865.

There are several companies running mini-cruises based on Barbados. Caribbean Safari Tours (Tel: 427 5100, Fax: 429 5446), organize day trips to St Lucia, Dominica, Grenada, Martinique and the Grenadines; they also do two and three night packages to these islands and to Trinidad, Tobago, St Vincent and Caracas. Some of these are quite competitively priced.

Geest Lines run a fortnightly service for bananas from Britain (Barry Port) to the Windwards via Barbados. This is a cheap and efficient method of freighting bulky items. There is also room for a few luxury passengers, but the fare is over £2,000, and booking is up to 18 months in advance. Thos and Jas Harrison Ltd's MV *Author* also calls at Bridgetown on its 6-week round trip from Liverpool; details are given in **Introduction and Hints**, Travel to and in the Caribbean—By Sea.

Airport Information

The airport is modern and well equipped. Clearing immigration can be a problem and it can take an hour to clear a 747. If three 747s arrive together expect delays of up to three hours. There is a Liat connection desk before immigration. There is a Tourist Board office, Barbados National Bank (very slow), (bureau de change in the arrivals and departure areas is open from 0800-2200), a post office, car hire agencies and quite a wide range of shops including an Inbound Duty Free Shop. *The Voyager* restaurant is fairly expensive. Taxis stop just outside customs, and there is a bus stop just across the car park, with buses running along the south coast to Bridgetown, or (over the road) to the *Crane* and *Sam Lord's Castle*. But you may have a long wait for a bus, and they often pass full in the rush hour.

Airlines

The Liat office is at St Michael's Plaza, St Michael's Row (Tel: 436 6224). BWIA (Tel: 426 2111); British Airways (Tel: 436 6413), Aeropostal (Tel: 427 7781) are all on Fairchild Street. American (Tel: 428 4170) and Cubana (Tel: 428 0060) have offices at the airport.

Helicopters

For those who want to make a lot of noise buzzing round the island, Bajan Helicopters do tours from US$70 per person. The heliport is near the deep water harbour at Bridgetown, Tel: 431 0069.

Road Transport

The island is fairly small (just over 21 miles from north to south) but it can take a surprisingly long time to travel from A to B as the rural roads are narrow and winding. Note that a new highway has been built from the airport to a point between Brighton and Prospect, north of Bridgetown. This road (called the ABC, or industrial access highway) skirts the eastern edge of the capital, giving access by various roads into the city.

Buses are cheap and frequent, but also crowded and unreliable. There is a flat fare of B$1.50 which will take you anywhere on the island. Around Bridgetown, there are plenty of small yellow minibuses; elsewhere, the big blue buses belong to the Transport Board. Almost all the routes radiate in and out of Bridgetown, so cross-country journeys are time-consuming if you are staying outside the city centre. The main Fairchild Street bus terminal, serving the south coast, is clean and modern. Other terminals at Lower Green and Princess Alice Highway serve the north and centre of the island. During the rush hour, all these terminals are chaotic, particularly during school term. Don't, whatever you do, try to get a bus to the airport (Route 12 to *Sam Lord's Castle*) if you have a plane to catch as this route is notorious. On most routes, the last bus leaves at midnight and the first bus at 0500.

However, travelling by bus can be fun. There are some circuits which work quite well; for example:

1. Any south coast bus to Oistins, then cross country College Savannah bus to the east coast, then direct bus back to Bridgetown.

2. Any west coast bus to Speightstown, then bus back to Bathsheba on the east coast, then direct bus back to Bridgetown. Out of town bus stops are marked simply 'To City' or 'Out of City'.

Bus Tours L E Williams (Tel: 427 1043), Bartic tours (Tel: 428 5980), Sunflower Tours (Tel: 429 8941), International Tour Services (Tel: 428 4803) and Blue Line (Tel: 423 9268) do round-the-island tours for US$25-40, including entrance fees to sites visited. Longer tours generally include lunch at the *Atlantic Hotel* in Bathsheba.

Taxis are expensive. There are plenty at the airport, the main hotels, and in Bridgetown. There are standard fares (Airport to Bridgetown US$15, or to Worthing US$12 for example). These are displayed just outside "arrivals" at the airport, and are also listed in the *Visitor* and the *Sunseeker*. Up to five people can travel for one fare. You may have to bargain hard for tours by taxi but always agree a fare in advance.

Motoring

Car Hire is efficient and generally reliable. Costs range upwards from B$120 per day for an open Mini Moke (not recommended in the rainy season). Small cars are often cheaper. Weekly rates work out lower, eg Sunny Isle Motors, Dayton, Worthing, Tel: 435 7979, car hire B$100/day or B$410/week, collision damage waiver B$60. Stoutes Car Rentals (Tel: 435 4456/7, Fax: 435 4435) are particularly helpful, and will arrange to meet you at the airport if you telephone in advance. L E Williams (Tel: 427 1043) has slightly lower rates for some vehicles. Other companies are listed in the Yellow Pages. There are often discounts available and tourist magazines frequently contain 10% vouchers.

It is also possible to hire a light

motorcycle or a **bicycle**. Fun Seekers, Rockley Main Road, Tel: 435 8206, have motor scooters B$61/day, B$155/week, bicycles B$19/day, B$73/week.

Drivers need a visitor's driving permit from Hastings, Worthing, or Holetown police stations (cost US$5). You will need this even if you have an International Driving Licence. Petrol costs B$1.27 per litre.

VIP Limo Services (Tel: 429 4617) hire a vehicle with driver for a whole-day tour at a cost of US$150 for up to 4 persons.

Where To Stay

There are over 175 hotels, although the Board of Tourism lists only 86 hotels and guest houses, and 50 apartment complexes. Rates in the larger hotels almost double in the peak season, which is from mid December to mid April. A 5% government tax and 10% service charge are generally added to the published rates and these rates are often quoted in US currency, which can be a pitfall for the unwary. The Barbados Hotel Association introduced a new charge in 1990, ranging from B$1 to B$4 per room per night. Rates quoted here are summer 1992.

Most of the accommodation offered is very pleasant to stay in, if not particularly cheap.

Super Luxury Most of these are on the west coast. *Sandy Lane*, US$220-540d EP summer rate, is Trust House Forte, extensively renovated in 1991 and quite nice of its type. Has a golf course. Watch out for extras on top of the astronomical room rate, golf, honeymoon packages available (Tel: 432-1311, Fax: 432 2954). *Glitter Bay*, US$175-295 EP (Tel: 422 4111, Fax: 422 3940), and *Royal Pavilion*, US$205-300d EP (Tel: 422 4444, Fax: 422 1685), are newer and just as smart, next to each other and under the same management. One is "Spanish Colonial Style", the other a pink palace. Perhaps better value to stay elsewhere and visit for a drink or afternoon tea. But well worth looking at, the guests as spectacular in some cases as the (faultless) interior design and landscaping. *Coral Reef Club*, St James (Tel: 422 2372, Fax: 422 1776), US$104-214d EP, member of Elegant Resorts of Barbados and Prestige Hotels, London, very highly regarded; also in St James, *Sandpiper Inn*. Tel: 422 2251, US$126-289d EP. Also on the west coast, good but not as luxurious, *Kings Beach Hotel*, US$120-140d EP (Tel: 422 1690, or 0932 849 462 in the UK or 800 223

1588 in the USA), at Mullins Bay, facilities for children and the handicapped.

Convenient for Bridgetown *Hilton*, US$137-266d EP, good location on a nice beach with gentle surf, good pool, concrete structure showing its age, restaurant not particularly recommended (Tel: 426 0200, Fax: 436 8946); *Grand Barbados*, US$100-300d EP (Tel: 426 0890, Fax: 436 9823); *Cunard Paradise Beach* (Tel: 424 0888, Fax: 424 0889). *Paradise Beach* has a better setting than the other two. *Hilton* does a good buffet lunch. *Blue Horizon*, Rockley, large hotel with pool, bar, restaurant, 100 yards from beach across main road, US$50-60d EP with kitchenette, rates double in winter, 10 minutes from Bridgetown.

Near the Airport *Shonlan Guest House* (US$30d, Tel: 428 0039) very mixed reports, noisy, nowhere near a beach, but only a mile from the terminal, although the taxi fare makes it no cheaper than a guest house further away. *Crane Beach*, US$110-200d EP, fairly near the airport, but definitely a taxi ride away. A spectacular cliff top setting, good beach, and good pool. Luxury prices and usually fairly quiet with only 18 rooms, but they are planning an extra 250 units (Tel: 423 6220).

Good Value Recommended are *Sandridge*, 1 mile from Speightstown, good-sized family apartments with cooking facilities, north-facing balconies overlook pool, friendly staff and management, good value barbecue evenings, excellent for families, US$55-80 EP, Tel: 422 2361. *Woodville Apartments*, Worthing, Tel: 435 6694, US$43-56 for studio apartment, US$60 1-bedroom, US$85 2-bedroom, summer rates. *Worthing Court Apartment Hotel*, Worthing, Tel: 435 7910, Fax: 435 7374, studios or one-bedroom connecting apartments, US$80-100d winter, US$55- 75d summer and *Casuarina*, Dover, US$75-160d, Tel: 428 3600. *Pegwell Inn*, US$40d, Oistins (Tel: 428 6150). Good for shops and airport buses, not brilliant for beaches. *Bona Vista*, on a side road off Golf Club Road, US$15s, US$30d, recommended, Tel: 435 6680. *Summer Home/ Place on Sea*, run by George de Mattos, US$20s, US$30d winter rate, Rydal Water, Worthing (Tel: 435 7424), rooms basic but clean, 2 rooms with cooking facilities available, very pleasant and good value, but both always seem to be booked up well in advance. Ring ahead. *Rydal Waters Guest House* in Worthing, US$20s, US$30d winter rate, breakfast US$4 extra, payment in cash preferred, recommended, pleasant beach (Tel: 435 7433). *Shells Guest House*, First Avenue, Worthing, Tel: 435 7253, US$18 with breakfast, excellent food in restaurant. *The Nook Apartments*, Dayrells Road in Rockley has 4 excellent 2-bedroom apartments for US$52-62 winter, with pool, maid service, clean, secure, convenient for shops and restaurants, highly recommended, discounts for airline staff and Caricom residents (Tel: 436 6494 0800-1600 Monday-Friday, 428 1033 evenings and weekends, Mr Harold Clarke). *Tree Haven*, Rockley, a short bus ride from the centre of town, US$35 low season, US$50 high season, excellent apartment opposite the beach, very clean, helpful and friendly owner. *Fred La Rose Bonanza*, Dover, from US$47 for a studio to US$67d (for 2 bedrooms (winter), US$21-43 in summer, helpful, quite convenient but not too clean, Tel: 428 9097. There are several other cheap places to stay in this area, all within walking distance of each other. *Woodbine*, B$45d summer rate, very pleasant, hot shower, use of kitchen, recommended but a short walk away from the beach (Tel: 427 7627 or 428 7356). Much more likely to have space available. All these are well served by the south coast bus routes. *Romans Beach Apartments*, Enterprise, studio US$45-60 winter rate, US$25-45 summer, Tel: 428 7635, friendly, comfortable. *Travellers Palm*, 265 Palm Ave, Sunset Crest, St James (Tel: 432 6666/7722), US$50-65 for 1-bedroom apartment with kitchen, winter rate, US$35 summer, roomy apartments, pool, 10 minutes walk to the beach, close to the underwater sea park. *Tower Hotel* in Paradise Village, Black Rock, north of Bridgetown on Princess Alice Highway, US$50-60 for 1-bedroom apartment, winter rate, US$30-40 summer, a/c, fridge, very pleasant (Tel: 424 3256).

Away from the main tourist areas *Atlantis*, Bathsheba, US$50-60d AP, Tel: 433 9445, and *Kingsley Club*, US$84d winter rate, Tel: 433 9422, both on the east coast, with a spectacular setting. Both do good food, pleasant, family-run hotels. *Edgewater Hotel*, Bathsheba, Tel/Fax: 433 9902, US$50-200 EP, pool overlooking sea, quiet and out of the way, popular with Venezuelans. *Sam Lord's Castle*, Marriott's fun-factory,

US$150-250d EP (Tel: 423 7350, Fax: 423 5918). Lots of new stuff round a cliff-top plantation house with some fairly spurious pirate legends attached. Good Sunday buffet, three swimming pools, and outdoor bars where they serve the drinks in plastic cups. *Ocean View Hotel*, south coast, US$95-175d EP winter rate, very old fashioned, with mahogany furniture and a dining terrace overlooking the sea but no beach (Tel: 427 7821). Mediocre food.

Villa Rental agents and property managers include Realtors Limited, Riverside House, River Road, St Michael, Tel: 426 4900, Fax: 426 6419; Bajan Services Ltd, Seascape Cottage, Gibbs, St Peter, Tel: 422 2618, Fax: 422 5366. Weekly rates for a small villa on the beach start at US$800 in the summer but can be twice the price in the winter, plus 8% tax.

Youth Hostel

Dumfries, run by the National Children's Home, Henry's Lane, Lower Collymore Rock, St Michael, PO Box 83 BH, Tel: 426 1449/4368, convenient for Bridgetown and the beach, parties of 4 or more welcome, US$7.50 pp per night, linen and towels extra, security deposit required (refundable).

Where To Eat

Barbados has a very wide range of places to eat. There is a good listing in the *Visitor*. Good places include:

Low prices fast food from Chefette chain, Pizza House chain or Del's chain. *Chicken Barn*, Broad Street and Rockley (big portions if you're hungry), *China Garden* (Bay Street). For those who like that sort of thing there are several *Kentucky Fried Chickens* and a *MacDonalds* in Rockley. In St Lawrence Gap is a *Pizza Hut* and the *Duke of Edinburgh Pub*. In Worthing the *Roti Hut* is cheap. *Granny's* in Oistins is more traditional and good value. *The Hotel School* in Marine House (Tel: 427 5420) does an excellent lunch at certain times of year, and a smarter evening meal on Tuesdays. Also drinks and snacks in the evening when they are running courses for bar staff. You could also try the canteens in the Light and Power Company on Bay Street and at Spring Gardens which are open to the public and do a huge traditional lunch. Good reports about *Kingsley Inn*, Cattlewash and *Little Edge*, Bathsheba (Tel: 433 9900), for breakfast and lunch. *Mangoes*, Holetown, on balcony overlooking beach, view spoilt by enormous satellite dish, better bet is small beach bar next door, delicious flying fish and good club sandwiches. There is a good cheap café in Mall 34, just behind Atlantis Submarine office in Bridgetown. The *Pirate's Bar* at the Animal Flower Caves has the best value coke on the island, B\$1.50 for ½ litre. Most sightseeing attractions have some kind of food available, eg Harrison Cave, fair snacks.

Middle price range *Waterfront Café* on the Careenage, interesting food, plenty to look at and a good social centre in the evenings. *The Quayside Centre* in Worthing is quite fun if you can't agree on what you want to eat: half a dozen counters with Caribbean, Italian, Chinese, Middle Eastern, etc, food arranged around a common eating area. There are some good beach bars, which do light meals and sometimes have a lively atmosphere; *Carib Beach Bar* at Worthing has inexpensive meals and drinks, barbecue once a week; even better is the Friday night barbecue at *Stowaways Beach Bar* at the Sheringham Hotel in Maxwell; *Sandy Banks* in Rockley; *The Boatyard* in Bay Street; *Coach House* and *Bamboo Beach Bar* in St James. These sometimes have live bands in the evenings. *The Ship/Captain's Carvery*, St Lawrence, has a good lunchtime buffet; in the evening there is usually a big crowd in the bar and often a live band. *Boomers* in St Lawrence Gap has quite good fast-food type dishes in a restaurant-type setting. *Sam's Lantern* and the *Pot and Barrel*, good inexpensive pizzas, just outside *Sam Lord's Castle* are worth a try. *Barclays Park Beach Bar* on the east coast does light meals (closed after 1900).

More expensive but worth it *The Treasure Beach Hotel* has the best food on the island, but at US\$50 a head. *Kokos* (Tel: 424 4557) has an interesting menu and a waterfront setting on the west coast. They will also do a good vegetarian meal if they have advance warning. *Brown Sugar* (Tel: 426 7684), Aquatic Gap, Bay Street, St Michael, buffet lunch B\$22, dinner, regional specialities, is good. So is *Reid's* (Tel: 432 7623) on the west coast (but they are quite capable of producing an already-opened bottle of wine at the table). *Josef's* (Tel: 435 6541/428 3379) on St Lawrence Gap, small, delightful, is well used by

Barbadians, you need to book well ahead, arrive early and have pre-dinner drinks on the lawn with the sea lapping the wall a few feet below you. *Pisces* (Tel: 428 6558), much larger, also on St Lawrence Gap, has some excellent and original fish dishes, and a perfect waterfront setting; *David's*, also on waterfront, in Worthing, very good with better service and friendlier. Another fish restaurant is *Fisherman's Wharf* (Tel: 436 7788), upstairs, on the Careenage in Bridgetown. *Da Luciano's* (Tel: 427 5518) is a good Italian restaurant, but avoid *Luigi's* which is very run down and serves Americanized Italian food at fancy prices. *The Taj* in Bay Street is a good Indian restaurant and not too expensive. Also good: *La Cage aux Folles*, St James; *Carambola*, St James; *Schooner* and *Golden Shell* in Grand Barbados.

Generally, eating out in Barbados is not cheap. There are some good places, but even the best are apt to fall down over some detail like the coffee, which can be annoying after an expensive meal.

Buffets are good value. Unlimited food for a fixed price, usually lunchtime only, certain days only. Try *Hilton, Colony Club* (buffet by the beach on Sunday B\$25) or *Sam Lord's*. *Atlantis Hotel* in Bathsheba has an enormous Sunday buffet, which is the place to try for traditional Barbadian cooking at its best (filling). Get up early and do a National Trust Sunday morning walk to work up an appetite.

Food And Drink

Fresh fish is excellent. The main fish season is December to May, when there is less risk of stormy weather at sea. Flying fish are a speciality and the national emblem, two or three to a plate. Dolphin (dorado, not a mammal in spite of its name) and kingfish are larger *steak-fish*. Snapper is excellent. *Sea eggs* are the roe of the white sea urchin, and are delicious but not often available. Fresh fish is sold at the fish markets in Oistins, Bridgetown and elsewhere in the late afternoon and evening, when the fishermen come in with their catch.

Cou-cou is a filling starchy dish made from breadfruit or corn meal. *Jug-jug* is a Christmas speciality made from guinea corn and supposedly descended from the haggis of the poor white settlers. Pudding and souse is a huge dish of pickled breadfruit, black pudding, and pork.

Barbados rum is probably the best in

the English-speaking Caribbean. It is worth paying a bit extra for a good brand such as VSOP or Old Gold, or for Sugar Cane Brandy, unless you are about to drown it in Coca Cola, in which case anything will do. *Falernum* is sweet, slightly alcoholic, with a hint of vanilla. *Corn and oil* is rum and falernum. *Mauby* is bitter, and made from tree bark. It can be refreshing. *Sorrel* is a bright red Christmas drink made with hibiscus sepals and spices; it is very good with white rum. Water is of excellent quality, it comes from inland springs.

Entertainment

Nightclubs There are quite a selection. Most charge US$10 for entry. It's worth phoning in advance to find out what is on offer. There are live bands on certain nights in some clubs, and on other nights drinks may be included in the cover charge. Most do not get lively until almost midnight, and close around 0400. Some have a complicated set of dress codes or admission rules, which is another reason for phoning ahead.

After Dark, St Lawrence Gap, recently redecorated, huge selection at the bar, very lively. *Pier 29* on Cavans Lane in Bridgetown is another good one but lacks adequate fire exits. *The Warehouse*, across the road has reopened after a fire and has a pleasant open air balcony to cool off. Others are *Harbour Lights* (lots of tourists and expats, open air on the beach, local and disco music) and *Septembers* on Bay Street (lots of Barbadians). *The Boatyard* is the sailor's pub in front of the anchorage at Carlisle Bay, Bay Street. *The Ship Inn* in St Lawrence has a big outdoor area and is often packed, especially at weekends and when there is a live band. The beach bars can be lively (see listings above), but pick your night. Cheap bars in St Lawrence Gap are *Harry's* and *Colonnade*. At *Shakey's Pizza Parlour* in Rockley they have a Karaoke sing-along machine nightly from 2100.

Dances For something less glossy and more Bajan, it might be worth trying one of the dances which are advertized in the *Nation* newspaper on Fridays. People hire a dance hall, charge admission (usually Bds$5), provide a disco, and keep the profits. There are very few foreigners, but the atmosphere is friendly, and the drinks a lot cheaper than in the smarter nightclubs. Unfortunately, there have been a few fights at 'Dub' fêtes and they are no longer as relaxed as they were.

Baxters Road in Bridgetown is another place to try. The one-roomed, ramshackle, rumshops are open all night (literally), and there's a lot of street life after midnight. Some of the rumshops sell fried chicken (the *Pink Star* is recommended) and there are women in the street selling fish, seasoned and fried in coconut oil over an open fire. Especially recommended if you are hungry after midnight.

If you drink in a rumshop, rum and other drinks are bought by the bottle. The smallest size is a mini, then a flask, then a full bottle. The shop will supply ice and glasses, you buy a mixer, and serve yourself. The same system operates in dances, though prices are higher; night clubs, of course, serve drinks by the glass like anywhere else. Wine, in a rumshop, usually means sweet British sherry. If you are not careful, it is drunk with ice and beer.

Shows The *Visitor* has a fairly full listing. Some of the better ones are: *The Off Off Off Broadway Revue*, Ocean View Hotel. Hollywood music with a twist. *Barbados Barbados*, Balls Plantation. Tuesdays. Dinner with musical show based on Barbadian history and culture. *1627 And All That*, Barbados Museum. Sunday and Thursday. Buffet dinner, folkdance drama, and museum tour. *Where the Rum Comes From*, guided tour of the West India Rum Refinery near the deep water port in Bridgetown on the Spring Garden Highway, with buffet lunch, free rum drinks and steel band entertainment every Wednesday, B$55, transport to/from hotels. The last three shows can be booked, Tel: 435 6900. All three provide transport to and from hotel.

Cinemas There are two cinemas in Bridgetown and a drive-in not far from the south coast. Fairly second-rate selection of features.

Theatres There are several good semi-professional theatre companies. Performances are advertized in the press. It is usually wise to buy tickets in advance. Most people dress quite formally for these performances.

Party Cruises The *Jolly Roger* (Tel: 436 6424) and *Bajan Queen* (Tel: 436 2149/2150) run four-hour daytime and evening cruises along the west coast to Holetown, near the Folkestone Underwater Park (where the fun and games take place) from the deepwater harbour. The drinks are unlimited (very).

There is also a meal, music, dancing, etc. On daytime cruises, there is swimming and snorkelling.

Security

Bridgetown is still much safer than some other Caribbean cities but crime rates have increased and both the UK and USA have raised a Travel Advisory on Barbados. Local people are now more cautious about where they go after dark and many no longer go to Nelson Street or some other run-down areas. Baxters Road, however, is generally quite safe. Unlike Jamaica, where crime is concentrated mainly in Kingston, crime has become prevalent in Barbados where tourists congregate, particularly at night. Care should be taken not to go for romantic walks along deserted beaches and to watch out for pickpockets and bag snatchers in tourist areas. Families with small children to care for at night rarely notice any crime and have commented on how secure they felt on Barbados.

Shopping

Prices are generally high, but the range of goods available is excellent. Travellers who are going on to other islands may find it useful to do some shopping here.

The best stocked supermarket is JB's Mastermart in Wildey. Big B in Worthing and Supercentre in Oistins and Holetown are also good, and are easier to reach by public transport. Food is not cheap but generally anything is available and good quality.

Duty-free shopping is well advertised. Visitors who produce passport and air ticket can take most duty-free goods away from the store for use in the island before they leave. Camera film and clothing for example are significantly cheaper duty-free, so don't go shopping without ticket and passport. But cameras and electrical goods may be much cheaper to buy in an ordinary discount store in the USA or Europe than duty free in Barbados.

The *Best of Barbados* shops (plus Walkers' Caribbean World, Caribbean Gifts and Great Gifts) sell high quality items made or designed in Barbados, including paintings and designs by Jill Walker, pottery, basketwork, island music and dolls. Locations include *Sandpiper Inn*, *Sam Lord's Castle*, Mall 34, Broad Street, St Lawrence Gap, Flower Forest. Other good displays of craft items are at Pelican Village on the Harbour Road. Origins on the Careenage in Bridgetown is a gallery with well-designed but expensive clothing, jewellery and ceramics. There is also a street market in Temple Yard where Rastafarians sell leather and other goods.

Street Vendors are very persistent but generally friendly even when you refuse their wares.

Bookshops are much better stocked than on other islands. The Cloister on the Wharf probably has the largest stock. The Book Place on Probyn Street specializes in Caribbean material and has a good secondhand section. Brydens and Cave Shepherd also have a good selection. Also Roberts Stationery, The Book Shop, The Bookstop.

Camera repairs Skeetes Repair Service on Milkmarket is a small workshop which repairs most brands of camera. Louis Bailey in Broad Street is well-equipped but more expensive.

Banks

Barclays Bank, the Royal Bank of Canada, Canadian Imperial Bank of Commerce, Scotiabank, Caribbean Commercial Bank, Bank of Credit and Commerce International, and Barbados National Bank all have offices in Bridgetown. The first five also have branches in the main south and west coast tourist centres. Opening hours for banks are 0800-1500 Monday to Thursday, and 0800-1200 and 1500-1700 on Fridays. Caribbean Commercial Bank in Hastings and Sunset Crest is also open on Saturdays from 0900 to 1200. The Barbados National Bank has a branch and a bureau de change at the airport; the latter is open from 0800-2200, but inaccessible unless you are actually arriving or departing.

Currency

The currency unit is the Barbados dollar, which is pegged at B$2.00 for US$1.00. Banks will of course charge a small commission on this rate. There is now a parallel market with Guyanese traders in

particular keen to buy US dollars as they can gain from arbitrage on the Guyanese cambios. Many tourist establishments quote prices in US dollars, if you are not careful a hotel room may end up costing twice as much as you bargained for. Rates offered by the banks for currencies other than the US dollar, sterling, and Deutschmark are not good. Credit cards are accepted in the large resorts, but their use is not widespread.

National Holidays

New Year's Day, 21 January (Errol Barrow Day), Good Friday, Easter Monday, 1 May, Whit Monday, Kadooment Day (first Monday in August), United Nations Day (first Monday in October), Independence Day (30 November), Christmas Day; Boxing Day.

Time Zone

Atlantic Standard Time, 4 hours behind GMT, 1 ahead of EST.

Electric Current

120 volts (American standard) and 50 cycles per second (British standard). Some houses and hotels also have 240-volt sockets for use with British equipment.

Telephone Service

Calls from a pay phone cost 25 cents for three minutes. Otherwise local calls are free. Many business places will allow you to use their telephone for local calls. International calls can be made from most hotels or (more cheaply) from Barbados External Telecommunications (Wildey). Telexes and Faxes can also be sent from and received at BET's office by members of the public. BET has a public office on the Wharf in Bridgetown for international calls, facsimile and telex.

Religion

Barbadians are a religious people and although the main church is Anglican, there are over 140 different faiths and sects, including Baptists, Christian Scientists, Jews, Methodists, Moravians and Roman Catholics. Times of services can be found in the *Visitor*.

To use the AT&T USADirect® Service from Barbados, look for specially marked telephones in airports, cruise docks and telephone centers.

AT&T USADirect® Service.

Newspapers

The Advocate, which also publishes *The Sunday Advocate*; *The Nation* (publisher also of *The Visitor* tourist weekly); *The Bajan* (monthly); *EC News* (weekly); *Caribbean Contact*, a weekly published by the Caribbean Conference of Churches.

Radio Stations

CBC Radio, medium wave 900 kHz; Voice of Barbados, medium wave 790 kHz; BBS, FM 90.7 MHz; Yess-Ten 4, FM 104.1 MHz; Radio Liberty, FM 98.1 MHz.

Addresses

British High Commission, Lower Collymore Rock, St Michael, Tel: 436 6694. Canadian High Commission, Bishop Court, Hill Pine Road, Tel: 429 3550. FDR Hon Consul, Tel: 427 1876. US Embassy, Broad Street, Tel: 436 4950; Brazilian Embassy, Fairchild Street, Tel: 427 1735; Venezuelan Embassy, Worthing, Tel: 435 7619. Trinidad and Tobago High Commission, Cockspur House, Nile Street, Bridgetown, Tel: 429 9600, issues visas (US$12) same day to those who need them.

Tourist Information

The Barbados Board of Tourism has its main office in Harbour Road, Bridgetown (PO Box 242, Tel: 427 2623, Fax: 426 4080). There are also offices at the deepwater harbour (Tel: 426 1718) and the airport (Tel: 428 0937). The Board of Tourism publishes a useful annual *Sports and Cultural Calendar*, which gives information on what to see throughout the year and the addresses of sporting organizations. Two good sources of information are *Visitor* and the *Sunseeker*, published weekly and distributed free by Barbados's two daily newspapers. *Ins and Outs of Barbados*, also free, is published annually, a glossy magazine with lots of advertising and distributed by hotels.

Exploring Historical Barbados, by Maurice Bateman Hutt, is quite good but perhaps slightly out of date as it was published in 1981.

Overseas the Board has offices in:

UK: 263 Tottenham Court Road, London W1P 9AA, Tel: 071-636 9448/9, Fax: 637 1496. **USA**: 800 Second Avenue, New York, NY 10017 Tel: 212-986 6516 or toll-free 800-221 9831, Fax: 212-573 9850; 3440 Wilshire Boulevard, Suite 1215, Los Angeles, CA 90010 Tel: 213-380 2198, toll free 800-221 9831, Fax: 213-384 2763).

Canada: 5160 Yonge Street, Suite 1800, North York, Ontario M2N GL9, Tel: 416-512 6569-71 or toll free 800-268 9122, Fax: 416-512 6581; 615 Dorchester Boulevard West, Suite 960, Montreal H3B 1P5, Tel: 514- 861 0085/ Fax: 514-861 7917). **Germany**: Rathenau Platz 1A, 6000 Frankfurt 1, Tel: 280 982/3, Fax: 49-69-294-782. **Sweden**: c/o Hotel Investors (Sweden) Ltd, Nybrogatan 87, S-114-41 Stockholm, Tel: 468-662-8584, Fax: 468-662-8775. **France** c/o Caribes 102, 102 Ave des Champs- Élysées, 75008 Paris, Tel: 45 62 62 62, Fax: 331-4074-0701.

The Barbados Embassy in Caracas can also provide tourist information.

The *Insight Guide to Barbados* has been recommended for further reading. Ordnance Survey Tourist Maps include Barbados in the series, 1:50,000 scale with inset of Bridgetown 1:10,000.

The Barbados chapter has been comprehensively revised by Patrick Dawson, of Trade & Travel Publications, who travelled there with his family in November 1991. For assistance during his visit, he would like to thank the Barbados Board of Tourism and Walter Forde, Manager of the *Sandridge Hotel*, Speightstown.

TRINIDAD AND TOBAGO

Introduction

TRINIDAD, the most southerly of the Caribbean islands, lying only seven miles off the Venezuelan coast, is one of the most colourful of the West Indian islands. It is an island of 1,864 square miles, traversed by two ranges of hills, the northern and southern ranges, running roughly east and west, and a third, the central range, running diagonally across the island. Apart from small areas in the northern range, of which the main peaks are Cerro del Aripo (3,083 feet) and El Tucuche (3,072 feet), all the land is below 1,000 feet. There are large areas of swamp on the east and west coasts. Trinidad is separated from the mainland of South America by the Boca del Dragón strait in the northwest (Dragon's Mouth) and Boca del Serpiente in the southwest (Serpent's Mouth, both named by Columbus).

Tobago (116 square miles) is only 21 miles by sea to the northeast. It is 26 miles long and only 9 miles wide, shaped like a cigar with a central 18-mile ridge of hills in the north (the Main Ridge, highest point 1,890 feet) running parallel with the coast. These northeastern hills are of volcanic origin; the southwest is flat or undulating and coralline. The coast itself is broken by any number of inlets and sheltered beaches. The population is concentrated in the western part of the island. There are small farms, but the main ridge is forested and quite wild. The climate is generally cooler and drier than most parts of Trinidad.

Trinidad has one of the world's most cosmopolitan populations. The emancipation of the slaves in 1834 and the adoption of free trade by Britain in 1846 resulted in far-reaching social and economic changes. To meet labour shortages over 150,000 immigrants were encouraged to settle from India, China and Madeira. Of today's population of approximately 1,259,000, about 40% are black and 40% East Indian. French and Spanish influences dominated for a long time (Catholicism is still strong) but gradually the English language and institutions prevailed and today the great variety of peoples has become a fairly harmonious entity, despite some tension betwen blacks and those of East Indian descent. Spanish is still spoken in small pockets in the northern mountains and French patois here and there. Tobago's population, mainly black, numbers about 47,000. The crime rate is much lower than on Trinidad and the people are noticeably helpful and friendly.

History
Trinidad was discovered by Columbus and claimed for Spain on his third voyage in 1498. Whether he named the island after the day of the Holy Trinity, or after a group of three hills that he spied from the sea is in dispute.

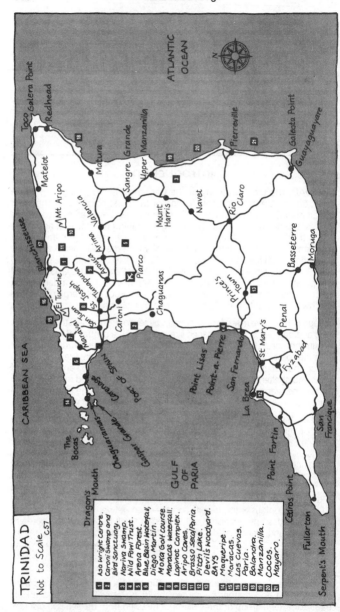

TRINIDAD
Not to Scale
C57

1 Asa Wright Centre.
2 Caroni Swamp and
  Bird Sanctuary.
3 Nariva Swamp.
4 Wild Fowl Trust.
5 Arena Forest.
6 Blue Basin Waterfall,
  Diego Martin.
7 Moka Golf course.
8 Maracas Waterfall.
9 Lopinot Complex.
10 Aripo Caves.
11 Brasso Seco/Paria.
12 Pitch Lake.
13 Devil's Woodyard.
BAYS
14 Maqueripe
15 Maracas.
16 Las Cuevas.
17 Paria.
18 Balandra.
19 Manzanilla.
20 Cocos.
21 Mayaro.

At that time there were at least seven tribes of Indians living on the island: the Arawaks, Chaimas, Tamanaques, Salives, Chaguanes, Quaquas and Caribs, the last being divided into four sub-groupings, the Nepoios, Yaios, Carinepagotos and Cumanagotos. The peaceful Arawaks were the majority and lived in the southern part of the island, having originally come from the upper regions of the Orinoco river. The northern part was populated by Indians of the Carib strain from the Amazon area who were aggressive and warlike. It was their hostility which prevented successful colonization until the end of the seventeenth century when Catalan Capuchin missionaries arrived. However, European diseases and the rigours of slavery took their toll of the Indian population; by 1824 there were only 893 Indians left on Trinidad and today there are none. The first Spanish governor was Don Antonio Sedeño who arrived in 1530, but failed to establish a permanent settlement because of Indian attacks. In 1592 the governor, Don Antonio de Berrio y Oruna, founded the town of San José de Oruna (now St Joseph), but it was destroyed by Sir Walter Raleigh in 1595 and not rebuilt until 1606. In 1783 a deliberate policy to encourage immigration of Roman Catholics was introduced, known as the Royal Cedula of Population, and it was from this date that organized settlement began with an influx of mostly French-speaking immigrants, particularly after the French Revolution.

British rule in Trinidad began in 1797 when an expedition led by Sir Ralph Abercromby captured the island. It was later ceded to Britain by Spain in 1802 under the Treaty of Amiens. At this time large numbers of African slaves were imported to work in the sugar fields introduced by the French. After the abolition of slavery in 1834, labour became scarce and the colonists looked for alternative sources of workers. Several thousands of immigrants from neighbouring islands came in 1834-48, many Americans from Baltimore and Pennsylvania came in 1841, Madeirans came seeking employment and religious freedom and were joined by European immigrants, namely the British, Scots, Irish, French, Germans and Swiss. There was also immigration of free West Africans in the 1840s, but by 1848 this had ceased as conditions improved in their own countries. In 1844 the British Government gave approval for the import of East Indian labour and the first indentured labourers arrived in 1845. By 1917, when Indian immigration ceased, 141,615 Indians had arrived for an indentured period of five years, and although many returned to India afterwards, the majority settled. The first Chinese arrived in 1849 during a lull in Indian immigration. Initially these were men only and this naturally encouraged intermarriage, but later arrivals included women. In 1866 the Chinese Government insisted on a return passage being paid, and this put an end to Chinese immigration.

Tobago is thought to have been discovered by Columbus in 1498, when it was occupied by Caribs. He is said to have called the island "Bella Forma"; the present name is a corruption of tobacco, which the Caribs used to grow there. In 1641 James, Duke of Courland (in the Baltic), obtained a grant of the island from Charles I and in 1642 a number of Courlanders settled on the north side. In 1658 the Courlanders were overpowered by the Dutch, who remained in possession of the island until 1662. In this year Cornelius Lampsius procured Letters Patent from Louis XIV creating him the Baron of Tobago under the Crown of France. After being occupied for short periods by the Dutch and the French, Tobago was ceded by France to Britain in 1763 under the Treaty of Paris. But it was not until 1802, after further invasions by the French and subsequent recapture by the British, that it was finally ceded to Britain, becoming a Crown Colony in 1877 and in 1888 being amalgamated politically with Trinidad.

The first political organizations in Trinidad and Tobago developed in the 1930s, when economic depression spurred the formation of labour movements. Full adult suffrage was introduced in 1946 and political parties began to develop. In 1956, the People's National Movement (PNM) was founded by the hugely influential Dr Eric Williams, who dominated local politics until his death in 1981. The party won control of the new Legislative Council, under the new constitutional arrangements which provided for self-government, and Dr Williams became the first Chief Minister. In 1958, Trinidad and Tobago became a member of the new Federation of the West Indies, but after the withdrawal of Jamaica in 1961 the colony was unwilling to support the poorer members of the Federation and Dr Williams sought the same rights for Trinidad and Tobago. The country became an independent member of the Commonwealth on 31 August, 1962 and became a republic within the Commonwealth on 1 August, 1976. Dr Williams remained Prime Minister, his party drawing on the support of the majority African elements of the population, while the opposition parties were supported mainly by the Indian minority.

In 1986, the National Alliance for Reconstruction (NAR) ended 30 years' rule by the PNM which had been hit by corruption scandals, winning 33 of the 36 parliamentary seats in the general election. Six NAR members defected in 1989 to form the United National Congress (UNC), led by former Deputy Prime Minister, Basdeo Panday. The popularity of the Prime Minister, A N R Robinson, was extremely low and he was seen as heading an uncaring administration which alienated voters by its economic policies of cutting the public sector and other costs.

On 27 July 1990 Trinidad was shaken by an attempted overthrow of the Government by a Muslim fundamentalist group, the Jamaat-al-Muslimeen, led by the Imam Yasin Abu Bakr. The rebels held the Prime Minister, A N R Robinson, eight of his Cabinet and other hostages, until their unconditional surrender on 1 August. A total of 23 people were killed in the disturbances and about 500 were injured (including the Prime Minister) during the bombing of the police headquarters, the takeover of the parliament building and TV station and subsequent rioting. Despite a promise of an amnesty 114 Jamaat members were arrested and charged with a number of offences, including murder and treason. After taking their case to the Privy Council in the UK their appeal was heard in 1992 and the amnesty was reinstated, leading to the release of prisoners.

General elections were held on 16 December 1991, bringing another about turn in political loyalties. Patrick Manning, of the PNM, led his party to victory, winning 21 seats, while the UNC won 13 and the NAR was left in the cold with only the two Tobago seats.

Government
Trinidad and Tobago became a republic within the Commonwealth on 1 August 1976 under a new constitution which provides for a President and a bicameral Parliament comprising a 31-seat Senate and a 36-seat House of Representatives. Noor Mohammed Hassanali took office as President in March 1987. Tobago has its own House of Assembly, which runs many local services.

The Economy
The soil in Trinidad is remarkably rich and the first settlers had no difficulty in raising a variety of crops, with tobacco, sugar and cocoa being the major exports. Today, however, agriculture contributes 2.2% of gross domestic

product and employs only 12% of the labour force. Agricultural exports have been broadened to include citrus fruits and coconut oils, but output of the traditional crops has plummetted. Trinidad is rich in mineral deposits including asphalt from the pitch lake at La Brea on the southwestern coast, lignite, gypsum, limestone, coal, sand, gravel, iron ore, argillite and fluorspar, but apart from the asphalt, which is used for road surfacing, they are not well developed. Petroleum and petroleum products still dominate the economy, providing about 27% of gdp, 43% of government revenue and 70% of foreign exchange earnings. There are two oil refineries, at Point-a-Pierre and Point Fortin. The island has substantial proven reserves of natural gas of 10 trillion cubic feet, and these are used to power several heavy industries such as an iron and steel mill, urea, methanol and ammonia plants. Dependence on oil has led to wide fluctuations in the rate of economic growth, with the 1970s a period of rapid expansion and rising real incomes as oil prices soared and the 1980s a decade of declining output and falling wages as the oil market retrenched. The recession in the oil industry exposed structural imbalances in the rest of the economy and the inability of agriculture, manufacturing or services to counter its effects.

Assistance was sought from the IMF in the context of debt rescheduling agreements with the Paris Club of creditor governments and with commercial banks. The Government also turned to the World Bank and Japan for the new lending to support structural adjustment of the economy. A slight improvement in economic activity towards the end of 1991 led to a fall in unemployment, to 17.4%. Unemployment remained most acute among the 15-19 age group, where 42.9% were unemployed, and crime increased noticeably. The second standby agreement expired on 31 March 1991 and the Government did not seek a third IMF programme. It was hoped that the economy would begin to grow in 1992 after nine consecutive annual declines in gdp. A liberalization of some foreign exchange controls in 1992 led to an easing of liquidity constraints and a return of some capital held overseas.

A concerted attempt is being made to diversify the economy and lessen the dependence on petroleum. Tourism is becoming an important source of foreign exchange and the Government is actively promoting both islands abroad. The tourist trade now generates about US$90m in annual foreign exchange earnings. A new cruise ship complex was opened in August 1989 at Port of Spain. A similar terminal is being constructed in Tobago as part of the Scarborough harbour re-development project. About 200 ships called at either Port of Spain or Scarborough in 1990, compared with 86 in 1989. A Tourism Development Authority has been established to replace the old Tourist Board and has full charge of matters relating to tourism.

Culture
The most exciting introduction to the vivid, cosmopolitan culture of this Republic is, of course, Carnival, or "De Mas", as locals refer to the annual "celebration of the senses". Background reading is a help for a visit at any time of the year. It is sensible to purchase books before departure, as prices are much higher in Trinidadian shops, even for locally produced reading matter. Some authors to investigate are the late C L R James, Samuel Selvon, Shiva Naipaul, V S Naipaul, the historian and past prime minister Dr Eric Williams, Earl Lovelace and newcomer Valerie Belgrave (whose *Ti Marie* has been described as the Caribbean *Gone with the Wind*). Although the tradition of performance poetry is not as strong here as in, say, Jamaica

(calypso fulfils some of its role), the monologues of Paul Keens-Douglas, some of which are on album or cassette, are richly entertaining and a great introduction to the local patois.

Alongside a strong oral/literary tradition goes a highly developed visual culture, reflecting the islands' racial melange. The most obvious examples are the inventive designs for the carnival bands, which often draw on craft skills like wire bending, copper beating, and the expressive use of fibreglass moulds. Fine painters and sculptors abound, too, although the only good galleries are small and commercial and located primarily in Port of Spain. Michel Jean Cazabon, born 1813, was the first great local artist (an illustrated biography by Aquarela Gallery owner Geoffrey MacLean is widely available). Contemporary work to look out for, often on the walls of the more enlightened hotels, restaurants and banks, includes paintings by Emheyo Bahabba, Pat Bishop, Isaiah Boodhoo, Francisco Cabral, LeRoy Clarke, Kenwyn Crichlow, Boscoe Holder and the fabled, controversial Mas' designer Peter Minshall.

Jewellery and fashion designers also figure strongly in the life of these islands, with exceptionally high standards of work demonstrated by jewellers like Barbara Jardine, Gillian Bishop and Rachel Ross. The doyenne of the fashion business is the gifted Meiling, but attractive original clothing by a growing number of native fashionmakers can be found in boutiques and shopping centres.

Carnival This extraordinary fete (see **Festivals** for dates) is considered by many to be safer, more welcoming to visitors and artistically more stimulating than its nearest rival in Rio de Janeiro. Commercialization is undermining many of the greatest Mas' traditions, and only some of the historical characters like the Midnight Robber and the Moko Jumbies can be glimpsed on J'Ouverte (pronounced joo-vay) morning and in small, independent bands of players. But it's a great party, enlivened by hundreds of thousands of costumed masqueraders and the homegrown music, calypso and steelband (usually referred to as "pan").

Calypsonians (or kaisonians, as the more historically-minded call them) are the commentators, champions and sometime conscience of the people. This unique musical form, a mixture of African, French and, eventually, British, Spanish and even East Indian influences dates back to Trinidad's first "shantwell", Gros Jean, late in the eighteenth century. Since then it has evolved into a popular, potent force, with both men and women (also children, of late) battling for the Calypso Monarch's crown, in a fierce competition that climaxes on Dimanche Gras, the Sunday immediately before the official beginning of Carnival. Calypsonians band together to perform in "tents" (performing halls) in the weeks leading up to the competition and are judged in semi-finals, which hones down the list to six final contenders. The season's calypso songs blast from radio stations and sound systems all over the islands and visitors should ask locals to interpret the sometimes witty and often scurrilous lyrics, for they are a fascinating introduction to the current state of the nation.

Pan music has a shorter history, developing this century from the tamboo-bamboo bands which made creative use of tins, dustbins and pans plus lengths of bamboo for percussion instruments. By the end of World War II (during which Carnival was banned) some ingenious souls discovered that huge oil drums could be converted into expressive instruments, their top surfaces tuned to all ranges and depths (eg the ping pong, or soprano pan embraces 28 to 32 notes, including both the diatonic and chromatic scales).

Aside from the varied pans, steelbands also include a rhythm section dominated by the steel, or iron men. For Carnival, the steelbands compete in the grand Panorama, playing calypsoes which are also voted on for the Road March of the Year. Biennally, the World Steelband Festival highlights the versatility of this music, for each of the major bands must play a work by a classical composer as well as a calypso of choice. On alternate years the National Schools Steelband Festival is held, similarly in late October/early November.

Other musical forms in this music-mad nation can be heard during the Yuletide season, when **parang** dominates all celebrations (part of the islands' Spanish heritage, parang is sung in Castillian and accompanied by guitar, cuatro, mandoline and tambourine) and, for the Hindi and Muslim festivals, East Indian drumming and vocal styles like chowtal.

The national **Best Village** competition, which runs from September to November, gives the smallest community a chance to display its finest drama, dance, music and crafts (price of tickets in the Queen's Park Savannah Grand Stand, TT$3 per night). Throughout the year, there are regular performances of plays and musicals, often by Caribbean dramatists, and concerts by fine choirs like the Lydian singers, sometimes accompanied by steelbands.

In short, Trinidad and Tobago boast some of the most impressive artists to be found anywhere in the region, and visitors can enjoy that art throughout the year, although many of the now internationally recognized performers tour abroad during the summer months.

Fauna and Flora

The Forestry Division of the Ministry of Agriculture, Land and Marine Resources (Long Circular Road, St James, Port of Spain, Tel: 622-7476, contact them for information on guided tours and hikes) has designated many parts of Trinidad and Tobago as national parks, wildlife reserves and protected areas. On Trinidad, the national parks are the Caroni and Nariva Swamps, Chaguaramas, and Madamas, Maracas and Matura in the northern range of hills. The Nariva Swamp, an area of 3,840 acres, contains hardwood forest, home to red howler monkeys and the weeping capuchin as well as 55 other species of mammal. Birds include the savannah hawk and the red-breasted blackbird. Access is by boat only. The Northern Range Sanctuary, Maracas, or El Tucuche Reserve, is a forest on the second highest peak, at 3,072 feet, covering 2,313 acres. It contains some interesting flora, such as giant bromeliad and orchids, as well as fauna, including the golden tree frog and the orange-billed nightingale-thrush. There are several hiking trails, the most popular of which is from Ortinola estate; guides can be hired. There are seven natural landmarks, three of which are described below (Blue Basin, the Pitch Lake and the Devil's Woodyard) and others include Tamana Hill in the central range, and Galera Point in the northeast. Twelve areas are scientific reserves (eg Trinity Hills, Galeota Point and the Aripo Savannas); twelve are nature conservation reserves: the Asa Wright Centre is described below, but also Cedros Peninsula and Godineau Swamp in the southwest, Manzanilla in the east and Valencia. The Valencia Wildlife Sanctuary covers 6,881 acres and contains at least 50 species of birds including antbirds and tanagers. Several mammals live here: deer, wild pig, agouti, tatoo. Near Valencia is the Arena Forest, one of ten recreation parks, while five areas have been designated scenic landscapes (Blanchisseuse, Maracas and Toco-Matelot on the north coast, Cocos Bay on the Atlantic, and Mount Harris on the Southern Road, south of Sangre Grande). Although about 50% of the island remains forested, there is much concern about the loss of wildlife habitats.

On Tobago, apart from two national parks (Buccoo Reef and the virgin and secondary forests of eastern Tobago), there are the Goldsborough natural landmark, the Kilgwyn scientific reserve, the Grafton nature conservation area, the Parlatuvier, Roxborough, scenic landscape, and three recreation parks (including Mount Irvine). Many of the small islands off the coasts of the two larger ones are reserves for wildlife and are important breeding grounds for red-billed tropic birds, frigate birds, man-o-war and other sea birds (for instance Saut d'Eau, Kronstadt Island and Soldado Rock off Trinidad, and Little Tobago, see below, St Giles and Marble Islands off Tobago).

Many flowering trees can be seen: pink and yellow poui, frangipani, cassia, pride of India, immortelle, flamboyant, jacaranda. Among the many types of flower are hibiscus, poinsettia, chaconia (wild poinsettia—the national flower), ixora, bougainvillea, over 700 species of orchid, ginger lily and heliconia. The Horticultural Society of Trinidad and Tobago (PO Box 252) has its office on Lady Chancellor Road, Port of Spain, Tel: 622-6423.

The islands boast 60 types of bat, and other mammals include the Trinidad capuchin and red howler monkeys, brown forest brocket (deer), collared peccary (quenk), manicou (opossum), agouti, rare ocelot and armadillo. Caymans live in the swamps.

Trinidad and Tobago together have more species of birds than any other Caribbean island, although the variety is South American, not West Indian. No species is endemic, but Tobago has 13 species of breeding birds not found on Trinidad. Most estimates say that there are 400 species of bird, including 41 hummingbirds (the aboriginal name for the island of Trinidad was Ieri, the land of the hummingbird). There are also 622 recorded species of butterfly. The most accessible bird-watching sites are the Caroni Bird Sanctuary, the Asa Wright Centre, the Caurita Plantation and the Wild Fowl Trust, all described elsewhere in this chapter.

Recommended is *A Guide to the Birds of Trinidad and Tobago*, by Richard Ffrench (Macmillan Caribbean). Those interested can also contact the Trinidad Field Naturalists Club, 1 Errol Park Road, St Anns, Port of Spain (Tel: 624-3321 evenings or weekends), secretary Miss Luisa Zuniaga. Each October Trinidad and Tobago hold Natural History Festivals to foster understanding of the islands flora and fauna.

Beaches and Watersports

The nearest beach to Port of Spain is Carenage, but it is badly polluted. To the northwest there are one or two pleasant swimming places in Chaguaramas Bay, with windsurfing and yachting, though you have to pay to use the beach here. Maqueripe Bay has a sheltered beach. Maracas Bay on the north coast over the hills, 10 miles/16 km from the capital, has a sheltered sandy beach fringed with coconut palms; despite small waves there can be a dangerous undertow here and at other beaches and drownings have occurred, do not swim far out and watch the markers (try the "shark and bread," a baked bread sandwich with shark meat in it, very tasty, especially after a drinking session at 0300, sold all along the beach for TT$5). Maracas Bay Village is scheduled for development. There are buses to Maracas Bay running every four hours (but they can be irregular) from the bus terminal. Difficulties in catching the bus have led travellers to recommend taxis: from Port of Spain costs TT$120 or there is a pick-up "route taxi" service from the centre of town, TT$10. Next to Maracas Bay is Tyrico Bay (surfing, lifeguard, another beach with a dangerous undertow and sandflies). Las Cuevas, also on the north coast (like Maracas Bay, surfing is good here but beware of the sandflies in the wet season), and Blanchisseuse have lovely beaches but are more difficult to reach (see below, under Arima). At the northeastern end, near Toco, are a number of bays, including Balandra for good bathing. Further down, the Atlantic coast from Matura to Mayaro is divided into three huge sweeping bays, with palm trees growing as high as 200 feet in some places. Of these bays Mayaro and Manzanilla both have beautiful sandy beaches; there are several beach houses to rent at Mayaro, heavily booked in peak holiday periods but the TDA can arrange in advance. In the southwest, near La Brea and the Pitch Lake is the resort of Vessigny. Generally, the beaches are difficult to get to except by taxi or hired car.

The only really safe place for diving off Trinidad is in the channels called the Bocas, between the islands off the northwest peninsula (The Dragon's Mouth). However, the currents are cold, so protective gear is essential. Contact the Diving Association of Trinidad, or Twin-Island Dives, Maraval.

Tobago Dive Experience at the *Blue Waters Inn*, Batteaux Bay, Speyside, Tel: 660-4341, Fax: 660-5195 (or the *Grafton*, Tel:639-0191), offers exciting drift diving, not recommended for novices although they will teach you. The only thing better than racing past dancing sea fans at three knots is to do it again at five knots. *(Blue Waters Inn* tends to be full throughout the year so book early.) *Man Friday Diving*, Charlotteville, Tel/Fax: 660-4676, covers the area from Charlotteville to Speyside. A fully-equipped, new dive shop has a classroom for PADI or NAUI training and equipment for hire. Diving is from two 28-foot, custom-built piroques one operating from Speyside and one from Charlotteville, taking no more than six in a group, single dive US$35, plus VAT, five dives US$150, hire of mask, snorkel and fins US$4/day, lots of courses on offer, accommodation can be arranged. Other dive operators include Dive Tobago Ltd (Jimmy Young), Pigeon Point, PO Box 53 (Scarborough), Tel: 639-2266/2385.

For boat trips to the islands north and west of Port of Spain Tel: 622-8974, Elton Pouchet, US$48 for 2.

Yachting has become big business in Trinidad and there are now two marinas: Trinidad Yacht Club at Bayshore and Yachting Association Marina at Chaguaramas.

Every July/August, there is a power boat race from Trinidad to Store Bay, Tobago. Each year Tobago has a sailing week; many crewing possibilities. The annual International Game Fishing Classic is held in February/March.

Other Sports

Cricket is very popular. Test matches are played at Queen's Park Oval, west of Queen's Park Savannah, Port of Spain; take a cushion, sunhat/umbrella and drinks if sitting in the cheap seats. Hockey and soccer are also played at the Oval. Also played are rugby, basketball, cycling and marathon running. There is horse-racing at Port of Spain (Queen's Park Savannah—see the horses exercising in the park), San Fernando and Arima. Horse-hire near Fort George. Swimming at the *Hilton Hotel*, US$4 (US$2 children); see below for swimming and golf at St Andrews (Moka) Golf Club; there are six other golf clubs on Trinidad, including a 9-hole public course at Chaguaramas; squash, Long Circular Mall, Tel: 622-1245, 0600-2200 (0900-1700 Saturday), US$3 for 40 minutes, advance booking essential; tennis, Country Club, Tel: 622-3470/2111/2113, US$1.50 for one week's membership, advance booking necessary, also at *Hilton Hotel*. The *Valley Vue Hotel*, Ariapita Road,

St Ann's has two squash courts with seating for 100 spectators per court, Tel: 624-0940, 627-8058/60, Fax: 627-8046.

On Tobago, golf and lawn tennis at Mount Irvine Bay, Tel: 639-8871: green fee US$20/day, tennis US$3 in day, US$6 at night. For hiking, bird-watching on- and off-shore, contact David Rooks, PO Box 58, Scarborough, Tel: 639-9408.

Festivals

Carnival takes place officially each year on the two days before Ash Wednesday which marks the beginning of the Christian season of Lent. In practice, the festivities start well in advance, with the Mas' camps abustle, the calypsonians performing most nights of the week and the impressive Panorama finals taking place with the competing steelbands at the Queen's Park Savannah stadium the week before Mas' proper. On Carnival Monday, the festivities start with "J'Ouverte" at 0400. This followed by "Ole Mas" which lasts until 0900. In the afternoon is "Lil Mas" when the bands start moving, followed by their lively and brightly dressed supporters. Tuesday is the more important day, however, when the bands all have their own troops of followers, there is a procession of floats and everyone is "jumping up" in the street (beware of pickpockets). For the stadium parades and band play-offs, try the North Stand. Tickets for all National Carnival Commission shows are sold at the Queen's Park Savannah, where the shows are held. You can join one of the Mas' camps by looking in the newspaper for the times and locations of the camps. If you are early enough you will be supplied with a costume which will allow you to participate in one of the 'tramps' through town. There is a lot of alcohol consumed during the road marches but there are no drunken brawls. Note that it is illegal to sell tapes of carnival artists but 'bootleg' tapes are inevitably sold on the streets.

The Hosay, or Hosein Festival, commemorating the murder of two Moslem princes, starts ten days after the first appearance of the new moon in the Moharrun month of the Moslem calendar. Colourful processions, hauling 10-to 30-foot-high miniature temples of wood, paper and tinsel, start the next day, heralded by moon dancers and accompanied by drum-beating. Also celebrated is the Moslem festival of Eid-ul-Fitr, to mark the end of Ramadan. Two principal Hindu festivals are Phagwa, or Holi, the colour, or spring, festival on the day of the full moon in the month of Phagun (February/March), and Divali, the festival of lights, usually in the last quarter of the year. On 29 August in Arima the feast of St Rose of Lima is celebrated; the parish church is dedicated to her. Descendants of the original Amerindians come from all over the island to walk in solemn procession round the church.

On Tobago, on Easter Monday and Tuesday, there are crab, goat and donkey races at Buccoo Village. The Tobago Heritage Festival lasts for the second fortnight of July, with historical re-enactments, variety shows and parades.

Trinidad

Port of Spain, with a population of 51,000 (350,000 including suburbs), lies on a gently sloping plain between the Gulf of Paria and the foothills of the Northern Range. The city has a pleasant atmosphere, but the streets and buildings are not well maintained. The streets are mostly at right-angles to one another; the buildings are a mixture of fretwork wooden architecture and modern concrete, interspersed with office towers and empty lots. Within easy reach of the port (King's Wharf and its extension) are many of the main buildings of interest. On the south side of Woodford Square, named after the former governor, Sir Ralph Woodford, is the fine Anglican Cathedral Church of the Holy Trinity (consecrated 1823), with an elaborate hammer-beam roof festooned with carvings. It was built during Woodford's governorship (1813-28) and contains a very fine monument to him. The Red House (completed 1907) contains the House of Representatives, the Senate and various government departments. It was the scene of an attempted overthrow of the Robinson Government by armed black Muslim rebels in July 1990. The rebels held the Prime Minister and several of his Cabinet captive for five days before surrendering to the Army. On the west side of the Red House, at the corner of St Vincent and Sackville Streets, can still be seen the skeletal remains of the former Police Headquarters, which the rebels firebombed before launching their assault on the Red House. The first Red House on this site was, ironically, destroyed by fire in 1903 during riots over an increase in water rates. On the opposite side of the Square to the Cathedral are the modern Hall of Justice (completed 1985), Central Library and City Hall (1961), with a fine relief sculpture on the front. The Square is Trinidad's equivalent to Speaker's Corner in London's Hyde Park.

At opposite ends of Independence Square (two blocks south of Woodford Square) are the Roman Catholic Cathedral of the Immaculate Conception, built in 1832, and the modern TSTT (Telecommunications) and Salvatori buildings. Behind the Cathedral is Columbus Square, with a small, brightly-painted statue of the island's discoverer. South of Independence Square, between Edward and St Vincent Streets is the financial centre, two tall towers and Eric Williams Plaza, housing the Central Bank and Ministry of Finance.

To the north of the city is Queen's Park Savannah, a large open space with many playing fields, a racecourse with grandstands, and plenty of joggers. Below the level of the Savannah are the Rock Gardens, with lily ponds and flowers. Opposite are the Botanic Gardens, founded in 1818 by Sir Ralph Woodford. There is an amazing variety of tropical and sub-tropical plants from southeast Asia and South America, as well as indigenous trees and shrubs.

Adjoining the Gardens is the small Emperor Valley Zoo, which specializes in animals living wild on the island. (Open 0930-1800, no tickets after 1730, adults TT$2, children 3-12, TT$1). Also next to the Gardens is the presidential residence: a colonial style building in an "L" shape in honour of Governor James Robert Longden (1870-74). Just off the Savannah (on St Ann's Road) is Queen's Hall, where concerts and other entertainments are given.

There are several other Victorian-colonial mansions along the west side of Queen's Park Savannah, known as the Magnificent Seven (after the film of the same name). From south to north, they are Queen's Royal College; Hayes Court, the residence of the Anglican Archbishop; Prada's House, or Mille Fleurs; Ambard's House, or Roomor; the Roman Catholic Archbishop's residence; White Hall, formerly the Prime Minister's office, now housing a few government departments; and Killarney, Mr Stollmeyer's residence (now owned by the Government). Apart from Hayes Court, which was built in 1910, all were built in 1904. A walk along the north and west sides of the Savannah can be made in the early morning (before it gets too hot), arriving outside Queen's Royal College as the students are arriving and the coconut sellers are turning up outside. The Anglican Church of All Saints at 13 Queen's Park West is also worth a visit. Knowsley, another 1904 building, and the *Queen's Park Hotel* (1895), both on the south side of the Savannah, are interesting buildings too.

Before leaving this area, pay a visit to the Lookout, 300 feet high, which gives superb views across the city to the Gulf of Paria. The turn off to the

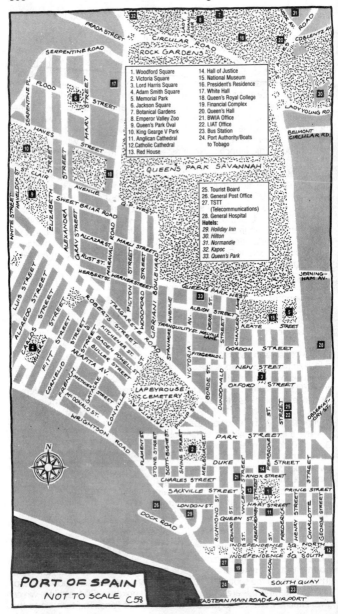

1. Woodford Square
2. Victoria Square
3. Lord Harris Square
4. Adam Smith Square
5. Memorial Park
6. Jackson Square
7. Botanical Gardens
8. Emperor Valley Zoo
9. Queen's Park Oval
10. King George V Park
11. Anglican Cathedral
12. Catholic Cathedral
13. Red House
14. Hall of Justice
15. National Museum
16. President's Residence
17. White Hall
18. Queen's Royal College
19. Financial Complex
20. Queen's Hall
21. BWIA Office
22. LIAT Office
23. Bus Station
24. Port Authority/Boats to Tobago

25. Tourist Board
26. General Post Office
27. TSTT (Telecommunications)
28. General Hospital
Hotels:
29. Holiday Inn
30. Hilton
31. Normandie
32. Kapoc
33. Queen's Park

PORT OF SPAIN
NOT TO SCALE   C.58

Lookout from the Savannah is near the zoo. Not safe at night.

Just off the Savannah, at the corner of Frederick and Keate Streets, is the small National Museum, in the former Royal Victoria Institute. It has sections on petroleum and other industries, Trinidad and Tobago's natural history, geology, archaeology and history, carnival costumes and photographs of kings and queens, and art exhibitions (including a permanent exhibition of the work of the 19th-century landscape artist, M J Cazabon; see **Culture** above). Entry free.

Away from the city centre, to the west of Port of Spain, is the suburb of St James where in Ethel Street is a large new Hindu temple, the Port of Spain Mandir. On the waterfront is the San Andres Fort built about 1785 to protect the harbour.

Excursions

There are pleasant drives in the hills around with attractive views of city, sea, and mountain: by Lady Chancellor Road to a look-out 600 feet above sea-level and to the Laventille Hills to see the view from the tower of the shrine of Our Lady of Laventille. From Fort George, a former signal station at 1,100 feet, there are also excellent views; to reach it take the St James route taxi from Woodford Square and ask to get off at Fort George Road; from there it is about 1 hour's walk uphill passing through some fairly tough residential territory. Midway along the Western Main Road to Chaguaramas a road runs off to the north, through the residential area of Diego Martin. The Blue Basin waterfall and natural landmark, on the Diego Martin river, is off this road, about a five-minute walk along a path from the town. (If you do leave your car to visit the fall, leave nothing of value in it. Also, you are advised to visit the falls in a group of five or six people if possible to avoid being robbed.) At River Estate, by Diego Martin, is a waterwheel which was once the source of power for a sugar plantation. The Western Main Road, with many pretty views, especially of the Five Islands, runs on to Carenage, where there is a remarkable little church, St Peter's Chapel, on the waterside, and to Chaguaramas, on the bay of the same name. From here you can take a launch to Gaspar Grande, one of the islands, on which are the Gasparee Caves. Also here is the Calypso Beach Resort (Gasparee Island).

North of Port of Spain is Maraval, just beyond which is the 18-hole St Andrews golf course at Moka (green fees US$16 for less than 5 people, cheaper for larger groups; there is also a swimming pool, US$3 for non-members). The North Coast Road branches off Saddle Road (which runs through Maraval back over the hills to meet the Eastern Main Road at San Juan), leading to Maracas Bay and Las Cuevas (see **Beaches** page 594).

The eastern corridor from Port of Spain is a dual carriageway and a priority bus route through the industrial and residential suburbs. At **St Joseph**, which was once the seat of government, is the imposing Jinnah Memorial Mosque. Nearby, high on a hill, is Mount St Benedict monastery, reached through Tunapuna. The monastery has a retreat, and a guest house, over US$40 (MAP), dinner US$6 extra. There are marvellous views over the Caroni Plain to the sea. A minibus from Port of Spain to Tunapuna takes at least 40 minutes, TT$2. There are several good, cheap Chinese restaurants in Tunapuna and a wide variety of fruits in the market. A little further along the Eastern Main Road, the Golden Grove Road branches south to Piarco international airport. If you turn north at this point (Arouca) a road winds 10 km up into the forested mountains to the Lopinot Complex, an estate built by the Comte de Lopinot at the turn of the 19th century. Originally called La Reconnaissance, it is now a popular picnic spot and destination for school trips; there is a small museum. Bar across the road, open "anyday, anytime".

Caurita Plantation and Nature Tours (c/o Gordon Dalla Costa, 143 Edward Street, Port of Spain) is set deep in the northern mountain range, some 1,200 feet above sea level. The 400 acres are rich in bird life, streams and other natural fauna and flora. There is lodging in four double rooms with bath and two without. Field trips are provided, in particular to the site of Amerindian inscriptions of rocks found only in this area.

Arima (the third largest city, 16 miles/25 km east of Port of Spain, population 26,000) has a small but interesting Amerindian museum at the Cleaver Woods Recreation Centre, on the west side of town. From Arima the road runs either to Toco at Trinidad's northeast tip (which is well worth a visit though its rocky shore defies bathing) or, branching off at Valencia, to the east coast. Take a bus or route taxi to Arima, from where the north coast can be reached at a couple of points. About 8 miles north of the town, off the Blanchisseuse Road, you can get (by car or taxi, TT$40) to the **Asa Wright Nature Centre**, an old plantation house overlooking a wooded valley and a must for bird-lovers. 16 rooms and full board are provided at the Asa Wright Centre, US$142 double per day (full board) for foreign tourists (Tel: 667-4655, Fax: 667-0493 for booking). There is swimming in a beautiful man-made pool, a network of trails and guided tours to see, for example, hummingbirds. The rare oil-birds in Dunstan Cave (also called Diablotin Cave) cannot at present be seen as the caves are closed indefinitely to visitors because the birds had been leaving. The centre is open daily 0900-1700; entrance charge TT$25.50 (US$6, US$4 children). It is wise to give 48 hours notice of your visit. This road carries on to Blanchisseuse (2 buses daily from Arima, TT$1.75). A nine-mile (14 km) walk from the road are the Aripo Caves (the longest system in Trinidad) with spectacular stalagmites and stalactites (in the wet season, June to December, a river runs through the caves).

From Arima you can take a bus, or hitchhike, to Brasso Seco and Paria (though the latter does not appear on some maps). From here the trail runs to Paria Bay, which is possibly the best beach on the island, about 8 miles/13 km, ask directions, or see the Tourism Development Authority's *Sites (trail guide)* book for the route. There is a primitive shelter on the beach but no other facilities so take provisions with you. At the beach, turn right to get to the bridge over the Paria River, from where it is a 5-minute walk inland to the spectacular Paria waterfall. Another path from the beach leads west to Blanchisseuse (7 miles/11 km), where the track forks; take the fork closer to the shore. A road continues west from Blanchisseuse to Las Cuevas.

Driving south you see dhoti-clad Indians in the rice fields, herds of water buffalo, Hindu temples and Moslem mosques. There are boat trips to the **Caroni Bird Sanctuary**, the home of scarlet ibis, whose numbers are dwindling as the swamp in which they live is encroached upon. The boats leave around 1600 so as to see the ibis returning to their roost at sunset. Egrets, herons and plovers can also be seen. Bus or route taxi from Port of Spain or San Fernando to Bamboo Grove Settlement no 1, on the Uriah Butler Highway, from where the boats leave, TT$2.50 or TT$5 respectively. Maxi taxi (green bands) from Independence Square. Ask to be dropped off at the Caroni Bird Sanctuary. Authorized boat operators in the swamp are Mr Winston Nanan (Tel: 645-1305), TT$25 pp, group rates available, and Mr David Ramsahai (Tel: 663-2207/645-4706), TT$20-25, children half price in each case; also enquire at the Asa Wright Centre for more detailed tours.

Tour operators in Port of Spain offer tours.

San Fernando on the southwest coast is a busy city (population 60,000), as yet not spoilt by tourism. An expressway connects Port of Spain with San Fernando, making it a half hour drive. In its neighbourhood are the principal industrial-development area of Point Lisas and the Pointe-a-Pierre oil refinery. Within the oil refinery is the 26-hectare Wild Fowl Trust, a conservation area with two lakes and breeding grounds for many endangered species (open 1000-1700, closed Saturday; entry TT$3, children TT$2. Tel: 637-5145, Ms Molly Gaskin or Mrs K Shepard on Tel: 662-4040, you must call 48 hours in advance to get permission to enter the compound (there are many entrances, it can be confusing).

A famous phenomenon to visit on the southwest coast near San Fernando is **Pitch Lake**, about 47 hectares of smooth surface resembling caked mud but which really is hot black tar; it is 41 metres deep. (It has been described by disappointed tourists, expecting something more dramatic, as looking like a parking lot.) If care is taken it is possible to walk on it, watching out for air holes bubbling up from the pressure under the ooze. The legend is that long ago the gods interred an entire tribe of Chaima Indians for daring to eat sacred hummingbirds containing the souls of their ancestors. In the place where the entire village sank into the ground there erupted a sluggish flow of black pitch gradually becoming an ever-refilling large pool. It provides a healthy, though recently decreasing, item in Trinidad's export figures. It can be reached by taking a bus from Port of Spain to San Fernando (TT$5 by air-conditioned express, by route taxi it costs TT$10) and then another from there to La Brea (TT$3). Official tours have been stopped but the former tour guides offer their services. Agree on a price in advance as there are no fixed rates any more. Sometimes there are crowds of guides who are difficult to avoid.

East of San Fernando, near Princes Town, is the Devil's Woodyard, one of 18 mud volcanoes on Trinidad, this one considered a holy site by some Hindus (it is also a natural landmark).

Warning: It is quite difficult to get beyond Arima and San Fernando by bus: you have to use route taxis, privately-operated maxi taxis, or hire a car or motorcycle.

Island Information—Trinidad

Airport Piarco International, 16 miles southeast of Port of Spain. Allow plenty of time to get there. The taxi fare to the centre of Port of Spain is US$20, (50% more after midnight). Taxi despatchers find taxis for new arrivals. Unlicensed taxis outside the main parking area charge about TT$50 (or less if business is bad). There is a direct bus, TT$1.50, 45 minutes-1 hour, from the airport to Port of Spain bus station, departing more or less every 30 minutes; buy tickets at the left luggage office at airport entrance. From the central bus terminal at the old railway station you will have to walk to Independence or Woodford Square for a route taxi for your ultimate destination. This is not advisable at night, especially if carrying luggage (ie take a taxi from the airport at night). If intending to take the bus to the airport, allow plenty of time to ensure arriving in time for checking in. Another possible route is bus, route or maxi taxi (TT$5) to Arouca, then route taxi (TT$2) to the airport. If waiting for a connection you can sleep overnight in the observation deck.

Transport Buses The bus service has been greatly improved by the addition of air-conditioned express buses, which run from Port of Spain to all the major population centres in Trinidad. Fares remain very reasonable, when compared with route taxis.

From Port of Spain to San Fernando costs TT$5, to Arima TT$3, to Tunapuna TT$2.50 and to Chaguanas TT$3. On all routes, you must purchase your ticket at the kiosk before boarding the bus; you may have to tender the exact fare. At the PTSC office in the old railway station on South Quay, you can get information showing how to reach the various sights by bus. The PTSC has been upgrading all services and plans to start excursions by bus. **Taxis** Most taxis set off from Independence Square, but those for St Ann's and St James leave from Woodford Square, for Carenage from St Vincent and Park Streets, and for Maraval from Duke and Charlotte Streets. Fares in town TT$2-3, further out TT$4-5. **Maxi-taxis** are minibuses which cover longer distances than route taxis; to the suburbs they are a bit cheaper than route taxis. They are colour coded and they set off mostly from Independence Square South (eg to Arima, TT$3; to Chaguanas, TT$3.50; to San Fernando, TT$5). Taxis to and from airport TT$65-75 (see above).

Where To Stay If you intend to stay in Trinidad for Carnival, when prices rise steeply, you must book a hotel well in advance. Some are booked a year ahead. If arriving without accommodation arranged at Carnival time, the tourist office at the airport may help to find you a room with a local family, though this like hotels will be expensive. You will be lucky to find anything. Prices are for 16 December 1991 to 15 April 1992, for a double room.

Hotels in the upper bracket in the **Port of Spain** area include: *Bel Air Piarco*, by the airport, Tel: 664-4771/3, Fax: add ext 15, US$68-87d for a small room, overpriced, typical airport hotel, swimming pool, good bar and restaurant but noise from planes; *Holiday Inn*, Wrightson Rd (PO Box 1017), Tel: 625-3361, Fax: 625-4166, in the business centre, US$105, all facilities; *Hilton*, on a rise at the corner of Lady Young and St Ann's Rds, northeast Queen's Park Savannah (PO Box 442), Tel: 624-3211, Fax: ext 6133, US$132-156, all facilities, restaurant excellent if pricey, including wide variety of lunch buffet, eating by the pool is not expensive, non-residents can eat/swim there, *Aviary Bar* for drinking and dancing; off St Ann's Rd, at the end of Nook Av (No 10) is *Normandie* (PO Box 851), Tel 624-1181/4, 52 rooms, a/c, US$70-90, but reduced rates for businessmen, swimming pool, in a complex with shops and restaurants, comfortable; *Kapok*, a Golden Tulip hotel, 16-18 Cotton Hill, St Clair (northwest Queen's Park Savannah, Tel: 622-6441, Fax: 622 9677), 71 rooms, a/c, TV, phone etc, US$78, restaurants, pool, shopping arcade; *Queen's Park Hotel*, 5-5a Queen's Park West (Tel: 625-1060/1, Fax: 624-1321), due to reopen after renovations in 1992; *Chaconia Inn*, 106 Saddle Rd, Maraval (Tel: 628-8603/5, Fax: 628-3214), US$75-85. *Tropical Hotel*, 6 Rookery Nook Road, Maraval, Tel: 622-5815/4249, US$50d, but US$80d during Carnival, a/c, pool, maid service, bar and restaurant attached, short walk from the Savannah, friendly, helpful, recommended. See **Excursions** above for accommodation at the St Benedict Monastery and Asa Wright Centre.

Guesthouses below US$20 a night are few and far between in the capital. The *Hillcrest Haven Guesthouse* is in this range (7A Hillcrest Rd, Cascade, Tel: 624-1344) but prices rise to US$30 during Carnival, minimum stay 6 nights, use of kitchen facilities, mixed reports. *Carr Rentals* (address above under **Car Rental**) offer accommodation, at special rates with car hire. *Zollna House*, 12 Ramlogan Development, La Seiva, Maraval, Tel: 628 3731, owned by Gottfried and Barbara Zollna, small guest house, food varied with local flavour, special diets catered for, US$50, breakfast and dinner per person US$5 and US$12 respectively. The Zollnas also manage the *Blue Waters Inn*, Batteaux Bay, Speyside, Tobago. *Copper Kettle Hotel*, 66-68 Edward Street, Tel: 625-4381, central, good, clean rooms with shower, US$20-36s, friendly and helpful staff, good restaurant; *Schultzi's Guest House and Pub*, 35 Fitt Street, Woodbrook, Tel: 622-7521, US$25 inc breakfast, kitchen, hot shower, good; *La Calypso Guest House*, 46 French Street, Woodbrook, Tel: 622-4077, US$25-30, clean, safe, efficient, car hire available; better, but under same management is *Alicia's Guest House*, 7 Coblentz Gardens, St Ann's, Tel: 623-2802, Fax: 623-8560, US$50d, including breakfast; *Trini House*, 5A Lucknow Street, St James, Tel/Fax: 638-7550, 4 rooms, US$30d including breakfast, English, German, Italian and French spoken by owners Michael Figuera and Margrit Lambrigger; *Valsayn Villa*, 34 Gilwell Road, Valsayn North, Tel: 645-1193, very large, modern, private house with beautifully furnished rooms, US$40, in one of the safest residential areas, 20 minutes by bus from down town Port of Spain, excellent home-cooked Indian meals available; *Errol J Lau Hotel*, 66 Edward St, US$22, clean and friendly, accepts Amex, recommended; *Kitty Peters*, 26 Warren Street, US$15pp, breakfast extra, immaculately clean, hot water showers, fans, quiet area, friendly; *Mardi Gras Guest House*, 134A Frederick Street, next to TDA building, Tel: 624-3897, from TT$65d (except carnival week), with private bath, dining room, bar; *The New City Cabs Guesthouse*, 93 Frederick St, Tel: 627-7372, cheap, but expect rats and intermittent water (US$10 without meals), "nutrition house" in basement with fruit and vegetable juices; *Bullet Guest House*, 6 Park Street, central, clean and safe, does not raise prices during carnival; *YWCA*, 8a Cipriani Blvd, under US$20. *Monique's Guest House*, 114 Saddle Road, Maravel, Tel: 628-3334, on road to Maracas Beach, US$35-40, clean, attractive, facilities for the disabled, Monique is helpful and hospitable. *Carnetta's House*, 28 Scotland Terrace, Analusia, Maraval, Tel: 628-2732, Fax: 628-7717, US$50-60 including breakfast, double that during carnival before tax, a/c, five rooms. *Naden's Court Guesthouse*, 32 St Augustine Circular Road, Tunapuna, Tel: 645-2937 (15-30 minutes to Port of Spain by bus on the priority route), US$35 with bath, less without, friendly, comfortable, safe and clean, laundry facilities, breakfast room where you can also get sandwiches in the evening, highly recommended. Halfway between the airport and Port of Spain near the St John's Road bus stop in the Saint Augustine district is the *Scarlet Ibis Hotel*, US$25 without shower, once upmarket, restaurant, pool, but now run down. At Longdenville, near Chaguanas, is the *Unique Hotel*, corner of Dam Road and Nelson Street, good service, TT$80 with bathroom, excellent meals, ask for the local Indian food, even at breakfast, recommended.

At mile post 23 on the Toco Main Road. north of **Balandra Bay** is Mr Hugh Lee Pow's *Green Acres Guest House*, TT$80, on a farm backed by the ocean, 3 good meals a day included, very kind and restful. At *Blanchisseuse* at Paradise Hill, Upper Village, Mrs Cooper offers bed and breakfast, not cheap but very good. *Surf's Country Inn*, in the same village, is a good restaurant and the owners plan to add some rooms, Tel: 669-2475. It can be hard to get a hotel room on the north coast in the low season when many places shut; self-catering may be difficult with few shops, no bank, no car rental.

In **San Fernando**, *Royal Hotel*, 46-54 Royal Road, Tel: 652-4881, Fax: 652-3924 US$55, a/c, kitchenette, lovely hilltop garden; *Farrell House Hotel*, Southern Main Road, Claxton Bay, near San Fernando, Tel: 659-2230, Fax: 659 2204, a/c, swimming pool, kitchenette, restaurant, good view of the Gulf of Paria, popular with visiting oil men, US$70. At Pointe-a-Pierre, near Guaracara cricket ground, *Blue Gardenia Guest House*, above a bar, basic, TT$20, "a real bargain", not much to do in the area but take-away food places and at *Mario's* nearby, prostitutes in the bar. At La Brea near the pitch lake is a hotel called *The Hideaway*, some rooms a/c, OK but not for the faint hearted, rooms available for 3, 12 or 24 hours.

At **Mayaro** on the southeast coast there are beach houses to rent which can be arranged through the TDA; the *Queen's Beach Hotel* is pleasant US$20, meals around US$10. Inland, the Victoria Regia Research Station, La Gloria Rd, Talparo, Mundo Nuevo, central Trinidad, Tel: Jack Price's wife 662-7113 or 662-5678, for all-inclusive accommodation and airport transfers, US$35 pp, or 7-night package including 5 guided tours, US$595 pp.

The Bed and Breakfast Association of Trinidad and Tobago, Diego Martin Post Office, Box 3231, Diego Martin (Tel: Miss Grace Steele 637-9329, Fax: 627-0856, or Mrs Barbara Zollna 628-3731, Fax: 625-6980), lists a number of establishments in Port of Spain, the suburbs, Carenage, Tunapuna, Arima and Blanchisseuse; prices from US$15 upwards double. It has a desk at the airport before immigration, very helpful.

Where To Eat In Port of Spain: at the main hotels, eg *Tiki Village* in the *Kapok Hotel*, serves good Polynesian and Chinese food; next door and owned by the *Kapok* is the *Café Savannah*, small and intimate (creole seafood, steak, good); in the *Normandie* complex, Nook Av, *La Fantasie* and *Café Trinidad*, both pricey. Also at 6 Nook Av is *Solimar*, Tel: 624-6267, Italian, reasonable prices, good service, outdoor dining, excellent food, reservations advisable and essential at weekends. *Mario's Pizza Place*, Tragarete Rd and other outlets; *Joe's Pizza*, St James, good, also other Italian dishes; *Wimpy*, 46a Independence Square; fast food at *Burger Boys and Pizza Boys*, Frederick St, and Ellerslie Plaza, Boissiere Village, Maraval (for take away Tel: 628-2697, good). *Kentucky Fried Chicken* in most cities and towns. The *Pelican Inn*, Coblenz Av, Cascade, serves food, but is mainly a pub, popular (with the gay community, too). *New Shay Shay Tian*, 81 Cipriani Blvd, recommended; *Monsoon*, 72 Tragarete Road, Indian dishes; *De Backyard*, 84 Picton Street, local dishes; *Hong Kong City Restaurant*, 86A Tragarete Road, Chinese; *Solimar*, 6 Nook Avenue, St Ann's, international food; *Michael's*, 143 Long Circular Road, Italian. If you've a yen for the best pepper shrimps in the Caribbean, the *Peninsular Restaurant* in Carenage is the place. For Chinese food in San Fernando, try *Soongs Great Wall*, 97 Circular Rd, round the corner from the *Royal Hotel*, very good, the distinctive, Trinidadian version of Chinese food. At the cruise ship harbour, *Coconut Village*, good food, cheap; *Breakfast Shed*, a big hall with several kitchens where locals eat, very cheap. At **Chaguaramas Anchorage**, Point Gourde Road for seafood. at **Blanchisseuse**, *Surf's Country Inn*, North Coast Road, Tel: 669-2475, good value, delicious meals.

Entertainment Trinidad abounds in evening entertainment, with calypso dancing eg *Sparrow's Hideaway*, limbo shows and international cabaret acts. Monday's local song and dance at the *Hilton* is less authentic in atmosphere than the steel band concerts on Fridays at the same venue. Entrance TT$10. For those wishing to visit the places where the local, rather than tourist, population go, anyone in the street will give directions. Though the atmosphere will be natural and hospitality generous, it will not be luxurious and the local rum is likely to flow. *Chaconia* on Saddle Rd has live music on Fridays and Saturdays. *Limelight* entertainment centre in Valpark Shopping Plaza has dancing and live floor shows; *Moon Over Bourbon Street*, West Mall, has a cocktail lounge and live local entertainment at weekends. The *Bel Air* near the airport has live entertainment on Saturday night. For spicier entertainment, go to the *International* (Wrightson Rd). *Mas Camp* club in Woodbrook has nightly entertainment including calypso and steel band (cover charge sometimes). *007 Club* nearby is good, open late (but lots of prostitutes who can be ignored). The Silver Stars Steel Orchestra (formed in the 1950s) can be seen in rehearsal Tuesdays, Wednesdays, Thursdays (check beforehand) at the Panyard, 56 Tragarete Road, Newtown, Woodbrook, Port of Spain. Silver Stars plays at the *Roxy*, at local parties, cruise ships or on the beach, workshops for individuals or groups can be arranged, contact Michael Figuera, Tel/Fax: 628-7550.

Theatres: Queen's Hall, 1-3 St Ann's Rd; Little Carib, White and Roberts Sts; Central Bank Auditorium, Eric Williams Plaza, Edward St. In San Fernando, Naparima Bowl reopened after a lengthy period of renovation; the folk theatre of the South National Institute of Performing Arts (Tel: 653-5355). See press for details of performances.

Tobago

Tobago is not as bustling as Trinidad but tourism is booming. The end of the oil boom in Trinidad and the growth of tourism in Tobago has narrowed the gap in living standards between the two islands. Nevertheless, it is ideal for those in search of relaxation. The tourist area is concentrated on the southwestern end, near the airport, and about six miles from the capital, **Scarborough**. In Scarborough itself there are interesting Botanic Gardens. Above the town is Fort King George (1770), which is well-maintained, has a small art gallery and good views along the coast. At the same location is a hospital. The town itself is pleasant but perhaps not worth an extended visit. Although there are some interesting buildings, such as the House of Assembly on James Park (built in 1925), and Gun bridge, with its rifle-barrel railings, the claim that "Except for the recently built Scarborough Mall there has been very little significant change in its appearance over 200 years" (Joan Bacchus-Xavier, *A Guide to Touring Tobago*) is exaggerated. There is plenty of new development with a new deep water harbour and cruise ship terminal. (NB The *Guide* is a handy book on the features of Tobago, it costs TT$20.)

Excursions

If you are driving around Tobago, the 1:50,000 map, usually available from the TDA office in Scarborough, at TT$20, is adequate, although note that many of the minor roads are only suitable for four-wheel drive. If you are hiking, get the three 1:25,000 sheets, not currently available in Tobago but you can get them from the Lands and Survey Division, Richmond Street, Port of Spain, or a good map shop abroad. East from Scarborough, on the Windward coast, is Bacolet Bay. Off the coastal road you can go to the Forest Reserve by taking a bus from Scarborough to Mount St George and then walking or hitching to Hillsborough Dam; from there continue northeast through the forest to Castara or Mason Hall. Directions, compass and supplies, including water, are essential. Birdwatching is excellent, but look out for snakes (none of them poisonous). By Mount St George (Tobago's first, short-lived principal town, then called George Town) is Studley Park House and Fort Granby which guards Barbados Bay. The road continues through Pembroke and Belle Garden, near where is Richmond Great House, now a hotel. Roxborough, the island's second town, also on the Windward coast, is worth a visit. The Argyll River waterfalls near Roxborough comprise four beautiful falls with a big green pool at the bottom, a ten minute walk upstream from the road. You can't miss them because of all the guides standing in the road.

Beyond Roxborough is King's Bay, with waterfalls near the road in which you can swim. From the fishing village of Speyside you can visit **Little Tobago**, an islet off the northeast coast, and sanctuary for birds. There are wild fowl and 58 species of other birds, including the red-billed tropic bird found here in the largest nesting colony in the north Atlantic. Boats across cost TT$35 (bargain; make sure the price includes return and a guided tour of the islet). Go early in the morning to see the birds. If you want to camp, you are supposed to have prior permission from the Forestry Division at Studley Park, Tel: 639-4468. They also have a rudimentary camp on the main ridge by the Roxborough-Parlaturies road, which can be used by arrangement. At Speyside, you can sling a hammock near the government centre on the beachfront: well-lit, a night-guard may keep your belongings under lock, but it may be windy. Buses from Scarborough to Charlotteville rarely go past Speyside even though the road is paved, because drivers do not like negotiating the hairpin bends

A trip to Charlotteville in the northeast (2 hours by bus from Scarborough, TT$2, be sure to check there is a bus back to Scarborough in the afternoon,

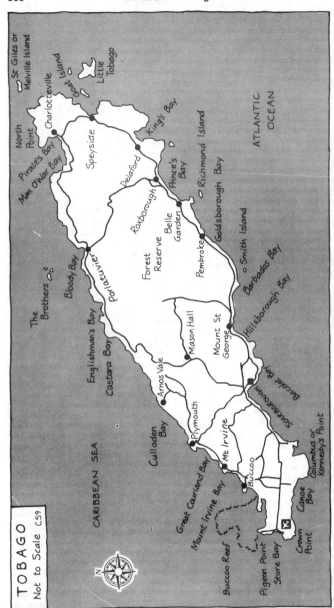

TOBAGO
Not to Scale C59

the timetable is unreliable; a route taxi is easier, TT$10, but not on Saturdays, when the Adventist drivers do not work) is recommended; there are magnificent views on the way and the village itself is on a fine horse-shoe bay with a good beach; swimming and snorkelling. On 29 June, the village celebrates St Peter's day with a festival. From Charlotteville, it is a 15-minute walk to Pirate's Bay, which is magnificent and unspoilt. Also adjacent is Man O'War Bay. It is fairly easy to hitch a ride from Charlotteville to Speyside.

At the southwest/tourist end of the island, many hotels and resorts are within walking distance of the airport. At Store Bay are the ruins of small Milford Fort, and brown pelicans frequent the beautiful beach, which is kept spotlessly clean and is a good place to watch the sunset. **Pigeon Point** has the island's most beautiful beach, clean and with calm water, though TT$10 is charged for adults and TT$3 for children for admission as the land is private; a wall has been built to stop you walking along the foreshore and groynes built by the owners have caused beach erosion. There are huts, tables and benches, lockers, bars, shopping, boat hire and water sports. It is another good place to watch the sunset. From Mount Irvine Bay (further north on the Caribbean coast), where there is an attractive, palm-fringed championship golf course (the hotel of the same name has a good beach—surfing) you can walk up to Bethel (about 2 miles), the island's highest village, for excellent views across the island. Another beach which is well worth a visit is Turtle Bay. The main town on this coast is Plymouth, with Fort James overlooking Great Courland Bay (site of the Courlander settlement in the 17th century). A much-quoted attraction in Plymouth is the enigmatic tombstone of Betty Stevens (25 November, 1783), which reads: "She was a mother without knowing it, and a wife, without letting her husband know, except by her kind indulgences to him." Hidden in the forest some miles from Arnos Vale is the Arnos Vale Sugarmill, dating from 1880; a recommended excursion, it is possible to hitchhike. It is difficult to continue along this coast by bus, Plymouth to Parlatuvier is not a recognized route. You have to go instead via Roxborough, with a lovely journey from there through the forest. Check that there is a bus back in the afternoon as there is nowhere to stay in Parlatuvier.

Buccoo Reef Glass-bottomed boats for visiting this undersea garden leave from Pigeon Point, Store Bay and the larger hotels nearby. Boats may be cheaper if hired from Buccoo Village. The charge is TT$30 for 2-2¼ hours, with shoes and snorkel provided; wear swimming costume and a hat. The dragging of anchors and greed of divers have tarnished the glory of this once marvellous reef, though. Elkhorn and other corals have been badly damaged by snorkellers and divers walking on them. The reef is now protected by law; it is forbidden to remove or destroy the corals or other marine life. Boat trips also include the Nylon Pool, an emerald-green pool in the Caribbean. Boats leave between 0900 and 1430, depending on the tide. Be selective in choosing which boat—and captain—you take for the trip; some are less than satisfactory (Selwyn's *Pleasure Girl* has been recommended, so has Archie and Mala's *Come to Starcheck*). From Scarborough to Buccoo by bus is TT$0.75. Taxis also go to Buccoo.

Island Information—Tobago

Transport To Tobago Almost all flights to Trinidad with BWIA can have a Tobago coupon added at no extra charge, dates can be open, worth booking on any trip. At least eight daily flights between Trinidad and Tobago; the crossing takes 12 minutes and costs TT$125 return, (adults), TT$62.50 children 2-12. Departures, however, are often subject to long delays and flights are heavily booked at weekends (at other times tickets can be bought the day before, even standby). BWIA also offer a one-day excursion, including lunch. Tobago's Crown Point airport has been extended to take international flights direct. There is a tourist office and a bank at the airport. **Boats** from Port of Spain to Tobago go once a day at 1400 Monday-Friday and 1100 on Sunday, no crossings on Saturday; all return crossings from Scarborough at 2300, but the schedule is modified monthly. The crossing is supposedly 5 hours. Hammocks can be slung at night. The trip can be rough. There are two vessels: M/F *Tobago*, on which all tickets cost TT$25 one way; and M/V *Panorama*, on which a cabin is TT$80 one way, tourist class TT$30 and economy TT$25. Tickets are sold at the Port Authority on the docks, office hours Monday-Friday 0700-1500, 1600-1800, 1900-2200 (buy passage in advance). You need a boarding pass and not just a ticket before you can board.

On Tobago (as on Trinidad), buy **bus** tickets in advance as drivers will not accept money. All buses originate in Scarborough. Buses every ½ hour between Crown Point (airport) and Scarborough, TT$0.75. Buy tickets from the grey hut outside the airport building where timetable is posted. Route taxis charge TT$4. **Taxi** fares are clearly displayed as you leave the airport: to Scarborough TT$25, the longest journey, to Charlotteville is TT$125. The Crown Point Airport route is the best, every 15-30 minutes, 0530-1830; Black Rock route is fair, every 30 minutes Monday-Friday 0530-2030, every 60-75 minutes Saturday and Sunday until 2000. There are less frequent and less reliable routes to Parlatuvier and Charlotteville.

Where To Stay In the vicinity of Crown Point: *Tropikist*, (Tel: 639-8512, Fax: 628-1110), rates on request, air conditioned rooms with balcony, pool, rocky beach, has been recommended; *Crown Point Beach Hotel*, PO Box 223, (Tel: 639-8781/3, Fax: 639-8731), studios and cabins, pool, US$55-85; *Jimmy's Holiday Resort*, Store Bay, Tel: 639-8292, US$200 per apartment, bars, eating places, shops nearby. If you turn right out of the airport, and take the first right, you come to *Store Bay Holiday Resort*, Tel: 639-8810, 5 minutes' walk, at US$30 about the cheapest in this area, but self-catering only, 15 apartments, clean, well-furnished, kitchen, gardens, small pool, friendly; next door is *Kariwak Village*, US$90, very nice, cabins, restaurant with excellent food, no beach, pool, PO Box 27 (Tel: 639-8545/8442, Fax: 639-8441); *Jetway Holiday Resort*, 100 metres from airport terminal, can be noisy until after 2200, pleasant self-contained units with cooking facilities, friendly, helpful, US$25d, a few minutes' walk to Pigeon Point and Store Bay, Tel: 639-8504; a bit further from the main road is *Golden Thistle* (Tel: 639-8521, Fax: 639-2213) US$50, quiet location. There are lots of guesthouses and small hotels along the road between the airport and Pigeon Point.

Accommodation in **Scarborough** is either in guesthouses or bed and breakfast (contact the *Association* c/o Mr Lloyd Anthony, *Tony's House*, Carnbee, Tel: 639-8836, or the Tourism Development Authority on Tobago; the brochure lists 14 properties, mostly in the southwest or near Scarborough, about US$20d). Highly recommended is *Glenco Guest House*, Glen Road, Scarborough (rates negotiable according to length of stay), clean, breakfast US$2-3, Tel: 639 2912. *Jacob's Guesthouse*, Scarborough, good, TT$30d, Tel: 639-2271, as is *Hope Cottage*, Fort Street, US$11 b&b; several others, eg *Della Mira*

Guest House, Windward Rd, Tel: 639-2531, US$31-45; *Miriam's Bed and Breakfast*, Federal Villa, Crooks River, Tel: 639-3926, six rooms, US$35d, shared bath, fan, modest but clean and comfortable, run by Miriam Edwards, secretary of the Bed and Breakfast Association. *Arnos Vale Hotel*, PO Box 208, Tel: 639-2881, Fax: 639-4629, 30 rooms, US$180, beautiful surroundings, hospitable, dive shop. Ten minutes drive from Scarborough is *Ocean View*, John Dial, Tel: 639-6796, US$30 pp, recommended; under same management is *Windy Edge*, Concordia, 12 minutes drive from the harbour, 600 feet above sea level overlooking the Atlantic and the Caribbean, spacious grounds, quiet, highly recommended, US$30 pp inc breakfast, evening meals by arrangement US$25-30, route taxis pass by, Tel: 639-5062. On the **Windward** coast, *Richmond Great House*, Tel: 660-4467, Fax: 639-2213, (**see page 605**) rates on request, overlooking Richmond Bay, lovely, airy, quiet, only three suites and two family rooms; one guest house in Roxborough, ask for Mrs Carter, Police Station Road, TT$25pp, 2 rooms, kitchen, shower, quiet, friendly; *Blue Waters Inn*, Batteaux Bay, Speyside, Tel: 660-4341, Fax: 660-5195, an isolated and delightfully unsophisticated hotel, US$90-220d, 29 rooms, 4 self-catering units for 4 people each, caters for people who want to sit on the beach, bird watchers and divers. At **Charlotteville** are *Man O'War Bay Cottages*, Tel/Fax: 660-4327, cottages US$50-125 a night, sleep 4, minimum 2 nights, spacious, well-equipped kitchen, right on beach with tropical gardens behind, barbeque facilities, expensive shop with limited range, check your shopping bill carefully; *Cholson's Chalet* has one-three bedroomed apartments separated from the beach by the road, TT$60-80, contact Hewitt Nicholson (Tel: 639-2847) or Pat Nicholson (Tel: 639-8553). *Alyne*, TT$50, very friendly, clean, comfortable; *Venizia*, TT$60-80, new, clean. Ask around for private accommodation, it is available, eg Mrs McCannon's house in Bellaire Road, not luxury but OK. At **Plymouth**, *Tante Loo*, old place but friendly; *Cocrico Inn*, Tel: 639-2961, Fax: 639-6565, US$55, swimming pool, MAP US$22 pp extra. *Mount Irvine Bay Hotel and Golf Course* (**see page 596** —PO Box 222, Tel: 639-8871, Fax: 639-8800) charges from US$195-350d, deluxe suites US$720 one-bedroom, US$1,000 two-bedrooms, reported badly run and overpriced. *Grafton Beach Resort*, Black Rock, Tel: 639-0191/9444, Fax: 639 0030, luxury, highly recommended, a/c, pool, TV, friendly and efficient service, excellent beach front location in Stonehaven Bay, US$195-220; *Palm Tree Village Hotel*, Little Rockly Bay, Milford Road, Tel: 639-4180, Fax: 623-5776, a/c, kitchenette, beach, US$120, US$240 2-bedroom villa, US$450 4-bedroomed villa; *Turtle Beach Hotel*, PO Box 201, Plymouth, Tel: 639-2851, Fax: 639-1495, pool, on beach, a/c, US$110-150, poor service, standards criticized, not recommended; *Arthur's On-Sea*, Crown Point, Tel: 639-0196, Fax: 639-4122, kind and helpful, a/c, pool, 4 minutes' walk from safe beach, US$60, recommended; *Bougainvillea Beach Towers*, Studley Park, swimming pool, a/c, kitchenette, on beach, US$36-48; *Coral Reef Guest House and Apartments*, Tel: 639-2536, Fax: 639-0770, a/c, pool, US$60; *Old Grange Inn*, Buccoo, Mt Irvine, Tel: 639-0275, a/c, US$50; *Samada Guest House*, Milford Road, a/c, kitchenette, US$32; *Credit Union Guest House*, Black Rock, clean, kitchen, bath, five minutes walk to the beach, US$10, contact office in Scarborough, Bacolet Street.

There are many cheap guesthouses throughout Tobago and many people take in visitors: ask at any village store (prices for room only).

Where To Eat The *Beach Bar* at Store Bay has music all day on Saturday, and an excellent barbecue from 2000-2400, for TT$15 per head. At the *Store Bay Resort* there are a number of restaurants, including *John Grant's*, many have tables outside near the beach, recommended is *Miss Jean's*, US$2 and less for all kind of 'ting', a full meal with drinks for two costs less than US$10, try crab and dumplings; the restaurant at the *Kariwak Village* has excellent food, well served; nearby is *Golden Spoon* (junction of roads to Scarborough and Pigeon Point, Tel: 639-8078, open for breakfast, lunch and dinner, local dishes) and *Columbus Snackette* (at the crossroads near Crown Reef Hotel). The *Papillon Restaurant* at the *Old Grange Inn*, Tel: 639-0275, and the *Sugar Mill* at Mt Irvine Bay Hotel have both been recommended for excellent meals. *Le Beau Rivage* at the Mt Irvine Golf Course, French and international cuisine; the *Conrado Beach Hotel*, Tel: 639-0145, has local dishes. The *Blue Crab*, Robinson Road, Scarborough, Tel: 639-2737, specializes in local food, good lunch, as do *Gemma's Sea View*, Speyside, Tel: 660-4066, on a tree top platform by the beach, good, filling lunch TT$20, closed Saturday (Adventists) and *Rouselles*, Bacolet Street, Tel: 639-4738. *La Tataruga*, Idlewild, near Scarborough, Tel: 639-1861, excellent Italian food, but they insist on advance booking; *Old Donkey Cart*, Bacolet, Tel: 639-3551, German wines, closed Wednesdays; *Dillon's Seafood Restaurant*, Crown Point, fresh fish, good service, generous portions. The bar/restaurant at Pigeon Point is good value, but closes at 1700. *Buddies Café* in the Mall, Scarborough, Tobago, is reasonable, Tel: 639-3355.

Crown Point Supermarket is well-stocked but expensive; small huts along Store Bay Road are cheaper.

Entertainment Though not as lively as Trinidad, Tobago offers dancing in its hotels. The Buccoo Folk Theatre gives an attractive show of dancing and calypso every Thursday at 2100. There is a Tobago Folk Performing Company. In Scarborough, *El Tropical* is a club frequented mostly by locals; it has a live show every Saturday night at about 2330. Also *JG's Disco*, nightly. The *Starting Gate Pub*, Shirvan Road, is recommended.

Information For Visitors

Documents
Passports are required by all visitors aged 16 and over. Passports issued by South Africa and Taiwan are not valid for entry into Trinidad and Tobago. US and Canadian citizens travelling on birth certificates for up to two months will be accepted if they have some form of identity with photograph. **Visas** are not required by nationals of most Commonwealth countries, West European countries (except Netherlands), Brazil, Colombia, Israel, Pakistan and Turkey; for US citizens for visits up to 2 months; and for Venezuelans for stays of up to 14 days. Some Commonwealth citizens do need visas, however; these include Australia, New Zealand, India, Sri Lanka, Nigeria, Uganda, Tanzania, and Papua New Guinea. A visa normally requires 48 hours' notice. A waiver for those with no visa can be obtained at the airport, but it costs US$26. **Entry permits** for one month are given on arrival; they can be extended at the immigration office in Port of Spain (at 67 Frederick Street) for TT$5. This is a time-consuming process, so try and get a 3-month entry permit if planning a long stay.

After 6 weeks visitors must get a tax clearance from the Inland Revenue office on Edward St. Even though you may not get asked for it all travellers need a return ticket to their country of origin, dated, not open-ended, proof that they can support themselves during their stay, an address at which they will be staying in Trinidad (the tourist office at the airport can help in this respect). Only those coming from an infected area need a yellow fever inoculation certificate. People going to Venezuela can obtain a tourist card (free of charge) at the Aeropostal office; this means buying a return ticket but this can be refunded or changed if an alternative

ticket out of Venezuela is later purchased.

How To Get There By Air
BWIA and LIAT link Trinidad with Tobago (several daily flights). **USA**: United Airlines (from New York); BWIA (Miami, New York); American Airlines (New York, Puerto Rico). **Canada**: Air Canada and BWIA from Toronto. **Europe**: British Airways (shared route from London with BWIA via Barbados); KLM (two flights a week from Amsterdam, one is via Paramaribo, Suriname, the other continues on to Paramaribo); BWIA (from Cologne/Bonn, Munich, Frankfurt, London, Stockholm, Zurich). **Venezuela**: United Airlines and Aeropostal from Caracas (book as far in advance as possible, ticket valid 7-17 days, you cannot buy it at Caracas airport). **Guyana**: BWIA daily flights from Georgetown. **Inter-Island**: BWIA, LIAT and ALM airlines connect Trinidad with other Caribbean islands including Antigua, Aruba, Barbados, Curaçao, Grenada, Jamaica (Kingston and Montego Bay), St Croix, St Kitts, St Lucia, St Maarten, St Vincent and San Juan, Puerto Rico (also American Airlines). There are flights to Tobago (Crown Point Airport) with Liat and/or BWIA from Aruba, Barbados, Frankfurt, Grenada, London, Miami, St Lucia and Stockholm, eliminating the need to change planes at Piarco airport. BWIA (and possibly other airlines) is reluctant to let you leave unless you have an onward ticket from your immediate destination to the next one.

Airline Offices
BWIA is at 30 Edward Street (Tel: 625-1010/1, 625-5866/8), opens for reservations at 0730; there is a separate desk for Tobago flights (take a number and wait in the queue; be prepared for a long wait, particularly for international tickets). BWIA at

Piarco airport, Tel: 664-4871/3400 (open later than Edward Street office for reservations for Tobago); also at Carlton Centre, San Fernando, Tel: 657-9712/1359, and at Crown Point airport, Tobago, Tel: 639-3130. Aeropostal, 13 Pembroke Street, Tel: 623-8201/6522. The following are at 90 Independence Square: American Airlines (Tel: 625-1661), British Airways (Tel: 625-18116); Air Canada is at 88 Independence Square (Tel: 625-2195). KLM and ALM, 1 Richmond Street, Tel: 625-1719. Guyana Airways, 44-48 Edward Street, Tel: 627- 2753/625- 1171. LIAT, CIC Building, 122-124 Frederick Street, Tel: 623-1837/4480. There is a 15% VAT on airline tickets purchased in Trinidad and Tobago.

There is a TT$50 exit tax.

How To Get There By Sea

The Geest Line started a service to Trinidad from Barry, South Wales, UK, in 1992, see page 12. A weekly passenger and cargo ferry service run by Windward Lines Limited sails from Trinidad to Güiria, Venezuela on Tuesday 2000, Wednesday 0700, returning Wednesday 2300. On Thursday 1600 it sets off for St Vincent, Barbados and St Lucia, arriving there Saturday 0700, returning Sunday 0700, getting back to Trinidad Tuesday 0700. For information and tickets contact United Caribbean Shipping Agency, Suite 106, Furness Building, 86B Independence Square, Port of Spain, Tel: 625-6328, Fax: 624-6865. For a round trip to St Lucia the fare, including cabin and VAT, is TT$621, return fare to Güiria TT$229 including VAT, no cabin, child reductions. Every Friday morning a boat carrying racing pigeons leaves for Güiria, Venezuela. Contact Francis Sagones, Tel: 632-0040; or talk to Siciliano Bottini in the Agencia Naviera in Güiria for sea transport in the other direction. Fishing boats and trading vessels ply this route frequently and can often be persuaded to take passengers. Be careful to get your passport stamped at both ends of the journey. A Trinidadian, Adrian Winter Roach, travels at least once a week with his boat El Cuchillo, and charges US$60 one way, US$100 return, he can be contacted in Venezuela through the Distribuidora Beirut, Calle Valdez 37, Güiria, Tel/Fax: 81677.

Customs

Duty-free imports: 200 cigarettes or 50 cigars or ½lb tobacco, 1 quart wine or spirits, and TT$50-worth of gifts. Perfume may not be imported free of duty, but may be deposited with Customs until departure. Passengers in transit, or on short visits, can deposit goods such as liquor with Customs at the airport and retrieve it later free of charge.

Taxis

Look for cars with first letter H on licence plates (no other markings). Agree on a price before the journey and determine whether the price is in TT or US dollars. Taxis are expensive, although route taxis (similar to colectivos) are very cheap. These cannot be distinguished from ordinary taxis, so ask the driver. They travel along fixed routes, like buses, but have no set stops, so you can hail them and be dropped anywhere along the route. During rush hour it is not easy to hail them, however, and in general it takes time to master how they work. On long-distance journeys, let the locals pay first so that you know you're not overcharged. (Be warned that route taxis are not covered by insurance so you cannot claim against the driver if you are involved in an accident.) There are also "pirate" taxis with the P registration of a private car, which cost the same as the ordinary taxis, although you can sometimes bargain with the drivers. "Ghost" taxis accept fares and drive off with your luggage as well—be warned. Be careful if hitching on Tobago as the cars that stop often prove to be pirate taxis.

Car Rentals

Car rental can be difficult on Trinidad, particularly at weekends, because of heavy demand from Trinidadians, many of whom cannot afford to buy but rent on a long term basis. Several companies do not accept credit cards, but require a considerable cash deposit which can be difficult to convert back into a hard currency. Small cars can be rented from TT$120 a day upwards, unlimited mileage, check tyres before driving off. Deposit TT$500-1,000 (varies from company to company, as does method of payment), book in advance. Insurance costs TT$6-7. Car rental firms include Hertz, at Hilton Hotel (Tel: 624-3316), Piarco Airport and on Tobago (639-8778); Auto Rentals Ltd, Richmond St/Tragarete Rd, Port of Spain (623-3063), Piarco (Tel: 664-3907), and in San Fernando (658-1470/1417); Bacchus Taxi and Car Rental, 37 Tragarete Rd (622-5588); Carr's, 34 Sydenham Av, St Ann's (624-1028); Wong's, 114 Belmont Circular Rd (624-5385); Singh's, 7-9 Wrightson Rd (625-4247) and at airport, reasonable rates. Also on Tobago: Rollocks, Tel: 639-0398; Williams, Tel: 660-4315/4377; Banana Rentals at Kariwak Village, cars and jeeps, TT$125/day, scooters TT$56/day (deposit

TT$350), bicycles TT$25/day (Tel: 639-8441/8545); Suzuki Jeep Rental (and small cars), and Cherry Scooter Rental at *Sandy Point Beach Club* (scooters and deposit cheaper than Banana); Tobago Travel, P O Box 163, (639-8778/8105), Baird's, Lower Sangster Hill Road (639-2528) and other agencies. Bicycles can be hired at the *Mount Irvine Bay Hotel*. Some companies only rent for a minimum of 3 days.

Driving is on the left and the roads are narrow, winding, and in places rather rough. On Tobago the roads are good in the south but badly maintained further north. The road between Charlotteville and Bloody Bay is for four-wheel drive vehicles only. International and most foreign driving licences are accepted for up to 90 days, after that the visitor must apply for a Trinidad and Tobago licence and take a test. Visitors must always carry their driving document with them.

Where To Stay

There are many hotels on the islands and the better known ones are expensive, but there are very good guest houses and smaller hotels which are reasonable. Information about accommodation can be obtained from Trinidad and Tobago Tourism Development Authority (TDA) at 134-138 Frederick Street, Port of Spain. Their office at Piarco airport is helpful. A 15% value added tax is charged at all hotels and in most a 10% service charge is added to the bill. Some, like the *Hilton*, add a 2% surcharge.

Camping

Camping on Trinidad is unsafe and is not recommended. Try the Boca Islands to the west. On Tobago, it is possible near the Mt Irvine beach. Ask the taxi drivers for advice on where to camp. *Canoe Bay Resorts* has 50 camp sites available, TT$20 per adult and TT$5 for children per night, includes toilet and shower but use of kitchen costs extra, Tel: 639-4055. At Store Bay and on the road to *Kariwak Village*, etc, there are small stores selling provisions.

Food

A wide variety of European, American and traditional West Indian dishes (these include pork souse, black pudding, roast sucking pig, sancoche and callaloo stews, and many others) is served at hotels and guest houses. Some also specialize in Créole cooking. There is also, of course, a strong East Indian influence in the local cuisine. Seafood, particularly crab, is excellent. Do not eat local oysters: their habitat has become polluted. Turtle meat is sold even though turtles are protected, do not buy it. The many tropical fruits and vegetables grown locally include the usual tropical fruits, and sapodillas, eddoes and yam tanias. The variety of juices and ice creams made from the fruit is endless. For those economizing, the *roti*, a pancake which comes in various forms, filled with peppery stew, for about TT$8, is very good. The best place for *roti* is probably the *Hot Shoppe for Hot Roti*, on Mucurapo St, west of downtown Port of Spain.*Buss up shut* (shut means shirt) is a curry, pickle and Indian bread, recommended. *Pelau*, savoury rice and meat, is also good, but when offered pepper, refuse unless you are accustomed to the hottest of curries or *chili* dishes. Try also *saheena*, deep-fried patties of spinach, dasheen, split peas and mango sauce. Dumplings are a must on Tobago, particularly good with crab. Eating out is fairly expensive in Trinidad and Tobago, other than in roti shops. The shopping malls offer a variety of places to eat, including Créole, Indian, Chinese, etc.

A local drink is mauby, like ginger beer, and the rum punches are recommended. Fresh lime juice is also recommended; it is sometimes served with a dash of Angostura bitters. Local beers are Carib ("each bottle tastes different") and Stag ("the recession fighter").

Tipping

If no service charge on bill, 10% for hotel staff and restaurant waiters; taxi drivers, 10% of fare, minimum of 25 cents (but no tip in route taxis); dock-side and airport porters, say 25 cents for each piece carried; hairdressers (in all leading hotels), 50 cents.

Shopping

The main Port of Spain shopping area is in Frederick Street, but pleasanter are Long Circular Mall at the junction of Long Circular Rd and Patna Street, St James and West Mall, Cocorite, Port of Spain, considered to be the best in the country. Purchases can be made at in-bond shops in Port of Spain and at the airport. Markets offer wide varieties of fruit. Handicrafts can also be purchased at markets. The Tourism Development Authority has a list of suppliers of traditional items such as batik and fabrics, straw and cane work, wood carvings, leather, ceramics, copper work and steelpans. A good place for souvenirs is Lakhan's Bazaar, 32 Western Main Road, St James. It has a branch at Piarco Airport. The Central Market is on the Beetham Highway. Do not purchase turtle shell, black coral, or other protected, shell items.

Bookshops

R I K Services Ltd, Frederick Street, Port of Spain, and 104 High Street, San Fernando; Cosmic Book Services, West Mall; Inprint Bookstore, 35 Independence Square; St Aubyns Book Services, Palm Plaza, Maraval.

Banks

In Port of Spain: Republic Bank of Trinidad and Tobago (formerly Barclays, gives cash on Visa card), Royal Bank of Trinidad and Tobago, Bank of Commerce, Bank of Nova Scotia, Trinidad Co-operative Bank, Citibank, Citicorp Merchant Bank, National Commercial Bank of Trinidad and Tobago (this bank has a branch at Piarco airport, open 0600-2200). All banks charge a fee for cashing travellers' cheques, some more than others, so check first. Banks generally will not change Venezuelan or other South American currencies.

Currency

The Trinidad and Tobago dollar, fixed at TT$2.40 = US$1 since 1976, was devalued to TT$3.60 = US$1 in December, 1985, then to TT$4.25 = US$1 in August, 1988. Notes are for TT$1, 5, 10, 20 and 100. Coins are for 1, 5, 10, 25 and 50 cents. A maximum of TT$200 may be taken out of the country. When changing money keep the receipt so that what remains unspent can be changed back, as long as there is no more money taken out than was brought in. Travellers' cheques and major credit cards are accepted almost everywhere.

Warning

The people of both islands are, as a rule, very friendly but downtown Port-of-Spain and the Queens Park area are no longer safe at night, especially for women. Care must be taken everywhere at night. The incidence of theft has risen sharply. The area east of Arima and south of Piarco airport should only be visited with residents or guides. Avoid the area around the port or bus terminal except when

making a journey. A favourite local saying is 'Tobago is Paradise, Trinidad is New York'. Take care accordingly.

Climate

The climate on the islands is tropical, but, thanks' to the trade winds, rarely excessively hot. Temperatures vary between 21° and 37°C, the coolest time being from December to April. There is a dry season from January to mid-May and a wet season from June to November, with a short break in September, but the rain falls in heavy showers and is rarely prolonged. Humidity is fairly high.

Clothing

Beachwear should be kept for the beach. In the evening people dress more smartly.

Business Hours

Government offices 0800-1600, Monday-Friday. Banks: 0900-1400, Monday-Thursday, 0900-1200, 1500- 1700, Friday. Businesses and shops: 0800- 1600/ 1630, Monday-Friday (shops 0800- 1200 on Saturday).

Public Holidays

Carnival Sunday, Monday and Tuesday, before Ash Wednesday, Good Friday, Easter Monday, Whit Monday, Eid ul-Fitr (17 April in 1991), Corpus Christi, Labour or Butler's Day (19 June), Eid ul-Azha (23 June in 1991), Discovery Day (first Mon in August), Independence Day (31 August), Yaum um-Nabi (20 September in 1991), Republic Day (24 September); Divali (18 October in 1991), Christmas Day, Boxing Day.

   Special Events: All· Souls' Day (2 November) is not a holiday, but is celebrated. The Hindu festival of Divali (Sept/Oct) is a holiday, but Phagwah (Feb/March) is not. Similarly, of the Moslem festivals, Eid ul-Fitr is a public holiday, but Eid ul-Azha (June/July) and Yaum um-Nabi (1 October, 1990) are not (all fall 10-11 days earlier each year).

Time Zone

Atlantic Standard Time, 4 hours behind GMT, 1 hour ahead of EST.

Useful Addresses

(Port of Spain) **Canadian** High Commission,

72 South Quay; **US** Embassy, 19 Queen's Park West (Tel: 622-6371/6), 0700-1700; **British** High Commission, 3rd floor, Furness House, 90 Independence Square (PO Box 778), Tel: 625-2861-6, 0730-1530; **New Zealand** Consulate, 69 Independence Square; **German** Embassy, 7-9 Marli St (Tel: 628-1630/2); **French** Embassy, Tatil Bldg, Maraval Rd, Tel: 622-7446/7; **Danish** Consulate General, 72-4 South Quay, PO Box 179, Tel: 623-4700; **Brazilian** Embassy, 18 Sweet Briar Rd, St Clair; **Argentine** Consulate, 16 Victoria Av; **Venezuelan** Embassy, 16 Victoria Av (Tel: 627-9823/4), 0900-1300, 1400-1600. Changes of address, and other representatives, can be checked at the Ministry of External Affairs, Tel: 623-4116/60.

Weights And Measures

Trinidad and Tobago have gone metric, so road signs are given in kilometres.

Electric Current

110 or 220 volts, 60 cycles AC.

Post And Telephones

The main Post Office is on Wrightson Road, Port of Spain, and is open 0700-1700, Monday-Friday. The main Telecommunications Services of Trinidad and Tobago Ltd (TSTT) office on Independence Square and 1 Edward St operates international telephone, cable, telex and fax, and is open 24 hours. There is a TSTT telephone office in Scarborough, Tobago. The service for international calls has improved greatly, with direct dialling to all countries but from anywhere other than the TSTT office it can be difficult and expensive. Fax and telex from main hotels. The internal telephone system is being improved.

Press

The two main daily papers are the *Trinidad and Tobago Express* and the *Trinidad Guardian*. There are several racier weekly papers which appear on Friday or Saturday.

Travel Agency

The Travel Centre Limited, Level 2, Uptown Mall, Edward Street, Port of Spain, Tel: 625-1636/4266, Fax: 623-5101 (P O Box 1254) is an American Express Travel Service Representative. The Davemar Reservations Agency, 2 Aylce Glen, Petit Valley, Tel: 637-7583, run by Marjorie Cowie, can arrange accommodation in hotels, guesthouses or self-catering and organize sightseeing tours.

Trinidad And Tobago Tourism Development Authority (TDA)

134-138 Frederick Street, Port of Spain, Tel: 623-1932/4, Fax: 623-3848, has lists of hotels, restaurants, tour operators, monthly schedule of events, etc. Piarco Tourist Bureau (at the airport), Tel: 664-5196, helpful with hotel or guest house reservations for your first night. In Tobago the Division of Tourism is in Scarborough, NIB Mall, there is a kiosk, and the head office is on the third level, next to *Buddy's Restaurant* (Tel: 639-2125/3566, or 639-INFO for information at Crown Point airport, Fax: 639-3566).

Overseas offices all have up-to-date hotel lists: **USA**: 15th floor, Forest Hills Tower, 118-35 Queen's Blvd, New York, NY 11375, Tel: (718) 575-3909 or 1-800-232-0082 (toll free), Fax: (718) 575-3518; Suite 310, 330 Biscayne Blvd, Miami, Florida 33122, Tel: (305) 374-2056, Fax: 372-8142. **UK**: Suite 1, 7th floor, 113 Upper Richmond Road, London SW15 2TL, Tel: (081) 780-0318, Fax: (081) 780-0319.

Our warmest thanks go to David Renwick of Port of Spain for updating this chapter.

THE GUIANAS

Introduction

LIKE the West Indians, the people of the three Guianas, Guyana (formerly British Guiana), Suriname (formerly Dutch Guiana) and French Guyane, are not regarded as belonging to Latin America. The explanation of these three non-Iberian countries on the South American continent goes back to the early days of the Spanish conquest of the New World. There was no gold or any other apparent source of wealth to attract the attention of the Spanish discoverers. This part of the coast, which Columbus had first sighted in 1498, seemed to them not only barren but scantily populated and seemingly uninhabitable. The English, the French and the Dutch, anxious to establish a foothold in this part of the world, were not so fastidious.

All three countries are geographically very similar: along the coast runs a belt of narrow, flat marshy land, at its widest in Suriname. This coastland carries almost all the crops and most of the population. Behind lies a belt of crystalline upland, heavily gouged and weathered. The bauxite, gold and diamonds are in this area. Behind this again is the massif of the Guiana Highlands. They reach a height of 3,000 feet (915 metres), in the Tumuc-Humac range, the divide between French Guyane and Suriname, and Brazil, and 9,219 feet (2,810 metres) at flat-topped Mount Roraima, where Guyana, Venezuela and Brazil all meet.

GUYANA

Introduction

GUYANA has an area of 83,000 square miles, nearly the size of Britain, but only about 0.5% (or 280,000 acres) is cultivated. About 90% of the population lives on the narrow coastal plain, either in Georgetown, the capital, or in villages along the main road running from Charity in the west to the Suriname border. Most of the plain is below sea level. Large wooden houses stand on stilts above the damp soil. A sea wall keeps out the Atlantic and the fertile clay soil is drained by a system of dykes. Sluice gates are opened to let out water at low tide; and separate irrigation channels are used to bring water back to the fields in dry weather. In several places fresh water is supplied by reservoirs, known as conservancies. Most of the western third of the coastal plain is undrained and uninhabited. The strange cultural mix: Dutch place names and drainage techniques, Hindu temples, mosques, coconut palms and calypso music, reflect the chequered history of the country.

Four major rivers cross the coastal plain, (from west to east) the Essequibo, the Demerara, the Berbice, and the Courantyne (which forms the frontier with Suriname). Only the Demerara is crossed by a bridge. Elsewhere ferries must be used. In the mouth of the Essequibo river are islands the size of Barbados. The lower reaches of these rivers are navigable; but waterfalls and rapids prevent them being used by large boats to reach the interior.

Inland from the coastal plain most of the country is covered by thick rain forest, although in the east there is a large area of grassland. Some timber has been extracted, but the main economic activity is mining: principally bauxite, but gold and diamonds are sifted from the river beds by miners using mercury (at considerable environmental cost). Large areas of rain forest are still undisturbed and even the more accessible areas have varied and spectacular wildlife, including brightly-plumaged birds. Towards the Venezuelan border the rain forest rises in a series of steep escarpments, with spectacular waterfalls, the highest and best-known of which are the Kaieteur Falls on the Potaro river. In the southwest of the country is the Rupununi Savanna, an area of open grassland more easily reached from Brazil than from Georgetown.

The area west of the Essequibo river, about 70% of the national territory, is claimed by Venezuela. Another area in the southeast, between the Koeroeni and New rivers, is claimed by Suriname.

Until the 1920s there was little natural increase in population, but the eradication of malaria and other diseases has since led to a rapid growth in population, particularly among the East Indians (Asian), who, according to most estimates comprise over 50% of the population. The 1980 census showed the following ethnic distribution: East Indian 51.4%; black (African Negro and Bush negro) 30.5%; mixed 11%; Amerindian 5.3% (Carib 3.7%, Arawak 1.4%); Chinese 0.2%; white (mostly Portuguese) 0.1%; other 1.5%. The total population in 1991 was put at 760,000. Descendants of the original Amerindian inhabitants are divided into nine ethnic groups, including the Akawaio, Makuxi and PeMonday. Some have lost their

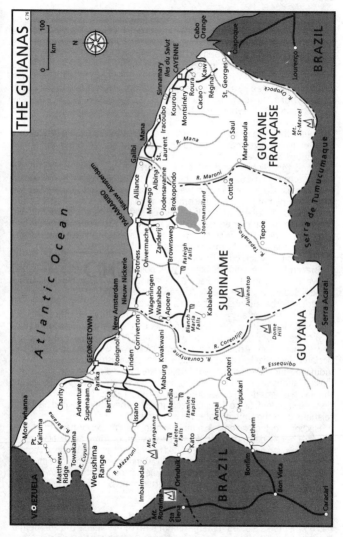

THE GUIANAS

isolation and moved to the urban areas, others keenly maintain aspects of their traditional culture and identity.

History

The country was first partially settled between 1616 and 1621 by the Dutch West India Company, who erected a fort and depot at Fort Kyk-over-al

(County of Essequibo). The first English attempt at settlement was made by Captain Leigh on the Oiapoque River (now French Guyane) in 1604, but he failed to establish a permanent settlement. Lord Willoughby, famous in the early history of Barbados, founded a settlement in 1663 at Suriname, which was captured by the Dutch in 1667 and ceded to them at the Peace of Breda in exchange for New York. The Dutch held the three colonies till 1796 when they were captured by a British fleet. The territory was restored to the Dutch in 1802, but in the following year was retaken by Great Britain, which finally gained it in 1814, when the three counties of Essequibo, Berbice and Demerara were merged to form British Guiana.

During the 17th century the Dutch and English settlers established posts up-river, in the hills, mostly as trading points with the Amerindian natives. Plantations were laid out and worked by slaves from Africa. Poor soil defeated this venture, and the settlers retreated with their slaves to the coastal area in mid-18th century: the old plantation sites can still be detected from the air. Coffee and cotton were the main crops up to the end of the 18th century, but sugar had become the dominant crop by 1820. In 1834 slavery was abolished. Many of the slaves scattered as small landholders, and the plantation owners had to look for another source of labour. It was found in indentured workers from India, a few Chinese, and some Portuguese labourers from the Azores and Madeira. At the end of their indentures many settled in Guyana.

The end of the colonial period was politically turbulent, with rioting between the mainly East Indian People's Progressive Party (PPP), led by Dr Cheddi Jagan, and the mainly African People's National Congress (PNC), under Mr Forbes Burnham. The PNC, favoured over the PPP by the colonial authorities, formed a government in 1964 and has retained office since.

On 26 May 1966 Guyana gained independence, and on 23 February 1970 it became a cooperative republic within the Commonwealth, adopting a new constitution. Another new constitution was adopted in 1980; this declared Guyana to be in transition from capitalism to socialism. Many industries, including bauxite and sugar, were nationalized in the 1970s and close relations with the USSR and Eastern Europe were developed. Following the death of President Forbes Burnham in August 1985, Mr Desmond Hoyte became President. Since then, overseas investors have been invited back and relations with the United States have improved.

Elections to the National Assembly and to the Presidency have been held regularly since independence, but have been widely criticized as fraudulent. The main opposition parties are the PPP, still led by Dr Jagan, and the Working People's Alliance, which attracts support from both East Indian and African communities. Elections, due to be held by May 1991, were postponed until a new electoral register was drawn up. Elections were expected to be held in October 1992.

Government
A Prime Minister and cabinet are responsible to the National Assembly, which has 65 members elected for a maximum term of five years. The President is Head of State. The country is divided into ten administrative regions.

The Economy
Apart from instant, temporary prosperity brought about by the brief non-oil commodities boom in the mid-1970s, which raised gdp growth to 10.4% in 1975, Guyana's economy was in almost permanent recession between 1970 and 1990, despite considerable, unexploited potential in hydroelectric

power, minerals and forestry. While Venezuela's long standing claim to the Essequibo region, within which most of these resources are situated, discouraged investment, other factors were more to blame. Inefficient management in the dominant state sector covering vital sugar and bauxite industries, an investment climate discouraging both domestic and foreign savings, and an acute foreign exchange shortage, resulted in poor performances from the key agricultural and mining sectors, and a largely moribund manufacturing sector.

In 1991, the economy experienced a dramatic turn around, with improvements in almost every sector, especially rice, sugar and gold, promoting 6.1% growth in gdp. Under an IMF-approved Economic Recovery Programme, a number of state-owned companies were privatized, with others earmarked for divestment. Major foreign investment in gold and timber were expected to increase these industries' foreign exchange earnings. Inflation was cut from a rate of 75% in 1991 to a forecast 20% in 1992.

Most agriculture is concentrated on the coastal plain. Sugar is the main crop, and has vied with bauxite and alumina as the most important source of export earnings. Rice is the second most important crop, and a useful foreign exchange earner, though significant quantities of rice production are bartered or export proceeds are undeclared through trade with South American neighbours, especially Suriname and Brazil.

Guyana is the world's largest producer of calcined bauxite, the highest grade of the mineral, and currently has roughly half the world market, though competition from China is becoming stronger.

A series of devaluations of the Guyana dollar between January 1987 and February 1991 culminated in the alignment of the official exchange rate with that of licensed exchange houses. These and other adjustment measures proved beneficial both for the current account and for government finances. The Government struggled to come to terms with the IMF, which declared Guyana ineligible for further assistance in May 1985 because of payment arrears. It was rewarded in June 1990 when the Bank for International Settlements and a group of donor countries provided funds to clear the country's arrears to the IMF and other creditors. This opened the way for lending from a variety of sources, including World Bank support for a Social Impact Amelioration Programme aimed at easing the hardship inflicted on lower income groups by the Economic Recovery Programme.

Guyana has suffered from serious economic problems for over 15 years. Wages are very low and many people depend on overseas remittances or "parallel market" activities to survive. There are frequent shortages of many basic items, although the country is basically self-sufficient for its food supply. Many foreign goods are readily available. The country's infrastructure is seriously run down. There are many electricity blackouts, but their duration has been cut to 10-20 minutes and their frequency reduced, at times every other day (remember to bring a good torch/flashlight with you). During these no water is available, except in larger hotels and businesses which have emergency generators and water pumps.

Georgetown

Georgetown, the capital, and the chief town and port, is on the right bank of the River Demerara, at its mouth. Its population is roughly 200,000. The climate is tropical, with a mean temperature of 27°C, but the trade winds often provide welcome relief. The city is built on a grid plan, with wide tree-lined streets and drainage canals following the layout of the old sugar estates. Despite being located on the Atlantic coast, Georgetown is known as the "Garden City of the Caribbean". Parts of the city are very attractive, with white-painted wooden nineteenth century houses raised on stilts and a profusion of flowering trees. In the evening the sea wall is crowded with strollers and at Easter it is a mass of colourful paper kites. Although part of the old city centre was destroyed by fire in 1945, there are some fine nineteenth century buildings, particularly on or near the Avenue of the Republic. The Gothic-style City Hall dates from 1887. St George's Anglican Cathedral, which dates from 1889 (consecrated 1894), is 44 metres (143 feet) high and is reputed to be the tallest wooden building in the world. The Public Buildings, which house Parliament, are an impressive neo-classical structure built in 1839. Much of the city centre is dominated by the imposing tower above Stabroek market (1880). At the head of Brickdam, one of the main streets, is an aluminium arch commemorating independence. Nearby is a monument to the 1763 slave rebellion, surmounted by an impressive statue of Cuffy, its best-known leader. Near the Forte Crest Georgetown Hotel on Seawall Road is the Umana Yana, a conical thatched structure built by a group of Wai Wai Amerindians using traditional techniques for the 1972 conference of the Non-Aligned Movement.

The **National Museum**, opposite the post office, houses an idiosyncratic collection of exhibits from Guyana and elsewhere, including a model of Georgetown before the 1945 fire. The Walter Roth Museum of Anthropology has a good collection of Amerindian artefacts.

The **Botanical Gardens** (entry free), covering 50 hectares, are beautifully laid out, with Victorian bridges and pavilions, palms and lily-ponds (run-down, but undergoing continual improvements). Near the southwest corner is the residence of the President and there is also a large mausoleum containing the remains of the former president, Forbes Burnham. Look out for the rare cannonball tree (Couroupita Guianensis), named after the appearance of its poisonous fruit. The zoo (being upgraded) has a fine collection of local animals and the manatees in the ponds will eat grass from your hand. It has a new aquarium and a recently-constructed Arapaima pond near the entrance, which houses Guyana's largest fresh water fish. The zoo boasts a breeding centre for endangered birds which are released into the wild. The police band gives a free concert on Thursdays, 1730-1830. There are also beautiful tropical plants in the Promenade Gardens on Middle Street and in the National Park on Carifesta Avenue. The National Park has a good public running track.

The **Georgetown Cricket Club** at Bourda has one of the finest cricket grounds in the tropics. Near the southeast corner of the Botanic Gardens is a well-equipped National Sports Centre. Nearby is the Cultural Centre, an impressive air-conditioned theatre with a large stage. Performances are also given at the Playhouse Theatre in Parade Street.

Local Information – Georgetown

Warning Georgetown is a dangerous city at night, especially during blackouts and periods of reduced electricity. There are frequent "choke and rob" attacks. Don't walk the streets at night; taxis are cheap and easy to find. Most areas are fairly safe by day, provided the usual precautions are taken (ie leave all valuables in your hotel). Particular care is required around the Stabroek Market area and on Main Street, day and night.

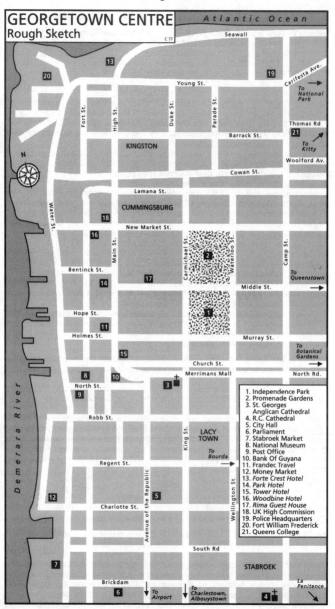

Avoid Albouystown (south of the centre) and Tiger Bay (along the Demerara River).

Where To Stay In the following large hotels foreigners have to pay in foreign currency (US, Canadian, East Caribbean, Barbadian or British); *Forte Crest Georgetown* (formerly the *Pegasus*, Trusthouse Forte), Seawall Road, PO Box 101147, Tel: 52853-9, Fax: 60532, US$95-185d, recently renovated and extended with new Kingston wing (US$160-250d), very safe, a/c, pool, restaurants, gym, tennis, business centre; *Park*, 37-38 Main St, Tel: 54912-5, US$45-75, a/c, secure, beautiful Victorian ballroom (worth a visit), new restaurant and health club due open 1992; *Tower*, 74-75 Main St, Tel: 72011-5, Fax: 65691, being renovated, US$75 EP, a/c, lively bar, very good restaurant, pool open to public, recommended; *Woodbine*, 41-42 New Market St, Tel: 59430-4, Fax: 58406, a/c, US$50-75, recommended; *Campala*, Camp St, Tel: 52951, 61920/51620, US$44 including breakfast, very clean, modern, a/c, near prison (other meals: lunch US$2, dinner US$2.50-6).

There are also many smaller, cheaper hotels which take payment in Guyanese dollars. Recommended are: *Waterchris*, Waterloo St, Tel: 71980, US$7.20-20, a/c, good restaurant, friendly; *Demico*, near Stabroek Market, Tel: 56372, US$10.40 with a/c, US$5.60 without; *Rima Guest House*, 92 Middle St, Tel: 57401, good area, modernized, well-run, US$7.60, good value, central, clean, safe, mosquito nets; *Van Ross*, North Road and Camp St, US$4.80, same management, very basic. Others include: *Belvedere*, Camp St, US$8, noisy; opposite is *Alpha Guest House*, US$7.20 pp, all rooms with double beds and mosquito nets, bar downstairs; *Trio La Chalet*, corner of Camp St and Hadfield St, US$8, popular with locals, 24-hour bar (breakfast US$1.30, other meals US$1.60; *Ariantze*, 176 Middle St, Tel: 57493, US$12d, simple, clean, under renovation, fans, dining room with TV and a/c, bar to open 1992; *Friends*, 82 Robb St, Tel: 72383, US$9, safe, small rooms, fan, shower; *German's*, 81 Robb St, with bath, no fan; *Dat Jean's Guest House*, Albert St, Queenstown, noisy but friendly, both under US$3. Many small hotels and guest houses are full of long-stay residents, while some are rented by the hour. Try to book in advance. If in doubt, go to a larger hotel for first night and look around next day in daylight.

Apartments *N and R*, 246 Anaida Ave, Eccles, East Bank Demerara, Tel: 60921 (reservations through N and R Apartment Rentals, 301 Church and Thomas Sts, Georgetown, Tel: 58079/664040), US$65 a day, one bedroom, a/c, TV, maid service, washer, dryer, guard service, generator.

Where To Eat Eating out is very cheap at present because of the favourable exchange rate. 10% service may be added to bill. At Hotels: *Forte Crest*, *El Dorado*, good food and atmosphere, Caribbean, Continental and Guyanese, *Café Demerara*, buffet lunch US$4; *Tower*, *Cazabon*, good food, US$7.50-9.20; very good breakfast at *Waterchris*. Best in town are *Del Casa* (fine food and atmosphere) and *Caribbean Rose* (very good), both on Middle St, (US$7.50-9.20); also recommended are *Palm Court*, Main St (many Chinese dishes, good food, poor service), and *Arawak Steak House*, in roof garden above *Demico Hotel* (casual atmosphere, good steak US$3.20-3.50, chicken US$2.80, prawn US$6.40). Good lunches for around US$3 at the *Rice Bowl* and *Country Pride*, both in Robb St, the *Coalpot* in New Town (no shorts allowed, cheaper cafeteria) and *Hack's Hallal* (only *Country Pride* serves dinner, US$4). Good Chinese: *Orient*, Camp and Middle Sts, nice atmosphere US$4-5, 10% service in VIP lounge, service at bit poor. Many Chinese restaurants (all pretty rough), including *Double Dragon*, Av of the Republic; and *Diamond Food House*, 9 Camp St. For late night eating there are several Chinese restaurants on Sheriff St including *Double Happiness*. For fast food, try *Red Rooster*, Regent St; *Arapaima*, Main St; *Idaho*, Brickdam; *Forest Hills*, Camp St; *Calypso*, Regent St. Cheaper counter lunches at *Guyana Stores*, Main St.

Night Life Georgetown is surprisingly lively at night, mainly with gold miners, traders and overseas Guyanese throwing US$ around. Liveliest disco is *Hollywood*, Camp St (entrance US$0.80, expensive); *The Library*, Camp St, very popular Wednesday night (ladies free), barbecue, beer garden, dance floor, bar (entrance US$0.80); *Blue Note*, Camp St, disco and beer garden; *Palm Court*, Main St, restaurant and beer garden, very lively Friday pm and holidays, no entrance fee; *Spectrum Club* in the Tower Hotel; *Mingles*, Crown St, is a good small club with excellent live music and dancing (entrance US$0.80, take a taxi there, US$1); *Trump Card*, Church St, near St George's, sometimes has a live band. Near the Kitty Market are *Jazzy Jacks*, Alexander St, and *Wee Place*, Lamaha St, but this area is unsafe unless you go with locals. Sheriff St is some way from the centre but is "the street that never sleeps" full of late night Chinese restaurants and has some good bars including *Tennessee Lounge*, *Burns Beat* and *Sheriff*. Most nightclubs sell imported, as well as local Banks beer.

Shopping Normal shopping hours are 0800-1600, Monday-Thursday, 0800-1700 Friday, 0800-1200 Saturday Market hours 0800-1600, Monday-Saturday, except Wednesday 0900-1200. The main shopping area is Regent St. The two main department stores are *Guyana Stores* in Church St, and *Fogarty's*, but neither has a wide range of goods. Most Guyanese do their regular shopping at the four big markets: Stabroek, Bourda, La Penitence and Kitty. Craft items are a good buy; Amerindian basketwork, hammocks, wood carvings, pottery, and small figures made out of Balata, a rubbery substance tapped from trees in the interior. *Houseproud*, on Avenue of the Republic has a good selection of craftwork, but there are many other craft shops including *Creations*, Water St. Gold is also sold widely, often at good prices but make sure you know what you are buying. Do not buy it on the street. Developing film takes time and is not always reliable: *Risans* on Main St recommended as quick and efficient.

Bookshops Some interesting books in *Houseproud*. Try also *GNTC* on Water St, *Argosy* and *Kharg* both on Regent St, *Dimension* on Cummings St, as well as *Guyana Stores* and *Fogarty's*.

Local Transport Car hire is available through *N and R Rentals*, 301 Church and Thomas Streets, Tel: 58079/66404, Toyota Camry and Corolla, Nissan Station Wagon, US$24/day, insurance US$2.40/day. **Minibuses** run regularly to most parts of the city, mostly from Stabroek market or Avenue of the Republic, standard fare US$0.20, very crowded. It is difficult to get a seat during rush hours. **Taxis** charge US$1.20 for short journeys, US$2.20 for longer runs, with higher rates at night and outside the city limits.

Exchange National Bank of Industry and Commerce; Guyana Bank of Trade and Industry; Bank of Baroda; Bank of Nova Scotia. Bank hours are 0800-1230 Monday-Friday, plus 1500-1700 on Friday. **Exchange houses** (*cambios*) in shops may be open longer hours. A good, safe *cambio* is Joe Chin Travel on Main Street. The *cambio* opposite the *Tower Hotel* accepts Thomas Cook travellers' cheques, but not at the best rates.

Post Office Main one on Avenue of the Republic, slow service.

Churches Anglican: St George's Cathedral, Christ Church, Waterloo Street; St Andrew's (Presbyterian), Avenue of the Republic; Roman Catholic Cathedral, Brickdam.

Travel Agencies Try Mr Mendoza at *Frandec Travel Service*, Main St, repeatedly recommended (no tours to the interior); *Wieting and Richter*, 78 Church and Carmichael Sts, very helpful (has Tourism Association of Guyana information desk). For **Tour Operators**, see below.

Bus Services There are regular services by minibuses and collective taxis to most coastal towns from the Stabroek Market. To **Rosignol** (for New Amsterdam, Springlands and Suriname), 2 hours, US$1.50; to **Parika** US$2; to **Linden** US$2.

Tour Operators The tourism sector is promoting ecotourism in the form of environmentally friendly resorts and camps on Guyana's rivers and in the rainforest. There is much tropical wildlife to be seen and operators are also promoting indigenous peoples as an attraction.

Tropical Adventures, c/o Forte Crest Georgetown, Seawall Road, Georgetown, Tel: 52853-9, Fax: 60532, offer day trips to Kaieteur and Orinduik Falls, Kamuni Creek and Santa Mission, Timberhead (see below), Double 'B' Exotic Gardens (see below) and city tours. Overnight tours to Timberhead, Shanklands (see below) and Essequibo River. Individual itineraries catered for. *Wonderland Tours*, Hotel Tower, Main Street, Georgetown, Tel: 72011-5, AH 65991, day trips to Kaieteur and Orinduik Falls, Santa Mission, Essequibo and Mazaruni Rivers, city tours; special arrangements for overnight stays available. *Torong Guyana*, 56 Coralita Avenue, Bel Air Park, Georgetown, Tel: 65298, trips to Kaieteur and Orinduik Falls and three-day Rupununi Safaris, including Kaieteur (US$450). *Hinterlander Tours*, 76 First Avenue, Subryanville, Tel: 62860, trips to Kaieteur and Orinduik Falls and Rupununi.

Resorts *Timberhead*, operated by Tropical Adventures (see above) in the Santa Amerindian Reserve, situated on a sandy hill overlooking Savannah and the Pokerero Creek, 3 native lodges with bath and kitchen facilities, well-run, good food, lovely trip up the Kamuni River to get there, US$80 pp for a day trip, US$120 pp for one night and two days (includes all transport, meals, bar, guide, accommodation). *Shanklands*, contact Joanne Jardim, Residence No 3, Thirst Park, Georgetown, Tel: 51586, on a cliff overlooking the Essequibo, colonial style cottages with verandah and kitchen, activities include swimming, walking, bird watching, croquet, fishing, water sports, about US$70 pp, not including transport. *The Gazebo*, on Kaow Island, contact Bibi Zackeryah, Willems Timber and Trading Co Ltd, PO Box 10443, Georgetown, Tel: 72046/7, 69252, Fax: 60983, the country home of the Willems family on 136-acre Kaow Island in the Essequibo River, facilities include a jungle walk, swimming, water sports, trekking, bird watching, room rates US$190d full board, most activities included, transport from Georgetown not included (air, 30 minutes, US$200; minibus and boat via Parika, 2 hours, US$125 or US$275, latter in cabin cruiser). *Arawak Resort and Double 'B' Exotic Gardens*, 58 Lamaha Gardens, Georgetown, Tel: 52023, Fax: 60997, contact Boyo Ramsaroop, near Timehri Airport, gardens open (specializing in heliconias), accommodation due for completion in 1993. *Sapodilla Health, Fitness and Organic Farm*, 86 miles from Timehri near the Berbice River, due for completion June 1992, contact Mr E Joseph, No 22 Bel Air, West Coast Berbice, Guyana, rates £350 pp per week.

Camps *Rainbow River Safari*, on the Mazaruni River, hammock camp, contact Junior Garrett, Tel: 70052, or Ted Sabat, 144 Duncan Street, Newtown, Georgetown. *Jacaranda Island Camp*, also on the Mazaruni River, 30 miles upriver from Bartica, set in an old jungle gold-mining camp, basic facilities, US$50 pp fully inclusive or US$30 pp self-catering (prices do not include transport), contact Tony Thorne, Forte Crest Hotel, Georgetown, Tel: 52853-9, or Captain Thunder, Bartica; there is river swimming, and a wildlife orphan rehabilitation programme funded by tourist income; gold mining still takes place nearby.

Note For visiting many parts of the interior, particularly Amerindian districts, a permit is required in advance from the Ministry of Public Works, Communications and Regional Development in Georgetown. If venturing out of Georgetown on your own, you must check beforehand whether you need a permit for where you intend to visit.

Southeast to Suriname

Linden (pop 35,000), the second-largest town in Guyana, is a bauxite mining town 70 miles/112 km south of Georgetown on the Demerara river. A good road connects the two towns. On the west bank of the river is a company mining town, across the river (bridge or ferry) are the poorer suburbs of Wismar and Christianburg. The town is dominated by a disused alumina plant and scarred by old bauxite pits. Accommodation is scarce (*Mackenzie Hotel*, pleasantly situated on the river, Tel: 04-2183, US$15; *Hotel Star Bonnett*, clean, good lunches).

New Amsterdam (pop 25,000) is 65 miles/104 km southeast of Georgetown on the east bank of the Berbice river, near its mouth. From Georgetown, take a minibus or collective taxi to Rosignol on the west bank of the Berbice, then cross the river by launch rather than the slow, smelly ferry (US$0.10; also takes vehicles). The town is run-down but picturesque.

Hotels *Church View Guest House*, including meals; *Hotel Embassy*, at Rose Hall; *Penguin*, Tel: 03-2012, a/c, all under US$20.

From New Amsterdam, it is sometimes possible to get a lift on a bauxite barge up the Berbice river to the small mining town of Kwakwani (there is a guesthouse, reasonable, check for vacancies at Guymine in Georgetown).

The road continues east from New Amsterdam (minibus, US$1), to **Springlands** and Skeldon at the mouth of the Courantyne river. The two towns are officially known as **Corriverton** (Courantyne River Town).

Hotels in Springlands: *Ambassador*, near point for ferry to Nieuw Nickerie; *Swiss Hotel*, Pakistani run, rough but helpful. In Skeldon: *Parapak*, US$10, no fan, no mosquito net, poor value; *Mahogany*, US$6, fan, clean, friendly, recommended; *Arawak*, under US$3, rough, avoid. Several good Chinese restaurants within a few blocks of Springlands town centre.

Exchange National Bank of Industry and Commerce; Guyana National Commercial Bank. *Cambio* (National Bank of Industry and Commerce) at Skeldon for arriving ferry passengers.

Crossing to Suriname
Before you leave Georgetown, check with the Suriname embassy whether you need a visa (without one, if required, you may be imprisoned before being sent back to Georgetown). From Springlands there is a daily ferry (not Sunday or national holidays of either country) to Nieuw Nickerie (foot passengers only). Queue at the booking office near the jetty from 0700, office opens 0800, booking fee US$0.25, all passports must be presented when booking, tickets are sold later on the ferry, Sf15 one way, payable in Suriname guilders only. Immigration and customs formalities (very slow and thorough) take place from 0900, ferry sails from 1100 depending on tides and weather, crossing time normally 2 hours. Change money at the stelling (ferry pier) before you travel. If you leave Georgetown at 0300 you should catch the ferry and reach Paramaribo by late afternoon.

West from Georgetown; Routes to Venezuela

Travelling west from Georgetown, the road crosses the Demerara bridge (toll) and continues to **Parika**, a small town on the east bank of the Essequibo river (minibus US$0.50). If you need accommodation, there are two small brothels where you can stay fairly safely. From here ferries cross the river to **Adventure** on the west bank at 1700 daily and 0830 Wednesday and Friday, returning at 0300 daily and 1330 Wednesday and Friday (See *Three Singles to Adventure* by Gerald Durrell). There are also three ferries a day to Leguan Island (½ hour, US$0.25); accommodation available at the *Hotel President*.

The northwestern coastal area is mainly accessible by boat only. From Adventure a road runs north through Anna Regina. Nearby is Lake Mainstay, a small resort (due for renovation), reached by taxi; it is also known as the hot and cold lake because it varies in temperature from one place to another. Then the road goes on to **Charity**, a pleasant little town with two small hotels and a lively market on Mondays.

Near the border with Venezuela is the small port of **Morawhanna** (Morajuana to the Venezuelans), which may be reached by an unreliable ferry from Georgetown. The journey is surprisingly rough and "you will have to fight for hammock space and watch your possessions like a hawk". From Morawhanna boats sail up the river to Port Kaituma, 40 miles/ 64 km inland, from where a small passenger railway connects with the isolated settlement of Matthews Ridge (more easily reached by chartered aircraft from Georgetown). The site of the Jonestown mass-suicide is nearby.

The Venezuelan border can be crossed at the River Cuyuni (at least from Venezuela into Guyana). On the Venezuelan side is San Martín, from which a narrow road goes to El Dorado on the road south to Brazil. It is possible to reach this border by boat from Georgetown (very infrequent), or by military plane, about 4 or 5 times a week, no schedule, US$60.

From Parika there is also a ferry up the Essequibo river to Bartica on Tuesday and Friday at 0700, Saturday 1330, returning on Monday and Thursday at 0930, Saturday 0815, US$1 one way. The 36 mile/ 58 km journey takes 6 hours, stopping at Fort Island (partially restored in 1991) where you can buy sweetcorn and pastries; small boats come out from riverside settlements to load up with fruit. Local people generally prefer to take a speedboat, US$5 pp, 1-2 hours, depending on horsepower.

Southwest from Georgetown: to Brazil

Bartica, at the junction of the Essequibo and Mazaruni rivers, is the "take-off" town for the gold and diamond fields, Kaieteur Falls, and the interior generally. Here an Amazon-like mass of waters meets, but with an effect vastly more beautiful, for they are coloured the "glossy copper" of all Guyanese rivers and not the dull mud-brown of most of the Amazon. Swimming very good. The *stelling* (wharf) and market are very colourful.

Where To Stay *Marin*; *The Nest* on Fifth Avenue, US$10, unsafe, very noisy, meals to be had from disco after 1730, or "Robbie's". *Modern*, near ferry, good food, noisy disco. Book ahead if possible. Mrs Payne's, near Hospital, basic, clean.

The Essequibo is navigable to large boats for some miles above Bartica. The Cuyuni flows into the Mazaruni 3 miles above Bartica, and above this confluence the Mazaruni is impeded for 120 miles by thousands of islands, rapids and waterfalls. To avoid this stretch of treacherous river a road has been built from Bartica to Issano, where boats can be taken up the more tranquil upper Mazaruni.

At the confluence of the Mazaruni and Cuyuni Rivers are the ruins of the Dutch stronghold Kyk-over-al, once the seat of government for the Dutch county of Essequibo. Nearby are the Marshall Falls where you can swim in the falls themselves ("a natural jacuzzi").

The **Kaieteur Falls**, on the Potaro river, rank with the Niagara, Victoria, and Iguazú Falls in majesty and beauty, but have the added attraction of being surrounded by unspoilt forest. The Falls, nearly five times the height of Niagara, with a sheer drop of 228 metres, are nearly 100 metres wide. They are unspoilt because of their isolation. In the dry months, April and October, the flow of the falls is reduced. A trip to the Kaieter Falls costs US$120; most agencies include the Orinduik Falls (see below) as well, US$150-180, including ground and air transport, meal, drinks and guide (book early, flights are often cancelled). Operators offering this service are *Tropical Adventures* at the *Forte Crest Hotel* (Tel: 52853-9, Fax: 60532), *Wonderland Tours* at *Hotel Tower* (Tel: 72011-5), Hinterlander Tours, 76 First Avenue Subryanville, Tel: 62860 and *Torang Guyana*, Mrs Chan-A-Sue in Georgetown, Tel: 65298. To charter a plane privately costs US$600-800. Overland routes to the falls are possible and take 7-10 days; seek information in Bartica.

The Kaieteur Falls lie within the **Kaieteur National Park**, where there is a variety of wildlife: tapirs, ocelots, monkeys, armadillos, anteaters, and jungle and river birds. The Pakaraima Mountains stretch from Kaieteur westwards to include the highest peak in Guyana, Mount Roraima, the possible inspiration for Conan Doyle's *Lost World*. Roraima is very difficult to climb from the Guyanese side.

There are several other spectacular waterfalls in the interior, including Imbaimadai and Orinduik, but none is very easy to reach. **Orinduik Falls** are on the Ireng River, which forms the border with Brazil; the river pours over steps and terraces of jasper, with a backdrop of the grass-covered Pakaraima Mountains. There is good swimming at the falls.

Precautions If going on your own, detailed planning and a guide are essential. Take adequate supplies of food and drink, a sleeping bag, a sheet and blanket, a mosquito net, and kerosene for Tilley lamps.

The **Rupununi Savanna** in the southwest is an extensive area of dry grassland with scattered trees, termite mounds and wooded hills. The freshwater creeks, lined with Ite palms, are good for swimming. The region is scattered with occasional Amerindian villages and a few large cattle ranches which date from the late nineteenth century: the descendants of some of the Scots settlers still live here. Links with Brazil are much closer than with the Guyanese coast; many people speak Portuguese and most trade, both legal and illegal, is with Brazil.

Avoid visiting the Rupununi in the wet season (May to June) as much of the Savanna is flooded and malaria mosquitoes widespread. The best time is the second half of the year. River bathing is good, but watch out for stingrays. Birds to look out for are macaws, tucan, parrots, love birds and hawks.

Lethem, a small but scattered town on the Brazilian frontier, is the service centre for the Rupununi and for trade with Brazil. There are a few stores, a small hospital, a police station and government offices which have radio telephone links with Georgetown. About 1½ miles/ 2½ km south of town at St Ignatius there is a Jesuit mission dating from 1911.

Where To Stay In Lethem: *Takutu Guest House*, near airfield, US$25 full board, or US$5 pp without food, run down, reports of theft; *Cacique Guesthouse*, US$7, full board also available, clean, good value, nice views, highly recommended; *Hotel Casila*, lots of mosquitoes; try also the government rest house next to Guyana Stores, good meals, clean, efficient, recommended. Eat at *Koo Foods*, or *Double Wheel* in Lethem. The *Manari Ranch Hotel*, 7 miles/11 km north of Lethem, US$20 pp full board, creek for swimming, recommended. Duane and Sandy de Freitas at the *Dadanawa Ranch*, 50 miles/80 km south of Lethem, takes guests and organizes tours, US$30 pp per day, as does Diane McTurk at *Karanambo Ranch*, 50 miles/80 km northeast of Lethem, US$120 pp per day; they can both be contacted via Peter Seabra in the offices of the Rupununi Livestock Producers' Association, above Gapoor's shop, America Street, Georgetown, Wendella Jackson, Tel: 53750, Georgetown (for *Karanambo*), or Johnette Gonsalves, Tel: 65759.

Exchange Mr Jardin, the Portuguese shopkeeper, may exchange travellers' cheques (technically illegal), at a poor rate; Mr Mahoney gives better rates for cash. Changing money is much better on the Brazilian side of the frontier.

Transport At *Koo Foods* bicycles can be hired for US$0.50/day; also there you can contact the birdwatching guide, Jason Foo. He will also help with jeep hire for bird watching and waterfalls in the nearby mountains.

Transport around the Rupununi is difficult; there are a few four-wheel drive vehicles, but ox-carts and bicycles are more common on the rough roads. From Lethem trucks can be hired for day-trips to the Moco-Moco Falls and the Kamu Falls and to the Kanuku Mountains. Trucks may also be hired to visit Aishalton, 70 miles/110 km south along a very bad road, 6 hour journey, US$260; and to Annai, 60 miles/96 km northeast along a better road, 3 hour journey, US$110. An interesting trip is to the Amerindian village of Yukupari, where the Alan Knight Training Centre, a theological college training Amerindians for the Anglican priesthood, is always happy to see visitors and can, on occasion, provide accommodation for stranded travellers. Truck-hire and tours can be arranged through Don and Shirley Melville, who run a bar near the air-strip in Lethem.

A road link between Georgetown and Lethem via Linden, Mabura Hill and

Kurupakari was opened in early 1991. From Georgetown to Mabura Hill is in good condition; Mabura Hill to Kurupakari is very bad but is being rebuilt and should be finished by early 1993; Kurupakari-Lethem is good. When complete there will be a through route Georgetown-Boa Vista (Brazil).

Truck Georgetown-Lethem: Frank Lissone (called Dutchie), 105 Brickdam Rd, Georgetown, in front of Telecom building, 2-3 days, take food and water, US$27.25, luggage US$0.15/kg (in Lethem, find Dutchie at *Takutu Guest House*); Ng-a-fook, on Church St, between Camp St and Waterloo St. (Care is needed on this route: dangerous driving and bandits reported.) Guyana Airways Corporation flies from Georgetown to Lethem and back Tuesday and Friday, US$50 one way; book well in advance at the GAC office on Main St, Georgetown. Regular charter planes link the town with Georgetown, about US$200 return.

Crossing to Brazil

Formalities are generally reported to be very lax on both sides of the border, but it is important to observe them as there are reports of people being refused entry to Guyana for not having the correct papers, including visa. In Lethem all procedures are dealt with at the police station (there is also immigration at the airport); report there also with a visa if arriving from Brazil. The Takutu river, the frontier between the two countries, is about 1 mile north of Lethem (taxis available, or pick-ups, US$1). There are small boats for foot passengers (US$0.25) and a pontoon for vehicles. Just over the river is a shop and the Brazilian customs post. From here it is 1½ mile/2½ km walk to the village of Bom Fim, from where a bus leaves for Boa Vista at 0800 every other day (from Boa Vista to Bom Fim at 1600), 3½ hours, US$10. It is possible to cycle across to Bom Fim with minimum formalities (5 km), but if you want to take a bus on to Boa Vista full passport/visas (if necessary) are required.

Information for Visitors

Documents

At the time of going to press, visa requirements were due to be relaxed. Visitors are advised to check with the nearest Embassy, Consulate or travel agent. All visitors require passports and all, apart from nationals of Caribbean Community countries, used to require visas, obtainable from Embassies, High Commissions and Consulates in London, Washington, New York (866 United Nations Plaza, 3rd floor, NY 10017, Tel: 527-3215), Port of Spain, Bridgetown, Caracas, Brasília, Paramaribo and elsewhere. To obtain a visa, two photos, an onward ticket and yellow fever certificate are required. Visas are charged strictly on a reciprocal basis, equivalent to the cost charged to a Guyanese visitor to the country concerned. Visitors arriving without visas are refused entry.

Customs

Baggage examination is very thorough. Duties are high on goods imported in commercial quantities.

How To Get There By Air

There are no direct flights to Guyana from Europe; from North America BWIA flies 4 times a week from New York, 5 times a week from Miami, 4 times a week from Toronto; most BWIA flights involve a change of planes in Port of Spain. Guyana Airways fly 3 times a week from New York, once from Miami and once from Toronto, all direct. BWIA flies to Guyana from Trinidad 15 times a week, 6 times a week from Barbados. LIAT flies daily from Barbados, and from Grenada, Antigua and St Lucia via Barbados. LIAT have connecting flights with British Airways in Barbados to/from London and Air Canada to Toronto. There are also twice weekly (Wednesday and Sunday) flights from Caracas by Aeropostal. Suriname Airways flies 3 times a week from Paramaribo, but these flights are difficult to book from outside the Guianas. ALM twice a week from Aruba.

Flights are often booked weeks in advance, especially at Christmas when overseas Guyanese return to visit relatives. Flights are frequently overbooked, so it is essential to reconfirm your outward flight, which can take some time, and difficult to change your travel plans at the last minute. Foreigners must pay for airline tickets in US$ or other specified currencies. Luggage should be securely locked as theft from checked-in baggage is common.

Airport Information

The international airport is at Timehri, 25 miles/40 km south of Georgetown. There is an exit tax of G$1,000, payable in Guyanese dollars, and a 10% tax on international airline tickets bought in the country. Exit tax can be paid when reconfirming your outward flight. Minibus No 42 to Georgetown US$0.80, taxi US$16. There is a small duty-free shop where local goods, but not rum, are reportedly slightly cheaper than in the capital and an exchange house, open usual business hours; if closed, plenty of parallel traders outside (find out from fellow passengers what the rate is). Internal flights go from Ogle airport; minibus from Market to Ogle US$0.20.

Internal Air Services

Guyana Airways has scheduled flights between Georgetown and Lethem on Tuesday and Friday. There are several charter companies, including Masaharally, Trans Guyana Airways, (Correia) and Kayman Sankar. Surplus seats on privately chartered flights are sometimes available and are advertised in the press. Ask the charter companies at Ogle airport for seats on cargo flights to any destination, they will help you to get in touch with the charterer. Prices vary, up to US$0.80 per pound. Returning to Ogle can be cheaper, even, if you are lucky, free.

Road Transport

Most coastal towns are linked by a good 185 mile road from Springlands in the east to Charity in the west; the Berbice and Essequibo rivers are crossed by ferries, the Demerara by a toll bridge, which is subject to frequent closures, near Georgetown. Apart from a good road connecting Georgetown and Linden, continuing as good dirt to Mabura Hill, most other roads in the interior are very poor. Car hire is available from N and R Rentals, see under Georgetown. There are shortages of car spares. Gasoline costs about US$1.42 a gallon. Traffic drives on the left. Minibuses and collective taxis run between Georgetown and most towns in the coastal belt.

River Transport

There are over 600 miles of navigable river,

which provide an important means of communication. Ferries and river boats are referred to in the text, but for further details contact the Transport and Harbours Department, Water St, Georgetown. Note that there is no vehicle ferry across the Courantyne to Suriname.

Accommodation

The largest hotels in Georgetown have their own emergency electricity generators and water pumps to deal with the frequent interruptions in supply. Other hotels usually provide a bucket of water in your room, fill this up when water is available. When booking an air-conditioned room, make sure it also has natural ventilation.

Food And Drink

The blend of different national influences (Indian, African, Chinese, Creole, English, Portuguese, Amerindian, North American) gives a distinctive flavour to Guyanese cuisine. One well-known dish, traditional at Christmas, is pepper-pot, meat cooked in bitter cassava juice with peppers and herbs. Seafood is plentiful and varied, as is the wide variety of tropical fruits and vegetables. Staple foods are rice and long thin bora beans. The food shortages and import ban of the early 1980s have ended, but they did have the positive effect of encouraging experimentation with local ingredients, sometimes with interesting results. In the interior wild meat is often available, try wild cow, or else labba (a small rodent).

Rum is the most popular drink. There is a wide variety of brands, all cheap, including the best which are very good and cost less than US$2 a bottle. High wine is a strong local rum. There is also local brandy and whisky (Diamond Club), which are worth trying. The local beer, Banks, made partly from rice is acceptable and cheap. There is a wide variety of fruit juices.

Currency

The unit is the Guyanese dollar. There are notes for 1, 5, 10, 20 and 100 dollars, though devaluation and inflation mean that even the largest of these is worth very little. Coins for amounts under a dollar exist but are of little practical use.

The devaluation of the Guyanese dollar in February 1991 aligned the official exchange rate with that offered by licensed exchange houses (known as *cambios*). Since that date the exchange rate was to be adjusted weekly in line with the market rate. In June 1992, this stood at G$125 = US$1. At present *cambios* only buy US or Canadian dollars and pounds sterling. Most *cambios* accept drafts (subject to verification), travellers' cheques and telegraphic transfers, but not credit cards. Rates vary slightly between *cambios* and from day to day and some *cambios* offer better rates for changing over US$100. Rates for changing travellers' cheques are not good in *cambios* or on the black market. A few banks accept Thomas Cook travellers' cheques. Note that to sell Guyanese dollars on leaving the country, you will need to produce your *cambio* receipt. The illegal black market on America Street ("Wall Street") in Georgetown still operates, but the rates offered are not significantly better than the *cambio* rate and there is a strong risk of being robbed or cheated. The black market also operates in Springlands, the entry point from Suriname.

Cost Of Living
The devaluation to the *cambio* rate means that, for foreigners, prices are low at present. Even imported goods may be cheaper than elsewhere and locally produced goods such as fruit are very cheap.

Health
There is a high risk of both types of malaria in the interior, especially in the wet season. Recommended prophylaxis is chloroquine 500 mg weekly plus paludrine 200 mg daily. Reports of chloroquine-resistant malaria in the interior (seek advice before going). If travelling to the interior for long periods carry drugs for treatment as these may not be available. Sleep under a mosquito net. Although there are plenty of mosquitoes on the coast, they are not malarial.

There is some risk of typhoid and water-borne diseases owing to low water pressure. Purification tablets are a good idea. Tapwater is usually brown and contains sediment, but this is not a cause for concern. The Georgetown Hospital is run down, understaffed and lacking equipment, but there are a number of well-equipped private hospitals, including St Joseph's on Parade St, Kingston; Prasad's on Thomas St; and the Davis Memorial Hospital on Lodge Backlands. Charges are US$2 to US$8 per day and medical consultations cost US$2 to US$4. If admitted to hospital you are expected to

provide your own sheets and food (St Joseph's provides all these).

In the interior, travellers should examine shower pipes, bedding, shoes and clothing for snakes.

Climate
Athough hot, is not unhealthy. Mean shade temperature throughout the year is 27°C; the mean maximum is about 31°C and the mean minimum 24°C. The heat is greatly tempered by cooling breezes from the sea and is most felt from August to October. There are two wet seasons, from May to June, and from December to the end of January, although they may extend into the months either side. Rainfall averages 2,300 mm a year in Georgetown.

Time Zone
4 hours behind GMT; one hour ahead of EST.

Public Holidays
1 January, New Years' Day; 23 February, Republic Day and Mashramani festival; Good Friday, Easter Monday; Labour Day, 1 May; Caricom Day, first Monday in July; Freedom Day, first Monday in August; Christmas Day, 25 December, and Boxing Day, 26 December.

The following public holidays are for Hindu and Muslim festivals; they follow a lunar calender, and dates should be checked as required: Phagwah, usually March; Eid el Fitr, end of Ramadan; Eid el Azah; Youm un Nabi; Deepavali, usually November.

Note that the Republic Day celebrations last about a week: during this time hotels in Georgetown are very full.

Weights And Measures
Although Guyana went metric in 1982, imperial measures are still widely used.

Voltage
100 v in Georgetown; 220 v in most other places, including some Georgetown suburbs.

Postal And Telephone Services
Overseas postal and telephone charges are very low. Telecommunications are rapidly improving. It is possible to dial direct to any country in the world. Public telephones in Georgetown only allow collect calls overseas. Some businesses and hotels may allow you to use their phone for local calls if you are buying something, usual charge about US$0.05. Overseas calls can be made from the

Guyana Telephone and Telegraph Company office in the Bank of Guyana building (arrive early and be prepared for a long wait), or from the *Tower Hotel* (more expensive but more comfortable). Travel agencies may allow you to make overseas collect calls when buying tickets.

Press

The Chronicle, daily except Monday, government-run; *The Mirror*, weekly, opposition PPP-run; *The Stabroek News*, daily except Monday, independent; *The Catholic Standard*, weekly, well-respected and widely read. Street vendors charge more than the cover price, this is normal and helps them make a living.

Embassies And Consulates

There is a surprisingly large number of embassies in Georgetown, including: **British High Commission** (44 Main St, PO Box 10849); **Canadian High Commission** (Young St) and the Embassies of the **United States** (Young St, Kingston, near *Forte Crest Hotel*), **Venezuela** (Thomas St), **Brazil** (308 Church St, Queenstown, Tel: 57970, visa issued next day, 90 days, 1 photo, US$12.75), **Cuba** (Main St) and **Suriname** (Bourda-2 passport photos, passport, US$20 and one week's wait needed).

Tourist Information

The combination of incentives, the stabilization of the economy and government recognition of the foreign exchange earning potential of tourism has led to many new ventures since 1990. The Ministry of Trade, Tourism and Industry has a Tourism Department which can provide information through its office at the corner of Urquart and Main Street, Georgetown, Tel: 65384/63182. Substantial private sector growth has led to the formation of the Tourism Association of Guyana (TAG), which covers all areas of tourism (hotels, airlines, restaurants, tour operators, etc). A TAG information desk can be found in Wieting and Richter Travel Agency, corner of Church and Carmichael Streets, Georgetown, Tel: 65121, or from PO Box 101147, Georgetown. An information desk is planned for Timehri International Airport for late 1992.

Maps of country and Georgetown (US$1.80) from Department of Lands and Surveys, Homestreet Ave, Dorban Backland (take a taxi). City maps also from *Guyana Store*, Water Street, next to the ice house (take a taxi).

We are deeply grateful to Tony Thorne (Georgetown) for a complete revision of the Guyana chapter, also, for their assistance, to Christopher Ram and Gavin O'Brien.

SURINAME

Introduction

SURINAME has a coast line on the Atlantic to the north; it is bounded on the west by Guyana and on the east by French Guyane; Brazil is to the south. Its area is 163,820 sq km. The principal rivers in the country are the Marowijne in the east, the Corantijn in the west, and the Suriname, Commewijne (with its tributary, the Cottica), Coppename, Saramacca and Nickerie. The country is divided into topographically quite diverse natural regions: the northern part of the country consists of lowland, with a width in the east of 25 km, and in the west of about 80 km. The soil (clay) is covered with swamps with a layer of humus under them. Marks of the old seashores can be seen in the shell and sand ridges, overgrown with tall trees. There follows a region, 5-6 km wide, of a loamy and very white sandy soil, then a slightly undulating region, about 30 km wide. It is mainly savanna, mostly covered with quartz sand, and overgrown with grass and shrubs. South of this lies the interior highland, almost entirely overgrown with dense tropical forest and intersected by streams. At the southern boundary with Brazil there are again savannas. These, however, differ in soil and vegetation from the northern ones. A large area in the southwest is in dispute between Guyana and Suriname. There is a less serious border dispute with Guyane in the southeast.

The 1980 census showed that the population had declined to 352,041, because of heavy emigration to the Netherlands. By 1991 it was estimated to have grown to 417,000. The 1983 population consisted of Indo-Pakistanis (known locally as Hindustanis), 37%; Creoles (European-African and other descent), 31%; Indonesians, 14%; Chinese, 3%; Bush Negroes, called locally "bosnegers" (retribalized descendants of slaves who escaped in the 17th century, living on the upper Saramacca, Suriname and Marowijne rivers), 8.5%; Europeans and others, 3%; Amerindians, 3% (some sources say only 1%). About 90% of the existing population live in or around Paramaribo or in the coastal towns; the remainder, mostly Carib and Arawak Indians and bosnegers, are widely scattered.

The Asian people originally entered the country as contracted estate labourers, and settled in agriculture or commerce after completion of their term. They dominate the countryside, whereas Paramaribo is a predominantly Creole city. One of Suriname's main problems is the racial tension between Creoles and Indo-Pakistanis.

The official language is Dutch. The native dialect, called negro English (Sranan Tongo) originally the speech of the Creoles, is now a *lingua franca* understood by all groups, and standard English is widely spoken and understood. The Asians still speak their own languages among themselves.

History

Although Amsterdam merchants had been trading with the "wild coast" of Guiana as early as 1613 (the name Parmurbo-Paramaribo was already known) it was not until 1630 that 60 English settlers came to Suriname under Captain Marshall and planted tobacco. The real founder of the colony was Baron Willoughby of Parham, governor of Barbados, who sent an expedition to Suriname in 1651 under Anthony Rowse to find a suitable place for settlement. Willoughbyland became an agricultural colony with 500 little sugar plantations, 1,000 white inhabitants and 2,000 African slaves. Jews from Holland and Italy joined them, as well as Dutch Jews ejected from Brazil after 1654. On 27 February 1667, Admiral Crynssen conquered the colony for the states of Zeeland and Willoughbyfort became the present Fort Zeelandia. By the Peace of Breda, 31 July 1667, it was agreed that Suriname should remain with the Netherlands, while Nieuw Amsterdam (New York) should be given to England. The colony was conquered by the British in 1799, and not until the Treaty of Paris in 1814 was it finally restored to the Netherlands. Slavery was forbidden in 1818 and formally abolished in 1863. Indentured labour from China and the East Indies took its place.

On 25 November 1975, the country became an independent republic, which signed a treaty with the Netherlands for an economic aid programme worth US$1.5bn until 1985. A military coup on 25 February 1980 overthrew the elected government. A state of emergency was declared, with censorship of the press, radio and TV. The military leader, Colonel Desi Bouterse, and his associates came under pressure from the Dutch and the USA as a result of dictatorial tendencies. After the execution of 15 opposition leaders on 8 December 1982, the Netherlands broke off relations and suspended its aid programme, although bridging finance was restored in 1988.

The ban on political parties was lifted in late 1985 and a new constitution was drafted. In 1986 guerrilla rebels (the Jungle Commando), led by a former bodyguard of Colonel Bouterse, Ronny Brunswijk, mounted a campaign to overthrow the government, disrupting both plans for political change, and the economy. Nevertheless, elections for the National Assembly were held in November 1987. A three-party coalition (the Front for Democracy and Development) gained a landslide victory over the military, winning 40 of the 51 seats. In January 1988, a former agriculture minister, Mr Ramsewak Shankar, was elected President by the Assembly for a 5-year term. Conflicts between President Shankar and Colonel Bouterse led to the deposition of the government in a bloodless coup on 24 December 1990 (the "telephone coup"). A military-backed government under the presidency of Johan Kraag was installed and elections for a new national assembly were held on 25 May 1991. The New Front of four traditional parties won 30 National Assembly seats. Twelve went to the army-backed National Democratic Party and nine to the Democratic Alternative, which favours closer links with The Netherlands. Ronald Venetiaan of the New Front was elected president on 6 September 1991. Both the Netherlands and the USA suspended aid after the coup, but meetings between Suriname and Netherlands ministers after the 1991 elections were expected to produce renewed aid in the second half of 1992. Although a basis for peace was drawn up in mid-1989 (the Kourou Accord), it was not until March 1991 that Colonel Bouterse and Brunswijk stated publicly that hostilities had ceased (Brunswijk had declared an end to his campaign in June 1990). No formal peace agreement had been signed by June 1992. The relationships between the different groups, government, army, Jungle Commando, bush blacks and Amerindians, were complex, with the added dimension of involvement by some groups in the cocaine trade undermining efforts to end the civil war.

Government

There is one legislative house, the National Assembly, which has 51 members. The President is both head of state and government. Suriname is divided into ten districts, of which the capital is one.

The Economy

Agriculture is restricted to some districts of the alluvial coastal zone, covering about 0.8m hectares and employing about 16.7% of the labour force. At least two-thirds of permanent crop and arable land is under irrigation. Farming (including forestry) accounts for 11.1% of gdp and about 15% of exports. The main crops are rice (the staple), bananas, sugar cane and citrus fruits, all of which are exported to Europe, along with small quantities of coffee. Apart from rice, Suriname is a net importer of food; priority is being given to rice and livestock. Between 1981 and 1983, the sector registered annual declines in output, but after 1984, positive growth was restored with the rice and shrimp sectors receiving new incentives. Suriname has vast timber resources, but exports account for less than 1% of the total and development has been hampered by a lack of investment. There is a small fishing industry, the chief catch being shrimps.

Manufacturing's contribution to gdp is 11.9%, employing 11.1% of the workforce. Import substitution, using both imported goods and local raw materials, is the main activity, with food processing accounting for 60% of the total.

Suriname is the world's sixth largest producer of bauxite, with reserves estimated at 1.9% of the world's total. The country has the capability to process the extracted ore into alumina and aluminium ingot. The bauxite/aluminium industry accounts for 74% of exports, while the mining sector as a whole contributes 3.8% of gdp and employs 4.7% of the workforce. Two companies control the industry, the Suriname Aluminium Company (Suralco), a subsidiary of Alcoa, and Billiton Maatschappij, part of Royal Dutch Shell. Their progressive merging of operations to improve competitiveness on world markets began to yield positive results in 1986 until the industry was severely disrupted by the civil war which started in that year.

Oil production from the Tambaredjo heavy oil deposit, operated by the state oil company, Staatsolie, is about 3,800 bpd. Exploratory wells in the Saramacca district have also yielded oil. Installed electricity generating capacity is 415 MW, of which 54% is thermal, 46% hydroelectric.

After five years of decline and a fall in gdp of 8.1% in 1987 alone, the economy began to recover, helped by resumption of activity in the bauxite industry, the attenuation of the domestic insurgency and the resumption of aid from the Dutch Government. Consistent improvement was not maintained and The Netherlands, the IMF and World Bank urged Suriname to unify the official and parallel exchange rates, reduce state involvement in the economy and cut the huge budget deficit to attract overseas investment.

Nature Reserves

Stinasu, the Foundation for Nature Preservation in Suriname, Jongbawstraat 14, Tel: 75845/71856, PO Box 436, Paramaribo, offers reasonably priced accommodation and provides tour guides on the extensive nature reserves throughout the country. One can see "true wilderness and wildlife" with them.

Raleighvallen/Voltzberg Nature Reserve (57,000 hectares) is rainforest park, including Foengoe Island and Voltzberg peak; climbing the mountain at sunrise is unforgettable. The **Coppename Estuary** is also a national park, protecting many bird colonies.

Only two or three hours by car from Paramaribo is the **Brownsberg National Park** (6,000 hectares). In this tropical rain-forest park live giant toads, communal spiders, monkeys, jaguars, peccaries, agoutis, and a variety of birds. Hiking maps are available at the Park office, and a guidebook to the birds of Brownsberg can be purchased in the Stinasu office in Paramaribo.

Two reserves are located on the northeast coast of Suriname. Known primarily as a major nesting site for sea turtles (five species including the huge leatherback turtle come ashore to lay their eggs) **Wia-Wia Nature Reserve** (36,000 hectares), also has nesting grounds for some magnificent birds. The nesting activity of sea turtles is best observed February-July. Since the beaches and consequently the turtles have shifted westwards out of the reserve, accommodation is now at **Matapica** beach, not in the reserve itself. (After a visit to the reserves please send any comments to Hilde Viane at Stinasu. Your support is needed to keep the reserve functioning.) There may also be mosquitoes and sandflies, depending on the season. A riverboat leaves Paramaribo daily at 0700 (buy ticket on board) and arrives in Alliance by way of the Commewijne River at 1100. You then transfer to a Stinasu motorboat for a one-hour ride to Matapica. The motorboat costs US$50 for 4 people, round trip. Suitable waterproof clothing should be worn. The beach hut accommodates 18 people in 4 rooms, and costs US$4 pp. Take your own bedding/food. Cooking facilities provided. Book the hut and boat through Stinasu and keep your receipts or you will be refused entry. Early booking is essential as the closure of the other reserves has made Matapica very popular.

The **Galibi Nature Reserve**, where there are more turtle-nesting places, is near the mouth of the Marowijne River. There are Carib Indian villages. From Albina it is a 3-hour (including ½ hour on the open sea) boat trip to Galibi.

Paramaribo

Paramaribo, the capital and chief port, lies on the Suriname river, 12 km from the sea. It has a population of about 192,000, mainly Creoles. There are many attractive colonial buildings.

The People's Palace (the old Governor's Mansion) is on Eenheidsplein (formerly Onafhankelijkheidsplein, and before that, Oranjeplein) and many beautiful 18th and 19th century buildings in Dutch (neo-Normanic) style are in the same area. The restored Fort Zeelandia used to house the Suriname Museum, but the fort has been repossessed by the military (the whole area is fenced off); very few exhibits remain in the old museum in the residential suburb of Zorg-en-Hoop, Commewijnestraat, 0700-1300. Look for Mr F Lim-A-Po-straat if you wish to see what Paramaribo looked like only a comparatively short time ago. The nineteenth-century Roman Catholic Peter and Paul cathedral (1885), built entirely of wood, is said to be the largest wooden building in the Americas, and is well worth a visit. Much of the old town, dating from the nineteenth century, and the churches have been restored. Other things to see are the colourful market and the waterfront, Hindu temples in Koningstraat, the Caribbean's largest mosque at Keizerstraat and the Synagogue (1854) at Heerenstraat (under renovation and closed since 1989). A new harbour has been constructed about 1½ km upstream. Two pleasant parks are the Palmentuin and the Cultuurtuin (with zoo, US$1.20, busy on Sunday), but the latter is quite a distance from the town and there are no buses to it. National dress is normally only worn by the Asians on national holidays and at wedding parties, but some Javanese women still go about in sarong and klambi. A university was opened in 1968. There is one public swimming pool at Weidestraat, US$0.60 pp. There is an exotic Asian flavour to the market and nearby streets. Cinemas show US, Indian and Chinese movies, with subtitles.

Local Information – Paramaribo

Where To Stay Prices are at official rate unless stated otherwise. Service charge at hotels is 10-15%. Over US$200: *Krasnapolsky* Domineestraat 39, Tel: 75050, Fax: 78524, ugly, swimming pool and shops, good breakfast, launderette on 1st floor, and bank (open until 1430); much nicer is *Torarica*, under US$70 at the parallel rate, very pleasant, book ahead, swimming pool, casino, nightclub, tropical gardens, fully air conditioned, central, superb breakfast US$6-12 (Tel: 71500, Fax: 11682); *Ambassador* (Tel: 77555, Fax: 77903), Sophie-Redmondstraat, prices as *Krasnapolsky*, quality as poor; *Riverclub*, at Leonsberg (8 km from city), Tel: 51959, Fax: 52981, same prices, many very-short-stay customers, swimming pool.

For budget travellers, best is the recently refurbished *YWCA Guesthouse* at Heerenstraat 14-16, Tel: 76981, (US$12 at official exchange rate, under US$3 parallel), cheaper weekly rates, clean, full of permanent residents, essential to book in advance (office open 0800-1400); if it's full try the *Graaf Van Zinzendorff-Herberg* at Gravenstraat 100, the same price as the YWCA. Advance booking advisable. Otherwise, try *Continental Inn*; *Fanna*, Princessestraat 31, Tel: 76789, safe, clean, friendly; *Au Soleil Levant*. *La Vida* on the way in from the airport is "cheap but nice". *Lisa's Guest House*, Buren Straat. *Balden*, Kwathweg 183, 2 km from centre on the road to Nickerie is probably the cheapest available accommodation; its Chinese restaurant serves cheap meals. Beware: many cheap hotels not listed above are "hot pillow" establishments. The *Salvation Army*, Saramaccastraat, will give the hard up a bed for Sf4.50 a night.

Where To Eat Main meals cost Sf60-100 pp. There are some good restaurants, mainly Indonesian and Chinese dishes. Try a *rijsttafel* in an Indonesian restaurant, eg *Sarinah* (open-air dining), Verlengde Gemenelandsweg 187. *La Bastille*, Kleine Waterstraat, opposite *Tocarica*, good, Tel: 73991; also *Golden Dragon*, Anamoestraat 22, *New Korean*, Mahonylaan, *Golden Crown*, David Simmonstraat and *New China*, Verlengde Gemenelandsweg. *Fa Tai*, Maagdenstraat 64, a/c; for the best Chinese food, but not cheap, try *Iwan's*, Grote Hofstraat. Many other Chinese restaurants. Cheap lunches and light meals at *Hofje*, Wagenwegstraat, and *Chalet Swiss*, Heerenstraat (more Chinese than Swiss.) Meat and noodles from stalls in the market costs Sf3. Javanese foodstalls on Waterkant are excellent and varied, lit at night by candles. Try *bami* (spicy noodles) for Sf1 and *petjil* (vegetables) for Sf0.50. Especially recommended on Sundays when the area is busiest. In restaurants a dish to try is *gadogado*, an Indonesian vegetable and peanut concoction, available for about Sf5. Good places for lunch include *Hola's Terrace*, Domineestraat. For breakfast, try *Klein Maar Fijn*, Watermolenstraat. The ice-cream parlour in Keizerstraat has been recommended as selling the best ice-cream in the Guianas.

Shopping *Arts & Crafts*, Neumanpad 13a. Amerindian goods, batik prints, carvings, basket work, drums are attractive. *Cultuurwinkel*, Anton de Kom Straat, bosneger carvings, also available at *Hotel Torarica*. Carvings are better value at the workshops on Nieuwe Dominee Straat and the Neumanpad. Old Dutch bottles US$10-25. **Bookshops** The two main bookshops are *Vaco* and *Kersten*, both on Domineestraat, and both sell English-language books. Also *Hoeksteen* (Gravenstraat 17) and the kiosk in *Krasnapolsky Hotel*. *Boekhandel Univers NV*, Gravenstraat 61, is recommended for nature, linguistic and scholarly books on Suriname. Second hand books, English and Dutch, are bought and sold in the market. Most bookshops sell a large map of Paramaribo, price US$7.

Local Transport Buses run regularly to most parts of the city; most services leave from Waterkant or Dr Sophie Redmondstraat. There are also privately run "wild buses", also known as "numbered buses" which run on fixed routes around the city. **Taxis** generally

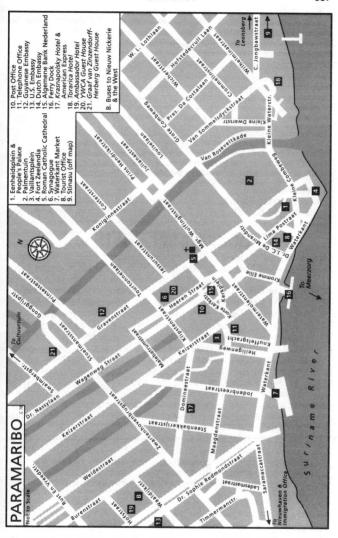

PARAMARIBO c78
Not to Scale

1. Eenheidsplein & People's Palace
2. Palmentuin
3. Vaillantsplein
4. Fort Zeelandia
5. Roman Catholic Cathedral
6. Synagogue
7. Waterkant Market
8. Tourist Office
9. Stinasu (off map)
10. Post Office
11. Telephone Office
12. Guyanese Embassy
13. U.S. Embassy
14. Dutch Embassy
15. Algemene Bank Nederland
16. Ferry Dock
17. Krasnapolsky Hotel & American Express
18. Torarica Hotel
19. Ambassador Hotel
20. YWCA Guest House
21. Graaf van Zinzendorf-Herberg Guest House
B. Buses to Nieuw Nickerie & the West

have no meters. The price should be agreed on beforehand to avoid trouble. A trip inside the city costs about Sf15. Recommended is Ally's Taxi service, Tel: 79434, English spoken.

Exchange Algemene Bank Nederland (Kerkplein 1), Surinaamse Bank and Hakrin Bank, 0700-1400. Surinaamse branch in *Hotel Krasnapolsky* open 0700-1430; 0800-1200 Saturday, Amex agents, charges Sf1.30 flat rate commission on each travellers cheque exchanged. Black market (illegal) around Waterkant market (see **Currency** in Information for Visitors).

Church The Anglican Church is St Bridget's, Hoogestraat 44 (Sunday 0900 service in English).

Tourist Agencies Mrs W J Robles-Cornelissen, *Independent Tours*, Rosenveltkade 20, Tel: 74770, and *Suriname Safari Tours* organize excursions to the interior. Trips take 3-5 days and cost about US$120 (parallel exchange), all inclusive. *Ram's Tours*, Neumandpad 30 Ben, Tel: 76011/76223. *Does Travel Service*, Domineestraat. *Saramaccan Jungle Safaris* (John Ligeon), PO Box 676, Zwartenhovenbrugstraat 19, Paramaribo, for visits by canoe to Saramaccan Bush Black villages and wildlife tours.

Bus Services To **Nickerie** from Dr Sophie Redmondstraat, last usually at 1200, Sf20 (extra for large bag). Other westbound services from Waaldijkstraat; to **Totness** at 1300. To **Afobaka** via Brokopondo, leaves from Saramaccastraat, at 0700. To **Brownsberg** at 0930. Also services eastwards to Albina via Moengo. For full details enquire at the tourist office (address in **Information for Visitors**).

Excursions

Powaka, about 90 minutes outside the capital, is a primitive village of thatched huts but with electric light and a small church. In the surrounding forest one can pick mangoes and other exotic fruit. An interesting half, or full day excursion is to take minibus 4, 0800, or taxi, to Leonsberg on the Suriname river, then ferry to *Nieuw Amsterdam*, the capital of the predominantly Javanese district of Commewijne. There is an open-air museum inside the old fortress (open only in mornings except Friday 1700-1900, Sf15), which guarded the confluence of the Suriname and Commewijne rivers. There are some old plantation mansions left in the Commewijne district which are of interest; Mariënburg is the last sugar estate in operation in Suriname. The return trip can be made by bus to Meerzorg on the river, taking the vehicle ferry back to Paramaribo.

By private car to *Jodensavanne* (Jews' Savanna, established 1639), south of Paramaribo on the opposite bank of the Suriname river, where part of one of the oldest synagogues in the Western Hemisphere has been restored. It has a small museum. You need permission from the Forestry Department (LBB), in Jongbawstraat, to use the ferry to Jodensavanne. There is a new guesthouse, with six rooms, at Blakkawatra, nearby. Accommodation is available through Stinasu (see above) and camping is possible. Some 4 km from the International Airport there is a resort called Cola Creek, so named for the colour of the water, but good swimming.

By bus or car to *Afobakka*, where there is a large hydro-electric dam on the Suriname river. There is a government guesthouse in nearby *Brokopondo*. The Brownsberg National Park is one hour by car from here. Transport can be arranged from Brownsweg, 14 km downhill from the Park. Accommodation in *Brownsweg*. A bus to Paramaribo leaves Brownsweg every morning.

West of Paramaribo

Totness is the largest village in the Coronie district, along the coast between Paramaribo and Nieuw Nickerie on the Guyanese border. There is a good government guesthouse. The road (bad, liable to flooding) leads through an extensive forest of coconut palms. Bus to Paramaribo at 0600. *Wageningen* is a modern little town, the centre of the Suriname rice-growing area. The road from Nickerie has recently been renewed. One of the largest fully mechanized rice farms in the world is found here. (*Hotel de Wereld*). The Bigi-Pan area of mangroves is a bird-watchers' paradise; boats may be hired from local fishermen.

Nieuw Nickerie, on the south bank of the Nickerie River 5 km from its mouth, opposite Guyana is the main town and port of the Nickerie district and is distinguished for its ricefields and for the number and voraciousness of its mosquitoes. The town has a population of more than 8,000, the district of 35,000, mostly East Indian. Paramaribo is 237 km away by road. Buses leave hourly or when full, Sf20 (extra for large bag) and take less time (5 hours) with the opening of the bridge than they did before. A special, late afternoon bus connecting with the ferry from Guyana may cost Sf40. Sit on the left-hand side of the bus to get the best views of the bird-life in the swamps.

Where To Stay *Ameerali*, G G Maynardstraat, Tel: 0316427/031212, Fax: 031066, near ferry, clean, over US$50 official rate about US$10 parallel; *De-Vesting*, similar quality, Balatastraat near ferry, Tel: 031265. *Dorien*, Tel: 031352, US$20 bed and breakfast; *Blue Hawaii*, central, US$10, reported to overcharge foreigners. On Gouverneurstraat are *Luxor* and *Tropical*, US$7-10, *President*, among the cheapest.

Where To Eat *Moksie Patoe*, Gouverneurstraat 115, run by Frenchman, Jean Amar, provides European and Indian dishes with items rarely found elsewhere in friendly atmosphere. *Ella*, Javanese food. *Tokyo*, rather basic. Good food at the Asanredjo foodstand (unmarked), ask to be directed, two blocks east of *Ajai*, on Oranjenassaustraat. Cheap filling meals can be obtained on the street for as little as US$1.50.

Exchange   The bank at the immigration office is reported to close at 1500 Monday-Friday, whether or not the ferry has arrived.

Ferry to Springlands, Guyana

Sf15, one way, 2 hours, no service Sunday or national holidays of either country, foot passengers only. Best to book 24 hours in advance, though you can book on day of departure. Book for same day departures by handing in your passport at the Immigration Office, 200 metres below ferry point, opens 0700, be there 0630. After booking, go to the stelling (ferry pier) and pass quite quickly through outgoing customs inspection and immigration. Book in advance either at Immigration Office or at military police station, corner of Maynardstraat and Bataviastraat, Monday-Friday 0900-1200, Saturday 0900-1100. Guyanese entry and currency forms available on ferry, US$0.50. For entry to Guyana a return ferry ticket will suffice as an onward ticket: without one you can be sent back on the next ferry. You will reach Springlands at 1000; take a minibus immediately to New Amsterdam, then launch, then minibus from Rossignol to get to Georgetown by 1400. Whole journey time 26 hours, overall cost US$5 (parallel rates).

Vast reserves of bauxite have been discovered in the Bakhuis Mountains, in the northern part of Nickerie District. A road has been built from Zanderij to **Apoera** on the Corantijn; it can also be reached by sea-going vessels. **Blanche Marie Falls**, 320 km from Paramaribo on the Apoera road, is a popular destination. There is a guesthouse, *Dubois*, US$35, contact Eldoradolaan 22, Paramaribo Tel: 76904/2. Camping is Sf30 tent/day. There is a good guesthouse at Apoera (US$25 with 3 meals, advance booking from Paramaribo advisable). **Washabo** near Apoera, which has an airstrip, is an Amerindian village. There is no public transport from Paramaribo to the Apoera-Bakhuis area, but many private cars and trucks go there and there are frequent charter flights to the Washabo airstrip. Irregular small boats go from Apoera to Nieuw Nickerie and to Springlands (Guyana). Try to rent a canoe to visit the Amerindian settlement of Orealla in Guyana or Kaboeri creek, 12 km downstream, where giant river otters may possibly be seen in October or March.

East of Paramaribo to Guyane

Moengo 160 km up the Cottica River from Paramaribo, is a bauxite mining and loading centre for the Suriname Aluminium Company (*Government Guesthouse*). Paranam, another loading centre, is on the left bank.

Albina the eastern frontier village, is 140 km from Paramaribo, 29 km from the mouth of the Marowijne River, the boundary with French Guyane. There is a park along the Marowijne river (about 15 minutes walk from the town centre) called Het Park with free hammock places. Opposite Albina, in French Guyane, is St-Laurent. Albina is the centre for trips by powered dugouts to Amerindian and bosneger villages on the Marowijne, Tapanahoni and Lawa rivers (about Sf50 plus). It takes 1½-2 days to get to the beautiful **Stoelmanseiland**, headquarters of Ronnie Brunswijk, on the Lawa River (guest house with full board, US$25, including meals. It and the bush negro villages and rapids in the area can be visited on excursions organized by tour operators. Price US$150 pp for 3 days (5 persons, minimum). They are more easily reached by river from St-Laurent du Maroni and Maripasoula in Guyane.

It is essential to get correct entry stamps from Immigration, not the police. If you do not, you will have real problems on departure.

Information for Visitors

Documents
Visitors must have a valid passport (one issued by the Hong Kong government, and a few others, will not be accepted), a visa, or tourist card. Visas cost US$30 and must be obtained in advance (up to 4 weeks wait not unusual) by citizens of all countries except Great Britain, Japan, Israel, The Gambia, South Korea, Denmark, Finland, Sweden, Switzerland, Netherlands Antilles, Brazil, Ecuador, Canada, Chile and Guyana (these require a tourist card, obtainable at the airport, US$14). There are consulates in Caracas, Brasília, Georgetown and Cayenne. Even with a visa to stay more than 10 days, you need a "blue card", issued by Immigration Office, van't Hogerhuystraat, Nieuwe Haven, Paramaribo. To get this you need a receipt for Sf10 from the Commissariat Combé, Van Sommelsdijkstraat, opposite *Torarica Hotel*, take passport and 2 passport photos, allow a week to get it. The same procedure applies for a re-entry stamp.

Customs
Duty-free imports include (if declared) 400 cigarettes or 100 cigars or ½ kg of tobacco, 2 litres of spirits and 4 litres of wine, 50 grams of perfume and 1 litre of toilet water, 8 rolls of still film and 60 metres of cinefilm, 100 metres of recording tape, and other goods up to a value of Sf40. Personal baggage is free of duty. Customs examination of baggage can be very thorough.

How To Get There By Air
Johann Pengel International Airport is served by SLM (Suriname Airways), KLM, Air France, ALM and Cruzeiro do Sul. SLM flies to Miami (twice a week), New York (once a week), Amsterdam (once a week), Belém, Curaçao, once a week each, Cayenne (once a week), and Georgetown (3 times a week). KLM flies from Amsterdam twice a week, once via Port of Spain; Air France flies from Cayenne once a week, Air Aruba once a week from Aruba, and ALM from Curaçao twice a week. Cruzeiro do Sul flies to Cayenne and Belém on Mondays. Additional services from Zorg en Hoop airfield to Guyane: SLM to Cayenne, once a week; Gum Air and Gonini, to Cayenne, Tuesday and Wednesday subject to demand; Gum Air to St-Laurent du Moroni (3 times a week). Many people go to Cayenne to take advantage of cheap Air France tickets to Europe as well as increased seat availability. Internal services are maintained by SLM and two small air charter firms.

Airport Information
The Johann Pengel International Airport (formerly Zanderij), is 45 km south of Paramaribo. Minibus or shared taxi to town costs Sf75; ordinary taxi, Sf150,

regular minibus, marked PZB or POZ, which leaves from the service station 15 minutes' walk from the centre on the south highway, US$0.30, daytime only. De Paarl minibus recommended as cheaper (Tel: 79600). Money exchange facilities, Hakrin Bank between Customs and Immigration (closed Sundays). There is an airport departure tax of US$15 (Sf30). There is a new guest house near the airport. Internal flights leave from Zorg-en-Hoop airfield in a suburb of Paramaribo.

Visa for Guyana
Nearly everyone needs a visa to enter Guyana, but see Guyana **Documents** in **Information for Visitors**. Visa free from the Guyanese Embassy at 82 Gravenstraat, open Monday, Wednesday, Friday, 0800-1300. Same day service if you make an early application. Take three passport photos and onward ticket from Guyana.

Internal Travel
There are 2,500 km of main roads, of which 850 km are paved. East-west roads: From Albina to Paramaribo to Nieuw Nickerie is open; buses and taxis are available (details in the text above). North-south: the road Paramaribo - Paranam - Afobaka - Pokigron is open. **Self-Drive Cars** City Taxi, Purperhart, Kariem, Intercar, and other agencies. Kentax (Tel: 72078) is open 24 hours a day. All driving licences accepted, but you need a stamp from the local police and a deposit of US$140-420. Gasoline/petrol is sold as "regular", or "extra" (more expensive). **Bicycles** Can be bought for about US$100 from A Seymonson, Rijwielhersteller, Rust en Vredestraat (cheaper in Guyana). Recommended rides from Paramaribo include to Nieuw Amsterdam, Marienburg, Alkmaar and back via Tamanredjo in the Javanese Commewijne district or from Rust en Werk to Spieringshoek to Reijnsdorp (3½ hours) and return to Leonsberg via ferry, whence it is a 30 minute ride to Paramaribo. Driving is on the left.
Local Shipping The three ferries across the main rivers operate only in daytime (the Paramaribo-Meerzorg ferry until 2200). The Suriname Navigation Co (SMS) has a daily service, leaving 0700, on the Commewijne river (a nice four-hour trip; one can get off at *De Nieuwe Grond*, a plantation owned by an English couple, and stay overnight). The SMS has a daily

service to Reynsdorp, leaving Paramaribo early in the morning. SMS also has infrequent services on other rivers (Wayombo and Cottica). SMS makes an interesting water trip, using inland waterways, to Nieuw Nickerie taking 36 hours; it leaves Paramaribo on Mondays at 0800, departs Nieuw Nickerie 1200 Wednesday (times subject to 2 hours variation due to tides), no cabins, only slatted seats, but there is hammock space; take food and drink; lots of mosquitoes.
Air: east-west, SLM flies 3 times daily, six days a week, from Zorg-en-Hoop (Paramaribo) to Nieuw Nickerie. North-south: the interior is currently open. Most settlements have an airstrip. Bush flights are operated by Gum-Air and Gonini to several Amerindian and bosneger villages. All flights are on demand.
Note It is advisable to check the weather conditions and probabilities of returning on schedule before you set out on a trip to the interior. Heavy rains can make it impossible for planes to land in some jungle areas; little or no provision is made for such delays and it can be a long and hungry wait for better conditions.

Accommodation
Hotels and restaurants are rare outside the capital, and you usually have to supply your own hammock and mosquito net, and food. A tent is less useful in this climate. Travelling is only cheap if you can change cash dollars on the black market, but taking your own hammock and food will reduce costs.

Warning
Those caught taking pictures of Fort Zeelandia, the People's Palace, police stations, military installations etc face confiscation of their film, at least. Be careful also when taking pictures from ferries.

Currency
The unit of currency is the Suriname guilder (Sf) divided into 100 cents. There are notes for 5, 10, 25, 100 and 500 guilders. Since end-1982 only notes showing the revolutionary symbol have been legal tender: do not accept the old ones. Coins are for 1 guilder and 5, 10, 25 (the 25-cent coin is usually known as a *kwartje*) and 50 cents. Suriname's monetary system is quite independent of Holland's; the Suriname guilder is valued officially against the US dollar at US$1 =

Sf1.78 (fixed), a rate which makes Suriname one of the most expensive in the world, but at the parallel rate of about US$1 = Sf14 (January 1992), it is one of the cheapest. Parallel trading is illegal. The easiest place to change is on the stelling (ferry pier) at Springlands (Guyana), where it's not against the law. In Paramaribo visit the market; traders will approach you. Find out the day's rate and go elsewhere to change money, eg a discreet shopkeeper or other contact (rates will be slightly worse). Foreign currency has to be declared on entry and on departure, so make sure that the amount you claim to have spent matches the official rate.

Health
No special precautions necessary except for a trip to the malarial interior; for free malaria prophylaxis contact the Public Health Department (BOG). Suriname Safari Tours provides malaria prophylaxis on its package tours. Chloroquine-resistant malaria in the interior. Mosquito nets should be used at night over beds in rooms not air-conditioned or screened. Outside Paramaribo drinking water should still be boiled despite protestations. In some coastal districts there is a risk of bilharzia (schistosomiasis). Vaccinations: yellow fever and tetanus advisable, typhoid only for trips into the interior. Swim only in running water because of poisonous fish. There is good swimming on the Marowijne river and at Matapica beach and on the Coppename river. There are 5 hospitals in Paramaribo, best is St Vincentius.

Climate And Clothing
Tropical and moist, but not very hot, since the north-east trade wind makes itself felt during the whole year. In the coastal area the temperature varies on an average from 23° to 31°C, during the day; the annual mean is 27°C, and the monthly mean ranges from 26° to 28°C, only. The mean annual rainfall is about 2,340 mm for Paramaribo and 1,930 mm for the western division. The seasons are: minor rainy season, November-February; minor dry season, February-April; main rainy season, April-August; main dry season, August-November. None of these seasons is, however, usually either very dry or very wet. The degree of cloudiness is fairly high and the average humidity is 82%. The climate of the interior is similar but with higher rainfall.

Except for official meetings, informal tropical clothing is worn, but not shorts.

An umbrella or plastic raincoat is very useful.

The **high seasons**, when everything is more expensive, are 15 March-15 May, July-September and 15 December-15 January.

Hours Of Business
Shops and Businesses: Monday-Thursday 0730-1630, Friday 0730-1300 and 1700-2000, Saturday 0730-1300. Government departments: Monday-Thursday 0700-1500, Friday 0700-1430. Banks are open Monday-Friday 0730-1400. The airport bank is open at flight arrival and departure times.

Public Holidays
1 January, New Year; Holi Phagwa (1 day in March); Good Friday; Easter (2 days); 1 May (Labour Day); 1 July (National Unity); 25 November (Independence Day); Christmas (2 days). For Moslem holidays see note under Guyana.

Time Zone
3 hours behind GMT.

Weights And Measures
The metric system is in general use.

Electricity Supply
127 volts AC, 60 cycles. Plug fittings are usually 2-pin round (European continental type). Lamp fittings are screw type.

Post, Telegraph, Telephone
Telegrams can be sent from 0700 until 2200 and from Government Telegraph Service, Gravenstraat, in urgent cases.

There is a telephone and telegraph office on Vaillantplein. Book and pay in advance, very time-consuming. Calls can be made to the US and UK via satellite. The office is open 0700-2000; calls booked before 2000 can be made up till midnight. USA Direct calls can be made from the *Hotel Torarica*. Best way to communicate abroad is by Fax at TeleSur, which can receive faxes for the public as well as send; number is 10555.

Newspapers
in Dutch, *De Ware Tijd* (morning) and *DeWest* (evening).

Embassies And Consulates
USA (Dr Sophie Redmondstraat 129, PO Box 1821, Tel: 72900), Netherlands, Belgium, Brazil, Cuba, France, Mexico, Venezuela, South Korea, India, Indonesia, Guyana, India, Japan, China (People's Republic), USSR. There are consuls-general, vice-consuls or consular agents for Canada, Denmark, Dominican

Republic, Ecuador, Finland, Germany, Haiti, UK, Mexico, Norway, Spain, and Sweden, all in Paramaribo. British Honorary Consul, Mr James Healy, Tel: 72870 office/74764 house, is very helpful.

Information
about Suriname can be had from: the Suriname Embassy, Alex Gogelweg 2, The Hague, Netherlands (Tel: 070-65-08-44) or the Tourist Board, Waterkant 8, PO Box 656 (Tel: 71163/78421; telex 292 Surair SN),

Paramaribo, useful handouts on lodgings and restaurants, free map of Paramaribo, English spoken, tours organized, or Stinasu, address under **Nature Reserves**. Also from embassies.

The *Surinam Planatlas* is available from the National Planning office on Dr Sophie Redmondstraat, Sf100; maps with natural environment and economic development topics, each with commentary in Dutch and English. Beautifully prepared and a real bargain.

GUYANE

Introduction

GUYANE, an Overseas Department of France, has its eastern frontier with Brazil formed partly by the River Oiapoque (Oyapoc in French) and its southern, also with Brazil, formed by the Tumuc-Humac mountains (the only range of importance). The western frontier with Suriname is along the River Maroni-Itani. To the north is the Atlantic coastline of 320 km. The area is estimated at 89,941 square km, or one-sixth that of France. The land rises gradually from a coastal strip some 15-40 km wide to the higher slopes and plains or savannas, about 80 km inland. Forests cover some 8 million hectares of the hills and valleys of the interior, and timber production is increasing rapidly. The territory is well watered, for over twenty rivers run to the Atlantic.

The population (120,000) consists of Creoles, who, by the widest measure, account for 72% of the population; Bush Negroes, 6.4%; Amerindians (including Arawak), 4.2%; Asians, Europeans and others (including Brazilians), 17.1%. There are an estimated 15,000 migrant workers from Haiti and nearby countries. The language is French, with officials not usually speaking anything else. The religion is predominantly Roman Catholic.

History

Several French and Dutch expeditions attempted to settle along the coast in the early 17th century, but were driven off by the native population. The French finally established a settlement at Sinnamary in the early 1660s but this was destroyed by the Dutch in 1665 and seized by the British two years later. Under the Treaty of Breda, 1667, Guyane was returned to France. Apart from a brief occupation by the Dutch in 1676, it remained in French hands until 1809 when a combined Anglo-Portuguese naval force captured the colony and handed it over to the Portuguese (Brazilians). Though the land was restored to France by the Treaty of Paris in 1814, the Portuguese remained until 1817. Gold was discovered in 1853, and disputes arose about the frontiers of the colony with Suriname and Brazil. These were settled by arbitration in 1891, 1899, and 1915. By the law of 19 March, 1946, the Colony of Cayenne, or Guyane Française, became the Department of Guyane, with the same laws, regulations, and administration as a department in metropolitan France. The seat of the Prefect and of the principal courts is at Cayenne. The colony was used as a prison for French convicts with camps scattered throughout the country; Saint-Laurent was the port of entry. After serving prison terms convicts spent an equal number of years in exile and were usually unable to earn their return passage to France. Those interested should read *Papillon* by Henri Charrière. Majority opinion seems to be in favour of greater autonomy: about 5% of the population are thought to favour independence.

Government

The head of state is the President of France; the local heads of government are a Commissioner of the Republic, for France, and the Presidents of the local General and Regional Councils. The General Council (19 seats) and the Regional Council (31 seats) are the two legislative houses. In regional council elections in March 1992, the Parti Socialiste Guyanais won 16 seats, while the other major party, the Front Democratique Guyanais, won 10. Guyane is divided into two *arrondissements*, Cayenne and St-Laurent du Maroni.

The Economy
Guyane has renewable natural riches in its timber forests (about 75,000 sq km) with 15 sawmills and mineral resources. Farming employs only 11.4% of the population and the country is very sparsely populated. An estimated 42 million tons of extractable bauxite have been located in the Kaw mountains to the southeast of Cayenne by Alcoa and Pechiney. Some 40m tonnes of kaolin have been located at St-Laurent du Maroni and gold is again being mined.

Guyane imports most of its foodstuffs and manufactured goods, of which about 60% come from France. The value of exports, mainly shrimps, rum, essence of rosewood, hardwoods and gold, is very low; France buys just under 50%, the remaining EC about 20%.

At end-1982 the French Government announced plans to step up the Department's development in consultation with local parties: the so-called Green Plan (Plan Vert), backed by the Société Financière de Développement de la Guyane. Under the plan local production of basic foodstuffs, such as meat and eggs, was to be raised, and areas of timber plantations doubled to 22,000 hectares. In recent years new building has taken place and facilities for visitors have been much improved.

Note The Amerindian villages in the Haut-Maroni and Haut-Oyapoc areas may only be visited with permission from the Préfecture in Cayenne *before* departure to Guyane.

Cayenne

Cayenne, the capital and the chief port, is on the island of Cayenne at the mouth of the Cayenne River. It is 645 km from Georgetown (Guyana) and 420 km from Paramaribo (Suriname) by sea. Population 42,000. There is an interesting museum, the Musée Departemental, in Rue de Remire, near the Place de Palmistes, which includes paintings of convict life on the Iles du Salut (Monday 1000-1300, Tuesday and Friday 0900-1300, 1600-1830, Wednesday 0900-1300, Saturday and Sunday 0900-1200; free admission). The Musée de L'Or, Impasse Buzaré, was closed for restoration in January, 1992. Also worth a visit are Crique, the colourful but dangerous area around the Canal Laussat (built by Malouet in 1777); the Jesuit-built residence (circa 1890) of the Prefect (L'Hôtel-de-Ville) in the Place de Grenoble; the Place des Amandiers (also known as the Place Auguste-Horth) by the sea; the Place des Palmistes, with assorted palms; a swimming pool; a municipal library and five cinemas. There are bathing beaches (water rather muddy) around the island, the best is Montjoly (no bus), but watch out for sharks.

Local Information – Cayenne

Where To Stay Between US$70 and 120: *Novotel Cayenne*, Tel: 303888, on beach, restaurant, a/c, very good; *Phigarita Studios*, 47 bis, rue F Arago, Tel: 30-66-00, friendly, helpful, breakfast 40F. Over US$45: *Amazonia*, Av Gen de Gaulle, good, friendly, a/c, luggage stored, central location, Tel: 30-03-02; *Central Hotel*, corner rue Mole and rue Becker, Tel: 31-30-00; *Guyane Studios*, 16 rue Mole, Tel: 30-25-11; *Le Baduel*, Tel: 30-51-58; *Ajoupa*, Tel: 30-33-08, Route Camp de Tigre, 2 km from town,

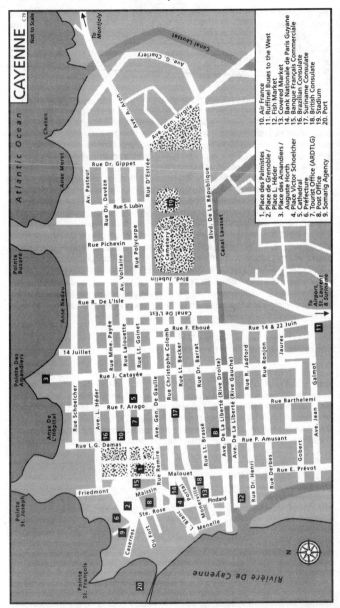

CAYENNE C.79
Not to Scale

Atlantic Ocean

1. Place des Palmistes
2. Place de Grenoble / Place L. Héder
3. Place des Amandiers / Auguste Horth
4. Place Victor Schoelcher
5. Cathedral
6. Préfecture
7. Tourist Office (ARDTLG)
8. Post Office
9. Somarig Agency
10. Air France
11. Ruffinel Buses to the West
12. Fish Market
13. Covered Market
14. Bank Nationale de Paris Guyane
15. Banque Français Commerciale
16. Brazilian Consulate
17. Surinaame Consulate
18. British Consulate
19. Stadium
20. Port

helpful. Over US$30: *Chez Mathilde*, 42 Av Gen de Gaulle, Tel: 30-25-13, hammock space, friendly, clean, noisy, not safe for left luggage, always full; *Madeleine*, Tel: 30-17-36, a/c, basic, clean, breakfast, 1 km out of town, friendly (good Surinamese snackbar nearby). *Neptima*, Rue F Eboué 21, Tel: 30-11-15 (15 rooms), US$25, best value, a/c, clean, friendly. Cheapest in town is *Foyer Paul VI*, Rue Yasim, Tel: 30-04-16, under US$10, cheap meals. *Hotel M*, a motel with air conditioned rooms and a small swimming pool; the owner hires out small cars, recommended for businessmen, breakfast, Tel: 35-41-00, Telex 010 310. Mme Izeros, Tel: 31-06-55, lets out rooms, about US$15, without breakfast. Most hotels do not add tax and service to their bill, but stick to prices posted outside or at the desk. Hotel rooms are expensive, none costs less than 150F a night double. Bed and breakfast accommodation is available for about 100F a night, contact the tourist office for details. Amex cards often not accepted but Visa OK.

Where To Eat And Drink   Main hotels. *L'Auberge des Amandiers*, Place Auguste-Horth, excellent, good value; *Armand Ti A Hing*, Place des Palmistes, French, excellent, 180F pp; *Cap St. Jacques*, Rue Docteur E Gippet, excellent Vietnamese food, reasonable. *Maxim'um*, Av Estrée. La Croix du Sud, 80, Av de Gaulle; *Le Snack Créole*, 17 Rue Eboué; *Palmiste*, 12 Av de Gaulle, central and spacious; *Frégate*, Av de Gaulle; *Le Traiteur de la Fôret*, Blvd Jubelin, friendly, good; *Marveen Snack Bar*, Rue Ch Colombe, near Canal de L'Est, food and staff pleasant, the patrons are very helpful regarding air travel and excursions (the elder of the two is a pilot for the Guyane Flying Club). *Ko Fei*, 18, Rue Lalouette, Tel: 312888, good Chinese; *Apsara*, 95 Rue Colombe, Chinese, good value. Along the Canal Laussant there are Javanese snack bars; try *bami* (spicy noodles) or *saté* (barbecued meat in a spicy peanut sauce). Vans around Place des Palmistes in evenings sell cheap, filling sandwiches. *Bar Cayenne Palace*, 45 Av de Gaulle, disco 80F with first drink. *Delifrance*, Av de Gaulle, hot chocolate and croissants; *Epi D'or*, Av Jubelin, good sweets and cakes, recommended. Food is expensive, probably 30% more than in metropolitan France.

Bookshops   *Librairie AJC*, 31 Boulevard Jubelin, has some stock in English. Also old maps and prints. Current map sold at *Librairie Alain* Pion, Av de Gaulle and in most bookshops.

Exchange   Banque Nacional de Paris-Guyane, 2 Place Schoelcher; no exchange facilities on Saturday. Banque Française Commerciale, 2 Place des Palmistes; Crédit Populaire Guyanais, 93 Rue Lalouette. Cambios give slightly better rates for US$ than banks. There are no exchange facilities at the airport; if in extreme need on Saturday you may be able to change money at Air France office in Place des Palmistes. Central drugstore may help when banks closed. Buy francs before arrival if possible.

Laundromat   Corner of Rue Lalouette and Rue Eboué, US$5 load all in.

Main Post Office   Route de Baduel, 2 km out from town (15F by taxi or 20 minutes on foot). Poste Restante letters are only kept for 2 weeks maximum. Also Poste Cayenne Cépéron, Place L Heder.

Travel Agent   *Takari Tour*, Colline du Montabo, Tel: 31-19-60 (BP 513). *Somarig*, Place L Heder, Tel: 31-29-80, is reported to be good for South American and European airline tickets. It also sells boat tickets to Ile Royale as well as meal tickets for the Auberge which are recommended. *JAL Voyages*, Tel: 38-23-70 and *Guyane Excursions*, Centre Commercial Simarouba, Tel: 32-05-41, both organize a varied programme of tours. *Agence Sainte-Claire*, 8 rue de Rémire, Tel: 30-00-38; *Havas*, 2 place du Marché, Tel: 30-26-22/31-27-26; *Minerve*, 65 rue Justin Catayéc, Tel: 31-89-00.

Bus   Bus terminal at corner of Rue Molé and Av de la Liberté. Regular urban services. Only westbound bus is run by Raffinel & Cie, 8 Av Galmot, Tel: 31-26-66 (Kourou 60F, St Laurent 150F) leaves 0530 (not Sunday) Service to *Mana* Monday and Thursday only. To Kaw, Wednesdays. Otherwise transport is by shared taxis (collectifs), which leave from Av de la Liberté, near the fish market early in the morning (Kourou 60F, St Laurent 150F).

West to Suriname

Kourou, 56 km west of Cayenne, where the main French space centre (Centre Spatial Guyanais), used for the European Space Agency's Ariane programme, is located, is referred to by the Guyanais as "white city" because of the number of metropolitan French families living there; its population is about 6,450. Tourist attractions include bathing, fishing, sporting and aero club, and a variety of organized excursions. The space centre occupies an area of about 4 km deep along some 30 km of coast, bisected by the Kourou river. It is open to the public on Monday-Thursday 0800-1200, Monday, Tuesday, Thursday 1400-1700. Phone 33-42-00 to reserve a place on a tour of the centre (in French only, max 40), often booked up days ahead; closed during Carnival. Kourou has its own port facilities, 4 km out of town. One can sometimes hitch a lift with the Space Centre bus to the cross roads 1 km from the port.

Local Information – Kourou

Where To Stay Over US$200: *Relais de Guyane* (*Hotel des Roches*), Les Roches, Tel: 32-00-66, pool, beach, good restaurants. Over US$100: *Hotel Manguiers*, Tel: 32-00-66. Over US$50: *Diamant*, Tel: 32-10-90; *Mme Moutton*, Rue Séraphin 56, studios with or without kitchen, friendly; *Studio Sodexho*, Place Newton, Tel: 32-06-11; *Centre D'Accueil*, de Gaulle, US$15, basic, clean, friendly.

Where To Eat Many, especially on de Gaulle including *Le Catouri*, *Cachiri*, *Auberge de Père Jean* (all creole), *Vieux Montmartre* and *L'Aubrevoir* (French). Cheapest in town is *La Légion*, very good value. Snack Bars: *La Cage*, Av Les Roches; *Felicio*, Allée des Tamanoirs. **Night Clubs**: *Bellevue* and *Club des Roches*, Av Les Roches, *Le Vieux Montmartre*, de Gaulle.

Exchange Banque National de Paris Guyane, Place Newton; Banque Française Commerciale, Place Jeanne d'Arc; Crédit Populaire Guyanais, de Gaulle.

Suriname Consulate 38 Rue Christophe Colomb.

Post Office Avenue des Frères Kennedy.

Tourist Office Avenue des Roches, Tel: 32-00-05.

Travel Agency *Guyane Excursions*, Tel: 32-05-41; *Floreal Tours*, Tel: 32-17-00; *Havas Voyages Kourou.*

Transport to Cayenne leaves from Shell service station. Raffinel buses Monday 0630, Tuesday-Saturday 0900, 70F; *taxis collectifs*, 0600 and 1400. Taxi to Cayenne or airport, 300F.

The *Iles du Salut* (many visitors at weekends), opposite Kourou, include the Ile Royale, the Ile Saint-Joseph, and the Ile du Diable. They were the scene of the notorious convict settlement built in 1852; the last prisoners left in 1953. The Ile du Diable ("Devil's Island"), a rocky palm-covered islet almost inaccessible from the sea, was where political prisoners, including Alfred Dreyfus, were held. There is a 60-bed hotel on Ile Royale, *Auberge Iles du Salut* (address Sothis, 97310 Kourou, Tel: 32-11-00), US$40-50, also dormitory accommodation US$15 pp, hammock US$10 pp; former guard's bungalow, main meals (excellent), minimum 180F, breakfast 40F (ex-mess hall for warders, with good food; bottled water sold). Camping is possible, but suitable sites are limited, the strong-hearted may try the old prison barracks; take food and water (you can also sling a hammock in the open); bread and water (check bottle is sealed) can be bought from the somewhat unfriendly hotel stall. You can see agoutis, turtles, humming birds and macaws, and there are many un-owned coconut palms. Beware the many open wells. Take a torch for visiting the ruins. Paintings of prison life are on show in the tiny church. Points of interest include the children's graveyard, hospital, mental asylum and death cells. Boat from next to *Hotel des Roches*, Kourou 150F return, leaves 0830, returns from island at 1700, 1 hour each way. Tickets may be obtained from Somarig Voyager,

Place Heder, Cayenne and from other tour agencies. Also boat from Pariacabo harbour 4 km out of town, or try hitching a lift at the yacht club. Four daily crossings (40F return) by small boat from Ile Royale to Ile Saint-Joseph, which is wilder and more beautiful, with a small beach (this island had solitary-confinement cells and the warders' graveyard). Surfing and swimming are possible between Ile Royale and Ile du Diable; strong currents at high tide. Boat owners are very reluctant to visit Ile du Diable except around July-August when the sea is calmer.

Between Kourou and Iracoubo, on the road west to St-Laurent, is **Sinnamary**, where Galibi Indians at a mission make artifical flowers from feathers, for sale to tourists. Scarlet ibis can be seen in numbers on the Sinnamary estuary.

    St-Laurent du Maroni, population 5,000, formerly a penal transportation camp, is now a quiet colonial town 250 km from Cayenne on the River Maroni, bordering Suriname. The old Camp de Transportation (the original penal centre) can be wandered round at will (an absolute must if visiting the country). (Nearby is St-Jean du Maroni, an Indian village.)

Local Information

Where To Stay Sinnamary *Sinnarive*, Tel: 34-55-55, and *Eldo Grill*, Tel: 34-51-41, both over US$60 or contact M Derain, Tel: 34-53-09, who lets out rooms, US$15 pp). St-Laurent *Hotel Toucan*, Boulevard de General de Gaulle, US$35, unfriendly, poor value. *Hotel Bacadel*, Avenue Felix Eboué, above *Le Saramarca* restaurant, US$25, but worth haggling, airy; the owner, Mme Bacadel, is friendly. *Star Hotel*, Rue Thiers, Tel: 34-10-84, US$35-50, a/c, pool, cheap restaurant, friendly, recommended. *Restaurants Vietnam* and *Le Point d'Intérrogation* have been recommended.

Tourist Office Rue August Boudinot Av de la Marne, Tel: 342398.

Transport Bus to Cayenne, 150F, 0500 daily (not Sunday); *taxis collectifs* to and from Cayenne, 140F a head, 3½-hour trip. Freight *pirogues* sometimes take passengers inland along the Maroni River. Avis has a car rental office in St-Laurent.

Crossing to Suriname The frontier was reopened in 1991; make sure you obtain proper entry stamps from immigration, not the police, to avoid problems when leaving. Ferry to Albina 5 daily, none Tuesday afternoon, 50F. GUM airways fly from St-Laurent to Paramaribo, 3 times a week, enquire at the *Star Hotel*.

40 km north of St-Laurent du Maroni is **Mana**, a delightful town with rustic architecture near the coast (*Gite d'Etape*, rooms OK, filthy kitchen, mosquitoes, disco next door; nuns next to the church rent beds and hammocks, US$10; Mme Hidair, Tel: 34-80-62, has rooms, US$25). 16 km west of Mana following the river along a single track access road is Les Hattes (*Gite Rureau*, US$35, clean) an Amerindian village (ask M Daniel for permission to stay in the church); 4 km further on is Les Hattes beach where leatherback-turtles lay their eggs at night; season April-August with its peak in June-July. No public transport to Les Hattes and its beach, but hitching possible at weekends; take food and water and mosquito repellent. In spite of the dryish climate Mana is a malaria region. The fresh water of the Maroni and Mana rivers makes sea bathing very pleasant. Very quiet during the week.

    Aouara, an Amerindian village with hammock places, is a few kilometres south east of Les Hattes. It also has a beach where the leatherback turtles lay their eggs; they take about three hours over it. Take mosquito nets, hammock and insect repellent.

    There are daily flights from Cayenne to **Maripasoula** (*Auberge Chez*

Dedè) up the Maroni from St-Laurent (2-4 day journey up river in *pirogue*). There may be freight canoes which take passengers (200F) or private boats (750F) which leave from St-Laurent; 5-day tour with Takari Tour US$450 pp. If going up the Maroni, take malaria prophylaxis.

Central Massif

Jef D Boeke of Boston, Mass, has recommended a visit to **Saül**, a remote gold-mining settlement in the "central massif". The main attractions are for the nature-loving tourist. Beautiful undisturbed tropical forests are accessible by a very well-maintained system of 90 km of marked trails, including several circular routes. The place has running water, a radiotelephone, and electricity. Ten-day expeditions are run by Christian Ball, "Vie Sauvage", 97314 Saül, 350F (30% in advance) per day with meals, maps of local trails provided, own hammock and bedding useful but not essential. It can be cold at night. Air service from Cayenne or via Maripasoula (see **Airport Information**); try at airport even if flight said to be full. By *pirogue* from Mana up Mana River, 9-12 days, then one day's walk to Saül, or from St-Laurent via Maripasoula along Moroni and Inini Rivers, 15 days and one day's walk to Saül, both routes expensive.

Southeast to Brazil

Southeast of Cayenne is the small town of **Roura** (Hotel La Pirogue, US$35, clean, good views), which has an interesting church; an excursion may be made to the Fourgassier Falls several km away. From Cayenne take a minibus to Stoupan, then catch the ferry across the River Comte (departs every hour 0730-1830). From Roura an unpaved road runs southeast towards the village of Kaw. At Km 36 from Cayenne is the *Hotel Relais de Patawa* (Tel: 31-93-95), US$25, or sling your hammock for 30F, cheaper rates for longer stays, highly recommended. The owners, M and Mme Baloué, who are entomologists, will show you their collection, take you on guided tours of local sights and introduce you to their pet anaconda and boa constrictors. At Km 59 on the road to Régina is the turn-off to **Cacao** (a further 13 km), a small, quiet village, where Hmong refugees from Laos are settled; they are farmers and produce fine traditional handicrafts. (Accommodation: *Restaurant La Lan*, one room, US$25, good value, good food; M Levessier, Tel: 30-51-22, has hammocks). Minibus from Cayenne, Monday 1200; Friday 1800. Halfway along the side road is the *Belle Vue* restaurant, which lives up to its name, because of the superb view over the tropical forest (hammock space available, 25F pp, bring your own); the restaurant is open at weekends or when hammock-guests are there. **Kaw**, at Km 83, is on an island amid swamps which are home to much rare wildlife including caymans. The village is reached by dugout either from the Cayenne road or from Régina; basic accommodation available (Mme Musron, Tel: 31-88-15), take insect repellent. Southwest of Kaw on the River Approuague is Régina, linked with Cayenne by an unpaved road.

St-Georges de l'Oyapoc is 15 minutes down river from Oiapoque (Brazil) US$2 pp (canoe), *Hotel Damas, Hotel Modestina*, US$10, restaurant, also *Theofila*, lunch US$3, other restaurants and a night club. Several duty-free shops with French specialities. Immigration (*gendarmerie*) some 200 metres. from the town hall, ½ km from docks, French and Spanish spoken. There is nowhere to change dollars into francs; if entering the country here, you must change money before arriving in St-Georges. There is a beautiful 19-metre waterfall one day's journey up the Oyapoc River at Saut Maripa.

For Air Guyane flights to Cayenne see below, **Airport Information**. The police check that those boarding flights who have arrived from Brazil have obtained their entry stamp. About once a week a small vessel, the *Sao Pedro*, sails to Cayenne, deck passengers 100F one way.

Information for Visitors

Documents
Passport not required by nationals of France and most French-speaking African countries carrying identity cards. No visa (45F) required for most nationalities (except for those of Guyana, Australia, some Eastern European countries, and Asian—not Japan—and other African countries) for a stay of up to 3 months, but an exit ticket out of the country is essential (a ticket out of one of the other Guianas is not sufficient); a deposit is required otherwise. If one stays more than three months, income tax clearance is required before leaving the country. Inoculation against yellow-fever officially required only for those staying in Guyane longer than 2 weeks, but advisable for all. Travel to certain Amerindian villages is restricted.

How To Get There By Air
Air France flies 3 times a week direct to Guyane from Paris, 5 times a week from Pointe-à-Pitre (Guadeloupe) and 5 times a week from Fort-de-France (Martinique), and once a week from Lima. Air Guadeloupe flies 5 times a week from Pointe-á-Pitre and Fort-de-France, Air Martinique 5 times a week from Fort-de-France. Cheapest flight from Europe is reported to be with Minerve (Paris Tel: 45-22-08-50), once a week from Paris. Cruzeiro do Sul fly to/from Paramaribo on Monday (Brazilian leg often booked 4-6 weeks in advance). Suriname Airways fly to Paramaribo once a week; for Georgetown you have to change in Paramaribo. **NB** Do not accept verbal confirmation of flights from Air France in Cayenne: insist on a time/date stamped confirmation to avoid later misunderstandings.

Airport Information
Cayenne-Rochambeau is 16 km from Cayenne, 20 minutes by taxi. No public transport; only taxis (100F daytime, 150F night, but you can probably bargain or share). Cheaper taxi: Richard Lugret, Tel: 31-29-89. Cheapest method of return to airport is by collective taxi from corner of

Av de la Liberté and Rue Malouet to Matoury (10 km) for 12F, then hitch or walk. Air France, 13, rue L G Damas, Place des Palmistes, Tel: 30-27-40; Air Guyane, 2 rue Lalouette, Tel: 31-72-00/35-65-55; Suriname Airways, 2 place Schoelcher, Tel: 31-72-98. Local air services: Air Guyane to all main centres. These flights are always heavily booked, so be prepared to wait or write or telephone Air Guyane in Cayenne (Tel: 317200). There are regular connections with Maripasoula, daily at 0930, 900F return; St-Georges, daily at 0745 and Monday, Tuesday, Thursday, and Friday, at 1500, 560F return; Saül on Monday, Tuesday, Thursday, and Friday, at 0930, 620F return; Régina, daily at 0745, 300F return. No services on Sunday.

Surface Transport To Guyane
The Compagnie Général Maritime runs a passenger service to France once a month via Martinique and a freight service every 3 months. Boat connections with Suriname recommenced in 1991. To Brazil by motorized dugout from St Georges to Oiapoque, no custom or immigration post but foreigners are still sometimes returned to Guyane if their papers are not in order. Make sure you get an exit stamp from Gendarmerie in St-Georges. This journey is possible in reverse.

Internal Surface Transport
There are about 1,000 km of road (65% asphalted). The main road, narrow but now paved, runs for 130 km from Pointe Macouris, on the roadstead of Cayenne, to Iracoubo. Another 117 km takes it to Mana and St-Laurent. There is a lack of public transport (details in the text above); car hire can be a great convenience; Renault 4s perform well on the rough roads. Gasoline/petrol costs 5.50F a litre. **Car Hire** There are 15 companies including both Hertz and Avis at airport. Full list available from ARDTLG (see **Tourist Office** below). An international driving licence is required. **Bicycle Hire** Rue J Catayee, Cayenne, 50F per day, 300F per week. **Hitching** is

reported to be easy and widespread. One-to three-ton boats which can be hauled over the rapids are used by the gold-seekers, the forest workers, and the rosewood establishments. There is a twice-a-month shipping service which calls at nearly all the coastal towns of Guyane. Ferries are free. Trips by motor-canoe (*pirogue*) up-river from Cayenne into the jungle can be arranged.

Accommodation

Details of hotels are given in the text. For information on *Gîtes* and *Chambres chez l'habitant* write to Agence Régionale de Dévélopement du Tourisme et des Loisirs de la Guyane (ARDTLG), 12, rue Lalouette, 97338, Cayenne Cedex, Tel: 30-09-00, Telex 910364 FG; also, for *Gîtes*, Association pour le Tourisme Vert en Guyane, 27, rue Justin Cataye, 97300 Cayenne, Tel: 31-10-11.

Food

Most is imported, except seafood; it is of very high quality but expensive.

Currency

The currency is the French franc (5.41F = US$1, mid-June 1992). Try to take francs with you as the exchange rate for dollars is low, many banks do not offer exchange facilities and most places demand cash. A better rate can be obtained by using Visa cards to withdraw cash from the Banque Nacionale de Paris Guyane, Place Victor Schoelcher, Cayenne.

Health

Tropical diseases, dysentery, malaria, etc, occur, but the country is fairly healthy. Malaria prophylaxis recommended. In 1987 there were 5 hospitals with 861 beds and 237 physicians.

Climate

Tropical with a very heavy rainfall. Average temperature at sea-level is 27°C, and fairly constant at that. Night and day temperatures vary more in the highlands. The rainy season is from November to July, with (sometimes) a short dry interruption in February and March. The great rains begin in May. The best months to visit are between August and November, which are the usual months for trips to the jungle.

Public Holidays

In addition to the feasts of the Church: 1 January, New Year's Day and 14 July, Fête Nationale. Moslem holidays are observed, but the dates vary because of the shorter Moslem year; see note under Guyana.

Time Zone

3 hours behind GMT.

Weights And Measures

The metric system is in use.

Telecommunications

There is telephone communication throughout the territory. International telephone calls via STD to Europe and French Antilles. Foreign telegraph communication is via Paramaribo or Fort-de-France, from the TSF station at Cayenne.

Consulates

British (Honorary), 16 Av Monnerville (BP 664, Cayenne 97300, Tel: 31-10-34/30-42-42, Fax: 30-40-94); Brazilian, 12 Rue L Héder, at corner of Place des Palmistes, near Air France offices (closed Saturdays Tel: 30-04-67); Suriname, 38 rue Christophe Colomb (Tel: 30-04-61), Monday-Friday 0900-1200, visa 150F, 2 photos needed.

Media

La Presse de la Guyane is the daily paper (circulation 1,500). *France - Guyane - Antilles* is a weekly newspaper with a good information page for the tourist.

Tourist Information

The French Government tourist offices generally have leaflets on Guyane; there is a special office in Paris, L'Office du Tourisme des Antilles et de la Guyane, 12 rue Auber, 75009 Paris, Tel: 268-11-07. The Cayenne offices, called Agence Régionale de Développement du Tourisme et des Loisirs de la Guyane (ARDTLG) are at 12, rue Lalouette, Cayenne (Telex 910356, Tel: 300900), free map and tourist guide *Guyane Poche*; Délégation Régionale, 10, rue L-Heder, 97307 Cayenne, Tel: 31-84-91; Syndicat d'Initiative de Cayenne, Jardin Botanique, PO Box 702, 97338 Cayenne, Tel: 31-29-19; St-Laurent du Maroni, 16, rue du Colonel Chandon, Tel: 34-10-86; Syndicat d'Initiative Rémire-Montjoly, Mairie de Rémire, 97305 Rémire, Tel: 35-41-10.

ISLA DE MARGARITA

Introduction

VENEZUELA has 2,800 kilometres of coastline on the Caribbean Sea. The country's total area is 912,050 square kilometres, and its population exceeds 19,700,000. It was given its name, "Little Venice", by the Spanish navigators, who saw in the Indian pile dwellings on Lake Maracaibo a dim reminder of the buildings along Venetian waterways.

When the Spaniards landed in eastern Venezuela in 1498, in the course of Columbus' third voyage, they found a poor country sparsely populated by Indians who had created no distinctive culture. Four hundred years later it was still poor, almost exclusively agrarian, exporting little, importing less. The miracle year which changed all that was 1914, when oil was discovered near Maracaibo. Today, Venezuela is said to be the richest country in Latin America and is one of the largest producers and exporters of oil in the world.

In the 1980s, the country faced economic difficulties resulting from a combination of falling oil prices and a large external debt. In consequence, the government has reappraised the potential of tourism as one of a number of means of earning foreign exchange. There is still much scope for improving every facet of tourist infrastructure.

Venezuela has 72 island possessions in the Caribbean, of which the largest and the most visited is Isla de Margarita. This island, and two close neighbours, Coche and Cubagua, form the state of Nueva Esparta. Most of the other islands are Federal Dependencies (whose capital is Los Roques) stretching in small groups of keys to the east of Bonaire. Two other sets of islands are incorporated in the national parks of Morrocoy (west of the country's capital, Caracas) and Mochima, east of Caracas.

Isla de Margarita

Isla de Margarita is in fact one island whose two sections are tenuously linked by the 18 kilometre sandspit which separates the sea from the Restinga lagoon. At its largest, Margarita is about 32 kilometres from north to south and 67 kilometres from east to west. Most of its people live in the developed eastern part, which has some wooded areas and fertile valleys. The western part, the Peninsula de Macanao, is hotter and more barren, with scrub, sand dunes and marshes. Wild deer, goats and hares roam the interior, but four-wheel drive vehicles are needed to penetrate it. The entrance to the Peninsula de Macanao is a pair of hills known as Las Tetas de María Guevara, a national monument covering 1,670 hectares.

The climate is exceptionally good, but rain is scant. Water is piped from the mainland. The roads are good, and a bridge connects the two parts. Nueva Esparta's population is over 200,000, of whom about 20,000 live in the main city, Porlamar (which is not the capital, that is La Asunción).

History

Christopher Columbus made landfall on the nearby Paria Peninsula in August 1498. Two years later, a settlement had been established at Santiago de Cubagua (later called Nueva Cádiz) to exploit the pearls which grew in its waters. Cubagua became a centre for pearling and for slavery, as the local Indians were used, under appalling duress, to dive into the oyster beds. By 1541, when Santiago was destroyed by an earthquake and tidal wave, the pearl beds had been almost exhausted, but the Greek word for pearl, *margarita*, was retained for the main island of the group.

Margarita, and the nearest town on the mainland, Cumaná, were strongholds of the forces for the independence of South America from Spain. Between 1810 and 1817, the island was the scene of revolts and harsh Spanish reprisals. The liberator Simón Bolívar declared the Third Republic, and was himself declared Commander in Chief of the Liberating Army, at Villa del Norte (now Santa Ana) in 1816. After the war, the name of Nueva Esparta (maintaining the Greek allusion) was conferred in recognition of the bravery of Margarita in the struggle. Subsequent events have been nothing like so heroic, with life revolving around fishing and small agriculture. After a regeneration of the the pearl industry at the end of the 19th century, it has gone into decline, the oyster beds having all but disappeared through disease.

The Economy

The island has enjoyed a boom since 1983, largely as a result of the fall in the value of the bolívar and the consequent tendency of Venezuelans to spend their holidays at home. Margarita's status as a duty-free zone also helps. Venezuelan shoppers go in droves for clothing, electronic goods and other consumer items. Gold and gems are good value, but many things are not. There has been extensive building in Porlamar, with new shopping areas and Miami-style hotels going up. A number of beaches are also being developed. The island has become expensive and travellers on a tight budget would be better advised to explore the mainland and islands in the Mochima National Park, described below.

Local industries are fishing and fibre work, such as hammocks and straw hats. Weaving, pottery and sweets are being pushed as handicraft items for the tourists. An exhibition centre has been opened at El Cercado, near Santa Ana, on Calle Principal, near the church.

Flora and Fauna

Despite the property boom and frenetic building on much of the coast and in Porlamar, much of the island has been given over to natural parks. Of these the most striking is the Laguna La Restinga. Launches provide lengthy runs around the mangrove swamps, but they create a lot of wash and noise. The mangroves are fascinating, with shellfish clinging to the roots. The launch will leave you on a shingle and shell beach (don't forget to arrange with your boatman to collect you), and you can rummage for shellfish in the

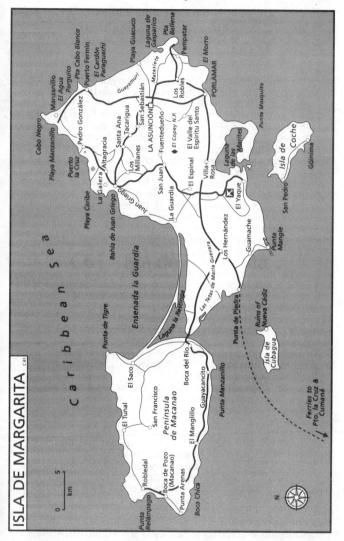

ISLA DE MARGARITA C-61

shallows (protection against the sun essential). Flamingos live in the lagoon.
There are mangroves also in the Laguna de las Marites Natural
Monument, west of Porlamar. Other parks are Las Tetas de María Guevara,
Cerro el Copey, 7,130 hectares, and Cerro Matasiete y Guayamurí, 1,672
hectares (both reached from La Asunción). Details of Inparques, the National

Parks office, are given in the **Information for Visitors.**

By boat from Porlamar you can go to the Isla de los Pájaros, or Morro Blanco, for both bird-spotting and underwater fishing. In Boca del Río there is a Museum of the Sea.

Beaches

Apart from the shopping, what attracts the holidaymakers from Venezuela and abroad are the beaches: long white stretches of sand bordered by palms, but rather hot, with little shade (sunscreen essential—local wisdom is that you can burn even when sitting in the shade). Topless bathing is not seen, but the tanga (*hilo dental*—dental floss) is fairly common.

In Porlamar, the beach by the *Concorde* hotel suffers from its popularity: calm shallow water, pedalos for hire, windsurf classes; but that by the *Bella Vista*, although crowded with foreign tourists, is kept clean. For a more Venezuelan atmosphere go northwest to **Pampatar**, which is set around a bay favoured as a summer anchorage by foreign yachtsmen escaping the hurricane season. A scale model of Columbus' *Santa María* is used for taking tourists on trips. (*Residencial Don Juan*, US$10 for room with bath and fan; apartments sleeping 6 are available, negotiate over price. Beach restaurant *Antonio's*, recommended; also *Trimar*, good value.) Pampatar has the island's largest fort, San Carlos Borromeo, and the smaller La Caranta, where the cannon show signs of having been spiked. Visit also the church of Cristo del Buen Viaje, the Library/Museum and the customs house (now the offices of Fondene, the local development agency). The beach at Pampatar is not very good, but there are lots of fishing boats and fishermen mending their nets. A fishing boat can be hired for US$12 for 2½ hours, 4-6 passengers; shop around for the best price. A fishing trip is good fun. New hotels are being built on this stretch. There is an amusement park to the southwest of Pampatar, called Isla Aventura, with ferris wheel, roller coaster, water slide, dodgems, etc, open Friday and Saturday 1800-2400, Sunday 1700-2400 and more frequently in peak holiday season. Entrance in peak season is US$5 adults, US$3.85 children, all rides included; in low season entrance is US$0.50 and each ride is US$0.30-0.60.

A number of good beaches are being developed on the eastern side. These are divided into ocean and calm beaches, according to their location in relation to the open sea. The former tend to be rougher (good surfing and windsurfing) and colder. Water is uniformly clear and unpolluted. Not all the beaches have local services yet, such as restaurants, though these, *churuatas* (bars built like indian huts), sunshades and deckchairs are becoming more widespread. (Hire charges are about US$1.30 per item.) It is still possible, even in high season, to find practically deserted beaches.

On the eastern coast are Playa Guacuco, reached from La Asunción by a road through the Guayamurí reserve: a lot of surf, fairly shallow (beware cross current when you are about waist deep, it gets very strong and can quickly carry you out to sea), palm trees, restaurant and parking lot, the liquor shop at La Sabana, 1 km before the beach, sells ice by the bucket, cheap; Parguito: long and open; Paraguachí: some *churuatas*. At **Playa del Agua** (45 minutes by bus from Porlamar, US$0.30), the sea is very rough for children, but fairly shallow. The beach is 4 km long, free of stones, white sand, with many kiosks which have installed palm-leaf covered shade areas. Two sun chairs under one of these costs US$7.70, under an umbrella US$4.60. This is by far the most popular beach on the island and during Venezuelan holidays, such as Semana Santa, it gets overcrowded. At other times it is a beautiful beach for sunbathing and walking. The fashionable part is at the southern end (interesting range of vendors on the beach—quail's eggs, caipirinha cocktails, coconuts, *cachapa* maize buns). Since the recent opening of the large, luxury *Playa El Agua Beach Resort* and *Miragua Club Resort* (about US$60), many of the beach restaurants stay open till 2100. Some that can be recommended are *Moisés* (Venezuelan owned), *Sueño Tropical* (French owned and very popular with Germans) and *Tinajón del Agua* (on the main road near the entrance to the beach, small, very good, popular). The restaurants which aim for the German market tend to be priced very high. *Restaurant El Paradiso* rents out cabins, US$12, small but comfortable; *Kiosko El Agua*, helpful, English spoken; *Posada Shangri-Lá*, recommended, and many other good seafood restaurants such as *Casa Vieja*, most are pricey but *La Dorada* is good value. The northern end is less touristy, with fewer facilities and less shade. *Residencias Miramar*, Av 31 de Julio—Carretera Manzanillo—esquina Calle Miragua, rooms from about US$15, 3 minutes from beach, 1 minute from supermarket, family-run, self-catering apartments, comfortable, clean, barbecue recommended; similar price range *Hotel FG*; *Casa Trudel*; Tel: 95-48-124, Fax: 95-61-3169, Apartado 106, 6301 Porlamar (Dan and Trudy O'Brien), small, US$36s-38d, bed and breakfast, no accommodation for small children, homely atmosphere and excellent breakfasts, German Dutch, Spanish and English spoken, recommended; *Vacacional El Agua*, Calle Miragua, Tel: (095) 48082, owned by Antonio J Sotillo, friendly, minimum 3 days stay, cheaper for longer stays and for groups, clean bathroom, good beds, fan, fridge, laundry facilities, 4 minutes walk from beach. **Manzanillo**: water gets deep rather suddenly, fishing huts, fish sold on beach, new apartments under construction, expensive restaurant, Playa Escondida at the far end; Puerto Fermín/El Tirano (Lope de Aguirre, the infamous conquistador, landed here in 1561 on his flight from Peru), El Caserío handicrafts museum is nearby; Punta Cabo Blanco: attractive limestone outcrop; El Cardón: some development (*Pahayda Villas*, US$25, new and nice apartments, large rooms, 2 baths for 4 people, sign at main road; 100 metres further on towards Playa Azul is a beach house with rooms to let and German-owned restaurant, good food).

The coast road is interesting, with glimpses of the sea and beaches to one side, inland vistas on the other. There are a number of clifftop look-out points. The road improves radically beyond Manzanillo, winding from one beach to the next. Playa Puerto la Cruz adjoins **Pedro González**, another fashionable spot with a broad sweeping beach, running from a promontory (easy to climb) to scrub and brush that reach down almost to the water's edge (ask for Antonietta Luciani at *Restaurant Pedrogonzález*, she has an apartment to rent, US$40 per day, sleeps 6, well-equipped, recommended as is her restaurant). The next bay is accessible by scrambling over rocks (major building work under way). One advantage of Pedro González beach is that there is a large lagoon on the other side of the coast road, so it will be impossible to spoil the bay with speculative building. There are a lot of pelicans and sea urchins (harmless).

Further west is **Juan Griego** bay and town, famous for its sunsets (tours go to see them). The town is marred by a number of cheap clothing bazaars and the beach has little sand. The bays to the north, however, are worth the walk. *Hotel La Galera*, recommended; *Fortín*, about US$10, a/c, cold water, opposite beach, most rooms have good views, good restaurant, tables on the beach; several others; also cabins for 5 with cooking facilities for US$20. *Restaurant Mi Isla* is recommended, also the Lebanese restaurant on the beach; *Viña del Mar*, opposite *Hotel Fortín*, a/c, attractive, excellent food; *Viejo Muelle*, next door, good restaurant, live music, outside beach bar. Playas Caribe and Galera are less spoilt (*Posada del Sol*, under US$20, bedroom, bath, kitchen, sitting area, clean, fan, fridge). Fortín La Galera is worth a visit for the view of Juan Griego and Galera bays; children will breathlessly recite the epic siege fought here during the wars of independence.

South of Juan Griego, the road goes inland to **San Juan**, then to Punta de Piedra (a pleasant stretch through cultivated land and farms at regular intervals). Near San Juan is Fuentedueño park which has special walks. A branch goes northwest to **La Guardia** at the eastern end of La Restinga. The dyke of broken seashells stretches to the Peninsula de Macanao: on its right a spotlessly clean beach, on its left the lagoon. At the far end is a cluster of fishermen's huts with landing stages from which the launches make trips into the labyrinth of canals in the lagoon (US$3.50 7 per boat taking 5 passengers; bus from Porlamar harbour front US$0.80, ask driver to drop you off).

The **Peninsula de Macanao** is quite underdeveloped, although it is hardly an untouched paradise. Construction companies are extracting large amounts of ballast for the building boom in Porlamar, while urban waste is simply being dumped in large quantities along the roadside. Some of the beaches, however, are highly regarded: Manzanilla, Guayaconcito, Boca de Pozo, Macanao, Punta Arenas and El Manglillo.

Festivals on Margarita
6-13 January at Altagracia; 20-27 January at Tacarigua (San Sebastian); 16-26 March at Paraguachí (*Feria de San José*); 3-10 May at Los Robles; 24-30 May at La Guardia; 6 June at Tacarigua (Sagrado Corazón de Jesús); 25-26 July at Santa Ana; 27 July at Punta de Piedras; 31 July (Batalla de Matasiete) and 14-15 August (Asunción de la Virgen) at La Asunción; 30 August-8 September at Villa Rosa; 8-15 September at El Valle; 11-12 (Fiesta del Virgen del Pilar) and 28 October (San Juan Tadeo) at Los Robles; 4-11 November at Boca del Río, 4-30 November at Boca del Pozo; 5-6 December at Porlamar; 15 December at San Francisco de Macanao; 27 December-3 January at Juan Griego. See map for locations.

The capital, **La Asunción** (population 8,000), is a few kilometres inland from Porlamar. It has several colonial buildings, a cathedral, and the fort of Santa Rosa, with a famous bottle dungeon (open Monday 0800-1500, other days 0800-1800). There is a museum in the Casa Capitular, and a local market, good for handicrafts. Nearby are the Cerro Matasiete historical site and the Félix Gómez look out in the Sierra Copuy.

Between La Asunción and Porlamar are the Parque Francisco Fajardo, beside the Universidad de Oriente, and **El Valle del Espíritu Santo**. Here is the church of the Virgen del Valle, a picturesque building with twin towers, painted white and pink. The Madonna is richly dressed (one dress has pearls, the other diamonds); the adjoining museum opens at 1400, it displays costumes and presents for the Virgin, including the "milagro de la pierna de perla", a leg-shaped pearl. A pilgrimage is held in early September. Proper dress is requested to enter the church.

Throughout the island, the churches are attractive: fairly small, with

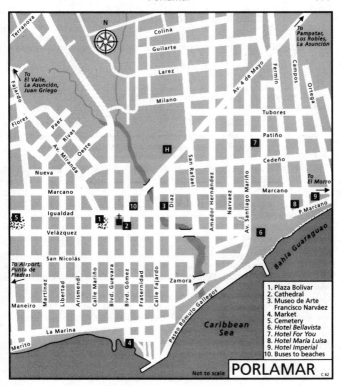

1. Plaza Bolívar
2. Cathedral
3. Museo de Arte Francisco Narváez
4. Market
5. Cemetery
6. *Hotel Bellavista*
7. *Hotel For You*
8. *Hotel María Luisa*
9. *Hotel Imperial*
10. Buses to beaches

PORLAMAR

baroque towers and adornments and, in many cases, painted pink.

Porlamar

Most of the hotels are at **Porlamar**, 11 kilometres from the airport and about 28 kilometres from **Punta de Piedra**, where most of the ferries dock. It has a magnificent cathedral. At Igualdad y Díaz is the Museo de Arte Francisco Narváez. The main, and most expensive, shopping area is Avenida Santiago Mariño; better bargains and a wider range of shops are to be found on Gómez and Guevara. At night everything closes by 2300; women alone should avoid the centre after dark. Note that in Porlamar there is a Calle Mariño and an Avenida Santiago Mariño in the centre.

Ferries go to the Isla de Coche (11 kilometres by 6), which has over 5,000 inhabitants and one of the richest salt mines in the country. They also go, on hire only, to Isla de Cubagua, which is totally deserted, but you can visit the ruins of Nueva Cádiz (which have been excavated).

Island Information—Isla de Margarita

How To Get There There are 18 flights a day from Caracas, with Avensa and Aeropostal, 45-minute flight; tickets are much cheaper if purchased in Venezuela in local currency (US$32.50 one way). Daily Avensa flight to Ciudad Guyana, about US$30, 1710, also Aeropostal at 1815, and daily Aereotuy to Ciudad Bolivar. Daily flight from Cumaná at 0700, Aeropostal, and 2020, Avensa. From Barcelona, US$19. Viasa, Av 4 de Mayo, Edificio Banco Royal, Porlamar (Tel: 32273, airport 691137); Avensa and Aeropostal are both on Calle Fajardo, Porlamar, opposite each other (Aeropostal hours 0800-1200, 1400-1800, Tel: 617064, airport 691128; Avensa Tel: 617111, airport 691021). (Airport: General Santiago Mariño, between Porlamar and Punta de Piedras; taxi US$6.)

Ferries (very busy at weekends and Mondays; in good condition, punctual): from Puerto La Cruz, Turismo Margarita, Los Boqueticos, Tel: 87-683, Pto La Cruz to Margarita 0700 and 1300, 4 hours (5-6 including check-in), depart Margarita (Punta de Piedra) 1000 and 1800; Conferries, Los Cocos terminal, Tel: 66-0389, and Meliá Hotel, Pto La Cruz to Margarita, 8 a day between 0300 and 2400 each way, 3½ hours, passengers US$7.50 1st class, US$3.75 2nd, cars US$14.35, jeeps US$15.85. From Cumaná, vehicle ferries of Conferry (Tel: 66-1462) and Naviarca at 0700 and 1600 daily, 3 hours, cars US$9, jeeps US$11.25, passengers US$4.50, ferry terminal is almost at mouth of the river. Faster, more expensive launch, *Gran Cacique I* (Turismo Margarita) twice daily to Punta de Piedra, 1½ hours, US$5.50. Several bus companies in Caracas sell through tickets from Caracas to Porlamar, arriving about midday. By car from Caracas, it takes about 4 hours, but will be reduced to 2½ when the Sucre motorway is opened.

Ferry Punta de Piedras-Isla de Coche Monday-Friday 1600, returns 1730, Saturday-Sunday 0800 and 1730, returns 0530 and 1730.

A ferry sails from Mercado Viejo to Chacopata on the mainland at 1000 and 1200, also takes cars.

Go to the Puerto de Pescadores, El Guamache, near Punta de Piedra, and ask boat captains about taking a boat to the Leeward or Windward Islands; eg US$50 pp to Martinique (very difficult to find boats willing to take passengers). A ferry to Grenada, *The Eastward*, sails once a month.

NB August and September are the vacation months when flights and hotels are fully booked.

Public Transport *Por Puestos* serve most of the island, leaving mainly from the corners of Plaza Bolívar in Porlamar. Fares: to Punta de Piedra, US$0.42, to the ferry terminal US$0.60; to La Asunción, US$0.20; to Pampatar, US$0.20; to La Restinga (from La Marina y Mariño), US$0.60; El Agua, US$0.40; Juan Griego, US$0.45. Taxi fares are published in the paper, *Mira*, are not uniformly applied by drivers. If you want to hire a taxi for a day you will be charged US$5-8 per hour. Always establish the fare before you get in the car. There is a 30% surcharge after 2100.

Car Hire An economic proposition for any number above one and probably the best way of getting around the island, from US$16.65 to US$66.65 per day depending on the make of car. To the cheapest rate add US$0.15/km and US$3.35 for each hour after the first day. With 150 km free rates are from US$33.35 to US$133.35, plus US$0.15 for each extra km and US$6.65 for each extra hour over the first day. Several competing offices at the airport, and at *Hotel Bella Vista* (including Avis, poor service), others also on Av Santiago Mariño. In all cases check the brakes. Scooters can also be hired for about US$14 a day from Diversion Rentals, Calle Amador Hernández, Maruba Motor Rentals, La Mariña (English spoken, good maps, highly recommended, US$16 bikes for 2, US$13 bikes for 1), or Auto Camping Margarita (boats and bicycles also for rent). Motor cycles may not be ridden between 2000 and 0500; although this (apparently) should not apply to tourists, police officers have been known to confiscate tourists' machines and impose heavy fines. **NB** remember to keep an eye on the fuel gauge; there are service stations in towns, but air conditioning is heavy on fuel.

Driving on Isla Margarita: the roads are generally good and most are paved. Sign posts are often poorly-positioned (behind bushes, round corners), which adds to the nighttime hazard of vehicles with badly adjusted lights. It is best not to drive outside Porlamar after dark.

Where To Stay At Porlamar *Margarita Hilton*, Calle Los Uveros, Tel: (95) 61-5822/5054, Fax: 61-4801, US$105-130d (+ 10% tax), new, health club, swimming pool, private beach with sailing dinghies for hire; other top class establishments, *Concorde*, Balúa de El Morro, and *Bella Vista*, Av Santiago, swimming pool, beach; *Cardón*, opposite old airport at Playa Cardón, peaceful, good rooms and restaurant, swimming pool, diving and snorkelling trips organized; *For You*, Patiño y Av Santiago Mariño, recommended, good breakfast. *Cabañas Turísticas*, Vía La Isleta, US$35 for a cabin sleeping 4, pool, restaurant. *Venus*, Tel: (095) 23722, Calle Milano y San Rafael, clean, a/c, safe, under US$30. *Colibrí*, Av Santiago Mariño, Tel: 616346, recommended; *Caribbean*, Via El Morro, pool, beach; *Vista Mar*, Urb Bella Vista, on the way to El Morro, beach; *Aguila Inn*, Narváez, about US$25, clean, swimming pool, restaurant, recommended; *Contemporáneo*, Calle Mariño entre Igualdad y Velázquez, US$15, modern, a/c, TV, clean, bar restaurant; *Italia*, San Nicolás, US$12 with bath, cold water, a/c, clean, safe, English spoken, recommended, although area is a bit rough. Under US$12 a night: *Dos Primos*, Calle Mariño entre Zamora y San Nicolás, clean and modern, recommended; on the Boulevard, *Brasilia*, San Nicolás, quiet, clean, nice new rooms at back, recommended; *Boston*, in the same block, US$7s with bath, fan, very clean; *María Luisa*, Vía El Morro, beach; *Evdama*, Bella Vista y Campos, helpful, also holiday flats with parking; *Imperial*, Av Raúl Leoni, Via El Morro, Tel: (095) 61-6420/4823, US$25, a/c, good showers, triple rooms available, clean, comfortable, safe, English spoken, recommended, but restaurant only average; next door is *Tamá*, (more with air conditioning, hot water, TV), excellent atmosphere and restaurant, bar is German-run, lots of languages spoken, highly recommended, Vía El Morro, beach; opposite is *Chez David*, air conditioning, on beach, modern; *Garland*, Av Miranda, good restaurant, convenient for *por puestos*; *Nueva Casa*, with bathroom and fan, clean and friendly. *La Opera*, Igualdad y Fraternidad, with bath (just off plaza), *Porlamar*, Igualdad y Fajardo, clean, good restaurant, a/c or fan, friendly; opposite is *Canadá*, recommended; *Chez Toni*, San Nicolás 14-56, English spoken, cheap restaurant, recommended; *Residencia Paraíso*, near main square, basic but clean, fan; *Residencia Don Francisco*, Igualdad, 2 blocks from plaza, more with bath, quiet, good; *Hotel España*, Mariño 6-35, hot shower, very clean, friendly, recommended; better value is *Rioja*, with fan and bath, clean, safe. Many others round Plaza Bolívar. Cheaper places on Maneiro, eg *Res Javi*, very basic, but friendly; *Maneiro*, No 13-17, poor value. For longer stays, Enrique and Elena Ganteaume rent apartments in Porlamar, Juan Griego and La Asunción (Av Principal 41, Urb Santa Lucía, La Asunción, Tel: 095-610467, friendly, English spoken).

Where To Eat *El Peñero*, Vía El Morro, service slow but food good; *Vecchia Marina*, Vía El Morro, good, but more expensive; *Bahía* bar-restaurant, Av Raúl Leoni y Vía El Morro, excellent value, live music; good breakfast at *Panadería*, Av 4 de Mayo y Fermín; *Sadaka*, Calle Fajardo, Lebanese, reasonable prices, good food, recommended; *Martín Pescador*, Av 4 de Mayo, lobster and other seafood, friendly, recommended; *Cheers*, Av 4 de Mayo, good bar, popular, recommended; *Centro Vegetariano Mariuxu*, Fermín 12-79 (yellow and green house, no sign), lunch only, recommended; *El Yate*, next to *Hotel For You* main entrance, highly recommended for food and service, superb steaks, US$20-25 for 2, but wine can double the bill; *Café de París*, outside *Hotel For You*, croissants and enormous ice creams, a good meeting place; also *París Croissant* on Blvd Santiago Mariño; *Los 3 Delfines*, Cedeño 26-9, seafood, recommended; *Guanaguanare*, pedestrian boulevard by sea, good food and service, reasonable prices. *La Isla*, Mariño y Cedeño, 8 fast food counters ranging from hamburgers to sausages from around the world. *La Cotorrera*, Av Santiago Mariño, steak, recommended, closed Sunday; *Flamingo*, 4 de Mayo (in hotel), cheap, good, but small portions; *Kiosco La Nena*, Av Raúl Leoni, Italian and local dishes; highly recommended for food and value if not atmosphere, try *pabellón margariteño* (white fish, rice, black beans, fried plantains, add sugar and chilli sauce to taste). *Jardín de Italo*, Calle Campos, French, classy, little atmosphere; *Cheers* (ask taxi driver to take you), meat dishes and crêpes, very popular and cheap.

Shopping Besides all duty-free shops, *Del Bellorín*, Cedeño, near Santiago Mariño, is good for handicrafts. Good selection of jewellery at *Sonia Gems*, on Cedeño; *Ivan Joyería* and *Inter Gold*, both on 4 de Mayo (latter is between *Ivan* and *Hotel Flamingo*);

many other places on the main street are overpriced. When purchasing jewellery, bargain hard, don't pay by credit card (surcharges are imposed), get a detailed guarantee of the item and, if unsure, get another jeweller to check its validity.

Entertainment *Mosquito Coast Club*, behind *Hotel Bella Vista*, disco with genuine Venezuelan feel, good *merengue* and rock music, bar outside. Discothèque for singles, *Village Club*, Av Santiago Mariño, recommended for good music with a variety of styles but expensive drinks, cover charge. Nightlife is generally good, but at European prices.

Exchange Banco Consolidado (American Express), Guevara y San Nicolás; banks generally slow with poor rates; best at Banco Construcción, Guevara or at *Hotel Contemporáneo* next to Banco Consolidado. *Casa de cambio* at Igualdad y Av Santiago Mariño. Amex office closed on Monday. Banks are open 0830-1130, 1400-1630. There are often long queues. Most shops accept credit cards.

Communications Post Office Calle Arismendi. **Phones** CANTV, Bolívar, between Fajardo and Fraternidad.

Information Tourist Office, Miranda, near cathedral, free city map. An outspoken and well-informed English-language newspaper, *Mira*, is published on the island; the editor/publisher acts also as an inexpensive tour guide; Av Santiago Mariño, Ed Carcaleo Suites, Apartamento 2-A, Porlamar (Tel: 095-613351). The best map is available from Corpoven.

Tourist Agents Turisol, Calle Hernández, friendly and helpful; Supertours, Calle Larez, Quinta Thaid, Tel: 618781, Fax: 617061, tours of the island and elsewhere; Zuluoya Tours, very helpful; Turismo Guaiquerí, Santiago Mariño y Marcano, English spoken, mixed reports.

Los Roques and the other Venezuelan Islands

Of Venezuela's other insular possessions, few are much visited. The overnight trip to **Los Roques** islands, directly north of La Guaira, is well worth it. Los Roques islands lie 150 km due north of Caracas; the atoll, of about 340 islets and reefs, constitutes one of Venezuela's loveliest National Parks (225,241 hectares). There are long stretches of white beaches (beware of sunburn as there is little shade), miles of coral reef with crystal-clear water ideal for snorkelling, and many bird nesting sites (eg the huge gull colonies on Cayo Francés and the pelicans, boobies and frigates on Selenqui). Small lizards, chameleons and iguanas, and cactus vegetation on some islets also add to the atoll's variety. Many of the islands' names seem strange because they are contractions of earlier names: eg 'Sarky' comes from Sister Key, 'Dos Mosquices' from Domus Key, where there is a Marine Biology Centre researching the coral reef and its ecology. For more information write to La Fundación Científica Los Roques, Apartado No 1, Av Carmelitas, Caracas 1010, Tel: 32-6771.

Gran Roque is the main and only inhabited island; here flights land near the scattered fishing village (population 900) which is Park Headquarters; average temperature 27°C with coolish nights. Private accommodation is available for US$6-9 including meals (small *pensión* run by Sra Carmen Zambrano), and you can negotiate with local fishermen for transport to other islands: you will need to take your own tent, food and (especially) water. There are some tiny beach houses on Cayo Rasqui, and Cayo Francés has an abandoned house and enough vegetation to provide shaded hammock sites, but otherwise there are no facilities. Cayo Francés is two islands joined by a sandspit, with calm lagoon waters on the south and rolling surf on the north; May is nesting time at the gull colonies here. For solitude, Los Roques are a "must" midweek: Venezuelans swarm here on long weekends and at school holidays. Tiny but irritating biting insects in the calmer months can make camping miserable.

It is sometimes possible to find a boat from La Guaira to Los Roques (6-8 hours); the more usual way is a 35-minute ride with Helicópteros del Caribe at Maiquetía; the helipad is at the east end of the International Terminal, Tel: (02) 821-7218 (return fare US$135-175; be prepared to wait at airport, ask for Rudi González who speaks English) or with Aereotuy (Tel: 02-262-1966), who fly to Gran Roque from Maiquetía, Porlamar and Barcelona daily except Mondays. Day excursion fare of US$100 including food, boat ride, insurance—and mask and snorkel! Good value. Another possibility is to hitchhike a lift from Aeroclub at La Carlota airport (often difficult). Best to go in the morning or weekends; several planes leave then and often have spare places if you ask. Tel: Caracas 952-1840/1/2 for flights. Planes chartered at La Carlota (Cessna 310) charge US$30 per hour, 1-5 passengers, you pay for 3 hours flight time if you leave in the morning and return same day; if picked up at a later date two full trips are charged. Not all pilots will fly to Gran Roque (dirt airstrip, no navigational facilities).

Also worth mentioning are the **Archipelago of Las Aves**, west of Los Roques, where fishing and diving are good. La Tortuga is Venezuela's second largest island, lying west of Margarita. Further out are La Blanquilla and La Orchila, both with coral reefs. About 500 kilometres north of Margarita, at the same latitude as Dominica, is Isla de Aves, 65 square kilometres of seabirds (sooty and brown noddy tern, frigate birds, gulls) surrounded by crystal clear water. The island is also a nesting site of the endangered green turtle. There is a Venezuelan coast guard station. For a full description of the island see *Audubon*, the magazine of the US National Audubon Society, January 1991, pages 72-81.

Much closer to the mainland are two areas of reefs and islands which have been designated national parks. There is no way to get to them other than by spending time in Venezuela itself.

The ***Morrocoy National Park*** was founded in 1974 to protect the large colonies of frigate birds, brown boobies and pelicans, and conserve the coral reefs and oyster beds in the mangrove swamps on the mainland coast between Tucacas and Chichiriviche. This region is 3½-4 hours by road west of Caracas and is a popular place for spending the weekend away from the capital. There are marinas, dive shops and boat hire in Tucacas, boat hire in Chichiriviche, and plenty of possibilities for bathing, beachcombing and camping. Tucacas is also on the road/ferry route between Caracas and the Netherlands Antilles, see **Information for Visitors**.

Tucacas is a small, hot, busy, dirty and expensive town with lots on new building in progress, where bananas and other fruit are loaded for Curaçao and Aruba, but offshore is the national park of Morrocoy, where there are hundreds of coral reefs, palm-studded islets, small cosy beaches and calm water for water-skiing, snorkelling, and skin-diving. (The Park is reached on foot from Tucacas; camping allowed, no facilities, no alcohol for sale, very crowded at weekends and, in the holiday season, with litter strewn all over the place.) With appropriate footwear it is possible to walk between some of the islands. The largest, cleanest and most popular of the islands is Cayo Sombrero (very busy at weekends). Even so it has some deserted beaches, with trees to sling hammocks. Playuela is equally beautiful and better for snorkelling, while Playa del Sol has no good beach and no palm trees. Boats are for hire (US$10-20 return to Cayo Sombrero, per boat, US$5.25 to nearer islands, ticket office to the left of the car entrance to the park; they will pick you up for the return journey, Pepe has been recommended). A more expensive way to organize a trip to any of the islands is through the travel agency Guili at Calle Sucre y Calle Silva No 1, Tel: 84661, Freddy speaks English, French and Spanish, Valentine speaks German and Russian; if you want to spend several days they will come and check on you every two days, also trips to Los Roques. Venezuelan skin-diving clubs come here for their contests. Scuba diving equipment can be hired from near the harbour for US$5 a day, but the diving is reported not very interesting. Try American-owned Submatur, run by Belgian André, for equipment hire, scuba courses (US$350) and trips. This is one of the two main fishing grounds of Venezuela; the other is off Puerto La Cruz.

Where To Stay *Hotel Manaure-Tucacas*, US$35, Av Silva, a/c, hot water, clean, restaurant; *Hotel Said*, at entrance, about US$10, swimming pool, good; *Greta*, under US$20, a/c, clean, friendly, recommended; *Palma*, US$10 without shower, fan, owner organizes boat trips; *La Suerte* on main street, under US$7.50s, but bargain, clean; seek out Carlos, who provides accommodation in his unnamed hotel, US$10s, safe, friendly. Cheap accommodation is difficult to find, especially in high season, hotels are generally more expensive than elsewhere in Venezuela.

Restaurant Fruti Mar, very good; *Cervezería Tito*, good food; many good bakeries. Camping gas available in Tucacas for camping in the Park. Bicycles can be hired in town. Banco Unión for exchange.

A few kilometres beyond, towards Coro, is the favourite beach resort of **Chichiriviche**; the town is filthy but offshore are numerous lovely islands and coral reefs. It is possible to hire a boat to any one of the islands; recommended for a weekend away from Caracas (note that prices posted on board, or on the jetty are per boat, not per person, from US$7.50-23, take a snorkel, no hire facilities; snorkel and mask can be bought from a shop near *Hotel Capri*). All-day cruises, stopping at three islands, cost US$60 per boat. There is no direct bus, but frequent *por puestos* from Puerto Cabello, US$1, and direct buses from Valencia to the turn-off to Chichiriviche. You may camp on the islands, but there are no facilities or fresh water (three islands have beach restaurants serving simple fish dishes, clean, good), and you require a permit from Inparques (Instituto Nacional de Parques, address in **Information for Visitors**). Take precautions against rats. Nearby is a vast nesting area for scarlet ibis, flamingoes and herons. Most of the flamingoes are in and around the estuary next to Chichiriviche, which is too shallow for boats, but you can walk there or take a taxi.

Hotels *Hotel Mario*, over US$30 including 3 meals, swimming pool, being upgraded in 1991 and like a builder's yard; *La Garza*, US$10 without food, full board available, comfortable, pleasant meals at low prices, popular, pool; *Vaya*, same price range, small, clean, restaurant; *Náutico*, under US$20 with breakfast and dinner, friendly, clean, good meals, fans but no a/c; *Villa Marina*, aparthotel, about US$10, good, clean, safe, pool; *Balaton*, fan; *Capri*, near docks, both under US$12 (bargain), shower, fan or a/c, clean, pleasant Italian-owned, good restaurant and supermarket; bakery opposite has tiny rooms, similar price, fan, shared bathroom. Restaurants (both near *Capri*), *Fregata*, expensive, recommended; *Falcón*, good, cheap, good coffee and juices. *El Juncal*, Calle Zamora, Edificio Falcón, good, cheap.

Venezuela's second Caribbean coastal National Park is **Mochima**, 55 kilometres from the port of Puerto la Cruz. This city is 320 kilometres, 5 hours east of Caracas. It is the main commercial centre in this part of the country, but is also a popular holiday centre with good watersports and yachting facilities. The park itself also includes the mainland coast between

Los Altos and Cumaná. The beaches and vistas of this stretch of the coast are beautiful. Since both Puerto La Cruz and Cumaná are ferry terminals for Margarita, Mochima can easily be incorporated into a visit to this part of Venezuela.

The easiest island to reach is **Isla de la Plata**, yet another supposed lair of the pirate Henry Morgan. It has a white sand beach, and clear waters which are ideal for snorkelling. There are food and drink stalls, but take drinking water as there is none on the island. Also take a hat and sunscreen. It's about 10 minutes by boat to the island, and the fare is about US$4 return per person. Further away, and larger, are the Chimana islands with beautiful beaches (Grande, Sur, del Oeste), in the waters around which there is snorkelling and good scuba diving (boat ride about US$14 return). In both cases, boats leave from the eastern end of Paseo Colón beach, next to the yacht club. Prices are fixed, payable in advance, arrange the time of return, reliable service.

Other islands in the vicinity are Monos (also good for scuba diving), La Borracha, El Borracho and Los Borrachitos, and Caracas de Oeste and Caracas del Este. All are in sheltered waters and are easy to explore by boat. There are diving and water sport shops in Puerto la Cruz.

Further east from Puerto La Cruz is **Sante Fe**, a good place to relax; it is not (yet) a tourist town, but there is plenty of loud music, a golf course on the dark red, sandy beach, and a market on Saturday. Hotel Cochaima, run by Margot (US$10 or so), is recommended as clean, friendly, with good food, fan, close to beach, ask for Diego who takes snorkelling or diving trips, US$6 for 6 hours snorkelling, all equipment provided; also family-run Hotel/Restaurant Chomena, Av Principal, which is cheaper. Gasoline is available; por puesto and bus to Cumaná and Puerto La Cruz. It is sometimes difficult to get the bus from Puerto La Cruz to stop at Santa Fe; a por puesto may be a better bet. Jeep, boat or diving tours are available. The village of Mochima, beyond Sante Fe, is 4 km off the main road, hitching difficult; bus to Cumaná at 1400, US$0.80. Here Sra Cellita Día and Doña Luisa both let rooms, under US$6; houses to rent for US$12 per day depending on length of stay; eat at Los Mochimeros, good and friendly; (try the empanadas with ice cold coconut milk), also Don Quijote, Av Bermúdez, very good. Boats to nearby beaches (such as Playa Marita and Playa Blanca) and around the islands, fares negotiable, about US$10 to one island, US$20 for a 2-hour trip round the islands (up to 6 people). **NB** At holiday times this coast is very busy.

Information for Visitors

Documents

Entry is by passport and visa, or by passport and tourist card. Tourist cards (tarjetas de ingreso) are valid only for those entering by air and are issued by most airlines to visitors from 25 countries including the USA, Canada, Japan and all Western European countries except Spain and Portugal. They are valid for 60 days with, theoretically, 2 extensions of 60 days each permissible, at a cost of US$25 each. On arrival in Venezuela your passport is stamped at immigration, but not necessarily with any indication of how long you can stay. Do not assume that if your visa is valid for one year you can stay that long. Overstaying your 60 days without an extension can lead to arrest and a fine when you try to depart. Renew at DIEX offices in Caracas (many other DIEX offices do not offer extensions), take passport and return ticket.

If you enter the country overland, you will be required to obtain a visa from a

Venezuelan consulate prior to arrival. Visas cost US$10 (£6 in UK), but US$3 to US citizens; you will need your passport, return ticket and letter of reference from your employer and bank. You must fill in an application form and the visa will take about three working days to come through, sometimes longer if authorization has to come from Venezuela. It appears that you cannot get a visa in advance in the USA or Canada, so to apply for an overland visa in Colombia you need: passport, one photo and an onward ticket. A tourist card issued by Viasa in Bogotá is only valid for arriving in Caracas by air from Bogotá, not if you travel overland. To extend a visa for one month, in any city, costs about US$25; it is best to leave the country (eg to Curaçao) and get a new one free. To change a tourist visa to a business visa, to obtain or to extend the latter, costs US$50 (£31 in UK). Tourist visas are multiple entry within their specified period. Transit passengers to another country can stay only 72 hours.

NB Carry your passport with you all the time you are in Venezuela as the police are increasing spot checks and anyone found without identification is immediately detained (carrying a certified copy for greater safety is permissible, though not always accepted by officials). A press card as identification is reported to work wonders. Border searches are very thorough.

Information for business visitors is given in "Hints to Exporters: Venezuela", issued by the DTI Export Publications, P O Box 55, Stratford-upon-Avon, Warwickshire, CV37 9GE. Businessmen on short visits are strongly advised to enter the country as tourists, otherwise they will have to obtain a tax clearance certificate (*solvencia*) before they can leave.

How To Get There
From Europe British Airways and Viasa fly from London to Simón Bolívar, the international airport for Caracas, the former twice a week direct. Viasa fly via Paris, and Porlamar. Viasa also serves Amsterdam, Frankfurt, Madrid, Milan, Porto, Rome, Santiago de Compostela and Zurich. The cheapest route from Europe is with Air Portugal from Lisbon to Caracas. There are also services from Europe by Air France, KLM, Iberia, Alitalia, Lufthansa and Avianca. Iberia has a weekly service to Tenerife, Canary Islands, from where connections can be made to various North and West African countries.

From North America By air, passengers may reach Venezuela by American Airlines (New York, Orlando, Miami), United Airlines (Boston, Miami, Chicago), Viasa (Houston, Miami, New York), and Avensa. Viasa and Air Canada fly to Toronto; there are also many charters at holiday times.

Within the Caribbean Aeropostal has services to Port of Spain (5 times a week from Caracas). Difficulties have been reported in entering Trinidad unless with a UK, US or Canadian passport. LIAT (once a week) and Aeropostal (twice) fly to Bridgetown, Barbados. BWIA (Oficentro Rovica, piso 1, Boulevar Sabana Grande, Tel: 718945/711307 or airport Tel: 552880) flies to Port of Spain, with onward connections; United flies daily to Port of Spain. Viasa and Aeropostal fly twice a week each Caracas-Havana (Viasa's outward flights London-Caracas connect with this service). Ideal Tours, Centro Capriles, Plaza Venezuela, Caracas offer trips to Cuba: US$366 for 4 days (with all transfers etc included), US$488 for 8 days.

To The Netherlands Antilles To Aruba from Caracas: Avensa, Servivensa and Aeropostal daily, Viasa 2 a week, Air Aruba 4 a week, US$112 return; from Las Piedras/Punto Fijo on the Paranaguá Peninsula, Avensa and Servivensa daily, Air Aruba 5 a week, US$90 return. To Curaçao from Caracas: ALM daily except Saturday, Aeropostal and Servivensa daily; from Las Piedras, Servivensa daily, (if you have no onward ticket from Curaçao, you must buy a return). Ferrys del Caribe sail from La Vela del Coro, on the western side of the Paranaguá Peninsula, to Curaçao and Aruba on the following schedule (subject to frequent change): Thursday 2000 Aruba-Curaçao, Friday 1200 Curaçao-Coro, Monday 2200 Coro-Curaçao, Wednesday 1000 Curaçao-Coro, Wednesday 2200 Coro-Aruba. One way fare is US$42.50, return US$75; an onward ticket from Curaçao or Aruba is essential. The ferry is not promoted for tourism since there are frequent delays and cancellations, you need to arrive 2-4 hours before sailing and refunds for unused portions of the ticket are hard to obtain. Ferrys del Caribe office in Coro is at Av Independencia, open Monday-Friday, Tel: (068) 51-0554/1956. Occasional cargo launches sail between La Vela del Coro and Curaçao, Tel: (068) 78922 and ask for Oscar Guerrero at

Oficina de Immigración. It is much simpler, unless transporting a car, to fly from Las Piedras (Punto Fijo).

Airport 28 km from Caracas, near the port of La Guaira: Maiquetía, for national flights, Simón Bolívar for international flights, adjacent to each other (5 minutes' walk, taxis take a circular route, fare US$1.15; Viasa and Avensa have shuttle buses). The Tourist Office at the international airport is reported unhelpful and only gives addresses of 4-5 star hotels; English spoken, open 0600-2400 Tel: 55-1060, passenger assistance Tel: 55-2424; police Tel: 55-2498. 3 *casas de cambio* open 24 hours (Italcambio, good rates, outside duty-free area). Check your change. There are cash machines for Visa, Amex and Mastercard. Pharmacy, bookshops, basement café (good value meals and snacks, open 0500-2400, hard to find); no seating in main terminal until you pass through security and check in. No official left luggage; ask for Paulo at the mini bar on the 1st floor of international terminal. Look after your belongings in both terminals. At Simón Bolívar, airline offices are in the basement, hard to find: Viasa information and ticket desk open 0500-2400 daily, others at flight times. In Caracas, Viasa, Esquina La Marrón, 2 blocks east of Plaza Bolívar; Avensa, Esquina El Conde, 1 block west of Plaza Bolívar; Aerolíneas Argentinas, Torre la Previsora (Mezzanine) at Plaza Venezuela metro.

Always allow plenty of time when going to the airport, whatever means of transport you are using: the route can be very congested and check-in procedures are very slow (2 hours in daytime, but only ½ hour at 0430). Allow at least 2 hours checking-in time before your flight, especially if flying Viasa. Taxi fares from airport to Caracas cost on average US$12-15, depending on part of city but overcharging is rife. Fares are supposedly controlled: the taxi office in the airport issues you with a ticket at the official fare. Give this to the driver after you have checked the fare. Insist that you are sold a prepaid ticket or you will be encouraged to get a taxi outside and pay more. After 2200 and at weekends a surcharge of 20% is included on the ticket, you may get charged up to US$40. Drivers may only surcharge you for luggage (US$0.50 per large bag). If you think the taxi driver is overcharging you, make a complaint to

Corpoturismo or tell him you will report him to the Departamento de Protección del Consumidor. The airport shuttle bus (blue and white with "Aeropuerto Internacional" on the side) leaves from east end of terminal, left out of exit for the city terminal (under the flyover at Bolívar and Av. Sur 17, 250 metres from Bellas Artes metro, poorly lit at night); regular service from 0600 to 0030, bus leaves when there are enough passengers and may not stop at international terminal if no flights due; go to start of route at national terminal, fare US$1.50. The bus is usually crowded so first time visitors may find a taxi good value. *Por puesto* airport, Caracas also US$1.50; from Caracas they are marked "Caracas Litoral", ask to be dropped off. When checking in, keep 10 bolívar bills handy to pay departure tax levied at most large airports.

Taxes
All tourists and diplomats leaving the country, except nationals of Denmark and transit passengers, must pay US$8.30 approx, Bs530 (Bs500 airport tax, Bs30 departure tax) at the airport or port of embarkation, payable in bolívares only. At Caracas airport this procedure is split between two desks; the form, or parts of it, may be required for up to 3 separate checks. Minors under twelve years of age do not pay the exit tax. Venezuelans, resident foreigners and holders of a *visa transeunte* have to pay Bs900 on departure. There is also an airport tax of US$0.80 for those passengers on internal flights.

Customs
You may bring into Venezuela, free of duty, 25 cigars and 200 cigarettes, 2 litres of alcoholic drinks, 4 small bottles of perfume, and gifts at the inspector's discretion.

Air Services
Most places of importance are served by Avensa (private) and/or Aeropostal (government-owned, both heavily overbooked always). Aeropostal and Avensa have international services (Viasa does not have domestic services). Both internal airlines offer special family discounts and student discounts, but this practice is variable (photocopies of ISTC card are useful as this allows officials to staple one to the ticket). Beware of overbooking during holiday time, especially at Caracas airport; it is

recommended that you check in two hours before departure, particularly at Easter. Internal night-time flights are scarce, and there is no late hour discount. If you travel with Viasa or any other airline for which Viasa is agent, it is possible to check in the day before flying out of Caracas by taking baggage, ticket and passport to their office at Centro Comercial Tamanaco, Nivel C2, "Predespacho", between 1500 and 2100 (cost US$0.40); take bus from Chacaíto. To avoid overbooking the Government now obliges airlines to post a passenger list, but it is important to obtain clear instructions from the travel agent regarding confirmation of your flight and checking-in time. Passengers leaving Caracas on international flights must reconfirm their reservations not less than 72 hours in advance, it is safer to do so in person than by telephone; not less than 24 hours for national flights (if you fail to do this, you lose all rights to free accommodation, food, transport, etc. if your flight is cancelled and you may lose your seat if the plane is fully booked). Beware of counterfeit tickets; buy only from agencies. If told by an agent that a flight is fully booked, try at the airport anyway. International passengers must check in two hours before departure or they may lose their seat to someone on a waiting list. Read carefully any notice you see posted with the relevant instructions. Handling charge for your luggage US$0.50. All flights are subject to delays or cancellation. Avensa operates an air-pass system, open only to non-residents and purchasable only outside Venezuela: unlimited travel for 21 days for US$139. Passengers are issued with an MCO (Miscellaneous Charges Order) in the country of purchase, this is exchanged in Caracas at Pasajes Avensa, Esquina El Conde, 1 block west of Plaza Bolívar. At the same time ask for a timetable of all Avensa flights. (In view of the cheapness of internal flights, the pass may not be worth buying.) For independent charter flights try Rudi González at Carlota aiport in the city of Caracas.

Road Transport

There are excellent (but slow) bus services between the major cities, but the colectivo taxis and minibuses, known in Venezuela as *por puesto*, seem to monopolize transport to and from smaller towns and villages. Outside Caracas, town taxis are relatively expensive.

Motoring

All visitors to Venezuela can drive if they are over 18 and have a valid driving licence from their own country; an international driving licence is preferred. If you have an accident and someone is injured, you will be detained as a matter of routine, even if you are not at fault. Do not drive at night if you can help it (if you do have to, do not drive fast). Carry insect spray if you do; if you stop and get out, the car will fill with biting insects. Self-drive tours, and fly-drive are now being marketed, the latter through National Car Rental, which has a wide network of offices. Car rental rates are given under Porlamar.

There are 5 grades of gasoline: "normal", 83 octane; 87 octane; 89 octane; 91 octane ; and "alta", 95 octane. Gasoline costs on average US$0.09 a litre; diesel costs US$0.05 a litre. Service stations are open 0500-2100, Monday-Saturday, except those on highways which are open longer hours. Only those designated to handle emergencies are open on Sunday. In the event of breakdown, Venezuelans are usually very helpful. There are many garages, even in rural areas; service charges are not high, nor are tyres, oil or accessories expensive, but being able to speak Spanish will greatly assist in sorting out problems. Carry spare battery water, fan belts, an obligatory breakdown triangle, a jack and spanners. Some cars have a security device to prevent the engine being started and this is recommended. The best road map is published by Lagoven, available from most service stations (not just Lagoven's), latest edition 1989. **Warning** There is an automatic US$20 fine for running out of fuel.

Hotel Reservations

Fairmont International, Torre Capriles, Planta Baja, Plaza Venezuela, Caracas, Tel: 782 8433, Telex 21232 SNRHO, Fax: 782 4407, will book hotel rooms both in Caracas and in other towns, where they have 102 hotels on their books. All, except luxury class hotels charge officially controlled prices. In 1988 a 10% tourist tax was added to hotel prices, not for the benefit of hoteliers but for the construction and maintenance of tourist amenities.

Camping

Camping in Venezuela is a popular recreation, for spending a weekend at the beach, on the islands, in the *llanos* and in the mountains. Camping is not however used by travellers as a substitute for hotels on the main highways, and no special camp sites are yet provided for this purpose. Wild camping is much easier with a car than with just a tent. If camping on the beach, for the sake of security, pitch your tent close to others, even though they play their radios loud.

Food And Drink

There is excellent local fish (we recommend *pargo* or red snapper), crayfish, small oysters and prawns, though sole, trout and large oysters are imported. Of true Venezuelan food there is *sancocho* (a stew of vegetables, especially yuca, with meat, chicken or fish); *arepas*, a kind of white maize bread, very bland in flavour; toasted *arepas* served with a wide selection of relishes, fillings or the local somewhat salty white cheese are cheap, filling and nutritious; *cachapas*, a maize pancake (soft, not hard like Mexican *tortillas*) wrapped around white cheese; *pabellón*, made of shredded meat, beans, rice and fried plantains; and *empanadas*, maize-flour pies containing cheese, meat or fish. At Christmas only there are *hallacas*, maize pancakes stuffed with chicken, pork, olives, etc boiled in a plantain leaf (but don't eat the leaf). The nearest thing to a boiled egg in most places is a *huevo tibio*. It comes without the shell because there are no eggcups. A *muchacho* (boy) on the menu is not a sign of cannibalism; it is a cut of beef. *Ganso* is also not goose but beef. *Solomo* and *lomito* are other cuts of beef. *Hervido* is chicken or beef with vegetables. *Contorno* with a meat of fish dish is a choice of chips, boiled potatoes, rice or yuca. *Caraotas* are beans; *cachitos* are *croissants* of bread. *Pasticho* is what the Venezuelans call Italian *lasagne*. The main fruits are bananas, oranges, grapefruit, mangoes, pineapple and papaya. N.B. Some Venezuelan variants of names for fruit: *lechosa* is papaya, *patilla* is water melon, *parchita* passion fruit, and *cambur* a small banana. A delicious sweet is *huevos chimbos*—egg yolk boiled and bottled in sugar syrup. Venezuelans dine late.

There is no good local wine though some foreign wines are bottled locally. Local wine is used only in cooking or in

sangría. Liqueurs are cheap; try the local *ponche crema*. There are four good local beers: Polar (the most popular), Regional (with a strong flavour of hops), Cardenal and Nacional (a *lisa* is a glass of keg beer; for a bottle of beer ask for a *tercio*), mineral waters, gin and excellent rum. The coffee is very good (*café con leche* has a lot of milk, *café marrón* much less); visitors should also try a *merengada*, a delicious drink made from fruit pulp, ice, milk and sugar; a *batido* is the same but with water, not milk. A *plus-café* is an after-dinner liqueur. Water is free in all restaurants even if no food is bought. Bottled water in *cervecerías* is often from the tap; no deception is intended, bottles are simply used as convenient jugs. Insist on seeing the bottle opened if you do not want a mouthful of chlorine with your whisky. *Chicha de arroz* is a sweet drink made of milk, rice starch, sugar and vanilla; fruit juices are very good. Gin and rum at about US$2 and coffee beans at US$1.50 per kilo are good buys.

Tipping

Taxi drivers are tipped if the taxi has a meter (hardly anywhere), but not if you have agreed the fare in advance. Usherettes are not tipped. Hotel porters, Bs 2; airport porters Bs 2 per piece of baggage. Restaurants, between 5% and 10% of bill.

Shopping

Goods in shops bear a label "PVP" followed by the price. This is the maximum authorized price; you may be able to negotiate a discount but should never pay more than the PVP price.

Currency

The unit of currency is the bolívar, which is divided into 100 céntimos. There are nickel alloy coins for 25 and 50 céntimos and 1, 2 and 5 bolívares, and notes for 1, 2, 5, 10, 20, 50, 100, 500 and 1,000 bolívares. In 1989, the official and free rates were unified. Change travellers' cheques or US dollar notes in a *casa de cambio* for optimum rates (if travelling off the beaten track, consider changing a substantial amount); of the banks, Banco Unión and Banco de Venezuela change cheques and cash, but the latter usually only change money after 1500. The majority of banks do not cash travellers' cheques; in major towns, one or two banks may, but this varies from branch to branch. American Express cheques are widely accepted as is the Visa card (Banco Consolidado is affiliated with American Express, no commission, some branches cash personal cheques from abroad on an Amex card; Banco Unión handles Visa transactions, and Banco Mercantil Mastercard). There are cash machines for Visa, Amex and Mastercard at Simón Bolívar airport. When changing dollars cash in banks, it is best to go in the morning. Have money sent to you by telex and not by post, which can take weeks. Rates of exchange in hotels are generally poor.

Popular names for coins: Fuerte, Bs 5; Real, Bs 0.50; Medio 0.25; Puya or Centavo, 0.05. The brown Bs100 note is sometimes referred to as a *marrón*, or a *papel*, the Bs500 note as an *orquidea*, because of its picture.

Security

Cameras and other valuables should not be exposed prominently. The police are increasing spot-checks and may confiscate pocket knives as "concealed weapons" if they find them, although they are sold legally in the shops. In Caracas, carry handbags, cameras etc on the side away from the street as motor-cycle purse-snatchers are notorious. Hotel thefts are becoming more frequent.

Health

Health conditions are good. Water in all main towns is heavily chlorinated, so safe to drink, although most people drink bottled water. Medical attention is good. State health care is free and said to be good (the Clínica Metropolitana in Caracas has been recommended). On the coast from Cumaná eastwards precautions against vampire bat bite are warranted since they can be rabies-carriers. Lights over hatches and windows are used by local fishermen to deter bats from entering boats and shore cabins. If bitten seek medical advice. Some rivers are infected with bilharzia and in some areas there are warning signs; check before bathing.

Climate

is tropical, with little change between season.

Hours Of Business

Banks are open from 0830 to 1130 and 1400 to 1630, Monday to Friday only. Government office hours vary, but 0800-1200 are usual morning hours. Government officials have fixed hours, usually 0900-1000 or 1500-1600, for receiving visitors. Business firms generally start work about 0800, and some continue until about 1800 with a midday break. Shops, 0900-1300, 1500-1900, Monday to Saturday. Generally speaking, Venezuelans start work early, and by seven in the morning everything is in full swing. Most firms and offices close on Saturday.

Holidays

There are two sorts of holidays, those enjoyed by everybody and those taken by employees of banks and insurance companies. Holidays applying to all businesses include: January 1, Carnival on the Monday and Tuesday before Ash Wednesday, Thursday-Saturday of Holy Week, 19 April, 1 May, 24 June, 5, 24 July, 12 October, 25 December. Holidays for banks and insurance companies only include all the above and also: 19 March and the nearest Monday to 6 January, Ascension Day, 29 June, 15 August, 1 November and 8 December. There are also holidays applying to certain occupations such as Doctor's Day or Traffic Policeman's Day. On New Year's Eve, everything closes and does not open for at least a day; public transport runs, but booking offices are not open. Queues for tickets, and traffic jams, are long. Business travellers should not visit during Holy Week or Carnival.

Official Time

Atlantic Standard Time, 4 hours behind GMT, 1 hour ahead of EST.

Weights And Measures

are metric.

Electric Current

110 volts, 60 cycles, throughout the country.

Postal Services

The postal service is extremely slow and unreliable. Air mail letters to the USA or Europe can take from one to four weeks and registered mail is no quicker. Important mail should be sent by air courier to a Venezuelan address. Internal mail also travels slowly, especially if there is no PO Box number. As in other countries, removing stamps from letters occurs; insist on seeing your letters franked, saying that you are a collector. Avoid the mail boxes in pharmacies as some no longer have collections. A private parcel delivery company, such as DHL, will charge around US$60 for parcels of up to 500g to Europe.

Telephone Service

All international and long distance calls are operated by CANTV in Caracas in the south building, Centro Simón Bolívar (facing Plaza Caracas), Tel: 41-8644, on the mezzanine of Centro Plaza on Francisco Miranda near US Embassy in east Caracas (corner of Andrés Bello between metros Parque del Este and Altamira), open 0800-2100, Tel: 284-7932, phone cards (tarjetas—see below) sold here.. Most major cities are now linked by direct dialling (Discado Directo), with a 3-figure prefix for each town in Venezuela. Otherwise CANTV offices deal with most long-distance and international calls in the cities outside Caracas. Collect calls are possible to some countries, at least from Caracas, though staff in offices may not be sure of this. Calls out of Venezuela are more expensive than calls into it and are subject to long delays. Local calls are troublesome and the connection is often cut in the middle of your conversation; calls are best made from hotels or CANTV offices, rather than from booths (of which there are few). Many public phones operate with phonecards (tarjetas), available from CANTV or shops for many different values up to US$8 equivalent, though many small shops impose a 25% handling charge and tarjetas may be out of stock. International calls are cheaper with a tarjeta, for example you can make 3 one-minute calls to Europe for US$8 with a tarjeta, but you have to pay for 3 minutes (at US$8) without one.

Tourist Information

may be obtained from Corpoturismo, Apartado 50.200, Caracas, main office for information is on floor 37, Torre Oeste, Parque Central. A useful publication is the Guía Turística y Hoteles de Venezuela, Colombia y el Caribe, published every July by Corpoturismo, which includes not only hotel details, but also road maps and tourist attractions. Also useful is the Guía Progreso, published by Seguros Progreso SA, available at the company offices and elsewhere, which is very detailed. The Guide to Venezuela (925 pages, updated and expanded 1989), by Janice Bauman, Leni Young and others, in English (freely available in Caracas) is a mine of information and maps, US$11.

For sailors, A Sailor's Guide to a Venezuelan Cruise, by Chris Doyle, is recommended, US$10 from Frances Punnett, PO Box 17, St Vincent, Tel: (809) 458 4246; it gives information on all the small islands as well as Margarita.

For information on the **National Parks** system, and to obtain necessary permits to stay in the parks, go to Instituto Nacional de Parques (Inparques), Avenida Rómulo Gallegos, Parque del Este (opposite Restaurante Carreta), Tel: 284-1956, Caracas, or to the local office of the guardaparques for each park. Further information can be had from the Ministerio del Ambiente y de los Recursos Naturales Renovables (MARNR) in the Centro Simón Bolívar in Caracas. The book: Guía de los Parques Nacionales y Monumentos Naturales de Venezuela, is obtainable in Audubon headquarters (open 0900-1230, 1430-1800), Las Mercedes shopping centre, Las Mercedes, Caracas, in the La Cuadra sector next to the car parking area (it is difficult to find), Tel: 91-3813. It is also available at Librería Noctúa, Villa Mediterránea, in the Centro Plaza Shopping Centre. The society will plan itineraries and make reservations.

We are deeply grateful to many travellers who wrote to The South American Handbook with updating material on the Venezuelan islands.

NETHERLANDS ANTILLES AND ARUBA THE ABCs

Introduction

THE NETHERLANDS ANTILLES consist of the islands of (Aruba – autonomous, see below, **Government**) Bonaire and Curaçao (popularly known as the ABCs) 60-80 km off the coast of Venezuela, outside the hurricane belt; 880 km further north (in the hurricane belt) are the "3 S's": Sint Eustatius (Statia), Saba, and the southern part of Sint Maarten (St-Martin) in what are generally known as the Leeward Islands. Because of the distance separating the northern islands from the other Dutch possessions, the 3 S's are described in a separate section earlier in the Handbook. There is some confusion regarding which islands are Leeward and which Windward: locals refer to the ABCs as "Leeward Islands", and the other three as "Windward", a distinction adopted from the Spaniards, who still speak of the *Islas de Sotovento* and *de Barlovento* with reference to the trade winds. Each island is different from the others in size, physical features, the structure of the economy and the level of development and prosperity.

Dutch is the official language, and many islanders also speak English or Spanish, but the *lingua franca* of the ABC islands is Papiamento, which originated with the Portuguese spoken by Jewish emigrants from Portugal, who were the most numerous settlers in the 17th century. Since then it has developed into a mixture of Portuguese, Dutch, Spanish, English, and some

African and Indian dialects. Papiamento has been in existence since at least the early 18th century, but has no fixed spelling, though it is becoming a written language.

History

The first known settlers of the islands were the Caiquetios, a tribe of peaceful Arawak Indians, who lived in small communities under a chieftain or a priest. They survived principally on fish and shellfish and collected salt from the Charoma saltpan to barter with their mainland neighbours for supplements to their diet. There are remains of Indian villages on Curaçao at Westpunt, San Juan, de Savaan and Santa Barbara, and on Aruba near Hooiberg. On each of the ABC islands there are cave and rock drawings. The Arawaks in this area had escaped attack by the Caribs but soon after the arrival of the Spaniards most were forcibly transported from Curaçao to work on Hispaniola. Although some were later repatriated, more fled when the Dutch arrived. The remainder were absorbed into the black or white population, so that by 1795, only five full-blooded Indians were to be found on Curaçao. On Aruba and Bonaire the Indians maintained their identity until about the end of the 19th century, but there were no full-blooded Indians left by the 20th century.

The islands were discovered in 1499 by a Spaniard, Alonso de Ojeda, accompanied by the Italian, Amerigo Vespucci and the Spanish cartographer Juan de la Cosa. The Spanish retained control over the islands throughout the 16th century, but because there was no gold, they were declared "useless islands". After 1621, the Dutch became frequent visitors looking for wood and salt and later for a military foothold. Curaçao's strategic position between Pernambuco and New Amsterdam within the Caribbean setting made it a prime target. In 1634, a Dutch fleet took Curaçao, then in 1636 they took Bonaire, which was inhabited by a few cattle and six Indians, and Aruba which the Spanish and Indians evacuated. Curaçao became important as a trading post and as a base for excursions against the Spanish. After 1654, Dutch refugees from Brazil brought sugar technology, but the crop was abandoned by 1688 because of the very dry climate. About this time citrus fruits were introduced, and salt remained a valuable commodity.

Wars between England and the Netherlands in the second half of the 17th century led to skirmishes and conquests in the Caribbean. The Peace of Nijmegen in 1678 gave the Dutch Aruba, Curaçao, Bonaire and the three smaller islands in the Leeward group, St Eustatius, Saba and half of St Martin. Further conflicts in Europe and the Americas in the 18th century led to Curaçao becoming a commercial meeting place for pirates, American rebels, Dutch merchants, Spaniards and créoles from the mainland. In 1800 the English took Curaçao but withdrew in 1803. They occupied it again from 1807 until 1816, when Dutch rule was restored, during when it was declared a free port. From 1828 to 1845, all Dutch West Indian colonies were governed from Surinam. In 1845 the Dutch Leeward Islands were joined to Willemstad in one colonial unit called Curaçao and Dependencies. The economy was still largely based on commerce, much of it with Venezuela, and there was a ship building industry, some phosphate mining and the salt pans, although the latter declined after the abolition of slavery in 1868.

In the 20th century the economy prospered with the discovery of oil in Venezuela and the subsequent decision by the Dutch-British Shell Oil Company to set up a refinery on Curaçao because of its political stability, its good port facilities and its better climate than around Lake Maracaibo. In 1924 another refinery was built on Aruba, which brought unprecedented wealth to that island and the population rose. The Second World War was another turning point as demand for oil soared and British, French and later US forces were stationed on the islands. The German invasion of Holland encouraged Dutch companies to transfer their assets to the Netherlands Antilles leading to the birth of the offshore financial centre. After the War, demands for autonomy from Holland began to grow.

Government

The organization of political parties began in 1936 and by 1948 there were four parties on Curaçao and others on Aruba and the other islands, most of whom endorsed autonomy. In 1948, the Dutch constitution was revised to allow for the transition to complete autonomy of the islands. In 1954 they were granted full autonomy in domestic affairs and became an integral part of the Kingdom of the Netherlands. The Crown continued to appoint the Governor, although since the 1960s this has gone to a native-born Antillian. Nevertheless, a strong separatist movement developed on Aruba and the island finally withdrew from the Netherlands Antilles in 1986, becoming an autonomous member of the Kingdom of the Netherlands, the same status as the whole of the Netherlands Antilles. Aruba will gain complete independence in 1996 unless proposed constitutional changes prompt a change of heart (see below).

The Netherlands Antilles now form two autonomous parts of the Kingdom of the Netherlands. The main part, comprising all the islands except Aruba, is a parliamentary federal democracy, the seat of which is in Willemstad, Curaçao, and each island has its own Legislative and Executive Council. Parliament (Staten) is elected in principle every four years, with 14 members from Curaçao, three from Bonaire, three from Sint Maarten and one each from Saba and St Eustatius. Ms Maria Liberia-Peters was re-elected Prime Minister of the five-island federation in 1990, as head of a coalition led by the National People's Party (Partido Nashonal di Pueblo-PNP) with ten of the Curaçao seats and the support of the five from Bonaire, Saba and St Eustatius in the 22-seat Parliament. Mr Nelson Aduber became Prime Minister of Aruba in 1989, as head of a coalition led by the People's Electoral Movement with 12 seats in the 21-seat Parliament. Separate status for some or all of the islands is a political issue, and while the majority favour continuing the Federation, there is a breakaway movement in Curaçao and St Maarten. The Netherlands Government's previous policy of encouraging independence has been reversed. The Hague is to draw up a new constitution governing relations between the Netherlands, the Antilles Federation and Aruba, which will be presented to the three parliaments for discussion. A round-table conference was due to be held in 1992 to establish the basis for future relations including financial support.

BONAIRE

Introduction

BONAIRE, second largest of the five islands comprising the Netherlands Antilles, is 38 km long and 6½-11½ km wide and 288 km square. It lies 80 km north of Venezuela, 50 km east of Curaçao, 140 km east of Aruba, at 12° 5' N and 86°25' W, outside the hurricane belt. The southern part of the crescent-shaped island is flat and arid, much of it given over to the production of salt. The northern end of the island is more hilly, the highest point being Mount Brandaris, and is a national park. There is little agriculture and most of the island is covered in scrub and a variety of cacti, many of which reach a height of six metres. Despite its lack of natural resources, it is, however, known as "Diver's Paradise", for its rich underwater life and is also valued by bird watchers. The windward coast is rough and windy, while the leeward coast is sheltered and calm.

Klein Bonaire, a small (608 hectares), flat, rocky and uninhabited islet one km off Bonaire's shores, is frequented by snorkellers and divers. It has sandy beaches but no natural shade and only a few shelters used by tour boats.

Bonaire is the least densely populated of the islands and the inhabitants, who number around 10,800 and are mostly of mixed Arawak, European and African descent, are a very friendly and hospitable people. The island is quiet, peaceful and very safe. As in Curaçao and Aruba, Dutch is the official language, Papiamento the colloquial tongue, and Spanish and English are both widely spoken.

The Economy

Bonaire has a fairly diversified economy with salt mining, oil trans-shipment, a textile factory, rice mill and radio communications industry. The Antilles International Salt Company has reactivated the long dormant salt industry, which benefits so greatly from the constant sunshine (with air temperatures averaging 27°C and water 26°C), scant rainfall (less than 560 mm a year), and refreshing trade winds. However, for foreign exchange, the island is overwhelmingly dependent on tourism, even if it is highly specialized. In 1991, tourist arrivals rose by 20% to 49,534 of which 42% came from the USA and 32% from Europe. Accommodation for tourists is split fairly evenly between hotels and villas, amounting to about 1,000 rooms. Financial assistance for the development of tourism has been provided by the EEC, which has financed the expansion of the airport and development of other infrastructure.

Flora and Fauna

The old salt pans of Pekelmeer, needed by the Salt Company, posed an ecological problem: Bonaire has one of the largest Caribbean flamingo colonies in the Western Hemisphere, and these birds build their conical mud nests in the salt pans. Pleas from wild-life conservationists convinced the company that it should set aside an area of 56 hectares for a flamingo sanctuary, with access strictly prohibited. The birds, initially rather startled by the sudden activity, have settled into a peaceful coexistence, so peaceful in fact that they have actually doubled their output and are now laying two eggs a year instead of their previous one. There are said to be over 15,000 flamingoes on the island, and they can be seen wading in Goto Meer Bay in the northwest, in the salt lake near Playa Grandi, and in Lac Bay on the southeast coast of Bonaire, feeding on algae which give them their striking rose-pink colour. It is an impressive sight to witness the flamingoes rising from the water in the evening as they prepare to overnight in Venezuela.

There are also two smaller bird sanctuaries at the Solar Salt Works and Goto Meer. At Pos'i Mangel, in the National Park, thousands of birds gather in the late afternoon. Bronswinkel Nell, also in the Park, is another good place to see hundreds of birds and giant cacti. The indigenous Bonaire Green Parrot can be seen at Onima. About 130 species of birds have been found on Bonaire as well as the flamingoes, and there are lots of iguanas and lizards of all shapes and sizes. The big blue lizards are endemic to Bonaire, while the Anolis, a tree lizard with a yellow dewlap, is related to the Windward Islands Anolis species rather than to the neighbouring Venezuelan species. The interior has scant vegetation but the enormous cacti provide perching places for yellow-winged parrots. The most common mammal you are likely to see is the goat, herds of which roam the island eating everything in sight except the cacti.

Beaches and Watersports

Bonaire is not noted for its beaches; the sand is usually full of coral and gritty, which is rather hard on the feet, and those on the leeward coast are narrow. Beaches in front of some hotels have been helped with extra sand. Recommended are Sorobon (a private, nudist resort where non-guests pay US$10 for admission), Lac Bay which has an area of mangroves at the north end of the bay, and in the northeast Playa Chiquito. Be careful at Playa Chiquito, or Chikito, there is a memorial plaque there for good reason. The surf is strong and it is dangerous to swim but it is pleasant for sunbathing. There were a few huts for shade but they are in a poor state of repair. Another reasonable, but shadeless beach is Pink Beach, south of Kralendijk, past the Salt Pier. In the Washington-Slagbaai National Park are two attractive bays: Playa Funchi, which is good for snorkelling, but has no sand and no facilities so the area is very smelly, and Boca Slagbaai, which is popular with tour boats for snorkelling and you can see flamingoes wading in the salinja behind the beach. At the latter, there are clean toilets and showers in a restored 19th century house and salt barn (ask the attendant to open them for you) and drinks and snacks are available. A very pleasant break in a hot and sweaty tour round the National Park. Fishing, sailing, windsurfing and waterskiing are all popular as an alternative to diving, which is what most people come to Bonaire to enjoy.

You can charter a fishing boat through your hotel and arrange half or full day trips with tackle and food included. Two independent charter companies are Piscatur, run by Captain Chris Morkos, Tel: 8774, Fax: 8380, half day US$275 for 4 people, US$425 full day in 30-foot diesel boat, or US$125 half day for 2 people, US$225 full day in 15-foot skiff; and *Slamdunk*, a 30-foot Topaz, Tel: 5111 Captain Rich at the Marina, same rates but for 6 people. There is an annual Bonaire International Fishing Tournament, held at the end of March, which attracts participants from throughout the Americas. The annual Bonaire Sailing Regatta is held in mid-October. This has grown into a world class event with races for seagoing yachts,

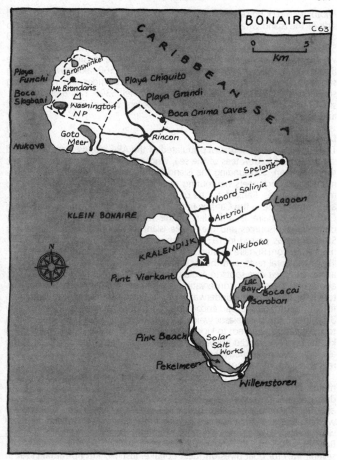

catamarans, sunfishes, windsurfers and local fishing boats. The smaller craft compete in Kralendijk Bay, while the larger boats race round Bonaire and Klein Bonaire. Held over five days, the event attracts crowds and hotel reservations need to be made well in advance. There is also an annual Nautical Race in November for small boats. Speed races are held in Kralendijk Bay. The Marina at *Harbour Village* is the only facility of its kind in Bonaire. There are 60 slips for boats up to 110 feet with showers, laundry, fuel, waste disposal etc, and has a 120-ton syncrolift and supply shop for repairs. Sailing trips with snorkelling and beach barbecue, often on Klein Bonaire, or sunset booze cruises, from US$20 pp, are offered on *Woodwind*, a trimaran based at the *Divi Flamingo Beach Resort*, Tel: 8285, and *Samur* (P O Box 287, Tel: 5252, Fax: 8240), a 56-foot Siamese junk, based at the *Sand Dollar Dive and*

Photo, with pick up service from most resorts. At Lac Bay on the windward side of the island where the water is calm and shallow, there is a constant onshore wind. Windsurfing Bonaire is based here, P O Box 301, Tel/Fax: 5363, free hotel pick up 0900 and 1300, instruction and board rental. Windsurfing rentals and instruction are also available at Great Adventures Bonaire at the *Harbour Village Beach Resort*, Tel: 7500, along with kayak, sunfish, mini speed boats, water skiing, sea biscuit rides and water taxi service to Klein Bonaire. *Sunset Beach Resort*, Tel: 5300, Fax: 8593, offers small hobie cat and sunfish rentals, waterscooters, waterskiing, hydrosliding and paddle boats.

Diving and Marine Life

The least developed and least populated of the ABC islands, Bonaire has a special appeal to devotees of the sea, whose treasures are unsurpassed in the Caribbean. Surrounding the island, with submarine visibility up to 60 metres, are coral reefs harbouring over a thousand different species of marine creatures. Ranked as one of the three top dive spots in the world, and number one in the Caribbean (followed by Grand Cayman Island and Cozumel), Bonaire is a leader in the movement for preservation of underwater resources and the whole island is a protected marine park. Stringent laws passed in 1971 ban spearfishing and the removal of any marine life from Bonaire's waters. It is a serious offence to disturb the natural life of the coral reefs, and the local diving schools have set up permanent anchors in their dive spots to avoid doing any unwarranted damage. With about 600 dives a day, conservation is essential. You are requested not to touch the coral or other underwater life, such as sea horses; not to feed the fish, as it is not natural and encourages the more aggressive species; not to drop litter, particularly plastic which does not decompose and can be harmful to sea creatures, and not to kick up sand with your fins as it can choke and kill the coral. Advanced buoyancy courses are available free of charge and are highly recommended for divers to train you to keep horizontal along the reef and limit fin damage to coral.

On the eastern side of the island there is a shelf and a drop-off about 12 metres from the shore down to a 30 metres coral shelf and then another drop down to the ocean floor. The sea is rather rough for most of the year although it sometimes calms down in October or November. Along the western side of the island there are numerous dive sites of varying depths with wrecks as well as reefs. The most frequently dived sites include, Calabas Reef, Pink Beach, Salt City, Angel City and the Town Pier. There are also several sites for boat dives off Klein Bonaire, just 1½ km from Kralendijk. The Bonaire Marine Park Guide is recommended and can be obtained from dive shops or from the environmental group, STINAPA.

Snorkelling is recommended at Nukove, Boca Slagbaai, Playa Funchi, Playa Benge (closed in 1991), Windsock Steep and Klein Bonaire. Salt Pier, where the wooden support pilings give shelter to small fish, and the *Divi Flamingo Hotel* pier encrusted with coral, are also popular. Dive boats usually take snorkellers along when dive sites are close to shore, about US$12 for 2-hour trip with divers on one tank. The snorkelling trail was wiped out by bad weather several years ago but will be replaced when the reef has recovered.

Whether you dive or snorkel, you are certain to enjoy the underwater world of Bonaire. Most visitors are tempted to take at least the one-day "resort" or crash diving course to get NAUI or PADI certificates (US$88 at Dive Bonaire). This enables you to decide if you'd like to continue, but one day will not make a diver of anyone. The main schools are Peter Hughes, Dive Bonaire (Tel: 8285, Fax: 8238, at the *Divi Flamingo Beach Resort*), Buddy Dive Resort (PO Box 231, Tel: 5080, Tel/ Fax: 8647), Captain Don's Habitat (Tel: 8290, Fax: 8240, P O Box 88), *Carib Inn* (PO Box 68, Tel: 8819, Fax: 5295), Dive Inn Bonaire (PO Box 362, Tel: 8761, Fax: 8513, at the *Sunset Inn*), Sand Dollar Dive and Photo at the *Sand Dollar Beach Club* (Tel: 5252, Fax: 8760, also has photo shop), Sunset Beach Dive Centre (P O Box 362, Tel: 5300 ext 278, Fax: 8513) at the *Sunset Beach Hotel*, Great Adventures Bonaire (P O Box 312, Tel: 7500, Fax: 7507) at the *Harbour Village Beach Resort*, with instruction in several languages, Neal Watson's Underwater Adventures (P O Box 380, Tel: 5580, Fax: 5680) at the *Coral Regency Resort* and Bonaire Scuba Centre (Tel: 8978, Fax: 8846, at the harbour, next to the shopping mall and at *Black Durgon Inn*). Prices are competitive, ranging from US$25-50 for a two tank dive if you have your own equipment. Dive Inn and Carib Inn are among the cheapest. All dive operations are well equipped and well staffed with a good safety record. If booking a package deal check whether their week-long dive packages include nightly night dives, or only one a week. For less experienced divers it is worth choosing a dive boat which keeps staff on board while the leader is underwater, in case you get into difficulties. Dive packages are available at the following hotels: *Captain Don's Habitat, Carib Inn, Coral Regency, Divi Flamingo, Harbour Village, Sand Dollar Beach Club, Sunset Beach Hotel, Sunset Inn, Sunset Oceanfront Apartments* and *Sunset Villas*.

Other Sports

There are tennis courts at the *Divi Flamingo Beach Resort*, open 0800-2200, Tel: 8285; *Sand Dollar Beach Club*, open 0900-2100, Tel: 8738; and at *Sunset Beach Hotel*, open 0800-1030, 1530-2100, Tel: 5300. There is also horse riding but little else in the way of land based sports. Walking and birdwatching are popular in the Washington/ Slagbaai National Park, particularly climbing up Mount Brandaris. A bridge club, Ups and Downs, almost opposite the *Divi Flamingo Beach Resort* on J A Abraham Boulevard 29, Tel: 8136, welcomes guest players, enroll before 1400, play starts 1930.

Kralendijk

Kralendijk, meaning coral dike, the capital of Bonaire, is a small, sleepy town with colourful buildings of one or two stories high. About 1,700 people live here and it is just a few blocks long with some streets projecting inland. Most of the shops are in the small Harbourside Shopping Mall and on the main street, the name of which changes from J A Abraham Boulevard to Kaya Grandi to Breedestraat. Places to visit include the Museum (Department of Culture), Sabana 14, Tel: 8868, open weekdays 0800-1200, 1300-1700, folklore, archaeology and a shell collection; the small Fort Oranje, the plaza called Wilhelminaplein, and the fish market built like a Greek temple.

Excursions

Hire a car if you do not want to go on an organized tour. The island can be toured in a day if you start early but it is more pleasant to do a northern tour on one day and a southern tour another. Take food and drinks, there is rarely any available along the way, and aim to picnic somewhere you can swim to cool off. North of Kralendijk the road passes most of the hotels and planned developments, past the Water Distillation Plant along the "scenic" road,

Key:
1. Wilhelminaplein
2. Fort Oranje
3. Protestant Church
4. Catholic Church
5. Museum
6. Tourist Office
7. Post Office
8. Police Station
9. Government offices
10. Customs
11. Hospital
12. Fish Market
13. Shopping Mall
14. Ro-Ro Pier
15. *Divi Flamingo Beach Resort*
16. *Sunset Inn and Dive Inn*

KRALENDIJK
ROUGH SKETCH   C63A

which offers several descents to the sea and some excellent spots for
snorkelling or diving along the rocky coastline. The first landmark is the radio
station which has masses of aerials. Note that the road is one way, do not
turn round, but beware of pot holes and watch out for lizards sunbathing.
At the National Parks Foundation building you can turn right on a better
road to Rincon, climbing to the top of the hill for a steep descent and a good
view of Rincon and the Windward coast. Alternatively, continue along to
the Bonaire Petroleum Company where the road turns inland to Goto Meer
Bay, the best place to see flamingoes, on another road to Rincon, Bonaire's
oldest village where the slaves' families lived. Past Rincon is a side road to
the Boca Onima caves with their Arawak Indian inscriptions. Indian
inscriptions in several caves around the island can still be seen, but they have
not been deciphered.

The road leading north from Rincon takes you to Washington/Slagbaai
National Park, which occupies the northern portion of the island, about
6,075 hectares, and contains more than 130 species of birds. The park is
open to the public daily (entrance fee US$2, children up to 15 free) from

0800 to 1700 (no entry after 1530). There is a small museum of local historical items opposite the office and a room with geological explanations, bird pictures and a shell collection behind the office. Toilet at the entrance. Bring food and water. No hunting, fishing, two-wheeled transport or camping is permitted. You can choose from a 34-km or a 24-km tour, the roads being marked by yellow or green arrows. The road is dirt, rough in parts, and the long route can be very hot and tiring unless you make several stops to swim and cool off. Do not expect much variation in vegetation, the overall impression is of miles of scrub and cactus, broken only by rocks or salinjas. You can drive to Goto Meer on the longer route but you can get a better view from the observation point outside the Park. The return to Kralendijk is inland through the villages of Noord Salinja and Antriol. It is not well marked but you are unlikely to get lost for long.

The tour south passes the airport and Trans World Radio's towering 213-metre antenna which transmits 3 million watts, making it the hemisphere's most powerful radio station. Its shortwave broadcasts can be picked up in almost any part of the world. The coastal area south of Kralendijk is being heavily developed for tourism with construction of time share apartments, villas and hotels. The salt pier dominates the view along the coastal road and the salt pans are a stunning pink/purple colour. Further on are the snow-white salt piles and the three obelisks: blue, white, and orange, dating from 1838, with the huts that sheltered the slaves who worked the saltpans. Remember the flamingoes are easily startled, so move quietly if near them. At the southern tip of the island is Willemstoren, Bonaire's lighthouse, which dates from 1837. Pass Sorobon Beach and the mangrove swamps to Boca Cai at landlocked Lac Bay, with its clear water excellent for underwater exploration. What seem to be snow-capped hills from a distance are great piles of empty conch shells left by the local fishermen at Boca Cai. Take the road back to Kralendijk through the village of Nikiboko.

Information for Visitors

Documents

See below under Curaçao Information for Visitors.

How To Get There

If you fly with ALM you are entitled to a free return flight to Curaçao as part of your ticket. KLM flies from Amsterdam once a week direct. ALM flies from Atlanta, Georgia and Miami and there are flights from Aruba with Air Aruba and ALM, from Curaçao with ALM, and from Caracas with Servivensa and ALM. There is a departure tax of US$5.75 (NAf 10) on local flights and US$10 (NAf 18) on international flights.

Local Transport

The best way of getting about is to hire a car. There are no public buses. Hitching is fairly easy. Bicycles are available to rent from most hotels' front desks.

Taxis

There are taxis at the airport but they are difficult to find around the island. Taxis do not "cruise" so you must telephone for one, Tel: 8100. Drivers carry list of officially approved rates, including touring and waiting time. The short trip from the airport to the *Divi Flamingo Beach Resort* is US$4; airport to *Sunset Beach Hotel*, US$8; fares increase by 25% 2000-midnight and by 50% from midnight-0600. Taxis have TX on their licence plates.

Self-Drive Cars

A B Car Rental at the airport, PO Box 339, Tel: 8980 and in town, Tel: 8667, also at *Divi Flamingo Beach Hotel*, Tel: 8285 ext 32, check cars carefully, brake failure reported, poor service. Dollar Rent A Car at Kaya Grandi No 86, Kralendijk, Tel: 8888 and at airport Tel: 5600 ext 41. Budget at Kaya L D Gerharts No 22, Kralendijk, Tel: 8300 ext 225, also at *Divi Flamingo Beach Hotel*, Tel: 8300 ext 234, at Shopping Gallery, Kaya Grandi, Tel: 8460, Airport, Tel: 8315, *Sunset Beach Hotel, Harbour Village Beach Resort*, and *Captain Don's Habitat*, Fax: 8865/ 8118.

Flamingo Car Rental, airport, Tel: 8313. Sunray Car Rental, Tel: 5600 ext 34. Trupial Car Rental, Kaya Grandi No 96, Tel: 8487. Camel Rent A Car, Kaya Betico Croes 28, Tel: 5120. Avis, Drive Yourself (Bonaire), J A Abraham Blvd 4, PO Box 20 Kralendijk, Tel: 5795/ 8922/ 5600, Fax: 5791. Daily rates, unlimited mileage start at US$26 for a minibus (dive car), US$30 for a Toyota Starlet, US$40 for a Suzuki jeep, not including insurance. At the busiest times of the year, it is best to reserve a car in advance.

Small motorcycles can be rented from US$12 a day, contact Bonaire Motorcycle Rentals, Gouverneur Debrotweg 28, Tel: 8488, or Happy Chappy Rentals at *Dive Inn*, Kaya C E B Hellmund 27, Tel: 8761.

The speed limit in built- up areas is 33 kph, outside towns it is 60 kph unless otherwise marked. Many of the roads in Kralendijk and the north of the island are one way.

Where To Stay

High season rates (December 16 to two weeks after Easter) are roughly double low- season 1992 rates quoted here in the more expensive hotels; the cheaper ones tend to charge the same all year round. A US$2.80 per person per night government tax and 10% service charge must be added. On the leeward coast, south of Kralendijk are *Sunset Inn*, P O Box 115, Tel: 8291/ 8118, only five rooms US$55d and two suites US$70d, some rooms with kitchenettes, bicycle rental, across the road from the sea, within easy walking distance of town, next to Dive Inn dive shop; *Divi Flamingo Beach Resort & Casino*, Tel: 8285, Fax: 8238, US$125-185d, third person US$20, is on a small artificial beach, snorkelling or diving just off the beach is excellent, Dive Bonaire and Photo Bonaire based here, dining is outdoors, some rooms in need of refurbishment, friendly staff but front office slow and inefficient, check your bill carefully, no food available after 2200 for late arrivals; next door is *Carib Inn*, Tel: 8819, Fax: 5295, PO Box 68, apartments US$49- 79d and suites US$99, a/ c, cable TV, pool, dive shop; a huge, luxury resort, *The Point*, was under construction by the airport in 1991, to have casino, dive shop, entertainment, disco, restaurants, much grander than other hotels but has not been recommended; further south are *Bonaire Beach Bungalows*, Tel: 8581/ 8585, by the airport on the way to the salt works,

six 2- bedroomed bungalows on the beach, US$85, a/c.

Two cheaper hotels in Kralendijk are *Hotel Rochaline*, Tel: 8286, 25 rooms, US$30-50d depending on which section you are in, functional, bar facing sea, restaurant, and *Leeward Inn*, 500m away, 5 rooms, US$60d, has been recommended.

Going north out of Kralendijk are *Harbour Village Beach Resort and Marina* on Playa Lechi, P O Box 312, Tel: 7500, Fax: 7507, 72 rooms and 30 condominiums, US$135-175d, suites US$275-410, a/c, cable TV, restaurants, bars, fitness centre, tennis, pool, Great Adventures Bonaire dive shop, and non-motorized watersports, casino planned for late 1992, a growing resort with more facilities coming on stream all the time, look out for promotional packages. *Sunset Beach Hotel*, on Playa Lechi, Tel: 8448, Fax: 8593, 148 rooms US$65-85d, Suites US$125, third person US$10, a/ c, tennis, watersports, dive shop, good breakfast, ideal for divers; *Sand Dollar Beach Club*, Tel: 8738, Fax: 8760, P O Box 175, 75 condominiums and 10 town houses US$125- 225, a/ c, beach, tennis, pool. Sand Dollar Dive and Photo, restaurant and delicatessen; *Buddy Dive Resort*, Tel: 8647/ 8065, 12 apartments US$120 weekly, a/ c, kitchen, pool, Buddy Watersports Center, planned timeshare apartments; *Coral Regency*, P O Box 380, Tel: 5580, Fax: 5680, opened 1991, 31 suites US$130-205, with kitchen, a/ c, cable TV, pool, restaurant, Neal Watson Undersea Adventures Dive Center, more suites and entertainment complex planned; *Captain Don's Habitat*, P O Box 88, Tel: 8290, Fax: 8240, rooms, US$145-185d, 11 cottages US$220 and 11 villas US$380-440 with more under construction, family packages, special excursions for children during their family month every August, pool, dive shop with world's youngest snorkelling instructor (the last three hotels are all in a row next to oil storage tanks); a little further along the coast is *Black Durgon Inn*, Tel: 8978, Fax: 8846, 1-bedroom apartments US$455 weekly, 2/3-bedroom villas US$130 pp weekly, with view of radio masts and oil storage tanks as well as the sea, a/ c, cable TV, Bonaire Scuba Center dive shop.

On the windward coast is the *Sorobon Beach Resort*, at Lac Bay, Tel: 8080, Fax:

5363, clothes optional, 23 chalets US$90-110d, snack bar, 6% charge for credit cards.

The Tourist Office has a more extensive list, including apartments and villas, of properties approved by Bonhata.

Where To Eat

International food at the major hotels varies on different nights of the week with barbecues or Indonesian nights, etc. Two good places to watch the fish are the *Green Parrot* at the *Sand Dollar Beach Club* and the *Chibi Chibi* at the *Divi Flamingo* (but do not feed them). Main courses in the upper- priced restaurants are about US$12- 20, but several restaurants do bar snacks if you want to economize. All food is imported, so even fruit and vegetables in the market are not cheap. Conch is recommended, either fried or in a stew, as is goat stew. The squeamish may not want to try iguana soup, which may also be on the menu. If you want to eat lobster, check where the restaurant gets its supplies, some lobster fishermen are reported to be unauthorized and disapproved of by divers and conservationists.

In Kralendijk, *Rendez- Vous*, Kaya L D Gerharts 3, Tel: 8454, is recommended, seafood specials, vegetarian choice, good vegetables, small and friendly; *Bistro des Amis*, opposite, French style, good but pricey; cheaper is *Mona Lisa*, on Kaya Grandi, Tel: 8412, closed Sunday, bar and restaurant, hamburgers and spaghetti as well as local dishes, large portions, popular; *Beefeater*, Kaya Grandi 12, Tel: 8773/ 8081, open 1830- 2300, closed Sunday, steak and seafood, pricey, small; *Raffles*, at the harbourside, Tel: 8617, open 1830- 2230, tiny, smokey dining room, nice terrace, reasonable prices at lunch, closed Monday, Indonesian and international; *Zeezicht*, on the waterfront, does breakfast, lunch and dinner, sandwiches and omelettes as well as fish and some Indonesian, food all right but service criticized; *Restaurant Lisboa*, in *Hotel Rochaline*, outdoor dining on waterfront, Tel: 8286, grills and seafood, lobster; in the new shopping mall upstairs is *Croccantino*, Italian, downstairs there is a pizza bar, *Cozzoli's Pizza*, for fast food; south of town, just past *Carib Inn* is *Richard's* waterfront dining, happy hour 1730- 1830, dinner 1830- 2230, closed Monday, seafood specialities, recommended when owner Richard Beady

is in attendance.

There are a few good Chinese restaurants in town, the best of which is probably the *China Garden* in an old restored mansion, which is open for lunch and dinner, Tel: 8480, closed Tuesday. *Mentor's*, about 1½ miles from *Sunset Beach*, is recommended, cheap, large portions of Chinese food. *Super Bon* vegetarian restaurant, open 0700- 1800, closed Saturday, good for snacks and juices, at Kaya Fraternan di Tilburg 2, Tel: 8337. There are several snack bars in Kralendijk.

Water comes from a desalinization plant and is safe to drink. Take water with you on excursions. Do not, however, wash in or drink water from outside taps. This is *sushi* water, treated sufficiently for watering plants but nothing more.

Camping

is possible on the beach, though fresh water is hard to obtain; there are no campsites.

Entertainment

Nightlife is not well developed but there are a few places to go. Late night dancing takes place at the *E Wowo* and *Dynamite* discos and at the *Zeezicht Bar and Restaurant*. There is a casino at the *Divi Flamingo Beach Resort* (open 2000 except Sunday) and others are planned at the *Harbour Village Resort* and at *The Point*. There is a modest cinema in Kralendijk.

Shops

Open 0800- 1200 and 1400- 1800, Monday- Saturday, and for a few hours on Sundays if cruise ships are in port. Bonaire is not a major shopping centre, though some shops do stock high quality low duty goods. The Harbourside Shopping Mall contains small boutiques and a 1- hr photo processing shop, Kodalux. Photo Bonaire at *Divi Flamingo* is good for underwater photographic equipment to buy or hire. Photo Tours on Kaya Grandi 68, Tel: 8060, also offers full underwater facilities. Local arts and crafts are largely shellwork, coral jewellery and fabrics. In Kralendijk there is a supermarket on Kaya L D Gerharts, just past the Exito bakery, well- stocked, good. Uncle Buddy's Sand Dollar Grocery is located in a small plaza in from of the *Sand Dollar Beach Club* along with *Lovers Ice Cream Parlour*. Near the *Divi Flamingo* a turning opposite leads to Jan's grocery and mini- market. Health food or snacks from Je- Mar Health shop, Kaya Grandi 5.

Banks

Open 0830- 1200, 1400- 1600, Monday-Friday. Algemene Bank Nederland NV, Kaya Grandi No 2, Tel: 8429; Maduro & Curiel's Bank (Bonaire) NV, Tel: 5520, with a branch in Rincon, Tel: 6266; Bank van de Nederlandse Antillen, Tel: 8507; Banco de Caribe NV, Tel: 8295.

Public Holidays

New Year's Day, Good Friday, Easter Monday, Queen's Birthday (30 April), Labour Day (1 May), Ascension Day, Bonaire Day (6 September), Christmas Day and Boxing Day.

Electric Current

127 volts, 50 cycles.

Hospital

The Hospital in Kralendijk has a decompression chamber, Tel: 8900/ 8445.

Post Office

J A Abraham Blvd, Kralendijk, on the corner of Plaza Reina Wilhelmina opposite the ABN bank, open 0730- 1200, 1330-1700 for stamps and postage, 1330- 1600 for money orders etc.

Tour Agency

Bonaire Sightseeing Tours, Tel: 8778 or 8300 ext. 225, 242, 229, Fax: 8118, head office Kaya L D Gerharts 22 or at any

Budget Rent A Car desk, 2- hour northern or southern tour, half or full day Washington Park tour, day trip to Curaçao.

Religious Services

Roman Catholic, San Bernardo Church, Kralendijk, Tel: 8304, Our Lady of Coromoto, Antriol, Tel: 4211, or San Ludovico Church, Rincon; United Protestant Church, Tel: 8086; Evangelical Alliance Mission, Tel: 6245; Jehova's Witnesses, Antriol; New Apostolic Church, Nikiboko, Tel: 8483; Seventh Day Adventist Church, Tel: 4254.

Tourist Office

Kaya Simón Bolívar 12, Kralendijk, Tel: 8322/ 8649. Limited tourist information and leaflets, no maps. In the USA, Resorts Management Inc, The Carriage House, 201½ East 29th Street, New York, NY 10016, Tel: (0800) 826-6247, (212) 696-4566, Fax: (212) 689-1598. In Canada, 512 Duplex Avenue, Toronto, Ontario, M4R 2E3, Tel: (416) 485-8724, Fax: (416) 485-8256.

Bonhata, the Bonaire Hotel and Tourist Association is actively engaged in promoting the island as a tourist destination, Tel: 5134, Fax: 8240, P O Box 358.

CURAÇAO

Introduction

CURAÇAO, the largest of the five islands comprising the Netherlands Antilles, lies in the Caribbean Sea 60 km off the Venezuelan coast at a latitude of 12°N, outside the hurricane belt. It is 65 km long and 11 km at its widest, with an area of 448 square km. The landscape is barren, because of low rainfall (560 mm a year) which makes for sparse vegetation (consisting mostly of cactus thickets), and although it is not flat, the only significant hill is Mount Christoffel in the northwest, which rises to a height of 375 metres. On a clear day you can see Aruba, Bonaire and Venezuela from the top. Deep bays indent the southern coast, the largest of which, Schottegat, provides Willemstad with one of the finest harbours in the Caribbean. On the island cactus plants grow up to 6 metres high, and the characteristic wind-distorted dividivi trees reach 3 metres, with another 3 metres or so of branches jutting out away from the wind at right angles to the trunk.

The population of 146,096 is truly cosmopolitan, and 79 nationalities are represented, of whom 16% were born outside the Netherlands Antilles.

The Economy

Curaçao has a more diversified economy than the other islands, yet even so, it suffered severe recession in the 1980s and unemployment is around 21% of the labour force. The major industry is the oil refinery dating back to 1917, now one of the largest in the world, to which the island's fortunes and prosperity are tied. Imports of crude oil and petroleum products make up two thirds of total imports, while exports of the same are 95% of total exports. That prosperity was placed under threat when Shell pulled out of the refinery in 1985, but the operation was saved when the island government purchased the plant, and leased it to Venezuela. Its future is in the balance again because of the need for a US$270m reconstruction, principally to reduce pollution. Bunkering has also become an important segment of the economy, and the terminal at Bullenbaai is one of the largest bunkering ports in the world. Besides oil, other exports include the famous Curaçao liqueur, made from the peel of the native orange. The island's extensive trade makes it a port of call for a great many shipping lines.

Coral reefs surrounding the island, constant sunshine, a mean temperature of 27°C (81°F), and refreshing trade winds lure visitors the year round, making tourism the second industry. Curaçao used to be a destination for tourists from Venezuela, but a devaluation of the bolívar in 1983 caused numbers to drop by 70% in just one year and several hotels had to be temporarily taken over by the Government to protect employment. A restructuring of the industry has led to a change of emphasis towards attracting US and European tourists and numbers are now increasing, with further hotel expansion planned. Despite the recession in the North American market, tourism was not severely affected in 1991, largely because of a 24% increase in the number of visitors from Europe. In 1991 there were 205,648 stopover visitors and 156,608 cruise ship

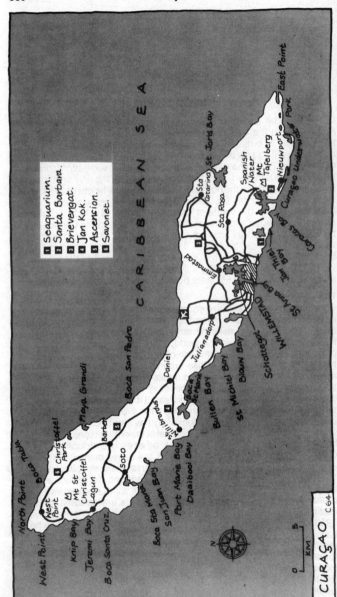

CURAÇAO C-64

passenger arrivals, a decline of 1% in both cases from 1990. Average hotel occupancy rose from 72% in 1990 to 78% in 1991 as visitors increased the length of their stay. Most rooms are in top grade hotels, with only a few in guest houses, but self-catering apartments, time share and condominiums are growing fast. In 1991 there were about 1,400 hotel rooms, with another 3,000 planned to be built in four years.

A third major foreign currency earner, the offshore financial sector, saw its operations severely curtailed in the 1980s. Once a centre for booking the issue of Eurobonds because of its favourable tax laws, the repeal of witholding tax in the USA in 1984 eliminated Curaçao's advantages and virtually wiped out the business. A second blow came with the cancellation by the USA, followed by similar action by the UK, of its double taxation treaty. These changes have led to greatly reduced income for the island's Government, although the offshore centre is actively seeking new areas of business, including captive insurance and mutual funds, in a highly competitive market. There are 61 banks, of which only 14 are licenced to carry out domestic business, the rest are offshore. After the crisis of the mid-1980s, assets in the offshore banks have risen steadily again.

Diving and Marine Life

The waters around Curaçao contain a wide variety of colourful fish and plant life and several wrecks which have foundered on the coral reef just offshore. The reef surrounds the island and consists generally of a gently sloping terrace to a depth of about ten metres, then a drop off and a reef slope with an angle of about 45°. Underwater visibility averages 24 metres and water temperature varies between 24-27°C. Scuba diving is becoming increasingly popular in Curaçao and many of the large resort hotels have dive shops on site. They have been encouraged by the establishment in 1983 of the Curaçao Underwater Park, managed by the Netherlands Antilles National Parks Foundation (Stinapa), which stretches from the *Princess Beach Hotel* to East Point. The Park extends out from the shore to a depth of 60 metres and covers 600 hectares of reef and 436 hectares of inner bays. Sixteen mooring buoys for boats have been placed at dive sites as part of Stinapa's programme for sustained utilization of the reef. A few of the sites can be dived from the shore, but most of the coastal strip is private property and boat dives are necessary. The *Guide to the Curaçao Underwater Park*, by Jeffrey Sybesma & Tom van't Hof, published in 1989 by Stinapa and available in bookshops locally, describes the sites and discusses conservation. No harpoons or spear guns are allowed and make sure you do not damage or remove coral or any other sea creatures.

There are several dive operators, not all of which are mentioned here, and it is worth shopping around before booking a package deal. In 1991 most operators offered a single boat dive for around US$25-30 and snorkelling trips including equipment for about US$12-15, but check when booking whether 10% service is included in the quoted price. Underwater Curaçao (Tel: 618131, Fax: 73507) at the *Lions Dive Hotel* next to the Seaquarium is one of the larger operations with two dive boats for 24 divers each and two scheduled dives a day. It has a large air station with a capacity to fill 1,000 tanks daily, a retail shop and offers several courses. Princess Diving and Watersports, Tel: 614944 ext 5047, boat dives, shore dives. PADI courses, fishing and sailing trips, windsurfing and jet skis, all at the *Princess Beach Hotel*. Divers Way of Curaçao at *Holiday Beach Hotel*, Tel: 627144, has a PADI 5-star training facility and a large retail dive shop, staff speak English,

German and Dutch. Coral Cliff Diving at Santa Martha Bay (P O Box 3782, Tel: 642822, Fax: 642237) also offers introductory or certification courses and package deals, also windsurfing US$10/hour, with sunfish, hobiecats and pedalboats available, prices not including 10% service. A smaller, more informal dive operation is at *Landhuis Daniel*. Dive Center Daniel (Tel/Fax: 648400) offers dive packages or individual dives from boat or car, photo equipment available, night diving on request. For independent divers and snorkellers without a boat there is the *Complete Guide to Landside Diving and Snorkelling Locations in Curaçao*, by Jeffrey Sybesma and Suzanne Koelega, including a map with the sites and roads to them.

The Seaquarium, southeast of Willemstad, just beyond the *Lions Dive Hotel*, has a large collection of undersea creatures and plants found around the island, which live in channelled sea water to keep them as close as possible to their natural environment. Some tanks are incorrectly marked, the inhabitants have obviously been moved. The Seaquarium was built in 1984, the lagoons and marina being excavated so as to leave the original coastline untouched and do minimal damage to the reef offshore. Open 0900-2200, entrance US$6, children under 15 and adults over 63 half price, after 1800 US$3 and US$1.50 respectively. Glass bottomed boat trips can also be arranged from the entrance, minimum five people, adults US$5.50, children and over 63 US$3. The water is frequently rough outside the marina, beware of seasickness. There is a restaurant, snack bar and shops selling shells and coral in marked contrast to the conservation efforts of the Underwater Park administration. The Seaquarium can be reached by bus marked Dominguito from the Post Office at 35 minutes past the hour (except for 1335), which passes the *Avila Beach Hotel*.

Beaches and Watersports

There are few really good beaches on Curaçao. The northwestern coast is rugged and rough for swimming, but the western coast offers some sheltered bays and beaches with excellent swimming and snorkelling. Windsurfing, waterskiing, yachting and fishing are available at resorts. Many of the beaches are private and make a small charge per car but in return you usually get some changing facilities, toilets and refreshments. Public beaches are free but most have no facilities and some are rather dirty and smelly round the edges. Topless sunbathing is not recommended on public beaches but is tolerated on private beaches. The only beach near Willemstad is the small, artificial one at the *Avila Beach Hotel*, where non-residents pay an entrance fee. The sand is very gritty at the water's edge and the sea is not calm enough to see much if you snorkel. You can get to the beach at Piscadera Bay near the *Curaçao Caribbean* or *Las Palmas* hotels by catching one of their shuttle buses from beside the Rif Fort in Otrabanda.

Southeast of Willemstad, by the *Princess Beach Hotel*, the *Lions Dive Hotel* and the Seaquarium (see above), is a 450-metre, man-made beach and marina with all watersports available. Entrance to the beach is US$1.50. There are also two high water slides and a smaller version for children, usually open at weekends only but may open at other times in high season. Showers and toilets. Past the Seaquarium is a residential area and private beach on Jan Thiel Bay, good swimming and snorkelling, entrance free for tourists, charge made per car, changing facilities, drinks and snacks, closed Tuesdays. Santa Barbara, located at the mouth of Spanish Water Bay on the Mining Company property, is a favourite with locals and has changing rooms, toilets and snack bars, open 0800-1800. Entrance free but US$3.33 per car. You can take a bus from the Post Office, get off at the Mining Company gate and hitchhike down to the beach, or take a taxi, it is too far to walk. Across the bay, which is one of the island's beauty spots, is the Curaçao Yacht Club, with a pleasant bar. There are four yacht clubs in Spanish Water.

Travelling northwest from Willemstad heading towards Westpoint, there are lots of coves and beaches worth exploring. A left turn soon after leaving town will take you to Blauw Bay, US$2.75 per car, facilities on the beach, good for snorkelling but there is too much coral and not enough sand for it to be nice to sit on, or to St Michiel's Bay, a fishing village and tanker clearing harbour (free). Further up the coast, Port Marie (private, charge per car) is sandy but there is no shade. San Juan, a private beach with lots of coral is off to the left of the main Westpoint road down a poor track, entrance fee charged. Boca Sta Martha, where the *Coral Cliff Resort* is located, is quiet with nice sea, beach entrance US$4.50 for non-residents, no pets or food allowed on the beach, some shade provided. Lagun is a lovely secluded beach in a small cove with cliffs surrounding it and small fishing boats pulled up on the sand. Jeremi, a private beach with a charge per car, is of the same design, slightly larger sandy beach with a steep drop to deep water and boats moored here, protected by the cliffs. Further up the coast, Knip is a more open, larger, sandy beach again with cliffs at either end. There are some facilities here and it is very popular at weekends when there is loud music and it gets crowded and noisy. A charge per car is being considered even though it is a public beach. Playa Abau is big, sandy, with beautiful clear water, surrounded by cliffs, some shade provided, toilets, well organized, popular at weekends and busy. Nearing the western tip, Playa Forti has dark sand and good swimming. There is a restaurant on the cliff top overlooking the sea which gets very busy at weekend lunchtimes. The beach at Westpoint below the church is stoney and littered, the only shade comes from the poisonous manchineel trees, but there is so much litter under them you would not be tempted to sit there. Fishing boats tie up at the pier but bathers prefer to go to Playa Forti. Beyond Westpoint is Kalki beach which is good for snorkelling and diving as well as bathing. Westpoint is the end of the road, about 45 minutes by car or one hour by bus from Otrabanda, US$0.85.

Many charter boats and diving operators go to Klein Curaçao, a small, uninhabited island off East Point which has sandy beaches and is good for snorkelling and scuba diving, a nice day trip with lunch provided.

The Curaçao International Sailing Regatta is held in March with competitions in three categories, short distance (windsurfers, hobie cats, sunfish etc), long distance (yachts race 112 km to Klein Curaçao and back) and open boat (trimarans, catamarans etc race 32 km to Spanish Water and back), all starting from the *Princess Beach Hotel*. For details, contact Timo Hilhorst at Uranusstraat 20, Curaçao, Tel: 613433.

Other Sports

Rancho Alegre, Tel: 81181, does horse riding for US$15/hour, including transport. Ashari's Ranch offers horses for hire by the hour inland, or 1½ hours including a swim at the beach, open 1000-1900, Groot Piscadera Kaya A-23, Tel: 86254, beginners as well as experienced riders, playground for children. There is a bowling alley on the island. The Curaçao Golf and Squash Club at Wilhelminalaan, Emmastad, has a 10-hole sand golf course open 0800-1230, green fee US$15 for 18-hole round, and two squash courts, US$7, open 0800-1800, Tel: 73590. Santa Catharina Sport and Country

Club, Tel: 677028/677030, Fax: 677026, has six hard tennis courts, a swimming pool, bar and restaurant. The large hotels have tennis courts: the *Curaçao Caribbean* and the *Princess Beach* have a pro, while *Las Palmas* is open 24 hours.

Carnival

Curaçao, Aruba and Bonaire all hold the traditional pre-Lent carnival. Curaçao's main parade is on the Sunday at 1000 and takes 3 hours to pass, starting at Otrabanda. There is a preview on the Friday night when the Holiday Hotel carnival passes through Punda. The following Monday and Tuesday see most shops closed and there is a Farewell Grand Parade on the Tuesday when the Rey Momo is burned.

Willemstad

Willemstad, capital of the Netherlands Antilles and of the island of Curaçao (population about 140,000), is full of charm and colour. The architecture is a joyous tropical adaptation of 17th-century Dutch, painted in storybook colours. Pastel shades of all colours are used for homes, shops and government buildings alike. Fanciful gables, arcades, and bulging columns evoke the spirit of the Dutch colonial burghers.

The earliest buildings in Willemstad were exact copies of Dutch buildings of the mid-17th century, high-rise and close together to save money and space. Not until the first quarter of the 18th century did the Dutch adapt their northern ways to the tropical climate and begin building galleries on to the façades of their houses, to give shade and more living space. The chromatic explosion is attributed to a Governor-General of the islands, the eccentric Vice-Admiral Albert Kikkert ("Froggie" to his friends), who blamed his headaches on the glare of white houses and decreed in 1817 that pastel colours be used. Almost every point of interest in the city is in or within walking distance of the shopping centre in Punda, which covers about five blocks. Some of the streets here are only five metres wide, but attract many tourists with their myriad shops offering international goods at near duty-free prices. The numerous jewellery shops in Willemstad have some of the finest stones to be found anywhere.

The Floating Market, a picturesque string of visiting Venezuelan, Colombian and other island schooners, lines the small canal leading to the Waaigat, a small yacht basin. Fresh fish, tropical fruit, vegetables and a limited selection of handicrafts are sold with much haggling. Visit early in the morning.

In the circular, concrete, public market building nearby there are straw hats and bags, spices, butcheries, fruit and vegetables for sale, while in the old market building behind, local food is cooked over charcoal and sold to office workers at lunchtime.

Nearby on Hanchi Snoa, is one of the most important historical sites on Curaçao, the **Mikvé Israel-Emanuel synagogue**, which dates back to 1732, making it the oldest in the Western Hemisphere. In the 1860s, several families broke away from the Mikvé Israel congregation to found a Sephardi Reform congregation which was housed in the Temple Emanuel (1867-1964) on the Wilhelminaplein. In 1964, however, they reunited to form the Mikvé Israel-Emanuel congregation, which is affiliated with both the Reconstructionist Foundation and the World Union for Progressive Judaism. Services are held Friday 1830 and Saturday 1000. Normally open

0900-1145 and 1430-1700, free, no photographs allowed. The big brass chandeliers are believed to be 300 years older than their syngogue, originating in Spain and Portugal, their candles are lit for Yom Kippur and special occasions. The names of the four mothers, Sara, Rebecca, Leah and Rachel are carved on the four pillars and there are furnishings of richly carved mahogany with silver ornamentation, blue stained glass windows and stark white walls. The traditional sand on the floor is sprinkled there daily, some say, to symbolize the wandering of the Israelites in the Egyptian desert during the Exodus. Others say it was meant to muffle the sound of the feet of those who had to worship secretly during the Inquisition period.

In the courtyard is the **Jewish Museum**, occupying two restored 18th century houses, which harbours a permanent exhibition of religious objects, most of which have been donated by local Jewish families. There are scrolls, silver, books, bibles, furniture, clothing and household items, many 18th century pieces and family bequeathments. Two circumcision chairs are still in use. Outside are some tombstones and a ritual bath excavated during restoration work. The Museum is open Monday-Friday 0900-1145, 1430-1700, closed Jewish and public holidays, entrance US$2. A small shop sells souvenirs, the Synagogue Guide Book and *Our Snoa*, papiamento for Synagogue, produced for the 250th anniversay in 1982. For those who want deeper research of the Jewish families there is the *History of the Jews of the Netherlands Antilles*, by Isaac S and Suzanne A Emmanuel, two volumes. West of the city, on the Schottegatweg Nord, is one of the two Jewish cemeteries, Bet Chayim (or Beth Haim), consecrated in 1659 and still in use. There are more than 1,700 tombstones from the 17th and 18th centuries, many still legible.

The 18th century Protestant church, the **Fortkerk**, located at the back of the square behind **Fort Amsterdam**, the Governor's palace, still has a British cannonball embedded in its walls. It was closed for renovation in 1991.

Two forts, **Rif Fort** and **Water Fort** were built at the beginning of the 19th century to protect the harbour entrance and replace two older batteries. All that is left of Rif Fort is a guard house dating from about 1840 but you can walk on the walls and eat at the restaurants in the vaults. The Water Fort Arches have been converted to house shops, bars and restaurants and the Tourist Information Office is here.

The swinging Queen Emma bridge spans St Anna Bay, linking the two parts of the city, Punda and Otrabanda (the latter means "the other side" in Papiamento). Built on sixteen great pontoons, it is swung aside some thirty times a day to let ships pass in and out of the harbour. The present bridge, the third on the site, was built in 1939. While the bridge is open, pedestrians are shuttled free by small ferry boats. The bridge is closed to vehicular traffic.

The new Queen Juliana fixed bridge vaults about 50 metres over the bay and connects Punda and Otrabanda by a four-lane highway. Taxis will often offer to stop at the bridge so you can get a panoramic view and photo of Willemstad.

In Otrabanda, on van Leeuwenhoekstraat, is the **Curaçao Museum**, founded in 1946 (housed in an old quarantine station built in 1853) with a small, interesting collection of artefacts of the Caiquetio Indian culture, as well as 19th and 20th century paintings, antique furniture, and other items from the colonial era. In the basement there is a children's museum of science, but it is limited and rather outdated, almost a museum piece in itself. On the roof is a 47-bell carillon, named The Four Royal Children after the four daughters of Queen Juliana of the Netherlands, which was brought

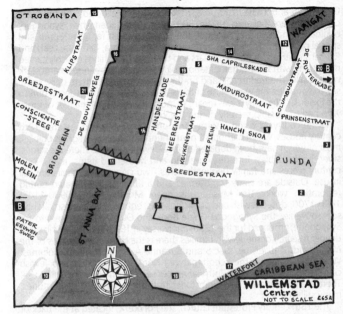

Willemstad Centre: Key to map

1. Wilhelminaplein; 2. Hendrikplein; 3. Pietermaaiplein; 4. Plaza Piar; 5. Plaza Jo Jo Correa; 6. Fort Amsterdam; 7. Government Palace; 8. Fortkerk; 9. Mikvé Israel-Emanuel Synagogue and Museum; 10. Riffort and Police Station; 11. Queen Emma Bridge; 12. Draw Bridge; 13. Public Market; 14. Floating Market; 15. Porto Paseo; 16. Harbour Ferry Docks; 17. Tourist Office; 18. *Van der Valk Plaza Hotel*; 19. Algemene Bank Nederland; 20. Post Office and Radio Holland Telephone Office (Off Map); 21. *Hotel Otrabanda*.

from Holland and installed in 1951. Lots of explanatory leaflets are given out at the museum, with a suggested route map. The museum is open daily, except Monday, admission NAf3 or US$1.50, NAf1.50 or US$0.75 for children under 14 (open 0900-1200 and 1400-1700, Tel: 623777).

Parts of Otrabanda are gradually being restored and there are many old houses here, both small, tucked away down alleys, and large mansions or town houses. Breedestraat is the main shopping street, the Basilica Santa Ana, founded in 1752 and made a Basilica in 1975 by Pope Paul VI, is just off here. The houses fronting on to the Pater Eeuwensweg, the highway heading west along the coast, once overlooked the Rifwater lagoon, now reclaimed land. Along St Anna Bay, past the ferry landing, is Porto Paseo, a restored area with bars and restaurants, popular on Friday evenings when there is music and dancing, or you can just sit and admire the view.

Another area within walking distance and worth exploring, is Scharloo, across the Wilhelmina bridge from the floating market. A former Jewish merchant housing area, now under renovation, there are many substantial properties with all the typical architectural attributes; note the green house

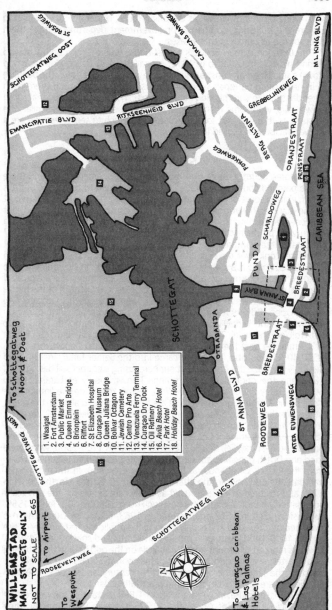

WILLEMSTAD
MAIN STREETS ONLY
NOT TO SCALE C65

1. Waaigat
2. Fort Amsterdam
3. Public Market
4. Queen Emma Bridge
5. Brionplein
6. Riffort
7. St Elizabeth Hospital
8. Curaçao Museum
9. Queen Juliana Bridge
10. Bolivar Octagon
11. Jewish Cemetery
12. Centro Pro Arte
13. Venezuela Ferry Terminal
14. Curaçao Dry Dock
15. Oil Refinery
16. Avila Beach Hotel
17. Park Hotel
18. Holiday Beach Hotel

with white trimmings known as the Cake House. Under a 5-10 year plan to restore the buildings, companies or government departments take them over for use as offices in many cases.

The Octagon, Simón Bolívar's sisters' house where Simón Bolívar stayed during his exile in Curaçao in 1812, is near the *Avila Beach Hotel* reached down a small road off Penstraat just before you get to the hotel. The building is in need of some repair work and looks neglected although there is an attendant (make sure his dogs are chained). There is one octagonal room downstairs, with some manuscripts, pictures and books, and a similar one upstairs, with a bed and some furniture; not much to see unless you are a Bolívar aficionado. Closed lunchtimes.

Excursions

The restored country estate houses, or *landhuizen*, emerge here and there in the parched countryside. Not all of them are open to the public but it is worth visiting some of those that are. Set in 503 hectares in the eastern part of the island is **Brievengat**. Its exact date of construction is unknown, but it is believed to date from the early 18th century. It was used in the 19th century to produce cattle, cochineal and aloe, but a hurricane in 1877 devastated the plantation and the house which were gradually abandoned. Shell later took over the property to extract water from the subsoil, but in 1954 when it was in a state of ruin Shell donated it to the Government who restored it to its former grandeur. The windows and the roof are typical of the local style but unusual are the arches extending the length of the house and the two towers at either side, which were once used to encarcerate slaves. Open daily 0930-1230, 1500-1800, bar and snacks, live music on Wednesday and Friday, open house last Sunday of the month 1000-1500 with folklore show, Tel: 78344. Take the bus marked Punda-Hato from Punda at 15 minutes past the hour and get off at the Sentro Deportivo Korsou, US$0.40. **Chobolobo**, at Salinja, came into the Senior family in 1948 and Senior & Co make the Curaçao liqueur here, using a copper still dating from 1896 and the original Valencia orange known locally as Laraha. Open Monday-Friday 0800-1200, 1300-1700, visitors may taste the liqueur. The clear, orange, amber, green and blue are for cocktails and all taste the same; others are chocolate, coffee, rum raisin. Entrance free, Tel: 78459. **Jan Kok** is the oldest landhouse on the island, dating from 1654 and overlooking the salt flats where flamingoes gather. It is open for private tours by reservation only Monday-Friday, Tel: 648087, open on Sundays 1100-2000, when local food and Dutch pancakes are served. Take the bus marked Lagun and Knip from the Riffort, Otrabanda, at half past the even hour in the morning or half past the odd hour in the afternoon, US$0.70. **Santa Martha**, built in 1700 and restored in 1979, is used as a day care centre for the physically and mentally handicapped but is open on Fridays, 0800-1600, Tel: 641559. **Ascension**, built in 1672 and restored in 1963, is used by Dutch marines stationed on the island and is only open to the public the first Sunday of the month 1000-1400, with local music, handicrafts and snacks, Tel: 641950. Take bus marked Westpunt from Otrabanda on the odd hour in the morning or a quarter past the odd hour in the afternoon, US$0.85. **Knip**, near the beach of the same name, is a restored 17th century landhouse where local handicrafts are on sale. On the same bus route as Jan Kok.

The Christoffel Park covers an area of 1,860 hectares in the west of the island, including Mount Christoffel at 375m, which was formerly three plantations. These plantations, Savonet, Zorgvlied and Zevenbergen, are the basis for a system of well-marked trails, blue (9km), green (7.5km or 12km) and yellow (11km), and there is a red walking trail up Mount Christoffel which takes about three hours there and back. You can see a wide range of fauna and flora, including orchids, the indigenous *wayacá* (*lignum vitae*) plant, acacias, aloe, many cacti, calabash and the tiny Curaçao deer. The ruins of the Zorgvlied landhouse can be seen off the green route. The Savonet route takes you to the coast and along to Amerindian rock drawings, painted between 500 and 2,000 years ago in terracotta, black and white. In this area there are also two caves (take a strong torch), one of which is about 125 metres long and you have to crawl in before you can stand up (lots of bats and lots of guano on the ground) and walk to the 'white chamber'(stalactites and stalagmites) and the 'cathedral'. The 17th century Savonet Plantation House is at the entrance to the Park on the Westpoint road, but it is not open to the public. However, several outbuildings are used; there is a small museum. The Park is open from 0800 Monday-Saturday, admission to the mountain side closes at 1500 and to the ocean side at 1600, although you can stay in until later. On Sundays the Park opens at 0600 and closes at 1500. Guided tours are available, special walks at dawn or dusk are organized at random, check in the newspapers, evening walking tours to see the Curaçao deer, maximum 8 people, reservations essential, Tel: 640363. Stinapa publishes an excellent *Excursion Guide to the Christoffel Park, Curaçao*, by Peer Reijns, 1984, which is available at the Park administration. A basic map of the trails is also provided. The bus Otrabanda-Westpunt passes the entrance to the Park.

Behind Spanish Water Bay on the south coast rises Mount Tafelberg, where phosphate mining used to take place. It can be visited on Tuesday and Friday when a special bus leaves the Mining Company entrance at 1400.

Information for Visitors

Documents

All visitors must have an onward ticket to a destination outside the Netherlands Antilles. US citizens do not need a passport; a birth certificate, alien registration card or naturalization papers are sufficient. Canadians must have a valid passport or birth certificate. Transit visitors and cruise ship visitors must have proof of identity for a 24-hour, or less, stay on the island. Immigration procedures at the airport are quick and easy.

How To Get There

Curaçao is very well served by airlines from Europe, the USA, Central and South America and the Caribbean, but the companies and their routes change frequently so check the latest flight guide. KLM flies direct from Amsterdam (so does Air Aruba) and has connecting flights to Caracas, Guayaquil, Quito, Lima, Guatemala City, Panama City and San José. TAP flies from Lisbon. There are flights from New York with Air Aruba, and from Miami with Air Aruba and ALM.

ALM also flies from Atlanta, Georgia. In high season there are more flights from the USA, eg American Airlines flies from Baltimore and San Juan, Puerto Rico and ALM flies from New York (JFK). Avianca flies from Barranquilla, Medellín and Bogotá, while ALM, Servivensa and Aeropostal fly from Caracas; ALM also flies from Barcelona, Barquisimeto and Valencia and Servivensa from Las Piedras and Maracaibo, Venezuela. ALM and Surinam Airways fly from Paramaribo. ALM flies from Georgetown, Guyana. Caribbean destinations include Aruba (Air Aruba, ALM), Bonaire (ALM), Kingston (ALM), Port au Prince (ALM), Port of Spain (ALM), Sint Maarten (ALM) and Santo Domingo in the Dominican Republic (ALM and Aeropostal).

ALM (Tel: 613033), KLM (Tel: 74777), BWIA (Tel: 612700) offices are at Gomezplein (Tel: 74777); American Airlines, Tel: 81081; Avianca, Tel: 80122; Aeropostal, Pietermaaiplein, Tel: 616776; Air Jamaica, Tel: 618307; Viasa, airport,

Tel: 81160, Plaza Piar, Tel: 613336; Dominicana, Tel: 80500; Air Portugal, Tel: 89045 Surinam Airways, Tel: 84360; Air Aruba, Tel: 83659.

There is an airport tax of US$5.65 on departure to the Netherlands Antilles or US$10 to Aruba or other destinations. This must be paid before you check in.

Ferry Service

There is a ferry to and from La Vela de Coro, Venezuela, and from Aruba once a week but the fare is similar to the airfare and hence little used. See the Aruba chapter, page 712 for details. Service is very unreliable, be prepared for delays of several hours. Drinks and sandwiches can be bought aboard. In Curaçao, customs and immigration formalities are carried out in the terminal.

Taxis

Taxis are easily identified by the signs on the roof and TX before the licence number. There are taxi stands at all hotels and at the airport, as well as in principal locations in Willemstad. It is not always possible to get a taxi to the airport early in the morning. Fares for sightseeing trips should be established at beginning of trip, the usual price is US$15 for the first hour and US$5 for each subsequent 15 minutes. Tipping is not strictly obligatory. There are collective taxis, called buses, and identified by an AC prefix on their licence plates. Airport displays taxi fares to main hotels. Taxis do not always go looking for business and it can be difficult to hail one. Best to telephone from a hotel lobby or restaurant/bar, one will arrive in a couple of minutes (Dispatch Tel: 616711, complaints Tel: 615577), or go to a taxi stand and just get into an empty car, the driver will then turn up. The rear windows of many taxis do not work, which makes the car uncomfortable in the hot climate. Courtesy vans operated by the hotels can be more comfortable.

Buses

Konvoois are big yellow buses which run to a schedule and serve outlying areas of Curaçao. There is a terminal at the Post Office in Punda and another at the Rif Fort in Otrabanda. To the airport get a bus marked Hato from Punda at 15 minutes past the hour from 0615 to 2315, or from Otrabanda at 35 minutes past the hour from 0635 to 2235, US$0.40. Buses to Westpunt leave from Otrabanda on the odd hour in the morning then at 15

minutes past the odd hour from 1515-2115, last bus 2245, US$0.85, return on the even hour in the morning and 15 minutes past the even hour from 1615. Buses to Dominguito (the Seaquarium) run at 35 minutes past the hour but minibuses also do this route. A bus marked Schottegat runs from Punda via the *Trupial Inn Hotel*, the Curaçao Golf and Squash Club, the Jewish cemetery and the Curaçao Museum to Otrabanda at 20 minutes past the hour in either direction. The Lagun and Knip bus route leaves Otrabanda at half past the even hour in the mornings and half past the odd hour in the afternoons via the Curaçao Museum, the University, Landhuis Jan Kok, Santa Cruz beach, Jeremi beach, Lagun Beach and Bahia beach, returning from Knip at half past the alternate hour. The standard city bus fare is US$0.40; *autobuses* (ie colectivos) charge US$0.85 before 2000, US$1 after.

Self- Drive Cars

There are about eight car rental agencies at the airport, all the offices are together so it is easy to pick up price lists for comparison. One or two companies usually have desks in each of the major hotels. Look in local tourist literature or newspapers for news of special deals on offer, there is lots of choice. Companies include Budget, Love Car Rentals, Europcar/National, Drive Yourself Inc (rep for Avis), Curaçao Car Rental, Buggy Rental Madeirense, Caribe Rentals, U Save Car Rental, Dollar Rent a Car. Prices start at about US$25 daily, unlimited mileage, including insurance, deposits from US$250, for a very small car, from US$35 for a jeep; minimokes, buggies, scooters and bikes also available. Foreign and international driving licences are accepted. Traffic moves on the right.

Where To Stay

There is a 5% government tax and 10% (sometimes 12%) service charge to be added to any quoted room rate and many hotels add an extra US$3 per day energy surcharge. In Willemstad, *Van der Valk Plaza*, very central, ugly, huge tower by the fortress walls, Tel: 612500, US$75 per room all year, including service, tax, breakfast, popular with the Dutch, good food, casino, games machines; *Otrabanda*, opened December 1990 and still rather sterile, on Breedestraat just by the bridge in Otrabanda, good for business travellers, standard rooms small but comfortable US$85d, single rooms US$75, suites are larger rooms with sofas US$100, coffee shop and restaurant with good view of Punda and floating bridge, casino, pool planned, Tel: 627400, Fax: 627299, or reservations through International Travel & Resorts, New York, Tel: 800- 223- 9815, Fax: 212- 545- 8467, or in Holland, Holland International, Tel: 70- 395 7957, Fax: 70- 395 7747; further west along the main road is the *Holiday Beach*, an ugly concrete block next to the brewery on a manmade beach, but elegant inside, Tel: 625400, Fax: 624397, 200 rooms, US$95- 105d winter 1990/91, a/c, phone, TV, casino and banks of gaming machines, pool, tennis, dive shop on site, conference rooms, reservations through ITR. 15 minutes walk east of the centre is the family- owned *Avila Beach*, Penstraat 130, P O Box 791, Tel: 614377, Fax: 611493, built in 1811 as Governor's residence but most rooms in an old hospital wing, small and with no sea view, US$90- 135d winter 1991/92, very popular, always full, cool reception area, service friendly but slow, no pool, lovely bar shaped like a ship's prow on the beach (rather gritty and painful on the feet at water's edge), great for evening cocktails, pleasant outdoor dining but food mediocre. A new extension has been built, called *La Belle Alliance*, 40 hotel rooms and some apartments, all rooms and suites with sea view, US$160- 200d.

The Tourist Board main office at Pietermaai 19 has a list of guesthouses and apartments (not all of which it recommends) including some cheap hotels such as *Stelaris* close to the *Otrabanda*, looking out over the floating market, seedy, Tel: 625337, from US$19 with fan, no bath, to US$37, a/c, with bath; *Estoril*, Breedestraat 181, Otrabanda, Tel: 625244, US$19- 27; in Scharloo, *Mirapunda*, Van der Brandhofstraat 12, Tel: 613995, 612392, US$30d, clean, friendly, recommended; *Central*, Scharlooweg 2, Tel: 613965, all rooms US$10; *Park*, on Frederikstraat 84, Tel: 623112, US$32d; *Bon Auberge*, Hoogstraat 63- 65, Tel: 627902, US$25- 37d, fans, only one room with private bath; *Pension Le Creole*, Saliña 2, P O Box 878, Tel/Fax: 613991, in Holland Tel: 020- 910134, US$15, fan or a/c, large rooms sleep four. Centrally located self- catering, *Pietersz Guesthouse & Apartments*, Roodeweg 1, in Otrabanda very near the hospital, Tel:

625222 0800- 1900, Tel: 82036 after 1900, clean, spacious rooms from US$45 with kitchenette, phone, a/c, TV, bathroom, 5 huge rooms also have sofabed and table for four, coffee shop downstairs; *Douglas Apartments*, Saliña 174, P O Box 3220, Tel: 614549, Fax: 614467, US$56d, a/c, cots available, towels and linen provided, minimum stay 2 nights; outside town, *Wayaca Apartments and Bungalows*, Gosieweg 153, Tel: 375589, Fax: 369797, US$37- 77, a/c, TV, phone, supermarket, launderette, tennis, min 1 week, car rental can be included; houses also available usually on weekly basis or longer.

East of Willemstad is the *Princess Beach*, in a rather desolate area 600 metres from the Seaquarium on a narrow beach, US$120- 200d, Tel: 614944, small pool, shops, casino, rather like a comfortable prison camp; next door is the *Lion's Dive*, attractive, not high rise, wooden balconies give it style, 72 rooms, TV, US$92- 110d including breakfast, tax and service, small pool, unlimited use of Seaquarium, dive shop on site, dive packages available, Tel: 611644, Fax: 618200.

Heading west of Willemstad along the coast are two Golden Tulip resorts overlooking Piscadera Bay: *Las Palmas*, rooms, suites and villas, US$105- 145d, telephone, a/c, TV, pool, tennis, diving and watersports, beach, casino, restaurant, Tel: 625200, Fax: 625962; and *Curaçao Caribbean*, 200 rooms and suites, a/c, US$145- 445d, casino, watersports, tennis, gym; two minutes from the airport is *Holland*, 40 rooms, a/c, TV, phone, business services, restaurant, pool, car rental, US$60d or US$100 for three nights including breakfast, tax and service, Tel: 88044, Fax: 88114; in the centre of the island, at Weg naar Westpunt Z/N, is the 17th century *Landhuis Daniel*, a small, friendly hotel popular with Europeans, children welcome, family rooms, 5 rooms in the landhouse (best) US$45d with a/c, US$37.50d with fans, and 4 small cabin rooms, US$30d, by the pool, basic, being upgraded gradually, good food, diving trips arranged, good shore dive sites close by, car, jeep and motor bike rental, US$30/day, Tel/Fax: 648400; *Coral Cliff*, a Golden Tulip resort on Santa Marta Bay, quiet beach, nice sea, some shade provided, entrance NAf8 for non-residents, sprawling, tatty, concrete block hotel in need of modernization, US$60-

75d, P O Box 3782, Tel: 641610, Fax: 641781, good sea view from restaurant on hill, dive shop on premises; *Bahia Inn*, near Lagun beach, small, basic, adequate, several beds in each room, US$32- 38d, P O Box 3501, Tel: 641000/84417, building work all along this coastal road; at Westpoint, *Jaanchie's* is a popular restaurant with 4 rooms to let, US$40-45d, a/c, bathroom, breakfast included, double beds, can fit extras in, Tel: 640126, 640354.

New hotel, villa or timeshare developments are springing up all over Curaçao. *Kadushi Cliff Resort*, at Westpoint is open although more building work is still to be done; several huge resorts are planned around Knip beach, Lagun, Cas Abou, Piscadera, Parasasa, Cornelis Bay and Jan Thiel. Be prepared for construction work.

Camping at *Brakkeput*, adjoining Spanish Waters, Arowakenweg 41A, P O Box 3291, Tel: 674428, school parties catered for, sports fields, showers and toilets, tents available, US$1.25 pp overnight with min charge US$18.75, cheaper for youth organizations. Camping is allowed on some beaches, but there are no facilities and you have to bring your own fresh water supplies.

Where To Eat

10% service is added to the bill in restaurants but an extra 5% is appreciated. One of the most highly regarded restaurants in Willemstad is *The Wine Cellar* on Concordiastraat, Tel: 612178/674909, owned by chef Nico Cornelisie, a master rotisseur, in small old house, only 8 tables, reservations recommended, open for lunch Tuesday-Friday, dinner Tuesday-Sunday; *Alouette*, in a restored house, Orionweg 12, Tel: 618222, very popular, reservations recommended, French-style food, low-calorie or vegetarian meals available, open 1200-1430, 1900-2200, later at weekends; *Larousse*, also in an old house on Penstraat 5, almost opposite the *Avila Beach*, Tel: 55418, French menu with local and imported North Sea fish, quiet, open 1800-2400, closed Mondays; *Fort Nassau* has a spectacular location with a panoramic view from the 200-year old fort, American-style menu using local ingredients, open Monday-Friday 1200-1400, Monday-Sunday 1830-2300, reservations Tel: 613086; *De Taveerne*, in an octagonal mansion, Landhuis Groot

Davelaar, Tel: 370669, beef and seafood, à la carte menu, antique furnishings, closed Sunday; *Bistro Le Clochard*, in the Rif Fort walls overlooking the harbour, French and Swiss cuisine, Tel: 625666/625667, open Monday-Friday 1200-1400, 1830 onwards, Saturday evenings only, open Sundays in December-March; *La Bistroëlle*, Promenade Shopping Centre, Salinja, Tel: 76929/370408, mainly a steakhouse with US imported beef but fish and local specialities available, open Monday-Saturday 1200-1400, Monday-Sunday 1900-2300; *Grand-Café Pietermaai* on Pietermaai 18, Tel: 617077, good for lunchtime salads and sandwiches as well as dinner, vegetarian meals also, terrace overlooks the sea with view of tankers and cruiseships, open daily 1000-2400, happy hour 1700-1900; same view but in the Waterfort Arches is *Seaview*, open air or indoors, bar and international restaurant, lunch 1200-1400, dinner 1800-2300 daily, Tel: 616688.

For an Indonesian meal it is best to make up a party to get the maximum number of dishes but this is not essential. The best and most popular restaurant is the *Indonesia*, Mercuriusstraat 13, Javanese food specializing in 16 or 25-dish rijstaffel, essential to book, often several days ahead, Tel: 612606/612999, open 1200-1400, 1800-2130 daily, dinner only on Sundays; the *Garuda* at the *Curaçao Caribbean* has also been recommended for a rijstaffel, open air dining overlooking the sea, Tel: 626519, open 1200-1400 daily except Saturday, 1830-2200, closed Monday; *Surabaya* in the Waterfort Arches has good food but no hot plates to keep it warm, vegetarian menu too, Tel: 617388, open Tuesday-Friday 1200-1400, Tuesday-Sunday 1800-2300.

The best place to try local food in Willemstad is the old market building beyond the round concrete market tower by the floating market, here many cooks offer huge portions of good, filling local food cooked in huge pots on charcoal fires, at reasonable prices, choose what you want to eat and sit down at the closest bench or one of the nearby tables having first ordered, takeaway available, very busy at lunchtimes, the best dishes often run out, make sure you have the right money available; the best restaurant for local food is *The Golden Star*, Socratesstraat 2, Tel:

54795/54865, informal, friendly, plastic table cloths and permanent Christmas decorations, tacky but fun, TV showing American sport, home cooking, very filling, popular with locals and tourists, open daily 1100-0100; outside town, *Martha Koosje* on the left on the Westpoint road, Colombian and local specialities particularly seafood, outdoor dining, family run, open 1500-2300, the bar is open until 0200, Tel: 648235; further along the same road, opposite the entrance to the Christoffel Park, is *Oasis*, seafood and creole dishes but also offering chicken and ribs, open 1200-2400, weekends 1030-0300, dinner served until 2100, dancing afterwards, Tel: 640085; *Playa Forti*, atop a cliff overlooking beach of same name, wonderful view, very popular lunchtime at weekends, Colombian and local dishes; further along the road in Westpoint is *Jaanchie's*, another weekend lunchtime favourite with local families although no sea view, huge, filling portions, see the bananaquits eating sugar, parties catered for, takeaway service, bus stops outside for return to Willemstad, Tel: 640126.

A good fish restaurant is *Pisces*, at the end of Caracasbaaiweg, reservations recommended, Tel: 672181; for steak try *Guacamaya Steakhouse*, Schottegatweg West 365, Tel: 89208, US grade beef, ribs and mixed grills, open 1200-1500, 1800-2300, closed Mondays; Chilean food at *El Entablao*, Indjuweg 47, in Rozenburg residential area, Tel: 614855, open Thursday-Sunday 1830-2330 for dinner, bar open later; Italian food at *Baffo & Bretella*, in the Seaquarium, homemade pasta, seafood, open 1200-1400, 1900-2300, closed Tuesdays, reservations required, Tel: 618700; *La Pergola*, in the Waterfort Arches, also serves Italian food, fish, pizza, terrace or a/c dining, Tel: 613482, open 1200-1400 Monday-Saturday, 1830-2230 daily; Chinese food at *Ho Wah*, Saturnusstraat 93, Tel: 615745; *Chung King*, Wilhelminaplein 1, Tel: 611855, open 1100-2145, closed Sunday; a good place for lunch is *Bon Appetit*, Hanchi di Snoa 4 at the end of Gomezplein, Tel: 616916, international and Dutch specialities, pancakes, charming but service has been criticized, open 0800-1900 Monday-Saturday; for drinks, snacks or cheap lunches, *Downtown Terrace*, also in Gomezplein, you can hear the chimes

from the Spritzer and Fuhrmann bells; if you are touring the island, *Landhuis Daniel* is a pleasant place to stop for a drink, snack or light lunch. There is plenty of fast food to cater for most tastes, including pancake houses, and *Pizza House* prides itself on having won awards. Late night fast food, local fashion, can be found at truk'i pans, bread trucks which stay open until 0400-0500 and sell sandwiches filled with conch, goat stew, salt fish and other Antillean specialities.

Food And Drink

Native food is filling and the meat dish is usually accompanied by several different forms of carbohydrate, one of which may be *funchi*, a corn meal bread in varying thickness but usually looking like a fat pancake. Goat stew is popular, slow cooked and mildly spicey, recommended. Soups (*sopi*) are very nourishing and can be a meal on their own, grilled fish or meat (*la paria*) is good although the fish may always be grouper, red snapper or conch, depending on the latest catch; meat, chicken, cheese or fish filled pastries (*pastechi*) are rather like the *empanadas* of South America or Cornish pasties.

While in the Netherlands Antilles, most visitors enjoy trying a *rijsttafel* (rice table), a sort of Asian *smørgasbørd* adopted from Indonesia, and delicious. Because *rijsttafel* consists of anywhere from 15 to 40 separate dishes, it is usually prepared for groups of diners, although some Curaçao restaurants will do a modified version of 10 or 15 dishes.

A limited selection of European and Californian wines is usually available in restaurants, although local waiters have little familiarity with them and it is advisable to examine your bottle well before allowing it to be opened. Table wine is likely to come in small bottles like you get on aeroplanes; it is usually awful. Curaçao's gold-medal-winning Amstel beer – the only beer in the world brewed from desalinated sea water – is very good indeed and available throughout the Netherlands Antilles. Amstel brewery tours are held on Tuesdays and Thursdays at 1000, Tel: 612944, 616922 for information. Some Dutch and other European beers can also be found. Fresh milk is difficult to get hold of and you are nearly always given evaporated milk with your tea or coffee. Curaçao's tap water is good; also distilled from the sea. Many hotels have no hot water taps, only cold.

This is because the water pipes in Curaçao are laid overground, the water in them being warmed by the sun during the day and cold at night.

Entertainment

For "night-owls", there are casinos. All the large hotels have them, with many gaming tables and rows and rows of fruit machines, open virtually all hours. There are many nightclubs and discothèques: *Infinity* is at Fort Nassau, open Friday and Saturday, 2100-0200, Tel: 613450; *Naick's Place*, Lindbergweg 32, Salinja, Tel: 614640, open Wednesday-Monday 2200-0400, live music Thursday-Friday; *Luigi's Club*, Waterfort Arches, Tel: 618680, open daily 2100-0400, merengue on Wednesday; *Blue Note Jazz Café*, Doormanweg 37, Tel: 370685, open Monday-Saturday from 1900; *De Fles*, Schottegatweg West 367, Tel: 84576, open daily 1800-0400, disco and restaurant; *The Pub*, Salinja, Tel: 612190, open daily from 2100, happy hour 2100-2200; *Jabulani African Bar*, Waterfort Arches, open 1400-0200, happy hour, 1800-1900. The Centro Pro Arte presents concerts, ballets and plays. While on the subject of entertainment, one of the most bizarre sights of Curaçao, not dealt with in the tourist brochures, is the government-operated red-light area, aptly named Campo Alegre. Close to the airport, it resembles a prison camp and is even guarded by a policeman.

Shops

Open on Sunday morning and lunchtimes if cruise ships are in port. Weekday opening is 0800-1200 and 1400-1800. The main tourist shopping is in Punda (see above). Willemstad's jewellery shops are noted for the quality of their stones.

Bookshops

Boekhandel Mensing in Punda has a limited selection of guide books and maps. Larger and more well stocked bookshops are out of the centre of Willemstad. Boekhandel Salas in the Foggerweg has good maps and guide book section as has Mensings' Caminada in the Schottegatweg and Van Dorp in the Promenade Shopping Centre. The public Library is a modern building in Scharloo, cross the bridge by the floating market, turn right along the water and it is on your left. The Reading Room has books in Dutch, English, Spanish, French and Papiamento.

Banks

Algemene Bank Nederland, Banco Popular Antilliano, Banco Venezolano Antillanc First National Bank of Boston, Maduro & Curiel Bank on Plaza Jojo Correa, Tel 611100, Banco di Caribe on Schottegatweg Oost, Tel: 616588 Banking hours are 0830-1200 and 1300-1630 Monday to Friday.

Currency

The currency is the guilder, divided into 100 cents. There are coins of 1, 2½, 5, 10 25 cents and 1 guilder, and notes of 1, 5 10, 25, 50, 100, 250 and 500 guilders. The exchange rate is US$1=NAf1.77 for bank notes, NAf1.79 for cheques, although the rate of exchange offered by shops and hotels ranges from NAf1.75-1.80. Credit cards and US dollars are widely accepted.

Warning

Beware of a tree with small, poisonous green apples that borders some beaches This is the manchineel (*manzanilla*) and it sap causes burns on exposed skin.

Health

The climate is healthy and non-malarial epidemic incidence is slight. Rooms without air-conditioning or window and door screens may need mosquito nets during the wetter months of November and December and sometimes May and June, and, although some spraying is done in tourist areas, mosquitoes are a problem Some anti-mosquito protection is recommended if you are outdoors any evening. The 550-bed St Elisabeth Hospital is a well-equipped and modern hospital with good facilities including a coronary unit and two decompression chambers For emergencies, Tel: 624900 (hospital) 625822 (ambulance). The Sentro Mediko Santa Rosa, at Santa Rosaweg 329, is open seven days a week, 0700-0000, laboratory on the premises, Tel: 676666, 672300.

Emergency

Emergency telephone numbers: Police and Fire Department Tel: 114 or 44444, ambulance 112, 625822, 89337 or 89266.

National Holidays

New Year's Day, Carnival Monday (February), Good Friday, Easter Monday, Queen's Birthday (30 April), Labour Day (1 May), Ascension Day, Flag Day (2 July), Christmas on 25 and 26 December.

Time Zone

Atlantic Standard Time, 4 hours behind GMT, 1 ahead of EST.

Electric Current

110/130 volts AC, 50 cycles.

Telecommunications

All American Cables & Radio Inc, Keukenstraat; Kuyperstraat; Radio Holland NV, De Ruytergade 51; Sita, Curaçao Airport.

Telephone rates abroad are published in the telephone book, but beware if phoning from a hotel, you can expect a huge mark up, check their rates before you call. To Europe, US$3.05 a minute, to the USA US$1.60, to Australia and Africa US$5.55, to the Netherlands Antilles US$0.55, Central America US$3.90, Venezuela US$1.10, Leeward and Windward Islands US$1.75.

Places of Worship

Curaçao has always had religious tolerance and as a result there are many faiths and denominations on the island. Details of services can be found in the official free guide, Curaçao Holiday, which lists Anglican, Catholic, Jewish, Protestant and other churches. Anglican Church, Leidenstraat, Tel: 53251; Holy Family Church (Roman Catholic), Mgr Neiwindstraat, Otrabanda, Tel: 62527; Methodist Church, Abr de Veerstraat 10, Tel: 75834; Mikvé Israel – Emanuel Synagogue, Hanchi Snoa 29, Punda, Tel: 611067; Ebenezer Church of the United Protestant Congregation, Oranjestraat, Tel: 53121; Christian Heritage Ministries (Evangelical), Polarisweg 27, Zeelandia, Tel: 615663; Church of Christ, 40 Schottegatweg West, Tel: 627628; Church of God Prophecy (Ecumenical), Caricauweg 35, Tel: 75306.

Tour Agencies

Harbour Tours, Tel: 611257, do 1-hour tours of Fort Nassau, Naval base, Container Harbour, dry dock and oil refinery on M/S Hilda Veronica and M/S Veronica 2, from Handels Kade, Punda, adults US$7, children US$4, also sea shuttle Willemstad - Seaquarium and Princess Beach, US$7 adults, US$4 children, and day trips to Bonaire. Daltino Tours do island coach tours eg to the east US$10, to the west US$16, day trips to Aruba, US$160, to Bonaire US$125, to Caracas US$195, Tel: 614888; Taber Tours do an eastern tour including the Seaquarium and glass bottomed boat trip for US$27.50 adults, US$17.50 children under 12, a western tour is US$12, children US$6, to Aruba US$135, Bonaire US$120. Old City Tours do a walking tour of Otrabanda, 1715-1900, US$5.55 including a drink, Tel: 613554.

Tourist Office

The main office of the Curaçao Tourism Development Bureau is at Pietermaai 19, Willemstad, PO Box 3266, Tel: 616000, Fax: 612305. However tourists should go to the offices at Waterfort Plaza, Tel: 613397 and the airport, Tel: 86789, offering helpful information, assistance in finding a hotel, brochures, maps, etc. There are also several Visitor Information Centres dotted round Willemstad and some booths sponsored by resort hotels, which have irregular hours. Curaçao Holiday is a useful, free guide, the walking tour of Willemstad described in the brochure is recommended. The Beach Herald, a weekly English language newspaper for tourists is available in hotels.

USA In New York: 400 Madison Avenue, suite 311, NY 10017, Tel: 212-751 8266.

Venezuela In Caracas: Avenida Francisco de Miranda, Centro Comercial Country, piso 2, Tel: 713403.

Holland: Benelux, Eendrachtsweg 69-C, 3012 LG Rotterdam, Tel: 010 414-2639.

ARUBA

Introduction

ARUBA, smallest and most westerly of the ABC group, lies 25 km north of Venezuela and 68 km west of Curaçao, at 12° 30'N, outside the hurricane belt. It is 31.5 km long, 10 km at its widest, with an area of 184 sq km. The average yearly temperature is 27.5°C, constantly cooled by northeasterly trade winds, with the warmest months being August and September, the coolest January and February. Average annual rainfall is less than 510 mm, and the humidity averages 76%. Like Curaçao and Bonaire, Aruba has scant vegetation, its interior or *cunucu* is a dramatic landscape of scruffy bits of foliage, mostly cacti, the weird, wind-bent dividivi trees and tiny bright red flowers called *fioritas*, plus huge boulders, caves and lots of dust.

Aruba is one of the very few Caribbean islands on which the Indian population was not exterminated although there are no full-blooded Indians now. The Aruban today is a descendant of the indigenous Arawak Indians, with a mixture of Spanish and Dutch blood from the early colonizers. There was no plantation farming in Aruba, so African slaves were never introduced. Instead, the Indians supervised the raising of cattle, horses, goats and sheep, and their delivery to the other Dutch islands. They were generally left alone and maintained regular contact with the mainland Indians. They lived mostly in the north at Ceru Cristal and then at Alto Vista, where in 1750 the first Catholic church was founded. The last Indians to speak an Indian language were buried in urns about 1800; later Indians lost their language and culture. When Lago Oil came to Aruba many workers from the British West Indies came to work in the refinery in San Nicolas, leading to Caribbean English becoming the colloquial tongue there instead of Papiamento. Of the total population today of about 65,500, including some 40 different nationalities, only about two-thirds were actually born on the island. The official language here, as in the other Netherlands Antilles, is Dutch, but Papiamento is the colloquial tongue. English and Spanish are widely spoken and the people are extremely welcoming. The crime rate is low and there are very few attacks on tourists.

The Economy

Gold was discovered in 1825, but the mine ceased to be economic in 1916. In 1929, black gold brought real prosperity to Aruba when Lago Oil and Transport Co, a subsidiary of Exxon, built a refinery at San Nicolas at the eastern end of the island. At that time it was the largest refinery in the world, employing over 8,000 people. In March 1985 Exxon closed the refinery, a serious shock for the Aruban economy, and one which the Government has striven to overcome. In 1989, Coastal Oil of Texas signed an agreement with the Government to reopen part of the refinery by 1991, with an initial capacity of 150,000 barrels a day, rising to perhaps 300,000 b/d by 1993, but plans were delayed because of the Gulf crisis. The project is to create 1,500 jobs.

Aruba has three ports. San Nicolas is used for the import and transshipment of crude oil and materials for the refinery and for the export of oil products. There are also two sea-berths at San Nicolas capable of handling the largest tankers in the world. Oranjestad is the commercial port

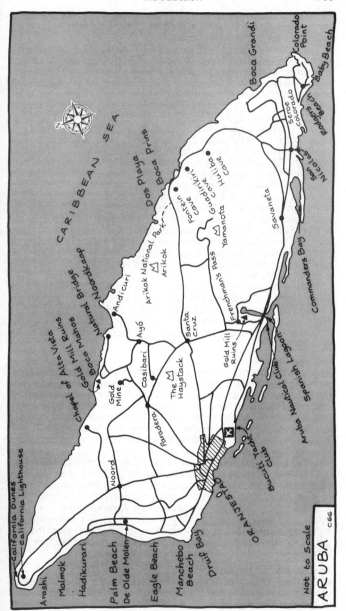

California Dunes
California Lighthouse
Arashi
Malmok
Hadikurari
Palm Beach
De Olde Molen
Eagle Beach
Manchebo Beach
Druif Bay

Chapel of Alta Vista
Gold Mill Ruins
Boca Nanos
Natural Bridge
Noordkaap

CARIBBEAN SEA

N

Andicuri
Ayó
Casibari
Gold Mine
The Haystack
Paradera
Noord

Dos Playa
Boca Prins

Arikok National Park
Arikok

Santa Cruz
Gold Mill Ruins

Fontein Cave
Guadirikiri Cave
Huliba Cave
Yamanota

Boca Grandi
Colorado Point
Baby Beach
Rodgers Beach
Seroe Colorado
Nicolas

Savaneta

Frenchman's Pass
Aruba Nautical Club
Spanish Lagoon
Commanders Bay

ORANJESTAD
Bucuti Yacht Club

Not to Scale

ARUBA c66

of Aruba, and it is open for day and night navigation. In 1962 the port of Barcadera was built to facilitate shipment of products from Aruba's new industrial zone on the leeward coast.

The economic crisis of 1985 forced the Government to turn to the IMF for help. The Fund recommended that Aruba promote tourism and increase the number of hotel rooms by 50%. The Government decided, however, to triple hotel capacity to 6,000 rooms, which it was estimated would provide employment for 20% of the population. Hotel construction has expanded rapidly and marketing efforts have attracted investors and visitors from as far afield as Japan. By 1990 tourist accommodation in fifteen major high rise and low rise hotels reached 3,326 rooms, with many more available in small hotels, guest houses and apartments. The economy is now overwhelmingly dependent on tourism for income, with 501,324 stayover visitors in 1991, a rise of 16% over 1990. Nearly 53% of tourists came from the USA; the next largest country of origin was Venezuela. A further 133,195 passengers arrived on cruiseships in 1991, a rise of 2.5% over 1990. Efforts are now being made to diversify away from a single source of revenues into areas such as re-exporting through the free trade zone, and offshore finance. Aruba is still dependent on the Netherlands for budget support and the aim is to reduce the level of financial assistance. New legislation has been approved to encourage companies to register on the island by granting tax and other benefits. Regulations are generally flexible and unrestricting on offshore business, although efforts are being made to ensure an efficient level of supervision.

There is no unemployment on Aruba and labour is imported for large projects such as the refinery and construction work. Turkish guest workers came to help get Coastal started and Philippinos work in the high rise hotels. The Government is encouraging skilled Arubans to return from Holland but is hampered by a housing shortage and a consequent boom in real estate prices.

Flora and Fauna

About 170 species of birds can be found on Aruba, about 50 species breed on the island. The most common birds are the trupiaal (with its bright orange colours), the chuchubi, the prikichi (a little parrot) and the barika geel (the little yellow-bellied bird you will find eating the sugar on the table in your hotel). An interesting site to see waterfowl is the Bubali Plassen, opposite the Olde Molen. Here you can often find cormorants, herons and fish eagle. Brown pelicans can be found along the southern shore. As well as various kinds of lizards. Aruba has large iguanas. These animals are hunted to prepare a typical Arubian soup. Two kinds of snakes can be found on Aruba: the Santanero, a harmless little snake (however, be careful when you pick it up, because it defecates in your hand) and the not so harmless rattle snake. Aruba's rattle snake is a unique subspecies and does not use its rattle. Rattle snakes live in the triangular area between the Yamanota, Fontein and San Nicolas. The best place to go looking for rattle snakes, if you really want to, is the area south of the Yamanota mountain. In the unlikely event that you get a bite from a rattle snake, go immediately to the hospital. They have anti-serum.

Beaches and Watersports

Of the three ABC islands, Aruba stands out as having the best beaches, all of which are public and free. There are good, sandy beaches on both sides of the island although fewer on the east side which is rough and not so good for swimming. Travelling northwards along the west coast from Oranjestad an excellent road takes you to the main resort areas where nearly all the hotels are gathered. Druif beach starts at the *Tamarijn Divi Beach Resort*, extending and widening along the coast to the sister hotel, the *Divi Divi*, with good windsurfing. At the *Best Western Manchebo* there is a huge expanse of sand, often seen in advertisements; Caribasurf, *Manchebo Beach Resort*, Tel: 23444, Fax: 32446, windsurfing boards and instruction. North of here is Eagle Beach, where the 'low rise' hotels are separated from the beach by the road, and then Palm Beach, where the 'high rise' hotels front directly on to the beach. These three sandy beaches extend for several miles, the water is calm, clear and safe for children, although watch out for watersports and keep within markers where provided.

North of Palm Beach is an area of very shallow water with no hotels to break the wind, known as Fisherman's Huts, which is excellent for very fast windsurfing. Surfers from all over the world come here to enjoy their sport and professionals often come here for photo sessions. Although speeds are high and there is a strong offshore wind, surfing is quite safe and there are several rescue boats to get you back if the wind blows you to Panama. This beach is called Malmok (southern end) or Arashi (northern end) and there are many villas and guesthouses across the road which cater for windsurfers. Windsurfing Aruba is a sympathetic small firm by the Heineken flags at the huts which rents equipment and gives lessons to beginners and intermediates at reasonable prices, Tel: 33472, Fax: 34407. There are other operators of high quality with higher prices: Roger's Windsurf Place, L G Smith Blvd 472, Tel/Fax: 21918, windsurf packages available, boards and accommodation; Sailboard Vacation, L G Smith Blvd 462, Tel: 21072, boards of different brands for rent. For information about the Aruba Hi-Winds Pro/Am boardsailing competitions at Eagle Beach, opposite *La Cabana Beach Hotel*, contact the B T A Group at L G Smith Boulevard 62, Tel: 35454, Fax: 37266. They usually take place around the same time as the Jazz and Latin Festival in June.

A residential area stretches up from Arashi to the lighthouse and the coast is indented with tiny rocky bays and sandy coves, the water is beautiful and good for snorkelling, while shallow and safe for children. It is also a fishing ground for the brown pelicans. At night they normally sleep in the shallow water close to the lighthouse. A little way after the lighthouse, if you follow the coastroad, there is a very spectacular place where high waves smash against the rocks at a small inlet. There is a blow hole, where water sometimes spouts up more than five metres.

At the other end of the island is Seroe Colorado, known as 'the colony', which used to be a residential area for Exxon staff but is currently used as temporary housing. You have to enter the zone through a guard post, but there is no entrance fee and no hindrance. There are two west facing beaches here worth visiting. Rodgers Beach has a snack bar, showers, yachts and is protected by a reef but is in full view of the refinery. Baby Beach, on the other hand, is round the corner, out of sight of the refinery, in a lovely sandy bay, protected by the reef, nice swimming and snorkelling, very busy on Sundays, with toilets but little shade. Sea Grape Grove and Boca Grandi, on the eastern coast of the southern tip has good snorkelling and swimming, being protected by a reef, and is popular with tours who come to see the largest elkhorn coral. Experienced windsurfers come here to wave jump. The prison is near here, remarkable for the pleasant sea view from the cells. Other beaches on the eastern side of the island are Boca Prins, where there are sand dunes, and further north from there, reached by a poor road, is Dos Playa where there is good surf for body surfing. The landscape is hilly and barren because of serious overgrazing by herds of goats. Andicouri is also popular with surfers, note that if you approach it through the coconut grove you will have to pay US$1 for crossing private land, but there is an alternative route which is free.

Virtually every type of watersport is available and most hotels provide extensive facilities. Activities which are not offered on site can be arranged through several tour agencies such as De Palm Tours, Tel: 24545 or ECO Destination Management. Caribbean Watersports, Tel: 29118, open 1000-1630, rents jetskis US$35, waterskis US$20 and snorkelling equipment US$15. Parasailing can be done from the high-rise hotels. Glass bottomed boat trips from various locations are around US$20, but can be more for a sunset cruise. Several yachts and catamarans offer cruises along the coast with stops for snorkelling and swimming. A morning cruise often includes lunch (about US$40), an afternoon trip will be drinks only – and then there are the sunset booze cruises (about US$20). *Pelican I* is a 50-foot catamaran running along the west coast from Pelican pier; *Wave Dancer*, another catamaran, departs from *Holiday Inn* beach, Tel: 25520; *Tranquilo*, a yacht, can be contacted through Mike, its captain Tel: 47533, or Pelican Tours Tel: 31228. *Mi Dushi* is an old sailing ship which starts cruises from the *Tamarijn Beach Resort*, morning and lunch US$35, snorkelling and sunset US$24, sunset booze cruise US$20, pirate sails and beach party US$40, Tel: 25842 or De Palm Tours.

Near Spanish Lagoon is the Aruba Nautical Club complex, with pier facilities offering safe, all-weather mooring for almost any size of yacht, plus gasoline, diesel fuel, electricity and water. For information, write to P O Box 161. A short sail downwind from there is the Bucuti Yacht Club with clubhouse and storm-proofed pier providing docking, electricity, water and other facilities. Write to P O Box 743.

Over a dozen charter boats are available for half or whole day deep sea fishing. The Tourist Office has a list so you can contact the captain direct, or else go through De Palm Tours or ECO Destination Management. Whole day trips including food and drinks range from US$350-480, depending on the number of people on board. Deep sea fishing tournaments are held in October and November at the Aruba Nautical Club and the Bucuti Yacht Club.

Diving and Marine Life

Visibility in Aruban waters is about 30 metres in favourable conditions and snorkelling and scuba diving is good, although not as spectacular as in the waters around Bonaire. A coral reef extends along the western side of the island from California reef in the north to Baby Beach reef in the south, with dives varying in depth from 5 to 45 metres. Organized boat trips regularly visit the two wrecks worth exploring, although they can get a bit crowded. One is a German freighter, the *Antilia*, which went down just after World War II was declared and is found in 20 metres of water off Malmok beach on the western coast. You can see quite a lot just snorkelling here as parts of the wreck stick up above the water. Snorkelling boat trips usually combine Malmok beach and the wreck. The other wreck is nearby in 10 metres of water, the *Pedernales*, a flat-bottomed oil tanker which was hit in a submarine attack in May 1941, while ferrying crude oil from Venezuela to Aruba.

There are several scuba diving operations and prices vary from US$30-40 for a single tank dive, US$35-45 for a night dive and US$55-65 for an introductory course and dive. Snorkelling is usually around US$15. *The Talk of the Town* has a beach bar and pool opposite the hotel and across the road, in full view of the airport runway; Hallo Aruba Dive Shop on the premises offers dive packages with wall diving, deep diving, drift diving or beach diving, Tel: 38270 or 23380 ext 254. Aruba Pro Dive is on the beach at *Playa Linda*, Tel: 25520. S E A Scuba, Charlie's Buddies, is at Savaneta, P O Box 97, Rondweg, Savaneta 196, Tel: 47930, Fax: 41640. Red Sail Sports, L G Smith Blvd 83, P O Box 218, Tel: 31603, and at hotels, sailing, snorkelling, diving with certification courses, windsurfing, waterskiing, hobie cats etc. Scuba Aruba has a retail operation in Seaport Village selling all watersports equipment, open Monday-Saturday 0900-1900, Tel: 34142.

The Atlantis Submarine has hourly dives 1000-1500 most days from the Seaport Village Marina. A catamaran takes you past the airport and the local garbage dump to where the submarine begins its one-hour tour of the Barcadera reef to a depth of 50 metres, turning frequently so that both sides can see. Recommended for those who are interested in marine life but do not scuba dive, but not for anyone who is claustrophobic. The submarine takes 46 passengers and is nearly always full, particularly when a cruise ship is in port, so book beforehand, US$58 adults, Arubans and children aged 4-12 US$29, no children under four allowed, Tel: 36090. Lunchtime is quite a good time to go, it is not so full then; Thursday is a bad day when a lot of cruise ships come in. Throwaway cameras with 400 ASA film, US$20, are available at the ticket office.

Other Sports
There is a nine-hole golf course with oiled sand greens and goats near San Nicolas, golf clubs for rent US$6, green fee US$10 for 18 holes, US$7.50 for 9 holes, Tel: 42006, Saturday and Sunday members only, open daily 0800-1700. At the *Holiday Inn* is an 18-hole mini-golf course. A mini golf course called Adventure Golf has been built opposite *La Cabana*, close to Bubali, in a nice garden. A large golf course is planned near the lighthouse, but the need to import water and completely alter the barren landscape will prevent it coming into operation before the turn of the century. There are tennis courts at most major hotels. Horseriding at Rancho El Paso, Washington 44, near Santa Ana Church, Tel: 23310 or 24244, Paso Fino horses, daily rides except Sunday, 1 hour through countryside or 2 hours part beach, part *cunucu*. The Eagle Bowling Palace at Pos Abou has 12 lanes, of which six are for reservation, open 1000-0200, US$9 from 1000-1500, US$10.50 from 1500-0200, US$1.20 shoe rental; also three racquetball courts available. Wings Over Aruba, at the airport, Tel: 37104, Fax: 37124, has a pilot school, with sightseeing flights, aerial photography, aircraft rental; sightseeing in a seaplane US$130/half hour, trial flying lesson US$120/90 minutes. Sailcarts available at a special rink not on the beach, Aruba Sailcart N V, Bushiri 213, Tel: 36005, open 0900-sunset, US$15/30 minutes for a single cart, US$20/30 minutes for a double cart. Drag races are held several times a year at the Palo Margo circuit near San Nicolas. A 10-km mini-marathon is held annually in June, contact the Tourist Office for details.

Festivals
The most important festival of the year is Carnival, held from the Sunday two weeks preceding Lent, starting with Children's Carnival. There are colourful parades and competitions for best musician, best dancer, best costume etc. The culmination is the Grand Parade on the Sunday preceding Lent. Other festive occasions during the year include New Year, when fireworks are let off

at midnight and musicians and singers go round from house to house (and hotel to hotel); National Anthem and Flag Day on 18 March, when there are displays of national dancing and other folklore, and St John's Day on 24 June, which is another folklore day: "Derramento di Gai". For visitors who do not coincide their trip with one of the annual festivals, there is a weekly Bonbini show in the courtyard of the Fort Zoutman museum on Tuesday 1830-2030, US$1, music, singing and dancing, interesting but overenthusiastic MC. In June there is a well-attended and popular festival of jazz and Latin American music, with many famous musicians and bands playing. Contact the Aruba Tourism Authority, PO Box 1019, Oranjestad, Tel: 23777, Fax: 34702, for information on the programme and package tours available. The International Theatre Festival takes place annually; for information contact CCA, Vondellaan 2, Tel: 21758. There is also a Dance Festival in October, for information Tel: 24581.

Oranjestad

Oranjestad, the capital of Aruba, population about 17,000, is a bustling little freeport town where "duty-free" generally implies a discount rather than a bargain. The main shopping area is on Caya G F (Betico) Croes, formerly named Nassaustraat, and streets off it; also shops in the Port of Call Market Place, Seaport Village Mall, Harbour Town, The Galleries, Strada I and II and the Holland Aruba Mall. Many of the buildings in the colourful Antillean style are actually modern and do not date from colonial times as in Willemstad, Curaçao.

There is a small museum in the restored 17th century Fort Zoutman/Willem III Tower, Zoutmanstraat, Tel: 26099, open Monday-Friday, 0900-1600, Saturday, 0900-1200, entrance Afl 1. Named the **Museo Arubano**, it contains items showing the island's history and geology, with fossils, shells, tools, furniture and products. The fort, next to the Parliament buildings, opposite the police station, dates from 1796 and marks the beginning of Oranjestad as a settlement. Built with four guns to protect commercial traffic, in 1810-1911 it sheltered the government offices. The tower was added around 1868 with the first public clock and a petrol lamp in the spire, which was first lit on King Willem III's birthday in 1869 and served as a lighthouse. The Fort was restored in 1974 and the tower in 1980-83. The **Archaeological Museum** on Zoutmanstraat 1, Tel: 28979, is open Monday-Friday 0800-1200, 1330-1630. Small, but cleverly laid out in three parts, Preceramic, Ceramic (from 500 AD) and Historic (from 1500-1800 AD when the Indians used European tools). The two main sites excavated are Canashitu and Malmok and most objects come from these. The descriptions are in English and Papiamento, easy to read and educational. Recommended, the best museum in the ABCs. A numismatic museum, **Mario's Worldwide Coin Collection**, J E Irausquin Plein No 2A, behind St Francis Church, beside Instituto di Cultura Aruba, Tel: 28831, has a large collection of coins from over 400 countries and coins from ancient Greece, Rome, Syria and Egypt. Interesting and well laid out, the museum is run by the daughter of the collector, Mario Odor; donations welcomed. Open

---

Oranjestad: Key to map

1. Wilhelmina Park; 2. Plaza Daniel Leo; 3. Protestant Church; 4. Roman Catholic Church; 5. Fort Zoutman and William III Tower; 6. Archaeological Museum; 7. Numismatic Museum; 8. Government Office and Parliament; 9. Court of Justice; 10. Customs House; 11. Tourism Bureau; 12. Telephone Exchange; 13. Post Office (off map); 14. Fruit Market; 15. Seaport Village Mall; 166. *Sonesta Hotel*; 17. Crystal Casino; 18. *Atlantis* Submarine.

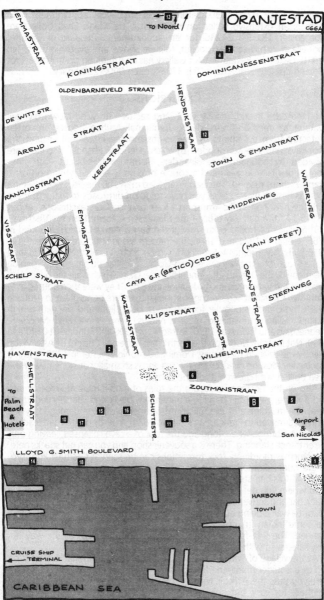

Monday-Friday, 0730-1630, Saturday and Sunday by appointment only. There is an extensive collection of shells at De Man's Shell Collection, Morgenster 18, Tel: 24246 for an appointment. The Cas di Cultura, Vondellaan 2, has concerts, ballet, folklore shows and art exhibitions, Tel: 21010. *Gasparito* Restaurant/Art Gallery has an exhibition of Aruban art for sale and display, Gasparito 3, Tel: 37044, open 0900-2300 daily.

Excursions

The landscape is arid, mostly scrub and cactus with wind blown divi divi (watapana) trees and very dusty. Traditional Aruban houses are often protected from evil spirits by 'hex' signs molded in cement around the doorways and are surrounded by cactus fences. Flashes of colour are provided by bougainvillea, oleanders, flamboyant, hibiscus and other tropical plants. You will need a couple of days to see everything on offer inland without rushing. The Esso Road Map marks all the sites worth seeing and it is best to hire a car as you have to go on dirt roads to many of them and there is no public transport. Tour agencies do excursions, about US$15-17 for a half day tour of the island, see **Information for Visitors**.

The village of Noord is known for the **Santa Anna Church**, founded in 1766, rebuilt in 1831 and 1886, the present stone structure was erected in 1916 by Father Thomas V Sadelhoff, whose portrait is on the twelfth station of the Cross. It has heavily carved neo-Gothic oak altar, pulpit and communion rails made by the Dutchman, Hendrik van der Geld, which were the prize work shown at the Vatican Council exhibition in 1870. They were then housed in St Anthony's Church at Scheveningen in Holland, before being given to Aruba in 1928. The church is popular for weddings, being light and airy with a high vaulted ceiling and stained glass windows. Services are held Mondays, Wednesdays and Fridays at 1830, Saturdays at 1900 and Sundays at 0730 and 1800. Not far from Noord on the north coast is the tiny **Chapel of Alto Vista**, built by the Spanish missionary, Domingo Antonio Silvester in 1750. It is in a spectacular location overlooking the sea and is so small that stone pews have been built in semi circles outside the Chapel.

Also on the north coast are the ruins of a gold mine at Seroe Gerard and a refinery at Bushiribana in a particularly bleak and sparsely vegetated area. The machinery at the mill, right on the coast, was damaged by sea spray and moved to Frenchman's Pass in 1824. A partly paved road leads to the natural bridge where long ago the roof of a cave collapsed, leaving only the entrance standing. There is a souvenir shop and you can get snacks here.

Inland, extraordinary rock formations can be seen at **Casibari** and **Ayó**, where huge, diorite boulders have been carved into weird shapes by the wind. At Casibari steps have been made so that you can climb to the top, from where you get a good view of the island and the Haystack. There is a snack bar and souvenir shop. Ayó does not have steps, you have to clamber up, but a wall is being built up around the rocks to keep out the goats. There are some Indian inscriptions. Toilets, a snack bar and souvenir shop are planned. The 541-foot **Hooiberg**, or Haystack, has steps all the way up. Very safe, even with children, the view is worth the effort.

At the village of **Santa Cruz**, just southeast of the Haystack, a cross on top of a boulder marks the first mission on the island. Travelling east from here you pass the **Arikok National Park**, where there are some well laid out trails for easy, but hot, walking. The road leads to Boca Prins (dune sliding) and the **Fontein** cave. Admission to the cave is free, you can hire helmets and flashlights. There is a large chamber at the entrance, with natural pillars, and a 100-metre tunnel leading off, halfway down which are Indian paintings. Despite the desolation of the area, there is a well near the caves with brackish water, which a Japanese man uses to cultivate vegetables for the Chinese restaurants on the island. Further along the coast are the **Guadirikiri** caves, two large chambers lit by sunlight, connected by passages and pillars, with a 100-metre tunnel, for which you need a torch. Bats live in this cave system. The road around the coast here is very bumpy and dusty, being used by quarry trucks. A third cave, **Huliba**, is known as the Tunnel of Love. Again, no entry fee but helmets (US$2.50) and torches available. The walk through the tunnel takes 20-30 minutes with a 10-minute return walk overground.

The road then takes you to *San Nicolas* where there is a strong smell of oil. After the closure of the oil refinery in 1985, San Nicolas was a ghost town, but now that Coastal Oil has taken over the refinery, activity is beginning to pick up. Old wooden houses are being demolished and new concrete houses built instead. A landmark is *Charlie's Bar*, which has been in operation since 1941; a good place to stop for refreshment to see the souvenirs hanging everywhere.

Returning northwest towards Oranjestad you pass through Savaneta, where the Dutch marines have a camp. Turn off to the left to *Brisas del Mar*, a good seafood restaurant open to the sea, very popular. At Pos Chiquito, a walkway leads through mangroves to *Isla di Oro*, a restaurant built like a ship where there is dancing at weekends and pedalos and watersports. A little further on a bay with shallow water and mangroves is ideal for snorkelling beginners. The view is not spectacular but you can see many colourful fish. **Spanish Lagoon**, once a pirates' hideout, is a seawater channel, at the mouth of which is the Aruba Nautical Club and the water desalination plant. At the other end is a bird sanctuary where parakeets breed and the ruins of the Balashi gold mill dating from 1899, where the machinery is better preserved than at Bushiribana. There is quicksand in the area around the bird sanctuary, so it is not advisable to walk there. Nearby is **Frenchman's Pass** where the French attacked the Indians in 1700. From here you can turn east again to drive up **Jamanota**, at 188 metres the highest elevation on the island.

Information for Visitors

Documents

US and Canadian citizens only require proof of identity, such as birth certificate, certificate of naturalization or voter registration card. Other nationalities need a passport. A return or onward ticket and proof of adequate funds are also required. Dogs and cats are permitted entry if they have a valid rabies and health certificate. However, no pets are allowed from South or Central America. Check with your hotel to see if they are allowed to stay.

How To Get There

KLM has direct flights from Amsterdam and on to Panama City or Lima. Air Aruba also flies direct from Amsterdam.

American Airlines (daily from JFK) and Air Aruba (six days a week from Newark) fly from New York; Air Aruba, BWIA, and ALM fly from Miami; American Airlines from Los Angeles, Chicago, Philadelphia and San Juan, Puerto Rico; Viasa from Houston; ALM, Key Airlines and Aeropostal from Atlanta, Aeropostal from Orlando; Key Airlines from Savannah, Georgia. Avianca flies from Barranquilla, Medellín and Bogotá, Servivensa and Air Aruba from Maracaibo and also Viasa, Aeropostal and Avensa from Caracas; from Las Piedras on the Paraguaná Peninsula with Air Aruba, Servivensa and Avensa. VASP flies from São Paulo via Manaus weekly, Air Aruba has a weekly flight from São Paulo via Belem and from Paramaribo.

Within the Caribbean, there are flights from Trinidad and Tobago (daily) with BWIA and from Santo Domingo and Sint Maarten with Air Aruba, as well as frequent flights from Bonaire and Curaçao with ALM and Air Aruba.

Airport tax US$10. Airline offices: Air Aruba at the airport, Tel: 22467; KLM/ ALM/ SLM/ VASP/ Air France/ BWIA/ Avianca information centre, Tel: 24800; American Airlines, Tel: 22700; Aeropostal/ Dominicana de Aviación, Tel: 26609; Avensa, Tel: 27779.

Ferry

There is a ferry service to Muaco terminal in La Vela de Coro leaving Aruba 2000 Thursday, arriving Curaçao 0800, leaving Curaçao Friday 1200, arriving Coro 1800, returning Coro Wednesday 2400 direct to Aruba, arriving Thursday 0800, round trip US$75, with car US$165. One way ticket to Venezuela US$42.50, only if you have air ticket out of Curaçao or Venezuela. Hut for the night US$3.50. Book ticket through Rufo U Winterdaal, Eman Trading Co, LG Smith Blvd 108, Oranjestad (PO Box 384), Tel: 21533/21156, Fax: 22135, Telex: 5027. The ferry is not promoted for tourists and used mainly for food and goods transport, it is shabby and the tradewinds make it bumpy, the return air fare is the same price and the flight takes only 20 minutes. Arriving at Oranjestad customs officers come aboard. The harbour is five minutes' walk from the town, there are a tourist information centre and some souvenir shops which open if a cruise ship is in. A fruit boat leaves once a week for Punto Fijo, Venezuela; check with Agencia Marítima La Confianza, Braziliëstraat 6 (Tel: 23814), Oranjestad.

Taxis

Telephone the dispatcher at Alhambra Bazaar or Boulevard Centre, Tel: 22116/ 21604. Drivers speak English, and individual tours can be arranged. Taxis do not have meters. Ask for flat rate tariffs. From the airport to Oranjestad is US$9, to the low rise hotels US$11 and to the high rise hotels US$12.

Buses

The bus station is behind Parliament on Zoutmanstraat. Bus No 1, every half hour until 1800 between town and the hotels on Eagle and Palm Beach; also to San Nicolas (schedules available at the hotels and the Tourist Office). One way fare is US$0.90. Otherwise there are "jitney cars" which operate like colectivos; the fare is US$1.00. A jitney or bus from Oranjestad to San Nicolas will drop you at the airport.

Self-Drive Cars

You must have a valid foreign or international driver's licence and be at least 21 to rent a car. Airways (Tel: 21845/ 29112), Hertz (Tel: 24545/ 24886), Avis (Tel: 28787/ 25496), Budget (Tel: 28600/ 25423), National (Tel: 21967/ 25451), Dollar (Tel: 22783/ 25651) and Thrifty (Tel: 35300/ 35335) have offices in Oranjestad and at the airport. Many companies also have desks in the hotels. Prices begin at US$35 daily, US$215 weekly, with unlimited mileage. Often when you rent a 4WD vehicle (recommended for getting to beaches like Dos Playa) you cannot take out all risks insurance. George Rental is the biggest 4WD rental company. Motorcycles, mopeds, and bicycles can also be rented; a 50cc moped or scooter costs around US$10-15 a day, a 250cc motorcycle US$35, a Harley Davidson SP1100 US$80 and a 10-speed touring bicycle US$8. The Tourist Office has a list of rental companies. Beware the local drivers, who are aggressive. Driving is on the right and all traffic, except bicycles, coming from the right should be given right of way, except at T junctions. Good maps are available at petrol stations, US$0.90.

Where To Stay

A cluster of glittering luxury hotels has sprung up along Druif Bay, and Eagle and Palm beaches; decent, cheap accommodation is now very difficult to find. High season winter rates (16 December to 15 April) quoted here are roughly double low season rates. A 5% government tax and 10-15% service charge must be added; some hotels also add a US$3-5/ day energy surcharge.

Closest to the airport, but only a 10-15 minute walk into town, is the **Best Western Talk of the Town**, L G Smith Blvd 2, Tel: 23380, Fax: 32446, convenient for business travellers, 63 rooms and suites built round a pool, US$100-170d winter 1990-91, children under 16 sharing free, large rooms, most with kitchenette, beach club and watersports centre across the road, guests may use facilities at the other Best Western hotels. In Oranjestad on the waterfront is the **Sonesta**, L G Smith Blvd 82, Tel: 36000, Fax: 34389, deluxe highrise, 300 rooms and 25 suites, US$170-610d, Seaport Village shops and Crystal casino on the premises, no beach at the hotel but guests may use a private island reached by motor launch from the hotel lobby which has watersports and all facilities, even a private honeymooners' beach, the only drawback being that the island is right at the end of the airport runway. A cheap hotel in town is *Central*, behind the main street, US$50, clean, basic, a/c, usually full of construction workers. Just outside town to the west in a rather unattractive industrial area immediately after the free zone, is the *Bushiri*, L G Smith Blvd 35, Tel: 25216, Fax: 26789, a 150-room hotel school and the only all-inclusive hotel, US$140-180pp, on man-made beach, gym, table tennis, lots of activities.

The low-rise resort hotel development starts on Punta Brabo Beach, Druif Bay, all hotels are on the beach and offer swimming pools, tennis, watersports, shops, restaurants etc. *Divi Tamarijn*, L G Smith Blvd 64, Tel: 24150, Fax: 34002, 236 rooms, time share apartments behind, US$205-225d, connected by trolley bus to the *Divi Divi* next along the beach, L G Smith Boulevard 93, Tel: 23300, Fax: 34002, 203 rooms, US$225-305d, shared facilities with *Tamarijn*, such as theatre, casino and shops. Next is the *Best Western Manchebo Beach Resort*, L G Smith Blvd 55, Tel: 23444, Fax: 32446, 70 rooms with balcony or terrace, US$140-150d, dive shop (Mermaid Divers, Tel: 35546) and windsurfing on huge expanse of beach; under same management with shared facilities is the *Bucuti Beach Resort*, same phone numbers, 63 rooms, some with kitchenette, some suites, balconies, sea view, US$170-220d. *Casa del Mar*, L G Smith Blvd 53, Tel: 27000, Fax: 26557, 107 luxury 2-bedroom (timeshare) apartments on the beach and 1-bedroom suites not on the beach, US$225-330, children's playground, gamesroom. The *Aruba Beach Club*, same address and phone numbers, 131 rooms with shared facilities, US$170-250d.

At Eagle Beach the road splits the hotels/ timeshare from the beach, where it is prohibited to build. *La Cabana*, L G Smith Blvd 250, Tel: 39000, Fax: 35474, studios and suites, racquetball, squash, fitness centre, waterslide, children's pool and playground, casino and condominiums under construction. *Amsterdam Manor*, L G Smith Blvd 252, Tel: 31492, Fax: 31463, 47 painted Dutch colonial style studios and apartments with sea view, kitchen, US$100-185 winter, pool, no restaurant. *Paradise Beach Villas*, Tel: 34000, Fax: 31662, 43 suites, US$150-230 winter, family oriented, pool,

tennis, racquetball, watersports. *La Quinta*, Tel: 35010, Fax: 26263, suites and rooms with kitchenette, from US$140 winter, pools, tennis, racquetball, expanding.

After the sewage treatment plant and Pos Chiquito the road curves round Palm Beach where all the high rise luxury hotels are. All have at least one smart restaurant and another informal bar/ restaurant, some have about five, all have shops, swimming pools, watersports, tennis and other sports facilities on the premises and can arrange anything else. Hotels with 300 rooms have casinos. The first one is the *Ramada Renaissance*, L G Smith Blvd 75, Tel: 37000, Fax: 39090, 300 rooms and suites, US$200-850d winter 1991/2, squash courts, fitness centre, all luxury facilities. *Aruba Concorde*, L G Smith Blvd 77, Tel: 24470, 500 rooms, US$170-680d winter, behind it is the restaurant *De Olde Molen*, an imported windmill around which a condominium resort *The Mill Resort* is being built, Tel: 35033, US$155-500 winter, waterslide, racquetball. *Aruba Palm Beach*, (used to be the *Sheraton*), L G Smith Blvd 79, Tel: 23900, Fax: 21941, 202 rooms and suites, olympic size swimming pool. The oldest hotel along here is the renewed and extended *Golden Tulip Aruba Caribbean*, L G Smith Blvd 81, Tel: 33555, Fax: 23260, 378 rooms and suites, not all with sea view, US$205-685d winter 1990-91, golf putting, usual luxury facilities. *Americana Aruba*, L G Smith Blvd 83, Tel: 24500, Fax: 23191, recently renovated, 421 rooms and suites with sea view and balcony, US$140-175d winter, Red Sails diving and watersports on site. The next hotel along is the new and glittering *Hyatt Regency Aruba*, L G Smith Blvd 85, Tel: (800) 233 1234 in the USA, 360 rooms and suites, US$240-365d winter 1990-91, designed for a luxury holiday or for business meetings and incentive trips, built around a huge three level pool complex with waterfalls, slides and salt water lagoon, in beautiful gardens, health and fitness centre, Red Sail diving and watersports, very popular, great for children or business travellers, always full. *Playa Linda*, L G Smith Blvd 87, Tel: 31000, Fax: 25210, a timeshare resort of suites and efficiencies, US$200-600d winter, health club, games room. *Holiday Inn Aruba*, L G Smith Blvd 230, Tel: 23600, Fax: 25165, 602 rooms with balcony, US$ 155-235d winter, usual facilities. Finally, *Plantation Bay*, L G Smith Blvd z/ n, Tel: 36847, Fax: 34775, 420 luxury suites to be ready September 1991, all sea view, US$205-780 per suite winter 1991-92, health and fitness club, racquetball, Red Sail diving and watersports, Velasurf windsurfing, just up the beach from here is excellent windsurfing.

The Aruba Tourism Authority publishes a list of apartments and guesthouses with photos. Weekly or monthly rates are more advantageous. If you arrive at a weekend the Tourist Office will be shut and you cannot get any help. In residential Oranjestad, *Aruba Apartments*, US$30. George Madurostraat 7, Tel: 24736; *Aulga's Place*, US$30, Seroe Blanco 31, Tel: 22717; *Camari Guesthouse*, US$20-25, Hospitaal 10, Tel: 28026; *Camacuri Apartments*, US$35-75, Fergusonstraat 46-B, Tel: 26805. In the district of Noord, *Cactus Apartments*, US$30, Matadera 5, Noord, Tel: 22903; *Coconut Inn*, US$25-50, Noord 31, Tel: 21298; *Turibana Plaza Apartments*, US$45-65, Noord 124, Tel: 27292, Fax: 32658; *Montaña Apartments*, US$20, Montaña 6-D, Noord, Tel: 24981. Near Malmok and convenient for windsurfing are *Malmok Apartments*, US$50-125, L G Smith Blvd 454, Malmok, run by the *Arubiana Inn Hotel*, US$45-70, Bubali 74, Tel: 26044, Fax: 24980; *Roger's (windsurf) Place*, US$35-85, L G Smith Blvd 472, P O Box 461, Malmok, Tel/ Fax: 21918; *Boardwalk Apartments*, US$65, Bakval 20, Noord, Tel/ Fax: 26654; *The Villas*, US$130-154, L G Smith Blvd 462, *The Boulevards*, US$60-105, L G Smith 486, and *The Edges Guesthouse*, US$60-105, L G Smith Blvd 458, all run by Sailboard Vacations Windsurf Villas, Tel: 31870.

Camping

Permit needed from police station, on Arnold Schuttrstraat, Oranjestad, who will advise on locations. It can take 10 days to get a permit and you must have a local address (ie hotel room). The permit costs one Afl4 stamp and it appears you can camp anywhere.

Where To Eat

With few exceptions, meals on Aruba are expensive and generally of the beef-and-seafood variety. Service charge on food and drinks is 15% at the hotels but at other places varies from 10% to 15%. Most tourists are on MAP at the hotels, many of which have a choice of formal or informal restaurants. Good wine is often difficult to find and always check that you get what you ordered, the waiter may not know that there is a difference between French and

Californian wines which bear the same name.

For Aruban specialities, *Gasparito*, Gasparito 3, Tel: 37044, Aruban and seafood, open daily 1200-1400, 1800-2300; *Mamas & Papas*, Dakota Shopping Centre, Tel: 26537, open 1200-1400; *Mi Cushina*, Noord Cura Cabai 24, Tel: 48335, Aruban and seafood, open 1200-1400, 1800-2200; *Brisas del Mar*, Savaneta 222A, Tel: 47718, seafood specialities, right on the sea, cool and airy, recommended, reasonable prices, open 1200-1430, 1830-2200; *La Nueva Marina Pirata*, seafood and Aruban dishes at Spanish Lagoon, Tel: 47150, open 1800-2300, Sunday 1200-2300, closed Tuesday, follow the main road to San Nicolas, turn right at *Drive Inn*. The hotels have some very good gourmet restaurants, such as *The French Room* at the *Golden Tulip Hotel*, Tel: 33555, but outside the hotels the best French restaurant is *Chez Mathilde*, Havenstraat 23, Tel: 34968, open 1830-2300, expect to pay over US$25pp; *Boonoonoonoos*, Wilhelminastraat 18A, Tel: 31888, open 1800-2300, has French and Caribbean specialities and the average price is around US$15; *De Olde Molen*, L G Smith Blvd 330, Tel: 22060, open 1700-2300, international food in an authentic windmill dating from 1804. For US prime steak and seafood, *Cattle Baron*, L G Smith Blvd 228, Tel: 22977, open 1200-1500, 1800-2400; *Twinkle Bone's*, Turibana Plaza, Noord 124, open 1800-2300, prices around US$18. Several Argentine restaurants serving steak, seafood and Argentine specialities, *El Gaucho*, Wilhelminastraat 80, Tel: 23677, open 1200-1500, 1800-2300; *Buenos Aires*, Noord 41, Tel: 27913, open 1800-2300; and *La Cabana Argentina*, Oude Schoolstraat 84, Tel: 27913, open 1800-2400. *The Steamboat*, opposite the *Hyatt* has a good brunch buffet for US$6 and lunch and dinner at reasonable prices.

Lots of Chinese restaurants, including the highly recommendable *Kowloon*, Emmastraat 11, Tel: 24950, open 1100-2230, regional specialities; *Dragon Phoenix*, Havenstraat 31, Tel: 21928, open 1100-2300; and *Astoria*, Crijnsenstraat 6, Tel: 45132, open 0800-2100, indoor and outdoor dining, low prices; in the Harbourtown shopping centre there is the *Japanese & Thai Dynasty*, Tel: 36288, open 1200-1430, 1830-2330, highly recommended but rather expensive. *Warung Djawa*, Wilhelminastraat, Tel: 34888, serves

Indonesian and Surinamese food, open 1200-1500, 1800-2300, US$10 for weekday rijstafel buffet lunch, all you can eat, many recommendations. There are plenty of Italian restaurants to choose from, *Cosa Nostra*, is on Scheopstraat 20, Tel: 33872, pizza, salads and other Italian dishes, open Monday-Friday 1200-0300, Saturday 1700-0100; *La Paloma*, Noord 39, Tel: 24611, open 1800-2400, Northern Italian and seafood; *Porto Bello*, Harbourtown, Tel: 35966, open 1130-2330, good for a cheap, light meal of pasta or pizza, specializes in huge ice creams; *Pizza Pub*, L G Smith Blvd 54, Tel: Tel: 29061, open daily around the clock, 24 hour delivery service. At the Alhambra Bazaar, *Roseland Buffet*, a good buffet meal for US$11, they also serve good pizzas (munchies) at a reasonable price. The *New York Deli*, Alhambra Bazaar, serves soup and oversized sandwiches, open 0800-0200; *Charlie's Bar*, Zeppenfeldtstraat 56, San Nicholas, Tel: 45086, is also good for Aruban light meals, open 1100-2400. *Café The Paddock* on L G Smith Blvd near *Wendy's* has outside seating. Amstel on draught and the *daghap* (dish of the day) for Afl 14.50; *The Silver Skate*, Caya G F Croes 42, is a *broodjeszaak* (sandwich shop) with imported Dutch cheese, chocolate milk, draught Amstel and bottled Grolsch beer, all at reasonable prices. There is a wide array of fast food outlets, including *Burger King*, *Kentucky Fried Chicken*, *McDonalds*, *Wendy's*, *Taco Bell*, *Dunkin Donuts*, *Subway* and *Domino Pizza*. For night owls in need of food the white trucks (mobile restaurants) serve local food and snacks from 2100-0500 at around US$5, located at Wilhelmina Park, the Post Office and the Courthouse.

Entertainment

The major attraction is gambling and there are many casinos on the island. Hotels must have 300 rooms before they can build one; those that do usually start at 1000 and operate two shifts. Their open air bars close around that time. Arubans are allowed in to casinos only four times a month. Some casinos also offer dancing and live bands. The place to be for a disco night out is *Visage*, next to the *Pizza Pub* at L G Smith Blvd 54. Other discothèques include *Blue Wave* on Shellstraat, Tel: 38856; *Chesterfield Night Club*, Zeppenfeldtstraat 57, San Nicolas, Tel: 45109; *Club L'Atmosphère*, L G Smith Blvd 152A, Tel: 36836; *Club Nouveau*, Wilhelminastraat 7, Tel: 24544; *Exit Nightclub*, Nassaustraat 152, Tel: 33839;

Isla de Oro, Pos Chiquito, Tel: 46; *Surfside Beach Club*, across the road from *Talk of the Town*, Tel: 23380. *The Plaza* at the Harbour Town Shopping Centre has a nice terrace and you can get a good, reasonably priced meal there. The *Coca Plum* on Caya Betico Croes serves a good meal and refreshing fruit juices on a terrace.

Shopping

A wide range of luxury items are imported from all over the world for re-sale to visitors at cut rate prices. Liquor rates are good, but prices for jewellery, silverware and crystal are only slightly lower than US or UK prices. There is no sales tax. There are also local handicrafts such as pottery and art work, try Artesanía Arubiano, on L G Smith Blvd 178, opposite *Tamarijn Hotel*, or ask the Institute of Culture, Tel: 22185, or the Aruba Tourism Authority, Tel: 23777, for more information.

Bookshops

Van Dorp in Naussaustraat is the main town centre bookshop. The light and airy Captains Log in the new Harbour Town development has a few books and reading material but is mostly souvenirs. Many bookshops in the hotels have some paperbacks.

Banks

Algemene Bank Nederland NV, Nassaustraat 89, Tel: 21515, Fax: 21856, also a branch on van Zeppen Feldstraat, San Nicolas and at the Port of Call shopping centre (close to the harbour where the cruise ships come in) on L G Smith Blvd. Aruba Bank NV, Nassaustraat 41, Tel: 21550, Fax: 29152, and at L G Smith Blvd 108, Tel: 31318; Banco di Caribe NV, L G Smith Blvd 90-92, Tel: 32168, Fax: 34222; Caribbean Mercantile Bank NV, Nassaustraat 53, Tel: 23118, Fax: 24373; Interbank, Nassaustraat 38, Tel: 31080, Fax: 24058; First National Bank, Nassaustraat 67, Tel: 33221, Fax: 21756. American Express representative for refunds, exchange or replacement of cheques or cards is SEL Maduro & Sons, Rockefellerstraat 1, Tel: 23888, open Monday-Friday 0800-1200, 1300-1700. Aruba Bank, Caribbean Mercantile Bank and Interbank are Visa/Mastercard representatives with cash advance.

Currency

Aruba has its own currency, the Aruban florin, not to be confused with the Antillean guilder, which is not accepted in shops and can only be exchanged at banks. The exchange rate is

Afl1.77=US$1, but shops' exchange rate is Afl1.80. US dollars and credit cards are widely accepted and the Venezuelan bolívar is also used.

Health

All the major hotels have a doctor on call. There is a well-equipped, 280-bed hospital (Dr Horacio Oduber Hospital, L G Smith Blvd, Tel: 24300) near the main hotel area with modern facilities and well-qualified surgeons and dentists. The emergency telephone number for the Ambulance and Fire Department is 115. Drinking water is distilled from sea water and consequently is safe. The main health hazard for the visitor is over-exposure to the sun. Be very careful from 1100-1430, and use plenty of high factor suntan lotion.

Climate

Aruba is out of the hurricane belt and the climate is dry. The hottest months are August-October and the coolest are December-February, but the temperature rarely goes over 90°F or below 80°F. A cooling trade wind can make the temperature deceptive. Average rainfall is 20 inches a year, falling in short showers during October-December.

Laundromat

Wash 'n Dry Laundromat, Turibana Plaza, Noord; Hop Long Laundromat, Grensweg 7, San Nicolas.

Clothing

Swim suits are not permitted in the shopping area. Most casinos require men to wear jackets and smart clothes are expected at expensive restaurants, otherwise casual summer clothes worn all year.

Hours Of Business

Banks are open 0800-1200, 1330-1600, Monday-Friday, although some banks remain open during lunch. Shops are open 0800-1830, Monday-Saturday, although some shut for lunch. Some shops open on Sundays or holidays when cruise ships are in port. Late night shopping at the Alhambra Bazaar 1700-2400.

National Holidays

New Year's Day, Carnival Monday (beginning of February), Flag Day (18 March), Good Friday, Easter Monday, Queen's Birthday (30 April), Labour Day (1 May), Ascension Day (May), Christmas Day, Boxing Day.

Time Zone

Atlantic Standard Time – 4 hours behind GMT, 1 ahead of EST.

Telecommunications

Modern telephone services with direct dialling are available. Aruba's country and area code is 2978. Hotels add a service charge on to international calls. The ITT office is on Boecoetiweg 33, Tel: 21458. Phone calls, telex, telegrams, electronic mailgram and mariphone calls at Servicio di Telecommunicacion di Aruba (Setar), next to the Post Office Building at Irausquinplein, Oranjestad. There are Teleshops in Oranjestad (Leoplein) and San Nicolas (Post Office), from where you can make international calls. Postal rates to the USA, Canada and the Netherlands are Afl 1, US$0.55 for letters, and Afl0.70, US$0.40 for post cards. The local television station is Tele-Aruba, but US programmes are also received.

Religion

A wide range of churches is represented on Aruba, including Catholic, Jewish and Protestant. There are Methodists, Baha'i, Baptists, Church of Christ, Evangelical, Jehovah's Witnesses and 7th Day Adventists. Check at your hotel for the times of services and the language in which they are conducted.

Electric Current

110 volts, 60 cycles AC.

Consulates

Brazil: E Pory Ierlandstraat 19, Tel: 21994; **Chile**: H de Grootstraat 1, Tel: 21085; **Costa Rica**: Savaneta 235-B, Tel: 47193; **Denmark**: L G Smith Blvd 82, Tel: 24622; **Dominican Republic**: J G Emanstraat 79, Tel: 36928; **Germany**: Scopetstraat 13, Tel: 21767; **Honduras**: Bilderdijkstraat 13, Tel: 21187; **Italy**: Caya G F Betico Croes 7, Tel: 22621; **Liberia**: Windstraat 20, Tel: 21171; **Panama**: Weststraat 15, Tel: 22908; **Peru**: Waterweg 3, Tel: 25355; **Portugal**: Seroe Colorado 73, Tel: 46178; **El Salvador**: H de Grootstraat 1, Tel: 21085; **Spain**: Madurostraat 9, Tel: 23163; **Sweden**: Havenstraat 33, Tel: 21821; **Venezuela**: Adriane Lacle Blvd 8, Tel: 21078.

Travel Agents

Pelican Tours P O Box 1194, Tel: 29134/ 31228, Fax: 32655, lobby desks in many hotels, also at Pelican Pier, Palm Beach, between *Holiday Inn* and *Playa Linda*, sightseeing trips, cruises, watersports. De Palm Tours, L G Smith Blvd 142, P O Box 656, Tel: 24400, Fax: 23012, also with offices in many hotels, sightseeing tours of the island and excursions to nearby islands or Venezuela. Their Mar-Lab Biological Tour, US$25 includes a visit to Seroe Colorado, and snorkelling at Boca Grandi. ECO Destination Management, Tel: 26034, for watersports, boating and excursions. Aruba Transfer Tours and Taxi, P O Box 723, L G Smith Blvd 82, Tel: 22116. Julio Maduro, Corvalou Tours, Tel: 21149, specializes in archaeological, geological, architectural, botanical and wildlife tours. For a combination 6-hour tour with lunch, US$35, call archaeologist E. Boerstra, Tel: 41513, or Julio Maduro, or Private Safaris educational tour, Tel: 34869.

Tourist Office

L G Smith Boulevard 172, Oranjestad, P O Box 1019, near the harbour, Tel: 23777, Fax: 34702. Also at airport and cruise dock.

USA: 521 5th Ave, 12th floor, New York, NY 10175, Tel: (212) 246 3030 or US toll free 1-800-To-ARUBA, Fax: (212) 557 1614; 85 Grand Canal Drive, Suite 200, Miami, Fl 33144, Tel: (305) 267 0404, Fax: (305) 267 0503. **Canada**: 86 Bloor Street West, Suite 204, Toronto, Ontario M5S 1M5, Tel: (416) 975 1950. **Venezuela**: Torre C, Piso 8, Oficina C-805, Chuao, Caracas, Tel: 959 1256. **Argentina**: Solis 370, Piso 3 '6', Buenos Aires, Tel: 814 4729, Fax: 814 4729. **Colombia**: Calle 100, No. 8A-49, Torre B, Edificio World Trade Center, Bogotá, Tel: 226 9013, Fax: 226 9038. **The Netherlands**: Amaliastraat 16, 2514 JC, Den Maag, Tel: (70) 3566220. **Germany**: Viktoriastrasse 28, D-6100, Darmstadt, Tel: 6151-23068.

We are most grateful to Dr Frank Eelens, Aruba, for his help in updating the Aruba chapter.

ISLANDS OF THE WESTERN CARIBBEAN

Introduction

CLOSE TO THE CARIBBEAN coast of Central America are several groups of islands which we describe below, from south to north. In most cases the islands can only be reached by air from the country to which they belong: Panama for the San Blas archipelago, Nicaragua for the Corn Islands and Belize for its Cayes. The exceptions are San Andrés, belonging to Colombia, which is a regular stop-over on flights from Miami or Central America to Colombia, the Bay Islands of Honduras, to which there are direct flights from three US cities, and Cancún and Cozumel, which are Mexican points of entry for flights originating in the USA and for package holidays. Sailors, of course, have greater flexibility in travelling to these islands.

These islands' close geographical and political links with Latin America have not eradicated their Caribbean nature. In fact, the mainland seaboard is invariably distinct from the countries' interior and Pacific regions. A strong English influence persists, the black population is larger, the island atmosphere is often un-Hispanic. Moreover, the San Blas islands, and the Nicaraguan and Honduran Mosquito Coast, are largely indigenous Indian areas. Unlike the Lesser and Greater Antilles, though, these island groups are not part of a chain, so they either retain a stronger sense of individuality, or they look to the mainland for their identity.

In view of the necessity of travelling to these islands via a South or Central American country, selective details on the points of access are given and a detailed Information for Visitors section is provided in each case.

SAN BLAS ISLANDS, PANAMA

The S-shaped isthmus of Panama, 80 km at its narrowest and no more than 193 km at its widest, is one of the great crossroads of the world. Its destiny has been entirely shaped by that fact. To it Panama owes its national existence, the make-up of its population and their distribution: two-fifths of the people are concentrated in the two cities which control the entry and exit of the canal.

The history of Panama is the history of its pass-route; its fate was determined on that day in 1513 when Balboa first glimpsed the Pacific. Panama City was of paramount importance for the Spaniards: it was the focus of conquering expeditions northwards and southwards along the Pacific coasts. All trade to and from these Pacific countries passed across the isthmus. Panama City was founded in 1519 after a trail had been discovered between it and the Caribbean. The trail became an established road to accommodate the Spanish traders; it was the route Henry Morgan took when he sacked Panama City in 1671; and it was the "road to hell" for the forty-niners on their way to the Californian goldfields. The goldrush brought a railway to the isthmus, which was superseded by the Panama Canal. On 15 August 1914, the first passage was made, by the ship *Ancón*.

The Canal Area, formerly Zone, is being gradually incorporated into Panamanian jurisdiction; this long process began in 1964, when Panama secured the right to fly its flag in the Zone alongside that of the USA, and is due for completion, with Panamanian operation of the Canal, by 2000.

Alongside this unique development and the vast influx of people that has accompanied it, only three Indian tribes have survived out of the sixty who inhabited the isthmus at the time of the Spanish Conquest. These are the Cunas of the San Blas Islands, the Guaymíes of the western provinces and the Chocóes of Darién.

San Blas Islands

We are concerned here with the San Blas Islands, an archipelago, which has 365 islands ranging in size from tiny ones with a few coconut palms to islands on which hundreds of Cuna Indians live. The islands vary in distance from the shore from 100 metres to several kilometres. They lie off the coast east of the Caribbean landfall for the passage of the Panama Canal, which is made at the twin cities of Cristóbal and Colón.

The Cuna are the most sophisticated and politically organized of the country's three major groups. They run the San Blas Territory virtually on their own terms, with internal autonomy and, uniquely among Panama's Indians, send their representative to the National Assembly. They have their own language, but Spanish is widely spoken. The women wear gold nose- and ear-rings, and costumes with unique designs based on local themes, geometric patterns, stylized flora and fauna, and pictorial representations of current events or political propaganda. They are outside the Panamanian tax zone and have negotiated a treaty perpetuating their long-standing trade with small craft from Colombia. Many men work on the mainland, but live on the islands.

Photographers need plenty of small change, as the set price for a Cuna to pose is US$0.25. *Molas* (decorative handsewn appliqué for blouse fronts) are very popular purchases; they cost upwards of US$5 each (also obtainable in many Panama City and Colón shops). You can also try the San Blas perfume, Kantule, similarly available in the city shops.

All Panamanian agencies run trips to El Porvenir, the island where the planes land; from there boats go to other islands, eg Wichub Huala, Nalunega and Corbisky, all close to each other (about 20 minutes by boat). There are hotels on the first three. A one-day tour costs US$110 (a recommended agent is Chadwick Travel, at the YMCA building in Balboa, Tel: 522741/522972, fluent English spoken). One night at **Posada Anai** (or *Hanay*) *Kantule* on Wichub Huala (Tel: 20-0746) costs US$55, bookable at the major Panama hotels (ask for Israel Hernández on arrival at El Porvenir). Other hotels near El Porvenir are **San Blas** (Tel: 62-5410) and **Residencial Turístico Yeri** (Tel: 62-3402); both charge US$25 a night. These trips are inclusive of food and sightseeing. Take your own drinks, because they are expensive on the islands (beer costs US$1). You can go to any island in the San Blas group, just asked to be dropped off by the pilot. The beaches and sea are inviting, but you must arrange when you will collected and bear in mind that there is no water or food available.

The nearest city on the Caribbean is Colón (population 54,469), the second largest in Panama. It was established in 1852 as the terminus of the railway across the isthmus and was originally called Aspinwall, after one of the founders of the railway. Despite its fine public buildings and well-stocked shops, it has some of the nastiest slums in Latin America, and is generally dirty. It has been described as having a "rough, but wonderful honky-tonk atmosphere". There is a curfew in Colón from 2100 to 0500. Cristóbal, Colón's twin city, came into being as the port of entry for the supplies used in building the Canal. The two cities merge into one another almost imperceptibly on Manzanillo Island at the entrance of the Canal; the island has now been connected with the mainland.

There are occasional boats to the San Blas islands from Colón or Portobelo (48 km north east of Colón—9 hours to San Blas), but there is no scheduled service and the trip can be rough. One ship that goes from time to time is the *Almirante*, try to find the captain, Figueres Cooper, who charges US$30 for the trip.

Isla Grande

Isla Grande, just off the coast, can be reached by boats hired from a car park, and a bus service; there are four hotels: *Isla Grande*, Tel: 61-4013, in huts scattered along an excellent sandy beach; *Jackson's*, cheaper, also huts; *Posada Villa Ensueño*, Tel: 68-2926/1425, and another to the right arriving by boat from the mainland. The island is a favourite of scuba divers and snorkellers.

The Panama Canal

It would be unusual, if in Panama, not to visit the Canal. Since the regular excursions to San Blas leave from Panama City's Paitilla airport, it would be simplest to travel through the Canal from there. Most people are surprised by the Canal. Few foresee that the scenery is so beautiful, and it is interesting to observe the mechanics of the passage. Since no tourist boat runs the length of the canal, and since the Panama City-Colón train journey is no longer running (and does not afford full views when it does), travellers are advised to take a bus to the Miraflores Locks (open 0900-1700, best between 0600-1000 for photographs and 1430-1800 for viewing – the sun is against you in the afternoon) if you want to see shipping. The viewing gallery is free. A detailed model of the canal, formerly in the Department of Transport at Ancón, is here and there is also a free slide show given throughout the day, with explanations in English. About 250 metres past the entrance to the Locks is a road (left) to the filtration plant and observatory, behind which is a picnic area and viewing point. Orange bus from Panama City to Miraflores Locks leaves from the bus station next to Plaza 5 de Mayo (direction Paraíso or Gamboa), 15 minutes, US$0.35. Ask the driver to let you off at the stop for "Esclusas de Miraflores", from where it's a 10-minute walk to the Locks. Another good way to see the Panama Canal area is to rent a car.

The very best way to see the Canal, though, is by boat. It is possible to traverse it as a linehandler (no experience necessary) on a yacht; the journey takes two days. Yachts are allowed into the canal on Tuesday and Thursday only. The yacht owners need 4 linehandlers. Go the day before to the Yacht Clubs in Cristóbal (downstairs from the building next to the wharf), or in Balboa (the port with the Canal Administration at the Pacific end), and ask people hanging around the bar. The Balboa Club offers good daily lunch special for US$2.15; a good place to watch canal traffic. 50 metres right of the Club is a small white booth which has a list of boat departures for the next day; ask here if you can go to the dock and take the motor boat which shuttles out to yachts preparing for passage. Ask to speak to captains from the launch and see if they'll let you "transit". However, don't expect too much, at times less than one private boat a week goes through the Canal.

Information for Visitors

Documents
Visitors must have a passport, together with a tourist card (issued for 30 days and renewable for another 60 in the Immigration Office, Panama City) or a visa (issued for 30 days, extendable to 90 days in Panama). Tourist cards are available at borders, from Panamanian consulates, Ticabus or airlines. To enter Panama you must have an onward flight ticket, travel agent confirmation of same, or, if entering by land, sufficient funds to cover your stay (US$550; US$300 may be asked for if you have an onward ticket). Once in Panama, you cannot get a refund on an onward flight ticket unless you have another exit ticket. Copa tickets can be refunded at any office in any country (in the currency of that country). **Customs at Paso Canoas,** at the border with Costa Rica, have been known to run out of tourist cards. If not

entering Panama at the main entry points (Tocumen airport, Paso Canoas), expect more complicated arrangements.

Neither visas nor tourist cards are required by nationals of Austria, Costa Rica, Finland, Germany, Honduras, Spain, Switzerland and the UK.

Citizens of the following countries need a visa which is free: USA, the Netherlands, Norway, Denmark, Colombia and Mexico. Before visiting Panama it is advisable to enquire at a Panamanian consulate whether you need a visa stamped in your passport, or whether a tourist card will suffice. Citizens of the United States, for example, may buy a tourist card at a border for US$2 instead of a visa. A visa costing the local equivalent of £10 must be obtained by citizens of Australia, New Zealand, Canada, Japan, France, Italy, Sweden, Israel, El Salvador,

Dominican Republic. Visas for citizens of many African, Eastern European and Asian countries require authorization from Panama, which takes 1 week (this includes Hong Kong, India, Poland, the former Soviet republics, and also Cuba and South Africa).

Immigration in Panama City is at Av Cuba y Calle 28E; the Ministerio de Hacienda y Tesoro is at Av Perú y Calle 35E.

How To Get There By Air

From London: British Airways, American, Continental or Virgin Atlantic to Miami, then by American, Copa, or LAB to Panama City. From elsewhere in North America: New York City, American (change in Miami), Ecuatoriana; from Los Angeles, Varig, Taca (via San Salvador), Lacsa (via San José), American (via Miami); from Houston, Continental, Taca. From Mexico, Aeroperú, Avensa, or connections with Lacsa via San José, Taca via San Salvador, or via Miami. From Central America, Copa, Lacsa (to San José, to connect with its Central American network and Los Angeles/ Mexico/Miami/New Orleans/ San Juan-Puerto Rico routes), Taca (including to Belize), Sahsa and Aeronica (to Managua, San José). Copa also flies to Kingston and Santo Domingo. From South America, Lacsa (Barranquilla, Caracas), Copa, (Barranquilla, Cartagena, Medellín). To Bogotá direct with Avianca and Aerolíneas Argentinas, or via Medellín by SAM, be at airport very early because it can leave before time; also to Cali with Avianca. To Guayaquil, Continental, Aerolíneas Argentinas, AeroPerú and Ecuatoriana, who also fly to Quito. Cubana flies direct to Havana on Monday. Other carriers are Avianca, Varig (to Manaus, as well as Rio and São Paulo), Avensa, Lloyd Aéreo Boliviano, SAM, Aerolíneas Argentinas, LAP, AeroPerú. From Europe, Iberia (Madrid via Santo Domingo), KLM (from Amsterdam via Aruba or Curaçao).

Taxes

An airport tax of US$15 has to be paid by all passengers. There is a 4% tax on air tickets purchased in Panama.

Airport

Tocumen, 27 km from Panama City. Taxi fares to/from city about US$20, colectivo US$8 pp (if staying for only a couple of days, it is cheaper to rent a car at the airport). Bus marked Tocumen, every 15 minutes, from Plaza 5 de Mayo, US$0.35, one hour's journey. Bus ("El Chorrillo") to Panama City from the crossing outside the airport (US$0.30), 45 minutes. There is a 24 hour left-luggage office near the Avis car rental desk for US$1 per article per day (worth it, since theft in the departure lounge is common). There are duty-free shops at the airport but more expensive than those downtown.

There is a small airport at La Paitilla (take a number 2 bus going to Boca La Caja, from Av Balboa at Calle 40), nearer Panama City, for domestic and private flights.

Customs

Even if you only change planes in Panama you must have the necessary papers for the airport officials. Cameras, binoculars, etc, 500 cigarettes or 500 grams of tobacco and 3 bottles of alcoholic drinks for personal use are taken in free. The Panamanian Customs are strict; drugs without a doctor's prescription and books deemed "subversive" are confiscated. In the latter case, a student's or teacher's card helps. **Note**: Passengers leaving Panama by land are *not* entitled to any duty-free goods, which are delivered only to ships and aircraft.

Shipping Services

From Panama there are frequent shipping services with the principal European and North American ports; with the Far East, New Zealand, and Australia, with both the east and west coast ports of South America and Central America, regularly with some, irregularly with others. For full information on shipping lines which carry passengers, contact Weider Travel, Charing Cross Shopping Concourse, The Strand, London WC2N 4HZ, Tel: 071-836 6363.

Internal Flights To San Blas Islands

The flights arranged by agencies leave Paitilla airport between 0600 and 0630, returning next day between 0700 and 0730 Monday to Saturday. If you can collect 9 people to fill the plane, you can leave at 0800 and return next day at 1600. Sunday flights must be booked privately. The airline serving the islands are Transpasa (Tel: 26-0932 or 26-0843), with single-engine, six-seater Cessnas, and Ansa (Tel: 26-7891 or 26-6881) with twin-engine Islanders. Both companies fly to any of the 20 airports in San Blas province (mainland and islands). A one-way fare to El Porvenir island is US$24.83 (including 5% tax), to Puerto Ooaldía on the mainland US$39.68. Passports must be taken on these flights since every so often someone tries to hijack a flight to Colombia.

There are local flights to most parts of Panama by the national airlines Ansa (Tel: 26-7891, Fax: 26-4070), Aeroperlas (Tel: 63-5363, Fax: 23-0606), Alas Chiricanas (Tel: 64-7759, Fax: 64-7190), Parsa (Tel: 26-3803, Fax: 26-3422), Aerotaxi (T64-8644), and others.

Rail

No passenger trains run between Panama City and Colón since the track, and especially the rolling stock, are in a very poor state. Station in Panama City is on Av de los Mártires, 1 km northwest of Plaza 5 de Mayo, not a pleasant area at night. When operating steel-car trains run roughly parallel to the Canal. Journey takes 1 hour 25-50 minutes. For information, Tel: 52-7720.

Local Transport

Taxis have no meters; charges are according to how many "zones" in town are traversed (about US$0.75-US$2). Try to settle fare beforehand if you can (you can often bargain down). Note that there are large taxis (*grandes*) and cheaper small ones (*chicos*). Taxis out of town charge US$10 per hour for tours to Miraflores locks and the Canal Area.

There are numerous small town buses nicknamed *chivas* (goats). These charge US$0.15, are not very comfortable but are very colourful, with blaring salsa music, and run along the major streets of the capital. Travel into the suburbs costs more. Yell "*parada*" to stop the bus.

Buses to all Canal Area destinations (Balboa, Summit, Paraíso, Kobbe, etc) leave from Canal Area bus station (SACA), next to Plaza 5 de Mayo. Panamá-Colón 1¾ hours, US$1.75, from Calle 26 Oeste y Av Central in Panama City, opposite San Miguel church.

Car Rental

At the airport (Hertz, Tel: 38-4081; Avis, Tel: 38-4069; National, Tel: 38-4144); rates about US$60/day, special rates if reservations made abroad. Cars in good condition. Other offices in El Cangrejo: Avis, C.55, Tel: 64-0722; International, C. 55, Tel: 64-4540; Barriga, Edif. Wonaga 1 B, Calle D, Tel: 69-0221; Gold, Calle 55, Tel: 64-1711. Hertz, Vía España 130, Tel:

64-1729; Budget Tel: 63-8777; Discount Tel: 23-6111.

Where To Stay

Some information on hotels on the San Blas islands is given above.

In Panama City there are many hotels to choose from in all price ranges. For instance: *El Marriott Caesar Park*, Vía Israel, Tel: 26-4077, Fax: 26-4262 US$125 for a double room; *Plaza Paitilla Inn* (former *Holiday Inn*), Punta Paitilla, PO Box 1807, Tel: 69-1122, Fax: 23-1470, US$105 double, US$95 single (not including tax), weekends rates US$69 available, restaurant, café, nightclub, swimming pool; a number on Vía España: *El Panamá*, Vía España y Calle 55, Tel: 69-5000, Fax: 69-5990, US$110; *Riande Continental*, Vía España, Tel: 63-9999, Fax: 69-4599, US$95 double; *Europa*, Vía España y Calle 42, Tel: 63-6911, Fax 63-6749, US$40 double; *California*, Vía España y Calle 43, Tel: 63-7844, US$27.50, a/c, TV, restaurant (breakfast US$1.75); *Gran Hotel Soloy*, Av Perú, Tel: 27-1133, Fax: 27-0884, US$44 double; nearby are *Acapulco*, Calle 30 Este, Tel: 25-3832, between Avs Perú and Cuba, US$27 a/c, clean, comfortable, TV, private bath, restaurant, conveniently located, recommended; *Aramo*, Vía Brasil y Abel Bravo, Tel: 69-2355, Fax: 69-2406, US$50, a/c, restaurant; around corner from *Soloy*, *Residencia Turístico Volcán*, Calle 29, with shower, under US$20, a/c, clean. *Central*, Plaza Catedral (Tel: 62-8044), US$12 with bath, under US$10 with shared bath, safe motorcycle parking, good cheap meals in restaurant, very run down.

Cheaper accommodation can be found in *pensiones*: *América*, Av Justo Arosemena and Av Ecuador, about US$10, back rooms best to avoid street noise, communal bathrooms, safe, clean and pleasant (airport bus stops outside, restaurant downstairs good value, proprietors can arrange safe parking at Hotel Costa Inn, 5-10 minutes away; *Foyo*, Calle 6, No 825, near Plaza Catedral, clean (but hang up all edibles to deter the mice), under US$12 with bath, cheaper without, colonial feel, noisy on street but good and central (restaurant *La Viña* nearby is good and cheap); *Las Palmeras*, Av Cuba between Calles 38-39, Tel: 25-0811, US$10-12, safe, clean; *Vásquez*, Av A, 2-47, close to the Palace of Justice, quiet, friendly, nice rooms and view of ocean and sand, US$9; many more, for example on Av México.

In **Colón**, the best is *Washington*, Av. del Frente final, Tel: 41-1868, followed by the *Carlton*, Calle 10 y Av. Meléndez, Tel: 45-0717, *Andros*, Tel: 41-0477/41-7923, US$15-20, safe; at the cheaper end, *Pensión Anita*, Av. Guerrero y Calle 10, US$6, US$8 with bath, very friendly, *Pensión Plaza*, Av Central, is clean, in the US$10-15 range.

NB There is a 10% tax on all hotel prices. All hotels are air-conditioned (but not necessarily *pensiones*). It may not be easy to find accommodation just before Christmas, as Central Americans tend to invade the capital to do their shopping, nor during Carnival. In the higher parts of Panama City, water shortages are common in summer, and electricity cuts are common in late summer everywhere.

Camping

The Panamanian Embassy in London advises that it is not safe for female travellers to camp in Panama (1992). There are no official sites but it is possible to camp on some beaches or, if in great need (they agree, but don't like it much) in the Balboa Yacht Club car park. Outside Panama City, camping requires prior arrangement.

What To Eat

Best hors d'oeuvre is *carimañola*, cooked mashed yuca wrapped round a savoury filling of chopped seasoned fried pork and fried a golden brown. The traditional stew, *sancocho*, made from chicken, yuca, dasheen, cut-up corn on the cob, plantain, potatoes, onions, flavoured with salt, pepper and coriander. *Ropa vieja*, shredded beef mixed with fried onions, garlic, tomatoes and green peppers and served with white rice, baked plantain or fried yuca. *Sopa borracha*, a rich sponge cake soaked in rum and garnished with raisins and prunes marinated in sherry. Panama is famous for its seafood: lobsters, corvina, shrimp, tuna, etc. Piquant *ceviche* is usually corvina or white fish seasoned with tiny red and yellow peppers, thin slices of onion and marinated in lemon juice; it is served very cold and has a bite. *Arroz con coco y tití* is rice with coconut and tiny dried shrimp. Plain coconut rice is also delicious. For low budget try *comida corriente* or *del día* (US$1.50 or so). Corn (maize) is eaten in various forms, depending on season, eg

tamales (or *bollos*), made of corn meal mash filled with cooked chicken or pork, olives and prunes; or *empanadas*, toothsome meat pies fried crisp. Plantain, used as a vegetable, appears in various forms. A fine dessert is made from green plantain flour served with coconut cream. Other desserts are *arroz con cacao*, chocolate rice pudding; *buñuelos de viento*, a puffy fritter served with syrup; *sopa de gloria*, sponge cake soaked in cooked cream mixture with rum added; *guanábana* ice cream is made from sweet ripe soursop.

Tipping

At hotels, restaurants: 10% of bill. Porters, 15 cents per item, but US$1 expected at the airport. Cloakroom, 25 cents. Hairdressers, 25 cents. Cinema usherettes, nothing. Taxi drivers don't expect tips; rates should be arranged before the trip.

Festivals

The *fiestas* in the towns are well worth seeing. That of Panama City at Carnival time, held on the four days before Ash Wednesday, is the best. During carnival women who can afford it wear the *pollera* dress, with its "infinity of diminutive gathers and its sweeping skirt finely embroidered", a shawl folded across the shoulders, satin slippers, tinkling pearl hair ornaments in spirited shapes and colours. The men wear a *montuno* outfit: native straw hats, embroidered blouses and trousers sometimes to below the knee only, and carry the *chácara*, or small purse. There is also a splendid local Carnival at Las Tablas, west of Panama City.

At the Holy Week ceremonies at Villa de Los Santos the farces and acrobatics of the big devils—with their debates and trials in which the main devil accuses and an angel defends the soul—the dance of the "dirty little devils" and the dancing drama of the Montezumas are all notable. The ceremonies at Pesé (near Chitré) are famous all over Panama. At Portobelo, near Colón, there is a procession of little boats in the canals of the city.

There are, too, the folk-tunes and dances. The music is cheerful, combining the rhythms of Africa with the melodic tones and dance-steps of Andalucía, to which certain characteristics of the Indian pentatonic scale have been added. The *tamborito* is the national dance. Couples dance separately and the song— which is sung by the women only, just as the song part of the *mejorana* or *socavón* is exclusively for male voices—is accompanied by the clapping of the audience and three kinds of regional drums. The *mejorana* is danced to the music of native guitars and in the interior are often heard the laments known as the *gallo* (rooster), *gallina* (hen), *zapatero* (shoemaker), or *mesano*. Two other dances commonly seen at *fiestas* are the *punto*, with its promenades and foot tapping, and the *cumbia*, of African origin, in which the dancers carry lighted candles and strut high.

Currency

Panama is one of the few countries in the world which issues no paper money; US banknotes are used exclusively, being called balboas instead of dollars. There are "silver" coins of 50c (called a *peso*), 25c, 10c, nickel of 5c (called a *real*) and copper of 1c. All the "silver" money is used interchangeably with US currency; each coin is the same size and material as the US coin of equivalent value. You can take in or out any amount of foreign or Panamanian currency.

Security

Panama City and Colón are not safe cities, particularly after dark. While most Panamanians are friendly and helpful, it is wise to take full precautions to protect your valuables.

Health

No particular precautions—water in Panama City and Colón is safe to drink.

Climate

The Isthmus is only 9° north of the equator, but prevailing winds reduce the discomfort, especially in the cool evenings of the dry season (January-April), though the humidity is high (the wet season is called *invierno*—winter, the dry *verano*—summer). Heavy rain falls sometimes in October and November.

The rate of deforestation in Panama has accelerated in the 1980s and early 1990s. Although more of the country is forested than any other Central American republic except Belize, the loss of forest in 1990 was estimated at 220,000 acres, against felling of up to 154,000 acres per year between 1985 and 1989. Deforestation is affecting the pattern of rainfall upon which depend not only the birds (over 800 species), animals, insects and plants, but also the Panama Canal. A further threat to the Canal is silting as a result of soil erosion.

Clothing

Lightweight tropical clothes for men, light cotton or linen dresses for women, for whom the wearing of trousers is quite OK.

Hours Of Business

Government departments, 0800-1200, 1230-1630 (Monday to Friday). Banks: open and close at different times, but are usually open all morning, but not on Saturday. Shops and most private enterprises: 0700 or 0800-1200 and 1400-1800 or 1900 every day, including Saturday.

Public Holidays

New Year's Day, National Mourning (9 January), Carnival (Shrove Tuesday), Good Friday, Labour Day (1 May: Republic), 15 August (Panama City only), National Revolution Day (11 October), National Anthem Day (1 November), All Souls (2 November), Independence Day (3 November), Flag Day (4 November), Independence Day (5 November: Colón only), First Call of Independence (10 November), Independence from Spain (28 November), Mothers' Day (8 December), Christmas Day. Many others are added at short notice.

Time Zone

Eastern Standard Time, 5 hours behind GMT.

Embassies And Consulates

Costa Rican, C. Gilberto Ortega y, Vía España, Tel: 64-2980 (open 0800-1430). **Nicaraguan**, Av. Federico Boyd y Calle 50, Tel: 23-0981 (0900-1300, 1500-1800). **Salvadorean**, Vía España, Edif. Citybank, piso 4, Tel: 23-3020, (0900-1300). **Guatemalan**, Calle 55, El Cangrejo, Condominio Abir, piso 6, Tel: 69-3475, open 0800-1300; **Honduran**, Av. Justo Arosemena y Calle 31, Edif. Tapia, piso 2, Tel: 25-8200, (0900-1400); **Mexican**, Ed. Bank of America, piso 5, Calle 50 y 53, Tel: 63-5021 (0830-1300). **Venezuelan**, Banco Unión Building, Av. Samuel Lewis, Tel: 69-1244 (0830-1200). **Colombian**, Calle Manuel María Icaza, Edif. Grobman, piso 6, Tel: 64-9266, open 0800-1200, 1400-1600; the **Chilean** and **Ecuadorean** embassies are housed in the same building, Tel: 23-8488 and 64-7820 respectively, neither is open in p.m.

US, Av. Balboa and 40, Edif. Macondo, piso 3, P.O. Box 1099, Tel: 27-1777 (0800-1700); **Canadian**, C.M.M. Icaza, Ed. Aeroperú, piso 5, Tel: 64-7014 (0800-1100). **British**, Torre Swiss Bank, Calle 53, Zona 1, Tel: 69-0866, Fax (507)

230730, Apartado 889 (0800-1200). **French**, Plaza Francia, Tel: 28-7835 (0830-1230). **German**, Edif. Bank of America, Calle 50 y 53, Tel: 63-7733 (0900-1200); **Netherlands**, Altos de Algemene Bank, Calle M.M. Icaza, 4, Tel: 64-7257 (0830-1300, 1400-1630); **Swedish**, Vía José Agustín Arango/Juan Díaz, Tel: 33-5883 (0900-1200, 1400-1600); **Swiss**, Av. Samuel Lewis y C. Gerardo Ortega, Ed. Banco Central, piso 4, Tel: 64-9731, P.O. Box 499, open 0815-1145. **Italian**, Calle 1, Parque Lefevre 42, Tel: 26-3111, open 0900-1200; **Danish**, C. Ricardo Arias, Ed. Ritz Plaza, piso 2, Tel: 63-5872, open 0800-1200, 1330-1630; **Spanish**, entre Av. Cuba y Av. Perú Calle 33A, Tel: 27-5122 (0900-1300); **Norwegian**, Av. Justo Arosemena y C. 35, Tel: 25-8217 (0900-1300, 1400-1630). **Japanese**, C. 50 y 61, Ed. Don Camilo, Tel: 63-6155 (0830-1200, 1400-1700); **Israeli Embassy**, Ed. Grobman, C. Manuel María Icaza, 5th floor, P.O. Box 6357, Tel: 64-8022/8257.

Weights And Measures

Both metric and the US system of weights and measures are used.

Electric Current

In modern homes and hotels, 220 volts. Otherwise 110 volt 3 phase, 60 cycles AC.

Foreign Postage

Great care should be taken to address all mail as "Republic of Panama" or "RP", otherwise it is returned to sender. Air mail takes 3-10 days, sea mail 3-5 weeks from Britain. Rates (examples) for air mail (up to 15 grams) are as follows: Central, North and South America and Caribbean, 30c; Europe, 37c up to 10 grams, 5c for every extra 5 grams; Africa, Asia, Oceania, 44c; all air letters require an extra 2c stamp. Parcels to Europe can only be sent from the post office in the El Dorado shopping centre in Panama City (bus from Calle 12 to Tumba Muerta).

Telecommunications

Telex is available at the airport, the cable companies and many hotels. Rate for a 3-minute call is US$14.40, and US$4.80 for each minute more. Telephone calls can be made between the UK and Panama any time, day or night. 3 minute minimum charge: US$10 station to station, but person to person, US$16 on weekdays, US$12 on Sunday plus tax of US$1 per call. To the USA the charge is US$4 for 3 minutes. Phone to Australia US$16 for 3 minutes (US$13 on Sunday).

Inter-continental contact by satellite is laid on by the Pan-American Earth Satellite Station. The local company is Intercomsa.

Tourist Bureau

Information office of the Instituto Panameño de Turismo (IPAT), in the Atlapa Convention Centre, Vía Israel opposite *Hotel Marriott* (0900 to 1600) issues good list of hotels, *pensiones*, motels and restaurants, and a free *Focus on Panama* guide (available at all major hotels, and airport). IPAT's address: aptdo 4421, Panama 5, RP; Tel: 26-7000/3544, ask for "información", helpful, English spoken.

Best **maps** from Instituto Geográfico Nacional Tommy Guardia (IGNTG), on Vía Simón Bolívar, opposite the National University (footbridge nearby, fortunately), take Transístmica bus from Calle 12 in Santa Ana: physical map of the country in 2 sheets, US$3.50 each; Panama City map in many sheets, US$1.50 per sheet (travellers will only need 3 or so). At the back of the Panama Canal Commission telephone books are good maps of the Canal Area, Panama City and Colón.

We are most grateful to Dr André Siraa and Carmen Rosa Robles of Panama City for updating information on the San Blas Islands.

CORN ISLANDS/ISLAS DEL MAIZ, NICARAGUA

Introduction

NICARAGUA, the largest Central American republic (128,000 square km) has a Caribbean coastline of 541 km. The zone inland from the coast is a wide belt of lowland through which a number of rivers flow from the central mountains into the Atlantic. Wet, warm winds off the Caribbean pour heavy rain onto this region, especially between May and December, with more than six metres annually.

Because of this heavy rainfall and the consequent unhealthiness, the forested eastern lowlands, together with about half the coastal area of Honduras, was never colonized by Spain. From 1687 to 1894 it was a British Protectorate known as the Miskito kingdom. It was populated then, as now, by Miskito Indians (some 75,000), but today there is strong African influence. The Afro-Nicaraguan people call themselves creoles (*criollos*). Other groups are Sumu (5,000), Rama, of whom only a few hundred remain, and Garifuna. The largest number of inhabitants of this zone are Spanish-speaking *mestizos*. English is widely spoken. The Sandinista revolution, like most other political developments in the Spanish-speaking part of Nicaragua, was met with mistrust, and many Indians engaged in fighting for self-determination. About half the Miskito population fled as refugees to Honduras, but most returned after 1985 when a greater understanding grew between the Sandinista government and the people of the East Coast. The Caribbean Coast (Autonomous Atlantic Region) was given the status of a self-governing region in 1987.

The British established several colonies of Jamaicans in the 18th century at Bluefields and San Juan del Norte (Greytown). But early this century the United Fruit Company of America (now United Brands) opened banana plantations inland from Puerto Cabezas, worked by blacks from Jamaica. Other companies followed suit along the coast, but the bananas were later attacked by Panama disease and exports today are small. A plan to re-establish banana plantations was announced in 1991. The local economy is now based on timber, fishing and mining.

The Corn Islands

The Corn Islands (Islas del Maíz) are two small beautiful islands fringed with white coral and slender coconut trees, though sadly many were blown down on the larger island by Hurricane Joan in October, 1988. They are approximately 70 ·km out into the Caribbean, opposite Bluefields, Nicaragua's main Caribbean port. The language of the islands is English. Local industries are the manufacture of coconut oil (devastated by the Hurricane), lobster fishing and shrimp-freezing plants.

The larger island is a popular Nicaraguan holiday resort; its surfing and bathing facilities make it ideal for tourists (best months March and April). Plans for developing the islands for larger-scale tourism before the Revolution never came to fruition. The best beach for swimming is Long Beach on Long Bay; walk across the island from Playa Coco. For fishing (barracuda, etc), contact Ernie Jenkie (about US$5/hour). If you climb the mountain, wear long trousers, as there are many ticks.

The smaller of the two islands escaped serious hurricane damage; it can be visited by boat from the larger island, but there are no facilities for tourists.

The atmosphere is very relaxed. However, the larger Corn Island suffered extensive damage when Hurricane Joan passed and, although some hotels survived, visitors must be prepared for very basic conditions and food shortages more severe than usual. There is a also a shortage of water and most drinks (except rum). Furthermore, you can expect power cuts and electricity generators to be turned off before midnight (pack a torch and/or candles). In general, the islands are expensive because everything has to be brought over from the mainland (except seafood, that is). Dollars are widely used and there is a dollartienda for the purchase of Western-style goods which are not available in normal Nicaraguan shops. The main market area is near Will Bowers wharf. The bank for exchange is 30 minutes walk from Will Bowers wharf, near the Promar lobster fleet offices. The local craftsmen work red and black coral, pearls, and tortoiseshell, but this and the black coral are prohibited imports in some countries, so think carefully before buying.

Bluefields

Bluefields, from where some transport goes to the Corn Islands, gets its name from the Dutch pirate Abraham Blaauwveld. It stands on a lagoon behind the bluff at the mouth of the Bluefields river (Río Escondido), which is navigable as far as Rama (96 km). From Rama a paved highway runs to the Nicaraguan capital, Managua, 290 km away, through Santo Tomás and Juigalpa. There are also flights (lasting 1 hour) to the capital.

Bananas, cabinet woods, frozen fish, shrimps and lobsters were the main exports until, tragically, in October 1988, Huricane Joan destroyed virtually all of Bluefields. The rebirth is well under way. Information on the region can be found at the Cidca office. Local bands practice above the Ivan Dixon Cultural Centre, beside the Library. There are several bars, a couple of reggae clubs, *comedores* and restaurants (2 with a/c) and a dollartienda. The atmosphere is relaxed and friendly.

Information for Visitors

Documents

Visitors must have a passport with 6 months validity (at least), and proof of US$500 (or equivalent in córdobas) in cash or cheques for their stay in the country—credit cards may be accepted as proof of adequate funds (according to the Nicaraguan Consulate in London—but see below). No visa is required by nationals of Guatemala, El Salvador, Chile, Bolivia, USA, Belgium, Denmark, Finland, Greece, Hungary, Ireland, Liechtenstein, Luxembourg, Netherlands, Norway, Spain, Sweden, Switzerland or the United Kingdom for a 90-day stay. Citizens of all other countries need a visa, which should be bought before arriving at the border, is valid for arrival within 30 days, and for a stay of up to 30 days; it costs US$25; 6 months validity on passport, 2 passport photographs and an onward ticket are required. In most cases a visa takes 48 hours to process; in some instances consultation with Managua is needed and this takes 1 week. Nationalities for whom consultation is necessary include: Israel, India, Dominican Republic, Haiti, Peru, Ecuador and Colombia. An air ticket can be cashed if not used, especially if issued by a large company, but bus tickets are sometimes difficult to encash. It is reported, however, that the Nicaraguan Embassy in a neighbouring country is empowered to authorize entry without the outward ticket, if the traveller has enough money to buy the ticket. Also, if you have a visa to visit another Central American country, you are unlikely to be asked to show an outward ticket. Only those visitors who have no tourist card and require a visa for entry need an exit permit. 72-hour transit visas are available (US$25), but they cannot be converted into full visas inside the country.

How To Get There By Air
From London: British Airways, Virgin Atlantic, American Airlines, Continental or Delta to Miami and connect to American, Aeronica, Central American Airlines, Lacsa, or Aviateca (via Guatemala City). Continental flies from Houston 4 times a week. Aeronica flies to Mexico City direct 4 days a week, Guatemala City (same schedule), San José and Panama City (4 days a week); Sahsa flies to Tegucigalpa, La Ceiba once a week, and San Pedro Sula and Belize City (twice a week), and Copa flies to Guatemala City, San José, San Salvador and Panama. From Europe, with Iberia to Managua Monday and Friday, or connect with KLM in San José. Cubana flies once a week to Havana (to fly to Havana you need an onward ticket). Aeroflot fly to Nicaragua from Moscow via Shannon, but it is *vital* to check that this service is in operation when you want to travel. All flight tickets purchased by non-residents must be paid in US dollars.

All passengers have to pay a sales tax of US$5 on all tickets issued in and paid for in Nicaragua; a transport tax of 1% on all tickets issued in Nicaragua to any destination; and an airport tax of US$10, payable in US dollars, on all departing passengers.

Transport To The Corn Islands
The state airline, Aeronica, flies from Managua to Bluefields on Tuesday, Thursday and Saturday, 1 hour, US$43 single. Under normal circumstances these flights continue to the Corn Islands, but in 1991 the landing strip's poor condition led to flights being suspended. When operating, air services between Bluefields and the Corn Islands should be booked well in advance and return booked immediately on arrival. Also, check your reservation continually; there is a waiting list and your chances depend on the size of the plane (either 22-or 26-seater; only 6 seats are allocated to tourists). Timetable seems to change weekly, so check.

Passenger-carrying cargo boats leave Bluefields for the Corn Islands from the docks of Copesnica, N of town, around a small bay and past the ruined church. Depart 0500, with a stop in El Bluff where foreigners must register with the police, US$3 one way. The water around Bluefields is dirty, muddy brown, soon becoming a clear, sparkling blue. Boats back to Bluefields leave from Will Bowers Wharf; tickets available in advance from nearby office. There are no regular sailings. It is possible to hitch a lift on a fishing boat, enquire at Inpesca at the port.

Airport
César Augusto Sandino, 12 km east of Managua, near Lake Managua. Bus 105 from the city to the airport, very crowded so may be better to take a taxi, US$5 from main road, US$15 from terminal, Taxis Unidos (slightly more expensive), regardless of number of passengers. Be early for international flights since formalities can take 2 hours. X-ray machines are reported unsafe for film.

Airlines
Around Plaza España in the capital: Sahsa, Aeronica (international flights; internal information at airport), Aeroflot, Iberia (MCOs only), KLM (300 metres east), Lufthansa and Continental; in Colonia Los Robles (Carretera a Masaya), Copa, Taca, Cubana (east of Plaza 19 de Julio, turn right on road opposite *Restaurant Lacmiel*, Tel: 73976).

Customs
Duty-free import of ½ kg of tobacco products, 3 litres of alcoholic drinks and 1 large bottle (or 3 small bottles) of perfume is permitted.

From Managua To Bluefields Overland
Take a bus from Mercado Ivan Montenegro/Oscar Benavides (Terminal Atlántico), on Pista José Angel Benavides, in the east of Managua to Rama, along the now-completed road (in poor condition near Rama), 6-7 hours, leaves 0200, to connect with boat, the "Bluefields Express", to Bluefields at 1200, Saturday, Sunday, Tuesday, Thursday (check in advance—bus US$5, boat US$4.40, book

24 hours in advance—it is very difficult to get a seat on this bus). Take your own food and drink, the river trip lasts 6 hours. On other days 5 or 6 buses from Managua and a fast boat (*pango*) can be hired for US$20 (takes 1½ hrs.) or hitch on a fishing boat. Return from Bluefields: boat at 0400, bus to Managua 1030 (combined tickets available, ticket office at Encab, near dock). Or take your car and park it in the compound at the Chinaman's store at Rama (opposite *Hotel Amy*) for US$0.50 a day. Other buses back to Managua leave Rama hourly from 0300 until 0600.

Internal Transport
Hitchhiking is widely accepted, but is difficult because everyone does it and there is little traffic—offer to pay ("pedir un ride"). Local buses are the cheapest in Central America, but are extremely crowded owing to a lack of vehicles and fuel. Better equipment was being introduced in 1992. Baggage that is loaded on to the roof or in the luggage compartment is charged for, usually half the rate for passengers.

Car Hire
Hertz, Avis and Budget. Rates are US$20-25 per day plus US$0.25 per km, not including tax and insurance. Only foreign exchange or credit cards accepted; special weekend rates available. Given the poor public transport and the decentralized layout of Managua, renting a car is often the best way to get around. Alternatively hire a taxi for long-distance trips; for journeys out of Managua, taxis need a special permit from an office opposite *Hotel Intercontinental* (opens 0930).

Motoring
Low octane gasoline costs US$2 a US gallon (shortages frequent, diesel US$1.20). Cars will be fumigated on entry, for which there is a US$2 charge. For motorcyclists, the wearing of crash helmets is compulsory. Service stations close at 1700-1800. Beware when driving at night, the national shortage of spare parts means that many cars have no lights. Unless left securely, unattended cars may be broken into.

Where To Stay And Eat On The Corn Islands
A 15% tax is levied on all hotel and restaurant bills, nevertheless, outside Managua, hotel accommodation is extremely cheap. An extra 10% service

charge is often added to restaurant bills.
There are four hotels: *Hospedaje Miramar*, recommended, meals served; *Hospedaje Playa Coco* also serves meals, and two others. One can find rooms for about US$2 (Miss Florence's house, *Casa Blanca*—although it is blue—at Playa Coco is recommended). The chief problem in all the hotels is rats, which may not be dangerous, but neither are they pleasant. For eating: *Comedor Blackstone*; *Mini Café*; ice cream parlour; several bars and reggae clubs. Ask around where meals are available; the restaurants serve mainly chicken and chop suey, but in private houses the fare is much better. Try banana porridge and sorrel drink (red, ginger flavoured).

Where To Stay In Bluefields
Costa Sur, about US$25 pp; *Caribbean*, under US$20 with bath, a/c, near centre of town, good cook (Angela), friendly, recommended; *Cuato*, damaged by the Hurricane, no running water, not rec. (yet); *El Dorado*, may offer floor space to late arrivals; *Marda Maus*, both about US$10. *Café Central* provides accommodation, has colour TV. Everywhere can be full if you arrive late, or are last off the ferry.

Where To Stay In Managua
There is a shortage of accommodation. Try to choose a central hotel (ie near *Intercontinental* or Plaza España) since transport to the outskirts is very difficult. 15% tax is added to hotel rates. There are, however, two good hotels near the airport: *Camino Real*, Tel: 31410, Apartado Postal C118, 2 km from terminal, about US$80 (low season), shuttlebus to the airport, free, good, no English spoken, restaurant, live music; and *Las Mercedes*, Tel: 32121/9, opposite the airport, a little cheaper, pleasant, swimming pool. There is regular water rationing and most hotels do not have large enough water tanks. The government stipulates a small additional charge for rooms with a telephone (whether used or not).

Intercontinental, 101 Octava Calle 50, Tel: (505-2) 23531/9, Fax: 25208, Apartado Postal 3278, is the city's major luxury hotel and a prominent landmark, US$95 single, US$105 double (corporate rates available) service poor, sauna, use of swimming pool for non-residents on Sunday, US$3, bookshop, handicrafts, buffet breakfast and lunch (see below), Amex and Visa cards accepted. There are a number of other hotels with rooms priced at US$20 double or over, eg *Estrella*, Pista de la Solidaridad (over US$45), air conditioning, swimming pool, with breakfast, long way from centre, book in advance as it's very popular; *Hotel Magut*, 1 block west of *Intercontinental*, US$30, with restaurant *La Fragata*; in same area, opposite Inturismo is *Hotel y Restaurant Nuevo Siete Mares*, Tel: 24670, US$35, Chinese food; *Casa de Fiedler*, 8a Calle Sur-Oeste 1320, with bath and air conditioning or fan, comfortable, good breakfasts; *Palace*, Av Pedro A Flores, US$30, with air conditioning and bath (US$23 without a/c), cold shower, run down, no restaurant, helpful, TV lounge, quiet; *Guest House Tres Laureles*, a few blocks west of *Intercontinental*, about 3 south of Ciné Cabrera, US$30 (US$20 single) with bath, fan, laundry facilities, only 3 rooms, friendly, filtered water, English spoken; on the same street, further west is *El Colibrí*, under US$20, single-storey, thatched walkway, shower, cold water, soap and towels but no toilet paper, restaurant spartan but reasonable, mice, often fully-booked.

For cheaper accommodation, US$12 or below: *El Pueblo*, in the old centre, with bath, good; *Royal*, near railway station (payable in córdobas), shared shower and toilet, nice family, always full; *Sultana* (basic), noisy, clean, recommended, if full, staff will arrange for you to stay at *Mi Siesta* on the other side of town (with bath and air conditioning, less without a/c), good, friendly, laundry facilities. Many hotels west of *Intercontinental Hotel* in the Barrio Martha Quezada and near the Ciné Dorado; apart from those listed above, cheaper places usually have very thin walls and are therefore noisy. This district, which also has a number of good eating places, is where many gringos congregate. For instance, on street leading to *Intercontinental Hotel*, *Casa de Huéspedes Santos* and, on same street, *Hospedaje Meza* (Tel: 22046); and many others.

Where To Eat In Managua

The *Hotel Intercontinental* serves enormous breakfasts (0600-1100) for US$8 (plus 15% tax and service charge), and an excellent lunch between 1200 and 1500, US$12 for as much as you can eat (best to dress smartly). Bill is made out in dollars, major credit cards accepted.

In the *Intercontinental*/Plaza España/Barrio Martha Quezada area there is a variety of eating places, including: *Antojitos*, opposite *Intercontinental*, Mexican, a bit overpriced, interesting photos of Managua pre-earthquake, good food and garden (open at 1200); a good piano bar next door; *Costa Brava*, north of Plaza España, excellent seafood; *Cipitío* is a Salvadorean restaurant in this area, 2½ blocks south of Ciné Cabrera.

Other areas for restaurants are on the Carretera Sur (*The Lobster's Inn*, Km 5.5, good for guess what; *El Tucán*, Km 7.5, recommended), and on the Carretera a Masaya (*Lacmiel*, Km 4.5, good value, real ice cream; *La Marseillaise*, Colonia Los Robles, French, excellent; vegetarian: *Soya Restaurant*, just off the Carretera on Pista de la Resistencia.

Tipping

10% of bill in hotels and restaurants (many restaurants add 10% service; 15% tax is added compulsorily); US$0.50 per bag for porters; no tip for taxi drivers.

Cost Of Living

In early 1992 Nicaragua was a relatively expensive country as far as hotel accommodation was concerned, but public transport was fairly cheap. For food, as a rough guide (early 1992) a *comida corrida* costs about US$2 outside Managua, US$2-3 in the capital (meals in restaurants US$6-10, breakfasts US$3-4); a beer US$0.75-1, a coke US$0.40-60 (depending on the establishment) and a newspaper US$0.30. During 1991, inflation forced weekly changes in local prices.

Currency

The unit is the córdoba oro (C$), divided into 100 centavos, introduced in July, 1990, at a par with the US dollar. The córdoba oro was devalued to 5 = US$1 in March 1991 and the old córdoba was withdrawn from circulation on 30 April 1991 (by March 1992 the dollar was fetching 5.3 córdobas oro on the black market). Notes in circulation are for ½, 1, 5, 10, 20, 500 and 100 córdobas oro. A decree, passed on 22 March 1991, permitted private banks to operate (the financial system was nationalized in 1979) The import and export of foreign and local currencies are unrestricted. Visa and Amex cards are beginning to be used in more places; Master Card is also used and, to a lesser extent, Cred-o-Matic and Diners

Club.

Changing travellers' cheques has been difficult; while the situation is improving, it is best to carry US dollar notes and sufficient local currency away from the bigger towns.

Security

Visitors to Nicaragua must carry their passports (or a photocopy) with them at all times. Border officials do not like army-type clothing on travellers, and may confiscate green or khaki rucksacks (backpacks), parkas, canteens. They usually inspect all luggage thoroughly on entering and leaving Nicaragua. Do not photograph any military personnel or installations.

Pickpocketing and bagslashing has increased greatly in Managua, especially in crowded places, and on buses throughout the country.

Working In Nicaragua

Volunteer work in Nicaragua is not as common after the 1990 elections as it was during the Sandinista years. Accepting foreigners on work brigades now seems to depend on which political party dominates the local council (in León, for example, the FSLN is keen that overseas volunteers should stay, but this is generally not the case). Certain skills are in demand, as elsewhere in the developing world; to discover the current situation, contact non-governmental organizations in your home country e.g. the Catholic Institute of International Relations—CIIR—in the UK, Nicaragua Network, 2025 I St NW, Suite 1117, Washington, DC 20006, Tel: 202-223 2328 in the USA, twin town/sister-city organizations and national solidarity campaigns (NSC, 23 Bevenden St., London N1 6BH; Dutch Nicaragua Komitee, Aptdo Postal 1922, Managua).

Health

Take the usual tropical precautions about food and drink. Tap water is not recommended for drinking generally and avoid uncooked vegetables and peeled fruit. Intestinal parasites abound; if requiring treatment, take a stool sample to a government laboratory before going to a doctor. Malaria risk especially in the wet season; take regular prophylaxis. Treatment in Centros de Salud, medical laboratories and dispensaries is free, although foreigners may have to pay. Private dentists are better-equipped than those in the national health service (but no

better trained). Medicines are in short supply, so you are advised to bring what you need from home.

Climate And Dress

There is a wide range of climates. Details of Atlantic conditions are given above, but note that it can get quite cold, especially after rain, in the Caribbean lowlands. Mid-day temperatures at Managua range from 30° to 36°C, but readings of 38° are not uncommon from March to May. Maximum daily humidity ranges from 90% to 100%.

Dress is informal; business men often shed jackets and wear sports shirts, but shorts are never worn. The wearing of trousers is perfectly OK for women.

Hours Of Business

0800-1200, 1430-1730 or 1800. Banks: 0830-1200, 1400-1600, but 0830-1130 on Saturday. Government offices are not normally open on Saturday in Managua, or in the afternoon anywhere.

Public Holidays

New Year's Day, Thursday of Holy Week and Good Friday (March or April), Labour Day (1 May), Revolution of 1979 (19 July), Battle of San Jacinto (14 September), Independence Day (15 September), All Souls' Day (Día de los Muertos—2 November), Immaculate Conception (Purísima—7 and 8 December), Christmas Day.

Businesses, shops and restaurants all close for most of Holy Week; many companies also close down during the Christmas-New Year period. Holidays which fall on a Sunday are taken the following Monday.

Time Zone

Eastern Standard Time, five hours behind GMT, as of the beginning of 1992.

Immigration

Pista de la Resistencia, Managua, about 1 km from Km 7 Carretera del Sur, bus No 118, open till 1400. **Customs** Km 5 Carretera del Norte, bus No 108.

Embassies

All in Managua: **USA**, Km 4½ Carretera del Sur (Tel: 23881); **Canada**, consul, 208/c del Triunfo, Frente Plazoleta Telcor Central, Tel: 24541; **German**, "al norte de" (to the north of) Plaza España; **French**, Km 12 Carretera del Sur, Tel: 26210/27011; **British**, El Reparto, "Los Robles", Primera Etapa, Entrada Principal de la Carretera a Masaya, Cuarta Casa a la mano derecha, Tel: 70034, Telex 2166, Apdo Aéreo 169, it is located on a right-turn off Carretera a Masaya; **Dutch**, from *Hotel Bolonia* (now closed) 2 blocks towards the Lake, Apartado 3534, Tel: (010-505-2) 664392/666175, Fax: 660364; **Swiss**, in emergency, at Hungarian Consul, Tel: 74173; **Swedish**, from Plaza España, 1 block west (Abajo), 2 blocks to the Lake, ½ block west (Abajo), Apartado Postal 2307, Tel: 60085; **Danish** Consulate General, Iglesia del Carmen, 2 cuadros al Oeste No 1610, Tel: 23189; **Panamanian** Consulate, near UCA, Plaza 19 de Julio; **Honduran** Consulate, Carretera del Sur, Km 15, Colonia Barcelona, open Monday-Friday, 0800-1400 (bus 118 from *Hotel Intercontinental*); **Venezuelan**, about Km 10 on the road to Masaya.

Weights And Measures

The metric system is official, but in domestic trade local terms are in use; for example, the *medio*, which equals a peck (2 dry gallons), and the *fanega*, of 24 *medios*. These are not used in foreign trade. The principal local weight is the *arroba*=25 lb and the *quintal* of 101.417 English lb. A random variety of other measures in use include US gallon for petrol, US quart and pint for liquids; *vara* (33 ins) for short distances and the lb for certain weights.

Electric Current

110 volts AC, 60 cycles.

Postal Services

Air-mail to Europe takes 2-4 weeks (US$0.60), from Europe 7-10 days.

Telecommunications

There are wireless transmitting stations at Managua, Bluefields and Cabo Gracias a Dios, and private stations at Puerto Cabezas, El Gallo, and Río Grande.

Phone lines are owned by the Government (Telcor). Rather unreliable automatic telephone services between Managua and main cities. A few telephones in Managua of the "big-ear" type (they take 1 córdoba coins). Calls to Europe in any major town at the Telcor office, open 0700-2200. Prices in early 1991 were US$12 for 3 minutes to USA, US$14 to Europe. You may have to wait a long time for a line, except for early in the morning on weekdays. Collect calls to the USA are easy ("a pagarse allá"), also possible to Europe. As with telephones, telex prices have been greatly increased.

Tourist Information

Inturismo in Managua 2 blocks east of *Hotel Intercontinental*, enter by side door. Standard information available, including on all types of transport in the country. Maps of Managua (almost up-to-date), with insets of León and Granada and whole country on reverse, US$5 (paid in dollars, no change given). Inturismo will help with finding accommodation with families, with full board. Turnica, Av 11 SO, 300 metres, or 2 minutes from Plaza España, Tel: 661387/660406, sells maps of Managua and of the country, and organizes tours of the capital, US$15 pp, and other cities, from US$30-50 pp (minimum 2 people, payable in dollars only).

SAN ANDRES AND PROVIDENCIA, COLOMBIA

Introduction

COLOMBIA'S Caribbean islands of the San Andrés and Providencia archipelago are 480 km north of the South American coast, 400 km southwest of Jamaica, and 180 km east of Nicaragua. This proximity has led Nicaragua to claim them from Colombia in the past. They are small and attractive, but very expensive by South American standards. Nevertheless, with their surrounding islets and cays, they are a popular holiday and shopping resort. Colombia itself encompasses a number of distinct regions, the most marked difference being between the sober peoples of the Andean highlands (in which the capital, Bogotá, is built) and the more light-hearted *costeños*, or people of the coast. The islands belong in the latter category, but, owing to their location, have more in common with the Caribbean's history of piracy, planters and their slaves than with Colombia's rich imperial past. The original inhabitants, mostly black, speak some English, but the population has swollen with unrestricted immigration from Colombia. There are also Chinese and Middle Eastern communities. The population in 1988 was officially put at 35,000, but it could now be about 65,000.

History and Economy
Before the European explorers and pirates came upon the islands, Miskito fisherman from Central America are known to have visited them. The date of European discovery is subject to controversy; some say Columbus found them in 1502, others that Alonso de Ojedo's landing in 1510 was the first. The earliest mention is on a 1527 map. Although the Spaniards were uninterested in them, European navies and pirates recognized the group's strategic importance. The first permanent settlement, called Henrietta, was not set up until 1629, by English puritans. The first slaves were introduced in 1633, to extract timber and plant cotton, but in that century, pirates held sway. Henry Morgan had his headquarters at San Andrés; the artificial Aury channel between Providencia and Santa Catalina is named after another pirate of that time. Although more planters arrived in the eighteenth century from Jamaica, England agreed in 1786 that the islands should be included in the Dominions of Spain. In 1822 they became Colombian possessions. After the abolition of slavery in 1837, coconut production replaced cotton and remained the mainstay of the economy until disease ruined the trade in the 1920s. In 1953, San Andrés was declared a freeport, introducing its present activities of tourism and commerce.

Apart from these areas, the main products are coconuts and vegetable oil. The main problem is deteriorating water and electricity supplies (in most hotels the water is salty—a desalination plant was installed in 1987). Being a customs-free zone, San Andrés is very crowded with Colombian shoppers looking for foreign-made bargains. Although alcoholic drinks are cheap,

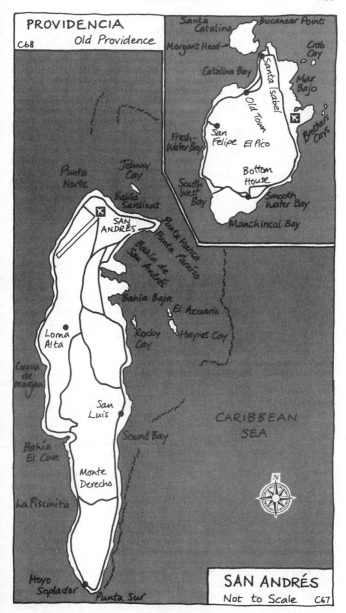

PROVIDENCIA
Old Providence
C68

Santa Catalina · Bucaneer Point
Morgan's Head
Catalina Bay
Santa Isabel
Crab Cay
Mar Bajo
Old Town
Fresh-Water Bay
San Felipe
El Pico
Brothers Cays
South West Bay
Bottom House
Smooth Water Bay
Manchineal Bay

Punta Norte
Johnny Cay
Bahía Sardinas
SAN ANDRÉS
Punta Hansa
Punta Paraíso
Bahía de San Andrés
Bahía Baja
El Acuario
Haynes Cay
Rocky Cay
Loma Alta
Cueva de Morgan
San Luis
Sound Bay
CARIBBEAN SEA
Bahía El Cove
Monte Derecho
La Piscinita
N
Hoyo Soplador
Punta Sur

SAN ANDRÉS
Not to Scale C67

essential goods are extremely costly, and electronic goods are more expensive than in the UK.

Culture
San Andrés and Providencia are famous in Colombia for their music, whose styles include the local form of calypso, soca, reggae and church music. A number of good local groups perform on the islands and in Colombia. Concerts are held at the Old Coliseum (every Saturday at 2100 in the high season); the Green Moon Festival is held in May. There is a cultural centre at Punta Hansa in San Andrés town (Tel: 5518).

Marine Life and Watersports
Diving off San Andrés is very good; depth varies from 10 to 100 feet, visibility from 30 to 100 feet. There are three types of site: walls of sea-weed and minor coral reefs, large groups of different types of coral, and underwater plateaux with much marine life. 70% of the insular platform is divable. Names of some of the sites are: The Pyramid, Big Channel, Carabela Blue, Blue Hole, Blowing Hole, The Cove and Small Mountain/La Montañita.

Diving trips to the reef cost US$50 with Pedro Montoya at Aquarium diving shop, Punta Hansa, Tel: 6649; also Buzos del Caribe, Centro Comercial Dann, Tel: 3712; both offer diving courses and equipment hire.

For the less-adventurous, take a morning boat (20 minutes, none in the afternoon) to the so-called Aquarium (US$2 return), off Haynes Key, where, using a mask and wearing sandals as protection against sea-urchins, you can see colourful fish. Snorkelling equipment can be hired on San Andrés for US$4-5, but it is better and cheaper on the shore than on the island.

Pedalos can be rented for US$4 per hour. Windsurfing and sunfish sailing rental and lessons are available from Bar Boat, road to San Luis (opposite the naval base), 1000-1800 daily (also has floating bar, English and German spoken), and Windsurf Spot, *Hotel Isleño*, Tel: 3990; water-skiing at Water Spot, *Hotel Aquarium*, Tel: 3120, and Jet Sky.

Beaches and Cays
Boats go in the morning from San Andrés to Johnny Key with a white beach and parties all day Sunday (US$2 return, you can go in one boat and return in another). Apart from those already mentioned, other cays and islets in the archipelago are Bolívar, Albuquerque, Algodón/Cotton (included in the Sunrise Park development in San Andrés), Rocky, the Grunt, Serrana, Serranilla and Quitasueño.

On San Andrés the beaches are in town and on the eastern coast (some of the most populated ones have been reported dirty). Perhaps the best is at San Luis and Sound Bay.

On Providencia the three main beaches are Manchincal Bay, the largest, most attractive and least developed, South West Bay and Freshwater Bay, all in the South West.

Festivals 20 July: independence celebrations on San Andrés with various events. Providencia holds its carnival in June.

San Andrés

San Andrés is of coral, some 11 km long, rising at its highest to 104 metres. The town, commercial centre, major hotel sector and airport are at the northern end. A picturesque road circles the island. Places to see, besides the beautiful cays and beaches on the eastern side, are the Hoyo Soplador

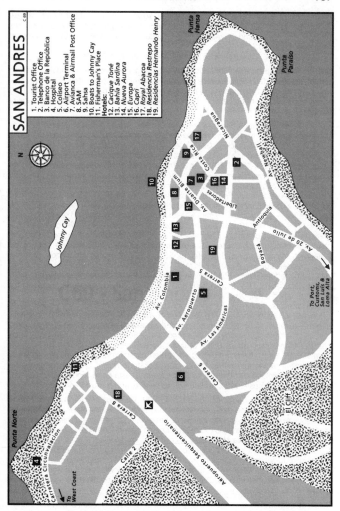

SAN ANDRES

1. Tourist Office
2. Telephone Office
3. Banco de la República
4. Hospital
5. Coliseo
6. Airport Terminal
7. Avianca & Airmail Post Office
8. SAM
9. Sahsa
10. Boats to Johnny Cay
11. Fisherman's Place

Hotels:
12. Cacique Toné
13. Bahía Sardina
14. Nueva Aurora
15. Europa
16. Capri
17. Royal Abacoa
18. Residencias Restrepo
19. Residencias Hernando Henry

(South End), a geyser-like hole through which the sea spouts into the air most surprisingly when the wind is in the right direction. The west side is less spoilt, but there are no beaches on this side. Instead there is The Cove, the island's deepest anchorage, and Morgan's Cave (yet another reputed hiding place for the pirate's treasure) which is penetrated by the sea through an underwater passage. At The Cove, the road either continues round the coast, or crosses the centre of the island back to town over La Loma, on which is a Baptist Church, built in 1847.

Island Travel Buses circle the island all day, US$0.25 (more at night and on holidays). A "tourist train" (suitably converted tractor and carriages) tours the island in 3 hours for US$2.50. **Taxis** round the island, US$8; to airport, US$3; in town, US$0.60; *colectivo* to airport, US$0.50.

Boat transport: Cooperativa de Lancheros, opposite *Hotel Abacoa*.

Vehicle Rental Bicycles are a popular way of getting around on the island and are easy to hire, eg opposite *El Dorado Hotel*—usually in poor condition, choose your own bike and check all parts thoroughly (US$1.10 per hour, US$6 per day); motorbikes also easy to hire, US$3.60 per hour. Cars can be hired for US$15 for 2 hours, with US$6 for every extra hour.

Where To Stay In the upper bracket (over US$60), *Tiuna*, Av Colombia No 3-59, air conditioning, swimming pool; *Royal Abacoa*, Av Colombia No 2-41, good restaurant, Tel: 4043. In the US$35-45 bracket: *Gran Internacional*, Av Atlántico, No 1A-49, Tel: 3043, air conditioning, swimming pool, 3 restaurants, largest on the island; *Nueva Aurora*, Av de las Américas No. 3-46, Tel: 3811, fan and private bath, pool, restaurant; *Bahía Marina*, road to San Luis, swimming pool, good restaurant; *Abacoa*, Av Colombia, T 4133/4, with bath and air conditioning; *Decameron*, Av Colombia, pool, a/c, TV, good restaurant, recommended; *Bahía Sardinas*, Av Colombia No 4-24, Tel: 3587, across the street from the beach, air conditioning, TV, fridge, good service, comfortable, clean, no swimming pool; *Cacique Toné*, Av Colombia, Carrera 5, deluxe, air conditioning, pool, on sea-front; *Capri*, Av Costa Rica No 1A-110, with bath and air conditioning, good value; *Isleño*, Av La Playa, great sea view; *El Dorado*, Av Colombia No 1A-25, Tel: 4155, air conditioning, restaurant, casino, swimming pool; *Coliseo*, Av Colombia No 1-59, Tel: 3330, friendly, noisy, good restaurant. *Verde Mar*, Av 20 de Julio, Tel: 5525, US$15-20, quiet and friendly, a/c, new, recommended; *Europa*, Av 20 de Julio No 1-101, US$25, with bath, clean. *Mediterráneo*, Av Los Libertadores, under US$20, clean, friendly, poor water supply; *Las Antillas*, Av 20 de Julio No 1A-81, US$15 with bath and fan, clean, safe, good water (including for drinking), safe deposit, good value.

Residencias Hernando Henry, under US$20, restaurant, fan, clean, good value, often full, on road from airport; *Residencia Restrepo*, "gringo hotel", Av 8 near airport—turn left to beach, then left, second left at fish restaurant and it's a hundred metres on left (no sign), noisy ("share a room with a Boeing 727"—till midnight), much cheaper than others, about US$5, or less for a hammock in the porch, clean, some rooms with bath, breakfast US$0.50, other meals US$ 1.50, good place for buying/selling unwanted return halves of air tickets to/from Central America or the Colombian mainland. On the way to *Restrepo* you pass a good food shop, breakfast, juices, snacks. Campsite at South End said to be dirty and mosquito-ridden.

Where To Eat *Oasis* (good), Av Colombia No 4-09; *Sea Food House*, Av 20 de Julio at Parque Bolívar, good food, not expensive, second floor terrace; *Popular*, on Av Bogotá, good square meal for US$4; *El Pimentón*, Av de las Américas, good and cheap; *El Zaguán de los Arrieros*, Av. 20 de Julio (50 m after cinema), good food and value; *Bahía*, good food; *Fonda Antioqueña Nos 1 and 2*, on Av Colombia near the main beach, and Av Colombia at Av Nicaragua, best value for fish; excellent fruit juices at *Jugolandia*, Calle 20 de Julio; *Jugosito*, Av Colombia, 1½ blocks from tourist office towards centre, cheap meals; *Fisherman's Place*, in the fishing cooperative at north end of main beach, very good, simple. Fish meals for US$2.50 can be bought at San Luis beach.

Exchange Banco de la República, Av Colón, will exchange dollars and travellers' cheques; Banco de Bogotá will advance pesos on a Visa card. Aerodisco shop at airport will change dollars cash anytime at rates slightly worse than banks, or try the Photo Shop on Av Costa Rica. Many shops will change US$ cash; it is impossible to change travellers' cheques at weekends. (Airport employees will exchange US$ cash at a poor rate.)

Providencia

Providencia, commonly called Old Providence (3,000 inhabitants), 80 km back to the north-northeast from San Andrés, is 7 km long and is more mountainous than San Andrés, rising to 610 metres. There are waterfalls, and the land drops steeply into the sea in places. Superb views can be had by climbing from Bottom House or Smooth Water to the peak. There are relics of the fortifications built on the island during its disputed ownership. Horse riding is available, and boat trips can be made to neighbouring islands such as Santa Catalina (an old pirate lair separated from Providencia by a channel cut for their better defence), and to the northeast, Crab Cay (beautiful swimming and snorkelling) and Brothers Cay. Trips from 1000-1500 cost about US$7 pp. On the west side of Santa Catalina is a rock formation called Morgan's Head; seen from the side it looks like a man's profile.

Like San Andrés, it is an expensive island. The sea food is good, water and fresh milk are generally a problem. Day tours are arranged by the Providencia office in San Andrés, costing US$35 inclusive. SAM fly from San Andrés, US$30, 25 minutes, up to five times a day, bookable only in San Andrés. (Return flight has to be confirmed at the airport, where there is a tourist office.) Boat trips from San Andrés take 8 hours, but are not regular.

Island Information—Providencia

Where To Stay Most of the accommodation is at Freshwater (Playa Agua Dulce): *Cabañas El Recreo* (Captain Brian's), *Cabañas El Paraíso*, *Cabañas Aguadulce* and *Hotel Royal Queen*; *Ma Elma's* recommended for cheap food; also *Morgan's Bar*, for fish meals and a good breakfast for US$2; at Santa Isabela on the north end of the island, *Flaming Trees Hotel*, clean, restaurant, good value, but a long way from the beach; at Smooth Water Bay, *Dutch Inn* (full board) and several houses take in guests. Camping is possible at Freshwater Bay. Truck drivers who provide transport on the island may be able to advise on accommodation.

Cartagena and Barranquilla

Mention should be made here of the two Caribbean cities on the mainland to which access is made from San Andrés, Cartagena and Barranquilla.

Cartagena, old and steeped in history, is one of the most interesting towns in South America, and should not be missed if you are taking this route. As well as the historical sites, Cartagena also has a popular beach resort at Bocagrande, a ten-minute bus ride from the city centre. Cartagena de Indias, to give it its full name, was founded on 13 January 1533, as one of the storage points for merchandise sent out from Spain and for treasure collected from the Americas to be sent back to Spain. A series of forts protecting the approaches from the sea, and the formidable walls built around the city, made it almost impregnable. All the same, it was challenged again and again by enemies. Sir Francis Drake, with 1,300 men, broke in successfully in 1586. The Frenchmen Baron de Pointis and Ducasse, with 10,000 men, sacked the city in 1697. But the strongest attack of all, by Sir Edward Vernon with 27,000 men and 3,000 pieces of artillery, failed in 1741 after besieging the city for 56 days. It was defended by the one-eyed, one-armed, one-legged hero Blas de Lezo.

A full description of the city, with its churches, forts, colonial streets and other attractions, is given in *The South American Handbook*.

Barranquilla (also described in detail in *The South American Handbook*) is Colombia's fourth city, with almost 2 million people. It is a modern, industrial sea and river port on the west bank of the Magdalena, one of the country's main waterways. The four-day Carnival in February is undoubtedly the best in Colombia.

Information for Visitors

Documents A passport and an onward ticket are always necessary. Visitors are sometimes asked to prove that they have US$20 for each day of their stay (US$10 for students). Nationals of the following countries do not need visas or tourist cards: Argentina, Austria, Barbados, Belgium, Bolivia, Brazil, Canada, Chile, Costa Rica, Denmark, Ecuador, Germany, Guatemala, Finland, France, Holland, Ireland, Israel, Italy, Japan, Liechtenstein, Luxemburg, Mexico, Norway, Panama, Peru, Portugal, St Vincent and the Grenadines, South Korea, Spain, Sweden, Switzerland, Trinidad and Tobago, UK, Uruguay, USA, Venezuela (this information was correct according to the Colombian consulate in London, April 1992. You must double-check before arrival: in 1991 Irish ·nationals required a visa despite consular information to the contrary). You are given 90 days permission to stay on entry. An extension (*salvoconducto*), a further 30 days can be applied for at the DAS office in any major city. Application must be made within 3 weeks of the expiry of the first 90 days and two weeks are needed for authorization from the Ministerio de Relaciones Exteriores in Bogotá. The 30-day extension runs from the day authorization is received by the DAS office (so if you apply on the last day of your 90 days you could get 45 days more). Leaving the country and re-entering to get a new permit is not always allowed. Citizens of those countries not listed above need a visa or a tourist card (free). Normal validity for either is 90 days; extensions must be applied for at the Ministerio de Relaciones Exteriores in Bogotá. Whether you need a tourist card or visa depends on your nationality, so check at a Colombian consulate in advance. Tourist cards are issued by Corporación · Nacional de Turismo (CNT) offices (in New York, or Caracas, for instance) or by Colombian airlines or authorized foreign carriers.

Visas are issued only by Colombian consulates. When a visa is required you must be prepared to show 1 photograph, an onward or return ticket, as well as a passport (allow 48 hours). Citizens of Asian, African, Middle Eastern and Socialist countries (including Cuba), must apply at least 4 weeks in advance for a visa. You may find that your onward ticket, which you must show before you can obtain a visa, is stamped "non-refundable". If you do not receive an entry card when flying in, the information desk will issue one, and restamp your passport for free. Note that to leave Colombia you must normally get an exit stamp from the DAS.

NB It is highly recommended that you have your passport photocopied and witnessed by a notary. This is a valid substitute (although some travellers report difficulties with this variant) and your passport can then be put into safe-keeping. Also, photocopy your travellers' cheques and any other essential documents. For more information, check with your consulate.

How To Get There By Air
San Andrés is a popular stopover on the routes Miami, or Central America to Colombia. By changing planes in San Andrés you can save money on flight fares. Avianca flies to Miami, SAM to Guatemala City and San José, Costa Rica, Sahsa to Tegucigalpa and Panama City. Note that Panama, Costa Rica and Honduras all require onward tickets which cannot be bought on San Andrés, but can be in Cartagena. SAM will not issue one way tickets to Central America. You buy a return and the SAM office on the mainland will refund once you show an onward ticket. The refund (less 15%) may not be immediate. Avianca, Aces and SAM have flights to most major Colombian cities: to Bogotá and Medellín with SAM (you can arrange a 72-hour stop-over in Cartagena).

Airport Information
San Andrés airport is 15 minutes' walk to town (taxi US$3 pp). All airline offices are in town (Avianca and SAM on Av Duarte Blum, Sahsa on Av Colombia), except Aces at the airport. The airport was being renewed in 1991. There is a customs tax of 15% on some items purchased if you are continuing to mainland Colombia.

There is an airport exit tax of US$15, from which only travellers staying less than 24 hours are exempt. When you arrive, ensure that all necessary documentation bears a stamp for your date of arrival; without it you will have to pay double the exit tax on leaving (with the correct stamp, you will only be charged half the exit ·tax if you have been in the country less than

30 days). Visitors staying more than 60 days have to pay an extra US$10 tax, which can only be avoided by bona-fide tourists who can produce the card given them on entry. There is a 15% tax on all international air tickets bought in Colombia for flights out of the country (7.5% on international return flights). Do not buy tickets for domestic flights to or from San Andrés island outside Colombia; they are much more expensive. When getting an onward ticket from Avianca for entry into Colombia, reserve a seat only and ask for confirmation in writing, otherwise you will pay twice as much as if purchasing the ticket inside Colombia.

Sunday flights are always heavily booked. In July and August, and December and January it is very difficult to get on flights into and out of San Andrés; book in advance if possible. If wait listed, do not give up hope, passengers usually get on a flight. Checking in for flights can be difficult because of queues of shoppers with their goods.

If flying from Guatemala to Colombia with SAM, via San Andrés, you have to purchase a round-trip ticket, refundable only in Guatemala. To get around this (if you are not going back to Guatemala) you will have to try to arrange a ticket swap with a traveller going in the other direction on San Andrés. There is, however, no difficulty in exchanging a round-trip ticket for a San Andrés-Colombian ticket with the airline, but you have to pay extra.

Flights to Colombia

British Airways has a twice-weekly service from London to **Bogotá**, via Caracas. Airlines with services from continental Europe are Air France, Alitalia, Iberia, and Lufthansa. Avianca, the Colombian national airline, flies from Frankfurt via Paris, Madrid and Caracas. Frequent services to and from the USA by Avianca and American.

Avianca flies from Miami and Newark to **Cartagena**; the same airline flies from **Barranquilla** to Miami (as does American, daily), Newark, Aruba, Curaçao and Santo Domingo.

Customs

Duty-free admission is granted for portable typewriters, radios, binoculars, personal and ciné cameras, but all must show use; 200 cigarettes or 50 cigars or 250 grams of tobacco or up to 250 grams of manufactured tobacco in any form, 2 bottles of liquor or wine per person.

How To Get There By Sea

Cruise ships and tours go to San Andrés; there are no other, official passenger services by sea. Cargo ships are not supposed to carry passengers to the mainland, but latest reports suggest that many do. If you want to leave by sea, speak only to the ship's captain. (Any other offer of tickets on ships to/from San Andrés, or of a job on a ship, may be a con trick.) Sometimes the captain may take you for free, otherwise he will charge anything between US$10-25; the sea crossing takes 3-4 days, depending on the weather. In Cartagena, ships leave from the Embarcadero San Andrés, opposite the Plaza de la Aduana.

Car Rental

National driving licences may be used by foreigners in Colombia, but must be accompanied by an official translation if in a language other than Spanish. International drivers licences are also accepted. Carry driving documents with you at all times. Even if you are paying in cash, a credit card may be asked for as proof of identity (Visa, Mastercard, American Express), in addition to passport and driver's licence.

Where To Stay

There is a tourist tax of 5% on rooms and an insurance charge, but no service charge, and tipping is at discretion. The more expensive hotels and restaurants also add on 10% VAT (IVA). The Colombian tourist office has lists of authorized prices for all hotels which are usually at least a year out of date. If you are overcharged the tourist office will arrange a refund. Most hotels in Colombia charge US$1 to US$6 for extra beds for children, up to a maximum (usually) of 4 beds per room.

Food

Colombia's food is very regional; it is quite difficult to buy in one area a dish you particularly liked in another. If you are economizing, ask for the "plato del día" or "plato corriente" (dish of the day). Of the Caribbean dishes, Cartagena's rice with coconut can be compared with rice *a la valenciana*; an egg *empanada*, consists of two layers of corn (maize) dough that open like an oyster-shell, fried with eggs in the middle, and try the *patacón*, a cake of mashed and baked plantain (green banana). *Huevos pericos*, eggs scrambled with onions and tomatoes, are a popular, cheap and nourishing snack for the impecunious—available almost anywhere. Throughout the country there is an abundance of fruits: bananas, oranges, mangoes, avocado pears, and (at least in the tropical zones) *chirimoyas, papayas*, and the delicious *pitahaya*, taken either as an appetizer or dessert and, for the wise, in moderation, because even a little of it has a laxative effect. Other fruits such as the *guayaba* (guava), *guanábana* (soursop), *maracuyá* (passion fruit), *lulo* (*naranjilla*), *mora* (blackberry) and *curuba* make delicious juices, sometimes with milk added to make a *sorbete*—but be careful of milk in Colombia. Fruit yoghurts are nourishing and cheap (try *Alpina* brand; *crema* style is best).

Drink

Tinto, the national small cup of black coffee, is taken ritually at all hours. Colombian coffee is always mild. (Coffee with milk is called *café perico; café con leche* is a mug of milk with coffee added.) *Agua de panela* is a common beverage (hot water with unrefined sugar), also made with limes, milk, or cheese. Many acceptable brands of beer are produced. The local rum is good and cheap; ask for *ron*, not *aguardiente*, because in Colombia the latter word is used for a popular drink containing aniseed (*aguardiente anisado*).

Warning

Great care should be exercised when buying imported spirits in shops. It has been reported that bottles bearing well-known labels have often been "recycled" and contain a cheap and poor imitation of the original contents. This can be dangerous to the health, and travellers are warned to stick to beer and rum. Also note that ice is usually not made from potable water.

Tipping

Hotels and restaurants 10%. Porters, cloakroom attendants, hairdressers and barbers, US$0.05-0.25. Taxi-drivers are not tipped.

Shopping

Local handicrafts are made from coral and coconut. Otherwise shopping is concentrated on the duty-free items so readily available. Typical Colombian products which are good buys: emeralds, leatherwork and handworked silver.

Currency The monetary unit is the peso, divided into 100 centavos. There are coins

of 50 centavos (rare) and of 1, 2, 5, 10, 20 and 50 pesos; there are notes of 100, 200, 500, 1,000, 2,000 and 5,000 pesos (a 10,000 peso note was planned for 1992). Large notes of over 1,000 pesos are often impossible to spend on small purchases as change is in short supply, especially in small cities, and in the morning. There is now a limit of 25,000 on the export of pesos. Travellers' cheques can in theory be exchanged in any bank, except the Banco de la República which, since June 1991, no longer undertakes exchange transactions. In practice, it is almost impossible to change dollars in a bank unless you hold an account. Therefore go to a *casa de cambio*, of which there are a few, legitimate ones; they are quicker to use than banks. Always check which rate of exchange is being offered. In mid-1992 the street rate was far worse than the official rate, owing to the amount of dollars in circulation. Hotels can give very poor rates of exchange, especially if you are paying in dollars. Owing to the quantity of counterfeit American Express travellers' cheques in circulation, travellers may experience difficulty in cashing these cheques, but the procedure is always slow, involving finger printing and photographs. It is also very difficult, according to our correspondents, to get reimbursement for lost American Express travellers' cheques. The best advice we can give is to take Thomas Cook's or a US bank's dollar traveller cheques' in small denominations. Sterling travellers' cheques are practically impossible to change in Colombia.

As it is unwise to carry large quantities of cash, **credit cards** are widely used, especially Diners' Club and Visa; Mastercard is less common, while American Express is only accepted in high-priced establishments in Bogotá. Many banks (e.g. Banco de Bogotá) advance pesos against Visa, and Banco de Occidente and Banco Industrial de Colombia give cash advances against Mastercard. In 1992 cash advances against credit cards gave the best rate of exchange.

Security

Carry your passport (or photocopy) at all times.

Avoid money changers on the street who offer over-favourable rates of exchange. They often short-change you or run off with your money, pretending that the police are coming. Beware of counterfeit dollars and pesos.

Colombia is part of a major drug-smuggling route. Police and customs activities have greatly intensified and smugglers increasingly try to use innocent carriers. Travellers are warned against carrying packages for other people without checking the contents (even taking your own boxes, packages or gift-wrapped parcels through customs may cause problems). Penalties run up to 12 years in none too comfortable jails. Be very polite if approached by policemen. If your hotel room is raided by police looking for drugs, try, if possible, to get a witness to prevent drugs being planted on you. Colombians who offer you drugs may well be setting you up for the police, who are very active on the north coast and San Andrés island.

If someone accosts you on the street, saying he's a plain-clothes policeman or drugs officer, and asks you to go to his office, offer to go with him to the nearest policeman (the tourist police where possible) or police station. He may well be a "confidence man" (if he doesn't ask to see your passport, he almost certainly is). These conmen usually work in pairs.

Health

Emergency medical treatment is given in hospitals: if injured in a bus accident, for example, you will be covered by insurance and treatment will be free. Take water sterilizer with you, or boil the water, or use the excellent mineral waters, when travelling outside the capital. Choose your food and eating places with care everywhere. Hepatitis is common; have a gamma-globulin injection before your trip. There is some risk of malaria and yellow fever in the coastal areas; prophylaxis is advised.

Climate And Clothing

Tropical clothing is needed in the hot and humid climate of the coast. Average temperature on the islands is 27-31°C.

Tourist Seasons

On the Caribbean coast and San Andrés and Providencia, high season is 15 December-30 April, 15 June-31 August.

Working Hours

Monday to Friday, commercial firms work 0800-1200 and from 1400-1730 or 1800. Government offices follow the same hours on the whole as the commercial firms, but generally prefer to do business with the public in the afternoon only. Embassy hours for the public are from 0900-1200 and from 1400-1700 (weekdays). Bank hours in San Andrés are 0800-1100, 1400-1500 Monday to Friday, Saturday morning only. Shopping hours are 0900-1230 and 1430-1830, including Saturday.

Public Holidays

Circumcision of our Lord (1 January), Epiphany* (6 January), St Joseph* (19 March), Maundy Thursday, Good Friday, Labour Day (1 May), Ascension Day*, Corpus Christi*, Sacred Heart*, SS Peter and Paul* (29 June), Independence Day (20 July), Battle of Boyacá (7 August), Assumption* (15 August), Discovery of America* (12 October), All Saints' Day* (1 November), Independence of Cartagena* (11 November), Immaculate Conception (8 December), Christmas Day (25 December).

When those marked with an asterisk do not fall on a Monday, or when they fall on a Sunday, they will be moved to the following Monday.

Time Zone

Eastern Standard Time—5 hours behind GMT.

Useful Addresses

DAS (immigration authorities) are at the San Andrés airport, Tel: 5540. (In Cartagena, DAS is just beyond Castillo San Felipe, behind the church; ask. In Barranquilla, DAS, Calle 54 No 41-113.) San Andrés Police, Tel: 6450; Red Cross, Tel: 3333; Panamanian Consulate, Av Atlántico No 1A-60, Tel: 6545. Other diplomatic representation in Barranquilla, Cartagena, or Bogotá.

Weights And Measures

Metric; weights should always be quoted in kilograms. Litres are used for liquid measures but US gallons are standard for the petroleum industry. Linear measures are usually metric, but the inch is quite commonly used by engineers and the yard on golf courses. For land measurement the hectare and cubic metre are officially employed but the traditional measures *vara* (80 centimetres) and *fanegada* (1,000 square *varas*) are still in common use. Food etc is often sold in *libras* (pounds), which are equivalent to ½ kilo.

Electric Current

120 volts AC. Transformer must be 110-150 volt AC, with flat-prong plugs (all of same size). Be careful with electrically heated showers.

Postal Services

Send all letters by airmail; there was reported to be no surface mail for overseas in 1992. Avianca controls all airmail services and has offices in provincial cities (Catalina Building, Av Duarte Blum in San Andrés). Correspondence with UK is good. It costs US$0.30 to send a letter or postcard to the US or Europe; a 1 kg package to Europe costs US$13 by air (Avianca).

Telecommunications

Systems have been automated; the larger towns are interconnected. Inter-city calls and cables must be made from Telecom offices unless you have access to a private phone (Telecom in San Andrés: Av Américas No 2A-23). Long-distance pay 'phones are located outside most Telecom offices, also at bus stations and airports. They take 20 peso coins. 1 peso coins for ordinary 'phones may be bought in 20 peso packets from Banco de la República. Fom the larger towns it is possible to telephone to Canada, the USA, the UK, and to several of the Latin American republics. International phone charges are high (about US$6 a minute to USA, US$8 to Europe, US$12 to Australia), but there is a 20% discount on Sunday; a deposit is required before the call is made which can vary between US$18 and US$36 (try bargaining it down), US$1 is charged if no reply, for person-to-person add an extra minute's charge to Canada, 2 minutes' to UK; all extra minutes' conversation cost ⅓ more. The best value is to purchase a phone card and dial direct yourself. AT&T USA Direct Service can be dialled on 900-11-0010. Collect, or reversed-charge, telephone calls are only possible from private telephones; make sure the operator understands what is involved or you may be billed in any case. It is also possible that the operator, once you have got through to him/her, may not call you back. The surest way of contacting home, assuming the facilities are available at each end, is to fax your hotel phone number to home and ask them to call you.

Tourist Information

In San Andrés, Corporación Nacional de Turismo (CNT), Avenida Colombia No 5-117, in front of *Hotel Isleño*, English spoken, maps, friendly, CNT has its headquarters at Calle 28, No 13A-15, **Bogotá** (Tel: 283-9466); it has branches in every departmental capital and other places of interest (in **Cartagena**, Carrera 3 No 36-57, Plaza Bolívar, Tel: 43400; in **Barranquilla**, Carrera 54 No 75-45, Tel: 454458).

They should be visited as early as possible not only for information on accommodation and transport, but also for details on areas which are dangerous to visit.

CNT also has offices in **New York**: 140 East 57th St, Tel: 688-0151; **Caracas**: Planta Baja 5 Av Urdaneta Ibarras a Pelota, Tel: 561-3592/5805; **Madrid**: Calle Princesa No 17 Tercero Izquierda, Tel: 248-5090/5690; and **Paris**: 9, Boulevard de la Madeleine, 75001 Paris, Tel: 260-3565.

BAY ISLANDS, HONDURAS

Introduction

The Central American republic of Honduras (population 5.0 million, capital Tegucigalpa) has a Caribbean coastline of 640 kilometres. Much of the country is mountainous: a rough plateau covered with volcanic ash and lava in the south, rising to peaks of over 2,000 metres in the Celaque range, but with intermont basins at between 900 and 1,800 metres. The volcanic detritus disappears to the north, revealing saw-toothed ranges which approach the coast at an angle; the one in the extreme north-west, along the border with Guatemala, disappears under the sea and shows itself again in an island group called the Bay Islands (Islas de la Bahía).

There are three main islands, Utila, Roatán and Guanaja, lying in an arc which curves away northeast from a point 32 km north of the port of La Ceiba. At the eastern end of Roatán are three small ones: Morat, Santa Elena and Barbareta; there are other islets and 65 cays. Today only Utila rests on the continental shelf, a deep trench separates it from Roatán.

Honduras possesses a number of other islands and cays: the Cayos Cochinos (Hog Cays), two islands and 13 cays 17 km from the Caribbean coast; Cayos Zapotillos, comprising Grass and Hunting Cays and one other, 42 km from the coast; the Swan Islands (Great Swan, Little Swan and Bobby Cay—Islas del Cisne, or Santanilla), 150 km northeast of Honduras; and 130 islets, cays and rocks off the swampy, densely-forested Mosquito coast, collectively called the Cayos Misquitos.

The total population of the Bay Islands is estimated at 21,550 (1988). There are English-speaking blacks who constitute the majority of the population, particularly on Roatán. Utila has a population which is roughly half black and half white, the latter of British stock descended mainly from settlers from Grand Cayman who arrived in 1830. Latin Hondurans have been moving to the islands from the mainland in recent years. There are also some Black Caribs, 5,000 of whom were deported from St Vincent in 1797 to Roatán. Many moved on to the mainland at a later date. The culture is very un-Latin American even though the government schools teach in Spanish. The population is bilingual.

The main industry is fishing, mostly for shellfish. Trade is also done in coconuts, bananas and plantains. Boat-building, once the principal occupation, is now dying.

Some of the things that you will *not* find on the Bay Islands are shopping centres, fast food, cruise ships, or crowds of tourists, and there is only one small stretch of paved road (on Roatán). There are telephones and television, including cable, now. Until 1988, wealthy Hondurans and the international and diplomatic community took most advantage of the islands' underwater potential, but the expansion of Roatán's airport to accommodate jets, will bring in many more visitors. Once landing rights have been granted to overseas carriers, the flow of tourists will increase further.

History

Columbus anchored off Guanaja in 1502, on his fourth voyage, but the islands had been inhabited for a long time before. Archaeologists have been busy on the islands but their findings are very confusing. The relationship between the Paya Indians who lived there and mainland groups has not been fully established. Clay vessels and figurines, articles of jade and stone, pendants, necklaces and amulets have been uncovered. In the 18th century European buccaneers, in the name of England or Spain, disputed the ownership of the islands. The ubiquitous Henry Morgan had a lair at Port Royal, Roatán and, according to local mythology, is buried on Utila. The British held the group for over a century before ceding the islands to Honduras in 1859.

Fauna

The Bay Islands' separation from the mainland permitted the development of a number of endemic animal species. Of the 106 species of sea bird reported on the islands, 20 (species and subspecies) are endemic, as are two lizards, the Roatán coral snake (poisonous) and a local type of *garrobo* (a reptile). The agouti found on Roatán is different from that found on the continent. The white-tailed deer is set to follow the islands' wild pig into extinction following indiscriminate hunting and the burning of vegetation. The Bay Islands Conservation Association (BICA) can be contacted through Charles George, "Vegas", Edificio Cooper, Calle Principal, Coxen's Hole, Roatán, Tel: (504) 45-1424, or Shelby McNab, c/o Robinson Crusoe Tours, or Troy Bodden, Troy's Dive Shop, Utila. Port Royal Park and Wildlife Refuge on Roatán is a highland reserve and unique Bay Island ecosystem. It contains the largest tract of the pine *pinus caribaea, var. hondurensis* and is home to many endemic species of flora and fauna (opossum, spiny lizard, coral snake, agouti, and a rare parrot). It also has precolumbian archaeological sites, and Port Royal harbour with its historical associations. BICA is seeking financial assistance to manage the Park and Refuge. At Sandy Bay, Roatán, is Carambola Botanical Gardens (Bill and Irma Brady, Tel: 45-1117), open daily 0700-1700, with flowering plants, ferns, spices, fruit trees, an orchid collection and archaeological sites. One can also see iguana and parrots.

Diving and Marine Life

The underwater environment is rich and extensive. Reefs surround the islands, often within swimming distance of the shore. They are a continuation of one of the largest barrier reefs in the world, stretching from reefs off Belize. Caves and caverns are a common feature, with a wide variety of sponges and the best collection of pillar coral in the Caribbean. 95% of the region's known corals can, it is claimed, be found in these waters. There is also great diversity in the fish, crustacea, turtles and other creatures. This wealth of marine life (and the dry land it surrounds) has inspired the Asociación Hondureña de Ecología (Honduran Ecology Association) to designate the following areas as sanctuaries or natural parks: all of Utila, except the island's settlements; the National Marine Park of Barbareta (comprising the islands of Barbareta, Morat, Santa Elena, mangrove swamps, the only remaining humid tropical forest (on Diamond Rock), unsurpassed coral reefs, and the eastern end of Roatán); West End, Roatán; 90% of Guanaja and its surrounding reefs. BICA manages the Sandy Bay Marine Reserve on West End, Roatán. The reserve contains coral reef ecosystems, which divers and snorkellers are permitted to visit under the control of BICA and local operators. Plans are under way to extend the reserve.

In addition, Honduras' other islands have been declared marine

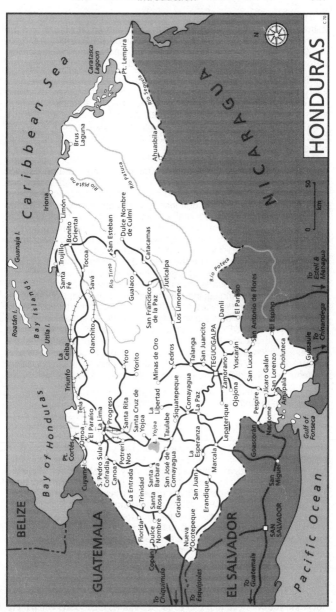

sanctuaries (Swan Islands, Cayos Cochinos) or biological reserves (Cayos Zapotillos and Misquitos), to protect the bird and aquatic life. (For more information, contact the Asociación Hondureña de Ecología, Apartado T-250, Toncontín, Tegucigalpa, or at its office on Boulevard Morazán, just before Centro Comercial Lomas del Boulevard.)

The islands are destined to become a major diving centre within a few years. Each of the three main islands offers a fascinating range of diving environments, from shallow, flat-bottomed dives to dramatic sheer reef walls. Jorge Valle-Aguiluz writes: "The reef area is so extensive and the dive resorts so few that there is very little chance that you will see another dive boat during your visit. Where the best diving is to be found is strictly a matter of opinion.

"Bay Islands coral formations are mostly close-fringing reefs with deeper areas near the shore creating extensive drop-offs, or walls, a short distance from the reef crest. A few areas near Utila, Cayos Cochinos and Pigeon Cays have a variety of patch, platform and bank reefs. An impressive feature of most Bay Islands reefs is the dramatic spur and grove systems associated with modern and ancient river drainage and local tide channels.

"Variations on this theme result in the development of numerous clefts, fissures, ledges, undercuts, overhangs, swim throughs, tunnels, caves, holes, and sizeable cathedral effects. Perhaps the most memorable example of this characteristic is Mary's Place on the south side of Roatán. Most island dive operations feature a number of special dive sites through wide or narrow cracks, with divers surrounded by huge masses of coral."

Snorkelling and diving equipment can be rented, and many of the hotels and resorts offer dive packages. It is difficult to arrange diving independently, although Bay Islands Divers give instruction to PADI certification level in individually structured courses. Prices start at US$215, Tel: Tegucigalpa 22-75-56 and ask for Bobby, or leave a message. Information on the Honduras Underwater Group can be obtained from Jorge Valle-Aguiluz at his *Café Allegro*, Av República de Chile 360-B, Colonia Palmira, Tegucigalpa. For more details of diving and boating possibilities, see text below.

Decompression Chamber and Ambulance are situated at "Cornerstone", at the entrance to *Anthony's Key Resort*, Sandy Bay, Tel: 45-15-15.

Utila

Utila (population 1,515) is only 32 km. from La Ceiba and is low lying, with only two hills, Pumpkin, and the smaller Stewarts with an aerial. The latter is nearer the main town, which is known locally as East Harbour. There are caves to which you can hike, one of them being reputed locally to have been a hideout for Henry Morgan. There is some evidence of Paya Indian culture. You can hike to Pumpkin Hill (45 minutes beyond *Bucket of Blood Bar*, on east side of the island) where there are some fresh water caves and a beach nearby (watch out for sharp coral), with a bar open in season. It can be very muddy after rain. Another 40-minute hike goes to the northern part of the island along a forested path. There are good views and a beach at the end, but it is rocky so sandals are needed. Utila is the cheapest and least developed of the islands to visit; there are no big resorts, but rather simpler dwellings where you can rent rooms. Take plenty of insect repellent; in February 1992 the island was sprayed against sandflies, with a 5 year guarantee. If it does not work, you will need to protect against sandflies on dry days when there

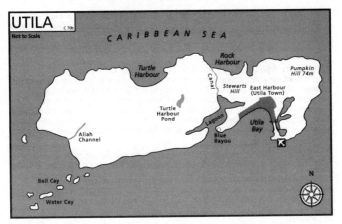

is no breeze. Coconut oil helps to keep them off. Sunbathing and swimming are not particularly good, but there is a swimming hole near the airport. At the left-hand end of the airstrip (from the town) is one of the best places for coral and quantity of fish. Snorkelling and diving equipment for hire. Going rate is US$30 for 2 dives, shop around for the best price (see below).

A 20-minute motorboat ride from East Harbour are the Cays, a chain of small islands populated by fisherfolk off the southwest coast of Utila. On the main Cay, a few families live; they are very friendly to foreigners, but there is nowhere to put a tent. 3 islands further out is Water Cay, one of the few places where you can camp, sling a hammock or, in emergency, sleep in, or under, the house of the caretaker; take food and fresh water. The caretaker collects a US$1 pp fee for landing. There are no facilities, but children sell cheap *pasteles de carne*. It is a coconut island with "white holes" (sandy areas with wonderful hot bathing in the afternoon) and some of the most beautiful underwater reefs in the world. The best snorkelling is off the S shore, a short walk from the beach, shallow water all around. To hire a *dory* (big motorized canoe) costs US$30 for four; many boatmen go and will collect you in the evening, recommended.

Island Information – Utila

Hotels on Utila The best hotel on the island is *Utila Lodge*, Tel: 45-3143, usually booked through US agent Tel: (904) 588-4131, an all-wooden building with decks and balconies, harbour view, US$50-67d, a/c, 8 rooms, clean and modern, run by Americans Shirley and Tom, meals only when they have guests; *Blue Bayou*, 25 minutes out of town, opposite end from airport (1 hour away), a beautiful spot for diving off the reef, US$10d, may be closed out of season, snacks and drinks available, restaurant only in high season, hammocks on the porch in the day, breeze usually keeps the mosquitoes away, bike rental US$2/day (take torch for night-time riding), rents canoes; *Trudy's*, 5 minutes from airport, US$4.60-6.50 pp with and without bath, comfortable, good breakfast and evening meals (but may be little room for non-residents), US satellite TV, diving equipment and boats for hire; *Palm Villa*, cabins at US$15 for 4, cooking facilities, good value, run by Willis Bodden; *Harbour View*, a few hundred metres past the bank on the left, US$4.50d, clean, fans, bathrooms clean, restaurant downstairs, owner takes diving and snorkelling trips; *Cross Creek* (see also **Diving** below), US$4.50, clean rooms, basic bathrooms, house rental US$40 for 2, US$45 for 3 and US$50 for 4; **Monkey Tail Inn**, US$1.30 pp, noisy, wooden building, cooking facilities, water all the time (beyond the *Bucket of Blood Bar*). Cheap and basic rooms at **Blueberry Hill** (US$1.15 pp), opposite *Bucket of Blood*, and **Dolores**; plenty of other houses and rooms for rent.

Restaurants *Toya's*, opposite the bank, popular, good; *Las Delicias*, small, go early, good fish; *Manhattan*, cheap, clean, main dishes greasy but good chocolate, spice and caramel cakes; *Bahía del Mar*, *Orma's*, simple but good food in nice little thatched bar overlooking the harbour; *Comedor El Teleño*, good food, meeting point; *The Cangaroo*, by Bancahsa; *Nolan's Place*, run by Dorothy, popular with locals, good food; *Selly's*, up the hill beyond *Bucket of Blood*, good seafood, cheap, self-service, popular with US divers and others, cable TV. *Mermaid's Corner Souvenir Shoppe* serves good pastries when it's open.

Bars *Bucket of Blood*, owned by Mr. Woods, a mine of information on the history of Utila and the Cays; *07* and *Casino* are both lively, as is *Captain Roy's*, next to the airport.

Arts and Crafts Günther, the dive master (see below), is a painter and sculptor with a gallery at his house (up the hill, near *Selly's* restaurant), good map of Utila, paintings, cards, wood carving and black coral jewellery; another sculptor is Bill Green, ask for him at *Casino Bar*.

Facilities There is a bank for changing dollars (Bancahsa) and you can get cash against a Visa card; another bank is under construction next door. Dollars are accepted on the island. There is a post office, a Hondutel office near *Utila Lodge*, and a good clinic. A paved road through the town is planned for 1992 and a 60-metre concrete jetty.

Tours Shelby McNab, who runs Robinson Crusoe Tours, takes visitors on half-day tours around the island (US$10 pp) explaining his theory that Daniel Defoe based his famous book on Robinson Crusoe on Utila (not Alexander Selkirk off Chile), fascinating. He also runs Gables Health Club, keep-fit, weight machines, steam bath and massages.

Diving Club Aqua Caribe, in front of *Harbour View Hotel*, run by Austrian Günther and American Terry Clymire, Tel: 45-3159, Fax 45-3106, fully qualified instructors, with a complete range of services, highly rec. Cross Creek, run by Ronald Janssen, Tel: or Fax 45-3134, scuba trips for beginners and certified divers, US$30 for 2 dives in one day, soft drink between dives, free accommodation for that day; 4-day beginner course (PADI, open water), including all boat dives and equipment, 4 nights' accommodation, US$175; advanced open water, 2 days, 5 dives US$150; rescue and dive master, 3 weeks, US$750; snorkel equipment (mask, snorkel and fins) US$2.50. Troy's Dive Shop, run by Troy Bodden, who also owns Bell Cay, a tiny immaculately-kept cay next to Water Cay (2 houses, fully self-contained, usually booked by groups, up to 14 people, US$50 per day pp, bookings through Caribbean Travel Agency in La Ceiba, Tel: 43-1360/1), Troy also hires out snorkel equipment and takes boat trips. Also recommended is Chris from the Utila Diving School, who is patient with beginners and speaks English.

Roatán

It is a few hours' sail to **Roatán**, the largest of the islands (population 10,245). It has a paved road running from West End to just beyond French Harbour, continuing unpaved to Oak Ridge and Punta Gorda; there are other, unmade roads. Renting a car or scooter gives access to many places that public transport does not reach. The capital of the department, Coxen's Hole, or Roatán City, is on the south-western shore. Besides being the seat of the local government, it has immigration, customs and the law courts. Port Royal, towards the eastern end of the island, and famous in the annals of buccaneering, is now just a community of private homes with no public facilities.

From Coxen's Hole to Sandy Bay, with the Sandy Bay Reserve and the

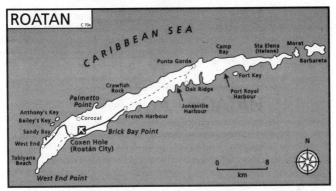

Carambolla Botanical Gardens, is a 2-hour walk, or a US$1 bus ride (airport employees try to charge US$12; it should only be US$2 from the airport). West End, a further 5 minutes by road beyond Sandy Bay, is a quiet community at the west tip of the island. There are several good restaurants as well as hotels with bungalows and rooms to rent. You can take a small motor boat from *Foster and Vivian's Restaurant* for a 10-minute ride to West Bay (US$1). West Bay is a beautiful, clean, unspoilt beach with excellent snorkelling at the far end; there are a couple of jetties where you can escape the sandflies which lurk in the powdery white sand. Take your own food and drinks, and insect repellent, because there are no facilities there. It is a stiff walk from Coxen's Hole over the hills (3 hours) to West End, or take the bus on the paved road for US$1, 20 minutes.

There are many minibuses which wait on Calle Principal in Coxen's Hole, going to points E and W; they usually leave on the hour or half-hour. At nightfall or on Sundays buses charge US$10 for express journeys. A frequent bus service goes to French Harbour (US$1.50), with its shrimping and lobster fleet the main fishing port of Roatán. There are two seafood packing plants: Mariscos Agua Azul and Mariscos Hybour. Two small boutiques are *The Brown Parrot*, just past *Buccaneer Inn*, and the one in the Yacht Club; there are also two grocery stores. The road passes *Coleman's Bakery*, where you can buy freshly-baked products.

The main road goes across the mountain ridge to Jonesville, Punta Gorda and Oak Ridge. Taking a bus on this route is the best way to see the island's hilly interior, with beautiful views from coast to coast. Jonesville is known for its mangrove canal, which is best reached by hiring a taxi boat in Oak Ridge. In Punta Gorda on the north coast, the oldest established community on Roatán, Black Caribs retain their own language, music, dance, food, crafts and religion. Carib Week, 8-12 April, is a good time to experience their customs. Oak Ridge, situated on a cay (US$0.40 crossing in a dory from the bus stop), is built around a deep inlet. It is a charming little fishing port, with rows of dwellings on stilts built on the water's edge (bus Coxen's Hole-Oak Ridge or Punta Gorda, 1 hour, US$1.60). You can hire a taxi boat to show you round. As well as its hotels, there is a grocery store and a couple of good restaurants.

Hire a boat for an hour's sail up the coast to Port Royal (also reached by good road from Oak Ridge); old British gun emplacements on Fort Cay. No bus from Port Royal to Oak Ridge, and it's a tough 3-hour walk. Note the Black Carib village of Punta Gorda on the north coast (probably the first non-Indian settlement on the islands). Beaches excellent; the best is said to be Camp Bay on the north coast at the eastern end (road sometimes too muddy to get there). Roatán is expensive, twice as dear as the mainland.

Island Information – Roatán

Hotels and Restaurants on Roatán At West End, *Roberts Hill*, US$20 with bath and fan, more basic rooms with shared bath US$10, clean, snorkelling, friendly, good value; *Lost Paradise*, Tel: 45-13-06, Fax 45-13-88, US$70, full board only, delicious meals (open to non-residents, book in advance), snorkelling equipment, transport back to airport; *Half Moon Bay Villages*, Tel: 45-1080/1382, US$25, bungalows and cabins with bath, burger-style restaurant to be built (same owner as *Coral* at Coxen's Hole); *Seaside Cottages*, US$25, individual cabins; *Seagrape Plantation*, Tel: 45-14-28, cabins, family atmosphere, friendly; *Jimmy Miller*, US$7, very friendly, cooking facilities, snorkelling gear available; *Sarina's*, similar price, reasonable rooms, meals around US$2.50, house for rent on beach US$100/month. Rooms for rent, about US$5d, some rather dingy.

Places to eat are scarce at West End, but *Foster and Vivian's Restaurant* is near *Roberts Hill*, good atmosphere and seafood, not cheap, built over the water, no sandflies, owned by Foster Diaz, his wife Vivian is the cook (they also jointly own a duplex on the beach, enquire at the restaurant, or to the other partner Robert Beels in Coral Gables, Florida, Tel: 305-448-5580). *Chino's* restaurant serves local meals and seafood, also has cabins, Tel: 45-1314; on the same property is the Diving Centre of Tyll Sass and Tokio Motorbike Rental (see below). *Sea View Restaurant*, highly recommended, be early since it's small and often runs out of food, large portions, home cooking; *Luna's Bay Café*, good for breakfast, downstairs at *Lucy's Minimart* for basic foodstuffs. Try the coconut bread which can be bought from the local women. There is a good gift shop, *Joanna's* next to *Robert's Hill*, with some good quality products.

At **Sandy Bay**, *Anthony's Key Resort*, Tel: 45-10-03, Fax 45-11-40 (US$75 full board), glorious situation, accommodation in small wooden cabins, launch and diving facilities (US$20, US$40 non-residents, the owner, Julio Galindo, is very serious about helping the environment and local community, the resort's own cay, Bailey's, has a small wildlife reserve (parrots, cockatoo, toucan, monkeys, agoutis, turtles), it has an interesting museum of some archaeological and colonial history, natural history laboratory, A-V lecture hall (entry for non-guests US$2), a dormitory lodge for study groups is to be built in 1992; it also has a dolphin enclosure in a natural pool, guests can swim with the dolphins for US$45, non-guests US$50); *Pirate's Den*, US$20-50, full board, poor service, beware of overcharging (well named); *Bamboo Inn*, US$15, clean and good (nice restaurant next door, reasonable prices); *Beth's Hostel*, on the hill above *Bamboo Inn*, US$10, owner, Beth Maglothin lives upstairs, use of kitchen, veranda with hammocks, no smokers, good supply of snorkelling equipment; *Quinn's*, reasonable.

At **French Harbour**, *Coral Reef Inn*; *Caribinn*, both US$15-20 range; *French Harbour Yacht Club*, Tel: 45-14-78, Fax 45-14-59, US$35, ocean-view rooms, cable TV in every room, reasonable rates, good food (especially lunch), friendly; *Buccaneer*, Tel: 45-10-32, Fax 45-1289, from US$55 to US$193 pp for a 3-day, 2-night package; *Fantasy Island Beach Resort*, Tel: 45-1222 (USA 813-251-5771), 80 rooms, luxurious on a cay, US$90-120, up to US$390 for package; *Coco View Resort*, Tel: 45-10-11; *Hotelito*, US$10, sometimes no water, in the village; *Brito's* (no sign, green) just before *Buccaneer Inn*, US$6-7, with fan, very good value. *Romeo's Restaurant*, Tel: 45-15-18, good for seafood.

At **Brick Bay**: *Caribbean Sailing Club*, modern hotel, US$55, with breakfast; *Island Garden*, Tel: 45-1585, Fax: 45-1588, US$50 pp in double room with breakfast, good European-run guest house (contact Edith Free, Tel: 45-1585), airport transfers, full board available, snorkelling, sailing, scuba diving US$20 pp per dive; *Romeo's Resort Dive and Yacht Club*, Tel: 45-11-27, Fax 45-15-94, US$30 and up, good.

At **Oak Ridge**, *Reef House Resort*, Tel: 45-2142/2297, in USA (512) 681-2888,

1-800-328-8897, Fax (512) 341-7942, US$130d, including meals, various packages, including diving, offered, wooden cabins with seaview balconies, seaside bar, private natural pool, good snorkelling from the shore, manager Carlos Acosta. *San José Hotel*, US$10, with bath (2 rooms), US$8 without (3 rooms), clean, pleasant, good value, good food, English-speaking owner, Louise Solórzano. There is a *pizzería* and, next door, a supermarket.

At **Port Royal**, *Camp Bay Resort*, over US$50; *Roatán Lodge*, Port Royal, luxury accommodation in cabins, hosts Brian and Lisa Blancher provide scuba diving and snorkelling expeditions; *Miss Merlee's Guest House*.

At **Coxen's Hole**: *Elizabethan Inn*, luxury, in Barrio El Ticket in front of Church of God; *Central*, US$10, basic but recommended, run by a doctor; *Coral*, owner Dr Jackeline Bush, US$10d, shared bath, clean, comfortable, Peace Corps favourite, basic; *Airport View* US$25 (less without bath or a/c); *Cay View*, Calle Principal, Tel: 45-12-02, Fax 45-1179, 15 rooms, US$16d, a/c, restaurant, bar, fishing, snorkelling, diving, cable TV; *El Paso*, next door, US$10, shared bath, restaurant (not cheap). Many of the cheaper hotels have water shortages.

Comedor Ray Monty, very cheap, set meal US$1.50 but avoid the meat, fish good; *Burger Hut*, opposite *Hotel Coral*, clean, good, chicken and fish, not expensive; *Hungry Diver*, pizzas and expensive seafood. *El Punto*, bar with one basic dish, very cheap. *H B Warren*, large well-stocked supermarket with cafetería, mainly lunch and snacks, open till 1800.

There are other, cheaper, places to stay, for example, Miss Effie's (near *Anthony's Key Resort*) and houses to let (at West End, Half Moon Bay, or Punta Gorda).

Facilities At Coxen's Hole are a post office, tourist information, *VIPs* duty free shop, groceries and several souvenir shops.

Discotheques 2 informal ones which come alive about midnight, *Paraguas* and *Harbour View*. They play mostly reggae, punta, calypso, salsa, country music and some rock.

Banks Banco Atlántida and Bancahsa in Coxen's Hole and French Harbour; also Banco Sogerín and Banffaa. Bancahsa in Oak Ridge, Tel: 45-22-10.

Car Rental National, *Hotel Fantasy Island*, Tel: 45-11-28; Amigo at the airport. Tokio Motorbike Rental, attached to *Chino's* at West End, US$21 pp per day.

Travel Agents *Bay Islands Tour and Travel Center*, in Coxen's Hole and French Harbour. *Tropical Travel*, in *Hotel Cay View*, Tel: 45-11-46; *Columbia Tours*, Barrio El Centro, Tel: 45-11-60.

Diving West End: Tyll v Sass, at *Chino's*, Tel: 45-1314 or in USA (813) 593-1259, one-tank dive US$20, windsurfing US$4 per hour, resort courses in both sports and charters available; Ocean Divers diving and snorkel hire, mask, snorkel and fin rental US$5 per day. Roatán Divers, Half Moon Bay, West End, Tino and Alejo Monterrosa, experienced, Spanish and English spoken, US$20 package dives, US$25 single dives, night dives, recommended. The *Bay Islands Aggressor* operates out of Roatán, US$1,395 for a 6-day cruise; contact The Aggressor Fleet, PO Drawer K, Morgan City, LA 70381, Tel: (504) 385-2416, Fax: (504) 384-0817 (1-800-348-2628). See also above under **Hotels and Restaurants**.

Excursion In glass-bottomed boat of Dennis, at *Foster and Vivian's Restaurant*, West End, to Hottest Sparrow Bay, for example, beyond *Anthony's Key Resort*, where the boat anchors for snorkelling, about US$4 pp in a group of 16, 4½ hours. He also takes charters and cruises all along the coast.

Guanaja

Columbus called Guanaja, the easternmost of the group, the Island of Pines, and the tree is still abundant. The locals call the island Bonacca, and it is also known as Isla Grande. The island's origins are both volcanic and coraline, so it has a variety of aspects. Marble Hill cave can be visited. Good (but sweaty) clambering on the island gives splendid views of the jungle and the sea. There are several attractive waterfalls. Much of Guanaja town, covering a small cay off the coast, is built on stilts above sea water: hence its nick-name, the "Venice of Honduras". Many other cays surround the coast and launches go to West End, Pine Ridge Bight, Michael Rock, Sandy Bay and Los Cayos. The island's population is 4,000. Bathing is made somewhat unpleasant by the many sandflies. These and mosquitoes cannot be escaped on the island, all the beaches are infected (coconut oil will help to ward off sandflies and doubles as sun protection). The cays are better, including Guanaja town. South West Caye is specially recommended. The diving and snorkelling in the clear waters compensates for any discomfort on the shore.

Island Information—Guanaja

Where To Stay and Eat *Alexander*, US$25, new (1990), Tel: 45-43-26, US$100 in 3-bed, 3-bathroom apartment; *Bayman Bay Club* (beautiful location on the north coast, Tel: 45-41-79) and *Posada del Sol* (on an outlying cay, beach, pool, tennis, Tel: 45-41-86), both have diving facilities and are in the US$120-150 range; *Miller*, US$25 (cheaper without air conditioning or bath, TV, restaurant, Tel: 45-42-02; *Harry Carter*, US$15, but "passed it", ask for a fan, all the a/c is broken down, clean however. *Rosaino*, US$25, with bath and a/c. *Club Guanaja Este*, full board available, many aquatic activities, and horseriding and hiking, reservations and information PO Box 40541, Cincinnati, Ohio 45240 or travel agents. *Casa Sobre El Mar*, on Bound Key, Tel: 45-41-80 (31-05-95 in Tegucigalpa), offers all-inclusive packages for US$75 per person. *Day Inn*, hotel and restaurant.

Where to Eat *Harbour Light*, through *Mountain View* discotheque, good food reasonably priced for the island; *The Nest*, Tel: 45-42-90, good eating in the evening; *Glenda's*, good standard meals for under US$1, small sandwiches

Facilities There are 3 banks, including Bancahsa and Banco Atlántida.

Cayos Cochinos

The Cayos Cochinos (Hog Islands), with lovely primeval hardwood forests, are 17 km north-east of La Ceiba (two small islands and thirteen palm-fringed cays): privately owned with reserved accommodation at Cayos del Sol. On the Isla de Cochino Grande is a dive resort; very beautiful. The owner of the largest island, Bobby Griffith, permits camping, especially if you can give him a news magazine or two.

Information for Visitors

Documents
A visa is not required, nor tourist card, for nationals of all West European countries, USA, Canada, Australia, New Zealand, or Japan. Citizens of other countries need either a tourist card which can be bought from Honduran consulates for US$2-3, occasionally less, or a visa, and they should enquire at a Honduran consulate in advance to see which they need. The price of a visa seems to vary per nationality, and according to where bought. It is imperative to check entry requirements in advance at a consulate.

Extensions of 30 days are easy to obtain (up to a maximum of 6 months' stay, cost US$5). There are immigration offices for

extensions at La Ceiba, San Pedro Sula and other towns, and all are more helpful than the Tegucigalpa office. A valid International Certificate of Vaccination against smallpox is required only from visitors coming from the Indian subcontinent, Indonesia and the countries of southern Africa. A ticket out of the country is necessary for air travellers (if coming from USA, you won't be allowed on the plane without one); onward tickets must be bought outside the country. It is not impossible to cash in the return half of the ticket in Honduras, but there is no guarantee and plenty of time is required.

NB To enter, you must *not* have in your

passport a stamp from a communist country (ie with which Honduras does not have diplomatic relations; this includes India); there is no official regulation concerning this, it is left to the individual judgement of border officials and therefore treatment may vary according to entry point.

There are no Customs duties on personal effects; 200 cigarettes or 100 cigars, or ½ kg of tobacco, and 2 quarts of spirit are allowed in free.

How To Get There

Sahsa has direct flights once a week, each to Roatán from Houston, Miami and New Orleans. On other days, the best flight connections from the USA are to San Pedro Sula, the second city, from Miami (American, Sahsa, Taca), then fly Isleña to the islands; or else go TAN-Sahsa to La Ceiba from Tegucigalpa and on from there (see **Transport to Roatán** below). There may be irregular boat connections with the Cayman Islands (see below). Flights to all three main islands originate in La Ceiba, with interconnection flights between Roatán and Guanaja only. Alternatively, you can go overland from either city (taking in some of mainland Honduras's sights on the way—see *The Mexico and Central American Handbook*). to the main port of access, La Ceiba, or to Puerto Cortés (which has a less frequent service).

Air Services To Honduras From London: British Airways, Delta, American, Continental or Virgin Atlantic to Miami, then American Airlines or Sahsa to Tegucigalpa. Also from Miami, Taca via San Salvador; to Tegucigalpa from New Orleans with Sahsa, or with Continental (via Houston) and Taca (via San Salvador); from Houston, besides Continental, Sahsa also flies 5 times a week; Lacsa flies to San Pedro Sula from New York (as does American), New Orleans (also Sahsa) and Los Angeles. Taca flies non-stop Miami-San Pedro Sula daily. Sahsa flies from Tegucigalpa to all Central American capitals, and to San Andrés Island; Lacsa flies to San José from San Pedro Sula direct; Taca flies to Mexico City and Guatemala as well as to San Salvador. Connections with Curaçao are made at Guatemala City (KLM/Taca). From Europe: subject to government approval Iberia's Thursday and Sunday. Madrid-Guatemala flights were to continue to San Pedro Sula; otherwise take a daily Iberia flight to Guatemala City and change to Sahsa;

alternatively fly KLM to Guatemala and a similar connection, or fly to Miami and on from there.

There is an airport tax and hospital tax of 3% on all tickets sold for domestic journeys, and a 10% tax on airline tickets for international journeys. There is an airport departure tax of 40 lempiras (US$7.35) and a customs tax of 20 lempiras (neither charged if in transit less than 9 hours). Note that the border offices close at 1700, not 1800 as in most other countries; there may be a fee charged after that time.

NB If you are flying from Honduras to a country that requires an onward ticket, Sahsa will not let you board their planes without it.

La Ceiba is reached by bus in 3 hours from San Pedro Sula (Tupsa, 2 Avenida N, 5-6 Calle, hourly from 0530, US$2.70); Puerto Cortés is 45 minutes by bus from San Pedro Sula (eg Impala, 2 Avenida, 4-5 Calle S O, No 23, several each hour, US$0.75). If going from the capital there is a direct bus to La Ceiba for US$5, or you have to go to San Pedro Sula and change buses there: take a Hedmán Alas bus (the best, US$4, 4½ hours, address in Tegucigalpa: 13-14 Calle, 11 Avenida, Comayagüela district, Tel: 37-71-43; in San Pedro Sula: 7-8 Avenida N O, 3 Calle, Casa 51, Tel: 53-13-61); other services between Tegucigalpa and San Pedro are cheaper at US$2.50.

Transport to Utila Isleña and Sahsa (apparently interchangeable) fly from **La Ceiba** for US$10 one way. Flights leave at 0600 and 1600, 15 minutes. Sosa fly from La Ceiba Monday-Saturday 0600 and 1530. Check all flight times in advance. There are no flights to the other islands. No need to take a taxi from Utila airport to town; US$2 for 300 metres.

Boats from **La Ceiba** to Utila charge US$5 single, 3 hours; some return overnight to **Puerto Cortés** (bunks available), US$5, times posted in main street. Take food and torch. Between Puerto Cortés and Utila, no regular schedule, US$10, continuing to Roatán. Fishing boats from La Ceiba charge US$10 to Utila.

Boats from Utila to Roatán can be chartered for about US$70; with enough passengers this can work out cheaper than flying back to La Ceiba and out to Roatán. Occasional freight boats, eg *Utila*

Tom, take passengers from Utila to Roatán. It's a 3-hour journey between the two islands and you and your possessions are liable to get soaked.

Transport to Roatán Take a plane to Coxen's Hole (airport is 20 minutes walk from town, taxi US$1.50) and launch up coast to French Harbour and Oak Ridge. Isleña and Sahsa fly from **La Ceiba** 6 times a day, US$16 one way (fewer on Sunday); Sahsa has a daily afternoon flight, except Saturday, from **Tegucigalpa** and **San Pedro Sula**, and a Sunday flight from Tegucigalpa and La Ceiba. Isleña flies twice a day from San Pedro Sula via La Ceiba. From the USA, Sahsa flies on Sat. from **Houston** via San Pedro Sula, on Sunday from **Miami** direct, and on Friday from **New Orleans** direct; Taca/Isleña connection from Miami via San Pedro Sula, Friday-Sunday. Sosa fly from La Ceiba to Roatán 0700 and 1300 Monday-Saturday, continuing to **Guanaja** (US$15 one way) about 10 minutes after arrival in Roatán. Roatán airport takes jets. Airlines: TACA, Edificio Shop and Save, Coxen's Hole, Tel: 45-12-36, at airport Tel: 45-13-87; TAN-Sahsa, Coxen's Hole Tel: 45-15-17, airport Tel: 45-10-85; Isleña, airport Tel: 45-10-88.

Boats go irregularly from Puerto Cortés to Roatán, US$5 plus US$0.50 dock charge for tourists. Boats most days at 1400 for La Ceiba, US$20. Fishing boats to La Ceiba for US$10 pp. Charter sailing yacht *Lusanda*, US$900 for 4 people for 4 nights/3 days, with transport to and from La Ceiba by air.

It is possible to **ship a vehicle to Roatán**, which costs US$150 from Puerto Cortés, about US$95 back from Roatán, but this is not recommended because of the carelessness of the boats' crews, lack of insurance of the boats, bureaucratic hassles and roughness of the sea crossing. Having said that, driving is fine when you get there.

Transport to Guanaja An airport on Bonacca Island, boat to Guanaja, US$1; Isleña has 3 flights daily except Saturday from La Ceiba, leaving at 0630, 1230 and 1600, US$20 each way. TAN-Sahsa Tel: 45-42-90. Other, non-scheduled flights are available.

The *Suyapa* sails between Guanaja, La Ceiba and Puerto Cortés. The *Miss Sheila* also does the same run and goes on to George Town (Grand Cayman). Cable Doly Zapata, Guanaja, for monthly sailing dates

to Grand Cayman (US$75 one way). Irregular sailings from Guanaja to Trujillo, twice a week, 5 hours, US$10. Irregular but frequent sailings in lobster boats for next to nothing to Puerto Lempira in Caratasco Lagoon, Mosquitia, or more likely, only as far as the Río Plátano.

Transport to Cayos Cochinos Take a bus from the stop 1 block from La Ceiba market to Nueva Armenia (US$1.50), then try to hitch on a dugout, or charter one (about US$10).

Where To Stay On The Mainland
Accommodation on the islands is given above.

If you have to spend the night in Tegucigalpa or San Pedro Sula, there are many hotels in each city in all price ranges. In Tegucigalpa, the cheaper ones tend to be in the Comayagüela district, which is most convenient for the bus terminals. The most expensive is the *Honduras Maya* in Colonia Palmira. In San Pedro Sula, the best is the *Gran Hotel Sula*, in the city; cheaper ones can be found between the bus terminals and the downtown market.

Accommodation is more limited in **La Ceiba**: the cheapest are beside the railway line leading from the central square to the pier; middle range hotels can be found on Avenida San Isidro (eg *Ceiba*, *Iberia*, *Dorita*, all reasonable); *Príncipe*, on 7 Calle between Av 14 de Julio and Av San Isidro, US$10 with bath and a/c, cheaper with fan, clean, recommended; the best in town is probably the *Colonial*, Av 14 de Julio, 6a y 7a Calle, Tel: 49-19-53, over US$20 a night, a/c, jacuzzi, nice atmosphere, or *Gran Hotel París*, Parque Central. *Hotel San Carlos* and its cafeteria is an information point for travel to the Bay Islands (cheap rooms).

Hotels in **Puerto Cortés** tend to be more basic, but in the US$30-40 range *International Mr Ggeerr* (Barrio El Centro) has been recommended; also *Costa Azul*, Playa El Faro, with restaurant, sports including horse riding, first class. Recommended at the cheaper end is *Formosa*, friendly Chinese owners, good food and value.

Tipping
Normally 10% of the bill.

Currency
The Honduran unit is the lempira, divided into 100 centavos. It was floated against the US dollar in 1990, having been fixed at a value of half the dollar since 1926. The

exchange rate on the now legalized parallel market is given in the Exchange Rate tables.

Health

Dysentery and stomach parasites are common and malaria is endemic in coastal regions, where a prophylactic regime should be undertaken and mosquito nets carried. Inoculate against typhoid and tetanus. Water is definitely not safe; drink bottled water. Salads and raw vegetables must be sterilized under personal supervision. There are hospitals at Tegucigalpa and all the larger towns.

Although the islands' climate is cooled by the trade winds, the sun is very strong (the locals bathe in T-shirts). Sand gnats and other insects are common, especially away from the resorts.

Climate

Average temperature is about 27°C, with easterly trade winds blowing all year. The wettest months are October to December; little rain falls February to May.

Public Holidays In Honduras

Most of the feast days of the Roman Catholic religion and also New Year's Day (1 January), Day of the Americas (14 April), Holy Week: Thursday, Friday, and Saturday before Easter Sunday, Labour Day (1 May), Independence Day (15 September), Francisco Morazán (3 October), Discovery of America (12 October), Army Day (21 October).

Time Zone

Local standard time is 6 hours behind GMT, 1 hour behind EST.

Weights And Measures

The metric system is in use.

Tourist Information

Instituto Hondureño de Turismo, Apartado Postal 154-C, Tegucigalpa, DC, Honduras (offices at Toncontín airport, in Barrio Guanacaste, Tegucigalpa, 15 minute walk from Parque Central, or take bus from Parque Central in direction of Colonia 21 de Octubre or Lomas de Guijarro, Edificio Inmosa, 3-4 Calle, 4 Avenida N O, San Pedro Sula, and Ramón Villeda Morales airport, San Pedro Sula). See above for the address of the Asociación Hondureña de Ecología.

In the USA: Honduras Information Service, 501 Fifth Avenue, New York 10017, Tel: (212) 490-0766.

We are most grateful to Huw Clough and Kate Hennessy (London NW), Ronald Janssen (resident on Utila) and Jorge Valle-Aguiluz (Tegucigalpa) for new information on the Bay Islands.

THE BELIZE CAYES

Introduction

BELIZE, formerly known as British Honduras, borders on Mexico and Guatemala, and has a land area of about 8,900 square miles, including numerous small islands, called cayes. Its greatest length (north-south) is 174 miles and its greatest width (east-west) is 68 miles. The capital is Belmopan, but the main commercial centre is Belize City on the coast.

The coastlands are low and swampy with much mangrove, many salt and fresh water lagoons and some sandy beaches. In the north the land is low and flat, but in the southwest there is a heavily forested mountain massif with a general elevation of between 2,000 and 3,000 feet. In the eastern part are the Maya Mountains, not yet wholly explored, and the Cockscomb Range which rises to a height of 3,675 feet at Victoria Peak. To the west are some 250 square miles of the Mountain Pine Ridge, with large open spaces and some of the best scenery in the country.

The most fertile areas of the country are in the northern foothills of the Maya Mountains: citrus fruit is grown in the Stann Creek valley, while in the valley of the Mopan, or upper Belize river, cattle raising and mixed farming are successful. The northern area of the country has long proved suitable for sugar cane production. In the south bananas and mangoes are cultivated. The lower valley of the Belize river is a rice-growing area as well as being used for mixed farming and citrus cultivation.

The population is estimated at 190,790 (1991 census). About 40% of them are of mixed ancestry, the so-called Creoles. They predominate in Belize City and along the coast, and on the navigable rivers. 33% of the population are mestizo; 7% are Indians, mostly Mayas, who predominate in the north between the Hondo and New rivers and in the extreme south and west. About 8% of the population are Garifuna (Black Caribs), descendants of the Black Caribs deported from St Vincent in 1797; they have a distinct language, and can be found in the villages and towns along the southern coast. They are good linguists, many speaking Mayan languages as well as Spanish and "Creole" English. They also brought much of their culture and customs from the West Indies, including religious practices and ceremonies, for example Yankanu (John Canoe) dancing at Christmas time. The remainder are of unmixed European ancestry (the majority Mennonites, who speak a German dialect, and are friendly and helpful) and a rapidly growing group of North Americans.

English is the official language, although about 75% speak mostly "Creole" English. Spanish is the mother tongue for about 15%. About 30% are bilingual, and 10% trilingual (see above). Spanish is widely spoken in the northern and western areas.

History

Throughout the country, especially in the forests of the centre and south are many ruins of the Classic Maya Period, which flourished here and in neighbouring Guatemala from the 4th to the 9th century and then

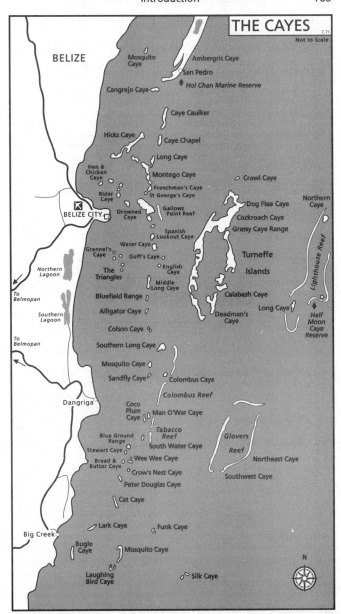

THE CAYES
C.71
Not to Scale

BELIZE

Mosquito Caye
Ambergris Caye
San Pedro
Hol Chan Marine Reserve

Cangrejo Caye

Caye Caulker

Hicks Caye
Caye Chapel

Long Caye

Hen & Chicken Caye
Montego Caye
Crawl Caye

Frenchman's Caye
St George's Caye

Rider Caye

BELIZE CITY
Drowned Caye
Gallows Point Reef
Dog Flea Caye
Northern Caye

Cockroach Caye

Spanish Lookout Caye
Grassy Caye Range

Water Caye
Turneffe Islands

Grennel's Caye
Goff's Caye

Northern Lagoon
The Triangles
English Caye

To Belmopan

Middle Long Caye

Bluefield Range
Calabash Caye

Long Caye

Southern Lagoon
Alligator Caye
Deadman's Caye

Half Moon Caye Reserve

To Belmopan
Colson Caye

Southern Long Caye

Mosquito Caye

Dangriga
Sandfly Caye
Columbus Caye

Columbus Reef

Coco Plum Caye
Man O'War Caye

Tabacco Reef
Glovers Reef

Blue Ground Range
Stewart Caye
South Water Caye
Northeast Caye

Bread & Butter Caye
Wee Wee Caye

Crow's Nest Caye
Southwest Caye

Peter Douglas Caye

Cat Caye

Big Creek
Lark Caye
Funk Caye

Bugle Caye
Mosquito Caye

Laughing Bird Caye
Silk Caye

N

somewhat mysteriously emigrated to Yucatán. It has been estimated that the population then was ten times what it is now.

The first settlers were Englishmen and their black slaves from Jamaica who came about 1640 to cut logwood, then the source of textile dyes. The British Government made no claim to the territory but tried to secure the protection of the wood-cutters by treaties with Spain. Even after 1798, when a strong Spanish force was decisively beaten off at St George's Cay, the British Government still failed to claim the territory, though the settlers maintained that it had now become British by conquest.

When they achieved independence from Spain in 1821, both Guatemala and Mexico laid claim to sovereignty over Belize as successors to Spain, but these claims were rejected by Britain. Long before 1821, in defiance of Spain, the British settlers had established themselves as far south as the river Sarstoon, the present southern boundary. Independent Guatemala claimed that these settlers were trespassing and that Belize was a province of the new republic. By the middle of the 19th century Guatemalan fears of an attack by the United States led to a *rapprochement* with Britain. In 1859, a Convention was signed by which Guatemala recognized the boundaries of Belize while, by Article 7, the United Kingdom undertook to contribute to the cost of a road from Guatemala City to the sea "near the settlement of Belize"; an undertaking which was never carried out.

Heartened by what it considered a final solution of the dispute, Great Britain declared Belize, still officially a settlement, a Colony in 1862, and a Crown Colony nine years later. Mexico, by treaty, renounced any claims it had on Belize in 1893, but Guatemala, which never ratified the 1859 agreement, renews its claims periodically.

Belize became independent on 21 September 1981, following a United Nations declaration to that effect. Guatemala refused to recognize the independent state, but in 1986, President Cerezo of Guatemala announced an intention to drop his country's claim to Belize. A British military force has been maintained in Belize since independence.

Belize was admitted into the OAS in 1991 following negotiations between Belize, Guatemala and Britain. As part of Guatemala's recognition of Belize as an independent nation Britain will recompense Guatemala by providing financial and technical assistance to construct road, pipeline and port facilities that will guarantee Guatemala access to the Atlantic. In Belize there will be a referendum to decide whether to accept the proposed Maritime Areas Bill which will delimit Belize's southern maritime borders in such a manner as to allow Guatemala uncontested and secure access to the high seas.

George Price, of the People's United Party, who had been re-elected continuously as Prime Minister since internal self-government was instituted in 1964, was defeated by Manuel Esquivel, of the United Democratic Party, in general elections held in December 1984 (the first since independence). General elections took place in 1989 and Mr George Price was returned as Prime Minister.

Government

Belize is a constitutional monarchy; the British monarch is the Chief of State, represented by a Governor-General. The head of government is the Prime Minister. There is a National Assembly, with a House of Representatives of 28 members elected by universal adult suffrage, and a Senate of 8: 5 appointed by the advice of the Prime Minister, 2 on the advice of the Leader of the Opposition, 1 by the Governor-General after consultation. General elections are held at intervals of not more than five years.

Flora and Fauna
Nature Conservation has become a high priority, with nature reserves sponsored by the Belize Audubon Society, the Government and various international agencies. "Nature tourism" is Belize's fastest growing industry. By 1992 18 national parks and reserves had been established, including: Half Moon Caye, Cockscomb Basin Wildlife Sanctuary (the world's only jaguar reserve), Crooked Tree Wildlife Sanctuary (swamp forests and lagoons with wildfowl), Community Baboon Sanctuary, Blue Hole National Park, Guanacaste Park, Society Hall Nature Reserve (a research area with Maya presence), Bladen Nature Reserve (watershed and primary forest), Hol Chan Marine Reserve (reef eco-system), Rio Bravo Conservation Area (managed by the Programme for Belize, 1 King Street, Belize City, Tel: 02-75616/7, or John Burton, Old Mission Hall, Sibton Green, Saxmundham, Suffolk, IP17 2JY), the Shipstern Nature Reserve (butterfly breeding, forest, lagoons, mammals and birds: contact PO Box 1694, Belize City, Tel: 08-22149 via BCL Radio phone, or International Tropical Conservation Foundation, Box 31, CH-2074 Marin-Ne, Switzerland). Five Blue Lakes National Park, based on an unusually deep karst lagoon in the far south near Guatemala was designated in April 1991. On 8 December 1991 the government created three new forest reserves and national parks: the Vaca Forest Reserve (52,000 acres), Chiquibul National Park (containing the Maya ruins of Caracol, 265,894 acres), both in Cayo District, and Laughing Bird Caye National Park (off Placencia). The first 8 listed are managed by the Belize Audubon Society, 29 Regent Street, Belize City (PO Box 1001), Tel: (02) 77369/78239.

NB A wildlife protection Act was introduced in 1982, which forbids the sale, exchange or dealings in wildlife, or parts thereof, for profit; the import, export, hunting or collection of wildlife is not allowed without a permit; only those doing scientific research or for educational purposes are eligible for exporting or collecting permits. Also prohibited are removing or exporting black coral, picking orchids, exporting turtle or turtle products, and spear fishing in certain areas or while wearing scuba gear.

Bird watchers are recommended to take Petersen's *Field Guide to Mexican Birds*.

The Cayes

From 10 to 40 miles off the coast an almost continuous, 150-mile line of reefs and cayes (meaning islands, pronounced "keys") provides shelter from the Caribbean and forms the longest barrier reef in the Western Hemisphere (the fifth-longest in the world). The overall area of the cayes is 212 square miles. Most of the cayes are quite tiny, but some have been developed as tourist resorts. Many have beautiful sandy beaches with clear, clean water, where swimming and diving are excellent. They are used by holiday campers from February to May and in August.

The larger ones are the Turneffe Islands and Ambergris and Caulker Cayes. Fishermen live on some cayes, coconuts are grown on others, but many are uninhabited swamps. The smaller cayes do not have much shade, so be careful if you go bathing on them. Sandflies infest some cayes (eg Caulker), the sandfly season is December to beginning of February; mosquito season is June, July, sometimes October.

Travel by boat to and between the islands is becoming increasingly regulated. Boats can only be hired for diving, fishing or sightseeing if they are licensed for the specific purpose by the government. This is intended to ensure that tourists travel on safe, reliable vessels and also to prevent the proliferation of self-appointed guides. The new licensing requirements will probably drive the cheaper boats out of business. In general, it is easier to arrange travel between the islands once there, than from Belize City. All authorized boats leave from Jan's Shell (A and R) Station on North Front Street, Belize City. Cargo boats are no longer allowed to carry passengers, too many have capsized with tourists on board, causing loss of life.

Fishing

The sea provides game fish such as sailfish, marlin, wahoo, barracuda and tuna. Tarpon, permit, grouper and snapper are also popular for sport fishing. On the flats, the most exciting fish for light tackle—the bonefish—are found in great abundance. In addition to the restrictions on turtle and coral extraction noted above, the following regulations apply: no person may take, buy or sell crawfish (lobster) between 15 March and 14 July, shrimp from 15 April to 14 August, or conch between 1 July and 30 September.

Fishing seasons: Billfish: blue marlin, all year (best November-March); white marlin, November-May; sailfish, March-May. Oceanic: yellowfin tuna, all year; blackfin tuna, all year; bonito, all year; wahoo, November-February; sharks, all year. Reef: kingfish, March-June; barracuda, all year; jackfish, all year; mackerel, all year; grouper, all year; snapper, all year; permit, all year; bonefish, November-April; tarpon, June-August River: tarpon, February-August; snook, February-August; snapper, year round.

Operators In Belize City: **Blackline Marine**, PO Box 332, Mile 2, Western Highway, Tel: 02-44155, Fax: 02-31975; **Sea Masters Company Ltd**, PO Box 59, Tel: 02-33185, Fax: 026-2028; **Caribbean Charter Services**, PO Box 752, Mile 5, Northern Highway, Tel: 02-45814 (have guarded car and boat park), fishing, diving and sightseeing trips to the Cayes. **Belize River Lodge**, PO Box 459, Tel: 025-2002, Fax: 025-2298, excellent reputation.

Diving

Old wrecks and other underwater treasures are protected by law and cannot be removed. Spear fishing, as a sport, is discouraged in the interests of conservation. Along the length of the barrier and outer reefs are spectacular dives, with canyons, caves, overhangs, ledges and walls. There are endless possibilities for underwater photography: schools of fish amid the hard and soft coral, sponges and fans. Boats can only be hired for diving, fishing or sightseeing if they are licensed for the specific purpose by the government. This is intended to ensure that tourists travel on safe, reliable vessels and also to prevent the proliferation of self-appointed guides. Try to see that the boat which is taking you to see the reef does not damage this attraction by dropping its anchor on, or in any other way destroying, the coral. Further details are given below. The Aggressor Fleet (PO Drawer K, Morgan City, LA 70581, Tel: 504-385-2416, Fax: 384-0817) offers 6-day, liveaboard cruises on the *Belize Aggressor II* around the barrier reef (1992 price US$1,395).

We describe the islands from north to south.

Ambergris Caye

This island (pronounced Ambergris), with its town of San Pedro, population 1,527, has grown rapidly over the last couple of years, with 50 hotels and guest houses registered on the island. Buildings are still restricted to no more than three storeys in height and the many wooden structures retain an authentic village atmosphere. It should be noted that, although sand is in abundance, there are few excellent beach areas around San Pedro town. The emphasis is on snorkelling on the nearby barrier reef and Hol Chan Marine Park, as well as the fine scuba diving, sailing, fishing and board sailing. A short distance to the north and south of San Pedro lie miles of deserted beach front, where picnic barbecues are popular for day-tripping snorkellers and birders who have visited nearby small cayes hoping to glimpse flamingoes or scarlet ibis. The British Ordnance Survey has published a Tourist Map of Ambergris Caye, scale 1:50,000, with a plan of San Pedro, 1:5,000.

Just south of Ambergris Caye, and not far from Caye Caulker, is the **Hol Chan Marine Park**, an underwater natural park for snorkelling. Entry BZ$3. Several boatmen in San Pedro offer snorkelling trips to the park, BZ$30 (not including entry fee), 2 hours. You can see shark, manta ray, many other fish and coral; a highly recommended trip. Only very experienced snorkellers should attempt to swim in the cutting between the reef and the open sea; seek advice on the tides.

Island Information – Ambergris Caye

Transport Several flights daily to and from Belize City municipal airport with Tropic, Island and Maya Air, BZ$70 return (about BZ$20 more from international airport). Universal Travel at San Pedro airfield helpful. More interesting than going by air are the boats from Shell station, Belize City, BZ$30, non-stop. Leaves at 1300, returns from Holiday Pier, San Pedro, at 0700, daily. From Southern Foreshore jetty boats leave for San Pedro Monday-Friday 1600, return 0700, Saturday 1300, return 0800, none on Sunday, BZ$20, 1½ hrs. Boats, irregular, between Ambergris and Caye Caulker, no set fare. Remember, pay on arrival. Bikes can be rented for BZ$4/hour. One cannot in practice walk north along the beach from San Pedro to Xcalak, Mexico.

Where To Stay *Ramon's Village Resort*, San Pedro Village, Tel: 026-2071/2213, Fax: 2214, or USA 601-649-1990, Fax: 601-425-2411 (PO Drawer 4407, Laurel, MS 39441), from US$110 to 225d, agree on which currency you are paying in, 61 rooms, a diving and beach resort, all meals and all diving, highly recommended even for non-divers (fishing, swimming, boating, snorkelling), very efficient, comfortable rooms, pool with beach club atmosphere; *Belize Yacht Club*, San Pedro town, PO Box 1, Tel: 026-2005/2060, Fax: 026-2331, all rooms are suites with fully-furnished kitchens, under US$200d, pool, docking facilities. The following three are under US$125d: *Sun Breeze*, San Pedro Town, Tel: 026-2347/2191/2345, Fax: 026-2346, near airport, Mexican style building, a/c, comfortable, all facilities, excellent restaurant, good dive shop, recommended; *Paradise Resort Hotel*, San Pedro, Tel: 026-2083, Fax: 026-2232, wide selection of rooms and villas, good location, villas better value, cheaper summer rates, all water sports; *Coral Beach*, San Pedro, Tel: 026-2013, Fax: 026-2001, central location, slightly run down but good local feel and excellent water sports facilities including dive boat charter, tours for fishing and scuba available. *San Pedro Holiday Hotel*, PO Box 1140, Belize City, Tel: 026-2014/2103, Fax: 026-2295, 16 rooms in good central location, US$63-90d, fun atmosphere with good facilities, reasonable value; *Spindrift Hotel*, San Pedro, Tel: 026-2018, Fax: 026-2251, 24 rooms, 4 apartments, about US$60, unattractive block but central location, good bar and restaurant, popular meeting place, trips up the Belize River, a/c, comfortable; *Rock's Inn Apartments*, San Pedro Town, Tel: 026-2326, Fax: 026-2358, good value and service, over US$70d.

Just outside San Pedro: *El Pescador*, on Punta Arena beach 3 miles north, PO Box 793, Belize City, Tel/Fax: 026-2398, over US$125, access by boat, specialist fishing lodge with good reputation, a/c, good food and service; *Journey's End*, PO Box 13, San Pedro, Tel: 026-2173, Fax: 026-2028, 4½ miles north, about US$150, excellent resort facilities including diving, resort club theme; *Captain Morgan's Retreat*, 3 miles north of town, Tel: 026-2567, Fax: 026-2616, similar price range, access by boat, thatched roofed cabañas with private facilities, pool, dock, secluded, recommended; *Victoria House*, PO Box 22, San Pedro, Tel: 026-2067/2240, Fax: 026-2429, including meals, 1½ km from town, three different types of room, from about US$75-150, excellent facilities, good dive shop and water sports, windsurfing BZ$30/hour, highly recommended; *Royal Palm*, PO Box 18, San Pedro, Tel: 026-2148/2244, Fax: 026-2329, good location near *Victoria House*, a little cheaper, 12 new villas with pool and full facilities just completed; *House of the Rising Sun*, Tel: 026-2336/2505, Fax: 026-2349, about US$50, nice location, reasonable rooms and value.

Other, cheaper hotels: *San Pedrano*, San Pedro, Tel: 026-2054/2093, over US$40, clean and good value. In the US$30-40 price range: *Conch Shell Inn*, facing sea, some rooms with kitchenette, Tel: 026-2062; *Hide Away Lodge*, PO Box 484, Belize City, Tel: 026-2141/2269, good value but a bit run down, popular with off-duty British military; *Lily's*, nice rooms with sea view, fan, clean, friendly, Tel: 026-2059; *Rubie's*, San Pedro Town on the beach, fan, private bath, good views, beach cabaña, central, recommended as best value in town, Tel: 026-2063/2434; *Martha's Hotel* (cheaper in low season), PO Box 27, San Pedro, Tel: 026-2054, Fax: 026-2589, good value, recommended; *La Joya del Caribe*, San Pedro Tel: 026-2050/2385, Fax: 026-2316, nice location just out of town, recommended; *Casa Blanca*, San Pedro town, Tel: 026-2630; *Pirate's Lantern*, in town, Tel: 026-2146; *Milo's*, Tel: 026-2033; *Seven Seas*, Tel: 026-2382/2137.

Where To Eat The *San Pedro Grill* is a good place to meet other travellers and swap information on boats, etc. Other eating places are: *Elvi's Kitchen*, popular, reasonable prices, good food; *Lily's Restaurant*, best seafood in town; *Jade Garden Restaurant*, Chinese, sweet and sour everything, drinks expensive; *The Hut*, Mexican, friendly. At Coral Beach, the Forman, Gómez, González and Paz families provide rooms and meals for BZ$18 each. At Sea Breeze, the Paz and Núñez families offer the same accommodation at the same price. In the same building complex as the *Spindrift* is the *Pier Restaurant*, very Mexican, dinners from BZ$20, also a branch of the Atlantic Bank, a post office and a chemist. *Big Daddy's Disco*, recommended.

Caye Caulker

A lobster-fishing island, which used to be relatively unspoilt, Caye Caulker, Corker or Cayo Hicaco is now popular with tourists. The houses are of wood, the majority built on stilts. It has been allowed to run down and the main landing jetty has been closed. It is said to be a drug centre. Some services are reported to have deteriorated, and theft and unpleasantness from some mainlanders who go to the caye with tourists occurs; on the other hand the islanders are friendly. The atmosphere seems to be much more relaxed out of the high tourist season; nevertheless, women should take care if alone at night. There are no beaches, but you can swim at the channel ("cutting", formed by a recent hurricane) or off one of the many piers. Diving is excellent because the caye is above one of the largest underwater cave systems in the world.

A reef museum has opened with enlarged photos of reef fish, free for school parties, tourists are asked for a US$2 donation to help expansion. There are only two vehicles on the island one of which is used solely to transport Belikin beer. Sandflies are ferocious in season (December-February), take trousers and a good repellent. Make sure you fix prices before going on trips or hiring equipment and it is clear whether you are talking US$ or BZ$.

A walk south along the shore takes you to the new airstrip, a gash across the island, and to mangroves where the rare black catbird (*melanoptila glabirostris*) can be seen and its sweet song heard. In this area there are lots of mosquitoes. A campaign to make the black catbird's habitat and the associated reef a Nature Reserve (called Siwa-Ban, after the catbird's Maya name) can be contacted at *Hiriarco Giftshop* (Ellen McCrea, near *Tropical Paradise*), or 143 Anderson, San Francisco, California.

Watersports and Diving

Reef trips, BZ$15-25 each (sometimes less) for 3-7 hours as long as there are four or more in a group. Protect against sunburn on reef trips, even while snorkelling. Mervin, a local man, is reliable for snorkelling trips, he will also take you to Belize City. Try "Bongo" for yacht trips to the reefs, "first mate" Donna (a Canadian) will guide first time snorkellers. Another is Ignacio, also Gamoosa, who will spend all day with you on the reef and then sometimes invites you to his house to eat the fish and lobster you have caught, prepared deliciously by his wife; she also offers a healthy breakfast of banana, yoghurt, granola and honey for BZ$5. Also recommended is Alfonso Rosardo, a Mexican, reef trips for up to six people, 5-6 hours, sometimes offers meals at his house afterwards. Also recommended is Lawrence (next to *Riva's Guest House*), Obdulio Lulu (a man) at *Tom's Hotel* goes to Hol Chan and San Pedro for a full day (if he catches a barracuda on the return, he will barbecue it at the hotel for BZ$1.50), Alex at *Aberdeen Restaurant*, relaxed, recommended; also Harrison (ask around for him, recommended). Lobster fishing and diving for conch is also possible. "Island Sun", near the "cutting", local husband and American wife, very conscientious; day tours to reef, plus snorkel hire (1000-1400); day tour to San Pedro and Hol Chan, plus snorkel hire, plus entry fee for reserve, recommended. A sailing boat also goes to Hol Chan, but the trip takes a long time, leaving only a short while for snorkelling, departs 1000 from in front of *Aberdeen* restaurant, US$12 for a day. Mask, snorkel and fins for BZ$5, cheapest (for instance at the post office, or *Sammie's Pastry Shop*).

Diving Frank and Janie Bounting (PO Box 667, Tel: 44307, ext 143 mainland side, past the football pitch) charge US$55 for two scuba dives, day and night, good value; they also offer a 4-day PADI certificate course for US$300, recommended. Ask about Belize Diving Service's 2 and 3-day trips to Lighthouse Reef on the *Reef Roamer*, highly recommended; the 3-day trip comprises 7 dives, including the Blue Hole, a visit to a bird reserve, good food and crew, US$290. Frenchie's Diving Service, Tel: 022-2234, charges US$330 for a 4-day PADI course, friendly and effective, 2-tank dive US$60, also advanced PADI instruction. For **sailing** charters, Jim and Dorothy Beveridge, "Seaing is Belizing", who also run scuba trips to Goff's Caye Park and the Turneffe Islands (5-10 days). They arrange slide shows of the reefs and the Jaguar Reserve (Cockscomb) at 2000, from time to time, US$2, excellent photography, personally narrated (they, too, have a book exchange); PO Box 374, Belize City, Tel: 022-2189. Ask Chocolate for all-day trips to the manatee reserve in the south of Belize, about US$25 pp for a group of at least eight. There is a sailing school, charging BZ$60 for a 5-hour, solo beginner's course. It may be possible to hire a boat for 6-8 people to Chetumal. There are also boats leaving for Placencia and Honduras from Caye Caulker, but be sure to get exit stamps and other documentation in Belize City first if going to Honduras.

Wind-surfing equipment hire opposite *Tropical Paradise Hotel* (also book exchange): BZ$8 an hour, BZ$20 ½ day, BZ$40 a day, lessons, BZ$10 excluding equipment. **Canoes** for hire from Salvador, at painted house behind *Marin's* restaurant, BZ$20 a day. Go **fishing** with Rolly Rosardo, 4 hours, US$45, up to five people, equipment, fresh bait and instruction provided.

Island Information – Caye Caulker

Transport Boats leave from behind A & R Shell Station on North Front Street, Belize City, for Caye Caulker, at 0630, then from 0900 until early afternoon daily (BZ$12-15 pp, BZ$10 on "sunrise boat", payable only on arrival at Caye Caulker, otherwise you'll be swindled), 45 minutes one way (boats depend on weather and number of passengers, can be "exciting" if it's rough), return boats from 0630 till pm (if booked in advance at some places, including *Edith's Hotel*, BZ$12). Jerry Pacheco's *Blue Wave* (recommended as fast and good, also snorkelling trips), Emilio Novelo's *Ocean Star* (good, cheaper than others) and "Chocolate's" *Soledad* are the currently authorized boats, but there are many others (including *Good Grief*, mixed reports, and *C Train*). Boats from San Pedro en route to Belize City 0700-0800, BZ$15. Incidentally, "Chocolate" is over 50 years old and has a white beard and moustache. Anyone else introducing himself as Chocolate is an imposter!

The airstrip has been newly constructed; Tropic Air, Island Air and Maya Air BZ$60 return from municipal airport (add BZ$20 from International airport).

Where To Stay The cheapest end of town is the south, but it is a long way from the "cutting" for swimming or snorkelling. A map which can be bought on arrival lists virtually everything on the island. Camping on the beach is forbidden. *Rainbow Hotel*, on the beach, Tel: 022-2123, 10 small bungalows, with shower, rooms also, US$25-35, hot water. Beach houses can also be rented for BZ$100-300 a month. *Tropical Paradise*, Tel: 022-2124, Fax: 022-2225 (PO Box 1206 Belize City), cabins, rooms US$22-35, restaurant (see below), good excursions; *CB's*, further south than *Tropical Paradise*, Tel: 022-2176, US$32 with bath, clean 12 beds, no advance bookings, good, small beds, restaurant; *Reef Hotel*, (Tel: 022-2196), US$25, small rooms, basic, but reasonable for the caye; *Shirley's Guest House*, Tel: 022-2145, US$20, south end of village, very relaxing, recommended; *Marin*, Tel: 022-44307 (also private hut) with bath, US$15, clean, helpful, recommended (the proprietor, John Marin, will take you out for a snorkelling trip on the reef for BZ$10); *Vega's Far Inn* rents 7 rooms, all doubles, Tel: 022-2142, US$15, with ceiling fan and fresh linen, flush toilets and showers (limited hot water) shared with camping ground, which is guarded, has drinking water, hot water, clean toilets, barbecue, can rent out camping gear (camping costs BZ$12 pp, overpriced).

Mira Mar, Tel: 022-44307, under US$12 pp, bargain if staying longer, helpful owner Melvin Badillo, he owns liquor store, his family runs a pastry shop and grocery store; *Deisy's*, Tel: 022-2150, US$10 with shower, toilet and fan, reductions for longer stays, cash travellers' cheques, good value; *Edith's*, US$8 per bed in room (whether occupied or not), good; *Hideaway*, round corner from *Deisy's*, US$10, clean, quiet, shared toilets and shower (cold, unpotable water), recommended; *Ignacio Beach Cabins*, Tel: 022-2212, (PO Box 1169, Belize City), small huts or hammocks just outside town, for double room, US$15 for a hut for 3-4, recommended, camping space BZ$12, plus BZ$2 for luggage store, toilet and shower facilities in private cabins only (Ignacio runs reef trips and he has equipment; he is principally a lobster fisherman); *Riva's Guest House*, Tel: 022-2127, US$10, basic accommodation, their reef trips in an attractive schooner are the longest, snorkelling equipment hire, BZ$5; *Sandy Lane Hotel*, Tel: 022-2217, one block back from main street, bungalow-type accommodation, US$10, clean, showers, run by Rico and Elma Novelo, recommended; *Tom's Hotel*, Tel: 022-2102, US$12, with shared bath and fan, up to US$25 in cabin with 3 beds, basic, clean, friendly, cold water, long walk from beach, laundry service US$5, safe deposit, barbecue, recommended. Tom's boat trips cost BZ$7, various destinations, including Hol Chan and coral gardens, and to Belize City.

Where To Eat *Rodriguez* for dinner at 1800 onwards for BZ$7 to 8, BZ$10 for lobster, very good (limited accommodation available). *Melvin's*, excellent lobster meals (opposite *Riva's*); *Tropical Paradise* for excellent seafood, slightly more expensive than others (also the only place selling ice cream). Cakes and pastries can be bought at houses displaying the sign, recommended are *Deisy's, Jessie's* (open 0830-1300, 1500-1700, behind *Riva's*; *Glenda's*, near *Hotel Marin*, try the delicious chicken "burritos", chicken, vegetables, chile and sauce wrapped in a tortilla for BZ$1, also good breakfast. *Island Yogurts* near the "cutting", sells granola, fruit and yogurt breakfast for BZ$4, owner, Bobby makes sailing trips. *Marin's*, good seafood in evening at reasonable prices; *Syd's* home cooking, big portions; *Aberdeen*, Chinese restaurant on main street, good food, yoghurt, reasonable prices. Many private houses serve food. Buy lobster or fish from the cooperative and cook up at the barbecue on the beach; beer is sold by the crate at the wholesaler on the dock by the generator; ice for sale at *Tropical Paradise*.

Services There are at least 4 small "markets" on the island where a variety of food can be bought; prices are 20-50% higher than the mainland. Better to buy food in Belize City beforehand, but rates for changing cash and travellers' cheques are reasonable; many places for exchange.

International telephone and Fax connections available on Caye Caulker (telephone exchange is open till 1600; Fax number at telephone exchange is 501-22-2239). The island also boasts two book swaps. Bookstore on opposite side of island to ferries has many different magazines, including *Time* and *Newsweek*.

Caye Chapel

40 minutes by boat from Belize City, this caye is free of sandflies and mosquitoes and there are several beaches, cleaned daily. It also has a landing strip used by local airlines. Be careful if you hire a boat for a day on Caye Chapel: the boatmen enjoy the bar on the island and your return journey can be unreasonably exciting. Also, there are very few fish now round this caye. On Caye Chapel is the *Pyramid Island Resort*, which has become run down and facilities are poor (prices over US$50, unhelpful staff, credit cards not accepted), it has an excellent beach, however, and good certification (PADI).

Long Caye

Long Caye is south of Caye Chapel, reached by boat from Jan's Shell Station in Belize City, US$7.50. The island is quiet, relaxing, with bird watching, snorkelling, fishing, although it gets a bit busy at the weekend when fishermen drop in for a drink and chat. There is birdwatching, snorkelling, alligator spotting and fishing, and a good supply of books in the one guesthouse. They charge US$45 double, or US$35 single, full board, superb food, clean, very friendly. If it is full, ask Bob and he will try and fit you in somewhere.

St George's Caye

Nine miles northeast of Belize City, St George's Caye was the capital of British Honduras from 1650 to 1784. It was the scene of the battle between Britain and Spain in 1798 which established British possession. *Cottage Colony*, PO Box 428, Belize City. Tel: 02-77051, Fax: 02-73253, colonial style cabañas with dive facilities, easy access from Belize City. *St George's Island Cottages*, PO Box 625, Belize City, 6 rooms. Boat fare is BZ$30.

English Caye

This beautiful island, 12 miles off Belize City, has no facilities (apart from a lighthouse); take a day trip only. It is part of the reef so you can snorkel right off the beach.

Small caye resorts within easy reach of Belize City: *Moonlight Shadows Lodge*, Middle Long Caye, Tel: 08-22587, still in early stages of development. *Ricardo's Beach Huts*, Blue Field Range (59 North Front St, PO Box 55, Belize City, Tel: 02-44970), recommended, charming and knowledgeable host, rustic, authentic fish camp feel, overnight camps to Rendez-vous Caye, English Caye and Sargeants Caye can be arranged with Ricardo, excellent food, snorkelling. *Spanish Bay Resort*, PO Box 35, Belize City, Tel: 02-77288, also in early stages of development, dive facilities. *The Wave*, Gallows Point Caye (9 Regent St, Belize City, Tel: 02-73054), 6 rooms, water sports facilities and diving.

Turneffe Islands

The Turneffe Islands are one of Belize's three atolls. On Big Caye Bokel, at the southern end of the group, is *Turneffe Islands Lodge*, PO Box 480, Belize City, which can accommodate 16 guests for week-long fishing and scuba packages. *Turneffe Flats*, 56 Eve St, Belize City, Tel: 02-45634, in a lovely location, also offers week-long packages, for fishing and scuba; it can take 12 guests, but is soon to expand. *Blackbird Caye Village*, 81 West Collet Canal St, Belize City, Tel: 02-77670, Fax: 02-73092, is a new, ecologically-oriented resort used by the Oceanic Society and is a potential site for a Biosphere Reserve 2 underwater project.

Half Moon Caye at Lighthouse Reef

Lighthouse Reef is the outermost of the three north-south reef systems off Belize, some 45 miles east of Belize City. Half Moon Caye is the site of the Red-Footed Booby Sanctuary, the first national reserve established in Belize (1982). Besides the booby, which is unusual in that almost all the individuals have the white colour phase (normally they are dull brown), magnificent frigate birds nest on the island. The seabirds nest on the western side, which has dense vegetation (the eastern side is covered mainly in coconut palms). Of the 98 other bird species recorded on Half Moon Caye, 77 are migrants. Iguana, the wish willy (smaller than the iguana) and the *anolis allisoni* lizard inhabit the caye, and hawksbill and loggerhead turtles lay their eggs on the beaches. The Belize Audubon Society, 29 Regent Street, maintains the sanctuary; there is a lookout tower and trail. A lighthouse on the caye gives fine views of the reef. Around sunset you can watch the boobies from the lookout as they return from fishing. They land beside their waiting mates at the rate of about 50 a minute. They seem totally unbothered by humans.

There are no facilities; take all food, drink and fuel. On arrival you must register with the warden near the lighthouse (the warden will provide maps and tell you where you can camp).

Twelve miles north of Half Moon Caye is the **Blue Hole**, an almost circular sinkhole 1,000 feet across and with depths exceeding 400 feet. It was studied by Jacques Cousteau in 1984. Stalagmites and stalactites can be found in the underwater cave. Scuba diving is outstanding at Lighthouse Reef, including two walls which descend almost vertically from 30-40 feet to several thousand.

Bobby takes passengers by sailing boat from Caye Caulker to Half Moon Caye and the Blue Hole for US$25 pp including food (bring your own tent and sleeping bag). To charter a motor boat in Belize City costs about US$50 pp if 10 people are going (6 hour journey). Bill Hinkis, in San Pedro Town, Ambergris Caye, offers three-day sailing cruises to Lighthouse Reef for US$150 (you provide food, ice and fuel). Bill and his boat *Yanira* can be found beside the lagoon off Back Street, just north of the football field. Other sailing vessels charge US$150-250 per day.

The Southern Cayes

Further south, the reef and cayes stretch down towards Guatemala and Honduras. There is a concentration of islets between the town of Dangriga and the Placencia/Mango Creek area. Among these are the Tobacco Range and Man of War Caye (a nesting site for frigate, or man of war, birds and boobies). **South Water Caye** is a private island, small, sandy, with snorkelling off the beach. It is partly taken up by *Blue Marlin Lodge* (PO Box 21, Dangriga, Tel: 05-22243, Fax: 05-22296), an excellent dive lodge which offers 8 day/7 night dive packages for about US$1,000 pp (less for non-divers, or 5 day/4 nights), or similar length fishing packages for US$1,300. It has a restaurant, runs tours to Twin Cayes (where manatees may be seen), the Smithsonian Marine Biology Institute Laboratory on Carrie Bow Caye, and mainland sites. *Leslie Cottages*, 2 rooms, US contact Tel: 800-548-5843 or 508-655-1461. Also based on South Water Caye is Coral Caye Conservation Ltd – Belize 90/95, a scientific survey of the reef ecosystem designed to establish a marine reserve. Expeditions are manned by volunteers who should apply to Dr Liam O'Toole or Jon Ridley, Sutton Business Centre, Restmoor Way, Wallington, Surrey, SM6 7AH, UK, Tel: 081-669 0011, Fax: 081-773 0406.

Tobacco Caye 1 hour by speedboat from Dangriga (BZ$25), this small island, quite heavily populated, has lots of local flavour and fishing camp charm. It is becoming a little commercialized, but still has an authentic feel. It sits right on the reef; you can snorkel from the beach although there are no large schools of fish. No sandflies on the beach; snorkelling equipment for rent. Boats go daily. *Reefs End Lodge*, PO Box 10, Dangriga, basic, small rooms, excellent host and food, boat transfer on request from Dangriga; *Island Camps*, PO Box 174 (51 Regent St, Belize City, Tel: 02-72109), owner Mark Bradley will pick up guests in Dangriga, neat, spacious campground, meals on request, reef excursions. Several families on the island take guests; accommodation very basic and grubby. A dive camp is scheduled to open on Tobacco Caye, in the meanwhile tank dives can be taken from nearby *Blue Marlin Lodge* on South Water Caye.

Still further south is **Wee Wee Caye**, a mangrove islet used as a field station by the Northeast Marine Environmental Institution, Inc (NEMEII, PO Box 660, Monument Beach, MA 02553, USA, Tel: 508-759 4055; it also has a station up the Sittee River, at Possum Point).

Outside the Barrier Reef in this area is **Glover's Reef**, about 45 miles off Dangriga, an atoll with beautiful diving. *Manta Reef Resort*, Glover's Reef Atoll, PO Box 215, 3 Eyre St, Belize City, Tel: 02-231895/232767, Fax: 02-322764; 9 individual cabins with full facilities, in perfect desert island setting, one week packages available only, reservations essential; excellent diving and fishing, good food, highly recommended (E6 photo lab available). On **Long Caye** is *Glover's Atoll Resort* (Gilbert, Marsha-Jo and Madeleine Lomont, PO Box 563, Belize City) with cabins for 2, US$15 a night, US$300 a month, plus 5% tax, with cooking facilities, cold shower, rainwater for drinking, fuel extra, meals available at advance notice. On **North East Caye** there are unfurnished cabins with wood burning stoves, US$15/night. Camping on either island US$3 pp. Boats for hire, with or without guide; snorkel and scuba rental; 4-day NAUI certification course US$250. Contact the Lomonts in advance to obtain a full breakdown of all services and costs. To get there take Saturday 1500 Z-Line bus from Venus terminal in Belize City (direction Punta Gorda); ask the driver to stop at Sittee River road (about 2000). For BZ$4 a truck takes you to *Glover's Atoll Guest House* at Sittee River Village, meals available with advance notice. Phone 08-22505, Bill or Sandy Leonard, to book space. At 0800 Sunday a boat leaves for the Reef 5 hours, US$15 pp one way, returns Friday. At other times, hitch to Sittee River Village and charter a boat (skiff or sailing boat, US$200 one way, up to 4 people, diesel sloop US$300, up to 20 people).

Points of access

Belize City is the old capital and chief town. Most of the houses are built of wood, often of charming design, with galvanized iron roofs; they stand for the most part on piles about seven feet above the ground, which is often swampy and flooded. Ground-floor rooms are used as kitchens, or for storage. Note the vast water butts outside many houses, with pipes leading to the domestic supply. Humidity is high, but the summer heat is tempered by the NE trades. The population (43,621) is just over a quarter of the total population, with the African strain predominating.

Haulover Creek divides the city; the swing bridge across the river is opened at 1730 daily to let boats pass. Among the commonest craft are sandlighters, whose lateen sails can be seen off Belize City. Three canals further divide the city. The main commercial area is either side of the swing bridge, although most of the shops are on the south side, many being located on Regent and Albert streets. The area around Central Park is always busy, but it is no distance to Southern Foreshore with its views of the rivermouth, harbour and out to sea. At the southern end of Regent Street, the Anglican Cathedral and Government House nearby are interesting; both were built in the early 19th century. In the days before the foundation of the Crown Colony the kings of the Mosquito Coast were crowned in the Cathedral. In the Cathedral, note the 19th century memorial plaques which give a harrowing account of early death from "country fever" (yellow fever) and other tropical diseases.

On the north side of the swing bridge, turn left up North Front Street for some of the cheaper hotels and the A and R Station, from which boats leave for the Cayes. Turn right for the Post Office, Tourist Office and roads which lead to Marine Parade (also with sea views). At the junction of Cork Street at Marine Parade is the *Fort George Hotel* whose new Club Wing, a copper-coloured glass tower, is a considerable landmark. Memorial Park on Marine Parade has a small obelisk, two cannon, concrete benches, and is peppered with the holes of landcrabs. The small park by the Fort George Lighthouse has a children's play area and is a popular meeting place.

Coming in by sea, after passing the barrier reef, Belize City is approached by a narrow, tortuous channel. This and the chain of mangrove cayes give shelter to what would otherwise be an open roadstead.

Some 48 miles from Belize City, near Belmopan, the narrow 52-mile Hummingbird Highway branches off southeast from the Western Highway, through beautiful jungle scenery to **Dangriga** (chief town of the Stann Creek District), some 105 miles from Belize City and 1¾-2½ hours drive from Belmopan. Dangriga's population is 6,838. In this, the most fertile area in the country, are grown citrus fruits, bananas, cassava, and general food crops. The town is on the seashore, and has an airstrip and cinema. Houses are built of wood, on piles. Mosquitoes and sand flies are a nuisance.

Local Holiday 18-19 November, Garifuna, or Settlement Day, re-enacting the landing of the Black Caribs in 1823; there is dancing all night and next day. It's a very popular festival. All transport to Dangriga is booked up a week in advance and hotel rooms impossible to find.

Placencia is a quiet, unspoilt little resort 30 miles south of Dangriga, reached by dugout, US$5 each way, 3 hours, or, now that the road from Dangriga is finished, by bus (leaves Dangriga at 1530, 1½ hours, US$3.50). There are no streets, just a concrete footpath and wooden houses under the palms. The atmosphere has been described as good, with lots of Jamaican music and lots of substances to make it tolerable for over one hour's listening. There is a police station. The people are very friendly and it's a good place for making excursions to the coral reef, 10 miles offshore (US$75-100 for 6 people). The only telephone is at the post office (good source of information on boats). The nearest bank in **Mango Creek** (Bank of Nova Scotia) open Friday only 0900-1200, but shops and market change travellers' cheques. Visa extensions obtainable in Mango Creek, which is a banana exporting port, 20 miles south of Dangriga.

Details of mainland excursions to Maya archaeological sites and the Mountain Pine Ridge area, near San Ignacio, are given in *The Mexico and Central American Handbook*. Most of the large hotels on the cayes and the mainland run tours to these places.

Information for Visitors

Documents

All nationalities need passports, as well as sufficient funds and, officially, an onward ticket. Visas are usually not required from nationals of all the countries of the EEC, some Commonwealth countries eg Australia, New Zealand, most Caribbean states (citizens of India do need a visa), USA, Canada, Liechtenstein, Mexico, Norway, Panama, Sweden, Turkey, Uruguay, Venezuela and Switzerland. Visas must be obtained from a consulate before arriving in the country; they cost US$10. They are not available at borders. It is possible that a visa may not be required if you have an onward ticket, but check all details at a consulate before arriving at the airport or border. Those going to other countries after leaving Belize should get any necessary visas in their home country. Visitors are initially granted 30 days' stay in Belize; this may be extended every 30 days up to 6 months at the Immigration Office, 115 Barrack Road, Belize City. At the end of 6 months, visitors must leave the country for at least 24 hours. Visitors must not engage in any type of employment, paid or unpaid, without first securing a work permit from the Department of Labour; if caught, the penalty for both the employer and the employee is severe. There have been reports that tourists carrying less than US$30 for each day of intended stay have been refused entry.

If arriving by boat, you must submit to the Customs Boarding Officer the vessel's certificate of registration, clearance from the last port of call, four copies of the crew and passenger list and of the stores list.

Customs

Clothing and articles for personal use are allowed in without payment of duty, but a deposit may be required to cover the duty payable on typewriters, dictaphones, cameras and radios. The duty, if claimed, is refunded when the visitor leaves the country. Import allowances are: 200 cigarettes or ½ lb of tobacco; 20 fluid ozs of alcohol; 1 bottle of perfume. Visitors can take in any amount of other currencies. No fruit or vegetables may be brought into Belize; searches are very thorough. Firearms may be imported only with prior arrangements. Pets must have proof of rabies inoculations and a vet's certificate of good health. CB radios are held by customs until a licence is obtained from Belize Communications Ltd.

How To Get There By Air

American Airlines, TAN Airlines, Taca International and Belize Trans Air from Miami. Other US points served: New Orleans (Sahsa, Taca), Houston (Continental, Taca, Sahsa) and Los Angeles (Taca). Also daily flights to San Pedro Sula (Sahsa), Tegucigalpa (TAN and Sahsa) San Salvador, San José, and Panama (all Taca). Sahsa has connections to Managua via Tegucigalpa. Tropic Air flies daily to Cancún (Mexico). Flights to Flores (Guatemala) and Guatemala City by Aerovías: in high season (December-March) flights daily leaving Belize International at 1330, BZ$170 Belize to Guatemala one way, BZ$122 Belize to Flores; same flight leaves Flores for Guatemala City at 1600, arriving 1700. Flights return from Guatemala City to Belize via Flores at 0700, Flores to Belize City at 0930. Out of season there are normally 5 flights weekly; check on arrival in Belize City as schedules fluctuate.

Departure Tax

US$10/BZ$20 on leaving from the international airport, but not for transit passengers who have spent less than 24 hours in the country. There is also a security screening charge of BZ$2.50. There is a land departure tax of US$1/BZ$2 except for those who have spent less than 24 hours in the country and for children under 12.

Airport

There is a 10-mile tarmac road from Belize City to the Phillip SW Goldson International Airport. Modern check-in facilities, a/c, toilets, restaurant, viewing deck and duty-free shop. Collective taxi US$15; make sure your taxi is legitimate. Any bus going up the Northern Highway passes the airport junction (US$0.50),

then 1½ mile walk. Shuttle bus service, Phillip Pou, Tel: 73977/77811, BZ$2, leaves Belize City 7 times a day 0530 to 1730, leaves airport 0600 to 1800; pick up points Pound Yard Bridge, corner Cemetery Road and Central American Blvd, corner Central American Blvd and Vernon Street, and bus stop by Pallotti High School. Bus service meets incoming flights taking passengers to downtown area. There is a municipal airstrip for local flights. Taxi from Belize City US$7.50, no bus.

Airline Offices

Local: Tropic Air, Belize City Tel: 02-45671, San Pedro Tel: 026-2012/2117/2029, Fax: 026-2338; Island Air, Belize City Tel: 02-31140, International airport Tel: 025-2219, San Pedro Tel: 026-2435/2484, Fax: 026-2192; Maya Air, 6 Fort St, Belize City Tel: 02-72312, municipal airport Tel: 02-44234/44032, International Tel: 025-2336, San Pedro Tel: 026-2611, Fax: 02-30585.

Taca (Belize Global Travel), 41 Albert St (Tel: 02-77363/77185, Fax: 75213), International Tel: 025-2163, Fax: 025-2453, also British Airways, Tel: 77363; Sahsa/TAN, New Road and Queen St, Tel: 02-77082/72057/77314, International Tel: 025-2060/2458. American, Valencia Building (Tel: 02-32522/3/4) and Continental Airlines, 32 Albert St, Tel: 02-78309/78463/78223, International Tel: 025-2263/2488. Aerovías, in *Mopan Hotel*, 55 Regent St, Tel: 02-75383/75445/6, Fax: 75383, for Flores/Guatemala; Belize Trans Air, Tel: 02-77666, for Miami.

How To Get There By Sea

The only regular boat service to Belize is from Punta Gorda, south of Mango Creek, to Puerto Barrios (and possibly Livingston), Guatemala (Tuesday and Friday at 1400-1500, 3 hours, US$5). Obtain all necessary exit stamps and visas before sailing (the nearest Guatemalan consulate is in Chetumal, Mexico). To Puerto Cortés, Honduras, from Belize City, you must charter a boat for US$360, 2-4 days, for 8 people. Motorized canoes go from Mango Creek to Puerto Cortés, Honduras, with no fixed schedule, but mostly Thursday-Sunday (Antonio Zabaneh at his store, Tel: 06-22011, knows when boats will arrive), US$50 one way, 7-9 hours (rubber protective sheeting is provided, hang on to it, usually not enough to go round, nor lifejackets, but you will still get wet unless wearing waterproofs, or just a swimming costume on hot days; it can be dangerous in rough weather). Remember to get an exit stamp (preferably in Belize City), obtainable at the police station in Mango Creek, not Placencia (the BZ$20 departure tax demanded here is not official).

Internal Travel

Air services to San Pedro, Caye Chapel and Caye Caulker with Tropic Air, Island Air and Maya Air, flights every hour 0700 to 1630, US$35 municipal airport to San Pedro return, US$30 to Caye Chapel and Caye Caulker (flights to these cayes from International airport cost about US$10 more). Fares to Big Creek for Placencia US$42, Dangriga US$25, Punta Gorda US$54 with Maya Air and Tropic Air, 5 flights daily from 0700, last return flight 1705 (one way fares).

Passenger transport between the main towns is by colectivo or bus. By law, buses are not allowed to carry standing passengers; some companies are stricter than others. Hitch hiking is very difficult as there is little traffic.

Bus If going overland to Mexico, take a bus to Chetumal, several daily each way between 0400 and 1100 (there is an express Batty Bus at 0600 stopping at Orange Walk and Corozal only), US$5, 3-4 hours, with 2 companies: Batty Bus, 54 East Collet Canal, Tel: 72025, and Venus, Magazine Rd, Tel: 73354. Bus Belize City to Dangriga, via Belmopan and the Hummingbird Highway, Z-line (Tel: 73937), from Venus bus station, daily, 1000, 1100, 1500, 1600, plus Monday 0600, US$9.50 to Dangriga (the 1000 bus connects with the 1530 Z-line bus to Punta Gorda); James Bus Line, Pound Yard Bridge (Collet Canal), unreliable, slow, 10-12 hours, US$9.50, to Punta Gorda via Dangriga and Mango Creek, Tuesday, Wednesday, Friday 0600, Monday, Saturday 0900. Return from Mango Creek Sunday, Friday at 1300, Sunday, Tuesday, Thursday 0600; US$6.50 (insect repellent imperative).

Taxis have green licence plates (drivers must also have identification card); within Belize City, US$2.50 for one person; for 2 or more passengers, US$1.75 pp. There is a taxi stand on Central Park opposite Barclays, another on the corner of Collet Canal Street and Cemetery Road. Outside Belize City, US$1.75 per mile, regardless of number of passengers. Check fare

before setting off. No meters. No tips necessary.

Car Hire

Car hire cost is high in Belize owing to heavy wear and tear on the vehicles. You can expect to pay between US$65 for a Suzuki Samuri to US$125 for an Isuzu Trooper per day. Cautious driving is advised in Belize as road conditions are generally poor except for the Northern and Western Highways and there is no street lighting in rural areas. Emory King's *Drivers Guide to Belize* is helpful when driving to the more remote areas.

Budget PO Box 863, 771 Bella Vista (near International Airport, can pick up and drop off car at airport, office almost opposite *Biltmore Plaza Hotel*), Tel: 32435, good service, well-maintained vehicles, good deals (Suzukis and Isuzu Troopers); **Crystal**, Mile 1.5 Northern Highway, Tel: 31600, Jay Crofton, cheapest deals in town, but not always most reliable, wide selection of vehicles including 30-seater bus, will release insurance papers for car entry to Guatemala and Mexico; **Pancho's**, 5747 Lizarraga Ave, Tel: 45554; **National**, International Airport, Tel: 31586 (Cherokee Chiefs); **Avis**, at *Fort George Hotel*, Tel: 78637, largest fleet, well-maintained, Daihatsus and Isuzu Troopers. **Smith & Sons**, 125 Cemetery Road, Tel: 73779 (less reliable than in the past); **Elijah Sutherland**, 127 Neal Pen Road, Tel: 73582, Mitsubishis. **Gilly's**, 31 Regent St, Tel: 77613; **Lewis**, 23 Cemetery Rd, Tel: 74461. CDW ranges from US$10 to US$20 per day.

Motorists should carry their own driving licence and certificate of vehicle ownership. Third party insurance is mandatory, and can be purchased at any border (about BZ$35 a week). There may be no one to collect it after 1900. Valid International Driving Licences are accepted in place of Belize driving permits. BZ$5 exit fee for car. Fuel costs BZ$5 for a US gallon. There is no unleaded gasoline in Belize.

Traffic drives on the right. When making a left turn, it is the driver's responsibility to ensure clearance of both oncoming traffic and vehicles behind; generally, drivers pull over to the far right, allow traffic from behind to pass, then make the left turn. Many accidents are caused by failure to observe this procedure. All major roads have been, or are being, improved.

Where To Stay On The Mainland

Accommodation on the **Cayes** is given above.

In **Belize City** Unless otherwise indicated, preface Belize City phone numbers with 02 (2 inside Belize). All hotels are subject to 5% government tax (on room rate only). The following is a selection; there are many others: *Radisson Fort George Hotel*, 2 Marine Parade (PO Box 321, Tel: 77400, Fax: 73820), in two wings (Club Wing and Colonial Section), each with excellent rooms, US$115-165, a/c, helpful staff, reservations should be made, safe parking, good restaurant, good pool (non-residents may use pool for BZ$20), recommended. *Ramada Royal Reef and Marina*, Newtown Barracks (PO Box 1248), Tel: 32677, Fax: 32360, US$149, on sea front (but not central), a/c, good food and service in restaurant and bar (a/c with sea views, expensive), pool; *Holiday Inn Villa*, 13 Cork St, Tel: 32800, Fax: 30276, a/c, TV, good restaurant (local and Lebanese), excellent rooftop bar with views of cayes and harbour, pool, nice gardens. *Belize Biltmore Plaza*, 3 Mile Northern Highway, Tel: 32302, Fax: 32301, US$100-160, comfortable rooms, a/c, restaurant (nice atmosphere, a/c, good selection), excellent English pub-style bar, pool, conference facilities, a long way from town (BZ$7 or more by taxi); *Bellevue*, 5 Southern Foreshore (Tel: 77051, Fax: 73253), US$83, a/c, private bath, good restaurant (nice atmosphere, good lunches with live music, steaks), leafy courtyard pool, nice bar with live music Friday and Saturday nights, good entertainment, recommended; *Chateau Caribbean*, 6 Marine Parade, by *Fort George* (Tel: 30800, Fax: 30900), US$79, a/c, with good bar, restaurant (excellent Chinese and seafood, sea view, good service) and discotheque, parking, recommended. *Belize International* , at Ladyville, 9 miles on Northern Highway, Tel: 025-2150 or 02-44001, 1½ miles from airport, tennis court, restaurant and bar; *Bakadeer Inn*, 74 Cleghorn Street, about US$35, private bath, breakfast included, a/c, new (1990) friendly, recommended; *Bliss*, 1 Water Lane (Tel: 72552), over US$30 with bath and a/c, cheaper with fan, good value; *El Centro*, 4 Bishop St, Tel: 72413, a/c, restaurant, good value; *Mopan*, 55 Regent Street (Tel: 77351), US$31.50 with bath, breakfast, a/c, in historic house, has restaurant and bar (owners Tom and Jean Shaw), pricey.

Four Fort Street (address as name, Tel:

30116, Fax: 78808), 6 rooms, all with four-poster beds and shared bath, charming, excellent restaurant, recommended; *Orchidia Guest House and Café*, 56 Regent St, Tel: 74266, Fax: 77600, US$42.50, colonial-style building, rooms with a/c or fan, charming, popular with backpackers, good juice bar; *Mom's Hotel and Restaurant* (formerly *Mom's Triangle Bar*), 11 Handyside St, Tel: 45073, Fax: 31975, PO Box 332, very popular restaurant, pricey; *Belize River Lodge*, Ladyville, PO Box 459 Belize City, Tel: 025-2002, Fax: 025-2298, 10 minutes from airport on Belize River, excellent accommodation, food and fishing (from lodge or cruises), also scuba facilities, numerous packages. *Sea Side Guest House*, 3 Prince Street, Tel: 78339, US$14, US$5 in bunk room, comfortable, quiet, very popular, very helpful American owners, German spoken, 6 rooms, breakfast only (good), repeatedly recommended; *Freddie's*, 86 Eve St, Tel: 44396, US$15 with shower and toilet, fan, hot water, clean, very nice, secure, very small. *North Front Street Guest House*, Tel: 77595, 1 block north of Post Office, 15 minutes walk from Batty bus station, 124 North Front St, US$12.50, US$5 pp in dormitory, no hot water, fan, book exchange, TV, clean, friendly, renovated in 1991, laundry, mice, French spoken, good information, keep windows closed at night and be sure to lock your door; *Bell's Hotel*, 140 North Front St, Tel: 31083, US$12.50, US$5 pp , owner Richard Clarke-Bell has a boat and can provide transport to the Cayes. *Bon Aventure*, 122 North Front St, Tel: 44248, (cheaper in dormitory), purified water available, a bit run down, but Hong Kong Chinese owners helpful, Spanish spoken, good meals at reasonable prices, safe to store luggage here; opposite are *Mira Rio*, similar prices, fan, toilet, clean, a bit noisy, and *Riverside*, Tel: 32397, 61 North Front St, Chinese run, same prices. *Marin Travel Lodge*, 6 Craig St, Tel: 45166, US$8, good, fans, shared hot showers, clean, safe, laundry facilities.

If going to the southern cayes and you want to stay on the mainland: hotels in **Dangriga** *Pelican Beach*, on the beach north of town (PO Box 14, Tel: 05-22044, Fax: 05-22570), over US$125, with private bath and a/c, good restaurant; *Bonefish*, Mahogany Street, Tel: 025-22165, on seafront on outskirts of town, US$60, a/c, colour TV with US cable, hot water, takes Visa, good; *Riverside*, 5 Commerce St, Tel: 05-22168, Fax: 05-22296,not always clean, US$15-20. *Hub Guest House*, 573 South Riverside, Tel: 05-22397, Fax: 05-22813, US$15-20 with bath, meals, helpful; *Cameleon*, 119 Commerce St, Tel: 05-22008, US$11, good and friendly. Cheaper lodgings in *Catalina*, 37 Cedar St, Tel: 05-22390, US$7.50, not too good; *Rio Mar*, 977 Southern Foreshore, OK, and in private homes (basic), eg Miss Caroline's. Unfurnished houses are rented out for US$20-30 a month.

Accommodation in Placencia (note that rooms may be hard to find in afternoon, eg after arrival of the bus from Dangriga) *Rancagua Lodge*, Tel: 06-23112, approx US$60, wooden cabins on the ocean, very clean; same range, *Placencia Cove*, PO Box 007, Tel: 06-22024; *E-Lee Placencia*, US$15 approx, full board US$7.50 extra (single meals available), créole cooking, run by Dalton Eiley and Jim Lee; they offer reef fishing, snorkelling, excursions to the jungle, Pine Ridge, Mayan ruins and into the mountains. If arriving by air at Big Creek, first contact Hubert Eiley, 3 Richard Sidewalk, Belize City (Tel: 3567) who will arrange for a boat to take you to Placencia. *Ran's Travel Lodge*, Tel: 06-22027, US$5, no meals, shared shower, toilet, friendly, fresh coconut bread baked next door (1000-1100). Ask at *Jennie's Restaurant*, or Tel: 06-23148, for lodgings at *Seaspray*, cheap, no private bath, good value, by post office. *Kitty's Place*, Tel: 06-22027, beach apartment, US$45 per day, US$135 per week, rooms US$20, camping US$5, hot showers, bar, restaurant and Placencia Dive Shop; Miss Jackson rents rooms, US$5, US$3.50 for 3 meals (book in advance if non-resident), cooking facilities, friendly (contact Bill, an American, here, for trips to the reef); Mrs Leslie at the Post Office rents houses at US$20 per day (4-6 people, fridge and cooker); she also has hammock space for 3, US$2.50 per night (noisy); Mrs Leslie's son Charles makes all arrangements for the boat to Puerto Cortés, Honduras (see above), and occasionally changes travellers' cheques; he also organizes trips to the reef, etc. Rooms for rent behind *Galley* restaurant, very basic but cheap, friendly owner; the *Galley* itself is a good place to eat (order meals 2-3 hours in advance) and has information on fishing and snorkelling. There are other hotels

and rooms for rent. Camping on the beach or under the coconut palms.

Where To Eat

Eating places on the Cayes are given above. In Belize City there are plenty of places to eat, with Créole, or Chinese food, burgers and sandwiches. *Golden Dragon*, Queen St, good, reasonably priced, recommended for Chinese food; *Four Fort Street* (at that address), near Memorial Park, nice atmosphere, sit out on the verandah, desserts a speciality, recommended, also has 6 rooms (see above); *Macy's*, 18 Bishop Street (Tel: 73419), recommended for well-prepared local game, Creole cooking, different fixed menu daily, charming host; *Barracks Restaurant and Bar*, 136 Barrack Rd, excellent value, much frequented by expatriot community and Belizeans alike, Chinese and Far Eastern cuisine; *Grill*, 164 Newtown Barracks (a short taxi ride from major hotels), English owner Richard Price, new, considered by many as best restaurant in the city, varied menu, Tel: 45020; *DIT's*, 50 King St, good, cheap; *GG's Café and Patio*, 2-3 King St, popular for lunches. *King's*, St Thomas St, good value; *Big Daddy's*, Pickstock St (2 blocks from North Front St), OK, cheap but limited, vegetarian food available, eat in or take-away; *Moms*, address above, large helpings, best breakfast selection in town, popular, good value, notice boards, good place for information, open 0600-2200, closed Saturday; *Pearl's*, next door, Italian and pizza, good value, friendly host Bill (ex-Placencia), no bar; *Marlin*, 11 Regent St West, overlooking Belize River, Tel: 73913, varied menu, good seafood.

Outside Belize City the restaurants tend to be simpler, but you can usually find good fare, especially the seafood.

Try the local drink, anise and peppermint, known as "A and P"; also the powerful "Old Belizeno" rum. The local beer, Belikin, is good, as is the "stout", strong and free of gas.

Camping

Camping on the beaches, in forest reserves, or in any other public place is not allowed. There are no tent camp sites. **NB** Butane gas in trailer/coleman stove size storage bottles is available in Belize.

Shopping

Handicrafts, woodcarvings, straw items, are all good buys. *Cottage Industries*, 26

Albert Street. *Admiral Burnaby's Coffee Shop*, Regent St, combination art gallery, book and craft shop, serving also coffee and juices. *The Holy Redeemer Book Centre*, North Front St, close to bridge and Catholic church, very good, has secondhand books and back issues of US magazines, front of shop sells T-shirts and souvenirs. *Belize Bookshop*, Regent St (opposite *Mopan Hotel*), ask at counter for "racy" British greetings cards. *Angelus Press*, 10 Queen Street, excellent selection of stationery supplies, books, cards, etc. *Go Tees*, 23 Regent St, Tel: 74082, excellent selection of T-shirts (printed on premises), arts and crafts from Belize, Guatemala and Mexico: jewellery, silver, wood carvings, clothes, paintings, etc; also has a branch at Belize Zoo, good zoo T-shirts and cuddly animals. Zericote (or Xericote) wood carvings can be bought in Belize City, for example at *Brodies Department Store* (Central Park end of Regent St), which also sells postcards, the Fort George Hotel, the small gift shop at *Four Fort Street*, or from Egbert Peyrefitte, 11a Cemetery Road. Such wood carvings are the best buy, but to find a carver rather than buy the tourist fare in shops, ask a taxi driver. (At the Art Centre, near Government House, the wood sculpture of Charles Gabb, who introduced carving into Belize, can be seen.) Wood carvers sell their work in front of the *Fort George* and *Holiday Inn Villa* hotels. A new craft centre at the southern end of the swing bridge, on the site of the old market, should be open by 1993. The market is by the junction of North Front St and Fort St. *Ro-Macs*, 27 Albert St, excellent supermarket including wide selection of imported foods and wines.

Exchange
All banks have facilities to arrange cash advance on Visa card. If you want US dollars against a credit card or travellers' cheques, you will be sent to get permission from the Central Bank, 2 Bishop Street, alternatively you may show proof that you are leaving the country; 3% commission is charged. The Belize Bank is particularly efficient and modern, BZ$1 commission on Amex cheques, gives cash on Visa and Mastercard; also Barclays Bank International, with some country branches, slightly better rates, no commission. Atlantic Bank, 6 Albert Street, or 16 New Road, quick efficient service, smaller queues than in others.

Bank of Nova Scotia. It is easy to have money telexed to Belize City. American Express at Global Travel, 41 Albert Street, Belize City (Tel: 77185/77363/4). Money changers at Batty Bus terminal just before departure of bus to Chetumal (the only place to change Mexican pesos). The black market is not recommended.

Currency
The monetary unit is the Belizean dollar, stabilized at BZ$2=US$1. Currency notes (Monetary Authority of Belize) are issued in the denominations of 100, 50, 20, 10, 5, 2, and 1 dollars, and coinage of 1 dollar, 50, 25, 10, 5 and 1 cent is in use. Notes marked Government of Belize, or Government of British Honduras, are only redeemable at a bank. The American expressions Quarter (25c), Dime (10c) and Nickel (5c) are common, although 25c is sometimes referred to as a shilling.

Security
Take good care of your possessions in Belize City. Do not trust the many self-appointed "guides" who also sell hotel rooms, boat trips to the Cayes, drugs, etc. Local advice is not even to say "no"; just shake your head and wag your finger if approached by a stranger. Street money changers are not to be trusted either. Recent government measures have increased the security presence in Belize City. It is wise to avoid small, narrow side streets and stick to major thoroughfares. Travel by taxi is cheap and advisable at night and in the rain. Outside the city the visitor should feel at no personal risk.

Health
Europeans leading a normal life and taking common precautions find the climate pleasant and healthy. Malaria was reportedly under control, but you are advised to take precautions when in Belize. It is advisable to carry mosquito repellent. Inoculation against yellow fever and tetanus is advisable but not obligatory. Tap water in Belize City is said to be safe to drink but bottled water is preferable. Out-patients' medical attention is free of charge.

Climate
Shade temperature is not often over 32°C on the coast, even in the hotter months of February to May (the "dry" season). Inland, in the west, day temperatures can exceed 38°C, but the nights are cooler. Between November and February there are cold spells during which the

temperature at Belize City may fall to 13°C. Humidity is high, making it "sticky" most of the time in the lowlands.

There are sharp annual variations of rainfall, there is even an occasional drought, but the average at Belize City is 65 inches, with about 50 inches in the north and a great increase to 170 inches in the south. Generally the driest months are April and May; in June and July there are heavy showers followed by blue skies; September and October tend to be overcast and there are lots of insects. Hurricanes can threaten the country from June to November, but there have been only four in the past thirty years. An efficient warning system has been established and there are hurricane shelters in most towns and large villages.

Clothing
The business dress for men is a short-sleeved cotton or poplin shirt or *guayabera* (ties not often worn) and trousers of some tropical weight material. Formal wear may include ties and jackets, but long-sleeved embroidered *guayaberas* are commoner. Women should not wear shorts in the cities and towns; acceptable only on the cayes and at resorts.

Business Hours
Retail shops are open 0800-1200, 1300-1600 and Friday 0900-2100, with a half day from 1200 on Wednesday. Small shops open additionally most late afternoons and evenings, and some on Sundays 0800-1000.

Government and commercial office hours are 0800-1200 and 1300-1600 Monday to Friday. Banking hours in Belize City: 0800-1300 Monday-Thursday, 0800-1200, 1500-1800 Friday (some variations elsewhere in the country).

Public Holidays
New Year's Day (1 January), Baron Bliss Day (9 March), Good Friday and Saturday, Easter Monday, Labour Day (1 May), Commonwealth Day (24 May), St George's Caye Day (10 September), Belize Independence Day (21 September), Pan American Day (12 October), Garifuna Settlement Day (19 November), Christmas and Boxing Day.

Note   Most services throughout the country close down Good Friday to Easter Monday: banks close at 1130 on the Thursday, buses run limited services Holy Saturday to Easter Monday, and boats to the Cayes are available. St George's Caye

Day celebrations in September start 2 or 3 days in advance and require a lot of energy.

Time Zone
6 hours behind GMT, 1 behind EST.

Consulates
Mexico, 20 North Park St, Tel: 30193/4 (open 0900-1300, Monday-Friday; if going to Mexico and requiring a visa, get it here, not at the border, tourist card given on the spot, long queues are normal, arrive early, get visa the afternoon before departure; **Honduras**, 91 North Front St, Tel: 45889, above *The Pub*; **El Salvador**, 120 New Road, Tel: 44318; **Panama**, 168 North Front Street. **Jamaica**, 26 corner Hyde's Lane and New Road, Tel: 245926, Fax: 223312. **USA**, 29 Gabourel Lane, Tel: 77161/2, consulate is round corner on Hutson Street; **Canada**, c/o Vogue Ltd, corner Queen and North Front Street, Tel: 245773/245769, PO Box 216; **Belgium**, Marcelo Ltd, Queen St, Tel: 45769; **The Netherlands**, 14 Central American Blvd, Tel: 275936; **Denmark**, 13 Southern Foreshore, Tel: 72172; **Sweden**, 13 Queen St, Tel: 77234; **Italy**, 18 Albert St, Tel: 77777; **Israel**, 4 Albert St, Tel: 30749/ Fax: 230750. **France**, 10 Queen Street, Tel: 245777; **German Honorary Consul**, 2 Cork Street, Tel: 77316.

Electric Current
110/220 volts single phase, 60 cycles for domestic supply.

Weights And Measures
Imperial and US standard weights and measures. The US gallon is used for gasoline and motor oil.

Telecommunications
There is a direct-dialling system between the major towns and to Mexico and USA. Belize Telecommunications Ltd, Church Street, next to Parcel Post Office, Belize City, open 0800-2100 Monday-Saturday, 0800-1200 Sunday and holidays, has an international telephone, telegraph and telex service. To make an international call from Belize costs far less than from neighbouring countries. US$12 for 3 minutes to UK and Europe (a deposit of US$15 required first); US$6.40 to USA and Canada; US$16 elsewhere. Collect calls to USA, Canada, Australia and UK only. Fax: US$4.80 minimum, plus US$2.50 service charge.

Airmail Postage
To UK 4-5 days, BZ$0.75 for a letter,

BZ$0.40 for a postcard; BZ$0.60 for a letter to USA, BZ$0.30 for a post card. **Post Office in Belize City**: letters, Queen Street and North Front Street; parcels, Church Street. Letters held for one month. Beautiful stamps sold.

Press

Belize Times; Amandala, People's Pulse, Reporter (weekly). Monthlies *Belize Today* and *Belize Review*; bi-monthly *Belize Currents.*

Tourist Information

Belize Tourist Bureau, 83 North Front Street, Belize City, PO Box 325, Tel: 2-77213/73255, Fax: 2-77490 (open 0800-1200, 1300-1700 Monday-Thursday, and till 1630 Friday), provides complete bus schedule as well as list of hotels and their prices. Also has a list of recommended taxi guides and tour operators, and free publications on the country and its Maya ruins, practical and informative. Excellent maps of the country for US$3 (postage extra). In the **USA**, 15 Penn Plaza, 415 Seventh Avenue, 18th floor, New York, NY 10001, Tel: 800-624-0686, 212-268-8798, Fax: 212-695-3018; **Canada**, Belize High Commission, 273 Patricia Avenue, Ottawa, K1Y V6C, Tel: 613-722-7187; **Germany**, Belize Tourist Board/WICRG, Lomenstr.-28, 2000 Hamburg 70, Tel: 49-40-695-8846, Fax: 49-40-380-0051. Suggested reading is *Hey Dad, this is Belize*, by Emory King, a collection of anecdotes, available in bookshops. Maps (US$3), books on Belizean fauna etc available at Angelus Press, Queen St. Above the Post Office is the Survey Office selling maps, 2-sheet, 1:250,000, US$8, dated, or more basic map US$2.

Belize Tourism Industry Association, private sector body for hotels, tour companies, etc, 99 Albert Street, Tel: 75717, Fax: 78710, brochures and information on all members throughout Belize. Enquire for details on all tour operators.

CANCUN, ISLA MUJERES AND COZUMEL, MEXICO

Introduction

OFF THE EASTERN, Caribbean coast of the Yucatán Peninsula, there are three Mexican islands which have been developed for tourism. All in the state of Quintana Roo, these are Cancún, the most recent and grandest of the resorts, Isla Mujeres and Cozumel (the largest island of the three). The islands are in fact a very small part of what the Yucatán has to offer the visitor. In Quintana Roo and the neighbouring state of Yucatán there are other beaches, magnificent archaeological sites in the form of Maya cities, and the important Spanish colonial city of Mérida. If visiting the region, you are strongly advised to make at least one excursion away from the beach. For an extended coverage of the whole area, consult *The Mexico and Central American Handbook*.

The proximity of all these attractions has helped Quintana Roo to become the largest tourist area in Mexico, with most tourists staying at the three island resorts. Since so many of the tourists coming to the coastal resorts know no Spanish, price hikes and short-changing have become very common there, making those places very expensive if one is not careful. In the peak, winter season, prices are increased anyway.

The peninsula of Yucatán is a flat land of tangled scrub in the drier northwest, merging into exuberant jungle and tall trees in the wetter southeast. There are no surface streams. The underlying geological foundation is a horizontal bed of limestone in which rainwater has dissolved enormous caverns. Here and there their roofs have collapsed, disclosing deep holes or *cenotes* in the ground, filled with water. Today this water is raised to surface-level by wind-pumps: a typical feature of the landscape. It is hot during the day but cool after sunset. Humidity is often high. All round the peninsula are splendid beaches fringed with palm groves and forests of coconut palms. The best time for a visit is from October to March.

The people are divided into two groups: the Maya Indians, the minority, and the *mestizos*, of mixed blood. The Maya women wear *huipiles*, or white cotton tunics (silk for *fiestas*) which may reach the ankles and are embroidered round the square neck and bottom hem. Ornaments are mostly gold. A few of the men still wear straight white cotton (occasionally silk) jackets and pants, often with gold or silver buttons, and when working protect this dress with aprons.

History
The Maya arrived in Yucatán from what is now Guatemala and Belize about AD 600 and later rebuilt their cities, but along different lines from those found further south, probably because of the arrival of Toltecs in the ninth and tenth centuries. Each city was autonomous, and in rivalry with other cities. Before the Spaniards arrived the Maya had developed a writing in

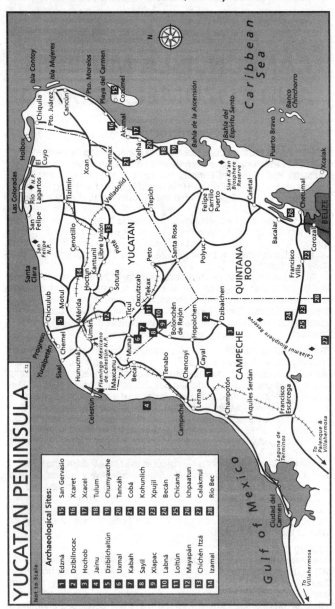

YUCATAN PENINSULA

Not to Scale

Archaeological Sites:

1 Edzná	8 Sayil	15 San Gervasio	22 Kohunlich
2 Dzibilnocac	9 Xlapac	16 Xcaret	23 Xpujil
3 Hochob	10 Labná	17 Xcacel	24 Becán
4 Jainu	11 Loltún	18 Tulum	25 Chicaná
5 Dzibilchaltún	12 Mayapán	19 Chumyaxche	26 Ichpaatun
6 Uxmal	13 Chichén Itzá	20 Tancáh	27 Calakmul
7 Kabah	14 Izamal	21 Cobá	28 Rio Bec

which the hieroglyphic was somewhere between the pictograph and the letter. Bishop Landa collected their books, wrote a very poor summary, the *Relación de las Cosas de Yucatán*, and with Christian but unscholar like zeal burnt all his priceless sources.

In 1511 some Spanish adventurers were shipwrecked on the coast. Two survived. One of them, Juan de Aguilar, taught a Maya girl Spanish. She became interpreter for Cortés after he had landed in 1519. The Spaniards found little to please them: no gold, no concentration of natives, but Mérida was founded in 1542 and the few natives handed over to the conquerors in *encomiendas*. The Spaniards found them difficult to exploit: even as late as 1847 there was a major revolt, mainly arising from the inhuman conditions in the *henequén* (sisal) plantations. In Yucatán and Quintana Roo, the economy has long been dependent on the export of *henequén* and chicle (for chewing gum), but both are facing heavy competition from substitutes and tourism is becoming ever more important.

Culture

Carnival is the year's most joyous occasion, with concerts, dances, processions. Yucatán's folk dance is the Jarana, the man dancing with his hands behind his back, the woman raising her skirts a little, and with interludes when they pretend to be bullfighting. During pauses in the music the man, in a high falsetto voice, sings *bambas* (compliments) to the woman.

The Maya are a courteous, gentle, strictly honest and scrupulously clean people. They drink little, except on feast days, speak Mayan, and profess Christianity laced with a more ancient nature worship.

NB The Yucatán peninsula falls within the hurricane zone, and was most recently affected in September 1988, when Hurricane Gilbert caused extensive damage on the eastern coast (especially on Isla Mujeres). The main tourist facilities have been quick to recover, although some smaller establishments may be out of business.

Cancún

Isla Mujeres, Cancún and the port of Puerto Juárez are all close to each other at the northeastern tip of the Yucatán Peninsula. It is perhaps stretching a point to call the famous resort of **Cancún** an island now. The hotel and beach sector, on a ribbon of land shaped a bit like the number seven, encompasses the Laguna Nichupté. A road connects it with Ciudad Cancún on the mainland. It is a thriving complex and town with skyscraper hotels, basically for the rich, and many smaller hotels with cheaper accommodation. In 1990, Cancún had 19,000 hotel rooms, with plans for 6,000 more by 1993. Its 87 hotels accommodate 20% of all Mexico's tourists. The computer which is said to have selected the site seems to have failed in two respects: (a) there are sharks; (b) there are undercurrents. So swimming in the sea is discouraged on several beaches.

Prices are higher on Cancún than elsewhere in Mexico because everything is brought in from miles outside. Hotels in Cancún town (or in Puerto Juárez, just 3 km away) are much cheaper than on the beach and there are buses running every five minutes for US$0.50. There are many new developments up to 30 km outside Cancún, but local infrastructure is poor. The population is about 30,000, almost all dedicated to servicing the tourist industry. On the island, there is an archaeological museum next to the Convention Centre with local finds, which also houses the excellent Ballet Folklórico shows in

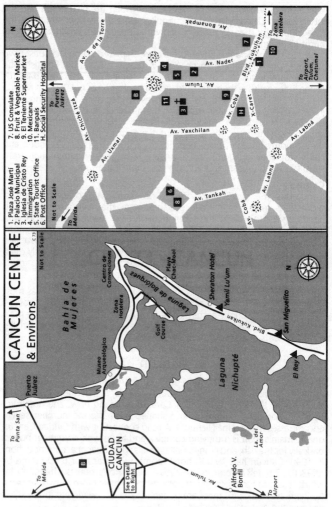

air-conditioned splendour. In the same area of the resort are five interconnecting shopping malls, while in town there are three supermarkets (one of them, Bodega El Teniente on Avenida Tulum, is good place for changing US dollar cash or cheques). Apart from the usual water sports facilities, there is an 18-hole, championship golf course. A free publication, *Cancún Tips*, issued twice a year from Avenida Tulum 29, Cancún, QR 77500, Mexico, gives details on what is available.

You can take an excursion to Isla Contoy (see below), which is a bird sanctuary to the north of Isla Mujeres; daily, once a day, US$70, including boat, food and snorkelling equipment.

Puerto Morelos (bus US$0.75), is not far south of Cancún. It has 3 hotels, two expensive, one basic, *Amor*, near the bus stop; also free and paying camping. The town is popular with scuba divers and snorkellers, but beware of sharks.

Local Information – Cancún

Where To Stay *Camino Real*, Tel: 30100, Fax: 31730; *Sheraton Cancún Resort and Towers*, and *Pirámide del Sol* (low season prices from US$155 to US$165 with ocean view, +10% tax), P.O. Box 834, Cancún, Quintana Roo 77500, Tel: 31988, Fax: (988) 50083; *Hyatt Cancún Caribe* (prices range from US$135-195 de luxe s or d, to U$150-280 ocean front, US$180-350 club, US$250-450 suite, depending on season) and *Hyatt Regency* (rates from US$170-220 de luxe US$190-240 ocean front, US$210-280 club, suites also available, breakfast included); *Best Western Playa Blanca*, Av Kukulkan Km 3.5, Tel: 303344, Fax: 30904, pool, marina, on beach, resort facilities, US$70-105, depending on room and season; and *Krystal* (Paseo Kukulkan, Lote 9, Tel: 31133, Fax: 31790), all in the super luxury bracket. Slightly less expensive are: *Aristos* (Tel: 30011, Fax: 30078), *Calinda Quality Inn*, US$85, Tel: 208-6733 or 800-900-00 in Mexico, or 800-228-5151 in USA for reservations), *Club Lagoon Caribe* (Tel: 31111, Fax: 31326), *Viva*, *Miramar Misión*. *El Presidente* (a member of the Stouffer hotel chain), is in the expensive bracket; it has 294 rooms, all a/c, 5 restaurant and bars, all medical, laundry and other services, facilities for the disabled, swimming, tennis, water sports and marina. At the far end of the island is the *Club Méditerranée* with its customary facilities (not recommended for children; local Tel: 988-42090; consult your local Club Med representative for rates).

Youth hostel, CREA (part of the national system), Km 3.2 Blvd Zona Hotelera, Tel: 31337, on the beach (taxi drivers know it), dormitory style, 12 people per room, under US$10 pp, filthy bathrooms, poor locations (also possible to put up tent for US$5).

Hotels in Cancún town: *Albatross*, with kitchen; *América*, *Atlantis*; slightly less expensive: *Antillano*, *Batab*, *Carillo*, *Handall*, *Konvasser* (a Mayan, not German name), *María de Lourdes*, *Plaza del Sol*, *Rivemar*, *Caribe Internacional*, *Soberanis*, *Villa Maya*, all in the US$20-35 range. Also in this range, *Parador*, Av Tulum, close to bus station, a/c, pool, clean; *María Isabel*, Palmera 595, Tel: 49015, also near bus station and Av Tulum (under US$20), fan and a/c, hot water, TV, small, clean; similar prices at *Cotty*, near bus station, a/c, TV, reports vary on cleanliness. Least expensive but acceptable still: *Arabe*, *Bonampak*, *Canto*, *Coral*, *Mar y Mar*, *Marufo*, *Villa Rossana* (US$12 and up), *San Carlos* (on Av Cedro), *Yaxchilán*, and *La Carreta Guest House*. Two or three cheap hotels on Calle 7 Oriente, near Av. Tulum/López Portillo (2 blocks from Supermarket Plaza 2000): *María Tere*, hot showers, fan, clean, friendly, can be noisy from bar/restaurant next door, and *Piña*, hot showers, fan, clean, recommended, cheaper, both under US$20. You'll be lucky to find much else below US$20 a night. If travelling on a budget, you can stay more cheaply in Puerto Juárez (see below) and spend the day on Cancún beach.

Camping Not permitted in Cancún except next to the CREA youth hostel. The nearest Trailer Park is between Puerto Juárez and Punta Sam.

Where To Eat There are about 200 restaurants apart from those connected with hotels. They range from hamburger stands to 5-star, gourmet places. The ones on the island are of slightly higher price and quality than those in the town and are scattered along Paseo Kukulkán, the main island drive, with a high concentration in the 5 shopping centres.

The best buys are on the side streets of Cancún town, while the largest selection can be found on the main street, Avenida Tulum. The best is said to be *100% Natural*, in front of *Hotel Caribe Internacional* on Yaxchilán; *Piemonte Pizzería*, Av Yaxchilán 52, good food and value; *Valladolid*, on Uxmal, is reasonable; many others on Uxmal, not too expensive. *Los Huarachos*, Yaxchilán y Uxmal, fast food, cheap *empanada* specials after 1300; *Bing*, Av Tulum y Uxmal, close to Banpais bank, best ice cream. The native Mexican restaurants in the workers' colonies are cheapest. The best bet is to buy food and beer in a store and take it to the beach, spending the day on a lounger. The market is at Av. Tulum 23.

Entertainment *La Boom*, disco near the Youth Hostel, free entry before 2200. Salsa club *Batacha* in *Miramar Misión* hotel, no entry charge during the week, about US$4 at weekends, popular with locals, good music. Crococun crocodile ranch, 30 km on road to Playa del Carmen (see below).

Bookshop *Fama*, Av Tulum 105, for international magazines in English, French and German.

Exchange Banpais. Several small *casas de cambio* which change cash and travellers' cheques (latter at poor rates) until 2100; best is *Cunex*, Av Tulum 13, close to Av Cobá.

Consulates Costa Rica, H Casa Maya, Suite 2105, Tel: 3-08-81; **Argentina**, Av. Cobá 18, Tel: 4-18-60. **USA**, Av. Cobá 30, Tel: 4-24-11; **Canada**, Plaza México, Tel: 4-37-16; **Germany**, *Hotel Club Lagoon*, Tel: 3-09-58, Est. 616; **Sweden**, Plaza Caribe 8, Tel: 4-11-75; **Spain**, Falmingos Real Estate, Plaza El Parián, Tel: 3-00-56; **Italy**, Calle Alcatraces 39, Tel: 4-12-72.

Travel Agent *Maritur*, director Vicente Posada Javier, Duraznos 32, SM2A, M 1, Retorno 3, Tel: 70011, English spoken, helpful, recommended.

Buses Local bus (Route No 1), US$0.50 (taxis are exorbitant). Buses along the beach front are crowded with pickpockets. Local bus to Puerto Juárez US$0.35, hourly between 0600-2300; taxi US$3.

Within easy reach are the sites of Chichén-Itzá (bus, 3½ hours, US$5), Tulum (US$3.50, 2 hours, 4 daily 1st class, 5 daily 2nd class, walk 1 km from bus stop), and many lesser known centres such as Cobá and Tablé. The road to Tulum is completely paved and continues paved to Chetumal, US$8.50 1st class, 0800-1600 hourly, takes 6 hours. To Mérida, US$7 1st class, US$6.25 2nd class, 4½ hours. (For details on some of these places, see below.) To Mexico City, ADO company, 1st class at 0615, 1215 and 1815.

Boat Services Expensive boats leave from the pier near *Calinda Quality Inn* in Cancún for Cozumel and Isla Mujeres; go instead to Puerto Juárez.

Car Hire Budget Rent-a-Car in Cancún has been recommended for good service.

Isla Mujeres

Isla Mujeres once epitomized the Caribbean island: long silver beaches, palm trees and clean blue water. Those who knew it even just a few years ago find it overbuilt, overpriced and disappointing. Moreover, almost all of the island's coconut palms have been lost to disease. Until a new, disease-resistant variety has matured, there is little shade. It is also suffering from the competition from Cancún and many hotels are now looking rather run-down. It is, nonetheless, touristy, with frequent instances of overpricing and unfriendliness. Having said that, its waters are still clear, in shades of turquoise and lapis-lazuli blue. The island got its name from the large number of female idols first found by the Spaniards. At the southern tip is an archaeological site known as El Observatorio, near the present lighthouse, 1 kilometre from Garrafón beach. In Maya times, Isla Mujeres was a centre for salt production.

The northern beach has dazzling white sand, so wear sunglasses. At the north end, the sea is cleaner away from the beach pollution of the town and the naval airstrip to the southwest of the town. **NB** Travellers are warned that there is a very dangerous beach on the ocean side near the north with strong undertows and cross-currents; there have been numerous drownings. It is just behind the *Bojórquez Hotel*. There are limestone (coral) cliffs and a rocky coast at the south end. A lagoon on the west side is now fouled up.

At Garrafón beach, 7 km from the town (mind your belongings, entry

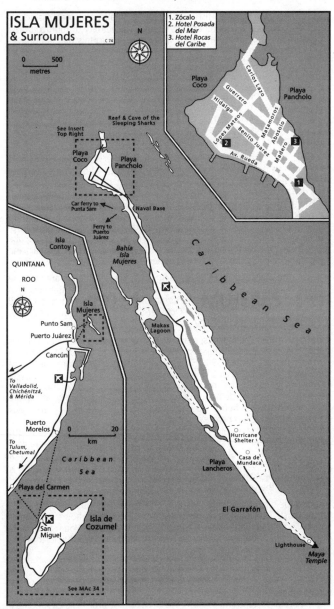

ISLA MUJERES
& Surrounds
C 74

N

0   500
metres

1. Zócalo
2. Hotel Posada del Mar
3. Hotel Rocas del Caribe

Carlos Lazo

Playa Coco

Guerrero

Hidalgo

López Mateos

Benito Juárez

Matamoros

Abasolo

Madero

Playa Pancholo

Av. Rueda

2

3

1

Reef & Cave of the Sleeping Sharks

See Insert Top Right

Playa Coco

Playa Pancholo

Car ferry to Punta Sam

Ferry to Puerto Juárez

Naval Base

Isla Contoy

QUINTANA

ROO

N

Bahía Isla Mujeres

Caribbean Sea

Isla Mujeres

Punto Sam

Puerto Juárez

Cancún

To Valladolid, Chichénitzá, & Mérida

Puerto Morelos

0   20
km

Makax Lagoon

To Tulum, Chetumal

Caribbean Sea

Hurricane Shelter

Casa de Mundaca

Playa Lancheros

Playa del Carmen

San Miguel

Isla de Cozumel

See MAc 34

El Garrafón

Lighthouse

Maya Temple

US$1) there is a tropical fish reserve on a small coral reef. Fishing is forbidden, so take a snorkel and swim among a variety of multicoloured tropical fish—they aren't at all shy. The coral, though, is dead and lacks colour. At peak times there can be more snorkellers than fish; swim before 0900 because it gets very crowded; at 1100 the music-boat from Cancún arrives. (Snorkel rental is US$3.75 a day from Buzco, near the pier, or outside the entry to the Park, flippers US$3, underwater camera US$20 —your tourist card will be asked for as security; to hire a locker costs US$1.50 at Garrafón, where drinks are twice the price of those in town). It's worth walking on from Garrafón up a track to the lighthouse. (Taxi to Garrafón US$3.25, may charge more for return journey; there is a bus which goes half-way there.) The Civil Guard patrol the beaches at night.

You can rent skin and scuba diving equipment, together with guide, from Divers of Mexico, on the waterfront north of the public pier: a boat and equipment costs about US$50 pp for half a day, check how many air tanks are included. They can set up group excursions to the Cave of the Sleeping Sharks; English spoken (their attitude to safety has been described as slapdash). Shop around for good deals. Deep sea fishing can be arranged for 10 in a boat from *Aguamundo*. In the opinion of an experienced diver, Erik Bernesson of Vaxtorp, Sweden, the underwater scene at Garrafón is much less interesting, and scuba diving more expensive, than at Cozumel or the Laguna Xelhá on the mainland further south; Belize, he says, is even better.

In town, the main activity in the evening takes place in the square near the church, where there are also a supermarket and a cinema. Between 1-8 December there is a fiesta for the Virgin of the island, with fireworks and dances until 0400 in the Plaza. In October there is a festival of music, with groups from Music and the USA performing in the main square.

If driving, respect speed limits, roads with new gravelling are tricky. There is public transport on Isla Mujeres: taxis at fixed prices (eg US$1.50 to the northern beach), and a US$0.15 bus service. You can walk from one end of the island to the other in 2½ hours. However, it is worth hiring a bicycle (wonderfully rickety), by the hour, US$0.75, or US$5 a day (about US$7 deposit), or a motorcycle hourly or for a day (US$25 from *Ciro's*), to explore the island in about 2 hours. Do check at the only rental shop if there is any damage to the bicycle *before* you hire.

One can cycle down to the southern end of the island to the curious remains of a pirate's domain, called Casa de Mundaca, a nature reserve with giant turtles at El Chequero, and the little   observatory. It is not signposted—mind you don't walk into the army firing range. Fine views. The island is best visited April to November, off-season (although one can holiday here the year round).

A trip to the bird and wildlife sanctuary on the unspoilt Isla Contoy (see also above) costs US$30, 8 hours with excellent lunch, two hours of fishing, snorkelling (equipment hire extra, US$2.50) and relaxing. You may be able to find cheaper boats; they may not leave until full. Also to the north of Isla Mujeres is the small island of Isla Blanca.

Local Information – Isla Mujeres

Where To Stay At Christmas hotel prices are increased steeply and the island can heave with tourists, especially in January. The island has several costly hotels and others, mainly in the US$12-20 range, and food is generally expensive. Plumbing in the Isla Mujeres hotels leaves a lot to be desired; it seems that there is no venting on drains so there are a lot of unpleasant smells.

Reasonable hotels to stay at on Isla Mujeres are: *Perla del Caribe*, Madero 2, Tel: 20444, US$30, highly recommended, on the ocean but the beach is dangerous, swimming pool, restaurant, laundry; *Posada del Mar*, Almirante Rueda 15, Tel: 20212, US$65 (including meals), has pleasant drinks terrace but expensive drinks, restaurant for residents only; *Berny*, Juárez y Abosolo, Tel: 20025, US$30 with bath and fan, basic, swimming pool; long-distance calls possible, residents only, but does not even honour confirmed reservations if a deposit for one night's stay has not been made. Under US$30: *Isla Mujeres*, next to church, with bath, renovated, run by pleasant Englishman; *Rocas del Caribe*, Madero 2, 100 metres from ocean, cool rooms, big balcony, clean, good service; *Osorio*, US$15, Madero, 1 block from waterfront, clean, fan, with bath and hot water, expensive bakery nearby; *El Peregrino* restaurant has an excellent Andean music group nightly, 1930-2230; *El Paso*, Morelos 13, with bath, clean, facing the pier, 2nd floor; *María José*, Madero 25, Tel: 20130, near seafront, US$25 with bath. *Vistalmar*, on promenade about 300 metres left from ferry dock, over US$20 (under US$20 for longer stays—negotiate), ask for rooms on top floor, bath, balcony, fan, insect screens, good value; *Carmelina*, Guerrero 9, US$15, central with bath, comfortable, safe, recommended. Under US$12: *Caribe Maya*, Madero 9, central, modern, fans, friendly, reasonable prices, clean, but noisy and smelly plumbing; *Caracol*, central, clean, good value; *Las Palmas*, US$15, central, Guerrero 20, 1 block from north beach, good, clean; *Isleñas*, about US$15 with bath, less without, very clean, helpful; *Poc-Na Hostal*, dormitory accommodation, is the cheapest (US$7), try for the central section where there are fans, no bedding, linen or mattresses, but all can be rented, gringo hang-out, café, video, take insect repellent (San Jorge laundry is just 1 block away, US$2 per kg).

There is a trailer park on the island, with a restaurant. At the south end of island is *Camping Los Indios* where you can put up your hammock. In town nobody seems to know (or want to know) about this place.

NB If you arrive late, book into any hotel the first night and set out to find what you want by 0700-0800, when the first ferries leave the next morning. If you arrive on the morning ferry, scrum for a cheap place.

Where To Eat Many beach restaurants close just before sunset. *El Limbo* at *Roca Mar Hotel* (Nicolás Bravo y Guerrero), excellent seafood, good view, reasonable prices; *Miriti*, opposite ferry, quite good value; *Rolandi's Pizza*, main shopping street, good (many *pizzerías* are expensive), good breakfast, popular; *Gomar* in town, expensive, possible to eat outside on verandah or in the colonial-style interior, popular; *Mano de Dios*, near beach, probably cheapest on island, quite good. *Eric's*, 1 block inland, very good inexpensive Mexican snacks; *Estrellita Marinera*, 1 block inland, clean, good Mexican food; *Tropicana*, 1 block from pier, simple, popular, cheap; *Cielito Lindo*, waterfront, open air, good service; *La Langosta*, 3 blocks south, good Mexican dishes, lovely view; *Bucanero*, downtown, steak, seafood, prime rib, classy for Isla Mujeres. *Sergio's* on main square, expensive, very good; next door is *La Peña*, reasonably-priced, good food and pizzas, recommended, so-called "happy hour" until 2200. *Giltri*, in town, good value; *Cito's*, good breakfast and health food; opposite is *Ciro's* which is not recommended. Small restaurants round the market are good value; try the local Poc-Chuc (pork and vegetables) dish. At Garrafón Beach: *El Garrafón*, *El Garrafón de Castilla*, *French Marías*, all 3 cater for tour boats from Cancún, pricey lobster on the magnificent tropical beach. Daily fish barbecue at El Paraíso beach.

Shopping Opposite the restaurant *Gomar* is a souvenir shop that sells good stone Maya carvings (copies), macramé hangings and colourful wax crayon "Maya" prints. *El Paso Boutique*, opposite the ferry, trades a small selection of English novels.

Entertainment Disco-bars *Tequila*, 1 block from *Poc-Na* and *Calipso*. *Bad Bones* has live rock-and-roll.

Exchange Banco del Atlántico, Av Juárez 5, 1% commission.

Puerto Juárez

Puerto Juárez is about 3 kilometres north of Cancún (taxi fare should be US$3, beware of overcharging). From the jetty opposite the bus terminal, a passenger ferry runs to Isla Mujeres nine times a day; can be erratic and sometimes leaves early (US$1.50, 1 hour). There are also small boats crossing, but these are more expensive (US$4 at least). There is a tourist kiosk at the ferry terminal, open 0900-1700.

A car ferry to Isla Mujeres sails from Punta Sam (a couple of kilometres north of Puerto Juárez; there are hourly buses from Puerto Juárez from 0500). About 75 vehicles are carried, six times a day between 0830 and 2200, returning between 0715 and 2200 (1 hour journey). (Facilities to store luggage at the jetty, US$0.25.) For the early morning return ferry from Isla Mujeres, tickets are sold anytime from about 0615. Get there early as it is popular. The boat trip across is US$6-7 for car, US$20 for trailer, US$1.50 pp.

Local Information – Puerto Juárez

Where To Stay And Eat *Hotel Caribel*, resort complex with bath and fan, about US$50; *Posada Zuemy*, 100 metres from bus terminal, on road to Cancún, US$15; *Isabel*, opposite the ferry terminal, about US$18, clean but noisy and overpriced; *Palmeras* is very cheap. Trailer park *Almirante de Gante*, hot showers, right on the beach, 4 km from the army camp and 1 km from Punta Sam. *Cabañas Punta Sam*, clean, comfortable, on the beach, with bath; irregular bus service there, or hitchhike from Puerto Juárez (check to see if restaurant is open evenings, no shops nearby; take mosquito repellent). *Restaurant Puerto Juárez* at bus terminal, friendly, good value.

Buses On the whole it is better to catch outgoing buses in Cancún rather than in Puerto Juárez: there are more of them. However, you can get buses from Puerto Juárez to Chichén-Itzá, Mérida, Tulum and Chetumal. Hourly service to Cancún, US$0.35.

Cozumel

Cozumel island is not only a marvellous place for snorkelling and scuba diving, but is described as a "jewel of nature, possessing much endemic wildlife including pygmy species of coati and raccoon; the bird life has a distinctly Caribbean aspect and many endemic forms also" (Jeffrey L White, Tucson, Arizona). Cozumel is by far the largest of Mexico's Caribbean islands, being about 45 kilometres at its longest (north-south) and 17 kilometres wide. A good map (*The Brown Map*), including reef locations, is available from stores and shops in the main town, San Miguel de Cozumel. In the shops, dollars are preferred to pesos, evidence of the island's popularity as a US holiday resort.

Maya pilgrims used to visit the shrine to the Goddess of Medicine, Ix Chel, which was located on the island. In all, there are some 34 archaeological sites on Cozumel. The easiest to see are the restored ruins of the Maya-Toltec period at San Gervasio in the north (7 km from Cozumel town, then 6 km to the left); Castillo Real, on the northeastern coast; El Cedral in the south (3 km from the main island road); and El Caracol, where the sun, in the form of a shell, was worshipped (1 km for the southernmost Punta Celarain). At Punta Celarain is an old lighthouse.

The best public beaches are some way from San Miguel town: in the north of the island they are sandy and wide, although those at the Zona Hotelera Norte were damaged in 1989 and are smaller than they used to be. South

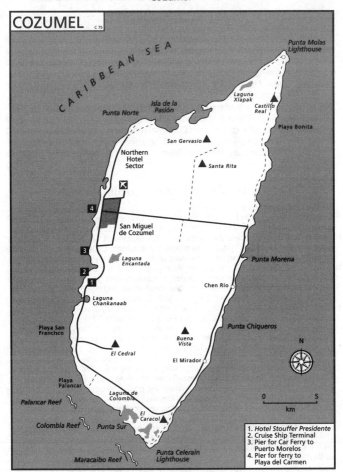

COZUMEL c75

CARIBBEAN SEA

Punta Molas
Lighthouse

Isla de la
Pasión

Punta Norte

Laguna
Xlapak

Castillo
Real

Playa Bonita

San Gervasio ▲

Northern
Hotel
Sector

▲ Santa Rita

San Miguel
de Cozumel

Punta Morena

Laguna
Encantada

Chen Río

Laguna Chankanaab

Playa San
Francisco

Buena
Vista ▲

Punta Chiqueros

El Cedral ▲

El Mirador ●

N

Playa
Palancar

Laguna de
Colombia

Palancar Reef

Colombia Reef   Punta Sur

El
Caracol ▲

0   5
km

Maracaibo Reef

Punta Celeraín
Lighthouse

1. Hotel Stouffer Presidente
2. Cruise Ship Terminal
3. Pier for Car Ferry to
   Puerto Morelos
4. Pier for ferry to
   Playa del Carmen

of San Miguel, San Francisco is good, but others are generally narrower and
rockier. All the main hotels are on the sheltered west coast. The east coast
is rockier; swimming and diving on the unprotected side is very dangerous
owing to ocean underflows.

The island is famous for the beauty of its underwater environment:
snorkel 9 km south of San Miguel de Cozumel at Parque Nacional
Chankanab (open 0800-1630, entrance US$3, taxi from San Miguel US$4),
where there is also a botanical garden, expensive restaurants and hire
facilities (mask and fins US$2, underwater camera and film US$20 a day,
lockers US$1). The snorkelling is good for beginners, but go early, otherwise
you will see only bodies and suntan lotion (which is killing the fish, do not

use if asked not to). The best reef for scuba diving is Palacar in the southwest, reached only by boat. Deportes Acuáticos Damián Piza on Calle 8 Norte, a diligent guide leads two dives separated by a cooked lunch and sunbake on Playa San Francisco—fascinating, US$45 out of season, recommended outfit. There are many diving agencies (Cozumel Divers recommended; Yucab Beach recommended, dive master Victor Brito); all charge US$50 for a resort course, US$250 for a certification course, including equipment.

There is a paved road on Cozumel but the bus service goes only to the expensive hotels north of town. It is best to hire a bicycle (quiet) when touring around the island. This way you can see wildlife—iguanas, turtles, birds—but if taking a motorbike (Rentadora Cozumel is not recommended) beware of policemen who take unguarded ones and then claim they were parked illegally; local police are strict and keen on fining so avoid illegal parking, U-turns, etc.

Local Information – Cozumel

Hotels (prices rise 50% around Christmas) *Maya Cozumel*, clean, friendly, pool, on Calle 5 Sur 4, Tel: 20011, US$40 (there is also *Meliá Mayan Cozumel*, 5 km from airport, Tel: 20411, over US$150); *Aguilar*, 3 Sur 98, Tel: 20307, US$40, pool, clean, central, a/c, recommended; *Marqués*, 5 Av Sur between 1 Sur and Adolfo Rosado Salas, Tel: 20677, similar price, recommended; also *López*, Calle Sur 7-A, Tel: 20108, hot showers, clean, main square, no meals; *La Plaza*, Blvd 11 y 20 Av Sur, US$40, Tel: 22152, pool, showers, a/c, fans, clean; *Blanquita*, 10-N, Tel: 2-11-90, US$20, clean, comfortable, friendly, owner speaks English, rents snorkelling gear and motor-scooters, recommended. The cheapest hotels on the island, all under US$30, are: *Pepita's*, Tel: 20098, a/c, fan, fridge, owner speaks English, Spanish, French, Italian, German and Mayan, highly recommended as best value on island; *Sao Lima*, Adolfo Rosado Salas, clean, fan, showers, recommended; *Flamingo*, Calle 6 Norte 81, Tel: 21264, showers, clean, fan; *José de León*, Av Pedro J Coldwell y 17 Calle Sur, fairly clean, showers; *Posada del Charro*, one block east of *José de León*, same owner, same facilities, being extended; *Paraíso Caribe*, 15 Av Norte y 10 Calle, fan, showers, clean; *Kary*, 25 Av Sur y A Rosado Salas, Tel: 22011, a/c, showers, pool, clean; *Posada Cozumel*, Calle 4, Norte 3, Tel: 20314, pool, showers, a/c, clean; *Yoli*, Calle 1 Sur 164 close to the Plaza, Tel: 20024, with bath and fan; *Al Marestal*, Calle 10 y 25 Av Norte, Tel: 20822, spacious, clean rooms, fan or a/c, cool showers, swimming pool, very good (from pier 5 blocks straight then 5 blocks left); *Flores*, Adolfo Rosado Salas 7, Tel: 20164, one block south of Plaza, ½ block east of waterfront, bargaining possible. First class hotels include: *Cabañas del Caribe* (Tel: 20072), *Cozumel Caribe* (Tel: 20100), *El Cozumeleño* (Tel: 20149), *El Stouffer Presidente* (Tel: 20322), *La Ceiba* (Tel: 20379), *Fiesta Americana*. The first-class hotels on the island charge about US$70-200 d a day and all are directly on the rocky shore except the *Fiesta Americana*, which has a tunnel under the road to the beach.

Camping is not permitted although there are two suitable sites on the south shore. Try asking for permission at the army base.

Restaurants In general, the further a place is from the beach the cheaper it is. *Las Palmeras*, at the pier (people-watching spot), recommended; *Morgans*, main square, elegant, expensive, good; *Plaza Leza*, main square, excellent and reasonable; *La Choza*, Adolfo Rosales Salas 198, reasonable, recommended; *Angelo's*, nearer the sea, more expensive; *Karen's*, pizza cheap, good; *Gato Pardo*, 10 Av 121, good pizzas and try their "tequila slammers"; *Café del Puerto*, 2nd floor by pier, South Seas style; *El Moro*, 75 Bis Norte 124, between 4 y 2, good, closed Thursday; *Santiago's Grill*, 15 Av Sur y A Rosado Salas, excellent, medium price-range, popular with divers; also popular with divers is *Las Tortugas*, 10 Av Norte, just north of square, good in the evening; *El Capi*, 2 locations: by market for lunch, and Calle 3 y 10 Av Sur, more up market, seafood at each; *La Yacatequita*, 9 Calle Sur y 10 Av Sur, genuine Mayan food, closes at 2130, best to go day before and discuss menu; *La Misión*, Av Benito

Juárez y 10 Av Norte, good food, friendly atmosphere; *Pepe's Grill*, waterfront, 2 blocks S of pier, expensive and excellent; *Costa Brava*, on waterfront, 5 blocks S of pier, good sea-food and breakfast, good value, rec. *Acuario*, on beach 6 blocks S of pier, famous for seafood, aquarium in restaurant (ask to see the tanks at the back. *Carlos and Charlie's* restaurant/bar, popular, 2nd floor on waterfront. *Pancho's Backyard*, Rafael Melgar 27, Mexican food and wine; *Tortas Denny*, Calle 1 Sur close to Plaza, good and reasonable; *El Sarape* and *El Focos* on same street, both specialise in tacos, *El Sarape* does a great *frijoles charros* soup; *Económico*, 10 Av Norte between Calle 1 Sur and Calle Salas, friendly, good Mexican food. *Naked Turtle*, on E side (has basic rooms to let); several other bar restaurants on the E side.

Nightclubs *Joman's* (very seedy), *Scaramouche* (the best), *Neptuno* (these two are state-of-the-art discos), all downtown, as well as hotel nightclubs.

Vehicle rental Many agencies for cars, jeeps, motorbikes/scooters and bicycles, e.g. Avis, Budget, Hertz, Thrifty, and local companies. Scooter rental is US$20-25 a day. One filling station, at Av Juárez y Av 30; beware overcharging.

Taxis all carry an official price list. Downtown fare US$3; San Francisco beach US$10; Maya ruins US$30; island tour including San Gervasio US$50. There are no public buses.

Museum On waterfront between Calles 4 and 6, history of the island, well laid-out. Rooftop restaurant has excellent food and views of sunset, good for breakfast, too. Recommended.

Film Two shops develop film, both quite expensive (about US$20 for 36 prints). Best to wait till you get home.

Playa del Carmen

On the mainland, opposite Cozumel, is *Playa del Carmen*, a fast-growing beach centre with many new hotels and restaurants, and resorts up and down the coast. Bathing is not safe beyond the point (to the left facing Cozumel) where there is nude bathing. Most atmosphere seems to have been lost and theft has been reported. The beaches are not always clean, though those to the north of town are the most pleasant (there are sandflies, though). There are some ruins nearby, unrestored (the Pole ruins) at *Xcaret*, a turnoff left on Route 307 to Tulum, after Playa del Carmen (a 2-hour walk along the beach from Playa del Carmen). You can go to a hand-forged chain over a 2 km bad road and pay whoever comes out of the house an entry fee and proceed down the road a few metres on foot. The ruins are near three linked *cenotes*, to their left; there are also lovely sea water lagoons—one can swim. Scuba and snorkelling equipment for rent at the bar. Pole was the departure point for Mayan voyages to Cozumel. There is a roadside restaurant which despite its looks is very clean (accepts Visa).

The present-day ferry for Cozumel goes from Playa del Carmen, US$3.20 one way, 40 minutes' journey, 9 a day from 0530-1930, returns between 0400 and 2000. A waterjet catamaran takes 25 minutes between Playa del Carmen and Cozumel, 0400-1830 from Cozumel, 0530-1930 to the island (US$8 one way, take seasickness pills). One report in early 1992 said the slow ferry had stopped running.

Local Information – Playa del Carmen

Hotels north of the town is *Blue Parrot*, on beach, with café, over US$45 in bungalow, highly recommended; *Rosa Mirador*, behind the *Blue Parrot*, from US$25 to US$40 depending on season, hot showers, fan, best views from 3rd floor, owner Alberto speaks English, recommended; *Las Molcas*, same price range as *Blue Parrot*, near beach, pool, luxurious, although restaurant is poor. About 6 km outside are: at Km 297/8, before

Playa del Carmen, **Cabañas Capitán Lafitte**, very good, pool, excellent cheap restaurant on barren beach; under same ownership is **Shangrilá del Caribe**, closer to town, equally good, excellent beach with diving and snorkelling; at Km 296, **El Marlín Azul**, swimming pool, good food (these 3 are over US$70); **Vista Azul**, at the end of the beach, US$40 with bath and balcony, ugly, overpriced; **Posada Lily**, US$15, with shower, fan, safe, clean, recommended, but noisy in am, 1 block from first-class bus station; **Maya Bric**, Av 5, turn left out of bus station and walk about ½ km, US$20, hot water, clean, friendly, pool, dive shop with equipment rental, snorkelling and fishing trips; **Hotel Nuevo Amanecer**, US$30, very attractive, fans, mosquito nets, clean; **Yax-Ha** cabins, Calle 10 Norte, US$25-50 (depending on size and season), excellent. **Cabañas Tuxatah**, 2 minutes from sea, 2 blocks from Av Principal (Apdo 45), German owner, Maria Weltin speaks English and French, US$30 with bath, clean, comfortable, hot water, laundry service, beautiful gardens, recommended, breakfast US$3; **Sian Ka'an**, Calle Siyan Can, 100 m from bus station, US$25, simple, clean, recommended. By the T-junction on the outskirts, at Route 307, is reasonable **Hotel Maranatha**, with café next door for breakfast and **Doña Juanita's** restaurant (good, opposite Pemex station). Campsite and **cabañas** close to bus station, US$3-4 per tent, US$2 for hammocks, cabins available. "**The Monastery**", 1 block from **Cabaña Banana**, US$15, better rates for longer stays, ask Sam, free use of kitchen and washing facilities, good restaurant with tame iguanas, English spoken, not fancy, but good (**Cabaña Banana** owns rooms, US$25); two doors away is **Mi Casa** (unmarked), US$7 pp with bath and fan, cold water, clean, friendly manager speaks English, mosquito coils necessary; **El Jardín Tropical**, under US$15, nice rooms with bed and hammock, a bit noisy from disco; **Cabañas La Ruina**, nice setting on beach, similar prices (US$2.50 to sling hammock), popular, noisy, recommended; **Cabañas Tucan**, at the end of the main sea side road, US$15, new, clean, good, mosquito net, highly recommended; **Costa del Mar**, on beach, pool. Lots of new places going up, none under US$10 a night. 8 km from Playa del Carmen you can camp at Xcalacoco for US$2.50 a night (US$15 for cabins). CREA Youth Hostel, quite comfortable but difficult to find, especially after dark (Tel: 525-2548).

Camping Small, "chaotic" site at **La Ruina**. Good camping with toilets and showers 100 metres N of main plaza on seashore, US$2-3 per tent, hammock space; camper vans taken if space, rooms from US$7-15 depending on number of people, laundry facilities.

Restaurants **El Herradero**, Calle 10, a few blocks up from beach, cheap and good; **Pez Vela**, good atmosphere, food, drinks and music; **Pollo Caribe**, near bus station, good chicken, cheap drinks, recommended; **Da China**, near **El Capitán**, cheap food, excellent fish. **Máscaras**, on beach, highly recommended. On Av 5: **Limones**, good food, popular, reasonable prices; **Chicago**, steakhouse, American-owned, also serves seafood and breakfast (US$2.50 on terrace with sea view), expensive, CNN TV; opposite is **Flippers**, good atmosphere, good food, moderately priced. **Belvedere**, on square between ferry and bus station, good pasta. **Bip Bip**, best pizza in town; **La Terraya**, at beach, excellent fish and good drinks, cheap, rec.; **Rincón Latino**, vegetarian, good coffee (ask for "hand made"), good yoghurts with granola and fruit, recommended. Various places serve breakfast close to Post Office. Many places have "happy hour" between 1600 and 1900.

Transport It is 68 km or one hour by bus to Tulum (US$1.50), 3½ hours to Chetumal (US$4.80, several between 0530 and 2030); also buses to Mérida (US$8.25), Cancún (US$1.35, 1 hour) and Puerto Juárez. From Mérida 1st class buses go via Cancún, 4 a day (co-ordinate with ferry to Cozumel), 2nd class buses 7 a day, 6 hours.

On the Mainland

The frequently mentioned **Tulum** is on the route between the northeastern Yucatán resorts and the Mexico/Belize border. It is a spectacular Maya-Toltec ruined city, dating from the 12th century, 128 km south of Cancún, 1 km off the main road. The city walls of white stone stand atop coastal cliffs (frescoes are still visible on the interior walls of temples). The temples were dedicated to the worship of the Falling God, or the Setting Sun, represented as a falling character over nearly all the west-facing doors (Cozumel was the home of the Rising Sun). The same idea is reflected in the buildings, which are wider at the top than at the bottom. Open 0800-1700, about two hours are needed to view the city at leisure (entry US$3.45, half-price for students if more than one in the group, Sunday free). Tulum is these days crowded with tourists (fewer in before 1100). Take towel and swimsuit if you wish to scramble down from the ruins to a beach for a swim. The reef is from 600 to 1,000 metres from the shore, so if you wish to snorkel you must either be a strong swimmer, or take a boat trip.

Tulum village is not very large and has neither a bank nor post office (nearest at Playa del Carmen or Felipe Carrillo Puerto, 98 km to the south). Beaches are beautiful but sometimes dirty, and there are beach camping spots and *cabañas* south of, but not at, the ruins.

There is a newly-laid road linking Tulum with the large but little-excavated city of **Cobá**, the ancient political capital of the area, with the largest ruins (entry US$3.45), about 50 km inland from Tulum. Still unspoiled, it is also being developed (tourist buses arrive at 1030, site opens 0800-1700); an unusual feature is the network of ancient roads, known as *sacbes*.

Another interesting place near Tulum is the beautiful clear lagoon, **Laguna Xelhá**, which is full of fish, but no fishing allowed as it is a national park (open 0800-1700), entry US$3.45—get a receipt if you want to leave and come back next day (12 km north, 45 minutes by bus from Playa del Carmen). Snorkelling gear can be rented at US$5 for a day, but it is often in poor repair; better to rent from your hotel. Arrive as early as possible to see fish as later buses full of tourists arrive from Cancún (you need to dive down about a metre because above that level the water is cold and fresh with few fish; below it is the warm, fish-filled salt water—watch out for sting-rays). There is a marvellous jungle path to one of the lagoon bays. Xelhá ruins (known also as Los Basadres) are located across the road from the beach of the same name. You may have to jump the fence to visit; there is a beautiful *cenote* at the end of the ruins where you can have a lovely swim. The small ruins of Ak are near Xelhá. Closer to Tulum, at Tancáh, are newly-discovered bright post-classical Maya murals but they are sometimes closed to the public.

20 km north of Tulum is the luxury resort of Akumal.

Chetumal, the capital of the state of Quintana Roo and border town with Belize, is now being developed for tourism (albeit slowly). It is a free port with clean wide streets, and a greatly improved waterfront with parks and trees. Accommodation may be a problem at holiday times, but in general there are plenty of places to stay and eat. Tourist information can be found at Avenida Héroes, helpful.

Buses The bus station is 2-3 km out of town at the intersection of Insurgentes y Belice (clean facilities, but poor food and mosquitoes); taxi from town US$0.65. You can change pesos into Belize dollars both at the bus station and at the border. Many buses go to the border, US$0.20; taxi from Chetumal to border, 20 minutes, US$5 for two.

To Belize Batty Bus and Venus Bus from bus terminal to Belize City (former each even hour, latter each odd hour), taking 4-5 hours, some buses "express", on a paved road, US$5 in pesos, US or Belize dollars. Be there in good time; they sometimes leave early if full.

From Chetumal you can make excursions into the lagoons which lie just north of the town. You can also visit the fascinating ruins that lie on the way to Francisco Escárcega (a town on the western side of the Yucatán): Kohunlich, Xpujil, Becán, and Chicana. Across the bay from Chetumal, at the very tip of Quintana Roo is **Xcalak**, which may be reached from Chetumal by private launch (2 hours), or by a long, scenic (recent) unpaved road from Limones (3½ hours, 120 km, suitable for passenger cars but needs skilled driver). Daily colectivos from 0700-1900 from 16 de Septiembre y Mahatma Ghandi, but the only one back is at 1300. Bus runs Friday 1600 and Sunday 0600, returning Saturday morning and Sunday afternoon (details from Chetumal tourist office). Xcalak is a fishing village (250 population) with a few shops with beer and basic supplies and one hotel. Do *not* try to walk from Xcalak along the coast to San Pedro, Belize; the route is virtually impassable. Rent a boat and explore Chetumal Bay and Banco Chinchorro, a group of unspoiled islands in the Caribbean.

If you are travelling from Belize into the Yucatán, or if you are staying at one of the coastal resorts, an excursion to some of the peninsula's other sites is recommended. These include **Mérida**, capital of Yucatán state. It was founded in 1542 on the site of the city of Tihoo. There are many colonial buildings, museums, parks and a good market where traditional crafts can be bought. The two most extensively excavated and restored cities in the region are Chichén-Itzá, 120 km southeast of Mérida, and Uxmal, 74 km south. Each deserves a day's exploration. Many other smaller sites can be visited, or, if you are tired of archaeology, you can investigate the north and west coasts. Our map shows the and other points of interest in the Yucatán; for more detail, see the International Travel Map of the region (1:1,000,000), ITM No 205, prepared by Kevin Healey (International Travel Map Productions, PO Box 2290, Vancouver BC, V6B 3W5, Canada). For a succinct introduction to Maya culture, read *The Maya*, by Michael D Coe (Pelican Books, 1971).

Information for Visitors

Documents

A passport is necessary, but US and Canadian citizens need only show birth certificate (or for US, a naturalization certificate). Tourists need the free **tourist card**, which can be obtained from any Mexican Consulate or Tourist Commission office, at the Mexican airport on entry, from the offices or on the aircraft of airlines operating into Mexico. Ask for at least 30 days (maximum 180 days); if you say you are in transit you may be charged US$8, with resulting paper work. NB Not all Mexican consuls in USA are aware of exact entry requirements; it is best to confirm details with airlines which fly to Mexico. Some nationalities appear no longer to need a tourist card. Best to say you are going to an inland destination. (Airlines may issue cards only to citizens of West European countries, most Latin American countries—not Cuba, Chile or Haiti—the USA, Canada, Australia, Japan and the Philippines.) There is a multiple

entry card valid for all visits within 6 months for US nationals. The normal validity for other nationals is 90 days, but sometimes only 30 days are granted at border crossings; insist you want more if wishing to stay longer.

Renewal of entry cards or visas must be done at the Secretaría de Gobernación, Dirección General de Servicios Migratorios, Albañiles 19, esquina Eduardo Molina, Colonia 20 de Noviembre, Mexico City, 1st floor, 1st door on right, takes 15 minutes, only 60 days given, open 0830-1500, Tel: 795-6166 (Metro San Lázaro) or at international airports. To renew a tourist card by leaving the country, you must stay outside Mexico for 72 hours. If you have proof of US$500 to cover each month of your intended stay, you may renew tourist cards at any immigration office. Take travellers' cheques as proof of finance. Travellers not carrying tourist cards need **visas** (Israelis and Finns need a visa); multiple entry not permitted, visa must be renewed before re-entry.

At border crossings make sure the immigration people don't con you to pay a dollar for the card or visa. It is free and the man typing it out is only doing his job. We would warn travellers that there have been several cases of tourist cards not being honoured, or a charge being imposed, or the validity being changed arbitrarily to 60 days or less. In this case, complaint should be made to the authorities in Mexico City. Some border stations do not issue tourist cards; you are therefore strongly advised, if travelling by land, to obtain a card before arriving at the border. Above all, do not lose your tourist card—you cannot leave the country without it and it takes at least a week to replace. If you want to return to Mexico after leaving there to visit Belize or Guatemala, remember that you will need a new visa/tourist card if yours is not marked for multiple entry.

At the land frontiers with Belize and Guatemala, you may be refused entry into Mexico if you have less than US$200 (or US$350 for each month of intended stay, up to a maximum of 180 days). This restriction does not officially apply to North American and European travellers. *Everyone* entering Mexico from Belize and Guatemala is given only 30 days entry, possibly renewable for up to 60 days.

Customs Regulations

The luggage of tourist-card holders is often passed unexamined. If flying into Mexico from South America, expect to be thoroughly searched (body and luggage) at the airport. US citizens can take in their own clothing and equipment without paying duty, but all valuable and non-US-made objects (diamonds, cameras, binoculars, typewriters, etc), should be registered at the US Customs office or the port of exit so that duty will not be charged on returning. Radios and television sets must be registered and taken out when leaving.

Tourists are allowed to take into Mexico duty-free 1 kg of tobacco and 400 cigarettes (or 50 cigars), 2 bottles of liquor, US$80 worth of gifts and 12 rolls of film, also portable TV, radio, typewriter, camera, tent and bicycle. There are no restrictions on the import or export of money apart from gold, but foreign gold coins are allowed into the US only if they are clearly

made into jewellery (perforated or otherwise worked on). Archaeological relics may not be taken out of Mexico. US tourists should remember that the US Endangered Species Act, 1973, prohibits importation into the States of products from endangered species, eg tortoise shell. The Department of the Interior issues a leaflet about this. The UK also forbids the import of products from endangered species.

How To Get There By Air

There are international airports at Cancún (very expensive shops and restaurant) and Cozumel, and a domestic airfield at Isla Mujeres. Only colectivos taxis run from the airport to Cancún town and hotel area, US$6.25; only taxis go to the airport, US$11. There is an irregular bus from Cancún to the airport four times a day.

Cancún is served by the national carriers Mexicana (to Chicago, Dallas, Los Angeles, Miami, New York/Newark, San Francisco, Flores-Guatemala, Mexico City and Guadalajara); Aeroméxico (to Houston, New Orleans, New York, Madrid, Paris, Mexico City and Mérida); and Aero Caribe (to Cozumel, Mérida, Oaxaca, Villahermosa and Flores-Guatemala). Regular US airlines to Cancún include: Continental (to Denver, Houston, Minneapolis, New York, Orange County, CA, and connections to other US cities); United Airlines (Chicago, Washington); American Airlines (to Dallas, Hartford, CT, Miami, Oklahoma, New York and Raleigh, North Carolina); North West Airlines (Detroit, Memphis, and Tampa). Lacsa flies from New Orleans, New York and San José (Costa Rica). Aero Quetzal flies to Guatemala City Tuesday and Saturday morning (book well in advance, office in Mexico City). Tropic Air flies to Belize City daily except Tuesday. LTU flies from Düsseldorf. Nouvelles Frontières fly charter Zürich-Cancún, 66 Blvd St Michel, 75006 Paris, France. There are many charters from North America and Germany.

Flights to Mexico City are heavily booked; try stand-by at the airport, or go instead to Mérida (from where other US and Mexican destinations can be reached).

Flight **Cozumel**-Mexico City with Mexicana, daily; this airline also flies daily to Dallas and 4 days a week to Miami from Cozumel. Continental goes to Houston direct and makes connections with other US cities. Aero Caribe's flight to Cancún is 9 times daily.

To Cuba

Return flight to Cuba, Saturday and Wednesday, with stop at Mérida if plane is not fully booked (Mexicana); Mexicana direct on Monday, Tuesday, Friday and Sunday, Cubana Monday and Friday. Cuba package tours with Mexicana cost (January 1992 prices) US$459-500 (Wednesday-Sunday) to US$501-651 (Sunday-Sunday) depending on hotel category and season, visa (US$9) included, but not tax, staying in Havana; "Sun, sea and sand" packages cost US$611-681. There are other packages available. In all cases, tours starting in Mérida cost US$165 less. High season is mid-December to early January, mid-to end-March and mid-July to mid-August. Cuba-Mex SA, Calle 63, No 500, Depto D, Edificio La Literaria, Mérida, Yucatán (Apdo Postal 508, CP 97000, Telex 753806 Cumeme, Tel: 23-91-99/97-25, Fax: 24-91-91), with branch at Manzanillo 123, D 104, esq Baja California, Colonia Roma Sur, Tel: 574-0813/584-2465, Fax 584-6814, México, DF. Also Cubana Tours, Reforma 400 C, local "B", Av Colón, Mérida, Tel: 25-79-91, Telex 75-36-22, or Baja California 255, Edif "B" Despacho 103, Col Hipódromo Condesa, México DF, Casilla Postal 06100, Tel: 564-7839/5208, Fax: 264-2865, Telex 176-1240. Ask around Hamburgo in Mexico City for cheap tickets: might pick them up for as little as US$120 or so. If you pay in dollars make sure the fact is noted on the ticket; if you pay in pesos and use the ticket later you may be surcharged if the peso price has risen meanwhile. Visas for Cuba available through Viñales Tours, Oaxaca 80, Colonia Roma, Tel: 208-99-00 (metro Insurgentes, very helpful), or other travel agencies; you have to show your return ticket for Cuba. Tourist visas only are issued in Mexico, valid for the length of your tour. To extend a tourist visa in Cuba will cost US$120. The Cuban consulate in Mexico City does not give visas to individual travellers.

Airport Departure Tax

US$12 on international flights; US$5 on internal flights.

Airline Addresses

All in Cancún: Aeroméxico, Av Cobá 80, Tel: 41186/airport 42639; Mexicana, Av Cobá 39, Tel: 74444, or Aeropuerto 42740; American Airlines, Aeropuerto, Tel: 42947; United Airlines, Centro El Parián, Tel: 42340. Mexicana in Cozumel, Avenida General Rafael E Melgar Sur 17, Tel: 20157, Aeropuerto 20405.

NB

VAT is payable on domestic plane tickets bought in Mexico. Domestic tax on Mexican flights is 10%, on international flights 3.75%.

Airport Taxis

To avoid overcharging, the Government has taken control of taxi services from airports to cities and only those with government licences are allowed to carry passengers from the airport. Sometimes one does not pay the driver but purchases a ticket from a booth on leaving the airport. No further tipping is then required, except when the driver handles luggage for you. The same system has been applied at bus stations but it is possible to pay the driver direct.

Travel In Mexico

Promotional packages for local tourism exist, with 30-40% discount, operated by hoteliers, restaurateurs, hauliers and Aeroméxico and Mexicana (the latter is more punctual). Their tickets are not interchangeable. Mexicana has 50% discounts on flights between 2300 and 0600.

Motoring

British AA and Dutch ANWB members are reminded that there are ties with the American Automobile Association (AAA), which extends cover to the US and entitles AA members to free travel information including a very useful book and map on Mexico. Holders of 180-day tourist cards can keep their cars in Mexico for that time.

Gasoline is either unleaded, 87 octane, called *magna sin*, which costs US$0.35/litre, and *nova*, leaded, 80 octane, US$0.25/litre. Unleaded petrol is supposed to be available every 80 km or so. It is signed on major roads, but filling stations sometimes run out, which is not much use for rental cars which often require it. Make sure you are given full value when you tank up, that the pump is set to zero before your tank is filled, that both they and you know what money you've proffered, that your change is correct, that the pump is correctly calibrated, and that your filler cap is put back on. The Free Assistance Service of the Mexican Tourist Department's green jeeps ("*ángeles verdes*") patrol most of Mexico's main roads. The drivers speak English, are trained to give first aid and to make minor auto repairs and deal with flat tyres. They carry gasoline and have radio connection. All help is completely free. Gasoline at cost price.

When entering Mexico from Belize by car point out to the authorities that you have a car with you, otherwise they may not note it and you could be arrested for illegally importing a car.

Tourists' cars cannot, *by law*, be sold in Mexico. This is very strictly applied. You may not leave the country without the car you entered in, except with written government permission with the car in bond.

Car Rental

It is cheaper to rent a car by arrangement in the USA or Europe than to do it in Mexico.

Where To Stay

Accommodation on the islands and neighbouring towns is given above.

Maximum rates are registered with the Government and advertised in the press, according to six zones around the country. Rates are set on 15 May and 15 December. Complaints about violations must be reported to the Department of Tourism, Presidente Masarik 172, Colonia Polanco, Mexico City, Tel: 250-1964 and 250-8555. English is spoken at the best hotels. The Secretaría de Turismo publishes a *Directorio Nacional de Hospedaje*, with hotel listings, tourist information, maps of the capital of each state, good value at about US$6.50 for 680 pages.

Casas de huéspedes are usually the cheapest places to stay, although they are often dirty with poor plumbing. Usually a flat rate for a room is charged, so sharing works out cheaper, say US$3-5 pp. There are very few places with double beds (*matrimonial*) under US$9 double. Sleeping out is possible anywhere, but is not advisable in urban areas. Choose a secluded, relatively invisible spot. Mosquito netting (*pabellón*) is available by the metre in textile shops and, sewn into a sheet sleeping bag, is ample protection against insects.

Beware of "helpfuls" who try to find you a hotel, as prices quoted at the hotel desk rise to give them a commission. If backpacking, it is best for one of you to watch over luggage while the other goes to book a room and pay for it; some hotels are put off by backpacks. During peak season (November-April), it may be hard to find a room and clerks do not always check to see whether a room is vacant. Insist, or if desperate, provide a suitable tip. The week after Semana Santa is normally a holiday, so prices remain high, but resorts are not as crowded as the previous week. When using a lift, remember PB (*Planta Baja*) stands for ground floor. Discounts on hotel prices can often be arranged in the low season (May-October), but this is more difficult in Yucatán. There is not a great price difference between single and double rooms in lower-priced establishments. When checking into a hotel, always ask if the doors are locked at night, preventing guests from entering if no nightguard is posted.

Motels and Auto-hotels are not usually places where guests stay the whole night (you can recognise them by curtains over the garage and red and green lights above the door to show if the room is free). If driving, and wishing to avoid a night on the road, they can be quite acceptable (clean, some have hot water, in the Yucatán they have a/c), and they tend to be cheaper than respectable establishments.

Camping

Most sites are called Trailer Parks, but tents are usually allowed. Beware of people stealing clothes, especially when you hang them up after washing. Paraffin oil (kerosene) for stoves is called *petróleo para lámparas* in Mexico; it is not a very good quality (dirty) and costs about US$0.05 per litre. It is available from an *expendio*, or *despacho de petróleo*, or from a *tlalalpería*, but not from gas stations. *Gasolina blanca* may be bought in *ferreterías* (ironmongers), prices vary widely; also for Coleman fuel. *Alcohol* for heating the burner can be obtained from supermarkets.

Youth Hostels

21 CREA *albergues* exist in Mexico, mostly in small towns, and generally of poor quality. The hostels take YHA members and non-members, who have to pay more. You have to pay a deposit for sheets, pillow and towel; make sure that this is written in the ledger or else you may not get your deposit back. Hostels have lockers for valuables; take good care of your other possessions.

Food

Usual meals are a light breakfast, and a heavy lunch between 1400 and 1500. Dinner, between 1800 and 2000, is light.

Many restaurants give foreigners the menu without the *comida corrida* (set meals), and so forcing them to order *à la carte* at double the price; watch this! Try to avoid eating in restaurants which don't post a menu. Meals cost about US$1-3 for breakfast, US$3-6 for lunch and US$4-10 for dinner (about US$7-17 a day on meals, depending on lavishness). In resort areas, where prices tend to be higher, the posh hotels include breakfast and dinner in many cases.

What To Eat

Tamales, or meat wrapped in maize and then banana leaves and boiled. Turkey, chicken and pork with exotic sauces—*mole de guajolote* and *mole poblano* (*chile* and chocolate sauce with grated coconut) are famous. *Tacos* (without *chiles*) and *enchiladas* (with all too many of them) are meat or chicken and beans rolled in *tortillas* (maize pancakes) and fried in oil; they are delicious. Try also spring onions with salt and lime juice in *taquerías*. Indian food is found everywhere: for instance, *tostadas* (toasted fried tortillas with chicken, beans and lettuce), or *gorditas*, fried, extra-thick tortillas with sauce and cheese. Black kidney beans (*frijoles*) appear in various dishes. Red snapper (*huachinango*), Veracruz style, is a famous fish dish, sautéed with *pimientos* and spices. Another excellent fish is the sea bass (*róbalo*). Fruits include a vast assortment of tropical types—avocados, bananas, pineapples, *zapotes*, pomegranates, guavas, limes and *mangos de Manila*, which are delicious. Don't eat fruit unless you peel it yourself, and avoid raw vegetables. Try *higos rebanados* (delicious fresh sliced figs), *guacamole* (a mashed avocado seasoned with tomatoes, onions, coriander and *chiles*) and of course, *papaya*, or pawpaw. Mexico has various elaborate regional cuisines. Chinese restaurants, present in most towns, generally give clean and efficient service. Fried eggs are known as *huevos estrellados*. On 6 January, Epiphany, the traditional *rosca*, a ring-shaped sweet bread with dried fruit and little plastic baby Jesuses inside, is eaten. The person who finds a baby Jesus in his piece must make a crib and clothes for Him, and invite everyone present to a *fiesta* on 2 February, Candelaria.

Drink

The beer is quite good. Brands include Dos Equis-XX, Montejo, Bohemia, Sol and Superior (the last two not as good). Negra Modelo is a dark beer, it has the same alcohol content as the other beers. Local wine, some of it quite good, is cheap. The native drinks are *pulque*, the fermented juice of the agave plant (those unaccustomed to it should not overindulge), *tequila*, made mostly in Jalisco and *mescal* from Oaxaca; the last two are distilled from agave plants. Mescal usually has a "gusano de maguey" (a worm) in the bottle, considered by Mexicans to be a particular speciality. Tequila and mescal rarely have an alcoholic content above 40-43%. Also available is the Spanish aniseed spirit, *anís*, which is made locally. Imported whiskies and brandies are expensive. Rum is cheap and good. There are always plenty of non-alcoholic soft drinks (*refrescos*)—try the *paletas*, safe and refreshing (those of Michoacán are everywhere)—and mineral water. Fresh juices, as long as not mixed with water, and milk shakes (*licuados*) are good and usually safe. If you don't like to drink out of a glass, ask for a straw (*popote*). Herbal teas, eg camomile, are available. There are few outdoor drinking places in Mexico except in tourist spots.

Tipping

More or less on a level of 10-15%; the equivalent of US$0.25 per bag for porters, the equivalent of US$0.20 for bell boys, theatre usherettes, and nothing for a taxi driver unless he gives some extra service. It is not necessary to tip the drivers of hired cars.

Cost Of Living

Budget travellers should note that there is a definite tourist economy, with high prices and, on occasion, unhelpful service. This can be avoided by seeking out those places used by locals; an understanding of Spanish is useful. The cost of living is one of the highest in Latin America and, according to a survey in 1989, only 8% lower than that of the USA. Nevertheless, for travellers, Mexico is much cheaper than the USA in terms of 1st class bus travel, town bus services and cheap hotel accommodation in city centres. High quality, seasonal tourist house rentals are expensive, owing to local shortages.

Film is reasonably cheap but developing is expensive and poor quality. Services are abundant. Doctors' and dentists' services are good, and their fees reasonable.

Exchange

Travellers' cheques from any well-known

bank can be cashed in most towns if drawn in US dollars; travellers' cheques in terms of sterling are harder to cash, and certainly not worth trying to change outside the largest of cities. The free rate of exchange changes daily and varies from bank to bank. Until the new day's rate is posted, at any time between 1000 and 1100, yesterday's rate prevails. Many banks only change foreign currency during a limited period (often between 1000 and 1200, but sometimes also 1600-1800 in Banamex), which should be remembered, especially on Fridays. *Casas de cambio* are generally quicker than banks for exchange transactions, but their rates are often not as good. Beware of short-changing at all times. American Express, Mastercard and Visa are generally accepted in Mexico and cash is obtainable with these credit cards at certain banks, eg Bancomer or Banamex, and travellers' cheques may be bought with Visa. Automatic Teller Machines (ATM) of Banamex accept Visa, Mastercard and ATM cards of the US Cirrus ATM network for withdrawals up to 1,500,000 pesos/US$500 daily. There have been instances of Banamex ATMs stating that cash cannot be given, "try again later", only for the cardholder to find that his/her account has been debited anyway. NB An American Express card issued in Mexico states "valid only in Mexico", and is used only for peso transactions. All other American Express cards are transacted in US dollars even for employees living in Mexico. Amex travellers' cheques are readily accepted.

Currency
The monetary unit is the Mexican peso (represented by a 'S' crossed with one vertical line, unlike 2 vertical lines on the US dollar sign), divided into 100 centavos. Owing to the rapid inflation of the past few years both coins and notes are being reissued. The smallest note is for 2,000, then 5,000, 10,000, 20,000, and 50,000 pesos. Coins have all been changed from silver and bronze to strange alloys that have various colours. Those in circulation are 20, 50, 100, 500, 1,000 and 5,000 pesos; there is a small 20-peso coin as well as an older, larger one, similarly with the 50-peso coins. It is wise to check the number on coins.

Health
The Social Security hospitals are restricted to members, but will take visitors in emergencies; they are more up to date than the Centros de Salud and Hospitales Civiles found in most centres, which are very cheap and open to everyone. There are many homeopathic physicians in all parts of Mexico. You are recommended to use bottled or mineral water for drinking, except in hotels which normally provide purified drinking water free. Ice is usually made from *agua purificada*. Coffee water is not necessarily boiled. Bottled water is available everywhere. Tehuacán mineral water is sold all over Mexico; both plain and flavoured are first class. Water-sterilizing tablets can be bought at pharmacies. Milk is only safe when in sealed containers marked *pasteurizado*. Raw salads and vegetables, and food sold on the streets and in cheap cafés, especially in Mexico City, may be dangerous. It is advisable to vaccinate against typhoid, paratyphoid and poliomyelitis if visiting the low-lying tropical zones, where there is also some risk of malaria.

Language
Speaking Spanish is a great asset in avoiding rip-offs for gringos and for making the most of cheap *comedores* and market shopping.

Best Season
For pleasure visits, between October and early April, when it hardly ever rains in most of the country. August is not a good time because it is a holiday month throughout Central America and most internal flights and other transport are heavily booked.

Clothing
Women visitors should not wear shorts other than at the seaside, though trousers are quite OK. Four musts are good walking shoes, sun hats, dark glasses, and flip-flops for the hot sandy beaches. Women are always escorted, except in the main streets of the larger cities. Men may need a jacket and tie in some restaurants. Topless bathing: ask first, or do as others do.

National Holidays
Sunday is a statutory holiday. Saturday is also observed as a holiday, except by the shops. There is no early-closing day. National holidays are as follows: New Year (1 January), Constitution Day (5 February), Birthday of Benito Juárez (21 March), Holy Thursday, Good Friday and Easter Saturday, Labour Day (1 May), Battle of Puebla (5 May), President's Annual Message (1 September), Independence Day (16 September), Discovery of America (12 October), Day of the Revolution (20 November), Christmas Day (25 December).

All Souls' Day (2 November), and Our Lady of Guadalupe (12 December), are not national holidays, but are widely celebrated.

Time Zone

Central Standard Time, 6 hours behind GMT, 1 behind EST.

Weights And Measures

The metric system is compulsory.

Postal Services

Rates are raised periodically in line with the peso's devaluation against the dollar. They are posted next to the windows where stamps are sold. Air mail letters to the USA take about six days, and to the UK (US$0.45) via the USA one to two weeks. *Poste restante* ("general delivery" in the USA) functions quite reliably, but you may have to ask under each of your names; if you wish to use this facilty it is known as *lista de correos*; mail is sent back after ten days. Address "*favor de retener hasta llegada*" on envelope.

Telecommunications

Telégrafos Nacionales maintains the national and international telegraph systems, separate from the Post Office. Pay telephones (black) for local calls take coin from 10 to 100 pesos, or *fichas*, also for collect long distance calls. Follow local procedures, then dial 02 for calls inside Mexico and 09 for international calls, and be patient. Telephone service to USA, Canada and Europe. AT&T's USA Direct service is available, for information in Mexico dial 412-553-7458, ext 359. From LADA phones (see below), dail **01, similar for AT&T credit cards. There is a heavy tax levied on all foreign long-distance calls originating and paid for in Mexico. *Casetas*, or booths, where you pay after phoning, are extremely expensive, and charges vary from place to place. It is better to call collect from private phones, but better still to use the LADA system. Collect calls on LADA can be made from any blue public phone, silver phones for local and direct long distance calls, some take coins (100, 500 and 1,000 pesos), other foreign credit cards (Visa, Mastercard—"a slot machine scenario", not all phones that say they take cards accept them, others that say they don't do), still others take plastic cards worth from 5,000 to 50,000 pesos, purchasable from phone company offices, supermarkets, etc). LADA numbers are: 91 long distance within Mexico, add city code and number (half-price Sunday); 92 long

distance in Mexico, person to person; 95 long distance to USA and Canada, add area code and number (29% discount Saturday 0700-1859, Sunday 1700-2359, Monday-Saturday 1900-2259, special nightly rate Monday-Saturday 2300-0659, Sunday 0000-1659); 96 to USA and Canada person to person for collect calls; 98 to rest of the world, add country code, city code and number; 99 to rest of the world, person to person. The *Directorio Telefónica Nacional Turístico* is full of useful information, including LADA details, federal tourist offices, time zones, yellow pages for each state, places of interest and maps. Fax services are common in main post offices, US$5 per page.

Press

The more important journals are in Mexico City. The most influential dailies are: *Excelsior, Novedades, El Día* (throughout Mexico), *Uno más Uno; The News* (in English, now available in all main cities); *El Universal (El Universal Gráfico); El Financiero*, the financial newspaper; *La Jornada* (more to the left); *La Prensa*, a popular tabloid, has the largest circulation. *El Nacional* is the mouthpiece of the Government. There are weekly magazines: *Epoca, Proceso*, and *Siempre*. The political satirical weekly is *Los Agachados*.

Local Information

All Mexican Government tourist agencies are now grouped in the Department of Tourism building at Avenida Masarik 172, near corner of Reforma, Mexico City. A few cities run municipal tourist offices to help travellers. Representatives of the Federal Tourism Department can be found at Avenida Tulum 81, Edificio Fira, planta baja, Cancún (PO Box 77550, Tel: 43238/43438), and Calle 61 No 470, Manzana 4a del Cuartel Primero, Mérida, Yucatán (PO Box 97000, Tel: 249431/249542). There is a state tourist office for Quintana Roo at Palacio de Gobierno, 2nd floor, Chetumal (PO Box 77009, Tel: 29100, ext 227), and for Yucatán at Edificio Planeación, planta baja, Calle 59 No 490 por Avenida Itzáes, Mérida (PO Box 97000, Tel: 15989/48925).

The Mexican Automobile Association (AMA) is at Chapultepec 276, México, DF; they sell an indispensable road guide, with good maps and very useful lists of hotels, with current prices. The ANA (Asociación Nacional Automobilística) sells similar but not such good material; offices in Insurgentes (Metro Glorieta) and Avenida

Jalisco 27, México 18 DF. For road conditions consult the AMA, which is quite reliable. A calendar of *fiestas* is published by *Mexico This Month*.

If you have any complaints about faulty goods or services, go to the Procuraduría Federal de Protección del Consumidor of which there is a branch in every city. Major cities also have a Procurador del Turista. The Tourist Office may also help with these, or criminal matters, while the Agente del Ministro Público (Federal or State District Attorney) will also deal with criminal complaints.

Maps

The Mexican Government Tourist Highway map is available free of charge at tourist offices (when in stock). If driving from the USA you get a free map if you buy your insurance at AAA or at Sanborn's in the border cities. The official map printers, Detenal, produce the only good large-scale maps of the country.

The Dirección General de Oceanografía in Calle Medellín 10, near Insurgentes underground station (Mexico City), sells excellent maps of the entire coastline of Mexico. Good detailed maps of the states of Mexico and the country itself from Dirección General de Geografía y Meteorología, Avenida Observatorio 192, México 18, DF, Tel: 515-15-27. The best road maps of Mexican states, free, on polite written request, are available from Ing Daniel Díaz Díaz, Director General de Programación, Xola 1755, 8° Piso, México 12 DF. Maps are also available from Instituto Nacional de Estadística, Geografía e Informática (INEGI), which has branches in Mexico City (Insurgentes Sur 795, planta baja, PO Box 03810, Tel: 687-4691/687-2911 ext 289) and 40 other cities around the country; in Quintana Roo: Lázaro Cárdenas 91, Chetumal; in Yucatán: Paseo Montejo 442, Edificio Oasis, Mérida (PO Box 97100).

Guidebooks

Travellers wanting more information than we have space to provide, on archaeological sites for instance, would do well to use the widely available Easy Guides written by Richard Bloomgarden, with plans and good illustrations. *A Field Guide to Mexican Birds*, Peterson and Chalif, Houghton Mifflin, 1973, has been recommended. For ornithologists: *Finding Birds in Mexico*, by Ernest P Edwards, Box AQ, Sweet Briar, Virginia 24595, USA, recommended as detailed and thorough. Highly recommended, practical and entertaining is *The People's Guide to Mexico* by Carl Franz (John Muir Publications, Santa Fe, NM), now in its 8th edition, 1990, *Back Country Mexico, A Traveller's Guide and Phrase Book*, by Bob Burlison and David H Riskind (University of Texas Press, Box 7819, Austin, Texas, 78713-7819) has been recommended. Also *Hidden Mexico* by Rebecca Burns.

We should like to thank all the correspondents who sent information to *The Mexico and Central American Handbook* for information on the Mexican islands.

Notes

Notes

CLIMATIC TABLES

The following table has been very kindly furnished by Mr. R.K. Headland, the notes by Mark Wilson. Each weather station is given with its altitude in metres (m). Temperatures (Centigrade) are given as averages for each month; the first line is the maximum and the second line is the minimum. The third line is the average number of wet days encountered in each month.

	Jan	Feb	Mar	Apr	May	June	July	Aug	Sept	Oct	Nov	Dec
Havana	26	27	28	29	30	31	31	32	31	29	27	26
49m.	18	18	19	21	22	23	24	24	24	23	21	19
	6	4	4	4	7	10	9	10	11	11	7	6
Kingston	30	29	30	30	31	31	32	32	32	31	31	30
7 m.	22	22	23	24	25	25	26	26	25	25	24	23
	3	2	3	3	5	6	3	6	6	12	5	3
Nassau	25	25	27	28	29	31	31	32	31	29	28	26
10m.	17	17	18	20	22	23	24	24	24	22	20	18
	6	5	5	6	9	12	14	14	15	13	9	6
Port-au-Prince	31	31	32	33	33	35	35	35	34	33	32	31
41m.	23	22	22	23	23	24	25	24	24	24	23	22
	3	5	7	11	13	8	7	11	12	12	7	3
Port of Spain	30	32	31	32	32	31	31	31	32	31	31	30
12m.	20	21	21	21	23	23	23	23	23	22	22	21
	11	8	2	8	9	19	23	17	16	13	17	16
San Juan, PR	27	27	27	28	29	29	29	29	30	30	28	27
14m.	21	21	22	22	23	24	24	24	24	24	23	22
	13	7	8	10	15	14	18	15	14	12	13	14
Santo Domingo	28	28	29	29	30	30	31	31	31	31	30	29
14m.	20	19	20	21	22	23	23	23	23	23	22	21
	7	6	5	7	11	12	11	11	11	11	10	8
Willemstad	28	29	29	30	30	31	31	31	32	31	30	29
23m.	24	23	23	24	25	26	25	26	26	26	24	24
	14	8	7	4	4	7	9	8	6	9	15	16

Use these tables with caution; variations within islands can be dramatic. On the mountainous islands, such as the Windwards, rainfall is generally about 3000 mm (120 inches) in the interior, but only 1500 mm (60 inches) in coastal rain shadow areas. Rain falls in intense showers, so even on a wet day there may be plenty of sunshine too. In most of the Caribbean, the wet season is from June to November, but there is plenty of fine weather at this time of year, and it is quite likely to rain in the dry season too. June to November is also the hurricane season, but most islands experience a hurricane on average only two or three times per century.

Temperatures are generally very steady. Nights are much warmer than in (for example) a Mediterranean summer. It generally feels much cooler on the windward (east) coasts; and it actually *is* a lot cooler in the mountains, where temperatures may fall to around 16°C (60°F). At high altitudes, there may be an almost continuous cover of low cloud at certain times of year. The winter season (January to March) is generally dry and not too hot. A possible hazard at this time of year are cold fronts or "northers", which can bring surprisingly cold winds and heavy rain to Jamaica and the northern Caribbean. Don't worry too much about the weather, the Caribbean's reputation is well deserved, and on most islands at most times of year, you can't go too far wrong.

TEMPERATURE CONVERSION TABLE

°C	°F	°C	°F	°C	°F	°C	°F	°C	°F
1	34	11	52	21	70	31	88	41	106
2	36	12	54	22	72	32	90	42	108
3	38	13	56	23	74	33	92	43	109
4	39	14	57	24	75	34	93	44	111
5	41	15	59	25	77	35	95	45	113
6	43	16	61	26	79	36	97	46	115
7	45	17	63	27	81	37	99	47	117
8	46	18	64	28	82	38	100	48	118
9	48	19	66	29	84	39	102	49	120
10	50	20	68	30	86	40	104	50	122

The formula for converting °C to °F is: °C x 9 ÷ 5 + 32 = °F

WEIGHTS AND MEASURES

Metric	**British and U.S.**

Weight:
1 kilogram (kg.) = 2,205 pounds
1 metric ton = 1.102 short tons
            = 0.984 long ton

1 pound (lb.) = 454 grams
1 short ton (2,000 lb.) = 0.907 metric ton
1 long ton (2,240 lb.) = 1.016 metric tons

Length:
1 millimetre (mm.) = 0.03937 inch
1 metre = 3.281 feet
1 kilometre (km.) = 0.621 mile

1 inch = 25.417 millimetres
1 foot (ft.) = 0.305 metre
1 mile = 1.609 kilometres

Area:
1 hectare = 2.471 acres
1 square km. (km²) = 0.386 sq. mile

1 acre = 0.405 hectare
1 square mile (sq. mile) = 2,590 km²

Capacity:
1 litre = 0.220 Imperial gallon
      = 0.264 U.S. gallon
    (5 Imperial gallons are approximately equal to 6 U.S. gallons)

1 Imperial gallon = 4.546 litres
1 U.S. gallon = 3.785 litres

Volume:
1 cubic metre (m³) = 35.31 cubic feet
              = 1.31 cubic yards

1 cubic foot (cu. ft) = 0.028 m³
1 cubic yard (cu. yd.) = 0.765 m³

N.B. The *manzana*, used in Central America, is about 0.7 hectare (1.73 acres).

ECONOMIC INDICATORS

COUNTRY	US$ GNP per head (1990)†	% change pa (1980-90)†	Annual Inflation*	Exchange rate/US$
ANGUILLA				2.7
ANTIGUA & BARBUDA	4,600	4.7%		2.7
ARUBA	9,320[1]		3.9%(11)	1.79
BAHAMAS	11,510	1.7%	6.5%(12)	1.0
BARBADOS	6,540	1.4%	8.1%(12)	2.0
BELIZE	1,970	2.5%	4.5%(12)	2.0
BERMUDA	24,346[2]	-0.1%	4.8%	1.0
CAYMAN ISLANDS	17,525[1]		7.8%(12)	0.83
COLOMBIA	1,240	1.1%	30.7%(2)	749.13
COSTA RICA	1,910	0.6%	26.8%(12)	129.9
CUBA				1.32
DOMINICA	1,940	3.0%	2.7%(11)	2.7
DOMINICAN REPUBLIC	820	-0.4%	4.0%(12)	13.0
GRENADA	2,120	5.1%	3.7%(9)	2.7
GUADELOUPE	over 6,000	n.a		5.41
HAITI	370	-2.3%	6.6%(11)	5.0
HONDURAS	590	-1.2%	24.6%(11)	5.44
JAMAICA	1,510	-0.4%	80.2%(12)	22.64
MEXICO	2,490	-0.9%	16.9%(3)	3,091.2
MONTSERRAT				2.7
NETH. ANTILLES	over 6,000	n.a	5.0%(10)	1.79
NICARAGUA	500-1,499	n.a	1183.2%(11)	5.0
PANAMA	1,830	-2.0%	1.2%(12)	1.0
PUERTO RICO	6,470	2.1%		1.0

[1]1988
[2]1989

ECONOMIC INDICATORS

COUNTRY	US$ GNP per head (1989)†	% change pa (1980-89) †	Annual Inflation*	Exchange rate/US$
ST KITTS & NEVIS	3,330	6.0%	4.5%	2.7
ST LUCIA	1,900	4.2%	5.2%(11)	2.7
ST VINCENT	1,600	5.7%	5.6%(11)	2.7
TRINIDAD & TOBAGO	3,470	-6.0%	2.3%(12)	4.25
TURKS & CAICOS				1.0
VENEZUELA	2,560	-2.0%	31.7%(3)	65.56
VIRGIN ISLANDS (UK)				1.0
VIRGIN ISLANDS (USA)	12,330	1.2%		1.0

† Source: World Bank
* 1991 latest month in brackets except Colombia, Mexico, and Venezuela, 1992; Caymans, Grenada, Netherlands Antilles, St Vincent, 1990; and Bermuda, 1991 average. Exchange rates at 29 May 1992.

The East Caribbean dollar, pegged at EC$2.70 = US$1, is used by:
  Anguilla
  Antigua & Barbuda
  Dominica
  Grenada
  Montserrat
  St Kitts & Nevis
  St Lucia
  St Vincent & the Grenadines

The US dollar is the currency of:
  British Virgin Islands
  Panama
  Puerto Rico
  Turks & Caicos
  US Virgin Islands

The French franc is the currency of:
  Guadeloupe
  Martinique
  St-Barthélémy
  St-Martin

The Netherlands Antilles guilder (or florin) at NAf1.79 = US$1, is the currency of:
  Bonaire
  Curaçao
  Saba
  Sint Eustatius
  Sint Maarten

INDEX TO PLACES

812

INDEX TO TOWN AND ISLAND MAPS

Notes

INDEX TO ADVERTISERS

AT&T USA Direct
This Service operates from:

Anguilla	400	Grenada	560
Antigua/Barbuda	372	Haiti	248
Aruba	716	Jamaica	200
Bahamas	120	Montserrat	412
Barbados	585	Saba	418
Bermuda	67	Sint Eustatius	425
Bonaire	684	Sint Maarten	434
British Virgin Islands	354	St Kitts/Nevis	392
Cayman Islands	169	St Lucia	519
Curaçao	701	Trinidad & Tobago	613
Dominica	497	Turks & Caicos Islands	224
Dominican Republic	290		

THOMAS COOK MASTERCARD TRAVELLERS CHEQUES

REFUND ASSISTANCE POINTS

Visitors to the Caribbean area should telephone Thomas Cook Princeton USA (1) 609-987-7300 (collect) – 24 hour service – or contact one of the following Thomas Cook MasterCard Refund Agents:-

WEST INDIES

Antigua

St John's	Alexander Parrish	Thomas Street	462-0638

Bahamas

Freeport	Royal Bank of Canada	East Mall & Expo Sts	352-6631
Nassau	Royal Bank of Canada	323 Bay St	322-8700

Barbados

Bridgetown	Paul Foster Travel	Independence Square	426-5160
	Royal Bank of Canada	Broad Street	426-5206

Cayman Islands

George Town	International Travel	Transnational Building West Bay Road	947-4323

Cuba

Havana	Banco Nacional de Cuba	Aguiar 411	61-9881

Dominica

Roseau	Musson Trading	Dorset House, Old Street	82550/6

Dominican Republic

La Romana	Banco del Comercio Dominicano	Calle Trinitaria 59 Esq EA Miranja	556-5151
Puerto Plata	Banco del Comercio Dominicano	Calle Duarte Esq Padre Castellanos	586-2350
Santo Domingo	Vimenca	Ave Abraham Lincoln 306	532-7381

Grenada

St George's	Grenada Bank of Commerce	Corner Cross & Halifax Streets	3521

Guadeloupe

Pointe à Pitre	Banque Français Commerciale	Rue Gambetta 21	82-27-90

Haiti

Port-au-Prince	Southerland Tours	30 Avenue Marie-James	3-1600

Jamaica

Kingston	Grace Kennedy Travel	19-21 Knutsford Boulevard	929-6290
Mandeville	Mutual Security Bank	9 Manchester Square	962-2886
May Pen	Mutual Security Bank	52 Main Street	986-2592
Montego Bay	Mutual Security Bank	4 Sam Sharp Square	952-3641
St. Elizabeth	Mutual Security Bank	High St. Black River	965-2207

Martinique

Fort de France	Laroc Voyages	1 Rue de la Liberté	63-66-66

Montserrat
Plymouth	Royal Bank of Canada	Parliament Street	2426

Netherlands Antilles
Bonaire	Maduro & Curiel's	Kerkstraat/Breedestraat Kraalendijk	8420
Curaçao	Mau-Assam Travel	37 Schottegatweg Oost Willemstad	37-05-55
St. Maarten	Windward Islands Bank	Philipsburg	5-22313

Puerto Rico
Hato Rey	Royal Bank of Canada	225 Ponce de Leon Ave	753-2000
Santurce	Thomas Cook	Luis Munoz Marim International Airport	791-1960

St. Kitts
Basseterre	Royal Bank of Canada	Fort & Bay Roads	465-2389

St. Lucia
Castries	St. Lucia Coop Bank	21 Bridge Street	2881
Vieux Fort	St Lucia Coop Bank	Commercial Street	6213

St. Vincent
Kingstown	Caribbean Banking Corp.	No. 81 South River Road	456-1501

Trinidad & Tobago
Port of Spain	National Commercial Bank	62 Independence Sq	62-52893
San Fernando	National Commercial Bank	High & Penitence Sts	652-2757

Visitors to South America, Mexico and Central America should also telephone Thomas Cook Princeton USA (1) 609-987-7300 (collect) – 24 hour service – for assistance.

In many Latin American countries there is a vigorous parallel (black) market for both travellers cheques and US Dollar notes. (This may be with or without Government permission). Rates are usually slightly better for notes but travellers cheques are obviously safer, which is especially important when theft is becoming more common.

You should shop around for rates since these may vary considerably. Hotel rates in particular tend to be poor.

Do not take currencies other than US Dollar. If accepted at all, the rate will be poor.

In some countries, only specific bank branches may deal in foreign exchange and you may have difficulty obtaining local currency when far from capital cities.

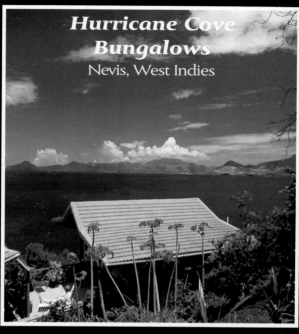